D1488601

Systematic Theology

Systematic Theology

Louis Berkhof

The Banner of Truth Trust

THE BANNER OF TRUTH TRUST
3 Murrayfield Road, Edinburgh EH12 6EL
PO Box 621, Carlisle, Pennsylvania 17013, USA

First Banner of Truth edition 1958
Reprinted 1960
Reprinted 1963
Reprinted 1966
Reprinted 1969
Reprinted 1971
Reprinted 1974
Reprinted 1976
Reprinted 1979
Reprinted 1981
Reprinted 1984
Reprinted 1988
Reprinted 1994
Reprinted 1998
Reprinted 2000
Reprinted 2003

ISBN 0 85151 056 6

*

Reprinted by photolithography in Great Britain
by The Bath Press, Bath

Preface

Now that my *Systematic Theology* is again being reprinted, the Preface can be very brief. It is not necessary to say much about the nature of the work, since it has been before the public for more than fifteen years and has been used extensively. I have every reason to be grateful for its kind reception, for the favourable testimony of many reviewers, and for the fact that the book is now used as a textbook in many Theological Seminaries and Bible Schools in our country, and that requests were even received from abroad for permission to translate it into other languages. These are blessings which I had not anticipated, and for which I am deeply grateful to God. To Him be all the honor. And if the work may continue to be a blessing in many sections of the Church of Jesus Christ, it will but increase my recognition of the abundant grace of God.

Grand Rapids, Michigan,   L. BERKHOF
August 1, 1949.

TABLE OF CONTENTS

Part One

THE DOCTRINE OF GOD

(The Being of God)

Part Three

THE DOCTRINE OF THE PERSON AND WORK OF CHRIST

The Person of Christ

The States of Christ

The Offices of Christ

Part Five

THE DOCTRINE OF THE CHURCH AND OF THE MEANS OF GRACE

The Church

The Means of Grace

Part Six

THE DOCTRINE OF THE LAST THINGS

Individual Eschatology

General Eschatology

Part One

———

THE DOCTRINE OF GOD

I. The Existence of God

A. Place of the Doctrine of God in Dogmatics.

WORKS on dogmatic or systematic theology generally begin with the doctrine of God. The prevailing opinion has always recognized this as the most logical procedure and still points in the same direction. In many instances even they whose fundamental principles would seem to require another arrangement, continue the traditional practice. There are good reasons for starting with the doctrine of God, if we proceed on the assumption that theology is the systematized knowledge of God, of whom, through whom, and unto whom, are all things. Instead of being surprised that Dogmatics should begin with the doctrine of God, we might well expect it to be a study of God *throughout* in all its ramifications, from the beginning to the end. As a matter of fact, that is exactly what it is intended to be, though only the first locus deals with God directly, while the succeeding ones treat of Him more indirectly. We start the study of theology with two presuppositions, namely (1) that God exists, and (2) that He has revealed Himself in His divine Word. And for that reason it is not impossible for us to start with the study of God. We can turn to His revelation, in order to learn what He has revealed concerning Himself and concerning His relation to His creatures. Attempts have been made in the course of time to distribute the material of Dogmatics in such a way as to exhibit clearly that it is, not merely in one locus, but in its entirety, a study of God. This was done by the application of the trinitarian method, which arranges the subject-matter of Dogmatics under the three headings of (1) the Father (2) the Son, and (3) the Holy Spirit. That method was applied in some of the earlier systematic works, was restored to favor by Hegel, and can still be seen in Martensen's *Christian Dogmatics*. A similar attempt was made by Breckenridge, when he divided the subject-matter of Dogmatics into (1) The Knowledge of God Objectively Considered, and (2) The Knowledge of God Subjectively Considered. Neither one of these can be called very successful.

Up to the beginning of the nineteenth century the practice was all but general to begin the study of Dogmatics with the doctrine of God; but a change came about under the influence of Schleiermacher, who sought to safeguard the scientific character of theology by the introduction of a new method. The religious consciousness of man was substituted for the Word

of God as the source of theology. Faith in Scripture as an authoritative revelation of God was discredited, and human insight based on man's own emotional or rational apprehension became the standard of religious thought.
Religion gradually took the place of God as the object of theology. Man
ceased to recognize the knowledge of God as something that was *given* in
Scripture, and began to pride himself on being a seeker after God. In course
of time it became rather common to speak of man's discovering God, as if
man ever discovered Him; and every discovery that was made in the process
was dignified with the name of "revelation." God came in at the end of a
syllogism, or as the last link in a chain of reasoning, or as the cap-stone of a
structure of human thought. Under such circumstances it was but natural
that some should regard it as incongruous to begin Dogmatics with the study
of God. It is rather surprising that so many, in spite of their subjectivism,
continued the traditional arrangement.

Some, however, sensed the incongruity and struck out in a different way.
Schleiermacher's dogmatic work is devoted to a study and analysis of the
religious consciousness and of the doctrines therein implied. He does not deal
with the doctrine of God connectedly, but only in fragments, and concludes his
work with a discussion of the Trinity. His starting point is anthropological
rather than theological. Some of the mediating theologians were influenced to
such an extent by Schleiermacher that they logically began their dogmatic
treatises with the study of man. Even in the present day this arrangement is
occasionally followed. A striking example of it is found in the work of O. A.
Curtis on *The Christian Faith.* This begins with the doctrine of man and concludes with the doctrine of God. Ritschlian theology might seem to call for
still another starting point, since it finds the objective revelation of God, not in
the Bible as the divinely inspired Word, but in Christ as the Founder of the
Kingdom of God, and considers the idea of the Kingdom as the central and
all-controlling concept of theology. However, Ritschlian dogmaticians, such as
Herrmann. Haering, and Kaftan follow, at least formally, the usual order. At
the same time there are several theologians who in their works begin the discussion of dogmatics proper with the doctrine of Christ or of His redemptive
work. T. B. Strong distinguishes between *theology* and *Christian theology,* defines the latter as "the expression and analysis of the Incarnation of Jesus Christ,"
and makes the incarnation the dominating concept throughout his *Manual of
Theology.*

B. Scripture Proof for the Existence of God.

For us the existence of God is the great presupposition of theology. There
is no sense in speaking of the knowledge of God, unless it may be assumed that
God exists. The presupposition of Christian theology is of a very definite type.
The assumption is not merely that there is something, some idea or ideal, some
power or purposeful tendency, to which the name of God may be applied, but
that there is a self-existent, self-conscious, personal Being, which is the origin

of all things, and which transcends the entire creation, but is at the same time immanent in every part of it. The question may be raised, whether this is a reasonable assumption, and this question may be answered in the affirmative. This does not mean, however, that the existence of God is capable of a logical demonstration that leaves no room whatever for doubt; but it does mean that, while the truth of God's existence is accepted by faith, this faith is based on reliable information. While Reformed theology regards the existence of God as an entirely reasonable assumption, it does not claim the ability to demonstrate this by rational argumentation. Dr. Kuyper speaks as follows of the attempt to do this: "The attempt to prove God's existence is either useless or unsuccessful. It is useless if the searcher believes that God is a rewarder of those who seek Him. And it is unsuccessful if it is an attempt to force a person who does not have this *pistis* by means of argumentation to an acknowledgment in a logical sense."

The Christian accepts the truth of the existence of God by faith. But this faith is not a blind faith, but a faith that is based on evidence, and the evidence is found primarily in Scripture as the inspired Word of God, and secondarily in God's revelation in nature. Scripture proof on this point does not come to us in the form of an explicit declaration, and much less in the form of a logical argument. In that sense the Bible does not prove the existence of God. The closest it comes to a declaration is perhaps in Heb. 11:6 . . . "for he that cometh to God must believe that He is, and that He is a rewarder of them that seek after Him." It presupposes the existence of God in its very opening statement, "In the beginning God created the heavens and the earth." Not only does it describe God as the Creator of all things, but also as the Upholder of all His creatures, and as the Ruler of the destinies of individuals and nations. It testifies to the fact that God works all things according to the counsel of His will, and reveals the gradual realization of His great purpose of redemption. The preparation for this work, especially in the choice and guidance of the old covenant people of Israel, is clearly seen in the Old Testament, and the initial culmination of it in the Person and work of Christ stands out with great clarity on the pages of the New Testament. God is seen on almost every page of Holy Writ as He reveals Himself in words and actions. This revelation of God is the basis of our faith in the existence of God, and makes this an entirely reasonable faith. It should be remarked, however, that it is only by faith that we accept the revelation of God, and that we obtain a real insight into its contents. Jesus said, "If any man will do his will, he shall know of the doctrine, whether it be of God, or whether I speak of myself," John 7:17. It is this intensive knowledge, resulting from intimate communion with God, which Hosea has in mind when he says, "And let us know, let us follow on to know the Lord," Hos. 6:3. The unbeliever has no real understanding of the Word of God. The words of Paul are very much to the point in this connection: "Where is the wise? where is the scribe? where is the disputer of this age (world)? Hath not God made foolish the wisdom of the

---

1. *Dict. Dogm., De Deo I*, p. 77 (translation mine — L. B.).

world? For, seeing that in the wisdom of God the world through its wisdom knew not God, it was God's good pleasure through the foolishness of the preaching to save them that believe," I Cor. 1:20,21.

C. Denial of the existence of God in its various forms.

Students of Comparative Religion and missionaries often testify to the fact that the idea of God is practically universal in the human race. It is found even among the most uncivilized nations and tribes of the world. This does not mean, however, that there are no individuals who deny the existence of God altogether, nor even that there is not a goodly number in Christian lands who deny the existence of God as He is revealed in Scripture, a self-existent and self-conscious Person of infinite perfections, who works all things according to a pre-determined plan. It is the latter denial that we have in mind particularly here. This may and has assumed various forms in the course of history.

1. ABSOLUTE DENIAL OF THE EXISTENCE OF GOD. As stated above, there is strong evidence for the universal presence of the idea of God in the human mind, even among tribes which are uncivilized and have not felt the impact of special revelation. In view of this fact some go so far as to deny that there are people who deny the existence of God, real atheists; but this denial is contradicted by the facts. It is customary to distinguish two kinds, namely, practical and theoretical atheists. The former are simply godless persons, who in their practical life do not reckon with God, but live as if there were no God. The latter are, as a rule, of a more intellectual kind, and base their denial on a process of reasoning. They seek to prove by what seem to them conclusive rational arguments, that there is no God. In view of the *semen religionis* implanted in every man by his creation in the image of God, it is safe to assume that no one is born an atheist. In the last analysis atheism results from the perverted moral state of man and from his desire to escape from God. It is deliberately blind to and suppresses the most fundamental instinct of man, the deepest needs of the soul, the highest aspirations of the human spirit, and the longings of a heart that gropes after some higher Being. This practical or intellectual suppression of the operation of the *semen religionis* often involves prolonged and painful struggles.

There can be no doubt about the existence of practical atheists, since both Scripture and experience testify to it. Psalm 10:4b declares of the wicked, "All his thoughts are, There is no God." According to Ps. 14:1 "The fool hath said in his heart, There is no God." And Paul reminds the Ephesians that they were formerly "without God in the world," Eph. 2:12. Experience also testifies abundantly to their presence in the world. They are not necessarily notoriously wicked in the eyes of men, but may belong to the so-called "decent men of the world," though respectably indifferent to spiritual things. Such people are often quite conscious of the fact that they are out of harmony with God, dread to think of meeting Him, and try to forget about Him. They seem to take a secret delight in parading their atheism when they have smooth sailing, but have been known to get down on their knees for prayer when their life was suddenly endangered.

At the present time thousands of these practical atheists belong to the *American Association for the Advancement of Atheism.*

Theoretical atheists are of a different kind. They are usually of a more intellectual type and attempt to justify the assertion that there is no God by rational argumentation. Prof. Flint distinguishes three kinds of theoretical atheism, namely, (1) *dogmatic atheism,* which flatly denies that there is a Divine Being; (2) *sceptical atheism,* which doubts the ability of the human mind to determine, whether or not there is a God; and (3) *critical atheism,* which maintains that there is no valid proof for the existence of God. These often go hand in hand, but even the most modest of them really pronounces all belief in God a delusion.[1] In this division, it will be noticed, agnosticism also appears as a sort of atheism, a classification which many agnostics resent. But it should be borne in mind that agnosticism respecting the existence of God, while allowing the possibility of His reality, leaves us without an object of worship and adoration just as much as dogmatic atheism does. However the real atheist is the *dogmatic atheist,* the man who makes the positive assertion that there is no God. Such an assertion may mean one of two things: either that he recognizes no god of any kind, sets up no idol for himself, or that he does not recognize the God of Scripture. Now there are very few atheists who do not in practical life fashion some sort of god for themselves. There is a far greater number who theoretically set aside any and every god; and there is a still greater number that has broken with the God of Scripture. Theoretical atheism is generally rooted in some scientific or philosophical theory. Materialistic Monism in its various forms and atheism usually go hand in hand. Absolute subjective Idealism may still leave us the idea of God, but denies that there is any corresponding reality. To the modern Humanist "God" simply means "the Spirit of humanity," "the Sense of wholeness," "the Racial Goal" and other abstractions of that kind. Other theories not only leave room for God, but also pretend to maintain His existence, but certainly exclude the God of theism, a supreme personal Being, Creator, Preserver, and Ruler of the universe, distinct from His creation, and yet everywhere present in it. Pantheism merges the natural and supernatural, the finite and infinite, into one substance. It often speaks of God as the hidden ground of the phenomenal world, but does not conceive of Him as personal, and therefore as endowed with intelligence and will. It boldly declares that all is God, and thus engages in what Brightman calls "the expansion of God," so that we get "too much of God," seeing that He also includes all the evil of the world. It excludes the God of Scripture, and in so far is clearly atheistic. Spinoza may be called "the God-intoxicated man," but his God is certainly not the God whom Christians worship and adore. Surely, there can be no doubt about the presence of theoretical atheists in the world. When David Hume expressed doubt as to the existence of a dogmatic atheist, Baron d'Holbach replied, "My dear sir, you are at this moment sitting at table with seventeen such persons." They who are agnostic respecting the existence

1. *Anti-Theistic Theories,* p. 4 f.

of God may differ somewhat from the dogmatic atheist, but they, as well as the latter, leave us without a God.

2. PRESENT DAY FALSE CONCEPTIONS OF GOD INVOLVING A DENIAL OF THE TRUE GOD. There are several false conceptions of God current in our day, which involve a denial of the theistic conception of God. A brief indication of the most important of these must suffice in this connection.

a. *An immanent and impersonal God.* Theism has always believed in a God who is both transcendent and immanent. Deism removed God from the world, and stressed His transcendence at the expense of His immanence. Under the influence of Pantheism, however, the pendulum swung in the other direction. It identified God and the world, and did not recognize a Divine Being, distinct from, and infinitely exalted above, His creation. Through Schleiermacher the tendency to make God continuous with the world gained a footing in theology. He completely ignores the transcendent God, and recognizes only a God that can be known by human experience and manifests Himself in Christian consciousness as Absolute Causality, to which a feeling of absolute dependence corresponds. The attributes we ascribe to God are in this view merely symbolical expressions of the various modes of this feeling of dependence, subjective ideas without any corresponding reality. His earlier and his later representations of God seem to differ somewhat, and interpreters of Schleiermacher differ as to the way in which his statements must be harmonized. Brunner would seem to be quite correct, however, when he says that with him the universe takes the place of God, though the latter name is used; and that he conceives of God both as identical with the universe and as the unity lying behind it. It often seems as if his distinction between God and the world is only an ideal one, namely, the distinction between the world as a unity and the world in its manifold manifestations. He frequently speaks of God as the "Universum" or the "Welt-All," and argues against the personality of God; though, inconsistently, also speaking as if we could have communion with Him in Christ. These views of Schleiermacher, making God continuous with the world, largely dominated the theology of the past century, and it is this view that Barth is combatting with his strong emphasis on God as "the Wholly Other."

b. *A finite and personal God.* The idea of a finite god or gods is not new, but as old as Polytheism and Henotheism. The idea fits in with Pluralism, but not with philosophical Monism or theological Monotheism. Theism has always regarded God as an absolute personal Being of infinite perfections. During the nineteenth century, when monistic philosophy was in the ascendant, it became rather common to identify the God of theology with the Absolute of philosophy. Toward the end of the century, however, the term "Absolute," as a designation of God, fell into disfavor, partly because of its agnostic and pantheistic implications, and partly as the result of the opposition to the idea of the "Absolute" in philosophy, and of the desire to exclude all metaphysics from theology. Bradley regarded the God of the Christian religion as a part of the Absolute, and James pleaded for a conception of God that was more in harmony with human experience than the idea of an infinite God. He eliminates from God the metaphysical attributes of self-existence, infinity, and immutability, and makes the moral attributes supreme. God has an environment, exists in time, and works out a history just like ourselves. Because of the evil that is in the world, He must be thought of as limited in knowledge or power, or in both. The condition of the world makes it impossible to believe in a good God infinite in knowledge and power. The existence of a larger power which is friendly to man and with which he can commune meets all the practical needs and experiences of religion. James conceived of this power as personal, but was not willing to express himself as to whether he believed in one finite God or a number of them. Bergson added to this conception of James the idea of a struggling and growing God, constantly drawing upon his environment. Others who defended the idea of a finite God, though in different ways, are Hobhouse, Schiller, James Ward, Rashdall, and H. G. Wells.

c. *God as the personification of a mere abstract idea.* It has become quite the vogue in modern liberal theology to regard the name "God" as a mere symbol, standing for some cosmic process, some universal will or power, or some lofty and comprehensive ideal. The statement is repeatedly made that, if God once created man in His image, man is now returning the compliment by creating God in his (man's) image. It is said of Harry Elmer Barnes that he once said in one of his laboratory classes: "Gentlemen, we shall now proceed to create God." That was a very blunt expression of a rather common idea. Most of those who reject the theistic view of God still profess faith in God, but He is a God of their own imagination. The form which He assumes at any particular time depends, according to Shailer Mathews, on the thought patterns of that day. If in pre-war times the controlling pattern was that of an autocratic sovereign, demanding absolute obedience, now it is that of a democratic ruler eager to serve all his subjects. Since the days of Comte there has been a tendency to personify the social order of humanity as a whole and to worship this personification. The so-called Meliorists or Social Theologians reveal a tendency to identify God in some way with the social order. And the New Psychologists inform us that the idea of God is a projection of the human mind, which in its early stages is inclined to make images of its experiences and to clothe them with quasi-personality. Leuba is of the opinion that this illusion of God has served a useful purpose, but that the time is coming when the idea of God will be no more needed. A few definitions will serve to show the present day trend. "God is the immanent spirit of the community" (Royce). He is "that quality in human society which supports and enriches humanity in its spiritual quest" (Gerald Birney Smith). "God is the totality of relations constituting the whole social order of growing humanity" (E. S. Ames). "The word 'god' is a symbol to designate the universe in its ideal forming capacity" (G. B. Foster). "God is our conception, born of social experience, of the personality-evolving and personally responsive elements of our cosmic environment with which we are organically related" (Shailer Mathews). It need hardly be said that the God so defined is not a personal God and does not answer to the deepest needs of the human heart.

D. The So-called Rational Proofs for the Existence of God.

In course of time certain rational arguments for the existence of God were developed, and found a foothold in theology especially through the influence of Wolff. Some of these were in essence already suggested by Plato and Aristotle, and others were added in modern times by students of the Philosophy of Religion. Only the most common of these arguments can be mentioned here.

1. THE ONTOLOGICAL ARGUMENT. This has been presented in various forms by Anselm, Descartes, Samuel Clarke, and others. It has been stated in its most perfect form by Anselm. He argues that man has the idea of an absolutely perfect being; that existence is an attribute of perfection; and that therefore an absolutely perfect being must exist. But it is quite evident that we cannot conclude from abstract thought to real existence. The fact that we have an idea of God does not yet prove His objective existence. Moreover, this argument tacitly assumes, as already existing in the human mind, the very knowledge of God's existence which it would derive from logical demonstration. Kant stressed the untenableness of this argument, but Hegel hailed it as the one great argument for the existence of God. Some modern Idealists suggested that it might better be cast into a somewhat different form, which Hocking called "the report of experience." By virtue of it we can say, "I have an idea of God, therefore I have an experience of God."

2. THE COSMOLOGICAL ARGUMENT. This has also appeared in several forms. In general it runs as follows: Every existing thing in the world must have an adequate cause; and if this is so, the universe must also have an adequate cause, that is a cause which is indefinitely great. However, the argument did not carry general conviction. Hume called the law of causation itself in question, and Kant pointed out that, if every existing thing has an adequate cause, this also applies to God, and that we are thus led to an endless chain. Moreover, the argument does not necessitate the assumption that the cosmos had a single cause, a personal and absolute cause, — and therefore falls short of proving the existence of God. This difficulty led to a slightly different construction of the argument, as, for instance, by B. P. Bowne. The material universe appears as an interacting system, and therefore as a unit, consisting of several parts. Hence there must be a unitary Agent that mediates the interaction of the various parts or is the dynamic ground of their being.

3. THE TELEOLOGICAL ARGUMENT. This is also a causal argument, and is really but an extension of the preceding one. It may be stated in the following form: The world everywhere reveals intelligence, order, harmony, and purpose, and thus implies the existence of an intelligent and purposeful being, adequate to the production of such a world. Kant regards this argument as the best of the three which were named, but claims that it does not prove the existence of God, nor of a Creator, but only of a great architect who fashioned the world. It is superior to the cosmological argument in that it makes explicit

what is not stated in the latter, namely, that the world contains evidences of intelligence and purpose, and thus leads on to the existence of a conscious, and intelligent, and purposeful being. That this being was the Creator of the world does not necessarily follow. "The teleological evidence," says Wright,[1] "merely indicates the probable existence of a Mind that is, at least in considerable measure, in control of the world process, — enough to account for the amount of teleology apparent in it." Hegel treated this argument as a valid but subordinate one. The Social Theologians of our day reject it along with all the other arguments as so much rubbish, but the New Theists retain it.

4. THE MORAL ARGUMENT. Just as the other arguments, this too assumed different forms. Kant took his startingpoint in the categorical imperative, and from it inferred the existence of someone who, as lawgiver and judge, has the absolute right to command man. In his estimation this argument is far superior to any of the others. It is the one on which he mainly relies in his attempt to prove the existence of God. This may be one of the reasons why it is more generally recognized than any other, though it is not always cast into the same form. Some argue from the disparity often observed between the moral conduct of men and the prosperity which they enjoy in the present life, and feel that this calls for an adjustment in the future which, in turn, requires a righteous arbiter. Modern theology also uses it extensively, especially in the form that man's recognition of a Highest Good and his quest for a moral ideal demand and necessitate the existence of a God to give reality to that ideal. While this argument does point to the existence of a holy and just being, it does not compel belief in a God, a Creator, or a being of infinite perfections.

5. THE HISTORICAL OR ETHNOLOGICAL ARGUMENT. In the main this takes the following form: Among all the peoples and tribes of the earth there is a sense of the divine, which reveals itself in an external cultus. Since the phenomenon is universal, it must belong to the very nature of man. And if the nature of man naturally leads to religious worship, this can only find its explanation in a higher Being who has constituted man a religious being. In answer to this argument, however, it may be said that this universal phenomenon may have originated in an error or misunderstanding of one of the early progenitors of the human race, and that the religious cultus referred to appears strongest among primitive races, and disappears in the measure in which they become civilized.

In evaluating these rational arguments it should be pointed out first of all that believers do not need them. Their conviction respecting the existence of God does not depend on them, but on a believing acceptance of God's self-revelation in Scripture. If many in our day are willing to stake their faith in the existence of God on such rational arguments, it is to a great extent due to the fact that they refuse to accept the testimony of the Word of God. Moreover, in using these arguments in an attempt to convince unbelievers, it will be well to bear in mind that none of them can be said to carry absolute conviction. No

---

1. *A Student's Philosophy of Religion*, p. 341.

one did more to discredit them than Kant. Since his day many philosophers and theologians have discarded them as utterly worthless, but to-day they are once more gaining favor and their number is increasing. And the fact that in our day so many find in them rather satisfying indications of the existence of God, would seem to indicate that they are not entirely devoid of value. They have some value for believers themselves, but should be called *testimonia* rather than arguments. They are important as interpretations of God's general revelation and as exhibiting the reasonableness of belief in a divine Being. Moreover, they can render some service in meeting the adversary. While they do not prove the existence of God beyond the possibility of doubt, so as to compel assent, they can be so construed as to establish a strong probability and thereby silence many unbelievers.

QUESTIONS FOR FURTHER STUDY. Why is modern theology inclined to give the study of man rather than the study of God precedence in theology? Does the Bible prove the existence of God or does it not? If it does, how does it prove it? What accounts for the general *sensus divinitatis* in man? Are there nations or tribes that are entirely devoid of it? Can the position be maintained that there are no atheists? Should present day Humanists be classed as atheists? What objections are there to the identification of God with the Absolute of philosophy? Does a finite God meet the needs of the Christian life? Is the doctrine of a finite God limited to Pragmatists? Why is a personified idea of God a poor substitute for the living God? What was Kant's criticism on the arguments of speculative reason for the existence of God? How should we judge of this criticism?

LITERATURE: Bavinck, *Geref. Dogm.* II, pp. 52-74; Kuyper, *Dict. Dogm. De Deo* I, pp. 77-123; Hodge, *Syst. Theol.* I, pp. 202-243; Shedd. *Dogm. Theol.* I, pp. 221-248; Dabney, *Syst. and Polem. Theol.*, pp. 5-26; Macintosh, *Theol. as an Empirical Science*, pp. 90-99; Knudson, *The Doctrine of God*, pp. 203-241; Beattie, *Apologetics*, pp. 250-444; Brightman, *The Problem of God*, pp. 139-165; Wright, *A Student's Phil. of Rel.*, pp. 339-390; Edward, *The Philosophy of Rel.*, pp. 218-305; Beckwith, *The Idea of God*, pp. 64-115; Thomson, *The Christian Idea of God*, pp. 160-189; Robinson, *The God of the Liberal Christian*, pp. 114-149; Galloway, *The Phil. of Rel.*, pp. 381-394.

II. The Knowability of God

A. God Incomprehensible but yet Knowable.

The Christian Church confesses on the one hand that God is the Incomprehensible One, but also on the other hand, that He can be known and that knowledge of Him is an absolute requisite unto salvation. It recognizes the force of Zophar's question, "Canst thou by searching find out God? Canst thou find out the Almighty unto perfection?" Job 11:7. And it feels that it has no answer to the question of Isaiah, "To whom then will ye liken God? or what likeness will ye compare unto Him?" Isa. 40:18. But at the same time it is also mindful of Jesus' statement, "And this is life eternal, that they should know Thee, the only true God, and Him whom thou didst send, even Jesus Christ," John 17:3. It rejoices in the fact that "the Son of God is come, and hath given us an understanding, that we know Him that is true, and we are in Him that is true, even in His Son Jesus Christ." I John 5:20. The two ideas reflected in these passages were always held side by side in the Christian Church. The early Church Fathers spoke of the invisible God as an unbegotten, nameless, eternal, incomprehensible, unchangeable Being. They had advanced very little beyond the old Greek idea that the Divine Being is absolute attributeless existence. At the same time they also confessed that God revealed Himself in the Logos, and can therefore be known unto salvation. In the fourth century Eunomius, an Arian, argued from the simplicity of God, that there is nothing in God that is not perfectly known and comprehended by the human intellect, but his view was rejected by all the recognized leaders of the Church. The Scholastics distinguished between the *quid* and the *qualis* of God, and maintained that we do not know what God is in His essential Being, but can know something of His nature, of what He is to us, as He reveals Himself in His divine attributes. The same general ideas were expressed by the Reformers, though they did not agree with the Scholastics as to the possibility of acquiring real knowledge of God, by unaided human reason, from general revelation. Luther speaks repeatedly of God as the *Deus Absconditus* (hidden God), in distinction from Him as the *Deus Revelatus* (revealed God). In some passages he even speaks of the *revealed* God as still a *hidden* God in view of the fact that we cannot fully know Him even through His special revelation. To Calvin, God in the depths of His being is past finding out. "His essence," he says, "is incomprehensible; so that His divinity wholly escapes all human senses." The Reformers do not deny that man can learn something of the nature of God from His creation, but maintain that he can acquire true knowledge of Him only from special revelation, under the illuminating influence of the Holy Spirit. Under the influence of the pantheizing theology of immanence, inspired by Hegel and Schleiermacher, a change came about. The transcendence of God is soft-pedaled, ignored, or explicitly denied. God is brought down to the level of the world, is made continuous with it, and is therefore regarded as less incomprehensible, though still shrouded in mystery. Special revelation in the sense of a direct communication of God to man is denied. Sufficient knowledge of God can be obtained without it, since man can discover God for himself in the depths of his own being, in the material universe, and above all in Jesus Christ, since these are all but outward manifestations of the immanent God. It is over against this trend in theology that Barth now raises his voice and points out that God is not to be found in nature, in history, or in human experience of any kind, but only in the special revelation that has reached us in the Bible. In his strong statements respecting the hidden God he uses the language of Luther rather than of Calvin.

Reformed theology holds that God can be known, but that it is impossible for man to have a knowledge of Him that is exhaustive and perfect in every way. To have such a knowledge of God would be equivalent to comprehending Him, and this is entirely out of the question: *"Finitum non possit capere infinitum."* Furthermore, man cannot give a definition of God in the proper sense of the word, but only a partial description. A logical definition is impossible, because God cannot be subsumed under some higher genus. At the same time it is maintained that man can obtain a knowledge of God that is perfectly adequate for the realization of the divine purpose in the life of man. However, true knowledge of God can be acquired only from the divine self-revelation, and only by the man who accepts this with childlike faith. Religion necessarily presupposes such a knowledge. It is the most sacred relation between man and his God, a relation in which man is conscious of the absolute greatness and majesty of God as the supreme Being, and of his own utter insignificance and subjection to the High and Holy One. And if this is true, it follows that religion presupposes the knowledge of God in man. If man were left absolutely in the dark respecting the being of God, it would be impossible for him to assume a religious attitude. There could be no reverence, no piety, no fear of God, no worshipful service.

B. Denial of the Knowability of God.

The possibility of knowing God has been denied on various grounds. This denial is generally based on the supposed limits of the human faculty of cognition, though it has been presented in several different forms. The fundamental position is that the human mind is incapable of knowing anything of that which lies beyond and behind natural phenomena, and is therefore necessarily ignorant of supersensible and divine things. Huxley was the first to apply to those who assume this position, himself included, the name "agnostics." They are entirely in line with the sceptics of former centuries and of Greek philosophy. As a rule agnostics do not like to be branded as atheists, since they do not deny absolutely that there is a God, but declare that they do not know whether He exists or not, and even if He exists, are not certain that they have any true knowledge of Him, and in many cases even deny that they can have any real knowledge of Him.

Hume has been called the father of modern agnosticism. He did not deny the existence of God, but asserted that we have no true knowledge of His attributes. All our ideas of Him are, and can only be, anthropomorphic. We cannot be sure that there is any reality corresponding to the attributes we ascribe to Him. His agnosticism resulted from the general principle that all knowledge is based on experience. It was especially Kant, however, who stimulated agnostic thought by his searching inquiry into the limits of the human understanding and reason. He affirmed that the theoretical reason knows only phenomena and is necessarily ignorant of that which underlies these phenomena, — the thing in itself. From this it followed, of course, that it is impossible for us to have any theoretical knowledge of God. But Lotze already pointed out that phenomena, whether physical or mental, are always connected with some substance lying back of them, and that in knowing the phenomena we also know the underlying substance, of which they are manifestations. The Scotch philosopher, Sir William Hamilton, while not in entire agreement with Kant, yet shared the intellectual agnosticism of the latter. He asserts that the human mind knows only that which is conditioned and exists in various relations, and that, since the Absolute and Infinite is entirely unrelated, that is exists in no relations, we can obtain no knowledge of it. But while he denies that the Infinite can be known by us, he does not deny its existence. Says he, "Through faith we apprehend what is beyond our knowledge." His views were shared in substance by Mansel, and were popularized by him. To him also it seemed utterly impossible to conceive of an infinite Being, though he also professed faith in its existence. The reasoning of these two men did not carry conviction, since it was felt that the Absolute or Infinite does not *necessarily* exist outside of all relations, but can enter into various relations; and that the fact that we know things only in their relations does not mean that the knowledge so acquired is merely a relative or unreal knowledge.

Comte, the father of Positivism, was also agnostic in religion. According to him man can know nothing but physical phenomena and their laws. His senses are the sources of all true thinking, and he can know nothing except the phenomena which they apprehend and the relations in which these stand to each other. Mental phenomena can be reduced to material phenomena, and in science man cannot get beyond these. Even the phenomena of immediate consciousness are excluded, and further, everything that lies behind the phenomena. Theological speculation represents thought in its infancy. No positive affirmation can be made respecting the existence of God, and therefore both theism and atheism stand condemned. In later life Comte felt the need of some religion and introduced the so-called "religion of Humanity." Even more than Comte, Herbert Spencer is recognized as the great exponent of modern scientific agnosticism. He was influenced very much by Hamilton's doctrine of the relativity of knowledge and by Mansel's conception of the Absolute, and in the light of these worked out his doctrine of the Unknowable, which was his designation of whatever may be absolute, first or ultimate in the order of the universe, including God. He proceeds on the assumption that there is some reality lying back of phenomena, but maintains that all reflection on it lands us in contradictions. This ultimate reality is utterly inscrutable. While we must accept·the existence of some ultimate Power, either personal or impersonal, we can form no conception of it. Inconsistently he devotes a great part of his *First Principles* to the development of the positive content of the Unknowable, as if it were well known indeed. Other agnostics, who were influenced by him, are such men as Huxley, Fiske, and Clifford. We meet with agnosticism also repeatedly in modern Humanism. Harry Elmer Barnes says: "To the writer it seems quite obvious that the agnostic position is the only one which can be supported by any scientifically-minded and critically-inclined person in the present state of knowledge."[1]

Besides the forms indicated in the preceding the agnostic argument has assumed several others, of which the following are some of the most important. (1) *Man knows only by analogy.* We know only that which bears some analogy to our own nature or experience: "*Similia similibus percipiuntur.*" But while it is true that we learn a great deal by analogy, we also learn by contrast. In many cases the differences are the very things that arrest our attention. The Scholastics spoke of the *via negationis* by which they in thought eliminated from God the imperfections of the creature. Moreover, we should not forget that man is made in the image of God, and that there are important analogies between the divine nature and the nature of man. (2) *Man really knows only what he can grasp in its entirety.* Briefly stated the position is that man cannot comprehend God, who is infinite, cannot have an exhaustive knowledge of Him, and therefore cannot know Him. But this position proceeds on the unwarranted assumption that partial knowledge cannot be real knowledge, an assumption which would really invalidate all our knowledge, since it always falls far short of completeness. Our knowledge of God, though not exhaustive, may yet be very real and perfectly adequate for our present needs. (3) *All predicates of God are negative and therefore furnish no real knowledge.* Hamilton says that the Absolute and the Infinite can only be conceived as a negation of the thinkable; which really means that we can have no conception of them at all. But though it is true that much of what we predicate to God is negative in form, this does not mean that it may not at the same time convey some positive idea. The aseity of God includes the positive idea of his self-existence and self-sufficiency. Moreover, such ideas as love, spirituality, and holiness, are positive. (4) *All our knowledge is relative to the knowing subject.* It is said that we know the objects of knowledge, not as they are objectively, but only as they are related to our senses and faculties. In the process of knowledge we distort and colour them. In a sense it is perfectly true that all our knowledge is subjectively conditioned,

---

1. *The Twilight of Christianity*, p. 260.

but the import of the assertion under consideration seems to be that, because we know things only through the mediation of our senses and faculties, we do not know them as they are. But this is not true; in so far as we have any real knowledge of things, that knowledge corresponds to the objective reality. The laws of perception and thought are not arbitrary, but correspond to the nature of things. Without such correspondence, not only the knowledge of God, but all true knowledge would be utterly impossible.

Some are inclined to look upon the position of Barth as a species of agnosticism. Zerbe says that practical agnosticism dominates Barth's thinking and renders him a victim of the Kantian unknowableness of the Thing-in-Itself, and quotes him as follows: "*Romans* is a revelation of the unknown God; God comes to man, not man to God. *Even after the revelation man cannot know God*, for He is always the unknown God. In manifesting Himself to us He is farther away than ever before. (Rbr. p. 53)".[1] At the same time he finds Barth's agnosticism, like that of Herbert Spencer, inconsistent. Says he: "It was said of Herbert Spencer that he knew a great deal about the 'Unknowable'; so of Barth, one wonders how he came to know so much of the 'Unknown God'."[2] Dickie speaks in a similar vein: "In speaking of a transcendent God, Barth seems sometimes to be speaking of a God of Whom we can never know anything."[3] He finds, however, that in this respect too there has been a change of emphasis in Barth. While it is perfectly clear that Barth does not mean to be an agnostic, it cannot be denied that some of his statements can readily be interpreted as having an agnostic flavor. He strongly stresses the fact that God is the hidden God, who cannot be known from nature, history, or experience, but only by His self-revelation in Christ, when it meets with the response of faith. But even in this revelation God appears only as the hidden God. God reveals Himself exactly as the hidden God, and through His revelation makes us more conscious of the distance which separates Him from man than we ever were before. This can easily be interpreted to mean that we learn by revelation merely that God cannot be known, so that after all we are face to face with an unknown God. But in view of all that Barth has written this is clearly not what he wants to say. His assertion, that in the light of revelation we see God as the hidden God, does not exclude the idea that by revelation we also acquire a great deal of useful knowledge of God as He enters into relations with His people. When He says that even in His revelation God still remains for us *the unknown God*, he really means, *the incomprehensible God*. The revealing God is God in action. By His revelation we learn to know Him in His operations, but acquire no real knowledge of His inner being. The following passage in *The Doctrine of the Word of God*,[4] is rather illuminating: "On this freedom (freedom of God) rests the *inconceivability* of God, the inadequacy of all knowledge of the revealed God. Even the three-in-oneness of God is revealed to us only in God's opera-

1. *The Karl Barth Theology*, p. 82.
2. *Ibid*, p. 84.
3. *Revelation and Response*, p. 187.
4. p. 426.

tions. Therefore the three-in-oneness of God is also inconceivable to us. Hence, too, the inadequacy of all our knowledge of the three-in-oneness. The conceivability with which it has appeared to us, primarily in Scripture, secondarily in the Church doctrine of the Trinity, is a creaturely conceivability. To the conceivability in which God exists for Himself it is not only relative: it is absolutely separate from it. Only upon the free grace of revelation does it depend that the former conceivability, in its absolute separation from its object, is yet not without truth. In this sense the three-in-oneness of God, as we know it from the operation of God, is truth."

C. Self-revelation the Prerequisite of all Knowledge of God.

1. GOD COMMUNICATES KNOWLEDGE OF HIMSELF TO MAN. Kuyper calls attention to the fact that theology as the knowledge of God differs in an important point from all other knowledge. In the study of all other sciences man places himself *above* the object of his investigation and *actively* elicits from it his knowledge by whatever method may seem most appropriate. but in theology he does not stand above but rather *under* the object of his knowledge. In other words, man can know God only in so far as the latter actively makes Himself known. God is first of all the subject communicating knowledge to man, and can only become an object of study for man in so far as the latter appropriates and reflects on the knowledge conveyed to him by revelation. Without revelation man would never have been able to acquire any knowledge of God. And even after God has revealed Himself objectively, it is not human reason that discovers God, but it is God who discloses Himself to the eye 'of faith. However, by the application of sanctified human reason to the study of God's Word man can. under the guidance of the Holy Spirit, gain an ever-increasing knowledge of God. Barth also stresses the fact that man can know God only when God comes to him in an act of revelation. He asserts that there is no way from man to God, but only from God to man, and says repeatedly that God is always the subject, and never an object. Revelation is always something purely subjective, and can never turn into something objective like the written Word of Scripture, and as such become an object of study. It is given once for all in Jesus Christ, and in Christ comes to men in the existential moment of their lives. While there are elements of truth in what Barth says, his construction of the doctrine of revelation is foreign to Reformed theology.

The position must be maintained, however, that theology would be utterly impossible without a self-revelation of God. And when we speak of revelation, we use the term in the strict sense of the word. It is not something in which God is passive, a mere "becoming manifest," but something in which He is actively making Himself known. It is not, as many moderns would have it, a deepened spiritual insight which leads to an ever-increasing discovery of God on the part of man; but a supernatural act of self-communication, a purposeful act on the part of the Living God. There is nothing surprising in the fact that God can be known only if. and in so far as, He reveals Himself. In a measure this is also true of man. Even after Psychology has made a rather exhaustive study of man, Alexis Carrell is still able to write a very convincing book on *Man the Unknown*. "For who among men," says Paul, "knoweth the things of a man, save the spirit of the man, which is in him? even so the things of God none knoweth, save the Spirit of God." I Cor. 2:11. The Holy Spirit searcheth all things, even the deep things of God, and reveals them unto man. God has made Himself known. Alongside of the archetypal knowledge of God, found in God Himself, there is also an ectypal knowledge of Him, given to man by revelation. The latter is related to the former as a copy is to the original, and therefore does not possess the same measure of clearness and perfection. All our knowledge of God is derived from His self-revelation in nature and in Scripture. Consequently, our knowledge of God is on the one hand ectypal and analogical, but on the other hand also true and accurate, since it is a copy of the archetypal knowledge which God has of Himself.

2. INNATE AND ACQUIRED KNOWLEDGE OF GOD (COGNITIO INSITA AND ACQUISTA). A distinction is usually made between innate and acquired knowledge of God. This is not a strictly logical distinction, because in the last analysis all human knowledge is acquired. The doctrine of innate ideas is philosophical rather than theological. The seeds of it are already found in Plato's doctrine of ideas, while it occurs in Cicero's *De Natura Deorum* in a more developed form. In modern philosophy it was taught first of all by Descartes, who regarded the idea of God as innate. He did not deem it necessary to consider this as innate in the sense that it was consciously present in the human mind from the start, but only in the sense that man has a natural tendency to form the idea when the mind reaches maturity. The doctrine finally assumed the form that there are certain ideas, of which the idea of God is the most prominent, which are inborn and are therefore present in human consciousness from birth. It was in this form that Locke rightly attacked the doctrine of innate ideas, though he went to another extreme in his philosophical empiricism. Reformed theology also rejected the doctrine in that particular form. And while some of its representatives retained the name "innate ideas," but gave it another connotation, others preferred to speak of a *cognitio Dei insita* (ingrafted or implanted knowledge of God). On the one hand this *cognitio Dei insita* does not consist in any ideas or formed notions which are present in man at the time of his birth; but on the other hand it is more than a mere capacity which enables man to know God. It denotes a knowledge that necessarily results from the constitution of the human mind, that is inborn only in the sense that it is acquired spontaneously, under the influence of the *semen religionis* implanted in man by his creation in the image of God, and that is not acquired by the laborious process of reasoning and argumentation. It is a knowledge which man, constituted as he is, acquires *of necessity*, and as such is distinguished from all knowledge that is conditioned by the will of man. Acquired knowledge, on the other hand, is obtained by the study of God's revelation. It does not arise spontaneously in the human mind, but results from the conscious and sustained pursuit of

knowledge. It can be acquired only by the wearisome process of perception and reflection, reasoning and argumentation. Under the influence of the Hegelian Idealism and of the modern view of evolution the innate knowledge of God has been over-emphasized; Barth on the other hand denies the existence of any such knowledge.

3. GENERAL AND SPECIAL REVELATION. The Bible testifies to a twofold revelation of God: a revelation in nature round about us, in human conscious- ness, and in the providential government of the world; and a revelation embodied in the Bible as the Word of God. It testifies to the former in such passages as the following: "The heavens declare the glory of God; and the firmanent showeth His handiwork. Day unto day uttereth speech, and night unto night showeth knowledge," Ps. 19:1,2. "And yet He left not Himself without witness, in that He did good and gave you from heaven rains and fruitful seasons, filling your hearts with food and gladness," Acts 14:17. "Because that which is known of God is manifest in them; for God manifested it unto them. For the invisible things of Him since the creation of the world are clearly seen, being perceived through the things that are made, even His everlasting power and divinity," Rom. 1:19, 20. Of the latter it gives abundant evidence in both the Old and the New Testament. "Yet Jehovah testified unto Israel, and unto Judah, by every prophet, and every seer, saying, Turn ye from your evil ways, and keep my commandments and my statutes, according to all the law which I commanded your fathers, and which I sent to you by my servants the prophets," I Kings 17:13. "He hath made known His ways unto Moses, His doings unto the children of Israel," Ps. 103:7. "No man hath seen God at any time; the only begotten Son, who is in the bosom of the Father, He hath declared Him," John 1:18. "God, having of old time spoken unto the fathers in the prophets by divers portions and in divers manners, hath at the end of these days spoken to us in His Son," Heb. 1:1,2.

On the basis of these scriptural data it became customary to speak of natural and supernatural revelation. The distinction thus applied to the idea of revela- tion is primarily a distinction based on the manner in which it is communicated to man; but in the course of history it has also been based in part on the nature of its subject-matter. The mode of revelation is natural when it is communicated through nature, that is, through the visible creation with its ordinary laws and powers. It is supernatural when it is communicated to man in a higher, super- natural manner, as when God speaks to him, either directly, or through super- naturally endowed messengers. The substance of revelation was regarded as natural, if it could be acquired by human reason from the study of nature; and was considered to be supernatural when it could not be known from nature, nor by unaided human reason. Hence it became quite common in the Middle Ages to contrast reason and revelation. In Protestant theology natural revelation was often called a *revelatio realis*, and supernatural revelation a *revelatio verbalis*, because the former is embodied in things, and the latter in words. In course of time, however, the distinction between natural and supernatural revelation was found to be rather ambiguous, since all revelation is supernatural in origin and, as a revelation of God, also in content. Ewald in his work on *Revelation: its Nature and Record*[1] speaks of the revelation in nature as *immediate* revelation, and of the revelation in Scripture, which he regards as the only one deserving the name "revelation" in the fullest sense, as *mediate revelation*. A more common distinction, however, which gradually gained currency, is that of *general* and *special* revelation. Dr. Warfield distinguishes the two as follows: "The one is addressed generally to all intelligent creatures, and is therefore accessible to all men; the other is addressed to a special class of sinners, to whom God would make known His salvation. The one has in view to meet and supply the natural need of creatures for knowledge of their God; the other to rescue broken and deformed sinners from their sin and its consequences."[2] General revelation is rooted in creation, is addressed to man as man, and more particularly to human reason, and finds its purpose in the realization of the end of his creation, to know God and thus enjoy communion with Him. Special revelation is rooted in the redemptive plan of God, is addressed to man as sinner, can be properly understood and appropriated only by faith, and serves the purpose of securing the end for which man was created in spite of the disturbance wrought by sin. In view of the eternal plan of redemption it should be said that this special revelation did not come in as an after-thought, but was in the mind of God from the very beginning.

There was considerable difference of opinion respecting the relation of these two to each other. According to Scholasticism natural revelation provided the necessary data for the construction of a scientific natural theology by human reason. But while it enabled man to attain to a scientific knowledge of God as the ultimate cause of all things, it did not provide for the knowledge of the mysteries, such as the Trinity, the incarnation, and redemption. This knowledge is supplied by special revelation. It is a knowledge that is not rationally demonstrable but must be accepted by faith. Some of the earlier Scholastics were guided by the slogan "Credo ut intelligam," and, after accepting the truths of special revelation by faith, considered it necessary to raise faith to understanding by a rational demonstration of those truths, or at least to prove their rationality. Thomas Aquinas, however, considered this impossible, except in so far as special revelation contained truths which also formed a part of natural revelation. In his opinion the mysteries, which formed the real contents of supernatural revelation, did not admit of any logical demonstration. He held, however, that there could be no conflict between the truths of natural and those of supernatural revelation. If there appears to be a conflict, there is something wrong with one's philosophy. The fact remains, however, that he recognized, besides the structure reared by faith on the basis of supernatural revelation, a system of scientific theology on the foundation of natural revelation. In the former one assents to something because it is revealed, in the latter because it

1. p. 5 f.
2. *Revelation and Inspiration*, p. 6.

is perceived as true in the light of natural reason. The logical demonstration, which is out of the question in the one, is the natural method of proof in the other.

The Reformers rejected the dualism of the Scholastics and aimed at a synthesis of God's twofold revelation. They did not believe in the ability of human reason to construct a scientific system of theology on the basis of natural revelation pure and simple. Their view of the matter may be represented as follows: As a result of the entrance of sin into the world, the handwriting of God in nature is greatly obscured, and is in some of the most important matters rather dim and illegible. Moreover, man is stricken with spiritual blindness, and is thus deprived of the ability to read aright what God had originally plainly written in the works of creation. In order to remedy the matter and to prevent the frustration of His purpose, God did two things. In His supernatural revelation He republished the truths of natural revelation, cleared them of misconception, interpreted them with a view to the present needs of man, and thus incorporated them in His supernatural revelation of redemption. And in addition to that He provided a cure for the spiritual blindness of man in the work of regeneration and sanctification, including spiritual illumination, and thus enabled man once more to obtain true knowledge of God, the knowledge that carries with it the assurance of eternal life.

When the chill winds of Rationalism swept over Europe, natural revelation was exalted at the expense of supernatural revelation. Man became intoxicated with a sense of his own ability and goodness, refused to listen and submit to the voice of authority that spoke to him in Scripture, and reposed complete trust in the ability of human reason to lead him out of the labyrinth of ignorance and error into the clear atmosphere of true knowledge. Some who maintained that natural revelation was quite sufficient to teach men all necessary truths, still admitted that they might learn them sooner with the aid of supernatural revelation. Others denied that the authority of supernatural revelation was complete, until its contents had been demonstrated by reason. And finally Deism in some of its forms denied, not only the necessity, but also the possibility and reality of supernatural revelation. In Schleiermacher the emphasis shifts from the objective to the subjective, from revelation to religion, and that without any distinction between natural and revealed religion. The term "revelation" is still retained, but is reserved as a designation of the deeper spiritual insight of man, an insight which does not come to him, however, without his own diligent search. What is called revelation from one point of view, may be called human discovery from another. This view has become quite characteristic of modern theology. Says Knudson: "But this distinction between natural and revealed theology has now largely fallen into disuse. The present tendency is to draw no sharp line of distinction between revelation and the natural reason, but to look upon the highest insights of reason as themselves divine revelations. In any case there is no fixed body of revealed truth, accepted on authority, that stands opposed to the truths of reason. All truth to-day rests on its power of appeal to the human mind."[1]

It is this view of revelation that is denounced in the strongest terms by Barth. He is particularly interested in the subject of revelation, and wants to lead the Church back from the subjective to the objective, from religion to revelation. In the former he sees primarily man's efforts to find God, and in the latter "God's search for man" in Jesus Christ. Barth does not recognize any revelation in nature. Revelation never exists on any horizontal line, but always comes down perpendicularly from above. Revelation is always God in action, God speaking, bringing something entirely new to man, something of which he could have no previous knowledge, and which becomes a real revelation only for him who accepts the object of revelation by a God-given faith. Jesus Christ is the revelation of God, and only he who knows Jesus Christ knows anything about revelation at all. Revelation is an act of grace, by which man becomes conscious of his sinful condition, but also of God's free, unmerited, and forgiving condescension in Jesus Christ. Barth even calls it *the reconciliation.* Since God is always sovereign and free in His revelation, it can never assume a factually present, objective form with definite limitations, to which man can turn at any time for instruction. Hence it is a mistake to regard the Bible as God's revelation in any other than a secondary sense. It is a witness to, and a token of, God's revelation. The same may be said, though in a subordinate sense, of the preaching of the gospel. But through whatever mediation the word of God may come to man in the existential moment of his life, it is always recognized by man as a word· directly spoken to him, and coming perpendicularly from above. This recognition is effected by a special operation of the Holy Spirit, by what may be called an individual *testimonium Spiritus Sancti.* The revelation of .God was given *once for all* in Jesus Christ: not in His historical appearance, but in the superhistorical in which the powers of the eternal world become evident, such as His incarnation and His death and resurrection. And if His revelation is also continuous — as it is —, it is such only in the sense that God continues to speak to individual sinners, in the existential moment of their lives, through the revelation in Christ, mediated by the Bible and by preaching. Thus we are left with mere flashes of revelation coming to individuals, of which only those individuals have absolute assurance; and fallible witnesses to, or tokens of, the revelation in Jesus Christ, — a rather precarious foundation for theology. It is no wonder that Barth is in doubt as to the possibility of constructing a doctrine of God. Mankind is not in possession of any infallible revelation of God, and of His unique revelation in Christ and its extension in the special revelations that come to certain men it has knowledge only through the testimony of fallible witnesses.

---

1. *The Doctrine of God,* p. 173.

QUESTIONS FOR FURTHER STUDY: In what sense can we speak of the hidden or unknown God in spite of the fact that He has revealed Himself? How did the Scholastics and the Reformers differ on this point? What is the position of modern theology? Why is revelation essential to religion? How does agnosticism differ theoretically from atheism? Is the one more favorable to religion than the other? How did Kant promote agnosticism? What was

Sir William Hamilton's doctrine of the relativity of knowledge? What form did agnosticism take in Positivism? What other forms did it take? Why do some speak of Barth as an agnostic? How should this charge be met? Is "revelation" an active or a passive concept? Is theology possible without revelation? If not, why not? Can the doctrine of innate ideas be defended? What is meant by "cognitio Dei insita?" How do natural and supernatural revelation differ? Is the distinction between general and special revelation an exact parallel of the preceding one? What different views were held as to the relation between the two? How does revelation differ from human discovery? Does Barth believe in general revelation? How does he conceive of special revelation?

LITERATURE: Bavinck, *Geref. Dogm.* II, pp. 1:74; Kuyper, *Dict. Dogm., De Deo* I, pp. 1-76; Hodge, *Syst. Theol.* I, pp. 191-240; 335-365; Shedd, *Dogm. Theol.* I, pp. 195-220; Thornwell, *Collected Works* I, pp. 74-142; Dorner, *System of Chr. Doct.*, I, pp. 79-159; Adeney, *The Christian Conception of God*, pp. 19-57; Steenstra, *The Being of God as Unity and Trinity*, pp. 1-25; Hendry, *God the Creator*; Gilson, *Reason and Revelation in the Middle Ages;* Baillie and Martin, *Revelation* (a *Symposium of Aulen, Barth, Bulgakoff, D'Arcy, Eliot, Horton, and Temple;* Warfield, *Revelation and Inspiration*, pp. 3-48; Orr, *Revelation and Inspiration*, pp.1-66; Camfield, *Revelation and the Holy Spirit*, pp. 11-127; Dickie, *Revelation and Response*, Warfield, *Calvin and Calvinism* (*Calvin's Doctrine of the Knowledge of God*).

III. Relation of the Being and Attributes of God

Some dogmaticians devote a separate chapter or chapters to the Being of God, before taking up the discussion of His attributes. This is done, for instance, in the works of Mastricht, Ebrard, Kuyper, and Shedd. Others prefer to consider the Being of God in connection with His attributes in view of the fact that it is in these that He has revealed Himself. This is the more common method, which is followed in the *Synopsis Purioris Theologiae*, and in the works of Turretin, à Marck, Brakel, Bavinck, Hodge, and Honig. This difference of treatment is not indicative of any serious fundamental disagreement between them. They are all agreed that the attributes are not mere names to which no reality corresponds, nor separate parts of a composite God, but essential qualities in which the Being of God is revealed and with which it can be identified. The only difference would seem to be that some seek to distinguish between the Being and the attributes of God more than others do.

A. The Being of God.

It is quite evident that the Being of God does not admit of any scientific definition. In order to give a logical definition of God, we would have to begin by going in search of some higher concept, under which God could be co-ordinated with other concepts; and would then have to point out the characteristics that would be applicable to God only. Such a *genetic-synthetic* definition cannot be given of God, since God is not one of several species of gods, which can be subsumed under a single genus. At most only an *analytical-descriptive* definition is possible. This merely names the characteristics of a person or thing, but leaves the essential being unexplained. And even such a definition cannot be complete but only partial, because it is impossible to give an exhaustive positive (as opposed to negative) description of God. It would consist in an enumeration of all the known attributes of God, and these are to a great extent negative in character.

The Bible never operates with an abstract concept of God, but always describes Him as the Living God, who enters into various relations with His creatures, relations which are indicative of several different attributes. In Kuyper's *Dictaten Dogmatiek*[1] we are told that God, personified as Wisdom, speaks of His *essence* in Prov. 8:14, when He ascribes to Himself *tushiyyach*, a Hebrew word rendered "wezen" in the Holland translation. But this rendering is very doubtful, and the English rendering "counsel" deserves preference. It has also been pointed out that the Bible speaks of the *nature* of God in II Pet. 1:4, but this can hardly refer to the essential Being of God, for

---

1. *De Deo* I, p. 28.

41

we are not made partakers of the divine essence. An indication of the very essence of God has been found in the name Jehovah, as interpreted by God Himself, "I am that I am." On the basis of this passage the essence of God was found in being itself, abstract being. And this has been interpreted to mean self-existence or self-contained permanence or absolute independence. Another passage is repeatedly quoted as containing an indication of the essence of God, and as the closest approach to a definition that is found in the Bible, namely, John 4:24, "God is Spirit: and they that worship Him must worship in spirit and truth." This statement of Christ is clearly indicative of the spirituality of God. The two ideas derived from these passages occur repeatedly in theology as designations of the very Being of God. On the whole it may be said that Scripture does not exalt one attribute of God at the expense of the others, but represents them as existing in perfect harmony in the Divine Being. It may be true that now one, and then another attribute is stressed, but Scripture clearly intends to give due emphasis to every one of them. The Being of God is characterized by a depth, a fullness, a variety, and a glory far beyond our comprehension, and the Bible represents it as a glorious harmonious whole, without any inherent contradictions. And this fullness of life finds expression in no other way than in the perfections of God.

Some of the early Church Fathers were clearly under the influence of Greek philosophy in their doctrine of God and, as Seeberg expresses it, did not advance "beyond the mere abstract conception that the Divine Being is absolute attributeless Existence." For some time theologians were rather generally inclined to emphasize the transcendence of God, and to assume the impossibility of any adequate knowledge or definition of the divine essence. During the trinitarian controversy the distinction between the one essence and the three persons in the Godhead was strongly emphasized, but the essence was generally felt to be beyond human comprehension. Gregory of Nazianze, however, ventures to say: "So far as we can discern, *ho on* and *ho theos* are somehow more than other terms the names of the (divine) essence, and of these *ho on* is the preferable." He regards this as a description of absolute being. Augustine's conception of the essence of God was closely akin to that of Gregory. In the Middle Ages too there was a tendency, either to deny that man has any knowledge of the essence of God, or to reduce such knowledge to a minimum. In some cases one attribute was singled out as most expressive of the essence of God. Thus Thomas Aquinas spoke of His aseity or self-existence, and Duns Scotus, of His infinity. It became quite common also to speak of God as *actus purus* in view of His simplicity. The Reformers and their successors also spoke of the essence of God as incomprehensible, but they did not exclude all knowledge of it, though Luther used very strong language on this point. They stressed the unity, simplicity, and spirituality of God. The words of the Belgic Confession are quite characteristic: "We all believe with the heart, and confess with the mouth, that there is one only simple and spiritual Being, which we call God."[1] Later on philosophers

---

1. Art. I.

and theologians found the essence of God in abstract being, in universal substance, in pure thought, in absolute causality, in love, in personality, and in majestic holiness or the numinous.

B. The Possibility of Knowing the Being of God.

From the preceding it already appears that the question as to the possibility of knowing God in His essential Being engaged the best minds of the Church from the earliest centuries. And the consensus of opinion in the early Church, during the Middle Ages, and at the time of the Reformation, was that God in His inmost Being is the Incomprehensible One. And in some cases the language used is so strong that it seemingly allows of no knowledge of the Being of God whatsoever. At the same time they who use it, at least in some cases, seem to have considerable knowledge of the Being of God. Misunderstanding can easily result from a failure to understand the exact question under consideration, and from neglecting to discriminate between "knowing" and "comprehending." The Scholastics spoke of three questions to which all the speculations respecting the Divine Being could be reduced, namely: *An sit Deus? Quid sit Deus?* and *Qualis sit Deus?* The first question concerns the existence of God, the second, His nature or essence, and the third, His attributes. In this paragraph it is particularly the second question that calls for attention. The question then is, What is God? What is the nature of His inner constitution? What makes Him to be what He is? In order to answer that question adequately, we would have to be able to comprehend God and to offer a satisfactory explanation of His Divine Being, and this is utterly impossible. The finite cannot comprehend the Infinite. The question of Zophar, "Canst thou by searching find out God? Canst thou find out the Almighty unto perfection?" (Job 11:7) has the force of a strong negative. And if we consider the second question entirely apart from the third, our negative answer becomes even more inclusive. Apart from the revelation of God in His attributes, we have no knowledge of the Being of God whatsoever. But in so far as God reveals Himself in His attributes, we also have some knowledge of His Divine Being, though even so our knowledge is subject to human limitations.

Luther uses some very strong expressions respecting our inability to know something of the Being or essence of God. On the one hand he distinguishes between the *Deus absconditus* (hidden God) and the *Deus revelatus* (revealed God); but on the other hand he also asserts that in knowing the *Deus revelatus*, we only know Him in his hiddenness. By this he means that even in His revelation God has not manifested Himself entirely *as He is essentially*, but as to His essence still remains shrouded in impenetrable darkness. We know God only in so far as He enters into relations with us. Calvin too speaks of the Divine essence as incomprehensible. He holds that God in the depths of His Being is past finding out. Speaking of the knowledge of the *quid* and of the *qualis* of God, he says that it is rather useless to speculate about the former, while our practical interest lies in the latter. Says he: "They are merely toying with frigid speculations whose mind is set on the question of what God is (*quid sit Deus*), when what it really concerns us to know is rather what kind of a person He is (*qualis sit*) and what is appropriate to His nature."[1] While he feels that God cannot be known to perfection, he does not deny that we can know something of His Being or nature. But this knowledge cannot be obtained by *a priori* methods, but only in an *a posteriori* manner through the attributes, which he regards as real determinations of the nature of God. They convey to us at least some knowledge of what God is, but especially of what He is in relation to us.

In dealing with our knowledge of the Being of God we must certainly avoid the position of Cousin, rather rare in the history of philosophy, that God even in the depths of His Being is not at all incomprehensible but essentially intelligible; but we must also steer clear of the agnosticism of Hamilton and Mansel, according to which we can have no knowledge whatsoever of the Being of God. We cannot comprehend God, cannot have an absolute and exhaustive knowledge of Him, but we can undoubtedly have a relative or partial knowledge of the Divine Being. It is perfectly true that this knowledge of God is possible only, because He has placed Himself in certain relations to His moral creatures and has revealed Himself to them, and that even this knowledge is humanly conditioned; but it is nevertheless real and true knowledge, and is at least a partial knowledge of the absolute nature of God. There is a difference between an absolute knowledge, and a relative or partial knowledge of an absolute being. It will not do at all to say that man knows only the relations in which God stands to His creatures. It would not even be possible to have a proper conception of these relations without knowing something of both God and man. To say that we can know nothing of the Being of God, but can know only relations, is equivalent to saying that we cannot know Him at all and cannot make Him the object of our religion. Dr. Orr says: "We may not know God in the depths of His absolute being. But we can at least know Him in so far as He reveals Himself in His relation to us. The question, therefore, is not as to the possibility of a knowledge of God in the unfathomableness of His being, but is: Can we know God *as He enters into relations* with the world and with ourselves? God has entered into relations with us in His revelations of Himself, and supremely in Jesus Christ; and we Christians humbly claim that through this Self-revelation we do know God to be the true God, and have real acquaintance with His character and will. Neither is it correct to say that this knowledge which we have of God is only a *relative knowledge*. It is in part a knowledge of the *absolute* nature of God as well."[2] The last statements are probably intended to ward off the idea that all our knowledge of God is merely relative to the human mind, so that we have no assurance that it corresponds with the reality as it exists in God.

C. The Being of God Revealed in His Attributes.

From the simplicity of God it follows that God and His attributes are one. The attributes cannot be considered as so many parts that enter into the com-

1. *Inst.* I. 2.2.
2. *Side-Lights on Christian Doctrine*, p. 11.

position of God, for God is not, like men, composed of different parts. Neither can they be regarded as something added to the Being of God, though the name, derived from *ad* and *tribuere*, might seem to point in that direction, for no addition was ever made to the Being of God, who is eternally perfect. It is commonly said in theology that God's attributes are God Himself, as He has revealed Himself to us. The Scholastics stressed the fact that God is, all that He has. He *has* life, light, wisdom, love, righteousness, and it may be said on the basis of Scripture that He *is* life, light, wisdom, love, and righteousness. It was further asserted by the Scholastics that the whole essence of God is identical with each one of the attributes, so that God's knowing is God, God's willing is God, and so on. Some of them even went so far as to say that each attribute is identical with every other attribute, and that there are no logical distinctions in God. This is a very dangerous extreme. While it may be said that there is an interpenetration of the attributes in God, and that they form a harmonious whole, we are moving in the direction of Pantheism, when we rule out all distinctions in God, and say that His self-existence is His infinity, His knowing is His willing, His love is His righteousness, and vice versa. It was characteristic of the Nominalists that they obliterated all real distinctions in God. They were afraid that by assuming real distinctions in Him, corresponding to the attributes ascribed to God, they would endanger the unity and simplicity of God, and were therefore motivated by a laudable purpose. According to them the perfections of the Divine Being exist only in our thoughts, without any corresponding reality in the Divine Being. The Realists, on the other hand, asserted the reality of the divine perfections. They realized that the theory of the Nominalists, consistently carried out, would lead in the direction of a pantheistic denial of a personal God, and therefore considered it of the utmost importance to maintain the objective reality of the attributes in God. At the same time they sought to safeguard the unity and simplicity of God by maintaining that the whole essence is in each attribute: God is All in all, All in each. Thomas Aquinas had the same purpose in mind, when he asserted that the attributes do not reveal what God is in Himself, in the depths of His Being, but only what He is in relation to His creatures.

Naturally, we should guard against separating the divine essence and the divine attributes or perfections, and also against a false conception of the relation in which they stand to each other. The attributes are real determinations of the Divine Being or, in other words, qualities that inhere in the Being of God. Shedd speaks of them as "an analytical and closer description of the essence."[1] In a sense they are identical, so that it can be said that God's perfections are God Himself as He has revealed Himself to us. It is possible to go even farther and say with Shedd, "The whole essence is in each attribute, and the attribute in the essence."[2] And because of the close relation in which the two stand to each other, it can be said that knowledge of the attri-

1. *Dogm. Theol.* I, p. 334.
2. *Ibid.* p. 334.

butes carries with it knowledge of the Divine Essence. It would be a mistake to conceive of the essence of God as existing by itself and prior to the attributes, and of the attributes as additive and accidental characteristics of the Divine Being. They are essential qualities of God, which inhere in His very Being and are co-existent with it. These qualities cannot be altered without altering the essential Being of God. And since they are essential qualities, each one of them reveals to us some aspect of the Being of God.

QUESTIONS FOR FURTHER STUDY: How can we distinguish between the being, the nature, and the essence of God? How do the philosophical views of the essential Being of God generally differ from the theological views? How about the tendency to find the essence of God in the absolute, in love, or in personality? What does Otto mean when he characterizes it as "the Holy" or "the Numinous"? Why is it impossible for man to comprehend God? Has sin in any way affected man's ability to know God? Is there any difference between Luther's and Barth's conception of the "hidden God"? Does Calvin differ from them on this point? Did Luther share the Nominalist views of Occam, by whom he was influenced in other respects? How did the Reformers, in distinction from the Scholastics, consider the problem of the existence of God? Could we have any knowledge of God, if He were pure attributeless being? What erroneous views of the attributes should be avoided? What is the proper view?

LITERATURE: Bavinck, Geref. Dogm. I, pp. 91-113.; Kuyper, Dict. Dogm., De Deo I, pp. 124-158; Hodge, Syst. Theol. I, pp. 335-374; Shedd, Dogm. Theol. I, pp. 152-194; Thornwell, Collected Works, I, pp. 104-172; Dorner, Syst. of Chr. Doct. I, pp. 187-212; Orr, Chr. View of God and the World, pp. 75-93; Otten, Manual of the Hist. of Dogmas I, pp. 254-260; Clarke, The Chr. Doct. of God, pp. 56-70; Steenstra, The Being of God as Unity and Trinity, pp. 1-88; Thomson, The Christian Idea of God, pp. 117-159; Hendry, God the Creator (from the Barthian standpoint); Warfield, Calvin and Calvinism, pp. 131-185 (Calvin's Doctrine of God).

IV. The Names of God

A. The Names of God in General.

While the Bible records several names of God, it also speaks of *the name* of God in the singular as, for instance in the following statements: "Thou shalt not take the name of the Lord thy God in vain," Ex. 20:7; "How excellent is thy name in all the earth," Ps. 8:1; "As is thy name, O God, so is thy praise," Ps. 48:10; "His name is great in Israel," Ps. 76:2; "The name of Jehovah is a strong tower; the righteous runneth into it and is safe," Prov. 18:10. In such cases "the name" stands for the whole manifestation of God in His relation to His people, or simply for the person, so that it becomes synonymous with God. This usage is due to the fact that in oriental thought a name was never regarded as a mere vocable, but as an expression of the nature of the thing designated. To know the name of a person was to have power over him, and the names of the various gods were used in incantations to exercise power over them. In the most general sense of the word, then, the name of God is His self-revelation. It is a designation of Him, not as He exists in the depths of His divine Being, but as He reveals Himself especially in His relations to man. For us the one general name of God is split up into many names, expressive of the many-sided Being of God. It is only because God has revealed Himself in His name (nomen editum), that we can now designate Him by that name in various forms (nomina indita). The names of God are not of human invention, but of divine origin, though they are all borrowed from human language, and derived from human and earthly relations. They are anthropomorphic and mark a condescending approach of God to man.

The names of God constitute a difficulty for human thought. God is the *Incomprehensible One*, infinitely exalted above all that is temporal; but in His names He descends to all that is finite and becomes like unto man. On the one hand we cannot name Him, and on the other hand He has many names. How can this be explained? On what grounds are these names applied to the infinite and incomprehensible God? It should be borne in mind that they are not of man's invention, and do not testify to his insight into the very Being of God. They are given by God Himself with the assurance that they contain in a measure a revelation of the Divine Being. This was made possible by the fact that the world and all its relations is and was meant to be a revelation of God. Because the Incomprehensible One revealed Himself in His creatures, it is possible for man to name Him after the fashion of a creature. In order to make Himself known to man, God had to condescend to the level of man, to accommodate Himself to the limited and finite human consciousness, and to speak in human language. If the naming of God with anthropomorphic names involves a limitation of God, as some say, then this must be true to an even greater degree of the revelation of God in creation. Then the world does not reveal, but rather conceals, God; then man is not related to God, but simply forms an antithesis to Him; and then we are shut up to a hopeless agnosticism.

From what was said about the name of God in general it follows that we can include under the names of God not only the appellatives by which He is indicated as an independent personal Being and by which He is addressed, but also the attributes of God; and then not merely the attributes of the Divine Being in general, but also those that qualify the separate Persons of the Trinity. Dr. Bavinck bases his division of the names of God on that broad conception of them, and distinguishes between nomina propria (proper names), nomina essentialia (essential names, or attributes), and nomina personalia (personal names, as Father, Son, and Holy Spirit). In the present chapter we limit ourselves to the discussion of the first class.

B. The Old Testament Names and their Meaning.

1. 'EL, 'ELOHIM, and 'ELYON. The most simple name by which God is designated in the Old Testament, is the name 'El, which is possibly derived from 'ul, either in the sense of being first, being lord, or in that of being strong and mighty. The name 'Elohim (sing. 'Eloah) is probably derived from the same root, or from 'alah, to be smitten with fear; and therefore points to God as the strong and mighty One, or as the object of fear. The name seldom occurs in the singular, except in poetry. The plural is to be regarded as intensive, and therefore serves to indicate a fulness of power. The name 'Elyon is derived from 'alah, to go up, to be elevated, and designates God as the high and exalted One, Gen. 14:19,20; Num. 24:16; Isa. 14:14. It is found especially in poetry. These names are not yet nomina propria in the strict sense of the word, for they are also used of idols, Ps. 95:3; 96:5, of men, Gen. 33:10; Ex. 7:1, and of rulers, Judg. 5:8; Ex. 21:6; 22:8-10; Ps. 82:1.

2. 'ADONAI. This name is related in meaning to the preceding ones. It is derived from either dun (din) or 'adan, both of which mean to judge, to rule, and thus points to God as the almighty Ruler, to whom everything is subject, and to whom man is related as a servant. In earlier times it was the usual name by which the people of Israel addressed God. Later on it was largely supplanted by the name Jehovah (Yahweh). All the names so far mentioned describe God as the high and exalted One, the transcendent God. The following names point to the fact that this exalted Being condescended to enter into relations with His creatures.

3. SHADDAI and 'EL-SHADDAI. The name Shaddai is derived from shadad, to be powerful, and points to God as possessing all power in heaven and on earth. Others, however, derive it from shad, lord. It differs in an important

point from *'Elohim,* the God of creation and nature, in that it contemplates God as subjecting all the powers of nature and making them subservient to the work of divine grace. While it stresses the greatness of God, it does not represent Him as an object of fear and terror, but as a source of blessing and comfort. It is the name with which God appeared unto Abraham, the father of the faithful, Ex. 6:2.

4. YAHWEH and YAHWEH TSEBHAOTH. It is especially in the name *Yahweh,* which gradually supplanted earlier names, that God reveals Himself as the God of grace. It has always been regarded as the most sacred and the most distinctive name of God, the incommunicable name. The Jews had a superstitious dread of using it, since they read Lev. 24:16 as follows: "He that nameth the name of *Yahweh* shall surely be put to death." And therefore in reading the Scriptures they substituted for it either *'Adonai* or *'Elohim;* and the Massoretes, while leaving the consonants intact, attached to them the vowels of one of these names, usually those of *'Adonai.* The real derivation of the name and its original pronunciation and meaning are more or less lost in obscurity. The Pentateuch connects the name with the Hebrew verb *hayah,* to be, Ex. 3:13,14. On the strength of that passage we may assume that the name is in all probability derived from an archaic form of that verb, namely, *hawah.* As far as the form is concerned, it may be regarded as a third person imperfect *qal* or *hiphil.* Most likely, however, it is the former. The meaning is explained in Ex. 3:14, which is rendered "I am that I am," or "I shall be what I shall be." Thus interpreted, the name points to the unchangeableness of God. Yet it is not so much the unchangeableness of His essential Being that is in view, as the unchangeableness of His relation to His people. The name contains the assurance that God will be for the people of Moses' day what He was for their fathers, Abraham, Isaac, and Jacob. It stresses the covenant faithfulness of God, is His proper name *par excellence,* Ex. 15:3; Ps. 83:19; Hos. 12:6; Isa. 42:8, and is therefore used of no one but Israel's God. The exclusive character of the name appears from the fact that it never occurs in the plural or with a suffix. Abbreviated forms of it, found especially in composite names, are *Yah* and *Yahu.*

The name *Yahweh* is often strengthened by the addition of *tsebhaoth.* Origen and Jerome regard this as an apposition, because *Yahweh* does not admit of a construct state. But this interpretation is not sufficiently warranted and hardly yields an intelligible sense. It is rather hard to determine to what the word *tsebhaoth* refers. There are especially three opinions:

a. *The armies of Israel.* But the correctness of this view may well be doubted. Most of the passages quoted to support this idea do not prove the point; only three of them contain a semblance of proof, namely, I Sam. 4:4; 17:45; II Sam. 6:2, while one of them, II Kings 19:31, is rather unfavorable to this view. While the plural *tsebhaoth* is used for the hosts of the people of Israel, the army is regularly indicated by the singular. This militates against the notion, inherent in this view, that in the name under consideration the term refers to the army of Israel. Moreover, it is clear that in the Prophets at least the name "Jehovah of hosts" does not refer to Jehovah as the God of war. And if the meaning of the name changed, what caused the change?

b. *The stars.* But in speaking of the host of heaven Scripture always uses the singular, and never the plural. Moreover, while the stars are called the host of heaven, they are never designated the host of God.

c. *The angels.* This interpretation deserves preference. The name *Yahweh tsebhaoth* is often found in connections in which angels are mentioned: I Sam. 4:4; II Sam. 6:2; Isa. 37:16; Hos. 12:4,5, Ps. 80:1,4 f.; Ps. 89; 6-8. The angels are repeatedly represented as a host that surrounds the throne of God, Gen. 28:12; 32:2; Jos. 5:14; I Kings 22:19; Ps. 68:17; 103:21; 148:2; Isa. 6:2. It is true that in this case also the singular is generally used, but this is no serious objection, since the Bible also indicates that there were several divisions of angels, Gen. 32:2; Deut. 33:2; Ps. 68:17. Moreover, this interpretation is in harmony with the meaning of the name, which has no martial flavor, but is expressive of the glory of God as King, Deut. 33:2; I Kings 22:19; Ps. 24:10; Isa. 6:3; 24:23; Zech. 14:16. Jehovah of hosts, then, is God as the King of glory, who is surrounded by angelic hosts, who' rules heaven and earth in the interest of His people, and who receives glory from all His creatures.

C. The New Testament Names and their Interpretation.

1. THEOS. The New Testament has the Greek equivalents of the Old Testament names. For *'El, 'Elohim,* and *'Elyon* it has *Theos,* which is the most common name applied to God. Like *'Elohim,* it may by accommodation be used of heathen gods, though strictly speaking it expresses essential deity. *'Elyon* is rendered *Hupsistos Theos,* Mark 5:7; Luke 1:32,35,75; Acts 7:48; 16:17; Heb. 7:1. The names *Shaddai* and *'El-Shaddai* are rendered *Pantokrator* and *Theos Pantokrator,* II Cor. 6:18; Rev. 1:8; 4:8; 11:17; 15:3; 16:7,14. More generally, however, *Theos* is found with a genitive of possession, such as *mou, sou, hemon, humon,* because in Christ God may be regarded as the God of all and of each one of His children. The national idea of the Old Testament has made place for the individual in religion.

2. KURIOS. The name *Yahweh* is explicated a few times by variations of a descriptive kind, such as "the Alpha and the Omega," "who is and who was and who is to come," "the beginning and the end," "the first and the last," Rev. 1:4,8,17; 2:8; 21:6; 22:13. For the rest, however the New Testament follows the Septuagint, which substituted *'Adonai* for it, and rendered this by *Kurios,* derived from *kuros,* power. This name does not have exactly the same connotation as *Yahweh,* but designates God as the Mighty One, the Lord, the Possessor, the Ruler who has legal power and authority. It is used not only of God, but also of Christ.

3. PATER. It is often said that the New Testament introduced a new name of God, namely, *Pater* (Father). But this is hardly correct. The name Father

is used of the Godhead even in heathen religions. It is used repeatedly in the Old Testament to designate the relation of God to Israel, Deut. 32:6; Ps. 103:13; Isa. 63:16; 64:8; Jer. 3:4,19; 31:9; Mal. 1:6; 2:10, while Israel is called the son of God, Ex. 4:22; Deut. 14:1; 32:19; Isa. 1:2; Jer. 31:20; Hos. 1:10; 11:1. In such cases the name is expressive of the special theocratic relation in which God stands to Israel. In the general sense of originator or creator it is used in the following New Testament passages: I Cor. 8:6; Eph. 3:15; Heb. 12:9; James 1:18. In all other places it serves to express either the special relation in which the first Person of the Trinity stands to Christ, as the Son of God either in a metaphysical or a mediatorial sense, or the ethical relation in which God stands to all believers as His spiritual children.

V. The Attributes of God in General

A. Evaluation of the Terms Used.

The name "attributes" is not ideal, since it conveys the notion of adding or assigning something to one, and is therefore apt to create the impression that something is added to the divine Being. Undoubtedly the term "properties" is better, as pointing to something that is proper to God and to God only. Naturally, in so far as some of the attributes are communicable, the absolute character of the proprium is weakened, for to that extent some of the attributes are not proper to God in the absolute sense of the word. But even this term contains the suggestion of a distinction between the essence or nature of God and that which is proper to it. On the whole it is preferable to speak of the "perfections" or "virtues" of God, with the distinct understanding, however, that in this case the term "virtues" is not used in a purely ethical sense. By so doing we (a) follow the usage of the Bible, which uses the term *arete*, rendered *virtues* or *excellencies*, in I Pet. 2:9; and (b) avoid the suggestion that something is added to the Being of God. His virtues are not added to His Being, but His Being is the *pleroma* of His virtues and reveals itself in them. They may be defined as *the perfections which are predicated of the Divine Being in Scripture, or are visibly exercised by Him in His works of creation, providence, and redemption.* If we still continue to use the name "attributes," it is because it is commonly used and with the distinct understanding that the notion of something added to the Being of God must be rigidly excluded.

B. Method of determining the attributes of God.

The Scholastics in their attempt to construct a system of natural theology posited three ways in which to determine the attributes of God, which they designated as the *via causalitatis, via negationis, and via eminentiae.* By the *way of causality* we rise from the effects which we see in the world round about us to the idea of a first Cause, from the contemplation of creation, to the idea of an almighty Creator, and from the observation of the moral government of the world, to the idea of a powerful and wise Ruler. *By way of negation* we remove from our idea of God all the imperfections seen in His creatures, as inconsistent with the idea of a Perfect Being, and ascribe to Him the opposite perfection. In reliance on that principle we speak of God as independent, infinite, incorporeal, immense, immortal, and incomprehensible. And finally, *by way of eminence* we ascribe to God *in the most eminent manner* the relative perfections which we discover in man, according to the principle that what exists in an effect, pre-exists in its cause, and even in the most absolute sense in God as the most perfect Being. This method may appeal to some, because it proceeds from the known to the unknown, but is not the proper method of dogmatic theology. It takes its startingpoint in man, and concludes from what it finds in man to what is found in God. And in so far as it does this it makes man the measure of God. This is certainly not a theological method of procedure. Moreover, it bases its knowledge of God on human conclusions rather than on the self-revelation of God in His divine Word. And yet this is the only adequate source of the knowledge of God. While that method might be followed in a so-called natural theology, it does not fit in a theology of revelation.

The same may be said of the methods suggested by modern representatives of experimental theology. A typical example of this may be found in Macintosh's *Theology as an Empirical Science*.[1] He also speaks of three methods of procedure. We may begin with our intuitions of the reality of God, those unreasoned certitudes which are firmly rooted in immediate experience. One of these is that the Object of our religious dependence is absolutely sufficient for our imperative needs. Especially may deductions be drawn from the life of Jesus and the "Christlike" everywhere. We may also take our starting point, not in man's certainties, but in his needs. The practically necessary postulate is that God is absolutely sufficient and absolutely dependable with reference to the religious needs of man. On that basis man can build up his doctrine of the attributes of God. And, finally, it is also possible to follow a more pragmatic method, which rests on the principle that we can learn to a certain extent what things and persons are, beyond what they are immediately perceived to be, by observing what they do. Macintosh finds it necessary to make use of all three methods.

Ritschl wants us to start with the idea that God is love, and would have us ask what is involved in this most characteristic thought of God. Since love is personal, it implies the personality of God, and thus affords us a principle for the interpretation of the world and of the life of man. The thought that God is love also carries with it the conviction that He can achieve His purpose of love, that is, that His will is supremely effective in the world. This yields the idea of an almighty Creator. And by virtue of this basic thought we also affirm God's eternity, since, in controlling all things for the realization of His Kingdom, He sees the end from the beginning. In a somewhat similar vein Dr. W. A. Brown says: "We gain our knowledge of the attributes by analyzing the idea of God which we already won from the revelation in Christ; and we arrange them in such a way as to bring the distinctive features of that idea to clearest expression."[2]

All these methods take their startingpoint in human experience rather than in the Word of God. They deliberately ignore the clear self-revelation of God in Scripture and exalt the idea of the human discovery of God. They who rely on such methods have an exaggerated idea of their own ability to find out God and to determine the nature of God inductively by approved "scientific methods."

---

1. p. 159 ff.
2. *Chr. Theol. in Outline*, p. 101.

At the same time they close their eyes to the only avenue through which they might obtain real knowledge of God, that is, His special revelation, apparently oblivious of the fact that only the Spirit of God can search and reveal the deep things of God and reveal them unto us. Their very method compels them to drag God down to the level of man, to stress His immanence at the expense of His transcendence, and to make Him continuous with the world. And as the final result of their philosophy we have a God made in the image of man. James condemns all intellectualism in religion, and maintains that philosophy in the form of scholastic theology fails as completely to define God's attributes in a scientific way as it does to establish His existence. After an appeal to the book of Job he says: "Ratiocination is a relatively superficial and unreal path to the deity." He concludes his discussion with these significant words: "In all sincerity I think we must conclude that the attempt to demonstrate by purely intellectual processes the truth of the deliverances of direct religious experiences is absolutely hopeless."[1] He has more confidence in the pragmatic method which seeks for a God that meets the practical needs of man. In his estimation it is sufficient to believe that "beyond each man and in a fashion continuous with him there exists a larger power which is friendly to him and to his ideals. All that the facts require is that the power should be other and larger than our conscious selves. Anything larger will do, if it only be large enough to trust for the next step. It need not be infinite, it need not be solitary. It might conceivably even be only a larger and more godlike self, of which the present self would then be the mutilated expression, and the universe might conceivably be a collection of such selves, of different degree and inclusiveness, with no absolute unity realized in it at all."[2] Thus we are left with the idea of a finite God.[3]

The only proper way to obtain perfectly reliable knowledge of the divine attributes is by the study of God's self-revelation in Scripture. It is true that we can acquire some knowledge of the greatness and power, the wisdom and goodness of God through the study of nature, but for an adequate conception of even these attributes it will be necessary to turn to the Word of God. In the theology of revelation we seek to learn from the Word of God which are the attributes of the Divine Being. Man does not elicit knowledge from God as he does from other objects of study, but God conveys knowledge of Himself to man, a knowledge which man can only accept and appropriate. For the appropriation and understanding of this revealed knowledge it is, of course, of the greatest importance that man is created in the image of God, and therefore finds helpful analogies in his own life. In distinction from the *a priori* method of the Scholastics, who deduced the attributes from the idea of a perfect Being, this method may be called *a posteriori*, since it takes its startingpoint, not in an abstract perfect Being, but in the fulness of the divine self-revelation, and in the light of this seeks to know the Divine Being.

1. *Varieties of Religious Experience*, p. 455
2. *Ibid.*, p. 525.
3. Cf. Baillie, *Our Knowledge of God*, p. 251 ff. on this matter.

C. Suggested Divisions of the Attributes.

The question of the classification of the divine attributes has engaged the attention of theologians for a long time. Several classifications have been suggested, most of which distinguish two general classes. These classes are designated by different names and represent different points of view, but are substantially the same in the various classifications. The following are the most important of these:

1. Some speak of *natural and moral attributes.* The former, such as self-existence, simplicity, infinity, etc., belong to the constitutional nature of God, as distinguished from His will. The latter, as truth, goodness, mercy, justice, holiness, etc., qualify Him as a moral Being. The objection to this classification is that the so-called moral attributes are just as truly natural (i.e. original) in God as the others. Dabney prefers this division, but admits, in view of the objection raised, that the terms are not felicitous. He would rather speak of moral and non-moral attributes.

2. Others distinguish between *absolute and relative attributes.* The former belong to the essence of God as considered in itself, while the latter belong to the divine essence considered in relation to His creation. The one class includes such attributes as self-existence, immensity, eternity; and the other, such attributes as omnipresence and omniscience. This division seems to proceed on the assumption that we can have some knowledge of God as He is in Himself, entirely apart from the relations in which He stands to His creatures. But this is not so, and therefore, properly speaking, all the perfections of God are relative, indicating what He is in relation to the world. Strong evidently does not recognize the objection, and gives preference to this division.

3. Still others divide the divine perfections into *immanent or intransitive and emanent or transitive* attributes. Strong combines this division with the preceding one, when he speaks of *absolute or immanent* and *relative or transitive* attributes. The former are those which do not go forth and operate outside of the divine essence, but remain immanent, such as immensity, simplicity, eternity, etc.; and the latter are such as issue forth and produce effects external to God, as omnipotence, benevolence, justice, etc. But if some of the divine attributes are purely immanent, all knowledge of them would seem to be excluded. H. B. Smith remarks that every one of them must be both immanent and transeunt.

4. The most common distinction is that between *incommunicable and communicable* attributes. The former are those to which there is nothing analogous in the creature, as aseity, simplicity, immensity, etc.; the latter those to which the properties of the human spirit bear some analogy, as power, goodness, mercy, righteousness, etc. This distinction found no favor with the Lutherans, but has always been rather popular in Reformed circles, and is found in such representative works as those of the Leyden Professors,[1] Mastricht and Turretin. It was felt from the very beginning, however,

---

1. *Synopsis Purioris Theologiae.*

that the distinction was untenable without further qualification, since from one point of view every attribute may be called communicable. None of the divine perfections are communicable in the infinite perfection in which they exist in God, and at the same time there are faint traces in man even of the so-called incommunicable attributes of God. Among more recent Reformed theologians there is a tendency to discard this distinction in favor of some other divisions. Dick, Shedd, and Vos retain the old division. Kuyper expresses himself as dissatisfied with it, and yet reproduces it in his *virtutes per antithesin* and *virtutes per synthesin;* and Bavinck, after following another order in the first edition of his Dogmatics, returns to it in the second edition. Honig prefers to follow the division given by Bavinck in his first edition. And, finally, the Hodges, H. B. Smith, and Thornwell follow a division suggested by the Westminster Catechism. However, the classification of the attributes under two main heads, as found in the distinction under consideration, is really inherent in all the other divisions, so that they are all subject to the objection that they apparently divide the Being of God into two parts, that first God as He is in Himself, God as the absolute Being, is discussed, and then God as He is related to His creatures, God as a personal Being. It may be said that such a treatment does not result in a unitary and harmonious conception of the divine attributes. This difficulty may be obviated, however, by having it clearly understood that the two classes of attributes named are not strictly co-ordinate, but that the attributes belonging to the first class qualify all those belonging to the second class, so that it can be said that God is one, absolute, unchangeable and infinite in His knowledge and wisdom, His goodness and love, His grace and mercy, His righteousness and holiness. If we bear this in mind, and also remember that none of the attributes of God are incommunicable in the sense that there is no trace of them in man, and that none of them are communicable in the sense that they are found in man as they are found in God, we see no reason why we should depart from the old division which has become so familiar in Reformed theology. For practical reasons it seems more desirable to retain it.

QUESTIONS FOR FURTHER STUDY: What objections are there to the use of the term attributes as applied to God? Do the same objections apply to the German "Eigenschaften" and the Holland "eigenschappen"? What name does Calvin use for them? What objection is there to the conception of the attributes as parts of God or as additions to the Divine Being? What faulty conceptions of the attributes were current in the Middle Ages? Did the Scholastics in their search for the attributes follow an *a priori* or an *a posteriori*, a deductive or an inductive method? Why is their method inherently foreign to the theology of revelation? What classifications of the attributes were suggested in addition to those mentioned in the text? Why is it virtually out of the question to give a faultless division? What division is suggested by the Westminster Catechism?

LITERATURE: Bavinck, *Geref. Dogm.* II, pp. 100-123; Kuyper, *Dict. Dogm., De Deo* I, pp. 268-287; Honig, *Geref. Dogm.,* pp. 182-185; Hodge, *Syst. Theol.* I, pp. 368-376; Shedd, *Dogm. Theol.* I, pp. 334-338; Thornwell, *Collected Works,* I, pp. 158-172; Dabney, *Lectures on Theol.,* pp. 147-151; Pieper, *Christl. Dogm.* I, pp. 524-536; Kaftan, *Dogm.,* pp. 168-181; Pope, *Chr. Theol.* I, pp. 287-291; Steenstra, *The Being of God as Unity and Trinity,* pp. 89-111.

VI. The Incommunicable Attributes

(God as the Absolute Being)

It has been quite common in theology to speak of God as the absolute Being. At the same time the term "absolute" is more characteristic of philosophy than it is of theology. In metaphysics the term "the Absolute" is a designation of the ultimate ground of all existence; and because the theist also speaks of God as the ultimate ground of all existence, it is sometimes thought that the Absolute of philosophy and the God of theism are one and the same. But that is not necessarily so. In fact the usual conception of the Absolute renders it impossible to equate it with the God of the Bible and of Christian theology. The term "Absolute" is derived from the Latin *absolutus*, a compound of *ab* (from) and *solvere* (to loosen), and thus means free as to condition, or free from limitation or restraint. This fundamental thought was worked out in various ways, so that the Absolute was regarded as that which is free from all conditions (the Unconditioned or Self-Existent), from all relations (the (Unrelated), from all imperfections (the Perfect), or free from all phenomenal differences or distinctions, such as matter and spirit, being and attributes, subject and object, appearance and reality (the Real, or Ultimate Reality).

The answer to the question, whether the Absolute of philosophy can be identified with the God of theology, depends on the conception one has of the Absolute. If Spinoza conceives of the Absolute as the one Self-subsistent Being of which all particular things are but transient modes, thus identifying God and the world, we cannot share his view of this Absolute as God. When Hegel views the Absolute as the unity of thought and being, as the totality of all things, which includes all relations, and in which all the discords of the present are resolved in perfect unity, we again find it impossible to follow him in regarding this Absolute as God. And when Bradley says that his Absolute is related to nothing, and that there cannot be any practical relation between it and the finite will, we agree with him that his Absolute cannot be the God of the Christian religion, for this God does enter into relations with finite creatures. Bradley cannot conceive of the God of religion as other than a finite God. But when the Absolute is defined as the First Cause of all existing things, or as the ultimate ground of all reality, or as the one self-existent Being, it can be considered as identical with the God of theology. He is the Infinite One, who does not exist in any *necessary* relations, because He is self-sufficient, but at the same time can *freely* enter into various relations with His creation as a whole and with His creatures. While the incommunicable attributes empha-

57

size the absolute Being of God, the communicable attributes stress the fact that He enters into various relations with His creatures. In the present chapter the following perfections of God come into consideration.

A. The Self-Existence of God.

God is self-existent, that is, He has the ground of His existence in Himself. This idea is sometimes expressed by saying that He is *causa sui* (His own cause), but this expression is hardly accurate, since God is the uncaused, who exists by the necessity of His own Being, and therefore necessarily. Man, on the other hand, does not exist necessarily, and has the cause of his existence outside of himself. The idea of God's self-existence was generally expressed by the term *aseitas*, meaning *self-originated*, but Reformed theologians quite generally substituted for it the word *independentia* (independence), as expressing, not merely that God is independent in His Being, but also that He is independent in everything else: in His virtues, decrees, works, and so on. It may be said that there is a faint trace of this perfection in the creature, but this can only mean that the creature, though absolutely dependent, yet has its own distinct existence. But, of course, this falls far short of being self-existent. This attribute of God is generally recognized, and is implied in heathen religions and in the Absolute of philosophy. When the Absolute is conceived of as the self-existent and as the ultimate ground of all things, which voluntarily enters into various relations with other beings, it can be identified with the God of theology. As the self-existent God, He is not only independent in Himself, but also causes everything to depend on Him. This self-existence of God finds expression in the name Jehovah. It is only as the self-existent and independent One that God can give the assurance that He will remain eternally the same in relation to His people. Additional indications of it are found in the assertion in John 5:26, "For as the Father hath life in Himself, even so gave He to the Son also to have life in Himself"; in the declaration that He is independent of all things and that all things exist only through Him, Ps. 94:8 ff.; Isa. 40:18 ff.; Acts 7:25; and in statements implying that He is independent in His thought, Rom. 11:33,34, and in His will, Dan. 4:35; Rom. 9:19; Eph. 1:5; Rev. 4:11, in His power, Ps. 115:3, and in His counsel, Ps. 33:11.

B. The Immutability of God.

The Immutability of God is a necessary concomitant of His aseity. It is that perfection of God by which He is devoid of all change, not only in His Being, but also in His perfections, and in His purposes and promises. In virtue of this attribute He is exalted above all becoming, and is free from all accession or diminution and from all growth or decay in His Being or perfections. His knowledge and plans, His moral principles and volitions remain forever the same. Even reason teaches us that no change is possible in God, since a change is either for better or for worse. But in God, as the absolute Perfection, improvement and deterioration are both equally impossible. This immutability of God is clearly taught in such passages of Scripture as Ex. 3:14; Ps. 102:26-28; Isa. 41:4; 48:12; Mal. 3:6; Rom. 1:23; Heb. 1:11,12; Jas. 1:17. At the same time there are many passages of Scripture which seem to ascribe change to God. Did not He who dwelleth in eternity pass on to the creation of the world, become incarnate in Christ, and in the Holy Spirit take up His abode in the Church? Is He not represented as revealing and hiding Himself, as coming and going, as repenting and changing His intention, and as dealing differently with man before and after conversion? Cf. Ex. 32:10-14; Jonah 3:10; Prov. 11:20; 12:22; Ps. 18:26,27. The objection here implied is based to a certain extent on misunderstanding. The divine immutability should not be understood as implying *immobility*, as if there were no movement in God. It is even customary in theology to speak of God as *actus purus*, a God who is always in action. The Bible teaches us that God enters into manifold relations with man and, as it were, lives their life with them. There is change round about Him, change in the relations of men to Him, but there is no change in His Being, His attributes, His purpose, His motives of action, or His promises. The purpose to create was eternal with Him, and there was no change in Him when this purpose was realized by a single eternal act of His will. The incarnation brought no change in the Being or perfections of God, nor in His purpose, for it was His eternal good pleasure to send the Son of His love into the world. And if Scripture speaks of His repenting, changing His intention, and altering His relation to sinners when they repent, we should remember that this is only an anthropopathic way of speaking. In reality the change is not in God, but in man and in man's relations to God. It is important to maintain the immutability of God over against the Pelagian and Arminian doctrine that God is subject to change, not indeed in His Being, but in His knowledge and will, so that His decisions are to a great extent dependent on the actions of man; over against the pantheistic notion that God is an eternal becoming rather than an absolute Being, and that the unconscious Absolute is gradually developing into conscious personality in man; and over against the present tendency of some to speak of a finite, struggling, and gradually growing God.

C. The Infinity of God .

The infinity of God is that perfection of God by which He is free from all limitations. In ascribing it to God we deny that there are or can be any limitations to the divine Being or attributes. It implies that He is in no way limited by the universe, by this time-space world, or confined to the universe. It does not involve His identity with the sum-total of existing things, nor does it exclude the co-existence of derived and finite things, to which He bears relation. The infinity of God must be conceived as intensive rather than extensive, and should not be confused with boundless extension, as if God were spread out through the entire universe, one part being here and another there, for God has no body and therefore no extension. Neither should it be regarded as a merely negative concept, though it is perfectly true that we cannot form a positive idea of it.

It is a reality in God fully comprehended only by Him. We distinguish various aspects of God's infinity.

1. HIS ABSOLUTE PERFECTION. This is the infinity of the Divine Being considered in itself. It should not be understood in a quantitative, but in a qualitative sense; it qualifies all the communicable attributes of God. Infinite power is not an absolute quantum, but an exhaustless potency of power; and infinite holiness is not a boundless quantum of holiness, but a holiness which is, qualitatively free from all limitation or defect. The same may be said of infinite knowledge and wisdom, and of infinite love and righteousness. Says Dr. Orr: "Perhaps we can say that infinity in God is ultimately: (a) internally and qualitatively, absence of all limitation and defect; (b) boundless potentiality."[1] In this sense of the word the infinity of God is simply identical with the perfection of His Divine Being. Scripture proof for it is found in Job 11:7-10; Ps. 145:3; Matt. 5:48.

2. HIS ETERNITY. The infinity of God in relation to time is called His eternity. The form in which the Bible represents God's eternity is simply that of duration through endless ages, Ps. 90:2; 102:12; Eph. 3:21. We should remember, however, that in speaking as it does the Bible uses popular language, and not the language of philosophy. We generally think of God's eternity in the same way, namely, as duration infinitely prolonged both backwards and forwards. But this is only a popular and symbolical way of representing that which in reality transcends time and differs from it essentially. Eternity in the strict sense of the word is abscribed to that which transcends all temporal limitations. That it applies to God in that sense is at least intimated in II Pet. 3:8. "Time," says Dr. Orr, "strictly has relation to the world of objects existing in succession. God fills time; is in every part of it; but His eternity still is not really this being in time. It is rather that to which time forms a contrast."[2] Our existence is marked off by days and weeks and months and years; not so the existence of God. Our life is divided into a past, present and future, but there is no such division in the life of God. He is the eternal "I am." His eternity may be defined as *that perfection of God whereby He is elevated above all temporal limits and all succession of moments, and possesses the whole of His existence in one indivisible present.* The relation of eternity to time constitutes one of the most difficult problems in philosophy and theology, perhaps incapable of solution in our present condition.

3. HIS IMMENSITY. The infinity of God may also be viewed with reference to space, and is then called His immensity. It may be defined as *that perfection of the Divine Being by which He transcends all spatial limitations, and yet is present in every point of space with His whole Being.* It has a negative and a positive side, denying all limitations of space to the Divine Being, and asserting that God is above space and fills every part of it *with His whole Being.* The last words are added, in order to ward off the idea that God is diffused through

---

1. *Side-Lights on Christian Doctrine*, p. 26.
2. *Ibid.*, p. 26.

space, so that one part of His Being is present in one place, and another part in some other place. We distinguish three modes of presence in space. Bodies are in space circumscriptively, because they are bounded by it; finite spirits are in space definitively, since they are not everywhere, but only in a certain definite place; and in distinction from both of these God is in space repletively, because He fills all space. He is not absent from any part of it, nor more present in one part than in another.

In a certain sense the terms "immensity" and "omnipresence," as applied to God, denote the same thing, and can therefore be regarded as synonymous. Yet there is a point of difference that should be carefully noted. "Immensity" points to the fact that God transcends all space and is not subject to its limitations, while "omnipresence" denotes that He nevertheless fills every part of space with His entire Being. The former emphasizes the transcendence, and the latter, the immanence of God. God is immanent in all His creatures, in His entire creation, but is in no way bounded by it. In connection with God's relation to the world we must avoid, on the one hand, the error of Pantheism, so characteristic of a great deal of present day thinking, with its denial of the transcendence of God and its assumption that the Being of God is really the substance of all things; and, on the other hand, the Deistic conception that God is indeed present in creation *per potentiam* (with His power), but not *per essentiam et naturam* (with His very Being and nature), and acts upon the world from a distance. Though God is distinct from the world and may not be identified with it, He is yet present in every part of His creation, not only *per potentiam*, but also *per essentiam*. This does not mean, however, that He is equally present and present in the same sense in all His creatures. The nature of His indwelling is in harmony with that of His creatures. He does not dwell on earth as He does in heaven, in animals as He does in man, in the inorganic as He does in the organic creation, in the wicked as He does in the pious, nor in the Church as He does in Christ. There is an endless variety in the manner in which He is immanent in His creatures, and in the measure in which they reveal God to those who have eyes to see. The omnipresence of God is clearly revealed in Scripture. Heaven and earth cannot contain Him, I Kings 8:27; Isa. 66:1; Acts 7:48,49; and at the same time He fills both and is a God at hand, Ps. 139:7-10; Jer. 23:23,24; Acts 17:27,28.

D. The Unity of God.

A distinction is made between the *unitas singularitatis* and the *unitas simplicitatis*.

1. THE *UNITAS SINGULARITATIS*. This attribute stresses both the oneness and the unicity of God, the fact that He is numerically one and that as such He is unique. It implies that there is but one Divine Being, that from the nature of the case there can be but one, and that all other beings exist of and through and unto Him. The Bible teaches us in several passages that there is but one true God. Solomon pleaded with God to maintain the cause of His people,

"that all the peoples of the earth may know that Jehovah, He is God; there is none else," I Kings 8:60. And Paul writes to the Corinthians, "But to us there is but one God, the Father, of whom are all things, and we in Him; and one Lord Jesus Christ, by whom are all things, and we in Him," I Cor. 8:6. Similarly he writes to Timothy, "For there is one God, and one Mediator between God and men, the man Christ Jesus," I Tim. 2:5. Other passages do not stress the numerical unity of God as much as they do His uniqueness. This is the case in the well known words of Deut. 6:4, "Hear, O Israel; Jehovah our God is one Jehovah." The Hebrew word 'echad, translated by "one" may also be rendered "an only," the equivalent of the German "einig" and the Dutch "eenig." And this would seem to be a better translation. Keil stresses that fact that this passage does not teach the numerical unity of God, but rather that Jehovah is the only God that is entitled to the name Jehovah. This is also the meaning of the term in Zech. 14:9. The same idea is beautifully expressed in the rhetorical question of Ex. 15:11, "Who is like unto thee, O Jehovah, among the gods? Who is like thee, glorious in holiness, fearful in praises, doing wonders?" This excludes all polytheistic conceptions of God.

2. THE UNITAS SIMPLICITATIS. While the unity discussed in the preceding sets God apart from other beings, the perfection now under consideration is expressive of the inner and qualitative unity of the Divine Being. When we speak of the simplicity of God, we use the term to describe the state or quality of being simple, the condition of being free from division into parts, and therefore from compositeness. It means that God is not composite and is not susceptible of division in any sense of the word. This implies among other things that the three Persons in the Godhead are not so many parts of which the Divine essence is composed, that God's essence and perfections are not distinct, and that the attributes are not superadded to His essence. Since the two are one, the Bible can speak of God as light and life, as righteousness and love, thus identifying Him with His perfections. The simplicity of God follows from some of His other perfections; from His Self-existence, which excludes the idea that something preceded Him, as in the case of compounds; and from His immutability, which could not be predicated of His nature, if it were made up of parts. This perfection was disputed during the Middle Ages, and was denied by Socinians and Arminians. Scripture does not explicitly assert it, but implies it where it speaks of God as righteousness, truth, wisdom, light, life, love, and so on, and thus indicates that each of these properties, because of their absolute perfection, is identical with His Being. In recent works on theology the simplicity of God is seldom mentioned. Many theologians positively deny it, either because it is regarded as a purely metaphysical abstraction, or because, in their estimation, it conflicts with the doctrine of the Trinity. Dabney believes that there is no composition in the substance of God, but denies that in Him substance and attributes are one and the same. He claims that God is no more simple in that respect than finite spirits.[1]

---

1. *Syst. and Polem. Theol.*, p. 43f.

QUESTIONS FOR FURTHER STUDY. What different conceptions of the Absolute do we meet with in philosophy? Can the Absolute of philosophy always be identified with the God of theology? How does Bradley distinguish between the two? How is the finite God of James, Schiller, Ward, Wells and others, related to the Absolute? How do the incommunicable attributes of God link up with the Absolute? Does the immutability of God exclude all movement in God? In how far does it exclude changes of action and relations? Should the absolute perfection of God be regarded as an attribute? Why does the Bible represent God's eternity as endless duration? Is it possible to harmonize the transcendence and the immanence of God? How is transcendence frequently interpreted in modern theology? What is implied in the simplicity of God?

LITERATURE: Bavinck, Geref. Dogm. II, pp. 137-171; Kuyper, Dict. Dogm., Deo I, pp. 287-318; Hodge, Syst. Theol. I, pp. 380-393; Shedd, Dogm. Theol. I, pp. 338-353; Dabney, Syst. and Polem. Theol., pp. 151-154; Thornwell, Collected Works I, pp. 189-205; Strong, Syst. Theol., pp. 254-260, 275-279; Pieper, Christl. Dogm. I, pp. 536-543, 547-549; Knudson, The Doct. of God, pp. 242-284; Steenstra, God as Unity and Trinity, pp. 112-139; Charnock, Existence and Attributes of God. pp. 276-405.

VII. The Communicable Attributes

(God as a Personal Spirit)

If the attributes discussed in the previous chapter stressed the absolute Being of God, those that remain to be considered emphasize His personal nature. It is in the communicable attributes that God stands out as a conscious, intelligent, free, and moral Being, as a Being that is personal in the highest sense of the word. The question has long engaged the attention of philosophers, and is still a subject of debate, whether personal existence is consistent with the idea of absoluteness. The answer to that question depends to a great extent on the meaning one ascribes to the word "absolute." The word has been used in three different senses in philosophy, which may be denominated as the agnostic, the logical, and the causal sense. For the agnostic the Absolute is the unrelated, of which nothing can be known, since things are known only in their relations. And if nothing can be known of it, personality cannot be ascribed to it. Moreover, since personality is unthinkable apart from relations, it cannot be identified with an Absolute which is in its very essence the unrelated. In the logical Absolute the individual is subordinated to the universal, and the highest universal is ultimate reality. Such is the absolute substance of Spinoza, and the absolute spirit of Hegel. It may express itself in and through the finite, but nothing that is finite can express its essential nature. To ascribe personality to it would be to limit it to one mode of being, and would destroy its absoluteness. In fact, such an absolute or ultimate is a mere abstract and empty concept, that is barren of all content. The causal view of the Absolute represents it as the ultimate ground of all things. It is not dependent on anything outside of itself, but causes all things to depend on it. Moreover, it is not necessarily completely unrelated, but can enter into various relations with finite creatures. Such a conception of the Absolute is not inconsistent with the idea of personality. Moreover, we should bear in mind that in their argumentation philosophers were always operating with the idea of personality as it is realized in man, and lost sight of the fact that personality in God might be something infinitely more perfect. As a matter of fact, perfect personality is found only in God, and what we see in man is only a finite copy of the original. Still more, there is a tri-personality in God, of which no analogy is found in human beings.

Several natural proofs, quite similar to those adduced for the existence of God, have been urged to prove the personality of God. (1) Human personality demands a personal God for its explanation. Man is not a self-existent and eternal, but a finite being that has a beginning and an end. The cause assumed must be sufficient to account for the whole of the effect. Since man is a personal product, the power originating him must also be personal. Otherwise there is something in the effect which is superior to anything that is found in the cause; and this would be quite impossible. (2) The world in general bears witness to the personality of God. In its whole fabric and constitution it reveals the clearest traces of an infinite intelligence, of the deepest, highest and tenderest emotions, and of a will that is all-powerful. Consequently, we are constrained to mount from the world to the world's Maker as a Being of intelligence, sensibility, and will, that is, as a person. (3) The moral and religious nature of man also points to the personality of God. His moral nature imposes on him a sense of obligation to do that which is right, and this necessarily implies the existence of a supreme Lawgiver. Moreover, his religious nature constantly prompts him to seek personal communion with some higher Being; and all the elements and activities of religion demand a personal God as their object and final end. Even so-called pantheistic religions often testify unconsciously to belief in a personal God. The fact is that all such things as penitence, faith and obedience, fellowship and love, loyalty in service and sacrifice, trust in life and death, are meaningless unless they find their appropriate object in a personal God.

But while all these considerations are true and have some value as *testimonia*, they are not the proofs on which theology depends in its doctrine of the personality of God. It turns for proof to God's Self-revelation in Scripture. The term "person" is not applied to God in the Bible, though there are words, such as the Hebrew *panim* and the Greek *prosopon*, that come very close to expressing the idea. At the same time Scripture testifies to the personality of God in more than one way. The presence of God, as described by Old and New Testament writers, is clearly a personal presence. And the anthropomorphic and anthropopathic representations of God in Scripture, while they must be interpreted so as not to militate against the pure spirituality and holiness of God, can hardly be justified, except on the assumption that the Being to whom they apply is a real person, with personal attributes, even though it be without human limitations. God is represented throughout as a personal God, with whom men can and may converse, whom they can trust, who sustains them in their trials, and fills their hearts with the joy of deliverance and victory. And, finally, the highest revelation of God to which the Bible testifies is a personal revelation. Jesus Christ reveals the Father in such a perfect way that He could say to Philip," He who hath seen me hath seen the Father," John 14:9. More detailed proofs will appear in the discussion of the communicable attributes.

A. The Spirituality of God.

The Bible does not give us a definition of God. The nearest approach to anything like it is found in the word of Christ to the Samaritan woman, "God is Spirit," John 4:24. This is at least a statement purporting to tell us in a single word what God is. The Lord does not merely say that God is *a* spirit, but that He is Spirit. And because of this clear statement it is but fitting that we should discuss first of all the spirituality of God. By teaching the spirituality of God theology stresses the fact that God has a substantial Being all His own and distinct from the world, and that this substantial Being is immaterial, invisible, and without composition or extension. It includes the thought that all the essential qualities which belong to the perfect idea of Spirit are found in Him: that He is a self-conscious and self-determining Being. Since He is Spirit in the most absolute, and in the purest sense of the word, there is in Him no composition of parts. The idea of spirituality of necessity excludes the ascription of anything like corporeity to God, and thus condemns the fancies of some of the early Gnostics and medieval Mystics, and of all those sectarians of our own day who ascribe a body to God. It is true that the Bible speaks of the hands and feet, the eyes and ears, the mouth and nose of God, but in doing this it is speaking anthropomorphically or figuratively of Him who far transcends our human knowledge, and of whom we can only speak in a stammering fashion after the manner of men. By ascribing spirituality to God we also affirm that He has none of the properties belonging to matter, and that He cannot be discerned by the bodily senses. Paul speaks of Him as "the King eternal, immortal, invisible" (I Tim. 1:17), and again as "the King of kings, and Lord of lords, who only hath immortality, dwelling in light unapproachable; whom no man hath seen, nor can see: to whom be honor and power eternal," I Tim. 6:15,16.

B. Intellectual Attributes.

God is represented in Scripture as Light. and therefore as perfect in His intellectual life. This category comprises two of the divine perfections. namely, the knowledge and the wisdom of God.

1. THE KNOWLEDGE OF GOD. The knowledge of God may be defined as *that perfection of God whereby He, in an entirely unique manner, knows Himself and all things possible and actual in one eternal and most simple act.* The Bible testifies to the knowledge of God abundantly, as, for instance, in I Sam. 2:3; Job 12:13; Ps. 94:9; 147:4; Isa. 29:15; 40:27,28. In connection with the knowledge of God several points call for consideration.

a. *Its nature.* The knowledge of God differs in some important points from that of men. It is *archetypal*, which means that He knows the universe as it exists in His own eternal idea previous to its existence as a finite reality in time and space; and that His knowledge is not, like ours, obtained from without. It is a knowledge that is characterized by *absolute perfection.* As such it is *intuitive* rather than demonstrative or discursive. It is *innate and immediate*, and does not result from observation or from a process of reasoning. Being perfect, it is also *simultaneous* and not successive, so that He sees things at once in their totality, and not piecemeal one after another. Furthermore, it is *complete and fully conscious*, while man's knowledge is always partial, frequently indistinct, and often fails to rise into the clear light of consciousness. A distinction is made between the *necessary* and *free* knowledge of God. The former is the knowledge which God has of Himself and of all things possible, a knowledge resting on the consciousness of His omnipotence. It is called *necessary knowledge*, because it is not determined by an action of the divine will. It is also known as *the knowledge of simple intelligence*, in view of the fact that it is purely an act of the divine intellect, without any concurrent action of the divine will. *The free knowledge of God* is the knowledge which He has of all things actual, that is, of things that existed in the past, that exist in the present, or that will exist in the future. It is founded on God's' infinite knowledge of His own all-comprehensive and unchangeable eternal purpose, and is called free knowledge, because it is determined by a concurrent act of the will. It is also called *scientia visionis*, knowledge of vision.

b. *Its extent.* The knowledge of God is not only perfect in kind, but also in its inclusiveness. It is called *omniscience*, because it is all-comprehensive. In order to promote a proper estimate of it, we may particularize as follows: God knows Himself and in Himself all things that come from Him (internal knowledge). He knows all things as they actually come to pass, past, present, and future, and knows them in their real relations. He knows the hidden essence of things, to which the knowledge of man cannot penetrate. He sees not as man sees, who observes only the outward manifestations of life, but penetrates to the depths of the human heart. Moreover, He knows what is possible as well as what is actual; all things that might occur under certain circumstances are present to His mind. The omniscience of God is clearly taught in several passages of Scripture. He is perfect in knowledge, Job 37:16, looketh not on outward appearance but on the heart, I Sam. 16:7; I Chron. 28:9,17; Ps. 139:1-4; Jer. 17:10, observes the ways of men, Deut. 2:7; Job 23:10; 24:23; 31:4; Ps. 1:6; 119:168, knows the place of their habitation, Ps. 33:13, and the days of their life, Ps. 37:18. This doctrine of the knowledge of God must be maintained over against all pantheistic tendencies to represent God as the unconscious ground of the phenomenal world, and of those who, like Marcion, Socinus and all who believe in a finite God, ascribe to Him only a limited knowledge.

There is one question, however, that calls for special discussion. It concerns God's foreknowledge of the free actions of men, and therefore of conditional events. We can understand how God can foreknow where necessity rules, but find it difficult to conceive of a previous knowledge of actions which man freely originates. The difficulty of this problem led some to deny the foreknowledge of free actions, and others to deny human freedom. It is perfectly evident that Scripture teaches the divine foreknowledge of contingent events, I Sam. 23:10-13; II Kings 13:19; Ps. 81:14,15; Isa. 42:9; 48:18; Jer. 2:2,3; 38:17-20; Ezek. 3:6; Matt. 11:21. Moreover, it does not leave us in doubt as to the freedom of man. It certainly does not permit the denial of either one of the terms of the problem. We are up against a problem here, which we cannot fully solve, though it is possible to make an approach to a solution. God has decreed all things, and has decreed them with their causes and conditions in the exact order in which they come to pass; and His foreknowledge of future things and also of contingent events rests on His decree. This solves the problem as far as the foreknowledge of God is concerned.

But now the question arises, Is the predetermination of things consistent with the free will of man? And the answer is that it certainly is not, if the freedom of the will be regarded as *indifferentia* (arbitrariness), but this is an unwarranted conception of the freedom of man. The will of man is not something altogether indeterminate, something hanging in the air that can be swung arbitrarily in either direction. It is rather something rooted in our very nature, connected with our deepest instincts and emotions, and determined by our intellectual considerations and by our very character. And if we conceive of our human freedom as *lubentia rationalis* (reasonable self-determination), then we have no sufficient warrant for saying that it is inconsistent with divine foreknowledge. Says Dr. Orr: "A solution of this problem there is, though our minds fail to grasp it. In part it probably lies, not in denying freedom, but in a revised conception of freedom. For freedom, after all, is not arbitrariness. There is in all rational action a *why* for acting — a reason which decides action. The truly free man is not the uncertain, incalculable man, but the man who is *reliable*. In short, freedom has its laws — spiritual laws — and the omniscient Mind knows what these are. But an element of mystery, it must be acknowledged, still remains."[1]

Jesuit, Lutheran, and Arminian theologians suggested the so-called *scientia media* as a solution of the problem. The name is indicative of the fact that it occupies a middle ground between the necessary and the free knowledge of God. It differs from the former in that its *object* is not all possible things, *but a special class of things actually future;* and from the latter in that its *ground* is not the eternal purpose of God, *but the free action of the creature as simply foreseen.*[2] It is called *mediate*, says Dabney, "because they suppose God arrives at it, not directly by knowing His own purpose to effect it, but indirectly by His infinite insight into the manner in which the contingent second cause will act, under given outward circumstances, foreseen or produced by God."[3] But this is no solution of the problem at all. It is an attempt to reconcile two things which logically exclude each other, namely, freedom of action in the Pelagian sense and a *certain* foreknowledge of that action. Actions that are in no way determined by God, directly or indirectly, but are wholly dependent on the arbitrary will of man, can hardly be the object of divine foreknowledge. Moreover, it is objectionable, because it makes the divine knowledge dependent on the choice of man, virtually annuls the certainty of the knowledge of future events, and thus implicitly denies the omniscience of God. It is also contrary to such passages of Scripture as Acts 2:23; Rom. 9:16; Eph. 1:11; Phil. 2:13.

2. THE WISDOM OF GOD. The wisdom of God may be regarded as a particular aspect of His knowledge. It is quite evident that knowledge and

---

1. *Side-Lights on Chr. Doct.*, p. 30.
2. A. A. Hodge, *Outlines of Theol.*, p. 147.
3. *Syst. and Polem. Theol.*, p. 156.

wisdom are not the same, though they are closely related. They do not always accompany each other. An uneducated man may be superior to a scholar in wisdom. Knowledge is acquired by study, but wisdom results from an intuitive insight into things. The former is theoretical, while the latter is practical, making knowledge subservient to some specific purpose. Both are imperfect in man, but in God they are characterized by absolute perfection. God's wisdom is His intelligence as manifested in the adaptation of means to ends. It points to the fact that He always strives for the best possible ends, and chooses the best means for the realization of His purposes. H. B. Smith defines the divine wisdom as "that attribute of God whereby He produces the best possible results with the best possible means." We may be a little more specific and call it *that perfection of God whereby He applies His knowledge to the attainment of His ends in a way which glorifies Him most.* It implies a final end to which all secondary ends are subordinate; and according to Scripture this final end is the glory of God, Rom. 11:33; 14:7,8; Eph. 1:11,12; Col. 1:16. Scripture refers to the wisdom of God in many passages, and even represents it as personified in Proverbs 8. This wisdom of God is seen particularly in creation, Ps. 19:1-7; 104:1-34; in providence, Ps. 33:10, 11; Rom. 8:28; and in redemption, Rom. 11:33; I Cor. 2:7; Eph. 3:10.

3. THE VERACITY OF GOD. Scripture uses several words to express the veracity of God: in the Old Testament *'emeth, 'amunah,* and *'amen,* and in the New Testament *alethes (aletheia), alethinos,* and *pistis.* This already points to the fact that it includes several ideas, such as truth, truthfulness, and faithfulness. When God is called the truth, this is to be understood in its most comprehensive sense. He is the truth first of all in a metaphysical sense, that is, in Him the idea of the Godhead is perfectly realized; He is all that He as God should be, and as such is distinguished from all so-called gods, which are called vanity and lies, Ps. 96:5; 97:7; 115:4-8; Isa. 44:9,10. He is also the truth in an *ethical* sense, and as such reveals Himself as He really is, so that His revelation is absolutely reliable, Num. 23:19; Rom. 3:4; Heb. 6:18. Finally, He is also the truth in a *logical* sense, and in virtue of this He knows things as they really are, and has so constituted the mind of man that the latter can know, not merely the appearance, but also the reality, of things. Thus the truth of God is the foundation of all knowledge. It should be borne in mind, moreover, that these three are but different aspects of the truth, which is one in God. In view of the preceding we may define the veracity or truth of God as *that perfection of His Being by virtue of which He fully answers to the idea of the Godhead, is perfectly reliable in His revelation, and sees things as they really are.* It is because of this perfection that He is the source of all truth, not only in the sphere of morals and religion, but also in every field of scientific endeavor. Scripture is very emphatic in its references to God as the truth, Ex. 34:6; Num. 23:19; Deut. 32:4; Ps. 25:10; 31:6; Isa. 65:16; Jer. 10:8, 10, 11; John 14:6; 17:3; Tit. 1:2; Heb. 6:18; I John 5:20, 21. There is still another aspect of this divine perfection, and one that is always

regarded as of the greatest importance. It is generally called His *faithfulness*, in virtue of which He is ever mindful of His covenant and fulfils all the promises which He has made to His people. This faithfulness of God is of the utmost practical significance to the people of God. It is the ground of their confidence, the foundation of their hope, and the cause of their rejoicing. It saves them from the despair to which their own unfaithfulness might easily lead, gives them courage to carry on in spite of their failures, and fills their hearts with joyful anticipations, even when they are deeply conscious of the fact that they have forfeited all the blessings of God. Num. 23:19; Deut. 7:9; Ps. 89:33; Isa. 49:7; I Cor. 1:9; II Tim. 2:13; Heb. 6:17, 18; 10:23.

C. Moral Attributes.

The moral attributes of God are generally regarded as the most glorious of the divine perfections. Not that one attribute of God is in itself more perfect and glorious than another, but relatively to man the moral perfections of God shine with a splendor all their own. They are generally discussed under three heads: (1) the goodness of God; (2) the holiness of God; and (3) the righteousness of God.

1. THE GOODNESS OF GOD. This is generally treated as a generic conception, including several varieties, which are distinguished according to their objects. The goodness of God should not be confused with His kindness, which is a more restricted concept. We speak of something as good, when it answers in all parts to the ideal. Hence in our ascription of goodness to God the fundamental idea is that He is in every way all that He as God should be, and therefore answers perfectly to the ideal expressed in the word "God." He is good in the metaphysical sense of the word, absolute perfection and perfect bliss in Himself. It is in this sense that Jesus said to the young ruler: "None is good save one, even God," Mark 10:18. But since God is good in Himself, He is also good for His creatures, and may therefore be called the *fons omnium bonorum*. He is the fountain of all good, and is so represented in a variety of ways throughout the Bible. The poet sings: "For with thee is the fountain of life; in thy light shall we see light," Ps. 36:9. All the good things which the creatures enjoy in the present and expect in the future, flow to them out of this inexhaustible fountain. And not only that, but God is also the *summum bonum*, the highest good, for all His creatures, though in different degrees and according to the measure in which they answer to the purpose of their existence. In the present connection we naturally stress the ethical goodness of God and the different aspects of it, as these are determined by the nature of its objects.

a. *The goodness of God towards His creatures in general.* This may be defined as *that perfection of God which prompts Him to deal bountifully and kindly with all His creatures.* It is the affection which the Creator feels towards His sentient creatures as such. The Psalmist sings of it in the well known words: "Jehovah is good to all; and His tender mercies are over all His works.

. . . The eyes of all wait for thee; and thou givest them their food in due season. Thou openest thy hand, and satisfiest the desire of every living thing," Ps. 145:9,15,16. This benevolent interest of God is revealed in His care for the creature's welfare, and is suited to the nature and the circumstances of the creature. It naturally varies in degree according to the capacity of the objects to receive it. And while it is not restricted to believers, they only manifest a proper appreciation of its blessings, desire to use them in the service of their God, and thus enjoy them in a richer and fuller measure. The Bible refers to this goodness of God in many passages, such as Ps. 36:6; 104:21; Matt. 5:45; 6:26; Luke 6:35; Acts 14:17.

b. *The love of God.* When the goodness of God is exercised towards His rational creatures, it assumes the higher character of love, and this love may again be distinguished according to the objects on which it terminates. In distinction from the goodness of God in general, it may be defined as *that perfection of God by which He is eternally moved to self-communication.* Since God is absolutely good in Himself, His love cannot find complete satisfaction in any object that falls short of absolute perfection. He loves His rational creatures for His own sake, or, to express it otherwise, He loves in them Himself, His virtues, His work, and His gifts. He does not even withdraw His love completely from the sinner in his present sinful state, though the latter's sin is an abomination to Him, since He recognizes even in the sinner His image-bearer. John 3:16; Matt. 5:44,45. At the same time He loves believers with a special love, since He contemplates them as His spiritual children in Christ. It is to them that He communicates Himself in the fullest and richest sense, with all the fulness of His grace and mercy. John 16:27; Rom. 5:8; I John 3:1.

c. *The grace of God.* The significant word "grace" is a translation of the Hebrew *chanan* and of the Greek *charis.* According to Scripture it is manifested not only by God, but also by men, and then denotes the favor which one man shows another, Gen. 33:8,10,18; 39:4; 47:25; Ruth 2:2; I Sam. 1:18; 16:22. In such cases it is not necessarily implied that the favor is undeserved. In general it can be said, however, that grace is the free bestowal of kindness on one who has no claim to it. This is particularly the case where the grace referred to is the grace of God. His love to man is always unmerited, and when shown to sinners, is even forfeited. The Bible generally uses the word to denote *the unmerited goodness or love of God to those who have forfeited it, and are by nature under a sentence of condemnation.* The grace of God is the source of all spiritual blessings that are bestowed upon sinners. As such we read of it in Eph. 1:6,7; 2:7-9; Tit. 2:11; 3:4-7. While the Bible often speaks of the grace of God as saving grace, it also makes mention of it in a broader sense, as in Isa. 26:10; Jer. 16:13. The grace of God is of the greatest practical significance for sinful men. It was by grace that the way of redemption was opened for them, Rom. 3:24; II Cor. 8:9, and that the message of redemption went out into the world, Acts 14:3. By grace sinners receive the gift of God in

Jesus Christ, Acts 18:27; Eph. 2:8. By grace they are justified, Rom. 3:24; 4:16; Tit. 3:7, they are enriched with spiritual blessings, John 1:16; II Cor. 8:9; II Thess. 2:16, and they finally inherit salvation, Eph. 2:8; Tit. 2:11. Seeing they have absolutely no merits of their own, they are altogether dependent on the grace of God in Christ. In modern theology, with its belief in the inherent goodness of man and his ability to help himself, the doctrine of salvation by grace has practically become a "lost chord," and even the word "grace" was emptied of all spiritual meaning and vanished from religious discourses. It was retained only in the sense of "graciousness," something that is quite external. Happily, there are some evidences of a renewed emphasis on sin, and of a newly awakened consciousness of the need of divine grace.

d. *The mercy of God.* Another important aspect of the goodness and love of God is His mercy or tender compassion. The Hebrew word most generally used for this is *chesed.* There is another word, however, which expresses a deep and tender compassion, namely, the word *racham,* which is beautifully rendered by "tender mercy" in our English Bible. The Septuagint and the New Testament employ the Greek word *eleos* to designate the mercy of God. If the grace of God contemplates man as guilty before God, and therefore in need of forgiveness, the mercy of God contemplates him as one who is bearing the consequences of sin, who is in a pitiable condition, and who therefore needs divine help. It may be defined as *the goodness or love of God shown to those who are in misery or distress, irrespective of their deserts.* In His mercy God reveals Himself as a compassionate God, who pities those who are in misery and is ever ready to relieve their distress. This mercy is bountiful, Deut. 5:10; Ps. 57:10; 86:5, and the poets of Israel delighted to sing of it as enduring forever, I Chron. 16:34; II Chron. 7:6; Ps. 136; Ezra 3:11. In the New Testament it is often mentioned alongside of the grace of God, especially in salutations, I Tim. 1:2; II Tim. 1:1; Titus 1:4. We are told repeatedly that it is shown to them that fear God, Ex. 20:2; Deut. 7:9; Ps. 86:5; Luke 1:50. This does not mean, however, that it is limited to them, though they enjoy it in a special measure. God's tender mercies are over all His works, Ps. 145:9, and even those who do not fear Him share in them, Ezek. 18:23,32; 33:11; Luke 6:35,36. The mercy of God may not be represented as opposed to His justice. It is exercised only in harmony with the strictest justice of God, in view of the merits of Jesus Christ. Other terms used for it in the Bible are "pity," "compassion," and "lovingkindness."

e. *The longsuffering of God.* The longsuffering of God is still another aspect of His great goodness or love. The Hebrew uses the expression *'erek 'aph,* which means literally "long of face," and then also "slow to anger," while the Greek expresses the same idea by the word *makrothumia.* It is *that aspect of the goodness or love of God in virtue of which He bears with the froward and evil in spite of their long continued disobedience.* In the exercise of this attribute the sinner is contemplated as continuing in sin, notwithstanding the admonitions and warnings that come to him. It reveals itself in the postponement of the merited judgment. Scripture speaks of it in Ex. 34:6; Ps. 86:15; Rom. 2:4; 9:22; I Pet. 3:20; II Pet. 3:15. A synonymous term of a slightly different connotation is the word "forbearance."

2. THE HOLINESS OF GOD. The Hebrew word for "to be holy," *quadash,* is derived from the root *qad,* which means to cut or to separate. It is one of the most prominent religious words of the Old Testament, and is applied primarily to God. The same idea is conveyed by the New Testament words *hagiazo* and *hagios.* From this it already appears that it is not correct to think of holiness primarily as a moral or religious quality, as is generally done. Its fundamental idea is that of a *position* or *relationship* existing between God and some person or thing.

a. *Its nature.* The Scriptural idea of the holiness of God is twofold. In its original sense it denotes that He is absolutely distinct from all His creatures, and is exalted above them in infinite majesty. So understood, the holiness of God is one of His transcendental attributes, and is sometimes spoken of as His central and supreme perfection. It does not seem proper to speak of one attribute of God as being more central and fundamental than another; but if this were permissible, the Scriptural emphasis on the holiness of God would seem to justify its selection. It is quite evident, however, that holiness in this sense of the word is not really a *moral* attribute, which can be co-ordinated with the others, such as love, grace and mercy, but is rather something that is co-extensive with, and applicable to, everything that can be predicated of God. He is holy in everything that reveals Him, in His goodness and grace as well as in His justice and wrath. It may be called the "majesty-holiness" of God, and is referred to in such passages as Ex. 15:11; I Sam. 2:2; Isa. 57:15; Hos. 11:9. It is this holiness of God which Otto, in his important work on *Das Heilige,*[1] regards as that which is most essential in God, and which he designates as "the *numinous.*" He regards it as part of the non-rational in God, which cannot be thought of conceptually, and which includes such ideas as "absolute unapproachability" and "absolute overpoweringness" or "aweful majesty." It awakens in man a sense of absolute nothingness, a "creature-consciousness" or "creature-feeling," leading to absolute self-abasement.

But the holiness of God also has a specifically ethical aspect in Scripture, and it is with this aspect of it that we are more directly concerned in this connection. The ethical idea of the divine holiness may not be dissociated from the idea of God's majesty-holiness. The former developed out of the latter. The fundamental idea of the ethical holiness of God is also that of separation, but in this case it is a separation from moral evil or sin. In virtue of His holiness God can have no communion with sin, Job 34:10; Hab. 1:13. Used in this sense, the word "holiness" points to God's majestic purity, or ethical majesty. But the idea of ethical holiness is not merely negative (separation from sin); it also has a positive content, namely, that of moral excellence, or ethical perfection. If man reacts to God's majestic-holiness with a feeling of utter insig-

---

1. Eng. tr. *The Idea of the Holy.*

nificance and awe, his reaction to the ethical holiness reveals itself in a sense of impurity, a consciousness of sin, Isa. 6:5. Otto also recognizes this element in the holiness of God, though he stresses the other, and says of the response to it: "Mere awe, mere need of shelter from the 'tremendum', has here been elevated to the feeling that man in his 'profaneness' is not *worthy* to stand in the presence of the Holy One, and that his entire personal unworthiness might defile even holiness itself."[1] This ethical holiness of God may be defined as *that perfection of God, in virtue of which He eternally wills and maintains His own moral excellence, abhors sin, and demands purity in his moral creatures.*

b. *Its manifestation.* The holiness of God is revealed in the moral law, implanted in man's heart, and speaking through the conscience, and more particularly in God's special revelation. It stood out prominently in the law given to Israel. That law in all its aspects was calculated to impress upon Israel the idea of the holiness of God, and to urge upon the people the necessity of leading a holy life. This was the purpose served by such symbols and types as the holy nation, the holy land, the holy city, the holy place, and the holy priesthood. Moreover, it was revealed in the manner in which God rewarded the keeping of the law, and visited transgressors with dire punishments. The highest revelation of it was given in Jesus Christ, who is called "the Holy and Righteous One," Acts 3:14. He reflected in His life the perfect holiness of God. Finally, the holiness of God is also revealed in the Church as the body of Christ. It is a striking fact, to which attention is often called, that holiness is ascribed to God with far greater frequency in the Old Testament than in the New, though it is done occasionally in the New Testament, John 17:11; I Pet. 1:16; Rev. 4:8; 6:10. This is probably due to the fact that the New Testament appropriates the term more particularly to qualify the third Person of the Holy Trinity as the One whose special task it is, in the economy of redemption, to communicate holiness to His people.

3. THE RIGHTEOUSNESS OF GOD. This attribute is closely related to the holiness of God. Shedd speaks of the justice of God as "a mode of His holiness"; and Strong calls it simply "transitive holiness." However, these terms apply only to what is generally called the *relative*, in distinction from the *absolute*, justice of God.

a. *The fundamental idea of righteousness.* The fundamental idea of righteousness is that of strict adherence to the law. Among men it presupposes that there is a law to which they must conform. It is sometimes said that we cannot speak of righteousness in God, because there is no law to which He is subject. But though there is no law above God, there is certainly a law in the very nature of God, and this is the highest possible standard, by which all other laws are judged. A distinction is generally made between the absolute and the relative justice of God. The former is *that rectitude of the divine nature, in virtue of which God is infinitely righteous in Himself,* while the latter is *that perfection*

---

1. *The Idea of the Holy*, p. 56.

of God by which He maintains Himself over against every violation of His holiness, and shows in every respect that He is the Holy One. It is to this righteousness that the term "justice" more particularly applies. Justice manifests itself especially in giving every man his due, in treating him according to his deserts. The inherent righteousness of God is naturally basic to the righteousness which He reveals in dealing with His creatures, but it is especially the latter, also called the justice of God, that calls for special consideration here. The Hebrew terms for "righteous" and "righteousness" are *tsaddik, tsedhek,* and *tsedhakah,* and the corresponding Greek terms, *dikaios* and *dikaiosune,* all of which contain the idea of conformity to a standard. This perfection is repeatedly ascribed to God in Scripture, Ezra 9:15; Neh. 9:8; Ps. 119:137; 145:17; Jer. 12:1; Lam. 1:18; Dan. 9:14; John 17:25; II Tim. 4:8; I John 2:29; 3:7; Rev. 16:5.

b. *Distinctions applied to the justice of God.* There is first of all a *rectoral justice* of God. This justice, as the very name implies, is the rectitude which God manifests as the Ruler of both the good and the evil. In virtue of it He has instituted a moral government in the world, and imposed a just law upon man, with promises of reward for the obedient, and threats of punishment for the transgressor. God stands out prominently in the Old Testament as the Lawgiver of Israel, Isa. 33:22, and of people in general, Jas. 4:12, and His laws are righteous laws, Deut. 4:8. The Bible refers to this rectoral work of God also in Ps. 99:4, and Rom. 1:32.

Closely connected with the rectoral is the *distributive justice* of God. This term usually serves to designate God's rectitude in the execution of the law, and relates to the distribution of rewards and punishments, Isa. 3:10,11; Rom. 2:6; I Pet. 1:17. It is of two kinds: (1) *Remunerative justice,* which manifests itself in the distribution of rewards to both men and angels, Deut. 7:9,12,13; II Chron. 6:15; Ps. 58:11; Micah 7:20; Matt. 25:21,34; Rom. 2:7; Heb. 11:26. It is really an expression of the divine love, dealing out its bounties, not on the basis of strict merit, for the creature can establish no absolute merit before the Creator, but according to promise and agreement, Luke 17:10; I Cor. 4:7. God's rewards are gracious and spring from a covenant relation which He has established. (2) *Retributive justice,* which relates to the infliction of penalties. It is an expression of the divine wrath. While in a sinless world there would be no place for its exercise, it necessarily holds a very prominent place in a world full of sin. On the whole the Bible stresses the reward of the righteous more than the punishment of the wicked; but even the latter is sufficiently prominent. Rom. 1:32; 2:9; 12:19; II Thess. 1:8, and many other passages. It should be noted that, while man does not merit the reward which he receives, he does merit the punishment which is meted out to him. Divine justice is originally and necessarily obliged to punish evil, but not to reward good, Luke 17:10; I Cor. 4:7; Job 41:11. Many deny the strict punitive justice of God and claim that God punishes the sinner to reform him, or to deter others from sin; but these positions are not tenable. The primary purpose of the punishment of sin is the maintenance of right and justice. Of course, it may incidentally serve, and may even, secondarily, be intended, to reform the sinner and to deter others from sin.

D. Attributes of Sovereignty.

The sovereignty of God is strongly emphasized in Scripture. He is represented as the Creator, and His will as the cause of all things. In virtue of His creative work heaven and earth and all that they contain belong to Him. He is clothed with absolute authority over the hosts of heaven and the inhabitants of the earth. He upholds all things with His almighty power, and determines the ends which they are destined to serve. He rules as King in the most absolute sense of the word, and all things are dependent on Him and subservient to Him. There is a wealth of Scripture evidence for the sovereignty of God, but we limit our references here to a few of the most significant passages: Gen. 14:19; Ex. 18:11; Deut. 10:14,17; I Chron. 29:11,12; II Chron. 20:6; Neh. 9:6; Ps. 22:28; 47:2,3,7,8; Ps. 50:10-12; 95:3-5; 115:3; 135:5,6; 145:11-13; Jer. 27:5; Luke 1:53; Acts 17:24-26; Rev. 19:6. Two attributes call for discussion under this head, namely (1) the sovereign will of God, and (2) the sovereign power of God.

1. THE SOVEREIGN WILL OF GOD.

a. *The will of God in general.* The Bible employs several words to denote the will of God, namely the Hebrew words *chaphets, tsebhu* and *ratson* and the Greek words *boule* and *thelema.* The importance of the divine will appears in many ways in Scripture. It is represented as the final cause of all things. Everything is derived from it; creation and preservation, Ps. 135:6; Jer. 18:6; Rev. 4:11, government, Prov. 21:1; Dan. 4:35, election and reprobation, Rom. 9:15,16; Eph. 1:11, the sufferings of Christ, Luke 22:42; Acts 2:23, regeneration, Jas. 1:18, sanctification, Phil. 2:13, the sufferings of believers, I Pet. 3:17, man's life and destiny, Acts 18:21; Rom. 15:32; Jas. 4:15, and even the smallest things of life, Matt. 10:29. Hence Christian theology has always recognized the will of God as the ultimate cause of all things, though philosophy has sometimes shown an inclination to seek a deeper cause in the very Being of the Absolute. However, the attempt to ground everything in the very Being of God generally results in Pantheism.

The word "will" as applied to God does not always have the same connotation in Scripture. It may denote (1) the whole moral nature of God, including such attributes as love, holiness, righteousness, etc.; (2) the faculty of self-determination, i.e. the power to determine self to a course of action or to form a plan; (3) the product of this activity, that is, the predetermined plan or purpose; (4) the power to execute this plan and to realize this purpose (the will in action or omnipotence); and (5) the rule of life laid down for rational creatures. It is primarily the will of God as the faculty of self-determination with which we are concerned at present. It may be defined as *that perfection of His Being whereby He, in a most simple act, goes out towards Himself as the highest good (i.e. delights in Himself as such) and towards His creatures for His own name's sake, and is thus the ground of their being and continued existence.* With reference to the universe and all the creatures which it contains this naturally includes the idea of causation.

b. *Distinctions applied to the will of God.* Several distinctions have been applied to the will of God. Some of these found little favor in Reformed theology, such as the distinction between an *antecedent* and a *consequent* will of God, and that between an *absolute* and a *conditional* will. These distinctions were not only liable to misunderstanding, but were actually interpreted in objectionable ways. Others, however, were found useful, and were therefore more generally accepted. They may be stated as follows: (1) *The decretive and the preceptive will of God.* The former is that will of God by which He purposes or decrees whatever shall come to pass, whether He wills to accomplish it effectively (causatively), or to permit it to occur through the unrestrained agency of His rational creatures. The latter is the rule of life which God has laid down for His moral creatures, indicating the duties which He enjoins upon them. The former is always accomplished, while the latter is often disobeyed. (2) *The will of eudokia and the will of eurestia.* This division was made, not so much in connection with the purpose to do, as with respect to the pleasure in doing, or the desire to see something done. It corresponds with the preceding, however, in the fact that the will of *eudokia*, like that of the decree, comprises what shall certainly be accomplished, while the will of *eurestia*, like that of the precept, embraces simply what God is pleased to have His creatures do. The word *eudokia* should not mislead us to think that the will of *eudokia* has reference only to good, and not to evil, cf. Matt. 11:26. It is hardly correct to say that the element of complacency or delight is always present in it. (3) *The will of the beneplacitum and the will of the signum.* The former again denotes the will of God as embodied in His hidden counsel, until He makes it known by some revelation, or by the event itself. Any will that is so revealed becomes a *signum.* This distinction is meant to correspond to that between the decretive and the preceptive will of God, but can hardly be said to do this. The good pleasure of God also finds expression in His preceptive will; and the decretive will sometimes also comes to our knowledge by a signum. (4) *The secret and the revealed will of God.* This is the most common distinction. The former is the will of God's decree, which is largely hidden in God, while the latter is the will of the precept, which is revealed in the law and in the gospel. The distinction is based on Deut. 29:29. The secret will of God is mentioned in Ps. 115:3; Dan. 4:17,25,32,35; Rom. 9:18,19; 11:33,34; Eph. 1:5,9,11; and His revealed will, in Matt. 7:21; 12:50; John 4:34; 7:17; Rom. 12:2. The latter is accessible to all and is not far from us, Deut. 30:14; Rom. 10:8. The secret will of God pertains to all things which He wills either to effect or to permit, and which are therefore absolutely fixed. The revealed will prescribes the duties of man, and represents the way in which he can enjoy the blessings of God.

c. *The freedom of God's will.* The question is frequently debated whether God, in the exercise of His will, acts necessarily or freely. The answer to this question requires careful discrimination. Just as there is a *scientia necessaria* and a *scientia libera*, there is also a *voluntas necessaria* (necessary will) and a *voluntas libera* (free will) in God. God Himself is the object of the former. He *necessarily* wills Himself, His holy nature, and the personal distinctions in the Godhead. This means that He necessarily loves Himself and takes delight in the contemplation of His own perfections. Yet He is under no compulsion, but acts according to the law of His Being; and this, while necessary, is also the highest freedom. It is quite evident that the idea of causation is absent here, and that the thought of complacency or self-approval is in the foreground. God's creatures, however, are the objects of His *voluntas libera*. God determines *voluntarily* what and whom He will create, and the times, places, and circumstances, of their lives. He marks out the path of all His rational creatures, determines their destiny, and uses them for His purposes. And though He endows them with freedom, yet His will controls their actions. The Bible speaks of this freedom of God's will in the most absolute terms, Job 11:10; 33:13; Ps. 115:3; Prov. 21:1; Isa. 10:15; 29:16; 45:9; Matt. 20:15; Rom. 9:15-18,20,21; I Cor. 12:11; Rev. 4:11. The Church always defended this freedom, but also emphasized the fact that it may not be regarded as absolute indifference. Duns Scotus applied the idea of a will in no sense determined to God; but this idea of a blind will, acting with perfect indifference, was rejected by the Church. The freedom of God is not pure indifference, but rational self-determination. God has reasons for willing as He does, which induce Him to choose one end rather than another, and one set of means to accomplish one end in preference to others. There is in each case a prevailing motive, which makes the end chosen and the means selected the most pleasing to Him, though we may not be able to determine what this motive is. In general it may be said that God cannot will anything that is contrary to His nature, to His wisdom or love, to His righteousness or holiness. Dr. Bavinck points out that we can seldom discern why God willed one thing rather than another, and that it is not possible nor even permissible for us to look for some deeper ground of things than the will of God, because all such attempts result in seeking a ground for the creature in the very Being of God, in robbing it of its contingent character, and in making it necessary, eternal, divine.[1]

d. *God's will in relation to sin.* The doctrine of the will of God often gives rise to serious questions. Problems arise here which have never yet been solved and which are probably incapable of solution by man.

(1) It is said that if the decretive will of God also determined the entrance of sin into the world, God thereby becomes the author of sin and really wills something that is contrary to His moral perfections. Arminians, to escape the

---

1. *Geref. Dogm.* II, p. 241.

difficulty, make the will of God to permit sin dependent on His foreknowledge of the course which man would choose. Reformed theologians, while maintaining on the basis of such passages as Acts 2:23; 3:8; etc., that God's decretive will also includes the sinful deeds of man, are always careful to point out that this must be conceived in such a way that God does not become the author of sin. They frankly admit that they cannot solve the difficulty, but at the same time make some valuable distinctions that prove helpful. Most of them insist on it that God's will with respect to sin is simply a will to permit sin and not a will to effectuate it, as He does the moral good. This terminology is certainly permissible, provided it is understood correctly. It should be borne in mind that God's will to permit sin carries certainty with it. Others call attention to the fact that, while the terms "will" or "to will" may include the idea of complacency or delight, they sometimes point to a simple determination of the will; and that therefore the will of God to permit sin need not imply that He takes delight or pleasure in sin.

(2) Again, it is said that the decretive and preceptive will of God are often contradictory. His decretive will includes many things which He forbids in His preceptive will, and excludes many things which He commands in His preceptive will, cf. Gen. 22; Ex. 4:21-23; II Kings 20:1-7; Acts 2:23. Yet it is of great importance to maintain both the decretive and the preceptive will, but with the definite understanding that, while they appear to us as distinct, they are yet fundamentally one in God. Though a perfectly satisfactory solution of the difficulty is out of the question for the present, it is possible to make some approaches to a solution. When we speak of the decretive and the preceptive will of God, we use the word "will" in two different senses. By the former God has determined what He will do or what shall come to pass; in the latter He reveals to us what we are in duty bound to do.[1] At the same time we should remember that the moral law, the rule of our life, is also in a sense the embodiment of the will of God. It is an expression of His holy nature and of what this naturally requires of all moral creatures. Hence another remark must be added to the preceding. The decretive and preceptive will of God do not conflict in the sense that in the former He does, and according to the latter He does not, take pleasure in sin; nor in the sense that according to the former He does not, and according to the latter He does, will the salvation of every individual *with a positive volition*. Even according to the decretive will God takes no pleasure in sin; and even according to the preceptive will He does not will the salvation of every individual *with a positive volition*.

2. THE SOVEREIGN POWER OF GOD. The sovereignty of God finds expression, not only in the divine will, but also in the omnipotence of God or the power to execute His will. Power in God may be called the effective energy of His nature, or *that perfection of His Being by which He is the absolute and highest causality*. It is customary to distinguish between a *potentia Dei absoluta*

---

1. Cf. Bavinck, *Geref. Dogm.* II, pp. 246 ff.; Dabney, *Syst. and Polem. Theol.*, p. 162

(absolute power of God) and a *potentia Dei ordinata* (ordered power of God). However, Reformed theology rejects this distinction in the sense in which it was understood by the Scholastics, who claimed that God by virtue of His absolute power could effect contradictions, and could even sin and annihilate Himself. At the same time it adopts the distinction as expressing a real truth, though it does not always represent it in the same way. According to Hodge and Shedd absolute power is the divine efficiency, as exercised without the intervention of second causes; while ordinate power is the efficiency of God, as exercised by the ordered operation of second causes.[1] The more general view is stated by Charnock as follows: "Absolute, is that power whereby God is able to do that which He will not do, but is possible to be done; ordinate, is that power whereby God doth that which He hath decreed to do, that is, which He hath ordained or appointed to be exercised; which are not distinct powers, but one and the same power. His ordinate power is a part of His absolute; for if He had not power to do everything that He could will, He might not have the power to do everything that He doth will."[2] The *potentia ordinata* can be defined as *that perfection of God whereby He, through the mere exercise of His will, can realize whatsoever is present in His will or counsel.* The power of God in actual exercise limits itself to that which is comprehended in His eternal decree. But the actual exercise of God's power does not represent its limits. God could do more than that, if He were so minded. In that sense we can speak of the *potentia absoluta*, or absolute power, of God. This position must be maintained over against those who, like Schleiermacher and Strauss, hold that God's power is limited to that which He actually accomplishes. But in our assertion of the absolute power of God it is necessary to guard against misconceptions. The Bible teaches us on the one hand that the power of God extends beyond that which is actually realized, Gen. 18:14; Jer. 32:27; Zech. 8:6; Matt. 3:9; 26:53. We cannot say, therefore, that what God does not bring to realization, is not possible for Him. But on the other hand it also indicates that there are many things which God cannot do. He can neither lie, sin, change, nor deny Himself, Num. 23:19; I Sam. 15:29; II Tim. 2:13; Heb. 6:18; Jas. 1:13,17. There is no absolute power in Him that is divorced from His perfections, and in virtue of which He can do all kinds of things which are inherently contradictory. The idea of God's omnipotence is expressed in the name *'El-Shaddai;* and the Bible speaks of it in no uncertain terms. Job 9:12; Ps. 115:3; Jer. 32:17; Matt. 19:26; Luke 1:37; Rom. 1:20; Eph. 1:19. God manifests His power in creation, Rom. 4:17; Isa. 44:24; in the works of providence, Heb. 1:3, and in the redemption of sinners, I Cor. 1:24; Rom. 1:16.

QUESTIONS FOR FURTHER STUDY. In what different senses can we speak of the foreknowledge of God? How do the Arminians conceive of this foreknowledge? What objections are there to the Jesuit idea of a *scientia media?* How must we judge of the modern emphasis on the love of God as the central and all-determining attribute of God? What is Otto's

1. Shedd, *Dogm. Theol.* I. pp. 361f., Hodge, *Syst. Theol.* 1. pp. 410f.

2. *Existence and Attributes of God* II. p. 12. Cf. also Bavinck, *Geref. Dogm.* II, p. 252; Kuyper, *Dict. Dogm., De Deo* I, pp. 412f.

conception of "the Holy" in God? What objection is there to the position that the punishments of God simply serve to reform the sinner, or to deter others from sin? What is the Socinian and the Grotian conception of retributive justice in God? Is it correct to say that God can do everything in virtue of His omnipotence?

LITERATURE: Bavinck, *Geref. Dogm.* II, pp. 171-259; Kuyper, *Dict. Dogm., De Deo* I, pp. 355-417; Vos, *Geref. Dogm.* I, pp. 2-36; Hodge, *Syst. Theol.* I, pp. 393-441; Shedd, *Dogm. Theol. I,* pp. 359-392; Dabney, *Syst. and Polem. Theol.,* pp. 154-174; Pope, *Chr. Theol.* I, pp. 307-358; Watson, *Theol. Inst.* Part II, Chap. II; Wilmers, *Handbook of the Chr. Religion,* pp. 171-181; Harris, *God, Creator and Lord of All,* I, pp. 128-209; Charnock, *The Existence and Attributes of God,* Discourse III, VII-IX; Bates, *On the Attributes;* Clarke, *The Christian Doctrine of God,* pp. 56-115; Snowden, *The Personality of God;* Adeney, *The Christian Conception of God,* pp. 86-152; Macintosh, *Theology as an Empirical Science,* pp. 159-194; Strong, *Syst. Theol.,* pp. 282-303.

VIII. The Holy Trinity

A. The Doctrine of the Trinity in History.

The doctrine of the Trinity has always bristled with difficulties, and therefore it is no wonder that the Church in its attempt to formulate it was repeatedly tempted to rationalize it and to give a construction of it which failed to do justice to the Scriptural data.

1. THE PRE-REFORMATION PERIOD. The Jews of Jesus' days strongly emphasized the unity of God, and this emphasis was carried over into the Christian Church. The result was that some ruled out the personal distinctions in the Godhead altogether, and that others failed to do full justice to the essential deity of the second and third persons of the Holy Trinity. Tertullian was the first to use the term "Trinity" and to formulate the doctrine, but his formulation was deficient, since it involved an unwarranted subordination of the Son to the Father. Origen went even farther in this direction by teaching explicitly that the Son is subordinate to the Father *in respect to essence,* and that the Holy Spirit is subordinate even to the Son. He detracted from the essential deity of these two persons in the Godhead, and furnished a stepping-stone to the Arians, who denied the deity of the Son and of the Holy Spirit by representing the Son as the first creature of the Father, and the Holy Spirit as the first creature of the Son. Thus the consubstantiality of the Son and the Holy Spirit with the Father was sacrificed, in order to preserve the unity of God; and the three persons of the Godhead were made to differ in rank. The Arians still retained a semblance of the doctrine of three persons in the Godhead, but this was sacrificed entirely by Monarchianism, partly in the interest of the unity of God and partly to maintain the deity of the Son. Dynamic Monarchianism saw in Jesus but a man and in the Holy Spirit a divine influence, while Modalistic Monarchianism regarded the Father, the Son, and the Holy Spirit, merely as three modes of manifestation successively assumed by the Godhead. On the other hand there were also some who lost sight of the unity of God to such an extent that they landed in Tritheism. Some of the later Monophysites, such as John Ascunages and John Philoponus, fell into this error. During the Middle Ages the Nominalist, Roscelinus, was accused of the same error. The Church began to formulate its doctrine of the Trinity in the fourth century. The Council of Nicea declared the Son to be co-essential with the Father (325 A.D.), while the Council of Constantinople (381 A.D.) asserted the deity of

the Holy Spirit, though not with the same precision. As to the interrelation of the three it was officially professed that the Son is generated by the Father, and that the Holy Spirit proceeds from the Father and the Son. In the East the doctrine of the Trinity found its fullest statement in the work of John of Damascus, and in the West, in Augustine's great work *De Trinitate*. The former still retains an element of subordination, which is entirely eliminated by the latter.

2. THE POST-REFORMATION PERIOD. We have no further development of the doctrine of the Trinity, but only encounter repeatedly some of the earlier erroneous constructions of it after the Reformation. The Arminians, Episcopius, Curcellæus, and Limborgh, revived the doctrine of subordination, chiefly again, so it seems, to maintain the unity of the Godhead. They ascribed to the Father a certain pre-eminence over the other persons, *in order, dignity, and power*. A somewhat similar position was taken by Samuel Clarke in England and by the Lutheran theologian, Kahnis. Others followed the way pointed out by Sabellius by teaching a species of Modalism, as, for instance, Emanuel Swedenborg, who held that the eternal God-man became flesh in the Son, and operated through the Holy Spirit; Hegel, who speaks of the Father as God in Himself, of the Son as God objectifying Himself, and of the Holy Spirit as God returning unto Himself; and Schleiermacher, who regards the three persons simply as three aspects of God: the Father is God as the underlying unity of all things, the Son is God as coming to conscious personality in man, and the Holy Spirit is God as living in the Church. The Socinians of the days of the Reformation moved along Arian lines, but even went beyond Arius, by making Christ merely a man and the Holy Spirit but a power or influence. They were the forerunners of the Unitarians and also of the liberal theologians who speak of Jesus as a divine teacher, and identify the Holy Spirit with the immanent God. Finally, there were also some who, since they regarded the statement of the doctrine of an ontological Trinity as unintelligible, wanted to stop short of it and rest satisfied with the doctrine of an economic Trinity, a Trinity as revealed in the work of redemption and in human experience, as Moses Stuàrt, W. L. Alexander, and W. A. Brown. For a considerable time interest in the doctrine of the Trinity waned, and theological discussion centered more particularly on the personality of God. Brunner and Barth have again called attention to its importance. The latter places it very much in the foreground, discussing it in connection with the doctrine of revelation, and devotes 220 pages of his Dogmatics to it. Materially, he derives the doctrine from Scripture, but, formally and logically, he finds that it is involved in the simple sentence, "God speaks." He is Revealer (Father), Revelation (Son) and Revealedness (Holy Spirit). He reveals Himself, He is the Revelation, and He is also the content of the Revelation. God and His revelation are identified. He remains God also in His revelation, absolutely free and sovereign. This view of Barth is not a species of Sabellianism, for he recognizes three

persons in the Godhead. Moreover, he does not allow for any subordination. Says he: "Thus, to the same God who in unimpaired unity is Revealer, Revelation, and Revealedness, is also ascribed in unimpaired variety in Himself precisely this threefold mode of being."[1]

B. God as Trinity in Unity.

The word "Trinity" is not quite as expressive as the Holland word "Drie-eenheid," for it may simply denote the state of being three, without any implication as to the unity of the three. It is generally understood, however, that, as a technical term in theology, it includes that idea. It goes without saying that, when we speak of the Trinity of God, we refer to a trinity in unity, and to a unity that is trinal.

1. THE PERSONALITY OF GOD AND THE TRINITY. As stated in the preceding, the communicable attributes of God stress His personality, since they reveal Him as a rational and moral Being. His life stands out clearly before us in Scripture as a personal life; and it is, of course, of the greatest importance to maintain the personality of God, for without it there can be no religion in the real sense of the word: no prayer, no personal communion, no trustful reliance and no confident hope. Since man is created in the image of God, we learn to understand something of the personal life of God from the contemplation of personality as we know it in man. We should be careful, however, not to set up man's personality as a standard by which the personality of God must be measured. The original form of personality is not in man but in God; His is archetypal, while man's is ectypal. The latter is not identical with the former, but does contain faint traces of similarity with it. We should not say that man is personal, while God is super-personal (a very unfortunate term), for what is super-personal is not personal; but rather, that what appears as imperfect in man exists in infinite perfection in God. The one outstanding difference between the two is that man is uni-personal, while God is tri-personal. And this tri-personal existence is a necessity in the Divine Being, and not in any sense the result of a choice of God. He could not exist in any other than the tri-personal form. This has been argued in various ways. It is very common to argue it from the idea of personality itself. Shedd bases his argument on the *general* self-consciousness of the triune God, as distinguished from the particular individual self-consciousness of each one of the Persons in the Godhead, for in self-consciousness the subject must know itself as an object, and also perceive that it does. This is possible in God because of His trinal existence. He says that God could not be self-contemplating, self-cognitive, and self-communing, if He were not trinal in His constitution.[2] Bartlett presents in an interesting way a variety of considerations to prove that God is *necessarily* tri-personal.[3] The argument from personality, to prove at least a plur-

---

1. *The Doctrine of the Word of God*, p. 344.
2. *Dogm. Theol.*, I, pp. 393 f., 251 ff., 178ff.
3. *The Triune God, Part Two.*

ality in God, can be put in some such form as this: Among men the ego awakens to consciousness only by contact with the non-ego. Personality does not develop nor exist in isolation, but only in association with other persons. Hence it is not possible to conceive of personality in God apart from an association of *equal* persons in Him. His contact with His creatures would not account for His personality any more than man's contact with the animals would explain his personality. In virtue of the tri-personal existence of God there is an infinite fulness of divine life in Him. Paul speaks of this *pleroma* (fulness) of the Godhead in Eph. 3:19 and Col. 1:9; 2:9. In view of the fact that there are three persons in God, it is better to say that God is personal than to speak of Him as a Person.

2. SCRIPTURAL PROOF FOR THE DOCTRINE OF THE TRINITY. The doctrine of the Trinity is very decidedly a doctrine of revelation. It is true that human reason may suggest some thoughts to substantiate the doctrine, and that men have sometimes on purely philosophical grounds abandoned the idea of a bare unity in God, and introduced the idea of living movement and self-distinction. And it is also true that Christian experience would seem to demand some such construction of the doctrine of God. At the same time it is a doctrine which we would not have known, nor have been able to maintain with any degree of confidence, on the basis of experience alone, and which is brought to our knowledge only by God's special self-revelation. Therefore it is of the utmost importance that we gather the Scriptural proofs for it.

a. *Old Testament proofs.* Some of the early Church Fathers and even some later theologians, disregarding the progressive character of God's revelation, gave the impression that the doctrine of the Trinity was completely revealed in the Old Testament. On the other hand Socinians and Arminians were of the opinion that it was not found there at all. Both were mistaken. The Old Testament does not contain a full revelation of the trinitarian existence of God, but does contain several indications of it. And this is exactly what might be expected. The Bible never deals with the doctrine of the Trinity as an abstract truth, but reveals the trinitarian life in its various relations as a living reality, to a certain extent in connection with the works of creation and providence, but particularly in relation to the work of redemption. Its most fundamental revelation is a revelation given in facts rather than in words. And this revelation increases in clarity in the measure in which the redemptive work of God is more clearly revealed, as in the incarnation of the Son and the outpouring of the Holy Spirit. And the more the glorious reality of the Trinity stands out in the facts of history, the clearer the statements of the doctrine become. The fuller revelation of the Trinity in the New Testament is due to the fact that the Word became flesh, and that the Holy Spirit took up His abode in the Church.

Proof for the Trinity has sometimes been found in the distinction of Jehovah and Elohim, and also in the plural Elohim, but the former is entirely unwarranted, and the latter is, to say the least, very dubious, though Rottenberg still maintains it in his work on *De Triniteit in Israels Godsbegrip.*[1] It is far more plausible that the passages in which God speaks of Himself in the plural, Gen. 1:26; 11:7, contain an indication of personal distinctions in God, though even these do not point to a trinity but only to a plurality of persons. Still clearer indications of such personal distinctions are found in those passages which refer to the Angel of Jehovah, who is on the one hand identified with Jehovah, and on the other hand distinguished from Him, Gen. 16:7-13; 18:1-21; 19:1-28; Mal. 3:1; and also in passages in which the Word or Wisdom of God is personified, Ps. 33:4, 6; Prov. 8:12-31. In some cases more than one person is mentioned, Ps. 33:6; 45:6, 7 (comp. Heb. 1:8, 9), and in others God is the speaker, and mentions both the Messiah and the Spirit, or the Messiah is the speaker who mentions both God and the Spirit, Isa. 48:16; 61:1; 63:9, 10. Thus the Old Testament contains a clear anticipation of the fuller revelation of the Trinity in the New Testament.

b. *New Testament proofs.* The New Testament carries with it a clearer revelation of the distinctions in the Godhead. If in the Old Testament Jehovah is represented as the Redeemer and Saviour of His people, Job. 19:25; Ps. 19:14; 78:35; 106:21; Isa. 41:14; 43:3,11,14; 47:4; 49:7,26; 60:16; Jer. 14:3; 50:14; Hos. 13:3, in the New Testament the Son of God clearly stands out in that capacity, Matt. 1:21; Luke 1:76-79; 2:17; John 4:42; Acts 5:3; Gal. 3:13; 4:5; Phil. 3:30; Tit. 2:13,14. And if in the Old Testament it is Jehovah that dwells among Israel and in the hearts of those that fear Him, Ps. 74:2; 135:21; Isa. 8:18; 57:15; Ezek. 43:7-9; Joel 3:17,21; Zech. 2:10, 11, in the New Testament it is the Holy Spirit that dwells in the Church, Acts 2:4, Rom. 8:9,11; I Cor. 3:16; Gal. 4:6; Eph. 2:22; Jas. 4:5. The New Testament offers the clear revelation of God sending His Son into the world, John 3:16; Gal. 4:4; Heb. 1:6; I John 4:9; and of both the Father and the Son, sending the Spirit, John 14:26; 15:26; 16:7; Gal. 4:6. We find the Father addressing the Son, Mark 1:11; Luke 3:22, the Son communing with the Father, Matt. 11:25,26; 26:39; John 11:41; 12:27,28, and the Holy Spirit praying to God in the hearts of believers, Rom. 8:26. Thus the separate persons of the Trinity are made to stand out clearly before our minds. At the baptism of the Son the Father speaks from heaven, and the Holy Spirit descends in the form of a dove, Matt. 3:16,17. In the great commission Jesus mentions the three persons: ". . . baptizing them into the name of the Father and of the Son and of the Holy Spirit," Matt. 28:19. They are also named alongside of each other in I Cor. 12:4-6; II Cor. 13:14; and I Peter 1:2. The only passage speaking of tri-unity is I John 5:7 (Auth. Ver.), but this is of doubtful genuineness, and is therefore eliminated from the latest critical editions of the New Testament.

---

1. pp. 19ff.

3. STATEMENT OF THE DOCTRINE OF THE TRINITY. The doctrine of the Trinity can best be discussed briefly in connection with various propositions, which constitute an epitome of the faith of the Church on this point.

a. *There is in the Divine Being but one indivisible essence (ousia, essentia).* God is one in His essential being or constitutional nature. Some of the early Church Fathers used the term "*substantia*" as synonymous with "essentia," but later writers avoided this use of it in view of the fact that in the Latin Church "*substantia*" was used as a rendering of "*hupostasis*" as well as of "*ousia*," and was therefore ambiguous. At present the two terms "substance" and "essence" are often used interchangeably. There is no objection to this, provided we bear in mind that they have slightly different connotations. Shedd distinguishes them as follows: "Essence is from *esse*, to be, and denotes energetic being. Substance is from *substare*, and denotes the latent possibility of being. . . . The term essence describes God as a sum-total of infinite perfections; the term substance describes Him as the underlying ground of infinite activities. The first is, comparatively, an active word; the last, a passive. The first is, comparatively, a spiritual, the last a material term. We speak of material substance rather than of material essence."[1] Since the unity of God was already discussed in the preceding, it is not necessary to dwell on it in detail in the present connection. This proposition respecting the unity of God is based on such passages as Deut. 6:4; Jas. 2:19, on the self-existence and immutability of God, and on the fact that He is identified with His perfections as when He is called life, light, truth, righteousness, and so on.

b. *In this one Divine Being there are three Persons or individual subsistences, Father, Son, and Holy Spirit.* This is proved by the various passages referred to as substantiating the doctrine of the Trinity. To denote these distinctions in the Godhead, Greek writers generally employed the term *hupostasis*, while Latin authors used the term *persona*, and sometimes *substantia*. Because the former was apt to be misleading and the latter was ambiguous, the Schoolmen coined the word *subsistentia*. The variety of the terms used points to the fact that their inadequacy was always felt. It is generally admitted that the word "person" is but an imperfect expression of the idea. In common parlance it denotes a separate rational and moral individual, possessed of self-consciousness, and conscious of his identity amid all changes. Experience teaches that where you have a person, you also have a distinct individual essence. Every person is a distinct and separate individual, in whom human nature is individualized. But in God there are no three individuals alongside of, and separate from, one another, but only personal self-distinctions within the Divine essence, which is not only generically, but also numerically, one. Consequently many preferred to speak of three hypostases in God, three different modes, not of manifestation, as Sabellius taught, *but of existence or subsistence.* Thus Calvin says: "By person, then, I mean a subsistence in the

---

1. *Dogm. Theol.*, I, p. 271.

Divine essence. — a subsistence which, while related to' the other two, is distinguished from them by incommunicable properties."[1] This is perfectly permissible and may ward off misunderstanding, but should not cause us to lose sight of the fact that the self-distinctions in the Divine Being imply an "I" and "Thou" and "He," in the Being of God, which assume personal relations to one another. Matt. 3:16; 4:1; John 1:18; 3:16; 5:20-22; 14:26; 15:26; 16:13-15.

c. *The whole undivided essence of God belongs equally to each of the three persons.* This means that the divine essence is not divided among the three persons, but is wholly with all its perfection in each one of the persons, so that they have a numerical unity of essence. The divine nature is distinguished from the human nature in that it can subsist *wholly* and *indivisibly* in more than one person. While three persons among men have only a *specific* unity of nature or essence, that is, share in the same kind of nature or essence, the persons in the Godhead have a *numerical* unity of essence, that is, possess the identical essence. Human nature or essence may be regarded as a species, of which each man has an individual part, so that there is a *specific* (from species) unity; but the divine nature is indivisible and therefore identical in the persons of the Godhead. It is numerically one and the same, and therefore the unity of the essence in the persons is a numerical unity. From this it follows that the divine essence is not an independent existence alongside of the three persons. It has no existence outside of and apart from the three persons. If it did, there would be no true unity, but a division that would lead into tetratheism. The personal distinction is one within the divine essence. This has, as it is usually termed, three modes of subsistence. Another conclusion which follows from the preceding, is that there can be no subordination *as to essential being* of the one person of the Godhead to the other, and therefore no difference in personal dignity. This must be maintained over against the subordinationism of Origen and other early Church Fathers, and the Arminians, and of Clarke and other Anglican theologians. The only subordination of which we can speak, is a subordination in respect to order and relationship. It is especially when we reflect on the relation of the three persons to the divine essence that all analogies fail us and we become deeply conscious of the fact that the Trinity is a mystery far beyond our comprehension. It is the incomprehensible glory of the Godhead. Just as human nature is too rich and too full to be embodied in a single individual, and comes to its adequate expression only in humanity as a whole so the divine Being unfolds itself in its fulness only in its three fold subsistence of Father, Son, and Holy Spirit.

d. *The subsistence and operation of the three persons in the divine Being is marked by a certain definite order.* There is a certain order in the ontological Trinity. In personal subsistence the Father is first, the Son second, and the Holy Spirit third. It need hardly be said that this order does not pertain to any priority of time or of essential dignity, but only to the logical order of

---

1. *Inst.* I, XIII, 6

derivation. The Father is neither begotten by, nor proceeds from any other person; the Son is eternally begotten of the Father, and the Spirit proceeds from the Father and the Son from all eternity. Generation and procession take place within the Divine Being, and imply a certain subordination as to the manner of personal subsistence, but no subordination as far as the possession of the divine essence is concerned. This ontological Trinity and its inherent order is the metaphysical basis of the economical Trinity. It is but natural, therefore, that the order existing in the essential Trinity should be reflected in the *opera ad extra* that are more particularly ascribed to each one of the persons. Scripture clearly indicates this order in the so-called *praepositiones distinctionales, ek, dia,* and *en,* which are used in expressing the idea that all things are out of the Father, through the Son, and in the Holy Spirit.

e. *There are certain personal attributes by which the three persons are distinguished.* These are also called *opera ad intra,* because they are works within the Divine Being, which do not terminate on the creature. They are personal operations, which are not performed by the three persons jointly and which are incommunicable. Generation is an act of the Father only; filiation belongs to the Son exclusively; and procession can only be ascribed to the Holy Spirit. As *opera ad intra* these works are distinguished from the *opera ad extra,* or those activities and effects by which the Trinity is manifested outwardly. These are never works of one person exclusively, but always works of the Divine Being as a whole. At the same time it is true that in the economical order of God's works some of the *opera ad extra* are ascribed more particularly to one person, and some more especially to another. Though they are all works of the three persons jointly, creation is ascribed primarily to the Father, redemption to the Son, and sanctification to the Holy Spirit. This order in the divine operations points back to the essential order in God and forms the basis for what is generally known as the economic Trinity.

f. *The Church confesses the Trinity to be a mystery beyond the comprehension of man.* The Trinity is a mystery, not merely in the Biblical sense that it is a truth, which was formerly hidden but is now revealed; but in the sense that man cannot comprehend it and make it intelligible. It is intelligible in some of its relations and modes of manifestation, but unintelligible in its essential nature. The many efforts that were made to explain the mystery were speculative rather than theological. They invariably resulted in the development of tritheistic or modalistic conceptions of God, in the denial of either the unity of the divine essence or the reality of the personal distinctions within the essence. The real difficulty lies in the relation in which the persons in the Godhead stand to the divine essence and to one another; and this is a difficulty which the Church cannot remove, but only try to reduce to its proper proportion by a proper definition of terms. It has never tried to explain the mystery of the Trinity, but only sought to formulate the doctrine of the Trinity in such a manner that the errors which endangered it were warded off.

4. VARIOUS ANALOGIES SUGGESTED TO SHED LIGHT ON THE SUBJECT. From the very earliest time of the Christian era attempts were made to shed light on the trinitarian Being of God, on the trinity in unity and the unity in trinity, by analogies drawn from several sources. While these are all defective, it cannot be denied that they were of some value in the trinitarian discussion. This applies particularly to those derived from the constitutional nature, or from the psychology, of man. In view of the fact that man was created in the image of God, it is but natural to assume that, if there are some traces of the trinitarian life in the creature, the clearest of these will be found in man.

a. Some of these illustrations or analogies were taken from inanimate nature or from plant life, as the water of the fountain, the creek, and the river, or of the rising mist, the cloud, and the rain, or in the form of rain, snow, and ice; and as the tree with its root, trunk, and branches. These and all similar illustrations are very defective. The idea of personality is, of course, entirely wanting; and while they do furnish examples of a common nature or substance, they are not examples of a common essence which is present, not merely in part, but in its entirety, in each of its constituent parts or forms.

b. Others of greater importance were drawn from the life of man, particularly from the constitution and the processes of the human mind. These were considered to be of special significance, because man is the image-bearer of God. To this class belong the psychological unity of the intellect, the affections, and the will (Augustine) ; the logical unity of thesis, antithesis, and synthesis (Hegel) ; and the metaphysical unity of subject, object, and subject-object (Olshausen, Shedd). In all of these we do have a certain trinity in unity, but no tri-personality in unity of substance.

c. Attention has also been called to the nature of love, which presupposes a subject and an object, and calls for the union of these two, so that, when love has its perfect work, three elements are included. But it is easy to see that this analogy is faulty, since it co-ordinates two persons and a relationship. It does not illustrate a tri-personality at all. Moreover, it only refers to a quality and not at all to a substance possessed in common by the subject and the object.

C. The Three Persons Considered Separately.

1. THE FATHER OR THE FIRST PERSON IN THE TRINITY.

a. *The name "Father" as applied to God.* This name is not always used of God in the same sense in Scripture. (1) Sometimes it is applied to the Triune God as the origin of all created things, I Cor. 8:6; Eph. 3:15; Heb. 12:9; Jas. 1:17. While in these cases the name applies to the triune God, it does refer more particularly to the first person, to whom the work of creation is more especially ascribed in Scripture. (2) The name is also ascribed to the triune God to express the theocratic relation in which He stands to Israel as

His Old Testament people, Deut. 32:6; Isa. 63:16; 64:8; Jer. 3:4; Mal. 1:6; 2:10: (3) In the New Testament the name is generally used to designate the triune God as the Father in an ethical sense of all His spiritual children, Matt. 5:45; 6:6-15; Rom. 8:16; I John 3:1. (4) In an entirely different sense, however, the name is applied to the first person of the Trinity in His relation to the second person, John 1:14,18; 5:17-26; 8:54; 14:12,13. The first person is the Father of the second in a metaphysical sense. This is the original fatherhood of God, of which all earthly fatherhood is but a faint reflection.

b. *The distinctive property of the Father.* The personal property of the Father is, negatively speaking, that He is not begotten or unbegotten, and positively speaking, the generation of the Son and the spiration of the Holy Spirit. It is true that spiration is also a work of the Son, but in Him it is not combined with generation. Strictly speaking, the only work that is peculiar to the Father exclusively is that of active generation.

c. *The opera ad extra ascribed more particularly to the Father.* All the *opera ad extra* of God are works of the triune God, but in some of these works the Father is evidently in the foreground, such as: (1) Designing the work of redemption, including election, of which the Son was Himself an object, Ps. 2:7-9; 40:6-9; Isa. 53:10; Matt. 12:32; Eph. 1:3-6. (2) The works of creation and providence, especially in their initial stages, I Cor. 8:6; Eph. 2:9. (3) The work of representing the Trinity in the Counsel of Redemption, as the holy and righteous Being, whose right was violated, Ps. 2:7-9; 40:6-9; John 6:37,38; 17:4-7.

2. THE SON OR THE SECOND PERSON IN THE TRINITY.

a. *The name "Son" as applied to the second person.* The second person in the Trinity is called "Son" or "Son of God" in more than one sense of the word. (1) *In a metaphysical sense.* This must be maintained over against Socinians and Unitarians, who reject the idea of a tri-personal Godhead, see in Jesus a mere man, and regard the name "Son of God" as applied to Him primarily as an honorary title conferred upon Him. It is quite evident that Jesus Christ is represented as the Son of God in Scripture, irrespective of His position and work as Mediator. (a) He is spoken of as the Son of God from a pre-incarnation standpoint, for instance in John 1:14,18; Gal. 4:4. (b) He is called the "only-begotten" Son of God or of the Father, a term that would not apply to Him, if He were the Son of God only in an official or in an ethical sense, John 1:14,18; 3:16,18; I John 4:9. Compare II Sam. 7:14; Job 2:1; Ps. 2:7; Luke 3:38; John 1:12. (c) In some passages it is abundantly evident from the context that the name is indicative of the deity of Christ, John 5:18-25; Heb. 1. (d) While Jesus teaches His disciples to speak of God, and to address Him as "our Father," He Himself speaks of Him, and addresses Him, simply as "Father" or "my Father," and thereby shows that He was conscious of a unique relationship to the Father, Matt. 6:9; 7:21; John 20:17. (e) According to Matt. 11:27, Jesus as the Son of God claims a unique knowledge of God, a knowledge such as no one else can possess. (f) The Jews certainly understood Jesus to claim that He was the Son of God in a metaphysical sense, for they regarded the manner in which He spoke of Himself as the Son of God as blasphemy, Matt. 26:63; John 5:18; 10:36. —— (2) *In an official or Messianic sense.* In some passages this meaning of the name is combined with the one previously mentioned. The following passages apply the name "Son of God" to Christ as Mediator, Matt. 8:29, 26:63 (where this meaning is combined with the other); 27:40; John 1:49; 11:27. This Messiah-Sonship is, of course, related to the original Sonship of Christ. It was only because He was the essential and eternal Son of God, that He could be called the Son of God as Messiah. Moreover, the Messiah-Sonship reflects the eternal Sonship of Christ. It is from the point of view of this Messiah-Sonship that God is even called the God of the Son, II Cor. 11:31; Eph. 1:3, and is sometimes mentioned as God in distinction from the Lord, John 17:3; I Cor. 8:6; Eph. 4:5,6. —— (3) *In a nativistic sense.* The name "Son of God" is given to Jesus also in view of the fact that He owed His birth to the paternity of God. He was begotten, according to His human nature, by the supernatural operation of the Holy Spirit, and is in that sense the Son of God. This is clearly indicated in Luke 1:32,35, and may probably be inferred also from John 1:13.

b. *The personal subsistence of the Son.* The personal subsistence of the Son must be maintained over against all Modalists, who in one way or another deny the *personal* distinctions in the Godhead. The personality of the Son may be substantiated as follows: (1) The way in which the Bible speaks of the Father and the Son alongside of each other implies that the one is just as personal as the other, and is also indicative of a personal relationship existing between the two. (2) The use of the appelatives "only-begotten" and "firstborn" imply that the relation between the Father and the Son, while unique, can nevertheless be represented approximately as one of generation and birth. The name "firstborn" is found in Col. 1:15; Heb. 1:6, and emphasizes the fact of the eternal generation of the Son. It simply means that He was before all creation. (3) The distinctive use of the term "Logos" in Scripture points in the same direction. This term is applied to the Son, not in the first place to express His relation to the world (which is quite secondary), but to indicate the intimate relation in which He stands to the Father, the relation like that of a word to the speaker. In distinction from philosophy, the Bible represents the Logos as personal and identifies Him with the Son of God, John 1:1-14; I John 1:1-3. (4) The description of the Son as the image, or even as the very image of God in II Cor. 4:4; Col. 1:15; Heb. 1:3. God clearly stands out in Scripture as a personal Being. If the Son of God is the very image of God, He too must be a person.

c. *The eternal generation of the Son.* The personal property of the Son is that He is eternally begotten of the Father (briefly called "filiation"), and shares with the Father in the spiration of the Spirit. The doctrine of the generation of the Son is suggested by the Biblical representation of the first and second persons of the Trinity as standing in the relation of Father and Son to each other. Not only do the names "Father" and "Son" suggest the generation of the latter by the former, but the Son is also repeatedly called "the only-begotten," John 1:14,18; 3:16,18; Heb. 11:17; I John 4:9. Several particulars deserve emphasis in connection with the generation of the Son: (1) *It is a necessary act of God.* Origen, one of the very first to speak of the generation of the Son, regarded it as an act dependent on the Father's will and therefore free. Others at various times expressed the same opinion. But it was clearly seen by Athanasius and others that a generation dependent on the optional will of the Father would make the existence of the Son contingent and thus rob Him of His deity. Then the Son would not be equal to and *homoousios* with the Father, for the Father exists necessarily, and cannot be conceived of as non-existent. The generation of the Son must be regarded as a necessary and perfectly natural act of God. This does not mean that it is not related to the Father's will in any sense of the word. It is an act of the Father's necessary will, which merely means that His concomitant will takes perfect delight in it. (2) *It is an eternal act of the Father.* This naturally follows from the preceding. If the generation of the Son is a *necessary* act of the Father, so that it is impossible to conceive of Him as not generating, it naturally shares in the eternity of the Father. This does not mean, however, that it is an act that was completed in the far distant past, but rather that it is a timeless act, the act of an eternal present, an act always continuing and yet ever completed. Its eternity follows not only from the eternity of God, but also from the divine immutability and from the true deity of the Son. In addition to this it can be inferred from all those passages of Scripture which teach either the pre-existence of the Son or His equality with the Father, Mic. 5:2; John 1:14,18; 3:16; 5:17,18,30,36; Acts 13:33; John 17:5; Col. 1:16; Heb. 1:3. The statement of Ps. 2:7, "Thou art my Son; this day have I begotten thee," is generally quoted to prove the generation of the Son, but, according to some, with rather doubtful propriety, cf. Acts 13:33; Heb. 1:5. They surmise that these words refer to the raising up of Jesus as Messianic King, and to the recognition of Him as Son of God in an official sense, and should probably be linked up with the promise found in II Sam. 7:14, just as they are in Heb. 1:5. (3) *It is a generation of the personal subsistence rather than of the divine essence of the Son.* Some have spoken as if the Father generated the essence of the Son, but this is equivalent to saying that He generated His own essence, for the essence of both the Father and the Son is exactly the same. It is better to say that the Father generates the personal subsistence of the Son, but thereby also communicates to Him the divine essence in its entirety. But in doing this we should guard against the idea that the Father first generated a second person, and then communicated the divine essence to this person, for that would lead to the conclusion that the Son was not generated out of the divine essence, but created out of nothing. In the work of generation there was a communication of essence; it was one indivisible act. And in virtue of this communication the Son also has life in Himself. This is in agreement with the statement of Jesus, "For as the Father hath life in Himself, even so gave He to the Son also to have life in Himself," John 5:26. (4) *It is a generation that must be conceived of as spiritual and divine.* In opposition to the Arians, who insisted that the generation of the Son necessarily implied separation or division in the divine Being, the Church Fathers stressed the fact that this generation must not be conceived in a physical and creaturely way, but should be regarded as spiritual and divine, excluding all idea of division or change. It brings *distinctio* and *distributio*, but no *diversitas* and *divisio* in the divine Being. (Bavinck) The most striking analogy of it is found in man's thinking and speaking, and the Bible itself seems to point to this, when it speaks of the Son as the Logos. (5) The following definition may be given of the generation of the Son: *It is that eternal and necessary act of the first person in the Trinity, whereby He, within the divine Being, is the ground of a second personal subsistence like His own, and puts this second person in possession of the whole divine essence, without any division, alienation, or change.*

d. *The deity of the Son.* The deity of the Son was denied in the early Church by the Ebionites and the Alogi, and also by the dynamic Monarchians and the Arians. In the days of the Reformation the Socinians followed their example, and spoke of Jesus as a mere man. The same position is taken by Schleiermacher and Ritschl, by a host of liberal scholars, particularly in Germany, by the Unitarians, and by the Modernists and Humanists of the present day. This denial is possible only for those who disregard the teachings of Scripture, for the Bible contains an abundance of evidence for the deity of Christ.[1] We find that Scripture (1) *explicitly asserts the deity of the Son* in such passages as John 1:1; 20:28; Rom. 9:5; Phil. 2:6; Tit. 2:13; I John 5:20; (2) *applies divine names to Him,* Isa. 9:6; 40:3; Jer. 23:5,6; Joel 2:32 (comp. Acts 2:21); I Tim. 3:16; (3) *ascribes to Him divine attributes,* such as eternal existence, Isa. 9:6; John 1:1,2; Rev. 1:8; 22:13, omnipresence, Matt. 18:20; 28:20; John 3:13, omniscience, John 2:24,25; 21:17; Rev. 2:23, omnipotence, Isa. 9:6; Phil. 3:21; Rev. 1:8, immutability, Heb. 1:10-12; 13:8, and in general every attribute belonging to the Father, Col. 2:9; (4) *speaks of Him as doing divine works,* as creation, John 1:3,10; Col. 1:16; Heb. 1:2,10, providence, Luke 10:22; John 3:35; 17:2; Eph. 1:22; Col. 1:17; Heb. 1:3, the forgiveness of sins, Matt. 9:2-7; Mark 2:7-10; Col. 3:13, resurrection and judgment, Matt. 25:31,32; John 5:19-29; Acts 10:42; 17:31; Phil. 3:21; II Tim. 4:1, the final dissolution and renewal of all things, Heb. 1:10-12; Phil. 3:21; Rev. 21:5,

---

1. This is very ably summed up in such works as Liddon's *The Divinity of Our Lord,* Warfield's *The Lord of Glory,* and Wm. C. Robinson's *Our Lord.*

and (5) *accords Him divine honour,* John 5:22,23; 14:1; I Cor. 15:19; II Cor. 13:13; Heb. 1:6; Matt. 28:19.

e. *The place of the Son in the economic Trinity.* It should be noted that the order of existence in the essential or ontological Trinity is reflected in the economic Trinity. The Son occupies the second place in the *opera ad extra.* If all things are *out of* the Father, they are *through* the Son, I Cor. 8:6. If the former is represented as the absolute cause of all things, the latter stands out clearly as the mediating cause. This applies in the natural sphere, where all things are created and maintained through the Son, John 1:3,10; Heb. 1:2,3. He is the light that lighteth every man that cometh into the world, John 1:9. It applies also to the work of redemption. In the Counsel of Redemption He takes upon Himself to be Surety for His people, and to execute the Father's plan of redemption, Ps. 40:7,8. He works this out more particularly in His incarnation, sufferings, and death, Eph. 1:3-14. In connection with His function the attributes of wisdom and power, I Cor. 1:24; Heb. 1:3, and of mercy and grace, are especially ascribed to Him, II Cor. 13:13; Eph. 5:2,25.

3. THE HOLY SPIRIT OR THE THIRD PERSON IN THE TRINITY.

a. *The name applied to the third person of the Trinity.* While we are told in John 4:24 that God is Spirit, the name is applied more particularly to the third person in the Trinity. The Hebrew term by which He is designated is *ruach,* and the Greek *pneuma,* both of which are, like the Latin *spiritus,* derived from roots which mean "to breathe." Hence they can also be rendered "breath," Gen. 2:7; 6:17; Ezek. 37:5, 6, or "wind," Gen. 8:1; I Kings 19:11; John 3:8. The Old Testament generally uses the term "spirit" without any qualification, or speaks of "the Spirit of God" or "the Spirit of the Lord," and employs the term "Holy Spirit" only in Ps. 51:11; Isa. 63:10,11, while in the New Testament this has become a far more common designation of the third person in the Trinity. It is a striking fact that, while the Old Testament repeatedly calls God "the Holy One of Israel," Ps. 71:22; 89:18; Isa. 10:20; 41:14; 43:3; 48:17, the New Testament seldom applies the adjective "holy" to God in general, but uses it frequently to characterize the Spirit. This is in all probability due to the fact that it was especially in the Spirit and His sanctifying work that God revealed Himself as the Holy One. It is the Holy Spirit that takes up His abode in the hearts of believers, that separates them unto God, and that cleanses them from sin.

b. *The personality of the Holy Spirit.* The terms "Spirit of God" or "Holy Spirit" do not suggest personality as much as the term "Son" does. Moreover, the person of the Holy Spirit did not appear in a clearly discernible personal form among men, as the person of the Son of God did. As a result the personality of the Holy Spirit was often called in question, and therefore deserves special attention. The personality of the Spirit was denied in the early Church by the Monarchians and the Pneumatomachians. In this denial they were followed by the Socinians in the days of the Reformation. Still later Schleiermacher, Ritschl, the Unitarians, present-day Modernists, and all modern Sabellians reject the personality of the Holy Spirit. It is often said in the present day that those passages which seem to imply the personality of the Holy Spirit simply contain personifications. But personifications are certainly rare in the prose writings of the New Testament and can easily be recognized. Moreover, such an explanation clearly destroys the sense of some of these passages, e.g. John 14:26; 16:7-11; Rom. 8:26. Scripture proof for the personality of the Holy Spirit is quite sufficient: (1) *Designations that are proper to personality are given to Him.* Though *pneuma* is neuter, yet the masculine pronoun *ekeinos* is used of the Spirit in John 16:14; and in Eph. 1:14 some of the best authorities have the masculine relative pronoun *hos.* Moreover, the name Parakletos is' applied to Him, John 14:26; 15:26; 16:7, which cannot be translated by "comfort," or be regarded as the name of any abstract influence. That a person is meant is indicated by the fact that the Holy Spirit as Comforter is placed in juxtaposition with Christ as the Comforter about to depart, to whom the same term is applied in I John 2:1. It is true that this term is followed by the neuters *ho* and *auto* in John 14:16-18, but this is due to the fact that *pneuma* intervenes. (2) *The characteristics of a person are ascribed to Him,* such as intelligence, John 14:26; 15:26; Rom. 8:16, will, Acts 16:7; I Cor. 12:11, and affections, Isa. 63:10; Eph. 4:30. Moreover, He performs acts proper to personality. He searches, speaks, testifies, commands, reveals, strives, creates, makes intercession, raises the dead, etc., Gen. 1:2; 6:3; Luke 12:12; John 14:26; 15:26; 16:8; Acts 8:29; 13:2; Rom. 8:11; I Cor. 2:10,11. What does all these things cannot be a mere power or influence, but must be a person. (3) *He is represented as standing in such relations to other persons as imply His own personality.* He is placed in juxtaposition with the apostles in Acts 15:28, with Christ in John 16:14, and with the Father and the Son in Matt. 28:19; II Cor. 13:13; I Pet. 1:1,2; Jude 20, 21. Sound exegesis requires that in these passages the Holy Spirit be regarded as a person. (4) *There are also passages in which the Holy Spirit is distinguished from His own power,* Luke 1:35; 4:14; Acts 10:38; Rom. 15:13; I Cor. 2:4. Such passages would become tautological, meaningless, and even absurd, if they were interpreted on the principle that the Holy Spirit is merely a power. This can be shown by substituting for the name "Holy Spirit" such a word as "power" or "influence."

c. *The relation of the Holy Spirit to the other persons in the trinity.* The early trinitarian controversies led to the conclusion that the Holy Spirit, as well as the Son, is of the same essence as the Father, and is therefore consubstantial with Him. And the long drawn dispute about the question, whether the Holy Spirit proceeded from the Father alone or also from the Son, was finally settled by the Synod of Toledo in 589 by adding the word "Filioque" to the Latin version of the Constantinopolitan Creed: *"Credimus in Spiritum*

Sanctum qui a Patre Filioque procedit" ("We believe in the Holy Spirit, who proceeds from the Father and the Son"). This procession of the Holy Spirit, briefly called spiration, is his personal property. Much of what was said respecting the generation of the Son also applies to the spiration of the Holy Spirit, and need not be repeated. The following points of distinction between the two may be noted, however: (1) Generation is the work of the Father only; spiration is the work of both the Father and the Son. (2) By generation the Son is enabled to take part in the work of spiration, but the Holy Spirit acquires no such power. (3) In logical order generation precedes spiration. It should be remembered, however, that all this implies no essential subordination of the Holy Spirit to the Son. In spiration as well as in generation there is a communication of the whole of the divine essence, so that the Holy Spirit is on an equality with the Father and the Son. The doctrine of the procession of the Holy Spirit from the Father and the Son is based on John 15:26, and on the fact that the Spirit is also called the Spirit of Christ and of the Son, Rom. 8:9; Gal. 4:6, and is sent by Christ into the world. Spiration may be defined as *that eternal and necessary act of the first and second persons in the Trinity whereby they, within the divine Being, become the ground of the personal subsistence of the Holy Spirit, and put the third person in possession of the whole divine essence, without any division, alienation or change.*

The Holy Spirit stands in the closest possible relation to the other persons. In virtue of His procession from the Father and the Son the Spirit is represented as standing in the closest possible relation to both of the other persons. From I Cor. 2:10,11, we may infer, not that the Spirit is the same as the self-consciousness of God, but that He is as closely connected with God the Father as the soul of man is with man. In II Cor. 3:17, we read, "Now the Lord is the Spirit, and where the Spirit of the Lord is, there is liberty." Here the Lord (Christ) is identified with the Spirit, not with respect to personality, but as to manner of working. In the same passage the Spirit is called "the Spirit of the Lord." The work for which the Holy Spirit was sent into the Church on the day of Pentecost was based on His unity with the Father and the Son. He came as the Parakletos to take the place of Christ and to do His work on earth, that is, to teach, proclaim, testify, bear witness, etc., as the Son had done. Now in the case of the Son this revelational work rested on His unity with the Father. Just so the work of the Spirit is based on His unity with the Father and the Son, John 16:14,15. Notice the words of Jesus in this passage: "He shall glorify me; for He shall take of mine, and shall declare it unto you. All things whatsoever the Father hath are mine: therefore said I, that He taketh of mine, and shall declare it unto you."

d. *The deity of the Holy Spirit.* The deity of the Holy Spirit may be established from Scripture by a line of proof quite similar to that employed in connection with the Son: (1) *Divine names are given to Him,* Ex. 17:7

(comp. Heb. 3:7-9); Acts 5:3,4; I Cor. 3:16; II Tim. 3:16 (comp. II Pet. 1:21). (2) *Divine perfections are ascribed to Him,* such as omnipresence, Ps. 139:7-10, omniscience, Isa. 40:13,14 (comp. Rom. 11:34); I Cor. 2:10,11, omnipotence, I Cor. 12:11; Rom. 15:19, and eternity, Heb. 9:14 (?). (3) *Divine works are performed by Him,* such as creation, Gen. 1:2; Job. 26:13; 33:4, providential renovation, Ps. 104:30, regeneration, John 3:5,6; Tit. 3:5, and the resurrection of the dead, Rom. 8:11. (4) *Divine honour is also paid to Him,* Matt. 28:19; Rom. 9:1; II Cor. 13:13.

e. *The work of the Holy Spirit in the divine economy.* There are certain works which are more particularly ascribed to the Holy Spirit, not only in the general economy of God, but also in the special economy of redemption. In general it may be said that it is the special task of the Holy Spirit to bring things to completion by acting immediately upon and in the creature. Just as He Himself is the person who completes the Trinity, so His work is the completion of God's contact with His creatures and the consummation of the work of God in every sphere. It follows the work of the Son, just as the work of the Son follows that of the Father. It is important to bear this in mind, for if the work of the Holy Spirit is divorced from the objective work of the Son, false mysticism is bound to result. The work of the Holy Spirit includes the following in the natural sphere: (1) *The generation of life.* As being is out of the Father, and thought through the Son, so life is mediated by the Spirit, Gen. 1:3; Job. 26:13; Ps. 33:6 (?); Ps. 104:30. In that respect He puts the finishing touch to the work of creation. (2) *The general inspiration and qualification of men.* The Holy Spirit inspires and qualifies men for their official tasks, for work in science and art, etc., Ex. 28:3; 31:2,3,6; 35:35; I Sam. 11:6; 16:13,14.

Of even greater importance is the work of the Holy Spirit in the sphere of redemption. Here the following points may be mentioned: (1) *The preparation and qualification of Christ for His mediatorial work.* He prepared Christ a body and thus enabled Him to become a sacrifice for sin, Luke 1:35; Heb. 10: 5-7. In the words "a body thou didst prepare for me," the writer of Hebrews follows the Septuagint. The meaning is: Thou hast enabled me by the preparation of a holy body to become a real sacrifice. At His baptism Christ was anointed with the Holy Spirit, Luke 3:22, and received the qualifying gifts of the Holy Spirit without measure, John 3:24. (2) *The inspiration of Scripture.* The Holy Spirit inspired Scripture, and thus brought to men the special revelation of God, I Cor. 2:13; II Pet. 1:21, the knowledge of the work of redemption which is in Christ Jesus. (3) *The formation and augmentation of the Church.* The Holy Spirit forms and increases the Church, the mystical body of Jesus Christ, by regeneration and sanctification, and dwells in it as the principle of the new life, Eph. 1:22,23; 2:22; I Cor. 3:16; 12:4 ff. (4) *Teaching and guiding the Church.* The Holy Spirit testifies to Christ and leads the Church in all the truth. By doing this He manifests the glory of God and of Christ, increases the knowledge of the Saviour, keeps the Church from error, and prepares her for her eternal destiny, John 14:26; 15:26; 16:13,14; Acts 5:32; Heb. 10:15; I John 2:27.

THE HOLY TRINITY

QUESTIONS FOR FURTHER STUDY. Does pagan literature contain any analogies of the doctrine of the Trinity? Does the development of the doctrine of the Trinity start from the ontological or from the economical Trinity? Can the economical Trinity be understood apart from the ontological? Why is the doctrine of the Trinity discussed by some as introductory to the doctrine of redemption? What is the Hegelian conception of the Trinity? How did Swedenborg conceive of it? Where do we find Sabellianism in modern theology? Why is it objectionable to hold that the Trinity is purely economical? What objections are there to the modern Humanitarian conception of the Trinity? Why does Barth treat of the Trinity in the Prolegomena to theology? What is the practical significance of the doctrine of the Trinity?

LITERATURE: Bavinck, *Geref Dogm.* II, pp. 260-347; Kuyper, *Dict. Dogm., De Deo* II, pp. 3-255; Vos. *Geref. Dogm.* I, pp. 36-81; Mastricht, *Godgeleerdheit* I, pp. 576-662; Turretin, *Opera, Locus Tertius;* Hodge, *Syst. Theol.* I, pp. 442-534; Dabney, *Syst. and Polem. Theol.,* pp. 174-211; Curtiss, *The Chr. Faith,* pp. 483-510; Harris, *God, Creator and Lord of All,* I, pp. 194-407; Illingworth, *The Doctrine of the Trinity;* Adeney, *The Christian Conception of God,* pp. 215-246; Steenstra, *The Being of God as Unity and Trinity,* pp. 159-269; Clarke, *The Chr. Doct. of God,* pp. 227-248; Bartlett, *The Triune God;* Liddon,*The Divinity of Our Lord;* Mackintosh, *The Doctrine of the Person of Jesus Christ;* Warfield, *The Lord of Glory; ibid, The Spirit of God in the Old Testament;* and *The Biblical Doctrine of the Trinity* (both in *Biblical Doctrines*), pp. 101 ff.; *ibid., Calvin's Doctrine of the Trinity* (in *Calvin and Calvinism*) ; Kuyper, *Het Werk van den Heiligen Geest,* cf. Index; Owen, *A Discourse Concerning the Holy Spirit,* cf. Index; Smeaton, *The Doct. of the Holy Spirit;* Pohle-Preuss, *The Divine Trinity.*

II

THE WORKS OF GOD

1. The Divine Decrees in General

A. The Doctrine of the Decrees in Theology.

Reformed theology stresses the sovereignty of God in virtue of which He has sovereignly determined from all eternity whatsoever will come to pass, and works His sovereign will in His entire creation, both natural and spiritual, according to His pre-determined plan. It is in full agreement with Paul when he says that God "worketh all things after the counsel of His will," Eph. 1:11. For that reason it is but natural that, in passing from the discussion of the Being of God to that of the works of God, it should begin with a study of the divine decrees. This is the only proper theological method. A theological discussion of the works of God should take its startingpoint in God, both in the work of creation and in that of redemption or recreation. It is only as issuing from, and as related to, God that the works of God come into consideration as a part of theology.

In spite of this fact, however, Reformed theology stands practically alone in its emphasis on the doctrine of the decrees. Lutheran theology is less theological and more anthropological. It does not consistently take its starting point in God and consider all things as divinely pre-determined, but reveals a tendency to consider things from below rather than from above. And in so far as it does believe in pre-determination, it is inclined to limit this to the good that is in the world, and more particularly to the blessings of salvation. It is a striking fact that many Lutheran theologians are silent, or all but silent, respecting the doctrine of the decrees of God in general and discuss only the doctrine of predestination, and regard this as *conditional* rather than absolute. In the doctrine of predestination Lutheran theology shows strong affinity with Arminianism. Krauth (an influential leader of the Lutheran Church in our country) even says: "The views of Arminius himself, in regard to the five points, were formed under Lutheran influences, and do not differ essentially from those of the Lutheran Church; but on many points in the developed system now known as Arminianism, the Lutheran Church has no affinity whatever with it, and on these points would sympathize far more with Calvinism, though she has never believed that in order to escape from Pelagianism, it is necessary to run into the doctrine of absolute predestination. The 'Formula of Concord' touches the five points almost purely on their practical sides, and on them arrays itself against Calvinism, rather by the negation of the inferences which result logically from that system, than by express condemnation of its fundamental theory in its abstract form."[1] In so far as Lutheran theologians include the doctrine of predestination in their system, they generally consider it in connection with Soteriology.

Naturally, Arminian theology does not place the doctrine of the decrees in the foreground. That of the decrees in general is usually conspicuous by its absence. Pope brings in the doctrine of predestination only in passing, and Miley introduces it as an issue for discussion. Raymond discusses only the doctrine of election, and Watson devotes considerable space to this in considering the extent of the atonement. One and all reject the doctrine of absolute predestination, and substitute for it a conditional predestination. Modern liberal theology does not concern itself with the doctrine of predestination, since it is fundamentally anthropological. In the "theology of crisis" it is again recognized, but in a form that is neither Scriptural nor historical. In spite of its appeal to the Reformers, it departs widely from the doctrine of predestination, as it was taught by Luther and Calvin.

B. Scriptural Names for the Divine Decrees.

From the purely immanent works of God (*opera ad intra*) we must distinguish those which bear directly on the creatures (*opera ad extra*). Some theologians, in order to avoid misunderstanding, prefer to speak of *opera immanentia* and *opera exeuntia*, and subdivide the former into two classes, *opera immanentia per se*, which are the *opera personalia* (generation, filiation, spiration), and *opera immanentia donec exeunt*, which are *opera essentialia*, that is, works of the triune God, in distinction from works of any one of the persons of the Godhead, but are immanent in God, until they are realized in the works of creation, providence, and redemption. The divine decrees constitute this class of divine works. They are not described in the abstract in Scripture, but are placed before us in their historical realization. Scripture uses several terms for the eternal decree of God.

1. OLD TESTAMENT TERMS. There are some terms which stress the intellectual element in the decree, such as *'etsah* from *ya'ats*, to counsel, to give advice, Job 38:2; Isa. 14:26; 46:11; *sod* from *yasad*, to sit together in deliberation (niphal), Jer. 23:18,22; and *mezimmah* from *zamam*, to meditate, to have in mind, to purpose, Jer. 4:28; 51:12; Prov. 30:32. Besides these there are terms which emphasize the volitional element, such as *chaphets*, inclination, will, good pleasure, Isa. 53:10; and *ratson*, to please, to be delighted, and thus denoting delight, good pleasure, or sovereign will, Ps. 51:19; Isa. 49:8.

2. NEW TESTAMENT TERMS. The New Testament also contains a number of significant terms. The most general word is *boule*, designating the decree in general, but also pointing to the fact that the purpose of God is based on counsel

---

1. *The Conservative Reformation and Its Theology*, pp. 127f.

and deliberation, Acts 2:23; 4:28; Heb. 6:17. Another rather general word is *thelema,* which, as applied to the counsel of God, stresses the volitional rather than the deliberative element, Eph. 1:11. The word *eudokia* emphasizes more particularly the freedom of the purpose of God, and the delight with which it is accompanied, though this idea is not always present, Matt. 11:26; Luke 2:14; Eph. 1:5,9. Other words are used more especially to designate that part of the divine decree that pertains in a very special sense to God's moral creatures, and is known as predestination. These terms will be considered in connection with the discussion of that subject.

C. The Nature of the Divine Decrees.

The decree of God may be defined with the Westminster Shorter Catechism as *"His eternal purpose according to the counsel of His will, whereby, for His own glory, He hath foreordained whatsoever comes to pass."*

1. THE DIVINE DECREE IS ONE. Though we often speak of the decrees of God in the plural, yet in its own nature the divine decree is but a single act of God. This is already suggested by the fact that the Bible speaks of it as a *prothesis,* a purpose or counsel. It follows also from the very nature of God. His knowledge is all immediate and simultaneous rather than successive like ours, and His comprehension of it is always complete. And the decree that is founded on it is also a single, all-comprehensive, and simultaneous act. As an eternal and immutable decree it could not be otherwise. There is, therefore, no series of decrees in God, but simply one comprehensive plan, embracing all that comes to pass. Our finite comprehension, however, constrains us to make distinctions, and this accounts for the fact that we often speak of the decrees of God in the plural. This manner of speaking is perfectly legitimate, provided we do not lose sight of the unity of the divine decree, and of the inseparable connection of the various decrees as we conceive of them.

2. THE RELATION OF THE DECREE TO THE KNOWLEDGE OF GOD. The decree of God bears the closest relation to the divine knowledge. There is in God, as we have seen, a necessary knowledge, including all possible causes and results. This knowledge furnishes the material for the decree; it is the perfect fountain out of which God drew the thoughts which He desired to objectify. Out of this knowledge of all things possible He chose, by an act of His perfect will, led by wise considerations, what He wanted to bring to realization, and thus formed His eternal purpose. The decree of God is, in turn, the foundation of His free knowledge or *scientia libera.* It is the knowledge of things as they are realized in the course of history. While the necessary knowledge of God logically precedes the decree, His free knowledge logically follows it. This must be maintained over against all those who believe in a conditional predestination (such as Semi-Pelagians and Arminians), since they make the pre-determinations of God dependent on His foreknowledge. Some of the words used to denote the divine decree point to an element of deliberation in the purpose of God. It would be

a mistake, however, to infer from this that the plan of God is the result of any deliberation which implies short-sightedness or hesitation, for it is simply an indication of the fact that there is no blind decree in God, but only an intelligent and deliberate purpose.

3. THE DECREE RELATES TO BOTH GOD AND MAN. The decree has reference, first of all, to the works of God. It is limited, however, to God's *opera ad extra* or transitive acts, and does not pertain to the essential Being of God, nor to the immanent activities within the Divine Being which result in the trinitarian distinctions. God did not decree to be holy and righteous, nor to exist as three persons in one essence or to generate the Son. These things are as they are *necessarily*, and are not dependent on the optional will of God. That which is essential to the inner Being of God can form no part of the contents of the decree. This includes only the *opera ad extra* or *excuntia*. But while the decree pertains primarily to the acts of God Himself, it is not limited to these, but also embraces the actions of His free creatures. And the fact that they are included in the decree renders them absolutely certain, though they are not all effectuated in the same manner. In the case of some things God decided, not merely that they would come to pass, but that He Himself would bring them to pass, either immediately, as in the work of creation, or through the mediation of secondary causes, which are continually energized by His power. He Himself assumes the responsibility for their coming to pass. There are other things, however, which God included in His decree and thereby rendered certain, but which He did not decide to effectuate Himself, as the sinful acts of His rational creatures. The decree, in so far as it pertains to these acts, is generally called God's permissive decree. This name does not imply that the futurition of these acts is not certain to God, but simply that He permits them to come to pass by the free agency of His rational creatures. God assumes no responsibility for these sinful acts whatsoever.

4. THE DECREE TO ACT IS NOT THE ACT ITSELF. The decrees are an internal manifestation and exercise of the divine attributes, rendering the futurition of things certain but this exercise of the intelligent volition of God should not be confounded with the realization of its objects in creation, providence, and redemption. The decree to create is not creation itself, nor is the decree to justify justification itself. A distinction must be made between the decree and its execution. God's so ordering the universe that man will pursue a certain course of action, is also quite a different thing from His commanding him to do so. The decrees are not addressed to man, and are not of the nature of a statute law; neither do they impose compulsion or obligation on the wills of men.

D. The Characteristics of the Divine Decree.

1. IT IS FOUNDED IN DIVINE WISDOM. The word "counsel," which is one of the terms by which the decree is designated, suggests careful deliberation and consultation. It may contain a suggestion of an intercommunion between the

three persons of the Godhead. In speaking of God's revelation of the mystery that was formerly hid in Him, Paul says that this was "to the intent that now unto the principalities and the powers in the heavenly places might be made known through the Church the manifold wisdom of God, according to the eternal purpose which He purposed in Christ Jesus our Lord," Eph. 3:10,11. The wisdom of the decree also follows from the wisdom displayed in the realization of the eternal purpose of God. The poet sings in Ps. 104:24, "O Jehovah, how manifold are thy works! In wisdom hast thou made them all." The same idea is expressed in Prov. 3:19, "Jehovah by wisdom founded the earth; by understanding He established the heavens." Cf. also Jer. 10:12; 51:15. The wisdom of the counsel of the Lord can also be inferred from the fact that it stands fast forever, Ps. 33:11; Prov. 19:21. There may be a great deal in the decree that passes human understanding and is inexplicable to the finite mind, but it contains nothing that is irrational or arbitrary. God formed his determination with wise insight and knowledge.

2. IT IS ETERNAL. The divine decree is eternal in the sense that it lies entirely in eternity. In a certain sense it can be said that all the acts of God are eternal, since there is no succession of moments in the Divine Being. But some of them terminate in time, as, for instance, creation and justification. Hence we do not call them eternal but temporal acts of God. The decree, however, while it relates to things outside of God, remains in itself an act within the Divine Being, and is therefore eternal in the strictest sense of the word. Therefore it also partakes of the simultaneousness and the successionlessness of the eternal, Acts 15:18; Eph. 1:4; II Tim. 1:9. The eternity of the decree also implies that the order in which the different elements in it stand to each other may not be regarded as temporal, but only as logical. There is a real chronological order in the events as effectuated, but not in the decree respecting them.

3. IT IS EFFICACIOUS. This does not mean that God has determined to bring to pass Himself by a direct application of His power all things which are included in His decree, but only that what He has decreed will certainly come to pass; that nothing can thwart His purpose. Says Dr. A. A. Hodge: "The decree itself provides in every case that the event shall be effected by causes acting in a manner perfectly consistent with the nature of the event in question. Thus in the case of every free act of a moral agent the decree provides at the same time — (a) That the agent shall be a free agent. (b) That his antecedents and all the antecedents of the act in question shall be what they are. (c) That all the present *conditions* of the act shall be what they are. (d) That the act shall be perfectly spontaneous and free on the part of the agent. (e) That it shall be certainly future. Ps. 33:11; Prov. 19:21; Isa. 46:10."[1]

4. IT IS IMMUTABLE. Man may and often does alter his plans for various reasons. It may be that in making his plan he lacked seriousness of purpose, that he did not fully realize what the plan involved, or that he is wanting the

---

1. *Outlines of Theology*, p. 203.

power to carry it out. But in God nothing of the kind is conceivable. He is not deficient in knowledge, veracity, or power. Therefore He need not change His decree because of a mistake of ignorance, nor because of inability to carry it out. And He will not change it, because He is the immutable God and because He is faithful and true. Job 23:13,14; Ps. 33:11; Isa. 46:10; Luke 22:22; Acts 2:23.

5. IT IS UNCONDITIONAL OR ABSOLUTE. This means that it is not dependent in any of its particulars on anything that is not part and parcel of the decree itself. The various elements in the decree are indeed mutually dependent but nothing in the plan is conditioned by anything that is not in the decree. The execution of the plan may require means or be dependent on certain conditions, but then these means or conditions have also been determined in the decree. God did not simply decree to save sinners without determining the means to effectuate the decree. The means leading to the pre-determined end were also decreed, Acts 2:23; Eph. 2:8; I Pet. 1:2. The absolute character of the decree follows from its eternity, its immutability, and its exclusive dependence on the good pleasure of God. It is denied by all Semi-Pelagians and Arminians.

6. IT IS UNIVERSAL OR ALL-COMPREHENSIVE. The decree includes whatsoever comes to pass in the world, whether it be in the physical or in the moral realm, whether it be good or evil, Eph. 1:11. It includes: (a) the good actions of men, Eph. 21:0; (b) their wicked acts, Prov. 16:4; Acts 2:23; 4:27,28; (c) contingent events, Gen. 45:8; 50:20; Prov. 16:33; (d) the means as well as the end, Ps. 119:89-91; II Thess. 2:13; Eph. 1:4; (e) the duration of man's life, Job 14:5; Ps. 39:4, and the place of his habitation, Acts 17:26.

7. WITH REFERENCE TO SIN IT IS PERMISSIVE. It is customary to speak of the decree of God respecting moral evil as permissive. By His decree God rendered the sinful actions of man infallibly certain without deciding to effectuate them by acting immediately upon and in the finite will. This means that God does not positively work in man "both to will and to do," when man goes contrary to His revealed will. It should be carefully noted, however, that this permissive decree does not imply a passive permission of something which is not under the control of the divine will. It is a decree which renders the future sinful act absolutely certain, but in which God determines (a) not to hinder the sinful self-determination of the finite will; and (b) to regulate and control the result of this sinful self-determination. Ps. 78:29; 106:15; Acts 14:16; 17:30.

E. Objections to the Doctrine of the Decrees.

As was said in the preceding, only Reformed theology does full justice to the doctrine of the decrees. Lutheran theologians do not, as a rule, construe it theologically but soteriologically, for the purpose of showing how believers can derive comfort from it. Pelagians and Socinians reject it as unscriptural; and Semi-Pelagians and Arminians show it scant favor: some ignoring it altogether; others stating it only to combat it; and still others maintaining only a decree conditioned by the foreknowledge of God. The objections raised to it are, in the main, always the same.

1. IT IS INCONSISTENT WITH THE MORAL FREEDOM OF MAN. Man is a free agent with the power of rational self-determination. He can reflect upon, and in an intelligent way choose, certain ends, and can also determine his action with respect to them. The decree of God however, carries with it necessity. God has decreed to effectuate all things or, if He has not decreed that, He has at least determined that they must come to pass. He has decided the course of man's life for him.[1] In answer to this objection it may be said that the Bible certainly does not proceed on the assumption that the divine decree is inconsistent with the free agency of man. It clearly reveals that God has decreed the free acts of man, but also that the actors are none the less free and therefore responsible for their acts, Gen. 50:19,20; Acts 2:23; 4:27,28. It was determined that the Jews should bring about the crucifixion of Jesus; yet they were perfectly free in their wicked course of action, and were held responsible for this crime. There is not a single indication in Scripture that the inspired writers are conscious of a contradiction in connection with these matters. They never make an attempt to harmonize the two. This may well restrain us from assuming a contradiction here, even if we cannot reconcile both truths.

Moreover, it should be borne in mind that God has not decreed *to effectuate by His own direct action* whatsoever must come to pass. The divine decree only brings certainty into the events, but does not imply that God will actively effectuate them, so that the question really resolves itself into this, whether previous certainty is consistent with free agency. Now experience teaches us that we can be reasonably certain as to the course a man of character will pursue under certain circumstances, without infringing in the least on his freedom. The prophet Jeremiah predicted that the Chaldeans would take Jerusalem. He knew the coming event as a certainty, and yet the Chaldeans freely followed their own desires in fulfilling the prediction. Such certainty is indeed inconsistent with the Pelagian liberty of indifference, according to which the will of man is not determined in any way, but is entirely indeterminate, so that in every volition it can decide in opposition, not only to all outward inducements, but also to all inward considerations and judgments, inclinations and desires, and even to the whole character and inner state of man. But it is now generally recognized that such freedom of the will is a psychological fiction. However, the decree is not necessarily inconsistent with human freedom in the sense of rational self-determination, according to which man freely acts in harmony with his previous thoughts and judgments, his inclinations and desires, and his whole character. This freedom also has its laws, and the better we are acquainted with them, the more sure we can be of what a free agent will do under certain circumstances. God Himself has established these laws. Naturally, we must

---

1. Cf. Watson, *Theological Institutes*, Part II, Chap. XXVIII; Miley, *Systematic Theology* II, pp. 271 ff.

guard against all determinism, materialistic, pantheistic, and rationalistic, in our conception of freedom in the sense of rational self-determination.

The decree is no more inconsistent with free agency than foreknowledge is, and yet the objectors, who are generally of the Semi-Pelagian or Arminian type, profess to believe in divine foreknowledge. By His foreknowledge God *knows* from all eternity the *certain futurition* of all events. It is based on His fore-ordination, by which He determined their future certainty. The Arminian will of course, say that he does not believe in a foreknowledge based on a decree which renders things certain, but in a foreknowledge of facts and events which are contingent on the free will of man, and therefore indeterminate. Now such a foreknowledge of the free actions of man may be possible, if man even in his freedom acts in harmony with divinely established laws, which again bring in the element of certainty; but it would seem to be impossible to foreknow events which are entirely dependent on the chance decision of an unprincipled will, which can at any time, irrespective of the state of the soul, of existing conditions, and of the motives that present themselves to the mind, turn in different directions. Such events can only be foreknown as bare possibilities.

2. IT TAKES AWAY ALL MOTIVES FOR HUMAN EXERTION. This objection is to the effect that people will naturally say that, if all things are bound to happen as God has determined them, they need not concern themselves about the future and need not make any efforts to obtain salvation. But this is hardly correct. In the case of people who speak after that fashion this is generally the mere excuse of indolence and disobedience. The divine decrees are not addressed to men as a rule of action, and cannot be such a rule, since their contents become known only through, and therefore after, their realization. There is a rule of action, however, embodied in the law and in the gospel, and this puts men under obligation to employ the means which God has ordained.

This objection also ignores the logical relation, determined by God's decree, between the means and the end to be obtained. The decree includes not only the various issues of human life, but also the free human actions which are logically prior to, and are destined to bring about, the results. It was absolutely certain that all those who were in the vessel with Paul (Acts 27) were to be saved, but it was equally certain that, in order to secure this end, the sailors had to remain aboard. And since the decree establishes an interrelation between means and ends, and ends are decreed only as the result of means, they encourage effort instead of discouraging it. Firm belief in the fact that, according to the divine decrees, success will be the reward of toil, is an inducement to courageous and persevering efforts. On the very basis of the decree Scripture urges us to be diligent in using the appointed means, Phil. 2:13; Eph. 2:10.

3. IT MAKES GOD THE AUTHOR OF SIN. This, if true, would naturally be an insuperable objection, for God cannot be the author of sin. This follows equally from Scripture, Ps. 92:15; Eccl. 7:29; Jas. 1:13; I John 1:5, from the law of God which prohibits all sin, and from the holiness of God. But the

charge is not true; the decree merely makes God the author of free moral beings, who are themselves the authors of sin. God decrees to sustain their free agency, to regulate the circumstances of their life, and to permit that free agency to exert itself in a multitude of acts, of which some are sinful. For good and holy reasons He renders these sinful acts certain, but He does not decree to work evil desires or choices efficiently in man. The decree respecting sin is not an efficient but a permissive decree, or a decree to permit, in distinction from a decree to produce, sin by divine efficiency. No difficulty attaches to such a decree which does not also attach to a *mere* passive permission of what He could very well prevent, such as the Arminians, who generally raise this objection, assume. The problem of God's relation to sin remains a mystery for us, which we are not able to solve. It may be said, however, that His decree to permit sin, while it renders the entrance of sin into the world certain, does not mean that He takes delight in it; but only that He deemed it wise, for the purpose of His self-revelation, to permit moral evil, however abhorrent it may be to His nature.

II. Predestination

In passing from the discussion of the divine decree to that of predestination, we are still dealing with the same subject, but are passing from the general to the particular. The word "predestination" is not always used in the same sense. Sometimes it is employed simply as a synonym of the generic word "decree." In other cases it serves to designate the purpose of God respecting all His moral creatures. Most frequently, however, it denotes "the counsel of God concerning fallen men, including the sovereign election of some and the righteous reprobation of the rest. In the present discussion it is used primarily in the last sense, though not altogether to the exclusion of the second meaning.

A. The Doctrine of Predestination in History.

Predestination does not form an important subject of discussion in history until the time of Augustine. Earlier Church Fathers allude to it, but do not as yet seem to have a very clear conception of it. On the whole they regard it as the prescience of God with reference to human deeds, on the basis of which He determines their future destiny. Hence it was possible for Pelagius to appeal to some of those early Fathers. "According to Pelagius," says Wiggers, "foreordination to salvation or to damnation, is founded on prescience. Consequently he did not admit an 'absolute predestination,' but in every respect a 'conditional predestination'."[1] At first, Augustine himself was inclined to this view, but deeper reflection on the sovereign character of the good pleasure of God led him to see that predestination was in no way dependent on God's foreknowledge of human actions, but was rather the basis of the divine foreknowledge. His representation of reprobation is not as unambiguous as it might be. Some of his statements are to the effect that in predestination God foreknows what He will Himself do, while He is also able to foreknow what He will not do, as all sins; and speak of the elect as subjects of predestination, and of the reprobate as subjects of the divine foreknowledge.[2] In other passages, however, he also speaks of the reprobate as subjects of predestination, so that there can be no doubt about it that he taught a double predestination. However, he recognized their difference, consisting in this that God did not predestinate unto damnation and the means unto it in the same way as He did to salvation, and that predestination unto life is purely sovereign, while predestination unto eternal

---

1. *Augustinism and Pelagianism*, p. 252.
2. Cf. Wiggers, ibid., p. 239; Dijk. *Om't Eeuwig Welbehagen*, pp. 39f.; Polman, *De Praedestinatieleer van Augustinus, Thomas van Aquino, en Calvijn*, pp. 149ff.

109

death is also judicial and takes account of man's sin.[1]

Augustine's view found a great deal of opposition, particularly in France, where the semi-Pelagians, while admitting the need of divine grace unto salvation, reasserted the doctrine of a predestination based on foreknowledge. And they who took up the defense of Augustine felt constrained to yield on some important points. They failed to do justice to the doctrine of a double predestination. Only Gottschalk and a few of his friends maintained this, but his voice was soon silenced, and Semi-Pelagianism gained the upper hand at least among the leaders of the Church. Toward the end of the Middle Ages it became quite apparent that the Roman Catholic Church would allow a great deal of latitude in the doctrine of predestination. As long as its teachers maintained that God willed the salvation of all men, and not merely of the elect, they could with Thomas Aquinas move in the direction of Augustinianism in the doctrine of predestination, or with Molina follow the course of Semi-Pelagianism, as they thought best. This means that even in the case of those who, like Thomas Aquinas, believed in an absolute and double predestination, this doctrine could not be carried through consistently, and could not be made determinative of the rest of their theology.

The Reformers of the sixteenth century all advocated the strictest doctrine of predestination. This is even true of Melanchton in his earliest period. Luther accepted the doctrine of absolute predestination, though the conviction that God willed that all men should be saved caused him to soft-pedal the doctrine of predestination somewhat later in life. It gradually disappeared from Lutheran theology, which now regards it either wholly or in part (reprobation) as conditional. Calvin firmly maintained the Augustinian doctrine of an absolute double predestination. At the same time he, in his defense of the doctrine against Pighius, stressed the fact that the decree respecting the entrance of sin into the world was a permissive decree, and that the decree of reprobation should be so construed that God was not made the author of sin nor in any way responsible for it. The Reformed Confessions are remarkably consistent in embodying this doctrine. though they do not all state it with equal fulness and precision. As a result of the Arminian assault on the doctrine, the Canons of Dort contain a clear and detailed statement of it. In churches of the Arminian type the doctrine of absolute predestination has been supplanted by the doctrine of conditional predestination.

Since the days of Schleiermacher the doctrine of predestination received an entirely different form. Religion was regarded as a feeling of absolute dependence, a Hinneigung zum Weltall, a consciousness of utter dependence on the causality that is proper to the natural order with its invariable laws and second causes, which predetermine all human resolves and actions. And predestination was identified with this predetermination by nature or the universal causal connection in the world. The scathing denunciation of this view by Otto is none too severe: "There can be no more spurious product of theological specu-

---

1. Cf. Dyk, *ibid.*, p. 40; Polman, *ibid.*, p. 158.

lation, no more fundamental falsification of religious conceptions than this; and it is certainly not against this that the Rationalist feels an antagonism, for it is itself a piece of solid Rationalism, but at the same time a complete abandonment of the real religious idea of 'predestination'."[1] In modern liberal theology the doctrine of predestination meets with little favor. It is either rejected or changed beyond recognition. G. B. Foster brands it as determinism; Macintosh represents it as a predestination of *all men* to be conformed to the image of Jesus Christ; and others reduce it to a predestination to certain offices or privileges.

In our day Barth has again directed attention to the doctrine of predestination, but has given a construction of it which is not even distantly related to that of Augustine and Calvin. With the Reformers he holds that this doctrine stresses the sovereign freedom of God in His election, revelation, calling, and so on.[2] At the same time he does not see in predestination a predetermined separation of men, and does not understand election like Calvin as particular election. This is evident from what he says on page 332 of his *Roemerbrief*. Camfield therefore says in his *Essay in Barthian Theology*, entitled *Revelation and the Holy Spirit*:[3] "It needs to be emphasized that predestination does not mean the selection of a number of people for salvation and the rest for damnation according to the determination of an unknown and unknowable will. That idea does not belong to predestination proper." Predestination brings man into crisis in the moment of revelation and decision. It condemns him in the relation in which he stands to God by nature, as sinner, and in that relation rejects him, but it chooses him in the relation to which he is called in Christ, and for which he was destined in creation. If man responds to God's revelation by faith, he is what God intended him to be, an elect; but if he does not respond, he remains a reprobate. But since man is always in crisis, unconditional pardon and complete rejection continue to apply to every one simultaneously. Esau may become Jacob, but Jacob may also become once more Esau. Says McConnachie: "For Barth, and as he believes, for St. Paul, the individual is not the object of election or reprobation, but rather the arena of election or reprobation. The two decisions meet within the same individual, but in such a way that, seen from the human side, man is always reprobate, but seen from the divine side, he is always elect. . . . The ground of election is faith. The ground of reprobation is want of faith. But who is he who believes? And who is he who disbelieves? Faith and unbelief are grounded in God. We stand at the gates of mystery."[4]

B. Scriptural Terms for Predestination.

The following terms come into consideration here:

1. THE HEBREW WORD *yada'* AND THE GREEK WORDS *ginoskein, proginoskein,* AND *prognosis.* The word *yada'* may simply mean "to know" or "to take

1. *The Idea of the Holy*, p. 90.
2. *The Doctrine of the Word of God*, p. 168; *Roemerbrief* (2nd ed.), p. 332.
3. p. 92.
4. *The Significance of Karl Barth*, pp. 240f.

cognizance" of someone or something, but may also be used in the more pregnant sense of "taking knowledge of one with loving care," or "making one the object of loving care or elective love." In this sense it serves the idea of election, Gen. 18:19; Amos 3:2; Hos. 13:5. The meaning of the words *proginoskein and prognosis* in the New Testament is not determined by their usage in the classics, but by the special meaning of *yada'*. They do not denote simple intellectual foresight or prescience, the mere taking knowledge of something beforehand, but rather a selective knowledge which regards one with favor and makes one an object of love, and thus approaches the idea of foreordination, Acts 2:23 (comp. 4:28); Rom. 8:29; 11:2; I Peter 1:2. These passages simply lose their meaning, if the words be taken in the sense of simply taking knowledge of one in advance, for God foreknows all men in that sense. Even Arminians feel constrained to give the words a more determinative meaning, namely, to foreknow one with absolute assurance in a certain state or condition. This includes the absolute certainty of that future state, and for that very reason comes very close to the idea of predestination. And not only these words, but even the simple *ginoskein* has such a specific meaning in some cases, I Cor. 8:3; Gal. 4:9; II Tim. 2:19.[1]

2. THE HEBREW WORD *bachar* AND THE GREEK WORDS *eklegesthai* AND *ekloge*. These words stress the element of choice or selection in the decree of God respecting the eternal destiny of sinners, a choice accompanied with good pleasure. They serve to indicate the fact that God selects a certain number of the human race and places them in a special relation to Himself. Sometimes they include the idea of a call to a certain privilege, or of the call to salvation; but it is a mistake to think, as some do, that this exhausts their meaning. It is perfectly evident that they generally refer to a prior and eternal election, Rom. 9:11; 11:5; Eph. 1:4; II Thess. 2:13.

3. THE GREEK WORDS *proorizein* AND *proorismos*. These words always refer to absolute predestination. In distinction from the other words, they really require a complement. The question naturally arises, Foreordained unto what? The words always refer to the foreordination of man to a certain end, and from the Bible it is evident that the end may be either good or bad, Acts 4:28; Eph. 1:5. However, the end to which they refer is not necessarily the final end, but is even more frequently some end in time, which is in turn a means to the final end, Acts 4:28; Rom. 8:29; I Cor. 2:7; Eph. 1:5,11.

4. THE GREEK WORDS *protithenai* AND *prothesis*. In these words attention is directed to the fact that God sets before Him a definite plan to which He steadfastly adheres. They clearly refer to God's purpose of predestinating men unto salvation in Rom. 8:29; 9:11; Eph. 1:9,11; II Tim. 1:9.

C. The Author and Objects of Predestination.

1. THE AUTHOR. The decree of predestination is undoubtedly in all its parts the concurrent act of the three persons in the Trinity, who are one in their

---

1. Cf. Article of C. W. Hodge on *"Foreknow, Foreknowledge"* in the *International Standard Bible Encyclopaedia*.

counsel and will. But in the economy of salvation, as it is revealed in Scripture, the sovereign act of predestination is more particularly attributed to the Father, John 17:6,9; Rom. 8:29; Eph. 1:4; I Pet. 1:2.

2. THE OBJECTS OF PREDESTINATION. In distinction from the decree of God in general, predestination has reference to God's rational creatures only. Most frequently it refers to fallen men. · Yet it is also employed in a wider sense, and we use it in the more inclusive sense here, in order to embrace all the objects of predestination. It includes all God's rational creatures, that is:

a. *All men, both good and evil.* These are included not merely as groups, but as individuals, Acts 4:28; Rom. 8:29,30; 9:11-13; Eph. 1:5,11.

b. *The angels, both good and evil.* The Bible speaks not only of holy angels, Mark 8:38; Luke 9:26, and of wicked angels, which kept not their first estate, II Pet. 2:4; Jude 6; but also makes explicit mention of elect angels, I Tim. 5:21, thereby implying that there were also non-elect angels. The question naturally arises, How are we to conceive of the predestination of angels? According to some it simply means that God determined in general that the angels which remained holy would be confirmed in a state of bliss, while the others would be lost. But this is not at all in harmony with the Scriptural idea of predestination. It rather means that God decreed, for reasons sufficient unto Himself, to give some angels, in addition to the grace with which they were endowed by creation and which included ample power to remain holy, a special grace of perseverance; and to withhold this from others. There are points of difference between the predestination of men and that of the angels: (1) While the predestination of men may be conceived of as infralapsarian, the predestination of the angels can only be understood as supralapsarian. God did not choose a certain number out of the fallen mass of angels. (2) The angels were not elected or predestined in Christ as Mediator, but in Him as Head, that is, to stand in a ministerial relation to Him.

c. *Christ as Mediator.* Christ was the object of predestination in the sense that (1) a special love of the Father, distinct from His usual love to the Son, rested upon Him from all eternity, I Pet. 1:20; 2:4; (2) in His quality as Mediator he was the object of God's good pleasure, I Pet. 2:4; (3) as Mediator He was adorned with the special image of God, to which believers were to be conformed, Rom. 8:29; and (4) the Kingdom with all its glory and the means leading to its possession were ordained for Him, that He might pass these on to believers, Luke 22:29.

D. The Parts of Predestination.

Predestination includes two parts, namely, election and reprobation, the predetermination of both the good and the wicked to their final end, and to certain proximate ends which are instrumental in the realization of their final destiny.

1. ELECTION.

a. *The Biblical Idea of Election.* The Bible speaks of election in more than one sense. There is (1) the election of Israel as a people for special privileges and for special service, Deut. 4:37; 7:6-8; 10:15; Hos. 13:5. (2) The election of individuals to some office, or to the performance of some special service, as Moses, Ex. 3, the priests, Deut. 18:5; the kings, I Sam. 10:24; Ps. 78:70, the prophets, Jer. 1:5, and the apostles, John 6:70; Acts 9:15. (3) The election of individuals to be children of God and heirs of eternal glory, Matt. 22:14; Rom. 11:5; I Cor. 1:27,28; Eph. 1:4; I Thess. 1:4; I Pet. 1:2; II Pet. 1:10. The last is the election that comes into consideration here as a part of predestination. It may be defined as *that eternal act of God whereby He, in His sovereign good pleasure, and on account of no foreseen merit in them, chooses a certain number of men to be the recipients of special grace and of eternal salvation.* More briefly it may be said to be God's eternal purpose to save some of the human race in and by Jesus Christ.

b. *The characteristics of election.* The characteristics of election are identical with the characteristics of the decrees in general. The decree of election: (1) *Is an expression of the sovereign will of God, His divine good pleasure.* This means among other things that Christ as Mediator is not the impelling, moving, or meritorious cause of election, as some have asserted. He may be called the mediate cause of the realization of election, and the meritorious cause of the salvation unto which believers are elected, but He is not the moving or meritorious cause of election itself. This is impossible, since He is Himself an object of predestination and election, and because, when He took His mediatorial work upon Him in the Counsel of Redemption, there was already a fixed number that was given unto Him. Election logically precedes the Counsel of Peace. The elective love of God precedes the sending of the Son, John 3:16; Rom. 5:8; II Tim. 1:9; I John 4:9. By saying that the decree of election originates in the divine good pleasure the idea is also excluded that it is determined by anything in man, such as foreseen faith or good works, Rom. 9:11; II Tim. 1:9. (2) *It is immutable, and therefore renders the salvation of the elect certain.* God realizes the decree of election by His own efficiency, by the saving work which He accomplishes in Jesus Christ. It is His purpose that certain individuals should believe and persevere unto the end, and He secures this result by the objective work of Christ and the subjective operations of the Holy Spirit, Rom. 8:29,30; 11:29; II Tim. 2:19. It is the firm foundation of God which standeth, "having this seal, The Lord knoweth them that are His." And as such it is the source of rich comfort for all believers. Their final salvation does not depend on their uncertain obedience, but has its guarantee in the unchangeable purpose of God. (3) *It is eternal, that is, from eternity.* This divine election should never be identified with any *temporal* selection, whether it be for the enjoyment of the special grace of God in this life, for special privileges and responsible services, or for the inheritance of glory hereafter, but must be regarded as eternal,

Rom. 8:29,30; Eph. 1:4,5. (4) *It is unconditional.* Election does not in any way depend on the foreseen faith or good works of man, as the Arminians teach, but exclusively on the sovereign good pleasure of God, who is also the originator of faith and good works, Rom. 9:11; Acts 13:48; II Tim. 1:9; I Pet. 1:2. Since all men are sinners and have forfeited the blessings of God, there is no basis for such a distinction in them; and since even the faith and good works of the believers are the fruit of the grace of God, Eph. 2:8,10; II Tim. 2:21, even these, as foreseen by God, could not furnish such a basis. (5) *It is irresistible.* This does not mean that man cannot oppose its execution to a certain degree, but it does mean that his opposition will not prevail. Neither does it mean that God in the execution of His decree overpowers the human will in a manner which is inconsistent with man's free agency. It does mean, however, that God can and does exert such an influence on the human spirit as to make it willing, Ps. 110:3; Phil. 2:13. (6) *It is not chargeable with injustice.* The fact that God favors some and passes by others, does not warrant the charge that He is guilty of injustice. We can speak of injustice only when one party has a claim on another. If God owed the forgiveness of sin and eternal life to all men, it would be an injustice if He saved only a limited number of them. But the sinner has absolutely no right or claim on the blessings which flow from divine election. As a matter of fact he has forfeited these blessings. Not only have we no right to call God to account for electing some and passing others by, but we must admit that He would have been perfectly just, if He had not saved any, Matt. 20:14,15; Rom. 9:14,15.

c. *The purpose of election.* The purpose of this eternal election is twofold: (1) *The proximate purpose is the salvation of the elect.* That man is chosen or elected unto salvation is clearly taught in the Word of God, Rom. 11:7-11; II Thess. 2:13. (2) *The final aim is the glory of God.* Even the salvation of men is subordinate to this. That the glory of God is the highest purpose of the electing grace is made very emphatic in Eph. 1:6,12,14. The social gospel of our day likes to stress the fact that man is elected unto service. In so far as this is intended as a denial of man's election unto salvation and unto the glory of God, it plainly goes contrary to Scripture. Taken by itself, however, the idea that the elect are predestined unto service or good works is entirely Scriptural, Eph. 2:10; II Tim. 2:21; but this end is subservient to the ends already indicated.

2. REPROBATION. Our confessional standards speak not only of election, but also of reprobation.[1] Augustine taught the doctrine of reprobation as well as that of election, but this "hard doctrine" met with a great deal of opposition. Roman Catholics, the great majority of Lutherans, Arminians, and Methodists, generally reject this doctrine in its absolute form. If they still speak of reprobation, it is only of a reprobation based on foreknowledge. That Calvin was deeply conscious of the seriousness of this doctrine, is perfectly evident from

---

1. *Conf. Belg.* Art. XVI; *Canons of Dort,* I, 15.

the fact that he speaks of it as a *"decretum horribile"* (dreadful decree).[1] Nevertheless, he did not feel free to deny what he regarded as an important Scriptural truth. In our day some scholars who claim to be Reformed balk at this doctrine. Barth teaches a reprobation which is dependent on man's rejection of God's revelation in Christ. Brunner seems to have a more Scriptural conception of election than Barth, but rejects the doctrine of reprobation entirely. He admits that it logically follows from the doctrine of election, but cautions against the guidance of human logic in this instance, since the doctrine of reprobation is not taught in Scripture.[2]

a. *Statement of the doctrine.* Reprobation may be defined as *that eternal decree of God whereby He has determined to pass some men by with the operations of His special grace, and to punish them for their sins, to the manifestation of His justice.* The following points deserve special emphasis: (1) *It contains two elements.* According to the most usual representation in Reformed theology the decree of reprobation comprises two elements, namely, *preterition* or the determination to pass by some men; and *condemnation* (sometimes called *precondemnation*) or the determination to punish those who are passed by for their sins. As such it embodies a twofold purpose: (a) to pass by some in the bestowal of regenerating and saving grace; and (b) to assign them to dishonor and to the wrath of God for their sins. The Belgic Confession mentions only the former, but the Canons of Dort name the latter as well. Some Reformed theologians would omit the second element from the decree of reprobation. Dabney prefers to regard the condemnation of the wicked as the foreseen and intended result of their preterition, thus depriving reprobation of its positive character; and Dick is of the opinion that the decree to condemn ought to be regarded as a separate decree, and not as a part of the decree of reprobation. It seems to us, however, that we are not warranted in excluding the second element from the decree of reprobation, nor to regard it as a different decree. The positive side of reprobation is so clearly taught in Scripture as the opposite of election that we cannot regard it as something purely negative, Rom. 9:21,22; Jude 4. However, we should notice several points of distinction between the two elements of the decree of reprobation: (a) Preterition is a sovereign act of God, an act of His mere good pleasure, in which the demerits of man do not come into consideration, while precondemnation is a judicial act, visiting sin with punishment. Even Supralapsarians are willing to admit that in condemnation sin is taken into consideration. (b) The reason for preterition is not known by man. It cannot be sin, for all men are sinners. We can only say that God passed some by for good and wise reasons sufficient unto Himself. On the other hand the reason for condemnation is known; it is sin. (c) Preterition is purely passive, a simple passing by without any action on man, but condemnation is efficient and positive. Those who are passed by are condemned on account

---

1. *Inst.* III. 23. 7.
2. *Our Faith*, pp. 32f.

of their sin. (2) We should guard against the idea, however, that as election and reprobation both determine with absolute certainty the end unto which man is predestined and the means by which that end is realized, they also imply that in the case of reprobation as well as in that of election God will bring to pass by His own direct efficiency whatsoever He has decreed. This means that, while it can be said that God is the author of the regeneration, calling, faith, justification, and sanctification, of the elect, and thus by direct action on them brings their election to realization, it cannot be said that He is also the responsible author of the fall, the unrighteous condition, and the sinful acts of the reprobate by direct action on them, and thus effects the realization of their reprobation. God's decree undoubtedly rendered the entrance of sin into the world certain, but He did not predestinate some unto sin, as He did others unto holiness. And as the holy God He cannot be the author of sin. The position which Calvin takes on this point in his Institutes is clearly indicated in the following deliverances found in *Calvin's Articles on Predestination*:

"Although the will of God is the supreme and first cause of all things and God holds the devil and all the impious subject to His will, God nevertheless cannot be called the cause of sin, nor the author of evil, neither is He open to any blame.

"Although the devil and reprobates are God's servants and instruments to carry out His secret decisions, nevertheless in an incomprehensible manner God so works in them and through them as to contract no stain from their vice, because their malice is used in a just and righteous way for a good end, although the manner is often hidden from us.

"They act ignorantly and calumniously who say that God is made the author of sin, if all things come to pass by His will and ordinance; because they make no distinction between the depravity of men and the hidden appointments of God."[1]
(3) It should be noted that that with which God decided to pass some men by, is not His common but his special, His regenerating, grace, the grace that changes sinners into saints. It is a mistake to think that in this life the reprobate are entirely destitute of God's favor. God does not limit the distribution of His natural gifts by the purpose of election. He does not even allow election and reprobation to determine the measure of these gifts. The reprobate often enjoy a greater measure of the natural blessings of life than the elect. What effectively distinguishes the latter from the former is that *they* are made recipients of the regenerating and saving grace of God.

b. *Proof for the doctrine of reprobation.* The doctrine of reprobation naturally follows from the logic of the situation. The decree of election inevitably implies the decree of reprobation. If the all-wise God, possessed of infinite knowledge, has eternally purposed to save some, then He *ipso facto*

---

1. Quoted by Warfield, *Studies in Theology*, p. 194.

also purposed not to save others. If He has chosen or elected some, then He has by that very fact also rejected others. Brunner warns against this argument, since the Bible does not in a single word teach a divine predestination unto rejection. But it seems to us that the Bible does not contradict but justifies the logic in question. Since the Bible is primarily a revelation of redemption, it naturally does not have as much to say about reprobation as about election. But what it says is quite sufficient, cf. Matt. 11:25,26; Rom. 9:13,17,18,21,22; 11:7; Jude 4; I Pet. 2:8.

E. Supra- and Infralapsarianism.

The doctrine of predestination has not always been presented in exactly the same form. Especially since the days of the Reformation two different conceptions of it gradually emerged, which were designated during the Arminian controversy as Infra- and Supralapsarianism. Already existing differences were more sharply defined and more strongly accentuated as the results of the theological disputes of that day. According to Dr. Dijk the two views under consideration were in their original form simply a difference of opinion respecting the question, whether the fall of man was also included in the divine decree. Was the first sin of man, constituting his fall, predestinated, or was this merely the object of divine foreknowledge? In their original form Supralapsarianism held the former, and Infralapsarianism, the latter. In this sense of the word Calvin was clearly a Supralapsarian. The later development of the difference between the two began with Beza, the successor of Calvin at Geneva. In it the original point in dispute gradually retires into the background, and other differences are brought forward, some of which turn out to be mere differences of emphasis. Later Infralapsarians, such as Rivet, Walaeus, Mastricht, Turretin, à Mark, and de Moor, all admit that the fall of man was included in the decree; and of the later Supralapsarians, such as Beza, Gomarus, Peter Martyr, Zanchius, Ursinus, Perkins, Twisse, Trigland, Voetius, Burmannus, Witsius and Comrie, at least some are quite willing to admit that in the decree of Reprobation God in some way took sin into consideration. We are concerned at present with Supra- and Infralapsarianism in their more developed form.

1. THE EXACT POINT AT ISSUE. It is quite essential to have a correct view of the exact point or points at issue between the two.

a. *Negatively, the difference is not found:* (1) *In divergent views respecting the temporal order of the divine decrees.* It is admitted on all hands that the decree of God is one and in all its parts equally eternal, so that it is impossible to ascribe any temporal succession to the various elements which it includes. (2) *In any essential difference as to whether the fall of man was decreed or was merely the object of divine foreknowledge.* This may have been, as Dr. Dijk says, the original point of difference; but, surely, anyone who asserts that the fall was not decreed but only foreseen by God, would now be said to be moving along Arminian rather than Reformed lines. Both Supra- and Infralapsarians admit that the fall is included in the divine decree, and that preterition is an act of God's sovereign will. (3) *In any essential difference as to the question, whether the decree relative to sin is permissive.* There is some difference of emphasis on the qualifying adjective. Supralapsarians (with few exceptions) are willing to admit that the decree relative to sin is permissive, but hasten to add that it nevertheless makes the entrance of sin into the world a certainty. And Infralapsarians (with few exceptions) will admit that sin is included in God's decree, but hasten to add that the decree, in so far as it pertains to sin, is permissive rather than positive. The former occasionally over-emphasize the positive element in the decree respecting sin, and thus expose themselves to the charge that they make God the author of sin. And the latter sometimes over-emphasize the permissive character of the decree, reducing it to a bare permission, and thus expose themselves to the charge of Arminianism. As a whole, however, Supralapsarians emphatically repudiate every interpretation of the decree that would make God the author of sin; and Infralapsarians are careful to point out explicitly that the permissive decree of God relative to sin makes sin certainly future. (4) *In any essential difference as to the question, whether the decree of reprobation takes account of sin.* It is sometimes represented as if God destined some men for eternal destruction, simply by an act of His sovereign will, without taking account of their sin; as if, like a tyrant, He simply decided to destroy a large number of His rational creatures, purely for the manifestation of His glorious virtues. But Supralapsarians abhor the idea of a tyrannical God, and at least some of them explicitly state that, while preterition is an act of God's sovereign will, the second element of reprobation, namely, condemnation, is an act of justice and certainly takes account of sin. This proceeds on the supposition that logically preterition precedes the decree to create and to permit the fall, while condemnation follows this. The logic of this position may be questioned, but it at least shows that the Supralapsarians who assume it, teach that God takes account of sin in the decree of reprobation.

b. *Positively, the difference does concern:* (1) *The extent of predestination.* Supralapsarians include the decree to create and to permit the fall in the decree of predestination, while Infralapsarians refer it to the decree of God in general, and exclude it from the special decree of predestination. According to the former, man appears in the decree of predestination, *not as created and fallen,* but *as certain to be created and to fall;* while according to the latter, he appears in it as already created and fallen. (2) *The logical order of the decrees.* The question is, whether the decrees to create and to permit the fall were means to the decree of redemption. Supralapsarians proceed on the assumption that in planning the rational mind passes from the end to the means in a retrograde movement, so that what is first in design is last in accomplishment. Thus they determine upon the following order: (a) The decree of God to glorify Himself, and particularly to magnify His grace and justice in the salvation of some and the perdition of other rational creatures, which exist in the divine mind as yet only as possibilities. (b) The decree to create those who were thus elected and reprobated. (c) The decree to permit them to fall. (d) The decree to justify the elect and to condemn the non-elect. On the other hand the Infralapsarians suggest a more historical order: (a) The decree to create man in holiness and blessedness. (b) The decree to permit man to fall by the self-determination of his own will. (c) The decree to save a certain number out of this guilty aggregate. (d) The decree to leave the remainder in their self-determination in sin, and to subject them to the righteous punishment which their sin deserves. (3) *The extension of the personal element of predestination to the decrees to create and to permit the fall.* According to Supralapsarians God, even in the decree to create and permit the fall, had His eye fixed on His elect individually, so that there was not a single moment in the divine decree, when they did not stand in a special relation to God as His beloved ones. Infralapsarians, on the other hand, hold that this personal element did not appear in the decree till after the decree to create and to permit the fall. In these decrees themselves the elect are simply included in the whole mass of humanity, and do not appear as the special objects of God's love.

2. THE SUPRALAPSARIAN POSITION.

a. *Arguments in favor of it:* (1) It appeals to all those passages of Scripture which emphasize the absolute sovereignty of God, and more particularly His sovereignty in relation to sin, such as Ps. 115:3; Prov. 16:4; Isa. 10:15; 45:9; Jer. 18:6; Matt. 11:25,26; 20:15; Rom. 9:17,19-21. Special emphasis is laid on the figure of the potter, which is found in more than one of these passages. It is said that this figure not merely stresses the sovereignty of God in general, but more especially His sovereignty in determining the quality of the vessels at creation. This means that Paul in Rom. 9 speaks from a pre-creation standpoint, an idea that is favored (a) by the fact that the potter's work is frequently used in Scripture as a figure of creation; and (b) by the fact that the potter determines each vessel for a certain use and gives it a corresponding quality, which might cause the vessel to ask, though without any right, Why didst Thou make me thus? (2) Attention is called to the fact that some passages of Scripture suggest that the work of nature or of creation in general was so ordered as to contain already illustrations of the work of redemption. Jesus frequently derives His illustrations for the elucidation of spiritual things from nature, and we are told in Matt. 13:35 that this was in fulfilment of the words of the prophet, "I will utter things hidden from the foundation of the world." Comp. Ps. 78:2. This is taken to mean that they were *hidden in nature*, but were brought to light in the parabolic teachings of Jesus. Ephesians 3:9 is also considered as an expression of the idea that the design of God in the creation of the world was directed to the manifestation of His wisdom, which would issue in the New Testament work of redemption. But the appeal to this passage seems, to say the least, very doubtful. (3) The order of the decrees, as accepted by the Supralapsarians, is regarded as the more ideal, the more logical and unified of the two. It clearly exhibits the rational order which exists between the ultimate end and the intermediate means. Therefore the Supralapsarians can, while the Infralapsarians cannot, give a specific answer to the question why God decreed to create the world and to permit the fall. They do full justice to the sovereignty of God and refrain from all futile attempts to justify God in the sight of men, while the Infralapsarians hesitate, attempt to prove the justice of God's procedure, and yet in the end must come to the same conclusion as the Supralapsarians, namely, that, in the last analysis, the decree to permit the fall finds its explanation only in the sovereign good pleasure of God.[1] (4) The analogy of the predestination of the angels would seem to favor the Supralapsarian position, for it can only be conceived as supralapsarian. God decreed, for reasons sufficient to Himself, to grant some angels the grace of perseverance and to withhold this from others; and to connect with this righteously the confirmation of the former in a state of glory, and the eternal perdition of the latter. This means, therefore, that the decree respecting the fall of the angels forms a part of their predestination. And it would seem impossible to conceive of it in any other way.

b. *Objections to it:* Notwithstanding its seeming pretensions, it does not give a solution of the problem of sin. It would do this, if it dared to say that God decreed to bring sin into the world *by His own direct efficiency.* Some Supralapsarians, it is true, do represent the decree as the efficient cause of sin, but yet do not want this to be interpreted in such a way that God becomes the author of sin. The majority of them do not care to go beyond the statement that God willed to permit sin. Now this is no objection to the Supralapsarian in distinction from the Infralapsarian, for neither one of them solves the problem. The only difference is that the former makes greater pretensions in this respect than the latter. (2) According to its representations man appears in the divine decree first as *creabilis et labilis* (certain to be created and to fall). The objects of the decree are first of all men considered as mere possibilities, as non-existent entities. But such a decree necessarily has only a provisional character, and must be followed by another decree. After the election and reprobation of these possible men follows the decree to create them and to permit them to fall, and this must be followed by another decree respecting these men whose creation and fall have now been definitely determined, namely, the decree to elect some and to reprobate the rest of those who now appear in the divine purpose as real men. Supralapsarians claim that this is no insuperable objection because, while it is true that on their position the actual existence of men has not yet been determined when they are elected and reprobated, they do exist in the divine idea. (3) It is said that Supralapsarianism makes the eternal punishment of the reprobate an object of the divine will in the same sense and in the same manner as the eternal salvation of the elect; and that it makes sin, which leads to eternal destruction, a means unto this end in the same manner and in the same sense as the redemption in Christ is a means unto

---

1. Bavinck, *Geref. Dogm.* II, p. 400.

salvation. If consistently carried through, this would make God the author of sin. It should be noted, however, that the Supralapsarian does not, as a rule, so represent the decree, and explicitly states that the decree may not be so interpreted as to make God the author of sin. He will speak of a predestination unto the grace of God in Jesus Christ, but not of a predestination unto sin. (4) Again, it is objected that Supralapsarianism makes the decree of reprobation just as absolute as the decree of election. In other words, that it regards reprobation as purely an act of God's sovereign good pleasure, and not as an act of punitive justice. According to its representation sin does not come into consideration in the decree of reprobation. But this is hardly correct, though it may be true of some Supralapsarians. In general, however, it may be said that, while they regard preterition as an act of God's sovereign good pleasure, they usually regard precondemnation as an act of divine justice which does take sin into consideration. And the Infralapsarian himself cannot maintain the idea that reprobation is an act of justice pure and simple, contingent on the sin of man. In the last analysis, he, too, must declare that it is an act of God's sovereign good pleasure, if he wants to avoid the Arminian camp. (5) Finally, it is said that it is not possible to construe a serviceable doctrine of the covenant of grace and of the Mediator on the basis of the Supralapsarian scheme. Both the covenant and the Mediator of the covenant can only be conceived as infralapsarian. This is frankly admitted by some Supralapsarians. Logically, the Mediator appears in the divine decree only after the entrance of sin; and this is the only point of view from which the covenant of grace can be construed. This will naturally have an important bearing on the ministry of the Word.

3. THE INFRALAPSARIAN POSITION.

a. *Arguments in favor of it.* (1) Infralapsarians appeal more particularly to those passages of Scripture in which the objects of election appear as in a condition of sin, as being in close union with Christ, and as objects of God's mercy and grace, such as Matt. 11:25,26; John 15:19; Rom. 8:28,30; 9:15.16; Eph. 1:4-12; II Tim. 1:9. These passages would seem to imply that in the thought of God the fall of man preceded the election of some unto salvation. (2) It also calls attention to the fact that in its representation the order of the divine decrees is less philosophical and more natural than that proposed by Supralapsarians. It is in harmony with the historical order in the execution of the decrees, which would seem to reflect the order in the eternal counsel of God. Just as in the execution, so there is in the decree a causal order. It is more modest to abide by this order, just because it reflects the historical order revealed in Scripture and does not pretend to solve the problem of God's relation to sin. It is considered to be less offensive in its presentation of the matter and to be far more in harmony with the requirements of practical life.[1] (3) While Supralapsarians claim that their construction of the doctrine of the decrees is the more logical of the two, Infralapsarians make the same claim for

1. Cf. Edwards, *Works* II, p. 543.

their position. Says Dabney: "The Supralapsarian (scheme) under the pretense of greater symmetry, is in reality the more illogical of the two."[1] It is pointed out that the supralapsarian scheme is illogical in that it makes the decree of election and preterition refer to non-entities, that is, to men who do not exist, except as bare possibilities, even in the mind of God; who do not yet exist in the divine decree and are therefore not contemplated as created, but only as creatable. Again, it is said that the supralapsarian construction is illogical in that it necessarily separates the two elements in reprobation, placing preterition before, and condemnation after, the fall. (4) Finally, attention is also called to the fact that the Reformed Churches in their official standards have always adopted the infralapsarian position, even though they have never condemned, but always tolerated, the other view. Among the members of the Synod of Dort and of the Westminster Assembly there were several Supralapsarians who were held in high honour (the presiding officer in both cases belonging to the number), but in both the Canons of Dort and the Westminster Confession the infralapsarian view finds expression.

b. *Objections to it.* The following are some of the most important objections raised against Infralapsarianism: (1) It does not give, nor does it claim to give a solution of the problem of sin. But this is equally true of the other view, so that, in a comparison of the two, this cannot very well be regarded as a real objection, though it is sometimes raised. The problem of the relation of God to sin has proved to be insoluble for the one as well as for the other. (2) While Infralapsarianism may be actuated by the laudable desire to guard against the possibility of charging God with being the author of sin, it is, in doing this, always in danger of overshooting the mark, and some of its representatives have made this mistake. They are averse to the statement that God *willed* sin, and substitute for it the assertion that He *permitted it.* But then the question arises as to the exact meaning of this statement. Does it mean that God merely took cognizance of the entrance of sin, without in any way hindering it, so that the fall was in reality a frustration of His plan? The moment the Infralapsarian answers this question in the affirmative, he enters the ranks of the Arminians. While there have been some who took this stand, the majority of them feel that they cannot consistently take this position, but must incorporate the fall in the divine decree. They speak of the decree respecting sin as a *permissive decree,* but with the distinct understanding that this decree rendered the entrance of sin into the world certain. And if the question be raised, why God decreed to permit sin and thus rendered it certain, they can only point to the divine good pleasure, and are thus in perfect agreement with the Supralapsarian. (3) The same tendency to shield God reveals itself in another way and exposes one to a similar danger. Infralapsarianism really wants to explain reprobation as an act of God's justice. It is inclined to deny either explicitly or implicitly that it is an act of the mere good pleasure of God. This really makes the decree of reprobation a conditional decree and leads into the Arminian fold. But infra-

---

1. *Syst. and Polem. Theol,* p. 233.

lapsarians on the whole do not want to teach a conditional decree, and express themselves guardedly on this matter. Some of them admit that it is a mistake to consider reprobation purely as an act of divine justice. And this is perfectly correct. Sin is not the ultimate cause of reprobation any more than faith and good works are the cause of election, for all men are by nature dead in sin and trespasses. When confronted with the problem of reprobation, Infralapsarians, too, can find the answer only in the good pleasure of God. Their language may sound more tender than that of the Supralapsarians, but is also more apt to be misunderstood, and after all proves to convey the same idea. (4) The Infralapsarian position does not do justice to the unity of the divine decree, but represents the different members of it too much as disconnected parts. First God decrees to create the world for the glory of His name, which means among other things also that He determined that His rational creatures should live according to the divine law implanted in their hearts and should praise their Maker. Then He decreed to permit the fall, whereby sin enters the world. This seems to be a frustration of the original plan, or at least an important modification of it, since God no more decrees to glorify Himself by the voluntary obedience of *all* His rational creatures. Finally, there follow the decrees of election and reprobation, which mean only a partial execution of the original plan.

4. From what was said it would seem to follow that we cannot regard Supra- and Infralapsarianism as absolutely antithetical. They consider the same mystery from different points of view, the one fixing its attention on the ideal or teleological; the other, on the historical, order of the decrees. To a certain extent they can and must go hand in hand. Both find support in Scripture. Supralapsarianism in those passages which stress the sovereignty of God, and Infralapsarianism in those which emphasize the mercy and justice of God, in connection with election and reprobation. Each has something in its favor: the former that it does not undertake to justify God, but simply rests in the sovereign and holy good pleasure of God; and the latter, that it is more modest and tender, and reckons with the demands and requirements of practical life. Both are necessarily inconsistent; the former because it cannot regard sin as a progression, but must consider it as a disturbance of creation, and speaks of a *permissive* decree; and the latter, since in the last analysis it must also resort to a permissive *decree*, which makes sin certain. But each one of them also emphasizes an element of truth. The true element in Supralapsarianism is found in its emphasis on the following: that the decree of God is a unit; that God had *one* final aim in view; that He willed sin in a certain sense; and that the work of creation was immediately adapted to the recreative activity of God. And the true element in Infralapsarianism is, that there is a certain diversity in the decrees of God; that creation and fall cannot be regarded merely as means to an end, but also had great independent significance; and that sin cannot be regarded as an element of progress, but should rather be considered as an element of disturbance in the world. In connection with the study of this profound subject we feel that our understanding is limited, and realize that we

grasp only fragments of the truth. Our confessional standards embody the infralapsarian position, but do not condemn Supralapsarianism. It was felt that this view was not necessarily inconsistent with Reformed theology. And the conclusions of Utrecht, adopted in 1908 by our Church, state that, while it is not permissible to represent the supralapsarian view as *the* doctrine of the Reformed churches in the Netherlands, it is just as little permissible to molest any one who cherishes that view for himself.

QUESTIONS FOR FURTHER STUDY. Is a foreknowledge of future events which is not based on the decree possible in God? What is the inevitable result of basing God's decree on His foreknowledge rather than *vice versa*, his foreknowledge on His decree? How does the doctrine of the decrees differ from fatalism and from determinism? Does the decree of predestination necessarily exclude the possibility of a universal offer of salvation? Are the decrees of election and reprobation equally absolute and unconditional or not? Are they alike in being causes from which human actions proceed as effects? How is the doctrine of predestination related to the doctrine of the divine sovereignty;— to the doctrine of total depravity;—to the doctrine of the atonement;—to the doctrine of the perseverance of the saints? Do the Reformed teach a predestination unto sin?

LITERATURE: Bavinck, *Geref. Dogm.* II, pp. 347-425; Kuyper, *Dict. Dogm., De Deo* III, pp. 80-258; Vos, *Geref. Dogm.* I, pp. 81-170; Hodge, *Syst. Theol.* I, pp. 535-549; II, pp. 315-321; Shedd, *Dogm. Theol.* I, pp. 393-462; Mastricht, *Godgeleerdheit,* I, pp. 670-757; Comrie en Holtius, *Examen van het Ontwerp van Tolerantie, Samenspraken* VI *and* VII; Turretin, *Opera,* I, pp. 279-382; Dabney,*Syst. and Polem Theol..* pp. 211-246; Miley, *Syst. Theol.* II, pp. 245-266; Cunningham, *Hist. Theol.,* II, pp. 416-489; Wiggers, *Augustinism and Pelagianism,* pp. 237- 254; Girardeau, *Calvinism and Evangelical Arminianism,* pp. 14-412; ibid., *The Will in its Theological Relations;* Warfield, *Biblical Doctrines,* pp. 3-67; ibid., *Studies in Theology,* pp. 117-231; Cole, *Calvin's Calvinism,* pp. 25-206; Calvin, *Institutes* III. Chap. XXI-XXIV; Dijk, *De Strijd over Infra-en Supralapsarisme in de Gereformeerde Kerken van Nederland;* ibid., *Om 't Eeuwig Welbehagen;* Fernhout, *De Leer der Uitverkiezing;* Polman, *De Praedestinatieleer van Augustinus, Thomas van Aquino en Calvijn.*

III. Creation in General

The discussion of the decrees naturally leads on to the consideration of their execution, and this begins with the work of creation. This is not only first in order of time, but is also a logical prius. It is the beginning and basis of all divine revelation, and consequently also the foundation of all ethical and religious life. The doctrine of creation is not set forth in Scripture as a philosophical solution of the problem of the world, but in its ethical and religious significance, as a revelation of the relation of man to his God. It stresses the fact that God is the origin of all things, and that all things belong to Him and are subject to Him. The knowledge of it is derived from Scripture only and is accepted by faith (Heb. 11:3), though Roman Catholics maintain that it can also be gathered from nature.

A. The Doctrine of Creation in History.

While Greek philosophy sought the explanation of the world in a dualism, which involves the eternity of matter, or in a process of emanation, which makes the world the outward manifestation of God, the Christian Church from the very beginning taught the doctrine of creation *ex nihilo* and as a *free* act of God. This doctrine was accepted with singular unanimity from the start. It is found in Justin Martyr, Irenaeus, Tertullian, Clement of Alexandria, Origen, and others. Theophilus was the first Church Father to stress the fact that the days of creation were literal days. This seems to have been the view of Irenaeus and Tertullian as well, and was in all probability the common view in the Church. Clement and Origen thought of creation as having been accomplished *in a single indivisible moment,* and conceived of its description as the work of several days merely as a literary device to describe the origin of things in the order of their worth or of their logical connection. The idea of an eternal creation, as taught by Origen, was commonly rejected. At the same time some of the Church Fathers expressed the idea that God was always Creator, though the created universe began in time. During the trinitarian controversy some of them emphasized the fact that, in distinction from the generation of the Son, which was a *necessary* act of the Father, the creation of the world was a *free* act of the triune God. Augustine dealt with the work of creation more in detail than others did. He argues that creation was eternally in the will of God, and therefore brought no change in Him. There was no time before creation, since the world was brought into being *with* time rather than *in* time. The question what God did in the many ages before creation is based on a misconception of eternity. While the Church in general still seems to have held that the world was created in six ordinary days, Augustine suggested a somewhat different view. He strongly defended the doctrine of *creatio ex nihilo*, but distinguished two moments of creation: the production of matter and spirits out of nothing, and the organization of the material universe. He found it difficult to say what kind of days the days of Genesis were, but was evidently inclined to think that God created all things *in a moment of time*, and that the thought of days was simply introduced to aid the finite intelligence. The Scholastics debated a great deal about the possibility of eternal creation; some, such as, Alexander of Hales, Bonaventura, Albertus Magnus, Henry of Ghent, and the great majority of the Scholastics denying this; and others, such as Thomas Aquinas, Duns Scotus, Durandus, Biel, and others affirming it. Yet the doctrine of creation with or in time carried the day. Erigena and Eckhart were exceptional in teaching that the world originated by emanation. Seemingly the days of creation were regarded as ordinary days, though Anselm suggested that it might be necessary to conceive of them as different from our present days. The Reformers held firmly to the doctrine of creation out of nothing by a free act of God in or with time, and regarded the days of creation as six literal days. This view is also generally maintained in the Post-Reformation literature of the sixteenth and seventeenth centuries, though a few theologians (as Maresius) occasionally speak of *continuous creation*. In the eighteenth century, however, under the dominating influence of Pantheism and Materialism, science launched an attack on the Church's doctrine of creation. It substituted the idea of evolution or development for that of absolute origination by a divine fiat. The world was often represented as a necessary manifestation of the Absolute. Its origin was pushed back thousands and even millions of years into an unknown past. And soon theologians were engaged in various attempts to harmonize the doctrine of creation with the teachings of science and philosophy. Some suggested that the first chapters of Genesis should be interpreted allegorically or mythically; others, that a long period elapsed between the primary creation of Gen. 1:1,2 and the secondary creation of the following verses; and still others, that the days of creation were in fact long periods of time.

B. Scriptural Proof for the Doctrine of Creation.

The Scriptural proof for the doctrine of creation is not found in a single and limited portion of the Bible, but is found in every part of the Word of God. It does not consist of a few scattered passages of doubtful interpretation, but of a large number of clear and unequivocal statements, which speak of the creation of the world as a historical fact. We have first of all the extended narrative of creation found in the first two chapters of Genesis, which will be discussed in detail when the creation of the material universe is considered. These chapters certainly appear to the unbiased reader as a historical narrative, and as the record of a historical fact. And the many cross-references scattered throughout the Bible do not regard them in any other light. They all refer to creation as a fact of history. The various passages in which they are found may be classified as follows: (1) Passages which stress the omnipotence of God in the work of creation, Isa. 40:26,28; Amos 4:13. (2) Passages which point to His exaltation above nature as the great and infinite God, Ps. 90:2; 102:26,27; Acts 17:24. (3) Passages which refer to the wisdom of God in the work of creation, Isa. 40:12-14; Jer. 10:12-16; John 1:3; (4) Passages regarding creation from the point of view of God's sovereignty and purpose in creation, Isa. 43:7; Rom. 1:25. (5) Passages that speak of creation as a fundamental work of God, I Cor. 11:9; Col. 1:16. One of the fullest and most beautiful statements is that found in Neh. 9:6: "Thou art Jehovah, even thou alone; thou hast made heaven, the heaven of heavens, with all their host, the earth and all things that are thereon, the seas and all that is in them, and thou preservest them all; and the host of heaven worshippeth thee." This passage is typical of several other, less extensive, passages that are found in the Bible, which emphasize the fact that Jehovah is the Creator of the universe, Isa. 42:5; 45:18; Col. 1:16; Rev. 4:11; 10:6.

C. The Idea of Creation.

The faith of the Church in the creation of the world is expressed in the very first article of the *Apostolic Confession of Faith*, "I believe in God the Father, Almighty, Maker of heaven and earth." This is an expression of the faith of the early Church, that God by His almighty power brought forth the universe out of nothing. The words "Maker of heaven and earth" were not contained in the original form of the creed, but represent a later addition. It ascribes to the Father, that is, to the first person in the Trinity, the origination of all things. This is in harmony with the representation of the New Testament that all things are of the Father, through the Son, and in the Holy Spirit. The word "Maker" is a rendering of the word *poieten*, found in the Greek form of the Apostolic Confession, while the Latin form has *creatorem*. Evidently, it is to be understood as a synonymous term for "Creator." "To create" was understood in the early Church in the strict sense of "to bring forth something out of nothing." It should be noted that Scripture does not always use the Hebrew word *bara'* and the Greek term *ktizein* in that absolute sense. It also employs these terms to denote a secondary creation, in which God made use of material that was already in existence but could not of itself have produced the result indicated, Gen. 1:21,27; 5:1; Isa. 45:7,12; 54:16; Amos 4:13; I Cor. 11:9; Rev. 10:6. It even uses them to designate that which comes into existence under the providential guidance of God, Ps. 104:30; Isa. 45:7,8; 65:18; I Tim. 4:4. Two other terms are used synonymously with the term "to create," namely, "to make" (Heb., *'asah*; Greek, *poiein*) and "to form" (Heb. *yatsar*; Greek, *plasso*). The former is clearly used in all the three senses indicated in the preceding: of primary creation in Gen. 2:4; Prov. 16:4; Acts 17:24; more frequently of secondary creation, Gen. 1:7,16,26; 2:22; Ps. 89:47; and of the work of providence in Ps. 74:17. The latter is used similarly of primary creation, Ps. 90:2 (perhaps the only instance of this use); of secondary creation, Gen. 2:7,19;

Ps. 104:26; Amos 4:13; Zech. 12:1; and of the work of providence, Deut. 32:18; Isa. 43:1,7,21; 45:7. All three words are found together in Isa. 45:7. Creation in the strict sense of the word may be defined as *that free act of God whereby He, according to His sovereign will and for His own glory, in the beginning brought forth the whole visible and invisible universe, without the use of pre-existent material, and thus gave it an existence, distinct from His own and yet always dependent on Him.* In view of the Scriptural data indicated in the preceding, it is quite evident, however, that this definition applies only to what is generally known as primary or immediate creation, that is, the creation described in Gen. 1:1. But the Bible clearly uses the word "create" also in cases in which God did make use of pre-existing materials, as in the creation of sun, moon, and stars, of the animals and of man. Hence many theologians add an element to the definition of creation. Thus Wollebius defines: *"Creation is that act by which God produces the world and all that is in it, partly out of nothing and partly out of material that is by its very nature unfit, for the manifestation of the glory of His power, wisdom, and goodness."* Even so, however, the definition does not cover those cases, also designated in Scripture as creative work, in which God works through secondary causes, Ps. 104:30; Isa. 45:7,8; Jer. 31:22; Amos 4:13, and produces results which only He could produce. The definition given includes several elements which call for further consideration.

1. CREATION IS AN ACT OF THE TRIUNE GOD. Scripture teaches us that the triune God is the author of creation, Gen. 1:1; Isa. 40:12; 44:24; 45:12, and this distinguishes Him from the idols, Ps. 96:5; Isa. 37:16; Jer. 10:11,12. Though the Father is in the foreground in the work of creation, I Cor. 8:6, it is also clearly recognized as a work of the Son and of the Holy Spirit. The Son's participation in it is indicated in John 1:3; I Cor. 8:6; Col. 1:15-17, and the activity of the Spirit in it finds expression in Gen. 1:2; Job 26:13; 33:4; Ps. 104:30; Isa. 40:12,13. The second and third persons are not dependent powers or mere intermediaries, but independent authors together with the Father. The work was not divided among the three persons, but the whole work, though from different aspects, is ascribed to each one of the persons. All things are at once *out of* the Father, *through* the Son, and *in* the Holy Spirit. In general it may be said that *being* is out of the Father, *thought* or the *idea* out of the Son, and *life* out of the Holy Spirit. Since the Father takes the initiative in the work of creation, it is often ascribed to Him economically.

2. CREATION IS A FREE ACT OF GOD. Creation is sometimes represented as a necessary act of God rather than as a free act determined by His sovereign will. The old theories of emanation and their modern counterpart, the Pantheistic theories, naturally make the world but a mere moment in the process of divine evolution (Spinoza, Hegel), and therefore regard the world as a necessary act of God. And the necessity which they have in mind is not a relative necessity resulting from the divine decree, but an absolute necessity which follows from the very nature of God, from his omnipotence (Origen) or from His love (Rothe).

However, this is not a Scriptural position. The only works of God that are inherently necessary with a necessity resulting from the very nature of God, are the *opera ad intra*, the works of the separate persons within the Divine Being: generation, filiation, and procession. To say that creation is a necessary act of God, is also to declare that it is just as eternal as those immanent works of God. Whatever necessity may be ascribed to God's *opera ad extra*, is a necessity conditioned by the divine decree and the resulting constitution of things. It is a necessity dependent on the sovereign will of God, and therefore no necessity in the absolute sense of the word. The Bible teaches us that God created all things, according to the counsel of His will, Eph. 1:11; Rev. 4:11; and that He is self-sufficient and is not dependent on His creatures in any way, Job 22:2,3; Acts 17:25.

3. CREATION IS A TEMPORAL ACT OF GOD.

a. *The teaching of Scripture on this point.* The Bible begins with the very simple statement, "In the beginning God created the heavens and the earth," Gen. 1:1. As addressed to all classes of people, it employs the ordinary language of daily life, and not the technical language of philosophy. The Hebrew term *bereshith* (lit. "in beginning") is itself indefinite, and naturally gives rise to the question, In the beginning of what? It would seem best to take the expression in the absolute sense as an indication of the beginning of all temporal things and even of time itself; but Keil is of the opinion that it refers to the beginning of the work of creation. Technically speaking, it is not correct to assume that time was already in existence when God created the world, and that He at some point in that existing time, called "the beginning" brought forth the universe. Time is only one of the forms of all created existence, and therefore could not exist before creation. For that reason Augustine thought it would be more correct to say that the world was created *cum tempore* (with time) than to assert that it was created *in tempore* (in time). The great significance of the opening statement of the Bible lies in its teaching that the world had a beginning. Scripture speaks of this beginning also in other places, Matt. 19:4,8; Mark 10:6; John 1:1,2; Heb. 1:10. That the world had a beginning is also clearly implied in such passages as Ps. 90:2, "Before the mountains were brought forth, or ever thou hadst formed the earth and the world, even from everlasting to everlasting thou art God"; and Ps. 102:25, "Of old didst thou lay the foundation of the earth; and the heavens are the work of thy hands."

b. *Difficulties which burden this doctrine.* Prior to the beginning mentioned in Gen. 1:1, we must postulate a beginningless eternity, during which God only existed. How must we fill up these blank ages in the eternal life of God? What did God do before the creation of the world? It is so far from possible to think of Him as a *Deus otiosus* (a God who is not active), that He is usually conceived of as *actus purus* (pure action). He is represented in Scripture as always working, John 5:17. Can we then say that He passed from a state of inactivity to one of action? Moreover, how is the transition from a non-creative to a creative state to be reconciled with His immutability? And if He had the eternal purpose to create, why did He not carry it out at once? Why did He allow a whole eternity to elapse before His plan was put into execution? Moreover, why did He select that particular moment for His creative work?

c. *Suggested solutions of the problem.* (1) *The theory of eternal creation.* According to some, such as Origen, Scotus Erigina, Rothe, Dorner, and Pfleiderer, God has been creating from all eternity, so that the world, though a creature and dependent, is yet just as eternal as God Himself. This has been argued from the omnipotence, the timelessness, the immutability, and the love of God; but neither one of these necessarily imply or involve it. This theory is not only contradicted by Scripture, but is also contrary to reason, for (a) creation from eternity is a contradiction in terms; and (b) the idea of eternal creation, as applied to the present world, which is subject to the law of time, is based on an identification of time and eternity, while these two are essentially different. (2) *The theory of the subjectivity of time and eternity.* Some speculative philosophers, such as Spinoza, Hegel, and Green, claim that the distinction of time and eternity is purely subjective and due to our finite position. Hence they would have us rise to a higher point of vantage and consider things *sub specie aeternitatis* (from the point of view of eternity). What exists for our consciousness as a time development, exists for the divine consciousness only as an eternally complete whole. But this theory is contradicted by Scripture just as much as the preceding one, Gen. 1:1; Ps. 90:2; 102:25; John 1:3. Moreover, it changes objective realities into subjective forms of consciousness, and reduces all history to an illusion. After all, time-development is a reality; there is a succession in our conscious life and in the life of nature round about us. The things that happened yesterday are not the things that are happening to-day.[1]

d. *Direction in which the solution should be sought.* In connection with the problem under consideration, Dr. Orr correctly says, "The solution must lie in getting a proper idea of the relation of eternity to time." He adds that, as far as he can see, this has not yet been satisfactorily accomplished. A great deal of the difficulty encountered here is undoubtedly due to the fact that we think of eternity too much as an indefinite extension of time, as, for instance, when we speak of the ages of comparative inaction in God before the creation of the world. God's eternity is no indefinitely extended time, but something essentially different, of which we can form no conception. His is a timeless existence, an eternal presence. The hoary past and the most distant future are both present to Him. He acts in all His works, and therefore also in creation, as the Eternal One, and we have no right to draw creation *as an act of God* into the temporal sphere. In a certain sense this can be called an eternal act, but only in the sense in which all the acts of God are eternal.

---

1. Cf. Orr, *Christian View of God and the World*, p. 130.

They are all *as acts of God*, works that are done in eternity. However, it is not eternal in the same sense as the generation of the Son, for this is an immanent act of God in the absolute sense of the word, while creation results in a temporal existence and thus terminates in time.[1] Theologians generally distinguish between active and passive creation, the former denoting creation as an act of God, and the latter, its result, the world's being created. The former is not, but the latter is, marked by temporal succession, and this temporal succession reflects the order determined in the decree of God. As to the objection that a creation in time implies a change in God, Wollebius remarks that "creation is not the Creator's but the creature's passage from potentiality to actuality."[2]

4. CREATION AS AN ACT BY WHICH SOMETHING IS BROUGHT FORTH OUT OF NOTHING.

a. *The doctrine of creation is absolutely unique.* There has been a great deal of speculation about the origin of the world, and several theories have been proposed. Some declared the world to be eternal, while others saw in it the product of an antagonistic spirit (Gnostics). Some maintained that it was made out of pre-existing matter which God worked up into form (Plato); others held that it originated by emanation out of the divine substance (Syrian Gnostics, Swedenborg); and still others regarded it as the phenomenal appearance of the Absolute, the hidden ground of all things (Pantheism). In opposition to all these vain speculations of men the doctrine of Scripture stands out in grand sublimity: "In the beginning God *created* the heavens and the earth."

b. *Scriptural terms for "to create."* In the narrative of creation, as was pointed out in the preceding, three verbs are used, namely, *bara'*, *'asah*, and *yatsar*, and they are used interchangeably in Scripture, Gen. 1:26,27; 2:7. The first word is the most important. Its original meaning is *to split, to cut, to divide;* but in addition to this it also means *to fashion, to create*, and in a more derivative sense, *to produce, to generate*, and *to regenerate*. The word itself does not convey the idea of bringing forth something out of nothing, for it is even used of works of providence, Isa. 45:7; Jer. 31:22; Amos 4:13. Yet it has a distinctive character: it is always used of divine and never of human production; and it never has an accusative of material, and for that very reason serves to stress the greatness of the work of God. The word *'asah* is more general, meaning *to do* or *to make*, and is therefore used in the general sense of *doing, making, manufacturing*, or *fashioning*. The word *yatsar* has, more distinctively, the meaning of *fashioning out of pre-existent materials*, and is therefore used of the potter's fashioning vessels out of clay. The New Testament words are *ktizein*, Mark 13:19, *poiein*, Matt. 19:4; *themelioun*, Heb. 1:10, *katartizein*, Rom. 9:22, *kataskeuazein*, Heb. 3:4, and *plassein*, Rom.

1. Bavinck, *Geref. Dogm.* II, p. 452.
2. Quoted by Warfield, *Calvin and Calvinism*, p. 294.

9:20. None of these words in themselves express the idea of creation out of nothing.

c. *Meaning of the term "creation out of nothing."* The expression "to create or bring forth out of nothing" is not found in Scripture. It is derived from one of the Apocrypha, namely, II. Macc. 7:28. The expression *ex nihilo* has been both misinterpreted and criticized. Some even considered the word *nihilum* (nothing) as the designation of a certain matter out of which the world was created, a matter without qualities and without form. But this is too puerile to be worthy of serious consideration. Others took the expression "to create out of nothing" to mean that the world came into being without a cause, and proceeded to criticize it as conflicting with what is generally regarded as an axiomatic truth, *ex nihilo nihil fit* (out of nothing comes nothing). But this criticism is entirely unwarranted. To say that God created the world out of nothing is not equivalent to saying that the world came into being without a cause. God Himself or, more specifically, the will of God is the cause of the world. Martensen expresses himself in these words: "The nothing out of which God creates the world are the eternal possibilities of His will, which are the sources of all the actualities of the world."[1] If the Latin phrase *"ex nihilo nihil fit"* be taken to mean that no effect can be without a cause, its truth may be admitted, but it cannot be regarded as a valid objection against the doctrine of creation out of nothing. But if it be understood to express the idea that nothing can originate, except out of previously existing material, it certainly cannot be regarded as a self-evident truth. Then it is rather a purely arbitrary assumption which, as Shedd points out, does not even hold true of man's thoughts and volitions, which are *ex nihilo*.[2] But even if the phrase does express a truth of common experience as far as human works are concerned, this does not yet prove its truth with respect to the work of the almighty power of God. However, in view of the fact that the expression "creation out of nothing" is liable to misunderstanding, and has often been misunderstood, it is preferable to speak of creation without the use of pre-existing material.

d. *Scriptural basis for the doctrine of creation out of nothing.* Gen. 1:1 records the beginning of the work of creation, and it certainly does not represent God as bringing the world forth out of pre-existent material. It was creation out of nothing, creation in the strict sense of the word, and therefore the only part of the work recorded in Gen. 1 to which Calvin would apply the term. But even in the remaining part of the chapter God is represented as calling forth all things by the word of His power, by a simple divine fiat. The same truth is taught in such passages as Ps. 33:6,9 and 148:5. The strongest passage is Heb. 11:3, "By faith we understand that the worlds have been framed by the word of God, so that what is seen hath not been made out of things which appear." Creation is here represented as a fact which we apprehend only by faith. By faith we understand (perceive, not comprehend) that the

---

1. *Christian Dogmatics,* p. 116.
2. *Dogm. Theol.* I, p. 467.

world was framed or fashioned by the word of God, that is, the word of God's power, the divine fiat, so that the things which are seen, the visible things of this world, were not made out of things which do appear, which are visible, and which are at least occasionally seen. According to this passage the world certainly was not made out of anything that is palpable to the senses. Another passage that may be quoted in this connection is Rom. 4:7, which speaks of God, "who quickeneth the dead, and calleth those things which be not as though they were" (Moffatt: "who makes the dead alive and calls into being what does not exist"). The apostle, it is true, does not speak of the creation of the world in this connection, but of the hope of Abraham that he would have a son. However, the description here given of God is general and is therefore also of a general application. It belongs to the very nature of God that He is able to call into being what does not exist, and does so call it into being.

5. CREATION GIVES THE WORLD A DISTINCT, YET ALWAYS DEPENDENT EXISTENCE.

a. *The world has a distinct existence.* This means that the world is not God nor any part of God, but something absolutely distinct from God; and that it differs from God, not merely in degree, but in its essential properties. The doctrine of creation implies that, while God is self-existent and self-sufficient, infinite and eternal, the world is dependent, finite, and temporal. The one can never change into the other. This doctrine is an absolute barrier against the ancient idea of emanation, as well as against all pantheistic theories. The universe is not the existence-form of God nor the phenomenal appearance of the Absolute; and God is not simply the life, or soul, or inner law of the world, but enjoys His own eternally complete life above the world, in absolute independence of it. He is the transcendent God, glorious in holiness, fearful in praises, doing wonders. This doctrine is supported by passages of Scripture which (1) testify to the distinct existence of the world, Isa. 42:5; Acts 17:24; (2) speak of the immutability of God, Ps. 102:27; Mal. 3:6; Jas. 1:17; (3) draw a comparison between God and the creature, Ps. 90:2; 102:25-27; 103:15-17; Isa. 2:21; 22:17, etc.; and (4) speak of the world as lying in sin or sinful, Rom. 1:18-32; I John 2:15-17, etc.

b. *The world is always dependent on God.* While God gave the world an existence distinct from His own, He did not withdraw from the world after its creation, but remained in the most intimate connection with it. The universe is not like a clock which was wound up by God and is now allowed to run off without any further divine intervention. This deistic conception of creation is neither biblical nor scientific. God is not only the transcendent God, infinitely exalted above all His creatures; He is also the immanent God, who is present in every part of His creation, and whose Spirit is operative in all the world. He is *essentially*, and not merely *per potentiam*, present in all His creatures, but He is not present in every one of them in the same manner. His immanence should not be interpreted as boundless extension throughout all the spaces of the universe, nor as a partitive presence, so that He is partly here and partly there. God is Spirit, and just because He is Spirit He is everywhere present *as a whole.* He is said to fill heaven and earth, Ps. 139:7-10; Jer. 23:24, to constitute the sphere in which we live and move and have our being, Acts 17:28, to renew the face of the earth by His Spirit, Ps. 104:30, to dwell in those that are of a broken heart, Ps. 51:11; Isa. 57:15, and in the Church as His temple, I Cor. 3:16; 6:19; Eph. 2:22. Both transcendence and immanence find expression in a single passage of Scripture, namely, Eph. 4:6, where the apostle says that we have "one God and Father of all, who is *over all,* and *through all,* and *in all.*" The doctrine of divine immanence has been stretched to the point of Pantheism in a great deal of modern theology. The world, and especially man, was regarded as the phenomenal manifestation of God. At present there is a strong reaction to this position in the so-called "theology of crisis." It is sometimes thought that this theology, with its emphasis on the "infinite qualitative difference" between time and eternity, on God as the "wholly Other" and the hidden God, and on the distance between God and man, naturally rules out the immanence of God. Brunner gives us the assurance, however, that this is not so. Says he, "Much nonsense has been talked about the 'Barthian theology' having perception only for the transcendence of God, not for His immanence. As if we too were not aware of the fact that God the Creator upholds all things by His power, that He has set the stamp of His divinity on the world and created man to be His own image."[1] And Barth says, "Dead were God Himself if He moved His world only from the outside, if He were a 'thing in Himself' and not the One in all, the Creator of all things visible and invisible, the beginning and the ending."[2] These men oppose the modern pantheistic conception of the divine immanence, and also the idea that, in virtue of this immanence, the world is a luminous revelation of God.

6. THE FINAL END OF GOD IN CREATION. The question of the final end of God in the work of creation has frequently been debated. In the course of history the question has received especially a twofold answer.

a. *The happiness of man or of humanity.* Some of the earlier philosophers, such as Plato, Philo, and Seneca, asserted that the goodness of God prompted Him to create the world. He desired to communicate Himself to His creatures; their happiness was the end He had in view. Though some Christian theologians chimed in with this idea, it became prominent especially through the Humanism of the Reformation period and the Rationalism of the eighteenth century. This theory was often presented in a very superficial way. The best form in which it is stated is to the effect that God could not make Himself the end of creation, because He is sufficient unto Himself and could need nothing. And if He could not make Himself the end, then this can be found only in the creature, especially in man, and ultimately in his supreme happiness. The

---

1. *The Word and the World,* p. 7.
2. *The Word of God and the Word of Man,* p. 291.

teleological view by which the welfare or happiness of man or humanity is made the final end of creation, was characteristic of the thinking of such influential men as Kant, Schleiermacher, and Ritschl, though they did not all present it in the same way. But this theory does not satisfy for several reasons: (1) Though God undoubtedly reveals His goodness in creation, it is not correct to say that His goodness or love could not express itself, if there were no world. The personal relations within the triune God supplied all that was necessary for a full and eternal life of love. (2) It would seem to be perfectly self-evident that God does not exist for the sake of man, but man for the sake of God. God only is Creator and the supreme Good, while man is but a creature, who for that very reason cannot be the end of creation. The temporal finds its end in the eternal, the human in the divine, and not *vice versa*. (3) The theory does not fit the facts. It is impossible to subordinate all that is found in creation to this end, and to explain all in relation to human happiness. This is perfectly evident from a consideration of all the sufferings that are found in the world.

b. *The declarative glory of God.* The Church of Jesus Christ found the true end of creation, not in anything outside of God, but in God Himself, more particularly in the external manifestation of His inherent excellency. This does not mean that God's receiving glory from others is the final end. The receiving of glory through the praises of His moral creatures, is an end included in the supreme end, but is not itself that end. God did not create first of all to receive glory, but to make His glory extant and manifest. The glorious perfections of God are manifested in His entire creation; and this manifestation is not intended as an empty show, a mere exhibition to be admired by the creatures, but also aims at promoting their welfare and perfect happiness. Moreover, it seeks to attune their hearts to the praises of the Creator, and to elicit from their souls the expression of their gratefulness and love and adoration. The supreme end of God in creation, the manifestation of His glory, therefore, includes, as subordinate ends, the happiness and salvation of His creatures, and the reception of praise from grateful and adoring hearts. This doctrine is supported by the following considerations: (1) It is based on the testimony of Scripture, Isa. 43:7; 60:21; 61:3; Ezek. 36:21,22; 39:7; Luke 2:14; Rom. 9:17; 11:36; I Cor. 15:28; Eph. 1:5,6,9,12,14; 3:9,10; Col. 1:16. (2) The infinite God would hardly choose any but the highest end in creation, and this end could only be found in Himself. If whole nations, as compared with Him, are but as a drop in a bucket and as the small dust of the balance, then, surely, His declarative glory is intrinsically of far greater value than the good of His creatures, Isa. 40:15,16. (3) The glory of God is the only end that is consistent with His independence and sovereignty. Everyone is dependent on whomsoever or whatsoever he makes his ultimate end. If God chooses anything in the creature as His final end, this would make Him dependent on the creature to that extent. (4) No other end would be sufficiently comprehensive to be the true end of all God's ways and works in creation. It has the advantage of comprising, in subordination, several other ends. (5) It is the only end that is actually and perfectly attained in the universe. We cannot imagine that a wise and omnipotent God would choose an end destined to fail wholly or in part, Job 23:13. Yet many of His creatures never attain to perfect happiness.

c. *Objections to the doctrine that the glory of God is the end of creation.* The following are the most important of these: (1) *It makes the scheme of the universe a selfish scheme.* But we should distinguish between selfishness and reasonable self-regard or self-love. The former is an undue or exclusive care for one's own comfort or pleasure, regardless of the happiness or rights of others; the latter is a due care for one's own happiness and well-being, which is perfectly compatible with justice, generosity, and benevolence towards others. In seeking self-expression for the glory of His name, God did not disregard the well-being, the highest good of others, but promoted it. Moreover, this objection draws the infinite God down to the level of finite and even sinful man and judges Him by human standards, which is entirely unwarranted. God has no equal, and no one can claim any right as over against Him. In making His declarative glory the end of creation, He has chosen the highest end; but when man makes himself the end of all his works, he is not choosing the highest end. He would rise to a higher level, if he chose the welfare of humanity and the glory of God as the end of his life. Finally, this objection is made primarily in view of the fact that the world is full of suffering, and that some of God's rational creatures are doomed to eternal destruction. But this is not due to the creative work of God, but to the sin of man, which thwarted the work of God in creation. The fact that man suffers the consequences of sin and insurrection does not warrant anyone in accusing God of selfishness. One might as well accuse the government of selfishness for upholding its dignity and the majesty of the law against all wilful transgressors. (2) *It is contrary to God's self-sufficiency and independence.* By seeking His honour in this way God shows that He needs the creature. The world is created to glorify God, that is, to add to His glory. Evidently, then, His perfection is wanting in some respects; the work of creation satisfies a want and contributes to the divine perfection. But this representation is not correct. The fact that God created the world for His own glory does not mean that He needed the world. It does not hold universally among men, that the work which they do not perform for others, is necessary to supply a want. This may hold in the case of the common laborer, who is working for his daily bread, but is scarcely true of the artist, who follows the spontaneous impulse of his genius. In the same way there is a good pleasure in God, exalted far above want and compulsion, which artistically embodies His thoughts in creation and finds delight in them. Moreover, it is not true that, when God makes His declarative glory the final end of creation, He aims primarily at receiving something. The supreme end which He had in view, was not to receive glory, but to manifest His inherent glory in the works of His hands.

It is true that in doing this, He would also cause the heavens to declare His glory, and the firmament to show His handiwork, the birds of the air and the beasts of the field to magnify Him, and the children of men to sing His praises. But by glorifying the Creator the creatures add nothing to the perfection of His being, but only acknowledge His greatness and ascribe to Him the glory which is due unto Him.

D. Divergent Theories Respecting the Origin of the World.

The Biblical doctrine is not the only view respecting the origin of the world. Three alternative theories, which were suggested, deserve brief consideration at this point.

1. THE DUALISTIC THEORY. Dualism is not always presented in the same form, but in its most usual form posits two self-existent principles, God and matter, which are distinct from and co-eternal with each other. Original matter, however, is regarded as but a negative and imperfect substance (sometimes regarded as evil), which is subordinate to God and is made the instrument of His will (Plato, Aristotle, the Gnostics, the Manichaeans). According to this theory God is not the creator, but only the framer and artificer of the world. This view is objectionable for several reasons. (a) It is wrong in its fundamental idea that there must have been some substance out of which the world was created, since *ex nihilo nihil fit*. This maxim is true only as an expression of the idea that no event takes place without a cause, and is false if it means to assert that nothing can ever be made except out of pre-existing material. The doctrine of creation does not dispense with a cause, but finds the all-sufficient cause of the world in the sovereign will of God. (b) Its representation of matter as eternal is fundamentally unsound. If matter is eternal, it must be infinite for it cannot be infinite in one way (duration) and finite in other respects. But it is impossible that two infinites or absolutes should exist side by side. The absolute and the relative may exist simultaneously, but there can be only one absolute and self-existent being. (c) It is unphilosophical to postulate two eternal substances, when one self-existent cause is perfectly adequate to account for all the facts. For that reason philosophy does not rest satisfied with a dualistic explanation of the world, but seeks to give a monistic interpretation of the universe. (d) If the theory assumes — as it does in some of its forms — the existence of an eternal principle of evil, there is absolutely no guarantee that good will triumph over evil in the world. It would seem that what is eternally necessary is bound to maintain itself and can never go down.

2. THE EMANATION THEORY IN VARIOUS FORMS. This theory is to the effect that the world is a necessary emanation out of the divine being. According to it God and the world are essentially one, the latter being the phenomenal manifestation of the former. The idea of emanation is characteristic of all pantheistic theories, though it is not always represented in the same way. Here,

again, we may register several objections. (a) This view of the origin of the
world virtually denies the infinity and transcendence of God by applying to
Him a principle of evolution, of growth and progress, which characterizes
only the finite and imperfect; and by identifying Him and the world. All
visible objects thus become but fleeting modifications of a self-existent, unconscious, and impersonal essence, which may be called God, Nature, or the
Absolute. (b) It robs God of His sovereignty by denuding Him of His power
of self-determination in relation to the world. He is reduced to the hidden
ground from which the creatures necessarily emanate, and which determines
their movement by an inflexible necessity of nature. At the same time it
deprives all rational creatures of their relative independence, of their freedom,
and of their moral character. (c) It also compromises the holiness of God
in a very serious manner. It makes God responsible for all that happens in
the world, for the evil as well as for the good. This is, of course, a very serious
consequence of the theory, from which Pantheists have never been able to
escape.

3. THE THEORY OF EVOLUTION. The theory of evolution is sometimes
spoken of as if it could be a substitute for the doctrine of creation. But this is
clearly a mistake. It certainly cannot be a substitute for creation in the sense
of absolute origination, since it presupposes something that evolves, and this
must in the last resort be either eternal or created, so that, after all, the
evolutionist must choose between the theory of the eternity of matter and the
doctrine of creation. At best, it might conceivably serve as a substitute for what
is called secondary creation, by which the substance already in existence is given
a definite form. (a) Some evolutionists, as, for instance, Haeckel, believe in
the eternity of matter, and ascribe the origin of life to spontaneous generation.
But belief in the eternity of matter is not only decidedly un-Christian and even
atheistic; it is also generally discredited. The idea that matter, with force as
its universal and inseparable property, is quite sufficient for the explanation
of the world, finds little favor to-day in scientific circles. It is felt that a
material universe, composed of finite parts (atoms, electrons, and so on) cannot
itself be infinite; and that that which is subject to constant change cannot be
eternal. Moreover, it has become increasingly clear that blind matter and
force or energy cannot account for life and personality, for intelligence and
free will. And the idea of spontaneous generation is a pure hypothesis, not only
unverified, but practically exploded. The general law of nature seems to be
"omne vivum e vivo" or "ex vivo." (b) Other evolutionists advocate what they
call theistic evolution. This postulates the existence of God back of the universe,
who works in it, as a rule according to the unalterable laws of nature and by
physical forces only, but in some cases by direct miraculous intervention, as,
for instance, in the case of the absolute beginning, the beginning of life, and
the beginning of rational and moral existence. This has often been called
derisively a "stop-gap" theory. It is really a child of embarrassment, which calls
God in at periodic intervals to help nature over the chasms that yawn at her

feet. It is neither the Biblical doctrine of creation, nor a consistent theory of evolution, for evolution is defined as "a series of gradual progressive changes *effected by means of resident forces*" (Le Conte). In fact, theistic evolution is a contradiction in terms. It is just as destructive of faith in the Biblical doctrine of creation as naturalistic evolution is; and by calling in the creative activity of God time and again it also nullifies the evolutionary hypothesis. Besides these two views we may also mention Bergson's Creative evolution, and C. Lloyd Morgan's Emergent evolution. The former is a vitalistic pantheist, whose theory involves the denial of the personality of God; and the latter in the end comes to the conclusion that he cannot explain his so-called emergents without positing some ultimate factor which might be called "God."

IV. Creation of the Spiritual World

A. Tlie Doctrine of the Angels in History.

There are clear evidences of belief in the existence of angels from the very beginning of the Christian era. Some of them were regarded as good, and others as evil. The former were held in high esteem as personal beings of a lofty order, endowed with moral freedom, engaged in the joyful service of God, and employed by God to minister to the welfare of men. According to some of the early Church Fathers they had fine ethereal bodies. The general conviction was that all angels were created good, but that some abused their freedom and fell away from God. Satan, who was originally an angel of eminent rank, was regarded as their head. The cause of his fall was found in pride and sinful ambition, while the fall of his subordinates was ascribed to their lusting after the daughters of men. This view was based on what was then the common interpretation of Gen. 6:2. Alongside of the general idea that the good angels ministered to the needs and welfare of believers, the specific notion of guardian angels for individual churches and individual men was cherished by some. Calamities of various kinds, such as sicknesses, accidents, and losses, were frequently ascribed to the baneful influence of evil spirits. The idea of a hierarchy of angels already made its appearance (Clement of Alexandria), but it was not considered proper to worship any of the angels.

As time went on the angels continued to be regarded as blessed spirits, superior to men in knowledge, and free from the encumbrance of gross material bodies. While some still ascribed to them fine ethereal bodies, there was an ever increasing uncertainty as to whether they had any bodies at all. They who still clung to the idea that they were corporeal did this, so it seems, in the interest of the truth that they were subject to spatial limitations. Dionysius the Areopagite divided the angels into three classes: the first class consisting of Thrones, Cherubim, and Seraphim; the second, of Mights, Dominions, and Powers; and the third, of Principalities, Archangels, and Angels. The first class is represented as enjoying the closest communion with God; the second, as being enlightened by the first; and the third, as being enlightened by the second. This classification was adopted by several later writers. Augustine stressed the fact that the good angels were rewarded for their obedience by the gift of perseverance, which carried with it the assurance that they would never fall. Pride was still regarded as the cause of Satan's fall, but the idea that the rest of the angels fell as the result of their lusting after the daughters of men, though still held by some, was gradually disappearing under the influence of a better exegesis of Gen. 6:2.

A beneficent influence was ascribed to the unfallen angels, while the fallen angels were regarded as corrupting the hearts of men, as stimulating to heresy. and as engendering diseases and calamities. The polytheistic tendencies of many of the converts to Christianity fostered an inclination to worship the angels. Such worship was formally condemned by a council which convened at Laodicea in the fourth century.

During the Middle Ages there were still a few who were inclined to assume that the angels have ethereal bodies, but the prevailing opinion was that they were incorporeal. The angelic appearances were explained by assuming that in such cases angels adopted temporal bodily forms for revelational purposes. Several points were in debate among the Scholastics. As to the time of the creation of the angels the prevailing opinion was that they were created at the same time as the material universe. While some held that the angels were created in the state of grace, the more common opinion was that they were created in a state of natural perfection only. There was little difference of opinion respecting the question, whether angels can be said to be in a place. The common answer to this question was affirmative, though it was pointed out that their presence in space is not circumscriptive but definitive, since only bodies can be in space circumscriptively. While all the Scholastics agreed that the knowledge of the angels is limited, the Thomists and Scotists differed considerably respecting the nature of this knowledge. It was admitted by all that the angels received infused knowledge at the time of their creation, but Thomas Aquinas denied, while Duns Scotus affirmed, that they could acquire new knowledge through their own intellectual activity. The former held that the knowledge of the angels is purely intuitive, but the latter asserted that it may also be discursive. The idea of guardian angels found considerable favor during the Middle Ages.

The period of the Reformation brought nothing new respecting the doctrine of the angels. Both Luther and Calvin had a vivid conception of their ministry, and particularly of the presence and power of Satan. The latter stresses the fact that he is under divine control, and that, while he is sometimes the instrument of God, he can only work within prescribed limits. Protestant theologians generally regarded the angels as pure spiritual beings, though Zanchius and Grotius still speak of them as having ethereal bodies. As to the work of the good angels the general opinion was that it is their special task to minister to the heirs of salvation. There was no general agreement, however, respecting the existence of guardian angels. Some favored this view, others opposed it, and still others refused to commit themselves on this point. Our Belgic Confession says in Article XII, which deals with creation: "He also created the angels good, to be His messengers and to serve His elect: some of whom are fallen from that excellency, in which God created them, into everlasting perdition; and the others have, by the grace of God, remained steadfast, and continued in their primitive state. The devils and evil spirits are so depraved that they are enemies of God and every good thing to the utmost of their power, as murderers watching to ruin the Church and every member thereof, and by their wicked stratagems to destroy all; and are therefore, by their own wickedness, adjudged to eternal damnation, daily expecting their horrible torments."

Up to the present time Roman Catholics generally regarded the angels as pure spirits, while some Protestants, such as Emmons, Ebrard, Kurtz, Delitzsch, and others, still ascribe to them some special kind of bodies. But even the great majority of the latter take the opposite view. Swedenborg holds that all angels were originally men and exist in bodily form. Their position in the angelic world depends on their life in this world. Eighteenth century Rationalism boldly denied the existence of angels and explained what the Bible teaches about them as a species of accommodation. Some modern liberal theologians consider it worthwhile to retain the fundamental idea expressed in the doctrine of the angels. They find in it a symbolic representation of the protecting care and helpfulness of God.

B. The Existence of the Angels.

All religions recognize the existence of a spiritual world. Their mythologies speak of gods, half-gods, spirits, demons, genii, heroes, and so on. It was especially among the Persians that the doctrine of the angels was developed, and many critical scholars assert that the Jews derived their angelology from the Persians. But this is an unproved and, to say the least, very doubtful theory. It certainly cannot be harmonized with the Word of God, in which angels appear from the very beginning. Moreover, some great scholars, who made special study of the subject, came to the conclusion that the Persian angelology was derived from that current among the Hebrews. The Christian Church has always believed in the existence of angels, but in modern liberal theology this belief has been discarded, though it still regards the angel-idea as useful, since it imprints upon us "the living power of God in the history of redemption, His *providentia specialissima* for His people, especially for the 'little ones.' "[1] Though such men as Leibnitz and Wolff, Kant and Schleiermacher, admitted the possibility of the existence of an angelic world, and some of them even tried to prove this by rational argumentation, it is quite evident that philosophy can neither prove nor disprove the existence of angels. From philosophy, therefore, we turn to Scripture, which makes no deliberate attempt to prove the existence of angels, but assumes this throughout, and in its historical books repeatedly shows us the angels in action. No one who bows before the authority of the Word of God can doubt the existence of angels.

C. The Nature of the Angels.

Under this heading several points call for consideration.

1. IN DISTINCTION FROM GOD THEY ARE CREATED BEINGS. The creation of the angels has sometimes been denied, but is clearly taught in Scripture. It is not certain that those passages which speak of the creation of the host of heaven

---

1. Foster, *Christianity in Its Modern Expression*, p. 114.

(Gen. 2:1; Ps. 33:6; Neh. 9:6) refer to the creation of the angels rather than to the creation of the starry host; but Ps. 148:2,5, and Col. 1:16 clearly speak of the creation of the angels, (comp. I Kings 22:19; Ps. 103:20,21). The time of their creation cannot be fixed definitely. The opinion of some, based on Job 38:7, that they were created before all other things, really finds no support in Scripture. As far as we know, no creative work preceded the creation of heaven and earth. The passage in the book of Job (38:7) teaches, indeed, in a poetic vein that they were present at the founding of the world just as the stars were, but not that they existed before the primary creation of heaven and earth. The idea that the creation of the heavens was completed on the first day, and that the creation of the angels was simply a part of the day's work, is also an unproved assumption, though the fact that the statement in Gen. 1:2 applies to the earth only would seem to favor it. Possibly the creation of the heavens was not completed in a single moment any more than that of the earth. The only safe statement seems to be that they were created before the seventh day. This at least follows from such passages as Gen. 2:1; Ex. 20:11; Job 38:7; Neh. 9:6.

2. THEY ARE SPIRITUAL AND INCORPOREAL BEINGS. This has always been disputed. The Jews and many of the early Church Fathers ascribed to them airy or fiery bodies; but the Church of the Middle Ages came to the conclusion that they are pure spiritual beings. Yet even after that some Roman Catholic, Arminian, and even Lutheran and Reformed theologians ascribed to them a certain corporeity, most subtle and pure. They regarded the idea of a purely spiritual and incorporeal nature as metaphysically inconceivable, and also as incompatible with the conception of a creature. They also appealed to the fact that the angels are subject to spatial limitations, move about from place to place, and were sometimes seen by men. But all these arguments are more than counter-balanced by the explicit statements of Scripture to the effect that the angels are *pneumata*, Matt. 8:16; 12:45; Luke 7:21; 8:2; 11:26; Acts 19:12; Eph. 6:12; Heb. 1:14. They have no flesh and bone, Luke 24:39, do not marry, Matt. 22:30, can be present in great numbers in a very limited space, Luke 8:30, and are invisible, Col. 1:16. Such passages as Ps. 104:4 (comp. Heb. 1:7) ; Matt. 22:30; and I Cor. 11:10 do not prove the corporeity of the angels. Neither is this proved by the symbolical descriptions of the angels in the prophecy of Ezekiel and in the book of Revelation, nor by their appearance in bodily forms, though it is difficult to say, whether the bodies which they assumed on certain occasions were real or only apparent. It is clear, however, that they are creatures and therefore finite and limited, though they stand in a freer relation to time and space than man. We cannot ascribe to them an *ubi repletivum*, nor an *ubi circumscriptivum*, but only an *ubi definitivum*. They cannot be in two or more places simultaneously.

3. THEY ARE RATIONAL, MORAL, AND IMMORTAL BEINGS. This means that they are personal beings endowed with intelligence and will. The fact that they are intelligent beings would seem to follow at once from the fact that they are

spirits; but it is also taught explicitly in Scripture, II Sam. 14:20; Matt. 24:36; Eph. 3:10; I Pet. 1:12; II Pet. 2:11. While not omniscient, they are superior to men in knowledge, Matt. 24:36. Moreover, they are possessed of moral natures, and as such are under moral obligation; they are rewarded for obedience, and are punished for disobedience. The Bible speaks of the angels which remained loyal as "holy angels," Matt. 25:31; Mark 8:38; Luke 9:26; Acts 10:22; Rev. 14:10, and pictures those who fell away as lying and sinning, John 8:44; I John 3:8-10. The good angels are also immortal in the sense that they are not subject to death. In that respect the saints in heaven are said to be like them, Luke 20:35,36. In addition to all this, great power is ascribed to them. They form the army of God, a host of mighty heroes, always ready to do the Lord's bidding, Ps. 103:20; Col. 1:16; Eph. 1:21; 3:10; Heb. 1:14; and the evil angels form the army of Satan, bent on destroying the work of the Lord, Luke 11:21; II Thess. 2:9; I Pet. 5:8.

4. THEY ARE PARTLY GOOD AND PARTLY EVIL. The Bible furnishes very little information respecting the original state of the angels. We read, however, that at the end of His creative work God saw everything that He had made and, behold, it was very good. Moreover, John 8:44; II Pet. 2:4; and Jude 6 presupposes an original good condition of all angels. The good angels are called elect angels in I Tim. 5:21. They evidently received, in addition to the grace with which all angels were endowed, and which was sufficient to enable them to retain their position, a special grace of perseverance, by which they were confirmed in their position. There has been a great deal of useless speculation about the time and character of the fall of the angels. Protestant theology, however, was generally satisfied with the knowledge that the good angels retained their original state, were confirmed in their position, and are now incapable of sinning. They are not only called holy angels, but also angels of light, II Cor. 11:14. They always behold the face of God, Matt. 18:10, are our exemplars in doing the will of God, Matt. 6:10, and possess immortal life, Luke 20:36.

D. The Number and Organization of the Angels.

1. THEIR NUMBER. The Bible contains no definite information respecting the number of the angels, but indicates very clearly that they constitute a mighty army. They are repeatedly called the host of heaven or of God, and this term itself already points to a goodly number. In Deut. 33:2 we read that "Jehovah came from Sinai . . . from the ten thousands of holy ones," and in Ps. 68:17 the poet sings, "The chariots of God are twenty thousand, even thousands upon thousands: the Lord is among them, as in Sinai, in the sanctuary." In reply to the question of Jesus addressed to an unclean spirit, the answer was, "my name is legion; for we are many," Mark 5:9,15. The Roman legion was not always the same, but varied at different times all the way from 3000 to 6000, In Gethsemane Jesus said to the band that came to take him captive, "Or thinkest thou that I cannot beseech my Father, and He shall even now send me more than twelve legions of angels?" Matt. 26:53. And, finally, we read in Rev. 5:11,

"And I saw, and I heard the voice of many angels round about the throne and the living creatures and the elders; and the number of them was ten thousand times ten thousand, and thousands of thousands." In view of all these data it is perfectly safe to say that the angels constitute an innumerable company, a mighty host. They do not form an organism like mankind, for they are spirits, which do not marry and are not born the one out of the other. Their full number was created in the beginning; there has been no increase in their ranks.

2. THEIR ORDERS. Though the angels do not constitute an organism, they are evidently organized in some way. This follows from the fact that, alongside of the general name "angel," the Bible uses certain specific names to indicate different classes of angels. The name "angel," by which we designate the higher spirits generally, is not a *nomen naturae* in Scripture, but a *nomen officii.* The Hebrew word *mal'ak* simply means messenger, and serves to designate one sent by men, Job 1:14; I Sam. 11:3, or by God, Hag. 1:13; Mal. 2:7; 3:1. The Greek term *aggelos* is also frequently applied to men, Matt. 11:10; Mark 1:2; Luke 7:24; 9:51; Gal. 4:14. There is no general distinctive name for all spiritual beings in Scripture. They are called sons of God, Job 1:6; 2:1; Ps. 29:1; 89:6, spirits, Heb. 1:14, saints, Ps. 89:5,7; Zech. 14:5; Dan. 8:13, watchers, Dan. 4:13,17,24. There are several specific names, however, which point to different classes of angels.

a. *Cherubim.* Cherubim are repeatedly mentioned in Scripture. They guard the entrance of paradise, Gen. 3:24, gaze upon the mercy-seat, Ex. 25:18; Ps. 80:1; 99:1; Isa. 37:16; Heb. 9:5, and constitute the chariot on which God descends to the earth, II Sam. 22:11; Ps. 18:10. In Ezek. 1 and Rev. 4 they are represented as living beings in various forms. These symbolical representations simply serve to bring out their extraordinary power and majesty. More than other creatures they were destined to reveal the power, the majesty, and the glory of God, and to guard His holiness in the garden of Eden, in tabernacle and temple, and in the descent of God to the earth.

b. *Seraphim.* A related class of angels are the Seraphim, mentioned only in Isa. 6:2,6. They are also symbolically represented in human form, but with six wings, two covering the face, two the feet, and two for the speedy execution of the Lord's commandments. In distinction from the Cherubim, they stand as servants round about the throne of the heavenly King, sing His praises, and are ever ready to do His bidding. While the Cherubim are the mighty ones, they might be called the nobles among the angels. While the former guard the holiness of God, they serve the purpose of reconciliation, and thus prepare men for the proper approach to God.

c. *Principalities, powers, thrones, and dominions.* In addition to the preceding the Bible speaks of certain classes of angels, which occupy places of authority in the angelic world, as *archai* and *exousiai* (principalities and powers), Eph. 3:10; Col. 2:10, *thronoi* (thrones), Col. 1:16, *kureotetoi* (dominions),

Eph. 1:21; Col. 1:16, and *dunameis* (powers), Eph. 1:21; I Pet. 3:22. These appellations do not point to different kinds of angels, but simply to differences of rank or dignity among them.

d. *Gabriel and Michael.* In distinction from all the other angels, these two are mentioned by name. Gabriel appears in Dan. 8:16; 9:21; Luke 1:19,26. The great majority of commentators regard him as a created angel, but some of these deny that the name Gabriel is a proper name and look upon it as common noun, meaning man of God, a synonym for angel. But this is an untenable position.[1] Some earlier and later commentators see in him an uncreated being, some even suggesting that he might be the third person of the Holy Trinity, while Michael was the second. But a simple reading of the passages in question shows the impossibility of this interpretation. He may be one of the seven angels that are said to stand before God in Rev. 8:2 (comp. Luke 1:19). It seems to have been his special task to mediate and interpret divine revelations.

The name Michael (lit., "who as God?") has been interpreted as a designation of the second person of the Trinity. But this is no more tenable than the identification of Gabriel with the Holy Spirit. Michael is mentioned in Dan. 10:13,21; Jude 9; Rev. 12:7. From the fact that he is called "the archangel" in Jude 9, and from the expression used in Rev. 12:7 it would seem that he occupies an important place among the angels. The passages in Daniel also point to the fact that he is a prince among them. We see in him the valiant warrior fighting the battles of Jehovah against the enemies of Israel and against the evil powers in the spirit-world. It is not impossible that the title "archangel" also applies to Gabriel and a few other angels.

E. The Service of the Angels.

We can distinguish between an ordinary and an extraordinary service of the angels.

1. THEIR ORDINARY SERVICE. This consists first of all in their praising God day and night, Job 38:7; Isa. 6; Ps. 103:20; 148:2; Rev. 5:11. Scripture gives the impression that they do this audibly, as at the birth of Christ, though we can form no conception of this speaking and singing of the angels. Since the entrance of sin into the world they are sent forth to minister to them that are heirs of salvation, Heb. 1:14. They rejoice at the conversion of a sinner, Luke 15:10, watch over believers, Ps. 34:7; 91:11, protect the little ones, Matt. 18:10, are present in the Church, I Cor. 11:10; I Tim. 5:21, learning from her the manifold riches of the grace of God, Eph. 3:10; I Pet. 1:12, and convey believers into the bosom of Abraham, Luke 16:22. The idea that some of them serve as guardians of individual believers finds no support in Scripture. The statement in Matt. 18:10 is too general to prove the point, though it seems to indicate that there is a group of angels who are particularly charged with the care of the little ones. Neither is it proved by Acts 12:15, for this passage

---

1. Cf. especially Kuyper, *De Engelen Gods*, p. 175.

merely goes to show that there were some even among the disciples of that early day who believed in guardian angels.

2. THEIR EXTRAORDINARY SERVICE. The extraordinary service of the angels was made necessary by the fall of man, and forms an important element in the special revelation of God. They often mediate the special revelations of God, communicate blessings to His people, and execute judgment upon His enemies. Their activity is most prominent in the great turning points of the economy of salvation, as in the days of the patriarchs, the time of the lawgiving, the period of the exile and of the restoration, and at the birth, the resurrection, and the ascension of the Lord. When the period of God's special revelation closed, the extraordinary service of the angels ceased, to be resumed only at the return of the Lord.

F. The Evil Angels.

1. THEIR ORIGIN. Besides the good there also are evil angels, who delight in opposing God and antagonizing His work. Though they are also creatures of God, they were not created as evil angels. God saw everything that He had created, and it was very good, Gen. 1:31. There are two passages in Scripture which clearly imply that some of the angels did not retain their original position, but fell from the state in which they were created, II Pet. 2:4; Jude 6. The special sin of these angels is not revealed, but has generally been thought to consist in this that they exalted themselves over against God, and aspired to supreme authority. If this ambition played an important part in the life of Satan and led to his downfall, it would at once explain why he tempted man on this particular point, and sought to lure him to his destruction by appealing to a possible similar ambition in man. Some of the early Church Fathers distinguished between Satan and the subordinate devils in explaining the cause of their fall. That of the fall of Satan was found in pride, but that of the more general fall in the angelic world, in fleshly lust, Gen. 6:2. That interpretation of Gen. 6:2 was gradually discarded, however, during the Middle Ages. In view of this it is rather surprising to find that several modern commentators are reiterating the idea in their interpretation of II Pet. 2:4 and Jude 6 as, for instance, Meyer, Alford, Mayor, Wohlenberg. It is an explanation, however, that is contrary to the spiritual nature of the angels, and to the fact that, as Matt. 22:30 would seem to imply, there is no sexual life among the angels. Moreover, on that interpretation we shall have to assume a double fall in the angelic world, first the fall of Satan, and then, considerably later, the fall resulting in the host of devils that now serves Satan. It is much more likely that Satan dragged the others right along with him in his fall.

2. THEIR HEAD. Satan appears in Scripture as the recognized head of the fallen angels. He was originally, it would seem, one of the mightiest princes of the angelic world, and became the leader of those that revolted and fell away from God. The name "Satan" points to him as "the Adversary," not in the first

place of man, but of God. He attacks Adam as the crown of God's handiwork, works destruction and is therefore called Apollyon (the Destroyer), and assaults Jesus when He undertakes the work of restoration. After the entrance of sin into the world he became Diabolos (the Accuser), accusing the people of God continually, Rev. 12:10. He is represented in Scripture as the originator of sin, Gen. 3:1,4; John 8:44; II Cor. 11:3; I John 3:8; Rev. 12:9; 20:2,10, and appears as the recognized head of those that fell away, Matt. 25:41; 9:34; Eph. 2:2. He remains the leader of the angelic hosts which he carried with him in his fall, and employs them in desperate resistance to Christ and His Kingdom. He is also called repeatedly "the prince of this (not, "of the") world, John 12:31; 14:30; 16:11, and even "the god of this world," II Cor. 4:4. This does not mean that he is in control of the world, for God is in control, and He has given all authority to Christ, but it does convey the idea that he is in control of this evil world, the world in so far as it is ethically separated from God. This is clearly indicated in Eph. 2:2, where he is called "the prince of the powers of the air, of the spirit that now worketh in the sons of disobedience." He is superhuman, but not divine; has great power, but is not omnipotent; wields influence on a large but restricted scale, Matt. 12:29; Rev. 20:2, and is destined to be cast into the bottomless pit, Rev. 20:10.

3. THEIR ACTIVITY. Like the good angels, the fallen angels, too, are possessed of superhuman power, but their use of it contrasts sadly with that of the good angels. While the latter perennially praise God, fight His battles, and serve Him faithfully, they as powers of darkness are bent on cursing God, battling against Him and His Anointed, and destroying His work. They are in constant revolt against God, seek to blind and mislead even the elect, and encourage sinners in their evil. But they are lost and hopeless spirits. They are even now chained to hell and pits of darkness, and though not yet limited to one place, yet, as Calvin says, drag their chains with them wherever they go, II Pet. 2:4; Jude 6.

V. Creation of the Material World

A. The Scriptural Account of Creation.

Other nations, as well as the Hebrews, had their accounts respecting the origin of the material universe, and of the way in which the original chaos was changed into a cosmos or habitable world. Some of those accounts reveal traces of similarity with the Biblical record, but contain even more striking dissimilarities. They are as a rule characterized by dualistic or polytheistic elements, represent the present world as the result of a fierce struggle among the gods, and are far removed from the simplicity and sobriety of the Biblical account. It may be advisable to preface our discussion of its details with a few general remarks.

1. THE POINT OF VIEW FROM WHICH THE BIBLE CONTEMPLATES THE WORK OF CREATION. It is a significant thing that the narrative of creation, while it mentions the creation of the heavens, devotes no further attention to the spiritual world. It concerns the material world only, and represents this primarily as the habitation of man and as the theater of his activities. It deals not with unseen realities such as spirits, but with the things that are seen. And because these things are palpable to the human senses, they come up for discussion, not only in theology, but also in other sciences and in philosophy. But while philosophy seeks to understand the origin and nature of all things by the light of reason, theology takes its starting point in God, allows itself to be guided by His special revelation respecting the work of creation, and considers everything in relation to Him. The narrative of creation is the beginning of God's self-revelation, and acquaints us with the fundamental relation in which everything, man included, stands to Him. It stresses the original position of man, in order that men of all ages might have a proper understanding of the rest of Scripture as a revelation of redemption. While it does not pretend to give us a complete philosophical cosmogony, it does contain important elements for the construction of a proper cosmogony.

2. THE ORIGIN OF THE ACCOUNT OF CREATION. The question as to the origin of the narrative of creation has been raised repeatedly, and the interest in it was renewed by the discovery of the Babylonian story of creation. This story, as it is known to us, took shape in the city of Babylon. It speaks of the generation of several gods, of whom Marduk proves supreme. He only was sufficiently powerful to overcome the primeval dragon Tiamat, and becomes the creator of the world, whom men worship. There are some points of similarity

between the narrative of creation in Genesis and this Babylonian story. Both speak of a primeval chaos, and of a division of the waters below and above the firmament. Genesis speaks of seven days, and the Babylonian account is arranged in seven tablets. Both accounts connect the heavens with the fourth epoch of creation, and the creation of man with the sixth. Some of these resemblances are of little significance, and the differences of the two accounts are far more important. The Hebrew order differs on many points from the Babylonian. The greatest difference is found, however, in the religious conceptions of the two. The Babylonian account, in distinction from that of Scripture, is mythological and polytheistic. The gods do not stand on a high level, but scheme and plot and fight. And Marduk succeeds only after a prolonged struggle, which taxes his strength, in overcoming the evil forces and reducing chaos to order. In Genesis, on the other hand, we encounter the most sublime monotheism, and see God calling forth the universe and all created things by the simple word of His power. When the Babylonian account was discovered, many scholars hastily assumed that the Biblical narrative was derived from the Babylonian source, forgetting that there are at least two other possibilities, namely, (a) that the Babylonian story is a corrupted reproduction of the narrative in Genesis; or (b) that both are derived from a common, more primit've, source. But however this question may be answered, it does not settle the problem of the origin of the narrative. How did the original, whether written or oral, come into existence? Some regard it simply as the natural product of man's reflection on the origin of things. But this explanation is extremely unlikely in view of the following facts: (a) the idea of creation is incomprehensible; (b) science and philosophy both equally oppose the doctrine of creation out of nothing; and (c) it is only by faith that we understand that the worlds have been framed by the word of God, Heb. 11:3. We therefore come to the conclusion that the story of creation was revealed to Moses or to one of the earlier patriarchs. If this revelation was pre-Mosaic, it passed in tradition (oral or written) from one generation to another, probably lost something of its original purity, and was finally incorporated in a pure form, under the guidance of the Holy Spirit, in the first book of the Bible.

3. THE INTERPRETATION OF GEN. 1:1,2. Some regard Gen. 1:1 as the superscription or title of the whole narrative of creation. But this is objectionable for three reasons: (a) because the following narrative is connected with the first verse by the Hebrew conjunction *waw* (and), which would not be the case if the first verse were a title; (b) because, on that supposition, there would be no account whatsoever of the original and immediate creation; and (c) since the following verses contain no account of the creation of heaven at all. The more generally accepted interpretation is that Gen. 1:1 records the original and immediate creation of the universe, Hebraistically called "heaven and earth." In this expression the word "heaven" refers to that invisible order of things in which the glory of God reveals itself in the most perfect manner. It cannot be regarded as a designation of the cosmical heavens, whether of the clouds or

of the stars, for these were created on the second and on the fourth day of the creative week. Then in the second verse the author describes the original condition of the earth (comp. Ps. 104:5,6). It is a debatable question, whether the original creation of matter formed a part of the work of the first day, or was separated from this by a shorter or longer period of time. Of those who would interpose a long period between the two, some hold that the world was originally a dwelling place of angels, was destroyed as the result of a fall in the angelic world, and was then reclaimed and turned into a fit habitation for men. We shall refer to this restitution theory in another connection.

B. The Hexaemeron, or the Work of the Separate Days.

After the creation of the universe out of nothing in a moment of time, the existing chaos was gradually changed into a cosmos, a habitable world, in six successive days. Before the work of the separate days is indicated, the question as to the length of the days of creation calls for a brief discussion.

1. CONSIDERATION OF THE THEORY THAT THEY WERE LONG PERIODS OF TIME. Some scholars assume that the days of Gen. 1 were long periods of time, in order to make them harmonize with the geological periods. The opinion that these days were not ordinary days of twenty-four hours was not entirely foreign to early Christian theology, as E. C. Messenger shows in detail in his learned work on *Evolution and Theology.* But some of the Church Fathers, who intimated that these days were probably not to be regarded as ordinary days, expressed the opinion that the whole work of creation was finished in a moment of time, and that the days merely constituted a symbolical frame-work, which facilitated the description of the work of creation in an orderly fashion, so as to make it more intelligible to finite minds. The opinion that the days of creation were long periods came to the foreground again in recent years, not, however, as the result of exegetical studies, but under the influence of the disclosures of science. Previous to the nineteenth century the days of Genesis were most generally regarded as literal days. But, of course, human interpretation is fallible, and may have to be revised in the light of later discoveries. If traditional exegesis conflicts, not merely with scientific theories — which are themselves interpretations —, but with well established facts, re-thinking and reinterpretation is naturally in order. It can hardly be maintained, however, that the assumed geological periods necessitate a change of front, since they are by no means generally recognized, even in scientific circles, as well established facts. Some Christian scholars, such as Harris, Miley, Bettex, and Geesink, assume that the days of Genesis are geological days, and both Shedd and Hodge call attention to the remarkable agreement between the record of creation and the testimony of the rocks, and are inclined to regard the days of Genesis as geological periods.

The question may be raised, whether it is exegetically possible to conceive of the days of Genesis as long periods of time. And then it must be admitted that the Hebrew word *yom* does not always denote a period of twenty-four hours in Scripture, and is not always used in the same sense even in the narrative of creation. It may mean daylight in distinction from darkness, Gen. 1:5,16,18; daylight and darkness together, Gen. 1:5,8,13 etc.; the six days taken together, Gen. 2:4; and an indefinite period marked in its entire length by some characteristic feature, as trouble, Ps. 20:1, wrath, Job 20:28, prosperity, Eccl. 7:14, or salvation II Cor. 6:2. Now some hold that the Bible favors the idea that.the days of creation were indefinite periods of time, and call attention to the following: (a) The sun was not created until the fourth day, and therefore the length of the previous days could not yet be determined by the earth's relation to the sun. This is perfectly true, but does not prove the point. God had evidently, even previous to the fourth day, established a rhythmic alternation of light and darkness, and there is no ground for the assumption that the days so measured were of longer duration than the later days. Why should we assume that God greatly increased the velocity of the earth's revolutions after the light was concentrated in the sun? (b) The days referred to are God's days, the archetypal days, of which the days of men are merely ectypal copies; and with God a thousand years are as a single day, Ps. 90:4; II Pet. 3:8. But this argument is based on a confusion of time and eternity. God ad intra has no days, but dwells in eternity, exalted far above all measurements of time. This is also the idea conveyed by Ps. 90:4; and II Pet. 3:8. The only actual days of which God has knowledge are the days of this time-space world. How does it follow from the fact that God is exalted above the limitations of time, as they exist in this world, where time is measured by days and weeks and months and years, that a day may just as well be a period of 100,000 years as one of twenty-four hours? (c) The seventh day, the day in which God rested from His labours, is said to continue up to the present time, and must therefore be regarded as a period of thousands of years. It is God's sabbath, and that sabbath never ends. This argument represents a similar confusion. The whole idea of God's beginning the work of creation at a certain point of time, and then ceasing it after a period of six days, does not apply to God as He is in Himself, but only to the temporal results of His creative activity. He is unchangeably the same from age to age. His sabbath is not an indefinitely prolonged period of time; it is eternal. On the other hand, the sabbath of the creation week was a day equal in length to the other days. God not only rested on that day, but He also blessed and hallowed it, setting it aside as a day of rest for man, Ex. 20:11. This would hardly apply to the whole period from the time of creation up to the present day.

2. CONSIDERATION OF THE VIEW THAT THEY WERE LITERAL DAYS. The prevailing view has always been that the days of Genesis 1 are to be understood as literal days. Some of the early Church Fathers did not regard them as real indications of the time in which the work of creation was completed, but rather as literary forms in which the writer of Genesis cast the narrative of creation, in order to picture the work of creation — which was really completed in a moment of time — in an orderly fashion for human intelligence. It was only after the comparatively new sciences of geology and palæontology

came forward with their theories of the enormous age of the earth, that theologians began to show an inclination to identify the days of creation with the long geological ages. To-day some of them regard it as an established fact that the days of Genesis 1 were long geological periods; others are somewhat inclined to assume this position, but show considerable hesitation. Hodge, Sheldon, Van Oosterzee, and Dabney, some of whom are not entirely averse to this view, are all agreed that this interpretation of the days is *exegetically* doubtful, if not impossible. Kuyper and Bavinck hold that, while the first three days may have been of somewhat different length, the last three were certainly ordinary days. They naturally do not regard even the first three days as geological periods. Vos in his *Gereformeerde Dogmatiek* defends the position that the days of creation were ordinary days. Hepp takes the same position in his *Calvinism and the Philosophy of Nature*.[1] Noortzij in *Gods Woord en der Eeuwen Getuigenis*,[2] asserts that the Hebrew word *yom* (day) in Gen. 1 cannot possibly designate anything else than an ordinary day, but holds that the writer of Genesis did not attach any importance to the concept "day," but introduces it simply as part of a frame-work for the narrative of creation, not to indicate historical sequence, but to picture the glory of the creatures in the light of the great redemptive purpose of God. Hence the sabbath is the great culminating point, in which man reaches his real destiny. This view reminds us rather strongly of the position of some of the early Church Fathers. The arguments adduced for it are not very convincing, as Aalders has shown in his *De Eerste Drie Hoofdstukken van Genesis*.[3] This Old Testament scholar holds, on the basis of Gen. 1:5, that the term *yom* in Gen. 1 denotes simply the period of light, as distinguished from that of darkness; but this view would seem to involve a rather unnatural interpretation of the repeated expression "and there was evening and there was morning." It must then be interpreted to mean, and there was evening preceded by a morning. According to Dr. Aalders, too, Scripture certainly favors the idea that the days of creation were ordinary days, though it may not be possible to determine their exact length, and the first three days may have differed somewhat from the last three.

The literal interpretation of the term "day" in Gen. 1 is favored by the following considerations: (a) In its primary meaning the word *yom* denotes a natural day; and it is a good rule in exegesis, not to depart from the primary meaning of a word, unless this is required by the context. Dr. Noortzij stresses the fact that this word simply does not mean anything else than "day," such as this is known by man on earth. (b) The author of Genesis would seem to shut us up absolutely to the literal interpretation by adding in the case of every day the words, "and there was evening and there was morning." Each one of the days mentioned has just one evening and morning, something that would hardly apply to a period of thousands of years. And if it should be said

---

1. p. 215.
2. pp. 79f.
3. pp. 232-240

that the periods of creation were extraordinary days, each one consisting of one long day and one long night, then the question naturally arises, What would become of all vegetation during the long, long night? (c) In Ex. 20:9-11 Israel is commanded to labor six days and to rest on the seventh, because Jehovah made heaven and earth in six days and rested on the seventh day. Sound exegesis would seem to require that the word "day" be taken in the same sense in both instances. Moreover the sabbath set aside for rest certainly was a literal day; and the presumption is that the other days were of the same kind. (d) The last three days were certainly ordinary days, for they were determined by the sun in the usual way. While we cannot be absolutely sure that the preceding days did not differ from them at all in length, it is extremely unlikely that they differed from them, as periods of thousands upon thousands of years differ from ordinary days. The question may also be asked, why such a long period should be required, for instance, for the separation of light and darkness.

3. THE WORK OF THE SEPARATE DAYS. We notice in the work of creation a definite gradation, the work of each day leads up to and prepares for the work of the next, the whole of it culminating in the creation of man, the crown of God's handiwork, entrusted with the important task of making the whole of creation subservient to the glory of God.

a. *The first day.* On the first day the light was created, and by the separation of light and darkness day and night were constituted. This creation of light on the first day has been ridiculed in view of the fact that the sun was not created until the fourth day, but science itself silenced the ridicule by proving that light is not a substance emanating from the sun, but consists of ether waves produced by energetic electrons. Notice also that Genesis does not speak of the sun as light (or), but as light-bearer (ma'or), exactly what science has discovered it to be. In view of the fact that light is the condition of all life, it was but natural that it should be created first. God also at once instituted the ordinance of the alternation of light and darkness, calling the light day and the darkness night. We are not told, however, how this alternation was effected. The account of each day's work closes with the words, "and there was evening and there was morning." The days are not reckoned from evening to evening, but from morning to morning. After twelve hours there was evening, and after another twelve hours there was morning.

b. *The second day.* The work of the second day was also a work of separation: the firmament was established by dividing the waters above and the waters below. The waters above are the clouds, and not, as some would have it, the sea of glass, Rev. 4:6; 15:2, and the river of life, Rev. 22:1. Some have discredited the Mosaic account on the supposition that it represents the firmament as a solid vault; but this is entirely unwarranted, for the Hebrew word *raqia* does not denote a solid vault at all, but is equivalent to our word "expanse."

c. *The third day.* The separation is carried still further in the separation of the sea from the dry land, cf. Ps. 104:8. In addition to that the vegetable kingdom of plants and trees was established. Three great classes are mentioned, namely, *deshe'*, that is flowerless plants, which do not fructify one another in the usual way; *'esebh*, consisting of vegetables and grain yielding seed; and *'ets peri* or fruit trees, bearing fruit according to their kind. It should be noted here: (1) That, when God said, "Let the earth put forth grass" etc., this was not equivalent to saying: Let inorganic matter develop *by its own inherent force* into vegetable life. It was a word of power by which God implanted the principle of life in the earth, and thus enabled it to bring forth grass and herbs and trees. That it was a creative word is evident from Gen. 2:9. (2) That the statement, "and the earth brought forth grass, herbs yielding seed after their kind, and trees bearing fruit, wherein is the seed thereof, after their kind" (vs. 12), distinctly favors the idea that the different species of plants were created by God, and did not develop the one out of the other. Each one brought forth seed after its kind, and could therefore only reproduce its kind. The doctrine of evolution, of course, negatives both of these assertions; but it should be borne in mind that both spontaneous generation and the development of one species from another, are unproved, and now largely discredited, assumptions.[1]

d. *The fourth day.* Sun, moon, and stars, were created as light-bearers, to serve a variety of purposes: (1) to divide the day and the night; (2) to be for signs, that is, to indicate the cardinal points, to presage changes of weather conditions, and to serve as signs of important future events and coming judgments; (3) to be for seasons, and for days and years, that is, to serve the purpose of effecting the change of seasons, the succession of years, and the regular recurrence of special festive days; and (4) to serve as lights for the earth and thus to make the development of organic life on earth possible.

e. *The fifth day.* This day brings the creation of the birds and the fishes, the inhabitants of the air and the waters. Birds and fishes belong together, because there is a great similarity in their organic structure. Moreover, they are characterized by an instability and mobility which they have in common with the element in which they move, in distinction from the solid ground. They also agree in their method of procreation. Notice that they, too, were created after their kind, that is, the species were created.

f. *The sixth day.* This day brings the climax of the work of creation. In connection with the creation of the animals the expression is once more used, "Let the earth bring forth," and this should again be interpreted as was indicated under (c). The animals did not naturally develop out of the earth, but were brought forth by the creative fiat of God. We are told distinctly in the 25th verse that God *made* the beasts of the earth, the cattle and the creeping things of the earth, after their kind. But even if the expression did refer to natural development, it would not be in harmony with the doctrine of evolution, since that does not teach that the animals developed directly out of the mineral world. The creation of man is distinguished by the solemn

---

1. Cf. O'Toole, *The Case Against Evolution*, p. 28.

counsel that precedes it: "Let us make man in our own image, after our likeness"; and this is no wonder, since all that preceded was but a preparation for the coming of man, the crowning work of God, the king of creation; and because man was destined to be the image of God. The words *tselem* and *demuth* do not denote exactly the same thing, but are nevertheless used interchangeably. When it is said that man is created in the image of God, this means that God is the archetype of which man is is the ectype; and when it is added that he is created according to the likeness of God, this merely adds the idea that the image is in every way like the original. In his entire being man is the very image of God.

Before passing on to the seventh day it may be well to call attention to the remarkable parallel between the work of the first, and that of the second three days of creation.

1.	4.
The creation of light.	The creation of light-bearers.

2.	5.
Creation of expanse and separation of waters.	Creation of fowls of the air and fishes of the sea.

3.	6.
Separation of waters and dry land, and preparation of the earth as a habitation for man and beast.	Creation of the beasts of the field, the cattle, and all creeping things; and man.

g. *The seventh day.* The rest of God on the seventh day contains first of all a negative element. God ceased from His creative work. But to this must be added a positive element, namely, that He took delight in His completed work. His rest was as the rest of the artist, after He has completed His masterpiece, and now gazes upon it with profound admiration and delight, and finds perfect satisfaction in the contemplation of His production. "And God saw everything that He had made, and, behold, it was very good." It answered the purpose of God and corresponded to the divine ideal. Hence God rejoices in His creation, for in it He recognizes the reflection of His glorious perfections. His radiant countenance shines upon it and is productive of showers of blessings.

4. No Second Account of Creation in Genesis 2. It is quite common for advanced higher criticism to assume that Gen. 2 contains a second and independent account of creation. The first account is regarded as the work of the Elohist, and the second as that of the Jehovist. The two, it is said, do not agree, but conflict on several points. According to the second account, as distinguished from the first, the earth is dry before the creation of plants; man is created before the animals, and that alone, not as man and woman; then God created

the animals, in order to see whether they will be fit companions for man; seeing that they fail in that respect, He creates woman as a helpmeet for man; and, finally, He places man in the garden which He had prepared for him. But this is clearly a complete misunderstanding of the second chapter. Genesis 2 is not, and does not pretend to be, a narrative of creation. The superscription *'eleh toledoth,* which is found ten times in Genesis, never refers to the birth or origin of things, but always to their births, that is, their later history. The expression dates from a time when history still consisted in the description of generations. The second chapter of Genesis begins the description of the history of man, arranges its material to suit this purpose, and only repeats so much of what was said in the previous chapter, without any consideration of chronological order, as is necessary for the author's purpose.

5. ATTEMPTS TO HARMONIZE THE NARRATIVE OF CREATION WITH THE FINDINGS OF SCIENCE.

a. *The ideal or allegorical interpretation.* This gives prominence to the idea rather than to the letter of the narrative. It regards Genesis 1 as a poetic description of the creative work of God, representing this from different points of view. But (1) it is quite evident that the narrative is intended as a record of history, and is clearly so regarded in Scripture, cf. Ex. 20:11; Neh. 9:6; Ps. 33:6,9; 145:2-6; (2) the opening chapter of Genesis "lacks nearly every element of acknowledged Hebrew poetry" (Strong); and (3) this narrative is inseparably connected with the succeeding history, and is therefore most naturally regarded as itself historical.

b. *The mythical theory of modern philosophy.* Modern philosophy has advanced beyond the preceding position. It rejects not only the historical narrative of creation, but also the idea of creation, and regards the contents of Genesis 1 as a myth embodying a religious lesson. There is no intentional allegory here, it is said, but only a naive mythical representation with a religious core or nucleus. This is also contrary to the fact that Gen. 1 certainly comes to us with the pretension of being a historical narrative, and in the cross references, referred to above, it certainly is not regarded as a myth.

c. *The restitution theory.* Some theologians attempted to reconcile the narrative of creation with the discoveries of science in the study of the earth by adopting the restitution theory. It was advocated by Chalmers, Buckland, Wisemann, and Delitzsch, and assumes that a long period of time elapsed between the primary creation mentioned in Gen. 1:1 and the secondary creation described in Gen. 1:3-31. This long period was marked by several catastrophic changes, resulting in the destruction supposedly described in the words "waste and void." The second verse should then read, "And the earth became waste and void." This destruction was followed by a restitution, when God changed the chaos into a cosmos, a habitable world for man. This theory might offer some explanation of the different strata of the earth, but it offers no explanation of the fossils in the rocks, unless it is assumed that there were also successive creations of animals, followed by mass destructions. This theory never found favor in scientific circles, and finds no support in Scripture. The Bible does not say that the earth *became*, but that it *was* waste and void. And even if the Hebrew verb *hayetha* can be rendered "became," the words "waste and void" denote an unformed condition, and not a condition resulting from destruction. Delitzsch combined with this theory the idea that the earth was originally inhabited by the angels, and that the fall in the angelic world was the cause of the destruction which resulted in the chaos referred to in verse 2. For some reason or other this view finds considerable favor among present day dispensationalists, who find support for it in such passages as Isa. 24:1; Jer. 4:23-26; Job. 9:4-7; II Pet. 2:4. But even a careful reading of these passages is sufficient to convince one that they do not prove the point in question at all. Moreover, the Bible clearly teaches us that God created heaven and earth "and all the host of them" in six days, Gen. 2:1; Ex. 20:11.

d. *The concordistic theory.* This seeks to harmonize Scripture and science by assuming that the days of creation were periods of thousands of years. In addition to what was said about this in discussing the days of creation, we may now add that the idea that the earth's strata positively point to long and successive periods of development in the history of its origin, is simply a theory of the geologists, and a theory based on unwarranted generalizations. We would call attention to the following considerations: (1) The science of geology is not only young, but it is still in bondage to speculative thought. It cannot be considered as an inductive science, since it is largely the fruit of *a priori* or deductive reasoning. Spencer called it "Illogical Geology" and ridiculed its methods, and Huxley spoke of its grand hypotheses as "not proven and not provable."[1] (2) Up to the present time it has done little more than scratch the surface of the earth, and that in a very limited number of places. As a result its conclusions are often mere generalizations, based on insufficient data. Facts observed in some places are contradicted by those found in others. (3) Even if it had explored large areas in all parts of the globe, it could only increase our knowledge of the present condition of the earth, but would never be able to give us perfectly reliable information respecting its past history. You cannot write the history of a nation on the basis of the facts observed in its present constitution and life. (4) Geologists once proceeded on the assumption that the strata of rocks were found in the same order all over the globe; and that by estimating the length of time required by the formation of each it could determine the age of the earth. But (a) it was found that the order of the rocks differs in various localities; (b) the experiments made to determine the time required for the formation of the different strata, led to widely different results; and (c) the uniformitarian theory of Lyell, that the physical and chemical action of today are safe guides in estimating those of all previous times, was found to be unreliable.[2] (5) When the attempt to determine the age of the various

1. Price, *The Fundamentals of Geology,* pp. 29, 32.
2. Cf. More, *The Dogma of Evolution,* p. 148.

strata or rocks by their mineral and mechanical make-up failed, geologists began to make the fossils the determining factor. Palæontology became the really important subject, and under the influence of the uniformitarian principle of Lyell developed into one of the important proofs of evolution. It is simply assumed that certain fossils are older than others; and if the question is asked on what basis the assumption rests, the answer is that they are found in the older rocks. This is just plain reasoning in a circle. The age of the rocks is determined by the fossils which they contain, and the age of the fossils by the rocks in which they are found. But the fossils are not always found in the same order; sometimes the order is reversed. (6) The order of the fossils as now determined by geology does not correspond to the order which the narrative of creation leads us to expect, so that even the acceptance of the geological theory would not serve the purpose of harmonizing Scripture and science.

6. THE DOCTRINE OF CREATION AND THE THEORY OF EVOLUTION. The question naturally arises in our day, How does the theory of evolution affect the doctrine of creation?

a. *The theory of evolution cannot take the place of the doctrine of creation.* Some speak as if the hypothesis of evolution offered an explanation of the origin of the world; but this is clearly a mistake, for it does no such thing. Evolution is development, and all development presupposes the prior existence of an entity or principle or force, out of which something develops. The non-existent cannot *develop* into existence. Matter and force could not have evolved out of nothing. It has been customary for evolutionists to fall back on the nebular hypothesis, in order to explain the origin of the solar system, though in present day science this is supplanted by the planetesimal hypothesis. But these only carry the problem one step farther back, and fail to solve it. The evolutionist must either resort to the theory that matter is eternal, or accept the doctrine of creation.

b. *The theory of naturalistic evolution is not in harmony with the narrative of creation.* If evolution does not account for the origin of the world, does it not at least give a rational account of the development of things out of primordial matter, and thus explain the origin of the present species of plants and animals (including man), and also the various phenomena of life, such as sentiency, intelligence, morality, and religion? Does it necessarily conflict with the narrative of creation? Now it is perfectly evident that naturalistic evolution certainly does conflict with the Biblical account. The Bible teaches that plants and animals and man appeared on the scene at the creative fiat of the Almighty; but according to the evolutionary hypothesis they evolved out of the inorganic world by a process of natural development. The Bible represents God as creating plants and animals after their kind, and yielding seed after their kind, that is, so that they would reproduce their own kind: but the theory of evolution points to natural forces, resident in nature, leading to the development of one species out of another. According to the narrative of creation, the vegetable and animal kingdoms and man were brought forth in a single week; but the hypothesis of evolution regards them as the product of a gradual development in the course of millions of years. Scripture pictures man as standing on the highest plane at the beginning of his career, and then descending to lower levels by the deteriorating influence of sin; the theory of evolution, on the other hand, represents original man as only slightly different from the brute, and claims that the human race has risen, through its own inherent powers, to ever higher levels of existence.

c. *The theory of naturalistic evolution is not well established and fails to account for the facts.* The conflict referred to in the preceding would be a serious matter, if the theory of evolution were an established fact. Some think it is and confidently speak of the *dogma* of evolution. Others, however, correctly remind us of the fact that evolution is still only a hypothesis. Even so great a scientist as Ambrose Fleming says that "the close analysis of the ideas connected with the term Evolution shows them to be insufficient as a philosophic or scientific solution of the problems of reality and existence."[1] The very uncertainty which prevails in the camp of the evolutionists is proof positive that evolution is only a hypothesis. Moreover, it is frankly admitted to-day by many who still cling to the principle of evolution that they do not understand its method of operation. It was thought at one time that Darwin had furnished the key to the whole problem, but that key is now rather generally discarded. The foundation pillars, on which the Darwinian structure was reared, such as the principle of use and disuse, the struggle for existence, natural selection, and the transmission of acquired characteristics, have been removed one after another. Such evolutionists as Weissmann, De Vries, Mendel, and Bateson, all contributed to the collapse of the Darwinian edifice. Nordenskioeld, in his *History of Biology*, speaks of the "dissolution of Darwinism" as an established fact. Dennert calls us to the deathbed of Darwinism, and O'Toole says, "Darwinism is dead, and no grief of mourners can resuscitate the corpse." Morton speaks of "the bankruptcy of evolution," and Price of the "phantom of organic evolution." Darwinism, then, has admittedly failed to explain the origin of species, and evolutionists have not been able to offer a better explanation. The Mendelian law accounts for variations, but not for the origin of new species. It really points away from the development of new species by a natural process. Some are of the opinion that the mutation theory of De Vries or Lloyd Morgan's theory of emergent evolution points the way, but neither one of these has proved to be a successful explanation of the origin of species by natural development pure and simple. It is now admitted that the mutants of De Vries are varietal rather than specific, and cannot be regarded as the beginnings of new species. And Morgan feels constrained to admit that he cannot explain his emergents without falling back upon some creative power that might be called God. Morton says:

----
1. *Evolution or Creation*, p. 29.

"The fact is that, besides creation, there is not even a theory of origins to hold the field to-day."[1]

The hypothesis of evolution fails at several points. It cannot explain the origin of life. Evolutionists sought its explanation in spontaneous generation, an unproved assumption, which is now discredited. It is a well established fact in science that life can only come from antecedent life. Further, it has failed utterly to adduce a single example of one species producing another distinct (organic as distinguished from varietal) species. Bateson said in 1921: "We cannot see how the differentiation in species came about. Variations of many kinds, often considerable, we daily witness, but no origin of species. . . . Meanwhile, though our faith in evolution stands unshaken, we have no acceptable account of the origin of species."[2] Neither has evolution been able successfully to cope with the problems presented by the origin of man. It has not even succeeded in proving the physical descent of man from the brute. J. A. Thomson, author of *The Outline of Science* and a leading evolutionist, holds that man really never was an animal, a fierce beastly looking creature, but that the first man sprang suddenly, by a big leap, from the primate stock into a human being. Much less has it been able to explain the psychical side of man's life. The human soul, endowed with intelligence, self-consciousness, freedom, conscience, and religious aspirations. remains an unsolved enigma.

d. *Theistic evolution is not tenable in the light of Scripture.* Some Christian scientists and theologians seek to harmonize the doctrine of creation, as taught by Scripture, and the theory of evolution by accepting what they call theistic evolution. It is a protest against the attempt to eliminate God, and postulates Him as the almighty worker back of the whole process of development. Evolution is regarded simply as God's method of working in the development of nature. Theistic evolution really amounts to this, that God created the world (the cosmos) by a process of evolution, a process of natural development, in which He does not miraculously intervene, except in cases where this is absolutely necessary. It is willing to admit that the absolute beginning of the world could only result from a direct creative activity of God; and, if it can find no natural explanation, will also grant a direct intervention of God in the origination of life and of man. It has been hailed as Christian evolution, though there is not necessarily anything Christian about it. Many, otherwise opposed to the theory of evolution, have welcomed it, because it recognizes God in the process and is supposed to be compatible with the Scriptural doctrine of creation. Hence it is freely taught in churches and Sunday Schools. As a matter of fact, however, it is a very dangerous hybrid. The name is a contradiction in terms, for it is neither theism nor naturalism, neither creation nor evolution in the accepted sense of the terms. And it does not require a great deal of penetration to see that Dr. Fairhurst is right

---

1. *The Bankruptcy of Evolution*, p. 182.
2. *Science*, Jan. 20, 1922.

in his conviction "that theistic evolution destroys the Bible as the inspired book of authority as effectively as does atheistic evolution."[1] Like naturalistic evolution it teaches that it required millions of years to produce the present habitable world; and that God did not create the various species of plants and animals, and that, so that they produced their own kind; that man, at least on his physical side, is a descendant of the brute and therefore began his career on a low level; that there has been no fall in the Biblical sense of the word, but only repeated lapses of men in their upward course; that sin is only a weakness, resulting from man's animal instincts and desires, and does not constitute guilt; that redemption is brought about by the ever-increasing control of the higher element in man over his lower propensities; that miracles do not occur, either in the natural or in the spiritual world; that regeneration, conversion, and sanctification are simply natural psychological changes, and so on. In a word, it is a theory that is absolutely subversive of Scripture truth.

Some Christian scholars of the present day feel that Bergson's theory of *Creative Evolution* commends itself to those who do not want to leave God out of consideration. This French philosopher assumes an *élan vital*, a vital impulse in the world, as the ground and animating principle of all life. This vital principle does not spring from matter, but is rather the originating cause of matter. It pervades matter, overcomes its inertia and resistance by acting as a living force on that which is essentially dying, and ever creates, not new material, but new movements adapted to ends of its own, and thus creates very much as the artist creates. It is directive and purposive and yet, though conscious, does not work according to a preconceived plan, however that may be possible. It determines evolution itself as well as the direction in which evolution moves. This ever creating life, "of which every individual and every species is an experiment," is Bergson's God, a God who is finite, who is limited in power, and who is seemingly impersonal, though Hermann says that "we shall, perhaps, not go far wrong in believing that he will be 'the ideal tendency of things' made personal."[2] Haas speaks of Bergson as a vitalistic pantheist rather than a theist. At any rate, his God is a God that is wholly within the world. This view may have a special appeal for the modern liberal theologian, but is even less in harmony with the narrative of creation than theistic evolution.

QUESTIONS FOR FURTHER STUDY. What is the real alternative to the doctrine of creation? Wherein lies the importance of the doctrine of creation? Should the first chapters of Genesis be allowed to have any bearing on the scientific study of the origin of things? Does the Bible in any way determine the time when the world was created? What extremes should be avoided as to the relation of God and the world to each other? Should the Bible always be interpreted in harmony with widely accepted scientific theories? What is the status of the hypothesis of evolution in the scientific world today? What is the characteristic element in the Darwinian theory of evolution? How do you account for its widesperad repudiation at the present time? How does Bergson's Creative Evolution or the Neo-vitalism of Hans Driesch

1. *Theistic Evolution*, p. 7.
2. *Eucken and Bergson*, p. 163.

affect the mechanistic view of the universe? In what respect is theistic evolution an improvement over naturalistic evolution?

LITERATURE. Bavinck, *Geref. Dogm.* II. pp. 426-543; ibid., *Schepping of Ontwikkeling;* Kuyper, *Dict. Dogm.*, *De Creatione*, pp. 3-127; *De Creaturis* A, pp. 5-54; B. pp. 3-42; ibid., *Evolutie;* Vos *Geref. Dogm.* I, *De Schepping;* Hodge. *Syst. Theol.* I, pp. 550-574; Shedd, *Dogm. Theol.* I, pp. 463-526; McPherson, *Chr. Dogm.*, pp. 163-174; Dabney, *Syst. and Polemic Theol.*, pp. 247-274; Harris, *God, Creator and Lord of All*, I, pp. 463-518; Hepp, *Calvinism and the Philosophy of Nature*, Chap. V; Honig, *Geref. Dogm.*, pp. 281-324; Noordtzij, *God's Woord en der Eeuwen Getuigenis*, pp. 77-98; Aalders, *De Goddelijke Openbaring in de Eerste Drie Hoofdstukken van Genesis;* Geesink, *Van's Heeren Ordinantien*, Inleidend Deel, pp. 216-332; various works of Darwin, Wallace, Weissman, Osborne, Spencer, Haeckel, Thomson, and others on Evolution; Dennert, *The Deathbed of Darwinism;* Dawson, *The Bible Confirmed by Science;* Fleming, *Evolution and Creation;* Hamilton, *The Basis of Evolutionary Faith;* Johnson, *Can the Christian Now Believe in Evolution?* McCrady, *Reason and Revelation;* More, *The Dogma of Evolution;* Morton, *The Bankruptcy of Evolution;* O'Toole, *The Case Against Evolution;* Price, *The Fundamentals of Geology;* ibid., *The Phantom of Organic Evolution;* Messenger, *Evolution and Theology;* Rimmer, *The Theory of Evolution and the Facts of Science.*

VI. Providence

Christian theism is opposed to both a deistic separation of God from the world and a pantheistic confusion of God with the world. Hence the doctrine of creation is immediately followed by that of providence, in which the Scriptural view of God's relation to the world is clearly defined. While the term "providence" is not found in Scripture, the doctrine of providence is nevertheless eminently Scriptural. The word is derived from the Latin *providentia*, which corresponds to the Greek *pronoia*. These words mean primarily prescience or foresight, but gradually acquired other meanings. Foresight is associated, on the one hand, with plans for the future, and on the other hand, with the actual realization of these plans. Thus the word "providence" has come to signify the provision which God makes for the ends of His government, and the preservation and government of all His creatures. This is the sense in which it is now generally used in theology, but it is not the only sense in which theologians have employed it. Turretin defines the term in its widest sense as denoting (1) foreknowledge, (2) foreordination, and (3) the efficacious administration of the things decreed. In general usage, however, it is now generally restricted to the last sense.

A. Providence in General.

1. HISTORY OF THE DOCTRINE OF PROVIDENCE. With its doctrine of providence the Church took position against both, the Epicurean notion that the world is governed by chance, and the Stoic view that it is ruled by fate. From the very start theologians took the position that God preserves and governs the world. However, they did not always have an equally absolute conception of the divine control of all things. Due to the close connection between the two, the history of the doctrine of providence follows in the main that of the doctrine of predestination. The earliest Church Fathers present no definite views on the subject. In opposition to the Stoic doctrine of fate and in their desire to guard the holiness of God, they sometimes over-emphasized the free will of man, and to that extent manifested a tendency to deny the absolute providential rule of God with respect to sinful actions. Augustine led the way in the development of this doctrine. Over against the doctrines of fate and chance, he stressed the fact that all things are preserved and governed by the sovereign, wise, and beneficent will of God. He made no reservations in connection with the providence of God, but maintained the control of God over the good and the evil that is in the world alike. By defending the reality of second causes. he safeguarded the holiness of God and upheld the responsibility of man.

During the Middle Ages there was very little controversy on the subject of divine providence. Not a single council expressed itself on this doctrine. The prevailing view was that of Augustine, which subjected everything to the will of God. This does not mean, however, that there were no dissenting views. Pelagianism limited providence to the natural life, and excluded the ethical life. And Semi-Pelagians moved in the same direction, though they did not all go equally far. Some of the Scholastics considered the conservation of God as a continuation of His creative activity, while others made a real distinction between the two. Thomas Aquinas' doctrine of divine providence follows in the main that of Augustine, and holds that the will of God, as determined by His perfections, preserves and governs all things; while Duns Scotus and such Nominalists as Biel and Occam made everything dependent on the arbitrary will of God. This was a virtual introduction of the rule of chance.

The Reformers on the whole subscribed to the Augustinian doctrine of divine providence, though they differed somewhat in details. While Luther believed in general providence, he does not stress God's preservation and government of the world in general as much as Calvin does. He considers the doctrine primarily in its soteriological bearings. Socinians and Arminians, though not both to the same degree, limited the providence of God by stressing the independent power of man to initiate action and thus to control his life. The control of the world was really taken out of the hands of God, and given into the hands of man. In the eighteenth and nineteenth centuries providence was virtually ruled out by a Deism which represented God as withdrawing Himself from the world after the work of creation; and by a Pantheism which identified God and the world, obliterated the distinction between creation and providence, and denied the reality of second causes. And while Deism may now be considered as a thing of the past, its view of the control of the world is continued in the position of natural science that the world is controlled by an iron-clad system of laws. And modern liberal theology, with its pantheistic conception of the immanence of God, also tends to rule out the doctrine of divine providence.

2. THE IDEA OF PROVIDENCE. Providence may be defined as *that continued exercise of the divine energy whereby the Creator preserves all His creatures, is operative in all that comes to pass in the world, and directs all things to their appointed end*. This definition indicates that there are three elements in providence, namely, preservation (*conservatio, sustentatio*), concurrence or cooperation (*concursus, co-operatio*), and government (*gubernatio*) Calvin, the Heidelberg Catechism, and some of the more recent dogmaticians (Dabney, the Hodges, Dick, Shedd, McPherson) speak of only two elements, namely, preservation and government. This does not mean, however, that they want to exclude the element of concurrence but only that they regard it as included in the other two as indicating the manner in which God preserves and governs the world. McPherson seems to think that only some of the great Lutheran

theologians adopted the threefold division; but in this he is mistaken, for it is very common in the works of Dutch dogmaticians from the seventeenth century on (Mastricht, à Marck, De Moor, Brakel, Francken, Kuyper, Bavinck, Vos, Honig). They departed from the older division, because they wanted to give the element of concurrence greater prominence, in order to guard against the dangers of both Deism and Pantheism. But while we distinguish three elements in providence, we should remember that these three are never separated in the work of God. While preservation has reference to the *being*, concurrence to the *activity*, and government to the *guidance* of all things, this should never be understood in an exclusive sense. In preservation there is also an element of government, in government an element of concursus, and in concursus an element of preservation. Pantheism does not distinguish between creation and providence, but theism stresses a twofold distinction: (a) Creation is the calling into existence of that which did not exist before, while providence continues or causes to continue what has already been called into existence. (b) In the former there can be no cooperation of the creature with the Creator, but in the latter there is a concurrence of the first Cause with second causes. In Scripture the two are always kept distinct.

3. MISCONCEPTIONS CONCERNING THE NATURE OF PROVIDENCE.

a. *Limiting it to prescience or prescience plus foreordination.* This limitation is found in some of the early Church Fathers. The fact is, however, that when we speak of the providence of God, we generally have in mind neither His prescience nor His foreordination, but simply His continued activity in the world for the realization of His plan. We realize that this cannot be separated from His eternal decree, but also feel that the two can and should be distinguished. The two have often been distinguished as immanent and transeunt providence.

b. *The deistic conception of divine providence.* According to Deism God's concern with the world is not universal, special and perpetual, but only of a general nature. At the time of creation He imparted to all His creatures certain inalienable properties, placed them under invariable laws, and left them to work out their destiny by their own inherent powers. Meanwhile He merely exercises a general oversight, not of the specific agents that appear on the scene, but of the general laws which He has established. The world is simply a machine which God has put in motion, and not at all a vessel which He pilots from day to day. This deistic conception of providence is characteristic of Pelagianism, was adopted by several Roman Catholic theologians, was sponsored by Socinianism, and was only one of the fundamental errors of Arminianism. It was clothed in a philosophic garb by the Deists of the eighteenth century, and appeared in a new form in the nineteenth century, under the influence of the theory of evolution and of natural science, with its strong emphasis on the uniformity of nature as controlled by an inflexible system of iron-clad laws.

c. *The pantheistic view of divine providence.* Pantheism does not recognize the distinction between God and the world. It either idealistically absorbs the world in God, or materialistically absorbs God in the world. In either case it leaves no room for creation and also eliminates providence in the proper sense of the word. It is true that Pantheists speak of providence, but their so-called providence is simply identical with the course of nature, and this is nothing but the self-revelation of God, a self-revelation that leaves no room for the independent operation of second causes in any sense of the word. From this point of view the supernatural is impossible, or, rather, the natural and the supernatural are identical, the consciousness of free personal self-determination in man is a delusion, moral responsibility is a figment of the imagination, and prayer and religious worship are superstition. Theology has always been quite careful to ward off the dangers of Pantheism, but during the last century this error succeeded in entrenching itself in a great deal of modern liberal theology under the guise of the doctrine of the immanence of God.[1]

4. THE OBJECTS OF DIVINE PROVIDENCE.

a. *The teachings of Scripture on this point.* The Bible clearly teaches God's providential control (1) over the universe at large, Ps. 103:19; Dan. 5:35; Eph. 1:11; (2) over the physical world, Job 37:5,10; Ps. 104:14; 135:6; Matt. 5:45; (3) over the brute creation, Ps. 104:21,28; Matt. 6:26; 10:29; (4) over the affairs of nations, Job 12:23; Ps. 22:28; 66:7; Acts 17:26; (5) over man's birth and lot in life, I Sam. 16:1; Ps. 139:16; Isa. 45:5; Gal. 1:15,16; (6) over the outward successes and failures of men's lives, Ps. 75:6,7; Luke 1:52; (7) over things seemingly accidental or insignificant, Prov. 16:33; Matt. 10:30; (8) in the protection of the righteous, Ps. 4:8; 5:12; 63:8; 121:3; Rom. 8:28; (9) in supplying the wants of God's people, Gen. 22:8,14; Deut. 8:3; Phil. 4:19; (10) in giving answers to prayer, I Sam. 1:19; Isa. 20:5,6; II Chron. 33:13; Ps. 65:2; Matt. 7:7; Luke 18:7,8; and (11) in the exposure and punishment of the wicked, Ps. 7:12,13; 11:6.

b. *General and special providence.* Theologians generally distinguish between general and special providence, the former denoting God's control of the universe as a whole, and the latter, His care for each part of it in relation to the whole. These are not two kinds of providence, but the same providence exercised in two different relations. The term "special providence," however, may have a more specific connotation, and in some cases refers to God's special care for His rational creatures. Some even speak of a very special providence (*providentia specialissima*) with reference to those who stand in the special relationship of sonship to God. Special providences are special combinations in the order of events, as in the answer to prayer, in deliverance out of trouble, and in all instances in which grace and help come in critical circumstances.

c. *The denial of special providence.* There are those who are willing to admit a general providence, an administration of the world under a fixed system

---

1. Cf. Randall, *The Making of the Modern Mind*, p. 538.

of general laws, but deny that there is also a special providence in which God concerns Himself with the details of history, the affairs of human life, and particularly the experiences of the righteous. Some hold that God is too great to concern Himself with the smaller things of life, while others maintain that He simply cannot do it, since the laws of nature bind His hands, and therefore smile significantly when they hear of God's answering man's prayers. Now it need not be denied that the relation of special providence to the uniform laws of nature constitutes a problem. At the same time it must be said that it involves a very poor, superficial, and un-Biblical view of God to say that He does not and cannot concern Himself with the details of life, cannot answer prayer, give relief in emergencies, or intervene miraculously in behalf of man. A ruler that simply laid down certain general principles and paid no attention to particulars, or a business man who failed to look after the details of his business, would soon come to grief. The Bible teaches that even the minutest details of life are of divine ordering. In connection with the question, whether we can harmonize the operation of the general laws of nature and special providence, we can only point to the following: (1) The laws of nature should not be represented as powers of nature absolutely controlling all phenomena and operations. They are really nothing more than man's, often deficient, description of the uniformity in variety discovered in the way in which the powers of nature work. (2) The materialistic conception of the laws of nature as a close-knit system, acting independently of God and really making it impossible for Him to interfere in the course of the world, is absolutely wrong. The universe has a personal basis, and the uniformity of nature is simply the method ordained by a personal agent. (3) The so-called laws of nature produce the same effects only if all the conditions are the same. Effects are not generally the results of a single power, but of a combination of natural powers. Even a man can vary the effects by combining one power of nature with some other power or powers, while yet each one of these powers works in strict accordance with its laws. And if this is possible for man, it is infinitely more possible for God. By all kinds of combinations He can bring about the most varied results.

B. Preservation.

1. BASIS FOR THE DOCTRINE OF PRESERVATION. Proof for the doctrine of preservation is both direct and inferential.

a. *Direct proof.* The divine preservation of all things is clearly and explicitly taught in several passages of Scripture. The following are but a few of the many passages that might be mentioned: Deut. 33:12,25-28; I Sam. 2:9; Neh. 9:6; Ps. 107:9; 127:1; 145:14,15; Matt. 10:29; Acts 17:28; Col. 1:17; Heb. 1:3. Very numerous are the passages that speak of the Lord as preserving His people, such as, Gen. 28:15; 49:24; Ex. 14:29,30; Deut. 1:30,31; II Chron. 20:15,17; Job 1:10; 36:7; Ps. 31:20; 32:6; 34:15,17,19; 37:15, 17,19,20; 91:1,3,4,7,9,10,14; 121:3,4,7,8; 125:1,2; Isa. 40:11; 43:2; 63:9;

Jer. 30:7,8,11; Ezek. 34:11,12,15,16; Dan. 12:1; Zech. 2:5; Luke 21:18; I Cor. 10:13; I. Pet. 3:12; Rev. 3:10.

b. *Inferential proof.* The idea of divine preservation follows from the doctrine of the sovereignty of God. This can only be conceived of as absolute; but it would not be absolute, if anything existed or occurred independently of His will. It can be maintained only on condition that the whole universe and all that is in it, is in its being and action absolutely dependent on God. It follows also from the dependent character of the creature. It is characteristic of all that is creature, that it cannot continue to exist in virtue of its own inherent power. It has the ground of its being and continuance in the will of its Creator. Only He who created the world by the word of His power, can uphold it by His omnipotence.

2. THE PROPER CONCEPTION OF DIVINE PRESERVATION. The doctrine of preservation proceeds on the assumption that all created substances, whether they be spiritual or material, possess real and permanent existence, distinct from the existence of God, and have only such active and passive properties as they have derived from God; and that their active powers have a real, and not merely an apparent, efficiency as second causes, so that they are able to produce the effects proper to them. Thus it guards against Pantheism, with its idea of a continued creation, which virtually, if not always expressly, denies the distinct existence of the world, and makes God the sole agent in the universe. But it does not regard these created substances as self-existent, since self-existence is the exclusive property of God, and all creatures have the ground of their continued existence in Him and not in themselves. From this it follows that they continue to exist, not in virtue of a merely negative act of God, but in virtue of a positive and continued exercise of divine power. The power of God put forth in upholding all things is just as positive as that exercised in creation. The precise nature of His work in sustaining all things in being and action is a mystery, though it may be said that, in His providential operations, He accommodates Himself to the nature of His creatures. With Shedd we say: "In the material world, God immediately works in and through material properties and laws. In the mental world, God immediately works in and through the properties of mind. Preservation never runs counter to creation. God does not violate in providence what He has established in creation."[1] Preservation may be defined as *that continuous work of God by which He maintains the things which He created, together with the properties and powers with which He endowed them.*

3. ERRONEOUS CONCEPTIONS OF DIVINE PRESERVATION. The nature of this work of God is not always properly understood. There are two views of it which ought to be avoided: (a) *That it is purely negative.* According to Deism divine preservation consists in this, that God does not destroy the work of His hands. By virtue of creation God endowed matter with certain properties, placed it under invariable laws, and then left it to shift for itself, independently

---

1. *Dogm. Theol.* I, p. 528.

of all support or direction from without. This is an unreasonable, irreligious, and an un-Biblical representation. It is unreasonable, because it implies that God communicated self-subsistence to the creature, while self-subsistence and self-sustenation are incommunicable properties, which characterize only the Creator. The creature can never be self-sustaining, but must be upheld from day to day by the almighty power of the Creator. Hence it would not require a positive act of omnipotence on the part of God to annihilate created existences. A simple withdrawal of support would naturally result in destruction. — This view is irreligious, because it removes God so far from His creation that communion with Him becomes a practical impossibility. History plainly testifies to the fact that it uniformly spells death for religion. — It is also un-Biblical, since it puts God altogether outside of His creation, while the Bible teaches us in many passages that He is not only transcendent but also immanent in the works of His hands. (b) *That it is a continuous creation.* Pantheism represents preservation as a continuous creation, so that the creatures or second causes are conceived as having no real or continuous existence, but as emanating in every successive moment out of that mysterious Absolute which is the hidden ground of all things. Some who were not Pantheists had a similar view of preservation. Descartes laid the basis for such a conception of it, and Malebranche pushed this to the farthest extreme consistent with theism. Even Jonathan Edwards teaches it incidentally in his work on Original Sin, and thus comes dangerously near to teaching Pantheism. Such a view of preservation leaves no room for second causes, and therefore necessarily leads to Pantheism. It is contrary to our original and necessary intuitions, which assure us that we are real, self-determining causes of action, and consequently moral agents. Moreover, it strikes at the very root of free agency, moral accountability, moral government, and therefore of religion itself. Some Reformed theologians also use the term "continuous creation,"[1] but do not thereby mean to teach the doctrine under consideration. They simply desire to stress the fact that the world is maintained by the same power which created it. In view of the the fact that the expression is liable to misunderstanding, it is better to avoid it.

C. **Concurrence.**

1. THE IDEA OF DIVINE CONCURRENCE AND SCRIPTURAL PROOF FOR IT.

a. *Definition and explanation.* Concurrence may be defined as *the co-operation of the divine power with all subordinate powers, according to the pre-established laws of their operation, causing them to act and to act precisely as they do.* Some are inclined to limit its operation, as far as man is concerned. to human actions that are morally good and therefore commendable; others. more logically, extend it to actions of every kind. It should be noted at the outset that this doctrine implies two things: (1) That the powers of nature do not work by themselves, that is, simply by their own inherent power, but that God is immediately operative in every act of the creature. This must be

1. Bavinck, *Geref. Dogm.* II. p. 654; Heppe, *Dogm.,* p. 190; McPherson. *Chr. Dogm..* p. 177.

maintained in opposition to the deistic position. (2) That second causes are real, and not to be regarded simply as the operative power of God. It is only on condition that second causes are real, that we can properly speak of a concurrence or co-operation of the First Cause with secondary causes. This should be stressed over against the pantheistic idea that God is the only agent working in the world.

b. *Scripture proof for divine concurrence.* The Bible clearly teaches that the providence of God pertains not only to the being but also to the actions or operations of the creature. The general truth that men do not work independently, but are controlled by the will of God, appears from several passages of Scripture. Joseph says in Gen. 45:5 that God rather than his brethren had sent him to Egypt. In Ex. 4:11,12 the Lord says that He will be with Moses' mouth and teach him what to say; and in Jos. 11:6 He gives Joshua the assurance that He will deliver the enemies to Israel. Proverbs 21:1 teaches us that "the king's heart is in the hand of Jehovah. . . . He turneth it whithersoever He will"; and Ezra 6:22, that Jehovah "had turned the heart of the king of Assyria" unto Israel. In Deut 8:18 Israel is reminded of the fact that it was Jehovah that gave it power to get wealth. More particularly, it is also evident from Scripture that there is some kind of divine co-operation in that which is evil. According to II Sam. 16:11 Jehovah bade Shimei to curse David. The Lord also calls the Assyrian "the rod of mine anger, the staff in whose hand is mine indignation," Isa. 10:5. Moreover, He provided for a lying spirit in the mouth of the prophets of Ahab, I Kings 22:20-23.

2. ERRORS THAT SHOULD BE AVOIDED. There are several errors against which we should guard in connection with this doctrine.

a. *That it consists merely in a general communication of power, without determining the specific action in any way.* Jesuits, Socinians, and Arminians maintain that the divine concurrence is only a general and indifferent co-operation, so that it is the second cause that directs the action to its particular end. It is common alike to all causes, quickening them into action, but in a way that is entirely indeterminate. While it stimulates the second cause, it leaves this to determine its own particular kind and mode of action. But if this were the situation, it would be in the power of man to frustrate the plan of God, and the First Cause would become subservient to the second. Man would be in control, and there would be no divine providence.

b. *That it is of such a nature that man does part of the work and God a part.* The co-operation of God and man is sometimes represented as if it were something like the joint efforts of a team of horses pulling together, each one doing his part. This is a mistaken view of the distribution of the work. As a matter of fact each deed is in its entirety both a deed of God and a deed of the creature. It is a deed of God in so far as there is nothing that is independent of the divine will, and in so far as it is determined from moment to moment by the will of God. And it is a deed of man in so far as God realizes it through the self-activity of the creature. There is interpenetration here, but no mutual limitation.

c. *That the work of God and that of the creature in concurrence are co-ordinate.* This is already excluded by what was said in the preceding. The work of God always has the priority, for man is dependent on God in all that he does. The statement of Scripture, "Without me ye can do nothing," applies in every field of endeavor. The exact relation of the two is best indicated in the following characteristics of the divine concurrence.

3. CHARACTERISTICS OF THE DIVINE CONCURRENCE.

a. *It is previous and pre-determining, not in a temporal but in a logical sense.* There is no absolute principle of self-activity in the creature, to which God simply joins His activity. In every instance the impulse to action and movement proceeds from God. There must be an influence of divine energy before the creature can work. It should be noted particularly that this influence does not terminate on the activity of the creature, but on the creature itself. God causes everything in nature to work and to move in the direction of a pre-determined end. So God also enables and prompts His rational creatures, as second causes, to function, and that not merely by endowing them with energy in a general way, but by energizing them to certain specific acts. He worketh all things in all, I Cor. 12:6, and worketh all things, also in this respect, according to the counsel of His will, Eph. 1:11. He gave Israel power to get wealth, Deut. 8:18, and worketh in believers both to will and to do according to His good pleasure, Phil. 2:13. Pelagians and Semi-Pelagians of all kinds are generally willing to admit that the creature cannot act apart from an influx of divine power, but maintain that this is not so specific that it determines the character of the action in any way.

b. *It is also a simultaneous concurrence.* After the activity of the creature is begun, the efficacious will of God must accompany it at every moment, if it is to continue. There is not a single moment that the creature works independently of the will and the power of God. It is in Him that we live *and move* and have our being, Acts 17:28. This divine activity accompanies the action of man at every point, but without robbing man in any way of his freedom. The action remains the free act of man, an act for which he is held responsible. This simultaneous concurrence does not result in an identification of the *causa prima* and the *causa secunda*. In a very real sense the operation is the product of both causes. Man is and remains the real subject of the action. Bavinck illustrates this by pointing to the fact that wood burns, that God only causes it to burn, but that formally this burning cannot be ascribed to God but only to the wood as subject. It is evident that this simultaneous action cannot be separated from the previous and pre-determining concurrence, but should be distinguished from it. Strictly speaking it, in distinction from the previous concurrence, terminates, not on the creature, but on its activity. Since it does not terminate on the creature, it can in the abstract be interpreted as having no ethical bearings. This explains that the Jesuits taught that the divine concurrence was simultaneous only, and not previous and pre-determining, and that some Reformed theologians limited the previous concurrence to the good deeds of men, and for the rest satisfied themselves with teaching a simultaneous concurrence.

c. *It is, finally, an immediate concurrence.* In His government of the world God employs all kinds of means for the realization of His ends; but He does not so work in the divine concurrence. When He destroys the cities of the plain by fire, this is an act of divine government in which He employs means. But at the same time it is His immediate concurrence by which He enables the fire to fall, to burn, and to destroy. So God also works in man in endowing him with power, in the determination of his actions, and in sustaining his activities all along the line.

4. THE DIVINE CONCURRENCE AND SIN. Pelagians, Semi-Pelagians, and Arminians raise a serious objection to this doctrine of providence. They maintain that a *previous* concurrence, which is not merely general *but predetermines man to specific actions*, makes God the responsible author of sin. Reformed theologians are well aware of the difficulty that presents itself here, but do not feel free to circumvent it by denying God's absolute control over the free actions of His moral creatures, since this is clearly taught in Scripture, Gen. 45:5; 50:19,20; Ex. 10:1,20; II Sam. 16:10.11; Isa. 10:5-7; Acts 2:23; 4:27.28. They feel constrained to teach: (a) that sinful acts are under divine control and occur according to God's pre-determination and purpose, but only by divine permission, so that He does not efficiently cause men to sin, Gen. 45:5; 50:20; Ex. 14:17; Isa. 66:4; Rom. 9:22; II Thess. 2:11; (b) that God often restrains the sinful works of the sinner, Gen. 3:6; Job 1:12; 2:6; Ps. 76:10; Isa. 10:15; Acts 7:51; and (c) that God in behalf of His own purpose overrules evil for good, Gen. 50:20; Ps. 76:10; Acts. 3:13.

This does not mean, however, that they all agree in answering the question, whether there is a direct, immediate and physical energizing of the active power of the creature, disposing and pre-determining it efficaciously to the specific act, and also enabling it to do that act. Dabney, for instance, while admitting such a physical concurrence in the lower creation, denies it with respect to free agents. The great majority, however, maintain it also in the case of free moral beings. Even Dabney agrees that God's control over all of the acts of His creatures is certain, sovereign, and efficacious; and therefore must, along with the others, face the question as to the responsibility of God for sin. He gives his conclusion in the following words: "This, then, is my picture of the providential evolution of God's purpose as to sinful acts; so to arrange and group events and objects around free agents by his manifold wisdom and power, as to place each soul, at every step, in the presence of those circumstances, which,

He knows, will be a sufficient objective inducement to it to do, of its own native, free activity, just the thing called for by God's plan. Thus the act is man's alone, though its occurrence is efficaciously secured by God. And the sin is man's only. God's concern in it is holy, first, because all His personal agency in arranging to secure its occurrence was holy; and second, His ends or purposes are holy. God does not will the sin of the act, for the sake of its sinfulness; but only wills the result to which the act is a means, and that result is always worthy of His holiness."[1] The vast majority of Reformed theologians, however, maintain the concursus in question, and seek the solution of the difficulty by distinguishing between the *materia* and the *forma* of the sinful act, and by ascribing the latter exclusively to man. The divine concursus energizes man and determines him efficaciously to the specific act, but it is man who gives the act its formal quality, and who is therefore responsible for its sinful character. Neither one of these solutions can be said to give entire satisfaction, so that the problem of God's relation to sin remains a mystery.

D. Government.

1. NATURE OF THE DIVINE GOVERNMENT. The divine government may be defined as *that continued activity of God whereby He rules all things teleologically so as to secure the accomplishment of the divine purpose.* This government is not simply a part of divine providence but, just as preservation and concurrence, the whole of it, but now considered from the point of view of the end to which God is guiding all things in creation, namely, to the glory of His name.

a. *It is the government of God as King of the universe.* In the present day many regard the idea of God as King to be an antiquated Old Testament notion, and would substitute for it the New Testament idea of God as Father. The idea of divine sovereignty must make place for that of divine love. This is thought to be in harmony with the progressive idea of God in Scripture. But it is a mistake to think that divine revelation, as it rises to ever higher levels, intends to wean us gradually from the idea of God as King, and to substitute for it the idea of God as Father. This is already contradicted by the prominence of the idea of the Kingdom of God in the teachings of Jesus. And if it be said that this involves merely the idea of a special and limited kingship of God, it may be replied that the idea of the Fatherhood of God in the Gospels is subject to the same restrictions and limitations. Jesus does not teach a universal Fatherhood of God. Moreover, the New Testament also teaches the universal kingship of God in such passages as Matt. 11:25; Acts 17:24; I Tim. 1:17; 6:15; Rev. 1:6; 19:6. He is both King and Father, and is the source of all authority in heaven and on earth, the King of kings and the Lord of lords.

b. *It is a government adapted to the nature of the creatures which He governs.* In the physical world He has established the laws of nature, and it is by means of these laws that He administers the government of the physical universe. In the mental world He administers His government mediately through

---

1. *Syst. and Polemic Theol.*, p. 288.

the properties and laws of mind, and immediately, by the direct operation of the Holy Spirit. In the government and control of moral agents He makes use of all kinds of moral influences, such as circumstances, motives, instruction, persuasion, and example, but also works directly by the personal operation of the Holy Spirit on the intellect, the will, and the heart.

2. THE EXTENT OF THIS GOVERNMENT. Scripture explicitly declares this divine government to be universal, Ps. 22:28,29; 103:17-19; Dan. 4:34,35; I Tim. 6:15. It is really the execution of His eternal purpose, embracing all His works from the beginning, all that was or is or ever shall be. But while it is general, it also descends to particulars. The most insignificant things, Matt. 10:29-31, that which is seemingly accidental, Prov. 16:33, the good deeds of men, Phil. 2:13, as well as their evil deeds, Acts 14:16, — they are all under divine control. God is King of Israel, Isa. 33:22, but He also rules among the nations, Ps. 47:9. Nothing can be withdrawn from His government.

E. Extraordinary Providences or Miracles.

1. THE NATURE OF MIRACLES. A distinction is usually made between *providentia ordinaria* and *providentia extraordinaria*. In the former God works through second causes in strict accordance with the laws of nature, though He may vary the results by different combinations. But in the latter He works immediately or without the mediation of second causes in their ordinary operation. Says McPherson: "A miracle is something done without recourse to the ordinary means of production, a result called forth directly by the first cause without the mediation, at least in the usual way, of second causes."[1] The distinctive thing in the miraculous deed is that it results from the exercise of the supernatural power of God. And this means, of course, that it is not brought about by secondary causes that operate according to the laws of nature. If it were, it would not be *supernatural* (above nature), that is, it would not be a miracle. If God in the performance of a miracle did sometimes utilize forces that were present in nature, He used them in a way that was out of the ordinary, to produce unexpected results, and it was exactly this that constituted the miracle.[2] Every miracle is above the established order of nature, but we may distinguish different kinds, though not degrees, of miracles. There are miracles which are altogether above nature, so that they are in no way connected with any means. But there are also miracles which are *contra media*, in which means are employed, but in such a way that something results which is quite different from the usual result of those means.

2. THE POSSIBILITY OF MIRACLES. Miracles are objected to especially on the ground that they imply a violation of the laws of nature. Some seek to escape the difficulty by assuming with Augustine that they are merely exceptions to nature *as we know* it, implying that, if we had a fuller knowledge of nature, we would be able to account for them in a perfectly natural way. But this is an

1. *Chr. Dogm.*, p. 183. Cf. also Hodge, *Outlines of Theol.*, p. 275.
2. Cf. Mead, *Supernatural Revelation*, p. 110.

untenable position, since it assumes two orders of nature, which are contrary to each other. According to the one the oil in the cruse would decrease, but according to the other it did not diminish; according to the one the loaves would gradually be consumed, but according to the other they multiplied. It must further suppose that the one system is superior to the other, for if it were not, there would merely be a collision and nothing would result; but if it were, it would seem that the inferior order would gradually be overcome and disappear. Moreover, it robs the miracle of its exceptional character, while yet miracles stand out as exceptional events on the pages of Scripture.

There is undoubtedly a certain uniformity in nature; there are laws controlling the operation of second causes in the physical world. But let us remember that these merely represent God's *usual* method of working in nature. It is His good pleasure to work in an orderly way and through secondary causes. But this does not mean that He cannot depart from the established order, and cannot produce an extraordinary effect, which does not result from natural causes, by a single volition, if He deems it desirable for the end in view. When God works miracles, He produces extraordinary effects in a supernatural way. This means that miracles are *above* nature. Shall we also say that they are contrary to nature? Older Reformed theologians did not hesitate to speak of them as a breach or a violation of the laws of nature. Sometimes they said that in the case of a miracle the order of nature was temporarily suspended. Dr. Bruin maintains that this view is correct in his *Het Christelijk Geloof en de Beoefening der Natuur-wetenschap*, and takes exception to the views of Woltjer, Dennert, and Bavinck. But the correctness of that older terminology may well be doubted. When a miracle is performed the laws of nature are not violated, but superseded at a particular point by a higher manifestation of the will of God. The forces of nature are not annihilated or suspended, but are only counteracted at a particular point by a force superior to the powers of nature.

3. THE PURPOSE OF THE MIRACLES OF SCRIPTURE. It may be assumed that the miracles of Scripture were not performed arbitrarily, but with a definite purpose. They are not mere wonders, exhibitions of power, destined to excite amazement, but have revelational significance. The entrance of sin into the world makes the supernatural intervention of God in the course of events necessary for the destruction of sin and for the renewal of creation. It was by a miracle that God gave us both, His special verbal revelation in Scripture, and His supreme factual revelation in Jesus Christ. The miracles are connected with the economy of redemption, a redemption which they often prefigure and symbolize. They do not aim at a violation, but rather at a restoration of God's creative work. Hence we find cycles of miracles connected with special periods in the history of redemption, and especially during the time of Christ's public ministry and of the founding of the Church. These miracles did not yet result in the restoration of the physical universe. But at the end of time another series of miracles will follow, which will result in the renewal of nature to the

glory of God, — the final establishment of the Kingdom of God in a new heaven and on a new earth.

QUESTIONS FOR FURTHER STUDY. Is the doctrine of divine providence an *articulus purus* or an *articulus mixtus*? Who was the first one of the Church Fathers to develop this doctrine? How do Luther and Calvin differ in their conception of divine providence? What accounts for the fact that the Arminians accept the Socinian position on this point? How must we judge of the assertion of some Reformed theologians that God is the only true cause in the world? What are second causes, and why is it important to maintain that they are real causes? Does the doctrine of divine concursus conflict with the free agency of man? What was Augustine's conception of miracles? Why is it important to maintain the miraculous? Do miracles admit of a natural explanation? Do they imply a suspension of the laws of nature? What is the special significance of the miracles of the Bible? Can miracles happen even now? Do they still happen? What about the miracles of the Roman Catholic Church?

LITERATURE: Bavinck, *Geref. Dogm.* II, pp. 635-670; Kuyper, *Dict. Dogm., De Providentia*, pp. 3-246; Vos, *Geref. Dogm.*, I, *De Voorzienigheid*; Hodge, *Syst. Theol.* I, pp. 575-636; Shedd, *Dogm. Theol.* I, pp. 527-545; Dabney, *Syst. and Polem. Theol.*, pp. 276-291; McPherson, *Chr. Dogm.*, pp. 174-184; Drummond, *Studies in Chr. Doct.*, pp. 187-202; Pope, *Chr. Theol.*, I, pp. 437-456; Raymond, *Syst. Theol.*, I, pp. 497-527; Valentine, *Chr. Theol.*, pp. 363-382; Pieper, *Christl. Dogm.*, I, pp. 587-600; Schmidt, *Doct. Theol. of the Ev. Luth. Church*, pp. 179-201; Dijk, *De Voorzienigheid Gods*; Mozley, *On Miracles*; Thomson, *The Christian Miracles and the Conclusions of Science*; Mead, *Supernatural Revelation*; Harris, *God, Creator and Lord of All*, I, pp. 519-579; Bruin, *Het Christelijke Geloof en de Beoefening der Natuurwetenschap*, pp. 108-138.

Part Two

———

THE DOCTRINE OF MAN IN RELATION TO GOD

MAN IN HIS ORIGINAL STATE

I. The Origin of Man

A. The Doctrine of Man in Dogmatics.

The transition from Theology to Anthropology, that is, from the study of God to the study of man, is a natural one. Man is not only the crown of creation, but also the object of God's special care. And God's revelation in Scripture is a revelation that is not only given to man, but also a revelation in which man is vitally concerned. It is not a revelation of God in the abstract, but a revelation of God in relation to His creatures, and particularly in relation to man. It is a record of God's dealings with the human race, and especially a revelation of the redemption which God has prepared for, and for which He seeks to prepare, man. This accounts for the fact that man occupies a place of central importance in Scripture, and that the knowledge of man in relation to God is essential to its proper understanding. The doctrine of man must follow immediately after the doctrine of God, since the knowledge of it is presupposed in all the following loci of Dogmatics. We should not confuse the present subject of study with general Anthropology or the science of mankind, which includes all those sciences which have men as the object of study. These sciences concern themselves with the origin and history of mankind, with the physiological structure and the psychical characteristics of man in general and of the various races of mankind in particular, with their ethnological, linguistic, cultural and religious development, and so on. Theological Anthropology is concerned only with what the Bible says respecting man and the relation in which he stands and should stand to God. It recognizes Scripture only as its source, and reads the teachings of human experience in the light of God's Word.

B. Scriptural Account of Origin of Man.

Scripture offers us a twofold account of the creation of man, the one in Gen. 1:26,27, and the other in Gen. 2:7,21-23. Higher criticism is of the opinion that the writer of Genesis pieced together two creation narratives, the first found in Gen. 1:1—2:3, and the second in Gen. 2:4-25; and that these two are independent and contradictory. Laidlaw in his work on *The Bible Doctrine of Man*[1] is willing to admit that the author of Genesis made use of two sources, but refuses to find here two different accounts of creation. He very properly denies that in the second chapter we have "a different account of creation, for the plain reason that it takes no account of the creation at large." In fact, the introductory words of the narrative beginning with Gen. 2:4, "These are the generations of the heavens and of the earth, when they were created," seen in

---

1. pp. 25f.

the light of the repeated use of the words "these are the generations" in the book of Genesis, point to the fact that we have something quite different here. The expression invariably points, not to the origin or beginning of those named, but to their family history. The first narrative contains the account of the creation of all things in the order in which it occurred, while the second groups things in their relation to man, without implying anything respecting the chronological order of man's appearance in the creative work of God, and clearly indicates that everything preceding it served to prepare a fit habitation for man as the king of creation. It shows us how man was situated in God's creation, surrounded by the vegetable and animal world, and how he began his history. There are certain particulars in which the creation of man stands out in distinction from that of other living beings:

1. MAN'S CREATION WAS PRECEDED BY A SOLEMN DIVINE COUNSEL. Before the inspired writer records the creation of man, he leads us back, as it were, into the council of God, acquainting us with the divine decree in the words, "Let us make man in our image, after our likeness," Gen. 1:26. The Church has generally interpreted the plural "us" on the basis of the trinitarian existence of God. Some scholars, however, regard it as a plural of majesty; others, as a plural of communication, in which God includes the angels with Himself; and still others, as a plural of self-exhortation. Of these three suggestions the first is very unlikely, since the plural of majesty originated at a much later date; the second is impossible, because it would imply that the angels were co-creators with God, and that man is also created in the image of the angels, which is an un-Scriptural idea; and the third is an entirely gratuitous assumption, for which no reason can be assigned. Why should such a self-exhortation be in the plural, except for the reason that there is a plurality in God.

2. THE CREATION OF MAN WAS IN THE STRICTEST SENSE OF THE WORD AN IMMEDIATE ACT OF GOD. Some of the expressions used in the narrative preceding that of the creation of man indicate mediate creation in some sense of the word. Notice the following expressions: "And God said, Let the earth put forth grass, herbs, yielding seed, and fruit-trees bearing fruit after their kind" — "Let the waters swarm with swarms of living creatures" . . . and, "Let the earth bring forth living creatures after their kind"; and compare these with the simple statement, "And God created man." Whatever indication of mediacy in the work of creation is contained in the former expressions, is entirely wanting in the latter. Evidently the work of God in the creation of man was not mediated in any sense of the word. He did make use of pre-existent material in forming the body of man, but even this was excluded in the creation of the soul.

3. IN DISTINCTION FROM THE LOWER CREATURES MAN WAS CREATED AFTER A DIVINE TYPE. With respect to fishes, birds, and beasts we read that God created them *after their kind*, that is, on a typical form of their own. Man, however, was not so created and much less after the type of an inferior creature.

With respect to him God said, "Let us make man *in our image, after our likeness.*" We shall see what this implies, when we discuss the original condition of man, and merely call attention to it here, in order to bring out the fact that in the narrative of creation the creation of man stands out as something distinctive.

4. THE TWO DIFFERENT ELEMENTS OF HUMAN NATURE ARE CLEARLY DISTINGUISHED. In Gen. 2:7 a clear distinction is made between the origin of the body and that of the soul. The body was formed out of the dust of the ground; in the production of it God made use of pre-existing material. In the creation of the soul, however, there was no fashioning of pre-existing materials, but the production of a new substance. The soul of man was a new production of God in the strict sense of the word. Jehovah "breathed into his (man's) nostrils the breath of life; and man became a living soul." In these simple words the twofold nature of man is clearly asserted, and their teaching is corroborated by other passages of Scripture, such as, Eccl. 12:7; Matt. 10:28; Luke 8:55; II Cor. 5:1-8; Phil. 1:22-24; Heb. 12:9. The two elements are the body and the breath or spirit of life breathed into it by God, and by the combination of the two man became "a living soul," which means in this connection simply "a living being."

5. MAN IS AT ONCE PLACED IN AN EXALTED POSITION. Man is represented as standing at the apex of all the created orders. He is crowned as king of the lower creation, and is given dominion over all the inferior creatures. As such it was his duty and privilege to make all nature and all the created beings that were placed under his rule, subservient to his will and purpose, in order that he and his whole glorious dominion might magnify the almighty Creator and Lord of the universe, Gen. 1:28; Ps. 8:4-9.

C. The Evolutionary Theory of the Origin of Man.

Among the various theories that have been broached to explain the origin of man, the theory of evolution at present holds the field, and therefore deserves brief consideration.

1. STATEMENT OF THE THEORY. The theory of evolution is not always stated in the same form. It is sometimes represented as if man is a direct descendant of one of the species of anthropoid apes now in existence, and then again, as if man and the higher apes have a common ancestry. But whatever difference of opinion there may be on this point, it is certain that, according to thorough-going naturalistic evolution, man descended from the lower animals, body and soul, by a perfectly natural process, controlled entirely by inherent forces. One of the leading principles of the theory is that of strict continuity between the animal world and man. It cannot allow for discontinuity anywhere along the line, for every break is fatal to the theory. Nothing that is absolutely new and unpredictable can appear in the process. What is now found in man must have been potentially present in the original germ out of

which all things developed. And the whole process must be controlled from start to finish by inherent forces. Theistic evolution, which seems more acceptable to many theologians, simply regards evolution as God's method of working. It is sometimes represented in a form in which God is merely called in to bridge the gaps between the inorganic and the organic, and between the irrational and the rational, creation. But to the extent to which a special operation of God is assumed, gaps are admitted which evolution cannot bridge, and something new is called into being, the theory naturally ceases to be a pure theory of evolution. It is sometimes held that only the body of man is derived by a process of evolution from the lower animals, and that God endowed this body with a rational soul. This view meets with considerable favor in Roman Catholic circles.

2. OBJECTIONS TO THE THEORY. Several objections can be raised against the theory of the evolutionary descent of man from the lower animals.

a. From the point of view of the theologian the greatest objection to this theory is, of course, that it is contrary to the explicit teachings of the Word of God. The Bible could hardly teach more clearly than it does that man is the product of a direct and special creative act of God, rather than of a process of development out of the simian stock of animals. It asserts that God formed man out of the dust of the ground, Gen. 2:7. Some theologians, in their eagerness to harmonize the teachings of Scripture with the theory of evolution, suggest that this may be interpreted to mean that God formed the body of man out of the body of the animals, *which is after all but dust.* But this is entirely unwarranted, since no reason can be assigned why the general expression "of the dust of the ground" should be used after the writer had already described the creation of the animals and might therefore have made the statement far more specific. Moreover, this interpretation is also excluded by the statement in Gen. 3:19, "In the sweat of thy face shalt thou eat bread, till thou return unto the ground: for out of it wast thou taken: for dust thou art, and unto dust shalt thou return." This certainly does not mean that man shall return to his former animal state. Beast and man alike return again to the dust. Eccl. 3:19,20. Finally, we are told explicitly in I Cor. 15:39 that "All flesh is not the same flesh: but there is one flesh of men, and another flesh of beasts." As to the spirit of man the Bible teaches explicitly that it came directly from God, Gen. 2:7, and therefore cannot be regarded as a natural development of some previously existing substance. In perfect harmony with this Elihu says, "The Spirit of God hath made me, and the breath of the Almighty giveth me life," Job 33:4. Furthermore, Scripture also teaches that man was at once separated from the lower creation by an enormous chasm. He at once stood on a high intellectual, moral, and religious level, as created in the image of God and was given dominion over the lower creation, Gen. 1:26,27,31; 2:19,20; Ps. 8:5-8. By his fall in sin, however, he fell from his high estate and became subject to a process of degeneration which sometimes results in bestiality. This is quite the opposite of what the evolutionary hypothesis teaches us. According to it man stood on the lowest level at the beginning of his career, but slightly removed from the brute, and has been rising to higher levels ever since.

b. The second great objection is that the theory has no adequate basis in well established facts. It should be borne in mind that, as was pointed out before, the evolutionary theory in general, though often represented as an established doctrine, is up to the present time nothing but an unproved working hypothesis, and a hypothesis that has not yet given any great promise of success in demonstrating what it set out to prove. Many of the most prominent evolutionists frankly admit the hypothetical character of their theory. They still avow themselves to be firm believers in the doctrine of descent, but do not hesitate to say that they cannot speak with any assurance of its method of operation. When Darwin published his works, it was thought that the key to the process was found at last, but in course of time it was found that the key did not fit the lock. Darwin truly said that his theory depended entirely on the possibility of transmitting acquired characteristics, and it soon became one of the corner-stones of Weismann's biological theory that acquired characteristics are not inherited. His opinion received abundant confirmation by the later study of genetics. On the basis of the assumed transmission of acquired characteristics, Darwin spoke with great assurance of the transmutation of species and envisaged a continuous line of development from the primordial cell to man; but the experiments of De Vries, Mendel, and others tended to discredit his view. The gradual and imperceptible changes of Darwin made place for the sudden and unexpected mutations of De Vries. While Darwin assumed endless variation in several directions, Mendel pointed out that the variations or mutations never take the organism outside of the species and are subject to a definite law. And modern cytology in its study of the cell. with its genes and chromosones as the carriers of the inherited characters, confirmed this idea. The so-called new species of the evolutionists were proved to be no true species at all, but only varietal species, that is varieties of the same species. Nordenskioeld in his *History of Biology* quotes the following sentence from a popular account of the results of heredity research, as reflecting the true state of affairs: "For the very reason of the great number of facts that modern heredity-research has brought to light, chaos prevails at present in regard to the views on the formation of species," p. 613. Prominent evolutionists now frankly admit that the origin of species is a complete mystery to them. And as long as that is so, there is not much chance of their explaining the origin of man.

Darwin in his attempt to prove the descent of man from a species of anthropoid apes relied on (1) the argument from the structural similarity between man and the higher animals; (2) the embryological argument; and (3) the argument from rudimentary organs. To these three were added later on, (4) the argument derived from blood tests; and (5) the palaeontological argument. But none of these arguments furnish the desired proof. The argument from structural likeness unwarrantably assumes that the similarity can be explained in only one way. Yet it can very well be accounted for by the assumption that God in creating the animal world made certain typical forms basic throughout, so as to have unity in variety, just as a great musician builds up his mighty composition on a single theme, which is repeated time and again, and at each repetition introduces new variations. The principle of preformation gives an adequate explanation of the similarities under consideration. The embryological similarity, such as it is, can be explained on the same principle. Moreover recent biological studies would seem to indicate that no structural similarity but only a genetic relationship can prove affinity or descent. As far as the rudimentary organs are concerned, more than one scientist has expressed doubt as to their vestigial character. Instead of being the useless remains of animal organs, it may very well be that they serve a definite purpose in the human organism. The blood tests in their original form, while pointing to a certain likeness between the blood of animals and man, do not prove genetic relationship, since in these tests only part of the blood, the sterile serum which contains no living matter, was used, while it is an established fact that the solid portion of the blood, containing the red and white cells, is the carrier of hereditary factors. Later tests, in which the spectroscope was called into use and the entire blood was examined, proved conclusively that there is an essential difference between the blood of animals and that of man. The palaeontological argument is equally inconclusive. If man really descended from the anthropoid apes, it might be expected that the intermediate forms would be in existence somewhere. But Darwin was not able to find this missing link any more than the thousands of missing links between the various species of animals. We are told that the early progenitors of man have long since died out. This being so, it was still possible that they might be found among the fossil remains. And to-day scientists actually claim that they have found some bones of very ancient men. They have reconstructed these men for us, and we can now enjoy looking at the imaginary photos of the reconstructed Java man (*Pithecanthropus erectus*), the Heidelberg man (*Homo Heidelbergensis* , the Neanderthal man (*Homo Neanderthalensis*), the Cro-Magnon, the Piltdown man, and others. These reconstructions seem to be taken seriously by some, but really have very little value. Since only a few bones were found of each, and even these were scattered in some cases, so that it is not certain that they belong to the same body, they merely testify to the ingenuity of the scientists who reconstructed them. In some cases the specialists are by no means agreed as to whether the bones in question belonged to a man or to an animal. Dr. Wood, professor of anatomy in the University of London, says in a booklet on the *Ancestry of Man*: "I find no occupation less worthy of the science of Anthropology than the not unfashionable business of modelling, painting, or drawing these nightmare pictures of the imagination, and lending them in the process, an utterly false value of apparent reality."[1] Fleming, one of the most prominent present day scientists, says: "The

---

1. Quoted by Allen, *Evolution in the Balances*. p. 110.

upshot of it all is that we cannot arrange all the known fossil remains of supposed 'man' in a lineal series gradually advancing in type or form from that of any anthropoid ape, or other mammal, up to the modern and now existing types of true man. Any supposition or statement that it can be done, and is true, is certainly incorrect. It is certainly misleading and unspeakably pernicious to put forward in popular magazines or other publications read by children pictures of gorillas or chimpanzees labelled 'Man's cousin' or 'Man's nearest relative,' or to publish perfectly imaginary and grotesque pictures of a supposed 'Java man' with brutish face as an ancestor of modern man, as is occasionally done. Those who do such things are guilty of ignorance or deliberate misrepresentation. Neither is it justifiable for preachers in the pulpit to tell their congregations that there is general agreement among scientific men as to the evolutionary origin of Man from an animal ancestor."[1] But the body of man does not even present the greatest difficulties to the evolutionist. These arise from the consideration of the spiritual element in man, or what is usually called "the origin of mind." It is at this point that his helplessness becomes most painfully apparent. In spite of all his attempts, he has signally failed to give a plausible explanation of the origin of the human mind, or intelligence (progressiveness), language, conscience, and religion. This might be pointed out in detail, but we do not deem it necessary. There are many who, like Dennert and Batison, still profess to believe in the doctrine of descent, but disown the Darwinian method of evolution and regard it as a well-nigh complete failure. Yet they know of no other method which might take its place. This means that for them evolution has ceased to be a science, and has become once more a mere philosophical theory. Batison said: "We read his (Darwin's) scheme of evolution as we would those of Lucretius or of Lamarck. . . . We are just about where Boyle was in the seventeenth century." The testimony of Dr. D. H. Scott is very similar. In a presidential address before the British Association for the Advancement of Science he made the following statements: "All is again in the melting-pot. . . . Is evolution, then, not a scientifically established fact? No, it is not . . . It is an act of faith — because there is no alternative." Creation, of course, is not to be thought of. He further said that there is in natural science "a return to pre-Darwinian chaos." Dr. Fleischmann of Erlangen writes: "The Darwinian theory has not a single fact to support it . . . is purely the product of the imagination." Even stronger is the assertion of Dr. B. Kidd: "Darwinism is a compound of astonishing presumption and incomparable ignorance."[2] Such scientists as Fleming, Dawson, Kelly, and Price do not hesitate to reject the theory of evolution and to accept the doctrine of creation. Respecting the origin of man, Sir William Dawson says: "I know nothing about the origin of man, except what I am told in the Scripture — that God created him. I do not know anything more than that, and I do not

---

1. *The Origin of Mankind*, p. 75.
2. Quotations taken from Zerbe, *Christianity and False Evolution*, pp. 271f.

know of anyone who does."[1] Fleming says: "All that science can say at present in the light of definitely ascertained and limited human knowledge is that it does not know, and has no certain proof,how, where, and when man was originated. If any true knowledge of it is to come to us, it must come from some source other than present modern anthropology."[2]

D. The Origin of Man and the Unity of the Roce.

1. SCRIPTURE TESTIMONY TO THE UNITY OF THE RACE. Scripture teaches that the whole human race descended from a single pair. This is the obvious sense of the opening chapters of Genesis. God created Adam and Eve as the beginning of the human species, and commanded them to be fruitful and multiply, and replenish the earth. Moreover, the subsequent narrative in Genesis clearly shows that the following generations down to the time of the flood stood in unbroken genetic relation with the first pair, so that the human race constitutes not only a specific unity, a unity in the sense that all men share the same human nature, but also a genetic or genealogical unity. This is also taught by Paul in Acts 17:26, "And God made of one every nation of man to dwell on all the face of the earth." The same truth is basic to the organic unity of the human race in the first transgression, and of the provision for the salvation of the race in Christ, Rom. 5:12,19; I Cor. 15:21,22. This unity of the race is not to be understood realistically, as it is represented by Shedd, who says: "Human nature is a specific or general substance created in and with the first individuals of a human species, which is not yet individualized, but which by ordinary generation is subdivided into parts, and those parts are formed into distinct and separate individuals of the species. The one specific substance, by propagation, is metamorphosed into millions of individual substances, or persons. An individual is a fractional part of human nature separated from the common mass, and constituted a particular person, having all the essential properties of human nature."[3] The objections to this view will be stated in another connection.

2. THE TESTIMONY OF SCIENCE TO THE UNITY OF THE RACE. Science in various ways confirms the testimony of Scripture as to the unity of the human race. Scientific men have not always believed in this. The ancient Greeks had their theory of autochtonism, to the effect that men sprang from the earth by a sort of spontaneous generation, a theory that has no solid foundation whatever, since spontaneous generation has never been proved but rather discredited. Agassiz propounded the theory of the Coadamites, which assumes that there were different centers of creation. As early as 1655 Peyrerius developed the theory of the Preadamites, which proceeds on the assumption that there were men before Adam was created. This theory was revived by Winchell, who did not deny the unity of the race, but regarded Adam as the first ancestor of

1. Quoted by W. Bell Dawson, *The Bible Confirmed by Science*, p. 146. Cf. also what the later Dawson says in Chap. VIII.
2. *The Origin of Mankind*, p. 76.
3. *Dogm. Theol.* II, p. 72.

the Jews rather than as the head of the human race. And in recent years Fleming, without being dogmatic in the matter, says that there are reasons to assume that there were inferior races of man preceding the appearance of Adam on the scene about 5500 B.C. While inferior to the Adamites, they already had powers distinct from those of the animals. The later Adamic man was endowed with greater and nobler powers and probably destined to bring the whole of the other existing humanity into allegiance to the Creator. He failed to preserve his own allegiance to God, and therefore God provided for the coming of a descendant who was human and yet far more than man, in order that He might accomplish what the Adamic man failed to do. The view which Fleming has been led to hold is "that the unquestionably Caucasian branch is alone the derivation by normal generation from the Adamic race, namely, from the God-worshipping members of the Adamic race which survived the flood — Noah and his sons and daughters."[1] But these theories, one and all, find no support in Scripture, and are contrary to Acts 17:26 and to all that the Bible teaches concerning the apostasy and deliverance of man. Moreover, science presents several arguments in favor of the unity of the human race, such as:

a. *The argument from history.* The traditions of the race of men point decisively to a common origin and ancestry in Central Asia. The history of the migrations of man tends to show that there has been a distribution from a single center.

b. *The argument from philology.* The study of the languages of mankind indicates a common origin. The Indo-Germanic languages are traced to a common primitive tongue, an old remnant of which still exists in the Sanskrit language. Moreover, there is evidence which goes to show that the old Egyptian is the connecting link between the Indo-European and the Semitic tongue.

c. *The argument from psychology.* The soul is the most important part of the constitutional nature of man, and psychology clearly reveals the fact that the souls of all men, to whatever tribes or nations they may belong, are essentially the same. They have in common the same animal appetites, instincts, and passions, the same tendencies and capacities, and above all the same higher qualities, the mental and moral characteristics that belong exclusively to man.

d. *The argument from natural science or physiology.* It is now the common judgment of comparative physiologists that the human race constitutes but a single species. The differences that exist between the various families of mankind are regarded simply as varieties of this one species. Science does not positively assert that the human race descended from a single pair, but nevertheless demonstrates that this may have been the case and probably is.

---

1. Cf. *The Origin of Mankind,* Chaps. VI and VII.

QUESTIONS FOR FURTHER STUDY: What can be said against the view that we have in Gen. 1 and 2 two different and more or less contradictory accounts of creation? Does it seem reasonable to think that the world existed millions of years before man appeared on the scene? Is the hypothesis of theistic evolution in harmony with the Scriptural account of the origin of man? Is the notion that the body of man at least is derived from the animals tenable in the light of Scripture? Has evolution established its case on this point? What has it proved in connection with the far more difficult question of the derivation of the human soul? What becomes of the doctrine of the fall in the theory of evolution? What is the theological significance of the doctrine of the unity of the human race?

LITERATURE: Bavinck, *Geref. Dogm.* II pp. 543-565,; Hodge, *Syst. Theol.* II, pp. 3-41; Litton, *Introd. to Dogm. Theol.*, pp. 107-113; Miley, *Syst. Theol.* I, pp. 355-392; Alexander, *Syst. of Bibl. Theol.* I, pp. 156-167; Laidlaw, *The Bible Doct. of Man*, pp. 24-46; Darwin, *Descent of Man*; Drummond, *The Ascent of Man*; Fleming, *The Origin of Mankind*; O'Toole, *The Case Against Evolution*, Part II, Chaps. II and III. Cf. further the works on Evolution referred to at the end of the previous chapter.

II. The Constitutional Nature of Man

The previous chapter is of a more or less introductory nature, and does not, strictly speaking, form an integral part of the systematic presentation of the doctrine of man in dogmatics. This explains why many treatises on systematic theology fail to devote a separate chapter to the origin of man. Yet it seemed desirable to insert it here, since it furnishes a fitting background for what follows. Under the present caption we shall consider the essential constituents of human nature, and the question of the origin of the soul in the individuals that constitute the race.

A. The Constituent Elements of Human Nature.

1. THE DIFFERENT VIEWS THAT WERE CURRENT IN HISTORY: DICHOTOMY AND TRICHOTOMY. It is customary, especially in Christian circles, to conceive of man as consisting of two, and only two, distinct parts, namely, body and soul. This view is technically called *dichotomy*. Alongside of it, however, another made its appearance, to the effect that human nature consists of three parts, body, soul, and spirit. It is designated by the term *trichotomy*. The tri-partite conception of man originated in Greek philosophy, which conceived of the relation of the body and the spirit of man to each other after the analogy of the mutual relation between the material universe and God. It was thought that, just as the latter could enter into communion with each other only by means of a third substance or an intermediate being, so the former could enter into mutual vital relationships only by means of a third or intermediate element, namely, the soul. The soul was regarded as, on the one hand, immaterial, and on the other, adapted to the body. In so far as it appropriated the *nous* or pneuma, it was regarded as immortal, but in so far as it was related to the body, as carnal and mortal. The most familiar but also the crudest form of trichotomy is that which takes the body for the material part of man's nature, the soul as the principle of animal life, and the spirit as the God-related rational and immortal element in man. The trichotomic conception of man found considerable favor with the Greek or Alexandrian Church Fathers of the early Christian centuries. It is found, though not always in exactly the same form, in Clement of Alexandria, Origen, and Gregory of Nyssa. But after Apollinaris employed it in a manner impinging on the perfect humanity of Jesus, it was gradually discredited. Some of the Greek Fathers still adhered to it, though Athanasius and Theodoret explicitly repudiated it. In the Latin Church the leading theologians distinctly favored the twofold division of

human nature. It was especially the psychology of Augustine that gave prominence to this view. During the Middle Ages it had become a matter of common belief. The Reformation brought no change in this respect, though a few lesser lights defended the trichotomic theory. The Roman Catholic Church adhered to the verdict of Scholasticism, but in the circles of Protestantism other voices were heard. During the nineteenth century trichotomy was revived in some form or other by certain German and English theologians, as Roos, Olshausen, Beck, Delitzsch, Auberlen, Oehler, White, and Heard; but it did not meet with great favor in the theological world. The recent advocates of this theory do not agree as to the nature of the *psuche,* nor as to the relation in which it stands to the other elements in man's nature. Delitzsch conceives of it as an efflux of the *pneuma,* while Beck, Oehler, and Heard, regard it as the point of union between the body and the spirit. Delitzsch is not altogether consistent and occasionally seems to waver, and Beck and Oehler admit that the Biblical representation of man is fundamentally dichotomic. Their defense of a Biblical trichotomy can hardly be said to imply the existence of three distinct elements in man. Besides these two theological views there were, especially in the last century and a half, also the philosophical views of absolute Materialism and of absolute Idealism, the former sacrificing the soul to the body, and the latter, the body to the soul.

2. THE TEACHINGS OF SCRIPTURE AS TO THE CONSTITUENT ELEMENTS OF HUMAN NATURE. The prevailing representation of the nature of man in Scripture is clearly dichotomic. On the one hand the Bible teaches us to view the nature of man as a unity, and not as a duality, consisting of two different elements, each of which move along parallel lines but do not really unite to form a single organism. The idea of a mere parallelism between the two elements of human nature, found in Greek philosophy and also in the works of some later philosophers, is entirely foreign to Scripture. While recognizing the complex nature of man, it never represents this as resulting in a twofold subject in man. Every act of man is seen as an act of the whole man. It is not the soul but man that sins; it is not the body but man that dies; and it is not merely the soul, but man, body and soul, that is redeemed in Christ. This unity already finds expression in the classical passage of the Old Testament — the first passage to indicate the complex nature of man — namely, Gen. 2:7: "And Jehovah God formed man of the dust of the ground, and breathed into his nostrils the breath of life; and man became a living soul." The whole passage deals with man: "God formed man . . . and man became a living soul." This work of God should not be interpreted as a mechanical process, as if He first formed a body of clay and then put a soul into it. When God formed the body, He formed it so that by the breath of His Spirit man at once became a living soul. Job 33:4; 32:8. The word "soul" in this passage does not have the meaning which we usually ascribe to it — a meaning rather foreign to the Old Testament — but denotes an animated being, and is a description of man as a whole. The very same Hebrew term, *nephesh chayyah*

(living soul or being) is also applied to the animals in Gen. 1:21,24,30. So this passage, while indicating that there are two elements in man, yet stresses the organic unity of man. And this is recognized throughout the Bible. At the same time it also contains evidences of the dual composition of man's nature. We should be careful, however, not to expect the later distinction between the body as the material element, and the soul as the spiritual element, of human nature, in the Old Testament. This distinction came into use later on under the influence of Greek philosophy. The antithesis — soul and body — even in its New Testament sense, is not yet found in the Old Testament. In fact, the Hebrew has no word for the body as an organism. The Old Testament distinction of the two elements of human nature is of a different kind. Says Laidlaw in his work on *The Bible Doctrine of Man:*[1] "The antithesis is clearly that of lower and higher, earthly and heavenly, animal and divine. It is not so much two elements, as two factors uniting in a single and harmonious result, — 'man became a living soul.' " It is quite evident that this is the distinction in Gen. 2:7. Cf. also Job 27:3; 32:8; 33:4; Eccl. 12:7. A variety of words is used in the Old Testament to denote the lower element in man or parts of it, such as "flesh," "dust," "bones," "bowels," "kidneys," and also the metaphorical expression "house of clay," Job 4:19. And there are also several words to denote the higher element, such as "spirit;" "soul," "heart," and "mind." As soon as we pass from the Old to the New Testament, we meet with the antithetic expressions that are most familiar to us, as "body and soul," "flesh and spirit." The corresponding Greek words were undoubtedly moulded by Greek philosophical thought, but passed through the Septuagint into the New Testament, and therefore retained their Old Testament force. At the same time the antithetic idea of the material and the immaterial is now also connected with them.

Trichotomists seek support in the fact that the Bible, as they see it, recognizes two constituent parts of human nature in addition to the lower or material element, namely, the soul (Heb., *nephesh;* Greek, *psuche*) and the spirit (Heb., *ruach;* Greek, *pneuma*). But the fact that these terms are used with great frequency in Scripture does not warrant the conclusion that they designate component parts rather than different aspects of human nature. A careful study of Scripture clearly shows that it uses the words interchangeably. Both terms denote the higher or spiritual element in man, but contemplate it from different points of view. It should be pointed out at once, however, that the Scriptural distinction of the two does not agree with that which is rather common in philosophy, that the soul is the spiritual element in man, as it is related to the animal world, while the spirit is that same element in its relation to the higher spiritual world and to God. The following facts militate against this philosophical distinction: *Ruach-pneuma,* as well as *nephesh-psuche,* is used of the brute creation, Eccl. 3:21; Rev. 16:3. The word *psuche* is even used with reference to Jehovah, Isa. 42:1; Jer. 9:9; Amos 6:8 (Heb.); Heb

1. p. 60.

10:38. The disembodied dead are called *psuchai*, Rev. 6:9;20:4. The highest exercises of religion are ascribed to the *psuche*, Mark 12:30; Luke 1:46; Heb. 6:18,19; Jas. 1:21. To lose the *psuche* is to lose all. It is perfectly evident that the Bible uses the two words interchangeably. Notice the parallelism in Luke 1:46,47: "My soul doth magnify the Lord, and my spirit hath rejoiced in God my Saviour." The Scriptural formula for man is in some passages "body and soul," Matt. 6:25; 10:28; and in others, "body and spirit," Eccl. 12:7; I Cor. 5:3,5. Death is sometimes described as the giving up of the soul, Gen. 35:18; I Kings 17:21; Acts 15:26; and then again as the giving up of the spirit, Ps. 31:5; Luke 23:46; Acts 7:59. Moreover both "soul" and "spirit" are used to designate the immaterial element of the dead, I Pet. 3:19; Heb. 12:23; Rev. 6:9; 20:4. The main Scriptural distinction is as follows: the word "spirit" designates the spiritual element in man as the principle of life and action which controls the body; while the word "soul" denominates the same element as the subject of action in man, and is therefore often used for the personal pronoun in the Old Testament, Ps. 10:1,2; 104:1; 146:1; Is. 42:1; cf. also Luke 12:19. In several instances it, more specifically, designates the inner life as the seat of the affections. All this is quite in harmony with Gen. 2:7, "And Jehovah God . . . breathed into his nostrils the breath of life; and man became a living soul." Thus it may be said that man *has* spirit, but *is* soul. The Bible therefore points to two, and only two, constitutional elements in the nature of man, namely, body and spirit or soul. This Scriptural representation is also in harmony with the self-consciousness of man. While man is conscious of the fact that he consists of a material and a spiritual element, no one is conscious of possessing a soul in distinction from a spirit.

There are two passages, however, that seem to conflict with the usual dichotomic representation of Scripture, namely, I Thess. 5:23, "And the God of peace Himself sanctify you wholly; and may your spirit and soul and body be preserved entire, without blame at the coming of our Lord Jesus Christ"; and Heb. 4:12, "For the word of God is living, and active, and sharper than any two-edged sword, and piercing even to the dividing of soul and spirit, of both joints and marrow, and quick to discern the thoughts and intents of the heart." But it should be noted that: (a) It is a sound rule in exegesis that exceptional statements should be interpreted in the light of the *analogia Scriptura*, the usual representation of Scripture. In view of this fact some of the defenders of trichotomy admit that these passages do not necessarily prove their point. (b) The mere mention of spirit and soul alongside of each other does not prove that, according to Scripture, they are two distinct substances, any more than Matt. 22:37 proves that Jesus regarded heart and soul and mind as three distinct substances. (c) In I Thess. 5:23 the apostle simply desires to strengthen the statement, "And the God of peace Himself sanctify you wholly," by an epexigetical statement, in which the different aspects of man's existence are summed up, and in which he feels perfectly free to mention soul and spirit alongside of each other, because the Bible distinguishes between the two. He cannot very well have thought of them as two different substances here, because he speaks elsewhere of man as consisting of two parts, Rom. 8:10; I Cor. 5:5; 7:34; II Cor. 7:1; Eph. 2:3; Col. 2:5. (d) Heb. 4:12 should not be taken to mean that the word of God, penetrating to the inner man, makes a separation between his soul and his spirit, which would naturally imply that these two are different substances; but simply as declaring that it brings about a separation in both between the thoughts and intents of the heart.[1]

3. THE RELATION OF BODY AND SOUL TO EACH OTHER. The exact relation of body and soul to each other has been represented in various ways, but remains to a great extent a mystery. The following are the most important theories relating to this point:

a. *Monistic.* There are theories which proceed on the assumption that body and soul are of the same primitive substance. According to Materialism this primitive substance is matter, and spirit is a product of matter. And according to absolute Idealism and Spiritualism the primitive substance is spirit, and this becomes objective to itself in what is called matter. Matter is a product of the spirit. The objection to this monistic view is that things so different as body and soul cannot be deduced the one from the other.

b. *Dualistic.* Some theories proceed on the assumption that there is an essential duality of matter and spirit, and present their mutual relations in various ways: (1) *Occasionalism.* According to this theory, suggested by Cartesius, matter and spirit each works, according to laws peculiar to itself, and these laws are so different that there is no possibility of joint action. What appears to be such can only be accounted for on the principle that, on the occasion of the action of the one, God by His direct agency produces a corresponding action in the other. (2) *Parallelism.* Leibnitz proposed the theory of pre-established harmony. This also rests on the assumption that there is no direct interaction between the material and the spiritual, but does not assume that God produces apparently joint actions by continual interference. Instead it holds that God made the body and the soul so that the one perfectly corresponds to the other. When a motion takes place in the body, there is a corresponding movement in the soul, according to a law of pre-established harmony. (3) *Realistic Dualism.* The simple facts to which we must always return, and which are embodied in the theory of realistic dualism, are the following: body and soul are distinct substances, which do interact, though their mode of interaction escapes human scrutiny and remains a mystery for us. The union between the two may be called a union of life: the two are organically related, the soul acting on the body and the body on the soul. Some of the actions of the body are dependent on the *conscious*

---

1. Cf. for a discussion of the psychology of Scripture especially, Bavinck, *Bijbelsche en Religionize Psychologie;* Laidlaw, *The Bible Doctrine of Man,* pp. 49-138; H. Wheeler Robinson, *The Christian Doctrine of Man,* pp. 4-150; Delitzsch, *System of Biblical Psychology;* Dickson, *St. Paul's Use of Terms Flesh and Spirit.*

operation of the soul, while others are not. The operations of the soul are connected with the body as its instrument in the present life; but from the continued conscious existence and activity of the soul after death it appears that it can also work without the body. This view is certainly in harmony with the representations of Scripture on this point. A great deal of present day psychology is definitely moving in the direction of materialism. Its most extreme form is seen in Behaviorism with its denial of the soul, of the mind, and even of consciousness. All that it has left as an object of study is human behavior.

B. The Origin of the Soul in the Individual.

1. HISTORICAL VIEWS RESPECTING THE ORIGIN OF THE SOUL. Greek philosophy devoted considerable attention to the problem of the human soul and did not fail to make its influence felt in Christian theology. The nature, the origin, and the continued existence of the soul, were all subjects of discussion. Plato believed in the pre-existence and transmigration of the soul. In the early Church the doctrine of the pre-existence of the soul was practically limited to the Alexandrian school. Origen was the chief representative of this view and combined it with the notion of a pre-temporal fall. Two other views at once made their appearance and proved to be far more popular in Christian circles. The theory of creationism holds that God creates a new soul at the birth of every individual. It was the dominant theory in the Eastern Church, and also found some advocates in the West. Jerome and Hilary of Pictavium were its most prominent representatives. In the Western Church the theory of Traducianism gradually gained ground. According to this view the soul as well as the body of man originates by propagation. It is usually wedded to the realistic theory that human nature was created in its entirety by God and is ever-increasingly individualized as the human race multiplies. Tertullian was the first to state this theory of Traducianism and under his influence it continued to gain favor in the North African and Western Church. It seemed to fit in best with the doctrine of the transmission of sin that was current in those circles. Leo the Great called it the teaching of the catholic faith. In the East it found no favorable reception. Augustine hesitated to choose between the two views. Some of the earlier Scholastics were somewhat undecided, though they regarded creationism as the more probable of the two; but in course of time it became the consensus of opinion among the Schoolmen that the individual souls were created. Says Peter the Lombard: "The Church teaches that souls are created at their infusion into the body." And Thomas Aquinas went even further by saying: "It is heretical to say that the intellectual soul is transmitted by way of generation." This remained the prevailing view in the Roman Catholic Church. From the days of the Reformation there was a difference of opinion among the Protestants. Luther expressed himself in favor of Traducianism, and this became the prevailing opinion in the Lutheran Church. Calvin, on the other hand, decidedly favored creationism. Says he in his

commentary on Gen. 3:16: "Nor is it necessary to resort to that ancient figment of certain writers, that souls are derived by descent from our first parents." Ever since the days of the Reformation this has been the common view in Reformed circles. This does not mean that there were no exceptions to the rule. Jonathan Edwards and Hopkins in New England theology favored Traducianism. Julius Mueller in his work on *The Christian Doctrine of Sin* again put up an argument in favor of the pre-existence of the soul, coupled with that of a pre-temporal fall, in order to explain the origin of sin.

2. PRE-EXISTENTIANISM. Some speculative theologians, among whom Origen, Scotus Erigena, and Julius Mueller are the most important, advocated the theory that the souls of men existed in a previous state, and that certain occurrences in that former state account for the condition in which those souls are now found. Origen looks upon man's present material existence, with all its inequalities and irregularities, physical and moral, as a punishment for sins committed in a previous existence. Scotus Erigena also holds that sin made its entrance into the world of humanity in the pre-temporal state, and that therefore man begins his career on earth as a sinner. And Julius Mueller has recourse to the theory, in order to reconcile the doctrines of the universality of sin and of individual guilt. According to him each person must have sinned willingly in that previous existence.

This theory is open to several objections. (a) It is absolutely devoid of both Scriptural and philosophical grounds, and is, at least in some of its forms, based on the dualism of matter and spirit as taught in heathen philosophy, making it a punishment for the soul to be connected with the body. (b) It really makes the body something accidental. The soul was without the body at first, and received this later on. Man was complete without the body. This virtually wipes out the distinction between man and the angels. (c) It destroys the unity of the human race, for it assumes that all individual souls existed long before they entered the present life. They do not constitute a race. (d) It finds no support in the consciousness of man. Man has absolutely no consciousness of such a previous existence; nor does he feel that the body is a prison or a place of punishment for the soul. In fact, he dreads the separation of body and soul as something that is unnatural.

3. TRADUCIANISM. According to Traducianism the souls of men are propagated along with the bodies by generation, and are therefore transmitted to the children by the parents. In the early Church Tertullian, Rufinus, Apollinarus, and Gregory of Nyssa were Traducianists. From the days of Luther Traducianism has been the prevailing view of the Lutheran Church. Among the Reformed it is favored by H. B. Smith and Shedd. A. H. Strong also prefers it.

a. *Arguments in favor of Traducianism.* Several arguments are adduced in favor of this theory. (1) It is said to be favored by the Scriptural representation (a) that God but once breathed into man's nostrils the breath of

life, and then left it to man to propagate the species, Gen. 1:28; 2:7; (b) that
the creation of Eve's soul was included in that of Adam, since she is said to
be "of the man" (I Cor. 11:8), and nothing is said about the creation of her
soul, Gen. 2:23; (c) that God ceased from the work of creation after He
had made man, Gen. 2:2; and (d) that descendants are said to be in the loins
of their fathers, Gen. 46:26; Heb. 7:9,10. Cf. also such passages as John 3:6;
1:13; Rom. 1:3; Acts 17:26. (2) It is supported by the analogy of vegetable
and animal life, in which the increase in numbers is secured, not by a continually increasing number of immediate creations, but by the natural derivation
of new individuals from a parent stock. But cf. Ps. 104:30. (3) It also seeks
support in the inheritance of mental peculiarities and family traits, which are
so often just as noticeable as physical resemblances, and which cannot be
accounted for by education or example, since they are in evidence even when
parents do not live to bring up their children. (4) Finally, it seems to offer
the best basis for the explanation of the inheritance of moral and spiritual
depravity, which is a matter of the soul rather than of the body. It is quite
common to combine with Traducianism the realistic theory to account for
original sin.

b. *Objections to Traducianism.* Several objections may be urged against
this theory. (1) It is contrary to the philosophical doctrine of the simplicity
of the soul. The soul is a pure spiritual substance that does not admit of
division. The propagation of the soul would seem to imply that the soul of
the child separates itself in some way from the soul of the parents. Moreover,
the difficult question arises, whether it originates from the soul of the father
or from that of the mother. Or does it come from both; and if so, is it not
a compositum? (2) In order to avoid the difficulty just mentioned, it must
resort to one of three theories: (a) that the soul of the child had a previous
existence, a sort of pre-existence; (b) that the soul is potentially present in
the seed of man or woman or both, which is materialism; or (c) that the
soul is brought forth, that is, created in some way, by the parents, thus making
them in a sense creators. (3) It proceeds on the assumption that, after the
original creation, God works only mediately. After the six days of creation
His creative work ceased. The continued creation of souls, says Delitzsch, is
inconsistent with God's relation to the world. But the question may be raised,
What, then, becomes of the doctrine of regeneration, which is not effected by
second causes? (4) It is generally wedded to the theory of realism, since this
is the only way in which it can account for original guilt. By doing this it
affirms the numerical unity of the substance of all human souls, an untenable
position; and also fails to give a satisfactory answer to the question, why men
are held responsible only for the first sin of Adam, and not for his later
sins, nor for the sins of the rest of their forebears. (5) Finally, in the form
just indicated it leads to insuperable difficulties in Christology. If in Adam
human nature as a whole sinned, and that sin was therefore the actual sin
of every part of that human nature, then the conclusion cannot be escaped

that the human nature of Christ was also sinful and guilty because it had actually sinned in Adam.

4. CREATIONISM. This view is to the effect that each individual soul is to be regarded as an immediate creation of God, owing its origin to a direct creative act, of which the time cannot be precisely determined. The soul is supposed to be created pure, but united with a depraved body. This need not necessarily mean that the soul is created first *in separation from the body,* and then polluted by being brought in contact with the body, which would seem to assume that sin is something physical. It may simply mean that the soul, though called into being by a creative act of God, yet is pre-formed in the psychical life of the fœtus, that is, in the life of the parents, and thus acquires its life not above and outside of, but under and in, that complex of sin by which humanity as a whole is burdened.[1]

a. *Arguments in favor of Creationism.* The following are the more important considerations in favor of this theory: (1) It is more consistent with the prevailing representations of Scripture than Traducianism. The original account of creation points to a marked distinction between the creation of the body and that of the soul. The one is taken from the earth, while the other comes directly from God. This distinction is kept up throughout the Bible, where body and soul are not only represented as different substances, but also as having different origins, Eccl. 12:7; Isa 42:5; Zech. 12:1; Heb. 12:9. Cf. Num. 16:22. Of the passage in Hebrews even Delitzsch, though a Traducianist, says, "There can hardly be a more classical proof text for creationism."[2] (2) It is clearly far more consistent with the nature of the human soul than Traducianism. The immaterial and spiritual, and therefore indivisible nature of the soul of man, generally admitted by all Christians, is clearly recognized by Creationism. The traducian theory on the other hand, posits a derivation of essence, which, as is generally admitted, necessarily implies separation or division of essence. (3) It avoids the pitfalls of Traducianism in Christology and does greater justice to the Scriptural representation of the person of Christ. He was very man, possessing a true human nature, a real body and a rational soul, was born of a woman, was made in all points like as we are, — and yet, without sin. He did not, like all other men, share in the guilt and pollution of Adam's transgression. This was possible, because he did not share the same numerical essence which sinned in Adam.

b. *Objections to Creationism.* Creationism is open to the following objections: (1) The most serious objection is stated by Strong in the following words: "This theory, if it allows that the soul is originally possessed of depraved tendencies, makes God the direct author of moral evil; if it holds the soul to have been created pure, it makes God indirectly the author of moral evil, by teaching that He put this pure soul into a body which will inevitably

---

1. Cf. Bavinck, *Geref. Dogm.* II, pp. 630 f.
2. *Bibl. Psych.,* p. 137.

corrupt it." This is undoubtedly a serious difficulty, and is generally regarded as the decisive argument against Creationism. Augustine already called attention to the fact that the Creationist should seek to avoid this pitfall. But it should be borne in mind that the Creationist does not, like the Traducianist, regard original sin entirely as a matter of inheritance. The descendants of Adam are sinners, not as a result of their being brought into contact with a sinful body, but in virtue of the fact that God imputes to them the original disobedience of Adam. And it is for that reason that God withholds from them original righteousness, and the pollution of sin naturally follows. (2) It regards the earthly father as begetting only the body of his child, — certainly not the most important part of the child, — and therefore does not account for the re-appearance of the mental and moral traits of the parents in the children. Moreover, by taking this position it ascribes to the beast nobler powers of propagation than to man, for the beast multiplies itself after its kind. The last consideration is one of no great importance. And as far as mental and moral similarities of parents and children are concerned, it need not necessarily be assumed that these can be accounted for only on the basis of heredity. Our knowledge of the soul is still too deficient to speak with absolute assurance on this point. But this similarity may find its explanation partly in the example of the parents, partly in the influence of the body on the soul, and partly in the fact that God does not create all souls alike, but creates in each particular case a soul adapted to the body with which it will be united and the complex relationship into which it will be introduced. (3) It is not in harmony with God's present relationship to the world and His manner of working in it, since it teaches a direct creative activity of God, and thus ignores the fact that God now works through secondary causes and ceased from His creative work. This is not a very serious objection for those who do not have a deistic conception of the world. It is a gratuitous assumption that God has ceased from all creative activity in the world.

5. CONCLUDING REMARKS.

a *Caution required in speaking on the subject.* It must be admitted that the arguments on both sides are rather well balanced. In view of this fact it is not surprising that Augustine found it rather hard to choose between the two. The Bible makes no direct statement respecting the origin of the soul of man, except in the case of Adam. The few Scriptural passages that are adduced as favoring the one theory or the other, can hardly be called conclusive on either side. And because we have no clear teaching of Scripture on the point in question, it is necessary to speak with caution on the subject. We ought not to be wise above that which is written. Several theologians are of the opinion that there is an element of truth in both of these theories, which must be recognized.[1] Dorner even suggests the idea that each one of the

---

1.   Cf. Smith, *Chr. Theol.*, p. 169; Dabney, *Syst. and Polemic Theol.*, pp. 320 f.; Martensen, *Chr. Dogm.*, p. 141; Bavinck, *Geref. Dogm.* II, p. 630; Raymond, *Syst. Theol.* II, pp. 35 f.

three theories discussed represents one aspect of the whole truth: "Traducianism, generic consciousness; Pre-existentianism, self-consciousness or the interest of the personality as a separate eternal divine thought; Creationism, God-consciousness."[1]

b. *Some form of Creationism deserves preference.* It seems to us that Creationism deserves the preference, because (1) it does not encounter the insuperable philosophical difficulty with which Traducianism is burdened; (2) it avoids the Christological errors which Traducianism involves; and (3) it is most in harmony with our covenant idea. At the same time we are convinced that the creative activity of God in originating human souls must be conceived as being most closely connected with the natural process in the generation of new individuals. Creationism does not claim to be able to clear up all difficulties, but at the same time it serves as a warning against the following errors: (1) that the soul is divisible; (2) that all men are numerically of the same substance; and (3) that Christ assumed the same numerical nature which fell in Adam.[2]

---

1. *Syst. of Chr. Doct.* II, p. 94.
2. For further study of this subject confer especially the study of Dr. Honig on *Creatianisme en Traducianisme.*

III. Man as the Image of God

A. Historical Views of the Image of God in Man.

According to Scripture man was created in the image of God, and is therefore God-related. Traces of this truth are found even in Gentile literature. Paul pointed out to the Athenians that some of their own poets have spoken of man as the offspring of God, Acts 17:28. The early Church Fathers were quite agreed that the image of God in man consisted primarily in man's rational and moral characteristics, and in his capacity for holiness; but some were inclined to include also bodily traits. Irenæus and Tertullian drew a distinction between the "image" and the "likeness" of God, finding the former in bodily traits, and the latter in the spiritual nature of man. Clement of Alexandria and Origen, however, rejected the idea of any bodily analogy, and held that the word "image" denoted the characteristics of man as man, and the word "likeness," qualities which are not essential to man, but may be cultivated or lost. This view is also found in Athanasius, Hilary, Ambrose, Augustine, and John of Damascus. According to Pelagius and his followers the image consisted merely in this, that man was endowed with reason, so that he could know God; with free will, so that he was able to choose and do the good; and with the necessary power to rule the lower creation. The distinction already made by some of the early Church Fathers between the image and the likeness of God, was continued by the Scholastics, though it was not always expressed in the same way. The former was conceived of as including the intellectual powers of reason and freedom, and the latter as consisting of original righteousness. To this was added another point of distinction, namely, that between the image of God as a natural gift to man, something belonging to the very nature of man as man, and the likeness of God, or original righteousness, as a supernatural gift, which served as a check on the lower nature of man. There was a difference of opinion as to whether man was endowed with this original righteousness at once at creation, or received it later on as a reward for a temporary obedience. It was this original righteousness that enabled man to merit eternal life. The Reformers rejected the distinction between the image and the likeness, and considered original righteousness as included in the image of God, and as belonging to the very nature of man in its original condition. There was a difference of opinion, however, between Luther and Calvin. The former did not seek the image of God in any of the natural endowments of man, such as his rational and moral powers, but exclusively in original righteousness, and therefore regarded it as entirely lost by sin. Calvin, on the other hand, expresses himself as follows, after stating that the image of God extends to everything in which the nature of man surpasses that of all other species of animals: "Accordingly, by this term ('image of God') is denoted the integrity with which Adam was endued when his intellect was clear, his affections subordinated to reason, all his senses duly regulated, and when he truly ascribed all his excellence to the admirable gifts of his Maker. And though the primary seat of the divine image was in the mind and the heart, or in the soul and its powers, there was no part even of the body in which some rays of glory did not shine."[1] It included both natural endowments and those spiritual qualities designated as original righteousness, that is, true knowledge, righteousness, and holiness. The whole image was vitiated by sin, but only those spiritual qualities were completely lost. The Socinians and some of the earlier Arminians taught that the image of God consisted only in man's dominion over the lower creation. Schleiermacher rejected the idea of an original state of integrity and of original righteousness as a necessary doctrine. Since, as he sees it, moral perfection or righteousness and holiness can only be the result of development, he regards it as a contradiction in terms to speak of man as being created in a state of righteousness and holiness. Hence the image of God in man can only be a certain receptivity for the divine, a capacity to answer to the divine ideal, and to grow into God-likeness. Such modern theologians as Martensen and Kaftan are quite in line with this idea.

B. Scriptural Data Respecting the Image of God in Man.

Scriptural teachings respecting the image of God in man warrant the following statements:

1. The words "image" and "likeness" are used synonymously and interchangeably, and therefore do not refer to two different things. In Gen. 1:26 both words are used, but in the twenty-seventh verse only the first. This is evidently considered sufficient to express the whole idea. In Gen. 5:1 only the word "likeness" occurs, but in the third verse of that chapter both terms are again found. Gen. 9:6 contains only the word "image" as a complete expression of the idea. Turning to the New Testament, we find "image" and "glory" used in I Cor. 11:7, "image" alone in Col. 3:10, and "likeness" only in Jas. 3:9. Evidently the two are used interchangeably in Scripture. This naturally implies that man was *created* also in the likeness of God, and that this likeness was not something with which he was endowed later on. The usual opinion is that the word "likeness" was added to "image" to express the idea that the image was most like, a perfect image. The idea is that by creation that which was archetypal in God became ectypal in man. God was the original of which man was made a copy. This means, of course, that man not only bears the image of God, but is His very image. This is clearly stated in I Cor. 11:7, but does not mean that he cannot also be said to bear the image of God, cf. I Cor. 15:49.

---

1. *Inst.* I. 15:3.

Some have considered the change of prepositions in Gen. 1:27, "*in* our image, *after* our likeness," as significant. Böhl even based on it the idea that we are created in the image as a sphere, but this is entirely unwarranted. While the first meaning of the Hebrew preposition *be* (rendered "in" here) is undoubtedly "in," it can also have the same meaning as the preposition *le* (rendered "after"), and evidently has that meaning here. Notice that we are said to be renewed "after the image" of God in Col. 3:10; and also that the prepositions used in Gen. 1:26 are reversed in Gen. 5:3.

2. The image of God in which man was created certainly includes what is generally called "original righteousness," or more specifically, true knowledge, righteousness, and holiness. We are told that God made man "very good," Gen. 1:31, and "upright," Eccl. 7:29. The New Testament indicates very specifically the nature of man's original condition where it speaks of man as being renewed in Christ, that is, as being brought back to a former condition. The condition to which he is restored in Christ is clearly not one of neutrality, neither good nor bad, in which the will is in a state of perfect equilibrium, but one of true knowledge, Col. 3:10, righteousness and holiness, Eph. 4:24. These three elements constitute the original righteousness, which was lost by sin, but is regained in Christ. It may be called the moral image of God, or the image of God in the more restricted sense of the word. Man's creation in this moral image implies that the original condition of man was one of positive holiness, and not a state of innocence or moral neutrality.

3. But the image of God is not to be restricted to the original knowledge, righteousness, and holiness which was lost by sin, but also includes elements which belong to the natural constitution of man. They are elements which belong to man as man, such as intellectual power, natural affections, and moral freedom. As created in the image of God man has a rational and moral nature, which he did not lose by sin and which he could not lose without ceasing to be man. This part of the image of God has indeed been vitiated by sin, but still remains in man even after his fall in sin. Notice that man even after the fall, irrespective of his spiritual condition, is still represented as the image of God, Gen. 9;6; I Cor. 11:7; Jas. 3:9. The crime of murder owes its enormity to the fact that it is an attack on the image of God. In view of these passages of Scripture it is unwarranted to say that man has completely lost the image of God.

4. Another element usually included in the image of God is that of spirituality. God is Spirit, and it is but natural to expect that this element of spirituality also finds expression in man as the image of God. And that this is so is already indicated in the narrative of man's creation. God "breathed into his nostrils the breath of life; and man became a living soul." Gen. 2:7. The "breath of life" is the principle of his life, and the "living soul" is the very being of man. The soul is united with and adapted to a body, but can, if need be, also exist without the body. In view of this we can speak of man as a spiritual being, and as also in that respect the image of God. In this connection

the question may be raised, whether the body of man also constitutes a part of the image. And it would seem that this question should be answered in the affirmative. The Bible says that man — not merely the soul of man — was created in the image of God, and man, the "living soul," is not complete without the body. Moreover, the Bible represents murder as the destruction of the body, Matt. 10:28, and also as the destruction of the image of God in man, Gen. 9:6. We need not look for the image in the material substance of the body; it is found rather in the body as the fit instrument for the self-expression of the soul. Even the body is destined to become in the end a spiritual body, that is, a body which is completely spirit-controlled, a perfect instrument of the soul.

5. Still another element of the image of God is immortality. The Bible says that God only hath immortality, I Tim. 6:16, and this would seem to exclude the idea of human immortality. But it is perfectly evident from Scripture that man is also immortal in some sense of the word. The meaning is that God alone hath immortality as an essential quality, has it in and of Himself, while man's immortality is an endowment, is derived from God. Man was created immortal, not merely in the sense that his soul was endowed with an endless existence, but also in the sense that he did not carry within himself the seeds of physical death, and in his original condition was not subject to the law of death. Death was threatened as a punishment for sin, Gen. 2:17, and that this included bodily or physical death is evident from Gen. 3:19. Paul tells us that sin brought death into the world, Rom. 5:12; I Cor. 15:20,21; and that death must be regarded as the wages of sin, Rom. 6:23.

6. There is considerable difference of opinion as to whether man's dominion over the lower creation also formed a part of the image of God. This is not surprising in view of the fact that Scripture does not express itself explicitly on this point. Some regard the dominion in question simply as an office conferred on man, and not as a part of the image. But notice that God mentions man's creation in the divine image and his dominion over the lower creation in a single breath, Gen. 1:26. It is indicative of the glory and honour with which man is crowned, Ps. 8:5,6.

C. Man as the Image of God.

According to Scripture the essence of man consists in this, that he is the image of God. As such he is distinguished from all other creatures and stands supreme as the head and crown of the entire creation. Scripture asserts that man was created in the image and after the likeness of God, Gen. 1:26,27; 9:6; Jas. 3:9, and speaks of man as being and as bearing the image of God, I Cor. 11:7; 15:49. The terms "image" and "likeness" have been distinguished in various ways. Some were of the opinion that "image" had reference to the body, and "likeness," to the soul. Augustine held that the former referred to the intellectual, and the latter, to the moral faculties of the soul. Bellarmin regarded "image" as a designation of the natural gifts of man, and "likeness" as a description of that which was supernaturally added to man. Still others asserted that "image" denoted the inborn, and "likeness," the acquired conformity to God. It is far more likely, however, as was pointed out in the preceding, that both words express the same idea, and that "likeness" is merely an epexegetical addition to designate the image as most like or very similar. The idea expressed by the two words is that of *the very image of God*. The doctrine of the image of God in man is of the greatest importance in theology, for that image is the expression of that which is most distinctive in man and in his relation to God. The fact that man is the image of God distinguishes him from the animal and from every other creature. As far as we can learn from Scripture even the angels do not share that honor with him, though it is sometimes represented as if they do. Calvin goes so far as to say that "it cannot be denied that the angels also were created in the likeness of God, since, as Christ declares (Matt. 22:30), our highest perfection will consist in being like them."[1] But in this statement the great Reformer does not have due regard for the point of comparison in the statement of Jesus. In many cases the assumption that the angels were also created in the image of God results from a conception of the image which limits it to our moral and intellectual qualities. But the image also includes the body of man and his dominion over the lower creation. The angels are never represented as lords of creation, but as ministering spirits sent out for the service of those that inherit salvation. The following are the most important conceptions of the image of God in man.

1. THE REFORMED CONCEPTION. The Reformed Churches, following in the footsteps of Calvin, have a far more comprehensive conception of the image of God than either the Lutherans or the Roman Catholics. But even they do not all agree as to its exact contents. Dabney, for instance, holds that it does not consist in anything absolutely essential to man's nature, for then the loss of it would have resulted in the destruction of man's nature; but merely in some *accidens*.[2] McPherson, on the other hand, asserts that it belongs to the essential nature of man, and says that "Protestant theology would have escaped much confusion and many needless and unconvincing doctrinal refinements, if it had not encumbered itself with the idea that it was bound to define sin as the loss of the image, or of something belonging to the image. If the image were lost man would cease to be man."[3] These two, then, would seem to be hopelessly at variance. Other differences are also in evidence in Reformed theology. Some would limit the image to the moral qualities of righteousness and holiness with which man was created, while others would include the whole moral and rational nature of man, and still others would also add the body. Calvin says that the proper seat of the image of God is in the soul, though some rays of its glory also shine in the body. He finds that the image consisted especially in that original integrity of man's

---

1. *Inst.* I. 15.3.
2. *Syst. and Polem. Theol.*, p. 293.
3. *Chr. Dogm.*, p. 203.

nature, lost by sin, which reveals itself in true knowledge, righteousness, and holiness. At the same time he adds further "that the image of God extends to everything in which the nature of man surpasses that of all other species of animals."[1] This broader conception of the image of God became the prevalent one in Reformed theology. Thus Witsius says: "The image of God consisted *antecendenter*, in man's spiritual and immortal nature; *formaliter*, in his holiness; *consequenter*, in his dominion."[2] A very similar opinion is expressed by Turretin.[3] To sum up it may be said that the image consists: (a) In the soul or spirit of man, that is, in the qualities of simplicity, spirituality, invisibility, and immortality. (b) In the psychical powers or faculties of man as a rational and moral being, namely, the intellect and the will with their functions. (c) In the intellectual and moral integrity of man's nature, revealing itself in true knowledge, righteousness, and holiness, Eph. 4:24; Col. 3:10. (d) In the body, not as a material substance, but as the fit organ of the soul, sharing its immortality; and as the instrument through which man can exercise dominion over the lower creation. (e) In man's dominion over the earth. In opposition to the Socinians, some Reformed scholars went too far in the opposite direction, when they regarded this dominion as something that did not belong to the image at all but was the result of a special disposal of God. In connection with the question, whether the image of God belongs to the very essence of man, Reformed theology does not hesitate to say that it *constitutes* the essence of man. It distinguishes, however, between those elements in the image of God which man cannot lose without ceasing to be man, consisting in the essential qualities and powers of the human soul; and those elements which man can lose and still remain man, namely, the good ethical qualities of the soul and its powers. The image of God in this restricted sense is identical with what is called original righteousness. It is the moral perfection of the image, which could be, and was, lost by sin.

2. THE LUTHERAN CONCEPTION. The prevailing Lutheran conception of the image of God differs materially from that of the Reformed. Luther himself sometimes spoke as if he had a broad conception of it, but in reality he had a restricted view of it.[4] While there were during the seventeenth century, and there are even now, some Lutheran theologians who have a broader conception of the image of God, the great majority of them restrict it to the spiritual qualities with which man was originally endowed, that is, what is called original righteousness. In doing this they do not sufficiently recognize the essential nature of man as distinct from that of the angels on the one hand, and from that of the animals on the other hand. In the possession of this image men are like the angels, who also possess it; and in comparison with what the two have in common, their difference is of little importance. Man lost the image of God entirely through sin, and what now distinguishes him from the animals has very little religious or theological significance. The great difference between the two lay in the image of God, and

1. *Inst.* I. 15.308.
2. *On the Covenants*, 1. 2. 11.
3. *Opera, De Creatione*, Quaestio X.
4. Koestlin, *The Theology of Luther* II, pp. 339-342.

this man has lost entirely. In view of this it is also natural that the Lutherans should adopt Traducianism, and thus teach that the soul of man originates like that of the animal, that is, by procreation. It also accounts for the fact that the Lutherans hardly recognize the moral unity of the human race, but emphasize strongly its physical unity and the exclusively physical propagation of sin. Barth comes closer to the Lutheran than to the Reformed position when he seeks the image of God in "a point of contact" between God and man, a certain conformity with God, and then says that this was not only ruined but even annihilated by sin.[1]

3. THE ROMAN CATHOLIC VIEW. Roman Catholics do not altogether agree in their conception of the image of God. We limit ourselves here to a statement of the prevailing view among them. They hold that God at creation endowed man with certain natural gifts, such as the spirituality of the soul, the freedom of the will, and the immortality of the body. Spirituality, freedom, and immortality, are *natural endowments*, and as such constitute the *natural image* of God. Moreover, God "attempered" (adjusted) the natural powers of man to one another, placing the lower in due subordination to the higher. The harmony thus established is called *justitia* — natural righteousness. But even so there remained in man a natural tendency of the lower appetites and passions to rebel against the authority of the higher powers of reason and conscience. This tendency, called concupiscence, is not itself sin, but becomes sin when it is consented to by the will and passes into voluntary action. In order to enable man to hold his lower nature in check, God added to the *dona naturalia* certain *dona supernaturalia*. These included the *donum superadditum* of original righteousness (the supernatural likeness to God), which was added as a foreign gift to the original constitution of man, either immediately at the time of creation, or at some later point as a reward for the proper use of the natural powers. These supernatural gifts, including the *donum superadditum* of original righteousness, were lost by sin, but their loss did not disrupt the essential nature of man.

4. OTHER VIEWS OF THE IMAGE OF GOD. According to the Socinians and some of the earlier Arminians the image of God consists in man's dominion over the lower creation, and in this only. Anabaptists maintained that the first man, as a finite and earthly creature, was not yet the image of God, but could become this only by regeneration. Pelagians, most of the Arminians, and Rationalists all, with little variation, find the image of God only in the free personality of man, in his rational character, his ethico-religious disposition, and his destiny to live in communion with God.

D. The Original Condition of Man as the Image of God.

There is a very close connection between the image of God and the original state of man, and therefore the two are generally considered together. Once again we shall have to distinguish between different historical views as to the original condition of man.

---

1. *The Doctrine of the Word of God*, p. 273.

1. THE PROTESTANT VIEW. Protestants teach that man was created in a state of relative perfection, a state of righteousness and holiness. This does not mean that he had already reached the highest state of excellence of which he was susceptible. It is generally assumed that he was destined to reach a higher degree of perfection in the way of obedience. He was, something like a child, perfect in parts, but not yet in degree. His condition was a preliminary and temporary one, which would either lead on to greater perfection and glory or terminate in a fall. He was *by nature* endowed with that original righteousness which is the crowning glory of the image of God, and consequently lived in a state of positive holiness. The loss of that righteousness meant the loss of something that belonged to the very nature of man in its ideal state. Man could lose it and still remain man, but he could not lose it and remain man in the ideal sense of the word. In other words, its loss would really mean a deterioration and impairment of human nature. Moreover, man was created immortal. This applies not only to the soul, but to the whole person of man; and therefore does not merely mean that the soul was destined to have a continued existence. Neither does it mean that man was raised above the possibility of becoming a prey to death; this can only be affirmed of the angels and the saints in heaven. It does mean, however, that man, as he was created by God, did not bear within him the seeds of death and would not have died *necessarily* in virtue of the original constitution of his nature. Though the possibility of his becoming a victim of death was not excluded, he was not liable to death as long as he did not sin. It should be borne in mind that man's original immortality was not something purely negative and physical, but was something positive and spiritual as well. It meant life in communion with God and the enjoyment of the favor of the Most High. This is the fundamental conception of life in Scripture, just as death is primarily separation from God and subjection to His wrath. The loss of this spiritual life would spell death, and would also result in physical death.[1]

2. THE ROMAN CATHOLIC VIEW. Roman Catholics naturally have a somewhat different view of the original condition of man. According to them original righteousness did not belong to the nature of man in its integrity, but was something supernaturally added. In virtue of his creation man was simply endowed with all the natural powers and faculties of human nature as such, and by the *justitia naturalis* these powers were nicely adjusted to each other. He was without sin and lived in a state of perfect innocency. In the very nature of things, however, there was a natural tendency of the lower appetites and passions to rebel against the higher powers of reason and conscience. This tendency, called *concupiscence*, was not itself sin, but could easily become the occasion and fuel for sin. (But cf. Rom. 7:8; Col. 3:5; I Thess. 4:5, Auth. Ver.). Man, then, as he was originally constituted, was by nature without positive holiness, but also without sin, though burdened with a tendency which might easily result in sin. But now God added to the natural constitution of man the supernatural gift of original righteousness, by which he was enabled

---

1. Cf. especially, Kennedy, *St. Paul's Conceptions of the Last Things*, Chap. III.

to keep the lower propensities and desires in due subjection. When man fell, he lost that original righteousness, but the original constitution of human nature remained intact. The natural man is now exactly where Adam was before he was endowed with original righteousness, though with a somewhat stronger bias towards evil.

3. RATIONALIZING VIEWS. Pelagians, Socinians, Arminians, Rationalists, and Evolutionists, all discount the idea of a primitive state of holiness altogether. The first four are agreed that man was created in a state of innocence, of moral and religious neutrality, but was endowed with a free will, so that he could turn in either direction. Evolutionists assert that man began his career in a state of barbarism, in which he was but slightly removed from the brute. Rationalists of all kinds believe that a concreated righteousness and holiness is a contradiction in terms. Man determines his character by his own free choice; and holiness can only result from a victorious struggle against evil. From the nature of the case, therefore, Adam could not have been created in a state of holiness. Moreover, Pelagians, Socinians, and Rationalists hold that man was created mortal. Death did not result from the entrance of sin into the world, but was simply the natural termination of human nature as it was constituted. Adam would have died in virtue of the original constitution of his nature.

QUESTIONS FOR FURTHER STUDY: What is the precise distinction which Delitzsch makes between the soul and the spirit in man? How does Heard make use of the tripartite conception of man in the interpretation of original sin, conversion, and sanctification? What accounts for the fact that Lutherans are prevailingly Traducianists, and Reformed prevailingly Creationists? How about the objection that Creationism virtually destroys the unity of the human race? What objections are there against realism with its assumption of the numerical unity of human nature? What criticism would you offer on Dorner's view, that the theories of Pre-existentianism, Traducianism, and Creationism, are simply three different aspects of the whole truth respecting the origin of the soul? How do Roman Catholics generally distinguish between the "image" and the "likeness" of God? Do they believe that man lost his *justitia* or natural righteousness by the fall or not? How do those Lutherans who restrict the image of God to man's original righteousness explain Gen. 9:6 and Jas. 3:9?

LITERATURE. Bavinck, Geref. Dogm., II, pp. 566-635; Kuyper, Dict. Dogm., De Creaturis C. pp. 3-131; Vos, Geref. Dogm. II, pp. 1-21; Hodge, Syst. Theol. II, pp. 42-116; Dabney, Syst. and Polem. Theol., pp. 292-302; Shedd, Dogm. Theol. II, pp. 4-114; Litton, Introd. to Dogm. Theol., pp. 107-122; Dorner, Syst, of Chr. Doct. II, pp. 68-96; Schmidt, Doct. Theol. of the Ev. Luth. Church, pp. 225-238; Martensen, Chr. Dogm., pp. 136-148; Pieper, Chr. Dogm. I, pp. 617-630; Valentine, Chr. Theol. I, pp. 383-415; Pope, Chr. Theol. I, pp. 421-436; Raymond, Syst. Theol. II, pp. 7-49; Wilmers, Handbook of the Chr. Rel., pp. 219-233; Orr, God's Image in Man, pp. 3-193; A. Kuyper, Jr., Het Beeld Gods, pp. 8-143; Talma, De Anthropologie van Calvijn, pp. 29-68; Heard, The Tri-partite Nature of Man; Dickson, St. Paul's Use of the Terms Flesh and Spirit, chaps. V-XI; Delitzsch, Syst. of Bibl. Psych., pp. 103-144; Laidlaw, The Bibl. Doct. of Man, pp. 49-108; H. W. Robinson, The Chr. Doct. of Man, pp. 4-150.

IV. Man in the Covenant of Works

The discussion of the original state of man, the *status integritatis*, would not be complete without considering the mutual relationship between God and man, and especially the origin and nature of the religious life of man. That life was rooted in a covenant, just as the Christian life is to-day, and that covenant is variously known as the covenant of nature, the covenant of life, the Edenic covenant, and the covenant of works. The first name, which was rather common at first, was gradually abandoned, since it was apt to give the impression that this covenant was simply a part of the natural relationship in which man stood to God. The second and third names are not sufficiently specific, since both of them might also be applied to the covenant of grace, which is certainly a covenant of life, and also originated in Eden, Gen. 3:15. Consequently the name "Covenant of Works" deserves preference.

A. The Doctrine of the Covenant of Works in History.

The history of the doctrine of the covenant of works is comparatively brief. In the early Church Fathers the covenant idea is seldom found at all, though the elements which it includes, namely, the probationary command, the freedom of choice, and the possibility of sin and death, are all mentioned. Augustine in his *de Civitates Dei* speaks of the relation in which Adam originally stood to God as a covenant (testamentum, pactum), while some others inferred the original covenant relationship from the well known passage of Hos. 6:7. In the scholastic literature and in the writings of the Reformers, too, all the elements which later on went into the construction of the doctrine of the covenant of works were already present, but the doctrine itself was not yet developed. Though they contain some expressions which point to the imputation of Adam's sin to his descendants, it is clear that on the whole the transmission of sin was conceived realistically rather than federally. Says Thornwell in his analysis of Calvin's *Institutes*: "Federal representation was not seized as it should be, but a mystic realism in place of it."[1] The development of the doctrine of the covenant of grace preceded that of the doctrine of the covenant of works and paved the way for it. When it was clearly seen that Scripture represented the way of salvation in the form of a covenant, the parallel which Paul draws in Rom. 5 between Adam and Christ soon gave occasion for thinking of the state of integrity also as a covenant. According to Heppe the first work which contained the federal representation of the way of salvation, was Bullinger's *Compendium of*

---

1. *Collected Writings* I. p. 619. Cf. Calvin. *Institutes* II, 1.

the Christian Religion; and Olevianus was the real founder of a well developed federal theology, in which the concept of the covenant became for the first time the constitutive and determinative principle of the entire system.[1] From the Reformed Churches of Switzerland and Germany federal theology passed over to thè Netherlands and to the British Isles, especially Scotland. Its earliest representatives in the Netherlands were Gomarus, Trelcatius, Ravensperger, and especially Cloppenburg. The latter is regarded as the forerunner of Coccejus, who is often mistakenly called "the father of federal theology." The real distinction of Coccejus lies, at least partly, in the fact that he sought to substitute for the usual scholastic method of studying theology, which was rather common in his day, what he considered a more Scriptural method. He was followed in that respect by Burmannus and Witsius. Coccejus and his followers were not the only ones to embrace the doctrine of the covenant of works. This was done by others as well, such as Voetius, Mastricht, à Marck, and De Moor. Ypeij and Dermout point out that in those days a denial of the covenant of works was regarded as a heresy.[2] The Socinians rejected this doctrine altogether, since they did not believe in the imputation of Adam's sin to his descendants; and some of the Arminians, such as Episcopius, Limborgh, Venema, and J. Alting, who called it a human doctrine, followed suit. About the middle of the eighteenth century, when the doctrine of the covenant in the Netherlands had all but passed into oblivion, Comrie and Holtius in their *Examen van het Ontwerp van Tolerantie* once more brought it to the attention of the Church. In Scotland several important works were written on the covenants, including the covenant of works, such as those of Fisher (*Marrow of Modern Divinity*), Ball, Blake, Gib, and Boston. Says Walker: "The old theology of Scotland might be emphatically described as *covenant theology.*"[3] The doctrine found official recognition in the *Westminster Confession*, and in the *Formula Consensus Helvetica*. It is significant that the doctrine of works met with very little response in Roman Catholic and Lutheran theology. This finds its explanation in their attitude to the doctrine of the *immediate imputation* of the sin of Adam to his descendants. Under the influence of Rationalism and of Placæus' theory of *mediate* imputation, which also found acceptance in New England theology, the doctrine of the covenant gradually suffered eclipse. Even such conservative scholars as Doedes and Van Oosterzee in the Netherlands rejected it; and in New England theology it was short-lived. In Scotland the situation is not much better. Hugh Martin already wrote in his work on *The Atonement* (published in 1887) : "It has come to pass, we fear, that the federal theology is at present suffering a measure of neglect which does not bode well for the immediate future of the Church amongst us."[4] And while in our own country such Presbyterian scholars as the Hodges, Thornwell, Breckenridge, and Dabney, take

1. Cf. the valuable chapter on *Die Foederaltheologie der Reformirten Kirche* in Heppe's *Geschichte des Pietismus*, pp. 204-240.
2. *Geschiedenis der Ned. Herv. Kerk, Aanteekeningen* I-11, p. 315.
3. *Scottish Theology and Theologians*, p. 73.
4. P. 25.

due account of the doctrine in their theological works, in the Churches which they represent it has all but lost its vitality. In the Netherlands there has been a revival of federal theology under the influence of Kuyper and Bavinck, and through the grace of God it still continues to be a living reality in the hearts and minds of the people.

B. The Scriptural Foundation for the Doctrine of the Covenant of Works.

The widespread denial of the covenant of works makes it imperative to examine its Scriptural foundation with care.

1. THE ELEMENTS OF A COVENANT ARE PRESENT IN THE EARLY NARRATIVE. It must be admitted that the term "covenant" is not found in the first three chapters of Genesis, but this is not tantamount to saying that they do not contain the necessary data for the construction of a doctrine of the covenant. One would hardly infer from the absence of the term "trinity" that the doctrine of the Trinity is not found in the Bible. All the elements of a covenant are indicated in Scripture, and if the elements are present, we are not only warranted but, in a systematic study of the doctrine, also in duty bound to relate them to one another, and to give the doctrine so construed an appropriate name. In the case under consideration two parties are named, a condition is laid down, a promise of reward for obedience is clearly implied, and a penalty for transgression is threatened. It may still be objected that we do not read of the two parties as coming to an agreement, nor of Adam as accepting the terms laid down, but this is not an insuperable objection. We do not read of such an explicit agreement and acceptance on the part of man either in the cases of Noah and Abraham. God and man do not appear as equals in any of these covenants. All God's covenants are of the nature of sovereign dispositions imposed on man. God is absolutely sovereign in His dealings with man, and has the perfect right to lay down the conditions which the latter must meet, in order to enjoy His favor. Moreover Adam was, even in virtue of his natural relationship, in duty bound to obey God; and when the covenant relation was established, this obedience also became a matter of self-interest. When entering into covenant relations with men, it is always God who lays down the terms, and they are very gracious terms, so that He has, also from that point of view, a perfect right to expect that man will assent to them. In the case under consideration God had but to announce the covenant, and the perfect state in which Adam lived was a sufficient guarantee for his acceptance.

2. THERE WAS A PROMISE OF ETERNAL LIFE. Some deny that there is any Scripture evidence for such a promise. Now it is perfectly true that no such promise is explicitly recorded, but it is clearly implied in the alternative of death as the result of disobedience. The clear implication of the threatened punishment is that in the case of obedience death would not enter, and this can only mean that life would continue. It has been objected that this would only mean a continuation of Adam's natural life, and not what Scripture calls life eternal. But the Scriptural idea of life is life in communion with God; and this is the life which Adam possessed, though in his case it was still amissible. If

Adam stood the test, this life would be retained not only, but would cease to be amissible, and would therefore be lifted to a higher plane. Paul tells us explicitly in Rom. 7:10 that the commandment, that is the law, was unto life. In commenting on this verse Hodge says: "The law was designed and adapted to secure life, but became in fact the cause of death." This is also clearly indicated in such passages as Rom. 10:5; Gal. 3:13. Now it is generally admitted that this glorious promise of unending life was in no way implied in the natural relation in which Adam stood to God, but had a different basis. But to admit that there is something positive here, a special condescension of God, is an acceptance of the covenant principle. There may still be some doubt as to the propriety of the name "Covenant of Works," but there can be no valid objection to the covenant idea.

3. BASICALLY, THE COVENANT OF GRACE IS SIMPLY THE EXECUTION OF THE ORIGINAL AGREEMENT BY CHRIST AS OUR SURETY. He undertook freely to carry out the will of God. He placed Himself under the law, that He might redeem them that were under the law, and were no more in a position to obtain life by their own fulfilment of the law. He came to do what Adam failed to do, and did it in virtue of a covenant agreement. And if this is so, and the covenant of grace is, as far as Christ is concerned, simply the carrying out of the original agreement, it follows that the latter must also have been of the nature of a covenant. And since Christ met the condition of the covenant of works, man can now reap the fruit of the original agreement by faith in Jesus Christ. There are now two ways of life, which are in themselves ways of life, the one is the way of the law: "the man that doeth the righteousness which is of the law shall live thereby," but it is a way by which man can no more find life; and the other is the way of faith in Jesus Christ, who met the demands of the law, and is now able to dispense the blessing of eternal life.

4. THE PARALLEL BETWEEN ADAM AND CHRIST. The parallel which Paul draws between Adam and Christ in Rom. 5:12-21, in connection with the doctrine of justification, can only be explained on the assumption that Adam, like Christ, was the head of a covenant. According to Paul the essential element in justification consists in this, that the righteousness of Christ is imputed to us, without any personal work on our part to merit it. And he regards this as a perfect parallel to the manner in which the guilt of Adam is imputed to us. This naturally leads to the conclusion that Adam also stood in covenant relationship to his descendants.

5. THE PASSAGE IN HOS. 6:7. In Hos. 6:7 we read: "But they like Adam have transgressed the covenant." Attempts have been made to discredit this reading. Some have suggested the reading "at Adam," which would imply that some well-known transgression occurred at a place called Adam. But the preposition forbids this rendering. Moreover, the Bible makes no mention whatever of such a well-known historical transgression at Adam. The Authorized Version renders "like men," which would then mean, in human fashion. To this it may be objected that there is no plural in the original, and that such

a statement would be rather inane, since man could hardly transgress in any other way. The rendering "like Adam" is after all the best. It is favored by the parallel passage in Job 31:33; and is adopted by the American Revised Version.

C. Elements of the Covenant of Works.

The following elements must be distinguished:

1. THE CONTRACTING PARTIES. On the one hand there was the triune God, the Creator and Lord, and on the other hand, Adam as His dependent creature. A twofold relationship between the two should be distinguished:

a. *The natural relationship.* When God created man, He by that very fact established a natural relationship between Himself and man. It was a relationship like that between the potter and the clay, between an absolute sovereign and a subject devoid of any claim. In fact, the distance between the two was so great that these figures are not even an adequate expression of it. It was such that a life in communion with each other seemed to be out of the question. As the creature of God man was naturally under the law, and was in duty bound to keep it. And while transgression of the law would render him liable to punishment, the keeping of it would not constitute an inherent claim to a reward. Even if he did all that was required of him, he would still have to say, I am but an unprofitable servant, for I have merely done that which it was my duty to do. Under this purely natural relationship man could not have merited anything. But though the infinite distance between God and man apparently excluded a life of communion with each other, man was created for just such communion, and the possibility of it was already given in his creation in the image of God. In this natural relationship Adam was the father of the human race.

b. *The covenant relationship.* From the very beginning, however, God revealed Himself, not only as an absolute Sovereign and Lawgiver, but also as a loving Father, seeking the welfare and happiness of His dependent creature. He condescended to come down to the level of man, to reveal Himself as a Friend, and to enable man to improve his condition in the way of obedience. In addition to the natural relationship He, by a positive enactment, graciously established a covenant relationship. He entered into a legal compact with man, which includes all the requirements and obligations implied in the creaturehood of man, but at the same time added some new elements. (1) Adam was constituted the representative head of the human race, so that he could act for all his descendants. (2) He was temporarily put on probation, in order to determine whether he would willingly subject his will to the will of God. (3) He was given the promise of eternal life in the way of obedience, and thus by the gracious disposition of God acquired certain conditional rights. This covenant enabled Adam to obtain eternal life for himself and for his descendants in the way of obedience.

2. THE PROMISE OF THE COVENANT. The great promise of the covenant of works was the promise of eternal life. They who deny the covenant of works generally base their denial in part on the fact that there is no record of such a promise in the Bible. And it is perfectly true that Scripture contains no explicit promise of eternal life to Adam. But the threatened penalty clearly implies such a promise. When the Lord says, "for in the day that thou eatest thereof thou shalt surely die," his statement clearly implies that, if Adam refrains from eating, he will not die, but will be raised above the possibility of death. The implied promise certainly cannot mean that, in the case of obedience, Adam would be permitted to live on in the usual way, that is, to continue the ordinary natural life, for that life was his already in virtue of his creation, and therefore could not be held out as a reward for obedience. The implied promise evidently was that of life raised to its highest development of perennial bliss and glory. Adam was indeed created in a state of positive holiness, and was also immortal in the sense that he was not subject to the law of death. But he was only at the beginning of his course and did not yet possess the highest privileges that were in store for man. He was not yet raised above the possibility of erring, sinning, and dying. He was not yet in possession of the highest degree of holiness, nor did he enjoy life in all its fulness. The image of God in man was still limited by the possibility of man's sinning against God, changing from good to evil, and becoming subject to the power of death. The promise of life in the covenant of works was a promise of the removal of all the limitations of life to which Adam was still subject, and of the raising of his life to the highest degree of perfection. When Paul says in Rom. 7:10 that the commandment was unto life, he means life in the fullest sense of the word. The principle of the covenant of works was: the man that does these things shall live thereby; and this principle is reiterated time and again in Scripture, Lev. 18:5; Ezek. 20:11,13,20; Luke 10:28; Rom. 10:5; Gal. 3:12.

3. THE CONDITION OF THE COVENANT. The promise in the covenant of works was not unconditional. The condition was that of implicit and perfect obedience. The divine law can demand nothing less than that, and the positive command not to eat of the fruit of the tree of the knowledge of good and evil, relating as it did, to a thing indifferent in itself, was clearly a test of pure obedience in the absolute sense of the word. Man was, of course, also subject to the moral law of God, which was written on the tablets of his heart. He knew this by nature, so that it did not have to be revealed supernaturally, as the special test was. Essentially, the moral law, as Adam knew it, was undoubtedly like the ten commandments, but the form was different. In its present form the moral law presupposes a knowledge of sin, and is therefore primarily negative; in Adam's heart, however, it must have had a positive character. But just because it was positive, it did not bring to his consciousness the possibility of sin. Therefore a negative commandment was added. Moreover, in order that the test of Adam might be a test of pure obedience, God deemed it necessary to add to the commandments of which Adam perceived the naturalness and reason-

ableness, a commandment which was in a certain sense arbitrary and indifferent. Thus the demands of the law were, so to say, concentrated on a single point. The great question that had to be settled was, whether man would obey God implicitly or follow the guidance of his own judgment. Dr. Bavinck says: "Het proefgebod belichaamde voor hem (Adam) het dilemma: God of de mensch, Zijn gezag of eigen inzicht, onvoorwaardelijke gehoorzaamheid of zelfstandig onderzoek, geloof of twijfel."[1]

4. THE PENALTY OF THE COVENANT. The penalty that was threatened was death, and what this means can best be gathered from the general meaning of the term as it is used in Scripture, and from the evils that came upon the guilty in the execution of the penalty. Evidently death in the most inclusive sense of the word is meant, including physical, spiritual, and eternal death. The fundamental Scriptural idea of death is not that of extinction of being, but that of separation from the source of life, and the resulting dissolution or misery and woe. Fundamentally, it consists in the separation of the soul from God, which manifests itself in spiritual misery, and finally terminates in eternal death. But it also includes the separation of body and soul and the consequent dissolution of the body. Undoubtedly the execution of the penalty began at once after the first transgression. Spiritual death entered instantly, and the seeds of death also began to operate in the body. The full execution of the sentence, however, did not follow at once, but was arrested, because God immediately introduced an economy of grace and restoration.

5. THE SACRAMENT(S) OF THE COVENANT. We have no definite information in Scripture respecting the sacrament(s) or seal(s) of this covenant. Hence there is a great variety of opinions on the subject. Some speak of four: the tree of life, the tree of the knowledge of good and evil, paradise, and the sabbath; others of three: the two trees and paradise; still others of two: the tree of life and paradise; and still others of one: the tree of life. The last opinion is the most prevalent one, and would seem to be the only one to find any support in Scripture. We should not think of the fruit of this tree as magically or medically working immortality in Adam's frame. Yet it was in some way connected with the gift of life. In all probability it must be conceived of as an appointed symbol or seal of life. Consequently, when Adam forfeited the promise, he was debarred from the sign. So conceived the words of Gen. 3:22 must be understood sacramentally.

D. The Present Status of the Covenant of Works.

With respect to the question, whether the covenant of works is still in force or was abrogated at the time of Adam's fall, there is considerable difference of opinion between Arminian and Reformed theologians.

1. THE ARMINIAN VIEW. Arminians claim that this legal covenant was wholly abrogated at the fall of Adam, and argue this as follows: (a) The promise was then revoked and thus the compact annulled, and where there is no compact

1. *Geref. Dog.*, II, p. 618.

there can be no obligation. (b) God could not continue to exact obedience of man, when the latter was by nature unable, and was not enabled by the grace of God, to render the required service. (c) It would be derogatory to God's wisdom, holiness, and majesty to call the depraved creature to a service of holy and undivided love. They maintain that God established a new covenant and enacted a new law, the law of faith and evangelical obedience, which man in spite of his impaired powers can keep when assisted by the enabling helps of common or sufficient grace. However, the following considerations militate against this view: (a) Man's obligation to God was never rooted merely in the covenant requirement, but fundamentally in the natural relation in which he stood to God. This natural relationship was incorporated in the covenant relationship. (b) Man's inability is self-induced, and therefore does not relieve him of his just obligation. His self-imposed limitations, his criminal and voluntary hostility to God did not deprive the sovereign Ruler of the universe of the right to demand the hearty and loving service which is His due. (c) The *reductio ad absurdum* of the Arminian view is that the sinner can gain complete emancipation from righteous obligations by sinning. The more a man sins, the more he becomes a slave of sin, unable to do that which is good; and the deeper he sinks into this slavery which robs him of his capacity for good, the less responsible he becomes. If man continues to sin long enough, he will in the end be absolved of all moral responsibility.

2. THE REFORMED VIEW. Even some Reformed theologians speak of the abrogation of the legal covenant, and seek proof for this in such passages as Heb. 8:13. This naturally raised the question, whether, and in how far, the covenant of works can be considered as a thing of the past; or whether, and in how far, it must be regarded as still in force. It is generally agreed that no change in the legal status of man can ever abrogate the authority of the law; that God's claim to the obedience of His creatures is not terminated by their fall in sin and its disabling effects; that the wages of sin continues to be death; and that a perfect obedience is always required to merit eternal life. This means with respect to the question under consideration:

a. *That the covenant of works is not abrogated:* (1) in so far as the natural relation of man to God was incorporated in it, since man always owes God perfect obedience; (2) in so far as its curse and punishment for those who continue in sin are concerned; and (3) in so far as the conditional promise still holds. God might have withdrawn this promise, but did not, Lev. 18:5; Rom. 10:5; Gal. 3:12. It is evident, however, that after the fall no one can comply with the condition.

b. *That the covenant of works is abrogated:* (1) in so far as it contained new positive elements, for those who are under the covenant of grace; this does not mean that it is simply set aside and disregarded, but that its obligations were met by the Mediator for His people; and (2) as an appointed means to obtain eternal life, for as such it is powerless after the fall of man.

MAN IN THE STATE OF SIN

I. The Origin of Sin

THE PROBLEM of the origin of the evil that is in the world has always been considered as one of the profoundest problems of philosophy and theology. It is a problem that naturally forces itself upon the attention of man, since the power of evil is both great and universal, is an ever present blight on life in all its manifestations, and is a matter of daily experience in the life of every man. Philosophers were constrained to face the problem and to seek an answer to the question as to the origin of all the evil, and particularly of the moral evil, that is in the world. To some it seemed to be so much a part of life itself that they sought the solution for it in the natural constitution of things. Others, however, were convinced that it had a voluntary origin, that is, that it originated in the free choice of man, either in the present or in some previous existence. These are much closer to the truth as it is revealed in the Word of God.

A. Historical Views Respecting the Origin of Sin.

The earliest Church Fathers do not speak very definitely on the origin of sin, though the idea that it originated in the voluntary transgression and fall of Adam in paradise is already found in the writings of Irenæus. This soon became the prevailing view in the Church, especially in opposition to Gnosticism, which regarded evil as inherent in matter, and as such the product of the Demiurge. The contact of the human soul with matter at once rendered it sinful. This theory naturally robbed sin of its voluntary and ethical character. Origen sought to maintain this by his theory of pre-existentianism. According to him the souls of men sinned voluntarily in a previous existence, and therefore all enter the world in a sinful condition. This Platonic view was burdened with too many difficulties to meet with wide acceptance. During the eighteenth and nineteenth centuries, however, it was advocated by Mueller and Rueckert, and by such philosophers as Lessing, Schelling, and J. H. Fichte. In general the Greek Church Fathers of the third and fourth centuries showed an inclination to discount the connection between the sin of Adam and those of his descendants, while the Latin Church Fathers taught with ever-increasing clearness that the present sinful condition of man finds its explanation in the first transgression of Adam in paradise. The teachings of the Eastern Church finally culminated in Pelagianism, which denied that there was any vital connection between the two, while those of the Western Church reached their culmination in Augustinianism which stressed the fact that we are both guilty and polluted in Adam. Semi-Pelagianism admitted the Adamic connection, but held that it accounted only for the pollution of sin. During the Middle Ages the connection was generally recognized. It was sometimes interpreted in an Augustinian, but more often in a Semi-Pelagian manner. The Reformers shared the views of Augustine, and the Socinians those of Pelagius, while the Arminians moved in the direction of Semi-Pelagianism. Under the influence of Rationalism and evolutionary philosophy the doctrine of the fall of man and its fatal effects on the human race was gradually discarded. The idea of sin was replaced by that of evil, and this evil was explained in various ways. Kant regarded it as something belonging to the supersensible sphere, which he could not explain. For Leibnitz it was due to the necessary limitations of the universe. Schleiermacher found its origin in the sensuous nature of man, and Ritschl, in human ignorance, while the evolutionist ascribes it to the opposition of the lower propensities to a gradually developing moral consciousness. Barth speaks of the origin of sin as the mystery of predestination. Sin originated in the fall, but the fall was not a historical event; it belongs to superhistory (Urgeschichte). Adam was indeed the first sinner, but his disobedience cannot be regarded as the cause of the sin of the world. The sin of man is in some manner bound up with his creatureliness. The story of paradise simply conveys to man the cheering information that he need not necessarily be a sinner.

B. Scriptural Data Respecting the Origin of Sin.

In Scripture the moral evil that is in the world stands out clearly as sin, that is, as transgression of the law of God. Man ever appears in it as a transgressor by nature, and the question naturally arises, How did he acquire that nature? What does the Bible reveal on that point?

1. GOD CANNOT BE REGARDED AS ITS AUTHOR. God's eternal decree certainly rendered the entrance of sin into the world certain, but this may not be interpreted so as to make God the cause of sin in the sense of being its responsible author. This idea is clearly excluded by Scripture. "Far be it from God, that He should do wickedness, and from the Almighty, that He should commit iniquity," Job 34:10. He is the holy God, Isa. 6:3, and there is absolutely no unrighteousness in Him, Deut. 32:4; Ps. 92:16. He cannot be tempted with evil, and He Himself tempteth no man, Jas. 1:13. When He created man, He created Him good and in His image. He positively hates sin, Deut. 25:16; Ps. 5:4; 11:5; Zech. 8:17; Luke 16:15, and made provision in Christ for man's deliverance from sin. In the light of all this it would be blasphemous to speak of God as the author of sin. And for that reason all those deterministic views which represent sin as a necessity inherent in the very nature of things should be rejected. They by implication make God the author of sin, and are contrary, not only to Scripture, but also to the voice of conscience, which testifies to the responsibility of man.

2. SIN ORIGINATED IN THE ANGELIC WORLD. The Bible teaches us that in the attempt to trace the origin of sin, we must even go back of the fall of man

as described in Gen. 3, and fix the attention on something that happened in the angelic world. God created a host of angels, and they were all good as they came forth from the hand of their Maker, Gen. 1:31. But a fall occurred in the angelic world, in which legions of angels fell away from God. The exact time of this fall is not designated, but in John 8:44 Jesus speaks of the devil as a murderer from the beginning (*kat' arches*), and John says in I John 3:8, that he sins from the beginning. The prevailing opinion is that this *kat' arches* means from the beginning of the history of man. Very little is said about the sin that caused the fall of the angels. From Paul's warning to Timothy, that no novice should be appointed as bishop, "lest being puffed up he fall into the condemnation of the devil," I Tim. 3:6, we may in all probability conclude that it was the sin of pride, of aspiring to be like God in power and authority. And this idea would seem to find corroboration in Jude 6, where it is said that the fallen angels "kept not their own principality, but left their proper habitation." They were not satisfied with their lot, with the government and power entrusted to them. If the desire to be like God was their peculiar temptation, this would also explain why they tempted man on that particular point.

3. The Origin of Sin in the Human Race. With respect to the origin of sin in the history of mankind, the Bible teaches that it began with the transgression of Adam in paradise, and therefore with a perfectly voluntary act on the part of man. The tempter came from the spirit world with the suggestion that man, by placing himself in opposition to God, might become like God. Adam yielded to the temptation and committed the first sin by eating of the forbidden fruit. But the matter did not stop there, for by that first sin Adam became the bond-servant of sin. That sin carried permanent pollution with it, and a pollution which, because of the solidarity of the human race, would affect not only Adam but all his descendants as well. As a result of the fall the father of the race could only pass on a depraved human nature to his offspring. From that unholy source sin flows on as an impure stream to all the generations of men, polluting everyone and everything with which it comes in contact. It is exactly this state of things that made the question of Job so pertinent, "Who can bring a clean thing out of an unclean? not one." Job 14:4. But even this is not all. Adam sinned not only as the father of the human race, but also as the representative head of all his descendants; and therefore the guilt of his sin is placed to their account, so that they are all liable to the punishment of death. It is primarily in that sense that Adam's sin is the sin of all. That is what Paul teaches us in Rom. 5:12: "Through one man sin entered into the world, and death through sin; and so death passed unto all men, for that all sinned." The last words can only mean that they all sinned in Adam, and sinned in such a way as to make them all liable to the punishment of death. It is not sin considered merely as pollution, but sin as guilt that carries punishment with it. God adjudges all men to be guilty sinners in Adam, just as He adjudges all believers to be righteous in Jesus

Christ. That is what Paul means, when he says: "So then as through one trespass the judgment came unto all men to condemnation; even so through one act of righteousness the free gift came unto all men to justification of life. For as through the one man's disobedience the many were made sinners, even so through the obedience of the one shall the many be made righteous," Rom. 5:18,19.

C. The Nature of the First Sin or the Fall of Man.

1. ITS FORMAL CHARACTER. It may be said that, from a purely formal point of view, man's first sin consisted in his eating of the tree of the knowledge of good and evil. We do not know what kind of tree this was. It may have been a date or a fig tree, or any other kind of fruit tree. There was nothing injurious in the fruit of the tree as such. Eating of it was not *per se* sinful. for it was not a transgression of the moral law. This means that it would not have been sinful, if God had not said, "Of the tree of the knowledge of good and evil thou shalt not eat." There is no unanimous opinion as to the reason why the tree was called the tree of the knowledge of good and evil. A rather common view is that the tree was so called, because the eating of it would impart a *practical* knowledge of good and evil; but this is hardly in keeping with the Scriptural representation that man by eating it would become *like God* in knowing good and evil, for God does not commit evil, and therefore has no *practical* knowledge of it. It is far more likely that the tree was so called, because it was destined to reveal (a) whether man's future state would be good or evil; and (b) whether man would allow God to determine for him what was good and evil, or would undertake to determine this for himself. But whatever explanation may be given of the name, the command given by God not to eat of the fruit of the tree simply served the purpose of testing the obedience of man. It was a test of pure obedience, since God did not in any way seek to justify or to explain the prohibition. Adam had to show his willingness to submit his will to the will of his God with implicit obedience.

2. ITS ESSENTIAL AND MATERIAL CHARACTER. The first sin of man was a typical sin, that is, a sin in which the real essence of sin clearly reveals itself. The essence of that sin lay in the fact that Adam placed himself in opposition to God, that he refused to subject his will to the will of God, to have God determine the course of his life; and that he actively attempted to take the matter out of God's hand, and to determine the future for himself. Man, who had absolutely no claim on God, and who could only establish a claim by meeting the condition of the covenant of works, cut loose from God and acted as if he possesed certain rights as over against God. The idea that the command of God was really an infringement on the rights of man seems to have been present already in the mind of Eve when, in answer to the question of Satan, she added the words, "Neither shall ye touch it," Gen. 3:3. She evidently wanted to stress the fact that the command had been rather unreasonable. Starting from the pre-supposition that he had certain rights as over against

God, man allowed the new center, which he found in himself, to operate against his Maker. This explains his desire to be like God and his doubt of the good intention of God in giving the command. Naturally different elements can be distinguished in his first sin. In the intellect it revealed itself as unbelief and pride, in the will, as the desire to be like God, and in the affections, as an unholy satisfaction in eating of the forbidden fruit.

D. The First Sin or the Fall as Occasioned by Temptation.

1. THE PROCEDURE OF THE TEMPTER. The fall of man was occasioned by the temptation of the serpent, who sowed in man's mind the seeds of distrust and unbelief. Though it was undoubtedly the intention of the tempter to cause Adam, the head of the covenant, to fall, yet he addressed himself to Eve, probably because (a) she was not the head of the covenant and therefore would not have the same sense of responsibility; (b) she had not received the command of God directly but only indirectly, and would consequently be more susceptible to argumentation and doubt; and (c) she would undoubtedly prove to be the most effective agent in reaching the heart of Adam. The course followed by the tempter is quite clear. In the first place he sows the seeds of doubt by calling the good intention of God in question and suggesting that His command was really an infringement of man's liberty and rights. When he notices from the response of Eve that the seed has taken root, he adds the seeds of unbelief and pride, denying that transgression will result in death, and clearly intimating that the command was prompted by the selfish purpose of keeping man in subjection. He asserts that by eating from the tree man would become like God. The high expectations thus engendered induced Eve to look intently at the tree, and the longer she looked, the better the fruit seemed to her. Finally, desire got the upper hand, and she ate and also gave unto her husband, and he ate.

2. INTERPRETATION OF THE TEMPTATION. Frequent attempts have been made and are still being made to explain away the historical character of the fall. Some regard the whole narrative in Gen. 3 as an allegory, representing man's self-depravation and gradual change in a figurative way. Barth and Brunner regard the narrative of man's original state and of the fall as a myth. Creation and the fall both belong, not to history, but to super-history (Urgeschichte), and therefore both are equally incomprehensible. The story in Genesis merely teaches us that, though man is now unable to do any good and is subject to the law of death, this is not necessarily so. It is possible for a man to be free from sin and death by a life in communion with God. Such is the life portrayed for us in the story of paradise, and it prefigures the life that will be granted to us in Him of whom Adam was but a type, namely, Christ. But it is not the kind of life that man now lives or ever has lived from the beginning of history. Paradise is not a certain locality to which we can point, but is there where God is Lord, and man and all other creatures are His willing subjects. The paradise of the past lies beyond the pale of human history. Says Barth: "When the history of man began; when man's

time had its beginning; when time and history commenced where man has the first and the last word, paradise had disappeared."[1] Brunner speaks in a similar vein when he says: "Just as in respect of the Creation we ask in vain: How, where and when has this taken place, so also is it with the Fall. The Creation and the Fall both lie behind the historical visible reality."[2]

Others who do not deny the historical character of the narrative in Genesis, maintain that the serpent at least should not be regarded as a literal animal, but merely as a name or a symbol for covetousness, for sexual desire, for erring reason, or for Satan. Still others assert that, to say the least, the speaking of the serpent should be understood figuratively. But all these and similar interpretations are untenable in the light of Scripture. The passages preceding and following Gen. 3:1-7 are evidently intended as a plain historical narrative. That they were so understood by the Biblical authors, can be proved by many cross-references, such as Job 31:33; Eccl. 7:29; Isa. 43:27; Hos. 6:7; Rom. 5:12,18,19; I Cor. 5:21; II Cor. 11:3; I Tim. 2:14, and therefore we have no right to hold that these verses, which form an integral part of the narrative, should be interpreted figuratively. Moreover, the serpent is certainly counted among the animals in Gen. 3:1, and it would not yield good sense to substitute for "serpent" the word "Satan." The punishment in Gen. 3:14,15 presupposes a literal serpent, and Paul conceives of the serpent in no other way, II Cor. 11:3. And while it may be possible to conceive of the serpent as saying something in a figurative sense by means of cunning actions, it does not seem possible to think of him as carrying on the conversation recorded in Gen. 3 in that way. The whole transaction, including the speaking of the serpent, undoubtedly finds its explanation in the operation of some superhuman power, which is not mentioned in Gen. 3. Scripture clearly intimates that the serpent was but the instrument of Satan, and that Satan was the real tempter, who was working in and through the serpent, just as at a later time he worked in men and swine, John 8:44; Rom. 16:20; II Cor. 11:3; Rev. 12:9. The serpent was a fit instrument for Satan, for he is the personification of sin, and the serpent symbolizes sin (a) in its cunning and deceptive nature, and (b) in its poisonous sting by which it kills man.

3. THE FALL BY TEMPTATION AND MAN'S SALVABILITY. It has been suggested that the fact that man's fall was occasioned by temptation from without, may be one of the reasons why man is salvable, in distinction from the fallen angels, who were not subject to external temptation, but fell by the promptings of their own inner nature. Nothing certain can be said on this point, however. But whatever the significance of the temptation in that respect may be, it certainly does not suffice to explain how a holy being like Adam could fall in sin. It is impossible for us to say how temptation could find a point of contact in a holy person. And it is still more difficult to explain the origin of sin in the angelic world.

---

1. *God's Search for Man,* p. 98.
2. *Man in Revolt,* p. 142.

E. The Evolutionary Explanation of the Origin of Sin.

Naturally, a consistent theory of evolution cannot admit the doctrine of the fall, and a number of liberal theologians have rejected it as incompatible with the theory of evolution. It is true, there are some rather conservative theologians, such as Denney, Gore, and Orr, who accept, though with reservations, the evolutionary account of the origin of man, and feel that it leaves room for the doctrine of the fall in some sense of the word. But it is significant that they all conceive of the story of the fall as a mythical or allegorical representation of an ethical experience or of some actual moral catastrophe at the beginning of history which resulted in suffering and death. This means that they do not accept the narrative of the fall as a real historical account of what occurred in the garden of Eden. Tennant in his Hulsean Lectures on *The Origin and Propagation of Sin*[1] gave a rather detailed and interesting account of the origin of sin from the evolutionary point of view. He realizes that man could not very well derive sin from his animal ancestors, since these had no sin. This means that the impulses, propensities, desires, and qualities which man inherited from the brute cannot themselves be called sin. In his estimation these constitute only the *material* of sin, and do not become actual sins until the moral consciousness awakens in man, and they are left in control in determining the actions of man, contrary to the voice of conscience, and to ethical sanctions. He holds that in the course of his development man gradually became an ethical being with an indeterminate will, without explaining how such a will is possible where the law of evolution prevails, and regards this will as the only cause of sin. He defines sin "as an activity of the will expressed in thought, word, or deed contrary to the individual's conscience. to his notion of what is good and right, his knowledge of the moral law and the will of God."[2] As the human race develops, the ethical standards become more exacting and the heinousness of sin increases. A sinful environment adds to the difficulty of refraining from sin. This view of Tennant leaves no room for the fall of man in the generally accepted sense of the word. As a matter of fact, Tennant explicitly repudiates the doctrine of the fall, which is recognized in all the great historical confessions of the Church. Says W. H. Johnson: "Tennant's critics are agreed that his theory leaves no room for that cry of the contrite heart which not only confesses to separate acts of sin, but declares: 'I was shapen in iniquity; there is a law of death in my members.' "[3]

F. The Results of the First Sin.

The first transgression of man had the following results:

1. The immediate concomitant of the first sin, and therefore hardly a result of it in the strict sense of the word, was the total depravity of human nature. The contagion of his sin at once spread through the entire man, leaving no part of his nature untouched, but vitiating every power and faculty

---

1. Chap. III.
2. p. 163.
3. *Can the Christian Now Believe in Evolution?* p. 136.

of body and soul. This utter corruption of man is clearly taught in Scripture, Gen. 6:5; Ps. 14:3; Rom. 7:18. Total depravity here does not mean that human nature was at once as thoroughly depraved as it could possibly become. In the will this depravity manifested itself as spiritual inability.

2. Immediately connected with the preceding was the loss of communion with God through the Holy Spirit. This is but the reverse side of the utter corruption mentioned in the preceding paragraph. The two can be combined in the single statement that man lost the image of God in the sense of original righteousness. He broke away from the real source of life and blessedness, and the result was a condition of spiritual death, Eph. 2:1,5,12; 4:18.

3. This change in the actual condition of man also reflected itself in his consciousness. There was, first of all, a consciousness of pollution, revealing itself in the sense of shame, and in the effort of our first parents to cover their nakedness. And in the second place there was a consciousness of guilt, which found expression in an accusing conscience and in the fear of God which it inspired.

4. Not only spiritual death, but physical death as well resulted from the first sin of man. From a state of *posse non mori* he descended to a state of *non posse non mori*. Having sinned, he was doomed to return to the dust from which he was taken, Gen. 3:19. Paul tells us that by one man death entered the world and passed on to all men, Rom. 5:12, and that the wages of sin is death, Rom. 6:23.

5. This change also resulted in a necessary change of residence. Man was driven from paradise, because it represented the place of communion with God, and was a symbol of the fuller life and greater blessedness in store for man, if he continued steadfast. He was barred from the tree of life, because it was the symbol of the life promised in the covenant of works.

QUESTIONS FOR FURTHER STUDY. What different theories are there as to the origin of sin? What Scriptural proof is there that sin originated in the angelic world? Can the allegorical interpretation of the narrative of the fall be maintained in the light of Scripture? Is there any place for the fall in the theory of evolution? Did God will the fall of man or did He merely permit it? Does our Reformed doctrine make God the author of sin? What objections are there to the notion that the souls of men sinned in a previous existence? Was God justified in making the spiritual state of mankind in general contingent on the obedience or non-obedience of the first man? What do Barth and Brunner mean when they speak of the fall of man as super-historical? Why is it that the doctrine of the covenant of works finds so little acceptance outside of Reformed circles? What accounts for the widespread neglect of this doctrine in our day? Why is it important to maintain this doctrine?

LITERATURE: Bavinck, *Geref. Dogm.* III. pp. 605-624; III, pp. 1-60; Kuyper, *Dict. Dogm.*, *De Foedere*, pp. 23-117; *De Peccato*, pp. 17-26; Vos, *Geref. Dogm.* II, pp. 32-54; Hodge, *Syst. Theol.*, pp. 117-129; Dabney, *Syst. and Polem Theol.*, pp. 332-339; Alexander, *Syst. of Bibl. Theol. I*, pp. 183-196; 216-232; Schmid, *Doct. Theol. of the Ev. Luth. Ch.*, pp. 239-242; Valentine, *Chr. Theol.* I, pp. 416-420; Litton, *Introd. to Dogm. Theol.*, pp. 133-136; Pope, *Chr. Theol.*, II, pp. 3-28; II, p. 108; Raymond, *Syst. Theol.* II, pp. 50-63; 99;111; *Macintosh, Theol. as an Empirical Science*, pp. 216-229; McPherson, *Chr. Dogm.*, pp. 220-242; Orr, *God's Image in Man*; pp. 197-240; Candlish, *The Bibl. Doct. of Sin*, pp. 82-89; Talma, *De Anthropologie van Calvijn*, pp. 69-91; Kuyper, *Uit het Woord, De Leer der Verbonden*, pp. 3-221; Tennant, *The Origin and Propagation of Sin; ibid, The Concept of Sin*.

II. The Essential Character of Sin

Sin is one of the saddest but also one of the most common phenomena of human life. It is a part of the common experience of mankind, and therefore forces itself upon the attention of all those who do not deliberately close their eyes to the realities of human life. Some may for a time dream of the essential goodness of man and speak indulgently of those separate words and actions that do not measure up to the ethical standards of good society as mere foibles and weaknesses, for which man is not responsible, and which readily yield to corrective measures; but as time goes on, and all measures of external reform fail, and the suppression of one evil merely serves to release another, such persons are inevitably disillusioned. They become conscious of the fact that they have merely been fighting the symptoms of some deep-seated malady, and that they are confronted, not merely with the problem of sins, that is, of separate sinful deeds, but with the much greater and deeper problem of sin. of an evil that is inherent in human nature. This is exactly what we are beginning to witness at the present time. Many Modernists at present do not hesitate to say that the doctrine of Rousseau respecting the inherent goodness of man has proved to be one of the most pernicious teachings of the Enlightenment, and now call for a greater measure of realism in the recognition of sin Thus Walter Horton, who pleads for a realistic theology and believes that this calls for the acceptance of some Marxian principles, says: "I believe that orthodox Christianity represents a profound insight into the whole human predicament. I believe that the basic human difficulty *is* that perversion of the will, that betrayal of divine trust, which is called sin; and I believe that sin *is* in a sense a racial disease, transmissible from generation to generation. In affirming these things the Christian Fathers and the Protestant Reformers spoke as realists, and could have assembled masses of empirical evidence to support their views."[1] In view of the fact that sin is real and that no man can get away from it in this present life, it is no wonder that philosophers as well as theologians undertook to grapple with the problem of sin, though in philosophy it is known as the problem of evil rather than as the problem of sin. We shall briefly consider some of the most important philosophical theories of evil before we state the Scriptural doctrine of sin.

A. **Philosophic Theories Respecting the Nature of Evil.**

1. THE DUALISTIC THEORY. This is one of the views that were current in Greek philosophy. In the form of Gnosticism it found entrance into the

---

1. *Realistic Theology*, p. 56.

early Church. It assumes the existence of an eternal principle of evil, and holds that in man the spirit represents the principle of good, and the body, that of evil. It is objectionable for several reasons: (a) The position is philosophically untenable, that there is something outside of God that is eternal and independent of His will. (b) This theory robs sin of its ethical character by making it something purely physical and independent of the human will, and thereby really destroys the idea of sin. (c) It also does away with the responsibility of man by representing sin as a physical necessity. The only escape from sin lies in deliverance from the body.

2. THE THEORY THAT SIN IS MERELY PRIVATION. According to Leibnitz the present world is the best possible one. The existence of sin in it must be considered as unavoidable. It cannot be referred to the agency of God, and therefore must be regarded as a simple negation or privation, for which no efficient cause is needed. The limitations of the creature render it unavoidable. This theory makes sin a necessary evil, since creatures are necessarily limited, and sin is an unavoidable consequence of this limitation. Its attempt to avoid making God the author of sin is not successful, for even if sin is a mere negation requiring no efficient cause, God is nevertheless the author of the limitation from which it results. Moreover, it tends to obliterate the distinction between moral and physical evil, since it represents sin as little more than a misfortune which has befallen man. Consequently, it has a tendency to blunt man's sense of the evil or pollution of sin, to destroy the sense of guilt, and to abrogate man's moral responsibility.

3. THE THEORY THAT SIN IS AN ILLUSION. For Spinoza, as for Leibnitz, sin is simply a defect, a limitation of which man is conscious; but while Leibnitz regards the notion of evil, arising from this limitation, as necessary, Spinoza holds that the resulting consciousness of sin is simply due to the inadequacy of man's knowledge, which fails to see everything *sub specie aeternitatis,* that is, in unity with the eternal and infinite essence of God. If man's knowledge were adequate, so that he saw everything in God, he would have no conception of sin; it would simply be non-existent for him. But this theory, representing sin as something purely negative, does not account for its terrible positive results, to which the universal experience of mankind testifies in the most convincing manner. Consistently carried through, it abrogates all ethical distinctions, and reduces such concepts as "moral character" and "moral conduct" to meaningless phrases. In fact, it reduces the whole life of man to an illusion: his knowledge, his experience, the testimony of conscience, and so on, for all his knowledge is inadequate. Moreover, it goes contrary to the experience of mankind, that the greatest intellects are often the greatest sinners, Satan being the greatest of all.

4. THE THEORY THAT SIN IS A WANT OF GOD-CONSCIOUSNESS, DUE TO MAN'S SENSUOUS NATURE. This is the view of Schleiermacher. According to him man's consciousness of sin is dependent on his God-consciousness. When

the sense of God awakens in man, he is at once conscious of the opposition of his lower nature to it. This opposition follows from the very constitution of his being, from his sensuous nature, from the soul's connection with a physical organism. It is therefore an inherent imperfection, but one which man feels as sin and guilt. Yet this does not make God the author of sin, since man wrongly conceives of this imperfection as sin. Sin has no objective existence, but exists only in man's consciousness. But this theory makes man constitutionally evil. The evil was present in man even in his original state, when the God-consciousness was not sufficiently strong to control the sensuous nature of man. It is in flagrant opposition to Scripture, when it holds that man wrongly adjudges this evil to be sin, and thus makes sin and guilt purely subjective. And though Schleiermacher wishes to avoid this conclusion, it does make God the responsible author of sin, for He is the creator of man's sensuous nature. It also rests upon an incomplete induction of facts, since it fails to take account of the fact that many of the most hateful sins of man do not pertain to his physical but to his spiritual nature, such as avarice, envy, pride, malice, and others. Moreover, it leads to the most absurd conclusions as, for instance, that asceticism, by weakening the sensuous nature, necessarily weakens the power of sin; that man becomes less sinful as his senses fail with age; that death is the only redeemer; and that disembodied spirits, including the devil himself, have no sin.

5. THE THEORY OF SIN AS WANT OF TRUST IN GOD AND OPPOSITION TO HIS KINGDOM, DUE TO IGNORANCE. Like Schleiermacher, Ritschl too stresses the fact that sin is understood only from the standpoint of the Christian consciousness. They who are outside of the pale of the Christian religion, and they who are still strangers to the experience of redemption, have no knowledge of it. Under the influence of the redemptive work of God man becomes conscious of his lack of trust in God and of his opposition to the Kingdom of God, which is the highest good. Sin is not determined by man's attitude to the law of God, but by his relation to the purpose of God, to establish the Kingdom. Man imputes his failure to make the purpose of God his own to himself as guilt, but God regards it merely as ignorance, and because it is ignorance, it is pardonable. This view of Ritschl reminds us by way of contrast of the Greek dictum that knowledge is virtue. It fails completely to do justice to the Scriptural position that sin is above all transgression of the law of God, and therefore renders man guilty in the sight of God and worthy of condemnation. Moreover, the idea that sin is ignorance goes contrary to the voice of Christian experience. The man who is burdened with the sense of sin certainly does not feel that way about it. He is grateful, too, that not only the sins which he committed in ignorance are pardonable, but all the others as well, with the single exception of the blasphemy against the Holy Spirit.

6. THE THEORY THAT SIN IS SELFISHNESS. This position is taken among others by Mueller and A. H. Strong. Some who take this position conceive

of selfishness merely as the opposite of altruism or benevolence; others understand by it the choice of self rather than God as the supreme object of love. Now this theory, especially when it conceives of selfishness as a putting of self in the place of God, is by far the best of the theories named. Yet it can hardly be called satisfactory. Though all selfishness is sin, and there is an element of selfishness in all sin, it cannot be said that selfishness is the essence of sin. Sin can be properly defined only with reference to the law of God, a reference that is completely lacking in the definition under consideration. Moreover, there is a great deal of sin in which selfishness is not at all the governing principle. When a poverty-stricken father sees his wife and children pine away for lack of food, and in his desperate desire to help them finally resorts to theft, this can hardly be called pure selfishness. It may even be that the thought of self was entirely absent. Enmity to God, hardness of heart, impenitence, and unbelief, are all heinous sins, but cannot simply be qualified as selfishness. And certainly the view that all virtue is disinterestedness or benevolence, which seems to be a necessary corollary of the theory under consideration, at least in one of its forms, does not hold. An act does not cease to be virtuous, when its performance meets and satisfies some demand of our nature. Moreover, justice, fidelity, humility, forbearance, patience, and other virtues may be cultivated or practiced, not as forms of benevolence, but as virtues inherently excellent, not merely as promoting the happiness of others, but for what they are in themselves.

7. THE THEORY THAT SIN CONSISTS IN THE OPPOSITION OF THE LOWER PROPENSITIES OF HUMAN NATURE TO A GRADUALLY DEVELOPING MORAL CONSCIOUSNESS. This view was developed, as we pointed out in the preceding, by Tennant in his Hulsean Lectures. It is the doctrine of sin constructed according to the theory of evolution. Natural impulses and inherited qualities, derived from the brute, form the material of sin, but do not actually become sin until they are indulged in contrary to the gradually awakening moral sense of mankind. The theories of McDowall and Fiske move along similar lines. The theory as presented by Tennant halts somewhat between the Scriptural view of man and that presented by the theory of evolution, inclining now to the one and anon to the other side. It assumes that man had a free will even before the awakening of his moral consciousness, so that he was able to choose when he was placed before a moral ideal; but does not explain how we can conceive of a free and indeterminate will in a process of evolution. It limits sin to those transgressions of the moral law, which are committed with a clear consciousness of a moral ideal and are therefore condemned by conscience as evil. As a matter of fact, it is merely the old Pelagian view of sin grafted into the theory of evolution, and is therefore open to all the objections with which Pelagianism is burdened.

The radical defect in all these theories is that they seek to define sin without taking into consideration that sin is essentially a breaking away from God, opposition to God, and transgression of the law of God. Sin should always be defined in terms of man's relation to God and to His will as expressed in the moral law.

B. The Scriptural Idea of Sin.

In giving the Scriptural idea of sin it is necessary to call attention to several particulars.

1. SIN IS A SPECIFIC KIND OF EVIL. At the present time we hear a great deal about evil, and comparatively little about sin; and this is rather misleading. Not all evil is sin. Sin should not be confused with physical evil, with that which is injurious or calamitous. It is possible to speak not only of sin but also of sickness as an evil, but then the word "evil" is used in two totally different senses. Above the physical lies the ethical sphere, in which the contrast between moral good and evil applies, and it is only in this sphere that we can speak of sin. And even in this sphere it is not desirable to substitute the word "evil" for "sin" without any further qualification, for the latter is more specific than the former. Sin is a moral evil. Most of the names that are used in Scripture to designate sin point to its moral character. *Chatta'th* directs attention to it as an action that misses the mark and consists in a deviation from the right way. *'Avel* and *'avon* indicate that it is a want of integrity and rectitude, a departure from the appointed path. *Pesha'* refers to it as a revolt or a refusal of subjection to rightful authority, a positive transgression of the law, and a breaking of the covenant. And *resha'* points to it as a wicked and guilty departure from the law. Furthermore, it is designated as guilt by *'asham*, as unfaithfulness and treason, by *ma'al*, as vanity, by *'aven*, and as perversion or distortion of nature (crookedness) by *'avah*. The corresponding New Testament words, such as *hamartia, adikia, parabasis, paraptoma, anomia, paranomia*, and others, point to the same ideas. In view of the use of these words, and of the way in which the Bible usually speaks of sin, there can be no doubt about its ethical character. It is not a calamity that came upon man unawares, poisoned his life, and ruined his happiness, but an evil course which man has deliberately chosen to follow and which carries untold misery with it. Fundamentally, it is not something passive, such as a weakness, a fault, or an imperfection, for which we cannot be held responsible, but an active opposition to God, and a positive transgression of His law, which constitutes guilt. Sin is the result of a free but evil choice of man. This is the plain teaching of the Word of God, Gen. 3:1-6; Isa. 48:8; Rom. 1:18-32; I John 3:4. The application of the philosophy of evolution to the study of the Old Testament led some scholars to the conviction that the ethical idea of sin was not developed until the time of the prophets, but this view is not borne out by the way in which the earliest books of the Bible speak of sin.

2. SIN HAS AN ABSOLUTE CHARACTER. In the ethical sphere the contrast between good and evil is absolute. There is no neutral condition between the two. While there are undoubtedly degrees in both, there are no gradations

between the good and the evil. The transition from the one to the other is not of a quantitative, but of a qualitative character. A moral being that is good does not become evil by simply diminishing his goodness, but only by a radical qualitative change, by turning to sin. Sin is not a lesser degree of goodness, but a positive evil. This is plainly taught in the Bible. He who does not love God is thereby characterized as evil. Scripture knows of no position of neutrality. It urges the wicked to turn to righteousness, and sometimes speaks of the righteous as falling into evil; but it does not contain a single indication that either the one or the other ever lands in a neutral position. Man is either on the right side or on the wrong side, Matt. 10:32,33; 12:30; Luke 11:23; Jas. 2:10.

3. SIN ALWAYS HAS RELATION TO GOD AND HIS WILL. The older dogmaticians realized that it was impossible to have a correct conception of sin without contemplating it in relation to God and His will, and therefore emphasized this aspect and usually spoke of sin as "lack of conformity to the law of God." This is undoubtedly a correct *formal* definition of sin. But the question arises, Just what is the material content of the law? What does it demand? If this question is answered, it will be possible to determine what sin is in a *material sense*. Now there is no doubt about it that the great central demand of the law is *love to God*. And if from the material point of view moral goodness consists in love to God, then moral evil must consist in the opposite. It is separation from God, opposition to God, hatred of God, and this manifests itself in constant transgression of the law of God in thought, word, and deed. The following passages clearly show that Scripture contemplates sin in relation to God and His law, either as written on the tablets of the heart, or as given by Moses, Rom. 1:32; 2:12-14; 4:15; Jas. 2:9; I John 3:4.

4. SIN INCLUDES BOTH GUILT AND POLLUTION. Guilt is the state of deserving condemnation or of being liable to punishment for the violation of a law or a moral requirement. It expresses the relation which sin bears to justice or to the penalty of the law. But even so the word has a twofold meaning. It may denote an inherent quality of the sinner, namely, his demerit, ill-desert, or guiltiness, which renders him worthy of punishment. Dabney speaks of this as "potential guilt." It is inseparable from sin, is never found in one who is not personally a sinner, and is permanent, so that once established, it cannot be removed by pardon. But it may also denote the obligation to satisfy justice, to pay the penalty of sin, "actual guilt," as Dabney calls it.[1] It is not inherent in man, but is the penal enactment of the lawgiver, who fixes the penalty of the guilt. It may be removed by the satisfaction of the just demands of the law personally or vicariously. While many deny that sin includes guilt, this does not comport with the fact that sin was threatened and is indeed visited with punishment, and clearly contradicts the plain statements of Scripture, Matt. 6:12;

---

1. *Christ Our Penal Substitute*, pp. 10 f.

Rom. 3:19; 5:18; Eph. 2:3. By pollution we understand the inherent corruption to which every sinner is subject. This is a reality in the life of every individual. It is not conceivable without guilt, though guilt as included in a penal relationship, is conceivable without *immediate* pollution. Yet it is always followed by pollution. Every one who is guilty in Adam is, as a result, also born with a corrupt nature. The pollution of sin is clearly taught in such passages as Job 14:4; Jer. 17:9; Matt. 7:15-20; Rom. 8:5-8; Eph. 4:17-19.

5. SIN HAS ITS SEAT IN THE HEART. Sin does not reside in any one faculty of the soul, but in the heart, which in Scriptural psychology is the central organ of the soul, out of which are the issues of life. And from this center its influence and operations spread to the intellect, the will, the affections, in short, to the entire man, including his body. In his sinful state the whole man is the object of God's displeasure. There is a sense in which it can be said that sin originated in the will of man, but then the will does not designate some actual volition as much as it does the volitional nature of man. There was a tendency of the heart underlying the actual volition when sin entered the world. This view is in perfect harmony with the representations of Scripture in such passages as the following: Prov. 4:23; Jer. 17:9; Matt. 15:19,20; Luke 6:45; Heb. 3:12.

6. SIN DOES NOT CONSIST EXCLUSIVELY IN OVERT ACTS. Sin does not consist only in overt acts, but also in sinful habits and in a sinful condition of the soul. These three are related to one another as follows: The sinful state is the basis of the sinful habits, and these manifest themselves in sinful deeds. There is also truth, however, in the contention that repeated sinful deeds lead to the establishment of sinful habits. The sinful acts and dispositions of man must be referred to and find their explanation in a corrupt nature. The passages referred to in the preceding paragraph substantiate this view, for they clearly prove that the state or condition of man is thoroughly sinful. And if the question should still be raised, whether the thoughts and affections of the natural man, called "flesh" in Scripture, should be regarded as constituting sin, it might be answered by pointing to such passages as the following: Matt. 5:22,28; Rom. 7:7; Gal. 5:17,24, and others. In conclusion it may be said that sin may be defined as *lack of conformity to the moral law of God, either in act, disposition, or state.*

C. The Pelagian View of Sin.

The Pelagian view of sin is quite different from that presented above. The only point of similarity lies in this that the Pelagian also considers sin in relation to the law of God, and regards it as a transgression of the law. But in all other particulars his conception differs widely from the Scriptural and Augustinian view.

1. STATEMENT OF THE PELAGIAN VIEW. Pelagius takes his startingpoint in the natural ability of man. His fundamental proposition is: God has com-

manded man to do that which is good; hence the latter must have the ability to do it. This means that man has a free will in the absolute sense of the word, so that it is possible for him to decide for or against that which is good, and also to do the good as well as the evil. The decision is not dependent on any moral character in man, for the will is entirely indeterminate. Whether a man will do good or evil simply depends on his free and independent will. From this it follows, of course, that there is no such thing as a moral development of the individual. Good and evil are located in the separate actions of man. From this fundamental position the doctrinal teaching of Pelagius respecting sin naturally follows. Sin consists only in the separate acts of the will. There is no such thing as a sinful nature, neither are there sinful dispositions. Sin is always a deliberate choice of evil by a will which is perfectly free, and can just as well choose and follow the good. But if this is so, then the conclusion inevitably follows that Adam was not created in a state of positive holiness, but in a state of moral equilibrium. His condition was one of moral neutrality. He was neither good nor bad, and therefore had no moral character; but he chose the course of evil, and thus became sinful. Inasmuch as sin consists only in separate acts of the will, the idea of its propagation by procreation is absurd. A sinful nature, if such a thing should exist, might be passed on from father to son, but sinful acts cannot be so propagated. This is in the nature of the case an impossibility. Adam was the first sinner, but his sin was in no sense passed on to his descendants. There is no such thing as original sin. Children are born in a state of neutrality, beginning exactly where Adam began, except that they are handicapped by the evil examples which they see round about them. Their future course must be determined by their own free choice. The universality of sin is admitted, because all experience testifies to it. It is due to imitation and to the habit of sinning that is gradually formed. Strictly speaking, there are, on the Pelagian standpoint, no sinners, but only separate sinful acts. This makes a religious conception of the history of the race utterly impossible.

2. OBJECTIONS TO THE PELAGIAN VIEW. There are several weighty objections to the Pelagian view of sin, of which the following are the most important:

a. The fundamental position that man is held responsible by God only for what he is able to do, is absolutely contrary to the testimony of conscience and to the Word of God. It is an undeniable fact that, as a man increases in sin, his ability to do good decreases. He becomes in an ever greater measure the slave of sin. According to the theory under consideration this would also involve a lessening of his responsibility. But this is equivalent to saying that sin itself gradually redeems its victims by relieving them of their responsibility. The more sinful a man, the less responsible he is. Against this position conscience registers a loud protest. Paul does not say that the hardened sinners, which he describes in Rom. 1:18-32 were virtually without responsibility, but regards them as worthy of death. Jesus said of the wicked Jews who gloried in their freedom, but manifested their extreme wickedness by seeking to kill Him, that they were bond-servants of sin, did not understand His speech, because they could not hear His word, and would die in their sins, John 8:21,22,34,43. Though slaves of sin, they were yet responsible.

b. To deny that man has by nature a moral character, is simply bringing him down to the level of the animal. According to this view everything in the life of man that is not a conscious choice of the will, is deprived of all moral quality. But the consciousness of men in general testifies to the fact that the contrast between good and evil also applies to man's tendencies, desires, moods, and affections, and that these also have a moral character. In Pelagianism sin and virtue are reduced to superficial appendages of man, in no way connected with his inner life. That the estimate of Scripture is quite different appears from the following passages: Jer. 17:9; Ps. 51:6,10; Matt. 15:19; Jas. 4:1,2.

c. A choice of the will that is in no way determined by man's character, is not only psychologically unthinkable, but also ethically worthless. If a good deed of man simply happens to fall out as it does, and no reason can be given why it did not turn out to be the opposite, in other words, if the deed is not an expression of man's character, it lacks all moral value. It is only as an exponent of character that a deed has the moral value that is ascribed to it.

d. The Pelagian theory can give no satisfactory account of the universality of sin. The bad example of parents and grandparents offers no real explanation. The mere abstract possibility of man's sinning, even when strengthened by the evil example, does not explain how it came to pass that all men actually sinned. How can it be accounted for that the will invariably turned in the direction of sin, and never in the opposite direction? It is far more natural to think of a general disposition to sin.

D. The Roman Catholic View of Sin.

Though the Canons and Decrees of the Council of Trent are somewhat ambiguous in the doctrine of sin, the prevailing Roman Catholic view of sin may be expressed as follows: Real sin always consists in a conscious act of the will. It is true that the dispositions and habits that are not in accord with the will of God, are of a sinful character; yet they cannot be called sins in the strict sense of the word. The indwelling concupiscence, which lies back of sin, gained the upper hand in man in paradise, and thus precipitated the loss of the *donum superadditum* of original righteousness, cannot be regarded as sin, but only as the *fomes* or fuel of sin. The sinfulness of Adam's descendants is primarily only a negative condition, consisting in the absence of something that ought to be present, that is, of original righteousness, which is not essential to human nature. Something essential is wanting only if, as some hold, the *justitia naturalis* was also lost.

The objections to this view are perfectly evident from what was said in connection with the Pelagian theory. A bare reminder of them would seem to be quite sufficient. In so far as it holds that real sin consists only in a deliberate choice of the will and in overt acts, the objections raised against Pelagianism are pertinent. The idea that original righteousness was supernaturally added to man's natural constitution, and that its loss did not detract from human nature, is an un-Scriptural idea, as was pointed out in our discussion of the image of God in man. According to the Bible concupiscence is sin, real sin, and the root of many sinful actions. This was brought out when the Biblical view of sin was considered.

QUESTIONS FOR FURTHER STUDY. Has philosophy succeeded in explaining the origin of sin? Does Scripture bear out the view that sin originally had no ethical quality? What objection is there to the view that sin is mere privation? Must we conceive of sin as a substance? With whose name is this view associated? Does this sin exist apart from the sinner? How can we prove that sin must always be judged by the law of God? Did Paul favor the old Greek dualism, when he spoke of "the body of sin" and used the term "flesh" to denote man's sinful nature? Is the present tendency to speak of 'evil' rather than of 'sin' commendable? What is meant by the social interpretation of sin? Does this recognize sin for what it is fundamentally?

LITERATURE: Bavinck, Geref. Dogm. III, pp. 121-158; Kuyper, Dict. Dogm., De Peccato, pp. 27-35; Hodge, Syst. Theol. II, pp. 130-192; Vos, Geref. Dogm, II, pp. 21-32; Dabney, Syst. and Polem. Theol., pp. 306-317; McPherson, Chr. Dogm., pp. 257-264; Pope, Chr. Theol. II, pp. 29-42; Orchard, Modern Theories of Sin; Moxon, The Doctrine of Sin; Alexander, Syst. of Bibl. Theol. I. pp. 232-265; Brown, Chr. Theol. in Outline, pp. 261-282; Clarke, An Outline of Chr. Theol. pp. 227-239; Orr, God's Image in Man, pp. 197-246; Mackintosh, Christianity and Sin, cf. Index; Candlish, The Bibl. Doct. of Sin. pp. 31-44; Talma, De Anthropologie van Calvijn, pp. 92-117; Tennant, The Concept of Sin.

III. The Transmission of Sin

Scripture and experience both teach us that sin is universal, and according to the Bible the explanation for this universality lies in the fall of Adam. These two points, the universality of sin, and the connection of Adam's sin with that of mankind in general, now call for consideration. While there has been rather general agreement as to the universality of sin, there have been different representations of the connection between the sin of Adam and that of his descendants.

A. Historical Review.

1. BEFORE THE REFORMATION. The writings of the Apologists contain nothing definite respecting original sin. while those of Irenaeus and Tertullian clearly teach that our sinful condition is the result of Adam's fall. But the doctrine of the direct imputation of Adam's sin to his descendants is foreign even to them. Tertullian had a realistic conception of mankind. The whole human race was potentially and numerically present in Adam, and therefore sinned when he sinned and became corrupt when he became corrupt. Human nature as a whole sinned in Adam, and therefore every individualization of that nature is also sinful. Origen, who was profoundly influenced by Greek philosophy, had a different view of the matter, and scarcely recognized any connection between the sin of Adam and that of his descendants. He found the explanation of the sinfulness of the human race primarily in the personal sin of each soul in a pre-temporal state, though he also mentions some mystery of generation. Augustine shared the realistic conception of Tertullian. Though he also spoke of "imputation," he did not yet have in mind the direct or immediate imputation of the guilt of Adam to his posterity. His doctrine of original sin is not entirely clear. This may be due to the fact that he hesitated to choose between Traducianism and Creationism. While he stresses the fact that all men were seminally present in Adam and actually sinned in him, he also comes very close to the idea that they sinned in Adam as their representative. However, his main emphasis was on the transmission of the *corruption of sin*. Sin is passed on by propagation, and this propagation of Adam's sin is at the same time a punishment for his sin. Wiggers states the idea very briefly in these words: "The corruption of human nature, in the whole race, was the righteous punishment of the transgression of the first man, in whom all men already existed."[1] Augustine's great opponent, Pelagius, denied such a connection between the sin of Adam and those of his posterity. As he saw it, the propagation of sin by generation involved the Traducianist theory of the origin of the soul, which he

---

1. *Augustinism and Pelagianism*, p. 88.

regarded as a heretical error; and the imputation of Adam's sin to anyone but himself would be in conflict with the divine rectitude.

The Pelagian view was rejected by the Church, and the Scholastics in general thought along the lines indicated by Augustine, the emphasis all the while being on the transmission of the pollution of Adam's sin rather than on that of his guilt. Hugo St. Victor and Peter the Lombard held that actual concupiscence stains the semen in the act of procreation, and that this stain in some way defiles the soul on its union with the body. Anselm, Alexander of Hales, and Bonaventura stressed the realistic conception of the connection between Adam and his posterity. The whole human race was seminally present in Adam, and therefore also sinned in him. His disobedience was the disobedience of the entire human race. At the same time generation was regarded as the *sine qua non* of the transmission of the sinful nature. In Bonaventura and others after him the distinction between original guilt and original pollution was more clearly expressed. The fundamental idea was, that the guilt of Adam's sin is imputed to all his descendants. Adam suffered the loss of original righteousness, and thereby incurred the divine displeasure. As a result all his descendants are deprived of original righteousness, and as such the objects of divine wrath. Moreover, the pollution of Adam's sin is in some way passed on to his posterity, but the manner of this transmission was a matter of dispute among the Scholastics. Since they were not Traducianists, and therefore could not say that the soul, which is after all the real seat of evil, was passed on from father to son by generation, they felt that something more had to be said to explain the transmission of inherent evil. Some said that it is passed on through the body, which in turn contaminates the soul as soon as it comes in contact with it. Others, sensing the danger of this explanation sought it in the mere fact that every man is now born in the state in which Adam was before he was endowed with original righteousness, and thus subject to the struggle between the unchecked flesh and the spirit. In Thomas Aquinas the realistic strain again appears rather strongly, though in a modified form. He pointed out that the human race constitutes an organism, and that, just as the act of one bodily member — say, the hand — is regarded as the act of the person, so the sin of one member of the organism of humanity is imputed to the whole organism.

2. AFTER THE REFORMATION. While the Reformers did not agree with the Scholastics as to the nature of original sin, their view of its transmission did not contain any new elements. The ideas of Adam as the representative of the human race, and of the "immediate" imputation of his guilt to his descendants are not yet clearly expressed in their works. According to Luther we are accounted guilty by God because of the indwelling sin inherited from Adam. Calvin speaks in a somewhat similar vein. He holds that, since Adam was not only the progenitor but the root of the human race, all his descendants are born with a corrupt nature; and that both the guilt of Adam's sin and their own inborn corruption are imputed to them as sin. The development of the federal

theology brought the idea of Adam as the representative of the human race to the foreground, and led to a clearer distinction between the transmission of the guilt and of the pollution of Adam's sin. Without denying that our native corruption also constitutes guilt in the sight of God, federal theology stressed the fact that there is an "immediate" imputation of Adam's guilt to those whom he represented as the head of the covenant.

Socinians and Arminians both rejected the idea of the imputation of Adam's sin to his descendants. Placeus, of the school of Saumur, advocated the idea of "mediate" imputation. Denying all immediate imputation, he held that because we inherit a sinful nature from Adam, we are deserving of being treated as if we had committed the original offense. This was something new in Reformed theology, and Rivet had no difficulty in proving this by collecting a long line of testimonies. A debate ensued in which "immediate" and "mediate" imputation were represented as mutually exclusive doctrines; and in which it was made to appear as if the real question was, whether man is guilty in the sight of God solely on account of Adam's sin, imputed to him, or solely on account of his own inherent sin. The former was not the doctrine of the Reformed Churches, and the latter was not taught in them before the time of Placeus. The teachings of the latter found their way into New England theology, and became especially characteristic of the New School (New Haven) theology. In modern liberal theology the doctrine of the transmission of sin from Adam to his posterity is entirely discredited. It prefers to seek the explanation of the evil that is in the world in an animal inheritance, which is not itself sinful. Strange to say, even Barth and Brunner, though violently opposed to liberal theology, do not regard the universal sinfulness of the human race as the result of Adam's sin. Historically, the latter occupies a unique place merely as the first sinner.

B. The Universality of Sin.

Few will be inclined to deny the presence of evil in the human heart, however much they may differ as to the nature of this evil and as to the way in which it originated. Even Pelagians and Socinians are ready to admit that sin is universal. This is a fact that forces itself upon the attention of every one.

1. THE HISTORY OF RELIGIONS AND OF PHILOSOPHY TESTIFY TO IT. The history of religions testifies to the universality of sin. The question of Job, "How shall a man be just with God?" is a question that was asked not merely in the realm of special revelation, but also outside of it in the Gentile world. The heathen religions testify to a universal consciousness of sin and of the need of reconciliation with a Supreme Being. There is a general feeling that the gods are offended and must be propitiated in some way. There is a universal voice of conscience, testifying to the fact that man falls short of the ideal and stands condemned in the sight of some higher Power. Altars reeking with the blood of sacrifices, often the sacrifices of dear children, repeated confessions of wrong-doing, and prayers for deliverance from evil, — all point to the consciousness

of sin. Missionaries find this wherever they go. The history of philosophy is indicative of the same fact. Early Greek philosophers were already wrestling with the problem of moral evil, and since their day no philosopher of name was able to ignore it. They were all constrained to admit the universality of it, and that in spite of the fact they were not able to explain the phenomenon. There was, it is true, a superficial optimism in the eighteenth century, which dreamt of the inherent goodness of man, but in its stupidity flew in the face of the facts and was sharply rebuked by Kant. Many liberal theologians were induced to believe and to preach this inherent goodness of man as gospel truth, but to-day many of them qualify it as one of the most pernicious errors of the past. Surely, the facts of life do not warrant such optimism.

2. THE BIBLE CLEARLY TEACHES IT. There are direct statements of Scripture that point to the universal sinfulness of man, such as I Kings 8:46; Ps. 143:2; Prov. 20:9; Eccl. 7:20; Rom. 3:1-12,19,20,23; Gal. 3:22; Jas. 3:2; I John 1:8,10. Several passages of Scripture teach that sin is the heritage of man from the time of his birth, and is therefore present in human nature so early that it cannot possibly be considered as the result of imitation, Ps. 51:5; Job 14:4; John 3:6. In Ephesians 2:3 Paul says of the Ephesians that they "were *by nature* children of wrath, even as the rest." In this passage the term "by nature" points to something inborn and original, as distinguished from what is subsequently acquired. Sin, then, is something original, in which all men participate, and which makes them guilty before God. Moreover, according to Scripture, death is visited even upon those who have never exercised a personal and conscious choice, Rom. 5:12-14. This passage implies that sin exists in the case of infants prior to moral consciousness. Since infants die, and therefore the effect of sin is present in their case, it is but natural to assume that the cause is also present. Finally, Scripture also teaches that all men are under condemnation and therefore need the redemption which is in Christ Jesus. Children are never made an exception to this rule, cf. the preceding passages and also John 3:3,5; I John 5:12. This is not contradicted by those passages which ascribe a certain righteousness to man, such as, Matt. 9:12,13; Acts 10:35; Rom. 2:14; Phil. 3:6; I Cor. 1:30, for this may be either civil righteousness, ceremonial or covenant righteousness, the righteousness of the law, or the righteousness which is in Christ Jesus.

C. The Connection of Adam's Sin with that of the Race.

1. THE DENIAL OF THIS CONNECTION. Some deny the causal connection of the sin of Adam with the sinfulness of the human race either wholly or in part.

a. Pelagians and Socinians deny absolutely that there is any necessary connection between our sin and the sin of Adam. The first sin was Adam's sin only and does not concern his posterity in any way. The most they will admit is that the evil example of Adam led to imitation.

b. Semi-Pelagians and the earlier Arminians teach that man inherited a natural inability from Adam, but is not responsible for this inability, so that no guilt attaches to it, and it may even be said that God is somewhat under obligation to provide a cure for it. The Wesleyan Arminians admit that this inborn corruption also involves guilt.

c. The New School (New Haven) theory teaches that man is born with an inherent tendency to sin, in virtue of which his moral preference is invariably wrong; but that this tendency cannot itself be called sin, since sin always consists exclusively in conscious and intentional transgression of the law.

d. The Theology of crisis stresses the solidarity of sin in the human race, but denies that sin originated in an act of Adam in paradise. The fall belongs to pre- or super-history, and is already a thing of the past when the historical Adam appears upon the scene. It is the secret of God's predestination. The story of the fall is a myth. Adam appears as the type of Christ in so far as it can be seen in him that life without sin is possible in communion with God. Says Brunner: "In Adam all have sinned — that is the Biblical statement; but how? The Bible does not tell us that. The doctrine of original sin is read into it."[1]

2. DIFFERENT THEORIES TO EXPLAIN THE CONNECTION.

a. *The realistic theory.* The earliest method of explaining the connection between the sin of Adam and the guilt and pollution of all his descendants was the realistic theory. This theory is to the effect that human nature constitutes, not only generically but numerically as well, a single unit. Adam possessed the whole human nature, and in him it corrupted itself by its own voluntary apostatizing act in Adam. Individual men are not separate substances, but manifestations of the same general substance; they are numerically one. This universal human nature became corrupt and guilty in Adam, and consequently every individualization of it in the descendants of Adam is also corrupt and guilty from the very beginning of its existence. This means that all men *actually* sinned in Adam before the individualization of human nature began. This theory was accepted by some of the early Church Fathers and by some of the Scholastics, and was defended in more recent times by Dr. Shedd. However, it is open to several objections: (1) By representing the souls of men as individualizations of the general spiritual substance that was present in Adam, it would seem to imply that the substance of the soul is of a material nature, and thus to land us inevitably in some sort of materialism. (2) It is contrary to the testimony of consciousness and does not sufficiently guard the interests of human personality. Every man is conscious of being a separate personality, and therefore far more than a mere passing wave in the general ocean of existence. (3) It does not explain why Adam's descendants are held responsible for his first sin only, and not for his later sins, nor for the sins of all the generations of forefathers that followed Adam. (4) Neither

---

1. *Man in Revolt*, p. 142.

does it give an answer to the important question, why Christ was not held responsible for the *actual* commission of sin in Adam, for He certainly shared the same human nature, the nature that *actually* sinned in Adam.

b. *The doctrine of the covenant of works.* This implies that Adam stood in a twofold relationship to his descendants, namely, that of the natural head of all mankind, and that of the *representative head* of the entire human race in the covenant of works. (1) *The natural relationship.* In his natural relationship Adam was the father of all mankind. As he was created by God he was subject to change, and had no rightful claim to an unchangeable state. He was in duty bound to obey God, and this obedience did not entitle him to any reward. On the other hand, if he sinned, he would become subject to corruption and to punishment, but the sin would be only his own, and could not be placed to the account of his descendants. Dabney holds that, according to the law that like begets like, his corruption would have passed on to his descendants. But however this may be — and it is rather useless to speculate about it — they certainly could not have been held responsible for this corruption. They could not have been considered guilty in Adam merely in virtue of the natural relationship in which Adam stood to the race. The usual Reformed representation is a different one. (2) *The covenant relationship.* To the natural relationship in which Adam stood to his descendants God graciously added a covenant relationship containing several positive elements: (a) *An element of representation.* God ordained that in this covenant Adam should not stand for himself only, but as the representative of all his descendants. Consequently, he was the head of the race not only in a parental, but also in a federal sense. (b) *An element of probation.* While apart from this covenant Adam and his descendants would have been in a continual state of trial, with a constant danger of sinning, the covenant guaranteed that persistent perseverance for a fixed period of time would be rewarded with the establishment of man in a permanent state of holiness and bliss. (c) *An element of reward or punishment.* According to the terms of the covenant Adam would obtain a rightful claim to eternal life, if he fulfilled the conditions of the covenant. And not only he, but all his descendants as well would have shared in this blessing. In its normal operation, therefore, the covenant arrangement would have been of incalculable benefit for mankind. But there was a possibility that man would disobey, thereby reversing the operation of the covenant, and in that case the results would naturally be correspondingly disastrous. Transgression of the covenant commandment would result in death. Adam chose the course of disobedience, corrupted himself by sin, became guilty in the sight of God, and as such subject to the sentence of death. And because he was the federal representative of the race, his disobedience affected all his descendants. In His righteous judgment God imputes the guilt of the first sin, committed by the head of the covenant, to all those that are federally related to him. And as a result they are born in a depraved and sinful condition as well, and this inherent corruption also involves guilt. This doctrine explains why only the first sin of Adam, and not his following sins nor the sins of our other forefathers, is imputed to us, and also safeguards the sinlessness of Jesus, for He was not a human person and therefore not in the covenant of works.

c. *The theory of mediate imputation.* This theory denies that the guilt of Adam's sin is *directly* imputed to his descendants, and represents the matter as follows: Adam's descendants derive their innate corruption from him by a process of natural generation, and only on the basis of that inherent depravity which they share with him are they also considered guilty of his apostasy. They are not born corrupt because they are guilty in Adam, but they are considered guilty because they are corrupt. Their condition is not based on their legal status, but their legal status on their condition. This theory, first advocated by Placeus, was adopted by the younger Vitringa and Venema, by several New England theologians, and by some of the New School theologians in the Presbyterian Church. This theory is objectionable for several reasons: (1) A thing cannot be mediated by its own consequences. The inherent depravity with which the descendants of Adam are born is already the result of Adam's sin, and therefore cannot be considered as the basis on which they are guilty of the sin of Adam. (2) It offers no objective ground whatsoever for the transmission of Adam's guilt and depravity to all his descendants. Yet there must be some objective legal ground for this. (3) If this theory were consistent, it ought to teach the mediate imputation of the sins of all previous generations to those following, for their joint corruption is passed on by generation. (4) It also proceeds on the assumption that there can be moral corruption that is not at the same time guilt, a corruption that does not in itself make one liable to punishment. (5) And finally, if the inherent corruption which is present in the descendants of Adam can be regarded as the *legal* ground for the explanation of something else, there is no more need of any mediate imputation.

IV. Sin in the Life of the Human Race

A. Original Sin.

The sinful state and condition in which men are born is designated in theology by the name *peccatum originale*, which is literally translated in the English "original sin." This term is better than the Holland name "erfzonde," since the latter, strictly speaking, does not cover all that belongs to original sin. It is not a proper designation of original guilt, for this is not inherited but imputed to us. This sin is called "original sin," (1) because it is derived from the original root of the human race; (2) because it is present in the life of every individual from the time of his birth, and therefore cannot be regarded as the result of imitation; and (3) because it is the inward root of all the actual sins that defile the life of man. We should guard against the mistake of thinking that the term in any way implies that the sin designated by it belongs to the original constitution of human nature, which would imply that God created man as a sinner.

1. HISTORICAL REVIEW. The early Church Fathers contain nothing very definite about original sin. According to the Greek Fathers there is a physical corruption in the human race, which is derived from Adam, but this is not sin and does not involve guilt. The freedom of the will was not affected directly by the fall, but is affected only indirectly by the inherited physical corruption. The tendency apparent in the Greek Church finally culminated in Pelagianism, which flatly denied all original sin. In the Latin Church a different tendency appeared especially in Tertullian, according to whom the propagation of the soul involves the propagation of sin. He regarded original sin as a hereditary sinful taint or corruption, which did not exclude the presence of some good in man. Ambrose advanced beyond Tertullian by regarding original sin as a state and by distinguishing between the inborn corruption and the resulting guilt of man. The free will of man was weakened by the fall. It is especially in Augustine that the doctrine of original sin comes to fuller development. According to him the nature of man, both physical and moral, is totally corrupted by Adam's sin, so that he cannot do otherwise than sin. This inherited corruption or original sin is a moral punishment for the sin of Adam. It is such a quality of the nature of man, that in his natural state, he can and will do evil only. He has lost the material freedom of the will, and it is especially in this respect that original sin constitutes a punishment. In virtue of this sin man is already under condemnation. It is not merely

corruption, but also guilt. Semi-Pelagianism reacted against the absoluteness of the Augustinian view. It admitted that the whole human race is involved in the fall of Adam, that human nature is tainted with hereditary sin, and that all men are by nature inclined to evil and not able, apart from the grace of God, to complete any good work; but denied the *total* depravity of man, the guilt of original sin, and the loss of the freedom of the will. This became the prevalent view during the Middle Ages, though there were some prominent Scholastics who were on the whole Augustinian in their conception of original sin. Anselm's view of original sin was altogether in harmony with that of Augustine. It represents original sin as consisting of the guilt of nature (the nature of the entire human race), contracted by a single act of Adam, and the resulting inherent corruption of human nature, handed down to posterity and manifesting itself in a tendency to sin. This sin also involves the loss of the power of self-determination in the direction of holiness (material freedom of the will), and renders man a slave of sin. The prevailing opinion among the Scholastics was that original sin is not something positive, but rather the absence of something that ought to be present, particularly the privation of original righteousness, though some would add a positive element, namely, an inclination to evil. Thomas Aquinas held that original sin, considered in its material element, is concupiscence, but considered in its formal element, is the privation of original justice. There is a dissolution of the harmony in which original justice consisted, and in this sense original sin can be called a languor of nature. Speaking generally, the Reformers were in agreement with Augustine, though Calvin differed from him especially on two points, by stressing the fact that original sin is not something purely negative, and is not limited to the sensuous nature of man. At the time of the Reformation the Socinians followed the Pelagians in the denial of original sin, and in the seventeenth century the Arminians broke with the Reformed faith, and accepted the Semi-Pelagian view of original sin. Since that time various shades of opinion were advocated in the Protestant Churches both in Europe and in America.

2. THE TWO ELEMENTS OF ORIGINAL SIN. Two elements must be distinguished in original sin, namely:

a. *Original guilt.* The word "guilt" expresses the relation which sin bears to justice or, as the older theologians put it, to the penalty of the law. He who is guilty stands in a penal relation to the law. We can speak of guilt in a twofold sense, namely, as *reatus culpae* and as *reatus poenae*. The former, which Turretin calls "potential guilt," is the intrinsic moral ill-desert of an act or state. This is of the essence of sin and is an inseparable part of its sinfulness. It attaches only to those who have themselves committed sinful deeds, and attaches to them permanently. It cannot be removed by forgiveness, and is not removed by justification on the basis of the merits of Jesus Christ, and much less by mere pardon. Man's sins are inherently ill-deserving even after he is justified. Guilt in this sense cannot be transferred from one person to another. The usual sense, however, in which we speak of guilt in theology, is that of *reatus poenae*. By this is meant desert of punishment, or obligation to render satisfaction to God's justice for self-determined violation of the law. Guilt in this sense is not of the essence of sin, but is rather a relation to the penal sanction of the law. If there had been no sanction attached to the disregard of moral relations, every departure from the law would have been sin, but would not have involved liability to punishment. Guilt in this sense may be removed by the satisfaction of justice, either personally or vicariously. It may be transferred from one person to another, or assumed by one person for another. It is removed from believers by justification, so that their sins, though inherently ill-deserving, do not make them liable to punishment. Semi-Pelagians and the older Arminians or Remonstrants deny that original sin involves guilt. The guilt of Adam's sin, committed by him as the federal head of the human race, is imputed to all his descendants. This is evident from the fact that, as the Bible teaches, death as the punishment of sin passes on from Adam to all his descendants. Rom. 5:12-19; Eph. 2:3; I Cor. 15:22.

b. *Original pollution.* Original pollution includes two things, namely, the absence of original righteousness, and the presence of positive evil. It should be noted: (1) That original pollution is not merely a disease, as some of the Greek Fathers and the Arminians represent it, but sin in the real sense of the word. Guilt attaches to it; he who denies this does not have a Biblical conception of original corruption. (2) That this pollution is not to be regarded as a substance infused into the human soul, nor as a change of substance in the metaphysical sense of the word. This was the error of the Manichæans and of Flacius Illyricus in the days of the Reformation. If the substance of the soul were sinful, it would have to be replaced by a new substance in regeneration; but this does not take place. (3) That it is not merely a privation. In his polemic with the Manichæans, Augustine not merely denied that sin was a substance, but also asserted that it was merely a privation. He called it a *privatio boni.* But original sin is not merely negative; it is also an inherent positive disposition toward sin. This original pollution may be considered from more than one point of view, namely, as total depravity and as total inability.

c. *Total depravity.* In view of its pervasive character, inherited pollution is called total depravity. This phrase is often misunderstood, and therefore calls for careful discrimination. Negatively, it does not imply: (1) that every man is as thoroughly depraved as he can possibly become; (2 that the sinner has no innate knowledge of the will of God, nor a conscience that discriminates between good and evil; (3) that sinful man does not often admire virtuous character and actions in others, or is incapable of disinterested affections and actions in his relations with his fellow-men; nor (4) that every unregenerate man will, in virtue of his inherent sinfulness, indulge in every form of sin: it often happens that one form excludes the other. Positively, it does indicate:

(1) that the inherent corruption extends to every part of man's nature, to all the faculties and powers of both soul and body; and (2) that there is no spiritual good, that is, good in relation to God, in the sinner at all, but only perversion. This total depravity is denied by Pelagians, Socinians, and seventeenth century Arminians, but is clearly taught in Scripture, John 5:42; Rom. 7:18,23; 8:7; Eph. 4:18; II Tim. 3:2-4; Tit. 1:15; Heb. 3:12.

d. *Total inability.* With respect to its effect on man's spiritual powers, it is called total inability. Here, again, it is necessary to distinguish. By ascribing total inability to the natural man we do not mean to say that it is impossible for him to do good in any sense of the word. Reformed theologians generally say that he is still able to perform: (1) natural good; (2) civil good or civil righteousness; and (3) externally religious good. It is admitted that even the unrenewed possess some virtue, revealing itself in the relations of social life, in many acts and sentiments that deserve the sincere approval and gratitude of their fellow-men, and that even meet with the approval of God to a certain extent. At the same time it is maintained that these same actions and feelings, when considered in relation to God, are radically defective. Their fatal defect is that they are not prompted by love to God, or by any regard for the will of God as requiring them. When we speak of man's corruption as total inability, we mean two things: (1) that the unrenewed sinner cannot do any act, however insignificant, which *fundamentally* meets with God's approval and answers to the demands of God's holy law; and (2) that he cannot change his fundamental preference for sin and self to love for God, nor even make an approach to such a change. In a word, he is unable to do any spiritual good. There is abundant Scriptural support for this doctrine: John 1:13; 3:5; 6:44; 8:34; 15:4,5; Rom. 7:18,24; 8:7,8; I Cor. 2:14; II Cor. 3:5; Eph. 2:1,8-10; Heb. 11:6. Pelagians, however, believe in the plenary ability of man, denying that his moral faculties were impaired by sin. Arminians speak of a gracious ability, because they believe that God imparts His common grace to all men, which enables them to turn to God and believe. The New School theologians ascribe to man natural as distinguished from moral ability, a distinction borrowed from Edwards' great work *On the Will.* The import of their teaching is that man in his fallen state is still in possession of all the natural faculties that are required for doing spiritual good (intellect, will, etc.), but lacks moral ability, that is, the ability to give proper direction to those faculties, a direction well-pleasing to God. The distinction under consideration is advanced, in order to stress the fact that man is *wilfully sinful,* and this may well be emphasized. But the New School theologians assert that man would be able to do spiritual good if he only wanted to do it. This means that the "natural ability" of which they speak, is after all an ability to do real spiritual good.[1] On the whole it may be said that the distinction between natural and moral ability is not a desirable one, for: (1) it has no warrant in Scripture, which teaches consistently that man

---

1. Cf. Hodge, *Syst. Theol.* II, p. 266.

is not able to do what is required of him; (2) it is essentially ambiguous and misleading: the possession of the requisite faculties to do spiritual good does not yet constitute an ability to do it; (3) "natural" is not. a proper antithesis of "moral," for a thing may be both at the same time; and the inability of man is also natural in an important sense, that is, as being incident to his nature in its present state as naturally propagated; and (4) the language does not accurately express the important distinction intended; what is meant is that it is moral, and not either physical or constitutional; that it has its ground, not in the want of any faculty, but in the corrupt moral state of the faculties, and of the disposition of the heart.

3. ORIGINAL SIN AND HUMAN FREEDOM. In connection with the doctrine of the total inability of man the question naturally arises, whether original sin then also involves the loss of freedom, or of what is generally called the *liberum arbitrium*, the free will. This question should be answered with discrimination for, put in this general way, it may be answered both negatively and positively. In a certain sense man has not, and in another sense he has, lost his liberty. There is a certain liberty that is the inalienable possession of a free agent, namely, the liberty to choose as he pleases, in full accord with the prevailing dispositions and tendencies of his soul. Man did not lose any of the constitutional faculties necessary to constitute him a responsible moral agent. He still has reason, conscience, and the freedom of choice. He has ability to acquire knowledge, and to feel and recognize moral distinctions and obligations; and his affections, tendencies, and actions are spontaneous, so that he chooses and refuses as he sees fit. Moreover, he has the ability to appreciate and do many things that are good and amiable, benevolent and just, in the relations he sustains to his fellow-beings. But man did lose his material freedom, that is, the rational power to determine his course in the direction of the highest good, in harmony with the original moral constitution of his nature. Man has by nature an irresistible bias for evil. He is not able to apprehend and love spiritual excellence, to seek and do spiritual things, the things of God that pertain to salvation. This position, which is Augustinian and Calvinistic, is flatly contradicted by Pelagianism and Socinianism, and in part also by Semi-Pelagianism and Arminianism. Modern liberalism, which is essentially Pelagian, naturally finds the doctrine, that man has lost the ability to determine his life in the direction of real righteousness and holiness, highly offensive, and glories in the ability of man to choose and do what is right and good. On the other hand the dialectical theology (Barthianism) strongly reasserts the utter inability of man to make even the slightest move in a Godward direction. The sinner is a slave of sin and cannot possibly turn in the opposite direction.

4. THE THEOLOGY OF CRISIS AND ORIGINAL SIN. It may be well at this point to define briefly the position of the Theology of Crisis or of Barthianism with respect to the doctrine of original sin. Walter Lowrie correctly says: "Barth has much to say about the Fall — but nothing about 'original sin.'

That man is *fallen* we can plainly see; but the Fall is not an event we can point to in history, it belongs decidedly to pre-history, *Urgeschichte*, in a meta-physical sense."[1] Brunner has something to say about it in his recent work on *Man in Revolt*.[2] He does not accept the doctrine of original sin in the traditional and ecclesiastical sense of the word. The first sin of Adam was not and could not be placed to the account of all his descendants; nor did this sin result in a sinful state, which is passed on to his posterity, and which is now the fruitful root of all actual sin. "Sin is never a state, but it is always an act. Even being a sinner is not a state but an act, because it is being a person." In Brunner's estimation the traditional view has an undesirable element of determinism in it, and does not sufficiently safeguard the responsibility of man. But his rejection of the doctrine of original sin does not mean that he sees no truth in it at all. It rightly stresses the solidarity of sin in the human race, and the transmission "of the spiritual nature, of the 'character,' from parents to children." However, he seeks the explanation of the universality of sin in something else than in "original sin." The man whom God created was not simply some one man, but a responsible person created in and for community with others. The isolated individual is but an abstraction. "In the Creation we are an individualized, articulated unity, one body with many members." If one member suffers, all the members suffer with it. He goes on to say: "If that is our origin, then our opposition to this origin cannot be an experience, an act, of the individual as an individual. . . . Certainly each individual is a sinner as an individual; but he is at the same time the whole in its united solidarity, the body, actual humanity as a whole." There was therefore solidarity in sinning; the human race fell away from God; but it belongs to the very nature of sin that we deny this solidarity in sin. The result of this initial sin is that man is now a sinner; but the fact that man is now a sinner should not be regarded as the cause of his individual sinful actions. Such a causal connection cannot be admitted, for every sin which man commits is a fresh decision against God. The state-ment that man is a sinner does not mean that he is in a state or condition of sin, but that he is actually engaged in rebellion against God. As Adam we turned away from God, and "he who commits this apostasy can do no other than repeat it continually, not because it has become a habit, but because this is the distinctive character of this act." Man cannot reverse the course, but continues to sin right along. The Bible never speaks of sin except as the act of turning away from God. "But in the very concept of 'being a sinner' this act is conceived as one which determines man's whole existence." There is much in this representation that reminds one of the realistic representation of Thomas Aquinas.

5. OBJECTIONS TO THE DOCTRINE OF TOTAL DEPRAVITY AND TOTAL INABILITY.

a. *It is inconsistent with moral obligation.* The most obvious and the most plausible objection to the doctrine of total depravity and total inability,

---

1. *Our Concern with the Theology of Crisis*, p. 187.
2. Chap. 6.

is that it is inconsistent with moral obligation. It is said that a man cannot be held justly responsible for anything for which he has not the required ability. But the general implication of this principle is a fallacy. It may hold in cases of disability resulting from a limitation which God has imposed on man's nature; but it certainly does not apply in the sphere of morals and religion, as already pointed out in the preceding. We should not forget that the inability under consideration is self-imposed, has a moral origin, and is not due to any limitation which God has put upon man's being. Man is unable as a result of the perverted choice made in Adam.

b. *It removes all motives for exertion.* A second objection is that this doctrine removes all motives for exertion and destroys all rational grounds for the use of the means of grace. If we know that we cannot accomplish a given end, why should we use the means recommended for its accomplishment? Now it is perfectly true that the sinner, who is enlightened by the Holy Spirit and is truly conscious of his own natural inability, ceases from work-righteousness. And this is exactly what is necessary. But it does not hold with respect to the natural man, for he is thoroughly self-righteous. Moreover, it is not true that the doctrine of inability naturally tends to foster neglect in the use of the means of grace ordained by God. On this principle the farmer might also say, I cannot produce a harvest; why should I cultivate my fields? But this would be utter folly. In every department of human endeavor the result depends on the co-operation of causes over which man has no control. The Scriptural grounds for the use of means remain: God commands the use of means; the means ordained by God are adapted to the end contemplated; ordinarily the end is not attained, except by the use of the appointed means; and God has promised to bless the use of those means.

c. *It encourages delay in conversion.* It is also asserted that this doctrine encourages delay in conversion. If a man believes that he cannot change his heart, cannot repent and believe the gospel, he will feel that he can only passively abide the time when it will please God to change the direction of his life. Now there may be, and experience teaches that there are, some who actually adopt that attitude; but as a rule the effect of the doctrine under consideration will be quite different. If sinners, to whom sin has grown very dear, were conscious of the power to change their lives at will, they would be tempted to defer it to the last moment. But if one is conscious of the fact that a very desirable thing is beyond the compass of his own powers, he will instinctively seek help outside of himself. The sinner who feels that way about salvation, will seek help with the great Physician of the soul, and thus acknowledge his own disability.

B. Actual Sin.

Roman Catholics and Arminians minimized the idea of original sin, and then developed doctrines, such as those of the washing away of original sin (though not only that) by baptism, and of sufficient grace, by which its seriousness is greatly obscured. The emphasis is clearly altogether on actual sins. Pelagians, Socinians, modern liberal theologians, and — strange as it may seem — also the Theology of Crisis, recognize only actual sins. It must be said, however, that this theology does speak of sin in the singular as well as in the plural, that is, it does recognize a solidarity in sin, which some of the others have not recognized. Reformed theology has always given due recognition to original sin and to the relation in which it stands to actual sins.

1. THE RELATION BETWEEN ORIGINAL AND ACTUAL SIN. The former originated in a free act of Adam as the representative of the human race, a transgression of the law of God and a corruption of human nature, which rendered him liable to the punishment of God. In the sight of God his sin was the sin of all his descendants, so that they are born as sinners, that is in a state of guilt and in a polluted condition. Original sin is both a state and an inherent quality of pollution in man. Every man is guilty in Adam, and is consequently born with a depraved and corrupt nature. And this inner corruption is the unholy fountain of all actual sins. When we speak of actual sin or *peccatum actuale*, we use the word "actual" or "actuale" in a comprehensive sense. The term "actual sins" does not merely denote those external actions which are accomplished by means of the body, but all those conscious thoughts and volitions which spring from original sin. They are the individual sins of act in distinction from man's inherited nature and inclination. Original sin is one, actual sin is manifold. Actual sin may be interior, such as a particular conscious doubt or evil design in the mind, or a particular conscious lust or desire in the heart; but they may also be exterior, such as deceit, theft, adultery, murder, and so on. While the existence of original sin has met with widespread denial, the presence of actual sin in the life of man is generally admitted. This does not mean, however, that people have always had an equally profound consciousness of sin. We hear a great deal nowadays about the "loss of the sense of sin," though Modernists hasten to assure us that, while we have lost the sense of *sin*, we have gained the sense of *sins*, in the plural, that is, of definite actual sins. But there is no doubt about it that people have to an alarming extent lost the sense of the heinousness of sin, as committed against a holy God, and have largely thought of it merely as an infringement on the rights of one's fellow-men. They fail to see that sin is a fatal power in their lives which ever and anon incites their rebellious spirits, which makes them guilty before God, and which brings them under a sentence of condemnation. It is one of the merits of the Theology of Crisis that it is calling attention once more to the seriousness of sin as a revolt against God, as a revolutionary attempt to be like God.

2. CLASSIFICATION OF ACTUAL SINS. It is quite impossible to give a unified and comprehensive classification of actual sins. They vary in kind and degree, and can be differentiated from more than one point of view. Roman Catholics

make a well-known distinction between venial and mortal sins, but admit that it is extremely difficult and dangerous to decide whether a sin is mortal or venial. They were led to this distinction by the statement of Paul in Gal. 5:21 that they "who do such things (as he has enumerated) shall not inherit the kingdom of God." One commits a mortal sin when one wilfully violates the law of God in a matter which one believes or knows to be important. It renders the sinner liable to eternal punishment. And one commits a venial sin when one transgresses the law of God in a matter that is not of grave importance, or when the transgression is not altogether voluntary. Such a sin is forgiven more easily, and even without confession. Forgiveness for mortal sins can be obtained only by the sacrament of penance. The distinction is not a Scriptural one, for according to Scripture every sin is essentially *anomia* (unrighteousness), and merits eternal punishment. Moreover, it has a deleterious effect in practical life, since it engenders a feeling of uncertainty, sometimes a feeling of morbid fear on the one hand, or of unwarranted carelessness on the other. The Bible does distinguish different kinds of sins, especially in connection with the different degrees of guilt attaching to them. The Old Testament makes an important distinction between sins committed presumptuously (with a high hand), and sins committed unwittingly, that is, as the result of ignorance, weakness, or error, Num. 15:29-31. The former could not be atoned by sacrifice and were punished with great severity, while the latter could be so atoned and were judged with far greater leniency. The fundamental principle embodied in this distinction still applies. Sins committed on purpose, with full consciousness of the evil involved, and with deliberation, are greater and more culpable than sins resulting from ignorance, from an erroneous conception of things, or from weakness of character. Nevertheless the latter are also real sins and make one guilty in the sight of God, Gal. 6:1; Eph. 4:18; I Tim 1:13; 5:24. The New Testament further clearly teaches us that the degree of sin is to a great extent determined by the degree of light possessed. The heathen are guilty indeed, but they who have God's revelation and enjoy the privileges of the gospel ministry are far more guilty, Matt. 10:15; Luke 12:47,48; 23:34; John 19:11; Acts 17:30; Rom. 1:32; 2:12; I Tim. 1:13,15,16.

3. THE UNPARDONABLE SIN. Several passages of Scripture speak of a sin that cannot be forgiven, after which a change of heart is impossible, and for which it is not necessary to pray. It is generally known as the sin or blasphemy against the Holy Spirit. The Saviour speaks of it explicitly in Matt. 12:31,32 and parallel passages; and it is generally thought that Heb. 6:4-6; 10:26,27, and John 5:16 also refer to this sin.

a. *Unwarranted opinions respecting this sin.* There has been quite a variety of opinions respecting the nature of the unpardonable sin. (1) Jerome and Chrysostom thought of it as a sin that could be committed only during Christ's sojourn on earth, and held that it was committed by those who were convinced in their hearts that Christ performed His miracles by the power of the Holy Spirit, but in spite of their conviction refused to recognize these miracles as such and ascribed them to the operation of Satan. However, this limitation is entirely unwarranted, as the passages in Hebrews and I John would seem to prove. (2) Augustine, the Melanchtonian dogmaticians of the Lutheran Church, and a few Scottish theologians (Guthrie, Chalmers) conceived of it as consisting in *impoenitentia finalis,* that is, impenitence persisted in to the end. A related view is that expressed by some in our own day, that it consists in continued unbelief, a refusal up to the very end to accept Jesus Christ by faith. But on this supposition it would follow that every one who died in a state of impenitence and unbelief had committed this sin, while according to Scripture it must be something of a very specific nature. (3) In connection with their denial of the perseverance of the saints, later Lutheran theologians taught that only regenerate persons could commit this sin, and sought support for this view in Heb. 6:4-6. But this is an un-Scriptural position, and the Canons of Dort reject, among others, also the error of those who teach that the regenerate can commit the sin against the Holy Spirit.

b. *The Reformed conception of this sin.* The name "sin against the Holy Spirit" is too general, for there are also sins against the Holy Spirit that are pardonable, Eph. 4:30. The Bible speaks more specifically of a "speaking against the Holy Spirit," Matt. 12:32; Mark 3:29; Luke 12:10. It is evidently a sin committed during the present life, which makes conversion and pardon impossible. The sin consists in the conscious, malicious, and wilful rejection and slandering, against evidence and conviction, of the testimony of the Holy Spirit respecting the grace of God in Christ, attributing it out of hatred and enmity to the prince of darkness. It presupposes, objectively, a revelation of the grace of God in Christ, and a powerful operation of the Holy Spirit; and, subjectively, an illumination and intellectual conviction so strong and powerful as to make an honest denial of the truth impossible. And then the sin itself consists, not in doubting the truth, nor in a simple denial of it, but in a contradiction of it that goes contrary to the conviction of the mind, to the illumination of the conscience, and even to the verdict of the heart. In committing that sin man wilfully, maliciously, and intentionally attributes what is clearly recognized as the work of God to the influence and operation of Satan. It is nothing less than a decided slandering of the Holy Spirit, an audacious declaration that the Holy Spirit is the spirit of the abyss, that the truth is the lie, and that Christ is Satan. It is not so much a sin against the person of the Holy Spirit as a sin against His official work in revealing, both objectively and subjectively, the grace and glory of God in Christ. The root of this sin is the conscious and deliberate hatred of God and of all that is recognized as divine. It is unpardonable, not because its guilt transcends the merits of Christ, or because the sinner is beyond the renewing power of the Holy Spirit, but because there are also in the world of sin certain laws and ordinances, established by God and maintained by Him. And the law in the case of this particular sin is, that it excludes all repentance, sears the conscience, hardens the sinner, and thus renders the sin unpardonable. In those who have committed this sin we may therefore expect to find a pronounced hatred to God, a defiant attitude to Him and all that is divine, delight in ridiculing and slandering that which is holy, and absolute unconcern respecting the welfare of their soul and the future life. In view of the fact that this sin is not followed by repentance, we may be reasonably sure that they who fear that they have committed it and worry about this, and who desire the prayers of others for them, have not committed it.

c. *Remarks on the passages in the Epistles that speak of it.* Except in the Gospels, this sin is not mentioned by name in the Bible. Thus the question arises, whether the passages in Heb. 6:4-6; 10:26,27,29, and I John 5:16 also refer to it. Now it is quite evident that they all speak of an unpardonable sin; and because Jesus says in Matt. 12:31, "Therefore I say unto you, Every sin and blasphemy shall be forgiven unto men; but the blasphemy against the Spirit shall not be forgiven," thereby indicating that there is but one unpardonable sin, it is but reasonable to think that these passages refer to the same sin. It should be noted, however, that Heb. 6 speaks of a specific form of this sin, such as could only occur in the apostolic age, when the Spirit revealed itself in extraordinary gifts and powers. The fact that this was not borne in mind, often led to the erroneous opinion that this passage, with its unusually strong expressions, referred to such as were actually regenerated by the Spirit of God. But Heb. 6:4-6, while speaking of experiences that transcend those of the ordinary temporal faith, yet do not necessarily testify to the presence of regenerating grace in the heart.

QUESTIONS FOR FURTHER STUDY. What objections are raised to the idea of the federal headship of Adam? What Scriptural ground is there for the imputation of Adam's sin to his descendants? Was Placeus' theory of mediate imputation in any way connected with Amyraldus' view of universal atonement? What objection does Dabney raise to the doctrine of immediate imputation? Is the doctrine of inherited evil the same as the doctrine of original sin, and if not, how do they differ? How do Pelagians, Semi-Pelagians, and Arminians differ in their view of original sin? How does the doctrine of original sin affect the doctrine of infant salvation? Does the Bible teach that one can be lost purely as the result of orginal sin? What is the connection between the doctrine of original sin and that of baptismal regeneration? What becomes of the doctrine of original sin in modern liberal theology? How do you account for the denial of original sin in Barthian theology? Can you name some additional classes of actual sins?

LITERATURE: Bavinck, *Geref. Dogm.* III, pp. 61-120; Kuyper, *Dict. Dogm., De Peccato,* pp. 36-50, 119-144; Vos, *Geref. Dogm.* II, pp. 31-76; Hodge, *Syst. Theol.* II, pp. 192-308; McPherson, *Chr. Dogma,* pp. 242-256; Dabney,*Syst. and Polem. Theol.,* pp. 321-351; Litton, *Intro. to Dogm. Theol.,* pp. 136-174; Schmid, *Doct. Theol. of the Ev. Luth. Ch.,* pp. 242-276; Valentine, *Chr. Theol.* I, pp. 420-476; Pope, *Chr. Theol.* II, pp. 47-86; Raymond, *Syst. Theol.* II, pp. 64-172; Wilmers, *Handbook of the Chr. Religion,* pp. 235-238; Mackintosh, *Christianity and Sin,* cf. Index; Girardeau,*The Will in its Theological Relations*; Wiggers, *Augustinism and Pelagianism*; Candlish, *The Bibl. Doct. of Sin,* pp. 90-128; Brunner, *Man in Revolt,* pp. 114-166.

V. The Punishment of Sin

Sin is a very serious matter, and is taken seriously by God, though men often make light of it. It is not only a transgression of the law of God, but an attack on the great Lawgiver Himself, a revolt against God. It is an infringement on the inviolable righteousness of God, which is the very foundation of His throne (Ps. 97:2), and an affront to the spotless holiness of God, which requires of us that we be holy in all manner of living (I Pet. 1:16). In view of this it is but natural that God should visit sin with punishment. In a word of fundamental significance He says: "I the Lord thy God am a jealous God, visiting the iniquity of the fathers upon the children unto the third and fourth generation of them that hate me," Ex. 20:5. The Bible abundantly testifies to the fact that God punishes sin both in this life and in the life to come.

A. Natural and positive penalties.

A rather common distinction applied to the punishments for sin, is that between natural and positive penalties. There are punishments which are the natural results of sin, and which men cannot escape, because they are the natural and necessary consequences of sin. Man is not saved from them by repentance and forgiveness. In some cases they may be mitigated and even checked by the means which God has placed at our disposal, but in other cases they remain and serve as a constant reminder of past transgressions. The slothful man comes to poverty, the drunkard brings ruin upon himself and his family, the fornicator contracts a loathsome and incurable disease, and the criminal is burdened with shame and even when leaving the prison walls finds it extremely hard to make a new start in life. The Bible speaks of such punishments in Job 4:8; Ps. 9:15; 94:23; Prov. 5:22; 23:21; 24:14; 31:3. But there are also positive punishments, and these are punishments in the more ordinary and legal sense of the word. They presuppose not merely the natural laws of life, but a positive law of the great Lawgiver with added sanctions. They are not penalties which naturally result from the nature of the transgression, but penalties which are attached to the transgressions by divine enactments. They are superimposed by the divine law, which is of absolute authority. It is to this type of punishment that the Bible usually refers. This is particularly evident in the Old Testament. God gave Israel a detailed code of laws for the regulation of its civil, moral, and religious life, and clearly stipulated the punishment to be meted out in the case of each transgression, cf. Ex. 20-23. And though many of the civil and religious regulations of this law were, in the form in which they were

255

couched, intended for Israel only, the fundamental principles which they embody also apply in the New Testament dispensation. In a Biblical conception of the penalty of sin we shall have to take into account both the natural and necessary outcome of wilful opposition to God and the penalty legally affixed and adjusted to the offense by God. Now there are some Unitarians, Universalists, and Modernists who deny the existence of any punishment of sin, except such consequences as naturally result from the sinful action. Punishment is not the execution of a sentence pronounced by the divine Being on the merits of the case, but simply the operation of a general law. This position is taken by J. F. Clarke, Thayer, Williamson, and Washington Gladden. The latter says: "The old theology made this penalty (penalty of sin) to consist in suffering inflicted upon the sinner by a judicial process in the future life . . . The penalty of sin, as the new theology teaches, consists in the natural consequences of sin. . . . The penalty of sin is sin. Whatsoever a man soweth *that* shall he also reap."[1] The idea is not new; it was present to the mind of Dante, for in his famous poem the torments of hell symbolize the consequences of sin; and Schelling had it in mind, when he spoke of the history of the world as the judgment of the world. It is abundantly evident from Scripture, however, that this is an entirely un-Biblical view. The Bible speaks of penalties, which are in no sense the natural result or consequences of the sin committed, for instance in Ex. 32:33; Lev. 26:21; Num. 15:31; I Chron. 10:13; Ps. 11:6; 75:8; Isa. 1:24,28; Matt. 3:10; 24:51. All these passages speak of a punishment of sin by a direct act of God. Moreover, according to the view under consideration there is really no reward or punishment; virtue and vice both naturally include their various issues. Furthermore, on that standpoint there is no good reason for considering suffering as punishment, for it denies guilt, and it is exactly guilt that constitutes suffering a punishment. Then, too, it is in many cases not the guilty that receives the severest punishment, but the innocent as, for instance, the dependents of a drunkard or a debauchee. And, finally, on this view, heaven and hell are not places of future punishment, but states of mind or conditions in which men find themselves here and now. Washington Gladden expresses this very explicitly.

B. Nature and Purpose of Punishments.

The word "punishment" is derived from the Latin poena, meaning punishment, expiation, or pain. It denotes pain or suffering inflicted because of some misdeed. More specifically, it may be defined as that pain or loss which is directly or indirectly inflicted by the Lawgiver, in vindication of His justice outraged by the violation of the law. It originates in the righteousness or punitive justice of God, by which He maintains Himself as the Holy One and neces- -sarily demands holiness and righteousness in all His rational creatures. Punishment is the penalty that is naturally and necessarily due from the sinner because of his sin; it is, in fact, a debt that is due to the essential justice of God. The punishments of sin are of two different kinds. There is a punishment

---

1. *Present Day Theology*, pp. 78-80.

that is the necessary concomitant of sin, for in the nature of the case sin causes separation between God and man, carries with it guilt and pollution, and fills the heart with fear and shame. But there is also a kind of punishment that is superimposed on man from without by the supreme Lawgiver, such as all kinds of calamities in this life and the punishment of hell in the future.

Now the question arises as to the object or the purpose of the punishment of sin. And on this point there is considerable difference of opinion. We should not regard the punishment of sin as a mere matter of vengeance and as inflicted with the desire to harm one who has previously done harm. The following are the three most important views respecting the purpose of punishment.

1. TO VINDICATE DIVINE RIGHTEOUSNESS OR JUSTICE. Turretin says: "If there be such an attribute as justice belonging to God, then sin must have its due, which is punishment." The law requires that sin be punished because of its inherent demerit, irrespective of all further considerations. This principle applies in the administration of both human and divine laws. Justice requires the punishment of the transgressor. Back of the law stands God, and therefore it may also be said that punishment aims at the vindication of the righteousness and holiness of the great Lawgiver. The holiness of God necessarily reacts against sin, and this reaction manifests itself in the punishment of sin. This principle is fundamental to all those passages of Scripture that speak of God as a righteous Judge, who renders unto every man according to his deserts. "He is the rock, His work is perfect: for all His ways are judgment: a God of truth and without iniquity, just and right is He," Deut. 32:4. "Far be it from God, that He should do wickedness; and from the Almighty, that He should commit iniquity. For the work of a man shall He render unto him, and cause every man to find according to his ways," Job. 34:10,11. "Thou renderest to every man according to his work," Ps. 62:12. "Righteous art thou, O Lord, and upright are thy judgments," Ps. 119:37. "I am the Lord which exercise lovingkindness, judgment, and righteousness in the earth," Jer. 9:24. "And if ye call on the Father, who without respect of persons judgest according to every man's work, pass the time of your sojourning here in fear," I Pet. 1:17. The vindication of the righteousness and holiness of God, and of that just law which is the very expression of His being, is certainly the primary purpose of the punishment of sin. There are two other views, however, which erroneously put something else in the foreground.

2. TO REFORM THE SINNER. The idea is very much in the foreground at the present time that there is no punitive justice in God which inexorably calls for the punishment of the sinner, and that God is not angry with the sinner but loves him, and only inflicts hardships upon him, in order to reclaim him and to bring him back to his Father's home. This is an un-Scriptural view, which obliterates the distinction between punishment and chastisement. The penalty of sin does not proceed from the love and mercy of the Lawgiver, but from His justice. If reformation follows the infliction of punishment, this is not due to the penalty as such, but is the fruit of some gracious operation of God by which

He turns that which is in itself an evil for the sinner into something that is beneficial. The distinction between chastisement and punishment must be maintained. The Bible teaches us on the one hand that God loves and chastens His people, Job 5:17; Ps. 6:1; Ps. 94:12; 118:18; Prov. 3:11; Isa. 26:16; Heb. 12:5-8; Rev. 3:19; and on the other hand, that He hates and punishes evil-doers, Ps. 5:5; 7:11; Nah. 1:2; Rom. 1:18; 2:5,6; 11 Thess. 1:6; Heb. 10:26,27. Moreover, a punishment must be recognized as just, that is, as according to justice, in order to be reformatory. According to this theory a sinner who has already reformed could no more be punished; nor could one beyond the possibility of reformation, so that there could be no punishment for Satan; the death penalty would have to be abolished, and eternal punishment would have no reason for existence.

3. To DETER MEN FROM SIN. Another theory rather prevalent in our day is that the sinner must be punished for the protection of society, by deterring others from the commission of similar offenses. There can be no doubt about it that this end is often secured in the family, in the state, and in the moral government of the world, but this is an incidental result which God graciously effects by the infliction of the penalty. It certainly cannot be the ground for the infliction of the penalty. There is no justice whatever in punishing an individual simply for the good of society. As a matter of fact the sinner is always punished for his sin, and incidentally this may be for the good of society. And here again it may be said that no punishment will have a deterring effect, if it is not just and right in itself. Punishment has a good effect only when it is evident that the person on whom it is afflicted really deserves punishment. If this theory were true, a criminal might at once be set free, if it were not for the possibility that others might be deterred from sin by his punishment. Moreover, a man might rightly commit a crime, if he were only willing to bear the penalty. According to this view punishment is in no sense grounded in the past, but is wholly prospective. But on that supposition it is very hard to explain how it invariably causes the repentant sinner to look back and to confess with contrite heart the sins of the past, as we notice in such passages as the following: Gen. 42:21; Num. 21:7; I Sam. 15:24,25; II Sam. 12:13; 24:10; Ezra 9:6,10, 13; Neh. 9:33-35; Job 7:21; Ps. 51:1-4; Jer. 3:25. These examples might easily be multiplied. In opposition to both of the theories considered it must be maintained that the punishment of sin is wholly retrospective in its primary aim, though the infliction of the penalty may have beneficial consequences both for the individual and for society.

C. The actual penalty of sin.

The penalty with which God threatened man in paradise was the penalty of death. The death here intended is not the death of the body, but the death of man as a whole, death in the Scriptural sense of the word. The Bible does not know the distinction, so common among us, between a physical, a spiritual, and an eternal death; it has a synthetic view of death and regards it as separation from God. The penalty was also actually executed on the day that man sinned, though the full execution of it was temporarily stayed by the grace of God. In a rather un-Scriptural way some carry their distinction into the Bible, and maintain that physical death should not be regarded as the penalty of sin, but rather as the natural result of the physical constitution of man. But the Bible knows of no such exception. It acquaints us with the threatened penalty, which is death in the comprehensive sense of the word, and it informs us that death entered the world through sin (Rom. 5:12), and that the wages of sin is death (Rom. 6:23). The penalty of sin certainly includes physical death, but it includes much more than that. Making the distinction to which we have grown accustomed, we may say that it includes the following:

1. SPIRITUAL DEATH. There is a profound truth in the saying of Augustine that sin is also the punishment of sin. This means that the sinful state and condition in which man is born by nature form part of the penalty of sin. They are, it is true, the immediate consequences of sin, but they are also a part of the threatened penalty. Sin separates man from God, and that means death, for it is only in communion with the living God that man can truly live. In the state of death, which resulted from the entrance of sin into the world, we are burdened with the guilt of sin, a guilt that can only be removed by the redemptive work of Jesus Christ. We are therefore under obligation to bear the sufferings that result from transgression of the law. The natural man carries the sense of the liability to punishment with him wherever he goes. Conscience is a constant reminder of his guilt, and the fear of punishment often fills the heart. Spiritual death means not only guilt, but also polution. Sin is always a corrupting influence in life, and this is a part of our death. We are by nature not only unrighteous in the sight of God, but also unholy. And this unholiness manifests itself in our thoughts, in our words, and in our deeds. It is always active within us like a poisoned fountain polluting the streams of life. And if it were not for the restraining influence of the common grace of God, it would render social life entirely impossible.

2. THE SUFFERINGS OF LIFE. The sufferings of life, which are the result of the entrance of sin into the world, are also included in the penalty of sin. Sin brought disturbance in the entire life of man. His physical life fell a prey to weaknesses and diseases, which result in discomforts and often in agonizing pains; and his mental life became subject to distressing disturbances, which often rob him of the joy of life, disqualify him for his daily task, and sometimes entirely destroy his mental equilibrium. His very soul has become a battle-field of conflicting thoughts, passions, and desires. The will refuses to follow the judgment of the intellect, and the passions run riot without the control of an intelligent will. The true harmony of life is destroyed, and makes way for the curse of the divided life. Man is in a state of dissolution, which often carries with it the most poignant sufferings. And not only that, but with and on account

of man the whole creation was made subject to vanity and to the bondage of corruption. The evolutionists especially have taught us to look upon nature as "red in tooth and claw." Destructive forces are often released in earthquakes, cyclones, tornadoes, volcanic eruptions, and floods, which bring untold misery on mankind. Now there are many, especially in our day, who do not see the hand of God in all this, and do not regard these calamities as a part of the penalty of sin. And yet that is exactly what they are in a general sense. However, it will not be safe to particularize, and to interpret them as special punishments for some grievous sins committed by those who live in the stricken areas. Neither will it be wise to ridicule the idea of such a causal connection as existed in the case of the Cities of the Plain (Sodom and Gomorrah), which were destroyed by fire from heaven. We should always bear in mind that there is a collective responsibility, and that there are always sufficient reasons why God should visit cities, districts or nations with dire calamities. It is rather a wonder that He does not more often visit them in His wrath and in His sore displeasure. It is always well to bear in mind what Jesus once said to the Jews who brought to Him the report of a calamity which had befallen certain Galileans, and evidently intimated that these Galileans must have been very sinful: "Think ye that these Galileans were sinners above all the Galileans, because they have suffered these things? I tell you, Nay: but except ye repent, ye shall all in like manner perish. Or those eighteen, upon whom the tower in Siloam fell, and killed them, think ye that they were offenders above all the men that dwell in Jerusalem? I tell you you, Nay: but, except ye repent, ye shall all likewise perish." Luke 13:2-5.

3. PHYSICAL DEATH. The separation of body and soul is also a part of the penalty of sin. That the Lord had this in mind also in the threatened penalty is quite evident from the explication of it in the words, "dust thou art, and unto dust thou shalt return," Gen. 3:19. It also appears from the whole argument of Paul in Rom. 5:12-21 and in I Cor. 15:12-23. The position of the Church has always been that death in the full sense of the word, including physical death, is not only the consequence but the penalty of sin. The wages of sin is death. Pelagianism denied this connection, but the North African General Synod of Carthage (418) pronounced an anathema against any man who says "that Adam, the first man, was created mortal, so that whether he sinned or not he would have died, not as the wages of sin, but through the necessity of nature." Socinians and Rationalists continued the Pelagian error, and in even more recent times it was reproduced in the systems of those Kantian, Hegelian, or Ritschlian theologians who virtually make sin a necessary moment in man's moral and spiritual development. Their views found support in present day natural science, which regards physical death as a natural phenomenon of the human organism. Man's physical constitution is such that he necessarily dies. But this view does not commend itself in view of the fact that man's physical organism is renewed every seven years, and that comparatively few people die in old age and from complete exhaustion. By far the greater number of them

die as the result of sickness and accidents. It is also contrary to the fact that man does not feel that death is something natural, but fears it as an unnatural separation of that which belongs together.

4. ETERNAL DEATH. This may be regarded as the culmination and completion of spiritual death. The restraints of the present fall away, and the corruption of sin has its perfect work. The full weight of the wrath of God descends on the condemned. Their separation from God, the source of life and joy, is complete, and this means death in the most awful sense of the word. Their outward condition is made to correspond with the inward state of their evil souls. There are pangs of conscience and physical pain. And the smoke of their torment goeth up for ever and ever. Rev. 14:11. The further discussion of this subject belongs to eschatology.

QUESTIONS FOR FURTHER STUDY. Why do many modern liberals deny all positive punishments for sin? Is the position at all tenable that the punishments of sin consist exclusively in the natural consequences of sin? What objections do you have to this position? How do you account for the widespread aversion to the idea that the punishment of sin is a vindication of the law and of the righteousness of God? Do the punishments of sin also serve as deterrents, and as means of reformation? What is the Biblical conception of death? Can you prove from Scripture that it includes physical death? Is the doctrine of eternal death consistent with the idea that the punishment of sin serves merely as a means of reformation, or as a deterrent?

LITERATURE: Bavinck, Geref. Dogm. III, pp. 150-198; Kuyper, Dict. Dogm., De Peccato, pp. 93-112; Strong, Syst. Theol., pp. 652-660; Raymond, Syst. Theol. II, pp. 175-184; Shedd, Doctrine of Endless Punishment; Washington Gladden, Present Day Theology, Chaps. IV and V; Kennedy, St. Paul's Conceptions of the Last Things, pp. 103-157; Dorner, Syst. of Chr. Doct. III, pp. 114-132.

MAN IN THE COVENANT OF GRACE

I. Name and Concept of the Covenant

A. The Name.

1. IN THE OLD TESTAMENT. The Hebrew word for covenant is always *berith*, a word of uncertain derivation. The most general opinion is that it is derived from the Hebrew verb *barah*, to cut, and therefore contains a reminder of the ceremony mentioned in Gen. 15:17. Some, however, prefer to think that it is derived from the Assyrian word *beritu*, meaning "to bind." This would at once point to the covenant as a bond. The question of the derivation is of no great importance for the construction of the doctrine. The word *berith* may denote a mutual voluntary agreement (dipleuric), but also a disposition or arrangement imposed by one party on another (monopleuric). Its exact meaning does not depend on the etymology of the word, nor on the historical development of the concept, but simply on the parties concerned. In the measure in which one of the parties is subordinate and has less to say, the covenant acquires the character of a disposition or arrangement imposed by one party on the other. *Berith* then becomes synonymous with *choq* (appointed statute or ordinance), Ex. 34:10; Isa. 59:21; Jer. 31:36; 33:20; 34:13. Hence we also find that *karath berith* (to cut a covenant) is construed not only with the prepositions *'am* and *ben* (with), but also with *lamedh* (to), Jos. 9:6; Isa. 55:3; 61:8; Jer. 32:40. Naturally, when God establishes a covenant with man, this monopleuric character is very much in evidence, for God and man are not equal parties. God is the Sovereign who imposes His ordinances upon His creatures.

2. IN THE NEW TESTAMENT. In the Septuagint the word *berith* is rendered *diatheke* in every passage where it occurs with the exception of Deut. 9:15 (*marturion*) and I Kings 11:11 (*entole*). The word *diatheke* is confined to this usage, except in four passages. This use of the word seems rather peculiar in view of the fact that it is not the usual Greek word for covenant, but really denotes a *disposition*, and consequently also a *testament*. The ordinary word for covenant is *suntheke*. Did the translators intend to substitute another idea for the covenant idea? Evidently not, for in Isa. 28:15 they use the two words synonymously, and there *diatheke* evidently means a pact or an agreement. Hence there is no doubt about it that they ascribe this meaning to *diatheke*. But the question remains, Why did they so generally avoid the use of *suntheke* and substitute for it a word which denotes a disposition rather than an agreement? In all probability the reason lies in the fact that in the Greek world the covenant idea expressed by *suntheke* was based to such an extent on

the legal equality of the parties, that it could not, without considerable modification, be incorporated in the Scriptural system of thought. The idea that the priority belongs to God in the establishment of the covenant, and that He sovereignly imposes His covenant on man was absent from the usual Greek word. Hence the substitution of the word in which this was very prominent. The word *diatheke* thus, like many other words, received a new meaning, when it became the vehicle of divine thought, This change is important in connection with the New Testament use of the word. There has been considerable difference of opinion respecting the proper translation of the word. In about half of the passages in which it occurs the Holland and the Authorized Versions render the word "covenant," while in the other half they render it "testament." The American Revised Version, however, renders it "covenant" throughout, except in Heb. 9:16,17. It is but natural, therefore, that the question should be raised, What is the New Testament meaning of the word? Some claim that it has its classical meaning of *disposition* or *testament,* wherever it is found in the New Testament, while others maintain that it means *testament* in some places, but that in the great majority of passages the *covenant* idea is prominently in the foreground. This is undoubtedly the correct view. We would expect *a priorily* that the New Testament usage would be in general agreement with that of the LXX; and a careful study of the relevant passages shows that the American Revised Version is undoubtedly on the right track, when it translates *diatheke* by "testament" only in Heb. 9:16,17. In all probability there is not a single other passage where this rendering would be correct, not even II Cor. 3:6,14. The fact that several translations of the New Testament substituted "testament" for "covenant" in so many places is probably due to three causes: (a) the desire to emphasize the priority of God in the transaction; (b) the assumption that the word had to be rendered as much as possible in harmony with Heb. 9:16,17; and (c) the influence of the Latin translation, which uniformly rendered *diatheke* by "testamentum."

B. The Concept.

The covenant idea developed in history before God made any formal use of the concept in the revelation of redemption. Covenants among men had been made long before God established His covenant with Noah and with Abraham, and this prepared men to understand the significance of a covenant in a world divided by sin, and helped them to understand the divine revelation, when it presented man's relation to God as a covenant relation. This does not mean, however, that the covenant idea originated with man and was then borrowed by God as an appropriate form for the description of the mutual relationship between Himself and man. Quite the opposite is true; the archetype of all covenant life is found in the trinitarian being of God, and what is seen among men is but a faint copy (ectype) of this. God so ordered the life of man that the covenant idea should develop there as one of the pillars of social life, and after it had so developed, He formally introduced it as an expression of the existing relation between Himself and man. The covenant relationship between

God and man existed from the very beginning, and therefore long before the formal establishment of the covenant with Abraham.

While the word *berith* is often used of covenants among men, yet it always includes a religious idea. A covenant is a pact or agreement between two or more parties. It may be, and among men most generally is, an agreement to which parties, which can meet on a footing of equality, voluntarily come after a careful stipulation of their mutual duties and privileges; but it may also be of the nature of a disposition or arrangement imposed by a superior party on one that is inferior and accepted by the latter. It is generally confirmed by a solemn ceremony as in the presence of God, and thereby obtains an inviolable character. Each one of the parties binds himself to the fulfilment of certain promises on the basis of stipulated conditions. Now we should not say that we cannot properly speak of a covenant between God and man, because the parties are too unequal, and therefore proceed on the assumption that the covenant of grace is nothing but the promise of salvation in the form of a covenant. By doing that we would fail to do justice to the covenant idea as it is revealed in Scripture. It is perfectly true that both the covenant of works and (as the sequel will show) the covenant of grace are monopleuric in origin, that they are of the nature of arrangements ordained and instituted by God, and that God has the priority in both; but they are nevertheless covenants. God graciously condescended to come down to the level of man, and to honor him by dealing with him more or less on the footing of equality. He stipulates His demands and vouchsafes His promises, and man assumes the duties thus imposed upon him voluntarily and thus inherits the blessings. In the covenant of works man could meet the requirements of the covenant in virtue of his natural endowments, but in the covenant of grace he is enabled to meet them only by the regenerating and sanctifying influence of the Holy Spirit. God works in man both to will and to do, graciously bestowing upon him all that He requires of him. It is called the covenant of grace, because it is an unparalleled revelation of the grace of God, and because man receives all its blessings as gifts of divine grace.

II. The Covenant of Redemption

A. Separate Discussion of this Desirable.

There are different representations respecting the parties in the covenant of grace. Some consider them to be the triune God and man, either without qualification, or qualified in some way, as "the sinner," "the elect," or "man in Christ"; others, God the Father, as representing the Trinity, and Christ as representing the elect;[1] and still others, since the days of Coccejus, distinguish two covenants, namely, the covenant of redemption (*pactum salutis*) between the Father and the Son, and, as based on this, the covenant of grace between the triune God and the elect, or the elect sinner. The second of these representations has a certain advantage from a systematic point of view. It may claim the support of such passages as Rom. 5:12-21 and I Cor. 15:21,22,47-49, and stresses the inseparable connection between the *pactum salutis* and the covenant of grace. It brings out the unity of the covenant in Christ, and is advocated among others by Boston, Gib, Dick, A. Kuyper Sr., H. Kuyper, and A. Kuyper, Jr. The third representation is more perspicuous, however, is easier to understand, and is therefore more serviceable in a practical discussion of the doctrine of the covenant. It escapes a great deal of confusion that is incidental to the other view, and is followed by the majority of Reformed theologians, such as Mastricht, à Marck, Turretin, Witsius, Heppe, the Hodges, Shedd, Vos, Bavinck, and Honig. There is no *essential* difference between these two representations. Says Dr. Hodge: "There is no doctrinal difference between those who prefer the one statement and those who prefer the other; between those who comprise all the facts of Scripture relating to the subject under one covenant between God and Christ as the representative of His people, and those who distribute them under two."[2] This being the case, the third mode of representing the whole matter undoubtedly deserves the preference. But in following it we should bear in mind what Shedd says: "Though this distinction (between the covenant of redemption and the covenant of grace) is favored by Scripture statements, it does not follow that there are two separate and independent covenants antithetic to the covenant of works. The covenant of grace and redemption are two modes or phases of the one evangelical covenant of mercy."[3]

---

1. *Westm. Larger Cat.*, Q. 31.
2. *Syst. Theol.* II, p. 358; cf. also Dabney, *Lect. on Theol.*, p. 432; Bavinck, *Geref. Dogm.* III, p. 240
3. *Dogm. Theol.* II, p. 360.

B. Scriptural Data for the Covenant of Redemption.

The name "counsel of peace" is derived from Zech. 6:13. Coccejus and others found in this passage a reference to an agreement between the Father and the Son. This was clearly a mistake, for the words refer to the union of the kingly and priestly offices in the Messiah. The Scriptural character of the name cannot be maintained, but this, of course, does not detract from the reality of the counsel of peace. The doctrine of this eternal counsel rests on the following Scriptural basis.

1. Scripture clearly points to the fact that the plan of redemption was included in the eternal decree or counsel of God, Eph. 1:4 ff.; 3:11; II Thess. 2:13; II Tim. 1:9; Jas. 2:5; I Pet. 1:2, etc. Now we find that in the economy of redemption there is, in a sense, a division of labor: the Father is the originator, the Son the executor, and the Holy Spirit the applier. This can only be the result of a voluntary agreement among the persons of the Trinity, so that their internal relations assume the form of a covenant life. In fact, it is exactly in the trinitarian life that we find the archetype of the historical covenants, a covenant in the proper and fullest sense of the word, the parties meeting on a footing of equality, a true *suntheke*.

2. There are passages of Scripture which not only point to the fact that the plan of God for the salvation of sinners was eternal, Eph. 1:4; 3:9,11, but also indicate that it was of the nature of a covenant. Christ speaks of promises made to Him before his advent, and repeatedly refers to a commission which He had received from the Father, John 5:30,43; 6:38-40; 17:4-12. And in Rom. 5:12-21 and I Cor. 15:22 He is clearly regarded as a representative head, that is, as the head of a covenant.

3. Wherever we have the essential elements of a covenant, namely, contracting parties, a promise or promises, and a condition, there we have a covenant. In Ps. 2:7-9 the parties are mentioned and a promise is indicated. The Messianic character of this passage is guaranteed by Acts 13:33; Heb. 1:5; 5:5. Again, in Ps. 40:7-9, also attested as Messianic by the New Testament (Heb. 10:5-7), the Messiah expresses His readiness to do the Father's will in becoming a sacrifice for sin. Christ repeatedly speaks of a task which the Father has entrusted to Him, John 6:38,39; 10:18; 17:4. The statement in Luke 22:29 is particularly significant: "I appoint unto you a kingdom, even as my Father appointed unto me." The verb used here is *diatithemi*, the word from which *diatheke* is derived, which means to appoint by will, testament or covenant. Moreover, in John 17:5 Christ claims a reward, and in John 17:6,9,24 (cf. also Phil. 2:9-11) He refers to His people and His future glory as a reward given Him by the Father.

4. There are two Old Testament passages which connect up the idea of the covenant immediately with the Messiah, namely, Ps. 89:3, which is based on II Sam. 7:12-14, and is proved to be a Messianic passage by Heb. 1:5; and Isa. 42:6, where the person referred to is the Servant of the Lord. The connection clearly shows that this Servant is not merely Israel. Moreover, there are

passages in which the Messiah speaks of God as *His God,* thus using covenant language, namely, Ps. 22:1, 2, and Ps. 40:8.

C. The Son in the Covenant of Redemption.

1. THE OFFICIAL POSITION OF CHRIST IN THIS COVENANT. The position of Christ in the covenant of redemption is twofold. In the first place He is Surety (Gr. egguos), a word that is used only in Heb. 7:22. The derivation of this word is uncertain, and therefore cannot aid us in establishing its meaning. But the meaning is not doubtful. A surety is one who engages to become responsible for it that the legal obligations of another will be met. In the covenant of redemption Christ undertook to atone for the sins of His people by bearing the necessary punishment, and to meet the demands of the law for them. And by taking the place of delinquent man He became the last Adam, and is as such also the Head of the covenant, the Representative of all those whom the Father has given Him. In the covenant of redemption, then, Christ is both Surety and Head. He took upon Himself the responsibilities of His people. He is also their Surety in the covenant of grace, which develops out of the covenant of redemption. The question has been raised, whether the suretyship of Christ in the counsel of peace was conditional or unconditional. Roman jurisprudence recognizes two kinds of suretyship, the one designated *fidejussor,* and the other *expromissor.* The former is conditional, and the latter unconditional. The former is a surety who undertakes to pay for another, provided this person does not himself render satisfaction. The burden of guilt remains on the guilty party until the time of payment. The latter, however, is a surety who takes upon himself unconditionally to pay for another, thus relieving the guilty party of his responsibility at once. Coccejus and his school maintained that in the counsel of peace Christ became a *fidejussor,* and that consequently Old Testament believers enjoyed no complete forgiveness of sins. From Rom. 3:25 they inferred that for those saints there was only a *paresis,* an overlooking of sin, and no *aphesis* or complete forgiveness, until Christ really made atonement for sin. Their opponents asserted, however, that Christ took upon Himself *unconditionally* to render satisfaction for His people, and therefore became a surety in the specific sense of an *expromissor.* This is the only tenable position, for: (a) Old Testament believers received full justification or forgiveness, though the knowledge of it was not as full and clear as it is in the New Testament dispensation. There was no essential difference between the status of the Old, and that of the New Testament believers, Ps. 32:1,2,5; 51:1-3, 9-11; 103:3,12; Isa. 43:25; Rom. 3:3,6-16; Gal. 3:6-9. The position of Coccejus reminds one of that of the Roman Catholics with their *Limbus Patrum.* (b) Coccejus' theory makes the work of God in making provision for the redemption of sinners dependent on the uncertain obedience of man in an entirely unwarranted way. There is no sense in saying that Christ became a conditional surety, as if it were still possible that the sinner should pay for himself. God's provision for the redemption of sinners is absolute. This is not the same as saying that He does not treat and address the sinner as personally

guilty until he is justified by faith, for this is exactly what God does do. (c) In Rom. 3:25, the passage to which Coccejus appeals, the apostle uses the word *paresis* (overlooking or passing over), not because the individual believers in the Old Testament did not receive full pardon of sin, but because during the old dispensation the forgiveness of sin assumed the form of a *paresis*, as long as sin had not been adequately punished in Christ, and the absolute righteousness of Christ had not been revealed in the cross.

2. THE CHARACTER THIS COVENANT ASSUMED FOR CHRIST. Though the covenant of redemption is the eternal basis of the covenant of grace, and, as far as sinners are concerned, also its eternal prototype, it was for Christ a covenant of works rather than a covenant of grace. For Him the law of the original covenant applied, namely, that eternal life could only be obtained by meeting the demands of the law. As the last Adam Christ obtains eternal life for sinners in reward for faithful obedience, and not at all as an unmerited gift of grace. And what He has done as the Representative and Surety of all His people, they are no more in duty bound to do. The work has been done, the reward is merited, and believers are made partakers of the fruits of Christ's accomplished work through grace.

3. CHRIST'S WORK IN THE COVENANT LIMITED BY THE DECREE OF ELECTION. Some have identified the covenant of redemption and election; but this is clearly a mistake. Election has reference to the selection of the persons destined to be the heirs of everlasting glory in Christ. The counsel of redemption, on the other hand, refers to the way in which and the means by which grace and glory are prepared for sinners. Election, indeed, also has reference to Christ and reckons with Christ, for believers are said to be elected in Him. Christ Himself is, in a sense, the object of election, but in the counsel of redemption He is one of the contracting parties. The Father deals with Christ as the Surety of His people. Logically, election precedes the counsel of redemption, because the suretyship of Christ, like His atonement, is particular. If there were no preceding election, it would necessarily be universal. Moreover, to turn this around would be equivalent to making the suretyship of Christ the ground of election, while Scripture bases election entirely on the good pleasure of God.

4. CONNECTION OF THE SACRAMENTS USED BY CHRIST WITH THE COVENANT. Christ used the sacraments of both the Old and the New Testament. It is evident, however, that they could not mean for Him what they do for believers. In His case they could be neither symbols nor seals of saving grace; nor could they be instrumental in strengthening saving faith. If we distinguish, as we are doing, between the covenant of redemption and the covenant of grace, then the sacraments were for Christ in all probability sacraments of the former rather than of the latter. Christ took upon Himself in the covenant of redemption to meet the demands of the law. These had assumed a definite form when Christ was on earth and also included positive religious regulations. The sacraments formed a part of this law, and therefore Christ had to subject Himself to them, Matt. 3:15. At the same time they could serve as seals of the promises

which the Father had given to the Son. The objection may be raised to this representation that the sacraments were indeed fit symbols and seals of the removal of sin and of the nourishment of spiritual life, but from the nature of the case could not have this meaning for Christ, who had no sin and needed no spiritual nourishment. The objection may be met, at least to a certain extent, by calling attention to the fact that Christ appeared on earth in a public and official capacity. Though He had no personal sin, and no sacrament could therefore signify and seal to Him its removal, yet He was made to be sin for His people, II Cor. 5:21, by being burdened with their guilt; and consequently the sacraments could signify the removal of this burden, according to the promise of the Father, after He had completed His atoning work. Again, though we cannot speak of Christ as exercising *saving faith* in the sense in which this is required of us, yet as Mediator He had to exercise faith in a wider sense by accepting the promises of the Father believingly, and by trusting the Father for their fulfilment. And the sacraments could serve as signs and seals to strengthen this faith as far as His human nature was concerned.

D. **Requirements and Promises in the Covenant of Redemption.**

1. REQUIREMENTS. The Father required of the Son, who appeared in this covenant as the Surety and Head of His people, and as the last Adam, that He should make amends for the sin of Adam and of those whom the Father had given Him, and should do what Adam failed to do by keeping the law and thus securing eternal life for all His spiritual progeny. This requirement included the following particulars:

a. That He should assume human nature by being born of a woman, and thus enter into temporal relations; and that He should assume this nature with its present infirmities, though without sin, Gal. 4:4,5; Heb. 2:10,11,14,15; 4:15. It was absolutely essential that He should become one of the human race.

b. That He, who as the Son of God was superior to the law, should place Himself under the law; that He should enter, not merely into the natural, but also into the penal and federal relation to the law, in order to pay the penalty for sin and to merit everlasting life for the elect, Ps. 40:8; Matt. 5:17,18; John 8:28,29; Gal. 4:4,5; Phil. 2:6-8.

c. That He, after having merited forgiveness of sins and eternal life for His own, should apply to them the fruits of His merits: complete pardon, and the renewal of their lives through the powerful operation of the Holy Spirit. By doing this He would render it absolutely certain that believers would consecrate their lives to God, John 10:16; John 16:14,15; 17:12,19-22; Heb. 2: 10-13; 7:25.

2. PROMISES. The promises of the Father were in keeping with His requirements. He promised the Son all that was required for the performance of His great and comprehensive task, thereby excluding all uncertainty in the operation of this covenant. These promises included the following:

a.   That He would prepare the Son a body, which would be a fit tabernacle for him; a body in part prepared by the immediate agency of God and uncontaminated by sin, Luke 1:35; Heb. 10:5.

b.   That He would endow Him with the necessary gifts and graces for the performance of His task, and particularly would anoint Him for the Messianic offices by giving Him the Spirit without measure, a promise that was fulfilled especially at the time of His baptism, Isa. 42:1,2; 61:1; John 3:31.

c.   That He would support Him in the performance of His work, would deliver Him from the power of death, and would thus enable Him to destroy the dominion of Satan and to establish the Kingdom of God, Isa. 42:1-7; 49:8; Ps. 16:8-11; Acts 2:25-28.

d.   That He would enable Him, as a reward for His accomplished work, to send out the Holy Spirit for the formation of His spiritual body, and for the instruction, guidance, and protection of the Church, John 14:26; 15:26; 16:13, 14; Acts 2:33.

e.   That He would give unto Him a numerous seed in reward for His accomplished work, a seed so numerous that it would be a multitude which no man could number, so that ultimately the Kingdom of the Messiah would embrace the people of all nations and tongues, Ps. 22:27; 72:17.

f.   That He would commit to Him all power in heaven and on earth for the government of the world and of His Church, Matt. 28:18; Eph. 1:20-22; Phil. 2:9-11; Heb. 2:5-9; and would finally reward Him as Mediator with the glory which He as the Son of God had with the Father before the world was, John 17:5.

E. The Relation of this Covenant to the Covenant of Grace.

The following points indicate the relation in which this covenant stands to the covenant of grace:

1.   The counsel of redemption is the eternal prototype of the historical covenant of grace. This accounts for the fact that many combine the two into a single covenant. The former is eternal, that is, from eternity, and the latter, temporal in the sense that it is realized in time. The former is a compact between the Father and the Son as the Surety and Head of the elect, while the latter is a compact between the triune God and the elect sinner in the Surety.

2.   The counsel of redemption is the firm and eternal foundation of the covenant of grace. If there had been no eternal counsel of peace between the Father and the Son, there could have been no agreement between the triune God and sinful men. The counsel of redemption makes the covenant of grace possible.

3.   The counsel of redemption consequently also gives efficacy to the covenant of grace, for in it the means are provided for the establishment and execution of the latter. It is only by faith that the sinner can obtain the

blessings of the covenant, and in the counsel of redemption the way of faith is opened. The Holy Spirit, which produces faith in the sinner, was promised to Christ by the Father, and the acceptance of the way of life through faith was guaranteed by Christ.

The covenant of redemption may be defined as *the agreement between the Father, giving the Son as Head and Redeemer of the elect, and the Son, voluntarily taking the place of those whom the Father had given Him.*

III. Nature of the Covenant of Grace

In a discussion of the nature of the covenant of grace several points come up for consideration, such as the distinction between it and the covenant of works, the contracting parties, the contents, the characteristics of the covenant, and the place of Christ in the covenant.

A. Comparison of the Covenant of Grace and the Covenant of Works.

1. POINTS OF SIMILARITY. The points of agreement are of a rather general nature. The two covenants agree as to (a) the author: God is the author of both; He only could establish such covenants; (b) the contracting parties, which are in both cases God and man; (c) the external form, namely, condition and promise; (d) the contents of the promise which is in both cases eternal life; and (e) the general aim, which is the glory of God.

2. POINTS OF DIFFERENCE. (a) In the covenant of works God appears as Creator and Lord; in the covenant of grace, as Redeemer and Father. The establishment of the former was prompted by God's love and benevolence; that of the latter, by His mercy and special grace. (b) In the covenant of works man appears simply as God's creature, rightly related to his God; in the covenant of grace he appears as a sinner who has perverted his ways, and can only appear as a party in Christ, the Surety. Consequently, there is no mediator in the former, while there is in the latter. (c) The covenant of works was contingent on the uncertain obedience of a changeable man, while the covenant of grace rests on the obedience of Christ as Mediator, which is absolute and certain. (d) In the covenant of works the keeping of the law is the way of life; in the covenant of grace, it is faith in Jesus Christ. Whatever faith was required in the covenant of works was a part of the righteousness of the law; in the covenant of grace, however, it is merely the organ by which we take possession of the grace of God in Jesus Christ. (e) The covenant of works was partly known by nature, since the law of God was written in the heart of man; but the covenant of grace is known exclusively through a special positive revelation.

B. The Contracting Parties.

Just as in the covenant of works, so in the covenant of grace God is the first of the contracting parties, the party that takes the initiative, and graciously determines the relation in which the second party will stand to Him. He appears in this covenant, however, not merely as a sovereign and a benevolent God, but also, and especially, as a gracious and forgiving Father, willing to pardon sin and to restore sinners to His blessed communion.

It is not easy to determine precisely who the second party is. In general it may be said that God naturally established the covenant of grace with fallen man. Historically, there is no definite indication of any limitation until we come to the time of Abraham. In course of time it became perfectly evident, however, that this new covenant relation was not meant to include all men. When God formally established the covenant with Abraham, He limited it to the patriarch and his seed. Consequently, the question arises as to the exact limits of the covenant.

Reformed theologians are not unanimous in answering this question. Some simply say that God made the covenant with the sinner, but this suggests no limitation whatsoever, and therefore does not satisfy. Others assert that He established it with Abraham and his seed, that is, his natural, but especially his spiritual, descendants; or, put in a more general form, with believers and their seed. The great majority of them, however, maintain that He entered into covenant relationship with the elect or the elect sinner in Christ. This position was taken by earlier as well as by later representatives of federal theology. Even Bullinger says the "covenant of God includes the entire seed of Abraham, that is, the believers." He finds this to be in harmony with Paul's interpretation of "the seed" in Gal. 3. At the same time he also holds that the children of believers are in a certain sense included in the covenant.[1] And Olevianus, co-author with Ursinus of the Heidelberg Catechism, says that God established the covenant with "all those whom God, out of the mass of lost men, has decreed to adopt as children by grace, and to endow them with faith."[2] This is also the position of Mastricht, Turretin, Owen, Gib, Boston, Witsius, à Marck, Francken, Brakel, Comrie, Kuyper, Bavinck, Hodge, Vos, and others.

But now the question arises, What induced these theologians to speak of the covenant as made with the elect in spite of all the practical difficulties involved? Were they not aware of these difficulties? It appears from their writings that they were fully conscious of them. But they felt that it was necessary to contemplate the covenant first of all in its most profound sense, as it is realized in the lives of believers. While they understood that others had a place in the covenant in some sense of the word, they nevertheless felt that it was a subordinate place, and that their relation to it was calculated to be subservient to the full realization of it in a life of friendship with God. And this is no wonder in view of the following considerations:

---

1. Cf. the quotations in A. J. Van 't Hooft, *De Theologie van Heinrich Bullinger*, pp. 47, 172.

2. *Van het Wezen des Genade-Verbondts Tusschen God ende de Uitverkorene*, Afd. I, par. 1.

1.   They who identified the covenant of redemption and the covenant of grace, and considered it un-Scriptural to distinguish the two, naturally thought of it first of all as a covenant established with Christ as the representative Head of all those whom the Father had given Him; a covenant in which He became the Surety of the elect and thus guaranteed their complete redemption. In fact, in the covenant of redemption only the elect come into consideration. The situation is practically the same in the case of those who distinguish two covenants, but insist on their close relationship and represent the covenant of redemption as the eternal basis of the covenant of grace, for in the former only the grace of God, as it is glorified and perfected in the elect, comes into consideration.

2.   Even in the history of the establishment of the covenant with Abraham, interpreted in the light of the rest of Scripture, Reformed theologians found abundant evidence that fundamentally the covenant of grace is a covenant established with those who are in Christ. The Bible distinguishes a twofold seed of Abraham. The beginning of this is distinctly found in Gen. 21:12, where we find God saying to Abraham, "In Isaac shall thy seed be called," thus ruling out Ishmael. Paul, in interpreting these words speaks of Isaac as a child of promise, and by "a child of promise" he does not simply mean a promised child, but a child that was not born in the ordinary way, but, in virtue of a promise, by a supernatural operation of God. He also connects with it the idea of a child to whom the promise belongs. According to him the expression, "in Isaac shall thy seed be called," indicates that "it is not the children of the flesh that are children of God; but the children of the promise are reckoned for a seed." Rom. 9:8. The same idea is expressed in Gal. 4:28, "Now we, brethren, as Isaac was, are children of promise," and as such also heirs of the promised blessings, cf. vs. 30. This is entirely in harmony with what the apostle says in Gal. 3:16: "Now to Abraham were the promises spoken, and to his seed. He saith not, And to seeds, as of many; but as of one, And to thy seed, which is Christ." But the seed is not limited to Christ, but includes all believers. "And if ye are Christ's, then are ye Abraham's seed, heirs according to promise." Gal. 3:29. W. Strong in his *Discourse of the Two Covenants* calls attention to the following subordination in the establishment of the covenant. He says that it was made "(1) first and immediately with Christ the second Adam: (2) in Him with all the faithful: (3) in them with their seed."[1]

3.   Still another factor should be taken into consideration. Reformed theologians were deeply conscious of the contrast between the covenant of works and the covenant of grace. They felt that in the former the reward of the covenant was dependent on the uncertain obedience of man and as a result failed to materialize, while in the covenant of grace the full realization of the promises is absolutely sure in virtue of the perfect obedience of Jesus Christ. Its realization is sure through the operation of the grace of God, but, of course,

---

1.   p. 193.

sure only for those who are partakers of that grace. They felt constrained to stress this aspect of the covenant especially over against the Arminians and Neonomians, who virtually changed it into a new covenant of works, and made salvation once more dependent on the work of man, that is, on faith and evangelical obedience. For this reason they stressed the close connection between the covenant of redemption and the covenant of grace, and even hesitated to speak of faith as the *condition* of the covenant of grace. Walker tells us that some of the Scottish divines were opposed to the distinction of two covenants, because they saw in it a "tendency . . . to Neonomianism, or, as the covenant of reconciliation (i.e., the covenant of grace as distinguished from that of redemption) was external in the visible Church, even a sort of bar to immediate dealing with the Saviour, and entrance by an appropriating faith into living union with Him."[1]

4. All in all it would seem safe to say that Reformed theology contemplated the covenant, not primarily as a means ministering to an end, but as an end in itself, a relation of friendship; not first of all as representing and including a number of external privileges, a set of promises, conditionally held out to man, a good merely offered unto him; but primarily as the expression of blessings freely given, of privileges improved by the grace of God for spiritual ends, of promises accepted by a faith which is the gift of God, and of a good realized, at least in principle, through the operation of the Holy Spirit in the heart. And because in its estimation all this was included in the covenant idea, and the blessings of the covenant are realized only in those that are actually saved, it stressed the fact that the covenant of grace was established between God and the elect. But in doing this it did not intend to deny that the covenant also has a broader aspect.

Dr. Vos says with reference to this view: "Het behoeft nauwelijks herinnerd to worden, hoe met dit alles geenszins bedoeld is, dat de verbondsbediening van de verkiezing uitgaat, noch ook dat alle niet-uitverkorenen buiten iedere relatie tot deze verbonds-bediening staan. Het is veelmeer zoo bedoeld, dat uit 't gesterkt verbonds-bewustzijn de zekerheid aangaande de verkiezing zich ontwikkelen moet; dat door heel de verbonds-bediening heen, ook de volstrekte, alomvattende beloften Gods, zooals zij uit de verkiezing voortvloeien moeten worden in het oog gehouden, bij Woord en Sacrament beide; dat eindelijk het wezen des verbonds, deszelfs volle realiseering slechts bij de ware kinderen Gods wordt aangetroffen, en dus niet wijder is dan de uit-verkiezing. Vooral op het tweede punt dient gelet te worden. Behalve dat er overal, waar Gods verbond bediend wordt, eene verzegeling is van dezen inhoud: In de vooronderstelling der aanwezigheid van geloof, wordt u het recht op alle verbondsgoederen verzekerd — behalve dat, zeggen wij, is er

---

1. *Scottish Theology and Theologians*, pp. 77 f.

steeds een plechtige betuiging en verzegeling, dat God in alle uitverkorenen den geheelen omvang des verbonds will verwerkelijken."[1]

The idea that the covenant is fully realized only in the elect is a perfectly Scriptural idea, as appears, for instance, from Jer. 31:31-34; Heb. 8:8-12. Moreover, it is also entirely in line with the relation in which the covenant of grace stands to the covenant of redemption. If in the latter Christ becomes Surety only for the elect, then the real substance of the former must be limited to them also. Scripture strongly emphasizes the fact that the covenant of grace, in distinction from the covenant of works, is an inviolable covenant, in which the promises of God are always realized, Isa. 54:10. This cannot be intended conditionally, for then it would be no special characteristic of the covenant of grace, but would apply to the covenant of works as well. And yet, this is exactly one of the important points in which the former differs from the latter, that it is no more dependent on the uncertain obedience of man, but only on the absolute faithfulness of God. The covenant promises will surely be realized, but — only in the lives of the elect.

But now the question arises, whether in the estimation of these Reformed theologians all the non-elect are outside of the covenant of grace *in every sense of the word.* Brakel virtually takes this position, but he is not in line with the majority. They realized very well that a covenant of grace, which in no sense of the word included others than the elect, would be purely individual, while the covenant of grace is represented in Scripture as an organic idea. They were fully aware of the fact that, according to God's special revelation in both the Old and the New Testament, the covenant as a historical phenomenon is perpetuated in successive generations and includes many in whom the covenant life is never realized. And whenever they desired to include this aspect of the covenant in their definition, they would say that it was established *with believers and their seed.* It should be borne in mind, however, that this description of the second party in the covenant does not imply that the covenant is established with men *in the quality of believers,* for faith itself is a fruit of the covenant. Dr. Bavinck correctly says: "Maar het verbond der genade gaat aan het geloof vooraf. Het geloof is geen voorwaarde *tot* het verbond, maar *in* het verbond; de weg, om al de andere goederen van dat verbond deelachtig

---

1. That is, "It need hardly be said that with all this it is not meant that the administration of the covenant originates from the election, nor that all who are not elect stand outside of every relation to this administration of the covenant. It is far more intended thus, that out of the strengthened covenant consciousness the certainty respecting the election must develop itself: that through the entire administration of the covenant, also the absolute, all-comprehensive promises of God, as they issue from the election, must be borne in mind in connection with both Word and Sacrament; that, finally, the essence of the covenant, its full realization, is found only in the true children of God, and therefore is not more extensive than the election. Attention should be paid especially to the second point. Besides that everywhere, where God's covenant is administered, there is a seal having this content: In the supposition of the presence of faith, you are assured of the right to all the blessings of the covenant, — besides that, we say, there is always a solemn testimony and seal, that God will realize the whole content of the covenant in the elect." *De Verbondsleer in de Gereformeerde Theologie,* pp. 46 f.

te worden en te genieten."[1] The description "believers and their seed" merely serves as a convenient practical designation of the limits of the covenant. The question of harmonizing these two aspects of the covenant will come up later on. The covenant of grace may be defined as *that gracious agreement between the offended God and the offending but elect sinner, in which God promises salvation through faith in Christ, and the sinner accepts this believingly, promising a life of faith and obedience.*

C. The Contents of the Covenant of Grace.

1. THE PROMISES OF GOD. The main promise of God, which includes all other promises, is contained in the oft-repeated words, "I will be a God unto thee, and to thy seed after thee." Gen. 17:7. This promise is found in several Old and New Testament passages which speak of the introduction of a new phase of the covenant life, or refer to a renewal of the covenant, Jer. 31:33; 32:38-40; Ezek. 34:23-25,30,31; 36:25-28; 37:26,27; II Cor. 6:16-18; Heb. 8:10. The promise is fully realized when at last the new Jerusalem descends out of heaven from God, and the tabernacle of God is pitched among men. Consequently we hear the last echo of it in Rev. 21:3. This grand promise is re-echoed time and again in the jubilant exaltation of those who stand in covenant relationship to God, "Jehovah is my God." This one promise really includes all other promises, such as (a) the promise of various temporal blessings, which often serve to symbolize those of a spiritual kind; (b) the promise of justification, including the adoption of children, and a claim to life eternal; (c) the promise of the Spirit of God for the application, full and free, of the work of redemption and of all the blessings of salvation; and (d) the promise of final glorification in a life that never ends. Cf. Job 19:25-27; Ps. 16:11; 73:24-26; Isa. 43:25; Jer. 31:33,34; Ezek. 36:27; Dan. 12:2,3; Gal. 4:5,6; Tit. 3:7; Heb. 11:7; Jas. 2:5.

2. THE RESPONSE OF MAN. The assent or response of man to these promises of God naturally appears in various forms, the nature of the response being determined by the promises. (a) In general the relation between the covenant God and the single believer or believers collectively is represented as the close relationship between man and wife, bridegroom and bride, a father and his children. This implies that the response of those who share the covenant blessings will be one of true, faithful, trustful, consecrated, and devoted love. (b) To the general promise, "I will be thy God," man responds by saying, "I will belong to thy people," and by casting his lot with the people of God. (c) And to the promise of justification unto the forgiveness of sins, the adoption of children, and eternal life, he responds by saving faith in Jesus Christ, by trust in Him for time and eternity, and by a life of obedience and consecration to God.

---

1. That is, "But the covenant of grace precedes faith. Faith is not a condition *to* the covenant, but *in* the covenant; the way to obtain possession of and to enjoy all the other blessings of the covenant." *Roeping en Wedergeboorte,* p. 108.

D. The Characteristics of the Covenant of Grace.

1. IT IS A GRACIOUS COVENANT. This covenant may be called a gracious covenant, (a) because in it God allows a Surety to meet our obligations; (b) because He Himself provides the Surety in the person of His Son, who meets the demands of justice; and (c) because by His grace, revealed in the operation of the Holy Spirit, He enables man to live up to His covenant responsibilities. The covenant originates in the grace of God, is executed in virtue of the grace of God, and is realized in the lives of sinners by the grace of God. It is grace from the beginning to the end for the sinner.

2. IT IS A TRINITARIAN COVENANT. The triune God is operative in the covenant of grace. It has its origin in the elective love and grace of the Father, finds its judicial foundation in the suretyship of the Son, and is fully realized in the lives of sinners only by the effective application of the Holy Spirit, John 1:16; Eph. 1:1-14; 2:8; I Pet. 1:2.

3. IT IS AN ETERNAL AND THEREFORE UNBREAKABLE COVENANT. When we speak of it as an eternal covenant, we have reference to a future rather than to a past eternity, Gen. 17:19; II Sam. 23:5; Heb. 13:20. Past eternity can be ascribed to it only, if we do not distinguish between it and the covenant of redemption. The fact that the covenant is eternal also implies that it is inviolable; and this is one of the reasons why it can be called a testament, Heb. 9:17. God remains forever true to His covenant and will invariably bring it to full realization in the elect. This does not mean, however, that man cannot and never will break the covenant relationship in which he stands.

4. IT IS A PARTICULAR AND NOT A UNIVERSAL COVENANT. This means (a) that it will not be realized in all men, as some Universalists claim, and also that God did not intend that it should be realized in the lives of all, as Pelagians, Arminians, and Lutherans teach; (b) that even as an external covenant relation it does not extend to all those to whom the gospel is preached, for many of them are not willing to be incorporated in the covenant; and (c) that the offer of the covenant does not come to all, since there have been many individuals and even nations who were never made acquainted with the way of salvation. Some of the older Lutherans claim that the covenant may be called universal, because there have been periods in history when it was offered to the human race as a whole, as for instance, in Adam, in Noah and his family, and even in the days of the apostles. But there is no ground for making Adam and Noah *representative* recipients of the offer of the covenant; and the apostles certainly did not evangelize the whole world. Some Reformed theologians, as Musculus, Polanus, and Wollebius, and others, spoke of a *foedus generale,* in distinction from the *foedus speciale ac sempiternum,* but in doing this they had in mind the general covenant of God with all creatures, men and beasts, established by Noah. The New Testament dispensation of the covenant may be called universal in the sense that in it the covenant is extended

to all nations, and is no more limited to the Jews, as it was in the old dispensation.

5. IT IS ESSENTIALLY THE SAME IN ALL DISPENSATIONS, THOUGH ITS FORM OF ADMINISTRATION CHANGES. This is contradicted by all those who claim that Old Testament saints were saved in another manner than New Testament believers, as for instance, Pelagians and Socinians, who hold that God gave additional help in the example and teachings of Christ; the Roman Catholics, who maintain that the Old Testament saints were in the *Limbus Patrum* until Christ's descent into hades; the followers of Coccejus, who assert that Old Testament believers enjoyed only a *paresis* (a passing over) and no *aphesis* (full forgiveness of sins); and present-day dispensationalists, who distinguish several different covenants (Scofield mentions 7; Milligan 9), and insist on the necessity of keeping them distinct. The unity of the covenant in all dispen- sations is proved by the following:

a. The summary expression of the covenant is the same throughout, both in the Old and New Testament: "I will be thy God." It is the expression of the essential content of the covenant with Abraham, Gen. 17:7, of the Sinaitic covenant, Ex. 19:5; 20:1, of the covenant of the Plains of Moab, Deut. 29:13, of the Davidic covenant, II Sam. 7:14, and of the new covenant, Jer. 31:33; Heb. 8:10. This promise is really an all-comprehensive summary and contains a guarantee of the most perfect covenant blessings. Christ infers from the fact that God is called the God of Abraham, Isaac, and Jacob, that those patriarchs are in possession of eternal life, Matt. 22:32.

b. The Bible teaches that there is but a single gospel by which men can be saved. And because the gospel is nothing but the revelation of the covenant of grace, it follows that there is also but one covenant. This gospel was already heard in the maternal promise, Gen. 3:15, was preached unto Abraham, Gal. 3:8, and may not be supplanted by any Judaistic gospel, Gal. 1:8,9.

c. Paul argues at length over against the Judaists that the way in which Abraham obtained salvation is typical for New Testament believers, no matter whether they be Jews or Gentiles, Rom. 4:9-25; Gal. 3:7-9,17,18. He speaks of Abraham as the father of believers, and clearly proves that the covenant with Abraham is still in force. It is perfectly clear from the argument of the apostle in Rom. 4 and Gal. 3 that the law has not annulled nor altered the covenant. Cf. also Heb. 6:13-18.

d. The Mediator of the covenant is the same yesterday, to-day, and forever, Heb. 13:8. In none other is there salvation, John 14:6; for neither is there any other name under heaven, that is given among men, whereby we must be saved, Acts 4:12. The seed promised to Abraham is Christ, Gal. 3:16, and those that are identified with Christ are the real heirs of the covenant, Gal. 3:16-29.

e. The way of salvation revealed in the covenant is the same. Scripture insists on the identical conditions all along, Gen. 15:6, compared with Rom. 4:11; Heb. 2:4; Acts 15:11; Gal. 3:6,7; Heb. 11:9. The promises, for the realization of which the believers hoped, were also the same, Gen. 15:6; Ps. 51:12; Matt. 13:17; John 8:56. And the sacraments, though differing in form have essentially the same signification in both dispensations, Rom. 4:11; I Cor. 5:7; Col. 2:11,12.

f. *It is both conditional and unconditional.* The question is repeatedly asked, whether the covenant is conditional or unconditional. This is a question that cannot be answered without careful discrimination, for the answer will depend on the point of view from which the covenant is considered.

On the one hand the covenant is unconditional. There is in the covenant of grace no condition that can be considered as *meritorious.* The sinner is exhorted to repent and believe, but his faith and repentance do not in any way merit the blessings of the covenant. This must be maintained in opposition to both the Roman Catholic and the Arminian position. Neither is it conditional in the sense that man is expected to perform in his own strength what the covenant requires of him. In placing him before the demands of the covenant, we must always remind him of the fact that he can obtain the necessary strength for the performance of his duty only from God. In a sense it may be said that God Himself fulfills the condition in the elect. That which may be regarded as a condition in the covenant, is for those who are chosen unto everlasting life also a promise, and therefore a gift of God. Finally, the covenant is not conditional in the sense that the reception of every separate blessing of the covenant is dependent on a condition. We may say that faith is the *conditio sine qua non of* justification, but the reception of faith itself in regeneration is not dependent on any condition, but only on the operation of the grace of God in Christ.

On the other hand the covenant may be called conditional. There is a sense in which the covenant is conditional. If we consider the basis of the covenant, it is clearly conditional on the suretyship of Jesus Christ. In order to introduce the covenant of grace, Christ had to, and actually did, meet the conditions originally laid down in the covenant of works, by His active and passive obedience. Again, it may be said that the covenant is conditional as far as the first conscious entrance into the covenant as a real communion of life is concerned. This entrance is contingent on faith, a faith, however, which is itself a gift of God. When we speak of faith as a condition here, we naturally refer to faith as a spiritual activity of the mind. It is only through faith that we can obtain a *conscious enjoyment* of the blessings of the covenant. Our experimental knowledge of the covenant life is entirely dependent on the exercise of faith. He who does not live a life of faith is, *as far as his conscious-ness is concerned*, practically outside of the covenant. If in our purview we include not only the beginning, but also the gradual unfolding and completion of the covenant life, we may regard sanctification as a condition in addition to faith. Both are conditions, however, within the covenant.

Reformed Churches have often objected to the use of the word "condition" in connection with the covenant of grace. This was largely due to a reaction against Arminianism, which employed the word "condition" in an un-Scriptural sense, and therefore to a failure to discriminate properly.[1] Bearing in mind what was said in the preceding, it would seem to be perfectly proper to speak of a condition in connection with the covenant of grace, for (1) the Bible clearly indicates that the entrance upon the covenant life is conditioned on faith, John 3:16,36; Acts 8:37 (not found in some MSS.); Rom. 10:9; (2) Scripture often threatens covenant children, but these threatenings apply exactly to those who ignore the condition, that is, who refuse to walk in the way of the covenant; and (3) if there were no condition, God only would be bound by the covenant, and there would be no "bond of the covenant" for man (but cf. Ezek. 20:37); and thus the covenant of grace would lose its character as a covenant, for there are two parts in all covenants.

g. *The covenant may in a sense be called a testament.* In view of the fact that a testament is an absolute declaration and knows of no conditions, the question is raised whether it is proper at all to apply the term "testament" to the covenant. There is but one passage in the New Testament where it seems to be justifiable to render the word *diatheke* by "testament," namely, Heb. 9:16,17. There Christ is represented as the testator, in whose death the covenant of grace, considered as a testament, becomes effective. There was a testamentary disposal of the blessings of the covenant, and this came into force through the death of Christ. This is the only passage in which the covenant is explicitly referred to as a testament. But the idea that believers receive the spiritual blessings of the covenant in a testamentary way is implied in several passages of Scripture, though the implied representation is slightly different from that in Heb. 9:16,17. It is God rather than Christ who is testator. In both the Old and the New Testament, but especially in the latter, believers are represented as children of God, legally by adoption, and ethically by the new birth, John 1:12; Rom. 8:15,16; Gal. 4:4-6; I John 3:1-3,9. Now the ideas of heirship and inheritance are naturally associated with that of sonship, and therefore it is no wonder that they are frequently found in Scripture. Paul says: "And if children, then heirs," Rom. 8:17; cf. also Rom. 4:14; Gal. 3:29; 4:1,7; Tit. 3:7; Heb. 6:17; 11:7; Jas. 2:5. In view of these passages there is no doubt that the covenant and the covenant blessings are represented in Scripture as an inheritance. But this representation is again based on the idea of a testament, with this difference, however, that the confirmation of the covenant does not imply the death of the testator. Believers are heirs of God (who cannot die) and joint-heirs with Christ, Rom. 8:17. It is perfectly evident that for the sinner the covenant has a testamentary side

1. Cf. Dick, *Theol. Lect.* XLVIII.

and can be regarded as an inheritance; but now the question arises, whether it can also assume this character for Christ. An affirmative answer would seem to be required in view of the fact that we are called *co-heirs* with Christ. Is He then also an heir? This question may be answered in the affirmative in view of the statement found in Luke 22:29. The inheritance referred to here is the mediatorial glory of Christ, which He received as an inheritance from the Father, and which He, in turn, communicates as an inheritance to all those that are His. But though there is undoubtedly a testamentary side to the covenant, this is but one side of the matter, and does not preclude the idea that the covenant is really a covenant. It can be called a testament, because (1) it is as a whole a gift from God; (2) the New Testament dispensation of it was ushered in by the death of Christ; (3) it is firm and inviolable; and (4) in it God Himself gives what He demands of man. Yet this should not be interpreted to mean that there are no two sides to the covenant, and that it is therefore absolutely monopleuric. However unequal the parties in themselves may be, God condescends to come down to the level of man and by His grace enables him to act as the second party in the covenant. A monopleuric covenant in the absolute sense of the word is really a *contradictio in adjecto*. At the same time those theologians who stress the monopleuric character of the covenant did this to emphasize an important truth, namely, that God and man do not meet each other half way in the covenant, but that God comes down to man and graciously establishes His covenant with him, freely giving all that He demands, and that man is really the only one that profits by the covenant. It is essential, however, that the dipleuric character of the covenant be maintained, because man really appears in it as meeting the demands of the covenant in faith and conversion, though it be only as God works in him both to will and to do, according to His good pleasure.

E. The Relation of Christ to the Covenant of Grace.

Christ is represented in Scripture as the Mediator of the covenant. The Greek word *mesites* is not found in classical Greek, but does occur in Philo and in later Greek authors. In the Septuagint it is found but once, Job 9:33. The English word "Mediator," as well as the Holland "Middelaar" and the German "Mittler," might lead us to think that it (*mesites*) simply designates one who arbitrates between two parties, an intermediary in the general sense of the word. It should be borne in mind, however, that the Scriptural idea is far more profound. Christ is Mediator in more than one sense. He intervenes between God and man, not merely to sue for peace and to persuade to it, but as armed with plenipotentiary power, to do all that is necessary to establish peace. The use of the word *mesites* in the New Testament justifies our speaking of a twofold Mediatorship of Christ, namely, that of surety and that of access (Gr. *prosagoge*, Rom. 5:2). In most of the passages in which the word is found in the New Testament, it is equal to *egguos*, and therefore points to Christ as one who, by taking upon Himself the guilt of sinners, terminated their penal relation to the law and restored them to the right legal relationship to God.

This is the meaning of the word in Heb. 8:6; 9:15, and 12:24. In Heb. 7:22 the term *egguos* itself is applied to Christ. There is one passage, however, in which the word *mesites* has a meaning that is more in accord with the ordinary sense of the word "mediator," as one who is called in to arbitrate between two parties and to reconcile them, namely, I Tim. 2:5. Here Christ is represented as Mediator in the sense that, on the basis of His sacrifice, He brings God and man together. The work of Christ, as indicated by the word *mesites*, is twofold. He labors in things pertaining to God and in things pertaining to man, in the objective legal sphere, and in the subjective moral sphere. In the former He propitiates the just displeasure of God by expiating the guilt of sin, makes intercession for those whom the Father has given Him, and actually makes their persons and services acceptable to God. And in the latter He reveals to men the truth concerning God and their relation to Him with the conditions of acceptable service, persuades and enables them to receive the truth, and directs and sustains them in all circumstances of life, so as to perfect their deliverance. In doing this work He employs the ministry of men, II Cor. 5:20.

IV. The Dual Aspect of the Covenant

In speaking of the contracting parties in the covenant of grace it was already intimated that the covenant may be considered from two different points of view. There are two different aspects of the covenant, and now the question arises, In what relation do these two stand to each other? This question has been answered in different ways.

A. An External and an Internal Covenant.

Some have distinguished between an external and an internal covenant. The external covenant was conceived as one in which a person's status depends entirely on the performance of certain external religious duties. His position is entirely correct, if he does what is required of him, somewhat in the Roman Catholic sense. Among Israel this covenant assumed a national form. Perhaps no one worked out the doctrine of an external covenant with greater consistency than Thomas Blake. The dividing line between the external and the internal covenant was not always represented in the same way. Some connected baptism with the external, and confession of faith and the Lord's Supper, with the internal covenant; others thought of baptism and confession as belonging to the external covenant, and of the Lord's Supper as the sacrament of the internal covenant. But the trouble is that this whole representation results in a dualism in the conception of the covenant that is not warranted by Scripture; it yields an external covenant that is not interpenetrated by the internal. The impression is created that there is a covenant in which man can assume an entirely correct position without saving faith; but the Bible knows of no such covenant. There are, indeed, external privileges and blessings of the covenant, and there are persons who enjoy these only; but such cases are abnormalities that cannot be systematized. The distinction between an external and an internal covenant does not hold.

This view must not be confused with another and related view, namely, that there is an external and an internal aspect of the covenant of grace (Mastricht and others). According to this some accept their covenant responsibilities in a truly spiritual way, from the heart, while others accept them only by an external profession with the mouth, and therefore are only apparently in the covenant. Mastricht refers to Judas Iscariot, Simon the sorcerer, those who have temporal faith, and others. But the trouble is that, according to this view, the non-elect and non-regenerate are merely external appendages to the covenant, and are simply regarded as children of the covenant *by us* because of our short-

284

sightedness, but are no covenant children at all *in the sight of God*. They are not really in the covenant, and therefore cannot really become covenant breakers either. It offers no solution of the problem in what sense the non-elect and non-regenerate, who are members of the visible Church, are children of the covenant *also in the sight of God*, and can therefore become covenant breakers.

B. The Essence and the Administration of the Covenant.

Others, as for instance, Olevianus and Turretin, distinguish between the essence and the administration of the covenant. According to Turretin the former corresponds to the internal calling and the invisible Church formed by means of this calling; and the latter, to the external calling and the visible Church, as consisting of those who are called externally by the Word. The administration of the covenant consists only in the offer of salvation in the preaching of the Word, and in the other external privileges in which all share who have a place in the Church, including many non-elect. The essence of the covenant, however, also includes the spiritual reception of all the blessings of the covenant, the life in union with Christ, and therefore extends to the elect only. This distinction certainly contains an element of truth, but is not altogether logical and clear. While essence and form would constitute an antithesis, essence and administration do not. They may refer to the invisible and the visible Church, as Turretin seems to intend, or to the final end or realization and the announcement of the covenant, as Olevianus understands the distinction. But if the former is meant, it would be better to speak of essence and revelation; and if the latter is intended, it would be preferable to speak of the aim and the means of its realization. Here, too, the question remains unanswered, whether and in how far the non-elect are covenant children *also in the sight of God*.

C. A Conditional and an Absolute Covenant.

Still others, as for instance, Koelman, speak of a conditional and an absolute covenant. Koelman emphasizes the fact that, when an external and an internal covenant are distinguished, only a single covenant is meant, and the terms "external" and "internal" simply serve to stress the fact that all are not in the covenant in exactly the same way. Some are in it merely by an external confession, to the enjoyment of external privileges, and others by a hearty acceptance of it, to the enjoyment of the blessings of salvation. Likewise, he wishes it to be clearly understood that, when he says that some are in the covenant externally and conditionally, he does not mean to assert that they are not really in the covenant, but only that they cannot obtain the promised blessings of the covenant, except by complying with the condition of the covenant. This representation, too, undoubtedly contains an element of truth, but in Koelman it is linked up in such a way with the notion of an external and an internal covenant, that he comes dangerously near to the error of accepting two covenants, especially when he claims that during the New Testament dispensation God incorporates whole nations and kingdoms in the covenant.

D. The Covenant as a Purely Legal Relationship and as a Communion of Life.

Reformed theologians, such as Kuyper, Bavinck, and Honig, speak of two sides of the covenant, the one external and the other internal. Dr. Vos uses terms that are more specific, when he distinguishes between the covenant as a purely legal relationship and the covenant as a communion of life. There is clearly a legal and a moral side to the covenant. The covenant may be regarded as an agreement between two parties, with mutual conditions and stipulations, and therefore as something in the legal sphere. The covenant in that sense may exist even when nothing is done to realize its purpose, namely the condition to which it points and for which it calls as the real ideal. The parties that live under this agreement are in the covenant, since they are subject to the mutual stipulations agreed upon. In the legal sphere everything is considered and regulated in a purely objective way. The determining factor in that sphere is simply the relation which has been established, and not the attitude which one assumes to that relation. The relation exists independently of one's inclination or disinclination, one's likes and dislikes, in connection with it. It would seem to be in the light of this distinction that the question should be answered, Who are in the covenant of grace? If the question is asked with the legal relationship, and that only, in mind, and really amounts to the query, Who are in duty bound to live in the covenant, and of whom may it be expected that they will do this? —the answer is, believers and their children. But if the question is asked with a view to the covenant as a communion of life, and assumes the quite different form, In whom does this legal relationship issue in a living communion with Christ? — the answer can only be, only in the regenerate, who are endowed with the principle of faith, that is, in the elect.

This distinction is warranted by Scripture. It is hardly necessary to cite passages proving that the covenant is an objective compact in the legal sphere, for it is perfectly evident that we have such a compact wherever two parties agree as in the presence of God to perform certain things affecting their mutual relation, or one party promises to bestow certain benefits on the other, provided the latter fulfills the conditions that are laid down. That the covenant of grace is such a compact is abundantly evident from Scripture. There is the condition of faith, Gen. 15:6, compared with Rom. 4:3 ff., 20 ff.; Hab. 2:4; Gal. 3:14-28; Heb. 11; and there is also the promise of spiritual and eternal blessings, Gen. 17:7; 12:3; Isa. 43:25; Ezek. 36:27; Rom. 4:5 ff.; Gal. 3:14,18. But it is also clear that the covenant in its full realization is something more than that, namely, a communion of life. This may be already symbolically expressed in the act of passing between the parts of the animals slain at the establishment of the covenant with Abraham, Gen. 15:9-17. Moreover, it is indicated in such passages as Ps. 25:14; Ps. 89:33,34; 103:17,18; Jer. 31:33,34 (Heb. 8:10-12); Ezek. 36:25-28; II Cor. 6:16; Rev. 21:2,3.

Now the question arises as to the relation between the sinner's being under the "bond of the covenant" as a legal relationship and his living in the communion of the covenant. The two cannot be conceived of as existing alongside of each other without some inner connection, but must be regarded as being most intimately related to each other, in order to avoid all dualism. When one takes the covenant relation upon himself voluntarily, the two must naturally go together; if they do not, a false relation ensues. But in the case of those who are *born* in the covenant the question is more difficult. Is the one then possible without the other? Is the covenant in that case a bare legal relationship, in which that which ought to be — but is not — takes the place of the glorious realities for which the covenant stands? Is there any reasonable ground to expect that the covenant relation will issue in a living communion; that for the sinner, who is of himself unable to believe, the covenant will actually become a living reality? In answer to this question it may be said that God undoubtedly desires that the covenant relationship shall issue in a covenant life. And He Himself guarantees by His promises pertaining to the seed of believers that this will take place, not in the case of every individual, but in the seed of the covenant collectively. On the basis of the promise of God we may believe that, under a faithful administration of the covenant, the covenant relation will, as a rule, be fully realized in a covenant life.

E. Membership in the Covenant as a Legal Relationship.

In discussing membership in the covenant as a legal relationship, it should be borne in mind that the covenant in this sense is not merely a system of demands and promises, demands that ought to be met, and promises that ought to be realized; but that it also includes a reasonable expectation that the external legal relationship will carry with it the glorious reality of a life in intimate communion with the covenant God. This is the only way in which the idea of the covenant is fully realized,

1. ADULTS IN THE COVENANT. Adults can only enter this covenant voluntarily by faith and confession. From this it follows that in their case, unless their confession be false, entrance into the covenant as a legal relationship and into the covenant as a communion of life coincide. They not merely take upon themselves the performance of certain external duties; nor do they merely promise in addition to this, that they will exercise saving faith in the future; but they confess that they accept the covenant with a living faith, and that it is their desire and intention to continue in this faith. They enter upon the full covenant life at once therefore, and this is the only way in which they can enter the covenant. This truth is implicitly or explicitly denied by all those who connect the confession of faith with a merely external covenant.

2. CHILDREN OF BELIEVERS IN THE COVENANT. With respect to the children of believers, who enter the covenant by birth, the situation is, of course, somewhat different. Experience teaches that, though by birth they enter the covenant as a legal relationship, this does not necessarily mean that they are also at once in the covenant as a communion of life. It does not even mean that the covenant relation will ever come to its full realization in their lives. Yet even in their case there must be a reasonable assurance that the covenant is not or

will not remain a mere legal relationship, with external duties and privileges, pointing to that which ought to be, but is also or will in time become a living reality. This assurance is based on the promise of God, which is absolutely reliable, that He will work in the hearts of the covenant youth with His saving grace and transform them into living members of the covenant. The covenant is more than the mere offer of salvation, more even than the offer of salvation plus the promise to believe the gospel. It also carries with it the assurance, based on the promises of God, who works in the children of the covenant "when, where, and how He pleaseth," that saving faith will be wrought in their hearts. As long as the children of the covenant do not reveal the contrary, we shall have to proceed on the assumption that they are in possession of the covenant life. Naturally, the course of events may prove that this life is not yet present; it may even prove that it is never realized in their lives. The promises of God are given to the seed of believers collectively, and not individually. God's promise to continue His covenant and to bring it to full realization in the children of believers, does not mean that He will endow every last one of them with saving faith. And if some of them continue in unbelief, we shall have to bear in mind what Paul says in Rom. 9:6-8. They are not all Israel who are of Israel; the children of believers are not all children of promise. Hence it is necessary to remind even children of the covenant constantly of the necessity of regeneration and conversion. The mere fact that one is in the covenant does not carry with it the assurance of salvation. When the children of believers grow up and come to years of discretion, it is, of course, incumbent on them to accept their covenant responsibilities voluntarily by a true confession of faith. Failure to do this is, strictly speaking, a denial of their covenant relationship. It may be said therefore that the legal relationship in which the children of believers stand, precedes the covenant as a communion of life and is a means to its realization. But in emphasizing the significance of the covenant as a means to an end, we should not stress exclusively, nor even primarily, the demands of God and the resulting duty of man, but especially the promise of the effectual operation of the grace of God in the hearts of covenant children. If we stress the covenant responsibilities only or excessively, and fail to give due prominence to the fact that in the covenant God gives whatsoever He demands of us, in other words, that His promises cover all His requirements, we are in danger of falling into the snare of Arminianism.

3. UNREGENERATE IN THE COVENANT. From the preceding it follows that even unregenerate and unconverted persons may be in the covenant. Ishmael and Esau were originally in the covenant, the wicked sons of Eli were covenant children, and the great majority of the Jews in the days of Jesus and the apostles belonged to the covenant people and shared in the covenant promises, though they did not follow the faith of their father Abraham. Hence the question arises, in what sense such persons may be regarded as being in the covenant. Dr. Kuyper says that they are not essential participants of the covenant, though they are really in it; and Dr. Bavinck says that they are *in foedere* (in the covenant),

but not *de foedere* (of the covenant). The following may be said regarding their position in the covenant:

a. They are in the covenant as far as their responsibility is concerned. Because they stand in the legal covenant relationship to God, they are in duty bound to repent and believe. If they do not turn to God and accept Christ by faith, when they come to years of discretion, they will be judged as breakers of the covenant. The special relationship in which they are placed to God, therefore, means added responsibility.

b. They are in the covenant in the sense that they may lay claim to the promises which God gave when He established His covenant with believers and their seed. Paul even says of his wicked kinsmen, "whose is the adoption, and the glory, and the covenants, and the giving of the law, and the service of God, and the promises," Rom. 9:4. As a rule God gathers the number of His elect out of those who stand in this covenant relationship.

c. They are in the covenant in the sense that they are subject to the ministrations of the covenant. They are constantly admonished and exhorted to live according to the requirements of the covenant. The Church treats them as covenant children, offers them the seals of the covenant, and exhorts them to a proper use of these. They are the guests who are first called to the supper, the children of the kingdom, to whom the Word must be preached first of all, Matt. 8:12; Luke 14:16-24; Acts 13:46.

d. They are in the covenant also as far as the common covenant blessings are concerned. Though they do not experience the regenerating influence of the Holy Spirit, yet they are subject to certain special operations and influences of the Holy Spirit. The Spirit strives with them in a special manner, convicts them of sin, enlightens them in a measure, and enriches them with the blessings of common grace, Gen. 6:3; Matt. 13:18-22; Heb. 6:4-6.

It should be noted that, while the covenant is an eternal and inviolable covenant, which God never nullifies, it is possible for those who are in the covenant to break it. If one who stands in the legal covenant relationship does not enter upon the covenant life, he is nevertheless regarded as a member of the covenant. His failure to meet the requirements of the covenant involves guilt and constitutes him a covenant breaker, Jer. 31:32; Ezek. 44:7. This explains how there may be, not merely a temporary, but a final breaking of the covenant, though there is no falling away of the saints.

V. The Different Dispensations of the Covenant

A. The Proper Conception of the Different Dispensations.

The question arises, whether we ought to distinguish two or three, or with the modern Dispensationalists, seven or even more dispensations.

1. THE DISPENSATIONAL VIEW. According to Scofield "a dispensation is a period of time during which man is tested in respect of obedience to some specific revelation of the will of God."[1] In further explanation of this he says on page 20 of his pamphlet on *Rightly Dividing the Word of Truth*: "Each of the dispensations may be regarded as a new test of the natural man, and each ends in judgment, — marking his failure." Every dispensation has a character of its own, and is so distinct that it cannot be commingled with any of the others. Seven such dispensations are usually distinguished, namely, the dispensation of innocency, of conscience, of human government, of promise, of the law, of grace, and of the kingdom. In answer to the question, whether God is then so fickle-minded that He must change His will as regards man seven times, Frank E. Gaebelein replies: "It is not God who has vacillated. Though there are seven dispensations, they are all one in principle, being throughout based upon the single test of obedience. And had man been found able to keep the conditions laid down by the first dispensation, the other six would have been unnecessary. But man failed. Yet, instead of casting off His guilty creature, God was moved with compassion, and gave him a fresh trial under new conditions. Thus each dispensation ends with failure, and each dispensation shows forth God's mercy."[2] There are serious objections to this view. (a) The word "dispensation" (*oikonomia*), which is a Scriptural term (cf. Luke 16:2-4; I Cor. 9:17; Eph. 1:10; 3:2,9; Col. 1:25; I Tim. 1:4) is here used in an un-Scriptural sense. It denotes a stewardship, an arrangement, or an administration, but never a testing time or a time of probation. (b) The distinctions are clearly quite arbitrary. This is evident already from the fact that dispensationalists themselves sometimes speak of them as overlapping. The second dispensation is called the dispensation of conscience, but according to Paul conscience was still the monitor of the Gentiles in his day, Rom. 2:14,15. The third is known as the dispensation of human government, but the specific command in it which was disobeyed and therefore rendered man liable to judgment, was not the command to rule the world for God — of which there is no trace—, but the command to replenish

---

1. *Scofield Bible*, p. 5.
2. *Exploring the Bible*, p. 95.

the earth. The fourth is designated the dispensation of promise and is supposed to terminate with the giving of the law, but Paul says that the law did not disannul the promise, and that this was still in effect in his own day, Rom. 4:13-17; Gal. 3:15-29. The so-called dispensation of the law is replete with glorious promises, and the so-called dispensation of grace did not abrogate the the law as a rule of life. Grace offers escape from the law only as a condition of salvation — as it is in the covenant of works —, from the curse of the law, and from the law as an extraneous power. (c) According to the usual representation of this theory man is on probation right along. He failed in the first test and thus missed the reward of eternal life, but God was compassionate and in mercy gave him a new trial. Repeated failures led to repeated manifestations of the mercy of God in the introduction of new trials, which, however, kept man on probation all the time. This is not equivalent to saying that God *in justice* holds the natural man to the condition of the covenant of works — which is perfectly true — but that God *in mercy and compassion* — and therefore seemingly to save — gives man one chance after another to meet the ever varying conditions, and thus to obtain eternal life by rendering obedience to God. This representation is contrary to Scripture, which does not represent fallen man as still on probation, but as an utter failure, totally unable to render obedience to God, and absolutely dependent on the grace of God for salvation. Bullinger, himself a dispensationalist, though of a somewhat different type, is right when he says: "Man was then (in the first dispensation) what is called 'under probation.' This marks off that Administration sharply and absolutely; for *man is not now under probation*. To suppose that he is so, is a popular fallacy which strikes at the root of the doctrines of grace. Man has been tried and tested, and has proved to be a ruin."[1] (d) This theory is also divisive in tendency, dismembering the organism of Scripture with disastrous results. Those parts of Scripture that belong to any one of the dispensations are addressed to, and have normative significance for, the people of that dispensation, and for no one else. This means in the words of Charles C. Cook "that in the Old Testament there is not one sentence that applies to the Christian as a Rule of Faith and Practice — not a single command that is binding on him, as there is not a single promise there given him at first hand, except what is included in the broad flow of the Plan of Redemption as there taught in symbol and prophecy."[2] This does not mean that we can derive no lessons from the Old Testament. The Bible is divided into two books, the Book of the Kingdom, comprising the Old Testament and part of the New, addressed to Israel; and the Book of the Church, consisting of the remainder of the New Testament, and addressed to us. Since the dispensations do not intermingle, it follows that in the dispensation of the law there is no revelation of the grace of God, and in the dispensation of grace there is no revelation of the law as binding on the New Testament people of

---

1. *How to Enjoy the Bible*, p. 65.
2. *God's Book Speaking For Itself*, p. 31.

God. If space permitted, it would not be difficult to prove that this is an entirely untenable position.

2. THE THEORY OF THREE DISPENSATIONS. Irenæus spoke of three covenants, the first characterized by the law written in the heart, the second, by the law as an external commandment given at Sinai, and the third, by the law restored to the heart through the operation of the Holy Spirit; and thus suggests the idea of three dispensations. Coccejus distinguished three dispensations of the covenant of grace, the first *ante legem*, the second *sub lege*, and the third *post legem*. He made a sharp distinction, therefore, between the administration of the covenant before and after Moses. Now it is undoubtedly true that there is considerable difference between the administration of the covenant before and after the giving of the law, but the similarity is greater than the difference, so that we are not justified in co-ordinating the work of Moses with that of Christ as a dividing-line in the administration of the covenant. The following points of difference may be noted:

a. *In the manifestation of the gracious character of the covenant.* In the patriarchal period the gracious character of the covenant stood out more prominently than in the later period. The promise was more in the foreground, Rom. 4:13; Gal. 3:18. Yet even this should not be stressed unduly, as if there were no legal burdens, both moral and ceremonial, before the time of Moses, and no gracious promises during the period of the law. The substance of the law was in force before Moses, and sacrifices were already required. And gracious promises are found in great abundance in the post-Mosaic writings. The only real point of difference is this: because the law constituted for Israel an explicit reminder of the demands of the covenant of works, there was a greater danger of mistaking the way of the law for the way of salvation. And the history of Israel teaches us that it did not escape the danger.

b. *In the emphasis on the spiritual character of the blessings.* The spiritual character of the blessings of the covenant stands out more clearly in the patriarchial period. Abraham, Isaac, and Jacob were mere sojourners in the land of promise, dwelling there as strangers and pilgrims. The temporal promise of the covenant was not yet fulfilled. Hence there was less danger of fixing the mind too exclusively on the material blessings, as the Jews did later on. The early patriarchs had a clearer understanding of the symbolical significance of those temporal possessions, and looked for a heavenly city, Gal. 4:25,26; Heb. 11:9,10.

c. *In the understanding of the universal destination of the covenant.* The universal destination of the covenant was more clearly evident in the patriarchal period. Abraham was told that in his seed all the nations of the world would be blessed, Gen. 22:18; Rom. 4:13-77; Gal. 3:8. The Jews gradually lost sight of this important fact, and proceeded on the assumption that the blessings of the covenant were to be restricted to the Jewish nation. The later prophets, however, stressed the universality of the promises, and thus revived the consciousness of the world-wide significance of the covenant.

But while these differences existed, there were several important points in which the pre- and post-Mosaic periods agreed, and in which they together differed from the Christian dispensation. While their difference from each other is simply one of degree, their common difference from the New Testament dispensation is one of contrast. As over against the Christian dispensation, the two Old Testament periods agree:

a. *In the representation of the Mediator as a seed that was still future.* The whole Old Testament points forward to the coming Messiah. This forward look characterizes the protevangel, the promise given to the patriarchs, the whole Mosaic ritual, and the central messages of the prophets.

b. *In prefiguring the coming Redeemer in ceremonies and types.* It is perfectly true that these increased after the giving of the law, but they were present long before that time. Sacrifices were offered as early as the days of Cain and Abel, and also had a piacular character, pointing forward to the great sacrifice of Jesus Christ. Those who served as priests foreshadowed the coming of the great High Priest. In distinction from the Old Testament, the New is commemorative rather than prefigurative.

c. *In prefiguring the vicissitudes of those who were destined to share in the spiritual realities of the covenant in the earthly career of those groups which stood in covenant relationship with God.* The pilgrimage of the patriarchs in the Holy Land, the servitude in Egypt, the entrance into Canaan, all pointed forward to higher spiritual things. In the New Testament all these types reach their fulfilment and therefore cease.

On the basis of all that has been said it is preferable to follow the traditional lines by distinguishing just two dispensations or administrations, namely, that of the Old, and that of the New Testament; and to subdivide the former into several periods or stages in the revelation of the covenant of grace.

B. The Old Testament Dispensation.

1. THE FIRST REVELATION OF THE COVENANT. The first revelation of the covenant is found in the protevangel, Gen. 3:15. Some deny that this has any reference to the covenant; and it certainly does not refer to any formal establishment of a covenant. The revelation of such an establishment could only follow after the covenant idea had been developed in history. At the same time Gen. 3:15 certainly contains a revelation of the essence of the covenant. The following points should be noted:

a. By putting enmity between the serpent and the woman God establishes a relation, as He always does in making a covenant. The fall brought man in league with Satan, but God breaks that newly formed alliance by turning man's friendship with Satan into enmity and re-establishing man in friendship with Himself; and this is the covenant idea. This rehabilitation of man included the promise of sanctifying grace, for it was only by such grace that man's friendship with Satan could be turned into enmity. God Himself had to reverse the condition by regenerating grace. In all probability He at once wrought the grace of the covenant in the hearts of our first parents. And when God by His saving power generates enmity to Satan in the heart of man, this implies that He chooses the side of man, that He becomes *man's confederate* in the struggle with Satan, and thus virtually establishes an offensive and defensive covenant.

b. This relationship between God and man on the one side and Satan on the other side, is not limited to the individuals, but extends to their seed. The covenant is organic in its operation and includes the generations. This is an essential element in the covenant idea. There will not only be a seed of man, but also a seed of the serpent, that is, of the devil, and there will be a prolonged struggle between the two, in which the seed of man will be victorious.

c. The struggle, then, will not be indecisive. Though the heel of the woman's seed will be bruised, the head of the serpent will be crushed. It can only bite the heel, and by doing this endangers its very head. There will be suffering on the part of the seed of the woman, but the deadly sting of the serpent will terminate in its own death. The death of Christ, who is in a pre-eminent sense the seed of the woman, will mean the defeat of Satan. The prophecy of redemption is still impersonal in the protevangel, but it is nevertheless a Messianic prophecy. In the last analysis the seed of the woman is Christ, who assumes human nature, and, being put to death on the cross, gains the decisive victory over Satan. It goes without saying that our first parents did not understand all this.

2. THE COVENANT WITH NOAH. The covenant with Noah is evidently of a very general nature: God promises that He will not again destroy all flesh by the waters of a flood, and that the regular succession of seed time and harvest, cold and heat, winter and summer, day and night will continue. The forces of nature are bridled, the powers of evil are put under greater restraint, and man is protected against the violence of both man and beast. It is a covenant conferring only natural blessings, and is therefore often called the covenant of nature or of common grace. There is no objection to this terminology, provided it does not convey the impression that this covenant is dissociated altogether from the covenant of grace. Though the two differ, they are also most intimately connected.

a. *Points of difference.* The following points of difference should be noted: (1) While the covenant of grace pertains primarily, though not exclusively, to spiritual blessings, the covenant of nature assures man only of earthly and temporal blessings. (2) While the covenant of grace in the broadest sense of the word includes only believers and their seed, and is fully realized only in the lives of the elect, the covenant with Noah was not only universal in its inception, but was destined to remain all-inclusive. Up to the days of the covenant transaction with Abraham there was no seal of the covenant of grace, but the covenant with Noah was confirmed by the token of the rainbow, a seal quite different from those that were later on connected with the covenant of grace.

b. *Points of connection.* Notwithstanding the differences just mentioned, there is a most intimate connection between the two covenants. (1) The covenant of nature also originated in the grace of God. In this covenant, just as in the covenant of grace, God bestows on man not only unmerited favors, but blessings that were forfeited by sin. By nature man has no claim whatsoever on the natural blessings promised in this covenant. (2) This covenant also rests on the covenant of grace. It was established more particularly with Noah and his seed, because there were clear evidences of the realization of the covenant of grace in this family, Gen. 6:9; 7:1; 9:9,26,27. (3) It is also a necessary appendage (Witsius: "aanhangsel") of the covenant of grace. The revelation of the covenant of grace in Gen. 3:16-19 already pointed to earthly and temporal blessings. These were absolutely necessary for the realization of the covenant of grace. In the covenant with Noah the general character of these blessings is clearly brought out, and their continuance is confirmed.

3. THE COVENANT WITH ABRAHAM. With Abraham we enter upon a new epoch in the Old Testament revelation of the covenant of grace. There are several points that deserve attention here:

a. Up to the time of Abraham there was no formal establishment of the covenant of grace. While Gen. 3:15 already contains the elements of this covenant, it does not record a formal transaction by which the covenant was established. It does not even speak explicitly of a covenant. The establishment of the covenant with Abraham marked the beginning of an institutional Church. In pre-Abrahamic times there was what may be called "the church in the house." There were families in which the true religion found expression, and undoubtedly also gatherings of believers, but there was no definitely marked body of believers, separated from the world, that might be called the Church. There were "sons of God" and "sons of men," but these were not yet separated by a visible line of demarcation. At the time of Abraham, however, circumcision was instituted as a sealing ordinance, a badge of membership, and a seal of the righteousness of faith.

b. In the transaction with Abraham the particularistic Old Testament administration of the covenant had its beginning, and it becomes perfectly evident that man is a party in the covenant and must respond to the promises of God by faith. The great central fact emphasized in Scripture, is that Abraham believed God and it was reckoned unto him for righteousness. God appears unto Abraham again and again, repeating His promises, in order to engender faith in his heart and to prompt its activity. The greatness of his faith was apparent in his believing against hope, in his trusting in the promise even when its fulfilment seemed to be a physical impossibility.

c. The spiritual blessings of the covenant of grace become far more apparent in the covenant with Abraham than they were before. The best Scriptural exposition of the Abrahamic covenant is contained in Rom. 3 and 4, and

Gal. 3. In connection with the narrative found in Genesis these chapters teach that Abraham received in the covenant justification, including the forgiveness of sins and adoption into the very family of God, and also the gifts of the Spirit unto sanctification and eternal glory.

d. The covenant with Abraham already included a symbolical element. On the one hand it had reference to temporal blessings, such as the land of Canaan, a numerous offspring, protection against and victory over the enemies; and on the other, it referred to spiritual blessings. It should be borne in mind, however, that the former were not co-ordinate with, but subordinate to, the latter. These temporal blessings did not constitute an end in themselves, but served to symbolize and typify spiritual and heavenly things. The spiritual promises were not realized in the natural descendants of Abraham as such, but only in those who followed in the footsteps of Abraham.

e. In view of this establishment of the covenant of grace with Abraham, he is sometimes considered as the head of the covenant of grace. But the word "head" is rather ambiguous, and therefore liable to misunderstanding. Abraham cannot be called the representative head of the covenant of grace, just as Adam was of the covenant of works, for (1) the Abrahamic covenant did not include the believers that preceded him and who were yet in the covenant of grace, and (2) he could not accept the promises for us nor believe in our stead, thereby exempting us from these duties. If there is a representative head in the covenant of grace, it can only be Christ (cf. Bavinck, *Geref. Dogm.* III, pp. 239,241); but, strictly speaking, we can consider Him as the Head only on the assumption that the covenant of redemption and the covenant of grace are one. Abraham can be called the head of the covenant only in the sense that it was formally established with him, and that he received the promise of its continuance in the line of his natural, but above all, of his spiritual, descendants. Paul speaks of him as "the father of all them that believe," Rom. 4:11. It is clear that the word "father" can only be understood figuratively here, for believers do not owe their spiritual life to Abraham. Says Dr. Hodge in his Commentary of Romans (4:11): "The word *father* expresses community of character, and is often applied to the head or founder of any school or class of men, whose character is determined by the relation to the person so designated; as Gen. 4:20,21. . . . Believers are called the children of Abraham, because of this identity of religious nature or character, as he stands out in Scripture as *the* believer; and because it was with him that the covenant of grace, embracing all the children of God, whether Jews or Gentiles, was re-enacted; and because they are his heirs, inheriting the blessings promised to him."

f. Finally, we must not lose sight of the fact that the stage of the Old Testament covenant revelation which is most normative for us in the New Testament dispensation, is not that of the Sinaitic covenant, but that of the covenant established with Abraham. The Sinaitic covenant is an interlude, covering a period in which the real character of the covenant of grace, that is, its free and gracious character, is somewhat eclipsed by all kinds of external ceremonies and forms which, in connection with the theocratic life of Israel, placed the demands of the law prominently in the foreground, cf. Gal. 3. In the covenant with Abraham, on the other hand, the promise and the faith that responds to the promise are made emphatic.

4. THE SINAITIC COVENANT. The covenant of Sinai was *essentially* the same as that established with Abraham, though the form differed somewhat. This is not always recognized, and is not recognized by present day dispensationalists. They insist on it that it was a different covenant, not only in form but in essence. Scofield speaks of it as a legal covenant, a "conditional Mosaic covenant of works,"[1] under which the point of testing was legal obedience as the condition of salvation.[2] If that covenant was a covenant of works, it certainly was not the covenant of grace. The reason why it is sometimes regarded as an entirely new covenant is that Paul repeatedly refers to the law and the promise as forming an antithesis, Rom. 4:13 ff.; Gal. 3:17. But it should be noted that the apostle does not contrast with the covenant of Abraham the Sinaitic covenant as a whole, but only the law as it functioned in this covenant, and this function only as it was misunderstood by the Jews. The only apparent exception to that rule is Gal. 4:21 ff., where two covenants are indeed compared. But these are not the Abrahamic and the Sinaitic covenants. The covenant that proceeds from Sinai and centers in the earthly Jerusalem, is placed over against the covenant that proceeds from heaven and centers in the Jerusalem that is above, that is, — the natural and the spiritual.

There are clear indications in Scripture that the covenant with Abraham was not supplanted by the Sinaitic covenant, but remained in force. Even at Horeb the Lord reminded the people of the covenant with Abraham, Deut. 1:8; and when the Lord threatened to destroy the people after they had made the golden calf, Moses based his plea for them on that covenant, Ex. 32:13. He also assured them repeatedly that, whenever they repented of their sins and returned unto Him, He would be mindful of His covenant with Abraham, Lev. 26:42; Deut. 4:31. The two covenants are clearly represented in their unity in Ps. 105:8-10: "He hath remembered His covenant forever, the word which He commanded to a thousand generations, the covenant which He made with Abraham, and His oath to Isaac, and confirmed the same unto Jacob for a statute, *to Israel for an everlasting covenant.*" This unity also follows from the argument of Paul in Gal. 3, where he stresses the fact that an unchangeable God does not arbitrarily alter the essential nature of a covenant once confirmed; and that the law was not intended to supplant but to serve the gracious ends of the promise, Gal. 3:15-22. If the Sinaitic covenant was indeed a covenant of works, in which legal obedience was the way of salvation, then it certainly was a curse for Israel, for it was imposed on a people that could not possibly obtain salvation by works. But this covenant is represented in Scripture as a blessing

---

1. Ref. Bib., p. 95.
2. Ibid, p. 1115.

bestowed upon Israel by a loving Father, Ex. 19:5; Lev. 26:44,45; Deut. 4:8; Ps. 148:20. But though the covenant with Abraham and the Sinaitic covenant were essentially the same, yet the covenant of Sinai had certain characteristic features.

a. At Sinai the covenant became a truly national covenant. The civil life of Israel was linked up with the covenant in such a way that the two could not be separated. In a large measure Church and State became one. To be in the Church was to be in the nation, and *vice versa;* and to leave the Church was to leave the nation. There was no spiritual excommunication; the ban meant cutting off by death.

b. The Sinaitic covenant included a service that contained a positive reminder of the strict demands of the covenant of works. The law was placed very much in the foreground, giving prominence once more to the earlier legal element. But the covenant of Sinai was not a renewal of the covenant of works; in it the law was made subservient to the covenant of grace. This is indicated already in the introduction to the ten commandments, Ex. 20:2; Deut. 5:6, and further in Rom. 3:20; Gal. 3:24. It is true that at Sinai a conditional element was added to the covenant, but it was not the salvation of the Israelite but his theocratic standing in the nation, and the enjoyment of external blessings that was made dependent on the keeping of the law, Deut. 28:1-14. The law served a twofold purpose in connection with the covenant of grace: (1) to increase the consciousness of sin, Rom. 3:20; 4:15; Gal. 3:19; and (2) to be a tutor unto Christ, Gal. 3:24.

c. The covenant with the nation of Israel included a *detailed* ceremonial and typical service. To some extent this was also present in the earlier period, but in the measure in which it was introduced at Sinai it was something new. A separate priesthood was instituted, and a *continuous* preaching of the gospel in symbols and types was introduced. These symbols and types appear under two different aspects: as the demands of God imposed on the people; and as a divine message of salvation to the people. The Jews lost sight of the latter aspect, and fixed their attention exclusively on the former. They regarded the covenant ever increasingly, but mistakenly, as a covenant of works, and saw in the symbols and types a mere appendage to this.

d. The law in the Sinaitic covenant also served Israel as a rule of life, so that the one law of God assumed three different aspects, designated as the moral, the civil, and the ceremonial or religious law. The civil law is simply the application of the principles of the moral law to the social and civic life of the people in all its ramifications. Even the social and civil relations in which the people stood to each other had to reflect the covenant relation in which they stood.

There have been several deviating opinions respecting the Sinaitic covenant which deserve attention.

a. Coccejus saw in the decalogue a summary expression of the covenant of grace, particularly applicable to Israel. When the people, after the establishment of this national covenant of grace, became unfaithful and made a golden calf, the legal covenant of the ceremonial service was instituted as a stricter and harsher dispensation of the covenant of grace. Thus the revelation of grace is found particularly in the decalogue, and that of servitude in the ceremonial law. Before the covenant of Sinai the fathers lived under the promise. There were sacrifices, but these were not obligatory.

b. Others regarded the law as the formula of a new covenant of works established with Israel. God did not really intend that Israel should merit life by keeping the law, since this had become utterly impossible. He simply wanted them to try their strength and to bring them to a consciousness of their own inability. When they left Egypt, they stood strong in the conviction that they could do all that the Lord commanded; but at Sinai they soon discovered that they could not. In view of their consciousness of guilt the Lord now re-established the Abrahamic covenant of grace, to which also the ceremonial law belonged. This reverses the position of Coccejus. The element of grace is found in the ceremonial law. This is somewhat in line with the view of present day dispensationalists, who regard the Sinaitic covenant as a "conditional Mosaic covenant of works" (Scofield), containing in the ceremonial law, however, some adumbrations of the coming redemption in Christ.

c. Still others are of the opinion that God established three covenants at Sinai, a national covenant, a covenant of nature or of works, and a covenant of grace. The first was made with all the Israelites, and was the continuation of the particularistic line which began with Abraham.   In it God demands external obedience, and promises temporal blessings. The second was a repetition of the covenant of works by the giving of a decalogue. And the last a renewal of the covenant of grace, as it was established with Abraham, in the giving of the ceremonial law.

These views are all objectionable for more than one reason: (1) They are contrary to Scripture in their multiplication of the covenants. It is un-Scriptural to assume that more than one covenant was established at Sinai, though it was a covenant with various aspects. (2) They are mistaken in that they seek to impose undue limitations on the decalogue and on the ceremonial law. It is very evident that the ceremonial law has a double aspect; and it is clear also that the decalogue, though placing the demands of the law clearly in the foreground, is made subservient to the covenant of grace.

C. The New Testament Dispensation.

Little need be said respecting the New Testament dispensation of the covenant. The following points should be noted:

1.   The covenant of grace, as it is revealed in the New Testament, is essentially the same as that which governed the relation of Old Testament believers

to God. It is entirely unwarranted to represent the two as forming an *essential* contrast, as is done by present day dispensationalism. This is abundantly evident from Rom. 4 and Gal. 3. If it is sometimes spoken of as a new covenant, this is sufficiently explained by the fact that its administration differs in several particulars from that of the Old Testament. The following points will indicate what is meant.

2. The New Testament dispensation differs from that of the Old in that it is universal, that is, extends to all nations. The covenant of grace was originally universal; its particularism began with Abraham, and was continued and intensified in the Sinaitic covenant. This particularism, however, was not intended to be permanent, but to disappear after it had served its purpose. Even during the period of the law it was possible for Gentiles to join the people of Israel and thus to share in the blessings of the covenant. And when Christ brought His sacrifice, the blessing of Abraham flowed out to the nations; — those that were afar off were brought nigh.

3. The New Testament dispensation places greater emphasis on the gracious character of the covenant. The promise is very much in the foreground. In fact, it is clearly brought out that in the covenant of grace God freely gives what He demands. In this respect the new dispensation connects up with the Abrahamic rather than with the Sinaitic covenant, as Paul clearly brings out in Rom. 4 and Gal. 3. This does not mean, however, that there were no gracious promises during the period of the law. When Paul in II Cor. 3 contrasts the ministry of the law with that of the gospel, he has in mind particularly the ministry of the law as it was understood by the later Jews, who turned the Sinaitic covenant into a covenant of works.

4. Finally, the New Testament dispensation brings richer blessings than the Old Testament dispensation. The revelation of God's grace reached its climax, when the Word became flesh and dwelt among men "full of grace and truth." The Holy Spirit is poured out upon the Church, and out of the fulness of the grace of God in Christ enriches believers with spiritual and eternal blessings. The present dispensation of the covenant of grace will continue until the return of Christ, when the covenant relation will be realized in the fullest sense of the word in a life of intimate communion with God.

QUESTIONS FOR FURTHER STUDY. How did the introduction of the doctrine of the covenant affect the presentation of the truth in Reformed theology? Why did this doctrine meet with little favor outside of Reformed circles? Who were the first to introduce this doctrine? What characterized the federal theology of Coccejus? Why did some insist on treating the covenant of redemption and the covenant of grace as a single covenant? Why do others prefer to treat them separately? What can be said in answer to the flippant rejection of the covenant idea as a legal fiction? How can Christ be both party and surety in the same covenant? What can be said against the idea of Blake that the covenant of grace is a purely external relationship? What objections are there to the idea of two covenants, the one external, and the other internal? Why does Kuyper maintain that Christ, and Christ only, is the second party in the covenant of grace? In what sense does he regard the covenant of grace as an eternal covenant? What must we think of the tendency of modern Premillennialism, to multiply the covenants and the dispensations? How did modern dispensationalism originate? How does it conceive of the relation between the Old and the New Testament? LITERATURE: Bavinck, *Geref. Dogm.* III, pp. 199-244; Kuyper, *Dict. Dogm., De Foedere,* pp. 118-154; ibid., *Uit het Woord, De Leér der Verbonden*; Vos, *Geref. Dogm.* II, pp. 76-140; ibid., *De Verbondsleer in de Geref. Theol.*; Hodge, *Syst. Theol.*, II, pp. 354-377; Dabney, *Syst. and Polem. Theol.*, pp. 429-463; H. H. Kuyper, *Hamabdil, van de Heiligheid van het Genadeverbond*; A. Kuyper, Jr., *De Vastigheid des Verbonds*; Van den Bergh, *Calvijn over het Genadeverbond*; Heppe, *Dogm. der Ev-Ref. Kirche,* pp. 268-293; ibid., *Dogm. des Deutschen Protestantismus,* II, pp. 215-221; ibid., *Geschichte des Pietismus.* pp. 205-240; Mastricht, *Godgeleerdheit,* II, pp. 363-412; a Marck, *Godgeleerdheid,* pp. 463-482; Witsius, De Verbonden, pp. 255-299; Turretin, *Opera, Locus* XII Q. 1-12; Brakel, *Redelijke Godsdienst,* I, pp. 351-382; Pictet, *Theol.,* pp. 280-284; Strong, *Discourse on the Covenant,* pp. 113-447; Owen, *The Covenant of Grace*; Boston, *The Covenant of Grace*; Girardeau, *The Federal Theology: Its Import and its Regulative Influence* (in the *Memorial Volume of the Semi-Centennial of Columbia Seminary*) ; W. L. Newton, *Notes on the Covenant, A Study in the Theology of the Prophets* (Roman Catholic) ; Aalders. *Het Verbond Gods.*

Part Three

———

THE DOCTRINE OF THE PERSON
and
THE WORK OF CHRIST

THE PERSON OF CHRIST

I. The Doctrine of Christ in History

A. The Relation between Anthropology and Christology.

THERE is a very close connection between the doctrine of man and the doctrine of Christ. The former deals with man, created in the image of God and endowed with true knowledge, righteousness and holiness, but through wilful transgression of the law of God despoiled of his true humanity and transformed into a sinner. It points to man as a highly privileged creature of God, still bearing some of the traces of his original glory, but yet as a creature that has lost its birthright, its true freedom, and its original righteousness and holiness. This means that it directs attention, not merely, nor even primarily, to the creatureliness, but to the sinfulness of man. It emphasizes the *ethical* distance between God and man, the distance resulting from the fall of man, which neither man nor angels can bridge; and is as such virtually a cry for divine help. Christology is in part the answer to that cry. It acquaints us with the objective work of God in Christ to bridge the chasm, and to remove the distance. It shows us God coming to man, to remove the barriers between God and man by meeting the conditions of the law in Christ, and to restore man to His blessed communion. Anthropology already directs attention to the gracious provision of God for a covenant of friendship with man, which provides for a life of blessed communion with God; but it is a covenant which is effective only in and through Christ. And therefore the doctrine of Christ, as the Mediator of the covenant, must necessarily follow. Christ, typified and predicted in the Old Testament as the Redeemer of man, came in the fulness of time, to tabernacle among men and to effect an eternal reconciliation.

B. The Doctrine of Christ before the Reformation.

1. UP TO THE COUNCIL OF CHALCEDON. In the early Christian literature Christ stands out as both human and divine, the Son of Man, but also the Son of God. His sinless character is maintained, and He is regarded as a proper object of worship. Naturally, the problem presented by Christ, as at once God and man, and the difficulties involved in such a conception, were not fully felt by the early Christian mind and only dawned on it in the light of contro- versy. It was but natural that Judaism, with its strong emphasis on monotheism, should exercise considerable influence on the early Christians of Jewish extraction. The Ebionites (or part of them) felt constrained, in the interest of

monotheism, to deny the deity of Christ. They regarded Him as a mere man, the son of Joseph and Mary, who was qualified at His baptism to be the Messiah, by the descent of the Holy Spirit upon Him. There were others in the early Church whose doctrine of Christ was constructed on similar lines. The Alogi, who rejected the writings of John, because they regarded his doctrine of the Logos as in conflict with the rest of the New Testament, also saw in Jesus a mere man, though miraculously born of a virgin, and taught that Christ descended on Him at baptism, conferring on Him supernatural powers. In the main this was also the position of the Dynamic Monarchians. Paul of Samosata, its main representative, distinguished between Jesus and the Logos. He regarded the former as a man like every other man, born of Mary, and the latter, as the impersonal divine reason, which took up its abode in Christ in a pre-eminent sense, from the time of His baptism, and thus qualified Him for His great task. In view of this denial it was part of the task of the early Apologetes to defend the doctrine of the deity of Christ.

If there were some who sacrificed the deity to the humanity of Christ, there were others who reversed the order. The Gnostics were profoundly influenced by the dualistic conception of the Greeks, in which matter as inherently evil is represented as utterly opposed to spirit; and by a mystic tendency to regard earthly things as allegorical representations of great cosmic redeeming processes. They rejected the idea of an incarnation, a manifestation of God in a visible form, since it involved a direct contact of spirit with matter. Harnack says that the majority of them regarded Christ as a Spirit consubstantial with the Father. According to some He descended upon the man Jesus at the time of His baptism, but left Him again before His crucifixion; while according to others He assumed a merely phantasmal body. The Modalistic Monarchians also denied the humanity of Christ, partly in the interest of His deity, and partly to preserve the unity of the Divine Being. They saw in Him merely a mode or manifestation of the one God, in whom they recognized no distinction of persons. The Anti-Gnostic and Alexandrian Fathers took up the defense of the deity of Christ, but in their defense did not altogether escape the error of representing Him as subordinate to the Father. Even Tertullian taught a species of subordination, but especially Origen, who did not hesitate to speak of a subordination *as to essence*. This became a stepping-stone for Arianism, in which Christ is distinguished from the Logos as the divine reason, and is represented as a pre-temporal, superhuman creature, the first of the creatures, not God and yet more than man. Athanasius took issue with Arius, and strongly defended the position that the Son is consubstantial with, and of the same essence as, the Father, a position that was officially adopted by the council of Nicea in 321. Semi-Arianism proposed a *via media* by declaring the Son to be of a *similar* essence as the Father.

When the doctrine of the deity of the Son was officially established, the question naturally arose as to the relation in which the two natures in Christ stand to each other. Apollinaris offered a solution of the problem. Accepting the Greek trichotomic conception of man as consisting of body, soul, and spirit, he took the position that the Logos took the place of the spirit (*pneuma*) in man, which he regarded as the seat of sin. His chief interest was to secure the unity of the person in Christ, without sacrificing His real deity; and also to guard the sinlessness of Christ. But he did so at the expense of the complete humanity of the Saviour, and consequently his position was explicitly condemned by the Council of Constantinople in 381. One of the things for which Apollinaris contended was the unity of the person in Christ. That this was really in danger became quite apparent in the position taken by the school of Antioch, which exaggerated the distinction of the two natures in Christ. Theodore of Mopsuestia and Nestorius stressed the complete manhood of Christ, and conceived of the indwelling of the Logos in Him as a mere moral indwelling, such as believers also enjoy, though not to the same degree. They saw in Christ a man side by side with God, in alliance with God, sharing the purpose of God, but not one with Him in the oneness of a single personal life, — a Mediator consisting of two persons. In opposition to them Cyril of Alexandria strongly emphasized the unity of the person in Christ, and in the estimation of his opponents denied the two natures. While they in all probability misunderstood him, Eutychus and his followers certainly appealed to him, when they took up the position that the human nature of Christ was absorbed by the divine, or that the two were fused into a single nature, a position involving the denial of the two natures in Christ. The Council of Chalcedon in 451 condemned both of these views and maintained the unity of the person as well as the duality of the natures.

2. AFTER THE COUNCIL OF CHALCEDON. For some time the Eutychian error was continued by the Monophysites and the Monothelites, but was finally overcome by the Church. The further danger that the human nature of Christ would be regarded as entirely impersonal was warded off by Leontius of Byzantium, when he pointed out that it is not impersonal but in-personal, having its personal subsistence in the person of the Son of God. John of Damascus, in whom the Christology of the East reached its highest development, added the idea that there is a circumincession of the divine and the human in Christ, a communication of the divine attributes to the human nature, so that the latter is deified and we may also say that God suffered in the flesh. He shows a tendency to reduce the human nature to the position of a mere organ or instrument of the Logos, yet he admits that there is a co-operation of the two natures, and that the one person acts and wills in each nature, though the human will is always subject to the divine.

In the Western Church Felix, bishop of Urgella, advocated adoptionism. He regarded Christ as to His divine nature, that is, the Logos, as the only-begotten Son of God in the natural sense, but considered Christ on His human side as a Son of God merely by adoption. He sought to preserve the unity of the person by stressing the fact that, from the time of His conception, the Son of Man was taken up into the unity of the person of the Son of God.

Thus a distinction was made between a natural and an adoptive sonship, and the latter did not begin with the natural birth of Christ, but had its inception at the time of His baptism and was consummated in the resurrection. It was a spiritual birth that made Christ the adopted Son of God. The Church saw the unity of the person in Christ once more endangered by this view, and therefore it was condemned by the Synod of Frankfort in 794 A.D.

The Middle Ages added very little to the doctrine of the person of Christ. Due to various influences, such as the emphasis on the imitation of Christ, the theories of the atonement, and the development of the doctrine of the mass, the Church retained a strong grasp on the full humanity of Christ. "The deity of Christ," says Mackintosh, "came into view rather as the infinite co-efficient raising human action and passion to an infinite value." And yet some of the Scholastics in their Christology set forth a docetic view of Christ. Peter the Lombard did not hesitate to say that in respect of His humanity Christ was nothing at all. But this Nihilism was condemned by the Church. Some new points were stressed by Thomas Aquinas. According to him the person of the Logos became composite at the incarnation, and its union with the manhood "hindered" the latter from arriving at an independent personality. The human nature of Christ received a twofold grace in virtue of its union with the Logos, (a) the *gratia unionis,* imparting to it a special dignity, so that it even became an object of worship, and (b) the *gratia habitualis,* which sustained it in its relationship to God. The human knowledge of Christ was twofold, namely, an infused and an acquired knowledge. There are two wills in Christ, but ultimate causality belongs to the divine will, to which the human will is always subject.

C. The Doctrine of Christ after the Reformation.

1. Up to the nineteenth century. The Reformation did not bring any great changes in the doctrine of the person of Christ. Both the Church of Rome and the Churches of the Reformation subscribed to the doctrine of Christ as it was formulated by the Council of Chalcedon. Their important and deep-seated differences lay elsewhere. There is one peculiarity of Lutheran Christology that deserves special mention. Luther's doctrine of the physical presence of Christ in the Lord's supper led to the characteristically Lutheran view of the *communicatio idiomatum,* to the effect "that each of Christ's natures permeates the other (perichoresis), and that His humanity participates in the attributes of His divinity."[1] It is held that the attributes of omnipotence, omniscience, and omnipresence were communicated to the human nature of Christ at the time of the incarnation. The question naturally arose, how this could be harmonized with what we know of the earthly life of Jesus. This question led to a difference of opinion among Lutheran theologians. Some held that Christ laid aside the divine attributes received in the incarnation, or used them only occasionally, while others said that He continued in possession of them during His entire earthly life, but concealed

---

1. Neve, *Lutheran Symbolics,* p. 132.

them or used them only secretly. Some Lutherans now seem inclined to discard this doctrine.

Reformed theologians saw in this Lutheran doctrine a species of Eutychianism or of the fusion of the two natures in Christ. Reformed theology also teaches a communication of attributes, but conceives of it in a different way. It believes that, after the incarnation, the properties of both natures can be attributed to the one person of Christ. The person of Christ can be said to be omniscient, but also, to have but limited knowledge; can be regarded as omnipresent, but also as being limited at any particular time to a single place. Hence we read in the Second Helvetic Confession: "We acknowledge, therefore, that there be in one and the same Jesus our Lord two natures — the divine and the human nature; and we say that these are so conjoined or united that they are not swallowed up, confounded, or mingled together, but rather united or joined together in one person (the properties of each being safe and remaining still), so that we do worship one Christ, our Lord, and not two. . . . Therefore we do not think nor teach that the divine nature in Christ did suffer, or that Christ, according to His human nature, is yet in the world, and so in every place."[1]

2. IN THE NINETEENTH CENTURY. About the beginning of the nineteenth century a great change took place in the study of the person of Christ. Up to that time the point of departure had been prevailingly theological, and the resulting Christology was theocentric; but during the last part of the eighteenth century there was a growing conviction that better results could be attained by starting closer at home, namely, with the study of the historical Jesus. Thus the so-called "second Christological period" was ushered in. The new point of view was anthropological, and the result was anthropocentric. It proved to be destructive of the faith of the Church. A far-reaching and pernicious distinction was made between the historical Jesus, delineated by the writers of the Gospels, and the theological Christ, who was the fruit of the fertile imagination of theological thinkers, and whose image is now reflected in the creeds of the Church. The supernatural Christ made way for a human Jesus; and the doctrine of the two natures, for the doctrine of a divine man.

Schleiermacher stood at the head of the new development. He regarded Christ as a new creation, in which human nature is elevated to the plane of ideal perfection. Yet his Christ can hardly be said to rise above the human level. The uniqueness of His person consists in the fact that He possesses a perfect and unbroken sense of union with the divine, and also realizes to the full the destiny of man in His character of sinless perfection. His supreme dignity finds its explanation in a special presence of God in Him, in His unique God-consciousness. Hegel's conception of Christ is part and parcel of his pantheistic system of thought. The Word become flesh means for him God become incarnate in humanity, so that the incarnation really expresses the oneness of God and man. The incarnation of Christ was, so it seems, merely

<hr/>
1. Chap. XI.

the culmination of a racial process. While mankind in general regards Jesus only as a human teacher, faith recognizes Him as divine and finds that by His coming into the world the transcendence of God is changed into immanence. Here we meet with a pantheistic identification of the human and the divine in the doctrine of Christ.

Something of this is also seen in the Kenotic theories, which represent a rather remarkable attempt to improve on the construction of the doctrine of the person of Christ. The term *kenosis* is derived from Phil. 2:7, which teaches that Christ "emptied (*ekenosen*) Himself, taking the form of a servant." The Kenoticists take this to mean that the Logos literally became, that is, was changed into a man by reducing (depotentiating) Himself, either wholly or in part, to the dimensions of a man, and then increased in wisdom and power until at last He again became God. This theory appeared in various forms, of which the most absolute is that of Gess, and for a time enjoyed considerable popularity. It aimed at maintaining the reality and integrity of the manhood of Christ, and to throw into strong relief the greatness of His humiliation in that He, being rich, for our sakes became poor. It involves, however, a pantheistic obliteration of the line of demarcation between God and man. Dorner, who was the greatest representative of the Mediating school, strongly opposed this view, and substituted for it the doctrine of a progressive incarnation. He saw in the humanity of Christ a new humanity with a special receptivity for the divine. The Logos, the principle of self-bestowal in God, joined Himself to this humanity; the measure in which He did this was determined at every stage by the ever-increasing receptivity of the human nature for the divine, and did not reach its final stage until the resurrection. But this is merely a new and subtle form of the old Nestorian heresy. It yields a Christ consisting of two persons.

With the exception of Schleiermacher, no one has exercised greater influence on present day theology than Albrecht Ritschl. His Christology takes its starting point in the work, rather than in the person of Christ. The work of Christ determines the dignity of His person. He was a mere man, but in view of the work which He accomplished and the service He rendered, we rightly attribute to Him the predicate of Godhead. He rules out the pre-existence, the incarnation, and the virgin birth of Christ, since this finds no point of contact in the believing consciousness of the Christian community. Christ was the founder of the kingdom of God, thus making the purpose of God His own, and now in some way induces men to enter the Christian community and to live a life that is motivated entirely by love. He redeems man by His teaching, example, and unique influence, and is therefore worthy to be called God. This is virtually a renewal of the doctrine of Paul of Samosata.

On the basis of the modern pantheistic idea of the immanence of God, the doctrine of Christ is to-day often represented in a thoroughly naturalistic way. The representations may vary greatly, but the fundamental idea is generally the same, that of an essential unity of God and man. The doctrine of the two natures of Christ has disappeared from modern theology, and instead we have a pantheistic identification of God and man. Essentially all men are divine, since they all have a divine element in them; and they are all sons of God, differing from Christ only in degree. Modern teaching about Christ is all based on the doctrine of the continuity of God and man. And it is exactly against this doctrine that Barth and those who are like-minded with him have raised their voice. There are in some circles to-day signs of a return to the two-nature doctrine. Micklem confesses in his *What Is the Faith?* that for many years he confidently asserted that the ascription to Christ of two natures in one person had to be abandoned, but now sees that this rested on a misunderstanding.[1]

QUESTIONS FOR FURTHER STUDY. What was the background of the Christological controversy in the early centuries? What ancient errors were revived by Roscelinus and Abelard? What was the Christological Nihilism in vogue among the disciples of Abelard? How did Peter the Lombard view Christ? Did the Scholastics bring any new points to the fore? Where do we find the official Lutheran Chrisiology? How can we account for the seemingly inconsistent representations of the formula of Concord? What objections are there to the Lutheran view that divine attributes may be predicated of the human nature? How did the Lutherans and the Reformed differ in their interpretation of Phil. 2:5-11? How does the Reformed Christology differ from the Lutheran? What is the main difference between recent and earlier Christologies? What objections are there to the Kenosis doctrine? What are the objectionable features of modern Christology? How do Barth and Brunner view Christ?

LITERATURE: *The Formula of Concord and the Second Helvetic Confession*; Seeberg, *History of Doctrine* II, pp. 65, 109 f., 154 f., 229 f., 321 f., 323 f., 374, 387; Hagenbach, *History of Doctrine* II, pp. 267-275; III, pp. 197-209, 343-353; Thomasius, *Dogmengeschichte* II, pp. 380-385; 388-429; Otten, *Manual of the History of Dogmas* II, pp. 171-195; Heppe, *Dogmatik des deutschen Protestantismus* II, pp. 78-178; Dorner, *History of Protestant Theology*, pp. 95 f., 201 f., 322 f.; Bruce, *The Humiliation of Christ*, pp. 74-355; Mackintosh, *The Doctrine of the Person of Jesus Christ*, pp. 223-284; Ottley, *The Doctrine of the Incarnation*, pp. 485-553, 587-671; Sanday, *Christologies Ancient and Modern*, pp. 59-83; Schweitzer, *The Quest of the Historical Jesus*; La Touche, *The Person of Christ in Modern Thought*.

---

1. p. 155.

II. The Names and Natures of Christ

A. The Names of Christ.

There are especially five names that call for a brief discussion at this point. They are partly descriptive of His natures, partly of His official position, and partly of the work for which He came into the world.

1. THE NAME JESUS. The name Jesus is the Greek form of the Hebrew *Jehoshua*, *Joshua*, Josh. 1:1; Zech. 3:1, or *Jeshua* (regular form in the post-exilic historical books), Ezra 2:2. The derivation of this common name of the Saviour is veiled in obscurity. The generally accepted opinion is that it is derived from the root *yasha'*, hiph., *hoshia'*, to save, but it is not easy to explain how *Jehoshua'* became *Jeshua'*. Probably *Hoshea'*, derived from the infinitive, was the original form (cf. Num. 13:8,16; Deut. 32:44), expressing merely the idea of redemption. The *yod*, which is the sign of the imperfect, may have been added to express the certainty of redemption. This would best agree with the interpretation of the name given in Matt. 1:21. For another derivation from *Jeho* (Jehovah) and *shua*, that is help (Gotthilf) cf. Kuyper, *Dict. Dogm.*[1] The name was borne by two well known types of Jesus in the Old Testament.

2. THE NAME CHRIST. If Jesus is the personal, Christ is the official, name of the Messiah. It is the equivalent of the Old Testament Mashiach (from *mashach*, to anoint), and thus means "the anointed one." Kings and priests were regularly anointed during the old dispensation, Ex. 29:7; Lev. 4:3; Judg. 9:8; I Sam. 9:16; 10:1; II Sam. 19:10. The King was called "the anointed of Jehovah," I Sam. 24:10. Only a single instance of the anointing of a prophet is recorded, I Kings 19:16, but there are probably references to it in Ps. 105:15 and Isa. 61:1. The oil used in anointing these officers symbolized the Spirit of God, Isa. 61:1; Zech. 4:1-6, and the anointing represented the transfer of the Spirit to the consecrated person, I Sam. 10:1,6,10; 16:13,14. The anointing was a visible sign of (a) an appointment to office; (b) the establishment of a sacred relationship and the consequent sacrosanctness of the person anointed, I Sam. 24:6; 26:9; II Sam. 1:14; and (c) a communication of the Spirit to the anointed one, I Sam. 16:13, cf. also II Cor. 1:21,22. The Old Testament refers to the anointing of the Lord in Ps. 2:2; 45:7, and the New Testament, in Acts 4:27 and 10:38. Formerly references to it were also found in Ps. 2:6 and Prov. 8:23, but to-day Hebraists assert that the word *nasak*, used in these passages, means "to set up" rather than "to anoint." But even

---

1. *De Christo*, I, pp. 56 f.

cf. also Isa. 11:2;.42:1. Christ was set up or appointed to His offices from
so the word points to the reality of the first thing symbolized in the anointing,
eternity, but historically His anointing took place when He was conceived
by the Holy Spirit, Luke 1:35, and when he received the Holy Spirit, especially
at the time of His baptism, Matt. 3:16; Mark 1:10; Luke 3:22; John 1:32;
3:34. It served to qualify Him for His great task. The name "Christ" was
first applied to the Lord as a common noun with the article, but gradually
developed into a proper noun, and was used without the article.

3. THE NAME SON OF MAN. In the Old Testament this name is found in
Ps. 8:4; Dan. 7:13, and frequently in the Prophecy of Ezekiel. It is also found
in the Apochrypha, Enoch 46 and 62, and II Esdras 13. The dependence of the
New Testament usage of it on the passage in Daniel is now quite generally
admitted, though in that prophecy it is merely a descriptive phrase, and not yet
a title. The transition from the one to the other was made later on, and was
apparently already an accomplished fact when the book of Enoch was written. It
was the most common self-designation of Jesus. He applied the name to Himself
on more than forty occasions, while others all but refrained from employing it.
The only exception in the Gospels is in John 12:34, where it appears in an
indirect quotation of a word of Jesus; and in the rest of the New Testament
only Stephen and John employ it, Acts 7:56; Rev. 1:13; 14:14.

Dr. Vos in his work on *The Self-Disclosure of Jesus* divides the passages in
which the name occurs into four classes: (a) Passages which clearly refer to
the eschatological coming of the Son of Man, as for instance, Matt. 16:27, 28;
Mark 8:38; 13:26, etc. and parallels. (b) Passages which speak particularly of
Jesus' sufferings, death, and (sometimes) resurrection, as, for instance, Matt.
17:22; 20:18,19,28; 12:40, etc. and parallels. (c) Passages in the Fourth Gospel,
in which the heavenly superhuman side and the pre-existence of Jesus is stressed,
as for instance, 1:51; 3:13,14; 6:27,53,62; 8:28, and so on. (d) A small
group of passages, in which Jesus reflects upon His human nature, Mark 2:27,
28; John 5:27; 6:27,51,62. It is hard to determine why Jesus preferred this
name as a self-designation. Formerly the name was generally regarded as a
cryptic title, by the use of which Jesus intended to veil rather than to reveal
His Messiahship. This explanation was discarded when more attention was
paid to the eschatological element in the Gospels, and to the use of the name
in the apocalyptic literature of the Jews. Dalman revived the idea and
regarded the title once more as "an intentional veiling of the Messianic
character under a title which affirms the humanity of Him who bore it."[1]
The supposed proof for this is found in Matt. 16:13; John 12:34. But the
proof is doubtful; the latter passage even shows that the people understood
the name Messianically. Dr. Vos is of the opinion that Jesus probably
preferred the name, because it stood farthest removed from every possible
Jewish prostitution of the Messianic office. By calling Himself the Son of Man,
Jesus imparted to the Messiahship His own heaven-centered spirit. And the

---

1. *Words of Jesus*, p. 253.

height to which He thus lifted His person and work may well have had something to do with the hesitancy of His early followers to name Him with the most celestial of all titles.[1]

4. THE NAME SON OF GOD. The name "Son of God" was variously applied in the Old Testament: (a) to the people of Israel, Ex. 4:22; Jer. 31:9; Hos. 11:1; (b) to officials among Israel, especially to the promised king of the house of David, II Sam. 7:14; Ps. 89:27; (c) to angels, Job 1:6; 2:1; 38:7; Ps. 29:1; 89:6; and (d) to pious people in general, Gen. 6:2; Ps. 73:15; Prov. 14:26. Among Israel the name acquired theocratic significance. In the New Testament we find Jesus appropriating the name, and others also ascribing it to Him. The name is applied to Jesus in four different senses, which are not always kept distinct in Scripture but are sometimes combined. The name is applied to Him:

a. *In the official or Messianic sense,* as a description of the office rather than of the nature of Christ. The Messiah could be called Son of God as God's heir and representative. The demons evidently understood the name Messianically, when they applied it to Jesus. It seems to have this meaning also in Matt. 24:36; Mark 13:32. Even the name, as uttered by the voice at the baptism of Jesus and at His transfiguration, Matt. 3:17; 17:5; Mark 1:11; 9:7; Luke 3:22; 9:35, can be so interpreted, but in all probability has a deeper meaning. There are several passages in which the Messianic sense is combined with the trinitarian sense, cf. under (b).

b. *In the trinitarian sense.* The name is sometimes used to denote the essential deity of Christ. As such it points to a pre-existent sonship, which absolutely transcends the human life of Christ and His official calling as Messiah. Instances of this use are found in Matt. 11:27; 14:28-33; 16:16, and parallels; 21:33-46, and parallels; 22:41-46; 26:63, and parallels. In some of these cases the idea of the Messianic sonship also enters more or less. We find the ontological and the Messianic sonship interwoven also in several Johannine passages, in which Jesus clearly intimates that He is the Son of God, though He does not use the name, as in 6:69; 8:16,18,23; 10:15,30; 14:20, and so on. In the Epistles Christ is frequently designated as the Son of God in the metaphysical sense, Rom. 1:3; 8:3; Gal. 4:4; Heb. 1:1, and many other passages. In modern liberal theology it is customary to deny the metaphysical sonship of Christ.

c. *In the nativistic sense.* Christ is also called the Son of God in virtue of His supernatural birth. The name is so applied to Him in the well known passage in the Gospel of Luke, in which the origin of His human nature is ascribed to the direct, supernatural paternity of God, namely, Luke 1:35. Dr. Vos also finds indications of this sense of the name in Matt. 1:18-24; John 1:13. Naturally, this meaning of the name is also denied by modern liberal theology, which does not believe in the virgin birth, nor in the supernatural conception of Christ.

---

1. *The Self-Disclosure of Jesus,* pp. 251 ff.

d. *In the ethico-religious sense.* It is in this sense that the name "sons" or "children of God" is applied to believers in the New Testament. It is possible that we have an example of the application of the name "Son of God" to Jesus in that ethico-religious sense in Matt. 17:24-27. This depends on the question, whether Peter is here represented as also exempt from the temple-tax. It is especially in this sense that modern liberal theology ascribes the name to Jesus. It finds that the sonship of Jesus is only an ethico-religious sonship, somewhat heightened indeed, but not essentially different from that of His disciples.

5. THE NAME LORD (*Kurios*). The name "Lord" is applied to God in the Septuagint, (a) as the equivalent of Jehovah; (b) as the rendering of *Adonai;* and (c) as the translation of a human honorific title applied to God (chiefly *Adon*), Josh. 3:11; Ps. 97:5. In the New Testament we find a somewhat similar threefold application of the name to Christ, (a) as a polite and respectful form of address, Matt. 8:2; 20:33; (b) as expressive of ownership and authority, without implying anything as to Christ's divine character and authority, Matt. 21:3; 24:42; and (c) with the highest connotation of authority, expressive of an exalted character, and in fact practically equivalent to the name "God," Mark 12:36,37; Luke 2:11; 3:4; Acts 2:36; I Cor. 12:3; Phil. 2:11. In some cases it is hard to determine the exact connotation of the title. Undoubtedly, after the exaltation of Christ, the name was generally applied to Him in the most exalted sense. But there are instances of its use even before the resurrection, where the specifically divine import of the title has evidently already been reached, as in Matt. 7:22; Luke 5:8; John 20:28. There is a great difference of opinion among scholars respecting the origin and development of this title as applied to Jesus. In spite of all that has been advanced to the contrary, there is no reason to doubt that the use of the name, as applied to Jesus, is rooted in the Old Testament. There is one constant element in the history of the conception, and that is the element of *authoritative ownership.* The Epistles of Paul suggest the additional idea that it is an authority and ownership *resting on antecedently acquired rights.* It is doubtful, whether this element is already present in the Gospels.

B. The Natures of Christ.

From the earliest times, and more particularly since the Council of Chalcedon, the Church confessed the doctrine of the two natures of Christ. The Council did not solve the problem presented by a person who was at once human and divine, but only sought to ward off some of the solutions which were offered and were clearly recognized as erroneous. And the Church accepted the doctrine of the two natures in one person, not because it had a complete understanding of the mystery, but because it clearly saw in it a mystery revealed by the Word of God. It was and remained ever since for the Church an article of faith, far beyond human comprehension. Rationalistic attacks on the doctrine were not entirely wanting, but the Church remained firm in the confession of this truth, in spite of the fact that it was once and again declared to be contrary to reason. In this confession Roman Catholics and Protestants stand shoulder to shoulder. But from the last part of the eighteenth century on this doctrine was made the butt of persistent attacks. The Age of Reason set in, and it was declared to be unworthy of man to accept on the authority of Scripture what was clearly contrary to human reason. That which did not commend itself to this new arbiter was simply declared to be erroneous. Individual philosophers and theologians now tried their hand at solving the problem presented by Christ, in order that they might offer the Church a substitute for the two-nature doctrine. They took their starting point in the human Jesus, and even after a century of painstaking research found in Jesus no more than a man with a divine element in Him. They could not rise to the recognition of Him as their Lord and their God. Schleiermacher spoke of a man with a supreme God-consciousness, Ritschl, of a man having the value of a God, Wendt, of a man standing in a continual inward fellowship of love with God, Beyschlag, of a God-filled man, and Sanday, of a man with an inrush of the divine in the sub-consciousness; — but Christ is and remains merely a man. To-day the liberal school represented by Harnack, the eschatological school of Weiss and Schweitzer, and the more recent school of comparative religion, headed by Bousset and Kirsopp Lake, all agree in denuding Christ of His true deity, and in reducing Him to human dimensions. To the first our Lord is merely a great ethical teacher; to the second, an apocalyptic seer; and to the third a peerless leader to an exalted destiny. They regard the Christ of the Church as the creation of Hellenism, or of Judaism, or of the two combined. To-day, however, the whole epistemology of the previous century is called in question, and the sufficiency of human reason for the interpretation of ultimate truth is seriously questioned. There is a new emphasis on revelation. And influential theologians, such as Barth and Brunner, Edwin Lewis and Nathaniel Micklem, do not hesitate to confess faith once more in the doctrine of the two natures. It is of the utmost importance to maintain this doctrine, as it was formulated by the Council of Chalcedon and is contained in our Confessional Standards.[1]

1. SCRIPTURE PROOFS FOR THE DEITY OF CHRIST. In view of the widespread denial of the deity of Christ, it is of the utmost importance to be thoroughly conversant with the Scripture proof for it. The proof is so abundant that no one who accepts the Bible as the infallible Word of God can entertain any doubt on this point. For the ordinary classification of the Biblical proofs, as derived from the divine names, the divine attributes, the divine works, and the divine honor ascribed to Him, we would refer to the chapter on the Trinity. A somewhat different arrangement is followed here in view of the recent trend of historical criticism.

a. *In the Old Testament.* Some have shown an inclination to deny that the Old Testament contains predictions of a divine Messiah, but this denial is quite untenable in view of such passages as Ps. 2:6-12 (Heb. 1:5) ; 45:6,7

---

1. *Conf. Belg.*, Art. XIX; *Heidelberg Cat.*, Qs. 15-18; *Canons of Dort* II, Art. IV.

(Heb. 1:8,9); 110:1 (Heb. 1:13); Isa. 9:6; Jer. 23:6; Dan. 7:13; Mic. 5:2; Zech. 13:7; Mal. 3:1. Several of the latest historical scholars strongly insist on the fact that the doctrine of a superhuman Messiah was native to pre-Christian Judaism. Some even find in it the explanation for the supernatural Christology of parts of the New Testament.

b. *In the writings of John and Paul.* It has been found quite impossible to deny that both John and Paul teach the deity of Christ. In the Gospel of John the most exalted view of the person of Christ is found, as appears from the following passages: John 1:1-3,14,18; 2:24,25; 3:16-18,35,36; 4:14,15; 5:18,20,21,22,25-27; 11:41-44; 20:28; I John 1:3; 2:23; 4:14,15; 5:5,10-13, 20. A similar view is found in the Pauline Epistles and in the Epistle to the Hebrews, Rom. 1:7; 9:5; I Cor. 1:1-3; 2:8; II Cor. 5:10; Gal. 2:20; 4:4; Phil. 2:6; Col. 2:9; I Tim. 3:16; Heb. 1:1-3,5,8; 4:14; 5:8, and so on. Critical scholars sought escape from the doctrine clearly taught in these writings in various ways as, for instance, by denying the historicity of the Gospel of John and the authenticity of many of the Epistles of Paul; by regarding the representations of John, Paul, and Hebrews as unwarranted interpretations, in the case of John and Hebrews especially under the influence of the Philonic Logos doctrine, and in the case of Paul under the same influence, or under that of his pre-Christian, Jewish views; or by ascribing to Paul a lower view than is found in John, namely, that of Christ as a pre-existent, heavenly man.

c. *In the Synoptics.* Some maintain that the Synoptics only furnish us with a true picture of Christ. They, it is said, portray the human, the truly historical Jesus, as contrasted with the idealized picture of the Fourth Gospel. But it is perfectly evident that the Christ of the Synoptics is just as truly divine as the Christ of John. He stands out as a supernatural person throughout, the Son of Man and the Son of God. His character and works justify His claim. Notice particularly the following passages: Matt. 5:17; 9:6; 11:1-6,27; 14:33; 16:16,17; 28:18; 25:31 ff.; Mark 8:38, and many similar and parallel passages. Dr. Warfield's *The Lord of Glory* is very illuminating on this point.

d. *In the self-consciousness of Jesus.* In recent years there has been a tendency to go back to the *self-consciousness of Jesus,* and to deny that He was conscious of being the Messiah or the Son of God. Naturally, it is not possible to have any knowledge of the consciousness of Jesus, except through His words, as these are recorded in the Gospels; and it is always possible to deny that they correctly express the mind of Jesus. For those who accept the Gospel testimony there can be no doubt as to the fact that Jesus was conscious of being the very Son of God. The following passages bear witness to this: Matt. 11:27 (Luke 10:22); 21:37,38 (Mk. 12:6; Luke 20:13); 22:41-46 (Mk. 13:35-37; Luke 20:41-44); 24:36 (Mk. 13:32); 28:19. Some of these passages testify to Jesus' Messianic consciousness; others to the fact that He was conscious of being the Son of God in the most exalted sense. There are several passages in Matthew and Luke, in which He speaks of the first person of the Trinity as "my Father," Matt. 7:21; 10:32,33; 11:27; 12:50; 15:13;

16:17; 18:10,19,35; 20:23; 25:34; 26:29,53; Luke 2:49; 22:29; 24:49. In the Gospel of John the consciousness of being the very Son of God is even more apparent in such passages as John 3:13; 5:17,18,19-27; 6:37-40,57; 8:34-36; 10:17,18,30,35,36, and other passages.

2. SCRIPTURE PROOF FOR THE REAL HUMANITY OF CHRIST. There has been a time, when the reality (Gnosticism) and the *natural* integrity (Docetism, Apollinarianism) of the human nature of Christ was denied, but at present no one seriously questions the real humanity of Jesus Christ. In fact, there is at present an extreme emphasis on His veritable humanity, an ever-growing humanitarianism. The only divinity many still ascribe to Christ, is simply that of His perfect humanity. This modern tendency is, no doubt, in part a protest against a one-sided emphasis on the deity of Christ. Men have sometimes forgotten the human Christ in their reverence for the divine. It is very important to maintain the reality and integrity of the humanity of Jesus by admitting his human development and human limitations. The splendor of His deity should not be stressed to the extent of obscuring His real humanity. Jesus called Himself man, and is so called by others, John 8:40; Acts 2:22; Rom. 5:15; I Cor. 15:21. The most common self-designation of Jesus, "the Son of Man," whatever connotation it may have, certainly also indicates the veritable humanity of Jesus. Moreover, it is said that the Lord came or was manifested in the flesh, John 1:14; I Tim. 3:16; I John 4:2. In these passages the term "flesh" denotes human nature. The Bible clearly indicates that Jesus possessed the essential elements of human nature, that is, a material body and a rational soul, Matt. 26:26,28,38; Luke 23:46; 24:39; John 11:33; Heb. 2:14. There are also passages which show that Jesus was subject to the ordinary laws of human development, and to human wants and sufferings, Luke 2:40,52; Heb. 2:10,18; 5:8. It is brought out in detail that the normal experiences of man's life were His, Matt. 4:2; 8:24; 9:36; Mk. 3:5; Lk. 22:44; John 4:6; 11:35; 12:27; 19:28,30; Heb. 5:7.

3. SCRIPTURE PROOF FOR THE SINLESS HUMANITY OF CHRIST. We ascribe to Christ not only natural, but also moral, integrity or moral perfection, that is sinlessness. This means not merely that Christ could avoid sinning (*potuit non peccare*), and did actually avoid it, but also that it was impossible for Him to sin (*non potuit peccare*) because of the essential bond between the human and the divine natures. The sinlessness of Christ has been denied by Martineau, Irving, Menken, Holsten, and Pfleiderer, but the Bible clearly testifies to it in the following passages: Luke 1:35; John 8:46; 14:30; II Cor. 5:21; Heb. 4:15; 9:14; I Pet. 2:22; I John 3:5. While Christ was made to be sin judicially, yet ethically He was free from both hereditary depravity and actual sin. He never makes a confession of moral error; nor does He join His disciples in praying, "Forgive us our sins." He is able to challenge His enemies to convince Him of sin. Scripture even represents Him as the one in whom the ideal man is realized, Heb. 2:8,9; I Cor. 15:45; II Cor. 3:18; Phil. 3:21.

Moreover, the name "Son of Man," appropriated by Jesus, seems to intimate that He answered to the perfect ideal of humanity.

4. THE NECESSITY OF THE TWO NATURES IN CHRIST. It appears from the preceding that, in the present day, many do not recognize the necessity of assuming two natures in Christ. To them Jesus is but a man; yet at the same time they feel constrained to ascribe to Him the value of a God, or to claim divinity for Him in virtue of the immanence of God in Him, or of the indwelling Spirit. The necessity of the two natures in Christ follows from what is essential to the Scriptural doctrine of the atonement.

a. *The necessity of His manhood.* Since man sinned, it was necessary that the penalty should be borne by man. Moreover, the paying of the penalty involved suffering of body and soul, such as only man is capable of bearing, John 12:27; Acts 3:18; Heb. 2:14; 9:22. It was necessary that Christ should assume human nature, not only with all its essential properties, but also with all the infirmities to which it is liable after the fall, and should thus descend to the depths of degradation to which man had fallen, Heb. 2:17,18. At the same time, He had to be a sinless man, for a man who was himself a sinner and who had forfeited his own life, certainly could not atone for others, Heb. 7:26. Only such a truly human Mediator, who had experimental knowledge of the woes of mankind and rose superior to all temptations, could enter sympathetically into all the experiences, the trials, and the temptations of man, Heb. 2:17,18; 4:15-5:2, and be a perfect human example for His followers, Matt. 11:29; Mk. 10:39; John 13:13-15; Phil. 2:5-8; Heb. 12:2-4; I Pet. 2:21.

b. *The necessity of His Godhead.* In the divine plan of salvation it was absolutely essential that the Mediator should also be very God. This was necessary, in order that (1) He might bring a sacrifice of infinite value and render perfect obedience to the law of God; (2) He might bear the wrath of God redemptively, that is, so as to free others from the curse of the law; and (3) He might be able to apply the fruits of His accomplished work to those who accepted Him by faith. Man with his bankrupt life can neither pay the penalty of sin, nor render perfect obedience to God. He can bear the wrath of God and, except for the redeeming grace of God, will have to bear it eternally, but he cannot bear it so as to open a way of escape, Ps. 49:7-10; 130:3.

QUESTIONS FOR FURTHER STUDY. What Old Testament persons bore the name 'Jesus,' and in what respect did they typify the Saviour? Is the bare title 'the Messiah,' without a genitive or a pronominal suffix, ever found in the Old Testament? How does Dalman account for its occurence in Jewish apocalyptic literature? Do the terms 'the anointed of Jehovah,' 'His anointed,' and 'my anointed' always have the same meaning in the Old Testament? Whence comes the idea that believers share the anointing of Christ? What about the idea that the name 'Son of Man,' reduced to its probable Aramaic original, simply means 'man'? How about the idea of Weiss and Schweitzer that Jesus employed the name only in a futuristic sense? Did He use it before Peter's confession at Cæsarea-Philippi? How do the liberals square their conception of Jesus as the Son of God only in a religious and ethical sense with the data of Scripture? What is the usual view of the origin of the *Kurios*-title? What theory was broached by Bousset and other liberal scholars? What accounts for the opposition to the two-natures doctrine? Is it a necessary doctrine, or is there some other doctrine that might take its place? What objections are there to the adoptionist doctrine;—to the Kenotic theories;—to the idea of a gradual incarnation;—to the Ritschlian view;—to Sanday's theory?

LITERATURE: Bavinck, *Geref. Dogm.* III, pp. 259-265, 328-335, 394-396: Kuyper, *Dict. Dogm., De Christo* I, pp. 44-61, 128-153; II, pp. 2-23; Hodge, *Syst. Theol.* II, pp. 378-387; Dabney, *Syst. and Polem. Theol.* pp. 464-477; Vos, *Geref. Dogm.* III, pp. 1-31; ibid. *The Self-Disclosure of Jesus,* pp. 104-256; ibid. on the *Kurios*-title, *Princeton Theol. Review,* Vol. XIII, pp. 151 ff.; Vol. XV, pp. 21 ff.; Dalman, *The Words of Jesus,* pp. 234-331; Warfield, *The Lord of Glory,* cf. Index; Liddon, *The Divinity of our Lord,* Lect. V; Rostron, *The Christology of St. Paul,* pp. 154 ff.; Machen, *The Origin of Paul's Religion,* pp. 293-317; Stanton. *The Jewish and the Christian* Messiah, pp. 239-250.

III. The Unipersonality of Christ

In the year 451 A.D. the Council of Chalcedon met and formulated the faith of the Church respecting the person of Christ, and declared Him "to be acknowledged in two natures, inconfusedly, unchangeably, indivisibly, inseperably; the distinction of the natures being in no wise taken away by the union, but rather the property of each nature being preserved, and concurring in one Person and one Subsistence, not parted or divided into two persons." This formulation is mainly negative, and simply seeks to guard the truth against various heretical views. It clearly states the faith of the early Church respecting the person of Christ, but makes no attempt to explain the mystery involved, a mystery that is not susceptible of a natural explanation. The great central miracle of history was permitted to stand forth in all its grandeur, the supreme paradox, to use Barthian language, God and man in one person. We are simply told what Jesus is, without any attempt to show how He became what He is. The great truth enunciated is that the eternal Son of God took upon Himself our humanity, and not, as Brunner reminds us, that the man Jesus acquired divinity. The deliverance of the Council of Chalcedon testifies to a movement from God to man, rather than vice versa. Centuries have gone by since that time, but, barring certain explications, the Church has really never gotten beyond the formula of Chalcedon. It has always recognized the incarnation as a mystery which defies explanation. And so it will remain, because it is the miracle of miracles. Several attempts have been made in course of time to give a psychological explanation of the person of Jesus Christ, but they were all bound to fail, because He is the Son of God, Himself very God, and a psychological explanation of God is out of the question. The following paragraphs are intended as a brief statement of the doctrine of the Church.

A. Statement of the Church's View Respecting the Person of Christ.

1. DEFINITION OF THE TERMS "NATURE" AND "PERSON." With a view to the proper understanding of the doctrine, it is necessary to know the exact meaning of the terms "nature" and "person," as used in this connection. The term "nature" denotes the sum-total of all the essential qualities of a thing, that which makes it what it is. A nature is a substance possessed in common, with all the essential qualities of such a substance. The term "person" denotes a complete substance endowed with reason, and, consequently, a responsible subject of its own actions. Personality is not an essential and integral part of a nature, but is, as it were, the terminus to which it tends. A person is a nature with something added, namely, independent subsistence, individuality. Now the

321

Logos assumed a human nature that was not personalized, that did not exist by itself.

2. PROPOSITIONS IN WHICH THE VIEW OF THE CHURCH MAY BE STATED.

a. There is but one person in the Mediator, the unchangeable Logos. The Logos furnishes the basis for the personality of Christ. It would not be correct, however, to say that the person of the mediator is divine only. The incarnation constituted Him a complex person, constituted of two natures. He is the God-man.

b. The human nature of Christ as such does not constitute a human person. The Logos did not adopt a human person, so that we have two persons in the Mediator, but simply assumed a human nature. Brunner declares that it is the mystery of the person of Jesus Christ that at the point where we have a sinful person, He has, or rather is, the divine person of the Logos.

c. At the same time it is not correct to speak of the human nature of Christ as impersonal. This is true only in the sense that this nature has no independent subsistence of its own. Strictly speaking, however, the human nature of Christ was not for a moment impersonal. The Logos assumed that nature into personal subsistence with Himself. The human nature has its personal existence in the person of the Logos. It is in-personal rather than impersonal.

d. For that very reason we are not warranted to speak of the human nature of Christ as imperfect or incomplete. His human nature is not lacking in any of the essential qualities belonging to that nature, and also has individuality, that is, personal subsistence, in the person of the Son of God.

e. This personal subsistence should not be confused with consciousness and free will. The fact that the human nature of Christ, in and by itself, has no personal subsistence, does not mean that it has no consciousness and will. The Church has taken the position that these belong to the nature rather than to the person.

f. The one divine person, who possessed a divine nature from eternity, assumed a human nature, and now has both. This must be maintained over against those who, while admitting that the divine person assumed a human nature, jeopardize the integrity of the two natures by conceiving of them as having been fused or mixed into a *tertium quid*, a sort of divine-human nature.

B. Scriptural Proof for the Unipersonality of Christ.

The doctrine of the two natures in one person transcends human reason. It is the expression of a supersensible reality, and of an incomprehensible mystery, which has no analogy in the life of man as we know it, and finds no support in human reason, and therefore can only be accepted by faith on the authority of the Word of God. For that reason it is doubly necessary to pay close attention to the teachings of Scripture on this point.

1. No EVIDENCE OF A DUAL PERSONALITY IN SCRIPTURE. In the first place there is a negative consideration of considerable importance. If there had been a dual personality in Jesus, we would naturally expect to find some traces of it in Scripture; but there is not a single trace of it. There is no distinction of an "I" and a "Thou" in the inner life of the Mediator, such as we find in connection with the triune Being of God, where one person addresses the other, Ps. 2:7; 40:7,8; John 17:1,4,5,21-24. Moreover, Jesus never uses the plural in referring to Himself, as God does in Gen. 1:26; 3:22; 11:7. It might seem as if John 3:11 were a case in point. The plural is peculiar, but in all probability refers to Jesus and those who were associated with Him, in opposition to Nicodemus and the group which he represented.

2. BOTH NATURES ARE REPRESENTED IN SCRIPTURE AS UNITED IN ONE PERSON. There are passages of Scripture which refer to both natures in Christ, but in which it is perfectly evident that only one person is intended, Rom. 1:3,4; Gal. 4:4,5; Phil. 2:6-11. In several passages both natures are set forth as united. The Bible nowhere teaches that divinity in the abstract, or some divine power, was united to, or manifested in, a human nature; but always that the divine nature in the concrete, that is, the divine person of the Son of God, was united to a human nature, John 1:14; Rom. 8:3; Gal. 4:4; 9:5; I Tim. 3:16; Heb. 2:11-14; I John 4:2,3.

3. THE ONE PERSON IS SPOKEN OF IN TERMS TRUE OF EITHER ONE OF THE NATURES. Repeatedly the attributes of one nature are predicated of the person, while that person is designated by a title derived from the other nature. On the one hand human attributes and actions are predicated of the person while he is designated by a divine title, Acts 20:28; I Cor. 2:8; Col. 1:13,14. And on the other hand divine attributes and actions are predicated of the person while he is designated by a human title, John 3:13; 6:62; Rom. 9:5.

C. The Effects of the Union of the Two Natures in One Person.

1. No ESSENTIAL CHANGE IN THE DIVINE NATURE. The doctrine of creation and the doctrine of the incarnation always constituted a problem in connection with the immutability of God. This was already pointed out in the discussion of that attribute. However this problem may be solved, it should be maintained that the divine nature did not undergo any essential change in the incarnation. This also means that it remained impassible, that is, incapable of suffering and death, free from ignorance, and insusceptible to weakness and temptation. It is well to stress the fact that the incarnation was a *personal act*. It is better to say that the *person* of the Son of God became incarnate than to say that the *divine nature* assumed human flesh. If Reformed theologians do occasionally speak of the divine nature as incarnate, they speak of it "not immediately but mediately," to use the language of scholastic theology; they consider this nature not absolutely and in itself, but in the person of the Son of God. The result of the incarnation was that the divine Saviour could be ignorant and weak, could

be tempted, and could suffer and die, not in His divine nature, but derivatively, by virtue of His possession of a human nature.

2. A THREEFOLD COMMUNICATION RESULTED FROM THE INCARNATION.

a. *A communicatio idiomatum, or communication of properties.* This means that the properties of both, the human and the divine natures, are now the properties of the person, and are therefore ascribed to the person. The person can be said to be almighty, omniscient, omnipresent, and so on, but can also be called a man of sorrows, of limited knowledge and power, and subject to human want and miseries. We must be careful not to understand the term to mean that anything peculiar to the divine nature was communicated to the human nature, or vice versa; or that there is an interpenetration of the two natures, as a result of which the divine is humanized, and the human is deified (Rome). The deity cannot share in human weaknesses; neither can man participate in any of the essential perfections of the Godhead.

b. *A communicatio apotelesmatum or operationum.* This means that the redemptive work of Christ, and particularly the final result of that work, the *apotelesma,* bears a divine-human character. Analyzing this, we can say that it means: (1) that the efficient cause of the redemptive work of Christ is the one undivided personal subject in Christ; (2) that it is brought about by the co-operation of both natures; (3) that each of these natures works with its own special *energeia;* and (4) that, notwithstanding this, the result forms an undivided unity, because it is the work of a single person.

c. *A communicatio charismatum or gratiarum.* This means that the human nature of Christ, from the very first moment of its existence, was adorned with all kinds of rich and glorious gifts, as for instance, (1) the *gratia unionis cum persona tou Logou,* that is, the grace and glory of being united to the divine Logos, also called the *gratia eminentiae,* by which the human nature is elevated high above all creatures, and even becomes the object of adoration; and (2) the *gratia habitualis,* consisting of those gifts of the Spirit, particularly of the intellect, of the will, and of power, by which the human nature of Christ was exalted high above all intelligent creatures. His impeccability, the *non posse peccare,* especially should be mentioned here.

3. THE GOD-MAN IS THE OBJECT OF PRAYER. Another effect of the union is, that the Mediator just as He now exists, that is, in both natures, is the object of our prayer. It should be borne in mind that the *honor adorationis* does not belong to the human nature as such, but belongs to it only in virtue of its union with the divine Logos, who is in His very nature *adorabilis.* We must distinguish between the object and the ground of this adoration. The object of our religious worship is the God-man Jesus Christ, but the ground on which we adore Him lies in the person of the Logos.

D. The Unipersonality of Christ a Mystery.

The union of the two natures in one person is a mystery which we cannot grasp, and which for that very reason is often denied. It has sometimes been compared with the union of body and soul in man; and there are some points of similarity. In man there are two substances, matter and spirit, most closely united and yet not mixed; so also in the Mediator. In man the principle of unity, the person, does not have its seat in the body but in the soul; in the Mediator, not in the human, but in the divine nature. As the influence of the soul on the body and of the body on the soul is a mystery, so also the connection of the two natures in Christ and their mutual influence on each other. Everything that happens in the body and in the soul is ascribed to the person; so all that takes place in the two natures of Christ is predicated of the person. Sometimes a man is denominated according to his spiritual element, when something is predicated of him that applies more particularly to the body, and *vice versa*. Similarly things that apply only to the human nature of Christ are ascribed to Him when He is named after His divine nature, and *vice versa*. As it is an honor for the body to be united with the soul, so it is an honor for the human nature of Christ to be united with the person of the Logos. Of course, the comparison is defective. It does not illustrate the union of the divine and the human, of the infinite and the finite. It does not even illustrate the unity of two spiritual natures in a single person. In the case of man the body is material and the soul is spiritual. It is a wonderful union, but not as wonderful as the union of the two natures in Christ.

E. The Lutheran Doctrine of the Communication of Attributes.

1. STATEMENT OF THE LUTHERAN POSITION. The Lutherans differ from the Reformed in their doctrine of the *communicatio idiomatum*. They teach that the attributes of one nature are ascribed to the other on the basis of an actual transference, and feel that it is only by such a transference that the real unity of the person can be secured. This position does not involve a denial of the fact that the attributes of both natures can be ascribed to the person, but adds something to that in the interest, as they see it, of the unity of the person. They did not always state their doctrine in the same form. Luther and some of the early Lutherans occasionally spoke of a communication in both directions, from the divine nature to the human, and also from the human to the divine. In the subsequent development of the doctrine, however, the communication from the human nature to the divine soon receded from sight, and only that from the divine to the human nature was stressed. A still greater limitation soon followed. Lutheran scholastics distinguished between the operative attributes of God (omnipotence, omnipresence, and omniscience), and His quiescent attributes (infinitude, eternity, etc.), and taught that only the former were transferred to the human nature. They were all agreed that the communication took place at the time of the incarnation. But the question naturally arose how this could be squared with the picture of Christ in the Gospels, which is not the picture of an omniscient and omnipresent man. This gave rise to a difference of opinion. According to some, Christ necessarily exercised these attributes during His humiliation, but did it secretly; but according to others their

exercise was subject to the will of the divine person, who voluntarily left them inoperative during the period of His humiliation. Opposition to this doctrine repeatedly manifested itself in the Lutheran Church. It was pointed out that it is inconsistent with the idea of a truly human development in the life of Christ, so clearly taught by Luther himself. The great Reformer's insistence on the communication of attributes finds its explanation partly in his mystical tendencies, and partly in his teachings respecting the physical presence of Christ in the Lord's Supper.

2. OBJECTIONS TO THIS LUTHERAN DOCTRINE. There are serious objections to the Lutheran doctrine of the *communicatio idiomatum.*

a. It has no Scriptural foundation. If it is inferred from such a statement as that in John 3:13, then, in consistency, it ought also to be concluded from I Cor. 2:8 that the ability to suffer was communicated to the divine nature. Yet the Lutherans shrink back from that conclusion.

b. It implies a fusion of the divine and the human natures in Christ. Lutherans speak as if the attributes can be abstracted from the nature, and can be communicated while the natures remain separate, but substance and attributes cannot be so separated. By a communication of divine attributes to the human nature that nature *as such* ceases to exist. Omnipresence and omniscience are not compatible with humanity. Such a communication results in a mixture of the divine and the human, which the Bible keeps strictly separate.

c. In the form in which the doctrine is now generally accepted by the Lutherans, the doctrine suffers from inconsistency. If the divine attributes are communicated to the human nature, the human must also be communicated to the divine. And if some attributes are communicated, they must all be communicated. But the Lutherans evidently do not dare to go the full length, and therefore stop half way.

d. It is inconsistent with the picture of the incarnate Christ during the time of His humiliation, as we find it in the Gospels. This is not the picture of a man who is omnipresent and omniscient. The Lutheran explanations of this inconsistency failed to commend themselves to the mind of the Church in general, and even to some of the followers of Luther.

e. It virtually destroys the incarnation. Lutherans distinguish between the *incarnatio and the exinanitio.* The Logos is the subject only of the former. He makes the human nature receptive for the inhabitation of the fulness of the Godhead and communicates to it some of the divine attributes. But by doing this He virtually abrogates the human nature by assimilating it to the divine. Thus only the divine remains.

f. It also practically obliterates the distinction between the state of humiliation and the state of exaltation. Brenz even says that these were not successive states, but states that co-existed during the earthly life of Christ. To escape the difficulty here, the Lutherans brought in the doctrine of the *exinanitio*, of which not the Logos but the God-man is the subject, to the effect that He practically emptied Himself, or laid aside the divine attributes. Some spoke of a constant but secret, and others of an intermittent use of them.

F. The Kenosis Doctrine in Various Forms.

About the middle of the nineteenth century a new form of Christology made its appearance in the Kenotic theories. It found favor especially among the Lutherans, but also with some Reformed theologians. It represents part of an attempt to bring the Lutheran and the Reformed sections of the Church closer together. The advocates of this new view desired to do full justice to the reality and integrity of the manhood of Christ, and to stress the magnitude of His self-denial and self-sacrifice.

1. STATEMENT OF THE DOCTRINE. The term "kenosis" is used in a two-fold sense in theology. Originally it was used by Lutheran theologians to denote the self-limitation, not of the Logos, but of the God-man, whereby He, in the interest of His humiliation, laid aside the actual use of His divine attributes. In the teachings of the Kenoticists, however, it signalized the doctrine that the Logos at the incarnation was denuded of His transitive or of all His attributes, was reduced to a mere potentiality, and then, in union with the human nature, developed again into a divine-human person. The main forms in which this doctrine were taught are the following:

a. *The theory of Thomasius, Delitzsch and Crosby.* Thomasius distinguishes between the absolute and essential attributes of God, such as absolute power, holiness, truth, and love, and His relative attributes, which are not essential to the Godhead, such as omnipotence, omnipresence, and omniscience; and maintains that the Logos while retaining His divine self-consciousness, laid the latter aside, in order to take unto Himself veritable human nature.

b. *The theory of Gess and H. W. Beecher.* This is far more thoroughgoing. La Touche speaks of it as "incarnation by divine suicide." The Logos so depotentiated Himself of all His divine attributes that He literally ceased from His cosmic functions and His eternal consciousness during the years of His earthly life. His consciousness became purely that of a human soul, and consequently He could and did take the place of the human soul in Christ. Thus the true manhood of Christ, even to the extent of His peccability, was secured.

c. *The theory of Ebrard.* Ebrard agrees with Gess in making the incarnate Logos take the place of the human soul. The eternal Son gave up the form of eternity, and in full self-limitation assumed the existence-form of a human life-center. But with him this self-reduction does not amount to a complete depotentiation of the Logos. The divine properties were retained, but were possessed by the God-man in the time-form appropriate to a human mode of existence.

d. *The theory of Martensen and Gore.* Martensen postulated the existence of a double life in the incarnate Logos from two non-communicating life-centers. As being in the bosom of God, He continued to function in the trinitarian life and also in His cosmic relations to the world as Creator and Sustainer. But at the same time He, as the depotentiated Logos, united with a human nature, knew nothing of His trinitarian and cosmic functions, and only knew Himself to be God in such a sense as that knowledge is possible to the faculties of manhood.

2. SUPPOSED •SCRIPTURAL BASIS FOR THE DOCTRINE. The Kenotics seek Scriptural support for their doctrine, especially in Phil. 2:6-8, but also in II Cor. 8:9 and John 17:5. The term "kenosis" is derived from the main verb in Phil. 2:7, *ekenosen*. This is rendered in the American Revised Version, "emptied Himself." Dr. Warfield calls this a mistranslation.[1] The verb is found in only four other New Testament passages, namely, Rom. 4:14; I Cor. 1:17; 9:15; II Cor. 9:3. In all of these it is used figuratively and means "to make void," "of no effect," "of no account," "of no reputation."[2] If we so understand the word here, it simply means that Christ made Himself of no account, of no reputation, did not assert His divine prerogative, but took the form of a servant. But even if we take the word in its literal sense, it does not support the Kenosis theory. It would, if we understood that which He laid aside to be the *morphe theou* (form of God), and then conceived of *morphe* strictly as the essential or specific character of the Godhead. In all probability *morphe* must be so understood, but the verb *ekenosen* does not refer to *morphe theou*, but to *einai isa theoi* (dat.) that is, His being on an equality with God. The fact that Christ took the form of a servant does not involve a laying aside of the form of God. There was no exchange of the one for the other. Though He pre-existed in the form of God, Christ did not count the being on an equality with God as a prize which He must not let slip, but emptied Himself, taking the form of a servant. Now what does His becoming a servant involve? A state of subjection in which one is called upon to render obedience. And the opposite of this is a state of sovereignty in which one has the right to command. The being on an equality with God does not denote a mode of being, but a state which Christ exchanged for another state.[3]

3. OBJECTIONS TO THE KENOSIS DOCTRINE.

a. The theory is based on the pantheistic conception that God and man are not so absolutely different but that the one can be transformed into the other. The Hegelian idea of *becoming* is applied to God, and the absolute line of demarcation is obliterated.

b. It is altogether subversive of the doctrine of the immutability of God, which is plainly taught in Scripture, Mal. 3:6; Jas. 1:17, and which is also implied in the very idea of God. Absoluteness and mutability are mutually exclusive; and a mutable God is certainly not the God of Scripture.

1. *Christology and Criticism*, p. 375.
2. Cf. Auth. Ver. in Phil. 2:7.
3. Cf. Kennedy, in *Exp. Gk. Test.;* Ewald, in *Zahn's Comm.;* Vos, *Notes on Christology of Paul;* Cooke, *The Incarnation and Recent Criticism*, pp. 201 ff.

c. It means a virtual destruction of the Trinity, and therefore takes away our very God. The humanized Son, self-emptied of His divine attributes, could no longer be a divine subsistence in the trinitarian life.

d. It assumes too loose a relation between the divine mode of existence, the divine attributes, and the divine essence, when it speaks of the former as if they might very well be separated from the latter. This is altogether misleading, and involves the very error that is condemned in connection with the Roman Catholic doctrine of transubstantiation.

e. It does not solve the problem which it was intended to solve. It desired to secure the unity of the person and the reality of the Lord's manhood. But, surely, the personal unity is not secured by assuming a human Logos as co-existent with a human soul. Nor is the reality of the manhood maintained by substituting for the human soul a depotentiated Logos. The Christ of the Kenotics is neither God nor man. In the words of Dr. Warfield His human nature is "just shrunken deity."

The Kenotic theory enjoyed great popularity in Germany for a while, but has now practically died out there. When it began to disappear in Germany, it found supporters in England in such scholars as D. W. Forrest, W. L. Walker, P. T. Forsyth, Ch. Gore, R. L. Ottley, and H. R. Mackintosh. It finds very little support at the present time.

G. The Theory of Gradual Incarnation.

Dorner was one of the first and the greatest of the opponents of the Kenosis doctrine. He set himself the task of suggesting another theory which, while escaping the errors of Kenoticism, would do full justice to the humanity of Christ. He proposed to solve the problem by the theory of a gradual or progressive incarnation. According to him the incarnation was not an act consummated at the moment of the conception of Jesus, but a gradual process by which the Logos joined Himself in an ever-increasing measure to the unique and representative Man (virtually a new creation), Christ Jesus, until the full union was finally consummated at the time of the resurrection. The union resulted in the God-man with a single consciousness and a single will. In this God-man the Logos does not supply the personality, but gives it its divine quality. This theory finds no support in Scripture, which always represents the incarnation as a momentary fact rather than as a process. It logically leads to Nestorianism or the doctrine of two persons in the Mediator. And since it finds the real seat of the personality in the man Jesus, it is utterly subversive of the real pre-existence of our Lord. Rothe and Bovon are two of the most important supporters of this doctrine.

The crucial difference between the ancient and the really modern theories respecting the person of Christ, lies in the fact that the latter, as appears also from the theory of Dorner, distinguish the person of the Logos, conceived as a special mode of the personal life of God, from the personality of Christ as a concrete human person uniquely divine in quality. According to modern views it is not the Logos but the man Jesus that constitutes the ego in Christ. The personality of Jesus is human in type of consciousness and also in moral growth, but at the same time uniquely receptive for the divine, and thus really the climax of an incarnation of which humanity itself is the general cosmic expression. This is true also of the theory suggested by Sanday in his *Christologies Ancient and Modern*, a theory which seeks to give a psychological explanation of the person of Jesus, which will do justice to both the human and the divine in Jesus. He stresses the fact that the subliminal consciousness is the proper seat of all divine indwelling, or divine action upon the human soul; and holds that the same or a corresponding subliminal self is also the proper seat or locus of the deity of the incarnate Christ. The ordinary consciousness of Jesus was the human consciousness, but there appeared in Him occasionally an uprush of the divine consciousness from the subliminal self. This theory has rightly been criticized severely. It ascribes a significance to the subliminal in the life of man which it does not possess, wrongly supposes that the deity can be located in some particular place in the person of Christ, and suggests a picture of Christ, as being only intermittently conscious of His deity, which is not in harmony with the data of Scripture. It reveals once more the folly of trying to give a psychological explanation of the person of Christ. Besides Sanday some of the more influential representatives of modern Christology are Kunze, Schaeder, Kaehler, Moberly, and Du Bose.

QUESTIONS FOR FURTHER STUDY. What change did the eighteenth century effect in Christology? What causes contributed to the present widespread denial of the deity of Christ? How do negative critics deal with the Scriptural proofs for the deity of Christ? Did the Liberal-Jesus-School succeed in presenting a tolerable picture of Jesus, which really squares with the facts? What is the distinction between the Jesus of history and the Christ of faith, and what purpose did it serve? What about the argument *aut Deus auto homo non bonus?* How is the reality of Christ's manhood sometimes endangered? Was there a single or a double self-consciousness in Christ? One or two wills? On what grounds is the Messianic consciousness of Jesus denied? How can it be defended? Did Jesus regard the Messiahship merely as a dignity that would be His in the future? Has the eschatological school any advantages over the liberal school? How do the Reformed, the Lutheran, and the Roman Catholic conceptions of the union of the two natures in Christ differ? What does the Formula Concordiae teach on this point? What was the Giessen-Tuebingen controversy? How did Kant, Hegel, and Schleiermacher conceive of this union? In what respect do the Kenosis theories reveal the influence of Hegel? How did the modern conception of the immanence of God affect more recent Christologies? Is Sanday's psychological theory an acceptable construction?

LITERATURE: Bavinck, *Geref. Dogm.*, III, pp. 264-349; Kuyper, *Dict. Dogm.*, De Christo I, pp. 62—II, p. 58; Vos, *The Self-Disclosure of Jesus*, pp. 35-103; Temple, *The Boyhood Consciousness of Christ*; Orr, *The Christian View of God and the World*, pp. 248-257; H. R. Mackintosh, *The Doct. of the Person of Jesus Christ*, pp. 141-284; Liddon, *The Divinity of our Lord*; Relton, *A Study in Christology*, pp. 3-222; Warfield, *Christology and Criticism*, Lectures VI-VIII; Rostron, *The Christology of St. Paul*, pp. 196-229; Schweitzer, *The Quest of the Historical Jesus*; La Touche, *The Person of Christ in Modern Thought*; Gore, *The Reconstruction of Belief*, pp. 297-526; Honig, *De Persoon Van den Middelaar in de Nieuwere Duitsche Dogmatiek*; Sheldon, *Hist. of Chr. Doct.* II, 134-137, 348-353; Krauth, *Conservative Reformation and Its Theology*, pp. 456-517; Bruce, *The Humiliation of Christ*, Lectures III, IV and V; Loofs, *What Is the Truth about Jesus Christ?* chap. VI; Sanday, *Christologies, Ancient and Modern*, Chaps. III, IV, VII; Cooke, *The Incarnation and Recent Criticism*, Chap. X; Brunner, *The Mediator*, especially Chap. XII.

THE STATES OF CHRIST

I. The State of Humiliation

A. Introductory: The Doctrine of the States of Christ in General.

1. THE DISTINCTION BETWEEN A STATE AND A CONDITION. It should be borne in mind that, though the word "state" is sometimes used synonymously with "condition," the word as applied to Christ in this connection denotes a relationship rather than a condition. In general a state and a condition may be distinguished as follows: A state is one's position or status in life, and particularly the forensic relationship in which one stands to the law, while a condition is the mode of one's existence, especially as determined by the circumstances of life. One who is found guilty in a court of justice is in a state of guilt or condemnation, and this is usually followed by a condition of incarceration with all its resulting deprivation and shame. In theology the states of the Mediator are generally considered as including the resulting conditions. In fact, the different stages of the humiliation and of the exaltation, as usually stated, have a tendency to make the conditions stand out more prominently than the states. Yet the states are the more fundamental of the two and should be so considered.[1] In the state of humiliation Christ was under the law, not only as a rule of life, but as the condition of the covenant of works, and even under the condemnation of the law; but in the state of exaltation He is free from the law, having met the condition of the covenant of works and having paid the penalty for sin.

2. THE DOCTRINE OF THE STATES OF CHRIST IN HISTORY. The doctrine of the states of Christ really dates from the seventeenth century, though traces of it are already found in the writings of the Reformers, and even in some of the early Church Fathers. It was first developed among the Lutherans when they sought to bring their doctrine of the *communicatio idiomatum* in harmony with the humiliation of Christ as it is pictured in the Gospels, but was soon adopted also by the Reformed. They differed, however, as to the real *subject* of the states. According to the Lutherans it is the human nature of Christ, but according to the Reformed, the person of the Mediator. There was considerable difference of opinion even among the Lutherans on the subject. Under the influence of Schleiermacher the idea of the states of the Mediator gradually disappeared from theology. By his pantheizing tendency the lines of demarcation between the Creator and the creature were practically obliterated. The emphasis was shifted from the transcendent to the immanent God; and the

---

1. Cf. Kuyper, *Dict. Dogm., De Christo* II, pp. 59 ff.

sovereign God whose law is the standard of right disappeared. In fact, the idea of objective right was banished from theology, and under such conditions it became impossible to maintain the idea of a judicial position, that is, of a state of the Mediator. Moreover, in the measure in which the humanity of Christ was stressed to the exclusion of His deity, and on the one hand His pre-existence, and on the other, His resurrection was denied, all speaking about the humiliation and exaltation of Christ lost its meaning. The result is that in many present day works on Dogmatics we look in vain for a chapter on the states of Christ.

3. THE NUMBER OF THE STATES OF THE MEDIATOR. There is a difference of opinion as to the number of the states of the Mediator. Some are of the opinion that, if we assume that the person of the Mediator is the subject of the states, strict logic requires that we speak of three states or modes of existence: the pre-existent state of eternal divine being, the earthly state of temporal human existence, and the heavenly state of exaltation and glory.[1] But since we can speak of the humiliation and exaltation of the person of Christ only in connection with Him as the God-man, it is best to speak of only two states. Reformed theologians do find an anticipation of both the humiliation and the exaltation of Christ in His pre-existent state: of His humiliation in that He freely took upon Himself in the *pactum salutis* to merit and administer our salvation; and of His exaltation in the glory which He as our prospective Mediator enjoyed before the incarnation, cf. John 17:5. The two states are clearly indicated in II Cor. 8:9; Gal. 4:4,5; Phil. 2:6-11; Heb. 2:9.

B. The State of Humiliation.

On the basis of Phil. 2:7,8, Reformed theology distinguishes two elements in the humiliation of Christ, namely, (1) the *kenosis* (emptying, *exinanitio*), consisting in this that He laid aside the divine majesty, the majesty of the sovereign Ruler of the universe, and assumed human nature in the form of a servant; and (2) the *tapeinosis* (*humiliatio*), consisting in that He became subject to the demands and to the curse of the law, and in His entire life became obedient in action and suffering to the very limit of a shameful death. On the basis of the passage in Philippians it may be said that the essential and central element in the state of humiliation is found in the fact that He who was the Lord of all the earth, the supreme Lawgiver, placed Himself under the law, in order to discharge its federal and penal obligations in behalf of His people. By doing this He became legally responsible for our sins and liable to the curse of the law. This state of the Saviour, briefly expressed in the words of Gal. 4:4, "born under the law," is reflected in the corresponding condition, which is described in the various stages of the humiliation. While Lutheran theology speaks of as many as eight stages in the humiliation of Christ, Reformed theology generally names only five, namely: (1) incarnation, (2) suffering, (3) death, (4) burial, and (5) descent into hades.

---

1. Cf. McPherson, *Chr. Dogm.*, p. 322; Valentine, *Chr. Theol.* II, p. 88.

1. THE INCARNATION AND BIRTH OF CHRIST. Under this general heading several points deserve attention.

a. *The subject of the incarnation.* It was not the triune God but the second person of the Trinity that assumed human nature. For that reason it is better to say that the Word became flesh than that God became man. At the same time we should remember that each of the divine persons was active in the incarnation, Matt. 1:20; Luke 1:35; John 1:14; Acts 2:30; Rom. 8:3; Gal. 4:4; Phil 2:7. This also means that the incarnation was not something that merely happened to the Logos, but was an active accomplishment on His part. In speaking of the *incarnation* in distinction from the *birth* of the Logos, His active participation in this historical fact is stressed, and His pre-existence is assumed. It is not possible to speak of the incarnation of one who had no previous existence. This pre-existence is clearly taught in Scripture: "In the beginning was the Word, and the Word was with God, and the Word was God," John 1:1. "I am come down from heaven," John 6:38. "For ye know the grace of our Lord Jesus Christ, that, though He was rich, yet for our sakes He became poor," II Cor. 8:9. "Who, existing in the form of God, counted not the being on an equality with God a thing to be grasped, but emptied Himself, taking the form of a servant, being made in the likeness of men," Phil. 2:6,7. "But when the fulness of the time came God sent forth His Son," Gal. 4:4. The pre-existent Son of God assumes human nature and takes to Himself human flesh and blood, a miracle that passes our limited understanding. It clearly shows that the infinite can and does enter into finite relations, and that the supernatural can in some way enter the historical life of the world.

b. *The necessity of the incarnation.* Since the days of Scholasticism the question has been debated, whether the incarnation should be regarded as involved in the idea of redemption, or as already involved in the idea of creation. Popularly stated, the question was, whether the Son of God would have come in the flesh even if man had not sinned. Rupert of Deutz was the first to assert clearly and positively that He would have become incarnate irrespective of sin. His view was shared by Alexander of Hales and Duns Scotus, but Thomas Aquinas took the position that the reason for the incarnation lay in the entrance of sin into the world. The Reformers shared this view, and the Churches of the Reformation teach that the incarnation was necessitated by the fall of man. Some Lutheran and Reformed scholars, however, such as Osiander, Rothe, Dorner, Lange, Van Oosterzee, Martensen, Ebrard, and Westcott, were of the contrary opinion. The arguments adduced by them are such as the following: Such a stupendous fact as the incarnation cannot be contingent, and cannot find its cause in sin as an accidental and arbitrary act of man. It must have been included in the original plan of God. Religion before and after the fall cannot be essentially different. If a Mediator is necessary now, He must have been necessary also before the fall. Moreover, Christ's work is not limited to the atonement and His saving operations. He is

Mediator, but also Head; He is not only the *arche*, but also the *telos* of creation, I Cor. 15:45-47; Eph. 1:10,21-23; 5:31,32; Col. 1:15-17.

However, it should be noted that Scripture invariably represents the incarnation as conditioned by human sin. The force of such passages as Luke 19:10; John 3:16; Gal. 4:4; I John 3:8; and Phil. 2:5-11 is not easily broken. The idea, sometimes expressed, that the incarnation in itself was fitting and necessary for God, is apt to lead to the pantheistic notion of an eternal self-revelation of God in the world. The difficulty connected with the plan of God, supposed to burden this view, does not exist, if we consider the matter *sub specie aeternitatis*. There is but one plan of God, and this plan includes sin and the incarnation from the very beginning. In the last analysis, of course, the incarnation, as well as the whole work of redemption was contingent, not on sin, but on the good pleasure of God. The fact that Christ also has cosmical significance need not be denied, but this too is linked up with His redemptive significance in Eph. 1:10,20-23; Col. 1:14-20.

c. *The change effected in the incarnation.* When we are told that the Word became flesh, this does not mean that the Logos ceased to be what He was before. As to His essential being the Logos was exactly the same before and after the incarnation. The verb *egeneto* in John 1:14 (the Word *became* flesh) certainly does not mean that the Logos changed into flesh, and thus altered His essential nature, but simply that He took on that particular character, that He acquired an additional form, without in any way changing His original nature. He remained the infinite and unchangeable Son of God. Again, the statement that the Word became *flesh* does not mean that He took on a human *person*, nor, on the other hand, merely that He took on *a human body*. The word *sarx* (flesh) here denotes human nature, consisting of body and soul. The word is used in a somewhat similar sense in Rom. 8:3; I Tim. 3:16; I John 4:2; II John 7 (comp. Phil. 2:7).

d. *The incarnation constituted Christ one of the human race.* In opposition to the teachings of the Anabaptists, our Confession affirms that Christ assumed His human nature from the substance of His mother. The prevailing opinion among the Anabaptists was that the Lord brought His human nature from heaven, and that Mary was merely the conduit or channel through which it passed. On this view His human nature was really a new creation, similar to ours, but not organically connected with it. The importance of opposing this view will be readily seen. If the human nature of Christ was not derived from the same stock as ours but merely resembled it, there exists no such relation between us and Him as is necessary to render His mediation available for our good.

e. *The incarnation effected by a supernatural conception and a virgin birth.* Our Confession affirms that the human nature of Christ was "conceived in the womb of the blessed virgin Mary by the power of the Holy Ghost, without the means of man." This emphasizes the fact that the birth of Christ was not at all an ordinary but a supernatural birth, in virtue of which He was called "the Son of God." The most important element in connection with the birth of Jesus was the supernatural operation of the Holy Spirit, for it was only through this that the virgin birth became possible. The Bible refers to this particular feature in Matt. 1:18-20; Luke 1:34,35; Heb. 10:5. The work of the Holy Spirit in connection with the conception of Jesus was twofold: (1) He was the efficient cause of what was conceived in the womb of Mary, and thus excluded the activity of man as an efficient factor. This was entirely in harmony with the fact that the person who was born was not a human person, but the person of the Son of God, who as such was not included in the covenant of works and was in Himself free from the guilt of sin. (2) He sanctified the human nature of Christ in its very inception, and thus kept it free from the pollution of sin. We cannot say exactly how the Holy Spirit accomplished this sanctifying work, because it is not yet sufficiently understood just how the pollution of sin ordinarily passes from parent to child. It should be noted, however, that the sanctifying influence of the Holy Spirit was not limited to the conception of Jesus, but was continued throughout His life, John 3:34; Heb. 9:14.

It was only through this supernatural conception of Christ that He could be born of a virgin. The doctrine of the virgin birth is based on the following passages of Scripture: Isa. 7:14; Matt. 1:18,20; Luke 1:34,35, and is also favored by Gal. 4:4. This doctrine was confessed in the Church from the earliest times. We meet with it already in the original forms of the Apostolic Confession, and further in all the great Confessions of the Roman Catholic and Protestant Churches. Its present denial is not due to the lack of Scriptural evidence for it, nor to any want of ecclesiastical sanction, but to the current general aversion to the supernatural. The passages of Scripture on which the doctrine is based are simply ruled out of court on critical grounds which are far from convincing; and that in spite of the fact that the integrity of the narratives is proved to be beyond dispute; and it is gratuitously assumed that the silence of the other New Testament writers respecting the virgin birth proves that they were not acquainted with the supposed fact of the miraculous birth. All kinds of ingenious attempts are made to explain how the story of the virgin birth arose and gained currency. Some seek it in Hebrew, and others in Gentile, traditions. We cannot enter upon a discussion of the problem here, and therefore merely refer to such works as Machen, *The Virgin Birth of Christ*; Orr, *The Virgin Birth of Christ*; Sweet, *The Birth and Infancy of Jesus Christ*; Cooke, *Did Paul Know the Virgin Birth?* Knowling, *The Virgin Birth.*

The question is sometimes asked, whether the virgin birth is a matter of doctrinal importance. Brunner declares that he is not interested in the subject at all. He rejects the doctrine of the miraculous birth of Christ and holds that it was purely natural, but is not sufficiently interested to defend his view at length. Moreover, he says: "The doctrine of the virgin birth would have been given up long ago were it not for the fact that it seemed as though dogmatic interests were concerned in its retention."[1] Barth recognizes the miracle of the virgin birth, and sees in it a token of the fact that God has creatively established a new beginning by condescending to become man.[2] He also finds in it doctrinal significance. According to him the "sin-inheritance" is passed on by the male parent, so that Christ could assume "creatureliness" by being born of Mary, and at the same time escape the "sin-inheritance" by the elimination of the human father.[3] In answer to the question, whether the virgin birth has doctrinal significance, it may be said that it would be inconceivable that God should cause Christ to be born in such an extraordinary manner, if it did not serve some purpose. Its doctrinal purpose may be stated as follows: (1) Christ had to be constituted the Messiah and the Messianic Son of God. Consequently, it was necessary that He should be born of a woman, but also that He should not be the fruit of the will of man, but should be born of God. What is born of flesh is flesh. In all probability this wonderful birth of Jesus was in the background of the mind of John when he wrote as he did in John 1:13. (2) If Christ had been generated by man, He would have been a human person, included in the covenant of works, and as such would have shared the common guilt of mankind. But now that His subject, His ego, His person, is not out of Adam, He is not in the covenant of works and is free from the guilt of sin. And being free from the guilt of sin, His human nature could also be kept free, both before and after His birth, from the pollution of sin.

f. *The incarnation itself part of the humiliation of Christ.* Was the incarnation itself a part of the humiliation of Christ or not? The Lutherans, with their distinction between the *incarnatio* and the *exinanitio*, deny that it was, and base their denial on the fact that His humiliation was limited to His earthly existence, while His humanity continues in heaven. He still has His human nature, and yet is no more in a state of humiliation. There was some difference of opinion on this point even among Reformed theologians. It would seem that this question should be answered with discrimination. It may be said that the incarnation, altogether in the abstract, the mere fact that God in Christ assumed a human nature, though an act of condescension, was not in itself a humiliation, though Kuyper thought it was.[4] But it certainly was a humiliation that the Logos assumed "flesh," that is, human nature as it is since the fall, weakened and subject to suffering and death, though free from the taint of sin. This would seem to be implied in such passages as Rom. 8:3; II Cor. 8:9; Phil. 2:6,7.

2. THE SUFFERINGS OF THE SAVIOUR. Several points should be stressed in connection with the sufferings of Christ.

a. *He suffered during His entire life.* In view of the fact that Jesus began to speak of His coming sufferings towards the end of His life, we are often inclined to think that the final agonies constituted the whole of His sufferings.

---

1. *The Mediator*, p. 324.
2. *The Doctrine of the Word of God*, p. 556; *Credo*, pp. 63 ff.; *Revelation*, pp. 65 f.
3. *Credo*, pp. 70 f.
4. *De Christo* II, pp. 68 ff.

Yet His whole life was a life of suffering. It was the servant-life of the Lord of Hosts, the life of the Sinless One in daily association with sinners, the life of the Holy One in a sin-cursed world. The way of obedience was for Him at the same time a way of suffering. He suffered from the repeated assaults of Satan, from the hatred and unbelief of His own people, and from the persecution of His enemies. Since He trod the wine-press alone, His loneliness must have been oppressive, and His sense of responsibility, crushing. His suffering was consecrated suffering, increasing in severity as He approached the end. The suffering that began in the incarnation finally reached its climax in the *passio magna* at the end of His life. Then all the wrath of God against sin bore down upon Him.

b. *He suffered in body and soul.* There has been a time when the attention was fixed too exclusively on the bodily sufferings of the Saviour. It was not the blind physical pain as such that constituted the essence of His suffering, but that pain accompanied with anguish of soul and with a mediatorial consciousness of the sin of humanity with which He was burdened. Later on it became customary to minimize the importance of the bodily sufferings, since it was felt that sin, being of a spiritual nature, could only be atoned for by purely spiritual sufferings. These one-sided views must be avoided. Both body and soul were affected by sin, and in both the punishment had to be borne. Moreover, the Bible clearly teaches that Christ suffered in both. He agonized in the garden, where His soul was "exceeding sorrowful, even unto death," and He was buffeted and scourged and crucified.

c. *His sufferings resulted from various causes.* In the last analysis all the sufferings of Christ resulted from the fact that He took the place of sinners vicariously. But we may distinguish several proximate causes, such as: (1) The fact that He who was the Lord of the universe had to occupy a menial position, even the position of a bond-servant or slave, and that He who had an inherent right to command was in duty bound to obey. (2) The fact that He who was pure and holy had to live in a sinful, polluted atmosphere, in daily association with sinners, and was constantly reminded of the greatness of the guilt with which He was burdened by the sins of His contemporaries. (3) His perfect awareness and clear anticipation, from the very beginning of His life, of the extreme sufferings that would, as it were, overwhelm Him in the end. He knew exactly what was coming, and the outlook was far from cheerful. (4) Finally, also the privations of life, the temptations of the devil, the hatred and rejection of the people, and the maltreatment and persecutions to which He was subjected.

d. *His sufferings were unique.* We sometimes speak of the "ordinary" sufferings of Christ, when we think of those sufferings that resulted from the ordinary causes of misery in the world. But we should remember that these causes were far more numerous for the Saviour than they are for us. Moreover, even these common sufferings had an extraordinary character in His case, and were therefore unique. His capacity for suffering was commensurate with the ideal character of His humanity, with His ethical perfection, and with His sense of righteousness and holiness and veracity. No one could feel the poignancy of pain and grief and moral evil as Jesus could. But besides these more common sufferings there were also the sufferings caused by the fact that God caused our iniquities to come upon Him like a flood. The sufferings of the Saviour were not purely natural, but also the result of a positive deed of God, Isa. 53:6,10. To the more special sufferings of the Saviour may also be reckoned the temptations in the desert, and the agonies of Gethsemane and Golgotha.

e. *His sufferings in temptations.* The temptations of Christ formed an integral part of His sufferings. They are temptations that are encountered in the pathway of suffering, Matt. 4:1-11 (and parallels); Luke 22:28; John 12:27; Heb. 4:15; 5:7,8. His public ministry began with a period of temptation, and even after that time temptations were repeated at intervals right on into dark Gethsemane. It was only by entering into the very trials of men, into their temptations, that Jesus could become a truly sympathetic High Priest and attain to the heights of a proved and triumphant perfection, Heb. 4:15; 5:7-9. We may not detract from the reality of the temptations of Jesus as the last Adam, however difficult it may be to conceive of one who could not sin as being tempted. Various suggestions have been made to relieve the difficulty, as for instance, that in the human nature of Christ, as in that of the first Adam, there was the *nuda possibilitas peccandi*, the bare abstract possibility of sinning (Kuyper); that Jesus' holiness was an ethical holiness, which had to come to high development through, and maintain itself in, temptation (Bavinck); and that the things with which Christ was tempted were in themselves perfectly lawful, and appealed to perfectly natural instincts and appetites (Vos). But in spite of all this the problem remains, How was it possible that one who *in concreto,* that is, as He was actually constituted, could not sin nor even have an inclination to sin, nevertheless be subject to real temptation?

3. THE DEATH OF THE SAVIOUR. The sufferings of the Saviour finally culminated in His death. In connection with this the following points should be emphasized:

a. *The extent of His death.* It is but natural that, when we speak of the death of Christ in this connection, we have in mind first of all physical death, that is, the separation of body and soul. At the same time we should remember that this does not exhaust the idea of death as it is represented in Scripture. The Bible takes a synthetic view of death, and regards physical death merely as one of its manifestations. Death is separation from God, but this separation can be viewed in two different ways. Man separates himself from God by sin, and death is the natural result, so that it can even be said that sin is death. But it was not in that way that Jesus became subject to death, since He had no personal sin. In this connection it should be borne in mind that death is not merely the natural consequence of sin, but above all the judicially imposed and inflicted punishment of sin. It is God's withdrawing

Himself with the blessings of life and happiness from man and visiting man in wrath. It is from this judicial point of view that the death of Christ must be considered. God imposed the punishment of death upon the Mediator judicially, since the latter undertook voluntarily to pay the penalty for the sin of the human race. Since Christ assumed human nature with all its weaknesses, as it exists after the fall, and thus became like us in all things, sin only excepted, it follows that death worked in Him from the very beginning and manifested itself in many of the sufferings to which He was subject. He was a man of sorrows and acquainted with grief. The Heidelberg Catechism correctly says that "all the time He lived on earth, but especially at the end of His life, He bore, in body and soul, the wrath of God against the sin of the whole human race."[1] These sufferings were followed by His death on the cross. But this was not all; He was subject not only to physical, but also to eternal death, though He bore this intensively and not extensively, when He agonized in the garden and when He cried out on the cross, "My God, my God, why hast thou forsaken me?" In a short period of time He bore the infinite wrath against sin to the very end and came out victoriously. This was possible for Him only because of His exalted nature. At this point we should guard against misunderstanding, however. Eternal death in the case of Christ did not consist in an abrogation of the union of the Logos with the human nature, nor in the divine nature's being forsaken of God, nor in the withdrawal of the Father's divine love or good pleasure from the person of the Mediator. The Logos remained united with the human nature even when the body was in the grave; the divine nature could not possibly be forsaken of God; and the person of the Mediator was and ever continued to be the object of divine favor. It revealed itself in the human consciousness of the Mediator as a feeling of God-forsakenness. This implies that the human nature for a moment missed the conscious comfort which it might derive from its union with the divine Logos, and the sense of divine love, and was painfully conscious of the fulness of the divine wrath which was bearing down upon it. Yet there was no despair, for even in the darkest hour, while He exclaims that He is forsaken, He directs His prayer to God.

b. *The judicial character of His death.* It was quite essential that Christ should die neither a natural nor an accidental death; and that He should not die by the hand of an assassin, but under a judicial sentence. He had to be counted with the transgressors, had to be condemned as a criminal. Moreover, it was providentially arranged by God that He should be tried and sentenced by a Roman judge. The Romans had a genius for law and justice, and represented the highest judicial power in the world. It might be expected that a trial before a Roman judge would serve to bring out clearly the innocence of Jesus, which it did, so that it became perfectly clear that He was not condemned for any crime which He had committed. It was a testimony to the fact that, as the Lord says, "He was cut off out of the land of the living for

---

1. Q. 37.

the transgression of my people, to whom the stroke was due." And when the Roman judge nevertheless condemned the innocent, he, it is true, also condemned himself and human justice as he applied it, but at the same time imposed sentence on Jesus as the representative of the highest judicial power in the world, functioning by the grace of God and dispensing justice in God's name. The sentence of Pilate was also the sentence of God, though on entirely different grounds. It was significant too that Christ was not beheaded or stoned to death. Crucifixion was not a Jewish but a Roman form of punishment. It was accounted so infamous and ignominious that it might not be applied to Roman citizens, but only to the scum of mankind, to the meanest criminals and slaves. By dying that death, Jesus met the extreme demands of the law. At the same time He died an accursed death, and thus gave evidence of the fact that He became a curse for us, Deut. 21:23; Gal. 3:13.

4. THE BURIAL OF THE SAVIOUR. It might seem that the death of Christ was the last stage of His humiliation, especially in view of one of the last words spoken on the cross, "It is finished." But that word in all probability refers to His active suffering, that is, the suffering in which He Himself took an active part. This was indeed finished when He died. It is clear that His burial also formed a part of His humiliation. Notice especially the following: (a) Man's returning to the dust from which he is taken, is represented in Scripture as part of the punishment of sin, Gen. 3:19. (b) Several statements of Scripture imply that the Saviour's abode in the grave was a humiliation. Ps. 16:10; Acts 2:27,31; 13:34,35. It was a descent into *hades*, in itself dismal and dreary, a place of corruption, though in it He was kept from corruption. (c) Burial is a going down, and therefore a humiliation. The burial of dead bodies was ordered by God to symbolize the humiliation of the sinner. (d) There is a certain agreement between the stages in the objective work of redemption and the order in the subjective application of the work of Christ. The Bible speaks of the sinner's being buried with Christ. Now this belongs to the putting off of the old man, and not to the putting on of the new, cf. Rom. 6:1-6. Consequently also the burial of Jesus forms a part of His humiliation. His burial, moreover, did not merely serve to prove that Jesus was really dead, but also to remove the terrors of the grave for the redeemed and to sanctify the grave for them.

5. THE SAVIOUR'S DESCENT INTO HADES.

a. *This doctrine in the Apostolic Confession.* After the Apostolic Confession has mentioned the sufferings, death, and burial, of the Lord, it continues with the words, "He descended into hell (hades)." This statement was not in the Creed as early nor as universally as the others. It was first used in the Aquileian form of the Creed (c. 390 A.D.), "*descendit in inferna*." Among the Greeks some translated "inferna" by "hades," and others by "lower parts." Some forms of the Creed in which these words were found did not mention the burial of Christ, while the Roman and Oriental forms generally mentioned the burial but not the descent into hades. Rufinus remarks that they contained the idea of the descent in the word "buried." Later on, however, the Roman form of the Creed added the statement in question after its mention of the burial. Calvin correctly argues that for those who added them after the word "buried," they must have denoted something additional.[1] It should be borne in mind that these words are not found in Scripture, and are not based on such direct statements of the Bible as the rest of the articles of the Creed.

b. *Scriptural basis for the expression.* There are especially four passages of Scripture that come into consideration here. (1) Eph. 4:9, "Now this, He ascended, what is it but that He also descended into the lower parts of the earth?" They who seek support in this passage take the expression "lower parts of the earth" as the equivalent of "hades." But this is a doubtful interpretation. The apostle argues that the ascent of Christ presupposes a descent. Now the opposite of the ascension is the incarnation, cf. John 3:13. Hence the majority of commentators take the expression as referring simply to the earth. The expression may be derived from Ps. 139:15 and refer more particularly to the incarnation. (2) I Peter 3:18,19, which speaks of Christ as "being put to death in the flesh, but made alive in the spirit, in which He also went and preached unto the spirits in prison." This passage is supposed to refer to the descent into hades and to state the purpose of it. The Spirit referred to is then understood to be the soul of Christ, and the preaching mentioned must have taken place between His death and resurrection. But the one is just as impossible as the other. The Spirit mentioned is not the soul of Christ but the quickening Spirit, and it was by that same life-giving Spirit that Christ preached. The common Protestant interpretation of this passage is that in the Spirit Christ preached through Noah to the disobedient that lived before the flood, who were spirits in prison when Peter wrote, and could therefore be designated as such. Bavinck considers this untenable and interprets the passage as referring to the ascension, which he regards as a rich, triumphant, and powerful preaching to the spirits in prison.[2] (3) I Pet. 4:4-6, particularly verse 6, which reads as follows: "For unto this end was the gospel preached even to the dead, that they might be judged indeed according to men in the flesh, but live according to God in the spirit." In this connection the apostle warns the readers that they should not live the rest of their life in the flesh to the lusts of men, but to the will of God, even if they should give offense to their former companions and be slandered by them, since they shall have to give an account of their doing to God, who is ready to judge the living and the dead. The "dead" to whom the gospel was preached were evidently not yet dead when it was preached unto them, since the purpose of this preaching was in part "that they might be judged according to men in the flesh." This could only take place during their life on earth. In all prob-

---

1. *Inst.* Bk. II, XVI, 8.; cf. also Pearson, *On the Creed.*
2. *Geref. Dogm.* III, p. 547. For still another interpretation, cf. Brown, *Comm. on Peter in loco.*

ability the writer refers. to the same spirits in prison of which he spoke in the preceding chapter. (4) Ps. 16:8-10 (comp. Acts 2:25-27,30,31). It is especially the 10th verse that comes into consideration here, "For thou wilt not leave my soul in Sheol; neither wilt thou suffer thy holy one to see corruption." From this passage Pearson concludes that the soul of Christ was in hell (hades) before the resurrection, for we are told that it was not left there.[1] But we should note the following: (a) The word *nephesh* (soul) is often used in Hebrew for the personal pronoun, and *sheol*, for the state of death. (b) If we so understand these words here, we have a clear synonymous parallelism. The idea expressed would be that Jesus was not left to the power of death. (c) This is in perfect harmony with the interpretation of Peter in Acts 2:30,31, and of Paul in Acts 13:34,35. In both instances the psalm is quoted to prove the resurrection of Jesus.

c. *Different interpretations of the creedal expression.* (1) The Catholic Church takes it to mean that, after His death, Christ went into the *Limbus Patrum*, where the Old Testament saints were awaiting the revelation and application of His' redemption, preached the gospel to them, and brought them out to heaven. (2) The Lutherans regard the descent into hades as the first stage of the exaltation of Christ. Christ went into the underworld to reveal and consummate His victory over Satan and the powers of darkness, and to pronounce their sentence of condemnation. Some Lutherans place this triumphal march between the death of Christ and His resurrection; others, after the resurrection. (3) The Church of England holds that, while Christ's body was in the grave, the soul went into hades, more particularly into paradise, the abode of the souls of the righteous, and gave them a fuller exposition of the truth. (4) Calvin interprets the phrase metaphorically,[2] as referring to the penal sufferings of Christ on the cross, where He really suffered the pangs of hell. Similarly, the Heidelberg Catechism.[3] According to the usual Reformed position the words refer not only to the sufferings on the cross, but also to the agonies of Gethsemane. (5) Scripture certainly does not teach a literal descent of Christ into hell. Moreover, there are serious objections to this view. He cannot have descended into hell according to the body, for this was in the grave. If He really did descend into hell, it can only have been as to His soul, and this would mean that only half of His human nature shared in this stage of His humiliation (or exaltation). Moreover, as long as Christ had not yet risen from the dead, the time had not come for a triumphal march such as' the Lutherans assume. And, finally, at the time of His death Christ commended His spirit to His Father. This seems to indicate that He would be passive rather than active from the time of His death until He arose from the grave. On the whole it seems best to combine two thoughts: (a) that Christ suffered the pangs' of hell before His death, in

---

1. *Expos. of the Creed, in loco.*
2. *Inst.* Bk. II, XVI, 8 ff.
3. Q. 44.

Gethsemane and on the cross; and (b) that He entered the deepest humiliation of the state of death.

QUESTIONS FOR FURTHER STUDY: How were state and condition related to each other in the case of Adam, when he fell? In the case of the Word becoming flesh? How are they related in the redemption of sinners? Do one's state and condition always correspond? How should the state of humiliation be defined? What does Kuyper mean, when he distinguishes between the *status generis* and the *status modi*? What stages does he distinguish in the state of humiliation? Is there any biblical proof for the virgin birth, except in the Gospels of Matthew and Luke? What are the doctrinal bearings of this doctrine? Have the theories of the mythical origin of the idea of the virgin birth been found adequate? What do we understand by Christ's subjection to the law? In what legal relation did He stand as Mediator during His humiliation? Was the human nature of Christ inherently subject to the law of death? Did eternal death in the case of Christ include all the elements that are included in the eternal death of sinners? How can the burial of the Saviour be conceived of as a proof that He really died?

LITERATURE: Bavinck, *Geref Dogm.* III, pp. 455-469; Kuyper, *Dict. Dogm., De Christo* II, pp. 59-108; ibid., *De Vleeschwording des Woords;* Hodge, *Syst. Theol.* II, pp. 612-625; Shedd, *Dogm. Theol.,* pp. 330-348; McPherson, *Chr. Dogm.,* pp. 321-326; Litton, *Introd to Dogm. Theol.,* pp. 175-191; Pieper, *Christl. Dogm.* II, pp. 358-378; Schmid, *Doct. Theol. of the Ev. Luth. Church,* pp. 383-406; Valentine, *Chr. Theol.* II, pp. 88-95; Heppe, *Dogm. der ev.-ref.* Kirche, pp. 351-356; Ebrard, *Christl. Dogm.* II, pp. 189-226; Mastricht, *Godgeleerdheit,* II, pp. 601-795; *Synopsis Purioris,* pp. 262-272; Turretin, *Opera, Locus* XIII, Q. IX-XVI; Machen, *The Virgin Birth of Christ;* Ort, *The Virgin Birth of Christ;* Sweet, *The Birth and Infancy of Jesus Christ;* Cooke, *Did Paul Know the Virgin Birth?* Knowling, *The Virgin Birth;* Barth, *Credo,* pp. 62-94; Brunner, *The Mediator,* pp. 303-376.

II. The State of Exaltation

A. General Remarks on the State of Exaltation.

1. THE SUBJECT AND NATURE OF THE EXALTATION. As already indicated in the preceding, there is a difference of opinion between Lutheran and Reformed theology on the subject of the states of Christ. The former deny that the Logos, and assert that the human nature of Christ, is the subject of the states of humiliation and exaltation. Hence they exclude the incarnation from the humiliation of Christ, and maintain that the state of humiliation consists in this, "that Christ for a time renounced (truly and really, yet freely) the plenary exercise of the divine majesty, which His human nature had acquired in the personal union, and, as a lowly man, endured what was far beneath the divine majesty (that He might suffer and die for the love of the world)."[1] They hold that the state of exaltation became manifest first of all to the *lower* world in the descent into hades, and further to *this* world in the resurrection and ascension, reaching its completion in the session at the right hand of God. The exaltation, then, consists in this that the human nature assumed the plenary exercise of the divine attributes that were communicated to it at the incarnation, but were used only occasionally or secretly. Reformed theology, on the other hand, regards the person of the Mediator, that is, the God-man, as the subject of the exaltation, but stresses the fact that it was, of course, the human nature in which the exaltation took place. The divine nature is not capable of humiliation or exaltation. In the exaltation the God-man, Jesus Christ, (a) passed from under the law in its federal and penal aspects, and consequently from under the burden of the law as the condition of the covenant of works, and from under the curse of the law; (b) exchanged the penal for the righteous relation to the law, and as Mediator entered into possession of the blessings of salvation which He merited for sinners; and (c) was crowned with a corresponding honor and glory. It had to appear also in His condition that the curse of sin was lifted. His exaltation was also His glorification.

2. THE EXALTATION OF CHRIST BOTH SCRIPTURAL AND REASONABLE. There is abundant Scriptural proof for the exaltation of Christ. The gospel story clearly shows us that the humiliation of Christ was followed by His exaltation. The classical passage to prove the latter is found in Phil. 2:9-11: "Wherefore also God highly exalted Him, and gave unto Him the name which

---

1. Baier, quoted by Schmid, *Doctrinal Theology of the Evangelical Lutheran Church,* p. 383.

is above every name; that in the name of Jesus every knee should bow, of things in heaven and things on earth, and that every tongue should confess that Jesus Christ is Lord, to the glory of God the Father." But in addition to this there are several others, such as Mark 16:19; Luke 24:26; John 7:39; Acts 2:33; 5:31; Rom. 8:17,34; Eph. 1:20; 4:10; I Tim. 3:16; Heb. 1:3; 2:9; 10:12. There is a close connection between the two states. The state of exaltation must be regarded as the judicial result of the state of humiliation. In His capacity as Mediator Christ met the demands of the law in its federal and penal aspects, paying the penalty of sin and meriting everlasting life. Therefore His justification had to follow and He had to be put in possession of the reward. Since He was a public person and accomplished His work publicly, justice required that the exaltation should also be a public matter. The exaltation of Christ has a threefold significance. Each one of the stages was a virtual declaration of God that Christ met the demands of the law, and was therefore entitled to His reward. The first two stages also had exemplary significance, since they symbolized what will take place in the life of believers. And, finally, all four stages were destined to be instrumental in the perfect glorification of believers.

3. THE STATE OF EXALTATION IN MODERN LIBERAL THEOLOGY. Modern liberal theology, of course. knows of no state of exaltation in the life of Christ. Not only has it discarded the legal idea of the states of Christ altogether, but it has also ruled out all the supernatural in the life of the Saviour. Rauschenbusch closes his *Theology for the Social Gospel* with a discussion of the death of Christ. Macintosh says that "the difficulties in the way of accepting the ordinary traditional notion of the 'resurrection' of Jesus, as a reanimation of the dead body, its miraculous transformation and final ascension to 'heaven,' are, to the scientific habit of thought, practically insuperable. . . . An undischarged burden of proof still rests upon those who maintain that it (the body of Christ) did not suffer disintegration, like the bodies of all others who have died."[1] Beckwith admits that the Bible, and particularly Paul, speaks of the exaltation of Christ, but says: "If we translate the Apostle's notion of exaltation into its modern equivalent, we shall find him saying that Christ is superior to all the forces of the universe and to all known orders of rational beings, even the highest, saving only the Father."[2] And George Burman Foster frankly declares: "According to orthodoxy, the Son of God laid aside his divine glory and then took it up again; he alienated from himself certain divine qualities, and then integrated them again. What is meant is at bottom good, namely, that the great and merciful God serves us, and is not too good for our daily human food. Perhaps the form of the orthodox doctrine was necessary when the doctrine was excogitated, but that terrible being, the modern man, cannot do anything with it."[3]

---

1. *Theology as an Empirical Science*, pp. 77,78.
2. *Realities of Christian Theology*, p. 138.
3. *Christianity in Its Modern Expression*, p. 144.

B. The Stages of the State of Exaltation.

Reformed theology distinguishes four stages in the exaltation of Christ.

1. THE RESURRECTION.

a. *The nature of the resurrection.* The resurrection of Christ did not consist in the mere fact that He came to life again, and that body and soul were re-united. If this were all that it involved, He could not be called "the first-fruits of them that slept," I Cor. 15:20, nor "the firstborn of the dead," Col. 1:18; Rev. 1:5, since others were restored to life before Him. It consisted rather in this that in Him human nature, both body and soul, was restored to its pristine strength and perfection and even raised to a higher level, while body and soul were re-united in a living organism. From the analogy of the change which, according to Scripture, takes place in the body of believers in the general resurrection, we may gather something as to the transformation that must have occurred in Christ. Paul tells us in I Cor. 15:42-44 that the future body of believers will be incorruptible, that is, incapable of decay; glorious, which means resplendent with heavenly brightness; powerful, that is, instinct with energy and perhaps with new faculties; and spiritual, which does not mean immaterial or ethereal, but adapted to the spirit, a perfect instrument of the spirit. From the Gospel story we learn that the body of Jesus had undergone a remarkable change, so that He was not easily recognized and could suddenly appear and disappear in a surprising manner, Luke 24:31,36; John 20:13,19; 21:7; but that it was nevertheless a material and very real body, Luke 24:39. This does not conflict with I Cor. 15:50, for "flesh and blood" is a description of human nature in its present material, mortal, and corruptible state. But the change that takes place in believers is not only bodily but also spiritual. Similarly, there was not only a physical but also a psychical change in Christ. We cannot say that any religious or ethical change took place in Him; but He was endowed with new qualities perfectly adjusted to His future heavenly environment. Through the resurrection He became the life-giving Spirit, I Cor. 15:45. The resurrection of Christ had a threefold significance: (1) It constituted a declaration of the Father that the last enemy had been vanquished, the penalty paid, and the condition on which life was promised, met. (2) It symbolized what was destined to happen to the members of Christ's mystical body in their justification, spiritual birth, and future blessed resurrection, Rom. 6:4,5,9; 8:11; I Cor. 6:14; 15:20-22; II Cor. 4:10,11,14; Col. 2:12; I Thess. 4:14. (3) It is also connected instrumentally with their justification, regeneration, and final resurrection, Rom. 4:25; 5:10; Eph. 1:20; Phil. 3:10; I Pet. 1:3.

b. *The Author of the resurrection.* In distinction from others who were raised from the dead, Christ arose through His own power. He spoke of Himself as the resurrection and the life, John 11:25, declared that He had the power to lay down His life, and to take it up again, John 10:18, and even predicted that He would rebuild the temple of His body, John 2:19-21. But the resurrection was not a work of Christ alone; it is frequently ascribed to the power of God in general, Acts 2:24,32; 3:26; 5:30; I Cor. 6:14; Eph. 1:20, or, more particularly, to the Father, Rom. 6:4; Gal. 1:1; I Pet. 1:3. And if the resurrection of Christ can be called a work of God, then it follows that the Holy Spirit was also operative in it, for all the *opera ad extra* are works of the triune God. Moreover, Rom. 8:11 also implies this.

c. *Objection to the doctrine of the resurrection.* One great objection is urged against the doctrine of a physical resurrection, namely, that after death the body disintegrates, and the various particles of which it is composed enter into the composition of other bodies, vegetable, animal, and human. Hence it is impossible to restore these particles to all the bodies of which, in the course of time, they formed a part. Macintosh asks, "What became of the atoms of carbon, oxygen, nitrogen, hydrogen and other elements which composed the earthly body of Jesus?"[1] Now we admit that the resurrection defies explanation. It is a miracle. But at the same time we should bear in mind that the identity of a resurrection body with the body that descended into the grave does not require that it be composed of exactly the same particles. The composition of our bodies changes right along, and yet they retain their identity. Paul in I Cor. 15 maintains the *essential* identity of the body that descends into the grave with that which is raised up, but also declares emphatically that the form changes. That which man sows in the earth passes through a process of death, and is then quickened; but in form the grain which he puts into the ground is not the same as that which he reaps in due time. God gives to each seed a body of its own. So it is also in the resurrection of the dead. It may be that there is some nucleus, some germ, that constitutes the essence of the body and preserves its identity. The argument of the apostle in I Cor. 15:35-38 seems to imply something of the kind.[2] It should be borne in mind that the real, the fundamental objection to the resurrection, is its supernatural character. It is not lack of evidence, but the fundamental tenet that miracles cannot happen, that stands in the way of its acceptance. Even liberal scholars admit that no fact is better attested than the resurrection of Christ — though others, of course, deny this. But this makes little difference to the modern scholar. Says Dr. Rashdall: "Were the testimony fifty times stronger than it is, any hypothesis would be more possible than that." Yet at the present time many eminent scientists frankly declare that they are not in a position to say that miracles cannot happen.

d. *Attempts to explain away the fact of the resurrection.* In their denial the anti-supernaturalists always run up against the story of the resurrection in the Gospels. The story of the empty tomb and of the appearances of Jesus after the resurrection present a challenge to them, and they accept the challenge and attempt to explain these without accepting the fact of the resurrection. The following attempts are some of the most important.

---

1. *Theology as an Empirical Science*, p. 77.
2. Cf. Kuyper, *E Voto* II, pp. 248 ff.; Milligan, *The Resurrection of the Dead*, pp. 117 ff.

(1) *The falsehood theory.* This is to the effect that the disciples practiced deliberate deception by stealing the body from the grave and then declaring that the Lord had risen. The soldiers who watched the grave were instructed to circulate that story, and Celsus already urged it in explanation of the empty tomb. This theory, of course, impugns the *veracity* of the early witnesses, the apostles, the women, the five hundred brethren, and others. But it is extremely unlikely that the faint-hearted disciples would have had the courage to palm off such a falsehood upon a hostile world. It is impossible to believe that they would have persisted in suffering for such a bare falsehood. Moreover, only the facts of the resurrection can explain the indomitable courage and power which they reveal in witnessing to the resurrection of Christ. These considerations soon led to the abandonment of this view.

(2) *The swoon theory.* According to this theory, Jesus did not really die, but merely fainted, while it was thought that He had actually died. But this naturally raises several questions that are not easy to answer. How can it be explained that so many people were deceived, and that the spear thrust did not kill Jesus? How could Jesus in His exhausted condition roll away the stone from the grave and then walk from Jerusalem to Emmaus and back. How is it that the disciples did not treat Him as a sick person, but saw in Him the powerful Prince of Life? And what became of Jesus after that? With the resurrection the ascension is naturally ruled out also. Did He then return to some unknown place and live in secret the rest of His life? This theory is burdened with so many improbabilities that even Strauss ridiculed it.

(3) *The vision theory.* This was presented in two forms. (a) Some speak of purely subjective visions. In their excited state of mind the disciples dwelt so much on the Saviour and on the possibility of His return to them, that at last they actually thought they saw Him. The spark was applied by the nervous and excitable Mary Magdalene, and soon the flame was kindled and spread. This has been the favorable theory for a long time, but it too is freighted with difficulties. How could such visions arise, seeing that the disciples did not expect the resurrection? How could they appear while the disciples were about their ordinary business and not given to prayer or meditation? Could the rapture or ecstacy required for the creation of subjective visions have started as early as the third day? Would not the disciples in such visions have seen Jesus, either as surrounded with a halo of heavenly glory, or just as they had known Him and eager to renew fellowship with them? Do subjective visions ever present themselves to several persons simultaneously? How can we account for the visionary conversations? (b) In view of the extreme weakness of this theory some scholars presented a different version of it. They claim that the disciples saw real objective visions, miraculously sent by God, to persuade them to go on with the preaching of the gospel. This does really avoid some of the difficulties suggested, but encounters others. It admits the supernatural; and if this is necessary, why not grant the resurrection, which certainly explains

all the facts? Moreover, this theory asks us to believe that these divinely sent visions were such as to mislead the apostles. Does God seek to work His ends by deception?

(4) *Mythical theories.* A new mythical school has come into existence, which discards, or at least dispenses with, theories of vision and apparition, and seeks to account for the resurrection legend by the help of conceptions imported into Judaism from Babylonia and other oriental countries. This school claims not only that the mythology of the ancient oriental religions contains analogies of the resurrection story, but that this story was actually derived from pagan myths. This theory has been worked out in several forms, but is equally baseless in all its forms. It is characterized by great arbitrariness in bolstering up a connection of the gospel story with heathen myths, and has not succeeded in linking them together. Moreover, it reveals an extreme disregard of the facts as they are found in Scripture.

e. *The doctrinal bearing of the resurrection.* The question arises, Does it make any difference, whether we believe in the physical resurrection of Christ, or merely in an ideal resurrection? For modern liberal theology the resurrection of Jesus, except in the sense of a spiritual survival, has no real importance for Christian faith. Belief in the bodily resurrection is not essential, but can very well be dropped without affecting the Christian religion. Barth and Brunner are of a different opinion. They do believe in the historical fact of the resurrection, but maintain that as such it is merely a matter of history, with which the historian may deal to the best of his ability, and not as a matter of faith. The important element is that in the resurrection the divine breaks into the course of history, that in it the *incognito* of Jesus is removed and God reveals Himself. The historian cannot describe it, but the believer accepts it by faith.

Belief in the resurrection certainly has doctrinal bearings. We cannot deny the physical resurrection of Christ without impugning the veracity of the writers of Scripture, since they certainly represent it as a fact. This means that it affects our belief in the trustworthiness of Scripture. Moreover the resurrection of Christ is represented as having evidential value. It was the culminating proof that Christ was a teacher sent from God (the sign of Jonah), and that He was the very Son of God, Rom. 1:4. It was also the supreme attestation of the fact of immortality. What is still more important, the resurrection enters as a constitutive element into the very essence of the work of redemption, and therefore of the gospel. It is one of the great foundation stones of the Church of God. The atoning work of Christ, if it was to be effective at all, had to terminate, not in death, but in life. Furthermore, it was the Father's seal on the completed work of Christ, the public declaration of its acceptance. In it Christ passed from under the law. Finally, it was His entrance on a new life as the risen and *exalted Head of the Church* and the *universal Lord.* This enabled Him to apply the fruits of His redemptive work.

2. THE ASCENSION.

a. The ascension of Christ does not stand out as boldly on the pages of the Bible as the resurrection does. This is probably due to the fact that the latter rather than the former was the real turning point in the life of Jesus. In a certain sense the ascension may be called the necessary complement and completion of the resurrection. Christ's transition to the higher life of glory, begun in the resurrection, was perfected in the ascension. This does not mean that the ascension was devoid of independent significance. But though the Scripture proof for the ascension is not as abundant as that for the resurrection, it is quite sufficient. Luke gives a double account of it, Luke 24:50-53, and Acts 1:6-11. Mark refers to it in 16:19, but this passage is contested. Jesus spoke of it time and again before His death, John 6:62; 14:2,12; 16:5,10,17,28; 17:5; 20:17. Paul refers to it repeatedly, Eph. 1:20; 4:8-10; I Tim. 3:16; and the Epistle to the Hebrews calls attention to its significance, 1:3; 4:14; 9:24.

b. *The nature of the ascension.* The ascension may be described as the visible ascent of the person of the Mediator from earth to heaven, according to His human nature. It was a local transition, a going from place to place. This implies, of course, that heaven is a place as well as earth. But the ascension of Jesus was not merely a transition from one place to another; it also included a further change in the human nature of Christ. That nature now passed into the fulness of heavenly glory and was perfectly adapted to the life of heaven. Some Christian scholars of recent date consider heaven to be a condition rather than a place, and therefore do not conceive of the ascension locally.[1] They will admit that there was a momentary lifting up of Christ in the sight of the Eleven, but regard this only as a symbol of the lifting up of our humanity to a spiritual order far above our present life. The local conception, however, is favored by the following considerations: (1) Heaven is represented in Scripture as the dwelling place of created beings (angels, saints, the human nature of Christ). These are all in some way related to space; only God is above all spatial relations. Of course, the laws that apply in heavenly space may differ from those that apply in earthly space. (2) Heaven and earth are repeatedly placed in juxta-position in Scripture. From this it would seem to follow that, if the one is a place, the other must be a place also. It would be absurd to put a place and a condition in juxta-position in that way. (3) The Bible teaches us to think of heaven as a place. Several passages direct our thought *upward* to heaven and *downward* to hell, Deut. 30:12; Jos. 2:11; Ps. 139:8; Rom. 10:6,7. This would have no meaning if the two were not to be regarded as local in some sense of the word. (4) The Saviour's entrance into heaven is pictured as an ascent. The disciples see Jesus ascending until a cloud intercepts Him and hides Him from their sight. The same local coloring is present to the mind of the writer of Hebrews in 4:14.

---

1. Cf. Milligan, *The Ascension and Heavenly Priesthood of our Lord*, pp. 24 ff; Swete, *The Ascended Christ*, pp. 8 f.; Gore, *The Reconstruction of Belief*, pp. 272 f.

c. *The Lutheran conception of the ascension.* The Lutheran conception of the ascension differs from that of the Reformed. They regard it, not as a local transition, but as a change of condition, whereby the human nature of Christ passed into the full enjoyment and exercise of the divine perfections, communicated to it at the incarnation, and thus became permanently omnipresent. In connection with the idea that Christ began His session at the right hand of God at the ascension, they maintain that this right hand (which is merely a symbol of power) is everywhere. Lutherans, however, do not all think alike on the subject of the ubiquity of Christ's human nature. Some deny it altogether, and others believe that, while the ascension resulted in the ubiquity of Christ, it also included a local movement, whereby Christ withdrew His visible presence from the earth.

d. *The doctrinal significance of the ascension.* Barth says that the question may well be asked why the ascension should have a place among the main articles of the Christian faith, seeing that it is mentioned less frequently and emphatically than the resurrection, and where it is mentioned appears only as a natural transition from the resurrection to the session at God's right hand. It is exactly in this transition that he finds the real significance of the ascension. Hence he does not care to stress the ascension as a visible exaltation, a "vertical elevation in space" before the eyes of the disciples, since that is evidently not the way to the session at the right hand of God, which is no place. Just as the historical facts of the virgin birth and of the resurrection are regarded by him merely as signs of a revelation of Christ, so too the ascension as a sign and wonder is merely a "*pointer* to the revelation, that occurred in the resurrection, of Jesus Christ as the bearer of all power in heaven and earth."[1]

It may be said that the ascension had a threefold significance. (1) It clearly embodied the declaration that the sacrifice of Christ was a sacrifice to God, which as such had to be presented to Him in the inner sanctuary; that the Father regarded the Mediatorial work of Christ as sufficient and therefore admitted Him to the heavenly glory; and that the Kingdom of the Mediator was not a kingdom of the Jews, but a universal kingdom. (2) It was also exemplary in that it was prophetic of the ascension of all believers, who are already set with Christ in heavenly places, Eph. 2:6, and are destined to be with Him forever, John 17:24; and also in that it revealed the initial restoration of the original kingship of man, Heb. 2:7,9. (3) Finally, it was also instrumental in preparing a place for those who are in Christ. The Lord Himself points to the necessity of going to the Father, in order to prepare a place for His disciples, John 14:2,3.

3. THE SESSION AT THE RIGHT HAND OF GOD.

a. *Scriptural proof for the session.* When Christ stood before the high priest He predicted that He would sit at the right hand of power, Matt. 26:64. Peter makes mention of it in his sermons, Acts 2:33-36; 5:31. In both of these passages the dative *tei dexiai* may have to be taken in its more usual instrumental sense, though in the first of the two the quotation in verse 34 favors the local

1. *Credo,* p. 113.

interpretation. It is also referred to in Eph. 1:20-22; Heb. 10:12; I Pet. 3:22; Rev. 3:21; 22:1. Besides these passages there are several that speak of Christ's reigning as King, Rom. 14:9; I Cor. 15:24-28; Heb. 2:7,8.

b. *The significance of the session.* Naturally, the expression "right hand of God" is anthropomorphic and cannot be taken literally. The expression, as used in this connection, is derived from Ps. 110:1, "Sit thou at my right hand, until I make thine enemies thy footstool." To be seated at the right hand of the king might be merely a mark of honour, I Kings 2:19, but might also denote participation in government, and consequently in honour and glory. In the case of Christ it was undoubtedly an indication of the fact that the Mediator received the reigns of government over the Church and over the universe, and is made to share in the corresponding glory. This does not mean that Christ was not King of Zion up to this time, but that He is now publicly inaugurated as God-man, and as such receives the government of the Church and of heaven and earth, and enters solemnly upon the actual administration of the power committed to Him. This is entirely in agreement with what Calvin says, namely, that the statement that Christ was seated at the right hand of God is equivalent to saying "that He was installed in the government of heaven and earth, and formally admitted to possession of the administration committed to Him, and not only admitted for once, but to continue until He descend to judgment."[1] It is perfectly evident that it would be a mistake to infer from the fact that the Bible speaks of Christ's "sitting" at the right hand of God, that the life to which the risen Lord ascended is a life of rest. It is and continues to be a life of constant activity. The statements of Scripture vary. Christ is not only represented as *sitting* at the right hand of God, but also simply as *being* at His right hand, Rom. 8:34; I Pet. 3:22, or as *standing* there, Acts 7:56, and even as *walking* in the midst of the seven golden candlesticks. And it would be equally wrong to conclude from the emphasis on the royal dignity and government of Christ, naturally suggested by the idea of His sitting at the right hand of God, that the work in which He is engaged during His heavenly session is exclusively governmental, and therefore neither prophetical nor priestly.

c. *The work of Christ during His session.* It deserves emphasis that Christ, while He is seated at the right hand of God, is not merely a passive recipient of divine dominion and power, majesty and glory, but is actively engaged in the continuation of His mediatorial work.

(1) Since the Bible most frequently connects the session with the kingly rule of Christ, it is natural to think first of all of His work as King. He rules and protects His Church by His Spirit, and also governs it through His appointed officers. He has all the forces of heaven under His command: the angels are His messengers, always ready to convey His blessings to the saints, and to guard them against surrounding dangers. He exercises authority over the forces of

---

1. *Inst.,* Bk. II. XVI. 15.

nature, and over all the powers that are hostile to the Kingdom of God; and will so continue to reign until He has subjected the last enemy.

(2)   However, His work is not limited to His kingly rule. He is priest forever after the order of Melchizedek. When He cried out on the cross, "It is finished," He did not mean to say that His priestly work was at an end, but only that His active suffering had reached its termination. The Bible also connects priestly work with Christ's session at the right hand of God, Zech. 6:13; Heb. 4:14; 7:24,25; 8:1-6; 9:11-15,24-26; 10:19-22; I John 2:2. Christ is continually presenting His completed sacrifice to the Father as the sufficient basis for the bestowal of the pardoning grace of God. He is constantly applying His sacrificial work, and making it effective in the justification and sanctification of sinners. Moreover, He is ever making intercession for those that are His, pleading for their acceptance on the basis of His completed sacrifice, and for their safe-keeping in the world, and making their prayers and services acceptable to God. The Lutherans stress the fact that the intercession of Christ is *vocalis et realis*, while the Reformed emphasize the fact that it consists primarily in the presence of Christ in man's nature with the Father, and that the prayers are to be considered as the presentation of legitimate claims rather than as supplications.

(3)   Christ also continues His prophetical work through the Holy Spirit. Before He parted with His disciples He promised them the Holy Spirit, to aid their memories, teach them new truths, guide them in all the truth, and enrich them out of the fulness of Christ, John 14:26; 16:7-15. The promise was fulfilled on the day of Pentecost; and from that day on Christ, through the Spirit, was active as our great Prophet in various ways: in the inspiration of Scripture; in and through the preaching of the apostles and of the ministers of the Word; in the guidance of the Church, making it the foundation and pillar of the truth; and in making the truth effective in the hearts and lives of believers.

4.   THE PHYSICAL RETURN OF CHRIST.

a.   *The return as a stage in the exaltation.* The return of Christ is sometimes omitted from the stages of His exaltation, as if the session at the right hand of God were the culminating point. But this is not correct. The highest point is not reached until He who suffered at the hands of man, returns in the capacity of Judge. He himself pointed to this as a special mediatorial prerogative, John 5:22,27, and so did the apostles, Acts 10:42; 17:31. Besides the passages that speak of Christ's appointment as Judge, there are several that refer to His judicial activity, Matt. 19:28; 25:31-34; Luke 3:17; Rom. 2:16; 14:9; II Cor. 5:10; II Tim. 4:1; Jas. 5:9.

b.   *Scriptural terms for the return.* Several terms are used to designate the future coming of Jesus Christ. The term *"parousia"* is the most common of these. It means in the first place simply "presence," but also serves to designate *a coming preceding a presence.* The latter is the common meaning of the term, when it is used in connection with the return of Jesus Christ, Matt. 24:3, 27,37,39; I Cor. 15:23; I Thess. 2:19; 3:13; 4:15; 5:23; II Thess. 2:1; Jas. 5:

354 DOCTRINE OF THE PERSON AND THE WORK OF CHRIST

7,8; II Pet. 3:4. A second term is *"apocalupsis,"* which stresses the fact that the return will be a *revealing* of Jesus Christ. It points to the uncovering of something that was previously hidden from view, in this case, of the concealed glory and majesty of Jesus Christ, II Thess. 1:7; I Pet. 1:7,13; 4:13. A third term is *"epiphaneia,"* the glorious appearing of the Lord. The implication is that what is uncovered is something glorious, II Thess. 2:8; I Tim. 6:14; II Tim. 4:1-8; Tit. 2:13.

c. *The manner of Christ's return.* Some place the return of Christ in the past, claiming that the promise of His coming again was realized when He returned in the Holy Spirit. They refer to the promise in John 14-16, and interpret the word *"parousia"* as meaning simply "presence."[1] Now it may be said that, in a sense, Christ did return in the Holy Spirit, and as such is now present in the Church. But this was a spiritual return, while the Bible teaches us to look for a physical and visible return of Christ, Acts. 1:11. Even after Pentecost we are taught to look forward to the coming of Christ, I Cor. 1:7; 4:5; 11:26; Phil. 3:20; Col. 3:4; I Thess. 4:15-17; II Thess. 1:7-10; Tit. 2:13; Rev. 1:7.

d. *The purpose of His return.* The second coming of Jesus Christ will be for the purpose of judging the world and perfecting the salvation of His people. Men and angels, the living and the dead, will appear before Him to be judged according to the record which was kept of them, Matt. 24:30,31; 25:31.32. It will be a coming with terrible judgments upon the wicked, but also with blessings of eternal glory for the saints, Matt. 25:33-46. While He will sentence the wicked to everlasting punishment, He will publicly justify His own and lead them into the perfect joy of His eternal Kingdom. This will signalize the completed victory of Jesus Christ.

e. *Objection to the doctrine of the return.* The great objection to the doctrine of the return of Jesus Christ is of a piece with the objection to the doctrine of the physical resurrection of Christ. If there can be no physical resurrection and ascension, there can be no physical return from heaven. Both are equally impossible, and the Biblical teachings respecting them are merely crude representations of an unscientific age. Jesus evidently shared the carnal views of His day, and these colored His prophetic delineations of the future. The only return of which we can speak and for which we can hope is a return in power, in the establishment of an ethical kingdom on earth.

QUESTIONS FOR FURTHER STUDY: What historical proofs have we for the resurrection of Christ? Does I Cor. 15:8 prove that the appearances were subjective visions? What myths are supposed to have entered into the shaping of the story of the resurrection? What light do the following passages shed on the post-resurrection condition of Jesus? I Cor. 6:17; II Cor. 3:17, 18; I Tim. 3:16; Rom. 1:3, 4; Heb. 9:14; I Pet. 3:18. What is the difference between a *soma psychicon,* a *soma pneumatikon,* and a *soma tes sarkos?* Are "spirit" and "spiritual" antithetical to "body" and "bodily" in the New Testament? Does science really make it impossible to think of heaven as a place? Is it true that in Scripture the words "heaven" and "heavenly" indicate a state rather than a place? Does modern theology think of heaven only as a condition to be entered upon after death? Does its position really find

---

1. Warren, *The Parousia;* J. M. Campbell, *The Second Coming of Christ,*

support in such a passage as Eph. 2:6? Does the Old Testament contain any references to the ascension and the session at the right hand of God? What serious objections are there to the Lutheran doctrine of the ubiquity of the human nature of Christ? Does the Bible teach us to regard the return of Christ as imminent?

LITERATURE: Bavinck, *Geref. Dogm.* III, pp. 469-504; Kuyper, *Dict. Dogm., De Christo* II, pp. 109-114; *E Voto* I, pp. 469-493; II, pp. 5-69; Mastricht, *Godgeleerdheit* III, pp. 1-100; *Synopsis Purioris Theol.*, pp. 272-281; Turretin, *Opera*, Locus XIII, Q. XVII-XIX; Hodge, *Syst. Theol.* II, pp. 626-638; Schmid, *Doct. Theol. of the Ev. Luth. Church*, pp. 385, 386, 406-413; Valentine, *Chr. Theol.* II, pp. 91-95; Milligan, *The Resurrection of our Lord;* Orr, *The Resurrection of Jesus;* Gore, *The Reconstruction of Belief*, pp. 226-273; Swete, *The Ascended Christ;* Milligan, *The Ascension and Heavenly Priesthood of Our Lord;* Tait, *The Heavenly Session of Our Lord;* A. M. Berkhoff, *De Wederkomst van Christus;* Brown, *The Second Advent;* Snowden, *The Coming of the Lord;* Brunner, *The Mediator*, pp. 561-590; Barth, *Credo*, pp. 95-126.

THE OFFICES OF CHRIST

I. Introduction; The Prophetic Office

A. Introductory Remarks on the Offices in General.

1. THE IDEA OF THE OFFICES IN HISTORY. It has become customary to speak of three offices in connection with the work of Christ, namely the prophetic, the priestly, and the kingly office. While some of the early Church Fathers already speak of the different offices of Christ, Calvin was the first to recognize the importance of distinguishing the three offices of the Mediator and to call attention to it in a separate chapter of his *Institutes*.[1] Among the Lutherans Gerhard was the first to develop the doctrine of the three offices, Quenstedt regarded the threefold distinction as rather unessential and called attention to the fact that some Lutheran theologians distinguished only two offices, combining the prophetical with the priestly office. Since the days of the Reformation the distinction was quite generally adopted as one of the commonplaces of theology, though there was no general agreement as to the relative importance of the offices, nor as to their interrelation. Some placed the prophetical, others the priestly, and still others the kingly, office in the foreground. There were those who applied the idea of a chronological succession to them, and thought of Christ functioning as prophet during his public ministry on earth, as priest in his final sufferings and death on the cross, and as king now that He is seated at the right hand of God. Others, however, correctly stressed the fact that He must be conceived as functioning in His threefold capacity both in His state of humiliation and in His state of exaltation. The Socinians really recognized only two offices: Christ functioned as prophet on earth, and functions as king in heaven. While they also spoke of Christ as priest, they subsumed His priestly under His kingly work, and therefore did not recognize His earthly priesthood.

In the Lutheran Church considerable opposition appeared to the doctrine of the three offices of Christ. Ernesti gives a summary of the objections that were raised. According to him the division is a purely artificial one; the terms prophet, priest, and king are not used in Scripture in the sense implied in this division; it is impossible to discriminate the one function clearly from the other in the work of Christ; and the terms as used in Scripture are applied to Christ only in a tropical sense, and therefore should not have precise meanings affixed to them, designating particular parts of the work of Christ. In answer to this it may be said that there is little force in the criticism of the use of the terms, since they are used throughout the Old Testament as designations of those who in the

---

1. Bk. II, Chap. XV.

offices of prophet, priest, and king typified Christ. The only really significant criticism is due to the fact that in Christ the three offices are united in one person. The result is that we cannot sharply discriminate between the different functions in the official work of Christ. The mediatorial work is always a work of the entire person; not a single work can be limited to any one of the offices. Of the later Lutheran theologians Reinhard, Doederlein, Storr and Bretschneider rejected the distinction. Ritschl also objected to it, and held that the term "vocation" should take the place of the misleading word "office." He further regarded the kingly function or activity of Christ as primary, and the priestly and prophetic as secondary and subordinate, the former indicating man's relation to the world, and the latter, his relation to God. He further stressed the fact that the prophetic and priestly kingship should be asserted equally of the state of humiliation and the state of exaltation. Haering follows Ritschl in his denial of the three offices, and in his emphasis on calling. Modern theology is averse to the whole idea, partly because it dislikes the terminology of the schools, and partly because it refuses to think of Christ as an *official* character. It is so much in love with Christ as the ideal Man, the loving Helper, and the Elder Brother, so truly human, that it fears to consider Him as a formal mediatorial functionary, since this would be apt to dehumanize Him.

2. IMPORTANCE OF THE DISTINCTION. The distinction of the three offices of Christ is a valuable one and ought to be retained, in spite of the fact that its consistent application to both of the states of Christ is not always easy and has not always been equally successful. The fact that Christ was anointed to a threefold office finds its explanation in the fact that man was originally intended for this threefold office and work. As created by God, he was prophet, priest, and king, and as such was endowed with knowledge and understanding, with righteousness and holiness, and with dominion over the lower creation. Sin affected the entire life of man and manifested itself not only as ignorance, blindness, error, and untruthfulness; but also as unrighteousness, guilt, and moral pollution; and in addition to that as misery, death, and destruction. Hence it was necessary that Christ, as our Mediator, should be prophet, priest, and king. As Prophet He represents God with man; as Priest He represents man in the presence of God, and as King He exercises dominion and restores the original dominion of man. Rationalism recognizes only His prophetic office; Mysticism, only His priestly office; and Chiliasm places a one-sided emphasis on His future kingly office.

B. The Prophetic Office.

1. THE SCRIPTURAL IDEA OF A PROPHET.

a. *The terms used in Scripture.* The Old Testament uses three words to designate a prophet, namely, *nabhi*, *ro'eh*, and *chozeh*. The radical meaning of the word *nabhi* is uncertain, but it is evident from such passages as Ex. 7:1 and Deut. 18:18 that the word designates one who comes with a message from God to the people. The words *ro'eh* and *chozeh* stress the fact that the prophet is one who receives revelations from God, particularly in the form of visions. These words are used interchangeably. Other designations are "man of God", "messenger of the Lord", and "watchman". These appellatives indicate that the prophets are in the special service of the Lord, and watch for the spiritual interests of the people. In the New Testament the word *prophetes* is used, which is composed of *pro* and *phemi*. The preposition is not temporal in this case. Consequently, the word *prophemi* does not mean "to speak beforehand", but "to speak forth". The prophet is one who speaks forth from God. From these names, taken together, we gather that a prophet is one who sees things, that is, who receives revelations, who is in the service of God, particularly as a messenger, and who speaks in His name.

b. *The two elements combined in the idea.* The classical passages, Ex. 7:1 and Deut. 18:18 indicate that there are two elements in the prophetic function, the one passive, and the other active, the one receptive, and the other productive. The prophet receives divine revelations in dreams, visions, or verbal communications; and passes these on to the people, either orally, or visibly in prophetical actions, Num. 12:6-8; Isa. 6; Jer. 1:4-10; Ezek. 3:1-4,17. Of these two elements the passive is the most important, because it controls the active element. Without receiving, the prophet cannot give, and he cannot give more than he receives. But the active is also an integral element. One who receives a revelation is not yet necessarily a prophet. Think of Abimelech, Pharaoh, and Nebuchadnezzar, who all received revelations. What constitutes one a prophet, is the divine calling, the instruction, to communicate the divine revelation to others.

c. *The duty of the prophets.* It was the duty of the prophets to reveal the will of God to the people. This might be done in the form of instruction, admonition and exhortation, glorious promises, or stern rebukes. They were the ministerial monitors of the people, the interpreters of the law, especially in its moral and spiritual aspects. It was their duty to protest against mere formalism, to stress moral duty, to urge the necessity of spiritual service, and to promote the interests of truth and righteousness. If the people departed from the path of duty, they had to call them back to the law and to the testimony, and to announce the coming terror of the Lord upon the wicked. But their work was also intimately related to the promise, the gracious promises of God for the future. It was their privilege to picture the glorious things which God had in store for His people. It is also evident from Scripture that the true prophets of Israel typified the great coming prophet of the future, Deut. 18:15, cf. Acts 3:22-24, and that He was already functioning through them in the days of the Old Testament, I Pet. 1:11.

2. DISTINCTIONS APPLIED TO THE PROPHETICAL WORK OF CHRIST. Christ functions as prophet in various ways:

a. *Both before and after the incarnation.* The Socinians were mistaken in limiting the prophetical work of Christ to the time of His public ministry. He was active as prophet even in the old dispensation, as in the special revelations of the angel of the Lord, in the teachings of the prophets, in whom He acted as the spirit of revelation (I Pet. 1:11), and in the spiritual illumination of believers. He appears in Proverbs 8 as wisdom personified, teaching the children of men. And after the incarnation He carries on His prophetical work in His teachings and miracles, in the preaching of the apostles and of the ministers of the Word, and also in the illumination and instruction of believers as the indwelling Spirit. He continues His prophetical activity from heaven through the operation of the Holy Spirit. His teachings are both verbal and factual, that is, He teaches not only by verbal communications, but also by the facts of revelation, such as the incarnation, His atoning death, the resurrection, and ascension; and even during the Old Testament period by types and ceremonies, by the miracles of the history of redemption, and by the providential guidance of the people of Israel.

b. *Both immediately and mediately.* He exercised His prophetical office immediately, as the Angel of the Lord in the Old Testament period, and as the incarnate Lord by His teachings and also by His example, John 13:15; Phil. 2:5; I Pet. 2:22. And He exercised it mediately through the operation of the Holy Spirit, by means of the teachings of the Old Testament prophets, and of the New Testament apostles, and exercises it even now through the indwelling Spirit in believers, and by the agency of the ministers of the gospel. This also means that He carries on His prophetical work both objectively and externally and subjectively and internally by the Spirit, which is described as the Spirit of Christ.

3. SCRIPTURE PROOF FOR THE PROPHETIC OFFICE OF CHRIST. Scripture testifies in more than one way to the prophetical office of Christ. He is foretold as a prophet in Deut. 18:15, a passage that is applied to Christ in Acts 3:22,23. He speaks of Himself as a prophet in Luke 13:33. Moreover, He claims to bring a message from the Father, John 8:26-28; 12:49,50; 14:10,24; 15:15; 17:8,20, foretells future things, Matt. 24:3-35; Luke 19:41-44, and speaks with singular authority, Matt. 7:29. His mighty works served to authenticate His message. In view of all this it is no wonder that the people recognized Him as a prophet, Matt. 21:11,46; Luke 7:16; 24:19; John 3:2; 4:19; 6:14; 7:40; 9:17.

4. MODERN EMPHASIS ON THE PROPHETIC OFFICE OF CHRIST. It is one of the main characteristics of the liberal school, both of the older liberalism, represented by Renan, Strauss, and Keim, and of the later liberalism, represented by such men as Pfleiderer, Weinel, Wernle, Wrede, Juelicher, Harnack, Bouset, and others, that it places the chief emphasis on Jesus as a teacher. His significance as such is emphasized to the exclusion of the other aspects of His person and work. There is a rather marked difference, however, between these two branches of liberalism. According to the older liberalism Jesus derives all His significance from His teachings, but according to the later liberalism it is the unique personality of Jesus that lends weight to His teachings. This is undoubtedly a welcome advance, but the gain is not as great as it may seem. In the words of La Touche: "Indeed, its recognition of the real significance of His personality

rather than His teaching is little more than an exaltation of pedagogy by example over pedagogy by precept." Christ is after all only a great teacher. Present day Modernism is entirely under the sway of this liberal school. Even in Barthian theology there is an emphasis which might seem to bring it very much in line with modern theology. Walter Lowrie correctly says: "It is characteristic of the Barthian Theology that it thinks predominantly of the Mediator as Revealer."[1] We are told repeatedly by Barth and Brunner that the revelation *is* the reconciliation, and sometimes it seems as if they regard the incarnation as in itself already the reconciliation. Then again the reconciliation is represented as the revelation. In the recent Symposium on *Revelation* Barth says: "Jesus Christ is the revelation, because in His existence He is *the reconciliation*. ...The existence of Jesus Christ is the reconciliation, and therefore the bridging of the gulf that has opened here."[2] The cross is sometimes defined as the revelation of the absolute contradiction, the final conflict between this world and the other. Consequently Zerbe says that the death of Christ, according to Barth, is not exactly an atonement of the second person of the Godhead for the sin of the world, but "a message of God to man, indeed the final message; the fundamental negation; the judgment on all human possibility, especially the religious." But while it is true that in Barthian theology the Mediator is primarily the Revealer, this does not mean that it fails to do justice to His sacrificial and atoning work.[3] Sydney Cave even says in his *The Doctrine of of the Work of Christ:* "For Barth the cross is central in the Christian message. 'Everything shines in the light of His death, and is illuminated by it.' "[4]

1. *Our Concern with the Theology of Crisis*, p. 152.
2. pp. 55 f.
3. Cf. especially Brunner, *The Mediator, Chapters* XVII-XXI.
4. p. 244.

II. The Priestly Office

A. The Scriptural Idea of a Priest.

1. THE TERMS USED IN SCRIPTURE. The Old Testament word for priest is almost without exception *kohen*. The only exceptions are found in passages which refer to idolatrous priests, II Kings 23:5; Hos. 10:5; Zeph. 1:4, where the word *chemarim* is found. The original meaning of *kohen* is uncertain. It is not impossible that in early times it could denote a civil as well as an ecclesiastical functionary, cf. I Kings 4:5; II Sam. 8:18; 20:26. It is clear that the word always denoted someone who occupied an honorable and responsible position, and was clothed with authority over others; and that it almost without exception serves to designate an ecclesiastical officer. The New Testament word for priest is *hiereus*, which originally seems to have denoted "a mighty one," and later on "a sacred person," "a person dedicated to God."

2. THE DISTINCTION BETWEEN A PROPHET AND A PRIEST. The Bible makes a broad but important distinction between a prophet and a priest. Both receive their appointment from God, Deut. 18:18 f; Heb. 5:4. But the prophet was appointed to be God's representative with the people, to be His messenger, and to interpret His will. He was primarily a religious teacher. The priest, on the other hand, was man's representative with God. He had the special privilege of approach to God, and of speaking and acting in behalf of the people. It is true that the priests were also teachers during the old dispensation, but their teaching differed from that of the prophets. While the latter emphasized the moral and spiritual duties, responsibilities, and privileges, the former stressed the ritual observances involved in the proper approach to God.

3. THE FUNCTIONS OF THE PRIEST AS INDICATED IN SCRIPTURE. The classical passage in which the true characteristics of a priest are given and his work is partly designated, is Heb. 5:1. The following elements are indicated here: (a) the priest is taken from among men to be their representative; (b) he is appointed by God, cf. verse 4; (c) he is active in the interest of men in things that pertain to God, that is, in religious things; (d) his special work is to offer gifts and sacrifices for sins. But the work of the priest included even more than that. He also made intercession for the people (Heb. 7:25), and blessed them in the name of God, Lev. 9:22.

4. SCRIPTURAL PROOF FOR THE PRIESTLY OFFICE OF CHRIST. The Old Testament predicts and prefigures the priesthood of the coming Redeemer. There are clear references to it in Ps. 110:4 and Zech. 6:13. Moreover, the Old Testa-

ment priesthood, and particularly the high priest, clearly pre-figured a priestly Messiah. In the New Testament there is only a single book in which He is called priest, namely, the Epistle to the Hebrews, but there the name is applied to Him repeatedly, 3:1; 4:14; 5:5; 6:20; 7:26; 8:1. At the same time many other New Testament books refer to the priestly work of Christ, as we shall see in the discussion of this subject.

B. The Sacrificial Work of Christ.

The priestly work of Christ was twofold according to Scripture. His foremost task was to offer an all-sufficient sacrifice for the sin of the world. It belonged to the office of a priest that he should offer gifts and sacrifices for sin.

1. THE SACRIFICIAL IDEA IN SCRIPTURE. The sacrificial idea occupies a very important place in Scripture. Various theories have been suggested as to the origin and development of this idea, of which the following are the most important:

a. *The gift-theory*, which holds that sacrifices were originally presents to the deity, given with the intention of establishing good relations and of securing favors. This is based on an extremely low conception of God, one that is altogether out of harmony with the Scriptural representation of God. Moreover, it does not explain why the gift should always be brought in the form of a slain animal. The Bible does speak of offering gifts to God (Heb. 5:1), but only as expressions of gratitude and not for the purpose of courting the favor of God.

b. *The sacramental-communion theory*, based on the totemistic idea of reverencing an animal which was supposed to share in the divine nature. On solemn occasions such an animal would be slain to furnish a meal for man, who would thus literally eat his God and assimilate the divine qualities. There is absolutely nothing in the book of Genesis, however, to suggest such an utterly unspiritual and crassly material view. It is totally at variance with the Biblical representation as a whole. This, of course, does not mean that some pagans may not have held that view later on, but it does mean that it is entirely unwarranted to regard this as the original view.

c. *The homage-theory*, according to which sacrifices were originally expressions of homage and dependence. Man was prompted to seek closer communion with God, not by a sense of guilt, but by a feeling of dependence and a desire to render homage to God. This theory does not do justice to the facts in the case of such early sacrifices as those of Noah and Job; nor does it explain why this homage should be rendered in the form of slaying an animal.

d. *The symbol-theory*, which regards the offerings as symbols of restored communion with God. The killing of the animal took place only to secure the blood, which as a symbol of life was brought upon the altar, signifying communion of life with God (Keil). This theory certainly does not square with the facts in the case of the sacrifices of Noah and Job, nor with those in the case of

Abraham, when he placed Isaac upon the altar. Neither does it explain why in later days so much importance was attached to the killing of the animal.

e. *The piacular theory*, which regards sacrifices as being originally expiatory or atoning. On this theory the fundamental idea in the slaying of the animal was that of vicarious atonement for the sins of the offerer. In the light of Scripture this theory certainly deserves preference. The idea that, whatever other elements may have been present, such as an expression of gratitude to God, or of communion with Him, the piacular element was also present and was even the most prominent element, is favored by the following considerations: (a) The recorded effect of Noah's burnt-offerings is expiatory, Gen. 8:21. (b) The occasion for the sacrifice of Job lay in the sins of his children, Job 1:5. (c) This theory accounts for the fact that the sacrifices were regularly brought in the form of slain animals, and that they were bloody, involving the suffering and death of the victim. (d) It is fully in harmony with the fact that the sacrifices which prevailed among heathen nations generally, were certainly regarded as expiatory. (e) It is further in perfect agreement with the undoubted presence of several promises of the coming Redeemer in the pre-Mosaic period. This should be borne in mind by those who regard the piacular idea of sacrifices as too advanced for that time. (f) Finally, it also fits in well with the fact that, when the Mosaic sacrificial ritual was introduced, in which the expiatory element was certainly the most prominent, it was in no way represented as something entirely new.

Among those who believe that the piacular element was present even in the pre-Mosaic sacrifices, there is a difference of opinion as to the origin of this type of sacrifices. Some are of the opinion that God instituted them by a direct divine command, while others hold that they were brought in obedience to a natural impulse of man, coupled with reflection. The Bible does not record any special statement to the effect that God commanded man to serve Him with sacrifices in those early days. And it is not impossible that man expressed His gratitude and devotion in sacrifices, even before the fall, led by the inner promptings of his own nature. But it would seem that the *expiatory* sacrifices after the fall could originate only in a divine appointment. There is considerable force in the arguments of Dr. A. A. Hodge. Says he: "(1) It is inconceivable that either the propriety or probable utility of presenting material gifts to the invisible God, and especially of attempting to propitiate God by the slaughter of His irrational creatures, should ever have occurred to the human mind as a spontaneous suggestion. Every instinctive sentiment and every presumption of reason must, in the first instance, have appeared to exclude them. (2) On the hypothesis that God intended to save men, it is inconceivable that He should have left them without instruction upon a question so vital as that concerned in the means whereby they might approach into His presence and conciliate His favor. (3) It is characteristic of all God's self-revelations, under every dispensation, that He discovers Himself as jealous of any use by man of unauthorized methods of worship or service. He uniformly insists upon this very point of His sovereign right of dictating methods of worship and service, as well as terms of acceptance. (4) As a matter of fact, the very first recorded instance of acceptable worship in the family of Adam brings before us bleeding sacrifices, and seals them with the divine approbation. They appear in the first act of worship, Gen. 4:3,4. They are emphatically approved by God as soon as they appear."[1] The Mosaic sacrifices were clearly of divine appointment.

2. THE SACRIFICIAL WORK OF CHRIST SYMBOLIZED AND TYPIFIED. The sacrificial work of Christ was symbolized and typified in the Mosaic sacrifices. In connection with these sacrifices the following points deserve attention.

a. *Their expiatory and vicarious nature.* Various interpretations have been given of the Old Testament sacrifices: (1) that they were gifts to please God, to express gratitude to Him, or to placate His wrath; (2) that they were essentially sacrificial meals symbolizing communion of man with God; (3) that they were divinely appointed means of confessing the heinousness of sin; or (4) that, in so far as they embodied the idea of substitution, they were merely symbolic expressions of the fact that God accepts the sinner, in lieu of actual obedience, in the sacrifice which expresses his desire to obey and his longing for salvation. However, Scripture testifies to the fact that all the animal sacrifices among Israel were piacular, though this feature was not equally prominent in all of them. It was most prominent in the sin- and trespass-offerings, less prominent in the burnt-offering, and least in evidence in the peace-offerings. The presence of that element in those sacrifices appears (1) from the clear statements in Lev. 1:4; 4:29,31,35; 5:10; 16:7; 17:11; (2) from the laying on of hands which, in spite of Cave's assertion to the contrary, certainly served to symbolize the transfer of sin and guilt, Lev. 1:4; 16:21,22; (3) from the sprinkling of the blood on the altar and on the mercy-seat as a covering for sin, Lev. 16:27; and (4) from the repeatedly recorded effect of the sacrifices, namely the pardoning of the sins of the offerer, Lev. 4:26,31,35. New Testament proofs could easily be added, but these will suffice.

b. *Their typico-prophetical nature.* The Mosaic sacrifices had not only ceremonial and symbolical, but also spiritual and typical significance. They were of a prophetical character, and represented the gospel in the law. They were designed to prefigure the vicarious sufferings of Jesus Christ and His atoning death. The connection between them and Christ is already indicated in the Old Testament. In Psalm 40:6-8 the Messiah is introduced as saying: "Sacrifice and offering thou hast no delight in: Mine eyes hast thou opened; burnt-offering and sin-offering hast thou not required. Then said I, Lo, I come; in the roll of the book it is written of me; I delight to do thy will O my God, yea thy law is within my heart." In these words the Messiah Himself substitutes His own great sacrifice for those of the Old Testament. The shadows pass away when the reality, which they adumbrated, arrives, Heb. 10:5-9. In the New Testament there are

---

1. *The Atonement,* pp. 123 f.

numerous indications of the fact that the Mosaic sacrifices were typical of the more excellent sacrifice of Jesus Christ. There are clear indications, and even express statements, to the effect that the Old Testament sacrifices prefigured Christ and His work, Col. 2:17, where the apostle clearly has the whole Mosaic system in mind; Heb. 9:23,24; 10:1; 13:11,12. Several passages teach that Christ accomplished for sinners in a higher sense what the Old Testament sacrifices were said to effect for those who brought them, and that He accomplished it in a similar way, II Cor. 5:21; Gal. 3:13; I John 1:7. He is called "the Lamb of God", John 1:29, clearly in view of Isa. 53 and of the paschal lamb, "a Lamb without blemish and without spot," I Pet. 1:19, and even "our Passover" that was slain for us, I Cor. 5:7. And because the Mosaic sacrifices were typical, they naturally shed some light on the nature of the great atoning sacrifice of Jesus Christ. A great many scholars under the influence of the Graf-Wellhausen school deny the penal and substitutionary character of the Old Testament sacrifices, though some of them are willing to admit that this character was sometimes ascribed to them during the Old Testament period, though at a comparatively late date and without sufficient warrant.

c. *Their purpose.* In view of the preceding it may be said that the Old Testament sacrifices had a twofold purpose. As far as the theocratic, the covenant, relation was concerned, they were the appointed means whereby the offender could be restored to the outward place and privileges, enjoyed as a member of the theocracy, which he had forfeited by neglect and transgression. As such they accomplished their purpose irrespective of the temper and spirit in which they were brought. However, they were not in themselves efficacious to expiate moral transgressions. They were not the real sacrifice that could atone for moral guilt and remove moral pollution, but only shadows of the coming reality. Speaking of the tabernacle, the writer of Hebrews says: "Which is a figure for the time present; according to which are offered both gifts and sacrifices that cannot, *as touching the conscience*, make the worshipper perfect", Heb. 9:9. In the following chapter he points out that they could not make the offerers perfect, 10:1, and could not take away sins, 10:4. From the spiritual point of view they were typical of the vicarious sufferings and death of Christ, and obtained forgiveness and acceptance with God only as they were offered in true penitence, and with faith in God's method of salvation. They had saving significance only in so far as they fixed the attention of the Israelite on the coming Redeemer and the promised redemption.

3. SCRIPTURAL PROOF FOR THE SACRIFICIAL WORK OF CHRIST. The striking thing in the Scriptural representations of the priestly work of Christ, is that Christ appears in them as both priest and sacrifice. This is in perfect harmony with the reality as we see it in Christ. In the Old Testament the two were necessarily separate, and in so far these types were imperfect. The priestly work of Christ is most clearly represented in the Epistle to the Hebrews, where the Mediator is described as our only real, eternal, and perfect High Priest, appointed by God, who takes our place vicariously, and by His self-sacrifice obtains a real and

perfect redemption, Heb. 5:1-10; 7:1-28; 9:11-15, 24-28; 10:11-14, 19-22; 12:24, and particularly the following verses, 5:5; 7:26; 9:14. This Epistle is the only one in which Christ is called priest, but His priestly work is also clearly represented in the Epistles of Paul, Rom. 3:24,25; 5:6-8; I Cor. 5:7; 15:3; Eph. 5:2. The same representation is found in the writings of John, John 1:29; 3:14, 15; I John 2:2; 4:10. The symbol of the brazen serpent is significant. As the brazen serpent was not itself poisonous, but yet represented the embodiment of sin, so Christ, the sinless One, was made sin for us. As the lifting up of the serpent signified the removal of the plague, so the lifting up of Christ on the cross effected the removal of sin. And as a believing look at the serpent brought healing, so faith in Christ heals to the saving of the soul. The representation of Peter, I Pet. 2:24; 3:18, and of Christ Himself, Mark 10:45, corresponds with the preceding. The Lord plainly tells us that His sufferings were vicarious.

4. THE PRIESTLY WORK OF CHRIST IN MODERN THEOLOGY. As was said in the preceding chapter, the doctrine of the offices of Christ does not meet with great favor in present day theology. As a matter of fact it is generally conspicuous by its absence. It can hardly be denied that the Bible speaks of Christ as prophet, priest, and king, but it is commonly held that these terms, as applied to Christ, are only so many figurative descriptions of the different aspects of Christ's work. Christ is not regarded as a *real* prophet, a *real* priest, and a *real* king. And if any one of the aspects of the work of Christ is made to stand out as pre-eminent, it is the prophetical rather than the priestly aspect. The modern spirit is quite averse to the official Christ, and while it may be greatly in love with the self-denying and self-sacrificing Jesus, it absolutely refuses to recognize His official priesthood. In view of this it should be emphasized at the outset that, according to Scripture, Jesus is a *real* priest. As over against the priests of the Old Testament, who were merely shadows and types, He may be called *the only real priest*. He was revealed among men as the truth, that is, the reality of all the shadows of the Old Testament, and therefore also of the Old Testament priesthood. The seventh chapter of the Epistle to the Hebrews stresses the fact that His priesthood is vastly superior to that of Aaron. Consequently it is a sad mistake to assume that He is priest only in some figurative sense, in the sense in which devotees of literature and art are sometimes called priests. This is an entirely unwarranted use of the word "priest", and one that is entirely foreign to Scripture. When Jehovah swore, "Thou art a priest forever after the order of Melchizedek," He constituted the Messiah a *real* priest.

III. The Cause and Necessity of the Atonement

The great and central part of the priestly work of Christ lies in the atonement, but this, of course, is not complete without the intercession. His sacrificial work on earth calls for His service in the heavenly sanctuary. The two are complementary parts of the priestly task of the Saviour. This and the following three chapters will be devoted to a discussion of the doctrine of the atonement, which is often called "the heart of the gospel."

A. The Moving Cause of the Atonement.

This lies:

1. IN THE GOOD PLEASURE OF GOD. It is sometimes represented as if the moving cause of the atonement lay in the sympathetic love of Christ for sinners. He was so good and loving that the very idea that sinners would be hopelessly lost, was abhorrent to Him. Therefore He offered Himself as a victim in their stead, paid the penalty by laying down His life for transgressors, and thus pacified an angry God. In some cases this view prompts men to laud Christ for His supreme self-sacrifice, but at the same time, to blame God for demanding and accepting such a price. In others it simply causes men to overlook God, and to sing the praises of Christ in unqualified terms. Such a representation is certainly all wrong, and often gives the opponents of the penal substitutionary doctrine of the atonement occasion to say that this doctrine presupposes a schism in the trinitarian life of God. On this view Christ apparently receives His due, but God is robbed of His honour. According to Scripture the moving cause of the atonement is found in the good pleasure of God to save sinners by a substitutionary atonement. Christ Himself is the fruit of this good pleasure of God. It was predicted that He would come into the world to carry out the good pleasure of God, . . . "and the pleasure of the Lord shall prosper in His hand", Isa. 53:10. At His birth the angels sang, "Glory to God in the highest, and on earth peace among men in whom He is well pleased", Luke 2:14. The glorious message of John 3:16 is that "God so loved the world, that He gave His only begotten Son, that whosoever believeth on Him should not perish, but have eternal life." Paul says that Christ "gave Himself for our sins, that He might deliver us out of this present evil world, *according to the will of our God and Father*", Gal. 1:4. And again, "For it was the good pleasure of the Father that in Him should all the fulness dwell; and through Him to reconcile all things unto Himself", Col. 1:19, 20. It would not be difficult to add other similar passages.

367

2. NOT IN THE ARBITRARY WILL OF GOD. The question may be raised, whether this good pleasure of God is to be regarded as an arbitrary will, or as a will that is rooted in the very nature of God and is in harmony with the divine perfections. It has been represented by Duns Scotus as if it were merely an arbitrary expression of the absolute sovereignty of God. But it is more in harmony with Scripture to say that the good pleasure of God to save sinners by a substitutionary atonement was founded in the love and justice of God. It was the love of God that provided a way of escape for lost sinners, John 3:16. And it was the justice of God which required that this way should be of such a nature as to meet the demands of the law, in order that God "might be just, and the justifier of him which believeth in Jesus," Rom. 3:26. In Rom. 3:24,25, we find both elements combined: "Being justified freely *by His grace* through the redemption that is in Christ Jesus: whom God set forth to be a propitiation through faith in His blood, *to declare His righteousness* for the remission of sins that are past, through the forbearance of God." This representation guards against the idea of an arbitrary will.

3. IN LOVE AND JUSTICE COMBINED. It is necessary to avoid all one-sidedness in this respect. If we represent the atonement as founded only in the righteousness and justice of God, we fail to do justice to the love of God as a moving cause of the atonement, and afford a pretext to those enemies of the satisfaction theory of the atonement who like to represent it as implying that God is a vindictive being, who is concerned only about His own honour. If, on the other hand, we consider the atonement purely as an expression of the love of God, we fail to do justice to the righteousness and veracity of God, and we reduce the sufferings and the death of Christ to an unexplained enigma. The fact that God gave up His only begotten Son to bitter sufferings and to a shameful death cannot be explained on the principle of His love only.

B. Historical Views respecting the Necessity of the Atonement.

On this subject there has been considerable difference of opinion. The following positions should be distinguished:

1. THAT THE ATONEMENT WAS NOT NECESSARY. The Nominalists of the Middle Ages generally regarded it as something purely arbitrary. According to Duns Scotus it was not inherently necessary, but was determined by the arbitrary will of God. He denied the infinite value of the sufferings of Christ, and regarded them as a mere equivalent for the satisfaction due, which God was pleased to accept as such. In his estimation God might have accepted any other substitute, and might even have carried on the work of redemption without demanding any satisfaction at all. Socinus also denied the necessity of the atonement. He removed the foundation pillar for such a necessity by the denial of such justice in God as required absolutely and inexorably that sin be punished. For him the justice of God meant only His moral equity and rectitude, by virtue of which there is no depravity or iniquity in any of His works. Hugo Grotius followed his denial on the basis of the consideration that the law of God was a positive enact-

ment of His will, which He could relax and could also set aside altogether. The Arminians shared his views on this point. One and all denied that it was necessary for God to proceed in a judicial way in the manifestation of His grace, and maintained that He might have forgiven sin without demanding satisfaction. Schleiermacher and Ritschl, who had a dominating influence on modern theology, broke completely with the judicial conception of the atonement. As advocates of the mystical and moral influence theories of the atonement, they deny the fact of an objective atonement, and therefore by implication also its necessity. With them and with modern liberal theology in general atonement becomes merely at-one-ment or reconciliation effected by changing the moral condition of the sinner. Some speak of a *moral* necessity, but refuse to recognize any *legal* necessity.

2. THAT IT WAS RELATIVELY OR HYPOTHETICALLY NECESSARY. Some of the most prominent Church Fathers, such as Athanasius, Augustine, and Aquinas, denied the absolute necessity of the atonement and ascribed to it merely a hypothetical necessity. Thomas Aquinas thus differed from Anselm on the one hand, but also from Duns Scotus on the other hand. This is also the position taken by the Reformers. Principal Franks says that Luther, Zwingli, and Calvin all avoided the Anselmian doctrine of the *absolute* necessity of the atonement, and ascribed to it only a relative or hypothetical necessity, based on the sovereign free will of God, or in other words, on the divine decree. This opinion is shared by Seeberg, Mosley, Stevens, Mackintosh, Bavinck, Honig, and others. Cf. also Turretin, on *The Atonement of Christ*, p. 14. Calvin says: "It deeply concerned us, that He who was to be our Mediator should be very God and very man. If the necessity be inquired into, it was not what is commonly called simple or absolute, but flowed from the divine decree, on which the salvation of man depended. What was best for us our Merciful Father determined."[1] The atonement was necessary, therefore, because God sovereignly determined to forgive sin on no other condition. This position naturally served to exalt the sovereign free will of God in making provision for the redemption of man. Some later theologians, such as Beza, Zanchius, and Twisse, shared this opinion, but according to Voetius the first of these changed his opinion in later life.

3. THAT IT WAS ABSOLUTELY NECESSARY. In the early Church Irenaeus already taught the absolute necessity of the atonement, and this was stressed by Anselm in the Middle Ages in his *Cur Deus Homo?* Reformed theology in general rightly shows a decided preference for this view. Whatever may be true of Beza in later life, it is certain that such scholars as Voetius, Mastricht, Turretin, à Marck, and Owen, all maintain the absolute necessity of the atonement and ground it particularly in the justice of God, that moral perfection by which He necessarily maintains His holiness over against sin and the sinner and inflicts due punishment on transgressors. They regard it as the only way

---

1. *Inst.* II, 12.1.

in which God could pardon sin and at the same time satisfy His justice. This is also the position of our Confessional Standards.[1] This view is undoubtedly the most satisfying, and would seem to be most in harmony with the teachings of Scripture. The denial of it really involves a denial of the punitive justice of God as one of the inherent perfections of the divine Being, though the Reformers, of course, did not mean to deny this at all.

C. Proofs for the Necessity of the Atonement.

The proofs for the necessity of the atonement are mostly of an inferential character, but are nevertheless of considerable importance.

1. It would seem to be the clear teaching of Scripture that God, in virtue of His divine righteousness and holiness, cannot simply overlook defiance to His infinite majesty, but must needs visit sin with punishment. We are told repeatedly that He will by no means clear the guilty, Ex. 34:7; Num. 14:18; Nah. 1:3. He hates sin with a divine hatred; His whole being reacts against it, Ps. 5:4-6; Nah. 1:2; Rom. 1:18. Paul argues in Rom. 3:25,26, that it was necessary that Christ should be offered as an atoning sacrifice for sin, in order that God might be just while justifying the sinner. The important thing was that the justice of God should be maintained. This clearly points to the fact that the necessity of the atonement follows from the divine nature.

2. This leads right on to the second argument. The majesty and absolute immutability of the divine law as inherent in the very nature of God made it necessary for Him to demand satisfaction of the sinner. The transgression of the law inevitably carries with it a penalty. It is inviolable exactly because it is grounded in the very nature of God and is not, as Socinus would have it, a product of His free will, Matt. 5:18. The general principle of the law is expressed in these words: "Cursed be he that confirmeth not the words of this law to do them," Deut. 27:26. And if God wanted to save the sinner, in spite of the fact that the latter could not meet the demands of the law, He had to make provision for a vicarious satisfaction as a ground for the sinner's justification.

3. The necessity of the atonement also follows from the veracity of God, who is a God of truth and cannot lie. "God is not a man, that He should lie; neither the son of man, that He should repent; hath He said it, and shall He not do it? or hath He spoken, and shall He not make it good?" Num. 23:19. "Let God be found true," says Paul, "but every man a liar." Rom. 3:4. When He entered into the covenant of works with man, He decreed that death would be the penalty of disobedience. That principle finds expression in many other words of Scripture, such as Ezek. 18:4; Rom. 6:23. The veracity of God demanded that the penalty should be executed, and if sinners were to be saved, should be executed in the life of a substitute.

---

1. *Heidelberg Catechism*, Q. 40; and *Canons of Dort* II, Art. 1.

4. The same conclusion may be drawn from the nature of sin as guilt. If sin were merely a moral weakness, a remnant of a pre-human state, which is gradually brought into subjection to the higher nature of man, it would require no atonement. But according to Scripture sin is something far more heinous than that. Negatively, it is lawlessness, and positively, transgression of the law of God, and therefore guilt, I John 3:4; Rom. 2:25,27, and guilt makes one a debtor to the law and requires either a personal or a vicarious atonement.

5. The amazing greatness of the sacrifice which God Himself provided also implies the necessity of the atonement. God gave His only-begotten Son, to be subjected to bitter sufferings and to a shameful death. Now it is not conceivable that God would do this unnecessarily. Dr. A. A. Hodge correctly says: "This sacrifice would be most painfully irrelevant if it were anything short of absolutely necessary in relation to the end designed to be attained— that is, unless it be indeed the only possible means to the salvation of sinful man. God surely would not have made His Son a wanton sacrifice to a bare point of will."[1] It is also worthy of note that Paul argues in Gal. 3:21 that Christ would not have been sacrificed, if the law could have given life. Scripture explicitly speaks of the sufferings of Christ as necessary in Luke 24:26; Heb. 2:10; 8:3; 9:22,23.

D. Objections to the Doctrine of the Absolute Necessity of the Atonement.

There are especially two objections that are often raised to the idea that God had to demand satisfaction, in order that He might be able to pardon sin, and because there was no other way, constituted His only begotten Son a sacrifice for the sin of the world.

1. THIS MAKES GOD INFERIOR TO MAN. Man can and often does freely forgive those who wrong him, but, according to the view under consideration, God cannot forgive until He has received satisfaction. This means that He is less good and less charitable than sinful men. But they who raise this objection fail to observe that God cannot simply be compared to a private individual, who can without injustice forget about his personal grievances. He is the Judge of all the earth, and in that capacity must maintain the law and exercise strict justice. A judge may be very kind-hearted, generous, and forgiving as a private individual, but in his official capacity he must see to it that the law takes its course. Moreover, this objection utterly ignores the fact that God was not under obligation to open up a way of redemption for disobedient and fallen man, but could with perfect justice have left man to his self-chosen doom. The ground of His determination to redeem a goodly number of the human race, and in them the race itself, can only be found in His good pleasure. The love to sinners revealed in it was not awakened by any consideration of satisfaction, but was entirely sovereign and free. The Mediator Himself was a gift of the Father's love, which naturally could not be contingent on the atonement.

---

1. *The Atonement*, p. 237.

And, finally, it should not be forgotten that God Himself wrought the atonement. He had to make a tremendous sacrifice, the sacrifice of His only begotten and beloved Son, in order to save His enemies.

2. The objection just considered often goes hand in hand with another, namely, that this view of the absolute necessity of the atonement assumes a schism in the trinitarian life of God, and this is a rather monstrous idea. Says David Smith, the author of *In the Days of His Flesh*: "It (the penal theory of satisfaction) places a gulf between God and Christ, representing God as the stern Judge who insisted on the execution of justice, and Christ as the pitiful Saviour who interposed and satisfied His legal demand and appeased His righteous wrath. They are not one either in their attitudes toward sinners or in the parts which they play. God is propitiated; Christ propitiates; God inflicts the punishment, Christ suffers it; God exacts the debt, Christ pays it."[1] This objection is also based on a misunderstanding, a misunderstanding for which those Christians are, at least in part, to blame who speak and sing as if Christ, rather than the triune God, were exclusively the author of their salvation. The Bible teaches us that the triune God provided freely for the salvation of sinners. There was nothing to constrain Him. The Father made the sacrifice of His Son, and the Son willingly offered Himself. There was no schism but the most beautiful harmony between the Father and the Son. Cf. Ps. 40:6-8; Luke 1:47-50,78; Eph. 1:3-14; 2:4-10; I Pet. 1:2.

---

1. *The Atonement in the Light of History and the Modern Spirit*, p. 106.

IV. The Nature of the Atonement

The doctrine of the atonement here presented is the penal substitutionary or satisfaction doctrine, which is the doctrine clearly taught by the Word of God.

A. Statement of the Penal Substitutionary Doctrine of the Atonement.

In the discussion of this view several particulars should be stressed.

1. THE ATONEMENT IS OBJECTIVE. This means that the atonement makes its primary impression on the person to whom it is made. If a man does wrong and renders satisfaction, this satisfaction is intended to influence the person wronged and not the offending party. In the case under consideration it means that the atonement was intended to propitiate God and to reconcile Him to the sinner. This is undoubtedly the primary idea, but does not imply that we can not also speak of the sinner's being reconciled to God. Scripture does this in more than one place, Rom. 5:10; II Cor. 5:19,20. But it should be borne in mind that this is not equivalent to saying that the sinner is atoned, which would mean that God made amends or reparation, that He rendered satisfaction to the sinner. And even when we speak of the sinner as being reconciled, this must be understood as something that is secondary. The reconciled God justifies the sinner who accepts the reconciliation, and so operates in his heart by the Holy Spirit, that the sinner also lays aside his wicked alienation from God, and thus enters into the fruits of the perfect atonement of Christ. In other words, the fact that Christ reconciles God to the sinner results in a reflex action on the sinner, in virtue of which the sinner may be said to be reconciled to God. Since the objective atonement by Christ is an accomplished fact, and it is now the duty of the ambassadors of Christ to induce sinners to accept the atonement and to terminate their hostility to God, it is no wonder that the secondary and subjective side of the reconciliation is somewhat prominent in Scripture. This statement of the objective character of the atonement is placed in the foreground, because it represents the main difference between those who accept the satisfaction doctrine of the atonement and all those who prefer some other theory.

Now the question arises, whether this conception of the atonement is supported by Scripture. It would seem to find ample support there. The following particulars should be noted:

a. The fundamental character of the priesthood clearly points in that direction. While the prophets represented God among men, the priests in their sacrificial and intercessory work represented men in the presence of God, and therefore looked in a Godward direction. The writer of Hebrews expresses it thus: "For every high priest, taken from among men, is ordained for men *in things pertaining to God,*" 5:1. This statement contains the following elements: (1) The priest is taken from among men, is one of the human race, so as to be able to represent men; (2) he is appointed for men, that is, to be active in the interests of men; and (3) he is appointed to represent men in things pertaining to God, that is, in things that have a Godward direction, that look to God, that terminate on God. This is a clear indication of the fact that the work of the priest looks primarily to God. It does not exclude the idea that the priestly work also has a reflex influence on men.

b. The same truth is conveyed by the general idea of the sacrifices. These clearly have an objective reference. Even among the Gentiles they are brought, not to men, but to God. They were supposed to produce an effect on God. The Scriptural idea of sacrifice does not differ from this in its objective reference. The sacrifices of the Old Testament were brought to God primarily to atone for sin, but also as expressions of devotion and gratitude. Hence the blood had to be brought into the very presence of God. The writer of Hebrews says that the "things pertaining to God" consist in offering "both gifts and sacrifices for sin." The friends of Job were urged to bring sacrifices, "lest I," says the Lord, "deal with you after your folly." Job 42:8. The sacrifices were to be instrumental in stilling the anger of the Lord.

c. The Hebrew word *kipper* (piel) expresses the idea of atonement for sin by the covering of sin or of the sinner. The blood of the sacrifice is interposed between God and the sinner, and in view of it the wrath of God is turned aside. It has the effect, therefore, of warding off the wrath of God from the sinner. In the Septuagint and in the New Testament the terms *hilaskomai* and *hilasmos* are used in a related sense. The verb means "to render propitious," and the noun, "an appeasing" or "the means of appeasing." They are terms of an objective character. In classical Greek they are often construed with the accusative of *theos* (God), though there is no example of this in the Bible. In the New Testament they are construed with the accusative of the thing (*hamartias*), Heb. 2:17, or with *peri* and the genitive of the thing (hamartion), I John 2:2; 4:10. The first passage is best interpreted in the light of the use of the Hebrew *kipper;* the last can be interpreted similarly, or with *theon* as the object understood. There are so many passages of Scripture which speak of the wrath of God and of God as being angry with sinners, that we are perfectly justified in speaking of a propitiation of God, Rom. 1:18; Gal. 3:10; Eph. 2:3; Rom. 5:9. In Rom. 5:10 and 11:28 sinners are called "enemies of God" (*echthroi*) in a passive sense, indicating, not that they are hostile to God, but that they are the objects of God's holy displeasure. In the former passage this sense is demanded by its connection with the previous verse; and in the latter by the fact that *echtroi* is contrasted with *agapetoi,* which does not mean "*lovers* of God," but "beloved of God."

d. The words *katalasso* and *katalage* signify "to reconcile" and "reconciliation." They point to an action by which enmity is changed to friendship, and surely have, first of all, an objective signification. The offender reconciles, not himself, but the person whom he has offended. This is clearly brought out in Matt. 5:23,24: "Therefore if thou bring thy gift before the altar, and there remember that thy brother hath aught against thee; leave thy gift there before the altar, and go thy way; first be reconciled to thy brother (which in this connection can only mean, *reconcile thy brother to thyself*, which is objective), and then come and offer thy gift." The brother who had done the supposed injury is called upon to remove the grievance. He must propitiate or reconcile his brother to himself by whatsoever compensation may be required. In connection with the work of Christ the words under consideration in some instances certainly denote the effecting of a change in the judicial relation between God and the sinner by removing the judicial claim. According to II Cor. 5:19 the fact that God reconciled the world to Himself is evident from this that He does not reckon unto them their sins. This does not point to any moral change in man, but to the fact that the demands of the law are met, and that God is satisfied. In Rom. 5:10,11 the term "reconciliation" can only be understood in an objective sense, for (1) it is said to have been effected by *the death of Christ*, while subjective reconciliation is the result of the work of the Spirit; (2) it was effected while we were yet enemies. that is, were still objects of God's wrath; and (3) it is represented in verse 11 as something objective which we receive.

e. The terms *lutron* and *antilutron* are also objective terms. Christ is the *Goel*, the liberator, Acts 20:28; I Cor. 6:20; 7:23. He redeems sinners from the demands of God's retributive justice. The price is paid to God by Christ as the representative of the sinner. Clearly, the Bible abundantly justifies us in ascribing an objective character to the atonement. Moreover, strictly speaking, atonement in the proper sense of the word is always objective. There is no such thing as subjective atonement. In atonement it is always the party that has done wrong that makes amends to the one who was wronged.

2. IT IS A VICARIOUS ATONEMENT.

a. *The meaning of the term "vicarious atonement."* There is a difference between personal and vicarious atonement. We are interested particularly in the difference between the two in connection with the atonement of Christ. When man fell away from God, he as such owed God reparation. But he could atone for his sin only by suffering eternally the penalty affixed to transgression. This is what God might have required in strict justice, and would have required, if He had not been actuated by love and compassion for the sinner. As a matter of fact, however, God appointed a vicar in Jesus Christ to take man's place, and this vicar atoned for sin and obtained an eternal redemption for man. Dr. Shedd calls attention to the following points of difference in this case: (1) Personal atonement is provided by the offending party; vicarious atonement by the offended party. (2) Personal atonement would have excluded the element of mercy; vicarious atonement represents the highest form of mercy. (3) Personal atonement would have been forever in the making and hence could not result in redemption; vicarious atonement leads to reconciliation and life everlasting.

b. *The possibility of vicarious atonement.* All those who advocate a subjective theory of the atonement raise a formidable objection to the idea of vicarious atonement. They consider it unthinkable that a just God should transfer His wrath against moral offenders to a perfectly innocent party, and should treat the innocent judicially as if he were guilty. There is undoubtedly a real difficulty here, especially in view of the fact that this seems to be contrary to all human analogy. We cannot conclude from the possibility of the transfer of a pecuniary debt to that of the transfer of a penal debt. If some beneficent person offers to pay the pecuniary debt of another, the payment must be accepted, and the debtor is *ipso facto* freed from all obligation. But this is not the case when someone offers to atone vicariously for the transgression of another. To be legal, this must be expressly permitted and authorized by the lawgiver. In reference to the law this is called relaxation, and in relation to the sinner it is known as remission. The judge need not, but can permit this; yet he can permit it only under certain conditions, as (1) that the guilty party himself is not in a position to bear the penalty through to the end, so that a righteous relation results; (2) that the transfer does not encroach upon the rights and privileges of innocent third parties, nor cause them to suffer hardships and privations; (3) that the person enduring the penalty is not himself already indebted to justice, and does not owe all his services to the government; and (4) that the guilty party retains the consciousness of his guilt and of the fact that the substitute is suffering for him. In view of all this it will be understood that the transfer of penal debt is well-nigh, if not entirely, impossible among men. But in the case of Christ, which is altogether unique, because in it a situation obtained which has no parallel, all the conditions named were met. There was no injustice of any kind.

c. *Scriptural proof for the vicarious atonement of Christ.* The Bible certainly teaches that the sufferings and death of Christ were vicarious, and vicarious in the strict sense of the word that He took the place of sinners, and that their guilt was imputed, and their punishment transferred, to Him. This is not at all what Bushnell means, when he speaks of the "vicarious sacrifice" of Christ. For him it simply means that Christ bore our sins "on His feeling, became inserted into their bad lot by His sympathy as a friend, yielded up Himself and His life, even, to an effort of restoring mercy; in a word that He bore our sins in just the same sense as He bore our sicknesses."[1] The sufferings of Christ were not just the sympathetic sufferings of a friend, but the substitutionary sufferings of the Lamb of God for the sin of the world. The Scriptural proofs for this may be classified as follows:

1. *Vicarious Sacrifice*, p. 46.

(1) The Old Testament teaches us to regard the sacrifices that were brought upon the altar as vicarious. When the Israelite brought a sacrifice to the Lord, he had to lay his hand on the head of the sacrifice and confess his sin. This action symbolized the transfer of sin to the offering, and rendered it fit to atone for the sin of the offerer, Lev. 1:4. Cave and others regard this action merely as a symbol of dedication.[1] But this does not explain how the laying on of hands made the sacrifice fit to make atonement for sin. Neither is it in harmony with what we are taught respecting the significance of the laying on of hands in the case of the scape-goat in Lev. 16:20-22. After the laying on of hands death was vicariously inflicted on the sacrifice. The significance of this is clearly indicated in the classical passage that is found in Lev. 17:11: "For the life of the flesh is in the blood; and I have given it to you to make atonement for your souls: for it is the blood that maketh atonement by reason of the life." Says Dr. Vos, "The sacrificial animal in its death takes the place of the death due to the offerer. It is forfeit for forfeit." The sacrifices so brought were pre-figurations of the one great sacrifice of Jesus Christ.

(2) There are several passages in Scripture which speak of our sins as being "laid upon" Christ, and of His "bearing" sin or iniquity, Isa. 53:6,12; John 1:29; II Cor. 5:21; Gal. 3:13: Heb. 9:28; I Pet. 2:24. On the basis of Scripture we can, therefore, say that our sins are imputed to Christ. This does not mean that our sinfulness was transferred to Him — something that is in itself utterly impossible — but that the guilt of our sin was imputed to Him. Says Dr. A. A. Hodge: "Sin may be considered (1) in its formal nature as transgression of the law, I John 3:4; or (2) as a moral quality inherent in the agent (macula), Rom. 6:11-13; or (3) in respect to its legal obligation to punishment (reatus). In this last sense alone is it ever said that the sin of one is laid upon or borne by another."[2] Strictly speaking, then, the guilt of sin *as liability to punishment* was imputed to Christ; and this could be transferred, because it did not inhere in the person of the sinner, but was something objective.

(3) Finally, there are several passages in which the prepositions *peri, huper,* and *anti* are used in connection with the work of Christ for sinners. The substitutionary idea is expressed least by the first, and most by the last preposition. But even in the interpretation of *huper* and *anti* we shall have to depend largely on the context, for while the former really means "in behalf of," it may, and in some cases does, express the idea of substitution, and while the latter may mean "instead of," it does not always have that meaning. It is rather interesting to notice that, according to Deissmann, several instances have been found on the inscriptions of the use of *huper* with the meaning "as representative of."[3] We find a similar use of it in Philemon 13. In such passages as Rom. 5:6-8; 8:32; Gal. 2:20; Heb. 2:9 it probably means "instead of," though

---

1. *The Scriptural Doctrine of Sacrifice.* pp. 129 f.
2. *Outlines of Theology,* p. 408.
3. *Light From the Ancient East,* p. 153.

it can also be rendered "in behalf of"; but in Gal. 2:13; John 11:50, and II Cor. 5:15 it certainly means "instead of." Robertson says that only violence to the text can get rid of that meaning here. The preposition *anti* clearly means "instead of" in Matt. 2:22; 5:38; 20:28; Mark 10:45. According to Robertson any other meaning of the term is out of the question here. The same idea is expressed in I Tim. 2:6.

d. *Objections to the idea of a vicarious atonement.* Several objections are raised against the idea of vicarious atonement.

(1) *Substitution in penal matters is illegal.* It is generally admitted that in cases of a pecuniary debt payment by a substitute is not only permissible, but must be accepted and at once cancels all further obligation on the part of the original debtor. However, it is said that penal debt is so personal that it does not admit of any such transfer. But it is quite evident that there are other than pecuniary cases in which the law has made provision for substitution. Armour in his work on *Atonement and Law* mentions three kinds of such cases. The first is that of substitution in cases of work for the public benefit required by law, and the second, that of substitution in the case of military service required in behalf of one's country. Respecting the third he says "Even in the case of *crime*, law, as understood and administered by men in all lands, provides that the penalty may be met by a substitute, in all cases in which the penalty prescribed is such that, a substitute may meet it consistently with the obligations he is already under."[1] It is perfectly evident that the law does recognize the principle of substitution, though it may not be easy to cite instances in which innocent persons were permitted to act as substitutes for criminals and to bear the penalties imposed on these. This finds a sufficient explanation in the fact that it is usually impossible to find men who meet all the requirements stated under (b) above. But the fact that it is impossible to find men who meet these requirements, is no proof that Jesus Christ could not meet them. In fact, He could and did, and was therefore an acceptable substitute.

(2) *The innocent is made to suffer for the wicked.* It is perfectly true that, according to the penal substitutionary doctrine of the atonement Christ suffered as "the righteous for the unrighteous" (I Pet. 3:18), but this can hardly be urged as an objection to the doctrine of vicarious atonement. In the form in which it is often stated it certainly has very little force. To say that this doctrine makes the innocent suffer the consequences of the guilt of the wicked, and is therefore unacceptable, is tantamount to raising an objection against the moral government of God in general. In actual life the innocent often suffer as a result of the transgression of others. Moreover, in this form the objection would hold against all the so-called theories of the atonement, for they all represent the sufferings of Christ as being in some sense the result of the sins of mankind. Sometimes it is said that a moral agent cannot become reasonably responsible for any sin, except by doing it personally; but this is

1. p. 129,

contradicted by the facts of life. One who hires another to commit a crime is held responsible; so are all accessories to a crime.

(3) *God the Father is made guilty of injustice.* It appears that all the objections are really variations on the same theme. The third is virtually the same as the second put in a more legal form. The doctrine of vicarious atonement, it is said, involves an injustice on the part of the Father in that He simply sacrifices the Son for the sins of mankind. This objection was already raised by Abelard, but loses sight of several pertinent facts. It was not the Father but the triune God that conceived the plan of redemption. There was a solemn agreement between the three persons in the Godhead. And in this plan the Son *voluntarily* undertook to bear the penalty for sin and to satisfy the demands of the divine law. And not only that, but the sacrificial work of Christ also brought immense gain and glory to Christ as Mediator. It meant for Him a numerous seed, loving worship, and a glorious kingdom. And, finally, this objection acts as a boomerang, for it returns with vengeance on the head of all those who, like Abelard, deny the necessity of an objective atonement, for they are all agreed that the Father sent the Son into the world for bitter suffering and a shameful death which, while beneficial, *was yet unnecessary.* This would have been cruel indeed!

4. *There is no such union as would justify a vicarious atonement.* It is said that, if a vicar is to remove the guilt of an offender there must be some real union between them which would justify such a procedure. It may be admitted that there must be some antecedent union between a vicar and those whom he represents, but the idea that this must be an organic union, such as the objectors really have in mind, cannot be granted. As a matter of fact the required union should be legal rather than organic, and provision was made for such a union in the plan of redemption. In the depths of eternity the Mediator of the new covenant freely undertook to be the representative of His people, that is, of those whom the Father gave unto Him. A federal relationship was established in virtue of which He became their Surety. This is the basic and the most fundamental union between Christ and His own, and on the basis of this a mystical union was formed, ideally in the counsel of peace, to be realized in the course of history in the organic union of Christ and His Church. Therefore Christ could act as the legal representative of His own, and being mystically one with them, can also convey to them the blessings of salvation.

3. IT INCLUDES CHRIST'S ACTIVE AND PASSIVE OBEDIENCE. It is customary to distinguish between the active and passive obedience of Christ. But in discriminating between the two, it should be distinctly understood that they cannot be separated. The two accompany each other at every point in the Saviour's life. There is a constant interpenetration of the two. It was part of Christ's active obedience, that He subjected Himself voluntarily to sufferings and death. He Himself says: "No man taketh my life from me, I lay it down of myself," John 10:18. On the other hand it was also part of Christ's passive obedience, that He lived in subjection to the law. His moving about in the form of a

servant constituted an important element of His sufferings. Christ's active and passive obedience should be regarded as complementary parts of an organic whole. In discussing it, account should be taken of a threefold relation in which Christ stood to the law, namely, the natural, the federal, and the penal relation. Man proved a failure in each one of these. He did not keep the law in its natural and federal aspects, and is not now in a position to pay the penalty, in order to be restored in the favor of God. While Christ naturally entered the first relation by His incarnation, He vicariously entered only the second and third relations. And it is with these that we are particularly concerned in this connection.

a. *The active obedience of Christ.* Christ as Mediator entered the federal relation in which Adam stood in the state of integrity, in order to merit eternal life for the sinner. This constitutes the active obedience of Christ, consisting in all that Christ did to observe the law in its federal aspect, as the condition for obtaining eternal life. The active obedience of Christ was necessary to make His passive obedience acceptable with God, that is, to make it an object of God's good pleasure. It is only on account of it that God's estimate of the sufferings of Christ differs from His estimate of the sufferings of the lost. Moreover, if Christ had not rendered active obedience, the human nature of Christ itself would have fallen short of the just demands of God, and He would not have been able to atone for others. And, finally, if Christ had suffered only the penalty imposed on man, those who shared in the fruits of His work would have been left exactly where Adam was before he fell. Christ merits more for sinners than the forgiveness of sins. According to Gal. 4:4,5 they are through Christ set free from the law as the condition of life, are adopted to be sons of God, and as sons are also heirs of eternal life, Gal. 4:7. All this is conditioned primarily on the active obedience of Christ. Through Christ the righteousness of faith is substituted for the righteousness of the law, Rom. 10:3,4. Paul tells us that by the work of Christ "the righteousness of the law is fulfilled in us," Rom. 8:3,4; and that we are made "the righteousness of God in Him," II Cor. 5:21.

According to Anselm Christ's life of obedience had no redemptive significance, since He owed this to God for Himself. Only the sufferings of the Saviour constituted a claim on God and were basic to the sinner's redemption. Thinking along somewhat similar lines Piscator, the seventeenth century Arminians, Richard Watson, R. N. Davies, and other Arminian scholars deny that the active obedience of Christ has the redemptive significance which we ascribe to it. Their denial rests especially on two considerations: (1) Christ needed His active obedience for Himself as man. Being under the law, He was in duty bound to keep it for Himself. In answer to this it may be said that Christ, though possessing a human nature, was yet a divine person, and as such was not subject to the law in its federal aspect, the law as the condition of life in the covenant of works. As the last Adam, however, He took the place of the first. The first Adam was by nature under the law of God, and the keeping of it as such gave him no claim to a reward. It was only when God graciously entered into a covenant with him and promised him life in the way of obedience, that the keeping of the law was made the condition of obtaining eternal life for himself and for his descendants. And when Christ voluntarily entered the federal relationship as the last Adam, the keeping of the law naturally acquired the same significance for Him and for those whom the Father had given Him. (2) God demands, or can demand, only one of two things of the sinner: either obedience to the law, or subjection to the penalty, but not both. If the law is obeyed, the penalty cannot be inflicted; and if the penalty is borne, nothing further can be demanded. There is some confusion here, however, which results in misunderstanding. This "either . . . or" applied to the case of Adam before the fall, but ceased to apply the moment he sinned and thus entered the penal relationship of the law. God continued to demand obedience of man, but in addition to that required of him that he pay the penalty for past transgression. Meeting this double requirement was the only way of life after sin entered the world. If Christ had merely obeyed the law and had not also paid the penalty, He would not have won a title to eternal life for sinners; and if He had merely paid the penalty, without meeting the original demands of the law, He would have left man in the position of Adam before the fall, still confronted with the task of obtaining eternal life in the way of obedience. By His active obedience, however, He carried His people beyond that point and gave them a claim to everlasting life.

b. *The passive obedience of Christ.* Christ as Mediator also entered the penal relation to the law, in order to pay the penalty in our stead. His passive obedience consisted in His paying the penalty of sin by His sufferings and death, and thus discharging the debt of all His people. The sufferings of Christ, which have already been described, did not come upon Him accidentally, nor as the result of purely natural circumstances. They were judicially laid upon Him as our representative, and were therefore really penal sufferings. The redemptive value of these sufferings results from the following facts: They were borne by a divine person who, only in virtue of His deity, could bear the penalty through to the end and thus obtain freedom from it. In view of the infinite value of the person who undertook to pay the price and to bear the curse, they satisfied the justice of God essentially and intensively. They were strictly moral sufferings, because Christ took them upon Himself voluntarily, and was perfectly innocent and holy in bearing them. The passive obedience of Christ stands out prominently in such passages as the following: Isa. 53:6; Rom. 4:25; I Pet. 2:24; 3:18; I John 2:2, while His active obedience is taught in such passages at Matt. 3:15; 5:17,18; John 15:10; Gal. 4:4,5; Heb. 10:7-9, in connection with the passages which teach us that Christ is our righteousness, Rom. 10:4; II Cor. 5:21; Phil. 3:9; and that He secured for us eternal life, the adoption of sons, and an eternal inheritance, Gal. 3:13,14; 4:4,5; Eph. 1:3-12; 5:25-27. Arminians are willing to admit that Christ, by His passive obedience merited for us the forgiveness of sins, but refuse to grant that He also merited for us positive acceptance with God, the adoption of children, and everlasting life.

B. Objections to the Satisfaction or Penal Substitutionary Doctrine of the Atonement.

There are many circles in which this doctrine of the atonement is not popular. There always has been opposition to it, and in our day the opposition is particularly strong. The main objections are the following:

1. Such an atonement was entirely unnecessary. Some hold that such an atonement was entirely unnecessary, either because sin is not guilt and therefore does not call for an atonement, or because there can be no obstacle to the free forgiveness of sin in God, who is our heavenly Father and is essentially a God of love. If a man can, and often does, forgive the penitent without demanding and receiving satisfaction, God, our perfect exemplar, surely can and will do this. This is the common objection of all those who advocate a purely subjective theory of the atonement. It may be answered, however, that the Bible certainly teaches us to regard sin as guilt; and because it is guilt, it makes man subject to the wrath of God and renders him liable to divine punishment. Moreover, the idea of a universal Fatherhood of God, in virtue of which He loves all men with a redemptive love, is entirely foreign to Scripture. And if God is a Father, He is also a Judge; if He is a God of love, He is also a God of justice and holiness. There is no one attribute in God which dominates and determines the expression of all the other divine perfections. And, finally, it should not be forgotten that what man can do as a private individual, he is not always able to do when acting in the capacity of a judge.

2. Such an atonement would derogate from the character of God. Closely connected with the preceding objection is that which holds that such an atonement would derogate from the character of God: from His justice, because He punishes the innocent for the guilty; from His love, because He acts as a stern, severe, and relentless being, who demands blood to appease His wrath; and from His pardoning grace, since He demands payment before He can or will forgive. But Christ *voluntarily* took the place of sinners, so that this substitution involved no injustice on the part of God. If God had been actuated by strict justice only, and not by compassionate love and mercy as well, He would have left the sinner to perish in His sin. Moreover, it is entirely incorrect to say that, according to the satisfaction doctrine of the atonement, the love and the pardoning grace of God could not flow forth until satisfaction was rendered, because God Himself provided the ransom, and by giving His Son already gave evidence of His infinite love and pardoning grace. His love precedes even the repentance of sinners and calls this into action.

3. Such an atonement assumes an impossible transfer of wrath. It is pointed out that this doctrine of the atonement holds that God transferred His wrath against the sinner to the Mediator, which is unthinkable; and that He also transferred the punishment of the sinner to Christ, which is manifestly illegal. In answer to this it may be said, however, that the wrath of God does

not partake of the nature of personal vindictiveness, such as we witness among men, and which they would find it hard to transfer from the object of their hatred to a perfectly innocent person. It is God's holy displeasure against sin, a displeasure to which the sinner is also exposed as long as the guilt of sin is not removed. It is also quite natural that, when the guilt of sin as liability to punishment was transferred to Jesus Christ, the wrath of God against sin was similarly transferred. Moreover, it cannot be said that the transfer of the punishment to Christ was manifestly illegal, because, as a matter of fact, He identified Himself with His people. He made satisfaction as the responsible Head of a community for those who in union with Him constituted one legal corporate body. This responsible union was constituted, says Hodge, (a) by His own voluntary assumption of the legal responsibilities of His people, (b) by the recognition of His sponsorship by God, and (c) by His assumption of our nature.

4. SUCH AN ATONEMENT IS NOT TAUGHT IN THE GOSPELS. Some are of the opinion that the Bible teaches no vicarious atonement or, if the Bible does, the Gospels certainly do not. And after all, it is what Jesus taught, and not what Paul said, that counts. We need not enter upon a lengthy discussion of this matter, since we have already shown that there is abundant proof for a vicarious atonement in Scripture. It is true that it does not stand out so clearly in the teachings of the Gospels as in those of the Epistles, but this is due to the fact (to express it in the words of Crawford) "that the purpose of our Lord's personal ministry in His life and death were not so much the *full preaching* of the atonement, as the *full accomplishment* of the atonement in order to the preaching of it."[1] Yet even the Gospels contain sufficient evidence for it, Matt. 20:28; John 1:29; 3:16; 10:11; 15:13; Matt. 26:27; John 6:51.

5. SUCH A DOCTRINE IS IMMORAL AND INJURIOUS. It is also claimed that this view of the atonement is immoral and injurious in its practical tendency. It is said to undermine the authority of the moral law, and to weaken, if not destroy, the force of our obligations and inducements to personal holiness. This objection was already made to the doctrine of free grace in the days of Paul. The charge is not true, however, for this theory more than any other upholds the majesty of the law, and in no way minimizes the obligation of the redeemed sinner to render full obedience to the law. On the contrary, it offers several incentives to personal holiness, by emphasizing the exceeding sinfulness of sin, by displaying the unspeakable love of God and of Jesus Christ, and by the assurance of divine aid in the struggle of life, and of the acceptance of our imperfect services in Christ.

---

1. *The Atonement*, p. 385.

V. Divergent Theories of the Atonement

Since the atonement is clearly something objective, something that has a Godward direction, strictly speaking only those theories can come into consideration here that represent the work of Christ as intended primarily to ward off the wrath of God and divine punishment from sinners rather than to change the sinner's attitude to God from one of hostility to one of friendship. Theories that are entirely subjective and conceive of the work of Christ exclusively as bearing on the sinner's moral condition might, in strict logic, be left out of consideration altogether. They might conceivably be considered as theories of reconciliation, but can hardly be regarded as theories of atonement. Miley argues that there really can be no more than two theories of atonement. He points out that the atonement, as an objective ground for the forgiveness of sins, must answer to a necessity which will naturally determine its nature. This necessity must lie, either in the requirement of an absolute justice which must punish sin, or in the rectoral office of justice as an obligation to conserve the interests of moral government. In the first case one arrives at the satisfaction theory; in the second, at the governmental theory, which is preferred by Miley and finds great favor with the Methodists in general. Alfred Cave ascribes an objective character also to the theory of the early Arminians, in which the death of Christ is regarded as a substitute for the penalty imposed on sinners; and to the theory of McLeod Campbell, which finds the real significance of the work of Christ in His vicarious repentance. And it is undoubtedly true that both of these do contain an objective element. But in addition to these there are several purely subjective theories. Though these are not, strictly speaking, theories of atonement, yet they call for consideration, since they are considered as such in many circles. The following are the most important theories:

A. Theories of the Early Church.

There were two theories in the early Church that call for brief mention.

1. THE RANSOM-TO-SATAN THEORY. This is based on the singular notion that the death of Christ constituted a ransom paid to Satan, in order to cancel the just claims which the latter had on man. Origen, one of the chief advocates of this theory, held that Satan was deceived in the bargain, since the outcome proved that he could not stand in the presence of the holy Christ, and was not able to retain his hold on Him. This theory found favor with several of the

early Church Fathers, though they did not always state it in exactly the same form. It proved to be rather tenacious, for the echo of it was still heard in the days of Anselm. Yet it was found to be so incongruous that it gradually disappeared for lack of intelligent support. Mackintosh speaks of this theory as the *exoteric* theory of the early Church.

2. THE RECAPITULATION THEORY. Irenæus, who also expresses the idea that the death of Christ satisfied the justice of God and thus liberated man, nevertheless gave great prominence to the recapitulation theory, that is, to the idea, as Orr expresses it, "that Christ recapitulates in Himself all the stages of human life, including those which belong to our state as sinners." By His incarnation and human life He reverses the course on which Adam by his sin started humanity and thus becomes a new leaven in the life of mankind. He communicates immortality to those who are united to Him by faith and effects an ethical transformation in their lives, and by His obedience compensates for the disobedience of Adam. This, according to Mackintosh, was the *esoteric* theory of the early Church.

B. The Satisfaction Theory of Anselm (Commercial Theory).

The theory of Anselm is sometimes identified with that of the Reformers, which is also known as the satisfaction theory, but the two are not identical. Some seek to prejudice others against it by calling it "the commercial theory." Anselm stressed the absolute necessity of the atonement by grounding it in the very nature of God. According to him sin consists in the creature's withholding from God the honor which is His due. By the sin of man God was robbed of His honor, and it was necessary that this should be vindicated. This could be done in either of two ways: by punishment or by satisfaction. The mercy of God prompted Him to seek it in the way of satisfaction, and more particularly through the gift of His Son, which was the only way, since an infinite satisfaction was required. Christ rendered obedience to the law, but since this was nothing more than His duty as man, it did not constitute any merit on His part. In addition to that, however, He also suffered and died in the performance of His duty; and since He as a sinless being was under no obligation to suffer and to die, He thus brought infinite glory to God. This was a work of supererogation on the part of Christ, which merited, and also brought, a reward; but since Christ as the Son of God needed nothing for Himself, the reward was passed on to sinners in the form of the forgiveness of sins and of future blessedness for all those who live according to the commandments of the gospel. Anselm was the first to work out a rather complete doctrine of the atonement, and in many respects his theory points in the right direction. However, it is open to several points of criticism.

1. It is not consistent in its representation of the necessity of the atonement. It ostensibly does not ground this necessity in the justice of God which cannot brook sin, but in the honor of God which calls for amends or reparation. He really starts out with the principle of "private law" or custom, according to which an injured party may demand whatever satisfaction he sees fit; and

yet argues for the necessity of the atonement in a way which only holds on the standpoint of public law.

2. This theory really has no place for the idea that Christ by suffering endured the *penalty* of sin, and that His suffering was strictly vicarious. The death of Christ is merely a tribute offered voluntarily to the honor of the Father. It constitutes a supererogatory merit, compensating for the demerits of others; and this is really the Roman Catholic doctrine of penance applied to the work of Christ.

3. The scheme is also one-sided and therefore insufficient in that it bases redemption exclusively on the death of Christ, conceived as a material contribution to the honor of God, and excludes the active obedience of Christ as a contributing factor to His atoning work. The whole emphasis is on the death of Christ, and no justice is done to the redemptive significance of His life.

4. In Anselm's representation there is merely an external transfer of the merits of Christ to man. It contains no indication of the way in which the work of Christ for man is communicated to man. There is no hint of the mystical union of Christ and believers, nor of faith as accepting the righteousness of Christ. Since the whole transaction appears to be rather commercial, the theory is often called the commercial theory.

C. The Moral Influence Theory.

This theory was first advocated by Abelard in opposition to Anselm, and since his day found many ardent supporters. The fundamental idea is always the same, though it has assumed different forms at the hands of such men as Young, Maurice, Bushnell, Stevens, David Smith, and many others. The fundamental idea is that there is no principle of the divine nature which necessarily calls for satisfaction on the part of the sinner; and that the death of Christ should not be regarded as an expiation for sin. It was merely a manifestation of the love of God, suffering in and with His sinful creatures, and taking upon Himself their woes and griefs. This suffering did not serve to satisfy the divine justice, but to reveal the divine love, so as to soften human hearts and to lead them to repentance. It assures sinners that there is no obstacle on the part of God which would prevent Him from pardoning their sins. Not only can He do this without receiving satisfaction, but He is even eager to do it. The only requirement is that sinners come to Him with penitent hearts. The following objections may be urged against this theory:

1. This theory is contrary to the plain teachings of Scripture, which represents the atoning work of Christ as necessary, not primarily to reveal the love of God, but to satisfy His justice; regards the sufferings and death of Christ as propitiatory and penal; and teaches that the sinner is not susceptible to the moral influence of the sacrificial work of Christ until the righteousness of Christ has become his own by faith.

2. While it is undoubtedly true that the cross of Christ was the supreme manifestation of the love of God, it can be regarded as such only from the point of view of the penal substitutionary doctrine of the atonement, according

to which the sufferings and death of Christ were absolutely necessary for the salvation of sinners. But according to the moral influence theory they merely served the purpose of making an impression on man, which God might have done in many other ways; and therefore were not necessary. And if they were not necessary, they were indeed a cruel manifestation of God's love, — a contradiction in terms. The sufferings and death of Christ were a manifestation of God's love only, if it was the only way to save sinners.

3. This theory robs the atonement of its objective character, and thereby ceases to be a real theory of the atonement. It is at most only a one-sided theory of reconciliation. In fact, it is not even that, for subjective reconciliation is only possible on the basis of an objective reconciliation. It really confounds God's method of saving man with man's experience of being saved, by making the atonement itself to consist in its effects in the life of the believer, in union with Christ.

4. Finally, this theory fails on its own principle. It is undoubtedly true that necessary suffering, that is, suffering for some saving purpose which could not be realized in any other way, is apt to make a deep impression. But the effect of a voluntary suffering, which is entirely unnecessary and uncalled for, is quite different. As a matter of fact, it is disapproved by the Christian conscience.

D. The Example Theory.

This theory was advocated by the Socinians in the sixteenth century, in opposition to the doctrine of the Reformers, that Christ vicariously atoned for the sin of mankind. Its fundamental principle is, that there is no retributive justice in God which requires absolutely and inexorably that sin be punished. His justice does not prevent Him from pardoning whom He will without demanding any satisfaction. The death of Christ did not atone for sin, neither did it move God to pardon sin. Christ saves men by revealing to them the way of faith and obedience as the way of eternal life, by giving them an example of true obedience both in His life and in His death, and by inspiring them to lead a similar life. This view really establishes no direct connection between the death of Christ and the salvation of sinners. Yet it holds that the death of Christ may be said to expiate the sins of man in view of the fact that Christ, as a reward for His obedience unto death, received power to bestow eternal life on believers. This theory is objectionable for various reasons.

1. It is really a revival and concoction of several ancient heresies: of Pelagianism, with its denial of human depravity and its assertion of the natural ability of man to save himself; of the adoptionist doctrine, with its belief that the man Christ was adopted to be the Messianic Son of God on account of His obedience; of the Scotist doctrine of an arbitrary will in God; and of the emphasis of some of the early Church Fathers on the saving efficacy of the example of Christ. Consequently it is open to all the objections that militate against these views.

2. It is entirely un-Scriptural in its conception of Christ as a mere man of exceptional qualities; in its view of sin, in which the character of sin as guilt, so strongly emphasized by the Word of God, is entirely ignored; in its one-sided emphasis on the redemptive significance of the life of Christ; and in its representation of the death of Christ as a martyr's death, while failing to account for the unmartyrlike anguish of Christ on the cross.

3. It fails to account for the salvation of those who lived before the incarnation and of infants. If the life and sufferings of Christ merely save men by their exemplary character, the question naturally arises, how they who lived prior to the coming of Christ, and they who die in infancy can derive any benefit from them. Yet there is clear Scriptural evidence for the fact that the work of Christ was also retrospective in its efficacy, and that little children also share in the benefits of His atoning death.

4. Moreover, while it is perfectly true that Christ is also represented as an example in Scripture, He is nowhere represented as an example after which unbelieving sinners must pattern, and which will save them if they do; and yet this is the necessary assumption of the theory under consideration. The example of Christ is one which only His people can follow, and to which even they can make but a slight approach. He is our Redeemer before He can be our example.

E. The Governmental Theory.

The governmental theory was intended to be a mean between the doctrine of the atonement, as taught by the Reformers, and the Socinian view. It denies that the justice of God necessarily demands that all the requirements of the law be met. The law is merely the product of God's will, and He can alter or even abrogate it, just as He pleases. While in strict justice the sinner deserved eternal death, that sentence is not strictly executed, for believers are set free. For them the penalty is set aside, and that without strict satisfaction. Christ did indeed render a certain satisfaction, but this was only a nominal equivalent of the penalty due to man; something which God was pleased to accept as such. If the question is asked, why God did not remit the penalty outright, as He might have done, the answer is that He had to reveal in some way the inviolable nature of the law and His holy displeasure against sin, in order that He, the moral Ruler of the universe, might be able to maintain His moral government. This theory, first advocated by Grotius, was adopted by Wardlaw and several New England theologians, and is also supported in such recent works as those of Dale, A. Cave, Miley, Creighton, and others. It is open to the following objections:

1. It clearly rests upon certain false principles. According to it the law is not an expression of the essential nature of God, but only of His arbitrary will, and is therefore subject to change; and the aim of the so-called penalty is not to satisfy justice, but only to deter men from future offenses against the law.

2. While it may be said to contain a true element, namely, that the penalty inflicted on Christ is also instrumental in securing the interests of the divine government, it makes the mistake of substituting for the main purpose of the atonement one which can, in the light of Scripture, only be regarded as a subordinate purpose.

3. It gives an unworthy representation of God. He originally threatens man, in order to deter him from transgression, and does not execute the threatened sentence, but substitutes something else for it in the punishment inflicted on Christ. And now He again threatens those who do not accept Christ. But how is it possible to have any assurance that He will actually carry out His threat?

4. It is also contrary to Scripture, which certainly represents the atonement of Christ as a necessary revelation of the righteousness of God, as an execution of the penalty of the law, as a sacrifice by which God is reconciled to the sinner, and as the meritorious cause of the salvation of sinners.

5. Like the moral influence and the example theories, it also fails to explain how the Old Testament saints were saved. If the punishment inflicted on Christ was merely for the purpose of deterring men from sin, it had no retroactive significance. How then were people saved under the old dispensation; and how was the moral government of God maintained at that time?

6. Finally, this theory, too, fails on its own principle. A real execution of the penalty might make a profound impression on the sinner, and might act as a real deterrent, if man's sinning or not sinning were, even in his natural state, merely contingent on the human will, which it is not; but such an impression would hardly be made by a mere sham exhibition of justice, designed to show God's high regard for the law.

F. The Mystical Theory.

The mystical theory has this in common with the moral influence theory, that it conceives of the atonement exclusively as exercising influence on man and bringing about a change in him. At the same time it differs from the moral influence theory in that it conceives of the change wrought in man, not primarily as an ethical change in the conscious life of man, but as a deeper change in the subconscious life which is brought about in a mystical way. The basic principle of this theory is that, in the incarnation, the divine life entered into the life of humanity, in order to lift it to the plane of the divine. Christ possessed human nature with its inborn corruption and predisposition to moral evil; but through the influence of the Holy Spirit He was kept from manifesting this corruption in actual sin, gradually purified human nature, and in His death completely extirpated this original depravity and reunited that nature to God. He entered the life of mankind as a transforming leaven, and the resulting transformation constitutes His redemption. This is in effect, though with differences of detail, the theory of Schleiermacher, Edward Irving, Menken, and Stier. Even Kohlbruegge seemed inclined to accept it in a measure. It is burdened, however, with the following difficulties:

1. It takes no account of the guilt of man. According to Scripture the guilt of man must be removed, in order that he may be purified of his pollution; but the mystical theory, disregarding the guilt of sin, concerns itself only with the expulsion of the pollution of sin. It knows of no justification, and conceives of salvation as consisting in subjective sanctification.

2. It rests upon false principles, where it finds in the natural order of the universe an exhaustive expression of the will and nature of God, regards sin exclusively as a power of moral evil in the world, which involves no guilt and deserves no punishment, and looks upon punishment as a mere reaction of the law of the universe against the transgressor, and not at all as a revelation of the personal wrath of God against sin.

3. It contradicts Scripture where it makes Christ share in the pollution of sin and hereditary depravity, and deduces the necessity of His death from the sinfulness of His own nature (not all do this). By doing this, it makes it impossible to regard Him as the sinless Saviour who, just because of His sinlessness, could take the place of sinners and pay the penalty for them.

4. It has no answer to the question, how those who lived before the incarnation can share in the redemption of Jesus Christ. If Christ in some realistic way drove out the pollution of sin during the time of His sojourn on earth, and now continues to drive it out; and if the salvation of man depends on this subjective process, how then could the Old Testament saints share in this salvation?

G. The Theory of Vicarious Repentance.

This theory of McLeod Cambell is also called the theory of sympathy and identification. It proceeds on the gratuitous assumption that a perfect repentance would have availed as a sufficient atonement for sin, if man had only been capable of an adequate repentance, which he was not. Now Christ offered to God, in behalf of humanity, the requisite repentance, and by so doing fulfilled the conditions of forgiveness. His work really consisted in the vicarious confession of sin in behalf of man. The question naturally arises, how the death of Christ is related to this vicarious repentance and confession. And the answer is that Christ, by His suffering and death, entered sympathetically into the Father's condemnation of sin, brought out the heinousness of sin and condemned sin; and this was viewed by the Father as a perfect confession of our sins. This condemnation of sin is also calculated to produce in man that holiness which God demands of sinful humanity. This theory labors under the following difficulties.

1. It can readily be understood that Christ as man could enter sympathetically into our afflictions and temptations, and into the feeling of our

infirmities; but it is not at all clear how the incarnation enabled Him to enter into a fellow-feeling with us *with respect to our sins*. He was sinless, a total stranger to sin as a corrupting power in His life, and therefore could hardly identify Himself in a moral sense with sinners.

2. While it may be admitted that, according to Scripture, Christ did sympathize with the sinners whom He came to save, this sympathy is certainly not represented as being the whole or even the most important part of His redemptive work. All the emphasis is on the fact that He vicariously endured the penalties that were due to sinners and met the requirements of the law in a life of obedience. Yet this theory, while recognizing the retributive justice of God and the demerit of sin, denies the necessity and possibility of penal substitution, and asserts that the work of Christ in behalf of sinners consisted, not in His suffering for them, but in the vicarious confession of their sins.

3. The theory proceeds on erroneous principles, namely, that sin does not necessarily make men liable to punishment; that the justice and holiness of God did not, as a matter of course, call for an objective atonement; and that the only necessity for redemptive help followed from the inability of man to repent in true fashion.

4. Finally, a vicarious confession, such as this theory implies, is really a contradiction in terms. Confession is something altogether subjective, and to be valid must be personal. It is the outcome of a personal consciousness of sin, and is also personal in its effects. It is hard to see how such a vicarious repentance can release others from the obligation to repent. Moreover, this theory has no Scriptural foundation.

VI. The Purpose and the Extent of the Atonement

A. The Purpose of the Atonement.

The atonement was destined to affect the relation of God to the sinner, the state and condition of Christ as the Mediatorial author of salvation, and the state and condition of the sinner.

1. ITS EFFECT WITH REFERENCE TO GOD. It should be emphasized first of all that the atonement effected no change in the inner being of God, which is unchangeable. The only change that was brought about was a change in the relation of God to the objects of His atoning love. He was reconciled to those who were the objects of His judicial wrath. This means that His wrath was warded off by the sacrificial covering of their sin. The atonement should not be represented as the moving cause of the love of God, for it was already an expression of His love. It is often represented as if, on the satisfaction theory, God could not love the sinner until His just demands were met. But then the fact is overlooked that Christ is already the gift of God's love, John 3:16. At the same time it is perfectly true that the atonement did remove obstacles to the manifestation of God's redeeming love in the pardoning of sinners and in their sanctification, by satisfying the justice of God and the demands of the law, both in its federal and penal aspects.

2. ITS EFFECT WITH RESPECT TO CHRIST. The atonement secured a manifold reward for Christ as Mediator. He was constituted the life-giving Spirit, the inexhaustible source of all the blessings of salvation for sinners. He received:

a. All that belonged to His glorification, including His present Messianic glory. Hence He prayed, when in His high priestly prayer He by anticipation already thought of His work as completed, "And now, O Father, glorify thou me with thine own self with the glory which I had with thee before the world was," John 17:5.

b. The fulness of those gifts and graces which He imparts to His people. Thus we read in Ps. 68:18: "Thou hast ascended on high, thou hast led captivity captive; thou hast received gifts for men; yea for the rebellious also, that the Lord might dwell among them." Paul applies this to Christ in Eph. 4:8.

c. The gift of the Holy Spirit for the formation of His mystical body and the subjective application of the fruits of His atoning work. This is evident from the words of Peter on the day of Pentecost: "Therefore being by the right hand of God exalted, and having received of the Father the promise of the Holy Spirit, He hath shed forth this which ye now see and hear," Acts 2:33.

d. The ends of the earth for His possession and the world for His dominion. This was one of the promises made unto Him: "Ask of me, and I shall give thee the heathen for thine inheritance, and the uttermost parts of the earth for thy possession," Ps. 2:8. That this promise was fulfilled is quite evident from Heb. 2:6-9.

3. ITS EFFECT AS FAR AS THE SINNER IS CONCERNED.

a. The atonement not only made salvation possible for the sinner, but actually secured it. On this point Calvinists join issue with the Roman Catholics, the Lutherans, the Arminians, and all those who teach a universal atonement. These hold that the atonement of Christ merely made salvation possible, and not certain, for those for whom it was offered. But the Calvinist teaches that the atonement meritoriously secured the application of the work of redemption to those for whom it was intended and thus rendered their complete salvation certain.

b. It secured for those for whom it was made: (1) A proper judicial standing through justification. This includes the forgiveness of sin, the adoption of children, and the right to an eternal inheritance. (2) The mystical union of believers with Christ through regeneration and sanctification. This comprises the gradual mortification of the old man, and the gradual putting on of the new man created in Christ Jesus. (3) Their final bliss in communion with God through Jesus Christ, in subjective glorification, and in the enjoyment of eternal life in a new and perfect creation. All this clearly obviates the objection so often raised against the penal substitutionary doctrine of the atonement, namely, that it has no ethical bearings and offers no basis for the ethical life of the redeemed. It may even be said that it is the only doctrine of the atonement that offers a secure basis for a real ethical life, a life that is rooted in the heart through the operation of the Holy Spirit. Justification leads right on to sanctification.

B. The Extent of the Atonement.

1. THE EXACT POINT AT ISSUE. The question with which we are concerned at this point is not (a) whether the satisfaction rendered by Christ was in itself sufficient for the salvation of all men, since this is admitted by all; (b) whether the saving benefits are actually applied to every man, for the great majority of those who teach a universal atonement do not believe that all are actually saved; (c) whether the bona fide offer of salvation is made to all that hear the gospel, on the condition of repentance and faith, since the Reformed Churches do not call this in question; nor (d) whether any of the fruits of the death of Christ accrue to the benefit of the non-elect in virtue

of their close association with the people of God, since this is explicitly taught by many Reformed scholars. On the other hand, the question does relate to the design of the atonement. Did the Father in sending Christ, and did Christ in coming into the world, to make atonement for sin, *do this with the design or for the purpose of saving only the elect or all men?* That is the question, and that only is the question.

2. STATEMENT OF THE REFORMED POSITION. The Reformed position is that Christ died for the purpose of actually and certainly saving the elect, and the elect only. This is equivalent to saying that He died for the purpose of saving only those to whom He actually applies the benefits of His redemptive work. Various attempts have been made in circles that claimed to be Reformed to modify this position. The Dutch Arminians maintained that Christ died for the purpose of making salvation possible for all men without exception, though they will not all be saved. Salvation is offered to them on lower terms than it was to Adam, namely on condition of faith and evangelical obedience, a condition which they can meet in virtue of God's gift of common or sufficient grace to all men. The Calvinistic Universalists sought to mediate between the Reformed position and that of the Arminians. They distinguished a twofold decree of God: (a) A decree to send Christ into the world to save all men by His atoning death on condition of faith in Him. However, because God saw that this purpose would fail, since no one would accept Christ by faith, He followed up the first by a second decree. (b) A decree to give a certain elect number special grace, in order to engender faith in their hearts and to secure their salvation. This dubious and very unsatisfactory view was held by the school of Saumur (Cameron, Amyraldus, and Testardus), and also by such English scholars as Wardlaw, John Brown, and James Richards. Some New England theologians, such as Emmons, Taylor, Park, and Beman held a somewhat similar view. The Marrow-men of Scotland were perfectly orthodox in maintaining that Christ died for the purpose of saving only the elect, though some of them used expressions which also pointed to a more general reference of the atonement. They said that Christ did not die for all men, but that He is dead, that is, available, for all. God's giving love, which is universal, led Him to make a deed of gift and grant to all men; and this is the foundation for the universal offer of salvation. His electing love, however, which is special, results in the salvation of the elect only. The most important of the Marrow-men were Hog, Boston, and the two Erskines.

3. PROOF FOR THE DOCTRINE OF A LIMITED ATONEMENT. The following proofs may be given for the doctrine of particular atonement:

a. It may be laid down, first of all, as a general principle, that the designs of God are always surely efficacious and cannot be frustrated by the actions of man. This applies also to the purpose of saving men through the death of our Lord Jesus Christ. If it had been His intention to save all men, this purpose could not have been frustrated by the unbelief of man. It is admitted on all hands that only a limited number is saved. Consequently, they are the only ones whom God has determined to save.

b. Scripture repeatedly qualifies those for whom Christ laid down His life in such a way as to point to a very definite limitation. Those for whom He suffered and died are variously called "His sheep," John 10:11,15, "His Church," Acts 20:28; Eph. 5:25-27, "His people," Matt. 1:21, and "the elect," Rom. 8:32-35.

c. The sacrificial work of Christ and His intercessory work are simply two different aspects of His atoning work, and therefore the scope of the one can be no wider than that of the other. Now Christ very definitely limits His intercessory work, when He says: "I pray not for the world, but for those whom thou hast given me." John 17:9. Why should He limit His intercessory prayer, if He had actually paid the price for all?

d. It should also be noted that the doctrine that Christ died for the purpose of saving all men, logically leads to absolute universalism, that is, to the doctrine that all men are actually saved. It is impossible that they for whom Christ paid the price, whose guilt He removed, should be lost on account of that guilt. The Arminians cannot stop at their half-way station, but must go all the way.

e. If it be said, as some do say, that the atonement was universal, but that the application of it is particular; that He made salvation possible for all, but actually saves only a limited number, — it should be pointed out that there is an inseparable connection between the purchase and the actual bestowal of salvation. The Bible clearly teaches that the design and effect of the atoning work of Christ is not merely to make salvation possible, but to reconcile God and man, and to put men in actual possession of eternal salvation, a salvation which many fail to obtain, Matt. 18:11; Rom. 5:10; II Cor. 5:21; Gal. 1:4; 3:13; Eph. 1:7.

f. And if the assertion be made that the design of God and of Christ was evidently conditional, contingent on the faith and obedience of man, attention should be called to the fact that the Bible clearly teaches that Christ by His death purchased faith, repentance, and all the other effects of the work of the Holy Spirit, for His people. Consequently these are no conditions of which the fulfilment is simply dependent on the will of man. The atonement also secures the fulfilment of the conditions that must be met, in order to obtain salvation, Rom. 2:4; Gal. 3:13,14; Eph. 1:3,4; 2:8; Phil. 1:29; II Tim. 3:5,6.

4. OBJECTIONS TO THE DOCTRINE OF A LIMITED ATONEMENT. These may be classified as follows:

a. There are passages which teach that Christ died for the world, John 1:29; 3:16; 6:33,51; Rom. 11:12,15; II Cor. 5:19; I John 2:2. The objection based on these passages proceeds on the unwarranted assumption that the word "world" as used in them means "all the individuals that constitute the human race." If this were not so, the objection based on them would have no point. But it is perfectly evident from Scripture that the term "world" has a variety of meanings, as a mere reading of the following passages will prove conclusively, Luke 2:1; John 1:10; Acts 11:28; 19:27; 24:5; Rom. 1:8; Col. 1:6. It also appears that, when it is used of men, it does not always include all men, John 7:4; 12:19; 14:22; 18:20; Rom. 11:12,15; in some of these passages it cannot possibly denote all men. If it had that meaning in John 6:33,51, it would follow that Christ *actually gives life to all men*, that is, *saves them all*. This is more than the opponents themselves believe. In Rom. 11:12, 15 the word "world" cannot be all-inclusive, since the context clearly excludes Israel; and because on that supposition these passages too would prove more than is intended, namely, *that the fruits of the atoning work of Christ are actually applied to all*. We do find in these passages, however, an indication of the fact that the word "world" is sometimes used to indicate that the Old Testament particularism belongs to the past, and made way for New Testament universalism. The blessings of the gospel were extended to all nations, Matt. 24:14; Mark 16:16; Rom. 1:5; 10:18. This is probably the key to the interpretation of the word "world" in such passages as John 1:29; 6:33,51; II Cor. 5:19; I John 2:2. Dr. Shedd assumes that the word means "all nations" in such passages as Matt. 26:13; John 3:16; I Cor. 1:21; II Cor. 5:19; and I John 2:2; but holds that in other passages it denotes the world of believers, or the Church, John 6:33,51; Rom. 4:13; 11:12,15. Kuyper and Van Andel also assume that this is the meaning of the word in some passages.

b.   Closely related to the passages to which we referred in the preceding, are those in which it is said that Christ died for all men, Rom. 5:18; I Cor. 15:22; II Cor. 5:14; I Tim. 2:4,6; Tit. 2:11; Heb. 2:9; II Pet. 3:9. Naturally, each of these passages must be considered in the connection in which it is found. For instance, the context clearly shows that the "all" or "all men" of Rom. 5:18, and I Cor. 15:22 includes only those who are in Christ, as contrasted with all who are in Adam. If the word "all" in these passages is not interpreted in a limited sense, they would teach, not merely that Christ made salvation possible for all men, but that He actually saves all without exception. Thus the Arminian would again be forced into the camp of the absolute Universalist, where he does not want to be. A similar limitation must be applied in the interpretation of II Cor. 5:14, and Heb. 2:9, cf. verse 10. Otherwise they would prove too much, and therefore prove nothing. In all these passages the "all" are simply all those who are in Christ. In the case of Tit. 2:11, which speaks of the appearance of the grace of God, "bringing salvation to all men," the context clearly shows that "all men" really means all classes of men. If the "all" is not restricted, this passage too would teach universal salvation. The passages in I Tim. 2:4-6, Heb. 2:9; II Pet. 3:9 refer to the revealed will of God that both Jews and Gentiles should be saved, but imply nothing as to the universal intent of the atonement. Even Moses Stuart, who believes in universal atonement, admits that in these cases the word "all" cannot be taken in a universal sense.

c. A third class of passages which seem to militate against the idea of a limited atonement consists of those which are said to imply the possibility that those for whom Christ died fail to obtain salvation. Rom. 14:15 and the parallel passage in I Cor. 8:11 may be mentioned first of all. Some commentators are of the opinion that these passages do not refer to eternal destruction, but it is more likely that they do. The apostle simply wants to bring the uncharitable conduct of some of the stronger brethren in the Church into strong relief. They were likely to offend the weaker brethren, to cause them to stumble, to override their conscience, and thus to enter upon the downward path, the natural result of which, if continued, would be destruction. While Christ paid the price of His life to save such persons, they by their conduct tended to destroy them. That this destruction will not actually follow, is evident from Rom. 14:4; by the grace of God they will be upheld. We have here then, as Dr. Shedd expresses it, "a supposition, for the sake of argument, of something that does not and cannot happen," just as in I Cor. 13:1-3; Gal. 1:8. Another, somewhat similar, passage is found in II Pet. 2:1, with which Heb. 10:29 may also be classed. The most plausible explanation of these passages is that given by Smeaton, as the interpretation of Piscator and of the Dutch annotations, namely, "that these false teachers are described according to their own profession and the judgment of charity. They gave themselves out as redeemed men, and were so accounted in the judgment of the Church while they abode in her communion."[1]

d. Finally, there is an objection derived from the *bona fide* offer of salvation. We believe that God "unfeignedly," that is, sincerely or in good faith, calls all those who are living under the gospel to believe, and offers them salvation in the way of faith and repentance. Now the Arminians maintain that such an offer of salvation cannot be made by those who believe that Christ died only for the elect. This objection was already raised at the time of the Synod of Dort, but its validity was not granted. The following remarks may be made in reply: (a) The offer of salvation in the way of faith and repentance does not pretend to be a revelation of the secret counsel of God, more specifically, of His design in giving Christ as an atonement for sin. It is simply the promise of salvation to all those who accept Christ by faith. (2) This offer, in so far as it is universal, is always conditioned by faith and conversion. Moreover, it is contingent on a faith and repentance such as can only be wrought in the heart of man by the operation of the Holy Spirit. (3) The universal offer of salvation does not consist in the declaration that Christ made atonement for every man that hears the gospel, and that God really intends to save each one. It consists in (a) an exposition of the atoning work of Christ as in itself sufficient for the redemption of all men; (b) a description

---

1. *The Doctrine of the Atonement as Taught by the Apostles,* p. 447.

of the real nature of the repentance and faith that are required in coming to Christ; and (c) a declaration that each one who comes to Christ with true repentance and faith will obtain the blessings of salvation. (4) It is not the duty of the preacher to harmonize the secret counsel of God respecting the redemption of sinners with His declarative will as expressed in the universal offer of salvation. He is simply an official ambassador, whose duty it is to carry out the will of the Lord in preaching the gospel to all men indiscriminately. (5) Dr. Shedd says: "The universal offer of the benefits of Christ's atonement springs out of God's will of complacency, Ezek. 33:11.... God may properly call upon the non-elect to do a thing that God delights in, simply because He does delight in it. The divine desire is not altered by the divine decree of preterition."[1] He also quotes a very similar statement from Turretin. (6) The universal offer of salvation serves the purpose of disclosing the aversion and obstinacy of man in his opposition to the gospel, and of removing every vestige of excuse. If it were not made, sinners might say that they would gladly have accepted the gift of God, if it only had been offered to them.

5. THE WIDER BEARING OF THE ATONEMENT. The question may be raised, whether the atonement wrought by Christ for the salvation of the elect, and of the elect only, has any wider bearing. The question is often discussed in Scottish theology, whether Christ did not die, *in some other than a saving sense*, also for the non-elect. It was discussed by several of the older theologians, such as Rutherford, Brown, Durham, and Dickson, but was answered by them in the negative. "They held, indeed," says Walker, "the intrinsic sufficiency of Christ's death to save the world, or worlds; but that was altogether irrespective of Christ's purpose, or Christ's accomplishment. The phrase that Christ died sufficiently for all was not approved, because the 'for' seemed to imply some reality of actual substitution."[2] Durham denied that any mercy bestowed upon the reprobate, and enjoyed by them, could be said to be the proper fruit of, or the purchase of, Christ's death; but at the same time maintained that certain consequences of Christ's death of an advantageous kind must reach wicked men, though it is doubtful whether these can be regarded as a blessing for them. This was also the position taken by Rutherford and Gillespie. The Marrow-men of Scotland, while holding that Christ died for the purpose of saving only the elect, concluded from the universal offer of salvation that the work of Christ also had a wider bearing, and that, to use their own words, "God the Father, moved by nothing but His free love to mankind lost, hath made a deed of gift and grant unto all men of His Son Jesus Christ." According to them all sinners are legatees under Christ's testament, not indeed in the essence but *in the administration* of the covenant of grace, but the testament becomes effectual only in the case of the elect. Their position was condemned by the Church of Scotland. Several Reformed theologians hold that, though Christ suffered and died only for the purpose of

1. *Dogm. Theol.* II, p. 484.
2. *Scottish Theology and Theologians*, p. 80.

saving the elect, many benefits of the cross of Christ do actually — and that also according to the plan of God — accrue to the benefit of those who do not accept Christ by faith. They believe that the blessings of common grace also result from the atoning work of Christ.[1]

That the atoning work of Christ also had significance for the angelic world would seem to follow from Eph. 1:10, and Col. 1:20. Things on earth and things in heaven are summed up in Christ as a Head (*anakephalaiosasthai*), Eph. 1:10, and are reconciled to God through the blood of the cross, Col. 1:20. Kuyper holds that the angelic world, which lost its head when Satan fell away, is reorganized under Christ as Head. This would reconcile or bring together the angelic world and the world of humanity under a single Head. Naturally, Christ is not the Head of the angels in the organic sense in which He is the Head of the Church. Finally, the atoning work of Christ will also result in a new heaven and a new earth in which dwelleth righteousness, a fit dwellingplace for the new and glorified humanity, and in the glorious liberty in which the lower creation will also share, Rom. 8:19-22.

---

1. Cf. Witsius, *De Verbonden* II, 9.4; Turretin, *Loc.* XIV, Q. 14, Sec. 11; Cunningham, *Hist. Theol.* II, p. 332; Hodge, *The Atonement*, 358 and elsewhere; Grosheide in the *Evangelical Quarterly*, April, 1940, p. 127. Cf. also Strong, *Syst. Theol.*, p. 772.

VII. The Intercessory Work of Christ

The priestly work of Christ is not limited to the sacrificial offering of Himself on the cross. The representation is sometimes given that, while Christ was a *Priest* on earth, He is a *King* in heaven. This creates the impression that His priestly work is finished, which is by no means correct. Christ is not only an earthly but also, and especially, a heavenly High Priest. He is even while seated at the right hand of God in heavenly majesty, "a minister of the sanctuary, and of the true tabernacle, which the Lord pitched, not man." Heb. 8:2. He only began His priestly work on earth, and is completing it in heaven. In the strict sense of the word He is not reckoned among the earthly priests, who were but shadows of a coming reality, Heb. 8:4. He is the *true*, that is, the *real* Priest, serving at the *real sanctuary*, of which the tabernacle of Israel was but an imperfect shadow. At the same time He is now the Priest upon the throne, our Intercessor with the Father.

A. Scriptural Proof for the Intercessory Work of Christ.

1. THE INTERCESSORY WORK OF CHRIST SYMBOLIZED. While the sacrificial work of Christ was symbolized primarily by the priestly functions at the brazen altar and the sacrifices that were brought upon it, His intercessory work was prefigured by the daily burning of incense on the golden altar in the Holy Place. The constantly rising cloud of incense was not only a symbol of the prayers of Israel, but also a type of the high priestly prayer of our great High Priest. This symbolic action of burning incense was not dissociated from, but most closely connected with, the bringing of the sacrifices at the brazen altar. It was connected with the application of the blood of the more important sin-offerings, which was applied to the horns of the golden altar, also called the altar of incense, was sprinkled towards the veil, and on the great Day of Atonement was even brought within the Holy of Holies and sprinkled upon the mercy-seat. This manipulation of the blood symbolized the presentation of the sacrifice to God, who dwelt between the cherubim. The Holy of Holies was clearly a symbol and type of the city four-square, the heavenly Jerusalem. There is still another connection between the sacrificial work at the brazen altar and the symbolical intercession at the golden altar. The fact that the incense might be burned only on living coals taken from the altar of burnt-offering was an indication of the fact that the intercession was based on the sacrifice and would be effective in no other way. This clearly indicates that the intercessory work of Christ in heaven is based on His accomplished sacrificial work, and is acceptable only on that basis.

400

2. NEW TESTAMENT INDICATIONS OF CHRIST'S INTERCESSORY WORK. The term *parakletos* is applied to Christ. The word is found only in John 14:16, 26; 15:26; 26:7; I John 2:1. It is rendered "Comforter" wherever it is found in the Gospel of John, but "Advocate" in the single passage in which it is found in the First Epistle of John. The form is a passive, and can therefore, says Westcott, "properly mean only 'one called to the side of another,' and that with the secondary notion of counseling or aiding him."[1] He points out that the word has that meaning in classical Greek, in Philo, and also in the writings of the Rabbis. Many of the Greek Fathers, however, gave the word an active sense, rendered it "Comforter," and thus gave undue prominence to what is but a secondary application of the term, though they felt that this meaning would not fit in I John 2:1. The word, then, denotes *one who is called in for aid, an advocate, one who pleads the cause of another and also gives him wise counsel.* Naturally, the work of such an advocate may bring comfort, and therefore he can also in a secondary sense be called a comforter. Christ is explicitly called our Advocate only in I John 2:1, but by implication also in John 14:16. The promise, "And I will pray the Father, and He shall give you *another* Comforter, that He may be with you forever," clearly implied that Christ was also a *parakletos.* The Gospel of John regularly applies the term to the Holy Spirit. There are therefore two Advocates, Christ and the Holy Spirit. Their work is partly identical and partly different. When Christ was on earth, He was the Advocate of the disciples, pleading their cause against the world and serving them with wise counsel, and the Holy Spirit is now continuing that work in the Church. In so far the work is identical, but there is also a difference. Christ as our Advocate pleads the believer's cause with the Father against Satan, the accuser (Zech. 3:1; Heb. 7:25; I John 2:1; Rev. 12:10), while the Holy Spirit not only pleads the cause of believers against the world (John 16:8), but also pleads the cause of Christ with believers and serves them with wise counsel, (John 14:26; 15:26; 16:14). Briefly, we can also say that Christ pleads our cause with God, while the Holy Spirit pleads God's cause with us. Other New Testament passages which speak of the intercessory work of Christ are found in Rom. 8:24; Heb. 7:25; 9:24.

B. The Nature of Christ's Intercessory Work.

It is evident that this work of Christ may not be dissociated from His atoning sacrifice, which forms its necessary basis. It is but the continuation of the priestly work of Christ, carrying it to completion. Compared with the sacrificial work of Christ His ministry of intercession receives but little attention. Even in evangelical circles the impression is often given, though perhaps without intending it, that the work accomplished by the Saviour on earth was far more important than the services which He now renders in heaven. It seems to be little understood that in the Old Testament the daily ministration at the

---

1. *Commentary on the Gospel of John, Additional Note after Chapter XVI.*

temple culminated in the burning of incense, which symbolized the ministry of intercession; and that the annual ritual on the great Day of Atonement reached its highest point, when the high priest passed beyond the veil with the atoning blood. Neither can it be said that the ministry of intercession is sufficiently understood. This may be the cause, but may also be the result, of the widespread failure of Christians to rivet the attention on it. The prevailing idea is that the intercession of Christ consists exclusively in the prayers which He offers for His people. Now it cannot be denied that these form an important part of the intercessory work of Christ, but they are not the whole of it. The fundamental point to remember is that the ministry of intercession should not be dissociated from the atonement, since they are but two aspects of the same redemptive work of Christ, and the two may be said to merge into one. Martin finds that the two constantly appear in juxtaposition and are so closely related in Scripture, that he feels justified in making the following statement: "The essence of the Intercession *is* Atonement; and the Atonement *is* essentially an Intercession. Or, perhaps, to put the paradox more mildly: The Atonement is real, — real sacrifice and offering, and not mere passive endurance, — because it is in its very nature an active and infallible intercession; while, on the other hand, the Intercession is real intercession, — judicial, representative, and priestly intercession, and not a mere exercise of influence, — because it is essentially an Atonement or substitutionary oblation, once perfected on Calvary, now perpetually presented and undergoing perpetual acceptance in heaven."[1] Analyzing it, we find the following elements in the intercession of Christ:

1. Just as the high priest on the great Day of Atonement entered the Holy of Holies with the completed sacrifice, to present it to God, so Christ entered the heavenly Holy Place with His completed, perfect, and all-sufficient sacrifice, and offered it to the Father. And just as the high priest, on entering the Holy Place, came into the presence of God, symbolically bearing the tribes of Israel on His breast, so Christ appeared before God as the representative of His people, and thus reinstated humanity in the presence of God. It is to this fact that the writer of Hebrews refers when he says: "For Christ entered not into a holy place made with hands, like in pattern to the true; but into heaven itself, now to appear before the face of God for us," Heb. 9:24. Reformed theologians often directed attention to it that the perpetual presence of the completed sacrifice of Christ before God contains in itself an element of intercession as a constant reminder of the perfect atonement of Jesus Christ. It is something like the blood of the passover, of which the Lord said: "And the blood shall be to you for a token upon the houses where ye are: and when I see the blood, I will pass over you." Ex. 12:13.

2. There is also a judicial element in the intercession, just as there is in the atonement. Through the atonement Christ met all the just demands of the law, so that no legal charges can justly be brought against those for whom He paid the price. However, Satan the accuser is ever bent on bringing charges

---

1. *The Atonement,* p. 115.

against the elect; but Christ meets them all by pointing to His completed work. He is the Paraklete, the Advocate, for His people, answering all the charges that are brought against them. We are reminded of this not only by the name "Paraklete," but also by the words of Paul in Rom. 8:33,34: "Who shall lay anything to the charge of God's elect? It is God that justifieth; who is he that condemneth? It is Jesus Christ that died, yea rather, that was raised from the dead, who is at the right hand of God, who also maketh intercession for us." Here the judicial element is clearly present. Cf. also Zech. 3:1,2.

3. Not only does the intercessory work of Christ bear on our judicial state; it also relates to our moral condition, our gradual sanctification. When we address the Father in His name, He sanctifies our prayers. They need this, because they are often so imperfect, trivial, superficial, and even insincere, while they are addressed to One who is perfect in holiness and majesty. And besides rendering our prayers acceptable, He also sanctifies our services in the Kingdom of God. This is also necessary, because we are often conscious of the fact that they do not spring from the purest motives; and that even when they do, they are far from that perfection that would make them, in themselves, acceptable to a holy God. The blight of sin rests upon them all. Therefore Peter says: "Unto whom coming, a living stone, rejected indeed of men, but with God elect, precious, ye also as living stones are built up a spiritual house, to be a holy priesthood, to offer up spiritual sacrifices, *acceptable to God through Jesus Christ.*" Christ's ministry of intercession is also a ministry of loving care for His people. He helps them in their difficulties, their trials, and their temptations. "For we have not a high priest which cannot be touched with the feeling of our infirmities; but one that hath been in all points tempted like as we are, yet without sin: for in that He himself hath suffered, being tempted, He is able to succor them that are tempted." Heb. 4:15; Heb. 2:18.

4. And in and through it all there is, finally, also the element of prayer for the people of God. If the intercession is of a piece with the atoning work of Christ, it follows that the prayer of intercession must have reference to the things pertaining to God (Heb. 5:1), to the completion of the work of redemption. That this element is included, is quite evident from the intercessory prayer in John 17, where Christ explicitly says that He prays for the apostles and for those who through their word will believe in Him. It is a consoling thought that Christ is praying for us, even when we are negligent in our prayer life; that He is presenting to the Father those spiritual needs which were not present to our minds and which we often neglect to include in our prayers; and that He prays for our protection against the dangers of which we are not even conscious, and against the enemies which threaten us, though we do not notice it. He is praying that our faith may not cease, and that we may come out victoriously in the end.

C. The Persons for Whom and the Things for Which He Intercedes.

1. THE PERSONS FOR WHOM HE INTERCEDES. The intercessory work is, as has been said, simply the complement of His redemptive priestly work, and

is therefore equal to it in extent. Christ intercedes for *all* those for whom He has made atonement, and for those *only*. This may be inferred from the limited character of the atonement, and also from such passages as Rom. 8:34; Heb. 7:25; 9:24, in every one of which the word "us" refers to believers. Moreover, in the high priestly prayer, recorded in John 17, Jesus tells us that He prays for His immediate disciples and "for them also that believe on me through their word," John 17:9, 20. In the 9th verse He makes a very explicit statement respecting the limitation of His high priestly prayer: "I pray for them: I pray not for the world, but for those whom thou hast given me." And from the 20th verse we can learn that He does not intercede for present believers only, but for all the elect, whether they are already believers, or will believe some time in the future. The intercessor is mindful of each one of those that are given unto Him, Luke 21:32; Rev. 3:5. Lutherans distinguish between a general intercession of Christ for all men, and a special intercession for the elect only. For proof they appeal to Luke 23:34, which contains Christ's prayer for His enemies, but that prayer need not be considered as a part of the official intercessory work of Christ. Dabney believes that it was, and that the objects of this prayer were later on converted. But it is also possible that this prayer was simply a prayer such as Christ taught all his followers to pray for their enemies, a prayer to ward off an immediate and terrible punishment for the enormous crime committed. Cf. Matt. 5:44.

2. THE THINGS FOR WHICH CHRIST INTERCEDES. Christ has a great deal to pray for in His intercessory prayer. We can only give a brief indication of some of the things for which He prays. He prays that the elect who have not yet come to Him may be brought into a state of grace; that those who have already come may receive pardon for their daily sins, that is, may experience the continued application to them of the fruits of justification; that believers may be kept from the accusations and temptations of. Satan; that the saints may be progressively sanctified, John 17:17; that their intercourse with heaven may be kept up, Heb. 4:14, 16; 10:21, 22; that the services of the people of God may be accepted, I Pet. 2:5; and that they may at last enter upon their perfect inheritance in heaven, John 17:24.

D. The Characteristics of His Intercession.

There are especially three characteristics of the intercessory work of Christ, to which attention should be directed:

1. THE CONSTANCY OF HIS INTERCESSION. We need not only a Saviour who has completed an objective work for us in the past, but also one who is daily engaged in securing for His own the subjective application of the fruits of the accomplished sacrifice, Tens of thousands of people call for His attention at once, and a moment's intermission would prove fatal to their interests. Therefore He is always on the alert. He is alive to all their wants, and none of their prayers escape Him.

2. THE AUTHORITATIVE CHARACTER OF HIS INTERCESSION. It is not altogether correct to represent Him as a suppliant at the throne of God, begging favors of His Father for His people. His prayer is not the *petition* of the creature to the Creator, but the *request* of the Son to the Father. "The consciousness of His equal dignity, of His potent and prevailing intercession, speaks out in this, that as often as He asks, or declares that He will ask, anything of the Father, it is always *eroto, eroteso*, an asking, that is, as upon equal terms (John 14:16; 16:26; 17:9,15,20), never *aiteo* or *aiteso*."[1] Christ stands before the Father as an authorized intercessor, and as one who can present legal claims. He can say: "Father, I desire that they also whom thou hast given me, be with me where I am," John 17:24.

3. THE EFFICACY OF HIS INTERCESSION. The intercessory prayer of Christ is a prayer that never fails. At the grave of Lazarus the Lord expressed the assurance that the Father always hears Him, John 11:42. His intercessory prayers for His people are based on His atoning work; He has merited all that He asks, and therein lies the assurance that those prayers are effective. They will accomplish all that He desires. The people of God may derive comfort from the fact that they have such a prevailing intercessor with the Father.

---

1. Trench, *New Testament Synonyms*, p. 136.

VIII. The Kingly Office

As the Second Person in the Holy Trinity, the eternal Son, Christ naturally shares the dominion of God over all His creatures. His throne is established in the heavens and His Kingdom ruleth over all, Ps. 103:19. This kingship differs from the mediatorial kingship of Christ, which is a conferred and economical kingship, exercised by Christ, not merely in His divine nature, but as Theanthropos (the God-man). The latter is not a kingship that was Christ's by original right, but one with which He is invested. It does not pertain to a new realm, one that was not already under His control as Son of God, for such a realm can nowhere be found. It is rather, to speak in the words of Dick, His original kingship, "invested with a new form, wearing a new aspect, administered for a new end." In general we may define the mediatorial kingship of Christ as His official power to rule all things in heaven and on earth, for the glory of God, and for the execution of God's purpose of salvation. We must distinguish, however, between a *regnum gratiae* and a *regnum potentiae*.

A. The Spiritual Kingship of Christ.

1. THE NATURE OF. THIS KINGSHIP. The spiritual kingship of Christ is His royal rule over the *regnum gratiae*, that is over His people or the Church. It is a spiritual kingship, because it relates to a spiritual realm. It is the mediatorial rule as it is established in the hearts and lives of believers. Moreover, it is spiritual, because it bears directly and immediately on a spiritual end, the salvation of His people. And, finally, it is spiritual, because it is administered, not by force or external means, but by the Word and the Spirit, which is the Spirit of truth and wisdom, of justice and holiness, of grace and mercy. This kingship reveals itself in the gathering of the Church, and in its government, protection, and perfection. The Bible speaks of it in many places, such as, Ps. 2:6; 45:6,7 (cf. Heb. 1:8,9); 132:11; Isa. 9:6,7; Jer. 23:5,6; Mic. 5:2; Zech. 6:13; Luke 1:33; 19:27,38; 22:29; John 18:36,37; Acts 2:30-36, and other places. The spiritual nature of this kingship is indicated, among others, by the fact that Christ is repeatedly called the Head of the Church, Eph. 1:22; 4:15; 5:23; Col. 1:18; 2:19. This term, as applied to Christ, is in some cases practically equivalent to "King" (Head in a figurative sense, one clothed with authority), as in I Cor. 11:3; Eph. 1:22; 5:23; in other cases, however, it is used in a literal and organic sense, Eph. 4:15; Col. 1:18; 2:19, and in part also Eph. 1:22. The word is never used (except it be in I Cor. 11:3) without the implication of this organic conception. The two ideas are most intimately connected. It is just because Christ is the Head of the Church that He can rule

it as King in an organic and spiritual way. The relation between the two may be indicated as follows: (1) The headship of Christ points to the mystical union between Christ and His body, the Church, and therefore belongs to the sphere of being. His kingship, however, implies that He is clothed with authority, and belongs to the judicial sphere. (2) The headship of Christ is subservient to His kingship. The Spirit which Christ, as the Head of the Church, imparts to it, is also the means by which He exercises His royal power in and over the Church. Present day Premillenarians strongly insist that Christ is the Head of the Church, but as a rule deny that He is its King. This is tantamount to saying that He is not the authoritative Ruler of the Church, and that the officers of the Church do not represent Him in the government of the Church. They not only refuse to admit that He is the King *of the Church,* but deny His present kingship altogether, except, perhaps, as a kingship *de jure,* a kingship which is His by right but has not yet become effective. At the same time their practice is better than their theory, for in practical life they do, rather inconsistently, recognize the authority of Jesus Christ.

2. THE KINGDOM OVER WHICH IT EXTENDS. This kingdom has the following characteristics:

a. *It is grounded in the work of redemption.* The *regnum gratiae* did not originate in the creative work of God but, as the name itself indicates, in His redeeming grace. No one is a citizen of this kingdom in virtue of his humanity. Only the redeemed have that honour and privilege. Christ paid the ransom for those that are His, and by His Spirit applies to them the merits of His perfect sacrifice. Consequently, they now belong to Him and recognize Him as their Lord and King.

b. *It is a spiritual Kingdom.* In the Old Testament dispensation this kingdom was adumbrated in the theocratic kingdom of Israel. Even in the old dispensation the reality of this kingdom was found only in the inner life of believers. The national kingdom of Israel, in which God was King, Lawgiver, and Judge, and the earthly king was only the vicegerent of Jehovah, appointed to represent the King, to carry out His will, and to execute His judgments, was only a symbol, and a shadow and type of that glorious reality, especially as it was destined to appear in the days of the New Testament. With the coming of the new dispensation all the Old Testament shadows passed away, and among them also the theocratic kingdom. Out of the womb of Israel the spiritual reality of the kingdom came forth and assumed an existence independent of the Old Testament theocracy. Hence the spiritual character of the kingdom stands forth far more clearly in the New Testament than it does in the Old. The *regnum gratiae* of Christ is identical with what the New Testament calls the kingdom of God or of heaven. Christ is its mediatorial King. Premillenarians mistakenly teach that the terms "kingdom of God" and "kingdom of heaven," as they are used in the Gospels, refer to two different realities, namely, to the universal kingdom of God and the future mediatorial kingdom of Christ. It is perfectly evident, as some of their own leaders feel constrained to admit, that the two terms are used interchangeably in the Gospels. This appears from the fact that, while Matthew and Luke often report the same statements of Jesus, the former represents Him as using the term "kingdom of heaven," and the latter substitutes for it the term "kingdom of God," compare Matt. 13 with Mark 4; Luke 8:1-10, and many other passages. The spiritual nature of the kingdom is brought out in several ways. Negatively, it is clearly indicated that the kingdom is not an external and natural kingdom of the Jews, Matt. 8:11,12; 21:43; Luke 17:21; John 18:36. Positively, we are taught that it can be entered only by regeneration, John 3:3,5; that it is like a seed cast into the earth, Mark 4:26-29, like a mustard seed, Mark 4:30, and like a leaven, Matt. 13:33. It is in the hearts of people, Luke 17:21, "is righteousness and peace and joy in the Holy Spirit," Rom. 14:17, and is not of this world, but a kingdom of the truth, John 18:36,37. The citizens of the kingdom are described as the poor in spirit, the meek, the merciful, the peacemakers, the pure in heart, and those that hunger and thirst for righteousness. The spiritual nature of the Kingdom should be stressed over against all those who deny the present reality of the mediatorial kingdom of God and hold that it will take the form of a re-established theocracy at the return of Jesus Christ.

In connection with the present day tendency to regard the kingdom of God simply as a new social condition, an ethical kingdom of ends, to be established by human endeavors, such as education, legal enactments, and social reforms, it is well to bear in mind that the term "kingdom of God" is not always used in the same sense. Fundamentally, the term denotes an abstract rather than a concrete idea, namely, the rule of God established and acknowledged in the hearts of sinners. If this is clearly understood, the futility of all human efforts and of all mere externals is at once apparent. By no mere human endeavors can the rule of God be established in the heart of a single man, nor can any man be brought to a recognition of that rule. In the measure in which God establishes His rule in the hearts of sinners, He creates for Himself a realm in which He rules and in which He dispenses the greatest privileges and the choicest blessings. And, again, in the proportion in which man responds to the rule of God and obeys the laws of the kingdom, a new condition of things will naturally result. In fact, if all those who are now citizens of the Kingdom would actually obey its laws in every domain of life, the world would be so different that it would hardly be recognized. In view of all that has been said, it causes no surprise that the term "kingdom of God" is used in various senses in Scripture, as, for instance, to denote the kingship of God or of the Messiah, Matt. 6:10; the realm over which this rule extends and the condition of things to which it gives rise, Matt. 7:21; 19:23,24; 8:12; the totality of the blessings and privileges that flow from the reign of God or of the Messiah, Matt. 13:44, 45; and the condition of things that marks the triumphant culmination of the reign of God in Christ, Matt. 22:2-14; Luke 14:16-24; 13:29.

c. *It is a kingdom that is both present and future.* It is on the one hand a present, ever developing, spiritual reality in the hearts and lives of men, and as such exercises influence in a constantly widening sphere. Jesus and the apostles clearly refer to the kingdom as already present in their time, Matt. 12:28; Luke 17:21; Col. 1:13. This must be maintained over against the great majority of present day Premillenarians. On the other hand it is also a future hope, an eschatological reality; in fact, the eschatological aspect of the kingdom is the more prominent of the two, Matt. 7:21,22; 19:23; 22:2-14; 25:1-13,34; Luke 22:29, 30; I Cor. 6:9; 15:50; Gal. 5:21; Eph. 5:5; I Thess. 2:12; II Tim. 4:18; Heb. 12:28; II Pet. 1:11. Essentially the future kingdom will consist, like that of the present, in the rule of God established and acknowledged in the hearts of men. But at the glorious coming of Jesus Christ this establishment and acknowledgment will be perfected, the hidden forces of the kingdom will stand revealed, and the spiritual rule of Christ will find its consummation in a visible and majestic reign. It is a mistake, however, to assume that the present kingdom will develop almost imperceptibly into the kingdom of the future. The Bible clearly teaches us that the future kingdom will be ushered in by great cataclysmic changes, Matt. 24:21-44; Luke 17:22-37; 21:5-33; I Thess. 5:2,3; II Pet. 3:10-12.

d. *It is closely related to the Church, though not altogether identical with it.* The citizenship of the kingdom is co-extensive with the membership in the invisible Church. Its field of operation, however, is wider than that of the Church, since it aims at the control of life in all its manifestations. The visible Church is the most important, and the only divinely instituted, external organization of the kingdom. At the same time it is also the God-given means *par excellence* for the extension of the kingdom of God on earth. It is well to note that the term "kingdom of God" is sometimes employed in a sense which makes it practically equivalent to the visible Church, Matt. 8:12; 13:24-30, 47-50. While the Church and the kingdom must be distinguished, the distinction should not be sought along the lines indicated by Premillennialism, which regards the kingdom as essentially a kingdom of Israel, and the Church as the body of Christ, gathered in the present dispensation out of Jews and Gentiles. Israel was the Church of the Old Testament and in its spiritual essence constitutes a unity with the Church of the New Testament, Acts 7:38; Rom. 11:11-24; Gal. 3:7-9,29; Eph. 2:11-22.

3. THE DURATION OF THIS KINGSHIP.

a. *Its beginning.* Opinions differ on this point. Consistent Premillenarians deny the present mediatorial kingship of Christ, and believe that He will not be seated upon the throne as Mediator until He ushers in the millennium at the time of His second advent. And the Socinians claim that Christ was neither priest nor king before His ascension. The generally accepted position of the Church is that Christ received His appointment as mediatorial King in the depths of eternity, and that He began to function as such immediately after the

fall, Prov. 8:23; Ps. 2:6. During the old dispensation He carried on His work as King partly through the judges of Israel, and partly through the typical kings. But though He was permitted to rule as Mediator even before His incarnation, He did not publicly and formally assume His throne and inaugurate His spiritual kingdom until the time of His ascension and elevation at the right hand of God, Acts 2:29-36; Phil. 2:5-11.

b. *Its termination* (?). The prevailing opinion is that the spiritual kingship of Christ over His Church will, as to its essential character, continue eternally, though it will undergo important changes in its mode of operation at the consummation of the world. The eternal duration of the spiritual kingship of Christ would seem to be explicitly taught in the following passages: Ps. 45:6 (comp. Heb. 1:8); 72:17; 89:36,37; Isa. 9:7; Dan. 2:44; II Sam. 7:13,16; Luke 1:33; II Pet. 1:11. The Heidelberg Catechism also speaks of Christ as "our eternal king." Similarly the Belgic Confession in article XXVII. Moreover, the kingship and the headship of Christ are inextricably bound up together. The latter is subservient to the former, and is sometimes clearly represented as including the former, Eph. 1:21,22; 5:22-24. But, surely, Christ will never cease to be the Head of His Church, leaving the Church as a body without a Head. Finally, the fact that Christ is a priest forever, after the order of Melchizedek, would also seem to argue in favor of the eternal duration of the spiritual kingship of Christ, since His mediatorial office is after all a unit. Dick and Kuyper, however, argue that this kingship of Christ will cease when He has accomplished the salvation of His people. The only passage of Scripture to which they appeal is I Cor. 15:24-28, but this passage evidently does not refer to Christ's spiritual kingship, but to His kingship over the universe.

B. The Kingship of Christ over the Universe.

1. THE NATURE OF THIS KINGSHIP. By the *regnum potentiae* we mean the dominion of the God-man, Jesus Christ, over the universe, His providential and judicial administration of all things in the interest of the Church. As King of the universe the Mediator so guides the destinies of individuals, of social groups, and of nations, as to promote the growth, the gradual purification, and the final perfection of the people which He has redeemed by His blood. In that capacity He also protects His own against the dangers to which they are exposed in the world, and vindicates His righteousness by the subjection and destruction of all His enemies. In this kingship of Christ we find the initial restoration of the original kingship of man. The idea that Christ now rules the destinies of individuals and nations in the interest of His blood-bought Church, is a far more comforting thought than the notion that He is now "a refugee on the throne of heaven."

2. THE RELATION OF THE REGNUM POTENTIAE TO THE REGNUM GRATIAE. The Kingship of Christ over the universe is subservient to His spiritual kingship. It is incumbent on Christ, as the anointed King, to establish the spiritual

kingdom of God, to govern it, and to protect it against all hostile forces. He must do this in a world which is under the power of sin and is bent on thwarting all spiritual endeavors. If that world were beyond His control, it might easily frustrate all His efforts. Therefore God invested Him with authority over it, so that He is able to control all powers and forces and movements in the world, and can thus secure a safe footing for His people in the world, and protect His own against all the powers of darkness. These cannot defeat His purposes, but are even constrained to serve them. Under the beneficent rule of Christ even the wrath of man is made to praise God.

3. THE DURATION OF THIS KINGSHIP. Christ was formally invested with this kingship over the universe when He was exalted at the right hand of God. It was a promised reward of His labors, Ps. 2:8,9; Matt. 28:18; Eph. 1:20-22; Phil. 2:9-11. This investiture was part of the exaltation of the God-man. It did not give Him any power or authority which He did not already possess as the Son of God; neither did it increase His territory. But the God-man, the Mediator, was now made the possessor of this authority, and His human nature was made to share in the glory of this royal dominion. Moreover, the government of the world was now made subservient to the interests of the Church of Jesus Christ. And this kingship of Christ will last until the victory over the enemies is complete and even death has been abolished, I Cor. 15:24-28. At the consummation of all things the God-man will give up the authority conferred on Him for a special purpose, since it will no more be needed. He will return His commission to God, that God may be all in all. The purpose is accomplished; mankind is redeemed; and thereby the original kingship of man is restored.

QUESTIONS FOR FURTHER STUDY: In whom was Christ typified as prophet in the Old Testament? How were the true prophets distinguished from the false? How did prophets and priests differ as teachers? What was characteristic of the priesthood after the order of Melchizedek? Were the sacrifices of Cain and Abel piacular? On what grounds do Jowett, Maurice, Young, and Bushnell deny the vicarious and typico-prophetical character of the Mosaic sacrifices? What is the difference between atonement, propitiation, reconciliation, and redemption? What accounts for the widespread aversion to the objective character of the atonement? What arguments are advanced to disprove the necessity of the atonement? Why is penal substitution practically impossible among men? Does the universal offer of salvation necessarily imply a universal atonement? What becomes of the doctrine of the atonement in modern liberal theology? What two *parakletoi* have we according to Scripture, and how does their work differ? What is the nature of the intercessory work of Christ? Are our intercessory prayers like those of Christ? Is Christ ever called "King of the Jews"? Do Premillenarians deny only the present spiritual kingship of Christ or also His Kingship over the universe?

LITERATURE: Bavinck, *Geref. Dogm.* III, pp. 394-455, 538-550; Kuyper, *Dict. Dogm.*, *De Christo*, III, pp. 3-196; Vos, *Geref. Dogm.* III, pp. 93-197; Hodge, *Syst. Theol.* II, pp. 455-609; Shedd, *Dogm. Theol.* II, pp. 353-489; Dabney, *Syst. and Polemic Theol.*, pp. 483-553; Dorner, *Syst. of Chr. Doct.* III, pp. 381-429; IV, pp. 1-154; Valentine, *Chr. Theol.* II, pp. 96-185; Pope, *Chr. Theol.* II, pp. 196-316; Calvin, *Institutes*, Bk. II, chaps. XV-XVII: Watson, *Institutes* II, pp. 265-496; Schmid, *Doct. Theol. of the Ev. Luth. Church*, pp. 344-382; Micklem, *What Is the Faith?*, pp. 188-205; Brunner, *The Mediator*, pp. 399-590; Stevenson, *The Offices of Christ*; Milligan, *The Ascension and Heavenly Priesthood of our Lord*; Meeter, *The Heavenly High-Priesthood of Christ*; A. Cave, *The Scriptural Doctrine of Sacrifice*; Faber, *The*

Origin of Expiatory Sacrifice; Davison, *The Origin and Intent of Primitive Sacrifice;* Symington, *Atonement and Intercession;* Stevens, *The Christian Doctrine of Salvation;* Franks, *History of the Doctrine of the Work of Christ* (2 vols.) ; D. Smith, *The Atonement in the Light of History and the Modern Spirit;* Mackintosh, *Historic Theories of the Atonement;* McLeod Campbell, *The Nature of the Atonement;* Bushnell, *Vicarious Sacrifice;* Denney, *The Christian Doctrine of Reconciliation;* Kuyper, *Dat de Genade Particulier Is;* Bouma, *Geen Algemeene Verzoening;* De Jong, *De Leer der Verzoening in de Amerikaansche Theologie;* S. Cave, *The Doctrine of the Work of Christ;* Smeaton, *Our Lord's Doctrine of the Atonement;* ibid., *The Apostles' Doctrine of the Atonement;* Cunningham, *Historical Theology* II, pp. 237-370; Creighton, *Law and the Cross;* Armour, *Atonement and Law;* Mathews, *The Atonement and the Social Process;* and further works on the Atonement by Martin, A. A. Hodge, Crawford, Dale, Dabney, Miley, Mozley, and Berkhof.

THE DOCTRINE OF THE APPLICATION
OF THE WORK OF REDEMPTION

I. Soteriology in General

A. Connection Between Soteriology and the Preceding Loci.

SOTERIOLOGY deals with the communication of the blessings of salvation to the sinner and his restoration to divine favor and to a life in intimate communion with God. It presupposes knowledge of God as the all-sufficient source of the life, the strength, and the happiness of mankind, and of man's utter dependence on Him for the present and the future. Since it deals with restoration, redemption, and renewal, it can only be understood properly in the light of the original condition of man as created in the image of God, and of the subsequent disturbance of the proper relationship between man and his God by the entrance of sin into the world. Moreover, since it treats of the salvation of the sinner wholly as a work of God, known to Him from all eternity, it naturally carries our thoughts back to the eternal counsel of peace and the covenant of grace, in which provision was made for the redemption of fallen men. It proceeds on the assumption of the completed work of Christ as the Mediator of redemption. There is the closest possible connection between Christology and Soteriology. Some, as, for instance, Hodge, treat of both under the common heading "Soteriology." Christology then becomes objective, as distinguished from subjective, Soteriology. In defining the contents of Soteriology, it is better to say that it deals with the *application of the work of redemption* than to say that it treats of the *appropriation of salvation*. The matter should be studied theologically rather than anthropologically. The work of God rather than the work of man is definitely in the foreground. Pope objects to the use of the former term, since in using it "we are in danger of the predestinarian error which assumes that the finished work of Christ is applied to the individual according to the fixed purpose of an election of grace." This is the very reason why a Calvinist prefers to use that term. To do Pope justice, however, it should be added that he also objects to the other term, because it "tends to the other and Pelagian extreme, too obviously making the atoning provision of Christ a matter of individual free acceptance or rejection." He prefers to speak of *"the administration of redemption,"* which is indeed a very good term.[1]

B. The Ordo Salutis, (Order of Salvation).

The Germans speak of *"Heilsaneignung,"* the Dutch, of *"Heilsweg"* and *"Orde des Heils,"* and the English, of the *"Way of Salvation."* The *ordo salutis* describes the process by which the work of salvation, wrought in Christ, is

---

1. *Christian Theology*, II, p. 319.

subjectively realized in the hearts and lives of sinners. It aims at describing in their logical order, and also in their interrelations, the various movements of the Holy Spirit in the application of the work of redemption. The emphasis is not on what man does in appropriating the grace of God, but on what God does in applying it. It is but natural that Pelagians should object to this view.

The desire to simplify the *ordo salutis* often led to unwarranted limitations. Weizsaecker would include in it only the operations of the Holy Spirit wrought in the heart of man, and holds that neither calling nor justification can properly be included under this category.[1] Kaftan, the most prominent Ritschlian dogmatician, is of the opinion that the traditional *ordo salutis* does not constitute an inner unity and therefore ought to be dissolved. He treats of calling under the Word as a means of grace; of regeneration, justification, and the mystical union, under the redemptive work of Christ; and relegates conversion and sanctification to the domain of Christian ethics. The result is that only faith is left, and this constitutes the *ordo salutis*.[2] According to him the *ordo salutis* should include only what is required on the part of man unto salvation, and this is faith, *faith only*, — a purely anthropological point of view, which probably finds its explanation in the tremendous emphasis of Lutheran theology on active faith.

When we speak of an *ordo salutis*, we do not forget that the work of applying the grace of God to the individual sinner is a unitary process, but simply stress the fact that various movements can be distinguished in the process, that the work of the application of redemption proceeds in a definite and reasonable order, and that God does not impart the fulness of His salvation to the sinner in a single act. Had He done this, the work of redemption would not have come to the consciousness of God's children in all its aspects and in all its divine fulness. Neither do we lose sight of the fact that we often use the terms employed to describe the various movements in a more limited sense than the Bible does.

The question may be raised, whether the Bible ever indicates a definite *ordo salutis*. The answer to that question is that, while it does not explicitly furnish us with a complete order of salvation, it offers us a sufficient basis for such an order. The nearest approach found in Scripture to anything like an *ordo salutis*, is the statement of Paul in Rom. 8:29,30. Some of the Lutheran theologians based their enumeration of the various movements in the application of redemption rather artificially on Acts 26:17,18. But while the Bible does not give us a clear-cut *ordo salutis*, it does do two things which enable us to construe such an order. (1) It furnishes us with a very full and rich enumeration of the operations of the Holy Spirit in applying the work of Christ to individual sinners, and of the blessings of salvation imparted to them. In doing this, it does not always use the very terms employed in Dogmatics, but frequently resorts to the use of other names and to figures of speech.

---

1. Cf. McPherson, *Chr. Dogm.*, p. 368.
2. *Dogm.*, p. 651.

Moreover, it often employs terms which have now acquired a very definite technical meaning in Dogmatics, in a far wider sense. Such words as *regeneration, calling, conversion,* and *renewal* repeatedly serve to designate the whole change that is brought about in the inner life of man. (2) It indicates in many passages and in various ways the relation in which the different movements in the work of redemption stand to each other. It teaches that we are justified by faith and not by works, Rom. 3:30; 5:1; Gal. 2:16-20; that, being justified, we have peace with God and access to Him, Rom. 5:1,2; that we are set free from sin to become servants of righteousness, and to reap the fruit of sanctification, Rom. 6:18,22; that when we are adopted as children, we receive the Spirit who gives us assurance, and also become co-heirs with Christ, Rom. 8:15-17; Gal. 4:4,5,6; that faith comes by the hearing of the word of God, Rom. 10:17; that death unto the law results in life unto God, Gal. 2:19,20; that when we believe, we are sealed with the Spirit of God, Eph. 1:13,14; that it is necessary to walk worthily of the calling with which we are called, Eph. 4:1,2; that having obtained the righteousness of God by faith, we share the sufferings of Christ, and also the power of His resurrection, Phil. 3:9,10; and that we are begotten again through the Word of God, I Pet. 1:23. These and similar passages indicate the relation of the various movements of the redemptive work to one another, and thus afford a basis for the construction of an *ordo salutis.*

In view of the fact that the Bible does not specify the exact order that applies in the application of the work of redemption, there is naturally considerable room for a difference of opinion. And as a matter of fact the Churches are not all agreed as to the *ordo salutis.* The doctrine of the order of salvation is a fruit of the Reformation. Hardly any semblance of it is found in the works of the Scholastics. In pre-Reformation theology scant justice is done to soteriology in general. It does not constitute a separate locus, and its constituent parts are discussed under other rubrics,, more or less as *disjecta membra.* Even the greatest of the Schoolmen, such as Peter the Lombard and Thomas Aquinas, pass on at once from the discussion of the incarnation to that of the Church and the sacraments. What may be called their soteriology consists of only two chapters, *de Fide et de Poenitentia.* The *bona opera* also receive considerable attention. Since Protestantism took its start from the criticism and displacement of the Roman Catholic conception of faith, repentance, and good works, it was but natural that the interest of the Reformers should center on the origin and development of the new life in Christ. Calvin was the first to group the various parts of the order of salvation in a systematic way, but even his representation, says Kuyper, is rather subjective, since it formally stresses the human activity rather than the divine.[1] Later Reformed theologians corrected this defect. The following representations of the order of salvation reflect the fundamental conceptions of the way of salvation that characterize the various Churches since the Reformation.

---

1. *Dict. Dogm., De Salute,* pp. 17 f.

1. THE REFORMED VIEW. Proceeding on the assumption that man's spiritual condition depends on his state, that is, on his relation to the law; and that it is only on the basis of the imputed righteousness of Jesus Christ that the sinner can be delivered from the corrupting and destructive influence of sin, — Reformed Soteriology takes its starting point in the union established in the *pactum salutis* between Christ and those whom the Father has given Him, in virtue of which there is an eternal imputation of the righteousness of Christ to those who are His. In view of this precedence of the legal over the moral some theologians, such as Maccovius, Comrie, A. Kuyper Sr., and A. Kuyper Jr., begin the *ordo salutis* with justification rather than regeneration. In doing this they apply the name "justification" also to the ideal imputation of the righteousness of Christ to the elect in the eternal counsel of God. Dr. Kuyper further says that the Reformed differ from the Lutherans in that the former teach justification *per justitiam Christi*, while the latter represent the justification *per fidem* as completing the work of Christ.[1] The great majority of Reformed theologians, however, while presupposing the imputation of the righteousness of Christ in the *pactum salutis*, discuss only justification by faith in the order of salvation, and naturally take up its discussion in connection with or immediately after that of faith. They begin the *ordo salutis* with regeneration or with calling, and thus emphasize the fact that the application of the redemptive work of Christ is in its incipiency a work of God. This is followed by a discussion of conversion, in which the work of regeneration penetrates to the conscious life of the sinner, and he turns from self, the world, and Satan, to God. Conversion includes repentance and faith, but because of its great importance the latter is generally treated separately. The discussion of faith naturally leads to that of justification, inasmuch as this is mediated to us by faith. And because justification places man in a new relation to God, which carries with it the gift of the Spirit of adoption, and which obliges man to a new obedience and also enables him to do the will of God from the heart, the work of sanctification next comes into consideration. Finally, the order of salvation is concluded with the doctrine of the perseverance of the saints and their final glorification.

Bavinck distinguishes three groups in the blessings of salvation. He starts out by saying that sin is guilt, pollution, and misery, for it involves a breaking of the covenant of works, a loss of the image of God, and a subjection to the power of corruption. Christ delivered us from these three by His suffering, His meeting the demands of the law, and His victory over death. Consequently, the blessings of Christ consist in the following: (a) He restores the right relation of man to God and to all creatures by justification, including the forgiveness of sins, the adoption of children, peace with God, and glorious liberty. (b) He renews man in the image of God by regeneration, internal calling, conversion, renewal, and sanctification. (c) He preserves man for his eternal inheritance, delivers him from suffering and death, and puts him in possession of eternal salvation by preservation, perseverance, and glorifi-

---

1. *Dict. Dogm., De Salute*, p. 69.

cation. The first group of blessings is granted unto us by the illumination of the Holy Spirit, is accepted by faith, and sets our conscience free. The second is imparted to us by the regenerating work of the Holy Spirit, renews us, and redeems us from the power of sin. And the third flows to us by the preserving, guiding, and sealing work of the Holy Spirit as the earnest of our complete redemption, and delivers us, body and soul, from the dominion of misery and death. The first group anoints us as prophets, the second, as priests, and the third, as kings. In connection with the first we look back to the completed work of Christ on the cross, where our sins were atoned; in connection with the second we look up to the living Lord in heaven, who as High Priest is seated at the right hand of the Father; and in connection with the third we look forward to the future coming of Jesus Christ, in which He will subject all enemies and will surrender the kingdom to the Father.

There are some things that should be borne in mind in connection with the *ordo salutis*, as it appears in Reformed theology.

a. Some of the terms are not always used in the same sense. The term *justification* is generally limited to what is called justification by faith, but is sometimes made to cover an objective justification of the elect in the resurrection of Jesus Christ, and the imputation of the righteousness of Christ to them in the *pactum salutis*. Again, the word *regeneration*, which now generally designates that act of God by which He imparts the principle of the new life to man, is also used to designate the new birth or the first manifestation of the new life, and in the theology of the seventeenth century frequently occurs as synonymous with *conversion* or even *sanctification*. Some speak of it as *passive* conversion in distinction from conversion proper, which is then called *active* conversion.

b. Several other distinctions also deserve attention. We should carefully distinguish between the judicial and the recreative acts of God, the former (as justification) altering the state, and the latter (as regeneration, conversion), the condition of the sinner; — between the work of the Holy Spirit in the subconscious (regeneration), and that in the conscious life (conversion) ; — between that which pertains to the putting away of the old man (repentance, crucifying of the old man), and that which constitutes the putting on of the new man (regeneration and in part sanctification) ; — and between the beginning of the application of the work of redemption (in regeneration and conversion proper), and the continuation of it (in daily conversion and sanctification).

c. In connection with the various movements in the work of application we should bear in mind that the judicial acts of God constitute the basis for His recreative acts, so that justification, though not temporally, is yet logically prior to all the rest; — that the work of God's grace in the subconscious, precedes that in the conscious life, so that regeneration precedes conversion; — and that the judicial acts of God (justification, including the forgiveness of sins and the adoption of children) always address themselves to the consciousness, while of the recreative acts one, namely, regeneration, takes place in the subconscious life.

2. THE LUTHERAN VIEW. The Lutherans, while not denying the doctrines of election, the mystical union, and the imputation of the righteousness of Christ, do not take their starting point in any one of these. They fully recognize the fact that the subjective realization of the work of redemption in the hearts and lives of sinners is a work of divine grace, but at the same time give a representation of the *ordo salutis* which places the main emphasis on what is done *a parte hominis* (on the part of man) rather than on what is done *a parte Dei* (on the part of God). They see in faith first of all a gift of God, but at the same time make faith, regarded more particularly as an active principle in man and as an activity of man, the all-determining factor in their order of salvation. Says Pieper: "So kommt denn hinsichtlich der Heilsaneignung alles darauf an, dass im Menschen der Glaube an das Evangelium entstehe."[1] Attention was already called to the fact that Kaftan regards faith as the whole of the *ordo salutis.* This emphasis on faith as an active principle is undoubtedly due to the fact that in the Lutheran Reformation the doctrine of justification by faith — often called the material principle of the Reformation — was very much in the foreground. According to Pieper the Lutheran takes his starting point in the fact that in Christ God is reconciled to the world of humanity. God announces this fact to man in the gospel and offers to put man subjectively in possession of that forgiveness of sins or justification which was objectively wrought in Christ. This calling is always accompanied with a certain measure of illumination and of quickening, so that man receives the power to not-resist the saving operation of the Holy Spirit. It frequently results in repentance, and this may issue in regeneration, by which the Holy Spirit endows the sinner with saving grace. Now all these, namely, calling, illumination, repentance, and regeneration, are really only preparatory, and are strictly speaking not yet blessings of the covenant of grace. They are experienced apart from any living relation to Christ, and merely serve to lead the sinner to Christ. "Regeneration is conditioned by the conduct of man with regard to the influence exerted upon him," and therefore "will take place at once or gradually, as man's resistance is greater or less."[2] In it man is endowed with a saving faith by which he appropriates the forgiveness or justification that is objectively given in Christ, is adopted as a child of God, is united to Christ in a mystical union, and receives the spirit of renewal and sanctification, the living principle of a life of obedience. The *permanent* possession of all these blessings depends on the continuance of faith, — on an active faith on the part of man. If man continues to believe, he has peace and joy, life and salvation; but if he ceases to exercise faith, all this becomes doubtful, uncertain, and amissible. There is always a possibility that the believer will lose all that he possesses.

---

1. *Christl. Dogm.* II, p. 477. Cf. also Valentine, *Chr. Theol.* II, pp. 258 ff.
2. Schmid, *Doct. Theol.,* p. 464.

3. THE ROMAN CATHOLIC VIEW. In Roman Catholic theology the doc-trine of the Church precedes the discussion of the *ordo salutis*. Children are regenerated by baptism, but they who first become acquainted with the gospel in later life receive a *gratia sufficiens*, consisting in an illumination of the mind and a strengthening of the will. Man can resist this grace, but can also assent to it. If he assents to it, it turns into a *gratia co-operans*, in which man co-operates to prepare himself for justification. This preparation consists of seven parts: (a) a believing acceptance of the Word of God, (b) an insight into one's sinful condition, (c) hope in the mercy of God, (d) the beginning of love to God, (e) an abhorrence of sin, (f) a resolve to obey the command-ments of God, and (g) a desire for baptism. It is quite evident that faith does not occupy a central place here, but is simply co-ordinated with the other preparations. It is merely an intellectual assent to the doctrines of the Church (*fides informis*) and acquires its justifying power only through the love that is imparted in the *gratia infusa* (*fides caritate· formata*). It can be called justifying faith only in the sense that it is the basis and root of all justification as the first of the preparations named above. After this preparation justi-fication itself follows in baptism. This consists in the infusion of grace, of supernatural virtues, followed by the forgiveness of sins. The measure of this forgiveness is commensurate with the degree in which sin is actually overcome. It should be borne in mind that justification is given freely, and is not merited by the preceding preparations. The gift of justification is preserved by obeying the commandments and by doing good works. In the *gratia infusa* man receives the supernatural strength to do good works and thus to merit (with a merit *de condigno*, that is, real merit) all following grace and even everlasting life. The grace of God thus serves the purpose of enabling man once more to merit salvation. But it is not certain that man will retain the forgiveness of sins. The grace of justification may be lost, not only through unbelief, but through any mortal sin. It may be regained, however, by the sacrament of penance, consisting of contrition (or, attrition) and confession, together with absolution and works of satisfaction. Both the guilt of sin and eternal punishment are removed by absolution, but temporal penalties can be canceled only by works of satisfaction.

4. THE ARMINIAN VIEW. The Arminian order of salvation, while osten-sibly ascribing the work of salvation to God, really makes it contingent on the attitude and the work of man. God opens up the possibility of salvation for man, but it is up to man to improve the opportunity. The Arminian regards the atonement of Christ "as an oblation and satisfaction for the sins of the whole world" (Pope), that is, for the sins of every individual of the human race. He denies that the guilt of Adam's sin is imputed to all his descendants, and that man is by nature totally depraved, and therefore unable to do any spiritual good; and believes that, while human nature is undoubtedly injured and deteriorated as the result of the fall, man is still able, by nature, to do that which is spiritually good and to turn to God. But because of the evil bias, the

perverseness, and the sluggishness of sinful human nature, God imparts to it gracious assistance. He bestows sufficient grace upon all men to enable them, if they choose, to attain to the full possession of spiritual blessings, and ultimately to salvation. The gospel offer comes to all men indiscriminately and exerts a merely moral influence on them, while they have it in their power to resist it or to yield to it. If they yield to it, they will turn to Christ in repentance and faith. These movements of the soul are not (as in Calvinism) the results of regeneration, but are merely introductory to the state of grace properly so called. When their faith really terminates in Christ, this faith is, for the sake of the merits of Christ, imputed to them for righteousness. This does not mean that the righteousness of Christ is imputed to them as their very own, but that, in view of what Christ did for sinners, their faith, which involves the principle of obedience, honesty of heart, and good dispositions, is accepted in lieu of a perfect obedience and is reckoned to them for righteousness. On this basis, then, they are justified, which in the Arminian scheme generally simply means that their sins are pardoned, and not that they are accepted as righteous. Arminians often put it in this form: The forgiveness of sins is based on the merits of Christ, but acceptance with God rests on man's obedience to the law or evangelical obedience. Faith not only serves to justify, but also to regenerate sinners. It insures to man the grace of evangelical obedience and this, if allowed to function through life, issues in the grace of perseverance. However, the grace of God is always resistible and amissible.

The so-called Wesleyan or Evangelical Arminian does not entirely agree with the Arminianism of the seventeenth century. While his position shows greater affinity with Calvinism than the original Arminianism does, it is also more inconsistent. It admits that the guilt of Adam's sin is imputed to all his descendants, but at the same time holds that all men are justified in Christ, and that therefore this guilt is at once removed, at birth. It also admits the entire moral depravity of man in the state of nature, but goes on to stress the fact that no man exists in that state of nature, since there is a universal application of the work of Christ through the Holy Spirit, by which the sinner is enabled to co-operate with the grace of God. It emphasizes the necessity of a *supernatural* (hyper-physical) work of grace to effect the sinner's renovation and sanctification. Moreover, it teaches the doctrine of Christian perfection or entire sanctification in the present life. It may be added that, while Arminius made the bestowal on man of an ability to co-operate with God a matter of justice, Wesley regarded this as a matter of pure grace. This is the type of Arminianism with which we mostly come in contact. We meet with it, not only in the Methodist Church, but also in large sections of other Churches, and especially in the many undenominational Churches of the present day.

II. The Operations of the Holy Spirit in General

A. Transition to the Work of the Holy Spirit.

As already intimated in the preceding, in passing from Christology to Soteriology, we pass from the objective to the subjective, from the work which God accomplished *for us* in Christ and which is in its sacrificial aspect a finished work, to the work which He realizes as time goes on *in the hearts and lives of believers,* and in which they are permitted, and also expected, to co-operate. And in the construction of this doctrine, too, we should be guided by Scripture. Dr. Bavinck calls attention to a difficulty that arises here, since the Bible seems to teach on the one hand that the whole work of redemption is finished in Christ, so that nothing remains for man to do; and on the other hand, that the really decisive thing must still be accomplished in and through man. Its teaching respecting the way of redemption seems to be both *autosoteric* and *heterosoteric*. Therefore it is necessary to guard against all one-sidedness, and to avoid both the Scylla of Nomism, as it appears in Pelagianism, Semi-Pelagianism, Arminianism, and Neonomism, and the Charybdis of Antino-mianism, as it reared its head, sometimes as a specific doctrine and sometimes as a mere doctrinal tendency, in some of the sects, such as the Nicolaitans, the Alexandrian Gnostics, the Brethren of the Free Spirit, the Anabaptists of the more fanatic type, the followers of Agricola, the Moravians, and some of the Plymouth brethren. Nomism denies the sovereign election of God by which He has infallibly determined, not on the basis of the foreseen attitude or works of men, but according to His good pleasure, who would and would not be saved; rejects the idea that Christ by His atoning death, not only made salvation possible, but actually secured it for all those for whom He laid down His life, so that eternal life is in the most absolute sense of the word a free gift of God, and in its bestowal human merits are not taken into consideration; and maintains, either that man can save himself without the aid of renewing grace (Pelagianism), or can accomplish this with the assistance of divine grace (Semi-Pelagianism and Arminianism). On the other hand Antinomianism, which is sometimes said to be favored by hyper-Calvinism, holds that the imputation of our sins to Christ made Him personally a sinner, and that the application of His righteousness to us makes us personally righteous, so that God sees no sin in us any more; that the union of believers with Christ is a "union of identity" and makes them in all respects one with Him; that the work of the Holy Spirit is quite superfluous, since the sinner's redemption was completed on the cross, or — even more extreme — that the work of Christ was also unnecessary, since the whole matter was settled in the eternal decree of God; that the sinner is justified in the resurrection of Christ or even in the counsel of redemption, and therefore does not need justification by faith or receives in this merely a declaration of a previously accomplished justification; and that believers are free from the law, not only as a condition of the covenant of works, but also as a rule of life. It virtually denies the personality and work of the Holy Spirit, and in some cases even the objective atonement through Christ. Both atonement and justification are from eternity. The penitent sinner wrongly proceeds on the assumption that God is angry with him and merely needs information on that point. Moreover, he should realize that whatever sins he may commit cannot affect his standing with God.

Scripture teaches us to recognize a certain economy in the work of creation and redemption and warrants our speaking of the Father and our creation, of the Son and our redemption, and of the Holy Spirit and our sanctification. The Holy Spirit has not only a personality of His own, but also a distinctive method of working; and therefore we should distinguish between the work of Christ in meriting salvation and the work of the Holy Spirit in applying it. Christ met the demands of divine justice and merited all the blessings of salvation. But His work is not yet finished. He continues it in heaven, in order to put those for whom He laid down His life in possession of all that He has merited for them. Even the work of application is a work of Christ, but a work which He accomplishes through the agency of the Holy Spirit. Though this work stands out in the economy of redemption as the work of the Holy Spirit, it cannot for a moment be separated from the work of Christ. It is rooted in the redemptive work of Jesus Christ and carries this to completion, and that not without the co-operation of the subjects of redemption. Christ Himself points out the close connection when He says: "Howbeit when He, the Spirit of truth, is come, He shall guide you into all the truth: for He shall not speak from Himself; but what things soever He shall hear, these shall He speak: and He shall declare unto you the things that are to come. He shall glorify me, for He shall take of mine, and shall declare it unto you." John 16:13,14.

B. General and Special Operations of the Holy Spirit.

Scripture clearly shows that not all the operations of the Holy Spirit are part and parcel of the saving work of Jesus Christ. Just as the Son of God is not only the Mediator of redemption, but also the Mediator of creation, so the Holy Spirit, as represented in Scripture, is operative, not only in the work of redemption, but also in the work of creation. Naturally, Soteriology is concerned with His redemptive work only, but for its proper understanding it is highly desirable to take some account of His more general operations.

1. THE GENERAL OPERATIONS OF THE HOLY SPIRIT. It is a well known fact that the trinitarian distinctions are not as clearly revealed in the Old Testament as in the New. The term "Spirit of God," as it is employed in the

Old Testament, does not always denote a person, and even in cases in which the personal idea is clearly present, does not always specifically point to the third person of the Holy Trinity. It is sometimes used figuratively to denote the breath of God, Job 32:8; Ps. 33:6, and in some instances is simply a synonym for "God," Ps. 139:7,8; Isa. 40:13. It serves very commonly to designate the power of life, the principle that causes the creatures to live, and that is in a unique way peculiar to God. The spirit dwelling in the creatures, and on which their very existence depends, is from God and binds them to God, Job 32:8; 33:4; 34:14,15; Ps. 104;29; Isa. 42:5. God is called the "God (or, "Father") of the spirits of all flesh," Num. 16:22; 27:16; Heb. 12:9. In some of these cases it is quite evident that the Spirit of God is not a mere power but a person. The very first passage in which the Spirit is mentioned, Gen. 1:2, already calls attention to this life-giving function, and this is particularized in connection with the creation of man, Gen. 2:7. The Spirit of God generates life and carries the creative work of God to completion, Job 33:4; 34:14,15; Ps. 104:29,30; Isa. 42:5. It is evident from the Old Testament that the origin of life, its maintenance, and its development depend on the operation of the Holy Spirit. The withdrawal of the Spirit means death.

Extraordinary exhibitions of power, feats of strength and daring, are also referred to the Spirit of God. The judges whom God raised up for the deliverance of Israel were evidently men of considerable ability and of unusual daring and strength, but the real secret of their accomplishments lay not in themselves, but in a supernatural power that came upon them. It is said repeatedly that "the spirit of Jehovah came (mightily) upon them," Judg. 3:10; 6:34; 11:29; 13:25; 14:6,19; 15:14. It was the Spirit of God that enabled them to work deliverance for the people. There is also a clear recognition of the operation of the Holy Spirit in the intellectual sphere. Elihu speaks of this when he says: "But there is a spirit in man, and the breath of the Almighty giveth them understanding." Job 32:8. Intellectual insight, or the ability to understand the problems of life, is ascribed to an illuminating influence of the Holy Spirit. The heightening of artistic skill is also ascribed to the Spirit of the Lord, Ex. 28:3; 31:3; 35:30 ff. Certain men, characterized by special endowments, were qualified for the finer work that was to be done in connection with the construction of the tabernacle and the adornment of the priestly garments, cf. also Neh. 9:20. Again, the Spirit of the Lord is represented as qualifying men for various offices. The Spirit was put, and rested, upon the seventy who were appointed to assist Moses in ruling and judging the people of Israel, Num. 11:17,25,26. These also received the spirit of prophecy temporarily, to attest their calling. Joshua was chosen as the successor of Moses, because he had the Spirit of the Lord, Num. 27:18. When Saul and David were anointed as kings, the Spirit of the Lord came upon them, to qualify them for their important task, I Sam. 10:6,10; 16:13,14. Finally, the Spirit of God also clearly operated in the prophets as the Spirit of revelation. David says, "The Spirit of Jehovah spake by me, and His word was upon my tongue," II Sam. 23:2. Nehemiah testifies in Neh. 9:30: "Yet many years didst thou bear with them, and testifiedst against them by thy Spirit through the prophets: yet they would not give ear." Ezekiel speaks of a vision by the Spirit of Jehovah, 11:24, and in Zech. 7:12 we read: "Yea, they made their heart as an adamant stone, lest they should hear the law, and the words which Jehovah of hosts had sent in His Spirit by the former prophets." Cf. also I Kings 22:24; I Pet. 1:11; II Pet. 1:21.

2. THE RELATION BETWEEN THE GENERAL AND THE SPECIAL OPERATIONS OF THE HOLY SPIRIT. There is a certain similarity between the general and the special operations of the Holy Spirit. By His general operations He originates, maintains, strengthens, and guides all life, organic, intellectual, and moral. He does this in different ways and in harmony with the objects concerned. Something similar may be said of His special operation. In the redemptive sphere He also originates the new life, fructifies it, guides it in its development, and leads it to its destiny. But in spite of this similarity, there is nevertheless an essential difference between the operations of the Holy Spirit in the sphere of creation and those in the sphere of redemption or re-creation. In the former He originates, maintains, develops and guides *the life of the natural creation*, restrains for the present the deteriorating and devastating influence of sin in the lives of men and of society, and enables men to maintain a certain order and decorum in their communal life, to do what is outwardly good and right in their relations to each other, and to develop the talents with which they were endowed at creation. In the latter, on the other hand, He originates, maintains, develops, and guides *the new life* that is born from above, is nourished from above, and will be perfected above, — a life that is heavenly in principle, though lived on earth. By His special operation the Holy Spirit overcomes and destroys the power of sin, renews man in the image of God, and enables him to render spiritual obedience to God, to be the salt of the earth, the light of the world, and a spiritual leaven in every sphere of life. While the work of the Holy Spirit in creation in general undoubtedly has a certain independent significance, yet it is made subordinate to the work of redemption. The entire life of the elect, also that preceding their new birth, is determined and governed by God with a view to their final destiny. Their natural life is so regulated that, when it is renewed, it will answer to the purpose of God.

C. The Holy Spirit as the Dispenser of Divine Grace.

As the covenant in which God made provision for the salvation of sinners is called the covenant of grace, and as the Mediator of the covenant is said to have appeared "full of grace," so that we can receive out of His fulness "grace for grace," John 1:16,17, so the Holy Spirit is called "the Spirit of grace," since He takes the "grace of Christ" and confers it on us.

1. THE BIBLICAL USE OF THE TERM "GRACE". The word "grace" is not always used in the same sense in Scripture, but has a variety of meanings. In the Old Testament we have the word *chen* (adj. *chanun*), from the root *chanan*. The noun may denote *gracefulness* or *beauty*, Prov. 22:11; 31:30, but most

generally means *favour* or *good-will*. The Old Testament repeatedly speaks of finding favour in the eyes of God or of man. The favour so found carries with it the bestowal of favours or blessings. This means that grace is not an abstract quality, but is an active, working principle, manifesting itself in beneficent acts, Gen. 6:8; 19:19; 33:15; Ex. 33:12; 34:9; I Sam. 1:18; 27:5; Esth. 2:7. The fundamental idea is, that the blessings graciously bestowed are *freely* given, and not in consideration of any claim or merit. The New Testament word *charis*, from *chairein*, "to rejoice," denotes first of all *a pleasant external appearance*, *"loveliness," "agreeableness," "acceptableness,"* and has some such meaning in Luke 4:22; Col. 4:6. A more prominent meaning of the word, however, is *favour* or *good-will*, Luke 1:30; 2:40,52; Acts 2:47; 7:46; 24:27; 25:9. It may denote the kindness or beneficence of our Lord, II Cor. 8:9, or the favour manifested or bestowed by God, II Cor. 9:8 (referring to material blessings); I Pet. 5:10. Furthermore, the word is expressive of the emotion awakened in the heart of the recipient of such favour, and thus acquires the meaning *"gratitude"* or *"thankfulness,"* Luke 4:22; I Cor. 10:30; 15:57; II Cor. 2:14; 8:16; I Tim. 1:12. In most of the passages, however, in which the word *charis* is used in the New Testament, it signifies the unmerited operation of God in the heart of man, effected through the agency of the Holy Spirit. While we sometimes speak of grace as an inherent quality, it is in reality the active communication of divine blessings by the inworking of the Holy Spirit, out of the fulness of Him who is "full of grace and truth," Rom. 3:24; 5:2,15, 17,20; 6:1; I Cor. 1:4; II Cor. 6:1; 8:9; Eph. 1:7; 2:5,8; 3:7; I Pet. 3:7; 5:12.

2. THE GRACE OF GOD IN THE WORK OF REDEMPTION. A discussion of the grace of God in connection with the work of redemption again calls for several distinctions, which should be borne in mind.

a. In the first place grace is an attribute of God, one of the divine perfections. It is God's free, sovereign, undeserved favour or love to man, in his state of sin and guilt, which manifests itself in the forgiveness of sin and deliverance from its penalty. It is connected with the mercy of God as distinguished from His justice. This is redemptive grace in the most fundamental sense of the word. It is the ultimate cause of God's elective purpose, of the sinner's justification, and of his spiritual renewal; and the prolific source of all spiritual and eternal blessings.

b. In the second place the term "grace" is used as a designation of the objective provision which God made in Christ for the salvation of man. Christ as the Mediator is the living embodiment of the grace of God. "The Word became flesh, and dwelt among us . . . full of grace and truth," John 1:14. Paul has the appearance of Christ in mind, when he says: "For the grace of God hath appeared, bringing salvation to all men," Tit. 2:11. But the term is applied not only to what Christ *is*, but also to what He *merited* for sinners. When the apostle speaks repeatedly in the closing salutations of his Epistles of "the grace of our Lord Jesus Christ," he has in mind the grace of which Christ is the meritorious cause. John says: "The law was given through Moses, but grace and truth came through Jesus Christ," John 1:17. Cf. also Eph. 2:7.

c. In the third place the word "grace" is used to designate the favour of God as it is manifested in the application of the work of redemption by the Holy Spirit. It is applied to the pardon which we receive in justification, a pardon freely given by God, Rom. 3:24; 5:2,21; Tit. 3:15. But in addition to that it is also a comprehensive name for all the gifts of the grace of God, the blessings of salvation, and the spiritual graces which are wrought in the hearts and lives of believers through the operation of the Holy Spirit, Acts 11:23; 18:27; Rom. 5:17; I Cor. 15:10; II Cor. 9:14; Eph. 4:7; Jas. 4:5,6; I Pet. 3:7. Moreover, there are clear indications of the fact that it is not a mere passive quality, but also an active force, a power, something that labours, I Cor. 15:10; II Cor. 12:9; II Tim. 2:1. In this sense of the word it is something like a synonym for the Holy Spirit, so that there is little difference between "full of the Holy Spirit" and "full of grace and power" in Acts 6:5 and 8. The Holy Spirit is called "the Spirit of grace" in Heb. 10:29. It is especially in connection with the teachings of Scripture respecting the application of the grace of God to the sinner by the Holy Spirit, that the doctrine of grace was developed in the Church.

3. THE DOCTRINE OF GRACE IN THE CHURCH. The teachings of Scripture respecting the grace of God stress the fact that God distributes His blessings to men *in a free and sovereign manner, and not in consideration of any inherent merit of men;* that men owe all the blessings of life to a beneficent, forbearing, and longsuffering God; and especially that all the blessings of the work of salvation are freely given of God, and are in no way determined by supposed merits of men. This is clearly expressed by Paul in the following words: "For by grace have ye been saved through faith; and that not of yourselves, it is the gift of God; not of works, that no man should glory," Eph. 2:8,9. He strongly emphasizes the fact that salvation is not by works, Rom. 3:20-28; 4:16; Gal. 2:16.

This doctrine did not go entirely unchallenged. In some of the early Church Fathers, particularly of the Eastern Church, we already meet with a strain of moralism that is not in harmony with the Pauline emphasis. The tendency that became apparent in that section of the Church, finally culminated in Pelagianism. Pelagius' conception of grace was rather unusual. According to Wiggers he comprehended under grace: (a) "The power of doing good (*possibilitas boni*), and therefore especially free will itself." (b) "The revelation, the law, and the example of Christ, by which the practice of virtue is made easier for man." (c) "Our being so made as to be able, by our own will, to abstain from sin, and in God's giving us the help of His law and His commands, and *in His pardoning the previous sins of those who return to Him.*" (d) "Supernatural influences on the Christian, by which his understanding is enlightened and the practice of virtue is rendered easy to him."[1] He recognized no *direct*

---

1. Augustinism and Pelagianism, pp. 179-183.

operation of the Spirit of God on the will of man, but only an *indirect* operation on the will through the enlightened conscience. In his view the operation of the grace of God was primarily, though not exclusively, external and natural. In opposition to the Pelagian view, that of Augustine is often designated as "the theology of grace." While Augustine admitted that the word "grace" could be used in a wider sense (natural grace), and that even in the state of integrity it was the grace of God that made it possible for Adam to retain his uprightness, his main emphasis is always on grace as the gift of God to fallen man, which manifests itself in the forgiveness of sin and in the renewal and sanctification of human nature. In view of the total depravity of man he regards this grace as absolutely necessary unto salvation. It is wrought in man by the operation of the Holy Spirit, who dwells and works in the elect and is the principle of all the blessings of salvation. He distinguished between *operating* or *prevenient*, and *co-operating* or *subsequent* grace. The former enables the will to choose the good, and the latter co-operates with the already enabled will, to do the good. In his struggle with Semi-Pelagianism Augustine emphasized the entirely gratuitous and irresistible character of the grace of God.

In the subsequent struggles the Augustinian doctrine of grace was only partly victorious. Seeberg expresses himself as follows: "Thus the doctrine of 'grace alone' came off victorious; but the Augustinian doctrine of predestination was abandoned. The irresistible grace of predestination was driven from the field by the sacramental grace of baptism."[1] During the Middle Ages the Scholastics paid considerable attention to the subject of grace, but did not always agree as to the details of the doctrine. Some approached the Augustinian, and others the Semi-Pelagian conception of grace. In general it may be said that they conceived of grace as mediated through the sacraments, and that they sought to combine with the doctrine of grace a doctrine of merit which seriously compromised the former. The emphasis was not on grace as the favor of God shown to sinners, but on grace as a quality of the soul, which might be regarded as both uncreated (i.e., as the Holy Spirit), or as increated, or wrought in the hearts of men by the Holy Spirit. This infused grace is basic to the development of the Christian virtues, and enables man to acquire merit with God, to merit further grace, though he cannot merit the grace of perseverance. This can only be obtained as a free gift of God. The Scholastics did not, like Augustine, maintain the logical connection between the doctrine of grace and the doctrine of predestination.

The Reformers went back to the Augustinian conception of grace, but avoided his sacramentarianism. They placed the emphasis once more on grace as the unmerited favour of God shown to sinners, and represented it in a manner which excluded all merit on the part of the sinner. Says Smeaton: "The term *grace*, which in Augustine's acceptation intimated the inward exercise of love, awakened by the operations of the Holy Spirit (Rom. 5:5), and which in the scholastic theology had come to denote a quality of the soul, or the

---

1. *History of Doctrine*, I, p. 382.

inner endowments, and infused habits of faith, love, and hope, was now taken in the more scriptural and wider sense for the free, the efficacious *favour* which is in the divine mind."[1] While the Reformers used the term *grace* in connection with justification, in other connections they often used the phrase, "the work of the Holy Spirit," instead of the term *grace*. While they all emphasized grace in the sense of the internal and saving operation of the Holy Spirit, Calvin especially developed the idea of common grace, that is, a grace which, while it is the expression of the favour of God, does not have a saving effect. According to the splendid dogma-historical study of Dr. H. Kuiper on *Calvin on Common Grace*,[2] he even distinguished three kinds of common grace, namely, universal common grace, general common grace, and covenant common grace. The Arminians departed from the doctrine of the Reformation on this point. According to them God gives sufficient (common) grace to all men, and thereby enables them to repent and believe. If the human will concurs or co-operates with the Holy Spirit and man actually repents and believes, God confers on man the further grace of evangelical obedience and the grace of perseverance. Thus the work of the grace of God is made to depend on the consent of the will of man. There is no such thing as irresistible grace. Says Smeaton in the work already quoted: "It was held that every one could obey or resist; that the cause of conversion was not the Holy Spirit so much as the human will concurring or co-operating; and that this was the immediate cause of conversion."[3] Amyraldus of the School of Saumur did not really improve on the Arminian position by his assumption, in connection with the general decree of God, that the sinner, while devoid of the moral ability, yet has the natural ability to believe, an unfortunate distinction, which was also carried over into New England by Edwards, Bellamy and Fuller. Pajon, a disciple of Amyraldus, denied the necessity of the work of the Holy Spirit in the internal illumination of sinners, in order to their saving conversion. The only thing which he regarded as necessary was that the understanding, which has in itself a sufficiency of clear ideas, should be struck by the light of external revelation. Bishop Warburton in his work on *The Doctrine of Grace, or the Office and Operations of the Holy Spirit* knows of no saving grace in the accepted sense of the word, but limits the word "grace" to the extraordinary operations of the Spirit in the apostolic age. And Junckheim in his important work denied the supernatural character of God's work in the conversion of the sinner, and affirmed that the moral power of the word effected all. The Methodist Revival in England and the Great Awakening in our own country brought with them a restoration of the doctrine of saving grace, though in some cases tinged more or less with Arminianism. For Schleiermacher the problem of the guilt of sin was practically non-existent, since he denied the objective existence of guilt. And consequently he knows little or nothing of the saving grace of God. Says

---

1. *The Doctrine of the Holy Spirit*, p. 346.
2. pp. 179 ff.
3. p. 357.

Mackintosh: "This central Biblical truth (of divine mercy to sinners) Schleiermacher for the most part passes by in silence, or mentions only in a perfunctory fashion that shows how little he understands it."[1] The doctrine of divine grace is also necessarily obscured in the theology of Albrecht Ritschl. And it may be said to be characteristic of the whole of modern liberal theology, with its emphasis on the goodness of man, that it has lost sight of the necessity of the saving grace of God. The word "grace" has gradually disappeared from the written and spoken word of many theologians, and many of the common people in our day attach no other meaning to the term than that of gracefulness or graciousness. Even Otto calls attention to it in his work on *The Idea of the Holy* that people fail to sense the deeper meaning of the word.[2] The Theology of Crisis deserves credit for stressing anew the need of divine grace, with the result that the word is once more coming into use.

QUESTIONS FOR FURTHER STUDY: On which elements of the *ordo salutis* did the emphasis fall in the first three centuries? In how far did these centuries reveal a drift towards moralism and ceremonialism? How was the doctrine of justification understood? How did Augustine conceive of it? What was his conception of faith? How many kinds of grace did he distinguish? Did grace exclude all merit in his system? Did he conceive of saving grace as amissible? What factors favored the development of the doctrine of good works? How did the Scholastics represent the doctrine of justification? How did the *ordo salutis* fare in the hands of the Antinomians? How did the rationalistic and pietistic neonomians conceive of it? What other than saving operations are ascribed to the Holy Spirit in Scripture? Which are the different meanings of the word 'grace' in Scripture? What does it designate in connection with the work of redemption? What is the relation between the doctrines of free will and grace in history?

LITERATURE: Bavinck, *Geref. Dogm.* III, pp. 551-690; Kuyper, *Dict. Dogm., De Salute*, pp. 15-20; McPherson, *Chr. Dogm.*, pp. 367-371; Kaftan, *Dogmatik*, pp. 525-532, 651-661; Warfield, *The Plan of Salvation*; Seeberg, *Heilsordnung* (Art. in Hauck's *Realencyclopaedie*); Pieper, *Christl. Dogm.* II, pp.. 473-498; H. Schmid, *Doct. Theol.*, pp. 413-416; K. Dijk, *Heilsorde* (Art. in *Chr. Enc.*); Pope, *Chr. Theol.* II, pp. 348-367; Neil, *Grace* (Art. in *A Protestant Dictionary*); Easton, *Grace* (Art. in the *Intern. Standard Bible Ec.*); Smeaton, *The Doctrine of the Holy Spirit*, pp. 1-99, 291-414; Buchanan, *The Doctrine of Justification*, pp. 339-364; Moffatt, *Grace in the New Testament*; Bryan, W. S., *An Inquiry into the Need of the Grace of God.*

---

1. *Types of Modern Theology*, p. 96.
2. pp. 32 ff., 145.

III.   Common Grace

In connection with the general operations of the Holy Spirit the subject of common grace also calls for attention. It should be understood, however, that Reformed theology does not, like Arminian theology, regard the doctrine of common grace as a part of Soteriology. At the same time it does recognize a close connection between the operations of the Holy Spirit in the sphere of creation and in that of redemption, and therefore feels that they should not be entirely dissociated.

A. Origin of the Doctrine of Common Grace.

1. THE PROBLEM WITH WHICH IT DEALS. The origin of the doctrine of common grace was occasioned by the fact that there is in the world, alongside of the course of the Christian life with all its blessings, a natural course of life, which is not redemptive and yet exhibits many traces of the true, the good, and the beautiful. The question arose, How can we explain the comparatively orderly life in the world, seeing that the whole world lies under the curse of sin? How is it that the earth yields precious fruit in rich abundance and does not simply bring forth thorns and thistles? How can we account for it that sinful man still "retains some knowledge of God, of natural things, and of the difference between good and evil, and shows some regard for virtue and for good outward behavior"? What explanation can be given of the special gifts and talents with which the natural man is endowed, and of the development of science and art by those who are entirely devoid of the new life that is in Christ Jesus? How can we explain the religious aspirations of men everywhere, even of those who did not come in touch with the Christian religion? How can the unregenerate still speak the truth, do good to others, and lead outwardly virtuous lives? These are some of the questions to which the doctrine of common grace seeks to supply the answer.

2. AUGUSTINE'S ATTITUDE TO THIS PROBLEM. Augustine did not teach the doctrine of common grace, though he did not use the word "grace" exclusively as a designation of saving grace. He spoke of a grace which Adam enjoyed before the fall, and even admitted that man's existing as a living, sentient, and rational being might be termed grace. But over against Pelagius, who stressed the natural ability of man and recognized no other grace than that consisting in the natural endowments of man, the law and the gospel, the example of Christ, and the illumination of the understanding by a gracious influence of God, — he emphasized the total inability of man and his absolute

dependence on the grace of God as an inner renewing power, which not only illumines the mind but also acts directly on the will of man, either as operating or as co-operating grace. He employs the word "grace" almost exclusively in this sense, and regards this grace as the necessary condition to the performance of each good act. When the Pelagians pointed to the virtues of the heathen, who "merely through the power of innate freedom" were often merciful, discreet, chaste, and temperate, he answered that these so-called virtues were sins, because they did not spring from faith. He admits that the heathen can perform certain acts which are in themselves good and from a lower point of view even praiseworthy, but yet considers these deeds, *as the deeds of unregenerate persons*, to be sin, because they do not spring from the motive of love to God or of faith, and do not answer to the right purpose, the glory of God.[1] He denies that such deeds are the fruit of any natural goodness in man.

3. THE VIEW THAT DEVELOPED DURING THE MIDDLE AGES. During the Middle Ages the Augustinian antithesis of *sin and grace* gave way to that of *nature and grace*. This was based on another antithesis which played an important part in Roman Catholic theology, namely, that of the natural and the supernatural. In the state of integrity man was endowed with the supernatural gift of original righteousness, which served as a bridle to hold the lower nature in check. As the result of the fall, man lost this supernatural gift, but his real nature remained or was but slightly affected. A sinful bias developed, but this did not prohibit man from producing much that was true, and good, and beautiful. However, without the infusion of the grace of God, all this did not suffice to give one a claim to life eternal. In connection with the antithesis of the natural and the supernatural, the Roman Catholic Church developed the distinction between the moral virtues of humility, obedience, meekness, liberality, temperance, chastity, and diligence in what is good, which men can gain for themselves by their own labors, and with the timely aid of divine grace; and the theological virtues of faith, hope, and charity, which are infused into man by sanctifying grace. Anabaptism and Socinianism suffer from the same antithesis, but with the distinction that the former exalts grace at the expense of nature, while the latter exalts nature at the expense of grace.

4. THE POSITION OF THE REFORMERS AND OF REFORMED THEOLOGY. On this, as on some other points of doctrine, Luther did not entirely escape the leaven of Roman Catholicism. While he did return to the Augustinian antithesis of sin and grace, he drew a sharp distinction between the lower earthly sphere and the higher spiritual sphere, and maintained that fallen man is by nature capable of doing much that is good and praiseworthy in the lower or earthly sphere, though he is utterly incapable of doing any spiritual good. With an appeal to Augustine the Augsburg Confession teaches "that man's will hath some liberty to work a civil righteousness, and to choose such things as reason can reach unto; but that it hath no power to work the righteousness of

1. Cf. Polman, *De Predestinatieleer van Augustinus, Thomas van Aquino en Calvijn*, pp. 77 f.; Shedd, *History of Christian Doctrine* II, pp. 75 f.

God."[1] The Article contains a quotation from Augustine, in which many of the good works pertaining to the present life, which the natural man can do, are named. Zwingli conceived of sin as pollution rather than as guilt, and consequently regarded the grace of God as sanctifying, rather than as pardoning, grace. This sanctifying influence, which penetrated in a measure even into the Gentile world, accounts for the true, the good, and the beautiful that is in the world. Calvin did not agree with the position of Luther, nor with that of Zwingli. He firmly maintained that the natural man can *of himself* do no good work whatsoever and strongly insisted on the particular nature of saving grace. He developed alongside of the doctrine of particular grace the doctrine of common grace. This is a grace which is communal, does not pardon nor purify human nature, and does not effect the salvation of sinners. It curbs the destructive power of sin, maintains in a measure the moral order of the universe, thus making an orderly life possible, distributes in varying degrees gifts and talents among men, promotes the development of science and art, and showers untold blessings upon the children of men. Since the days of Calvin the doctrine of common grace was generally recognized in Reformed theology, though it also met with occasional opposition. For a long time, however, little was done to develop the doctrine. This was in all probability due to the fact that the rise and prevalence of Rationalism made it necessary to place all emphasis on special grace. Up to the present Kuyper and Bavinck did more than any one else for the development of the doctrine of common grace.

B. Name and Concept of Common Grace.

1. NAME. The name "common grace" as a designation of the grace now under discussion cannot be said to owe its origin to Calvin. Dr. H. Kuiper in his work on *Calvin on Common Grace* says that he found only four passages in Calvin's works in which the adjective "common" is used with the noun "grace," and in two of these the Reformer is speaking of saving grace.[2] In later Reformed theology, however, the name *gratia communis* came into general use to express the idea that this grace extends to all men, in contrast with the *gratia particularis* which is limited to a part of mankind, namely, to the elect. In course of time it became evident that the term "communis" admitted of various interpretations. In Dutch theology it is often regarded as equivalent to "general," and as a result it became customary to speak of "general grace" (*algemeene genade*) in the Netherlands. Strictly speaking, however, the term *communis*, as applied to grace, while implying that it is general in some sense of the word, stresses the fact that this grace is communal, that is, possessed in common by all creatures, or by all men, or by those who live under the administration of the gospel. Thus Dr. H. Kuiper classifies the common grace of which Calvin speaks under three heads, namely: (1) Universal Common Grace, a grace that extends to all creatures; (2) General Common

---

1. Art. XVIII.
2. Cf. p. 178.

Grace, that is a grace which applies to mankind in general and to every member of the human race; and (3) Covenant Common Grace, a grace that is common to all those who live in the sphere of the covenant, whether they belong to the elect or not. It is quite evident that Reformed theologians also subsumed under the term "common grace" a grace that is not general, namely, the external privileges of those who are living under the administration of the gospel, including the external universal calling. At the same time they point out that this grace, in distinction from general common grace, belongs to the economy of redemption.[1] Finally, it should be noted that the term *gratia communis* is susceptible of, and has actually received, not only a quantitative, but also a qualitative interpretation. It may denote a grace that is common in the sense of *ordinary*. The ordinary, in distinction from the special, operations of the Holy Spirit are called common. His natural or usual operations are contrasted with those which are unusual and supernatural. This is the meaning of the term "common" in the *Westminister Confession* X. 4; and the *Westminster Larger Catechism*, Q. 60. W. L. Alexander declares of the common grace enjoyed by those who live under the gospel: "The grace thus bestowed is common, not in the sense of being given to all men in common, but in the sense of producing effects which are ordinary, and may fall short of a real saving efficacy."[2] So understood, the grace of God may be common without being general or universal.

2. CONCEPT. The distinction between common and special grace is not one that applies to grace as an attribute in God. There are no two kinds of grace in God, but only one. It is that perfection of God in virtue of which he shows unmerited and even forfeited favour to man. This one grace of God manifests itself, however, in different gifts and operations. The richest manifestation of it is seen in those gracious operations of God which aim at, and result in, the removal of the guilt, the pollution, and the punishment of sin, and the ultimate salvation of sinners. But while this is the crowning work of the grace of God, it is not its only manifestation. It appears also in the natural blessings which God showers upon man in the present life, in spite of the fact that man has forfeited them and lies under the sentence of death. It is seen in all that God does to restrain the devastating influence and development of sin in the world, and to maintain and enrich and develop the natural life of mankind in general and of those individuals who constitute the human race. It should be emphasized that these natural blessings are manifestations of the *grace* of God to man in general. Some prefer to say that they are expressions of His goodness, kindness, benevolence, mercy, or longsuffering, but seem to forget that He could not be good, kind, or benevolent to the *sinner* unless He were first of all *gracious*. It should be borne in mind, however, that the term *gratia communis*, though generally designating a grace that is common to the whole of mankind, is also used to denote a grace that is common to the elect

---

1. Cf. Mastricht, *God geleerdheit* I, p. 441; Brakel, *Redelijke Godsdienst* I, pp. 729 f.; Hodge, *Syst. Theol.* II, p. 654; A. A. Hodge, *Outlines of Theol.*, p. 449; Shedd, *Calvinism Pure and Mixed*, pp. 98 f.; Vos, *Geref. Dogm.* IV, pp. 13 f.
2. *System of Bib. Theol.* II, p. 352.

and the non-elect that are living under the gospel, such as the external gospel call that comes to both alike, and that inner illumination and those gifts of the Spirit of which we read in Heb. 6:4-6. It is understood, however, that these privileges can be called common grace only in the sense that they are enjoyed by the elect and the reprobate indiscriminately, and that they do not constitute special, in the sense of saving, grace. In distinction from the more general manifestations of common grace they, while they do not constitute a part of the grace of God that necessarily leads to salvation, are nevertheless related to the soteriological process. They are sometimes called "special" grace, but then "special" is not equivalent to "saving." In general it may be said that, when we speak of "common grace," we have in mind, either (a) *those general operations of the Holy Spirit whereby He, without renewing the heart, exercises such a moral influence on man through His general or special revelation, that sin is restrained, order is maintained in social life, and civil righteousness is promoted;* or, (b) *those general blessings, such as rain and sunshine, food and drink, clothing and shelter, which God imparts to all men indiscriminately where and in what measure it seems good to Him.*

The following points of distinction between special (in the sense of saving) and common grace should be noted:

a. The extent of special grace is determined by the decree of election. This grace is limited to the elect, while common grace is not so limited, but is granted to all men indiscriminately. The decree of election and reprobation has no determining influence on it. It cannot even be said that the elect receive a greater measure of common grace than the non-elect. It is a matter of common knowledge, and has frequently been observed, that the wicked often possess a greater measure of common grace and have a greater share in the natural blessings of life than the pious.

b. Special grace removes the guilt and penalty of sin, changes the inner life of man, and gradually cleanses him from the pollution of sin by the supernatural operation of the Holy Spirit. Its work invariably issues in the salvation of the sinner. Common grace, on the other hand, never removes the guilt of sin, does not renew human nature, but only has a restraining effect on the corrupting influence of sin and in a measure mitigates its results. It does not effect the salvation of the sinner, though in some of its forms (external calling and moral illumination) it may be closely connected with the economy of redemption and have a soteriological aspect.

c. Special grace is irresistible. This does not mean that it is a deterministic force which compels man to believe against his will, but that by changing the heart it makes man perfectly willing to accept Jesus Christ unto salvation and to yield obedience to the will of God. Common grace is resistible, and as a matter of fact is always more or less resisted. Paul shows in Rom. 1 and 2 that neither the Gentiles nor the Jews were living up to the light which they had. Says Shedd: "In common grace the call to believe and repent is invariably ineffectual, because man is averse to faith and repentance and in bondage to sin."¹ It is ineffectual unto salvation because it leaves the heart unchanged.

d. Special grace works in a spiritual and re-creative way, renewing the whole nature of man, and thus making man able and willing to accept the offer of salvation in Jesus Christ, and to produce spiritual fruits. Common grace, to the contrary, operates only in a rational and moral way by making man in a general way receptive for the truth, by presenting motives to the will, and by appealing to the natural desires of man. This is equivalent to saying that special (saving) grace is immediate and supernatural, since it is wrought directly in the soul by the immediate energy of the Holy Spirit, while common grace is mediate, since it is the product of the mediate operation of the Holy Spirit through the truth of general or special revelation and by moral persuasion.

This conception of common grace should be carefully distinguished from that of the Arminians, who regard common grace as a link in the *ordo salutis* and ascribe to it *saving* significance. They hold that, in virtue of the common grace of God, the unregenerate man is perfectly able to perform a certain measure of spiritual good, to turn to God in faith and repentance, and thus to accept Jesus unto salvation. They go even farther than that, and maintain that common grace by the illumination of the mind and the persuasive influence of the truth incites the sinner to accept Jesus Christ and to turn to God in faith and repentance, and will certainly achieve this end, unless the sinner obstinately resists the operation of the Holy Spirit. The Canons of Dort have this in mind where they reject the error of those who teach "that the corrupt and natural man can so well use the common grace (by which they understand the light of nature), or the gifts still left him after the fall, that he can gradually gain by their good use a greater, that is, the evangelical or saving grace, and salvation itself."²

C. Common Grace and the Atoning Work of Christ.

The question naturally arises, whether the manifestation of common grace is in any way connected with the atoning work of Christ. As far as we know, Dr. Kuyper does not posit such a connection. According to him Christ as the Mediator of creation, the light that lighteth every man coming into the world, is the source of common grace. This means that the blessings of common grace flow from the work of creation. But this hardly suffices to answer the question, how it is to be explained that a holy and just God extends grace to, and bestows favors upon, sinners who have forfeited everything, even when they have no share in the righteousness of Christ and prove finally impenitent. The question is exactly, How can God continue to bestow those blessings of creation on men who are under the sentence of death and condemnation? As far as the elect are concerned this question is answered by the cross of Christ, but how about the reprobate? Perhaps it can be said that it is not necessary to assume a specific judicial basis for the bestowal of common grace on man in view of

1. *Calvinism Pure and Mixed*, p. 99.
2. III-IV. Rejection of errors 5.

the fact (a) that it does not remove the guilt of sin and therefore does not carry pardon with it; and (b) that it does not lift the sentence of condemnation, but only postpones the execution. Perhaps the divine good pleasure to stay the revelation of His wrath and to endure "with much longsuffering vessels of wrath fitted unto destruction," offers a sufficient explanation for the blessings of common grace.

Reformed theologians generally hesitate to say that Christ by His atoning blood merited these blessings for the impenitent and reprobate. At the same time they do believe that important natural benefits accrue to the whole human race from the death of Christ, and that in these benefits the unbelieving, the impenitent, and the reprobate also share. In every covenant transaction recorded in Scripture it appears that the covenant of grace carries with it not only spiritual but also material blessings, and those material blessings are generally of such a kind that they are naturally shared also by unbelievers. Says Cunningham: "Many blessings flow to mankind at large from the death of Christ, collaterally and incidentally, in consequence of the relation in which men, viewed collectively, stand to each other."[1] And it is but natural that this should be so. If Christ was to save an elect race, gradually called out of the world of humanity in the course of centuries, it became necessary for God to exercise forbearance, to check the course of evil, to promote the development of the natural powers of man, to keep alive within the hearts of men a desire for civil righteousness, for external morality and good order in society, and to shower untold blessings upon mankind in general. Dr. Hodge expresses it thus: "It is very plain that any plan designed to secure the salvation of an elect portion of a race propagated by generation and living in association, as is the case with mankind, cannot secure its end without greatly affecting, for better or for worse, the character and destiny of all the rest of the race not elected." He quotes Dr. Candlish to the effect that "the entire history of the human race, from the apostasy to the final judgment, is a dispensation of forbearance in respect to the reprobate, in which many blessings, physical and moral, affecting their characters and destinies forever, accrue even to the heathen, and many more to the educated and refined citizens of Christian communities. These come to them through the mediation of Christ, and coming to them now, must have been designed for them from the beginning."[2] These general blessings of mankind, indirectly resulting from the atoning work of Christ, were not only foreseen by God, but designed by Him as blessings for all concerned. It is perfectly true, of course, that the design of God in the work of Christ pertained primarily and directly, not to the temporal well-being of men in general, but to the redemption of the elect; but secondarily and indirectly it also included the natural blessings bestowed

---

1. *Hist. Theol.* II, p. 333.
2. *The Atonement,* pp. 358 f.

on mankind indiscriminately. All that the natural man receives other than curse and death is an indirect result of the redemptive work of Christ.[1]

D. The Relation Between Special and Common Grace.

Several questions may be raised respecting this relation, of which the following are some of the most important.

1. DO SPECIAL AND COMMON GRACE DIFFER ESSENTIALLY OR ONLY IN DEGREE? Arminians recognize alongside of sufficient (common) grace the grace of evangelical obedience, but aver that these two differ only in degree and not in essence. They are both soteriological in the sense that they form part of the saving work of God. The former makes it possible for man to repent and believe, while the latter, in co-operation with the will, causes man to repent and believe. Both can be resisted, so that even the latter is not necessarily effectual unto salvation. Reformed theology, however, insists on the *essential* difference between common and special grace. Special grace is supernatural and spiritual: it removes the guilt and pollution of sin and lifts the sentence of condemnation. Common grace, on the other hand, is natural; and while some of its forms may be closely connected with saving grace, it does not remove sin nor set man free, but merely restrains the outward manifestations of sin and promotes outward morality and decency, good order in society and civic righteousness, the development of science and art, and so on. It works only in the natural, and not in the spiritual sphere. It should be maintained therefore that, while the two are closely connected in the present life, they are yet *essentially* different, and do not differ merely in degree. No amount of common grace can ever introduce the sinner into the new life that is in Christ Jesus. However, common grace does sometimes reveal itself in forms that can hardly be distinguished by man from the manifestations of special grace as, for instance, in the case of temporal faith. Dr. Shedd does not seem to bear the essential difference between the two in mind especially when he says: "The non-elect receives common grace, and common grace would incline the human will if it were not defeated by the human will. If the sinner should make no hostile opposition, common grace would be equivalent to saving grace." In a note he adds: "To say that common grace, if not resisted by the sinner, would be equivalent to regenerating grace, is not the same as to say that common grace, if *assisted* by the sinner, would be equivalent to regenerating grace. In the first instance, God would be the sole author of regeneration; in the second He would not be."[2] This reminds one of Lutheran theology, but the author's meaning is not entirely clear, for elsewhere he also ascribes the non-resistance of the sinner to the operation of the Holy Spirit.[3]

2. WHICH ONE OF THE TWO IS PRIMARY, COMMON OR SPECIAL GRACE? To this question it must be answered that in a temporal sense neither one of

---

1. Cf Turretin. *Opera. Locus* XIV, Q. XIV, par. XI; Witsius, *De Verbonden*, B. II, Kap. 9, s. 4; Cunningham, *Hist. Theol.* II, p. 332; Symington, *Atonement and Intercession*, p. 255; Bavinck, *Geref. Dogm.* III, p. 535; Vos, *Ger. Dogm.* III, p. 150,
2. *Dogm. Theol.* II, p. 483.
3. *Calvinism Pure and Mixed*, p. 101.

them can be said to be prior to the other. The third chapter of Genesis clearly reveals that both of them go into operation at once after the fall. Logical priority should be ascribed to special grace, however, because common grace is made subservient to this in its operation in the world.

3. DOES COMMON GRACE SERVE AN INDEPENDENT PURPOSE OR NOT? It cannot be doubted that common grace finds its purpose in part in the redemptive work of Jesus Christ; it is subservient to the execution of the plan of God in the life of the elect and in the development of the Church. But in addition to that it also serves an independent purpose, namely, to bring to light and to harness for the service of man the hidden forces of nature, and to develop the powers and talents that are latent in the human race, in order that man may ever-increasingly exercise dominion over the lower creation, to the glory of God the Creator.[1]

4. DO SPECIAL AND COMMON GRACE EACH HAVE A PECULIAR SPHERE ENTIRELY DISTINCT FROM THAT OF THE OTHER? It may be said that in a certain sense special grace has its own peculiar sphere in the organized Church, though it is not necessarily limited to this, and common grace is also operative in the Church for it is granted to all men. Both operate in the world, but while common grace in the more usual sense of the term pertains to the things of the natural world and this present life, special grace bears on the things of the new creation. They cannot but influence each other. Common grace enriches the Church with its blessings; and the Church raises the fruits of common grace to a higher level by bringing them under the influence of the regenerate life.

E. The Means by Which Common Grace Operates.

Several means can be distinguished by which common grace effects its work. Calvin suggests some of these when he, in speaking of the restraining influence of common grace says: "Hence, how much soever men may disguise their impurity, some are restrained only by shame, others by fear of the laws, from breaking out into many kinds of wickedness. Some aspire to an honest life, as deeming it most conducive to their interest, while others are raised above the vulgar lot, that, by the dignity of their station, they may keep inferiors to their duty. Thus God by his providence, curbs the perverseness of nature, preventing it from breaking forth into action, yet without rendering it inwardly pure."[2] The following are some of the most important means through which common grace effects its work.

1. THE LIGHT OF GOD'S REVELATION. This is fundamental for without it all other means would be impossible, and even if possible, would fail to function properly. We have in mind here primarily the light of God's revelation that shines in nature and lightens every man coming into the world. It is itself the fruit of common grace, but in turn becomes a means for the further manifestation of it, since it serves to guide the conscience of the natural man. Paul speaks of the Gentiles who do by nature the things of the law, "in that they

1. Cf. Kuyper, *Gemeene Gratie* II, pp. 622,628,633; Bavinck, *De Algemeene Genade*, p. 45.
2. *Inst.* II. 3,3.

show the word of the law written in their hearts, their conscience bearing witness therewith, and their thoughts one with another accusing or else excusing them." Rom. 2:14,15. Calvin in commenting on this passage says that such Gentiles "prove that there is imprinted on their hearts a discrimination and judgment by which they distinguish between what is just and unjust, between what is honest and dishonest."[1] In addition to this, however, it may be said that common grace in a more restricted sense also operates in the light of God's special revelation, which is not itself the fruit of common, but of special, grace.

2. GOVERNMENTS. Of these too it may be said that they are at once the fruit and the means of common grace. According to Rom. 13 governments are ordained of God, to maintain good order in society. To resist them is to resist the ordinance of God. The ruler, says Paul, "is a minister of God to thee for good." Rom. 13:4. He finds support in the conscience of man (verse 5) and for the rest "beareth not the sword in vain." On this point the Belgic Confession says: "We believe that our gracious God, because of the depravity of mankind, hath appointed kings, princes, and magistrates, willing that the world should be governed by certain laws and policies; to the end that the dissoluteness of men might be restrained, and all things carried on among them with good order and decency."[2]

3. PUBLIC OPINION. The natural light that shines in the hearts of men, especially when re-enforced by the influence of God's special revelation, results in the forming of a public opinion that is in external conformity with the law of God; and this has a tremendous influence on the conduct of men who are very sensitive to the judgment of public opinion. Naturally public opinion will be a means of common grace only when it is formed under the influence of God's revelation. If it is not controlled by conscience, acting in harmony with the light of nature, or by the Word of God, it becomes a mighty influence for evil.

4. DIVINE PUNISHMENTS AND REWARDS. The providential arrangements of God, whereby He visits the iniquity of men upon them in this life, and rewards deeds that are in outward conformity with the divine law, serve an important purpose in curbing the evil that is in the world. The punishments have a deterring effect, and the rewards serve as incentives. By these means, whatever there is of moral goodness in the world is greatly encouraged. Many shun evil and seek that which is good, not because they fear the Lord, but because they feel that good brings its own reward and best serves their interests.

F. The Fruits of Common Grace.

In the preceding it was already intimated that what is left to us of the light of nature, is still operative only in virtue of the common grace of God. It is one of the most important fruits of common grace, without which some of the others would not be conceivable. The following fruits may be mentioned here:

1. *Comm. on Romans in loco.*
2. Art. XXXVI.

1. THE EXECUTION OF THE SENTENCE IS STAYED. God pronounced the sentence of death on the sinner. Speaking of the tree of the knowledge of good and evil, He said. "In the day that thou eatest thereof thou shalt surely die." Man did eat of it, and the sentence went into execution to a certain extent, but clearly was not fully executed at once. It is due to common grace that God did not at once fully execute the sentence of death on the sinner, and does not do so now, but maintains and prolongs the natural life of man and gives him time for repentance. He does not at once cut short the life of the sinner, but affords him an opportunity to repent, thereby removing all excuse and justifying the coming manifestation of His wrath upon those who persist in sin unto the end. That God acts on this principle is abundantly evident from such passages as Isa. 48:9; Jer. 7:23-25; Luke 13:6-9; Rom. 2:4; 9:22; II Peter 3:9.

2. THE RESTRAINT OF SIN. Through the operation of common grace sin is restrained in the lives of individuals and in society. The element of corruption that entered the life of the human race is not permitted, for the present, to accomplish its disintegrating work. Calvin says: "But we ought to consider that, notwithstanding the corruption of our nature, there is some room for divine grace, such grace as, without purifying it, may lay it under internal restraint. For, did the Lord let every mind loose to wanton in its lusts, doubtless there is not a man who would not show that his nature is capable of all the crimes with which Paul charges it, (Rom. 3 compared with Ps. 14:3 ff)."[1] This restraint may be external or internal or both, but does not change the heart. There are passages of Scripture which speak of a striving of the Spirit of God with men which does not lead to repentance, Gen. 6:3; Isa. 63:10; Acts 7:51; of operations of the Spirit that are finally withdrawn, I Sam. 16:14; Heb. 6:4-6; and of the fact that in some cases God finally gives up men to the lusts of their own hearts, Ps. 81:12; Rom. 1:24,26,28. In addition to the preceding passages there are some which are clearly indicative of the fact that God restrains sin in various ways, such as Gen. 20:6; 31:7; Job 1:12; 2:6; II Kings 19:27,28; Rom. 13:1-4.

3. THE PRESERVATION OF SOME SENSE OF TRUTH, MORALITY AND RELIGION. It is due to common grace that man still retains some sense of the true, the good, and the beautiful, often appreciates these to a rather surprising degree, and reveals a desire for truth, for external morality, and even for certain forms of religion. Paul speaks of Gentiles who "show the work of the law written in their hearts, their conscience bearing witness therewith, and their thoughts one with another accusing or else excusing them," Rom. 2:15, and even says of those who gave free vent to their wicked lives that they knew the truth of God, though they hindered the truth in unrighteousness and exchanged it for a lie, Rom. 1:18-25. To the Athenians, who were devoid of the fear of God, he said, "Ye men of Athens, in all things I perceive that ye are very religious," Acts 17:22. The Canons of Dort express themselves as follows on this point: "There remain, however, in man since the fall, the glimmerings of natural light,

1. *Inst.* II. 3,3.

whereby he retains some knowledge of God, of natural things, and of the difference between good and evil, and shows some regard for virtue and for good outward behavior. But so far is this light of nature from being sufficient to bring him to a saving knowledge of God and true conversion that he is incapable of using it aright even in things natural and civil. Nay, further, this light, such as it is, man in various ways renders wholly polluted, and hinders in unrighteousness, by doing which he becomes inexcusable before God." III-IV. 4.

4. THE PERFORMANCE OF OUTWARD GOOD AND CIVIL RIGHTEOUSNESS. Common grace enables man to perform what is generally called *justitia civilis*, that is, that which is right in civil or natural affairs, in distinction from that which is right in religious matters, natural good works especially in social relations, works that are outwardly and objectively in harmony with the law of God, though entirely destitute of any spiritual quality. This is in harmony with our Reformed Confession. Art. XIV of the Belgic Confession speaks in its title of man's incapacity to perform what is *truly* good, says that man retained only small remains of his excellent gifts, so as to render him without excuse, and rejects only the Pelagian error that man can of himself perform spiritual or saving good. The Canons of Dort III-IV, Art. 3, speak in a similar vein: "Therefore all men are conceived in sin, and are by nature children of wrath, incapable of *saving* good" etc. It may be objected that the Heidelberg Catechism speaks in absolute terms when it says in Question 8 that we are incapable of doing any good unless we are regenerated. But it is quite evident from the Commentary of Ursinus himself that he would not deny that man can do civil good, but only that he cannot perform good works such as are defined in Question 91 of the Catechism. Reformed theologians generally maintain that the unregenerate can perform natural good, civil good, and outwardly religious good.[1] They call attention to the fact, however, that, while such works of the unregenerate are good from a material point of view, as works which God commanded, they cannot be called good from a formal point of view, since they do not spring from the right motive and do not aim at the right purpose. The Bible repeatedly speaks of works of the unregenerate as good and right, II Kings 10:29,30; 12:2 (comp. II Chron. 24:17-25); 14:3,14-16,20,27 (comp. II Chron. 25:2); Luke 6:33; Rom. 2:14,15.

5. MANY NATURAL BLESSINGS. To common grace man further owes all the natural blessings which he receives in the present life. Though he has forfeited all the blessings of God, he receives abundant tokens of the goodness of God from day to day. There are several passages of Scripture from which it appears abundantly that God showers many of His good gifts on all men indiscriminately, that is, upon the good and the bad, the elect and the reprobate, such as: Gen. 17:20 (comp. vs. 18); 39:5; Ps. 145:9,15,16; Matt. 5:44,45; Luke

1. Cf. Calvin, *Inst.* III. 14,2; Van Mastricht, *Godgeleerdheid*, Bk. IV. 4,11,12; Voetius, *Catechisatie* I, p. 168-172; Ursinus, *Comm. on the Catechism, Lord's Day* II, p. 77; Charnock, *On the Attributes* II, pp. 303,304; Brakel, *Redelijke Godsdienst* I, p. 338.

6:35,36; Acts 14:16,17; I Tim. 4:10. And these gifts are intended as blessings, not only for the good but also for the evil. In the light of Scripture the position is untenable that God never blesses the reprobate, though He does give them many gifts which are good in themselves. In Gen. 39:5 we read that "Jehovah blessed the Egyptian's house for Joseph's sake; and the blessing of Jehovah was upon all that he had in the house and in the field." And in Matt. 5:44,45 Jesus exhorts His disciples in these words, "Bless those that curse you . . . that ye may be children of your Father who is in heaven." This can only mean one thing, namely, that God also blesses those who curse Him. Cf. also Luke 6:35,36; Rom. 2:4.

G. Objections to the Reformed Doctrine of Common Grace.

Several objections have been and are even now raised by some against the doctrine of common grace as it is presented in the preceding. The following are some of the most important of these:

1. Arminians are not satisfied with it, because it does not go far enough. They regard common grace as an integral part of the saving process. It is that sufficient grace that enables man to repent and believe in Jesus Christ unto salvation, *and which in the purpose of God is intended to lead men to faith and repentance,* though it may be frustrated by men. A grace that is not so intended and does not actually minister to the salvation of men is a contradiction in terms. Hence Pope, a Wesleyan Arminian, speaks of common grace in the Calvinistic system as "being universal and not particular; being necessarily, or at least actually, inoperative for salvation in the purpose of God," and calls this a "wasted influence." He further says: "Grace is no more grace, if it does not include the saving intention of the Giver."[1]   But, surely, the Bible does not so limit the use of the term "grace." Such passages as Gen. 6:8; 19:19; Ex. 33:12,16; Num. 32:5; Luke 2:40, and many others do not refer to what we call "saving grace," nor to what the Arminian calls "sufficient grace."

2. It is sometimes argued that the Reformed doctrine of common grace involves the doctrine of universal atonement, and therefore leads into the Arminian camp. But there is no good ground for this assertion. It neither says nor implies that it is the purpose of God to save all men through the atoning blood of Jesus Christ. The objection is based particularly on the universal proclamation of the gospel, which is considered possible only on the basis of a universal atonement. It was already suggested by the Arminians themselves at the time of the Synod of Dort, when they asserted that the Reformed with their doctrine of particular atonement could not preach the gospel to all men indiscriminately. But the Synod of Dort did not recognize the implied contradiction. The Canons teach particular atonement,[2] and also require the universal proclamation of the gospel.[3]   And this is in perfect harmony with Scripture, which teaches on the one hand, that Christ

---

1. *Christian Theology* II, pp. 387 f.
2. II. 8.
3. II. 5 and III. 8.

atoned only for the elect, John 10:15; Acts 20:28; Rom. 8:32,33; cf. also John 17:9; and on the other hand, that the gospel call must be extended to all men indiscriminately, Matt. 22:2-14; 28:19; Mark 16:15,16. If it be objected that we cannot fully harmonize the indiscriminate and sincere offer of salvation on condition of faith and repentance with the doctrine of particular atonement, this may be admitted but with the distinct understanding that the truth of a doctrine does not depend on our ability to harmonize it with every other doctrine of Scripture.

3. Another objection to the doctrine of common grace is that it presupposes a certain favorable disposition in God even to reprobate sinners, while we have no right to assume such a disposition in God. This stricture takes its starting point in the eternal counsel of God, in His election and reprobation. Along the line of His election God reveals His love, grace, mercy, and long-suffering, leading to salvation; and in the historical realization of His reprobation He gives expression only to His aversion, disfavor, hatred, and wrath, leading to destruction. But this looks like a rationalistic over-simplification of the inner life of God, which does not take sufficient account of His self-revelation. In speaking on this subject we ought to be very careful and allow ourselves to be guided by the explicit statements of Scripture rather than by our bold inferences from the secret counsel of God. There is far more in God than we can reduce to our logical categories. Are the elect in this life the objects of God's love only, and never in any sense the objects of His wrath? Is Moses thinking of the reprobate when he says: "For we are consumed in thine anger, and in thy wrath are we troubled"? Ps. 90:7. Does not the statement of Jesus that the wrath of God *abideth* on them that obey not the Son imply that it is removed from the others when, *and not until,* they submit to the beneficent rule of Christ? John 3:36. And does not Paul say to the Ephesians that they "were by nature children of wrath even as the rest"? Eph. 2:3. Evidently the elect can not be regarded as *always* and *exclusively* the objects of God's love. And if they who are the objects of God's redeeming love can also in some sense of the word be regarded as the objects of His wrath, why should it be impossible that they who are the objects of His wrath should also in some sense share His divine favor? A father who is also a judge may loathe the son that is brought before him as a criminal, and feel constrained to visit his judicial wrath upon him, but may yet pity him and show him acts of kindness while he is under condemnation. Why should this be impossible in God? General Washington hated the traitor that was brought before him and condemned him to death, but at the same time showed him compassion by serving him with the dainties from his own table. Cannot God have compassion even on the condemned sinner, and bestow favors upon him? The answer need not be uncertain, since the Bible clearly teaches that He showers untold blessings upon all men and also clearly indicates that these are the expression of a favorable disposition in God, which falls short, however, of the positive volition to pardon their sin, to lift their sentence, and to grant them salvation. The following passages

clearly point to such a favorable disposition: Prov. 1:24; Isa. 1:18; Ezek. 18:23,32; 33:11; Matt. 5:43-45; 23:37; Mark 10:21; Luke 6:35: Rom. 2:4; I Tim. 2:4. If such passages do not testify to a favorable disposition in God, it would seem that language has lost its meaning, and that God's revelation is not dependable on this subject.

4. Anabaptists object to the doctrine of common grace, because it involves the recognition of good elements in the natural order of things, and this is contrary to their fundamental position. They regard the natural creation with contempt, stress the fact that Adam was of the earth earthy, and see only impurity in the natural order as such. Christ established a new supernatural order of things, and to that order the regenerate man, who is not merely a renewed, but an entirely new man, also belongs. He has nothing in common with the world round about him and should therefore take no part in its life: never swear an oath, take no part in war, recognize no civil authority, avoid worldly clothing, and so on. On this position there is no other grace than saving grace. This view was shared by Labadism, Pietism, the Moravian brethren, and several other sects. Barth's denial of common grace seems to be following along these same lines. This is no wonder, since for him too creaturliness and sinfulness are practically identical. Brunner gives the following summary of Barth's view: "It follows from the acknowledgment of Christ as the only saving grace of God that there exists no creative and sustaining grace which has been operative ever since the creation of the world and which manifests itself to us in God's maintenance of the world, since in that case we should have to recognize two or even three kinds of grace, and that would stand in contradistinction with the singleness of the grace of Christ. . . . Similarly, the new creation is in no wise a fulfilment but exclusively a replacement accomplished by a complete annihilation of what went before, a *substitution* of the new man for the old. The proposition, *gratia non tollit naturam sed perficit*, is not true in any sense but is altogether an arch-heresy."[1] Brunner rejects this view and is more in line with the Reformed thought on this point.

QUESTIONS FOR FURTHER STUDY: Do the Hebrew and Greek words for 'grace' always denote saving grace? Are they ever used as a designation of what we call 'common grace'? Does the doctrine of common grace presuppose the doctrine of universal atonement? Does it imply a denial of the fact that man is by nature subject to the wrath of God? Does it involve a denial of man's total depravity, and of his inability to do spiritual good? Is the good which the natural man can do good only in the sight of man or also in the sight of God? Does the doctrine of common grace destroy the antithesis between the world and the kingdom of God? If not, how do you explain this?

LITERATURE: Calvin, *Institutes* II. 2 and 3; Kuyper, *De Gemeene Gratie*; Bavinck, *De Algemeene Genade*; ibid., *Calvin and Common Grace* (in, *Calvin and the Reformation*); Shedd, *Calvinism Pure and Mixed*, pp. 96-106; ibid., *Dogm. Theol.* I, pp. 432, 435; II, pp. 483 ff.; Hodge, *Syst. Theol.* II, pp. 654-675; Vos, *Geref. Dogm.* IV, pp. 11-17; Alexander, *Syst. of Bib. Theol.* II. pp. 343-361; Dabney, *Syst. and Polem. Theol.*, pp. 583-588; ibid., *Discussions*, pp. 282-313 (*God's Indiscriminate Proposals of Mercy*); H. Kuiper, *Calvin on Common Grace*; Berkhof, *De Drie Punten in Alle Deelen Gereformeerd*; Hepp, Art. *Gemeene Gratie* in the *Christelijke Encyclopaedie*.

1. *Natur und Gnade*, p. 8.

IV. The Mystical Union

Calvin repeatedly expresses the idea that the sinner cannot share in the saving benefits of Christ's redemptive work, unless he be in union with Him, and thus emphasizes a very important truth. As Adam was the representative head of the old humanity, so Christ is the representative head of the new humanity. All the blessings of the covenant of grace flow from Him who is the Mediator of the covenant. Even the very first blessing of the saving grace of God which we receive already presupposes a union with the Person of the Mediator. It is exactly at this point that we find one of the most characteristic differences between the operations and blessings of special and those of common grace. The former can be received and enjoyed only by those who are in union with Christ, while the latter can be and are enjoyed also by those who are not reckoned in Christ, and therefore are not one with Him. Every spiritual blessing which believers receive flows to them out of Christ. Hence Jesus in speaking of the coming Paraklete could say unto His disciples: "He shall glorify me; for He shall take of mine, and shall declare it unto you," John 16:14. Subjectively, the union between Christ and believers is effected by the Holy Spirit in a mysterious and supernatural way, and for that reason is generally designated as the *unio mystica* or mystical union.

A. Nature of the Mystical Union.

Lutherans generally treat the doctrine of the mystical union *anthropologically,* and therefore conceive of it as established by faith. Hence they naturally take it up at a later point in their soteriology. But this method fails to do full justice to the idea of our union with Christ, since it loses sight of the eternal basis of the union and of its objective realization in Christ, and deals exclusively with the subjective realization of it in our lives, and even so only with our personal conscious entrance into this union. Reformed theology, on the other hand, deals with the union of believers with Christ *theologically,* and as such does far greater justice to this important subject. In doing so it employs the term "mystical union" in a broad sense as a designation not only of the subjective union of Christ and believers, but also of the union that lies back of it, that is basic to it, and of which it is only the culminating expression. namely, the federal union of Christ and those who are His in the counsel of redemption, the mystical union ideally established in that eternal counsel, and the union as it is objectively effected in the incarnation and the redemptive work of Christ.

447

1. THE FEDERAL UNION OF CHRIST WITH THOSE WHOM THE FATHER HAS GIVEN HIM, IN THE COUNSEL OF REDEMPTION. In the counsel of peace Christ voluntarily took upon Himself to be the Head and Surety of the elect, destined to constitute the new humanity, and as such to establish their righteousness before God by paying the penalty for their sin and by rendering perfect obedience to the law and thus securing their title to everlasting life. In that eternal covenant the sin of His people was imputed to Christ, and His righteousness was imputed to them. This imputation of the righteousness of Christ to His people in the counsel of redemption is sometimes represented as a justification from eternity. It is certainly the eternal basis of our justification by faith, and is the ground on which we receive all spiritual blessings and the gift of life eternal. And this being so, it is basic to the whole of soteriology, and even to the first stages in the application of the work of redemption, such as regeneration and internal calling.

2. THE UNION OF LIFE IDEALLY ESTABLISHED IN THE COUNSEL OF REDEMPTION. In the case of the first Adam there was not only a federal, but also a natural and organic union between him and his descendants. There was the tie of a common life between him and all his progeny, and this made it possible that the blessings of the covenant of works, if these had eventuated, could have been passed on to the whole organism of mankind in an organic way. A somewhat similar situation obtained in the case of the last Adam as the representative Head of the covenant of redemption. Like the first Adam. He did not represent a conglomeration of disjointed individuals, but a body of men and women who were to derive their life from Him, to be united by spiritual ties, and thus to form a spiritual organism. Ideally this body, which is the Church, was already formed in the covenant of redemption, and formed in union with Christ, and this union made it possible that all the blessings merited by Christ could be passed on to those whom He represented in an organic way. They were conceived of as a glorious body, a new humanity, sharing the life of Jesus Christ. It was in virtue of that union, as it was realized in the course of history, that Christ could say: "Behold, I and the children whom God hath given me," Heb. 2:13.

3. THE UNION OF LIFE OBJECTIVELY REALIZED IN CHRIST. In virtue of the legal or representative union established in the covenant of redemption Christ became incarnate as the substitute for His people, to merit all the blessings of salvation for them. Since His children were sharers in flesh and blood, "He also in like manner partook of the same; that through death He might bring to nought him that had the power of death, that is the devil; and might deliver all them who through fear of death were all their lifetime subject to bondage," Heb. 2:14,15. He could merit salvation for them just because He already stood in relation to them as their Surety and Mediator, their Head and Substitute. The whole Church was included in Him as her Head. In an objective sense she was crucified with Christ, she died with Him, she arose in Him from the dead, and was made to sit with Him in the heavenly places. All the blessings of saving

grace lie ready for the Church in Christ; man can add nothing to them; and they now only await their subjective application by the operation of the Holy Spirit, which is also merited by Christ and is sure of progressive realization in the course of history.

4. THE UNION OF LIFE SUBJECTIVELY REALIZED BY THE OPERATION OF THE HOLY SPIRIT. The work of Christ was not finished when He had merited salvation for His people and had obtained actual possession of the blessings of salvation. In the counsel of redemption He took it upon Himself to put all His people in possession of all these blessings, and He does this through the operation of the Holy Spirit, who takes all things out of Christ, and gives them unto us. We should not conceive of the subjective realization of the mystical union in the Church atomistically, as if it were effected by bringing now this and then that individual sinner to Christ. It should be seen from the point of view of Christ. Objectively, the whole Church is in Him, and is born out of Him as the Head. It is not a mechanism, in which the parts precede the whole, but an organism, in which the whole is prior to the parts. The parts come forth out of Christ through the regenerating work of the Holy Spirit, and then continue in living relationship with Him. Jesus calls attention to this organic relationship when He says: "I am the vine, ye are the branches: he that abideth in me and I in him, the same beareth much fruit: for apart from me ye can do nothing," John 15:5. In view of what was said, it is quite evident that it is not correct to say that the mystical union is the fruit of man's believing acceptance of Christ, as if faith were not one of the blessings of the covenant which flow unto us from the fulness of Christ, but a condition which man must meet partly or wholly in his own strength, in order to enter into living relationship with Jesus Christ. Faith is first of all a gift of God, and as such a part of the treasures that are hidden in Christ. It enables us to appropriate on our part what is given unto us in Christ, and to enter ever-increasingly into conscious enjoyment of the blessed union with Christ, which is the source of all our spiritual riches.

This union may be defined as *that intimate, vital, and spiritual union between Christ and His people, in virtue of which He is the source of their life and strength, of their blessedness and salvation.* That it is a very intimate union appears abundantly from the figures that are used in Scripture to describe it. It is a union as of the vine and the branches, John 15:5, as of a foundation and the building that is reared on it, I Pet. 2:4,5, as of husband and wife, Eph. 5:23-32, and as of the head and the members of the body, Eph. 4:15,16. And even these figures fail to give full expression to the reality. It is a union that passes understanding. Says Dr. Hodge: "The technical designation of this union in theological language is 'mystical,' because it so far transcends all the analogies of earthly relationships, in the intimacy of its connection, in the transforming power of its influence, and in the excellence of its consequences."[1] If the discussion of this aspect of the mystical union is taken up first of all in the *ordo salutis*, it should be borne in mind (a) that it would seem

---

1. *Outlines of Theology*, p. 483.

to be desirable to consider it in connection with what precedes it, ideally in the counsel of redemption, and objectively in the work of Christ; and (b) that the order is logical rather than chronological. Since the believer is "a new creature" (II Cor. 5:17), or is "justified" (Acts 13:39) only in Christ, union with Him logically precedes both regeneration and justification by faith, while yet, chronologically, the moment when we are united with Christ is also the moment of our regeneration and justification.

B. Characteristics of the Mystical Union.

From the preceding it appears that the term "mystical union" can be, and often is, used in a broad sense, including the various aspects (legal, objective, subjective) of the union between Christ and believers. Most generally, however, it denotes only the crowning aspect of that union, namely, its subjective realization by the operation of the Holy Spirit, and it is this aspect of it that is naturally in the foreground in soteriology. All that is said in the rest of this chapter bears on this subjective union. The following are the main characteristics of this union:

1. IT IS AN ORGANIC UNION. Christ and the believers form one body. The organic character of this union is clearly taught in such passages as John 15:5; I Cor. 6:15-19; Eph. 1:22,23; 4:15,16; 5:29,30. In this organic union Christ ministers to the believers, and the believers minister to Christ. Every part of the body serves and is served by every other part, and together they are subservient to the whole in a union that is indissoluble.

2. IT IS A VITAL UNION. In this union Christ is the vitalizing and dominating principle of the whole body of believers. It is none other than the life of Christ that indwells and animates believers, so that, to speak with Paul, "Christ is formed" in them, Gal. 4:19. By it Christ becomes the formative principle of their life, and leads it in a Godward direction, Rom. 8:10; II Cor. 13:5; Gal. 4:19,20.

3. IT IS A UNION MEDIATED BY THE HOLY SPIRIT. The Holy Spirit was in a special capacity a part of the Mediator's reward, and as such was poured out on the day of Pentecost for the formation of the spiritual body of Jesus Christ. Through the Holy Spirit Christ now dwells in believers, unites them to Himself, and knits them together in a holy unity, I Cor. 6:17; 12:13; II Cor. 3:17,18; Gal. 3:2,3.

4. IT IS A UNION THAT IMPLIES RECIPROCAL ACTION. The initial act is that of Christ, who unites believers to himself by regenerating them and thus producing faith in them. On the other hand, the believer also unites himself to Christ by a conscious act of faith, and continues the union, under the influence of the Holy Spirit, by the constant exercise of faith, John 14:23; 15:4,5; Gal. 2:20; Eph. 3:17.

5. IT IS A PERSONAL UNION. Every believer is personally united directly to Christ. The representation that the life which is in the Church through Christ flows from the Church into the individual believer is decidedly un-

THE MYSTICAL UNION 451

Scriptural, not only in its sacramentarian but also in its pantheistic form (Rome, Schleiermacher, and many modern theologians). Every sinner who is regenerated is directly connected with Christ and receives his life from Him. Consequently the Bible always emphasizes the bond with Christ, John 14:20; 15:1-7; II Cor. 5:17; Gal. 2:20; Eph. 3:17,18.

6. IT IS A TRANSFORMING UNION. By this union believers are changed into the image of Christ *according to his human nature*. What Christ effects in His people is in a sense a replica or reproduction of what took place with Him. Nor only objectively, but also in a subjective sense they suffer, bear the cross, are crucified, die, and are raised in newness of life, with Christ. They share in a measure the experiences of their Lord, Matt. 16:24; Rom. 6:5; Gal. 2:20; Col. 1:24; 2:12; 3:1; I Pet. 4:13.

C. Erroneous Conceptions of the Mystical Union.

There are several erroneous conceptions of the mystical union, against which we should be on our guard. Errors on this point should not be regarded as inconsequential and therefore unimportant, for they are fraught with danger for a true understanding of the Christian life.

1. RATIONALISTIC ERROR. We must avoid the error of the Rationalist who would identify the mystical union with the union of Christ as the Logos with the whole creation or with the immanence of God in all human spirits. This is found in the following statement, which A. H. Strong quotes from Campbell, *The indwelling Christ*: "In the immanence of Christ in nature we find the ground of his immanence in human nature. . . . A man may be out of Christ, but Christ is never out of him. Those who banish him he does not abandon." In this view the mystical union is robbed of its soteriological significance.

2. MYSTICAL ERROR. Another dangerous error is that of the Mystics who understand the mystical union as an identification of the believer with Christ. According to this view there is in it a union of essence, in which the personality of the one is simply merged into that of the other, so that Christ and the believer do not remain two distinct persons. Even some of the Lutherans went to that extreme. One extremist did not hesitate to say, "I am Christ Jesus, the living Word of God; I have redeemed thee by my sinless sufferings."

3. SOCINIAN AND ARMINIAN ERROR. Quite another extreme is found in the teachings of Socinians and Arminians, who represent the mystical union as a mere moral union, or a union of love and sympathy, like that existing between a teacher and his pupils or between friend and friend. Such a union does not involve any interpenetration of the life of Christ and that of believers. It would involve no more than loving adherence to Christ, friendly service freely rendered to him, and ready acceptance of the message of the Kingdom of God. It is a union that does not call for a Christ within us.

4. SACRAMENTARIAN ERROR. Another error to be avoided is that of the sacramentarians, represented by the Roman Catholic Church and by some Luth-

erans and High Church Episcopalians. Strong speaks of this as "perhaps the most pernicious misinterpretation of the nature of this union." It makes the grace of God something substantial, of which the Church is the depositary, and which can be passed on in the sacraments; and completely loses sight of the fact that the sacraments cannot effect this union, because they already presuppose it.

D. The Significance of the Mystical Union.

1. The mystical union in the sense in which we are now speaking of it is not the judicial ground, on the basis of which we become partakers of the riches that are in Christ. It is sometimes said that the merits of Christ cannot be imputed to us as long as we are not in Christ, since it is only on the basis of our oneness with Him that such an imputation could be reasonable. But this view fails to distinguish between our legal unity with Christ and our spiritual oneness with Him, and is a falsification of the fundamental element in the doctrine of redemption, namely, of the doctrine of justification. Justification is always a declaration of God, not on the basis of an existing condition, but on that of a gracious imputation, — a declaration which is not in harmony with the existing condition of the sinner. The judicial ground for all the special grace which we receive lies in the fact that the righteousness of Christ is freely imputed to us.

2. But this state of affairs, namely, that the sinner has nothing in himself and receives everything freely from Christ, must be reflected in the consciousness of the sinner. And this takes place through the mediation of the mystical union. While the union is effected when the sinner is renewed by the operation of the Holy Spirit, he does not become cognizant of it and does not actively cultivate it until the conscious operation of faith begins. Then he becomes aware of the fact that he has no righteousness of his own, and that the righteousness by which he appears just in the sight of God is imputed to him. But even so something additional is required. The sinner must feel his dependence on Christ in the very depths of his being, — in the sub-conscious life. Hence he is incorporated in Christ, and as a result experiences that all the grace which he receives flows from Christ. The constant feeling of dependence thus engendered, is an antidote against all self-righteousness.

3. The mystical union with Christ also secures for the believer the continuously transforming power of the life of Christ, not only in the soul but also in the body. The soul is gradually renewed in the image of Christ, as Paul expresses it, "from glory to glory, even as by the Spirit of the Lord." II Cor. 3:18. And the body is consecrated in the present to be a fit instrument of the renewed soul, and will at last be raised up in the likeness of Christ's glorified body, Phil. 3:21. Being in Christ, believers share in all the blessings which He merited for his people. He is for them a perennial fountain springing into everlasting life.

4. In virtue of this union believers have fellowship with Christ. Just as Christ shared the labours, the sufferings, and the temptations of His people, they are now made to share His experiences. His sufferings are, in a measure, reproduced and completed in the lives of His followers. They are crucified with Him, and also arise with Him in newness of life The final triumph of Christ also becomes their triumph. Rom. 6:5,8; 8:17; II Cor. 1:7; Phil. 3:10; I Pet. 4:13.

5. Finally, the union of believers with Christ furnishes the basis for the spiritual unity of all believers, and consequently for the communion of the saints. They are animated by the same spirit, are filled with the same love, stand in the same faith, are engaged in the same warfare, and are bound for the same goal. Together they are interested in the things of Christ and His Church, of God and His Kingdom. John 17:20,21; Acts 2:42; Rom. 12:15; Eph. 4:2,3; Col. 3:16; I Thess. 4:18; 5:11; Heb. 3:13; 10:24,25; Jas. 5:16; I John 1:3,7.

QUESTIONS FOR FURTHER STUDY: What is the meaning of the term 'mystical' as applied to the union with Christ? What is the relation between grace in the legal, and that in the moral sphere? How should we answer the contention that the sinner cannot become a participant in the blessings of God's special grace until he is subjectively incorporated in Christ? What can be said in reply to the assertion that faith precedes regeneration, because it effects the union with Christ, while regeneration is the fruit of this union? Does the mystical union suppress or does it preserve the personality of man? Cf. Eph. 4:13. Do all believers derive equal benefits from this union? If this union is indissoluble, how must John 15:1-7 be understood? What is Schleiermacher's conception of the believer's union with Christ?

LITERATURE: Bavinck, *Geref. Dogm.* III, pp. 594 f.; IV, pp. 114, 226 f., 268 f.; Kuyper, *Het Werk van den Heiligen Geest* II, pp. 163-182; Dabney, *Syst. and Polem. Theol.*, pp. 612-617; Strong, *Syst. Theol.*, pp. 795-808; Dick, *Theol.*, pp. 36-365; Hodge, *Outlines*, pp. 482-486; ibid., *The Atonement*, pp. 198-211; McPherson, *Chr. Theol.*, pp. 402-404; Valentine, *Chr. Theol.* II, pp. 275-277; Schmid, *Doct. Theol.*, pp. 485-491; Litton, *Introd. to Dogm. Theol.*, pp. 321-322.

V. Calling in General and External Calling

A. Reasons for Discussing Calling First.

The question of the relative order of calling and regeneration has frequently been discussed, and the discussion has often suffered from a lack of discrimination and a resulting misunderstanding. The terms "calling" and "regeneration" were not always used in the same sense. Consequently, it was possible to maintain, without inconsistency, on the one hand that calling precedes regeneration, and on the other, that regeneration is prior to calling. We shall briefly consider (1) the representations found in Scripture and in our confessional standards: (2) the order generally followed by Reformed theologians; and (3) the reasons that may be advanced in favor of a separate discussion of the external calling through the Word, as preceding both regeneration and internal calling.

1. THE BIBLICAL REPRESENTATION. The Biblical order is chiefly indicated in a few well known passages. There is first of all the vision of the dry bones in Ezekiel 37:1-14. While Ezekiel prophesied over the dry bones of the house of Israel, the breath of life came into them. This passage refers to the civil restoration and the spiritual revival of the house of Israel, and probably also contains a hint respecting the resurrection of its dead. It represents the prophetic word as preceding the origin of the new life of the people of Israel. Naturally, this does not yet mean that the former was causally related to the latter. . . . A very instructive passage is found in Acts 16:14, which speaks of the conversion of Lydia. During the preaching of Paul the Lord opened the heart of Lydia to give heed to the things that were spoken by the apostle. It is clearly intimated that the opening of the heart is preceded by the external, and is followed by the internal calling. The unity of the twofold calling is clearly seen. . . . The statement of Paul in Rom. 4:17 is also frequently quoted in this connection, but can hardly be considered relevant, because it does not refer to either the external or the internal calling by the preaching of the Word of God, but either to the creative fiat of God, by which things are called into being, or to His command issued to things that are not, as though they were, and reaching even the dead. . . . Another passage is found in James 1:18, "Of His own will He brought us forth by the word of truth, that we should be a kind of firstfruits of His creatures." It can hardly be doubted that the word of truth mentioned here is the word of preaching, and the assumption is that this word precedes the new birth and is in some sense instrumental to it. . . . And, finally, there is a well known passage in I Pet. 1:23, in which the apostle speaks of believers as "having been begotten again, not of corruptible seed, but of incorruptible, through the word

CALLING IN GENERAL AND EXTERNAL CALLING   455

of God, which liveth and abideth." In view of verse 25 the word here referred to can hardly be anything else than the word of the gospel preached among the readers. This word of Peter too implies that the word of preaching precedes regeneration and is instrumentally connected with it. In view of these passages the conclusion is perfectly warranted that in the case of adults external calling by the preaching of the word generally precedes regeneration. Whether they also warrant the assertion that internal calling is prior to the implanting of the new life, is a question that need not be considered at this point.

2. THE VIEW REPRESENTED IN OUR CONFESSIONAL STANDARDS. Our confessional standards also imply that in the case of adults the preaching of the word precedes regeneration, but it should be borne in mind that they do not use the word "regeneration" in the limited sense in which it is employed to-day. The Belgic Confession says in Art. XXIV: "We believe that this true faith, being wrought in man by the hearing of the Word of God and the operation of the Holy Ghost, doth regenerate and make him a new man, causing him to live a new life, and freeing him from the bondage of sin." Faith is wrought in man by the hearing of the Word and, in turn, works regeneration, that is, the renewal of man in conversion and sanctification. The Canons of Dort contain a somewhat more detailed description in III and IV, Articles 11 and 12: "But when God accomplishes His good pleasure in the elect, or works in them true conversion, He not only causes the gospel to be externally preached to them, and powerfully illumines their minds by His Holy Spirit, that they may rightly understand and discern the things of the Spirit of God, but by the efficacy of the same regenerating Spirit He pervades the innermost recesses of the man; . . . And this is the regeneration so highly celebrated in Scripture and denominated a new creation: a resurrection from the dead; a making alive, which God works in us without our aid. But this is nowise effected merely by the external preaching of the gospel, by moral suasion, or such a mode of operation that, after God has performed His part, it still remains in the power of man to be regenerated or not, to be converted or to continue unconverted," etc. In these articles the words "regeneration" and "conversion" are used interchangeably. It is quite evident, however, that they denote the fundamental change in the governing disposition of the soul as well as the resulting change in the outward manifestations of life. And this change is brought about not merely, but at least in part, by the preaching of the gospel. Consequently this precedes.

3. THE ORDER GENERALLY FOLLOWED BY REFORMED THEOLOGIANS. Among the Reformed it has been quite customary to place calling before regeneration, though a few have reversed the order. Even Maccovius, Voetius, and Comrie, all Supralapsarians, follow the usual order. Several considerations prompted Reformed theologians in general to place calling before regeneration.

a. *Their doctrine of the covenant of grace.* They considered the covenant of grace as the great and all-comprehensive good which God in infinite mercy grants unto sinners, a good including all the blessings of salvation, and therefore also regeneration. But this covenant is inseparably connected with the gospel. It is announced and made known in the gospel, of which Christ is the living center, and therefore does not exist without it. Where the gospel is not known the covenant is not realized, but where it is preached God establishes His covenant and glorifies His grace. Both the preaching of the gospel and the administration of the covenant precede the saving operations of the Holy Spirit, and the believer's participation in the salvation wrought by Christ.

b. *Their conception of the relation between the work of Christ and that of the Holy Spirit.* The Anabaptists failed to do justice to this relation. Christ and His redemptive work are presented to us in the gospel. And it is from Christ, as the Mediator of God and man and as the meritorious cause of our salvation, that the Holy Spirit derives everything which He communicates to sinners. Consequently, He joins His work to the preaching of the gospel and operates in a saving way only where the divine message of redemption is brought. The Holy Spirit does not work apart from the Christ presented in the gospel.

c. *Their reaction against the mysticism of the Anabaptists.* The Anabaptists proceeded on the assumption that regeneration effected not merely a renewal of human nature, but an entirely new creation. And this being so, they regarded it as impossible that anything belonging to this natural creation as, for instance, the human language in which the Word of God is brought to man, could in any way be instrumental in communicating the new life to sinners. As they saw it, regeneration *eo ipso* excluded the use of the Word as a means, since this was after all only a dead letter. This mystical tendency was strongly opposed by Reformed theologians.

d. *Their experience in connection with the spiritual renewal of adults.* While it was a settled opinion that covenant children who die in infancy are reborn and therefore saved, there was no unanimous opinion as to the time when those who grew up became partakers of the grace of regeneration. Some shared the opinion of Voetius that all elect children are regenerated before baptism, and that the new life can, even in adults, remain concealed for many years. The great majority, however, were loath to take that position, and held that the new life, if present, would reveal itself in some way. Experience taught them that many gave no evidences of the new life until after they had heard the gospel for many years.

4. REASONS FOR A SEPARATE DISCUSSION OF EXTERNAL CALLING AS PRECEDING REGENERATION.

a. *Clearness of presentation.* External and internal calling are essentially one; yet they can and should be carefully distinguished. A dispute may arise respecting the one that does not directly concern the other. It may be doubted, whether internal calling logically precedes regeneration in the case of adults, while there is no uncertainty whatsoever in this respect concerning the external calling through the gospel. Hence it may be considered desirable to treat of the external calling first, and then to take up the discussion of internal calling in connection with that of regeneration.

b. *The preparatory nature of external calling.*. If we proceed on the assumption that the *ordo salutis* deals with the effective application of the redemption wrought by Christ, we feel at once that the external calling by the Word of God can, strictly speaking, hardly be called one of its stages. As long as this calling does not, through the accompanying operation of the Holy Spirit, turn into an internal and effectual calling, it has only a preliminary and preparatory significance. Several Reformed theologians speak of it as a kind of common grace, since it does not flow from the eternal election and the saving grace of God, but rather from His common goodness; and since, while it sometimes produces a certain illumination of the mind, it does not enrich the heart with the saving grace of God.[1]

c. *The general nature of external calling.* While all the other movements of the Holy Spirit in the *ordo salutis* terminate on the elect only, the external calling by the gospel has a wider bearing. Wherever the gospel is preached, the call comes to the elect and the reprobate alike. It serves the purpose, not merely of bringing the elect to faith and conversion, but also of revealing the great love of God to sinners in general. By means of it God maintains His claim on the obedience of all His rational creatures, restrains the manifestation of sin, and promotes civic righteousness, external morality, and even outward religious exercises.[2]

B. Calling in General.

Since external calling is but an aspect of calling in general, we shall have to consider this briefly before entering upon a discussion of external calling.

1. THE AUTHOR OF OUR CALLING. Our calling is a work of the triune God. It is first of all a work of the Father, I Cor. 1:9; I Thess. 2:12; I Pet. 5:10. But the Father works all things through the Son; and so this calling is also ascribed to the Son, Matt. 11:28; Luke 5:32; John 7:37; Rom. 1:6(?). And Christ, in turn, calls through His Word and Spirit, Matt. 10:20; John 15:26; Acts 5:31,32.

2. VOCATIO REALIS AND VERBALIS. Reformed theologians generally speak of a *vocatio realis*, as distinguished from the *vocatio verbalis*. By this they mean the external call that comes to men through God's general revelation, a revelation of the law and not of the gospel, to acknowledge, fear, and honour God as their Creator. It comes to them in things (*res*) rather than in words: in nature and history, in the environment in which they live, and in the experiences and vicissitudes of their lives, Ps. 19:1-4; Acts 16:16,17; 17:27; Rom. 1:19-21; 2:14,15. This call knows nothing of Christ, and therefore cannot lead to salvation. At the same time it is of the greatest importance in connection with the restraint of sin, the development of the natural life, and the maintenance of good

---

1. Cf. references above, pp. 304 f. and also a Marck, *Godgeleerdheid.* XXIII. 3.
2. Cf. Bavinck, *Geref. Dogm.* IV, pp. 7 f.

order in society. This is not the calling with which we are concerned at present. In soteriology only the *vocatio verbalis* comes into consideration; and this may be defined as *that gracious act of God whereby He invites sinners to accept the salvation that is offered in Christ Jesus.*

3. DIFFERENT CONCEPTIONS OF THE VOCATIO VERBALIS. The *vocatio verbalis* is, as the term itself suggests, the divine call that comes to man through the preaching of the Word of God. According to Roman Catholics it can also come to man through the administration of baptism. In fact, they regard the sacrament as the most important means in bringing man to Christ, and ascribe a decidedly subordinate significance to the preaching of the gospel. Not the pulpit, but the altar is central with Rome. In course of time considerable difference of opinion became apparent on the question, why the gospel call proves efficacious in some cases and not in others. Pelagius sought the explanation for this in the arbitrary will of man. Man has by nature a perfectly free will, so that he can accept or reject the gospel, as he sees fit, and thus either obtain or fail to obtain the blessings of salvation. Augustine, on the other hand, ascribed the difference to the operation of the grace of God. Said he: "The hearing of the divine call, is produced by divine grace itself, in him who before resisted; and then the love of virtue is kindled in him when he no longer resists." Semi-Pelagianism sought to mediate between the two and to avoid both the Augustinian denial of free will and the Pelagian depreciation of divine grace. It assumed the presence of the seeds of virtue in man, which of themselves tended to bear good fruit, but held that these needed the fructifying influence of divine grace for their development. The grace necessary for this is given to all men gratuitously, so that they are with the aid of it able to accept the gospel call unto salvation. The call will therefore be effective provided man, aided by divine grace, accepts it. This became the prevailing doctrine of the Roman Catholic Church. Some later Roman Catholics, of whom Bellarmin was one of the most important, brought in the doctrine of congruism, in which the acceptance of the gospel call is made dependent on the circumstances in which it comes to man. If these are congruous, that is, fit or favorable, he will accept it, but if not, he will reject it. The character of the circumstances will, of course, largely depend on the operation of prevenient grace. Luther developed the idea that, while the law worked repentance, the gospel call carried with it the gift of the Holy Spirit. The Holy Spirit is in the Word, and therefore the call is in itself always sufficient and in its intention always efficacious. The reason why this call does not always effect the desired and intended result lies in the fact that men in many cases place a stumblingblock in the way, so that, after all, the result is determined by the negative attitude of man. While some Lutherans still speak of external and internal calling, they insist on it that the former never comes to man apart from the latter. The call is essentially always efficacious, so that there is really no room for the distinction. Luther's strong insistence on the efficacious character of the gospel call was due to the Anabaptist depreciation of it. The Anabaptists virtually set aside

the Word of God as a means of grace, and stressed what they called the internal word, the "inner light," and the illumination of the Holy Spirit. To them the external word was but the letter that killeth, while the internal word was spirit and life. External calling meant little or nothing in their scheme. The distinction between external and internal calling is already found in Augustine, was borrowed from him by Calvin, and thus made prominent in Reformed theology. According to Calvin the gospel call is not in itself effective, but is made efficacious by the operation of the Holy Spirit, when He savingly applies the Word to the heart of man; and it is so applied only in the hearts and lives of the elect. Thus the salvation of man remains the work of God from the very beginning. God by His saving grace, not only enables, but causes man to heed the gospel call unto salvation. The Arminians were not satisfied with this position, but virtually turned back to the Semi-Pelagianism of the Roman Catholic Church. According to them the universal proclamation of the gospel is accompanied by a universal sufficient grace, — "gracious assistance actually and universally bestowed, sufficient to enable all men, if they choose, to attain to the full possession of spiritual blessings, and ultimately to salvation."[1] The work of salvation is once more made dependent on man. This marked the beginning of a rationalistic return to the Pelagian position, which entirely denies the necessity of an internal operation of the Holy Spirit unto salvation.

C. External Calling.

The Bible does not use the term "external," but clearly speaks of a calling that is not efficacious. It is presupposed in the great commission, as it is found in Mark 16:15,16, "Go ye into all the world, and preach the gospel to the whole creation. He that believeth and is baptized shall be saved; but he that disbelieveth shall be condemned." The parable of the marriage feast in Matt. 22:2-14 clearly teaches that some who were invited did not come, and concludes with the well-known words: "For many are called, but few chosen." The same lesson is taught in the parable of the great supper, Luke 14:16-24. Other passages speak explicitly of a rejection of the gospel, John 3:36; Acts 13:46; II Thess. 1:8. Still others speak of the terrible sin of unbelief in a way which clearly shows that it was committed by some, Matt. 10:15; 11:21-24; John 5:40; 16:8,9; I John 5:10. The external call consists in *the presentation and offering of salvation in Christ to sinners, together with an earnest exhortation to accept Christ by faith, in order to obtain the forgiveness of sins and life eternal.*

1. THE ELEMENTS COMPRISED IN IT.

a. *A presentation of the gospel facts and of the doctrine of redemption.* The way of redemption revealed in Christ must be set forth clearly in all its relations. God's plan of redemption, the saving work of Christ, and the renewing and transforming operations of the Holy Spirit, should all be interpreted in their mutual relations. It should be borne in mind, however, that a mere presentation of the truths of redemption, no matter how well done, does not yet

---

1. Cunningham, *Hist. Theol.* II, p. 396.

constitute the gospel call. It is not only fundamental to it, but even constitutes a very important part of it. At the same time it is by no means the whole of that call. According to our Reformed conception the following elements also belong to it.

b. *An invitation to accept Christ in repentance and faith.* The representation of the way of salvation must be supplemented by an earnest invitation (II Cor. 5:11,20) and even a solemn command (John 6:28,29; Acts 19:4) to repent and believe, that is to accept Christ by faith. But, in order that this coming to Christ may not be understood in a superficial sense, as it is often represented by revivalists, the true nature of the repentance and the faith required should be clearly set forth. It must be made perfectly clear that the sinner cannot of himself truly repent and believe, but that it is God who worketh in him "both to will and to work, for His good pleasure."

c. *A promise of forgiveness and salvation.* The external call also contains a promise of acceptance for all those who comply with the conditions, not in their own strength, but by the power of the grace of God wrought in their hearts by the Holy Spirit. They who by grace repent of their sins and accept Christ by faith receive the assurance of the forgiveness of sins and of eternal salvation. This promise, it should be noticed, is never absolute, but always conditional. No one can expect its fulfilment, except in the way of a faith and repentance that is truly wrought by God.

From the fact that these elements are included in external calling, it may readily be inferred that they who reject the gospel not merely refuse to believe certain facts and ideas, but resist the general operation of the Holy Spirit, which is connected with this calling, and are guilty of the sin of obstinate disobedience. By their refusal to accept the gospel, they increase their responsibility, and treasure up wrath for themselves in the day of judgment, Rom. 2:4,5. That the above elements are actually included in the external calling, is quite evident from the following passages of Scripture: (a) According to Acts 20:27 Paul considers the declaration of the whole counsel of God as a part of the call; and in Eph. 3:7-11 he recounts some of the details which he had declared unto the readers. (b) Examples of the call to repent and believe are found in such passages as Ezek. 33:11; Mark 1:15; John 6:29; II Cor. 5:20. (c) And the promise is contained in the following passages, John 3:16-18,36; 5:24,40.[1]

2. THE CHARACTERISTICS OF EXTERNAL CALLING.

a. *It is general or universal.* This is not to be understood in the sense in which it was maintained by some of the old Lutheran theologians, namely, that that call actually came to all the living more than once in the past, as, for instance, in the time of Adam, in that of Noah, and in the days of the apostles. McPherson correctly says: "A universal call of this kind is not a fact, but a

---

1. Cf. also the *Canons of Dort* II, 5,6; III and IV, 8.

mere theory invented for a purpose."[1] In this representation the terms "general" or "universal" are not used in the sense in which they are intended, when it is said that the gospel call is general or universal. Moreover, the representation is at least in part contrary to fact. External calling is general only in the sense that it comes to all men to whom the gospel is preached, indiscriminately. It is not confined to any age or nation or class of men. It comes to both the just and the unjust, the elect and the reprobate. The following passages testify to the general nature of this call: Isa. 55:1, "Ho, every one that thirsteth, come ye to the waters, and he that hath no money; :ome ye, buy and eat; yea, come, buy wine and milk without money and without price," cf. also verses 6,7. In connection with this passage one might conceivably say that only spiritually qualified sinners are called; but this certainly cannot be said of Isa. 45:22, "Look unto me, and be ye saved, all the ends of the earth; for I am God, and there is none else." Some also interpret the familiar invitation of Jesus in Matt. 11:28, "Come unto me, all ye that labor and are heavy laden, and I will give you rest," as limited to such as are truly concerned about their sins and really repentant; but there is no warrant for such a limitation. The last book of the Bible concludes with a beautiful general invitation: "And the Spirit and the bride say, Come. And he that heareth, let him say, Come. And he that is athirst, let him come: he that will, let him take of the water of life freely," Rev. 22:17. That the gospel invitation is not limited to the elect, as some hold, is quite evident from such passages as Ps. 81:11-13; Prov. 1:24-26; Ezek. 3:19; Matt. 22:2-8,14; Luke 14:16-24.

The general character of this calling is also taught in the *Canons of Dort*.[2] Yet this doctrine repeatedly met with opposition by individuals and groups in the Reformed Churches. In the Scottish Church of the seventeenth century some denied the indiscriminate invitation and offer of salvation altogether, while others wanted to limit it to the confines of the visible Church. Over against these the Marrow men, such as Boston and the Erskines, defended it. In the Netherlands this point was disputed especially in the eighteenth century. They who maintained the universal offer were called preachers of the *new light*, while they who defended the particular offer, the offer to those who already gave evidence of a measure of special grace and could therefore be reckoned as among the elect, were known as the preachers of the *old light*. Even in the present day we occasionally meet with opposition on this point. It is said that such a general invitation and offer is inconsistent with the doctrine of predestination and of particular atonement, doctrines in which, it is thought, the preacher should take his starting point. But the Bible does not teach that the preacher of the gospel should take his starting point in these doctrines, however important they may be. His starting point and warrant lie in the commission of his King: "Go ye into all the world, and preach the gospel to every creature. He that believeth and is baptized shall be saved:

---

1. *Chr. Dogm.* p. 377.
2. II, 5; III and IV, 8.

but he that believeth not shall be damned." Mark 16:15,16. Moreover, it is an utter impossibility that anyone, in preaching the gospel, should limit himself to the elect, as some would have us do, since he does not know who they are. Jesus did know them, but He did not so limit the offer of salvation, Matt. 22:3-8,14; Luke 14:16-21; John 5:38-40. There would be a real contradiction between the Reformed doctrines of predestination and particular atonement on the one hand, and the universal offer of salvation on the other hand, if this offer included the declaration that God purposed to save every individual hearer of the gospel, and that Christ really atoned for the sins of each one of them. But the gospel invitation involves no such declaration. It is a gracious calling to accept Christ by faith, and a *conditional* promise of salvation. The condition is fulfilled only in the elect, and therefore they only obtain eternal life.

b. *It is a bona fide calling.* The external calling is a calling in good faith, a calling that is seriously meant. It is not an invitation coupled with the hope that it will not be accepted. When God calls the sinner to accept Christ by faith, He earnestly desires this; and when He promises those who repent and believe eternal life, His promise is dependable. This follows from the very nature, from the veracity, of God. It is blasphemous to think that God would be guilty of equivocation and deception, that He would say one thing and mean another, that He would earnestly plead with the sinner to repent and believe unto salvation, and at the same time not desire it in any sense of the word. The *bona fide* character of the external call is proved by the following passages of Scripture: Num. 23:19; Ps. 81:13-16; Prov. 1:24; Isa. 1:18-20; Ezek. 18:23,32; 33:11; Matt. 21:37; II Tim. 2:13. The Canons of Dort also assert it explicitly in III and IV, 8. Several objections have been offered to the idea of such a *bona fide* offer of salvation. (1) One objection is derived from the veracity of God. It is said that, according to this doctrine, He offers the forgiveness of sins and eternal life to those for whom He has not intended these gifts. It need not be denied that there is a real difficulty at this point, but this is the difficulty with which we are always confronted, when we seek to harmonize the decretive and the preceptive will of God, a difficulty which even the objectors cannot solve and often simply ignore. Yet we may not assume that the two are really contradictory. The decretive will of God determines what will most certainly come to pass (without necessarily implying that God really takes delight in all of it. as, for instance, in all kinds of sin), while the preceptive will is man's rule of life, informing him as to what is well pleasing in the sight of God. Furthermore, it should be borne in mind that God does not offer sinners the forgiveness of sins and eternal life unconditionally, but only in the way of faith and conversion; and that the righteousness of Christ, though not intended for all, is yet sufficient for all. (2) A second objection is derived from the spiritual inability of man. Man, as he is by nature, cannot believe and repent, and therefore it looks like mockery to ask this of him. But in connection with this objection we should remember that in the last analysis man's inability in spiritual things is rooted in his unwillingness to serve God. The actual condition of things is not such that many would like to repent and believe in Christ, if they only could. All those who do not believe are not willing to believe, John 5:40. Moreover, it is no more unreasonable to require repentance and faith in Christ of men than it is to demand of them that they keep the law. Very inconsistently some of those who oppose the general offer of salvation on the basis of man's spiritual inability, do not hesitate to place the sinner before the demands of the law and even insist on doing this.

3. THE SIGNIFICANCE OF EXTERNAL CALLING. The question may be asked, why God comes to all men indiscriminately, including even the reprobate, with the offer of salvation. This external calling answers more than one purpose.

a. In it God maintains His claim on the sinner. As the sovereign Ruler of the universe He is entitled — and this is a matter of absolute right — to the service of man. And though man tore away from God in sin and is now incapable of rendering spiritual obedience to his rightful Sovereign, his wilful transgression did not abrogate the claim of God on the service of His rational creatures. The right of God to demand absolute obedience remains, and He asserts this right in both the law and the gospel. His claim on man also finds expression in the call to faith and repentance. And if man does not heed this call, he disregards and slights the just claim of God and thereby increases his guilt.

b. It is the divinely appointed means of bringing sinners to conversion. In other words, it is the means by which God gathers the elect out of the nations of the earth. As such it must necessarily be general or universal, since no man can point out the elect. The final result is, of course, that the elect, and they only, accept Christ by faith. This does not mean that missionaries can go out and give their hearers the assurance that Christ died for each one of them and that God intends to save each one; but it does mean that they can bring the joyful tidings that Christ died for sinners, that He invites them to come unto Him, and that He offers salvation to all those who truly repent of their sins and accept him with a living faith.

c. It is also a revelation of God's holiness, goodness, and compassion. In virtue of His holiness God dissuades sinners everywhere from sin, and in virtue of His goodness and mercy He warns them against self-destruction, postpones the execution of the sentence of death, and blesses them with the offer of salvation. There is no doubt about it that this gracious offer is in itself a blessing and not, as some would have it, a curse for sinners. It clearly reveals the divine compassion for them, and is so represented in the Word of God, Ps. 81:13; Prov. 1:24; Ezek. 18:23,32; 33:11; Amos 8:11; Matt. 11:20-24; 23:37. At the same time it is true that man by his opposition to it may turn even this blessing into a curse. It naturally heightens the responsibility of the sinner, and, if not accepted and improved, will increase his judgment.

d. Finally, it clearly accentuates the righteousness of God. If even the revelation of God in nature serves the purpose of forestalling any excuse which sinners might be inclined to make, Rom. 1:20, this is all the more true of the special revelation of the way of salvation. When sinners despise the forbearance of God and reject His gracious offer of salvation, the greatness of their corruption and guilt, and the justice of God in their condemnation, stands out in the clearest light.

QUESTIONS FOR FURTHER STUDY: In what cases do the Reformed assume that regeneration precedes even external calling? How do they connect external calling up with the doctrine of the covenant? On what grounds did the Arminians at the time of the Synod of Dort assert that the Reformed churches could not consistently teach that God seriously calls sinners indiscriminately to salvation? How do Roman Catholics conceive of the calling by the Word? What is the Lutheran conception of calling? Is it correct to say (with Alexander, *Syst. Theol.* II, pp. 357 ff.) that the Word by itself is adequate to effect a spiritual change, and that the Holy Spirit merely removes the obstruction to its reception?

LITERATURE: Bavinck, *Geref. Dogm.* IV, pp. 1-15; ibid., *Roeping en Wedergeboorte* Kuyper, *Dict. Dogm., De Salute,* pp. 84-92; Mastricht, *Godgeleerdheit* III, pp. 192-214; Marck, *Godgeleerdheid,* pp. 649-651; Witsius, *De Verbonden* III, c. 5; Hodge, *Syst. Theol* II. pp. 639-653; Dabney, *Theology.,* pp. 553-559; Schmid, *Doct. Theol.,* pp. 448-456; Valentine *Chr. Theol.* II, pp. 194-204; Pope, *Chr. Theol.* II, pp. 335-347; W. L. Alexander, *Syst. of Bibl. Theol.* II, pp. 357-361.

VI.   Regeneration and Effectual Calling

A. The Scriptural Terms for Regeneration and Their Implications.

1. THE TERMS THAT COME INTO CONSIDERATION. The Greek word for "regeneration" (*palingenesia*) is found only in Matt. 19:28 and Titus 3:5; and only in the last named passage does it refer to the beginning of the new life in the individual Christian. The idea of this beginning is more commonly expressed by the verb *gennao* (with *anothen* in John 3:3), or its compositum *anagennao*. These words mean either *to beget, to beget again*, or *to bear or give birth*, John 1:13; 3:3,4,5,6,7,8; I Pet. 1:23; I John 2:29; 3:9; 4:7; 5:1,4,18. In one passage, namely, Jas. 1:18, the word *apokueo, to bear* or *bring forth*, is employed. Furthermore, the thought of the production of a new life is expressed by the word *ktizo, to create*, Eph. 2:10, and the product of this creation is called a *kaine ktisis* (a new creature), II Cor. 5:17; Gal. 6:15, or a *kainos anthropos* (a new man), Eph. 4:24. Finally, the term *suzoopoieo, to make alive with, to quicken with*, is also used in a couple of passages, Eph. 2:5; Col. 2:13.

2. THE IMPLICATIONS OF THESE TERMS. These terms carry with them several important implications, to which attention should be directed. (a) Regeneration is a creative work of God, and is therefore *a work in which man is purely passive*, and in which there is no place for human co-operation. This is a very important point, since it stresses the fact that salvation is wholly of God. (b) The creative work of God produces a *new life*, in virtue of which man, made alive with Christ, shares the resurrection life, and can be called a new creature, "created in Christ Jesus for good works, which God afore prepared that we should walk in them," Eph. 2:10. (c) Two elements must be distinguished in regeneration, namely, *generation or the begetting of the new life*, and *bearing or bringing forth*, by which the new life is brought forth out of its hidden depths. Generation implants the principle of the new life in the soul, and the new birth causes this principle to begin to assert itself in action. This distinction is of great importance for a proper understanding of regeneration.

B. The Use of the Term "Regeneration" in Theology.

1. IN THE EARLY CHURCH AND IN ROMAN CATHOLIC THEOLOGY. In the mind of the early Church the term "regeneration" did not stand for a sharply defined concept. It was used to denote a change closely connected with the washing away of sins, and no clear distinction was made between regeneration and justification. As identified with baptismal grace, the former was understood especially as a designation of the remission of sin, though the idea of a

certain moral renovation was not excluded. Even Augustine did not draw a sharp line here, but did distinguish between regeneration and conversion. To him regeneration included, in addition to the remission of sin, only an *initial* change of the heart, followed by conversion later on. He conceived of it as a strictly monergistic work of God, in which the human subject cannot co-operate, and which man cannot resist. For Pelagius, of course, "regeneration" did not mean the birth of a new nature, but the forgiveness of sins in baptism, the illumination of the mind by the truth, and the stimulation of the will by divine promises. The confusion of regeneration and justification, already apparent in Augustine, became even more pronounced in Scholasticism. In fact, justification became the more prominent concept of the two, was thought of as including regeneration, and was conceived of as an act in which God and man co-operate. Justification, according to the common representation, included the infusion of grace, that is, the birth of a new creature or regeneration, and the forgiveness of sin and the removal of the guilt attaching to it. There was a difference of opinion, however, as to which of these two elements is the logical prius. According to Thomas Aquinas the infusion of grace is first, and the forgiveness of sins is, at least in a certain sense, based on this; but according to Duns Scotus the forgiveness of sin is first, and is basic to the infusion of grace. Both elements are effected by baptism *ex opere operato*. The opinion of Thomas Aquinas gained the upper hand in the Church. Up to the present time there is a certain confusion of regeneration and justification in the Roman Catholic Church, which is, no doubt, largely due to the fact that justification is not conceived as a forensic act, but as an act or process of renewal. In it man is not *declared* but *made* just. Says Wilmers in his *Handbook of the Christian Religion*: "As justification is a spiritual renewal and regeneration, it follows that sin is really *destroyed* by it, and not, as the Reformers maintained, merely *covered*, or *no longer imputed*."

2. BY THE REFORMERS AND IN THE PROTESTANT CHURCHES. Luther did not entirely escape the confusion of regeneration with justification. Moreover, he spoke of regeneration or the new birth in a rather broad sense. Calvin also used the term in a very comprehensive sense as a designation of the whole process by which man is renewed, including, besides the divine act which originates the new life, also conversion (repentance and faith) and sanctification.[1] Several seventeenth century authors fail to distinguish between regeneration and conversion, and use the two terms interchangeably, treating of what we now call regeneration under vocation or effectual calling. The Canons of Dort also use the two words synonymously,[2] and the Belgic Confession seems to speak of regeneration in an even wider sense.[3] This comprehensive use of the term "regeneration" often led to confusion and to the disregard of very necessary distinctions. For instance, while regeneration and conversion were identified, regeneration was yet declared to be monergistic, in spite of the fact that in conversion man certainly

1. *Inst.* III. 3,9.
2. III and IV. 11,12.
3. Art. XXIV.

co-operates. The distinction between regeneration and justification had already become clearer, but it gradually became necessary and customary also to employ the term "regeneration" in a more restricted sense. Turretin defines two kinds of conversion: first, a "habitual" or passive conversion, the production of a disposition or habit of the soul, which, he remarks, might better be called "regeneration"; and, secondly, an "actual" or "active" conversion, in which this implanted habit or disposition becomes active in faith and repentance. In present day Reformed theology the word "regeneration" is generally used in a more restricted sense, as a designation of that divine act by which the sinner is endowed with new spiritual life, and by which the principle of that new life is first called into action. So conceived, it includes both the "begetting again" and the "new birth," in which the new life becomes manifest. In strict harmony, however, with the literal meaning of the word "regeneration" the term is sometimes employed in an even more limited sense, to denote simply the implanting of the new life in the soul, apart from the first manifestations of this life. In modern liberal theology the term "regeneration' acquired a different meaning. Schleiermacher distinguished two aspects of regeneration, namely, conversion and justification, and held that in regeneration "a new religious consciousness is produced in the believer by the common Christian spirit of the community, and new life, or 'sanctification,' is prepared for." (Pfleiderer.) That "Christian spirit of the community" is the result of an influx of the divine life, through Christ, into the Church, and is called "the Holy Spirit" by Schleiermacher. The Modern view is well stated in these words of Youtz: "Modern interpretation inclines to return to the symbolical use of the conception of Regeneration. Our ethical realities deal with transformed characters. Regeneration expresses thus a radical, vital, ethical change, rather than an absolutely new metaphysical beginning. Regeneration is a vital step in the natural development of the spiritual life, a radical readjustment to the moral processes of life."[1] Students of the Psychology of Religion generally fail to distinguish between regeneration and conversion. They regard it as a process in which man's attitude to life changes from the autocentric to the heterocentric. It finds its explanation primarily in the sub-conscious life, and does not necessarily involve anything supernatural. James says: "To be converted, to be regenerated, to receive grace, to experience religion, to gain an assurance, are so many phrases which denote the process, gradual or sudden, by which a self hitherto divided, and consciously wrong, inferior and unhappy, becomes unified and consciously right, superior and happy, in consequence of its firmer hold upon religious realities."[2] According to Clark, "Students have agreed in discerning three distinct steps in conversion: (1) A period of 'storm and stress,' or sense of sin, or feeling of inward disharmony, known to theology as 'conviction of sin' and designated by James as 'soul sickness.' (2) An emotional crisis which marks a turning point. (3) A succeeding relaxation attended by a sense of peace, rest, inner harmony,

---

1. *A Dictionary of Religion and Ethics*, Art. *Regeneration*.
2. *Varieties of Religious Experience*, p. 189.

acceptance with God, and not infrequently motor and sensory reflexes of various sorts."[1]

C. The Essential Nature of Regeneration.

Relative to the nature of regeneration there are several misconceptions which should be avoided. It may be well to mention these first, before stating the positive qualifications of this re-creative work of God.

1. MISCONCEPTIONS. (a) Regeneration is not a change in the *substance* of human nature, as was taught by the Manichæans and in the days of the Reformation by Flacius Illyricus, who conceived of original sin as a substance, to be replaced by another substance in regeneration. No new physical seed or germ is implanted in man; neither is there any addition to, or subtraction from, the faculties of the soul. (b) Neither is it simply a change in *one or more of the faculties* of the soul, as, for instance, of the emotional life (feeling or heart), by removing the aversion to divine things, as some evangelicals conceive of it; or of the intellect, by illuminating the mind that is darkened by sin, as the Rationalists regard it. It affects the heart, understood in the Scriptural sense of the word, that is, as the central and all-controlling organ of the soul, out of which are the issues of life. This means that it affects human nature as a whole. (c) Nor is it a complete or perfect change of the whole nature of man, or of any part of it, so that it is no more capable of sin, as was taught by the extreme Anabaptists and by some other fanatical sects. This does not mean that it does not in principle affect the entire nature of man, but only that it does not constitute the whole change that is wrought in man by the operation of the Holy Spirit. It does not comprise conversion and sanctification.

2. POSITIVE CHARACTERISTICS OF REGENERATION. The following positive assertions may be made respecting regeneration:

a. Regeneration consists in the implanting of the *principle* of the new spiritual life in man, in a radical change of the governing disposition of the soul, which, under the influence of the Holy Spirit, gives birth to a life that moves in a Godward direction. In principle this change affects the whole man: the intellect, I Cor. 2:14,15; II Cor. 4:6; Eph. 1:18; Col. 3:10; the will, Ps. 110:3; Phil. 2:13; II Thess. 3:5; Heb. 13:21; and the feelings or emotions, Ps. 42:1,2; Matt. 5:4; I Pet. 1:8.

b. It is an *instantaneous* change of man's nature, affecting at once the whole man, intellectually, emotionally, and morally. The assertion that regeneration is an instantaneous change implies two things: (1) that it is not a work that is gradually prepared in the soul, as the Roman Catholics and all Semi-Pelagians teach; there is no intermediate stage between life and death; one either lives or is dead; and (2) that it is not a gradual process like sanctification. It is true that some Reformed authors have occasionally used the term "regeneration" as including even sanctification, but that was in the days when the *ordo salutis* was not as fully developed as it is to-day.

---

1. *The Psychology of Religious Awakening*, p. 38.

c. It is in its most limited sense a change that occurs in the *sub-conscious* life. It is a secret and inscrutable work of God that is never *directly* perceived by man. The change may take place without man's being conscious of it momentarily, though this is not the case when regeneration and conversion coincide; and even later on he can perceive it *only in its effects.* This explains the fact that a Christian may, on the one hand, struggle for a long time with doubts and uncertainties, and can yet, on the other hand, gradually overcome these and rise to the heights of assurance.

3. DEFINITION OF REGENERATION. From what was said in the preceding respecting the present use of the word "regeneration," it follows that regeneration may be defined in two ways. In the strictest sense of the word we may say: *Regeneration is that act of God by which the principle of the new life is implanted in man, and the governing disposition of the soul is made holy.* But in order to include the idea of the new birth as well as that of the "begetting again," it will be necessary to complement the definition with the following words: . . . *"and the first holy exercise of this new disposition is secured."*

D. Effectual Calling in Relation to External Calling and Regeneration.

1. ITS INSEPARABLE CONNECTION WITH EXTERNAL CALLING. The calling of God may be said to be one, and the distinction between an external and an internal or effectual calling merely calls attention to the fact that this one calling has two aspects. This does not mean that these two aspects are always united and always go together. We do not aver with the Lutherans that "the inner call is always concurrent with the hearing of the word."[1] It does mean, however, that where the inner call comes to adults, it is mediated by the preaching of the Word. It is the same Word that is heard in the external call, and that is made effective in the heart in the internal calling. Through the powerful application of the Holy Spirit the external call passes right into the internal.[2] But while this calling is closely connected with the external call and forms a unit with it, there are certain points of difference: (a) It is a calling by the Word, *savingly applied by the operation of the Holy Spirit,* I Cor. 1:23,24; I Pet. 2:9; (b) it is a *powerful* calling, that is, a calling that is effectual unto salvation, Acts 13:48; I Cor. 1:23,24; and (c) it is *without repentance,* that is, it is a call that is not subject to change and that is never withdrawn, Rom. 11:29.

2. CHARACTERISTICS OF THE INTERNAL CALL. The following characteristics should be noted:

a. *It works by moral suasion plus the powerful operation of the Holy Spirit.* The question arises, whether in this calling (as distinguished from regeneration) the Word of God works in a creative way, or by moral suasion. Now there is no doubt about it that the Word of God is sometimes said to work in a creative manner, Gen. 1:3; Ps. 33:6,9; 147:15; Rom. 4:17 (though this may be interpreted differently). But these passages refer to the word of God's

---

1. Valentine, *Chr. Theol.* II, pp. 197 f.
2. Bavinck, *Roeping en Wedergeboorte,* p. 215.

power, to His authoritative command, and not to the word of preaching with which we are concerned here. The Spirit of God operates through the preaching of the Word only in a morally persuasive way, making its persuasions effective, so that man listens to the voice of his God. This follows from the very nature of the Word, which addresses itself to the understanding and the will.[1] It should be borne in mind, however, that this moral suasion does not yet constitute the whole of the internal call; there must be in addition to this a powerful operation of the Holy Spirit, applying the Word to the heart.

b. *It operates in the conscious life of man.* This point is most intimately connected with the preceding. If the word of preaching does not operate creatively, but only in a moral and persuasive way, it follows that it can work only in the conscious life of man. It addresses the understanding, which the Spirit endows with spiritual insight into the truth, and through the understanding influences the will effectively, so that the sinner turns to God. The internal calling necessarily issues in conversion, that is, in a conscious turning away from sin in the direction of holiness.

c. *It is teleological.* Internal calling is of a teleological character, that is, it calls man to a certain end: to the great goal to which the Holy Spirit is leading the elect, and, consequently also to the intermediate stages on the way to this final destiny. It is a calling to the fellowship of Jesus Christ, I Cor. 1:9; to inherit blessing, I Pet. 3:9; to liberty, Gal. 5:13; to peace, I Cor. 7:15; to holiness, I Thess. 4:7; to one hope, Eph. 4:4; to eternal life, I Tim. 6:12; and to God's kingdom and glory, I Thess. 2:12.

3. THE RELATION OF EFFECTUAL CALLING TO REGENERATION.

a. *The identification of the two in seventeenth century theology.* It is a well known fact that in seventeenth century theology effectual calling and regeneration are often identified, or if not entirely identified, then at least in so far that regeneration is regarded as included in calling. Several of the older theologians have a separate chapter on calling, but none on regeneration. According to the Westminster Confession, X. 2, effectual calling includes regeneration. This view finds some justification in the fact that Paul, who uses the term "regeneration" but once, evidently conceives of it as included in calling in Rom. 8:30. Moreover, there is a sense in which calling and regeneration are related as cause and effect. It should be borne in mind, however, that in speaking of calling as including, or as being causally related to, regeneration, we do not have in mind merely what is technically termed internal or effectual calling, but calling in general, including even a creative calling. The extensive use in Post-Reformation times of the term "calling" rather than "regeneration," to designate the beginning of the work of grace in the life of sinners, was due to a desire to stress the close connection between the Word of God and the operation of His grace. And the prevalence of the term "calling"

---

1. Bavinck, *Roeping en Wedergeboorte*, pp. 217,219,221.

in the apostolic age finds its explanation and justification in the fact that, in the case of those who were in that missionary period gathered into the Church, regeneration and effectual calling were generally simultaneous, while the change was reflected in their conscious life as a powerful calling from God. In a systematic presentation of the truth, however, we should carefully discriminate between calling and regeneration.

b. *Points of difference between regeneration and effectual calling.* Regeneration in the strictest sense of the word, that is, as *the begetting again,* takes place in the sub-conscious life of man, and is quite independent of any attitude which he may assume with reference to it. Calling, on the other hand, addresses itself to the consciousness, and implies a certain disposition of the conscious life. This follows from the fact that regeneration works from within, while calling comes from without. In the case of children we speak of regeneration rather than calling. Furthermore, regeneration is a creative, a hyper-physical operation of the Holy Spirit, by which man is brought from one condition into another, from a condition of spiritual death into a condition of spiritual life. Effectual calling, on the other hand, is teleological, draws out the new life and points it in a God-ward direction. It secures the exercises of the new disposition and brings the new life into action.

c. *The relative order of calling and regeneration.* This is perhaps best understood, if we note the following stages: (1) Logically, the external call in the preaching of the Word (except in the case of children) generally precedes or coincides with the operation of the Holy Spirit, by which the new life is produced in the soul of man. (2) Then by a creative word God generates the new life, changing the inner disposition of the soul, illuminating the mind, rousing the feelings, and renewing the will. In this act of God the ear is implanted that enables man to hear the call of God to the salvation of his soul. *This is regeneration in the most restricted sense of the word.* In it man is entirely passive. (3) Having received the spiritual ear, the call of God in the gospel is now heard by the sinner, and is brought home effectively to the heart. The desire to resist has been changed to a desire to obey, and the sinner yields to the persuasive influence of the Word through the operation of the Holy Spirit. *This is the effectual calling through the instrumentality of the word of preaching, effectively applied by the Spirit of God.* (4) This effectual calling, finally, secures, through the truth as a means, the first holy exercises of the new disposition that is born in the soul. The new life begins to manifest itself; the implanted life issues in the new birth. *This is the completion of the work of regeneration in the broader sense of the word, and the point at which it turns into conversion.*

Now we should not make the mistake of regarding this logical order as a temporal order that will apply in all cases. The new life is often implanted in the hearts of children long before they are able to hear the call of the gospel; yet they are endowed with this life only where the gospel is preached.

There is, of course, always a creative call of God by which the new life is produced. In the case of those who live under the administration of the gospel the possibility exists that they receive the seed of regeneration long before they come to years of discretion and therefore also long before the effectual calling penetrates to their consciousness. It is very unlikely, however, that, being regenerated, they will live in sin for years, even after they have come to maturity, and give no evidences at all of the new life that is in them. On the other hand, in the case of those who do not live under the administration of the covenant, there is no reason to assume an interval between the time of their regeneration and that of their effectual calling. In the effectual call they at once become conscious of their renewal, and immediately find the seed of regeneration germinating into the new life. This means that regeneration, effective calling, and conversion all coincide.

E. The Necessity of Regeneration.

1. THIS NECESSITY IS DENIED BY MODERN LIBERAL THEOLOGY. The necessity of regeneration, as this is understood by the Christian Church, is naturally denied in modern liberal theology. It is not in accord with the teaching of Rousseau, that man is by nature good. Any *radical change* or complete turnabout in the life of a man who is *essentially* good, would be a change for the worse. Liberals speak of salvation by character, and the only regeneration of which they know is a regeneration conceived as "a vital step in the natural development of the spiritual life, a radical readjustment to the moral processes of life." (Youtz.) Many teach a series of ethical renewals. Emerton says: "The character thus gained and proven and held fast *is* redemption. There is no other worthy definition of the word. It is the redemption of man's lower self by the domination of his higher self. It is the spiritual redeeming the material, the divine that is in every man redeeming the animal."[1]

2. IT FOLLOWS FROM WHAT SCRIPTURE TEACHES CONCERNING THE NATURAL CONDITION OF MAN. Holiness or conformity to the divine law is the indispensable condition of securing divine favor, attaining peace of conscience, and enjoying fellowship with God. Heb. 12:14. Now the condition of man by nature is, according to Scripture, both in disposition and act, exactly the opposite of that holiness which is so indispensable. Man is described as dead through trespasses and sins, Eph. 2:1, and this condition calls for nothing less than a restoration to life. A radical internal change is necessary, a change by which the whole disposition of the soul is altered.

3. IT IS ALSO EXPRESSLY ASSERTED BY SCRIPTURE. Scripture does not leave us in doubt about the necessity of regeneration, but asserts this in the clearest terms. Jesus says: "Verily, verily, I say unto thee, Except a man be born again he cannot see the kingdom of God," John 3:3.[2] This statement of the Saviour is absolute and leaves no room for exceptions. The

---

1. *Unitarian Thought,* p. 193.
2. Cf. also the verses 5-7.

same truth is clearly brought out in some of the statements of Paul, as, for instance, in I Cor. 2:14: "But the natural man receiveth not the things of the Spirit of God, for they are foolishness unto him: neither can he know them, because they are spiritually discerned"; Gal. 6:15: "For in Christ Jesus neither is circumcision anything, nor uncircumcision, but a new creature." Cf. also Jer. 13:23; Rom. 3:11; Eph. 2:3,4.

F. The Efficient Cause of Regeneration.

There are only three fundamentally different views that come into consideration here, and all the others are modifications of these.

1. THE HUMAN WILL. According to the Pelagian conception regeneration is solely an act of the human will, and is practically identical with self-reformation. With some slight differences this is the view of modern liberal theology. A modification of this view is that of the Semi-Pelagian and Arminian, who regard it as, at least in part, an act of man, co-operating with divine influences applied through the truth. This is the synergistic theory of regeneration. Both of these views involve a denial of the total depravity of man, so plainly taught in the Word of God, John 5:42; Rom. 3:9-18; 7:18,23; 8:7; II Tim. 3:4, and of the Scripture truth that it is God who inclines the will, Rom. 9:16; Phil. 2:13.

2. THE TRUTH. According to this view the truth as a system of motives, presented to the human will by the Holy Spirit, is the immediate cause of the change from unholiness to holiness. This was the view of Lyman Beecher and of Charles G. Finney. It assumes that the work of the Holy Spirit differs from that of the preacher only in degree. Both work by persuasion only. But this theory is quite unsatisfactory. The truth can be a motive to holiness only if it is loved, while the natural man does not love the truth, but hates it, Rom. 1:18,25. Consequently the truth, presented externally, cannot be the efficient cause of regeneration.

3. THE HOLY SPIRIT. The only adequate view is that of the Church of all ages, that the Holy Spirit is the efficient cause of regeneration. This means that the Holy Spirit works directly on the heart of man and changes its spiritual condition. There is no co-operation of the sinner in this work whatsoever. It is the work of the Holy Spirit directly and exclusively, Ezek. 11:19; John 1:13; Acts 16:14; Rom. 9:16; Phil. 2:13. Regeneration, then, is to be conceived monergistically. God alone works, and the sinner has no part in it whatsoever. This, of course, does not mean, that man does not co-operate in later stages of the work of redemption. It is quite evident from Scripture that he does.

G. The Use of the Word of God as an Instrument in Regeneration.

The question arises, whether the Word of God is used as a means in regeneration or not; or, as it is frequently put, whether regeneration is mediate or immediate.

1. THE PROPER IMPORT OF THE QUESTION. Careful discrimination is required, in order to avoid misunderstanding.

a. When the older Reformed theologians insisted on the *immediate* character of regeneration, they often gave the term "immediate" a connotation which it does not have to-day. Some of the representatives of the school of Saumur, as Cameron and Pajon, taught that in regeneration the Holy Spirit supernaturally illumines and convinces the mind or the intellect in such a powerful manner that the will cannot fail to follow the prevalent dictate of the practical judgment. He works immediately only on the intellect, and through this mediately on the will. *According to them there is no immediate operation of the Holy Spirit on the will of man.* In opposition to these men, Reformed theologians generally stressed the fact that in regeneration the Holy Spirit also *operates directly on the will of man,* and not merely through the mediation of the intellect. To-day the question of mediate or immediate regeneration is a slightly different, though related, one. It is the question of the use of the Word of God as a means in the work of regeneration.

b. The exact form of the question ought to be carefully noted. The question is not, whether God works regeneration by means of a *creative* word. It is generally admitted that He does. Neither is it, whether He employs the word of truth, the word of preaching in the *new birth*, as distinguished from *the divine begetting* of the new man, that is, in securing the first holy exercises of the new life. The real question is, whether God, in implanting or generating the new life, employs the word of Scripture or the word of preaching as an instrument or means. The discussion of this matter often suffered in the past from the lack of proper discrimination.

2. CONSIDERATIONS THAT FAVOR A NEGATIVE ANSWER. Dr. Shedd says: "The influence of the Holy Spirit is distinguishable from that of the truth; from that of man upon man; and from that of any instrument or means whatever. His energy acts directly upon the human soul itself. It is the influence of spirit upon spirit; of one of the trinitarian persons upon a human person. Neither the truth, nor a fellow-man, can thus operate directly upon the essence of the soul itself."[1] The following considerations favor this view:

a. Regeneration is a creative act, by which the spiritually dead sinner is restored to life. But the truth of the gospel can only work in a moral and persuasive way. Such an instrument has no effect on the dead. To assert its use would seem to imply a denial of the spiritual death of man; which, of course, is not intended by those who take this position.

b. Regeneration takes place in the sphere of the sub-conscious, that is, outside of the sphere of conscious attention, while the truth addresses itself to the consciousness of man. It can exercise its persuasive influence only when man's attention is fixed on it.

---

1. *Dogm. Theol.* II, p. 500.

c. The Bible distinguishes the influence of the Holy Spirit from that of the Word of God, and declares that such an influence is necessary for the proper reception of the truth, John 6:64,65; Acts 16:14; I Cor. 2:12-15; Eph. 1:17-20. Notice particularly the case of Lydia, of whom Luke says: "She heard us (*ekouen*, impf.), whose heart the Lord opened (*dienoixen*, aor., single act), that she attended (*prosechein*, inf. of result or purpose) unto the things which were spoken of Paul."

3. SCRIPTURE PASSAGES THAT SEEM TO PROVE THE CONTRARY.

a. In James 1:18 we read: "Of his own will he brought us forth by the word of truth, that we should be a kind of firstfruits of His creatures." This passage does not prove that the new generation is mediated by the Word of God, for the term here used is *apokuesen*, which does not refer to begetting, but to giving birth. They who believe in immediate regeneration do not deny that the new birth, in which the new life first becomes manifest, is secured by the Word.

b. Peter exhorts believers to love one another fervently in view of the fact that they have been "begotten again, not of corruptible seed, but of incorruptible, through the Word of God, which liveth and abideth." I Pet. 1:23. It is not correct to say, as some have done, that "the Word" in this verse is the creative word, or the second person in the Trinity, for Peter himself informs us that he has in mind the word that was preached unto the readers, vs. 25. But it is perfectly in order to point out that even *gennao* (the word here used) does not always refer to the masculine begetting, but may also denote the feminine giving birth to children. This is perfectly evident from such passages as Luke 1:13,57; 23:29; John 16:21; Gal. 4:24. Consequently, there is no warrant for the assertion that Peter in this passage refers to the initial act in regeneration, namely, the begetting. And if it refers to regeneration in a broader sense, then the passage offers no difficulty whatsoever in connection with the matter under consideration. The idea that it refers to the new birth here, is favored by the fact that the readers are represented as having been born again out of a seed that was evidently already implanted in the soul, cf. John 1:13. It is not necessary to identify the seed with the Word.

c. The Parable of the Sower is sometimes urged in favor of the idea that regeneration takes place through the Word. The seed in this parable is the word of the kingdom. The argument is that the life is in the seed and comes forth out of the seed. Consequently, the new life comes forth out of the seed of the Word of God. But, in the first place, this is over-shooting the mark, for it will hardly do to say that the Spirit or the principle of the new life is shut up in the Word, just as the living germ is shut up in the seed. This reminds one somewhat of the Lutheran conception of calling, according to which the Spirit is in the Word so that the call would always be effective, if man did not put a stumbling-block in the way. And, in the second place, this is pressing a point which is not at all in the *tertium comparationis*. The Saviour wants to explain in this parable how it comes about that the seed of the Word bears fruit in some cases, and not in others. It bears fruit only in those cases in which it falls in good ground, in hearts so prepared that they understand the truth.

4. THE RELEVANT TEACHINGS OF OUR CONFESSIONAL STANDARDS. The following passages come into consideration here: *Conf. Belg.*, Articles XXIV and XXXV; *Heid. Cat.*, Q. 54; *Canons of Dort*, III and IV, Articles 11,12,17; and, finally, the *Conclusions of Utrecht*, adopted by our Church in 1908. From these passages it is perfectly evident that our confessional writings speak of regeneration in a broad sense, as including both the origin of the new life and its manifestation in conversion. We are even told that faith regenerates the sinner.[1] There are passages which seem to say that the Word of God is instrumental in the work of regeneration.[2] Yet they are couched in such language that it still remains doubtful, whether they actually teach that the principle of the new life is implanted in the soul by the instrumentality of the Word. They fail to discriminate carefully between the various elements which we distinguish in regeneration. In the *Conclusions of Utrecht* we read: "As far as the third point, that of *immediate regeneration*, is concerned, Synod declares that this expression can be used in a good sense, in so far as our churches have always confessed, over against the Lutheran and the Roman Catholic Church, that regeneration is not effected through the Word or the Sacraments as such, but by the almighty regenerating work of the Holy Spirit; that this regenerating work of the Holy Spirit, however, may not in that sense be divorced from the preaching of the Word, as if both were separated from each other; for, although our Confession teaches that we need not be in doubt respecting the salvation of our children which die in infancy, though they have not heard the preaching of the gospel, and our confessional standards nowhere express themselves as to the manner in which regeneration is effected in the case of these and other children, — yet it is, on the other hand, certain that the gospel is a power of God unto salvation for every one who believes, and that in the case of adults the regenerating work of the Holy Spirit accompanies the preaching of the gospel."[3]

H. Divergent Views of Regeneration.

1. THE PELAGIAN VIEW. According to the Pelagians man's freedom and personal responsibility implies that he is at all times just as able to desist

---

1. *Conf. Belg.*, Art. XXIV.
2. *Conf. Belg.*, Art XXIV, and especially Art. XXVI; *Canons of Dort* III and IV, Articles 12,17.
3. The following Reformed theologians teach immediate regeneration; *Synopsis Puriosis Theologie* (of the Leyden Professors), 31:9; Mastricht, *Godgeleerdheit* VI. 3,26; Brakel, *Redelijke Godsdienst* I, p. 738. These three authorities, however, apparently use the term "immediate" in a different sense. Further: Turretin, *Opera* XV. 4,23 f.; Shedd, *Dogm. Theol.* II, pp. 500, 506; Hodge, *Syst. Theol.* III, p. 31; Kuyper, *Dict Dogm., De Salute*, p. 74; Bavinck, *Roeping en Wedergeboorte*, pp. 219 ff.; Vos, *Geref. Dogm.* IV, pp. 46 ff.

from sin as to commit sin. Only acts of conscious volition are regarded as sin. Consequently, regeneration simply consists in moral reformation. It means that the man who formerly chose to transgress the law, now chooses to live in obedience to it.

2. BAPTISMAL REGENERATION. This is not always represented in the same way.

a. *In the Church of Rome.* According to the Roman Catholic Church regeneration includes not only spiritual renewal, but also justification or the forgiveness of sins, and is effected by means of baptism. In the case of children the work of regeneration is always effective; not so in the case of adults. These can gratefully accept and utilize the grace of regeneration, but can also resist it and make it ineffective. Moreover, it is always possible that they who have appropriated it will lose it again.

b. *In the Anglican Church.* The Church of England is not unanimous on this point, but represents two different tendencies. The so-called Puseyites are in essential agreement with the Church of Rome. But there is also an influential party in the Church which distinguishes two kinds of regeneration: the one consisting merely in a change of one's relation to the Church and the means of grace; and the other, in a fundamental change of human nature. According to this party only the former is effected by baptism. This regeneration includes no spiritual renewal. By means of it man merely enters into a new relation to the Church, and becomes a child of God in the same sense in which the Jews became children of God through the covenant of which circumcision was a seal.

c. *In the Lutheran Church.* Luther and his followers did not succeed in purging their Church from the leaven of Rome on this point. On the whole the Lutherans maintain, in opposition to Rome, the monergistic character of regeneration. They regard man as entirely passive in regeneration and incapable of contributing anything to it, though adults can resist it for a long time. At the same time some teach that baptism, working *ex opere operato,* is the usual means by which God effects regeneration. It is the *usual,* but *not the only* means, for the preaching of the Word may also produce it. They speak of two kinds of regeneration, namely, *regeneratio prima,* by which the new life is begotten, and the *regeneratio secunda* or *renovatio,* by which the new life is led in a God-ward direction. While children receive the *regeneratio prima* by means of baptism, adults, who receive the first regeneration by means of the Word, become partakers of the *regeneratio secunda* through baptism. According to the Lutherans regeneration is amissible. But through the grace of God it can be restored in the heart of the penitent sinner, and that without re-baptism. Baptism is a pledge of God's continued readiness to renew the baptized and to pardon his sins. Moreover, regeneration is not always accomplished at once, but is often a gradual process in the life of adults.

3. THE ARMINIAN VIEW. According to the Arminians regeneration is not exclusively a work of God, nor exclusively a work of man. It is the fruit of man's choice to co-operate with the divine influences exerted by means of the truth. Strictly speaking, the work of man is prior to that of God. They do not assume that there is a preceding work of God by which the will is inclined to the good. Naturally, they also believe that the grace of regeneration can be lost. The Wesleyan Arminians altered this view in so far that they stress the fact that regeneration is the work of the Holy Spirit, be it in co-operation with the human will. They do assume a prior operation of the Holy Spirit to enlighten. awaken, and draw man. However, they also believe that man can resist this work of the Holy Spirit, and that. as long as he does this, he remains in his unregenerate condition.

4. THE VIEW OF THE MEDIATING THEOLOGIANS. This is cast in a pantheistic mold. After the incarnation there are no two separate natures in Christ, but only a divine-human nature, a fusion of divine and human life. In regeneration a part of that divine-human life passes over into the sinner. This does not require a separate operation of the Holy Spirit whenever a sinner is regenerated. The new life has been communicated to the Church once for all, is now the permanent possession of the Church, and passes from the Church into the individual. Communion with the Church also insures participation of the new life. This view ignores the legal aspect of the work of Christ entirely. Moreover, it makes it impossible to hold that any one could be regenerated before the divine-human life of Christ came into existence. The Old Testament saints cannot have been regenerated. Schleiermacher is the father of this view.

5. THE TRICHOTOMIC VIEW. Some theologians constructed a peculiar theory of regeneration on the basis of the trichotomic view of human nature. This view proceeds on the assumption that man consists of three parts, — body, soul, and spirit. It is generally assumed, though there are variations on this point, that sin has its seat only in the soul, and not in the spirit (*pneuma*). If it had penetrated to the spirit, man would have been irretrievably lost, just as the devils, who are pure spiritual beings. The spirit is the higher, divine life in man, destined to control the lower life. By the entrance of sin into the world the influence of the spirit on the lower life is weakened very much; but by regeneration it is strengthened again and harmony is restored in the life of man. This is, of course, a purely rationalistic theory.[1]

6. THE VIEW OF MODERN LIBERALISM. The liberal theologians of the present day do not all have the same view of regeneration. Some of them speak in terms that remind one of Schleiermacher. More generally, however, they sponsor a purely naturalistic view. They are averse to the idea that regeneration is a supernatural and recreative work of God. In virtue of the immanent God every man has a divine principle within him and thus possesses potentially all that is necessary unto salvation. The one thing that is necessary, is

---

1. Cf. Heard, *The Tripartite Nature of Man.*

that man become conscious of his potential divinity, and that he consciously yield to the guidance of the higher principle within him. Regeneration is simply an ethical change of character.

QUESTIONS FOR FURTHER STUDY: What other terms and expressions does the Bible use to designate the work of regeneration? Does the Bible sharply distinguish between calling, regeneration, conversion, and sanctification? How do you account for it that the Roman Catholic Church includes even justification in regeneration? How do regeneration and conversion differ? Is there such a thing as prevenient grace, preceding and preparing for regeneration? What is active, as distinguished from passive, regeneration? Does man's passivity in regeneration last for any length of time? Does not the view that the Word of God is not instrumental in effecting regeneration, make the preaching of the Word seem futile and quite unnecessary? Does it not lead to the verge of mysticism?

LITERATURE: Kuyper, *Dict. Dogm., De Salute*, pp. 70-83; ibid., *Het Werk van den Heiligen Geest*, II, pp. 140-162; Bavinck, *Geref. Dogm*, IV, pp. 11-82; ibid., *Roeping en Wedergeboorte*; Mastricht, *Godgeleerdheit*, VI, 3; Dick, *Theology*, Lect. LXVI; Shedd, *Dogm. Theol.* II, pp. 490-528; Dabney, *Syst. and Polem. Theol.*, Lect. XLVII; Vos, *Geref. Dogm.* IV, pp. 32-65; Hodge, *Syst. Theol.* III, pp. 1-40; McPherson, *Chr. Dogma*, pp. 397-401; Alexander, *Syst. of Bib. Theol.* II, pp. 370-384; Litton, *Introd. to Dogm. Theol.*, pp. 313-321; Schmid, *Doct. Theol. of the Ev. Luth. Church*, pp. 463-470; Valentine, *Chr. Theol.* II, pp. 242-271; Raymond, *Syst. Theol.* II, pp. 344-359; Pope, *Chr. Theol.* III, pp. 5-13; Strong, *Syst. Theol.*, pp. 809-828; Boyce, *Abstract of Syst. Theol.*, pp. 328-334; Wilmers, *Handbook of the Chr. Rel.*, pp. 314-322; Anderson, *Regeneration*.

VII. Conversion

From the discussion of regeneration and effectual calling there is a natural transition to that of conversion. By a special operation of the Holy Spirit the former issues in the latter. Conversion may be a sharply marked crisis in the life of the individual, but may also come in the form of a gradual process. In the psychology of religion the two are generally identified. All this points to the close relation between the two.

A. The Scriptural Terms for Conversion.

1. THE OLD TESTAMENT WORDS. The Old Testament employs especially two words for conversion, namely:

a. *Nacham*, which serves to express a deep feeling, either of sorrow (niphal) or of relief (piel). In *niphal* it means *to repent*, and this repentance is often accompanied with a change of plan and of action, while in *piel* it signifies *to comfort* or *to comfort one's self*. As a designation of repentance—and this is the meaning with which we are concerned here—it is used not only of man but also of God, Gen. 6:6,7; Ex. 32:14; Judg. 2:18; I Sam. 15:11.

b. *Shubh*, which is the most common word for conversion, means *to turn, to turn about*, and *to return*. It is often used in a literal sense of both God and man, but soon acquired a religious and ethical signification. This meaning is most prominent in the prophets, where it refers to Israel's return to the Lord, after it has departed from Him. The word clearly shows that, what the Old Testament calls conversion, is a return to Him from whom sin has separated man. This is a very important element in conversion. It finds expression in the words of the prodigal son, "I will return, and go to my father."

2. THE NEW TESTAMENT WORDS. There are especially three words that come into consideration here:

a. *Metanoia* (verbal form, *metanoeo*). This is the most common word for conversion in the New Testament, and is also the most fundamental of the terms employed. The word is composed of *meta* and *nous*, which is again connected with the verb *ginosko* (Lat. *noscere*; Eng., *to know*), all of which refers to the conscious life of man. In the English Bible the word is translated "repentance," but this rendering hardly does justice to the original, since it gives undue prominence to the emotional element. Trench points out that in the classics the word means: (1) *to know after, after-knowledge*; (2) *to change the mind as the result of this after-knowledge*; (3) in consequence of this change of mind, *to regret the course pursued*; and (4) *a change of conduct for the future*, springing from all the preceding. It might indicate a change for the worse as well as for the better, however, and did not necessarily include a *resipiscentia* — a becoming wise again. In the New Testament, however, its meaning is deepened, and it denotes primarily a change of mind, taking a *wiser* view of the past, including regret for the ill then done, and leading to a change of life for the better. Here the element of *resipiscentia* is present. Walden in his work on *The Great Meaning of Metanoia* comes to the conclusion that it conveys the idea of "a *general* change of mind, which becomes in its fullest development an *intellectual and moral regeneration*."[1] While maintaining that the word denotes primarily a change of mind, we should not lose sight of the fact that its meaning is not limited to the intellectual, theoretical consciousness, but also includes the moral consciousness, the conscience. Both the mind and the conscience are defiled, Tit. 1:15, and when a person's *nous* is changed, he not only receives new knowledge, but the direction of his conscious life, its moral quality, is also changed. To become more particular, the change indicated by his word has reference, (1) *to the intellectual life*, II Tim. 2:25, to a better knowledge of God and His truth, and a saving acceptance of it (identical with the action of faith); (2) *to the conscious volitional life*, Acts 8:22, to a turning from self to God (thus again including an action of faith); and (3) *to the emotional life*, in so far as this change is accompanied with godly sorrow, II Cor. 7:10, and opens new fields of enjoyment for the sinner. In all these respects *metanoia* includes a conscious opposition to the former condition. This is an essential element in it, and therefore deserves careful attention. To be converted, is not merely to pass from one conscious direction to another, but to do it with a clearly perceived aversion to the former direction. In other words *metanoia* has not only a positive but also a negative side; it looks backward as well as forward. The converted person becomes conscious of his ignorance and error, his wilfulness and folly. His conversion includes both faith and repentance. Sad to say, the Church gradually lost sight of the original meaning of *metanoia*. In Latin theology Lactantius rendered it *"resipiscentia,"* a becoming-wise-again, as if the word were derived from *meta* and *anoia*, and denoted a return from madness or folly. The majority of Latin writers, however, preferred to render it *"poenitentia,"* a word that denotes the sorrow and regret which follows when one has made a mistake or has committed an error of any kind. This word passed into the Vulgate as the rendering of *metanoia*, and, under the influence of the Vulgate, the English translators rendered the Greek word by "repentance," thus stressing the emotional element and making *metanoia* equivalent to *metameleia*. In some cases the deterioration went even farther. The Roman Catholic Church externalized the idea of repentance in its sacrament of penance so that the *metanoeite* of the Greek Testament (Matt. 3:2) became *poenitentiam agite*, — "do penance," in the Latin Version.

b. *Epistrophe* (verbal form, *epistrepho*). This word is next in importance to *metanoia*. While in the Septuagint *metanoia* is one of the renderings of

---

1. p. 107.

nacham, the words *epistrophe* and *epistrepho* serve to render the Hebrew words *teshubhah* and *shubh.* They are constantly used in the sense of *turning again,* or *turning back.* The Greek words must be read in the light of the Hebrew, in order to bring out the important point that the turning indicated is in reality a *re-turning.* In the New Testament the noun *epistrophe* is used but once, Acts 15:3, while the verb occurs several times. It has a somewhat wider signification than *metanoeo,* and really indicates the final act of conversion. It denotes not merely a change of the *nous* or mind, but stresses the fact that a new relation is established, that the active life is made to move in another direction. This must be borne in mind in the interpretation of Acts 3:19, where the two are used alongside of each other. Sometimes *metanoeo* contains the idea of repentance only, while *epistrepho* always includes the element of faith. *Metanoeo* and *pisteuein* can be used alongside of each other; not so *epistrepho* and *pisteuein.*

c. *Metameleia* (verbal form, *metamelomai*). Only the verbal form is used in the New Testament, and literally means *to become a care to one afterwards.* It is one of the renderings of the Hebrew *nicham* in the Septuagint. In the New Testament it is found only five times, namely, in Matt. 21:29,32; 27:3; II Cor. 7:10; Heb. 7:21. It is evident from these passages that the word stresses the element of repentance, though this is not necessarily *true* repentance. In it the negative, retrospective and emotional element is uppermost, while *metanoeo* also includes a volitional element and denotes an energetic turn-about of the will. While *metanoeo* is sometimes used in the imperative, this is never the case with *metamelomai.* The feelings do not permit themselves to be commanded. This word corresponds more nearly to the Latin *poenitentia* than does *metanoeo.*

B. The Biblical Idea of Conversion. Definition.

The doctrine of conversion is, of course, like all other doctrines, based on Scripture and should be accepted on that ground. Since conversion is a conscious experience in the lives of many, the testimony of experience can be added to that of the Word of God, but this testimony, however valuable it may be, does not add to the certainty of the doctrine taught in the Word of God. We may be grateful that in recent years the Psychology of Religion paid considerable attention to the fact of conversion, but should always bear in mind that, while it has brought some interesting facts to our attention, it did little or nothing to *explain* conversion as a *religious phenomenon.* The Scriptural doctrine of conversion is based not merely on the passages containing one or more of the terms mentioned in the preceding, but also on many others in which the phenomenon of conversion is described or represented concretely in living examples. The Bible does not always speak of conversion in the same sense. We may distinguish the following:

1. NATIONAL CONVERSIONS. In the days of Moses, Joshua, and the Judges, the people of Israel repeatedly turned their backs upon Jehovah, and after experiencing the displeasure of God, repented of their sin and returned unto the

Lord; there was a national conversion in the kingdom of Judah in the days of Hezekiah and again in the days of Josiah. Upon the preaching of Jonah the Ninevites repented of their sins and were spared by the Lord, Jonah 3:10. These national conversions were merely of the nature of moral reformations. They may have been accompanied with some real religious conversions of individuals, but fell far short of the true conversion of all those that belonged to the nation. As a rule they were very superficial. They made their appearance under the leadership of pious rulers, and when these were succceeded by wicked men, the people at once fell back into their old habits.

2. TEMPORARY CONVERSIONS. The Bible also refers to conversions of individuals that represent no change of the heart, and are therefore of only passing significance. In the parable of the sower Jesus speaks of such as hear the word and at once receive it with joy, but have no root in themselves, and therefore endure but for a while. When tribulations and trials and persecutions come, they are speedily offended and fall away. Matt. 13:20,21. Paul makes mention of Hymenaeus and Alexander, who "made shipwreck concerning the faith," I Tim. 1:19,20. Cf. also II Tim. 2:17,18. And in II Tim. 4:10 he refers to Demas who left him, because the love of the present world gained the upper hand. And the writer of Hebrews speaks of some as falling away "who were once enlightened and tasted of the heavenly gift, and were made partakers of the Holy Spirit, and tasted the good word of God, and the powers of the age to come," Heb. 6.4-6. Finally, John says of some who had turned their backs upon the faithful: "They went out from us, but they were not of us; for if they had been of us, they would have continued with us," I John 2:19. Such temporary conversions may for a time have the appearance of true conversions.

3. TRUE CONVERSION (CONVERSIS ACTUALIS PRIMA). True conversion is born of godly sorrow, and issues in a life of devotion to God, II Cor. 7:10. It is a change that is rooted in the work of regeneration, and that is effected in the conscious life of the sinner by the Spirit of God; a change of thoughts and opinions, of desires and volitions, which involves the conviction that the former direction of life was unwise and wrong and alters the entire course of life. There are two sides to this conversion, the one active and the other passive; the former being the act of God, by which He changes the conscious course of man's life, and the latter, the result of this action as seen in man's changing his course of life and turning to God. Consequently, a twofold definition must be given of conversion: (a) Active conversion is *that act of God whereby He causes the regenerated sinner, in His conscious life, to turn to Him in repentance and faith.* (b) Passive conversion is *the resulting conscious act of the regenerated sinner whereby he, through the grace of God, turns to God in repentance and faith.* This true conversion is the conversion with which we are primarily concerned in theology. The Word of God contains several striking examples of it, as, for instance, the conversions of Naaman, II Kings 5:15; Manasseh, II Chron. 33:12,13; Zaccheus, Luke 19:8,9; the man born blind, John 9:38; the Samaritan woman, John 4:29,39;

the eunuch, Acts 8:30 ff.; Cornelius, Acts 10:44 ff.; Paul, Acts 9:5 ff.; Lydia, Acts 16:14. and others.

4. REPEATED CONVERSION. The Bible also speaks of a repeated conversion, in which a converted person, after a temporary lapse into the ways of sin, turns back to God. Strong prefers not to use the word "conversion" for this change, but to employ such words and phrases as "breaking off, forsaking, returning from, neglects or transgressions," and "coming back to Christ, trusting Him anew." But Scripture itself uses the word "conversion" for such cases, Luke 22:32; Rev. 2:5,16,21,22; 3:3,19. It should be understood, however, that conversion in the strictly soteriological sense of the word is never repeated. They who have experienced a true conversion may temporarily fall under the spell of evil and fall into sin; they may at times even wander far from home; but the new life is bound to re-assert itself and will eventually cause them to return to God with penitent hearts.

C. The Characteristics of Conversion.

Conversion is simply one part of the saving process. But because it is a part of an organic process, it is naturally closely connected with every other part. Sometimes a tendency becomes apparent, especially in our country, to identify it with some of the other parts of the process or to glorify it as if it were by far the most important part of the process. It is a well known fact that some, in speaking of their redemption, never get beyond the story of their conversion and forget to tell about their spiritual growth in later years. This is undoubtedly due to the fact that in their experience conversion stands out as a sharply marked crisis, and a crisis which called for action on their part. In view of the present day tendency to lose sight of the lines of demarcation in the saving process, it is well to remind ourselves of the truth of the old Latin adage, "*Qui bene distinguet, bene docet.*" We should note the following characteristics of conversion:

1. Conversion belongs to the re-creative rather than to the judicial acts of God. It does not alter the state but the condition of man. At the same time it is closely connected with the divine operations in the judicial sphere. In conversion man becomes conscious of the fact that he is worthy of condemnation and is also brought to a recognition of that fact. While this already presupposes faith, it also leads to a greater manifestation of faith in Jesus Christ, a confident trusting in Him for salvation. And this faith, in turn, by appropriating the righteousness of Jesus Christ, is instrumental in the sinner's justification. In conversion man awakens to the joyous assurance that all his sins are pardoned on the basis of the merits of Jesus Christ.

2. As the word *metanoia* clearly indicates, conversion takes place, not in the subconscious, but in the conscious life of the sinner. This does not mean that it is not rooted in the subconscious life. Being a direct effect of regeneration, it naturally includes a transition in the operations of the new life ·from

the subconscious to the conscious life. In view of this it may be said that conversion begins below consciousness, but that, as a completed act, it certainly falls within the range of the conscious life. This brings out the close connection between regeneration and conversion. A conversion that is not rooted in regeneration is no true conversion.

3. Conversion marks the conscious beginning, not only of the putting away of the old man, a fleeing from sin, but also of the putting on of the new man, a striving for holiness of life. In regeneration the sinful principle of the old life is already replaced by the holy principle of the new life. But it is only in conversion that this transition penetrates into the conscious life, turning it into a new and Godward direction. The sinner consciously forsakes the old sinful life and turns to a life in communion with and devoted to God. This does not mean, however, that the struggle between the old and the new is at once ended; it will continue as long as man lives.

4. If we take the word "conversion" in its most specific sense, it denotes a momentary change and not a process like sanctification. It is a change that takes place once and that cannot be repeated, though, as stated above, the Bible also speaks of the Christian's return to God, after he has fallen into sin, as conversion. It is the believer's turning to God and holiness again, after he has temporarily lost sight of these. In connection with regeneration we cannot possibly speak of repetition; but in the conscious life of the Christian there are ups and downs, seasons of close communion with God and seasons of estrangement from Him.

5. Over against those who think of conversion only as a definite crisis in life, it should be noted that, while conversion may be such a sharply marked crisis, it may also be a very gradual change. Older theology has always distinguished between sudden and gradual conversions (as in the cases of Jeremiah, John the Baptist, and Timothy); and in our day the psychology of conversion stresses the same distinction. Crisis conversions are most frequent in days of religious declension, and in the lives of those who have not enjoyed the privileges of a real religious education, and who have wandered far from the path of truth, of righteousness, and of holiness.

6. Finally, in our day, in which many psychologists show an inclination to reduce conversion to a general and natural phenomenon of the adolescent period of life, it becomes necessary to point out that, when we speak of conversion, we have in mind a *supernatural* work of God, resulting in a *religious change*. The psychologists sometimes intimate that conversion is but a natural phenomenon by calling attention to the fact that sudden changes also occur in the intellectual and moral life of man. Some of them hold that the emergence of the idea of sex plays an important part in conversion. Over against this rationalistic and naturalistic tendency the specific character of religious conversion must be maintained.

D. The Different Elements in Conversion.

It already appears from the preceding that conversion comprises two elements, namely, repentance and faith. Of these the former is retrospective, and the latter prospective. Repentance is directly connected with sanctification, while faith is closely, though not exclusively, related to justification. In view of the fact that faith will be discussed in a separate chapter, we limit ourselves to repentance here, and define it as *that change wrought in the conscious life of the sinner, by which he turns away from sin.*

1. THE ELEMENTS OF REPENTANCE. We distinguish three elements in repentance:

a. *An intellectual element.* There is a change of view, a recognition of sin as involving personal guilt, defilement, and helplessness. It is designated in Scripture as *epignosis hamartias* (knowledge of sin), Rom. 3:20, cf. 1:32. If this is not accompanied by the following elements, it may manifest itself as fear of punishment, while there is as yet no hatred of sin.

b. *An emotional element.* There is a change of feeling, manifesting itself in sorrow for sin committed against a holy and just God, Ps. 51:2,10,14. This element of repentance is indicated by the word *metamelomai.* If it is accompanied by the following element, it is a *lupe kata theou* (godly sorrow), but if it is not so accompanied, it is a *lupe tou kosmou* (sorrow of the world), manifesting itself in remorse and despair, II Cor. 7:9,10; Matt. 27:3; Luke 18:23.

c. *A volitional element.* There is also a volitional element, consisting in a change of purpose, an inward turning away from sin, and a disposition to seek pardon and cleansing, Ps. 51:5,7,10; Jer. 25:5. This includes the two other elements, and is therefore the most important aspect of repentance. It is indicated in Scripture by the word *metanoia*, Acts 2:38; Rom. 2:4.

2. THE SACRAMENT OF PENANCE IN THE CHURCH OF ROME. The Church of Rome has externalized the idea of repentance entirely. The most important elements in its sacrament of penance are *contrition, confession, satisfaction,* and *absolution.* Of these four *contrition* is the only one that properly belongs to repentance, and even from this the Romanist excludes all sorrow for inborn sin, and retains only that for personal transgressions. And because only few experience real *contrition*, he is also satisfied with *attrition.* This is "the mental conviction that sin deserves punishment, but does not include trust in God and a purpose to turn away from sin. It is the fear of hell."[1] Confession in the Roman Catholic Church is confession to the priest, who absolves, not declaratively, but judicially. Moreover, satisfaction consists in the sinner's doing penance, that is, enduring something painful, or performing some difficult or distasteful task. The central thought is that such outward performances really constitute a satisfaction for sin.

---

1. Schaff, *Our Fathers' Faith and Ours*, p. 358.

3. THE SCRIPTURAL VIEW OF REPENTANCE. Over against this external view of repentance the Scriptural idea should be maintained. According to Scripture repentance is wholly an inward act, and should not be confounded with the change of life that proceeds from it. Confession of sin and reparation of wrongs are *fruits* of repentance. Repentance is only a negative condition, and not a positive means of salvation. While it is the sinner's present duty, it does not offset the claims of the law on account of past transgressions. Moreover, true repentance never exists except in conjunction with faith, while, on the other hand, wherever there is true faith, there is also real repentance. The two are but different aspects of the same turning, — a turning away from sin in the direction of God. Luther sometimes spoke of a repentance preceding faith, but seems nevertheless to have agreed with Calvin in regarding true repentance as one of the fruits of faith. Lutherans are wont to stress the fact that repentance is wrought by the law and faith by the gospel. It should be borne in mind, however, that the two cannot be separated; they are simply complementary parts of the same process.

E. The Psychology of Conversion.

During recent years psychologists have made a special study of the phenomena of conversion.

1. THE NATURE OF THIS STUDY. The nature of this study can best be learned from such works as those of Coe, *The Spiritual Life;* Starbuck, *The Psychology of Religion;* James, *Varieties of Religious Experience;* Ames, *The Psychology of Religious Experience;* Pratt, *The Religious Consciousness;* Clark, *The Psychology of Religious Awakening;* Hughes, *The New Psychology and Religious Experience;* and Horton, *The Psychological Approach to Theology.* For a long time Psychology neglected the facts of the religious life altogether, but for more than a quarter of a century now it has taken notice of them. At first the attention was focussed primarily — not to say exclusively — on what must have appeared to be the great central fact of religious experience, the fact of conversion. Psychologists have studied many cases of conversion inductively and have attempted to classify the various forces at work in conversion, to distinguish the different types of religious experience, to determine the period of life in which conversion is most apt to occur, and to discover the laws that control the phenomena of conversion. While they presented their study as a purely inductive investigation into the phenomena of religion as shown in individual experience, and in some cases expressed the laudable desire and intention to keep their own philosophical and religious convictions in the background, they nevertheless in several instances clearly revealed a tendency to look upon conversion as a purely natural process, just as amenable to the ordinary laws of psychology as any other psychical fact; and to overlook, if not to deny explicitly, its supernatural aspect. The more careful scholars among them ignore, but do not deny, the supernatural in conversion. They explain their silence respecting the deeper aspects of this

central fact in religious experience by calling attention to their limitations as psychologists. They can only deal with observed facts and the psychical laws which evidently control them, but have no right to probe into the possible or probable spiritual background, in which these facts find their explanation. They have pointed out that conversion is not a specifically Christian phenomenon, but is also found in other religions; and that it is not necessarily a religious phenomenon, but also occurs in non-religious spheres. In fact, it is but one of the many changes that occur in the period of adolescence, "a sudden readjustment to a larger spiritual environment," a surrender of the old self to a truer one. "At its best," says Starbuck, "it is the individual will coming into harmony with what it feels to be the divine will."[1] As Pratt understands it, "the essential thing about conversion is just the unification of character, the achievement of a new self."[2] As to the question, whether there is anything supernatural about conversion, there is a difference of opinion among the psychologists. Coe puts the question: "Shall we therefore conclude that conversion is practically an automatic performance?" And he answers: "Not unless we first define conversion so as to ignore its profound relation to God and to the principle of a good life.... The substance of religious experiences as far transcends their emotional forms as a man transcends the clothes he wears."[3] James feels that an orthodox Christian might ask him, whether his reference of the phenomena of conversion to the subliminal self does not exclude the notion of the direct presence of the Deity in it altogether; and he replies in these words: "I have to say frankly that as a psychologist I do not see why it necessarily should."[4] He finds that, "if there are higher powers able to impress us, they may gain access only through the subliminal door."[5] The representatives of the New Psychology, that is, of the Behaviourist School and of the School of Psychoanalysis, frankly take the position that conversion may come about in a perfectly natural way, without any supernatural influence. James and others hold that the real secret of the sudden change in conversion lies in some activity of the subliminal self, which may or may not be subject to some divine influence. Students of Psychology are rather generally agreed that there are three distinct steps in conversion, which Ames describes as follows: "First, a sense of perplexity and uneasiness; second, a climax and turning point; and third, a relaxation marked by rest and joy."[6] It is quite generally agreed that there are at least two outstanding types of conversion, which are designated in various ways. Speaking of these two kinds of conversion, Starbuck says that the one is accompanied with a violent sense of sin, and the other, with a feeling of incompleteness, a struggle after a larger life, and a desire for spiritual illumination. A distinction is made between childhood and adult conversion, between gradual and sudden (violent) conversions, and between intellectual and emotional con-

1. *The Psychology of Religion*, p. 162.
2. *The Religious Consciousness*, p. 123.
3. *The Spiritual Life*, p. 140.
4. *The Varieties of Religious Experience*, p. 242.
5. p. 243.
6. *The Psychology of Religious Experience*, p. 258.

versions. These are but different names for the two recognized types of conversion. While conversion in general may be regarded as a rather normal experience, it is sometimes found to take on an abnormal aspect, especially during revivals, and then becomes a pathological phenomenon. As far as the time of conversion is concerned, it is pointed out that conversion does not occur with the same frequency at all periods of life, but belongs almost exclusively to the years between 10 and 25, and is extremely rare after 30. This means that it is peculiarly characteristic of the period of adolescence. Environment, education, and religious training, all affect the nature and the frequency of its occurrence.

2. EVALUATION OF THESE STUDIES. The value of these psychological studies of conversion need not be denied. It would be folly to brush them aside as of little or no significance, or to ignore them just because they do not take due account of the supernatural in conversion. They shed a welcome light on some of the laws that apply in the psychical life of man, on some of the phenomena that accompany the spiritual crisis in the conscious life of man, and on the various types of conversion and the factors that determine these. They deepen our insight into the different types of conversion, which have always been recognized in Reformed theology, confirm our conviction respecting the three elements that are found in conversion, and are quite in agreement with the theological conviction that conversion is rooted in the subconscious life; though they do not explicitly affirm, and in some cases even deny that it finds its explanation in a divine work of the Holy Spirit below the threshold of consciousness, — the work of regeneration. At the same time we should not overrate these studies. Some of them, as, for instance, the work of James is decidedly one-sided, since it is based entirely on the study of extraordinary conversions, which he found most interesting. Moreover, they have not escaped the danger of carrying the idea of the operation of psychical law in conversion too far, and of overlooking the divine and supernatural side of the important process of conversion. James deals with it all as a moral change and defines it in a general way as "the process, gradual or sudden, by which a self hitherto divided, and consciously wrong, inferior and unhappy, becomes unified and consciously right, superior, and happy, in consequence of its firmer hold upon religious realities."[1] Others reduce it to a purely natural phenomenon, and even explain it materialistically, as controlled by physical laws. They do not, and even from the nature of the case cannot, go down to the root of the matter, do not and cannot penetrate to the hidden depths from which conversion springs. There is an obvious tendency to challenge the old, orthodox idea of conversion, regarding it as unscientific to teach that the religious nature of man is miraculously implanted. They do not accept the light of the Word of God, and therefore have no standard by which to judge the deeper things of life. Snowden says: "As some psychologists have tried to work out a psychology of the soul without any soul, so some of them have endeavored to construct a psychology of religion without religion. Under their treatment of

1. *Op. cit.*, p. 189.

it religion has evaporated into a mere subjective feeling or delusion without any objective reality, and such a psychology of religion is baseless and worthless both as psychology and as religion."[1]

F. The Author of Conversion.

1. GOD THE AUTHOR OF CONVERSION. God only can be called the author of conversion. This is the clear teaching of Scripture. In Ps. 85:4 the poet prays, "Turn us, O God of our salvation," and in Jer. 31:18 Ephraim prays, "Turn thou me, and I shall be turned." A similar prayer is found in Lam. 5:21. In Acts 11:18 Peter calls attention to the fact that God has granted unto the Gentiles repentance unto life. A similar statement is found in II Tim. 2:25. There is a twofold operation of God in the conversion of sinners, the one moral and the other hyper-physical. In general it may be said that He works repentance by means of the law, Ps. 19:7; Rom. 3:20, and faith by means of the gospel, Rom. 10:17. Yet we cannot separate these two, for the law also contains a presentation of the gospel, and the gospel confirms the law and threatens with its terrors, II Cor. 5:11. But God also works in an immediate, hyperphysical manner in conversion. The new principle of life that is implanted in the regenerate man, does not issue into conscious action by its own inherent power, but only through the illuminating and fructifying influence of the Holy Spirit. Cf. John 6:44; Phil. 2:13. To teach otherwise would be Lutheran and Arminian.

2. MAN CO-OPERATES IN CONVERSION. But though God only is the author of conversion, it is of great importance to stress the fact, over against a false passivity, that there is also a certain co-operation of man in conversion. Dr. Kuyper calls attention to the fact that in the Old Testament *shubh* is used 74 times of conversion as a deed of man, and only 15 times, of conversion as a gracious act of God; and that the New Testament represents conversion as a deed of man 26 times. and speaks of it only 2 or 3 times as an act of God.[2] It should be borne in mind, however, that this activity of man always results from a previous work of God in man, Lam. 5:21; Phil. 2:13. That man is active in conversion is quite evident from such passages as Isa. 55:7; Jer. 18:11; Ezek. 18:23,32; 33:11; Acts 2:38; 17:30, and others.

G. The Necessity of Conversion.

The Bible speaks in absolute terms of the necessity of regeneration; not so of the necessity of conversion. It tells us plainly that, "Except a man be born again (anew, or, from above), he cannot see the kingdom of God," John 3:3, but does not speak of the need of conversion in the same general way, which allows of no exceptions. Naturally, they who identify the two cannot admit this distinction. Undoubtedly there are passages of Scripture which contain a call to conversion, in order to enjoy the blessings of God, such as Ezek. 33:11; Isa. 55:7, and these imply the necessity of conversion in the case

---

1. *The Psychology of Religion*, p. 20.
2. *Dict. Dogm., De Salute*, p. 94.

of those addressed or mentioned there. The passage that comes nearest to an absolute declaration is found in Matt. 18:3, "Verily, I say unto you, Except ye turn and become as little children, ye shall in no wise enter into the kingdom of heaven." But even in this case one might insist that this refers only to the persons addressed. The expressed or implied exhortations to turn about, found in Scripture, come only to those to whom they are addressed and do not necessarily mean that every one must pass through a conscious conversion, in order to be saved. The question as to the necessity of conversion should be answered with discrimination. Those who die in infancy must be regenerated, in order to be saved, but cannot very well experience conversion, a conscious turning from sin unto God. In the case of adults, however, conversion is absolutely essential, but it need not appear in each one's life as a strongly marked crisis. Such a definite crisis can, as a rule, be expected only in the lives of those who, after a life of sin and shame, are arrested in their evil course by the regenerating power of the Holy Spirit and by the effectual call to conversion. In them the life of conscious enmity is at once transformed into a life of friendship with God. It can hardly be looked for, however, in the lives of those who, like John the Baptist and Timothy, served the Lord from early youth. At the same time, conversion is necessary in the case of all adults in the sense that its elements, namely, repentance and faith must be present in their lives. This means that they must in some form experience the essence of conversion.

H. Relation of Conversion to other Stages of the Saving Process.

1. To REGENERATION. This has already been indicated to some extent. The two words "regeneration" and "conversion" are used synonymously by some. Yet in present day theology they generally refer to different, though closely related matters. The principle of the new life implanted in regeneration comes into active expression in the conscious life of the sinner when he is converted. The change that is effected in the subconscious life in regeneration passes into the conscious life in conversion. Logically, conversion follows regeneration. In the case of those who are regenerated in infancy, there is necessarily a temporal separation of the two, but in the case of those who are regenerated after they have come to years of discretion, the two generally coincide. In regeneration the sinner is entirely passive, but in conversion he is both passive and active. The former can never be repeated, but the latter can to a certain extent, though the *conversio actualis prima* occurs but once.

2. To EFFECTUAL CALLING. Conversion is the direct result of internal calling. As an effect in man, internal calling and the beginning of conversion really coincide. The situation is not such that God calls the sinner, and that then the sinner in his own strength turns to God. It is exactly in the internal calling that man becomes conscious of the fact that God is working conversion in him. The truly converted man will feel all along that his conversion is the work of God. This distinguishes him from the man who aims at superficial moral improvement. The latter works in his own strength.

3. To FAITH. As already indicated, conversion consists in repentance and faith, so that faith is really a part of conversion. Yet we should distinguish here. There are two kinds of true faith, each having a distinct object, namely, (a) a recognition of the truth of God's revelation of redemption, not merely in a detached, historical sense, but in such a way that it is recognized as a reality that cannot be ignored with impunity, because it affects life in a vital way; and (b) a recognition and acceptance of the salvation offered in Jesus Christ, which is saving faith in the proper sense of the word. Now there is no doubt that faith in the former sense is present at once in conversion. The Holy Spirit causes the sinner to see the truth as it applies to his own life, so that he comes under "conviction," and thus becomes conscious of his sin. But he may remain in this stage for some time, so that it is hard to say in how far saving faith, that is, trust in Christ unto salvation, is at once included in conversion. There is no doubt that, logically, repentance and the knowledge of sin precedes the faith that yields to Christ in trusting love.

QUESTIONS FOR FURTHER STUDY: Why did Beza prefer to call conversion *resipiscentia* rather than *poenitentia?* Why is the term 'repentance' inadequate to express the idea of conversion? How did Luther's conception of repentance differ from that of Calvin? Is conversion always preceded by 'conviction of sin'? Can we speak of prevenient grace relative to conversion? Is conversion an instantaneous act or is it a process? What is meant by the term 'daily conversion'? What is the proper view of the necessity of conversion? Does covenant preaching have a tendency to silence the call to conversion? What is the Methodist conception of conversion? Are the methods of the revival meetings commendable? What about the lasting character of the conversions of which they boast? Do the statistics of the Psychology of conversion give us any information on this point?

LITERATURE: Bavinck, *Geref. Dogm.* IV, pp. 127-181; Kuyper, *Dict. Dogm., De Salute,* pp. 93-97; ibid., *Het Werk van den Heiligen Geest* II, pp. 197-203; A. A. Hodge, *Outlines of Theology,* pp. 487-495; Strong, *Syst. Theol.,* pp. 829-849; McPherson, *Chr. Dogm.,* pp. 393-397; Shedd, *Dogm. Theol.* II, pp. 529-537; Alexander, *Syst. of Bib. Theol.* II, pp. 38-384; Litton, *Introd. to Dogm. Theol.,* pp. 249-258; Vos, *Geref. Dogm.* IV, pp. 66-81; Pope, *Chr. Dogm.* II, pp. 367-376; Schmid, *Doct. Theol. of the Ev. Luth. Church,* pp. 465, 466, 470-484; Drummond, *Studies in Chr. Doct.,* pp. 488-491; Macin'osh, *Theol. as an Empirical Science,* pp. 134-136; Mastricht, *Godgeleerdheit,* IV, 4; Walden, *The Great Meaning of Metanoia;* Jackson, *The Fact of Conversion;* Coe, *The Spiritual Life;* Starbuck, *The Psychology of Religion;* James, *The Varieties of Religious Experience,* pp. 189-258; Ames, *The Psychology of Religious Experience,* pp. 257-276; Clark, *The Psychology of Religious Awakening;* Pratt, *The Religious Consciousness.* pp. 122-164; Steven, *The Psychology of the Christian Soul,* pp. 142-298; Hughes, *The New Psychology and Religious Experience,* pp. 213-241; Snowden, *The Psychology of Religion,* pp. 143-199.

VIII. Faith

The preceding chapter dealt with conversion in general, and also gave a brief description of the negative element of conversion, namely, repentance. The present chapter will be devoted to a discussion of the positive element, which is faith. This is of such central significance in soteriology that it calls for separate treatment. It is best taken up at this point, not only because faith is a part of conversion, but also because it is instrumentally related to justification. Its discussion forms a natural transition to the doctrine of justification *by faith*.

A. Scriptural Terms for Faith.

1. THE OLD TESTAMENT TERMS AND THEIR MEANING. The Old Testament contains no noun for faith, unless *emunah* be so considered in Hab. 2:4. This word ordinarily means "faithfulness," Deut. 32:4; Ps. 36:5; 37:3; 40:11, but the way in which the statement of Habakkuk is applied in the New Testament, Rom. 1:17; Gal. 3:11; Heb. 10:38, would seem to indicate that the prophet used the term in the sense of faith. The most common Old Testament word for "to believe" is *he'emin*, the hiphil form of *'aman*. In *qal* it means "to nurse" or "to nourish"; in *niphal*, "to be firm" or "established," "steadfast"; and in *hiphil*, "to consider established," "to regard as true," or "to believe." The word is construed with the prepositions *beth* and *lamedh*. Construed with the former, it evidently refers to a confident resting on a person or thing or testimony; while, with the latter, it signifies the assent given to a testimony, which is accepted as true. — The word next in importance is *batach*, which is construed with *beth* and means "to confide in," "to lean upon," or "to trust." It does not emphasize the element of intellectual assent, but rather that of confident reliance. In distinction from *he'emin*, which is generally rendered by *pisteuo* in the Septuagint, this word is usually translated by *elpizo* or *peithomai*. The man who trusts in God is one who fixes all his hope for the present and for the future on Him. — There is still another word, namely, *chasah*, which is used less frequently, and means "to hide one's self," or "to flee for refuge." In this, too, the element of trust is clearly in the foreground.

2. THE NEW TESTAMENT TERMS AND THEIR MEANING. Two words are used throughout the New Testament, namely, *pistis* and the cognate verb *pisteuein*. These do not always have exactly the same connotation.

a. *The different meanings of pistis.* (1) *In classical Greek.* The word *pistis* has two meanings in classical Greek. It denotes: (a) a conviction based on confidence in a person and in his testimony, which as such is distinguished from knowledge resting on personal investigation; and (b) the confidence itself on which such a conviction rests. This is more than a mere intellectual conviction that a person is reliable; it presupposes a personal relation to the object of confidence, a going out of one's self, to rest in another. The Greeks did not ordinarily use the word in this sense, to express their relation to the gods, since they regarded these as hostile to men, and therefore as objects of fear rather than of trust.—(2) *In the Septuagint.* The transition from the use of the word *pistis* in classical Greek to the New Testament usage, in which the meaning "confidence" or "trust" is all-important, is found in the Septuagint use of the verb *pisteuein* rather than in that of the noun *pistis*, which occurs in it but once with anything like its New Testament meaning. The verb *pisteuein* generally serves as a rendering of the word *he'emin*, and thus expresses the idea of faith both in the sense of assent to the Word of God and of confident trusting in Him. — (3) *In the New Testament.* There are a few instances in which the word has a passive meaning, namely, that of "fidelity" or "faithfulness," which is its usual meaning in the Old Testament, Rom. 3:3; Gal. 5:22; Tit. 2:10. It is generally used in an active sense. The following special meanings should be distinguished: (a) an intellectual belief or conviction, resting on the testimony of another, and therefore based on trust in this other rather than on personal investigation, Phil. 1:27; II Cor. 4:13; II Thess. 2:13, and especially in the writings of John; and (b) a confiding trust or confidence in God or, more particularly, in Christ with a view to redemption from sin and to future blessedness. So especially in the Epistles of Paul, Rom. 3:22,25; 5:1,2; 9:30,32; Gal. 2:16; Eph. 2:8; 3:12, and many other passages. This trust must be distinguished from that on which the intellectual trust mentioned under (a) above, rests. The order in the successive stages of faith is as follows: (a) general confidence in God and Christ; (b) acceptance of their testimony on the basis of that trust; and (c) yielding to Christ and trusting in Him for the salvation of the soul. The last is specifically called saving faith.

b. *The different constructions of pisteuein and their meaning.* We have the following constructions: (1) *Pisteuein with the dative.* This generally denotes believing assent. If the object is a person, it is ordinarily employed in a somewhat pregnant sense, including the deeply religious idea of a devoted, believing trust. When the object is a thing, it is usually the Word of God, and when it is a person, it is generally either God or Christ, John 4:50; 5:47; Acts 16:34; Rom. 4:3; II Tim. 1:12. — (2) *Pisteuein followed by hoti.* In this construction the conjunction generally serves to introduce what is believed. On the whole this construction is weaker than the preceding. Of the twenty passages in which it is found, fourteen occur in the writings of John. In a couple of cases the matter believed hardly rises into the religious sphere, John 9:18; Acts 9:26, while in some of the others it is decidedly of soteriological import, Matt. 9:28; Rom. 10:9; I Thess. 4:14. — (3) *Pisteuein with prepositions.* Here the deeper meaning of the word, that of firm trustful reliance, comes to its full rights. The following constructions come into consideration: (a) *Construction with en.* This is the most frequent construction in the Septua-gint, though it is all but absent from the New Testament. The only certain case is Mark 1:15, where the object is the gospel. Other possible instances are John 3:15; Eph. 1:13, where the object would be Christ. The implication of this construction seems to be that of a firmly fixed confidence in its object. (b) *Construction with epi and the dative.* It is found only in the quotation from Isa. 28:16, which appears in three passages, namely, Rom. 9:33; 10:11; I Pet. 2:6, and in Luke 24:25; I Tim. 1:16. It expresses the idea of a steady and restful repose, a reliance on its object. (c) *Construction with epi and the accusative.* This is used seven times in the New Testament. In a couple of cases the object is God, as He operates in the saving of the soul in Christ; in all the others it is Christ. This construction includes the idea of moral motion, of mental direction towards the object. The main idea is that of turning with confident trust to Jesus Christ. (d) *Construction with eis.* This is the most characteristic construction of the New Testament. It occurs forty-nine times. About fourteen of these instances are Johannine, and the remainder Pauline. Except in one case, the object is always a person, rarely God, and most com-monly Christ. This construction has a very pregnant meaning, expressing, as it does, "an absolute transference of trust from ourselves to another, a complete self-surrender to God." Cf. John 2:11; 3:16,18,36; 4:39; 14:1; Rom. 10:14; Gal. 2:16; Phil. 1:29.

B. Figurative Expressions Used to Describe the Activity of Faith.

There are several figurative expressions of the activity of faith in Scripture. The following are some of the most important.

1. It is spoken of as a looking to Jesus, John 3:14,15 (comp. Num. 21:9). This is a very appropriate figure, because it comprises the various elements of faith, especially when it refers to a steadfast looking to anyone, as in the passage indicated. There is in it an act of perception (intellectual element), a deliberate fixing of the eye on the object (volitional element), and a certain satisfaction to which this concentration testifies (emotional element).

2. It is also represented as a hungering and thirsting, an eating and drinking, Matt. 5:6; John 6:50-58; 4:14. When men really hunger and thirst spiritually, they feel that something is wanting, are conscious of the indis-pensable character of that which is lacking, and endeavor to obtain it. All this is characteristic of the activity of faith. In eating and drinking we not only have the conviction that the necessary food and drink is present, but also the confident expectation that it will satisfy us, just as in appropriating Christ by faith we have a certain measure of confidence that He will save us.

3. Finally, there are also the figures of coming to Christ and receiving Him, John 5:40; 7:37 (cf. vs. 38); 6:44,65; 1:12. The figure of coming to Christ pictures faith as an action in which man looks away from himself and his

own merits, to be clothed with the righteousness of Jesus Christ; and that of receiving Christ stresses the fact that faith is an appropriating organ.

C. The Doctrine of Faith in History.

1. BEFORE THE REFORMATION. From the very earliest times of the Christian Church faith stood out in the minds of the leaders as the one great condition of salvation. Alongside of it repentance also soon became rather prominent. At the same time there was little reflection at first on the nature of faith and but little understanding of the relation of faith to the other parts of the *ordo salutis*. There was no current definition of faith. While there was a tendency to use the word "faith" to denote the acceptance of the truth on testimony, it was also in some cases employed in a deeper sense, so as to include the idea of self-surrender to the truth intellectually received. The Alexandrians contrasted *pistis* and *gnosis*, and regarded the former primarily as initial and imperfect knowledge. Tertullian stressed the fact that faith accepts a thing on authority, and not because it is warranted by human reason. He also used the term in an objective sense, as a designation of that which must be believed, — the *regula fidei*. Even up to the time of Augustine little attention was devoted to the nature of faith, though it was always acknowledged to be the pre-eminent means in the appropriation of salvation. Augustine, however, gave the matter a greater measure of consideration. He spoke of faith in more than one sense. Sometimes he regarded it as nothing more than intellectual assent to the truth. But he conceived of evangelical or justifying faith as including also the elements of self-surrender and love. This faith is perfected in love and thus becomes the principle of good works. He did not have a proper conception, however, of the relation between faith and justification. This is partly due to the fact that he did not carefully distinguish between justification and sanctification. The deeper conception of faith that is found in Augustine was not shared by the Church in general. There was a tendency to confound faith with orthodoxy, that is, with the holding of an orthodox faith. The Scholastics distinguished between a *fides informis*, that is, a mere intellectual assent to the truth taught by the Church, and a *fides formata* (*charitate*), that is, a faith informed (given a characteristic form) by love, and regarded the latter as the only faith that justifies, since it involves an infusion of grace. It is only as *fides formata* that faith becomes active for good and becomes the first of the theological virtues by which man is placed in the right relation to God. Strictly speaking it is the love by which faith is perfected that justifies. Thus in faith itself a foundation was laid for human merit. Man is justified, not exclusively by the imputation of the merits of Christ, but also by inherent grace. Thomas Aquinas defines the virtue of faith as a "habit of the mind, by reason of which eternal life has its inception in us, inasmuch as it causes the intellect to give its assent to things that are not seen."

2. AFTER THE REFORMATION. While the Roman Catholics stressed the fact that justifying faith is merely assent and has its seat in the understanding,

the Reformers generally regarded it as *fiducia* (trust), having its seat in the will. On the relative importance of the elements in faith there have been differences, however, even among Protestants. Some regard the definition of Calvin as superior to that of the Heidelberg Catechism. Says Calvin: "We shall now have a full definition of faith if we say that it is a firm and sure knowledge of the divine favour toward us, founded on the truth of a free promise in Christ, and revealed to our minds, and sealed in our hearts, by the Holy Spirit."[1] The Heidelberg Catechism, on the other hand, also brings in the element of confidence when it answers the question, "What is true faith?" as follows: "True faith is not only a sure knowledge whereby I hold for truth all that God has revealed to us in His Word, but also a firm confidence which the Holy Spirit works in my heart by the gospel, that not only to others, but to me also, remission of sins, everlasting righteousness and salvation are freely given by God, merely of grace, only for the sake of Christ's merits."[2] But it is quite evident from the connection that Calvin means to include the element of confidence in the "firm and sure knowledge" of which he speaks. Speaking of the boldness with which we may approach God in prayer, he even says: "Such boldness springs only from confidence in the divine favour and salvation. So true is this, that the term *faith* is often used as equivalent to *confidence*."[3] He absolutely rejects the fiction of the Schoolmen who insist "that faith is an assent with which any despiser of God may receive what is delivered in Scripture."[4] But there is an even more important point of difference between the Reformers' conception of faith and that of the Scholastics. The latter recognized in faith itself some real and even meritorious efficacy (*meritum ex congruo*) in disposing to, and in procuring or obtaining justification. The Reformers, on the other hand, were unanimous and explicit in teaching that justifying faith does not justify by any meritorious or inherent efficacy of its own, but only as the instrument for receiving or laying hold on what God has provided in the merits of Christ. They regarded this faith primarily as a gift of God and only secondarily as an activity of man in dependence on God. The Arminians revealed a Romanizing tendency, when they conceived of faith as a meritorious work of man, on the basis of which he is accepted in favor by God. Schleiermacher, the father of modern theology, hardly mentions saving faith and knows absolutely nothing of faith as childlike trust in God. He says that faith "is nothing but the incipient experience of the satisfaction of our spiritual need by Christ." It is a new psychological experience, a new consciousness, rooted in a feeling, not of Christ, nor of any doctrine, but of the harmony of the Infinite, of the Whole of things, in which the soul finds God. Ritschl agreed with Schleiermacher in holding that faith springs up as the result of contact with the divine reality, but finds its object, not in any idea or doctrine, nor in the whole of things, but in the Person of Christ, as

---

1. *Inst.* III. 2,7.
2. Q. 21.
3. *Ibid.*, III. 2,15.
4. *Ibid.* III. 2,8.

the supreme revelation of God. It is not a passive assent, but an active principle. In it man makes God's self-end, that is, the kingdom of God, his own, begins to work for the kingdom, and in doing this finds salvation. The views of Schleiermacher and Ritschl characterize a great deal of modern liberal theology. Faith, in this theology, is not a heaven-wrought experience, but a human achievement; not the mere receiving of a gift, but a meritorious action; not the acceptance of a doctrine, but a "making Christ Master" in an attempt to pattern one's life after the example of Christ. This view met with strong opposition, however, in the theology of crisis, which stresses the fact that saving faith is never a merely natural psychological experience, is strictly speaking an act of God rather than of man, never constitutes a permanent possession of man, and is in itself merely a *hohlraum* (empty space), quite incapable of effecting salvation. Barth and Brunner regard faith simply as the divine response, wrought in man by God, to the Word of God in Christ, that is, not so much to any doctrine, as to the divine command or the divine act in the work of redemption. It is the affirmative answer, the "yes" to the call of God, a "yes" that is elicited by God Himself.

D. The Idea of Faith in Scripture.

1. IN THE OLD TESTAMENT. Evidently the New Testament writers, in stressing faith as the fundamental principle of the religious life, were not conscious of shifting ground and of departing from the Old Testament representation. They regard Abraham as the type of all true believers (Rom. 4; Gal. 3; Heb. 11; Jas. 2), and those who are of faith as the true sons of Abraham (Rom. 2:28,29; 4:12,16; Gal. 3:9). Faith is never treated as a novelty of the new covenant, nor is any distinction drawn between the faith of the two covenants. There is a sense of continuity, and the proclamation of faith is regarded as the same in both dispensations, John 5:46; 12:38,39; Hab. 2:4; Rom. 1:17; 10:16; Gal. 3:11; Heb. 10:38. In both Testaments faith is the same radical self-commitment to God, not merely as the highest good of the soul, but as the gracious Saviour of the sinner. The only difference that is apparent, is due to the progressive work of redemption, and this is more or less evident even within the confines of the Old Testament itself.

a. *In the patriarchal period.* In the earlier portions of the Old Testament there is but little in the line of abstract statement respecting the way of salvation. The essence of the religion of the patriarchs is exhibited to us in action. The promise of God is in the foreground, and the case of Abraham is designed to set forth the idea that the proper response to it is that of faith. The whole life of Noah was determined by trust in God and in His promises, but it is especially Abraham that is set before us as the typical believer, who commits himself to God with unwavering trust in His promises and is justified by faith.

b. *In the period of the law.* The giving of the law did not effect a fundamental change in the religion of Israel, but merely introduced a change in its external form. The law was not substituted for the promise; neither was faith supplanted by works. Many of the Israelites, indeed, looked upon the law in a purely legalistic spirit and sought to base their claim to salvation on a scrupu-lous fulfilment of it as a body of external precepts. But in the case of those who understood its real nature, who felt the inwardness and spirituality of the law, it served to deepen the sense of sin and to sharpen the conviction that salvation could be expected only from the grace of God. The essence of real piety was ever-increasingly seen to consist in a confident trust in the God of salvation. While the Old Testament clearly stresses the fear of the Lord, a large number of expressions, such as hoping, trusting, seeking refuge in God, looking to Him, relying on Him, fixing the heart on Him, and cleaving to Him — make it abun-dantly evident that this fear is not a craven but a child-like, reverent fear, and emphasize the necessity of that loving self-commitment to God which is the essence of saving faith. Even in the period of the law faith is distinctly soterio-logical, looking to the Messianic salvation. It is a trusting in the God of salva-tion, and a firm reliance on His promises for the future.

2. IN THE NEW TESTAMENT. When the Messiah came in fulfilment of the prophecies, bringing the hoped-for salvation, it became necessary for the vehicles of God's revelation to direct God's people to the person of their Re-deemer. This was all the more necessary in view of the fact that the fulfilment came in a form which many did not expect, and which apparently did not correspond with the promise.

a. *In the Gospels.* The demand for faith in Jesus as the Redeemer, prom-ised and hoped for, appeared as something characteristic of the new age. "To believe" meant to become a Christian. This demand seemed to create a gulf between the old dispensation and the new. The beginning of the latter is even called "the coming of faith," Gal. 3:23,25. It is the characteristic thing of the Gospels that in them Jesus is constantly offering Himself as the object of faith, and that in connection with the highest concerns of the soul. The Gospel of John stresses the higher aspects of this faith more than the Synoptics.

b. *In the Acts.* In the Acts of the Apostles faith is required in the same general sense. By the preaching of the apostles men are brought to the obedience of faith in Christ; and this faith becomes the formative principle of the new community. Different tendencies developed in the Church and gave rise to the different modes of dealing with faith that became apparent in the writings of the New Testament.

c. *In the Epistle of James.* James had to rebuke the Jewish tendency to conceive of the faith that was well pleasing to God as a mere intellectual assent to the truth, a faith that did not yield appropriate fruit. His idea of the faith that justifies does not differ from that of Paul, but he stresses the fact that this faith must manifest itself in good works. If it does not, it is a dead faith, and is, in fact, non-existent.

d. *In the Epistles of Paul.* Paul had to contend particularly with the ingrained legalism of Jewish thought. The Jew boasted of the righteousness of the law. Consequently, the apostle had to vindicate the place of faith as the only instrument of salvation. In doing this, he naturally dwelt a great deal on

Christ as the object of faith, since it is from this object only that faith derives its efficacy. Faith justifies and saves only because it lays hold on Jesus Christ.

e. *In the Epistle to the Hebrews.* The writer of Hebrews also regards Christ as the proper object of saving faith, and teaches that there is no righteousness except through faith, 10:38; 11:7. But the danger against which the writer of this letter had to guard was not that of falling from faith into works, but rather that of falling from faith into despair. He speaks of faith as "the assurance of things hoped for, the conviction of things not seen," 11:1. He exhorts the readers to an attitude of faith, which will enable them to rise from the seen to the unseen, from the present to the future, from the temporal to the eternal, and which will enable them to be patient in the midst of sufferings.

f. *In the Epistles of Peter.* Peter also writes to readers that were in danger of becoming discouraged, though not of falling back into Judaism. The circumstances in which they found themselves prompted him to lay special emphasis on the relation of faith to the consummated salvation, in order to quicken within their hearts the hope that would sustain them in their present trials, the hope of an unseen and eternal glory. The Second Epistle stresses the importance of the knowledge of faith as a safeguard against prevailing errors.

g. *In the Writings of John.* John had to contend with an incipient Gnosticism, which falsely emphasized knowledge (*gnosis*) and despised simple faith. The former was supposed to carry with it a far greater degree of blessedness than the latter. Hence John makes it a point to magnify the blessings of faith. He insists, not so much on the certainty and glory of the future inheritance which faith secures, as on the fulness of the present enjoyment of salvation which it brings. Faith embraces knowledge as a firm conviction and makes believers at once possessors of the new life and of eternal salvation. Meanwhile John does not neglect the fact that it also reaches out into the future.

E. Faith in General.

The word "faith" is not exclusively a religious and theological term. It is often used in a general and non-religious sense, and even so has more than one connotation. The following uses of the term deserve particular attention. It may denote:

1. FAITH AS LITTLE MORE THAN MERE OPINION. The word "faith" is sometimes used in a rather loose and popular sense, to denote a persuasion of the truth which is stronger than mere opinion, and yet weaker than knowledge. Even Locke defined faith as "the assent of the mind to propositions which are probably, but not certainly, true." In popular language we often say of that of which we are not absolutely sure, but which we at the same time feel constrained to recognize as true: "I believe that, but I am not sure of it." Consequently some philosophers have found the distinguishing characteristic of faith in the lesser degree of certainty which it yields—Locke, Hume, Kant, and others.

2. FAITH AS IMMEDIATE CERTAINTY. In connection with science faith is often spoken of as *immediate* certainty. There is a certainty which man obtains by means of perception, experience, and logical deduction, but there is also an intuitive certainty. In every science there are axioms that cannot be demonstrated and intuitive convictions that are not acquired by perception or logical deduction. Dr. Bavinck says "Het gebied der onmiddelijke zekerheid is veel grooter dan dat der demonstratieve, en deze laatste is altijd weer op de eerste gebouwd, en staat en valt met deze. Ook is deze intuitieve zekerheid niet minder maar grooter dan die, welke langs den weg van waarneming en logische demonstratie verkregen wordt." The sphere of immediate certainty is greater than that of demonstrative certainty. In both cases now mentioned faith is regarded exclusively as an activity of the intellect.

3. FAITH AS A CONVICTION BASED ON TESTIMONY AND INCLUDING TRUST. In common parlance the word "faith" is often used to denote the conviction that the testimony of another is true, and that what he promises will be done; a conviction based only on his recognized veracity and fidelity. It is really a believing acceptance of what another says on the basis of the confidence which he inspires. And this faith, this conviction based on confidence, often leads to a further confidence: trust in a friend in time of need, in the ability of a doctor to give aid in times of sickness, and in that of a pilot to guide the vessel into the harbor, and so on. In this case faith is more than a mere matter of the intellect. The will is brought into play, and the element of trust comes to the foreground.

F. Faith in the Religious Sense and Particularly Saving Faith.

The distinguishing characteristics of faith in the theological sense have not always been stated in the same way. This will become evident, when we consider the concept, the elements, the object, and the ground of faith.

1. THE CONCEPT OF FAITH: FOUR KINDS OF FAITH DISTINGUISHED. As a psychological phenomenon faith in the religious sense does not differ from faith in general. If faith in general is a persuasion of the truth founded on the testimony of one in whom we have confidence and on whom we rely, and therefore rests on authority, Christian faith in the most comprehensive sense is man's persuasion of the truth of Scripture on the basis of the authority of God. The Bible does not always speak of religious faith in the same sense, and this gave rise to the following distinctions in theology.

a. *Historical faith.* This is a purely intellectual apprehension of the truth, devoid of any moral or spiritual purpose. The name does not imply that it embraces only historical facts and events to the exclusion of moral and spiritual truths; nor that it is based on the testimony of history, for it may have reference to contemporaneous facts or events, John 3:2. It is rather expressive of the idea that this faith accepts the truths of Scripture as one might accept a history in which one is not personally interested. This faith may be the result of tradition, of education, of public opinion, of an insight into the moral grandeur of Scripture, and so on, accompanied with the general operations of the Holy Spirit. It may be very orthodox and Scriptural, but is not rooted in the heart, Matt. 7:26; Acts 26:27,28; Jas. 2:19. It is a *fides humana*, and not a *fides divina*.

b. *Miraculous faith*. The so-called miraculous faith is a persuasion wrought in the mind of a person that a miracle will be performed by him or in his behalf. God can give a person a work to do that transcends his natural powers and enable him to do it. Every attempt to perform a work of that kind requires faith. This is very clear in cases in which man appears merely as the instrument of God or as the one who announces that God will work a miracle, for such a man must have full confidence that God will not put him to shame. In the last analysis God only works miracles, though He may do it through human instrumentality. *This is faith of miracles in the active sense*, Matt. 17:20; Mark 16:17,18. It is not necessarily, but may be, accompanied with saving faith. *The faith of miracles may also be passive*, namely, the persuasion that God will work a miracle in one's behalf. It, too, may or may not be accompanied with saving faith, Matt. 8:10-13; John 11:22 (comp. verses 25-27); 11:40; Acts 14:9. The question is often raised, whether such a faith has a legitimate place in the life of man to-day. Roman Catholics answer this question affirmatively, while Protestants are inclined to give a negative answer. They point out that there is no Scriptural basis for such a faith, but do not deny that miracles may still occur. God is entirely sovereign also in this respect, and the Word of God leads us to expect another cycle of miracles in the future.

c. *Temporal faith*. This is a persuasion of the truths of religion which is accompanied with some promptings of the conscience and a stirring of the affections, but is not rooted in a regenerate heart. The name is derived from Matt. 13:20,21. It is called a temporary faith, because it is not permanent and fails to maintain itself in days of trial and persecution. This does not mean that it may not last as long as life lasts. It is quite possible that it will perish only at death, but then it surely ceases. This faith is sometimes called a hypocritical faith, but that is not entirely correct, for it does not necessarily involve conscious hypocrisy. They who possess this faith usually believe that they have the true faith. It might better be called an imaginary faith, seemingly genuine, but evanescent in character. It differs from historical faith in the personal interest it shows in the truth and in the reaction of the feelings upon it. Great difficulty may be experienced in attempting to distinguish it from true saving faith. Christ says of the one who so believes: "He hath no root in himself," Matt. 13:21. It is a faith that does not spring from the root implanted in regeneration, and therefore is not an expression of the new life that is embedded in the depths of the soul. In general it may be said that temporal faith is grounded in the emotional life and seeks personal enjoyment rather than the glory of God.

d. *True Saving faith.* True saving faith is a faith that has its seat in the heart and is rooted in the regenerate life. A distinction is often made between the *habitus* and the *actus* of faith. Back of both of these, however, lies the *semen fidei.* This faith is not first of all an activity of man, but a potentiality wrought by God in the heart of the sinner. The seed of faith is implanted in man in regeneration. Some theologians speak of this as the *habitus* of faith, but others more correctly call it the *semen fidei.* It is only after God has implanted the seed of faith in the heart that man can exercise faith. This is apparently what Barth has in mind also, when he, in his desire to stress the fact that salvation is exclusively a work of God, says that God rather than man is the subject of faith. The conscious exercise of faith gradually forms a *habitus,* and this acquires a fundamental and determining significance for the further exercise of faith. When the Bible speaks of faith, it generally refers to faith as an activity of man, though born of the work of the Holy Spirit. Saving faith may be defined as *a certain conviction, wrought in the heart by the Holy Spirit, as to the truth of the gospel, and a hearty reliance (trust) on the promises of God in Christ.* In the last analysis, it is true, Christ is the object of saving faith, but He is offered to us only in the gospel.

2. THE ELEMENTS OF FAITH. In speaking of the different elements of faith we should not lose sight of the fact that faith is an activity of man as a whole, and not of any part of man. Moreover, the soul functions in faith through its ordinary faculties, and not through any special faculty. It is an exercise of the soul which has this in common with all similar exercises, that it appears simple, and yet on closer scrutiny is found to be complex and intricate. And therefore. in order to obtain a proper conception of faith, it is necessary to distinguish between the various elements which it comprises.

a. *An intellectual element (notitia).* There is an element of knowledge in faith, in connection with which the following points should be considered:

(1) *The character of this knowledge.* The knowledge of faith consists in a positive recognition of the truth, in which man accepts as true whatsoever God says in His Word, and especially what He says respecting the deep depravity of man and the redemption which is in Christ Jesus. Over against Rome the position must be maintained that this sure knowledge belongs to the essence of faith; and in opposition to such theologians as Sandeman, Wardlaw, Alexander, Chalmers, and others, that a mere intellectual acceptance of the truth is not the whole of faith. On the one hand it would be an over-estimation of the knowledge of faith, if it were regarded as a complete comprehension of the objects of faith. But on the other hand it would also be an under-estimation of it, if it were considered as a mere taking notice of the things believed, without the conviction that they are true. Some modern liberals take this view and consequently like to speak of faith as a venture. It is a spiritual insight into the truths of the Christian religion that find response in the heart of the sinner.

(2) *The certainty of this knowledge.* The knowledge of faith should not
be regarded as less certain than other knowledge. Our Heidelberg Catechism
assures us that true faith is among other things also "a *certain* (sure, incontest-
able) knowledge."[1] This is in harmony with Heb. 11:1, which speaks of it
as "the assurance of things hoped for, a conviction of things not seen"
It makes future and unseen things subjectively real and certain for the believer.
The knowledge of faith is mediated for, and imparted to, us by the testimony
of God in His Word, and is accepted by us as certain and reliable on the basis
of the veracity of God. The certainty of this knowledge has its warrant in God
Himself, and consequently nothing can be more certain. And it is quite
essential that this should be so, for faith is concerned with spiritual and eternal
things, in which certainty is needed, if anywhere. There must be certainty
as to the reality of the object of faith; if there is not, faith is in vain. Machen
deplores the fact that many lose sight of this fact in the present day. Says he:
"The whole trouble is that faith is being considered as a beneficent quality of
the soul without respect to the reality or unreality of its object; and the moment
faith comes to be considered in that way, in that moment it is destroyed."[2]

(3) *The measure of this knowledge.* It is impossible to determine with
precision just how much knowledge is absolutely required in saving faith.
If saving faith is the acceptance of Christ as He is offered in the gospel, the
question naturally arises, How much of the gospel must a man know, in order
to be saved? Or, to put it in the words of Dr. Machen: "What, to put it baldly,
are the minimum doctrinal requirements, in order that a man may be a
Christian?"[3] In general it may be said that it must be sufficient to give
the believer some idea of the object of faith. All true saving faith must
contain at least a minimum of knowledge, not so much of the divine revelation
in general as of the Mediator and His gracious operations. The more real
knowledge one has of the truths of redemption, the richer and fuller one's faith
will be, if all other things are equal. Naturally one who accepts Christ by a
true faith, will also be ready and willing to accept God's testimony as a whole.
It is of the utmost importance, especially in our day, that the churches should
see to it that their members have a fairly good, and not merely a hazy, understanding of the truth. Particularly in this undogmatic age, they should be far
more diligent than they are in the indoctrination of their youth.

b. *An emotional element (assensus).* Barth calls attention to the fact
that the time when man accepts Christ by faith is the existential moment of his
life, in which he ceases to consider the object of faith in a detached and
disinterested way, and begins to feel a lively interest in it. It is not necessary
to adopt Barth's peculiar construction of the doctrine of faith, to admit the
truth of what he says on this point. When one embraces Christ by faith, he
has a deep conviction of the truth and reality of the object of faith, feels that
it meets an important need in his life, and is conscious of an absorbing interest

1. Q. 21.
2. *What Is Faith?* p. 174.
3. *Op cit.,* p. 155.

in it, — and this is assent. It is very difficult to distinguish this assent from the knowledge of faith just described, because, as we have seen, it is exactly the distinguishing characteristic of the knowledge of saving faith, that it carries with it a conviction of the truth and reality of its object. Hence some theologians have shown an inclination to limit the knowledge of faith to a mere taking cognizance of the object of faith; but (1) this is contrary to experience, for in true faith there is no knowledge that does not include a hearty conviction of the truth and reality of its object and an interest in it; and (2) this would make the knowledge in saving faith identical with that which is found in a purely historical faith, while the difference between historical and saving faith lies in part exactly at this point. Because it is so difficult to make a clear distinction, some theologians prefer to speak of only two elements in saving faith, namely, knowledge and personal trust. These are the two elements mentioned in the Heidelberg Catechism when it says that true faith "is not only *a certain knowledge* whereby I hold for true all that God has revealed to us in His Word, but also *a hearty trust* which the Holy Ghost works in me by the gospel."[1] It probably deserves preference to regard knowledge and assent simply as two aspects of the same element in faith. Knowledge may then be regarded as its more passive and receptive side, and assent as its more active and transitive side.

c. *A volitional element (fiducia).* This is the crowning element of faith. Faith is not merely a matter of the intellect, nor of the intellect and the emotions combined; it is also a matter of the will, determining the direction of the soul, an act of the soul going out towards its object and appropriating this. Without this activity the object of faith, which the sinner recognizes as true and real and entirely applicable to his present needs, remains outside of him. And in saving faith it is a matter of life and death that the object be appropriated. This third element consists in a personal trust in Christ as Saviour and Lord, including a surrender of the soul as guilty and defiled to Christ, and a reception and appropriation of Christ as the source of pardon and of spiritual life. Taking all these elements in consideration, it is quite evident that the seat of faith cannot be placed in the intellect, nor in the feelings, nor in the will exclusively, but only in the heart, the central organ of man's spiritual being, out of which are the issues of life. In answer to the question whether this *fiducia* (trust) necessarily includes an element of personal assurance, it may be said, in opposition to the Roman Catholics and Arminians, that this is undoubtedly the case. It naturally carries with it a certain feeling of safety and security, of gratitude and joy. Faith, which is in itself certainty, tends to awaken a sense of security and a feeling of assurance in the soul. In the majority of cases this is at first more implicit and hardly penetrates into the sphere of conscious thought; it is something vaguely felt rather than clearly perceived. But in the measure in which faith grows and the activities of faith increase, the consciousness of the security and safety which it brings also

---

1. Q. 21.

becomes greater. Even what theologians generally call "refuge-seeking trust" (toevluchtnemend vertrouwen) conveys to the soul a certain measure of security. This is quite different from the position of Barth, who stresses the fact that faith is a constantly repeated act, is ever anew a leap of despair and a leap in the dark, and never becomes a continuous possession of man; and who therefore rules out the possibility of any subjective assurance of faith.

3. THE OBJECT OF FAITH. In giving an answer to the question as to what is the object of true saving faith, we shall have to speak with discrimination, since it is possible to speak of this faith in a general and in a special sense. There is:

a. *A fides generalis.* By this is meant saving faith in the more general sense of the word. Its object is the whole divine revelation as contained in the Word of God. Everything that is explicitly taught in Scripture or can be deduced from it by good and necessary inference, belongs to the object of faith in this general sense. According to the Church of Rome it is incumbent on its members to believe whatsoever the *ecclesia docens* declares to be a part of God's revelation, and this includes the so-called apostolic tradition. It is true that the "teaching church" does not claim the right to make new articles of faith, but it does claim the right to determine authoritatively what the Bible teaches and what, according to tradition, belongs to the teachings of Christ and His apostles. And this affords a great deal of latitude.

b. *A fides specialis.* This is saving faith in the more limited sense of the word. While true faith in the Bible as the Word of God is absolutely necessary, that is not yet the specific act of faith which justifies and therefore saves directly. It must and as a matter of fact does lead on to a more special faith. There are certain doctrines concerning Christ and His work, and certain promises made in Him to sinful men, which the sinner must receive and which must lead him to put his trust in Christ. The object of special faith, then, is Jesus Christ and the promise of salvation through Him. The special act of faith consists in receiving Christ and resting on Him as He is presented in the gospel, John 3:15,16,18; 6:40. Strictly speaking, it is not the act of faith as such, but rather that which is received by faith, which justifies and therefore saves the sinner.

4. THE GROUND OF FAITH. The ultimate ground on which faith rests, lies in the veracity and faithfulness of God, in connection with the promises of the gospel. But because we have no knowledge of this apart from the Word of God, this can also be, and frequently is, called the ultimate ground of faith. In distinction from the former, however, it might be called the proximate ground. The means by which we recognize the revelation embodied in Scripture as the very Word of God is, in the last analysis, the testimony of the Holy Spirit, I John 5:7 (Am. Rev. Version): "And it is the Spirit which beareth witness because the Spirit is the truth." Cf. also Rom. 4:20,21; 8:16; Eph. 1:13; I John 4:13; 5:10. Roman Catholics find the ultimate ground of faith in the Church; Rationalists acknowledge only reason as such; Schleiermacher

seeks it in Christian experience; and Kant, Ritschl, and many modern liberals place it in the moral needs of human nature.

G. Faith and Assurance.

A very important question arises here, namely, whether assurance belongs to the essence of faith, or is something additional that is not included in faith. Because the expression "assurance of faith" is not always used in the same sense, it is necessary to discriminate carefully. There is a twofold assurance, namely, (1) The objective assurance of faith, which is "the certain and undoubting conviction that Christ is all He professes to be, and will do all He promises." It is generally agreed that this assurance is of the essence of faith. (2) The subjective assurance of faith, or the assurance of grace and salvation, which consists in a sense of security and safety, rising in many instances to the height of an "assured conviction that the individual believer has had his sins pardoned and his soul saved." As to the relation of this assurance to the essence of faith opinions differ.

1. The Roman Catholic Church denies, not only that personal assurance belongs to the essence of faith, but even that this is an *actus reflexus* or fruit of faith. It teaches that believers cannot be sure of their salvation, except in those rare cases in which assurance is given by special revelation. This is a natural result of the Semi-Pelagianism and of the confessional system of Rome. The early Arminians, who shared the Semi-Pelagian position of Rome, took a very similar stand. Their view was condemned by the Synod of Dort.

2. The Reformers reacted against the unsound and pernicious position of the Church of Rome. In their protest they occasionally stressed assurance one-sidedly as the most important element of faith. They sometimes spoke as if one who lacks the assurance of salvation, the positive conviction that his sins are forgiven, did not possess true faith. The *fiducia* of faith was sometimes represented by them as the assured trust of the sinner that all his sins are pardoned for the sake of Christ. Yet it is quite evident from their writings, (a) that they did not mean to teach that this *fiducia* did not include other elements; and (b) that they did not intend to deny that true children of God must frequently struggle with all kinds of doubts and uncertainties.[1]

3. The Reformed confessional standards vary somewhat. The Heidelberg Catechism teaches, also in reaction to Rome, that the *fiducia* of faith consists in the assurance of the forgiveness of sins. It places itself entirely on the standpoint of the Reformers, and conceives of the assurance of salvation as belonging to the essence of faith. The Canons of Dort take the position that this assurance in the elect is not the fruit of a special revelation, but springs from faith in God's promises, from the testimony of the Holy Spirit, and from the exercise of a good conscience and the doing of good works, and is enjoyed according to the measure of faith. This certainly implies that it belongs in some measure to the essence of faith. It is explicitly stated, however, that

---

1. Cf. my *The Assurance of Faith*, pp. 23 f.

believers frequently have to struggle with carnal doubts, so that they are not always sensible of the assurance of faith. The Westminster Confession, speaking of the full assurance of faith, asserts that this does not so belong to the essence of faith that a true believer may not have to wait for it a long time. This has given some Presbyterian theologians occasion to deny that personal assurance belongs to the essence of faith. Yet the Confession does not say this, and there are reasons to think that it did not intend to teach this. The Marrow-men in Scotland certainly gave a different interpretation of its position.[1]

4. After the confessional period there were several departures from this position.

a. Antinomians considered this assurance to be the whole of the essence of faith. They ignored all other activities of faith, and regarded faith simply as an intellectual acceptance of the proposition: Thy sins are forgiven thee. De Labadie (Dutch theologian) recognized no one as a member of the Church who was not fully assured.[2]

b. On the other hand a pietistic Nomism asserted that assurance does not belong to the very being, but only to the well-being of faith; and that it can be secured, except by special revelation, only by continuous and conscientious introspection. All kinds of "marks of the spiritual life," derived not from Scripture but from the lives of approved Christians, became the standard of self-examination. The outcome proved, however, that this method was not calculated to produce assurance, but rather tended to lead to ever-increasing doubt, confusion, and uncertainty.

c. The Methodists aim at a methodical conversion that carries immediate certainty with it. They place men before the law, cause them to see their utter sinfulness and terrible guilt, and frighten them with the terrors of the Lord. And after they have thus brought them under the terrifying influence of the law, they at once introduce them to the full and free gospel of redemption, which merely calls for a willing acceptance of Christ as their Saviour. In a single moment sinners are transported on waves of emotion from the deepest sorrow into the most exalted joy. And this sudden change carries with it an immediate assurance of redemption. He who believes, is also sure that he is redeemed. This does not mean, however, that he is also certain of ultimate salvation. This is a certainty to which the consistent Methodist cannot attain since he believes in a falling away of the saints.

d. Among Reformed theologians there is a difference of opinion. Many Presbyterians deny that faith itself includes assurance; and in Reformed circles some share this denial. Kuyper, Bavinck, and Vos, however, correctly hold that true faith, as including trust, carries with it a sense of security, which may vary in degree. There is also an assurance of faith, however, that is the fruit of reflection. It is possible to make faith itself an object of reflection, and thus

1. Cf. *The Assurance of Faith*, pp. 24-29.
2. Cf. Heppe, *Geschichte des Pietismus*, pp. 240-374.

to arrive at a subjective assurance that does not belong to the essence of faith. In that case we conclude from what we experience in our own life to the presence of the work of the Holy Spirit within us, cf. I John 2:9-11; 3:9,10, 18,19; 4:7,20.[1]

H. The Roman Catholic Conception of Faith.

Three points deserve our attention here:

1. The Church of Rome obliterates the distinction between historical and saving faith by teaching that faith consists in a mere assent to the doctrines of the Church. This faith is one of the seven preparations for justification in baptism, and therefore necessarily precedes this; but as a purely intellectual activity it naturally does not lead to salvation. A man may have true, that is, Biblical faith, and yet be lost. In so far the Church of Rome applies her principle of externalization also to faith.

2. It has also virtually removed the element of knowledge from faith. One may be considered a true believer, if one is but ready to believe what the Church teaches, without really knowing what this is. Such a faith is called a *fides implicita* in distinction from the *fides explicita*, which includes knowledge. By teaching that it is sufficient to believe what the *ecclesia docens* teaches, the Roman Catholic Church applies the principle of clericalism.

3. There is still another point which characterizes the Roman Catholic doctrine of faith, namely, the distinction between a *fides informis* and a *fides formata*. The former is the mere assent to the doctrine of the Church, while the other is a faith which includes love as a formative principle and is perfected in love. This is the faith that really justifies.

QUESTIONS FOR FURTHER STUDY: What was the conception of faith in the early Church? Did Augustine's view differ from that of the earlier fathers? How did the distinction between a *fides informis* and a *fides formata* arise? How did Luther and Calvin differ as to the order of faith and repentance? Do the Lutherans and the Reformed agree as to the order of faith and regeneration? Why is it important to maintain the proper order? How did the distinction between the *actus* and the *habitus* of faith arise, and why is it important? Can the proposition, "I am saved," ever be the object of saving faith? What conception of faith is found in Schleiermacher and Ritschl? Why is it very appropriate that salvation should be contingent on faith? How does the excessive *activism* of Barth affect his doctrine of faith? What does he mean when he says that man is never a believer or a Christian, but always a sinner? How do you account for his denial that faith includes assurance?

LITERATURE: Bavinck, *Geref. Dogm.* IV, pp. 83-127; Kuyper, *Dict. Dogm.*, *De Salute*, pp. 98-131; ibid., *Het Werk van den Heiligen Geest* II, pp. 233-297; Vos, *Geref. Dogm.* IV., pp. 82-154; Hodge, *Syst. Theol.* III, pp. 41-113; Shedd, *Dogm. Theol.* II, pp. 531-534; Dabney, *Syst. and Polem. Theol.*, pp. 600-612; McPherson, *Chr. Dogm.*, pp. 388-393; Schmid, *Doct. Theol. of the Ev. Luth. Ch.*, pp. 416-430; Valentine, *Chr. Theol.* II. pp. 232-241; Kaftan, *Dogm.*. pp. 656-681; Litton, *Introd. to Dogm. Theol.*. pp. 282-296: Pope, *Chr. Theol.* II. pp. 376-385; Pictet, *Theol.*. pp. 298-309; Inge, *Faith and Its Psychology*; Machen, *What is Faith?*; O'Brian, *The Nature and Effects of Faith*; Moehler, *Symbolism or Doctrinal Differences*; Bavinck, *De Zekerheid des Geloofs*; Berkhof, *The Assurance of Faith*; Wernecke, *"Faith" in the New Testament*; Warfield, *The Biblical Doctrine of Faith* (in *Biblical Doctrines*, VIII).

1. Cf. further, *The Assurance of Faith*, chap. III.

IX. Justification.

A. The Scriptural Terms for Justification and Their Meaning.

1. THE OLD TESTAMENT TERM. The Hebrew term for "to justify" is *hitsdik*, which in the great majority of cases means "to declare judicially that one's state is in harmony with the demands of the law, Ex. 23:7; Deut. 25:1; Prov. 17:15; Isa. 5:23. The *piel tsiddek* occasionally has the same meaning, Jer. 3:11; Ezek. 16:50,51. The meaning of these words is therefore strictly forensic or legal. Since Roman Catholics, such representatives of the moral influence theory of the atonement as John Young of Edinburgh and Horace Bushnell, and also the Unitarians and modern liberal theologians, deny the legal meaning of the term "to justify," and ascribe to it the moral sense of "to make just or righteous," it becomes important to take careful notice of the considerations that may be urged in favor of the legal meaning. That this is the proper denotation of the word appears (a) from the terms placed in contrast with it, as, for instance "condemnation," Deut. 25:1; Prov. 17:15; Isa. 5:23; (b) from the correlative terms placed in juxtaposition with it and which often imply a process of judgment, Gen. 18:25; Ps. 143:2; (c) from the equivalent expressions that are sometimes used, Gen. 15:6; Ps. 32:1,2; and (d) from the fact that a passage like Prov. 17:15 would yield an impossible sense, if the word meant "to make just." The meaning would then be: He who morally improves the life of the wicked is an abomination to the Lord. There are a couple of passages, however, in which the word means more than simply "to declare righteous," namely, Isa. 53:11; Dan. 12:3. But even in these cases the sense is not "to make good or holy," but rather "to alter the condition so that man can be considered righteous."

2. THE NEW TESTAMENT TERMS AND THEIR USE. Here we have:

a. *The verb dikaio-o.* This verb means in general "to declare a person to be just. Occasionally it refers to a personal declaration that one's moral character is in conformity with the law, Matt. 12:37; Luke 7:29; Rom. 3:4. In the Epistles of Paul the soteriological meaning of the term is clearly in the foreground. It is "to declare forensically that the demands of the law as a condition of life are fully satisfied with regard to a person, Acts 13:39; Rom. 5:1,9; 8:30-33; I Cor. 6:11; Gal. 2:16; 3:11. In the case of this word, just as in that of *hitsdik*, the forensic meaning of the term is proved by the following facts: (a) in many instances it can bear no other sense, Rom. 3:20-28; 4:5-7; 5:1; Gal. 2:16; 3:11; 5:4; (b) it is placed in antithetic relation to "condemnation" in Rom. 8:33,34; (c) equivalent and interchangeable expressions convey a judicial or legal idea, John 3:18; 5:24; Rom. 4:6,7; II Cor. 5:19; and (d) if it does not bear this meaning, there is no distinction between justification and sanctification.

b. *The word dikaios.* This word, connected with the verb just discussed, is peculiar in that it never expresses what a thing is in itself, but always what it is in relation to something else, to some standard outside of it, to which it ought to correspond. In that respect it differs from *agathos.* In classical Greek, for instance, *dikaios* is applied to a wagon, a horse, or something else to indicate that it is fit for its intended use. *Agathos* expresses the idea that a thing in itself answers to the ideal. In Scripture a man is called *dikaios* when, in the judgment of God, his relation to the law is what it ought to be, or when his life is such as is required by his judicial relation to God. This may include the idea that he is good, but only from a certain point of view, namely, that of his judicial relation to God.

c. *The noun dikaiosis, justification.* This is found in only two places in the New Testament, namely, Rom. 4:25; 5:18. It denotes the act of God's declaring men free from guilt and acceptable to Him. The resulting state is denoted by the word *dikaiosune.*

3. *The resulting idea of justification.* Our word *justification* (from the Latin *justificare,* composed of *justus* and *facere,* and therefore meaning "to make righteous"), just as the Holland *rechtvaardigmaking,* is apt to give the impression that justification denotes a change that is brought about in man, which is not the case. In the use of the English word the danger is not so great, because the people in general do not understand its derivation, and in the Holland language the danger may be averted by employing the related words *rechtvaardigen* and *rechtvaardiging.* "To justify" in the Scriptural sense of the word, is to effect an objective relation, the state of righteousness, by a judicial sentence. This can be done in a twofold way: (a) by bringing into account the actual subjective condition of a person (to justify the just or the righteous), Jas. 2:21; or (b) by imputing to a person the righteousness of another, that is, by accounting him righteous though he is inwardly unrighteous. The latter is the usual sense of justification in the New Testament.

B. The Doctrine of Justification in History.

The doctrine of justification by faith was not always clearly understood. In fact, it did not find its classical expression until the days of the Reformation. We shall briefly consider:

1. THE DOCTRINE BEFORE THE REFORMATION. Some of the earliest Church Fathers already speak of justification by faith, but it is quite evident that they had no clear understanding of it and of its relation to faith. Moreover, they did not sharply distinguish between regeneration and justification. A rather common representation was that regeneration takes place in baptism

and includes the forgiveness of sins. Even Augustine does not seem to have had an accurate understanding of justification as a legal act, as distinguished from the moral process of sanctification, though it is quite evident from the whole tenor of his teachings and also from separate statements, that he regarded the grace of God in the redemption of sinners as free, sovereign, and efficacious, and in no way dependent on any merits of men. The confounding of justification and sanctification continued into the Middle Ages and gradually acquired a more positive and doctrinal aspect. According to the prevailing teachings of the Scholastics, justification includes two elements: man's sins are forgiven, and he is made just or righteous. There was a difference of opinion as to the logical order of these two elements, some reversing the order just indicated. This was also done by Thomas Aquinas, and his view became the prevalent one in the Roman Catholic Church. Grace is infused in man, whereby he is made just, and partly on the basis of this infused grace, his sins are pardoned. This was already an approach to the evil doctrine of merit, which was gradually developed in the Middle Ages in connection with the doctrine of justification. The idea found favor ever-increasingly that man is justified in part on the basis of his own good works. The confounding of justification and sanctification also led to divergent opinions on another point. Some of the Scholastics speak of justification as an instantaneous act of God, while others describe it as a process. In the Canons and Decrees of the Council of Trent we find the following in Chap. XVI, Canon IX: "If any one saith, that by faith alone the impious is justified in such wise as to mean, that nothing else is required to co-operate in order to the obtaining of the grace of justification, and that it is not in any way necessary, that he be prepared and disposed by the movement of his own will: let him be anathema." And Canon XXIV speaks of an increase in justification and therefore conceives of it as a process: "If any one saith, that the justice received is not preserved and also increased before God through good works; but that the said works are merely the fruits and signs of justification obtained, but not a cause of the increase thereof: let him be anathema."

2. THE DOCTRINE AFTER THE REFORMATION. The doctrine of justification was the great material principle of the Reformation. With respect to the nature of justification the Reformers corrected the error of confounding justification with sanctification by stressing its legal character and representing it as an act of God's free grace, whereby He pardons our sins and accepts us as righteous in His sight, but does not change us inwardly. As far as the ground of justification is concerned, they rejected the idea of Rome that this lies, at least in part, in the inherent righteousness of the regenerate and in good works, and substituted for it the doctrine that it is found only in the imputed righteousness of the Redeemer. And in connection with the means of justification they emphasized the fact that man is justified freely by that faith which receives and rests in Christ only for salvation. Moreover, they rejected the doctrine of a progressive justification, and held that it was instantaneous and

complete, and did not depend for its completion on some further satisfaction for sin. They were opposed by the Socinians, who held that sinners obtain pardon and acceptance with God, through His mercy, on the ground of their own repentance and reformation. The Arminians do not all agree on the subject, but in general it may be said that they limit the scope of justification, so as to include only the forgiveness of sins on the basis of the passive obedience of Christ, and to exclude the adoption of the sinner in favor by God on the basis of the imputed righteousness of Jesus Christ. The sinner is accounted righteous only on the basis of his faith or his life of obedience. The Neonomians in England were in general agreement with them on this point. For Schleiermacher and Ritschl justification meant little more than the sinner's becoming conscious of his mistake in thinking that God was angry with him. And in modern liberal theology we again meet with the idea that God justifies the sinner by the moral improvement of his life. This conception of it is found, for instance, in Bushnell's *Vicarious Sacrifice* and in Macintosh's *Theology as an Empirical Science.*

C. The Nature and Characteristics of Justification

Justification is a judicial act of God, in which He declares, on the basis of the righteousness of Jesus Christ, that all the claims of the law are satisfied with respect to the sinner. It is unique in the application of the work of redemption in that it is a judicial act of God, a declaration respecting the sinner, and not an act or process of renewal, such as regeneration, conversion, and sanctification. While it has respect to the sinner, it does not change his inner life. It does not affect his condition, but his state, and in that respect differs from all the other principal parts of the order of salvation. It involves the forgiveness of sins, and restoration to divine favor. The Arminian holds that it includes only the former, and not the latter; but the Bible clearly teaches that the fruit of justification is much more than pardon. They who are justified have "peace with God," "assurance of salvation," Rom. 5:1-10, and an "inheritance among them that are sanctified," Acts 26:18. The following points of difference between justification and sanctification should be carefully noted:

1. Justification removes the guilt of sin and restores the sinner to all the filial rights involved in his state as a child of God, including an eternal inheritance. Sanctification removes the pollution of sin and renews the sinner ever-increasingly in conformity with the image of God.

2. Justification takes place outside of the sinner in the tribunal of God, and does not change his inner life, though the sentence is brought home to him subjectively. Sanctification, on the other hand, takes place in the inner life of man and gradually affects his whole being.

3. Justification takes place once for all. It is not repeated, neither is it a process; it is complete at once and for all time. There is no more or less in justification; man is either fully justified, or he is not justified at all. In

distinction from it sanctification is a continuous process, which is never completed in this life.

4. While the meritorious cause of both lies in the merits of Christ, there is a difference in the efficient cause. Speaking economically, God the Father declares the sinner righteous, and God the Holy Spirit sanctifies him.

D. The Elements of Justification.

We distinguish two elements in justification, the one negative, and the other positive.

1. *The negative element.* There is first of all a negative element in justification, namely, the remission of sins on the ground of the atoning work of Jesus Christ. This element is based more particularly, though not exclusively, on the passive obedience of the Saviour. Calvin and some of the older Reformed theologians occasionally speak as if this were the whole of justification. This is partly due to the Old Testament representation, in which this side of justification is decidedly in the foreground, Ps. 32:1; Isa. 43:25; 44:22; Jer. 31:34, and partly to their reaction against Rome, which did not do justice to the element of grace and free pardon. In opposition to Arminianism, however, Reformed theology has always maintained that justification is more than pardon. That the forgiveness of sins is an important element in justification is evident, not only from the Old, but also from the New Testament, as appears from such passages as Rom. 4:5-8; 5:18,19; Gal. 2:17.

The pardon granted in justification applies to all sins, past, present, and future, and thus involves the removal of all guilt and of every penalty. This follows from the fact that justification does not admit of repetition, and from such passages as Rom. 5:21; 8:1,32-34; Heb. 10:14; Ps. 103:12; Isa. 44:22, which assure us that no one can lay anything to the charge of the justified man, that he is exempt from condemnation, and that he is constituted an heir of eternal life. It is also implied in the answer to the 60th question of our Heidelberg Catechism. This conception of justification, though eminently Scriptural, is not devoid of difficulty. Believers continue to sin after they are justified, Jas. 3:2; I John 1:8, and, as Scripture examples clearly show, frequently fall into grievous sins. Hence it is no wonder that Barth likes to stress the fact that the justified man remains a sinner, though a justified sinner. Christ taught His disciples to pray daily for the forgiveness of sins, Matt. 6:12, and the Bible saints are often pleading for pardon and obtaining it, Ps. 32:5; 51:1-4; 130:3,4. Consequently it is not surprising that some felt constrained to speak of a repeated justification. The Church of Rome infers from the data to which we called attention that believers must in some way atone for sins committed after baptism, and therefore also believes in an increasing justification. Antinomians, on the other hand, desiring to honour the unlimited pardoning grace of God, maintain that the sins of believers are not accounted as such to the new man but only to the old, and that it is quite unnecessary for them to pray for the forgiveness of sins. For fear of this Antinomian position even some Reformed theologians had scruples about teaching that the future sins of believers are also pardoned in justification, and spoke of a repeated and even daily justification.[1] The usual position of Reformed theology, however, is that in justification God indeed removes the guilt, but not the culpability of sin, that is, He removes the sinner's just amenability to punishment, but not the inherent guiltiness of whatever sins he may continue to perform. The latter remains and therefore always produces in believers a feeling of guilt, of separation from God, of sorrow, of repentance, and so on. Hence they feel the need of confessing their sins, even the sins of their youth, Ps. 25:7; 51:5-9. The believer who is really conscious of his sin feels within him an urge to confess it and to seek the comforting assurance of forgiveness. Moreover, such confession and prayer is not only a subjectively felt need, but also an objective necessity. Justification is essentially an objective declaration respecting the sinner in the tribunal of God, but it is not merely that; it is also an *actus transiens*, passing into the consciousness of the believer. The divine sentence of acquittal is brought home to the sinner and awakens the joyous consciousness of the forgiveness of sins and of favor with God. Now this consciousness of pardon and of a renewed filial relationship is often disturbed and obscured by sin, and is again quickened and strengthened by confession and prayer, and by a renewed exercise of faith.

2. THE POSITIVE ELEMENT. There is also a positive element in justification which is based more particularly on the active obedience of Christ. Naturally they who, like Piscator and the Arminians, deny the imputation of the active obedience of Christ to the sinner, thereby also deny the positive element in justification. According to them justification leaves man without any claim on life eternal, simply places him in the position of Adam before the fall, though according to the Arminians under a different law, the law of evangelical obedience, and leaves it to man to merit acceptance with God and eternal life by faith and obedience. But it is quite evident from Scripture that justification is more than mere pardon. Unto Joshua, the high priest, who stood, as the representative of Israel, with filthy garments before the Lord, Jehovah said: "Behold, I have caused thine iniquity to pass from thee (negative element), and I will clothe thee with rich apparel" (positive element), Zech. 3:4. According to Acts 26:18 we obtain by faith "remission of sins *and an inheritance among them that are sanctified.*" Romans 5:1,2 teaches us that justification by faith brings not only peace with God, *but also access to God and joy in the hope of glory.* And according to Gal. 4:5 Christ was born under the law also *"that we might receive the adoption of sons."* In this positive element two parts may be distinguished:

a. *The adoption of children.* Believers are first of all children of God by adoption. This implies, of course, that they are not children of God by nature, as modern liberals would have us believe, for one cannot well adopt

1. Cf. Brakel, *Redelijke Godsdienst* I, pp. 876 ff.

his own children. This adoption is a legal act, whereby God places the sinner in the status of a child, but does not change him inwardly any more than parents by the mere act of adoption change the inner life of an adopted child. The change that is effected concerns the relation in which man stands to God. By virtue of their adoption believers are as it were initiated into the very family of God, come under the law of filial obedience, and at the same time become entitled to all the privileges of sonship. The sonship by adoption should be carefully distinguished from the moral sonship of believers, their sonship by regeneration and sanctification. They are not only adopted to be children of God, but are also born of God. Naturally these two cannot be separated. They are mentioned together in John 1:12; Rom. 8:15,16; Gal. 3:26,27; 4:5,6. In Rom. 8:15 the term *huiothesia* (from *huios* and *tithenai*) is used, which literally means "placing as a son," and in classical Greek is always employed to denote an objective placing in the status of a child. The following verse contains the word *tekna* (from *tikto*, "to beget"), which designates believers as those who are begotten of God. In John 1:12 the idea of adoption is expressed by the words, "But as many as received Him, to them gave He the right (*exousian edoken*) to become children of God." The Greek expression here used means "to give legal right." Immediately thereafter, in the 13th verse, the writer speaks of ethical sonship by regeneration. The connection between the two is clearly brought out in Gal. 4:5,6 . . . "that we might receive the adoption of sons. And because ye are sons (by adoption), God sent forth the Spirit of His Son into our hearts, crying, Abba, Father." That Spirit regenerates and sanctifies us and prompts us to address God full of confidence as Father.

b. *The right to eternal life.* This element is virtually included in the preceding one. When sinners are adopted to be children of God, they are invested with all the legal filial rights, and become heirs of God and co-heirs with Christ, Rom. 8:17. This means first of all that they become heirs of all the blessings of salvation in the present life, the most fundamental of which is described in the words, "the promise of the Spirit," that is, the promised blessing in the form of the Spirit, Gal. 3:14; and in the slightly different phrase, "the Spirit of His Son," Gal. 4:6. And in and with the Spirit they receive all the gifts of Christ. But this is not all; their inheritance also includes the eternal blessings of the future life. The glory of which Paul speaks in Rom. 8:17 follows after the sufferings of the present time. According to Rom. 8:23 the redemption of the body, which is there called "the adoption," also belongs to the future inheritance. And in the *ordo salutis* of Rom. 8:29,30 glorification connects up immediately with justification. Being justified by faith, believers are heirs of life eternal.

E. **The Sphere in which Justification Occurs.**

The question as to the sphere in which justification occurs, must be answered with discrimination. It is customary to distinguish between an *active* and a *passive,* also called an *objective* and a *subjective,* justification, each having its own sphere.

1. ACTIVE OR OBJECTIVE JUSTIFICATION. This is justification in the most fundamental sense of the word. It is basic to what is called subjective justification, and consists in a declaration which God makes respecting the sinner, and this declaration is made in the tribunal of God. This declaration is not a declaration in which God simply acquits the sinner, without taking any account of the claims of justice, but is rather a divine declaration that, in the case of the sinner under consideration, the demands of the law are met. The sinner is declared righteous in view of the fact that the righteousness of Christ is imputed to him. In this transaction God appears, not as an absolute Sovereign who simply sets the law aside, but as a righteous Judge, who acknowledges the infinite merits of Christ as a sufficient basis for justification, and as a gracious Father, who freely forgives and accepts the sinner. This active justification logically precedes faith and passive justification. We *believe* the forgiveness of sins.

2. PASSIVE OR SUBJECTIVE JUSTIFICATION. Passive or subjective justification takes place in the heart or conscience of the sinner. A purely objective justification that is not brought home to the sinner would not answer the purpose. The granting of a pardon would mean nothing to a prisoner, unless the glad tidings were communicated to him and the doors of the prison were opened. Moreover, it is exactly at this point that the sinner learns to understand better than anywhere else that salvation is of free grace. When the Bible speaks of justification, it usually refers to what is known as passive justification. It should be borne in mind, however, that the two cannot be separated. The one is based on the other. The distinction is simply made to facilitate the proper understanding of the act of justification. Logically, passive justification follows faith; we are justified by faith.

F. The Time of Justification.

Some theologians separate active and passive justification temporally. The active justification is then said to have taken place in eternity or in the resurrection of Christ, while passive justification takes place by faith and therefore, it is said, follows the other in a temporal sense. We shall consider successively justification from eternity, justification in the resurrection of Christ, and justification by faith.

1. JUSTIFICATION FROM ETERNITY. The Antinomians held that the justification of the sinner took place in eternity, or in the resurrection of Christ. They either confounded it with the eternal decree of election, or with the objective justification of Christ when He was raised from the dead. They did not properly distinguish between the divine purpose in eternity and its execution in time, nor between the work of Christ in procuring, and that of the Holy Spirit in applying the blessings of redemption. According to this position we

are justified even before we believe, though we are unconscious of it, and faith simply conveys to us the declaration of this fact. Moreover, the fact that our sins were imputed to Christ made Him personally a sinner, and the imputation of His righteousness to us makes us personally righteous, so that God can see no sin in believers at all. Some Reformed theologians also speak of justification from eternity, but at the same time refuse to subscribe to the Antinomian construction of this doctrine. The grounds on which they believe in justification from eternity deserve brief consideration.

a. *Grounds for the doctrine of justification from eternity.*

(1) Scripture speaks of a grace or mercy of God which is from everlasting, Ps. 25:6; 103:17. Now all grace or mercy that is from eternity must have as its judicial or legal basis a justification that is from eternity. But in answer to this it may be said that there are eternal mercies and lovingkindnesses of God which are not based on any justification of the sinner, as, for instance, His plan of redemption, the gift of His Son, and the willing suretyship of Christ in the *pactum salutis*.

(2) In the *pactum salutis* the guilt of the sins of the elect was transferred to Christ, and the righteousness of Christ was imputed to them. This means that the burden of sin was lifted from their shoulders and that they were justified. Now there is no doubt about it that there was a certain imputation of the righteousness of Christ to the sinner in the counsel of redemption, but not all imputation can be called justification in the Scriptural sense of the term. We must distinguish between what was merely ideal in the counsel of God and what is realized in the course of history.

(3) The sinner receives the initial grace of regeneration on the basis of the imputed righteousness of Christ. Consequently, the merits of Christ must have been imputed to him before his regeneration. But while this consideration leads to the conclusion that justification logically precedes regeneration, it does not prove the priority of justification in a temporal sense. The sinner can receive the grace of regeneration on the basis of a justification, ideally existing in the counsel of God and certain to be realized in the life of the sinner.

(4) Children also need justification, in order to be saved, and yet it is quite impossible that they should experience justification by faith. But though it is perfectly true that children, who have not yet come to maturity, cannot experience passive justification, they can be actively justified in the tribunal of God and thus be in possession of that which is absolutely essential.

(5) Justification is an immanent act of God, and as such must be from eternity. It is hardly correct, however, to speak of justification as an *actus immanens* in God; it is rather an *actus transiens*, just as creation, incarnation, and so on. The advocates of justification from eternity feel the weight of this consideration, and therefore hasten to give us the assurance that they do not

mean to teach that the elect are justified from eternity *actualiter*, but only in the intention of God, in the divine decree. This leads us back to the usual distinction between the counsel of God and its execution. If this justification in the intention of God warrants our speaking of a justification from eternity, then there is absolutely no reason why we should not speak of a creation from eternity as well.

b. *Objections against the doctrine of justification from eternity.*

(1) The Bible teaches uniformly that justification takes place by faith or out of faith. This, of course, applies to passive or subjective justification, which, however, cannot be separated temporally from active or objective justification except in the case of children. But if justification takes place by faith, it certainly does not precede faith in a temporal sense. Now it is true that the advocates of a justification from eternity also speak of a justification by faith. But in their representation this can only mean that man by faith becomes conscious of what God has done in eternity.

(2) In Rom. 8:29,30, where we find some of the *scalae* of the *ordo salutis*, justification stands between two acts of God in time, namely, calling and glorification, which begins in time but is completed in a future eternity. And these three together are the result of two others which are explicitly indicated as eternal. Dr. Kuyper is not warranted in saying that Rom. 8:30 refers to what took place with the regenerated before they were born, as even Dr. De Moor, who also believes in a justification from eternity, is quite willing to admit.[1]

(3) In teaching justification from eternity, the decree of God respecting the justification of the sinner, which is an *actus immanens*, is identified with justification itself, which is an *actus transiens*. This only leads to confusion. What took place in the *pactum salutis* cannot be identified with what results from it. All imputation is not yet justification. Justification is one of the fruits of Christ's redemptive work, applied to believers by the Holy Spirit. But the Spirit did not and could not apply this or any other fruit of the work of Christ from eternity.

2. JUSTIFICATION IN THE RESURRECTION OF CHRIST. The idea that sinners are in some sense of the word justified in the resurrection of Christ was stressed by some Antinomians, is taught by those Reformed theologians who believe in a justification from eternity, and is also held by some other Reformed scholars. This view is based on the following grounds:

a. By His atoning work Christ satisfied all the demands of the law for His people. In the resurrection of Jesus Christ from the dead the Father publicly declared that all the requirements of the law were met for all the elect and thereby justified them. But here too careful distinction is required. Even though it be true that there was an objective justification of Christ and of the

1. Cf. his *De Rechtvaardigmaking Van Eeuwigheid*, p. 20.

whole body of Christ in His resurrection, this should not be confounded with the justification of the sinner of which Scripture speaks. It is not true that, when Christ rendered full satisfaction to the Father for all His people, their guilt naturally terminated. A penal debt is not like a pecuniary debt in this respect. Even after the payment of a ransom, the removal of guilt may depend on certain conditions, and does not follow as a matter of course. The elect are not personally justified in the Scriptural sense until they accept Christ by faith and thus appropriate His merits.

b. In Rom. 4:25 we read that Christ was "raised up for (*dia*, causal, on account of) our justification," that is, to effect our justification. Now it is undoubtedly true that *dia* with the accusative is causal here. At the same time it need not be retrospective, but can also be prospective and therefore mean "with a view to our justification," which is equivalent to saying, "in order that we may be justified." The retrospective interpretation would be in conflict with the immediately following context, which clearly shows (1) that Paul is not thinking of the objective justification of the whole body of Christ, but of the personal justification of sinners; and (2) that he conceives of this as taking place through faith.

c. In II Cor. 5:19 we read: "God was in Christ reconciling the world unto Himself, not reckoning unto them their trespasses." From this passage the inference is drawn that the objective reconciliation of the world in Christ involves the non-imputation of sin to the sinner. But this interpretation is not correct. The evident meaning of the apostle is: God was in Christ reconciling the world unto Himself, as appears from the fact that He does not impute to men their sins, and that He has entrusted to His servants the word of reconciliation. Notice that *me logizomenos* (present tense) refers to what is constantly going on. This cannot be conceived as a part of the objective reconciliation, for then the following clause, "and having committed to us the word of reconciliation," would also have to be so interpreted, and this is quite impossible.

In connection with this matter it may be said that we can speak of a justification of the body of Christ as a whole in His resurrection, but this is purely objective and should not be confounded with the personal justification of the sinner.

3. JUSTIFICATION BY FAITH.

a. *The relation of faith to justification.* Scripture says that we are justified *dia pisteos, ek pisteos, or pistei* (dative), Rom. 3:25,28,30; 5:1; Gal. 2:16; Phil. 3:9. The preposition *dia* stresses the fact that faith is the instrument by which we appropriate Christ and His righteousness. The preposition *ek* indicates that faith logically precedes our personal justification, so that this, as it were, originates in faith. The dative is used in an instrumental sense. Scripture never says that we are justified *dia ten pistin*, on account of faith. This means that faith is never represented as the ground of our justification. If this were the case, faith would have to be regarded as a meritorious work of man. And this would be the introduction of the doctrine of justification by works, which the apostle opposes consistently, Rom. 3:21,27,28; 4:3,4; Gal. 2:16,21; 3:11. We are told indeed that Abraham's faith was reckoned unto him for righteousness, Rom. 4:3,9,22; Gal. 3:6, but in view of the whole argument this surely cannot mean that in his case faith itself as a work took the place of the righteousness of God in Christ. The apostle does not leave it doubtful that, strictly speaking, only the righteousness of Christ imputed to us, is the ground of our justification. But faith is so thoroughly receptive in the appropriation of the merits of Christ, that it can be put figuratively for the merits of Christ which it receives. "Faith" then is equivalent to the contents of faith, that is, to the merits or the righteousness of Christ.

It is often said, however, that the teachings of James conflict with those of Paul on this point, and clearly support the doctrine of justification by works in Jas. 2:14-26. Various attempts have been made to harmonize the two. Some proceed on the assumption that both Paul and James speak of the justification of the sinner, but that James stresses the fact that a faith which does not manifest itself in good works is no true faith, and therefore is not a faith that justifies. This is undoubtedly true. The difference between the representations of Paul and James is unquestionably due partly to the nature of the adversaries with which they had to deal. Paul had to contend with legalists who sought to base their justification, at least in part, on the works of the law. James, on the other hand, joined issue with Antinomians, who claimed to have faith, but whose faith was merely an intellectual assent to the truth (2:19), and who denied the necessity of good works. Therefore he stresses the fact that faith without works is a dead faith, and consequently not at all a faith that justifies. The faith that justifies is a faith that is fruitful in good works. But it may be objected that this does not explain the whole difficulty, since James explicitly says in verse 24 that a man is justified by works and not only by faith, and illustrates this by the example of Abraham, who was "justified by works in that he offered up Isaac" (verse 21). "Thou seest," says he in verse 24, "that faith wrought with his works, and by works was faith made perfect." It is quite evident, however, that in this case the writer is not speaking of the justification of the sinner, for Abraham the sinner was justified long before he offered up Isaac (cf. Gen. 15), but of a further justification of the believing Abraham. True faith will manifest itself in good works, and these works will testify before men of the righteousness (that is, the righteousness of life) of him that possesses such a faith. The justification of the just by works confirms the justification by faith. If James actually meant to say in this section of his letter that Abraham and Rahab were justified with the *justificatio peccatoris*, on the basis of their good works, he would not only be in conflict with Paul, but would also be self-contradictory, for he explicitly says that Abraham was justified by faith.

b. *Theological terms to express the relation of faith to justification.* There are especially three terms that come into consideration here.

(1) *Instrumental cause.* This name was very generally used at first, but afterwards met with considerable opposition. The question was raised, whether it was God's instrument or man's. And it was said: It cannot be God's, since the faith referred to is not God's faith; neither can it be man's, for justification is not a deed of man, but of God. We should bear in mind, however, (a) that according to the plain teaching of the Bible we are justified by faith, *dia pisteos*, and that this *dia* can only be understood in an instrumental sense, Rom. 3:28; Gal. 3:8; (b) that the Bible explicitly says that *God* justifies the sinner by faith, and therefore represents faith as God's instrument, Rom. 3:30; and (c) that faith is also represented as the instrument of man, as the means by which he receives justification, Gal. 2:16. Faith can be regarded as the instrument of God in a twofold sense. It is a gift of God wrought in the sinner unto justification. Moreover, by working faith in the sinner, God carries the declaration of pardon into his heart or conscience. But faith is also an instrument of man by which he appropriates Christ and all His precious gifts, Rom. 4:5; Gal. 2:16. This is also the representation of the matter which we find in the *Belgic Confession*,[1] and in the *Heidelberg Catechism*.[2] By faith we embrace Christ and remain in contact with Him who is our righteousness. The name "instrumental cause" is regularly used in Protestant Confessions. Yet some Reformed theologians prefer to avoid it, in order to guard themselves against the danger of giving the impression that justification is in any way dependent on faith as a work of man.

(2) *Appropriating organ.* This name expresses the idea that by faith the sinner appropriates the righteousness of Christ and establishes a conscious union between himself and Christ. The merits of Christ constitute the *dikaioma*, the legal basis on which the formal declaration of God in justification rests. By faith the sinner appropriates the righteousness of the Mediator already imputed to him ideally in the *pactum salutis;* and on the basis of this he is now formally justified before God. Faith justifies in so far as it takes possession of Christ. The name "appropriating organ" includes the instrumental idea, and is therefore perfectly in harmony with the statements found in our confessional standards. It has an advantage over the more common name in that it excludes the idea that faith is in any sense the basis for justification. It can be called an appropriating organ in a twofold sense: (a) It is the organ by which we lay hold on and appropriate the merits of Christ, and accept these as the meritorious ground of our justification. As such it logically precedes justification. (b) It is also the organ by which we consciously apprehend our justification and obtain possession of subjective justification. In this sense it logically follows justification. On the whole this name deserves preference, though it should be borne in mind that, strictly speaking, faith is the organ by which we

1. Art. XXII.
2. Questions 60 and 61.

appropriate the righteousness of Christ as the ground of our justification, rather than the organ by which we appropriate justification itself.

(3) *Conditio sine qua non.* This name, suggested by some Reformed theologians, did not meet with great favor. It expresses the idea, which is perfectly true in itself, that man is not justified apart from faith, and that faith is an indispensable condition of justification. The name expresses nothing positive, and is, moreover, liable to misunderstanding.

G. The Ground of Justification.

One of the most important points of controversy between the Church of Rome and the Reformers, and between Reformed theology and the Arminians, concerned the ground of justification. With respect to this the Reformers taught:

1. Negatively, that this cannot be found in any virtue of man, nor in his good works. This position must also be maintained at present over against Rome and the Pelagianizing tendencies of various Churches. Rome teaches that the sinner is justified on the basis of the inherent righteousness that has been infused into his heart, and which, in turn, is the fruit of the co-operation of the human will with prevenient grace. This applies to what is called the first justification; in all following justification the good works of man come into consideration as the formal cause or ground of justification. It is impossible, however, that the inherent righteousness of the regenerate man and his good works should constitute the ground of his justification, for (a) this righteousness is and remains during this life a very imperfect righteousness; (b) it is itself already the fruit of the righteousness of Christ and of the grace of God; and (c) even the best works of believers are polluted by sin. Moreover, Scripture teaches us very clearly that man is justified freely by the grace of God, Rom. 3:24, and that he cannot possibly be justified by the works of the law, Rom. 3:28; Gal. 2:16; 3:11.

2. Positively, that the ground of justification can be found only in the perfect righteousness of Jesus Christ, which is imputed to the sinner in justification. This is plainly taught in several passages of Scripture, such as Rom. 3:24; 5:9,19; 8:1; 10:4; I Cor. 1:30; 6:11; II Cor. 5:21; Phil. 3:9. In the passive obedience of Christ, who became a curse for us (Gal. 3:13) we find the ground for the forgiveness of sins; and in His active obedience, by which He merited all the gifts of grace, including eternal life, the ground for the adoption of children, by which sinners are constituted heirs of life eternal. The Arminian goes contrary to Scripture when he maintains that we are accepted in favor by God only on the ground of our faith or evangelical obedience.

H. Objections to the Doctrine of Justification.

Modern liberal theology, with its rationalizing tendencies, raises several objections to the doctrine of justification as such, which deserve brief consideration.

1. Some, who still believe in salvation by grace, ostensibly object to justification in the interest of the recognition of the grace of God. Justification, it is said, is a legal transaction and as such excludes grace, while the Bible clearly

teaches that the sinner is saved by grace. But it can easily be shown that justification with all its antecedents and consequents is a gracious work of God. The substitute allowed for guilty sinners, the vicarious sufferings and obedience of Christ, the imputation of His righteousness to unworthy transgressors, and God's dealing with believers as righteous, — it is all free grace from start to finish.

2. Justification is sometimes called an impious procedure, because it declares sinners to be righteous contrary to fact. But this objection does not hold, because the divine declaration is not to the effect that these sinners are righteous in themselves, but that they are clothed with the perfect righteousness of Jesus Christ. This righteousness wrought by Christ, is freely imputed to them. It is not the personal subjective righteousness of Christ, but His vicarious covenant righteousness, that is imputed to those who are in themselves unrighteous, and all to the glory of God.

3. It is often said this doctrine is ethically subversive, because it leads to licentiousness. But there is no truth in this whatsoever, as even the lives of the justified clearly show. In justification the sure foundation is laid for that vital spiritual union with Christ which secures our sanctification. It really leads right on to the only conditions under which we can be truly holy in principle. The man who is justified also receives the spirit of sanctification, and is the only one who can abound in good works which will glorify God.

I. Divergent Views of Justification.

1. THE ROMAN CATHOLIC VIEW. The Roman Catholic view confounds justification and sanctification. It includes the following elements in justification (a) the expulsion of indwelling sin; (b) the positive infusion of divine grace; and (c) the forgiveness of sins. The sinner is prepared for justification by prevenient grace, without any merits on his part. This prevenient grace leads the sinner to a *fides informis*, to conviction of sin, to repentance, to a confident reliance on the grace of God in Christ, to the beginnings of a new life, and to a desire for baptism. Justification really consists in the infusion of new virtues after the pollution of sin has been removed in baptism. After the expulsion of indwelling sin, the forgiveness of sin or the removal of the guilt of sin necessarily follows. And after that the Christian advances from virtue to virtue, is able to perform meritorious works, and receives as a reward a greater measure of grace and a more perfect justification. The grace of justification can be lost, but can also be restored by the sacrament of penance.

2. THE VIEW OF PISCATOR. Piscator taught that only the passive obedience of Christ is imputed to the sinner in justification, unto the forgiveness of sins; and that His active obedience could not possibly be imputed to him, unto the adoption of children and an eternal inheritance, because the man Christ Jesus owed this to God for Himself. Moreover, if Christ had fulfilled the law for us, we could no more be held responsible for the keeping of the law. Pisca-

tor regarded the bearing of the penalty of sin and the keeping of the law as alternatives, of which the one excludes the other. He left the door open for regarding the sinner's own personal obedience as the only ground of his future hope. This view is very much like that of the Arminians, and is quite in line with the doctrine of Anselm in the Middle Ages.

3. THE VIEW OF OSIANDER. Osiander revealed a tendency to revive in the Lutheran Church the essentials of the Roman Catholic conception of justification, though with a characteristic difference. He asserted that justification does not consist in the imputation of the vicarious righteousness of Christ to the sinner, but in the implanting of a new principle of life. According to him the righteousness by which we are justified is the eternal righteousness of God the Father, which is imparted to or infused into us by His Son Jesus Christ.

4. THE ARMINIAN VIEW. The Arminians hold that Christ did not render strict satisfaction to the justice of God, but yet offered a real propitiation for sin, which was graciously accepted and acted on as satisfactory by God in pardoning sin and thus justifying the sinner. While this only squares past accounts, God also makes provision for the future. He just as graciously imputes the believer's faith to him for righteousness, that faith, namely, as including the entire religious life of the believer, — his evangelical obedience. On this view faith is no more the mere instrument of the positive element of justification, but the graciously admitted ground on which it rests. Justification, then, is not a judicial but a sovereign act of God.

5. THE BARTHIAN VIEW. While Barth does speak of justification as a momentary act, yet he does not regard it as an act accomplished once for all, and which is then followed by sanctification. According to him justification and sanctification go hand in hand all along the line. Pauck says that according to Barth justification is not a growth or an ethical development; it occurs ever anew, whenever man has reached the point of complete despair as to the beliefs and values upon which he has built his life. Thurneysen also rejects the view that justification takes place once for all, calls it the view of Pietism, and claims that it is fatal to the doctrine of the Reformation.

QUESTIONS FOR FURTHER STUDY: What does the verb *dikaio-o* mean in classical Greek? Is justification a creative or a declarative act? Is it possible to think of justification with respect to past sins in any other sense than that of a judicial acquittal? Should justification be thought of exclusively as something objective and external to man? What is meant in theology by the *formal* cause of justification? How do the Romanists and Protestants differ on this point? Is the justification of the Roman Catholics by the *fides formata* really a justification by faith, or a justification by love under the guise of faith? What is the Antinomian doctrine of justification from eternity? Is the distinction made by Buchanan and Cunningham between active and passive justification as being actual and declarative justification correct or not? Can we say that in declarative justification (passive justification) God simply declares the sinner to be what he is? What becomes of the doctrine of justification in Schleiermacher, Ritchl, and modern liberal theology?

LITERATURE: Bavinck, *Geref. Dogm.*, IV, pp. 182-245; Kuyper, *Dict. Dogm.*, *De Salute*, pp. 45-69; ibid., *Het Werk van den Heiligen Geest* II, pp. 204-232; Comrie, *Brief over de Rechtvaardigmaking*; Hodge, *Syst. Theol.* III, pp. 114-212; Shedd, *Dogm. Theol.* II, pp. 538-552; Dick, *Theology, Lectures* LXXI-LXXIII; Dabney, *Syst and Polem. Theol.*, pp. 618-650; Mastricht, *Godgeleerdheit* VI. 6 and 7; Buchanan, *The Doctrine of Justification*; Owen, *On Justification*; Litton, *Introd. to Dogm. Theol.*, pp. 259-313; Girardeau, *Calvinism and Evangelical Arminianism*, pp. 413-566; Pieper, *Christl. Dogm.* II, pp. 606-672; Vos, *Geref. Dogm.* IV., pp. 154-210; Schmid, *Doct. Theol. of the Ev. Luth. Church*, pp. 430-448; Valentine, *Chr. Theol.* II, pp. 214-241; Strong, *Syst. Theol.*, pp. 849-868; Dorner, *Syst. of Chr. Doct.* IV, pp. 194-238; Watson, *Theological Institutes*, II, pp. 406-475; De Moor, *Rechtvaardigmaking van Eeuwigheid*.

X. Sanctification.

A. The Scriptural Terms for Sanctification and Holiness.

1. THE OLD TESTAMENT TERMS. The Old Testament word for 'to sanctify' is *qadash*, a verb that is used in the *niphal, piel, hiphil,* and *hithpa'el* species. The corresponding noun is *qodesh*, while the adjective is *qadosh*. The verbal forms are derived from the nominal and adjectival forms. The original meaning of these words is uncertain. Some are of the opinion that the word *qadash* is related to *chadash*, meaning 'to shine.' This would be in harmony with the qualitative aspect of the Biblical idea of holiness, namely, that of purity. Others, with a greater degree of probability, derive the word from the root *qad*, meaning 'to cut.' This would make the idea of separation the original idea. The word would then point to aloofness, separateness, or majesty. Though this meaning of the words 'sanctification' and 'holiness' may seem unusual to us, it is in all probability the fundamental idea expressed by them. Says Girdlestone: "The terms 'sanctification' and 'holiness' are now used so frequently to represent moral and spiritual qualities, that they hardly convey to the reader the idea of *position or relationship* as existing between God and some person or thing consecrated to Him; yet this appears to be the real meaning of the word."[1] Similarly, Cremer-Koegel calls attention to the fact that the idea of separation is fundamental to that of holiness. "Heiligkeit ist ein verhaeltnisbegriff." At the same time it is admitted that the two ideas of holiness and separation do not merge, are not absorbed in each other, but that the former in a measure serves to qualify the latter.[2]

2. THE NEW TESTAMENT TERMS.

a. *The verb hagiazo and its various meanings.* The verb *hagiazo* is a derivative of *hagios*, which like the Hebrew *qadosh* expresses primarily the idea of separation. It is used in several different senses, however, in the New Testament. We may distinguish the following: (1) It is used in a mental sense of persons or things, Matt. 6:9; Luke 11:2; I Pet. 3:15. In such cases it means "to regard an object as holy," "to ascribe holiness to it," or "to acknowledge its holiness by word or deed." (2) It is also employed occasionally in a ritual sense, that is, in the sense of "separating from ordinary for sacred purposes," or of "setting aside for a certain office," Matt. 23:17,19; John 10:36; II Tim. 2:21. (3) Again it is used to denote that operation of God by which He, especially through His Spirit, works in man the subjective quality of holiness, John 17:17;

---

1. *Old Testament Synonyms,* p. 283.
2. *Biblisch-Theologisches Woerterbuch* (10th ed.) p. 41.

Acts 20:32; 26:18; I Cor. 1:2; I Thess. 5:23. (4) Finally, in the Epistle to the Hebrews it seems to be used in an expiatory sense, and also in the related sense of the Pauline *dikaio-o*, Heb. 9:13; 10:10,29; 13:12.[1]

b. *The adjectives expressive of the idea of holiness.* (1) *Hieros.* The word that is used least and that is also the least expressive, is the word *hieros*. It is found only in I Cor. 9:13; II Tim. 3:15, and then not of persons but of things. It does not express moral excellence, but is expressive of the inviolable character of the thing referred to, which springs from the relation in which it stands to God. It is best translated by the English word "sacred." (2) *Hosios.* The word *hosios* is of more frequent occurrence. It is found in Acts 2:27; 13:34,35; I Tim. 2:8; Tit. 1:8; Heb. 7:26; Rev. 15:4; 16:5, and is applied not only to things, but also to God and to Christ. It describes a person or thing as free from defilement or wickedness, or more actively (of persons) as religiously fulfilling every moral obligation. (3) *Hagnos.* The word *hagnos* occurs in II Cor. 7:11; 11:2; Phil. 4:8; I Tim. 5:22; Jas. 3:17; I Pet. 3:2; I John 3:3. The fundamental idea of the word seems to be that of freedom from impurity and defilement in an ethical sense. (4) *Hagios.* The really characteristic word of the New Testament, however, is *hagios*. Its primary meaning is that of separation in consecration and devotion to the service of God. With this is connected the idea that what is set aside from the world for God, should also separate itself from the world's defilement and share in God's purity. This explains the fact that *hagios* speedily acquired an ethical signification. The word does not always have the same meaning in the New Testament. (a) It is used to designate an external official relation, a being set aside from ordinary purposes for the service of God, as for instance, when we read of "holy prophets," Luke 1:70, "holy apostles," Eph. 3:5, and "holy men of God" II Pet. 1:21. (b) More often, however, it is employed in an ethical sense to describe the quality that is necessary to stand in close relation to God and to serve Him acceptably, Eph. 1:4; 5:27; Col. 1:22; I Pet. 1:15,16. It should be borne in mind that in treating of sanctification we use the word primarily in the latter sense. When we speak of holiness in connection with sanctification, we have in mind both an external relation and an inner subjective quality.

c. *The nouns denoting sanctification and holiness.* The New Testament word for sanctification is *hagiasmos*. It occurs ten times, namely, in Rom. 6:19, 22; I Cor. 1:30; I Thess. 4:3,4,7; II Thess. 2:13; I Tim. 2:15; Heb. 12:14; I Pet. 1:2. While it denotes ethical purification, it includes the idea of separation, namely, "the separation of the spirit from all that is impure and polluting, and a renunciation of the sins towards which the desires of the flesh and of the mind lead us." While *hagiasmos* denotes the work of sanctification, there are two other words that describe the result of the process, namely, *hagiotes* and *hagiosune*. The former is found in I Cor. 1:30 and Heb. 12:10; and the latter in Rom. 1:4; II Cor. 7:1, and I Thess. 3:13. These passages show that the

---

1. Cf. Denney, *The Death of Christ*, p. 220; Kennedy, *The Theology of the Epistles*, p. 214.

quality of holiness or freedom from pollution and impurity is essential to God, was exhibited by Jesus Christ, and is imparted to the Christian.

B. The Doctrine of Sanctification in History.

1. BEFORE THE REFORMATION. In the historical unfolding of the doctrine of sanctification, the Church concerned itself primarily with three problems: (a) the relation of the grace of God in sanctification to faith; (b) the relation of sanctification to justification; and (c) the degree of sanctification in this present life. The writings of the early Church Fathers contain very little respecting the doctrine of sanctification. A strain of moralism is quite apparent in that man was taught to depend for salvation on faith and good works. Sins committed before baptism were washed away in baptism, but for those after baptism man must provide by penance and good works. He must lead a life of virtue and thus merit the approval of the Lord. "Such dualism," says Scott in his *The Nicene Theology*,[1] "left the domain of sanctification only indirectly related to the redemption of Christ; and this was the field in which grew up, naturally, defective conceptions of sin, legalism, Sacramentarianism, priestcraft, and all the excesses of monkish devotion." Asceticism came to be regarded as of the greatest importance. There was also a tendency to confound justification and sanctification. Augustine was the first one to develop rather definite ideas of sanctification, and his views had a determining influence on the Church of the Middle Ages. He did not clearly distinguish between justification and sanctification, but conceived of the latter as included in the former. Since he believed in the total corruption of human nature by the fall, he thought of sanctification as a new supernatural impartation of divine life, a new infused energy, operating exclusively within the confines of the Church and through the sacraments. While he did not lose sight of the importance of personal love to Christ as a constituent element in sanctification, he manifested a tendency to take a metaphysical view of the grace of God in sanctification, — to regard it as a deposit of God in man. He did not sufficiently stress the necessity of a constant preoccupation of faith with the redeeming Christ, as the most important factor in the transformation of the Christian's life. The tendencies apparent in the teachings of Augustine came to fruitage in the theology of the Middle Ages, which is found in its most developed form in the writings of Thomas Aquinas. Justification and sanctification are not clearly distinguished, but the former is made to include the infusion of divine grace, as something substantial, into the human soul. This grace is a sort of *donum superadditum,* by which the soul is lifted to a new level or a higher order of being, and is enabled to achieve its heavenly destiny of knowing, possessing, and enjoying God. The grace is derived from the inexhaustible treasury of the merits of Christ and is imparted to believers by the sacraments. Looked at from the divine point of view, this sanctifying grace within the soul secures the remission of original sin, imparts a permanent habit of inherent righteousness, and carries within itself the potency of further development, and even of perfection. Out of it the new life develops

---

1. p. 200.

with all its virtues. Its good work can be neutralized or destroyed by mortal sins; but the guilt contracted after baptism can be removed by the eucharist in the case of venial sins, and by the sacrament of penance in the case of mortal sins. Considered from the human point of view, the supernatural works of faith working through love have merit before God, and secure an increase of grace. Such works are impossible, however, without the continuous operation of the grace of God. The result of the whole process was known as justification rather than as sanctification; it consisted in making man just before God. These ideas are embodied in the Canons and Decrees of the Council of Trent.

2. AFTER THE REFORMATION. The Reformers in speaking of sanctification emphasized the antithesis of sin and redemption rather than that of nature and supernature. They made a clear distinction between justification and sanctification, regarding the former as a legal act of divine grace, affecting the judicial status of man, and the latter, as a moral or re-creative work, changing the inner nature of man. But while they made a careful distinction between the two, they also stressed their inseparable connection. While deeply convinced that man is justified by faith alone, they also understood that the faith which justifies is not alone. Justification is at once followed by sanctification, since God sends out the Spirit of His Son into the hearts of His own as soon as they are justified, and that Spirit is the Spirit of sanctification. They did not regard the grace of sanctification as a supernatural essence infused in man through the sacraments, but as a supernatural and gracious work of the Holy Spirit, primarily through the Word and secondarily through the sacraments, by which He delivers us more and more from the power of sin and enables us to do good works. Though in no way confounding justification and sanctification, they felt the necessity of preserving the closest possible connection between the former, in which the free and forgiving grace of God is strongly emphasized, and the latter, which calls for the co-operation of man, in order to avoid the danger of work-righteousness. In Pietism and Methodism great emphasis was placed on constant fellowship with Christ as the great means of sanctification. By exalting sanctification at the expense of justification, they did not always avoid the danger of self-righteousness. Wesley did not merely distinguish justification and sanctification, but virtually separated them, and spoke of entire sanctification as a second gift of grace, following the first, of justification by faith, after a shorter or longer period. While he also spoke of sanctification as a process, he yet held that the believer should pray and look for full sanctification at once by a separate act of God. Under the influence of Rationalism and of the moralism of Kant sanctification ceased to be regarded as a supernatural work of the Holy Spirit in the renewal of sinners, and was brought down to the level of a mere moral improvement by the natural powers of man. For Schleiermacher it was merely the progressive domination of the God-consciousness within us over the merely sentient and ever morally defective world-consciousness. And for Ritschl it was the moral perfection of the Christian life to which we attain by fulfilling our vocation as members of the Kingdom of God. In a great deal

of modern liberal theology sanctification consists only in the ever-increasing redemption of man's lower self by the domination of his higher self. Redemption by character is one of the slogans of the present day, and the term "sanctification" has come to stand for mere moral improvement.

C. The Biblical Idea of Holiness and Sanctification.

1. IN THE OLD TESTAMENT. In Scripture the quality of holiness applies first of all to God, and as applied to Him its fundamental idea is that of unapproachableness. And this unapproachableness is based on the fact that God is divine and therefore absolutely distinct from the creature. Holiness in this sense is not merely an attribute to be co-ordinated with others in God. It is rather something that is predicable of everything that is found in God. He is holy in His grace as well as in His righteousness, in His love as well as in His wrath. Strictly speaking, holiness becomes an attribute only in the later ethical sense of the word. The ethical meaning of the term developed out of the majesty-meaning. This development starts with the idea that a sinful being is more keenly conscious of the majesty of God than a sinless being. The sinner becomes aware of his impurity as over against the majestic purity of God, cf. Isa. 6. Otto speaks of holiness in the original sense as the numenous, and proposes to call the characteristic reaction to it "creature-feeling, or creature-consciousness," a disvaluation of self into nothingness, while he speaks of the reaction to holiness in the derived ethical sense as a "feeling of absolute profaneness." Thus the idea of holiness as majestic purity or ethical sublimity was developed. This purity is an active principle in God, that must vindicate itself and uphold its honor. This accounts for the fact that holiness is represented in Scripture also as the light of the divine glory turned into a devouring fire. Isa. 5:24; 10:17; 33:14,15. Over against the holiness of God man feels himself to be, not merely insignificant, but positively impure and sinful, and as such an object of God's wrath. God revealed His holiness in the Old Testament in various ways. He did it in terrible judgments upon the enemies of Israel, Ex. 15:11,12. He did it also by separating unto Himself a people, which He took out of the world, Ex. 19:4-6; Ezek. 20:39-44. By taking this people out of the impure and ungodly world, He protested against that world and its sin. Moreover, He did it repeatedly in sparing His unfaithful people, because He did not want the unholy world to rejoice at what it might consider the failure of His work, Hos. 11:9.

In a derivative sense the idea of holiness is also applied to things and persons that are placed in a special relation to God. The land of Canaan, the city of Jerusalem, the temple-mount, the tabernacle and temple, the sabbaths and the solemn feasts of Israel, — they are all called holy, since they are consecrated to God and are placed within the radiance of His majestic holiness. Similarly, the prophets, the Levites, and the priests are called holy as persons that were set aside for the special service of the Lord. Israel had its sacred places, its sacred seasons, its sacred rites, and its sacred persons. This is not yet the ethical idea of holiness, however. One might be a sacred person, and yet be entirely devoid of the grace of God in his heart. In the old dispensation, as well as in the new, ethical holiness results from the renewing and sanctifying influence of the Holy Spirit. It should be remembered, however, that even where the conception of holiness is thoroughly spiritualized, it is always expressive of a relation. The idea of holiness is never that of moral goodness, considered in itself, but always that of ethical goodness seen in relation to God.

2. In the New Testament. In passing from the Old Testament to the New we become aware of a striking difference. While in the Old Testament there is not a single attribute of God that stands out with anything like the same prominence as His holiness, in the New Testament holiness is seldom ascribed to God. Except in a few Old Testament quotations, it is done only in the writings of John, John 17:11; I John 2:20; Rev. 6:10. In all probability the explanation for this lies in the fact that in the New Testament holiness stands forth as the special characteristic of the Spirit of God, by whom believers are sanctified, are qualified for service, and are led to their eternal destiny, II Thess. 2:13; Tit. 3:5. The word *hagios* is used in connection with the Spirit of God well nigh a hundred times. The conception of holiness and sanctification, however, is no other in the New Testament than it is in the Old. In the former as well as in the latter holiness is ascribed in a derived sense to man. In the one as well as in the other ethical holiness is not mere moral rectitude, and sanctification is never mere moral improvement. These two are often confused in the present day, when people speak of salvation by character. A man may boast of great moral improvement, and yet be an utter stranger to sanctification. The Bible does not urge moral improvement pure and simple, but moral improvement in relation to God, for God's sake, and with a view to the service of God. It insists on sanctification. At this very point much ethical preaching of the present day is utterly misleading; and the corrective for it lies in the presentation of the true doctrine of sanctification. Sanctification may be defined as *that gracious and continuous operation of the Holy Spirit, by which He delivers the justified sinner from the pollution of sin, renews his whole nature in the image of God, and enables him to perform good works.*

D. The Nature of Sanctification.

1. It is a supernatural work of God. Some have the mistaken notion that sanctification consists merely in the drawing out of the new life, implanted in the soul by regeneration, in a persuasive way by presenting motives to the will. But this is not true. It consists fundamentally and primarily in a divine operation in the soul, whereby the holy disposition born in regeneration is strengthened and its holy exercises are increased. It is essentially a work of God, though in so far as He employs means, man can and is expected to co-operate by the proper use of these means. Scripture clearly exhibits the supernatural character of sanctification in several ways. It describes it as a work of God, I Thess. 5:23; Heb. 13:20,21, as a fruit of the union of life with Jesus Christ,

John 15:4; Gal. 2:20; 4:19, as a work that is wrought in man from within and which for that very reason cannot be a work of man, Eph. 3:16; Col. 1:11, and speaks of its manifestation in Christian virtues as the work of the Spirit, Gal. 5:22. It should never be represented as a merely natural process in the spiritual development of man, nor brought down to the level of a mere human achievement, as is done in a great deal of modern liberal theology.

2. IT CONSISTS OF TWO PARTS. The two parts of sanctification are represented in Scripture as:

a. *The mortification of the old man, the body of sin.* This Scriptural term denotes that act of God whereby the pollution and corruption of human nature that results from sin is gradually removed. It is often represented in the Bible as the crucifying of the old man, and is thus connected with the death of Christ on the cross. The old man is human nature in so far as it is controlled by sin, Rom. 6:6; Gal. 5:24. In the context of the passage of Galatians Paul contrasts the works of the flesh and the works of the Spirit, and then says: "And they who are of Christ Jesus have crucified the flesh with the passions and the lusts thereof." This means that in their case the Spirit has gained predominance.

b. *The quickening of the new man, created in Christ Jesus unto good works.* While the former part of sanctification is negative in character, this is positive. It is that act of God whereby the holy disposition of the soul is strengthened, holy exercises are increased, and thus a new course of life engendered and promoted. The old structure of sin is gradually torn down, and a new structure of God is reared in its stead. These two parts of sanctification are not successive but contemporaneous. Thank God, the gradual erection of the new building need not wait until the old one is completely demolished. If it had to wait for that, it could never begin in this life. With the gradual dissolution of the old the new makes its appearance. It is like the airing of a house filled with pestiferous odors. As the old air is drawn out, the new rushes in. This positive side of sanctification is often called "a being raised together with Christ," Rom. 6:4,5; Col. 2:12; 3:1,2. The new life to which it leads is called "a life unto God," Rom. 6:11; Gal. 2:19.

3. IT AFFECTS THE WHOLE MAN: BODY AND SOUL; INTELLECT, AFFECTIONS AND WILL. This follows from the nature of the case, because sanctification takes place in the inner life of man, in the heart, and this cannot be changed without changing the whole organism of man. If the inner man is changed, there is bound to be change also in the periphery of life. Moreover, Scripture clearly and explicitly teaches that it affects both body and soul, I Thess. 5:23; II Cor. 5:17; Rom. 6:12; I Cor. 6:15,20. The body comes into consideration here as the organ or instrument of the sinful soul, through which the sinful inclinations and habits and passions express themselves. The sanctification of the body takes place especially in the crisis of death and in the resurrection of the dead. Finally, it also appears from Scripture that sanctification affects all the powers or faculties of the soul: the understanding, Jer. 31:34; John 6:45; — the will,

Ezek. 36:25-27; Phil. 2:13; — the passions, Gal. 5:24; — and the conscience, Tit. 1:15; Heb. 9:14.

4. IT IS A WORK OF GOD IN WHICH BELIEVERS CO-OPERATE. When it is said that man takes part in the work of sanctification, this does not mean that man is an independent agent in the work, so as to make it partly the work of God and partly the work of man; but merely, that God effects the work in part through the instrumentality of man as a rational being, by requiring of him prayerful and intelligent co-operation with the Spirit. That man must co-operate with the Spirit of God follows: (a) from the repeated warnings against evils and temptations, which clearly imply that man must be active in avoiding the pitfalls of life, Rom. 12:9,16,17; I Cor. 6:9,10; Gal. 5:16-23; and (b) from the constant exhortations to holy living. These imply that the believer must be diligent in the employment of the means at his command for the moral and spiritual improvement of his life, Micah 6:8; John 15:2,8,16; Rom. 8:12,13; 12:1,2,17; Gal. 6:7,8,15.

E. The Characteristics of Sanctification.

1. As appears from the immediately preceding, sanctification is a work of which God and not man is the author. Only the advocates of the so-called free will can claim that it is a work of man. Nevertheless, it differs from regeneration in that man can, and is in duty bound to, strive for ever-increasing sanctification by using the means which God has placed at his disposal. This is clearly taught in Scripture, II Cor. 7:1; Col. 3:5-14; I Pet. 1:22. Consistent Antinomians lose sight of this important truth, and feel no need of carefully avoiding sin, since this affects only the old man which is condemned to death, and not the new man which is holy with the holiness of Christ.

2. Sanctification takes place partly in the subconscious life, and as such is an immediate operation of the Holy Spirit; but also partly in the conscious life, and then depends on the use of certain means, such as the constant exercise of faith, the study of God's Word, prayer, and association with other believers.

3. Sanctification is usually a lengthy process and never reaches perfection in this life. At the same time there may be cases in which it is completed in a very short time or even in a moment, as, for instance, in cases in which regeneration and conversion are immediately followed by temporal death. If we may proceed on the assumption that the believer's sanctification is perfect immediately after death — and Scripture seems to teach this as far as the soul is concerned —, then in such cases the sanctification of the soul must be completed almost at once.

4. The sanctification of the believer must, it would seem, be completed either at the very moment of death, or immediately after death, as far as the soul is concerned, and at the resurrection in so far as it pertains to the body. This would seem to follow from that fact that, on the one hand, the Bible teaches that in the present life no one can claim freedom from sin, I Kings 8:46; Prov.

20:9; Rom. 3:10,12; Jas. 3:2; I John 1:8; and that, on the other hand, those who have gone before are entirely sanctified. It speaks of them as "the spirits of just men made perfect," Heb. 12:23, and as "without blemish," Rev. 14:5. Moreover, we are told that in the heavenly city of God there shall in no wise enter "anything unclean or he that maketh an abomination and a lie," Rev. 21:27; and that Christ at His coming will "fashion anew the body of our humiliation, that it may be conformed to the body of His glory," Phil. 3:21.

F. The Author and Means of Sanctification.

Sanctification is a work of the triune God, but is ascribed more particularly to the Holy Spirit in Scripture, Rom. 8:11; 15:16; I Pet. 1:2. It is particularly important in our day, with its emphasis on the necessity of approaching the study of theology anthropologically and its one-sided call to service in the kingdom of God, to stress the fact that God, and not man, is the author of sanctification. Especially in view of the Activism that is such a characteristic feature of American religious life, and which glorifies the work of man rather than the grace of God, it is necessary to stress the fact over and over again that sanctification is the fruit of justification, that the former is simply impossible without the latter, and that both are the fruits of the grace of God in the redemption of sinners. Though man is privileged to co-operate with the Spirit of God, he can do this only in virtue of the strength which the Spirit imparts to him from day to day. The spiritual development of man is not a human achievement, but a work of divine grace. Man deserves no credit whatsoever for that which he contributes to it instrumentally. In so far as sanctification takes place in the subconscious life, it is effected by the immediate operation of the Holy Spirit. But as a work in the conscious life of believers it is wrought by several means, which the Holy Spirit employs.

1. THE WORD OF GOD. In opposition to the Church of Rome it should be maintained that the principal means used by the Holy Spirit is the Word of God. The truth in itself certainly has no adequate efficiency to sanctify the believer, yet it is naturally adapted to be the means of sanctification as employed by the Holy Spirit. Scripture presents all the objective conditions for holy exercises and acts. It serves to excite spiritual activity by presenting motives and inducements, and gives direction to it by prohibitions, exhortations, and examples, I Pet. 1:22; 2:2; II Pet. 1:4.

2. THE SACRAMENTS. These are the means *par excellence* according to the Church of Rome. Protestants regard them as subordinate to the Word of God, and sometimes even speak of them as the "visible Word." They symbolize and seal to us the same truths that are verbally expressed in the Word of God, and may be regarded as an acted word, containing a lively representation of the truth, which the Holy Spirit makes the occasion for holy exercises. They are not only subordinate to the Word of God, but cannot exist without it, and are therefore always accompanied by it, Rom. 6:3; I Cor. 12:13; Tit. 3:5; I Pet. 3:21.

3. PROVIDENTIAL GUIDANCE. God's providences, both favorable and adverse, are often powerful means of sanctification. In connection with the operation of the Holy Spirit through the Word, they work on our natural affections and thus frequently deepen the impression of religious truth and force it home. It should be borne in mind that the light of God's revelation is necessary for the interpretation of His providential guidances, Ps. 119:71; Rom. 2:4; Heb. 12:10.

G. Relation of Sanctification to Other Stages in the Ordo Salutis.

It is of considerable importance to have a correct conception of the relation between sanctification and some of the other stages in the work of redemption.

1. TO REGENERATION. There is both difference and similarity here. Regeneration is completed at once, for a man cannot be more or less regenerated; he is either dead or alive spiritually. Sanctification is a process, bringing about gradual changes, so that different grades may be distinguished in the resulting holiness. Hence we are admonished to perfect holiness in the fear of the Lord, II Cor. 7:1. The Heidelberg Catechism also presupposes that there are degrees of holiness, when it says that even "the holiest men, when in this life, have only a small beginning of this obedience."[1] At the same time regeneration is the beginning of sanctification. The work of renewal, begun in the former, is continued in the latter, Phil. 1:6. Strong says: "It (sanctification) is distinguished from regeneration as growth from birth, or as the strengthening of a holy disposition from the original impartation of it."[2]

2. TO JUSTIFICATION. Justification precedes and is basic to sanctification in the covenant of grace. In the covenant of works the order of righteousness and holiness was just the reverse. Adam was created with a holy disposition and inclination to serve God, but on the basis of this holiness he had to work out the righteousness that would entitle him to eternal life. Justification is the judicial basis for sanctification. God has the right to demand of us holiness of life, but because we cannot work out this holiness for ourselves, He freely works it within us through the Holy Spirit on the basis of the righteousness of Jesus Christ, which is imputed to us in justification. The very fact that it is based on justification, in which the free grace of God stands out with the greatest prominence, excludes the idea that we can ever merit anything in sanctification. The Roman Catholic idea that justification enables man to perform meritorious works is contrary to Scripture. Justification as such does not effect a change in our inner being and therefore needs sanctification as its complement. It is not sufficient that the sinner stands righteous before God; he must also be holy in his inmost life. Barth has a rather unusual representation of the relation between justification and sanctification. In order to ward off all self-righteousness, he insists on it that the two always be considered jointly. They go together and should not be considered quantitatively, as if the one followed the other. Justification is not a station which one passes, an accomplished fact on the basis

---

1. Q. 114.
2. *Syst. Theol.*, p. 871.

of which one next proceeds to the highway of sanctification. It is not a completed fact to which one can look back with definite assurance, but occurs
ever anew whenever man has reached the point of complete despair, and then
goes hand in hand with sanctification. And just as man remains a sinner even
after justification, so he also remains a sinner in sanctification, even his best
deeds continue to be sins. Sanctification does not engender a holy disposition,
and does not gradually purify man. It does not put him in possession of any
personal holiness, does not make him a saint, but leaves him a sinner. It
really becomes a declarative act like justification. McConnachie, who is a very
sympathetic interpreter of Barth, says: "Justification and sanctification are,
therefore, to Barth, two sides of one act of God upon men. Justification is the
pardon of the sinner (*justificatio impii*), *by which* God declares the sinner
righteous. Sanctification is the sanctification of the sinner (*sanctificatio impii*),
by which God declares the sinner 'holy'." However laudable the desire of Barth
to destroy every vestige of work-righteousness, he certainly goes to an unwarranted extreme, in which he virtually confuses justification and sanctification,
negatives the Christian life, and rules out the possibility of confident assurance.

3. To FAITH. Faith is the mediate or instrumental cause of sanctification
as well as of justification. It does not merit sanctification any more than it does
justification, but it unites us to Christ and keeps us in touch with Him as the
Head of the new humanity, who is the source of the new life within us, and
also of our progressive sanctification, through the operation of the Holy Spirit.
The consciousness of the fact that sanctification is based on justification, and is
impossible on any other basis, and that the constant exercise of faith is necessary, in order to advance in the way of holiness, will guard us against all
self-righteousness in our striving to advance in godliness and holiness of life. It
deserves particular attention that, while even the weakest faith mediates a per-
fest justification, the degree of sanctification is commensurate with the strength
of the Christian's faith and the persistence with which he apprehends Christ.

H. The Imperfect Character of Sanctification in This Life.

1. SANCTIFICATION IMPERFECT IN DEGREE. When we speak of sanctification as being imperfect in this life, we do not mean to say that it is imperfect
in parts, as if only a part of the holy man that originates in regeneration were
affected. It is the whole, but yet undeveloped new man, that must grow into
full stature. A new-born child is, barring exceptions, perfect in parts, but not
yet in the degree of development for which it is intended. Just so the new man
is perfect in parts, but remains in the present life imperfect in the degree of
spiritual development. Believers must contend with sin as long as they live, I
Kings 8:46; Prov. 20:9; Eccl. 7:20; Jas. 3:2; I John 1:8.

2. DENIAL OF THIS IMPERFECTION BY THE PERFECTIONISTS.

a. *The doctrine of perfectionism.* Speaking generally, this doctrine is to
the effect that religious perfection is attainable in the present life. It is taught
in various forms by Pelagians, Roman Catholics or Semi-Pelagians, Arminians,

Wesleyans, such mystical sects as the Labadists, the Quietists, the Quakers, and others, some of the Oberlin theologians, such as Mahan and Finney, and Ritschl. These all agree in maintaining that it is possible for believers in this life to attain to a state in which they comply with the requirements of the law *under which they now live*, or under that law *as it was adjusted to their present ability and needs*, and, consequently, to be free from sin. They differ, however: (1) In their view of sin, the Pelagians, in distinction from all the rest, denying the inherent corruption of man. They all agree, however, in externalizing sin. (2) In their conception of the law which believers are now obliged to fulfill, the Arminians, including the Wesleyans, differing from all the rest in holding that this is not the original moral law, but the gospel requirements or the new law of faith and evangelical obedience. The Roman Catholics and the Oberlin theologians maintain that it is the original law, but admit that the demands of this law are adjusted to man's deteriorated powers and to his present ability. And Ritschl discards the whole idea that man is subject to an externally imposed law. He defends the autonomy of moral conduct, and holds that we are under no law but such as is evolved out of our own moral disposition in the course of activities for the fulfilment of our vocation. (3) In their idea of the sinner's dependence on the renewing grace of God for the ability to fulfill the law. All, except the Pelagians, admit that he is in some sense dependent on divine grace, in order to the attainment of perfection.

It is very significant that all the leading perfectionist theories (with the sole exception of the Pelagian, which denies the inherent corruption of man) deem it necessary to lower the standard of perfection and do not hold man responsible for a great deal that is undoubtedly demanded by the original moral law. And it is equally significant that they feel the necessity of externalizing the idea of sin, when they claim that only conscious wrong-doing can be so considered, and refuse to recognize as sin a great deal that is represented as such in Scripture.

b. *Scriptural proofs adduced for the doctrine of perfectionism.*

(1) The Bible commands believers to be holy and even to be perfect, I Pet. 1:16; Matt. 5:48; Jas. 1:4, and urges them to follow the example of Christ who did no sin, I Pet. 2:21 f. Such commands would be unreasonable, if it were not possible to reach sinless perfection. But the Scriptural demand to be holy and perfect holds for the unregenerate as well as for the regenerate, since the law of God demands holiness from the start and has never been revoked. If the command implies that they to whom it comes can live up to the requirement, this must be true of every man. However, only those who teach perfectionism in the Pelagian sense can hold that view. The measure of our ability cannot be inferred from the Scriptural commandments.

(2) Holiness and perfection are often ascribed to believers in Scripture, Song of Sol. 4:7; I Cor. 2:6; II Cor. 5:17; Eph. 5:27; Heb. 5:14; Phil. 4:13; Col. 2:10. When the Bible speaks of believers as holy and perfect, however, this does not necessarily mean that they are without sin, since both words are

often used in a different sense, not only in common parlance, but also in the Bible. Persons set aside for the special service of God are called holy in the Bible, irrespective of their moral condition and life. Believers can be and are called holy, because they are objectively holy in Christ, or because they are in principle subjectively sanctified by the Spirit of God. Paul in his Epistles invariably addresses his readers as saints, that is "holy ones," and then proceeds in several cases to take them to task for their sins. And when believers are described as perfect, this means in some cases merely that they are full-grown, I Cor. 2:6; Heb. 5:14, and in others that they are fully equipped for their task, II Tim. 3:17. All this certainly does not give countenance to the theory of sin less perfection.

(3) There are, it is said, Biblical examples of saints who led perfect lives, such as Noah, Job, and Asa, Gen. 6:9; Job 1:1; I Kings 15:14. But, surely, such examples as these do not prove the point for the simple reason that they are no examples of sinless perfection. Even the most notable saints of the Bible are pictured as men who had their failings and who sinned, in some cases very grievously. This is true of Noah, Moses, Job, Abraham, and all the others. It is true that this does not necessarily prove that their lives remained sinful as long as they lived on earth, but it is a striking fact that we are not introduced to a single one who was without sin. The question of Solomon is still pertinent: "Who can say, I have made my heart clean, I am pure from my sin?" Prov. 20:9. Moreover, John says: "If we say that we have no sin, we deceive ourselves, and the truth is not in us," I John 1:8.

(4) The apostle John declares explicitly that they who are born of God do not sin, I John 3:6,8,9; 5:18. But when John says that they who are born of God do not sin, he is contrasting the two states, represented by the old and the new man, as to their essential nature and principle. One of the essential characteristics of the new man is that he does not sin. In view of the fact that John invariably uses the present to express the idea that the one born of God does not sin, it is possible that he desires to express the idea that the child of God does not *go on sinning habitually*, as the devil does, I John 3:8.[1] He certainly does not mean to assert that the believer never commits an act of sin, cf. I John 1:8-10. Moreover, the Perfectionist cannot very well use these passages to prove his point, since they would prove too much for his purpose. He does not make bold to say that all believers are actually sinless, but only that they can reach a state of sinless perfection. The Johannine passages, however, would prove, on his interpretation, that all believers are without sin. And more than that, they would also prove that believers never fall from the state of grace (for this is sinning); and yet the Perfectionists are the very people who believe that even perfect Christians may fall away.

c. *Objections to the theory of Perfectionism.*

(1) In the light of Scripture the doctrine of Perfectionism is absolutely untenable. The Bible gives us the explicit and very definite assurance that there

---

1. Cf. Robertson, *The Minister and His Greek Testament*, p. 100.

is no one on earth who does not sin, I Kings 8:46; Prov. 20:9; Eccl. 7:20; Rom. 3:10; Jas. 3:2; I John 1:8. In view of these clear statements of Scripture it is hard to see how any who claim to believe the Bible as the infallible Word of God can hold that it is possible for believers to lead sinless lives, and that some actually succeed in avoiding all sin.

(2) According to Scripture there is a constant warfare between the flesh and the Spirit in the lives of God's children, and even the best of them are still striving for perfection. Paul gives a very striking description of this struggle in Rom. 7:7-26, a passage which certainly refers to him in his regenerate state. In Gal. 5:16-24 he speaks of that very same struggle as a struggle that characterizes all the children of God. And in Phil. 3:10-14 he speaks of himself, practically at the end of his career, as one who has not yet reached perfection, but is pressing on toward the goal.

(3) Confession of sin and prayer for forgiveness are continually required. Jesus taught all His disciples without any exception to pray for the forgiveness of sins and for deliverance from temptation and from the evil one, Matt. 6:12,13. And John says: "If we confess our sins, He is faithful and righteous to forgive us our sins, and to cleanse us from all unrighteousness," I John 1:9. Moreover, Bible saints are constantly represented as confessing their sins, Job 9:3,20; Ps. 32:5; 130:3; 143:2; Prov. 20:9; Isa. 64:6; Dan. 9:16; Rom. 7:14.

(4) The Perfectionists themselves deem it necessary to lower the standard of the law and to externalize the idea of sin, in order to maintain their theory. Moreover, some of them have repeatedly modified the ideal to which, in their estimation, believers can attain. At first the ideal was "freedom from all sin"; then, "freedom from all conscious sin," next, "entire consecration to God," and, finally, "Christian assurance." This is in itself a sufficient condemnation of their theory. We naturally do not deny that the Christian can attain to the assurance of faith.

I. Sanctification and Good Works.

Sanctification and good works are most intimately related. Just as the old life expresses itself in works of evil, so the new life, that originates in regeneration and is promoted and strengthened in sanctification, naturally manifests itself in good works. These may be called the fruits of sanctification, and as such come into consideration here.

1. THE NATURE OF GOOD WORKS.

a. *Good works in the specifically theological sense.* When we speak of good works in connection with sanctification, we do not refer to works that are perfect, that answer perfectly to the requirements of the divine moral law, and that are of such inherent worth as to entitle one to the reward of eternal life under the conditions of the covenant of works. We do mean, however, works that are essentially different in moral quality from the actions of the unregenerate, and that are the expressions of a new and holy nature, as the principle from which they spring. These are works which God not only approves, but in a certain sense also rewards. The following are the characteristics of works that are spiritually good: (1) They are the fruits of a regenerate heart, since without this no one can have the disposition (to obey God) and the motive (to glorify God) that is required, Matt. 12:33; 7:17,18. (2) They are not only in external conformity with the law of God, but are also done in conscious obedience to the revealed will of God, that is, because they are required by God. They spring from the principle of love to God and from the desire to do His will, Deut. 6:2; I Sam. 15:22; Isa. 1:12; 29:13; Matt. 15:9. (3) Whatever their proximate aim may be, their final aim is not the welfare of man, but the glory of God, which is the highest conceivable aim of man's life, I Cor. 10:31; Rom. 12:1; Col. 3:17,23.

b. *Good works in a more general sense.* Though the term "good works" is generally used in theology in the strict sense just indicated, it remains true that the unregenerate can also perform works that may be called good in a superficial sense of the word. They often perform works that are in outward conformity with the law of God and may be called objectively good, in distinction from flagrant transgressions of the law. Such works answer to a proximate aim that meets with the approval of God. Moreover, in virtue of the remains of the image of God in the natural man and of the light of nature, man may be guided in his relation to other men by motives which are laudable and in so far bear the stamp of God's approval. Those good works, however, cannot be regarded as fruits of the corrupt heart of man. They find their explanation only in the common grace of God. Furthermore, we should bear in mind that, though these works can be called good in a certain sense and are so called in the Bible, Luke 6:33, they are yet essentially defective. The deeds of the unregenerate are divorced from the spiritual root of love to God. They represent no inner obedience to the law of God and no subjection to the will of the sovereign Ruler of heaven and earth. They have no spiritual aim, since they are not performed for the purpose of glorifying God, but only bear on the relations of the natural life. The real quality of the act is, of course, determined by the quality of its final aim. The ability of the unregenerate to perform good works in some sense of the word has often been denied. Barth goes one step further when he goes to the extreme of denying that believers can do good works, and asserts that all their works are sins.

2. THE MERITORIOUS CHARACTER OF GOOD WORKS. Even from the earliest ages of the Christian Church there was a tendency to ascribe a certain merit to good works, but the doctrine of merit was really developed in the Middle Ages. At the time of the Reformation it was very prominent in Roman Catholic theology and was pushed to ridiculous extremes in practical life. The Reformers at once joined issue with the Church of Rome on this point.

a. *The position of Rome on the point in question.* The Roman Catholic Church distinguishes between a *meritum de condigno*, which represents inherent dignity and worth, and a *meritum de congruo*, which is a sort of quasi-merit, something fit to be rewarded. The former attaches only to works done after regeneration by the aid of divine grace, and is a merit which intrinsically deserves the reward it receives from the hand of God. The latter attaches to those dispositions or works which a man may develop or do before regeneration, in virtue of a mere prevenient grace, and is a merit which makes it congruous or fitting for God to reward the agent by infusing grace into his heart. Since the decisions of the Council of Trent are rather dubious on this point, there is some uncertainty, however, as to the exact position of the Church. The general idea seems to be that the ability to perform good works in the strict sense of the word springs from grace infused into the sinner's heart for the sake of Christ; and that afterwards these good works merit, that is, give man a just claim to, salvation and glory. The Church goes even farther than that, and teaches that believers can perform works of supererogation, can do more than is necessary for their own salvation and can thus lay by a store of good works, which may accrue to the benefit of others.

b. *The Scriptural position on this point.* Scripture clearly teaches that the good works of believers are not meritorious in the proper sense of the word. We should bear in mind, however, that the word "merit" is employed in a twofold sense, the one strict and proper, and the other loose. Strictly speaking, a meritorious work is one to which, on account of its intrinsic value and dignity, the reward is justly due from commutative justice. Loosely speaking, however, a work that is deserving of approval and to which a reward is somehow attached (by promise, agreement, or otherwise) is also sometimes called meritorious. Such works are praiseworthy and are rewarded by God. But, however this may be, they are surely not meritorious in the strict sense of the word. They do not, by their own intrinsic moral value, make God a debtor to him who performs them. In strict justice the good works of believers merit nothing. Some of the most conclusive passages of Scripture to prove the point under consideration are the following: Luke 17:9,10; Rom. 5:15-18; 6:23; Eph. 2:8-10; II Tim. 1:9; Tit. 3:5. These passages clearly show that believers do not receive the inheritance of salvation because it is due to them in virtue of their good works, but only as a free gift of God. It stands to reason also that such works cannot be meritorious, for: (1) Believers owe their whole life to God and therefore cannot merit anything by giving God simply what is His due, Luke 17:9,10. (2) They cannot perform good works in their own strength, but only in the strength which God imparts to them from day to day; and in view of that fact they cannot expect the credit for these works, I Cor. 15:10; Phil. 2:13. (3) Even the best works of believers remain imperfect in this life, and all good works together represent only a partial obedience, while the law demands perfect obedience and can be satisfied with nothing less, Isa. 64:6; Jas. 3:2. (4) Moreover, the good works of believers are out of all proportion to the eternal reward of glory. A temporal and imperfect obedience can never merit an eternal and perfect reward.

3. THE NECESSITY OF GOOD WORKS. There can be no doubt about the necessity of good works properly understood. They cannot be regarded as necessary to merit salvation, nor as a means to retain a hold on salvation, nor even as the only way along which to proceed to eternal glory, for children enter salvation without having done any good works. The Bible does not teach that no one can be saved apart from good works. At the same time good works necessarily follow from the union of believers with Christ. "He that abideth in me and I in him, the same beareth much fruit," John 15:5. They are also necessary as required by God, Rom. 7:4; 8:12.13; Gal. 6:2, as the fruits of faith, Jas. 2:14,17,20-22, as expressions of gratitude, I Cor. 6:20, unto the assurance of faith, II Peter 1:5-10, and to the glory of God, John 15:8; I Cor. 10:31. The necessity of good works must be maintained over against the Antinomians, who claim that, since Christ not only bore the penalty of sin, but also met the positive demands of the law, the believer is free from the obligation to observe it, an error that is still with us to-day in some of the forms of dispensationalism. This is a thoroughly false position, for it is only the law as a system of penalty and as a method of salvation that is abolished in the death of Christ. The law as the standard of our moral life is a transcript of the holiness of God and is therefore of permanent validity also for the believer, though his attitude to the law has undergone a radical change. He has received the Spirit of God, which is the Spirit of obedience, so that, without any constraint, he willingly obeys the law. Strong sums it up well, when he says: Christ frees us "(1) from the law as a system of curse and penalty; this He does by bearing the curse and penalty Himself . . . ; (2) from the law with its claims as a method of salvation; this He does by making His obedience and merits ours . . . ; (3) from the law as an outward and foreign compulsion; this He does by giving us the spirit of obedience and sonship, by which the law is progressively realized within."[1]

QUESTIONS FOR FURTHER STUDY: How was theocratic, related to ethical, holiness among Israel? How were the ritual purifications related to sanctification? Who is the subject of sanctification, the old man or the new, or neither of the two? Does sanctification in this life affect all parts of man equally? Where does the process of sanctification begin? Do all Christians experience a steady progress in sanctification? What is the difference between sanctification and moral improvement? Does the fact that sanctification is never complete in this life necessarily lead to the doctrine of purgatory, or to that of the continuation of sanctification after death? How did Wesley conceive of "entire sanctification"? Does Barth also ascribe holiness as an ethical quality to the believer? What Scripture proof is there that the Christian is not free from the law as a rule of life? Do Protestants in general teach that good works are not necessary? How do Roman Catholics and Protestants differ as to the necessity of good works? Is it wise to say without any qualification that good works are necessary unto salvation? If all Christians inherit eternal life, in what sense will their good works be the standard of their reward?

LITERATURE: Bavinck, *Geref. Dogm.* IV, pp. 245-288; Kuyper, *Dict. Dogm., De Salute,* pp. 134-157; ibid., *Het Werk van den Heiligen Geest* III, pp. 1-123; Vos, *Geref. Dogm.* IV, pp. 211-248; Hodge, *Syst. Theol.* III, pp. 213-258; Shedd, *Dogm. Theol.* II, pp. 553-560; Dabney, *Syst. and Polem. Theol.,* pp. 660-687; Strong, *Syst. Theol.,* pp. 869-881; Alexander, *Syst. of Bibl. Theol.* II, pp. 428-459; Litton, *Introd. to Dogm. Theol.,* pp. 322-337; Schmid, *Doct.*

1. *Syst. Theol.,* p. 876.

Theol. of the Ev. Luth. Church, pp. 491-503; Valentine, *Chr. Theol.* II, pp. 272-277; Pieper, *Chr. Dogmatik* III, pp. 1-106; Watson, *Theol. Institutes* III, pp. 197-206; Curtiss, *The Chr. Faith*, pp. 373-393; Pope, *Chr. Theol.* III, pp. 28-99; Candlish, *The Chr. Salvation*, pp. 110-133; Impeta, *De Leer der Heiliging and Volmaking bij Wesley and Fletcher*; Clarke, *An Outline of Chr. Theol.*, pp. 409-427; Wilmers, *Handbook of the Chr. Rel.*, pp. 293-304; Moehler, *Symbolism*, pp. 157-175; Finney, *Syst. Theol.* pp. 402-481; Starbuck, *The Psych. of Rel.*, pp. 375-391; Koberle, *The Quest of Holiness*; Warfield, *Studies in Perfectionism* (2 vols.); Newton Flew, *The Idea of Perfection in Christian Theology*.

XI. Perseverance of the Saints.

A. The Doctrine of the Perseverance of the Saints in History.

The doctrine of the perseverance of the saints is to the effect that they whom God has regenerated and effectually called to a state of grace, can neither totally nor finally fall away from that state, but shall certainly persevere therein to the end and be eternally saved. This doctrine was first explicitly taught by Augustine, though he was not as consistent on this point as might have been expected of him as a strict predestinarian. With him the doctrine did not assume the form just stated. He held that the elect could not so fall away as to be finally lost, but at the same time considered it possible that some who were endowed with new life and true faith could fall from grace completely and at last suffer eternal damnation. The Church of Rome with its Semi-Pelagianism, including the doctrine of free will, denied the doctrine of the perseverance of the saints and made their perseverance dependent on the uncertain obedience of man. The Reformers restored this doctrine to its rightful place. The Lutheran Church, however, makes it uncertain again by making it contingent on man's continued activity of faith, and by assuming that true believers can fall completely from grace. It is only in the Calvinistic Churches that the doctrine is maintained in a form in which it affords absolute assurance. The Canons of Dort, after calling attention to the many weaknesses and failures of the children of God, declare: "But God, who is rich in mercy, according to His unchangeable purpose of election, does not wholly withdraw the Holy Spirit from His own people even in their grievous falls; nor suffers them to proceed so far as to lose the grace of adoption and forfeit the state of justification, or to commit the sin unto death or against the Holy Spirit; nor does He permit them to be totally deserted, and to plunge themselves into everlasting destruction."[1] The Arminians rejected this view and made the perseverance of believers dependent on their will to believe and on their good works. Arminius himself avoided that extreme, but his followers did did not hesitate to maintain their synergistic position with all its consequences. The Wesleyan Arminians followed suit as did several of the sects. The Reformed or Calvinistic Churches stand practically alone in giving a negative answer to the question, whether a Christian can completely fall from the state of grace and be finally lost.

B. Statement of the Doctrine of Perseverance.

The doctrine of perseverance requires careful statement, especially in view of the fact that the term "perseverance of the saints" is liable to misunder-

---

1. V, Art. 6.

standing. It should be noted first of all that the doctrine is not merely to the effect that the elect will certainly be saved in the end, though Augustine has given it that form, but teaches very specifically that they who have once been regenerated and effectually called by God to a state of grace, can never completely fall from that state and thus fail to attain to eternal salvation, though they may sometimes be overcome by evil and fall in sin. It is maintained that the life of regeneration and the habits that develop out of it in the way of sanctification can never entirely disappear. Moreover, we should guard against the possible misunderstanding that this perseverance is regarded as an inherent property of the believer or as a continuous activity of man, by means of which he perseveres in the way of salvation. When Strong speaks of it as "the voluntary continuance, on the part of the Christian, in faith and well-doing," and as "the human side or aspect of that spiritual process which, as viewed from the divine side, we call sanctification," — this is certainly liable to create the impression that perseverance depends on man. The Reformed, however, do not consider the perseverance of the saints as being, first of all, a disposition or activity of the believer, though they certainly believe that man co-operates in it just as he does in sanctification. They even stress the fact that the believer would fall away, if he were left to himself. It is, strictly speaking, not man but God who perseveres. Perseverance may be defined as *that continuous operation of the Holy Spirit in the believer, by which the work of divine grace that is begun in the heart, is continued and brought to completion.* It is because God never forsakes His work that believers continue to stand to the very end.

C. Proof for the Doctrine of Perseverance.

The doctrine of perseverance may be proved by certain statements of Scripture and by inference from other doctrines.

1. DIRECT STATEMENTS OF SCRIPTURE. There are some important passages of Scripture that come into consideration here. In John 10:27-29 we read: "My sheep hear my voice, and I know them, and they follow me; and I give unto them eternal life; and they shall never perish, and no one shall snatch them out my hand. My Father, who hath given them unto me, is greater than all; and no one is able to snatch them out of the Father's hand." Paul says in Rom. 11:29: "For the gifts and the calling of God are not repented of." This means that the grace of God revealed in His calling is never withdrawn, as though He repented of it. This is a general statement, though in the connection in which it is found it refers to the calling of Israel. The apostle comforts the believing Philippians with the words: "Being confident of this very thing, that He who began a good work in you will perfect it unto the day of Jesus Christ," Phil. 1:6. In II Thess. 3:3 he says: "But the Lord is faithful, who shall establish you, and guard you from the evil one." In II Tim. 1:12 he sounds a note of rejoicing: "For I know Him whom I have believed, and I am persuaded that He is able to guard that which I have committed unto Him against that day." And in 4:18 of the same Epistle he glories in the fact that

the Lord will deliver him from every evil work and will save him unto His heavenly kingdom.

2. INFERENTIAL PROOFS. The doctrine of perseverance may also be proved in an inferential way.

a. *From the doctrine of election.* Election does not merely mean that some will be favored with certain external privileges and *may be saved,* if they do their duty, but that they who belong to the number of the elect shall finally be saved and can never fall short of perfect salvation. It is an election unto an end, that is, unto salvation. In working it out God endows believers with such influences of the Holy Spirit as to lead them, not only to accept Christ, but to persevere unto the end and to be saved unto the uttermost.

b. *From the doctrine of the covenant of redemption.* In the covenant of redemption God gave His people to His Son as the reward for the latter's obedience and suffering. This reward was fixed from eternity and was not left contingent on any uncertain faithfulness of man. God does not go back on His promise, and therefore it is impossible that they who are reckoned as being in Christ, and as forming a part of His reward, can be separated from Him (Rom. 8:38,39), and that they who have entered the covenant as a communion of life should fall out.

c. *From the efficacy of the merits and intercession of Christ.* In His atoning work Christ paid the price to purchase the sinner's pardon and acceptance. His righteousness constitutes the perfect ground for the justification of the sinner, and it is impossible that one who is justified by the payment of such a perfect and efficacious price should again fall under condemnation. Moreover, Christ makes constant intercession for those who are given Him of the Father, and His intercessory prayer for His people is always efficacious, John 11:42; Heb. 7:25.

d. *From the mystical union with Christ.* They who are united to Christ by faith become partakers of His Spirit, and thus become one body with Him, pulsating with the life of the Spirit. They share in the life of Christ, and because He lives they live also. It is impossible that they should again be removed from the body, thus frustrating the divine ideal. The union is permanent, since it originates in a permanent and unchangeable cause, the free and eternal love of God.

e. *From the work of the Holy Spirit in the heart.* Dabney correctly says: "It is a low and unworthy estimate of the wisdom of the Holy Spirit and of His work in the heart, to suppose that He will begin the work now, and presently desert it; that the vital spark of heavenly birth is an *ignis fatuus,* burning for a short season, and then expiring in utter darkness; that the spiritual life communicated in the new birth, is a sort of spasmodic or galvanic vitality, giving the outward appearance of life in the dead soul, and then dying."[1]

1. *Syst. and Polem. Theol.,* p. 692.

According to Scripture the believer is already in this life in possession of salvation and eternal life, John 3:36; 5:24; 6:54. Can we proceed on the assumption that eternal life will not be everlasting?

f. *From the assurance of salvation.* It is quite evident from Scripture that. believers can in this life attain to the assurance of salvation, Heb. 3:14; 6:11; 10:22; II Pet. 1:10. This would seem to be entirely out of the question, if it were possible for believers to fall from grace at any moment. It can be enjoyed only by those who stand in the firm conviction that God will perfect the work which He has begun.

D. Objections to the Doctrine of Perseverance.

1. IT IS INCONSISTENT WITH HUMAN FREEDOM. It is said that the doctrine of perseverance is inconsistent with human freedom. But this objection proceeds on the false assumption that real freedom consists in the liberty of indifference, or the power of contrary choice in moral and spiritual matters. This is erroneous, however. True liberty consists exactly in self-determination in the direction of holiness. Man is never more free than when he moves consciously in the direction of God. And the Christian stands in that liberty through the grace of God.

2. IT LEADS TO INDOLENCE AND IMMORALITY. It is confidently asserted that the doctrine of perseverance leads to indolence, license, and even immorality. A false security is said to result from it. This is a mistaken notion, however, for, although the Bible tells us that we are kept by the grace of God, it does not encourage the idea that God keeps us without constant watchfulness, diligence, and prayer on our part. It is hard to see how a doctrine which assures the believer of a perseverance in holiness can be an incentive for sin. It would seem that the certainty of success in the active striving for sanctification would be the best possible stimulus to ever greater exertion.

3. IT IS CONTRARY TO SCRIPTURE. The doctrine is frequently declared to be contrary to Scripture. The passages adduced to prove this contention can be reduced to three classes.

a. There are warnings against apostasy which would seem to be quite uncalled for, if the believer could not fall away, Matt. 24:12; Col. 1:23; Heb. 2:1; 3:14; 6:11; I John 2:6. But these warnings regard the whole matter from the side of man and are seriously meant. They prompt self-examination, and are instrumental in keeping believers in the way of perseverance. They do not prove that any of those addressed will apostatize, but simply that the use of means is necessary to prevent them from committing this sin. Compare Acts 27:22-25 with verse 31 for an illustration of this principle.

b. There are also exhortations, urging believers to continue in the way of sanctification, which would appear to be unnecessary if there is no doubt about it that they will continue to the end. But these are usually found in connection with such warnings as those referred to under (a), and serve exactly the same purpose. They do not prove that any of the believers exhorted will not persevere, but only that God uses moral means for the accomplishment of moral ends.

c. Again, it is said that Scripture records several cases of actual apostasy, I Tim. 1:19,20; II Tim. 2:17,18; 4:10; II Peter 2:1,2; cf. also Heb. 6:4-6. But these instances do not prove the contention that real believers, in possession of true saving faith, can fall from grace, unless it be shown first that the persons indicated in these passages had true faith in Christ, and not a mere temporal faith, which is not rooted in regeneration. The Bible teaches us that there are persons who profess the true faith, and yet are not of the faith, Rom. 9-6; I John 2:19; Rev. 3:1. John says of some of them, "They went out from us," and adds by way of explanation, "but they were not of us; for if they had been of us, they would have remained with us," I John 2:19.

E. The Denial of this Doctrine Makes Salvation Dependent on Man's Will.

The denial of the doctrine of perseverance virtually makes the salvation of man dependent on the human will rather than on the grace of God. This consideration will, of course, have no effect on those who share the Pelagian conception of salvation as autosoteric — and their numbers are great — but certainly ought to cause those to pause who glory in being saved by grace. The idea is that, after man is brought to a state of grace by the operation of the Holy Spirit alone, or by the joint operation of the Holy Spirit and the will of man, it rests solely with man to continue in faith or to forsake the faith, just as he sees fit. This renders the cause of man very precarious and makes it impossible for him to attain to the blessed assurance of faith. Consequently, it is of the utmost importance to maintain the doctrine of perseverance. In the words of Hovey, "It may be a source of great comfort and power, — an incentive to gratitude, a motive to self-sacrifice, and a pillar of fire in the hour of danger."

QUESTIONS FOR FURTHER STUDY: What is the real question concerning perseverance: is it whether the *elect*, or whether the *regenerate* persevere? Do Augustine and the Lutherans also teach that the *elect* may finally be lost? How does the analogy of the natural life favor the doctrine of perseverance? Do not such passages as Heb. 6:4-6; 10:29; II Pet. 2:1 prove the possibility of falling away? How about John 15:1-6? Is the grace of perseverance something innate, necessarily given with the new nature, or is it the fruit of a special, gracious, and preserving activity of God? Does the doctrine imply that one may be living in habitual and intentional sin, and yet be in a justified state? Does it preclude the idea of lapses into sin?

LITERATURE: Bavinck, *Geref. Dogm. IV*, pp. 289-294; Vos, *Geref. Dogm. IV.*, pp. 248-260; Dabney, *Syst. and Polem. Theol.*, pp. 687-698; Dick, *Theology, Lect. LXXIX*; Litton, *Introd. to Dogm. Theol.*, pp. 338-343; Finney, *Syst. Theol.*, pp. 544-619; Hovey, *Manual of Theology and Ethics*, pp. 295-299; Pieper, *Christ. Dogm. III*, pp. 107-120; Pope *Chr. Theol.* III, pp. 131-147; Meijering, *De Dordtsche Leerregels*, pp. 256-354; Bos, *De Dordtsche Leerregelen*, pp. 199-255.

THE DOCTRINE OF THE CHURCH AND
OF THE MEANS OF GRACE

THE CHURCH

Introduction

The doctrine of the application of the merits of Christ naturally leads on to the doctrine of the Church, for the Church consists of those who are partakers of Christ and of the blessings of salvation that are in Him. The Reformed conception is that Christ, by the operation of the Holy Spirit, unites men with Himself, endows them with true faith, and thus constitutes the Church as His body, the *communio fidelium* or *sanctorum*. In Roman Catholic theology, however, the discussion of the Church takes precedence over everything else, preceding even the discussion of the doctrine of God and of divine revelation. The Church, it is said, has been instrumental in producing the Bible and therefore takes precedence over it; it is moreover the dispenser of all supernatural graces. It is not Christ that leads us to the Church, but the Church that leads us to Christ. All the emphasis falls, not on the invisible Church as the *communio fidelium,* but on the visible Church as the *mater fidelium.* The Reformation broke with this Roman Catholic view of the Church and centered attention once more on the Church as a spiritual organism. It emphasized the fact that there is no Church apart from the redemptive work of Christ and from the renewing operations of the Holy Spirit; and that, therefore, the discussion of these logically precedes the consideration of the doctrine of the Church.

It seems rather peculiar that practically all the outstanding Presbyterian dogmaticians of our country, such as the two Hodges, H. B. Smith, Shedd, and Dabney, have no separate locus on the Church in their dogmatical works and, in fact, devote very little attention to it. Only the works of Thornwell and Breckenridge form an exception to the rule. This might create the impression that, in their opinion, the doctrine of the Church should not have a place in dogmatics. But this is extremely unlikely, since none of them raise a single objection to its inclusion. Moreover, Turretin and their Scottish forbears, on whose foundation they are building, devote a great deal of attention to the Church. Walker says: "There is perhaps no country in the world in which all kinds of Church questions have been so largely discussed as in our own."[1] And, finally, Dr. A. A. Hodge informs us that his father lectured to his various classes on the subjects of Ecclesiology, practically covered the entire ground,

---

1. *Scottish Theology and Theologians,* p. 95; cf. also McPherson, *The Doctrine of the Church in Scottish Theology,* pp. 1 ff.

and intended to complete his Systematic Theology by the publication of a fourth volume on the Church; but was prevented by the infirmities incident to his advanced age.[1] Dabney says that he omitted the doctrine of the Church, because this was ably treated in another department of the Seminary in which he labored.[2] Shedd in giving his scheme asserts that the Church comes into consideration in connection with the means of grace.[3] However, he devotes very little attention to the means of grace and does not discuss the doctrine of the Church. And the editor of Smith's *System of Christian Theology* incorporated into this work the author's views on the Church, as expressed in other works.[4]

---

1. *Preface* to Hodge's work on *Church Polity*.
2. *Lect. on Theol.*, p. 726.
3. *Dogm. Theol.* I, p. 10.
4. pp. 590 ff.

I. Scriptural Names of the Church and the Doctrine
of the Church in History

A. Scriptural Names for the Church.

I. IN THE OLD TESTAMENT. The Old Testament employs two words to designate the Church, namely *qahal* (or *kahal*), derived from an obsolete root *qal* (or *kal*), meaning "to call"; and *'edhah*, from *ya'adh*, "to appoint" or "to meet or come together at an appointed place." These two words are some-times used indiscriminately, but were not, at first, strictly synonymous. *'Edhah* is properly a gathering by appointment, and when applied to Israel, denotes the society itself formed by the children of Israel or their representative heads, whether assembled or not assembled. *Qahal*, on the other hand, properly denotes the actual meeting together of the people. Consequently we find occasionally the expression *qehal 'edhah*, that is, "the assembly of the congre-gation" Ex. 12:6; Num. 14:5; Jer. 26:17. It seems that the actual meeting was sometimes a meeting of the representatives of the people, Deut. 4:10; 18:16, comp. 5:22,23; I Kings 8:1,2,3,5; II Chron. 5:2-6. *'Edhah* is by far the more common word in Exodus, Leviticus, Numbers, and Joshua, but is wholly absent from Deuteronomy, and is found but rarely in the later books. *Qahal*, abounds in Chronicles, Ezra, and Nehemiah. *Sunagoge* is the usual, almost universal, rendering of the former in the Septuagint, and is also the usual rendering of the latter in the Pentateuch. In the later books of the Bible, however, *qahal* is generally rendered by *ekklesia*. Schuerer claims that later Judaism already pointed to the distinction between *sunagoge* as a desig-nation of the congregation of Israel as an empirical reality, and *ekklesia* as the name of that same congregation ideally considered. He is followed in this by Dr. Bavinck. Cremer-Koegel, however, takes exception to this. Hort says that after the exile the word *qahal* seems to have combined the shades of meaning belonging to both it and *'edhah;* and that consequently "*ekklesia*, as the primary Greek representative of *qahal*, would naturally, for Greek-speaking Jews, mean the congregation of Israel quite as much as an assembly of the congregation."[1]

2. IN THE NEW TESTAMENT. The New Testament also has two words, derived from the Septuagint, namely, *ekklesia*, from *ek* and *kaleo*, "to call out," and *sunagoge*, from *sun* and *ago*, meaning "to come or to bring together." The latter is used exclusively to denote either the religious gatherings of the Jews or the buildings in which they assembled for public worship, Matt. 4:23; Acts 13:43; Rev. 2:9; 3:9. The term *ekklesia*, however, generally designates

---

1. *The Christian Ekklesia*, p. 7.

the Church of the New Testament, though in a few places it denotes common civil assemblies. Acts 19:32,39,41. The preposition *ek* in *ekklesia* (*ekkaleo*) is often interpreted to mean "out from among the common mass of the people," and to indicate in connection with the Scriptural use of *ekklesia*, that the Church consists of the elect, called out of the world of humanity. This interpretation is rather doubtful, however, for the preposition originally simply denoted that the Greek citizens were called out of their houses. Now it would not have been unnatural if that entirely Scriptural idea had been put into the word in God's revelation. But, as a matter of fact, we have no proof that this was actually done. The compound verb *ekkaleo* is never so used, and the word *ekklesia* never occurs in a context which suggests the presence of that particular thought in the mind of the writer. Deissmann would simply render *ekklesia* as "the (convened) assembly," regarding God as the convener. Because the idea of the Church is a many-sided concept, it is quite natural that the word *ekklesia*, as applied to it, does not always have exactly the same connotation. Jesus was the first one to use the word in the New Testament, and He applied it to the company that gathered about Him, Matt. 16:18, recognized Him publicly as their Lord, and accepted the principles of the Kingdom of God. It was the *ekklesia* of the Messiah, the true Israel. Later on, as a result of the extension of the Church, the word acquired various significations. Local churches were established everywhere, and were also called *ekklesiai*, since they were manifestations of the one universal Church of Christ. The following are the most important uses of the word:

a. Most frequently the word *ekklesia* designates a circle of believers in some definite locality, a local church, irrespective of the question whether these believers are or are not assembled for worship. Some passages contain the added idea that they are assembled, Acts 5:11; 11:26; I Cor. 11:18; 14:19,28,35, while others do not, Rom. 16:4; I Cor. 16:1; Gal. 1:2; I Thess. 2:14, etc.

b. In some cases the word denotes what may be called a domestic *ekklesia*, the church in the house of some individual. It seems that in apostolic times wealthy or otherwise important persons often set aside a large room in their homes for divine worship. Instances of this use of the word are found in Rom. 16:23; I Cor. 16:19; Col. 4:15; Philemon 2.

c. If the reading of Tisschendorf is correct (as is now generally taken for granted), then the word is found at least once in the singular to denote a group of churches, namely, the churches of Judea, Galilee, and Samaria. The passage in which it is so used is Acts 9:31. Naturally, this does not yet mean that they together constituted an organization such as we now call a denomination. It is not impossible that the church of Jerusalem and the church of Antioch in Syria also comprised several groups that were accustomed to meet in different places.

d. In a more general sense the word serves to denote the whole body, throughout the world, of those who outwardly profess Christ and organize for purposes of worship, under the guidance of appointed officers. This meaning of the word is somewhat in the foreground in the First Epistle to the Corinthians, 10:32; 11:22; 12:28, but was, it would seem, present also in the mind of Paul, when he wrote the letter to the Ephesians, though in that letter the emphasis is on the Church as a spiritual organism, cf. especially Eph. 4:11-16.

e. Finally, the word in its most comprehensive meaning signifies the whole body of the faithful, whether in heaven or on earth, who have been or shall be spiritually united to Christ as their Saviour. This use of the word is found primarily in the Epistles of Paul to the Ephesians and the Colossians, most frequently in the former, Eph. 1:22; 3:10,21; 5:23-25, 27, 32; Col. 1:18,24.

We should bear in mind that the names "Church," "Kerk" and "Kirche" are not derived from the word *ekklesia*, but from the word *kuriake*, which means "belonging to the Lord." They stress the fact that the Church is the property of God. The name *to kuriakon* or *he kuriake* first of all designated the place where the Church assembled. This place was conceived of as belonging to the Lord, and was therefore called *to kuriakon*. But the place itself was empty and did not really become manifest as *to kuriakon* until the Church gathered for worship. Consequently, the word was transferred to the Church itself, the spiritual building of God.

3. OTHER BIBLICAL DESIGNATIONS OF THE CHURCH. The New Testament contains several figurative designations of the Church, each one of which stresses some particular aspect of the Church. It is called:

a. *The body of Christ.* Some in our day seem to regard this appellation as a complete definition of the New Testament Church, but it is not so intended. The name is applied not only to the Church universal, as in Eph. 1:23; Col. 1:18, but also to a single congregation, I Cor. 12:27. It stresses the unity of the Church, whether local or universal, and particularly the fact that this unity is organic, and that the organism of the Church stands in vital relationship to Jesus Christ as her glorious head.

b. *The temple of the Holy Spirit or of God.* The church of Corinth is called "a temple of God," in which the Holy Spirit dwelleth, I Cor. 3:16. In Ephesians 2:21,22 Paul speaks of believers as growing into "a holy temple in the Lord," and as being built together for "a habitation of God in the Spirit." There the name is applied to the ideal Church of the future, which is the church universal. And Peter says that believers as living stones are built up "a spiritual house," I Pet. 2:5. The connection clearly shows that he is thinking of a temple. This figure emphasizes the fact that the Church is holy and inviolable. The indwelling of the Holy Spirit imparts to her an exalted character.

c. *The Jerusalem that is above, or the new Jerusalem, or the heavenly Jerusalem.* All three of these forms are found in the Bible, Gal. 4:26; Heb. 12:22; Rev. 21:2, cf. the verses 9 and 10. In the Old Testament Jerusalem is represented as the place where God dwelt between the cherubim and where He symbolically established contact with His people. The New Testament evidently regards the Church as the spiritual counterpart of the Old Testament Jerusalem, and therefore applies to it the same name. According to this representation the Church is the dwelling place of God, in which the people of God are brought into communion with Him; and this dwelling place, while still in part on earth, belongs to the heavenly sphere.

d. *Pillar and ground of the truth.* There is just one place in which that name is applied to the Church, namely, I Tim. 3:15. It clearly refers to the Church in general, and therefore also applies to every part of it. The figure is expressive of the fact that the Church is the guardian of the truth, the citadel of the truth, and the defender of the truth over against all the enemies of the Kingdom of God.

B. The Doctrine of the Church in History.

1. THE DOCTRINE OF THE CHURCH BEFORE THE REFORMATION.

a. *In the patristic period.* By the Apostolic Fathers and by the Apologetes the Church is generally represented as the *communio sanctorum*, the people of God which He has chosen for a possession. The necessity for making distinctions was not at once apparent. But as early as the latter part of the second century there was a perceptible change. The rise of heresies made it imperative to name some characteristics by which the *true* catholic Church could be known. This tended to fix the attention on the outward manifestation of the Church. The Church began to be conceived as an external institution, ruled by a bishop as a direct successor of the apostles, and in possession of the true tradition. The catholicity of the Church was rather strongly emphasized. Local churches were not regarded as so many separate units, but simply as parts of the one universal Church. The increasing worldliness and corruption of the Church gradually led to reaction and gave rise to the tendency of various sects, such as Montanism in the middle of the second, Novatianism in the middle of the third, and Donatism at the beginning of the fourth century, to make the holiness of its members the mark of the true Church. The early Church Fathers, in combating these sectaries, emphasized ever increasingly the episcopal institution of the Church. Cyprian has the distinction of being the first to develop fully the doctrine of the episcopal Church. He regarded the bishops as the real successors of the apostles and ascribed to them a priestly character in virtue of their sacrificial work. They together formed a college, called the episcopate, which as such constituted the unity of the Church. The unity of the Church was thus based on the unity of the bishops. They who do not subject themselves to the bishop forfeit the fellowship of the Church and also their salvation, since there is no salvation outside of the Church. Augustine was not altogether consistent in his conception of the Church. It was his struggle with the Donatists that compelled him to reflect more deeply on the nature of the Church. On the one hand he shows himself to be the predestinarian, who conceives of the Church as the company of the elect, the *communio sanctorum*, who have the Spirit of God and are therefore characterized by true love. The important thing is to be a living member of the Church so conceived, and not to belong to it in a merely external sense. But on the other hand he is the Church-man, who adheres to the Cyprianic idea of the Church at least in its general aspects. The true Church is the catholic Church, in which the apostolic authority is continued by episcopal succession. It is the depositary of divine grace, which it distributes through the sacraments. For the present this Church is a mixed body, in which good and evil members have a place. In his debate with the Donatists he admitted, however, that the two were not in the Church in the same sense. He also prepared the way for the Roman Catholic identification of the Church and the Kingdom of God.

b. *In the Middle Ages.* The Scholastics have very little to say about the Church. The system of doctrine developed by Cyprian and Augustine was fairly complete and needed but a few finishing touches to bring it to its final development. Says Otten (Roman Catholic historian): "This system was taken over by the Scholastics of the Middle Ages, and then was handed down by them, practically in the same condition in which they had received it, to their successors who came after the Council of Trent."[1] Incidentally a few points were somewhat further developed. But if there was very little development in the *doctrine* of the Church, the Church itself actually developed more and more into a close-knit, compactly organized, and absolute hierarchy. The seeds of this development were already present in the Cyprianic idea of the Church and in one aspect of the Church as represented by Augustine. The other and more fundamental idea of that great Church Father, that of the Church as the *communio sanctorum*, was generally disregarded and thus remained dormant. This is not saying that the Scholastics denied the spiritual element altogether, but merely that they did not give it due prominence. The emphasis was very definitely on the Church as an external organization or institution. Hugo of St. Victor speaks of the Church and the State as the two powers instituted by God for the government of the people. Both are monarchical in constitution, but the Church is the higher power, because she ministers to the salvation of men, while the State only provides for their temporal welfare. The king or emperor is the head of the state, but the Pope is the head of the Church. There are two classes of people in the Church with well defined rights and duties: the clerics, dedicated to the service of God, who constitute a unit; and the laics consisting of people from every domain of life, who constitute a separate class altogether. Step by step the doctrine of the papacy came to development, until at last the Pope became virtually an absolute monarch. The growth of this doctrine was in no small measure aided by the development of the idea that the Catholic Church was the Kingdom of God on earth, and that

---

1. *Manual of the History of Dogmas*, II, p. 214.

therefore the Roman bishopric was an earthly kingdom. This identification of the visible and organized Church with the Kingdom of God had far-reaching consequences: (1) It required that everything be brought under the control of the Church: the home and the school, science and art, commerce and industry, and so on. (2) It involved the idea that all the blessings of salvation come to man only through the ordinances of the Church, particularly through the sacraments. (3) It led to the gradual secularization of the Church, since the Church began to pay more attention to politics than to the salvation of sinners, and the Popes finally claimed dominion also over secular rulers.

2. THE DOCTRINE OF THE CHURCH DURING AND AFTER THE REFORMATION.

a. *During the period of the Reformation.* The Reformers broke with the Roman Catholic conception of the Church, but differed among themselves in some particulars. The idea of an infallible and hierarchical Church, and of a special priesthood, which dispenses salvation through the sacraments, found no favor with Luther. He regarded the Church as the spiritual communion of those who believe in Christ, and restored the Scriptural idea of the priesthood of all believers. He maintained the unity of the Church, but distinguished two aspects of it, the one visible and the other invisible. He was careful to point out that these are not two churches, but simply two aspects of the same Church. The invisible Church becomes visible, not by the rule of bishops and cardinals, nor in the headship of the Pope, but by the pure administration of the Word and of the sacraments. He admitted that the visible Church will always contain a mixture of pious and wicked members. However, in his reaction against the Roman Catholic idea of the domination of the Church over the State, he went to another extreme, and virtually made the Church subject to the State in everything except the preaching of the Word. The Anabaptists were not satisfied with his position, and insisted on a Church of believers only. They, in many instances, even scorned the visible Church and the means of grace. Moreover, they demanded the complete separation of Church and State. Calvin and Reformed theologians were at one with Luther in the confession that the Church is essentially a *communio sanctorum*, a communion of saints. However, they did not, like the Lutherans, seek the unity and the holiness of the Church primarily in the objective ordinances of the Church, such as the offices, the Word, and the sacraments, but most of all in the subjective communion of believers. They, too, distinguished between a visible and an invisible aspect of the Church, though in a slightly different way. Moreover, they found the true marks of the Church, not only in the true administration of the Word and of the sacraments, but also in the faithful administration of Church discipline. But even Calvin and the Reformed theologians of the seventeenth century in a measure fostered the idea of the subjection of the Church to the state. However, they established a form of government in the Church which made for a greater degree of ecclesiastical independence and power than was known in the Lutheran Church. But while both Lutheran and Reformed theologians sought to maintain the proper connection between the visible and the invisible Church, others lost sight of this. The Socinians and the Arminians of the seventeenth century, though indeed speaking of an invisible Church, forgot all about it in actual life. The former conceived of the Christian religion simply as an acceptable doctrine, and the latter made the Church primarily a visible society and followed the Lutheran Church by yielding the right of discipline to the State and retaining for the Church only the right to preach the gospel and to admonish the members of the Church. The Labadists and Pietists, on the other hand, manifested a tendency to disregard the visible Church, seeking a Church of believers only, showing themselves indifferent to the institutional Church with its mixture of good and evil, and seeking edification in conventicles.

b. *During and after the eighteenth century.* During the eighteenth century Rationalism made its influence felt also in the doctrine of the Church. It was indifferent in matters of faith and lacked enthusiasm for the Church, which it placed on a par with other human societies. It even denied that Christ intended to found a church in the received sense of the word. There was a pietistic reaction to Rationalism in Methodism, but Methodism did not contribute anything to the development of the doctrine of the Church. In some cases it sought strength in casting reflection on the existing Churches, and in others it adapted itself to the life of these Churches. For Schleiermacher the Church was essentially the Christian community, the body of believers who are animated by the same spirit. He had little use for the distinction between the visible and the invisible Church, and found the essence of the Church in the spirit of Christian fellowship. The more the Spirit of God penetrates the mass of Christian believers, the fewer divisions there will be, and the more they will lose their importance. Ritschl substituted for the distinction between the invisible and the visible Church that between the Kingdom and the Church. He regarded the Kingdom as the community of God's people acting from the motive of love, and the Church as that same community met for worship. The name "Church" is therefore restricted to an external organization *in the one function of worship;* and this function merely enables believers to become better acquainted with one another. This is certainly far from the teaching of the New Testament. It leads right on to the modern liberal conception of the Church as a mere social center, a human institution rather than a planting of God.

QUESTIONS FOR FURTHER STUDY: Does the history of the Church begin at or before the day of Pentecost? If it existed before, how did the Church preceding that day differ from the Church following it? To what Church does Jesus refer in Matt. 18:17? Did Augustine identify the Church as a spiritual organism, or the Church as an external institution, with the Kingdom of God? How do you account for the Roman Catholic emphasis on the Church as an external organization? Why did not the Reformers insist on entire freedom of the Church from the State? How did Luther and Calvin differ in this respect? What controversies respecting the Church arose in Scotland? What accounts for the different conceptions of the Church in England and in Scotland? How did Rationalism affect the doctrine of the Church? What great dangers are threatening the Church at the present time?

LITERATURE: Bavinck, *Geref. Dogm.* IV, pp. 302-319; Innes, *Church and State;* Cunningham, *Historical Theology,* two volumes, cf. the Index; Hauck, *Real-Encyclopaedie,* Art. *Kirche* by Koestlin; *Histories of Dogma,* especially those of Harnack, Seeberg, Sheldon, and Otten, cf. the Indices.

II. Nature of the Church

A. The Essence of the Church.

1. THE ROMAN CATHOLIC CONCEPTION. The early Christians spoke of the Church as the *communio sanctorum*, and thus already, though without having thought the matter through, gave expression to the essence of the Church. But even as early as the end of the second century, as the result of the rise of heresies, the question as to the true Church forced itself upon them and caused them to fix their attention upon certain characteristics of the Church as an external institution. From the days of Cyprian down to the Reformation the essence of the Church was sought ever increasingly in its external visible organization. The Church Fathers conceived of the catholic Church as comprehending all true branches of the Church of Christ, and as bound together in an external and visible unity, which had its unifying bond in the college of bishops. The conception of the Church as an external organization became more prominent as time went on. There was an ever growing emphasis on the hierarchical organization of it, and the capstone was added with the institution of the Papacy. Roman Catholics now define the Church as: *"The congregation of all the Faithful, who, being baptized, profess the same faith, partake of the same sacraments, and are governed by their lawful pastors, under one visible head on earth."* They make a distinction between the *ecclesia docens* and the *ecclesia audiens*, that is, between "the Church consisting of those who rule, teach, and edify" and "the Church which is taught, governed, and receives the sacraments." In the strictest sense of the word it is not the *ecclesia audiens* but the *ecclesia docens* that constitutes the Church. The latter shares *directly* in the glorious attributes of the Church, but the former is adorned with them only indirectly. Catholics are willing to admit that there is an invisible side to the Church, but prefer to reserve the name "Church" for the visible communion of believers. They frequently speak of the "soul of the Church," but do not seem to be altogether agreed as to the exact connotation of the term. Devine defines the soul of the Church as "the society of those who are called to faith in Christ, and who are united to Christ by supernatural gifts and graces."[1] Wilmers, however, finds it in "all those spiritual, supernatural graces which constitute the Church of Christ, and enable its members to attain their last end." Says he: "What we call *soul* in general is that pervading principle which gives life to a body and enables its members to perform their peculiar functions. To the soul of the Church belong faith, the common aspiration of

---

1. *The Creed Explained*, p. 259.

all to the same end, the invisible authority of superiors, the inward grace of sanctification, the supernatural virtues, and other gifts of grace."[1] The former writer finds the soul of the Church in certain qualified persons, while the latter regards it as an all-pervading principle, something like the soul in man. But whatever Roman Catholics may be ready to grant, they will not admit that what may be called "the invisible Church" logically precedes the visible. Moehler says: "The Catholics teach: the visible Church is first,—then comes the invisible: the former gives birth to the latter." This means that the Church is a *mater fidelium* (mother of believers) before she is a *communio fidelium* (community of believers). Moehler grants, however, that there is one sense in which "the internal Church" is prior to "the exterior one," namely in the sense that we are not *living* members of the latter until we belong to the former. He discusses the whole subject of the relation of those two to each other in his *Symbolism or Doctrinal Differences*.[2] He stresses the identity of the visible Church with Christ: "Thus, the visible Church, from the point of view here taken, is the Son of God, everlastingly manifesting himself among men in a human form, perpetually renovated, and eternally young — the permanent incarnation of the same, as in Holy Writ, even the faithful are called 'the body of Christ.' "[3]

2. THE GREEK ORTHODOX CONCEPTION. The Greek Orthodox conception of the Church is closely related to that of the Roman Catholics, and yet differs from it in some important points. That Church does not recognize the Roman Catholic Church as the *true* Church, but claims that honor for itself. There is but one true Church, and that Church is the Greek Orthodox. While it acknowledges with greater frankness than the Roman Catholics the two different aspects of the Church, the visible and the invisible, it nevertheless places the emphasis on the Church as an external organization. It does not find the essence of the Church in her as the community of the saints, but in the Episcopal hierarchy, which it has retained, while rejecting the Papacy. The infallibility of the Church is maintained, but this infallibility resides in the bishops, and therefore in the ecclesiastical councils and synods. "As invisible," says Gavin, "she (the Church) is the bearer of divine gifts and powers, and is engaged in transforming mankind into the Kingdom of God. As visible, she is constituted of men professing a common faith, observing common customs, and using visible means of grace." At the same time the idea is rejected of "an invisible and ideal Church, of which the various bodies of Christians formed into distinct organizations and calling themselves 'Churches,' are partial and incomplete embodiments." The Church is "an actual, tangible, visible entity, not an unrealized and unrealizable ideal."[4]

3. THE PROTESTANT CONCEPTION. The Reformation was a reaction against the externalism of Rome in general, and in particular, also against its

---

1. *Handbook of the Christian Religion*, p. 103.
2. Chap. V, especially in the paragraphs XLVI-XLVIII.
3. p. 59.
4. *Greek Orthodox Thought*, pp. 241-242.

external conception of the Church. It brought the truth to the foreground once more that the essence of the Church is not found in the external organization of the Church, but in the Church as the *communio sanctorum*. For both Luther and Calvin the Church was simply the community of the saints, that is, the community of those who believe and are sanctified in Christ, and who are joined to Him as their Head. This is also the position taken in the Reformed confessional standards. Thus the Belgic Confession says: "We believe and profess one catholic or universal Church, which is a holy congregation of true Christian believers, all expecting their salvation in Jesus Christ, being washed by His blood, sanctified and sealed by the Holy Spirit."[1] The Second Helvetic Confession expresses the same truth by saying that the Church is "a company of the faithful, called and gathered out of the world; a communion of all saints, that is, of them who truly know and rightly worship and serve the true God, in Jesus Christ the Saviour, by the word of the Holy Spirit, and who by faith are partakers of all those good graces which are freely offered through Christ."[2] And the Westminster Confession, defining the Church from the point of view of election, says: "The catholic or universal Church, which is invisible, consists of the whole number of the elect, that have been, are, or shall be gathered into one, under Christ the head thereof; and is the spouse, the body, the fulness of Him that filleth all in all."[3] The Church universal, that is, the Church as it exists in the plan of God, and as it is realized only in the course of the ages, was conceived as consisting of the whole body of the elect, who are in course of time called unto life eternal. But the Church as it actually exists on earth was regarded as the community of the saints. And it was not only the invisible Church that was so regarded, but the visible Church as well. These are not two Churches but one, and therefore have but a single essence. The one as well as the other is *essentially* the *communio sanctorum*, but the invisible Church is the Church as God sees it, a Church which contains only believers, while the visible Church is the Church as man sees it, consisting of those who profess Jesus Christ with their children and therefore adjudged to be the community of the saints. This may and always does contain some who are not yet regenerated — there may be chaff among the wheat —, but may not tolerate public unbelievers and wicked persons. Paul addresses his Epistles to empirical churches, and does not hesitate to address them as "saints," but also insists on the necessity of putting away the wicked and those who give offense from among them, I Cor. 5; II Thess. 3:6,14: Tit. 3:10. The Church forms a spiritual unity of which Christ is the divine Head. It is animated by one Spirit, the Spirit of Christ; it professes one faith, shares one hope, and serves one King. It is the citadel of the truth and God's agency in communicating to believers all spiritual blessings. As the body of Christ it is destined to reflect the glory of God as manifested in the work of redemption. The Church in its ideal sense, the Church as God intends it to be

1. Art. XXVII.
2. Chap. XVII.
3. Chap. XXV.

and as it will once become, is an object of faith rather than of knowledge. Hence the confession: "I believe one holy catholic Church."

B. The Many-sided Character of the Church.

In speaking of the Church several distinctions come into consideration.

1. THAT OF A MILITANT AND A TRIUMPHANT CHURCH. The Church in the present dispensation is a militant Church, that is, she is called unto, and is actually engaged in, a holy warfare. This, of course, does not mean that she must spend her strength in self-destroying internecine struggles, but that she is duty bound to carry on an incessant warfare against the hostile world in every form in which it reveals itself, whether in the Church or outside of it, and against all the spiritual forces of darkness. The Church may not spend all her time in prayer and meditation, however necessary and important these may be, nor may she rest on her oars in the peaceful enjoyment of her spiritual heritage. She must be engaged with all her might in the battles of her Lord, fighting in a war that is both offensive and defensive. If the Church on earth is the militant Church, the Church in heaven is the triumphant Church. There the sword is exchanged for the palm of victory, the battle-cries are turned into songs of triumph, and the cross is replaced by the crown. The strife is over, the battle is won, and the saints reign with Christ forever and ever. In these two stages of her existence the Church reflects the humiliation and exaltation of her heavenly Lord. Roman Catholics speak, not only of a militant and triumphant, but also of a *suffering* Church. This Church, according to them, includes all those believers who are no more on earth, but have not yet entered the joys of heaven, and are now being purified in purgatory of their remaining sins.

2. THAT BETWEEN A VISIBLE AND AN INVISIBLE CHURCH. This means that the Church of God is on the one hand visible, and on the other invisible. It is said that Luther was the first to make this distinction, but the other Reformers recognized and also applied it to the Church. This distinction has not always been properly understood. The opponents of the Reformers often accused them of teaching that there are two separate Churches. Luther perhaps gave some occasion for this charge by speaking of an invisible *ecclesiola* within the visible *ecclesia*. But both he and Calvin stress the fact that, when they speak of a visible and an invisible Church, they do not refer to two different Churches, but to two aspects of the one Church of Jesus Christ. The term "invisible" has been variously interpreted as applying (a) to the triumphant Church; (b) to the ideal and completed Church as it will be at the end of the ages; (c) to the Church of all lands and all places, which man cannot possibly see; and (d) to the Church as it goes in hiding in the days of persecution, and is deprived of the Word and the sacraments. Now it is undoubtedly true that the triumphant Church is invisible to those who are on earth, and that Calvin in his Institutes also conceives of this as included in the invisible Church, but the distinction was undoubtedly primarily intended to apply to the militant Church. As a rule it is so applied in Reformed theology. It stresses the fact that the Church as it exists on earth is both visible and invisible. This Church is said

to be invisible, because she is essentially spiritual and in her spiritual essence cannot be discerned by the physical eye; and because it is impossible to determine infallibly who do and who do not belong to her. The union of believers with Christ is a mystical union; the Spirit that unites them constitutes an invisible tie; and the blessings of salvation, such as regeneration, genuine conversion, true faith, and spiritual communion with Christ, are all invisible to the natural eye; — and yet these things constitute the real *forma* (ideal character) of the Church. That the term "invisible" should be understood in this sense, is evident from the historical origin of the distinction between the visible and the invisible Church in the days of the Reformation. The Bible ascribes certain glorious attributes to the Church and represents her as a medium .of saving and eternal blessings. Rome applied this to the Church as an external institution, more particularly to the *ecclesia representativa* or the hierarchy as the distributor of the blessings of salvation, and thus ignored and virtually denied the immediate and direct communion of God with His children, by placing a human mediatorial priesthood between them. This is the error which the Reformers sought to eradicate by stressing the fact that the Church of which the Bible says such glorious things is not the Church as an external institution, but the Church as the spiritual body of Jesus Christ, which is essentially invisible at present, though it has a relative and imperfect embodiment in the visible Church and is destined to have a perfect visible embodiment at the end of the ages.

The invisible Church naturally assumes a visible form. Just as the human soul is adapted to a body and expresses itself through the body, so the invisible Church, consisting, not of mere souls but of human beings having souls and bodies, necessarily assumes a visible form in an external organization through which it expresses itself. The Church becomes visible in Christian profession and conduct, in the ministry of the Word and of the sacraments, and in external organization and government. By making this distinction between the invisible and the visible Church, McPherson says, "Protestantism sought to find the proper mean between the magical and supernatural externalism of the Romish idea and the extravagant depreciation of all outward rites, characteristic of fanatical and sectarian spiritualism."[1] It is very important to bear in mind that, though both the invisible and the visible Church can be considered as universal, the two are not in every respect commensurate. It is possible that some who belong to the invisible Church never become members of the visible organization, as missionary subjects who are converted on their deathbeds, and that others are temporarily excluded from it, as erring believers who are for a time shut out from the communion of the visible Church. On the other hand there may be unregenerated children and adults who, while professing Christ, have no true faith in Him, in the Church as an external institution; and these, as long as they are in that condition, do not belong to the invisible Church.

---

1. *Chr. Dogmatics*, p. 417.

Good definitions of the visible and invisible Church may be found in the Westminster Confession.

3. THAT BETWEEN THE CHURCH AS AN ORGANISM AND THE CHURCH AS AN INSTITUTION. This distinction should not be identified with the preceding one, as is sometimes done. It is a distinction that applies to the *visible* Church and that directs attention to two different aspects of the Church considered as a visible body.[1] It is a mistake to think that the Church becomes visible only in the offices, in the administration of the Word and the sacraments, and in a certain form of Church government. Even if all these things were absent, the Church would still be visible in the communal life and profession of the believers, and in their joint opposition to the world. But while emphasizing the fact that the distinction under consideration is a distinction within the visible Church, we should not forget that both the Church as an organism and the Church as an institution (also called *apparitio* and *institutio*) have their spiritual background in the invisible Church. However, though it is true that these are two different aspects of the one visible Church, they do represent important differences. The Church as an organism is the *coetus fidelium*, the communion of believers, who are united in the bond of the Spirit, while the Church as an institution is the *mater fidelium*, the mother of believers, a *Heilsanstalt*, a means of salvation, an agency for the conversion of sinners and the perfecting of the saints. The Church as an organism exists charismatic: in it all kinds of gifts and talents become manifest and are utilized in the work of the Lord. The Church as an institution, on the other hand, exists in an institutional form and functions through the offices and means which God has instituted. The two are co-ordinate in a sense, and yet there is also a certain subordination of the one to the other. The Church as an institution or organization (*mater fidelium*) is a means to an end, and this is found in the Church as an organism, the community of believers (*coetus fidelium*).

C. Various Definitions of the Church.

The Church being a many-sided entity has naturally also been defined from more than one point of view.

1. FROM THE POINT OF VIEW OF ELECTION. According to some theologians the Church is *the community of the elect*, the *coetus electorum*. This definition is apt to be somewhat misleading, however. It applies only to the Church *ideally considered*, the Church as it exists in the idea of God and as it will be completed at the end of the ages, and not to the Church as a present empirical reality. Election includes all those who belong to the body of Christ, irrespective of their present actual relation to it. But the elect who are yet unborn, or who are still strangers to Christ and outside of the pale of the Church, cannot be said to belong to the Church *realiter*.

1. Cf. Kuyper, *Enc. III*, p. 204; Bavinck, *Geref. Dogm.* IV., p. 331; Ten Hoor, *Afscheiding of Doleantie*, pp. 88 f.; Doekes, *De Moeder der Geloovigen*, pp. 10 f.; Steen, *De Kerk*, pp. 51 ff.

2. From the point of view of effectual calling. To escape the objection raised to the preceding definition, it gradually became customary to define the Church from the point of view of some subjective spiritual characteristic of those who belong to it, especially effectual calling or faith, either by naming such a characteristic in addition to election, or by substituting it for election. Thus the Church was defined as the company of the elect who are called by the Spirit of God (*coetus electorum vocatorum*), as the body of those who are effectually called (*coetus vocatorum*), or, even more commonly, as the community of the faithful or believers (*coetus fidelium*). The first two of these definitions serve the purpose of designating the Church as to its invisible essence, but give no indication whatsoever of the fact that it also has a visible side. This is done, however, in the last named definition, for faith reveals itself in confession and conduct.

3. From the point of view of baptism and profession. From the point of view of baptism and profession the Church has been defined as the community of those who are baptized and profess the true faith; or as the community of those who profess the true religion *together with their children*. It will readily be seen that this is a definition of the Church according to its external manifestation. Calvin defines the visible Church as "the multitude of men diffused through the world, who profess to worship one God in Christ; are initiated into this faith by baptism; testify their unity in doctrine and charity by participating in the Supper; have consent in the Word of God, and for the preaching of that Word maintain the ministry ordained of Christ."[1]

D. The Church and the Kingdom of God.

1. The idea of the Kingdom of God. The Kingdom of God is primarily an eschatological concept. The fundamental idea of the Kingdom in Scripture is not that of a restored theocratic kingdom of God in Christ — which is essentially a kingdom of Israel—, as the Premillenarians claim; neither is it a new social condition, pervaded by the Spirit of Christ, and realized by man through such external means as good laws, civilization, education, social reforms, and so on, as the Modernists would have us believe. The primary idea of the Kingdom of God in Scripture is that of the rule of God established and acknowledged in the hearts of sinners by the powerful regenerating influence of the Holy Spirit, insuring them of the inestimable blessings of salvation, — a rule that is realized in principle on earth, but will not reach its culmination until the visible and glorious return of Jesus Christ. The present realization of it is spiritual and invisible. Jesus took hold of this eschatological concept and made it prominent in His teachings. He clearly taught the present spiritual realization and the universal character of the Kingdom. Moreover, He Himself effected that realization in a measure formerly unknown and greatly increased the present blessings of the Kingdom. At the same time He held out the blessed hope of the future appearance of that Kingdom in external glory and with the perfect blessings of salvation.

---

1. *Institutes* IV., 1,7.

2. HISTORICAL CONCEPTIONS OF THE KINGDOM. In the early Church Fathers the Kingdom of God, the greatest good, is primarily regarded as a future entity, the goal of the present development of the Church. Some of them regarded it as the coming millennial rule of the Messiah, though history does not bear out the exaggerated claims of some Premillenarian writers as to their number. Augustine viewed the kingdom as a present reality and identified it with the Church. For him it was primarily identical with the pious and holy, that is, with the Church as a community of believers; but he used some expressions which seem to indicate that he also saw it embodied in the episcopally organized Church. The Roman Catholic Church frankly identified the Kingdom of God with their hierarchical institution, but the Reformers returned to the view that it is in this dispensation identical with the invisible Church. Under the influence of Kant and especially of Ritschl it was robbed of its religious character and came to be regarded as an ethical kingdom of ends. It is often defined at present as a new principle introduced into society and destined to transform it in all its relations, or as the moral organization of mankind through action from the motive of love, the final end of creation.

3. THE KINGDOM OF GOD AND THE INVISIBLE CHURCH. While the Kingdom of God and the invisible Church are in a measure identical, they should nevertheless be carefully distinguished. Citizenship in the one and membership in the other are equally determined by regeneration. It is impossible to be in the Kingdom of God without being in the Church as the mystical body of Jesus Christ. At the same time it is possible to make a distinction between the point of view from which believers are called the Kingdom and that from which they are called the Church. They constitute a Kingdom in their relation to God in Christ as their Ruler, and a Church in their separateness from the world in devotion to God, and in their organic union with one another. As a Church they are called to be God's instrument in preparing the way for, and in introducing, the ideal order of things; and as a Kingdom they represent the initial realization of the ideal order among themselves.

4. THE KINGDOM OF GOD AND THE VISIBLE CHURCH. Since the Roman Catholics insist indiscriminately on the identification of the Kingdom of God and the Church, their Church claims power and jurisdiction over every domain of life, such as science and art, commerce and industry, as well as social and political organizations. This is an altogether mistaken conception. It is also a mistake to maintain, as some Reformed Christians do, in virtue of an erroneous conception of the Church as an organism, that Christian school societies, voluntary organizations of younger or older people for the study of Christian principles and their application in life, Christian labor unions, and Christian political organizations, are manifestations of the Church as an organism, for this again brings them under the domain of the visible Church and under the direct control of its officers. Naturally, this does not mean that the Church has no responsibility with respect to such organizations. It does mean, however, that they are manifestations of the Kingdom of God, in which groups of Christians

seek to apply the principles of the Kingdom to every domain of life. The visible Church and the Kingdom, too, may be identified to a certain extent. The visible Church may certainly be said to belong to the Kingdom, to be a part of the Kingdom, and even to be the most important visible embodiment of the forces of the Kingdom. It partakes of the character of the invisible Church (the two being one) as a means for the realization of the Kingdom of God. Like the visible Church, the Kingdom also shares in the imperfections to which a sinful world exposes it. This is quite evident from the parable of the wheat and the tares, and that of the fishnet. In so far as the visible Church is instrumental in the establishment and extension of the Kingdom, it is, of course, subordinate to this as a means to an end. The Kingdom may be said to be a broader concept than the Church, because it aims at nothing less than the complete control of all the manifestations of life. It represents the dominion of God in every sphere of human endeavor.

E. The Church in the Different Dispensations.

1. IN THE PATRIARCHAL PERIOD. In the patriarchial period the families of believers constituted the religious congregations; the Church was best represented in the pious households, where the fathers served as priests. There was no regular cultus, though Gen. 4:26 seems to imply a public calling upon the name of the Lord. There was a distinction between the children of God and the children of men, the latter gradually gaining the upper hand. At the time of the flood the Church was saved in the family of Noah, and continued particularly in the line of Shem. And when true religion was again on the point of dying out, God made a covenant with Abraham, gave unto him the sign of circumcision, and separated him and his descendants from the world, to be His own peculiar people. Up to the time of Moses the families of the patriarchs were the real repositories of the true faith, in which the fear of Jehovah and the service of the Lord was kept alive.

2. IN THE MOSAIC PERIOD. After the exodus the people of Israel were not only organized into a nation, but were also constituted the Church of God. They were enriched with institutions in which not only family devotion or tribal faith but the religion of the nation could find expression. The Church did not yet obtain an independent organization, but had its institutional existence in the national life of Israel. The particular form which it assumed was that of a Church-State. We cannot say that the two coalesced altogether. There were separate civil and religious functionaries and institutions within the bounds of the nation. But at the same time the whole nation constituted the Church; and the Church was limited to the one nation of Israel, though foreigners could enter it by being incorporated into the nation. In this period there was a marked development of doctrine, an increase in the quantity of the religious truth known, and greater clearness in the apprehension of the truth. The worship of God was regulated down to the minutest details, was largely ritual and ceremonial, and was centered in one central sanctuary.

3. In the New Testament. The New Testament Church is essentially one with the Church of the old dispensation. As far as their essential nature is concerned, they both consist of true believers, and of true believers only. And in their external organization both represent a mixture of good and evil. Yet several important changes resulted from the accomplished work of Jesus Christ. The Church was divorced from the national life of Israel and obtained an independent organization. In connection with this the national boundaries of the Church were swept away. What had up to this time been a national Church now assumed a universal character. And in order to realize the ideal of world-wide extension, it had to become a missionary Church, carrying the gospel of salvation to all the nations of the world. Moreover, the ritual worship of the past made place for a more spiritual worship in harmony with the greater privileges of the New Testament.

The representation given in the preceding proceeds on the assumption that the Church existed in the old dispensation as well as in the new, and was *essentially* the same in both, in spite of acknowledged institutional and administrative differences. This is in harmony with the teachings of our confessional standards. The Belgic Confession says in Art. XXVII: "This Church has been from the beginning of the world, and will be to the end thereof; which is evident from the fact that Christ is an eternal King, which without subjects He cannot be." In full agreement with this the Heidelberg Catechism says in Lord's Day XXI: "That the Son of God, out of the whole human race, from the beginning to the end of the world, gathers, defends, and preserves for Himself, by His Spirit and Word, in the unity of the true faith, a Church chosen to everlasting life." The Church is essentially, as was pointed out in the preceding, the community of believers, and this community existed from the beginning of the old dispensation right down to the present time and will continue to exist on earth until the end of the world. On this point we cannot agree with those Premillenarians who, under the influence of a divisive dispensationalism, claim that the Church is exclusively a New Testament institution, which did not come into existence until the outpouring of the Holy Spirit on the day of Pentecost and will be removed from the earth before the beginning of the millennium. They like to define the Church as "the body of Christ," which is a characteristically New Testament name, and seem to forget that it is also called "the temple of God" and "Jerusalem," which are very decidedly names with an Old Testament flavor, cf. I Cor. 3:16,17; II Cor. 6:16; Eph. 2:21; Gal. 4:26; Heb. 12:22. We should not close our eyes to the patent fact that the name "Church" (Heb. *qahal*, rendered *ekklesia* in the Septuagint) is applied to Israel in the Old Testament repeatedly, Josh. 8:35; Ezra 2:65; Joel 2:16. The fact that in our translations of the Bible the Old Testament rendering of the original is "gathering," "assembly," or "congregation," while the New Testament rendering of it is "Church," may have given rise to misunderstanding on this point; but the fact remains that in the Old Testament as well as in the New the original word denotes a congregation or an assembly of the people of God, and as such serves to designate the essence of the Church. Jesus on the one hand said that He would found the Church in the future, Matt. 16:18, but also recognized it as an already existing institution, Matt. 18:17. Stephen speaks of "the Church in the wilderness," Acts 7:38. And Paul clearly testifies to the spiritual unity of Israel and the Church in Rom. 11:17-21, and in Eph. 2:11-16. In essence Israel constituted the Church of God in the Old Testament, though its external institution differed vastly from that of the Church in the New Testament.

F. The Attributes of the Church.

According to Protestants the attributes of the Church are ascribed primarily to the Church as an invisible organism, and only secondarily to the Church as an external institution. Roman Catholics, however, ascribe them to their hierarchical organization. The former speak of three attributes, but to these three the latter add a fourth.

1. THE UNITY OF THE CHURCH.

a. *The Roman Catholic conception.* Roman Catholics ordinarily recognize only the hierarchically organized *ecclesia* as the Church. The unity of this Church manifests itself in its imposing world-wide organization, which aims at including the Church of all nations. Its real center is not found in the believers, but in the hierarchy with its concentric circles. There is first of all the broad circle of the lower clergy, the priests and other inferior functionaries; then the smaller circle of the bishops; next the still narrower one of the archbishops; and, finally, the most restricted circle of the cardinals; — the entire pyramid being capped by the Pope, the visible head of the whole organization, who has absolute control of all those that are under him. Thus the Roman Catholic Church presents to the eye a very imposing structure.

b. *The Protestant conception.* Protestants assert that the unity of the Church is not primarily of an external, but of an internal and spiritual character. It is the unity of the mystical body of Jesus Christ, of which all believers are members. This body is controlled by one Head, Jesus Christ, who is also the King of the Church, and is animated by one Spirit, the Spirit of Christ. This unity implies that all those who belong to the Church share in the same faith, are cemented together by the common bond of love, and have the same glorious outlook upon the future. This inner unity seeks and also acquires, relatively speaking, outward expression in the profession and Christian conduct of believers, in their public worship of the same God in Christ, and in their participation in the same sacraments. There can be no doubt about the fact that the Bible asserts the unity, not only of the invisible, but also of the visible Church. The figure of the body, as it is found in I Cor. 12:12-31, implies this unity. Moreover, in Eph. 4:4-16, where Paul stresses the unity of the Church, he evidently also has the visible Church in mind, for he speaks of the appointment of office-bearers in the Church and of their labors in behalf of the ideal unity of the Church. Because of the unity of the Church one local church was admonished to supply the needs of another, and the council of Jerusalem undertook to settle a question that arose in Antioch. The Church of Rome strongly emphasized the unity of the visible Church and expressed it in its hierarchical organization. And when the Reformers broke with Rome, they did not deny the unity of the visible Church but maintained it. However, they did not find the bond of union in the ecclesiastical organization of the Church, but in the true preaching of the Word and the right administration of the sacraments. This is also the case in the Belgic Confession.[1] We quote only the following statements from it: "We believe and profess one catholic or universal Church, which is a holy congregation of true believers, all expecting their salvation in Jesus Christ, being washed by His blood, sanctified and sealed by the Holy Spirit."[2] The marks by which the true Church is known are these: "If the pure doctrine of the Gospel is preached therein; if it maintains the pure administration of the sacraments as instituted by Christ; if Church discipline is exercised in punishing sin; in short, if all things are managed according to the pure Word of God; all things contrary thereto rejected, and Jesus Christ acknowledged as the only Head of the Church. Hereby the true Church may certainly be known, from which no man has a right to separate himself."[3] The unity of the visible Church was also taught by Reformed theologians of the post-Reformation period, and was always very strongly emphasized in Scottish theology. Walker even says: "True Churches of Christ, side by side with one another, forming separate organizations, with separate governments, seemed to them (Scottish theologians) utterly inadmissible, unless it might be in a very limited way, and for some reason of temporary expediency."[4] In the Netherlands this doctrine was eclipsed in recent years in the measure in which the multi- or pluriformity of the Churches was emphasized in deference to the facts of history and the existing condition. At present it is again stressed in some of the current discussions. In view of the present divisions of the Church, it is quite natural that the question should arise, whether these do not militate against the doctrine of the unity of the visible Church. In answer to this it may be said that some divisions, such as those caused by differences of locality or of language, are perfectly compatible with the unity of the Church; but that others, such as those which originate in doctrinal perversions or sacramental abuses, do really impair that unity. The former result from the providential guidance of God, but the latter are due to the influence of sin: to the darkening of the understanding, the power of error, or the stubbornness of man; and therefore the Church will have to strive for the ideal of overcoming these. The question may still arise, whether the one invisible Church ought not to find expression in a single organization. It can hardly be said that the Word of God explicitly requires this, and history has shown this to be infeasible and also of questionable worth. The only attempt that was made so far to unite the whole Church in one great external organization, did not prove productive of good results, but led to externalism, ritualism, and legalism. Moreover, the multiformity of Churches, so

---

1. Articles XXVII - XXIX.
2. Art. XXVII.
3. Art. XXIX.
4. *Scottish Theology and Theologians*, pp. 97 f.

characteristic of Protestantism, in so far as it resulted from the providential guidance of God and in a legitimate way, arose in the most natural manner, and is quite in harmony with the law of differentiation, according to which an organism in its development evolves from the homogeneous to the heterogeneous. It is quite possible that the inherent riches of the organism of the Church find better and fuller expression in the present variety of Churches than they would in a single external organization. This does not mean, of course, that the Church should not strive for a greater measure of external unity. The ideal should always be to give the most adequate expression to the unity of the Church. At the present time there is a rather strong Church union movement, but this movement, as it has developed up to this time, though undoubtedly springing from laudable motives on the part of some, is still of rather doubtful value. Whatever external union is effected must be the natural expression of an existing inner unity, but the present movement partly seeks to fabricate an external union where no inner unity is found, forgetting that "no artificial aggregation that seeks to unify natural disparities can afford a guarantee against the strife of parties within the aggregation." It is un-Scriptural in so far as it has been seeking unity at the expense of the truth and has been riding the wave of subjectivism in religion. Unless it changes colour and strives for greater unity *in the truth*, it will not be productive of real unity but only of uniformity, and while it may make the Church more efficient from a business point of view, it will not add to the true spiritual efficiency of the Church. Barth sounds the right note when he says: "The quest for the unity of the Church must in fact be identical with the quest for Jesus Christ as the concrete Head and Lord of the Church. The blessing of unity cannot be separated from Him who blesses, in Him it has its source and reality, through His Word and Spirit it is revealed to us, and only in faith can it become a reality among us."[1]

2. THE HOLINESS OF THE CHURCH.

a. *The Roman Catholic conception.* The Roman Catholic conception of the holiness of the Church is also primarily of an external character. It is not the inner holiness of the members of the Church through the sanctifying work of the Holy Spirit, but the outer ceremonial holiness that is placed in the foreground. According to Father Devine the Church is holy first of all "in her dogmas, in her moral precepts, in her worship, in her discipline," in which "all is pure and irreproachable, all is of such a nature as is calculated to remove evil and wickedness, and to promote the most exalted virtue."[2] Only secondarily is the holiness of the Church conceived of as moral. Father Deharbe says that the Church is also holy, "because there were in her at all times saints whose holiness God has also confirmed by miracles and extraordinary graces."[3]

b. *Protestant conception.* Protestants, however, have quite a different conception of the holiness of the Church. They maintain that the Church is

---

1. *The Church and the Churches*, p. 28.
2. *The Creed Explained*, p. 285.
3. *Catechism of the Catholic Religion*, p. 140.

absolutely holy in an objective sense, that is, as she is considered in Jesus Christ. In virtue of the mediatorial righteousness of Christ, the Church is accounted holy before God. In a relative sense they also regard the Church as being subjectively holy, that is, as actually holy in the inner principle of her life and destined for perfect holiness. Hence she can truly be called a community of saints. This holiness is first of all a holiness of the inner man, but a holiness which also finds expression in the outer life. Consequently, holiness is also attributed, secondarily, to the visible Church. That Church is holy in the sense that it is separated from the world in consecration to God, and also in the ethical sense of aiming at, and achieving in principle, a holy conversation in Christ. Since visible local churches consist of believers and their seed, they are supposed to exclude all open unbelievers and wicked persons. Paul does not hesitate to address them as churches of the saints.

3. THE CATHOLICITY OF THE CHURCH.

a. *Roman Catholic conception.* The attribute of catholicity is appropriated by the Roman Catholic Church, as if it only has the right to be called catholic. Like the other attributes of the Church, it is applied by her to the visible organization. She claims the right to be considered as the one really catholic Church, because she is spread over the whole earth and adapts herself to all countries and to all forms of government; because she has existed from the beginning and has always had subjects and faithful children, while sects come and go; because she is in possession of the fulness of truth and grace, destined to be distributed among men; and because she surpasses in number of members all dissenting sects taken together.

b. *Protestant conception.* Protestants, again, apply this attribute primarily to the invisible Church, which can be called catholic in a far truer sense than any one of the existing organizations, not even the Church of Rome excepted. They justly resent the arrogance of the Roman Catholics in appropriating this attribute for their hierarchical organization, to the exclusion of all other Churches. Protestants insist that the invisible Church is primarily the real catholic Church, because she includes all believers on earth at any particular time, no one excepted; because, consequently, she also has her members among all the nations of the world that were evangelized; and because she exercises a controlling influence on the entire life of man in all its phases. Secondarily, they also ascribe the attribute of catholicity to the visible Church. In our discussion of the unity of the visible Church, it already became apparent that the Reformers and the Reformed Confessions expressed their belief in a catholic visible Church, and this opinion has been reiterated by Dutch, Scottish, and American Reformed theologians right up to the present time, though in recent years some in the Netherlands expressed doubt about this doctrine. It must be admitted that this doctrine presents many difficult problems, which still call for solution. It is not easy to point out with precision just where this one catholic visible Church is. Furthermore, such questions as these arise: (1) Does this doctrine carry with it a wholesale condemnation of denominationalism, as Dr. Henry Van Dyke seems to think? (2) Does it mean that some one denomination is the *true* Church, while all others are *false*, or is it better to distinguish between Churches of more or less pure formation? (3) At what point does a local church or a denomination cease to be an integral part of the one visible Church? (4) Is a single external institution or organization essential to the unity of the visible Church, or not? These are some of the problems that still call for further study.

G. The Marks of the Church.

1. THE MARKS OF THE CHURCH IN GENERAL.

a. *The need of such marks.* Little need was felt for such marks as long as the Church was clearly one. But when heresies arose, it became necessary to point to certain marks by which the *true* Church could be recognized. The consciousness of this need was already present in the early Church, was naturally less apparent in the Middle Ages, but became very strong at the time of the Reformation. At that time the one existing Church was not only divided into two great sections, but Protestantism itself was divided into several Churches and sects. As a result it was felt ever increasingly that it was necessary to point out some marks by which the true Church could be distinguished from the false. The very fact of the Reformation proves that the Reformers, without denying that God maintains His Church, were yet deeply conscious of the fact that an empirical embodiment of the Church may become subject to error, may depart from the truth, and may totally degenerate. They assumed the existence of a standard of truth to which the Church must correspond, and recognized as such the Word of God.

b. *The marks of the Church in Reformed theology.* Reformed theologians differed as to the number of the marks of the Church. Some spoke of but one, the preaching of the pure doctrine of the Gospel (Beza, Alsted, Amesius, Heidanus, Maresius); others, of two, the pure preaching of the word and the right administration of the sacraments (Calvin, Bullinger, Zanchius, Junius, Gomarus, Mastricht, à Marck) and still others added to these a third, the faithful exercise of discipline (Hyperius, Martyr, Ursinus, Trelcatius, Heidegger, Wendelinus). These three are also named in our Confession;[1] but after making mention of them, the Confession combines them all into one by saying: "in short, if all things are managed according to the pure Word of God." In course of time a distinction was made, especially in Scotland, between those features which are absolutely necessary to the *being* of a Church, and those which are only necessary to its *well-being*. Some began to feel that, however necessary discipline might be to the health of the Church, it would be wrong to say that a church without discipline was no Church at all. Some even felt the same way about the right administration of the sacraments, since they did not feel free to unchurch either the Baptists or the Quakers. The effect of this is seen in the

----

1. Art. XXIX.

Westminster Confession, which mentions as the only thing that is indispensable to the *being* of the Church "the profession of the true religion," and speaks of other things, such as purity of doctrine or worship, and of discipline as excellent qualities of particular churches, by which the degree of their purity may be measured.[1] Dr. Kuyper recognizes only the *praedicatio verbi* and the *administratio sacramenti* as real marks of the Church, since they only: (1) are specific, that is, are characteristics of the Church and of no other body; (2) are instruments through which Christ works with His grace and Spirit in the Church; and (3) are formative elements that go into the constitution of the Church. Discipline is also found elsewhere and cannot be co-ordinated with these two. Bearing this in mind, he has no objection, however, to regard the faithful exercise of discipline as one of the marks of the Church. Now it is undoubtedly true that the three marks usually named are not really co-ordinate. Strictly speaking, it may be said that the true preaching of the Word and its recognition as the standard of doctrine and life, is the one mark of the Church. Without it there is no Church, and it determines the right administration of the sacraments and the faithful exercise of Church discipline. Nevertheless, the right administration of the sacraments is also a real mark of the Church. And though the exercise of discipline may not be peculiar to the Church, that is, is not found in it exclusively, yet it is absolutely essential to the purity of the Church.

2. THE MARKS OF THE CHURCH IN PARTICULAR.

a. *The true preaching of the Word.* This is the most important mark of the Church. While it is independent of the sacraments, these are not independent of it. The true preaching of the Word is the great means for maintaining the Church and for enabling her to be the mother of the faithful. That this is one of the characteristics of the true Church, is evident from such passages as John 8:31,32,47; 14:23; I John 4:1-3; II John 9. Ascribing this mark to the Church does not mean that the preaching of the Word in a Church must be perfect before it can be regarded as a true Church. Such an ideal is unattainable on earth; only relative purity of doctrine can be ascribed to any Church. A church may be comparatively impure in its presentation of the truth without ceasing to be a true church. But there is a limit beyond which a Church cannot go in the misrepresentation or denial of the truth, without losing her true character and becoming a false Church. This is what happens when fundamental articles of faith are publicly denied, and doctrine and life are no more under the control of the Word of God.

b. *The right administration of the sacraments.* The sacraments should never be divorced from the Word, for they have no content of their own, but derive their content from the Word of God; they are in fact a visible preaching

1. Chap. XXV, paragraphs 2, 4. 5.

of the Word. As such they must also be administered by lawful ministers of the Word, in accordance with the divine institution, and only to properly qualified subjects, the believers and their seed. A denial of the central truths of the gospel will naturally affect the proper administration of the sacraments; and the Church of Rome certainly departs from the right mode, when it divorces the sacraments from the Word, ascribing to them a sort of magical efficacy; and when it allows midwives to administer baptism in time of need. That the right administration of the sacraments is a characteristic of the true Church, follows from its inseparable connection with the preaching of the Word and from such passages as Matt. 28:19; Mark 16:15,16; Acts 2:42; I Cor. 11:23-30.

c. *The faithful exercise of discipline.* This is quite essential for maintaining the purity of doctrine and for guarding the holiness of the sacraments. Churches that are lax in discipline are bound to discover sooner or later within their circle an eclipse of the light of the truth and an abuse of that which is holy. Hence a Church that would remain true to her ideal in the measure in which this is possible on earth, must be diligent and conscientious in the exercise of Christian discipline. The Word of God insists on proper discipline in the Church of Christ, Matt. 18:18; I Cor. 5:1-5,13; 14:33,40; Rev. 2:14,15,20.

QUESTIONS FOR FURTHER STUDY: What is the meaning of the word *ekklesia* in Matt. 16:18; 18:17? When and how did the term *kuriake* come into use for the Church? How do the Dutch words 'kerk' and 'gemeente' differ, and how are they related to the Greek term? Are there passages in Scripture in which the word *ekklesia* is undoubtedly used to denote as a unity the whole body of those throughout the world who outwardly profess Christ? Is the word ever used as the designation of a group of churches under a common government, such as we call a denomination? Does the visibility of the Church consist merely in the visibility of its members? If not, in what does it become visible? Does the visible Church stand in any other than a mere outward relation to Christ, and does it enjoy any other than mere outward promises and privileges? Does the essence of the visible Church differ from that of the invisible Church? What objections have been raised to the distinction between the Church as an institution and the Church as an organism? What is the fundamental difference between the Roman Catholic and the Reformed conception of the Church?

LITERATURE: Bavinck, *Geref. Dogm.* IV, pp. 295-354; Kuyper, *Dict. Dogm.*, *De Ecclesia*, pp. 3-267; id., *Tractaat Van de Reformatie der Kerken;* ibid., *E Voto*, II, pp. 108-151; Vos, *Geref. Dogm.* V, pp. 1-31; Bannerman, *The Church of Christ*, I, pp. 1-67; *Ten Hoor, Afscheiding en Doleantie* and *Afscheiding of Doleantie;* Doekes, *De Moeder der Geloovigen*, pp. 7-64; Steen, *De Kerk*, pp. 30-131; McPherson, *The Doctrine of the Church in Scottish Theology*, pp. 54-128; Van Dyke, *The Church, Her Ministry and Sacraments*, pp. 1-74; Hort, *The Christian Ecclesia*, especially pp. 1-21, 107-122; Pieper, *Christl. Dogm.* III, pp. 458-492; Valentine, *Chr. Dogm.* II, pp. 362-377; Pope, *Chr. Theol.* III, pp. 259-287; Litton, *Introd. to Dogm. Theol.*, pp. 357-378; Strong, *Syst. Theol.*, pp. 887-894; Devine, *The Creed Explained*, pp. 256-295; Wilmers, *Handbook of the Chr. Rel.*, pp. 102-119; Moehler, *Symbolism*, pp. 310-362; Schaff, *Our Fathers' Faith and Ours*, pp. 213-239; Morris, *Ecclesiology*, pp. 13-41; W. A. Visser 't Hooft and J. H. Oldham, *The Church and its Function in Society.*

III. The Government of the Church

A. Different Theories Respecting the Government of the Church.

1. THE VIEW OF QUAKERS AND DARBYITES. It is a matter of principle with the Quakers and Darbyites to reject all Church Government. According to them every external Church formation necessarily degenerates and leads to results that are contrary to the spirit of Christianity. It exalts the human element at the expense of the divine. It neglects the divinely given charisms and substitutes for them offices instituted by man, and consequently offers the Church the husk of human knowledge rather than the vital communications of the Holy Spirit. Therefore they regard it as not only unnecessary but decidedly sinful to organize the visible Church. Thus the offices fall by the way, and in public worship each simply follows the promptings of the Spirit. The tendency that becomes apparent in these sects, which gives clear evidence of the leaven of Mysticism, must be regarded as a reaction against the hierarchical organization and the formalism of the Established Church of England. In our country some of the Quakers have regularly ordained ministers and conduct their worship very much as other Churches do.

2. THE ERASTIAN SYSTEM, NAMED AFTER ERASTUS, 1524-1583. Erastians regard the Church as a society which owes its existence and form to regulations enacted by the State. The officers of the Church are merely instructors or preachers of the Word, without any right or power to rule, except that which they derive from the civil magistrates. It is the function of the State to govern the Church, to exercise discipline and to excommunicate. Church censures are civil punishments, though their application may be entrusted to the legal officers of the Church. This system has been variously applied in England, Scotland, and Germany (Lutheran Churches). It conflicts with the fundamental principle of the Headship of Jesus Christ, and does not recognize the fact that Church and State are distinct and independent in their origin, in their primary objects, in the power they exercise, and in the administration of that power.

3. THE EPISCOPALIAN SYSTEM. The Episcopalians hold that Christ, as the Head of the Church, has entrusted the government of the Church directly and exclusively to an order of prelates or bishops, as the successors of the apostles; and that He has constituted these bishops a separate, independent, and self-perpetuating order. In this system the *coetus fidelium* or community of believers has absolutely no share in the government of the Church. In the early centuries this was the system of the Roman Catholic Church. In England it is

combined with the Erastian system. But the Bible does not warrant the existence of such a separate class of superior officers, who have the inherent right of ordination and jurisdiction, and therefore do not represent the people nor, in any sense of the word, derive their office from them. Scripture clearly shows that the apostolic office was not of a permanent nature. The apostles did form a clearly distinct and independent class, but it was not their special task to rule and administer the affairs of the churches. It was their duty to carry the gospel to unevangelized districts, to found churches, and then to appoint others from among the people for the task of ruling these churches. Before the end of the first century the Apostolate had disappeared entirely.

4. THE ROMAN CATHOLIC SYSTEM. This is the Episcopal system carried to its logical conclusion. The Roman Catholic system pretends to comprise, not only successors of the apostles, but also a successor to Peter, who is said to have had the primacy among the apostles, and whose successor is now recognized as the special representative of Christ. The Church of Rome is of the nature of an absolute monarchy, under the control of an infallible Pope, who has the right to determine and regulate the doctrine, worship, and government, of the Church. Under him there are inferior classes and orders, to whom special grace is given, and whose duty it is to govern the Church in strict accountability to their superiors and to the supreme Pontiff. The people have absolutely no voice in the government of the Church. This system also conflicts with Scripture, which recognizes no such primacy of Peter as that on which the system is built, and distinctly recognizes the voice of the people in ecclesiastical affairs. Moreover, the claim of the Roman Catholic Church, that there has been an unbroken line of succession from the time of Peter down to the present day, is contradicted by history. The papal system is, both exegetically and historically, untenable.

5. THE CONGREGATIONAL SYSTEM. This is also called the system of independency. According to it each church or congregation is a complete church, independent of every other. In such a church the governing power rests exclusively with the members of the church, who are entitled to regulate their own affairs. Officers are simply functionaries of the local church, appointed to teach and to administer the affairs of the church, and have no governing power beyond that which they possess as members of the church. If it is considered expedient that the various churches should exercise communion with one another, as is sometimes the case, this fellowship finds expression in ecclesiastical councils and in local or provincial conferences, for the consideration of their common interests. But the actions of such associated bodies are held to be strictly advisory or declarative, and are not binding on any particular church. This theory of popular government, making the office of the ministry altogether dependent on the action of the people, is certainly not in harmony with what we learn from the Word of God. Moreover, the theory that each church is independent of every other church, fails to express the unity of the Church of Christ, has a disintegrating effect, and opens the door for all kinds

of arbitrariness in church government. There is no appeal from any of the decisions of the local church.

6. THE NATIONAL-CHURCH SYSTEM. This system, also called the Collegial system (which supplanted the Territorial system) was developed in Germany especially by C. M. Pfaff (1686-1780), and was later on introduced into the Netherlands. It proceeds on the assumption that the Church is a voluntary association, equal to the State. The separate churches or congregations are merely sub-divisions of the one national Church. The original power resides in a national organization, and this organization has jurisdiction over the local churches. This is just the reverse of the Presbyterian system, according to which the original power has its seat in the consistory. The Territorial system recognized the *inherent* right of the State to reform public worship, to decide disputes respecting doctrine and conduct, and to convene synods, while the Collegial system ascribes to the State only the right of supervision as an *inherent right*, and regards all other rights, which the State might exercise in Church matters, as rights which the Church by a tacit understanding or by a formal pact conferred upon the State. This system disregards altogether the autonomy of the local churches, ignores the principles of self-government and of direct responsibility to Christ, engenders formalism, and binds a professedly spiritual Church by formal and geographical lines. Such a system as this, which is akin to the Erastian system, naturally fits in best with the present-day idea of the totalitarian State.

B. The Fundamental Principles of the Reformed or Presbyterian System.

Reformed Churches do not claim that their system of Church government is determined in every detail by the Word of God, but do assert that its fundamental principles are directly derived from Scripture. They do not claim a *jus divinum* for the details, but only for the general fundamental principles of the system, and are quite ready to admit that many of its particulars are determined by expediency and human wisdom. From this it follows that, while the general structure must be rigidly maintained, some of the details may be changed in the proper ecclesiastical manner for prudential reasons, such as the general profit of the churches. The following are its most fundamental principles.

1. CHRIST IS THE HEAD OF THE CHURCH AND THE SOURCE OF ALL ITS AUTHORITY. The Church of Rome considers it of the greatest importance to maintain the headship of the Pope over the Church. The Reformers maintained and defended the position, in opposition to the claims of the Papacy, that Christ is the only Head of the Church. They did not entirely avoid the danger, however, of recognizing, the one more and the other less, the supremacy of the State over the Church. Consequently the Presbyterian and Reformed Churches had to fight another battle later on, the battle for the Headship of Jesus Christ in opposition to the unwarranted encroachments of the State. This battle was fought first of all in Scotland, and later on also in The Netherlands. The very

fact that it was fought against such external powers as the Papacy and the State or the King, both of whom claimed to be the head of the visible Church, clearly implies that they who were engaged in this battle were particularly interested in establishing and maintaining the position that Christ is the only lawful Head of the *visible* Church, and is therefore the only supreme Law-giver and King of the Church. Naturally, they also recognized Christ as the *organic* Head of the *invisible* Church. They realized that the two could not be separated, but, since the Pope and the King could hardly claim to be the organic head of the invisible Church, this was not really the point in question. Respecting the Scottish teachers Walker says: "They meant that Christ is the real King and Head of the Church, as a visible organisation, ruling it by His statutes, and ordinances, and officers, and forces, as truly and literally as David or Solomon ruled the covenant people of old."[1]

The Bible teaches us that Christ is Head over all things: He is the Lord of the universe, not merely as the second person of the Trinity, but in His media-torial capacity, Matt. 28:18; Eph. 1:20-22; Phil. 2:10,11; Rev. 17:14; 19:16. In a very special sense, however, He is the Head of the Church, which is His body. He stands in a vital and organic relation to it, fills it with His life, and controls it spiritually, John 15:1-8; Eph. 1:10,22,23; 2:20-22; 4:15; 5:30; Col. 1:18; 2:19; 3:11. Premillenarians claim that this is the only sense in which Christ is the Head of the Church, for they deny the very point for which our Reformed Fathers contended. namely, that Christ is the *King* of the Church, and therefore the only supreme authority to be recognized in it. Scripture plainly teaches, however, that Christ is the Head of the Church, not only in virtue of His vital relationship to it, but also as its Legislator and King. In the organic and vital sense He is the Head primarily, though not exclusively, of the invisible Church, which constitutes His spiritual body. But He is also the Head of the visible Church, not only in the organic sense, but also in the sense that He has authority and rule over it, Matt. 16:18,19; 23:8,10; John 13:13; I Cor. 12:5; Eph. 1:20-23; 4:4,5,11,12; 5:23,24. This Headship of Christ over the visible Church is the principal part of the dominion bestowed upon Him as the result of His sufferings. His authority is manifested in the following points: (a) He instituted the Church of the New Testament, Matt. 16:18, so that it is not, as many regard it in our day, a mere voluntary society, which has its only warrant in the consent of its members. (b) He instituted the means of grace which the Church must administer, namely, the Word and the sacra-ments, Matt. 28:19,20; Mark 16:15,16; Luke 22:17-20; I Cor. 11:23-29. In these matters no one else has the right to legislate. (c) He gave to the Church its constitution and officers, and clothed them with divine authority, so that they can speak and act in His name, Matt. 10:1; 16:19; John 20:21-23; Eph. 4:11,12. (d) He is ever present in the Church when it meets for worship, and speaks and acts through its officers. It is Christ as King that warrants them in speaking and acting with authority, Matt. 10:40; II Cor. 13:3.

---

1. *Scottish Theology and Theologians*, p. 130.

2. CHRIST EXERCISES HIS AUTHORITY BY MEANS OF HIS ROYAL WORD. The reign of Christ is not in all respects similar to that of earthly kings. He does not rule the Church by force, but *subjectively* by His Spirit, which is operative in the Church, and *objectively* by the Word of God as the standard of authority. All believers are unconditionally bound to obey the word of the King. As Christ is the only sovereign Ruler of the Church, His word is the only word that is law in the absolute sense. Consequently, all despotic power is contraband in the Church. There is no ruling power independent of Christ. The Pope of Rome stands condemned in that he, while professing to be Christ's vicar on earth, virtually supplants Christ and supersedes His word by human innovations. He not only places tradition on an equal footing with Scripture, but also claims to be the infallible interpreter of both when speaking *ex cathedra* in matters of faith and morals. Scripture and tradition may be the mediate or remote rules of faith, the immediate rule is the teaching of the Church, which has its guarantee in papal infallibility.[1] The word of the Pope is the word of God. But while it is true that Christ exercises His authority in the Church through the officers, this is not to be understood in the sense that He *transfers* His authority to His servants. He Himself rules the Church through all the ages, but in doing this, He uses the officers of the Church as His organs. They have no absolute or independent, but only a derived and ministerial power.

3. CHRIST AS KING HAS ENDOWED THE CHURCH WITH POWER. A rather delicate question arises at this point, namely, Who are the first and proper subjects of Church power? To whom has Christ committed this power in the first instance? Roman Catholics and Episcopalians answer: to the officers as a separate class, in contradistinction from the ordinary members of the Church. This view has also been held by some eminent Presbyterian divines, such as Rutherford and Baillie. Diametrically opposed to this is the theory of the Independents, that this power is vested in the Church at large, and that the officers are merely the organs of the body as a whole. The great Puritan divine, Owen, adopts this view with some modifications. In recent years some Reformed theologians apparently favored this view, though without subscribing to the separatism of the Independents. There is another view, however, representing a mean between these two extremes, which would seem to deserve preference. According to it ecclesiastical power is committed by Christ to the Church as a whole, that is to the ordinary members and the officers alike; but in addition to that the officers receive such an additional measure of power as is required for the performance of their respective duties in the Church of Christ. They share in the original power bestowed upon the Church, and receive their authority and power as officers directly from Christ. They are representatives, but not mere deputies or delegates of the people. Older theologians often say: "All Church power, in *actu primo*, or fundamentally, is in the Church itself; in *actu secundo*, or its exercise, in them that are specially called thereto." This

---

1. Cf. Wilmers, *Handbook of the Christian Religion*, p. 134.

is substantially the view held by Voetius, Gillespie (in his work on Ceremonies), Bannerman, Porteous, Bavinck, and Vos.

4. CHRIST PROVIDED FOR THE SPECIFIC EXERCISE OF THIS POWER BY REPRESENTATIVE ORGANS. While Christ committed power to the Church as a whole, He also provided for it that this power should be exercised ordinarily and specifically by representative organs, set aside for the maintenance of doctrine, worship, and discipline. The officers of the Church are the representatives of the people chosen by popular vote. This does not mean, however, that they receive their authority from the people, for the call of the people is but the confirmation of the inner call by the Lord Himself; and it is from Him that they receive their authority and to Him that they are responsible. When they are called representatives, this is merely an indication of the fact that they were chosen to their office by the people, and does not imply that they derive their authority from them. Hence they are no deputies or tools that merely serve to carry out the wishes of the people, but rulers whose duty it is to apprehend and apply intelligently the laws of Christ. At the same time they are in duty bound to recognize the power vested in the Church as a whole by seeking its assent or consent in important matters.

5. THE POWER OF THE CHURCH RESIDES PRIMARILY IN THE GOVERNING BODY OF THE LOCAL CHURCH. It is one of the fundamental principles of Reformed or Presbyterian government, that the power or authority of the Church does not reside first of all in the most general assembly of any Church, and is only secondarily and by derivation from this assembly, vested in the governing body of the local Church; but that it has its original seat in the consistory or session of the local Church, and is by this transferred to the major assemblies, such as classes (presbyteries) and synods or general assemblies. Thus the Reformed system honors the autonomy of the local church, though it always regards this as subject to the limitations that may be put upon it as the result of its association with other churches in one denomination, and assures it the fullest right to govern its own internal affairs by means of its officers. At the same time it also maintains the right and duty of the local church to unite with other similar churches on a common confessional basis, and form a wider organization for doctrinal, judicial, and administrative purposes, with proper stipulations of mutual obligations and rights. Such a wider organization undoubtedly imposes certain limitations on the autonomy of the local churches, but also promotes the growth and welfare of the churches, guarantees the rights of the members of the Church, and serves to give fuller expression to the unity of the Church.

C. The Officers of the Church.

Different kinds of officers may be distinguished in the Church. A very general distinction is that between extraordinary and ordinary officers.

1. EXTRAORDINARY OFFICERS.

a. *Apostles.* Strictly speaking, this name is applicable only to the Twelve chosen by Jesus and to Paul; but it is also applied to certain apostolic men, who assisted Paul in his work, and who were endowed with apostolic gifts and graces, Acts 14:4,14; I Cor. 9:5,6; II Cor. 8:23; Gal. 1:19 (?). The apostles had the special task of laying the foundation for the Church of all ages. It is only through their word that believers of all following ages have communion with Jesus Christ. Hence they are the apostles of the Church in the present day as well as they were the apostles of the primitive Church. They had certain special qualifications. They (a) received their commission directly from God or from Jesus Christ, Mark 3:14; Luke 6:13; Gal. 1:1; (b) were witnesses of the life of Christ and especially of His resurrection, John 15:27; Acts 1:21,22; I Cor. 9:1; (c) were conscious of being inspired by the Spirit of God in all their teaching, both oral and written, Acts 15:28; I Cor. 2:13; I Thess. 4:8; I John 5:9-12; (d) had the power to perform miracles and used this on several occasions to ratify their message, II Cor. 12:12; Heb. 2:4; and (e) were richly blessed in their work as a sign of the divine approval of their labors, I Cor. 9:1,2; II Cor. 3:2,3; Gal. 2:8.

b. *Prophets.* The New Testament also speaks of prophets, Acts 11:28; 13.1,2; 15:32; I Cor. 12:10; 13:2; 14:3; Eph. 2:20; 3:5; 4:11; I Tim. 1:18; 4:14; Rev. 11:6. Evidently the gift of speaking for the edification of the Church was highly developed in these prophets, and they were occasionally instrumental in revealing mysteries and predicting future events. The first part of this gift is permanent in the Christian Church, and was distinctly recognized by the Reformed Churches (prophesyings), but the last part of it was of a charismatic and temporary character. They differed from ordinary ministers in that they spoke under special inspiration.

c. *Evangelists.* In addition to apostles and prophets, evangelists are mentioned in the Bible, Acts 21:8; Eph. 4:11; II Tim. 4:5. Philip, Mark, Timothy, and Titus belonged to this class. Little is known about these evangelists. They accompanied and assisted the apostles, and were sometimes sent out by these on special missions. Their work was to preach and baptize, but also to ordain elders, Tit. 1:5; I Tim. 5:22, and to exercise discipline, Tit. 3:10. Their authority seems to have been more general and somewhat superior to that of the regular ministers.

2. ORDINARY OFFICERS.

a. *Elders.* Among the common officers of the Church the *presbuteroi* or *episkopoi* are first in order of importance. The former name simply means "elders," that is, older ones, and the latter, "overseers." The term *presbuteroi* is used in Scripture to denote old men, and to designate a class of officers somewhat similar to those who functioned in the synagogue. As a designation of office the name was gradually eclipsed and even superseded by the name *episkopoi.* The two terms are often used interchangeably, Acts 20:17,28; I Tim. 3:1; 4:14; 5:17,19; Tit. 1:5,7; I Pet. 5:1,2. *Presbuteroi* are first mentioned in Acts 11:30, but the office was evidently well known already when Paul and Barnabas went to Jerusalem, and may have been in existence even before the institution of the diaconate. At least the term *hoi neoteroi* in Acts 5 seems to point to a distinction between these and the *presbuteroi.* Frequent mention is made of them in the book of Acts, 14:23; 15:6,22; 16:4; 20:17,28; 21:18. Probably the presbyterial or episcopal office was first instituted in the churches of the Jews, Jas. 5:14; Heb. 13:7,17, and then, shortly after, also in those of the Gentiles. Several other names are applied to these officers, namely, *proistamenoi,* Rom. 12:8; I Thes. 5:12; *kuberneseis,* I Cor. 12:28; *hegoumenoi,* Heb. 13:7,17,24; and *poimenes,* Eph. 4:11. These officers clearly had the oversight of the flock that was entrusted to their care. They had to provide for it, govern it, and protect it, as the very household of God.

b. *Teachers.* It is clear that the elders were not originally teachers. There was no need of separate teachers at first, since there were apostles, prophets, and evangelists. Gradually, however, the *didaskalia* was connected more closely with the episcopal office; but even then the teachers did not at once constitute a separate class of officers. Paul's statement in Eph. 4:11, that the ascended Christ also gave "pastors and teachers," mentioned as a single class, to the Church, clearly shows that these two did not constitute two different classes of officers, but one class having two related functions. I Tim. 5:17 speaks of elders who labor in the Word and in teaching, and according to Heb. 13:7 the *hegoumenoi* were also teachers. Moreover, in II Tim. 2:2 Paul urges upon Timothy the necessity of appointing to office faithful men who shall also be able to teach others. In course of time two circumstances led to a distinction between the elders or overseers that were entrusted only with the government of the Church, and those that were also called upon to teach: (1) when the apostles died and heresies arose and increased, the task of those who were called upon to teach became more exacting and demanded special preparation, II Tim. 2:2; Tit. 1:9; and (2) in view of the fact that the laborer is worthy of his hire, those who were engaged in the ministry of the Word, a comprehensive task requiring all their time, were set free from other work, in order that they might devote themselves more exclusively to the work of teaching. In all probability the *aggeloi* who were addressed in the letters to the seven churches of Asia Minor, were the teachers or ministers of those churches, Rev. 2:1,8,12,18; 3:1,7,14. In Reformed circles the ministers now rule the churches together with the elders, but in addition to that administer the Word and the sacraments. Together they make the necessary regulations for the government of the Church.

c. *Deacons.* Besides the *presbuteroi* the *diakonoi* are mentioned in the New Testament, Phil. 1:1; I Tim. 3:8,10,12. According to the prevailing opinion Acts 6:1-6 contains the record of the institution of the diaconate. Some modern scholars doubt this, however, and regard the office mentioned in

Acts 6, either as a general office in which the functions of elders and deacons were combined, or as a merely temporal office serving a special purpose. They call attention to the fact that some of the seven chosen, as Philip and Stephen, evidently engaged in teaching; and that the money collected at Antioch for the poor in Judea was delivered into the hands of the *elders*. No mention is made of deacons whatsoever in Acts 11:30, though these, if they had existed as a separate class, would have been the natural recipients of that money. And yet in all probability Acts 6 does refer to the institution of the diaconate, for: (1) The name *diakonoi*, which was, previous to the event narrated in Acts 6, always used in the general sense of servant, subsequently began to be employed, and in course of time served exclusively, to designate those who were engaged in works of mercy and charity. The only reason that can be assigned for this is found in Acts 6. (2) The seven men mentioned there were charged with the task of distributing properly the gifts that were brought for the *agapae*, a ministry that is elsewhere more particularly described by the word *diakonia*, Acts 11:29, Rom. 12:7; II Cor. 8:4; 9:1,12,13; Rev. 2:19. (3) The require-ments for the office, as mentioned in Acts 6, are rather exacting, and in that respect agree with the demands mentioned in I Tim. 3:8-10,12. (4) Very little can be said in favor of the pet idea of some critics that the diaconate was not developed until later, about the time when the episcopal office made its appearance.

3. THE CALLING OF THE OFFICERS AND THEIR INDUCTION INTO OFFICE. A distinction should be made between the calling of the extraordinary officers, such as apostles, and that of the ordinary officers. The former were called in an extraordinary way with an immediate calling from God, and the latter, in the ordinary manner and through the agency of the Church. We are concerned more particularly with the calling of the ordinary officers.

a. *The calling of the ordinary officers.* This is twofold:

(1) *Internal calling.* It is sometimes thought that the internal calling to an office in the Church consists in some extraordinary indication of God to the effect that one is called, — a sort of special revelation. But this is not correct. It consists rather in certain ordinary providential indications given by God, and includes especially three things: (a) the consciousness of being impelled to some special task in the Kingdom of God, by love to God and His cause; (b) the conviction that one is at least in a measure intellectually and spiritually qualified for the office sought; and (c) the experience that God is clearly paving the way to the goal.

(2) *External calling.* This is the call that comes to one through the instrumentality of the Church. It is not issued by the Pope (Roman Catholic), nor by a bishop or a college of bishops (Episcopalian), but by the local church. Both the officers and the ordinary members of the church have a part in it. That the officers have a guiding hand in it, but not to the exclusion of the people, is evident from such passages as Acts 1:15-26; 6:2-6; 14:23. The

people were recognized even in the choice of an apostle, according to Acts 1:15-26. It would seem that in the apostolic age the officers guided the choice of the people by calling attention to the necessary qualifications that were required for the office, but allowed the people to take part in the choosing, Acts 1:15-26; 6:1-6; I Tim. 3:2-13. Of course, in the case of Matthias God Himself made the final choice.

b. *The officers' induction into office.* There are especially two rites connected with this:

(1) *Ordination.* This presupposes the calling and examination of the candidate for office. It is an act of the classis or the presbytery (I Tim. 4:14). Says Dr. Hodge: "Ordination is the solemn expression of the judgment of the Church, by those appointed to deliver such judgment, that the candidate is truly called of God to take part in this ministry, thereby authenticating to the people the divine call."[1] This authentication is, under all ordinary circumstances, the necessary condition for the exercise of the ministerial office. It may briefly be called a public acknowledgement and confirmation of the candidate's calling to this office.

(2) *Laying on of hands.* Ordination is accompanied with the laying on of hands. Clearly, the two went hand in hand in apostolic times, Acts 6:6; 13:3; I Tim. 4:14; 5:22. In those early days the laying on of hands evidently implied two things: it signified that a person was set aside for a certain office, and that some special spiritual gift was conferred upon him. The Church of Rome is of the opinion that these two elements are still included in the laying on of hands, that it actually confers some spiritual grace upon the recipient, and therefore ascribes to it sacramental significance. Protestants maintain, however, that it is merely a symbolical indication of the fact that one is set aside for the ministerial office in the Church. While they regard it as a Scriptural rite and as one that is entirely appropriate, they do not regard it as absolutely essential. The Presbyterian Church makes it optional.

D. The Ecclesiastical Assemblies.

1. The governing bodies (Church courts) in the Reformed system. Reformed Church government is characterized by a system of ecclesiastical assemblies in an ascending or a descending scale, according to the point of view from which they are considered. These are the consistory (session), the classis (presbytery), the synod(s), and (in some cases) the general assembly. The consistory consists of the minister (or, ministers) and the elders of the local church. The classis is composed of one minister and one elder of each local church within a certain district. This is somewhat different in the Presbyterian Church, however, where the presbytery includes all the ministers within its boundaries, and one elder from each of its congregations. The synod, again, consists of an equal number of ministers and elders from each classis or presbytery. And, finally, the general assembly is (in the case of the Presbyter-

---

1. *Church Polity*, p. 349.

ians) composed of an equal delegation of ministers and elders from each of the presbyteries, and not, as might be expected, from each of the particular synods.

2. THE REPRESENTATIVE GOVERNMENT OF THE LOCAL CHURCH AND ITS RELATIVE AUTONOMY.

a. *The representative government of the local church.* Reformed churches differ, on the one hand, from all those churches in which the government is in the hands of a single prelate or presiding elder, and on the other hand, from those in which it rests with the people in general. They do not believe in any one man rule, be he an elder, a pastor, or a bishop; neither do they believe in popular government. They choose ruling elders as their representatives, and these, together with the minister(s), form a council or consistory for the government of the local church. Very likely the apostles were guided by the venerated custom of having elders in the synagogue rather than by any direct commandment, when they ordained elders in the various churches founded by them. The Jerusalem church had elders, Acts 11:30. Paul and Barnabas ordained them in the churches which they organized on the first missionary journey, Acts 14:23. Elders were evidently functioning at Ephesus, Acts 20:17, and at Philippi, Phil. 1:1. The Pastoral Epistles repeatedly make mention of them, I Tim. 3:1,2; Tit. 1:5,7. It deserves attention that they are always spoken of in the plural, I Cor. 12:28; I Tim. 5:17; Heb. 13:7,17,24; I Pet. 5:1. The elders are chosen by the people as men who are specially qualified to rule the Church. Scripture evidently intends that the people shall have a voice in the matter of their selection, though this was not the case in the Jewish synagogue, Acts 1:21-26; 6:1-6; 14:23. In the last passage, however, the word *cheirotoneo* may have lost its original meaning of *appointing by stretching out the hand*, and may simply mean *to appoint*. At the same time it is perfectly evident that the Lord Himself places these rulers over the people and clothes them with the necessary authority, Matt. 16:19; John 20:22,23; Acts 1:24,26; 20:28; I Cor. 12:28; Eph. 4:11,12; Heb. 13:17. The election by the people is merely an external confirmation of the inner calling by the Lord Himself. Moreover, the elders, though representatives of the people, do not derive their authority from the people, but from the Lord of the Church. They exercise rule over the house of God in the name of the King, and are responsible only to Him.

b. *The relative autonomy of the local church.* Reformed Church government recognizes the autonomy of the local church. This means:

(1) That every local church is a complete church of Christ, fully equipped with everything that is required for its government. It has absolutely no need of it that any government should be imposed upon it from without. And not only that, but such an imposition would be absolutely contrary to its nature.

(2) That, though there can be a proper affiliation or consolidation of contiguous churches, there may be no union which destroys the autonomy of the local church. Hence it is better not to speak of classes and synods as higher,

but to describe them as major or more general assemblies. They do not represent a higher, but the very same, power that inheres in the consistory, though
exercising this on a broader scale. McGill speaks of them as *higher* and
remoter tribunals.[1]

(3)   That the authority and prerogatives of the major assemblies are
not unlimited, but have their limitation in the rights of the sessions or consistories. They are not permitted to lord it over a local church or its members,
irrespective of the constitutional rights of the consistory; nor to meddle with
the internal affairs of a local church under any and all circumstances. When
churches affiliate, their mutual rights and duties are circumscribed in a Church
Order or Form of Government. This stipulates the rights and duties of the
major assemblies, but also guarantees the rights of the local church. The idea
that a classis (presbytery) or synod can simply impose whatever it pleases on
a particular church is essentially Roman Catholic.

(4)   That the autonomy of the local church has its limitations in the
relation in which it stands to the churches with which it is affiliated, and in
the general interests of the affiliated churches. The Church Order is a sort of
Constitution, solemnly subscribed to by every local church, as represented by its
consistory. This on the one hand guards the rights and interests of the local
church, but on the other hand also, the collective rights and interests of the
affiliated churches. And no single church has the right to disregard matters
of mutual agreement and of common interest. The local group may be even
called upon occasionally to deny itself for the far greater good of the Church
in general.

3.   THE MAJOR ASSEMBLIES.

a.   *Scripture warrant for major assemblies.* Scripture does not contain an
explicit command to the effect that the local churches of a district must form
an organic union. Neither does it furnish us with an example of such a union.
In fact, it represents the local churches as individual entities without any
external bond of union. At the same time the essential nature of the Church,
as described in Scripture, would seem to call for such a union. The Church
is described as a spiritual organism, in which all the constituent parts are
vitally related to one another. It is the spiritual body of Jesus Christ, of which
He is the exalted Head. And it is but natural that this inner unity should
express itself in some visible manner, and should even, as much as possible in
this imperfect and sinful world, seek expression in some corresponding external
organization. The Bible speaks of the Church not only as a spiritual body,
but also as a tangible body, as a temple of the Holy Spirit, as a priesthood, and
as a holy nation. Every one of these terms points to a visible unity. Congrega
tionalists or Independents and Undenominationalists lose sight of this important
fact. The existing divisions in the visible Church at the present time should
not cause us to lose sight of the fact that there are certain passages of Scripture

---

1.   *Church Government*, p. 457.

which seem to indicate rather clearly that, not only the invisible Church, but also the visible Church is a unity. The word *ekklesia* is used in the singular as an indication of the visible church in a wider sense than that of the purely local hurch, Acts 9:31 (according to the now accepted reading), I Cor. 12:28, and probably also I Cor. 10:32. In the descriptions of the Church in I Cor. 12:12-50 and Eph. 4:4-16 the apostle also has its visible unity in mind. Moreover, there are reasons for thinking that the Church at Jerusalem and at Antioch consisted of several separate groups, which together formed a sort of unity. And, finally, Acts 15 acquaints us with the example of the council of Jerusalem. This council was composed of apostles and elders, and therefore did not constitute a proper example and pattern of a classis or synod in the modern sense of the word. At the same time it was an example of a major assembly, and of one that spoke with authority and not merely in an advisory capacity.

b. *The representative character of the major assemblies.* In the abstract it may be said that the major assemblies might have been composed of *all* the representatives of all the local churches under their jurisdiction; but, on account of the number of the churches represented, such a body would in most cases prove unwieldy and inefficient. In order to keep the number of representatives down to reasonable proportions, the principle of representation is carried through also in connection with the major assemblies. Not the local churches, but the classes or presbyteries, send their representatives to Synods. This affords the gradual contraction that is necessary for a well-compacted system. The immediate representatives of the people who form the consistories or sessions, are themselves represented in classes or presbyteries; and these in turn are represented in synods or general assemblies. The more general the assembly, the more remote it is from the people; yet none of them is too remote for the expression of the unity of the Church, for the maintenance of good order, and for the general effectiveness of its work.

c. *The matters that fall under their jurisdiction.* The ecclesiastical char-acter of these assemblies should always be borne in mind. It is because they are Church assemblies, that purely scientific, social, industrial, or political matters do not, as such, fall under their jurisdiction. Only ecclesiastical mat-ters belong to their province, such as matters of doctrine or morals, of church government and discipline, and whatever pertains to the preservation of unity and good order in the Church of Jesus Christ. More particularly, they deal with (1) matters which, as to their nature, belong to the province of a minor assembly, but for some reason or other cannot be settled there; and (b) matters which, as to their nature, belong to the province of a major assembly, since they pertain to the churches in general, such as matters touching the Confession, the Church Order, or the liturgy of the Church.

d. *The power and authority of these assemblies.* The major assemblies do not represent a higher kind of power than is vested in the consistory or session. The Reformed churches know of no higher kind of ecclesiastical power than that which resides in the consistory. At the same time their authority is greater in degree and wider in extent than that of the consistory. Church power is represented in greater measure in the major assemblies than in the consistory, just as apostolic power was represented in greater measure in twelve than in a single apostle. Ten churches certainly have more authority than a single church; there is an accumulation of power. Moreover, the authority of the major assemblies does not apply to a single church only, but extends to all the affiliated churches. Consequently, the decisions of a major assembly carry great weight and can never be set aside at will. The assertion sometimes made that they are only of an advisory character and therefore need not be carried out, is a manifestation of the leaven of Independency. These decisions are authoritative, except in cases where they are explicitly declared to be merely advisory. They are binding on the churches as the sound interpretation and application of the law, — the law of Christ, the King of the Church. They cease to be binding only when they are shown to be contrary to the Word of God.

QUESTIONS FOR FURTHER STUDY: What is the difference between the New Testament meaning of the word *episkopos* and its later connotation? Why are regular offices necessary in the Church? Does Scripture favor the idea that the people should have some part in the government of the Church? What is the chief characteristic of Prelatism? What is the Roman Catholic distinction between a hierarchy of order and a hierarchy of jurisdiction? How did the Territorial and the Collegial systems originate, and how do they differ? What system did the Arminians adopt, and how did this affect their position? What is the present form of Church government in the Lutheran Church? How does the idea that Christ is the Head of the Church only in an organic sense affect the offices and the authority of the Church? What important practical bearing does the Headship of Christ (including His kingship) have on the life, the position, and the government of the Church? Can any Church be considered autonomous in the absolute sense of the word? How do Reformed major assemblies differ from Congregational conferences and general councils?

LITERATURE: Bavinck, *Geref. Dogm.* IV, pp. 354-424; Kuyper, *Dict. Dogm., De Ecclesia,* pp. 268-293; id., *Tractaat van de Reformatie der Kerken,* pp. 41-82; Vos, *Geref. Dogm.,* V, pp. 31-39, 49-70; Hodge, *Church Polity,* cf. Index; Bannerman, *The Church* II, pp. 201-331; McGill, *Church Government,* pp. 143-522; McPherson, *Presbyterianism;* Heyns, *Handbook for Elders and Deacons,* pp. 13-70; Bouwman, *Geref. Kerkrecht,* cf. Index; Rieker, *Grundsaetze reformierter Kirchenverfassung;* Hoffmann, *Kirchenverfassungsrecht;* Lechler, *Geschichte der Presbyterial—und Synodalverfassung seit der Reformation;* Morris, *Ecclesiology,* pp. 80-151; Hatch, *The Organisation of the Early Christian Churches;* Sillevis Smitt, *De Organisatie van de Christelijke Kerk;* Lindsay, *The Church and the Ministry in the Early Centuries;* J. Cunningham, *The Growth of the Church,* pp. 1-77; Van Dyke, *The Church, Her Ministry and Sacraments,* pp. 115-161; Pieper, *Christl. Dogm.* III, pp. 501-534; Litton, *Introd. to Dogm. Theol.,* pp. 376-410; Wilson, *Free Church Principles,* pp. 1-65; Wilmers, *Handbook of the Chr. Rel.,* pp. 77-101; Devine, *The Creed Explained,* pp. 302-340; Boynton, *The Congregational Way;* W. A. Visser 't Hooft and J. H. Oldham, *The Church and its Function in Society.*

IV. The Power of the Church

A. The Source of Church Power.

Jesus Christ not only founded the Church, but also endowed it with the necessary power or authority. He is the Head of the Church, not only in an organic, but also in an administrative sense, that is, He is not only the Head of the body, but also the King of the spiritual commonwealth. It is in His capacity as King of the Church that He has clothed her with power or authority. He Himself spoke of the Church as founded so firmly upon a rock that the gates of hell cannot prevail against her, Matt. 16:18; and on the same occasion — the very first on which He made mention of the Church — He also promised to endow her with power, when He said unto Peter: "I will give unto thee the keys of the Kingdom of heaven, and whatsoever thou shalt bind on earth shall be bound in heaven; and whatsoever thou shalt loose on earth shall be loosed in heaven," Matt. 16:19. It is quite evident that the terms 'Church' and 'Kingdom of Heaven' are used interchangeably here. Keys are an emblem of power (cf. Isa. 22:15-22), and in the keys of the Kingdom of Heaven Peter receives power to bind and to loose, which in this connection would seem to mean, to determine what is forbidden and what is permitted in the sphere of the Church.[1] And the judgment he passes — in this case not on persons, but on actions — will be sanctioned in heaven. Peter receives this power as the representative of the apostles, and these are the nucleus and foundation of the Church in their capacity as teachers of the Church. The Church of all ages is bound by their word, John 17:20; I John 1:3. That Christ endowed not only Peter but all the apostles with power and with the right to judge, and that not merely actions but also persons, is quite evident from John 20:23: "Whose soever sins ye forgive, they are forgiven unto them; whose soever sins ye retain, they are retained." Christ gave this power first of all and in the fullest degree to the apostles, but He also extends it, though in a lesser degree, to the Church in general. The Church has the right to excommunicate an unrepentant sinner. But it can do this only because Jesus Christ Himself dwells in the Church and through the agency of the apostles has supplied the Church with a proper standard of judgment. That Christ has given power to the Church as a whole, is quite evident from several passages of the New Testament, Acts 15:23-29; 16:4; I Cor. 5:7,13; 6:2-4; 12:28; Eph. 4:11-16. The officers in the Church receive their authority from Christ and not from men, even though the congregation is instrumental in putting

---

Cf. Vos, *The Kingdom of God and the Church*, p. 147; Grosheide, *Comm. on Matthew,* in loco.

them into office. This means on the one hand that they do not obtain it at the hands of any civil authority, which has no power in ecclesiastical matters, and therefore cannot bestow any; but on the other hand also, that they do not derive it from the people in general, though they are representatives of the people. Porteous correctly remarks: "That the presbyter is termed the people's representative shows that he is their chosen ruler. The way in which the office is acquired, but not the source of its power, is designated by the title of representative."[1]

B. The Nature of this Power.

1. A SPIRITUAL POWER. When the power of the Church is called a spiritual power, this does not mean that it is altogether internal and invisible, since Christ rules both body and soul, His Word and sacraments address the whole man, and the ministry of the diaconate even has special references to physical needs. It is a spiritual power, because it is given by the Spirit of God, Acts 20:28, can only be exercised in the name of Christ and by the power of the Holy Spirit, John 20:22,23; I Cor. 5:4, pertains exclusively to believers, I Cor. 5:12, and can only be exercised in a moral and spiritual way, II Cor. 10:4.[2] The State represents the government of God over the outward and temporal estate of man, while the Church represents His government of man's inward and spiritual estate. The former aims at assuring its subjects of the possession and enjoyment of their external and civil rights, and is often constrained to exercise coercive power over against human violence. The latter is founded in opposition to an evil spirit and for the purpose of delivering men from spiritual bondage by imparting to them the knowledge of the truth, by cultivating in them spiritual graces, and by leading them to a life of obedience to the divine precepts. Since the power of the Church is exclusively spiritual, it does not resort to force. Christ intimated on more than one occasion that the administration of His Kingdom on earth involved a spiritual and not a civil power, Luke 12:13 ff.; Matt. 20:25-28; John 18:36,37. The Church of Rome loses sight of this great fact, when it insists on the possession of temporal power and is bent on bringing the entire life of the people under its sway.

2. A MINISTERIAL POWER. It is abundantly evident from Scripture that the power of the Church is no independent and sovereign power, Matt. 20:25,26; 23:8,10; II Cor. 10:4,5; I Pet. 5:3, but a *diakonia leitourgia*, a ministerial power, Acts 4:29,30; 20:24; Rom. 1:1, derived from Christ and subordinate to His sovereign authority over the Church, Matt. 28:18. It must be exercised in harmony with the Word of God and under the direction of the Holy Spirit, through both of which Christ governs His Church, and in the name of Christ Himself as the King of the Church, Rom. 10:14,15; Eph. 5:23; I Cor. 5:4. Yet it is a very real and comprehensive power, consisting in the administration of the Word and the sacraments, Matt. 28:19, the determination of what is and what is not permitted in the Kingdom of God, Matt. 16:19, the forgiving

---

1. *The Government of the Kingdom of God*, p. 322.
2. Bavinck, *Dogm.* IV, p. 452.

and retaining of sin, John 20:23, and the exercise of discipline in the Church, Matt. 16:18; 18:17; I Cor. 5:4; Tit. 3:10; Heb. 12:15-17.

C. Different Kinds of Church Power.

In connection with the three offices of Christ there is also a threefold power in the Church, namely, the *potestas dogmatica* or *docendi,* the *potestas gubernans* or *ordinans* of which the *potestas iudicans* or *disciplinae* is a subdivision, and the *potestas* or *ministerium misericordiae.*

1. THE POTESTAS DOGMATICA OR DOCENDI. The Church has a divine task in connection with the truth. It is her duty to be a witness to the truth to those who are without, and both a witness and a teacher to those that are within. The Church must exercise this power:

a. *In the preservation of the Word of God.* By giving His Word to the Church, God constituted the Church the keeper of the precious deposit of the truth. While hostile forces are pitted against it and the power of error is everywhere apparent, the Church must see to it that the truth does not perish from the earth, that the inspired volume in which it is embodied be kept pure and unmutilated, in order that its purpose may not be defeated, and that it be handed on faithfully from generation to generation. It has the great and responsible task of maintaining and defending the truth against all the forces of unbelief and error, I Tim. 1:3,4; II Tim. 1:13; Tit. 1:9-11. The Church has not always been mindful of this sacred duty. During the last century too many of the leaders of the Church have even welcomed the assaults of a hostile criticism upon the Bible, and have rejoiced in the fact that it was brought down to the level of a purely human production, a mixture of truth and error. They have shown little of the determination which caused Luther to cry out: "Das Wort sollen Sie stehen lassen."

b. *In the administration of the Word and of the sacraments.* It is not only the duty of the Church to preserve the Word of God, but also to preach it in the world and in the assembly of the people of God, for the conversion of sinners and for the edification of the saints. The Church has an evangelistic or missionary task in the world. The King, clothed with all authority in heaven and on earth, gave her the great commission: "Go ye, therefore, and make disciples of all the nations, baptizing them in the name of the Father and of the Son and of the Holy Spirit, teaching them to observe whatsoever I commanded you." Through the ministry of the Church the Son is ceaselessly gathering out of the whole human race a Church chosen to everlasting life. The empirical Church of any particular time must be actively engaged in the enlargement and expansion of the Church through missionary endeavors, must be instrumental in bringing in the elect out of all the nations of the world, adding living stones to the spiritual temple that is in process of construction, and must in that manner promote the completion of the number who will ultimately constitute the ideal Church of the future, the perfect bride of Christ, the new Jerusalem of Revelation 21. If the Church of Jesus Christ should be derelict in the performance of this great task, she would prove unfaithful to her Lord. That work must be continued and must be completed before the glorious return of the Saviour, Matt. 24:14. And the great means at the disposal of the Church for the accomplishment of this work is, not education, civilization, human culture, or social reforms, though all these may have subsidiary significance, but the gospel of the Kingdom, which is none other, in spite of what Premillenarians may say, than the gospel of free grace, of redemption through the blood of the Lamb. But the Church may not rest satisfied with bringing sinners to Christ through the instrumentality of the gospel; she must also engage in preaching the word in the assemblies of those who have already come to Christ. And in the performance of this task it is not her main task to call sinners unto Christ, though the invitation to come to Christ may not be wanting even in organized churches, but to edify the saints, to strengthen their faith, to lead them on in the way of sanctification, and thus to solidify the spiritual temple of the Lord. Paul has this in mind when he says that Christ gave the teaching officers to the Church "for the perfecting of the saints, unto the work of ministering, unto the building up of the body of Christ: till we all attain unto the unity of the faith, and of the knowledge of the Son of God, unto a full-grown man, unto the measure of the stature of the fulness of Christ." Eph. 4:1213. The Church may not rest satisfied with teaching the first principles of faith, but must press on to higher ground, in order that those who are babes in Christ may become full-grown men and women in Christ, Heb. 5:11-6:3. Only a Church that is really strong, that has a firm grasp of the truth, can in turn become a powerful missionary agency and make mighty conquests for the Lord. Thus the task of the Church is a comprehensive task. She must point out the way of salvation, must warn the wicked of their coming doom, must cheer the saints with the promises of salvation, must strengthen the weak, encourage the faint-hearted and comfort the sorrowing. And in order that all this work may be done in every land and among all nations, she must see to it that the Word of God is translated into all languages. The ministry of the sacraments must, of course, go hand in hand with the ministry of the Word. It is merely the symbolical presentation of the gospel, addressed to the eye rather than to the ear. The duty of the Church to preach the Word is plainly taught in many passages of Scripture, such as Isa. 3:10,11; II Cor. 5:20; I Tim. 4:13; II Tim. 2:15; 4:2; Tit. 2:1-10. In view of the clear instructions of her King she may never allow any totalitarian government to dictate to her what she must preach; neither may she accommodate herself, as far as the contents of her message is concerned, to the demands of a naturalistic science, or to the requirements of a culture that reflects the spirit of the world. Modernists have done just that during the past decades by the suicidal efforts to adapt themselves in their preaching to the demands of a rationalistic higher criticism, of biology and psychology, of sociology and economics, until at last they completely lost the message of the King. Many of them are now coming to the discovery that the message recommended in *Rethinking Missions* and in Vernon White's *A New*

Theology for Missions is quite different from the original message and contains little that is peculiar to the pulpit; and that, as things now stand in their circles, the Church has no message of its own. Frantic attempts are made by Modernists to discover for themselves some message which they might bring to the churches, while they should seek to recover the original message and humbly take their place at the feet of Jesus.

c.   *In the framing of symbols and confessions.* Every Church must strive for self-consciousness in the confession of the truth. In order to accomplish this, it will not only have to reflect deeply on the truth, but also to formulate its expression of what it believes. By doing this it will engender in its members a clear conception of their faith, and convey to outsiders a definite understanding of its doctrines. The necessity of doing this was greatly enhanced by the historical perversions of the truth. The rise of heresies invariably called for the construction of symbols and confessions, for clearly formulated statements of the faith of the Church. Even the apostles sometimes found it necessary to restate with greater precision certain truths because of errors that had crept in. John restates the central truth of Christ's manifestation in the world in view of an incipient Gnosticism (cf. his Gospel and his First Epistle); Paul restates the doctrine of the resurrection, which was denied by some (I Cor. 15; I Tim. 1:20; II Tim. 2:17,18), and also that of the second coming of Christ, which was misunderstood (II Thess. 2); and the council of Jerusalem found it necessary to re-assert the doctrine of Christian liberty (Acts 15). Naturally, the Bible contains no example of a creed. Creeds are not given by revelation, but are the fruit of the Church's reflection on revealed truth. In our day many are averse to symbols and confessions, and sing the glories of a creedless Church. But the objections raised against them are not at all insuperable. Creeds are not, as some insinuate, regarded as equal in authority to the Bible, and much less as superior to it. They do not, either by express statements or by implication add to the truth of Scripture. They do not militate against the freedom of the conscience, nor do they retard the progress of scientific theological study. Neither can they be regarded as the cause of the divisions in the Church, though they may be expressive of these. The divisions were there first and gave rise to the various creeds. As a matter of fact, they serve to a great extent to promote a measure of unity in the visible Church. Moreover, if a Church does not want to be silent, it is bound to develop a creed, be it written or unwritten. All this does not mean, however, that creeds cannot be abused.

d.   *In the cultivation of the study of theology.* The Church may not rest on its oars and be satisfied with the knowledge of the divine truth to which it has attained and which it has formulated in its confessions. It must seek to dig ever deeper into the mine of Scripture, in order to bring to light its hidden treasures. Through scientific study it must seek an ever deeper knowledge, an ever better understanding, of the words of life. It owes this to the truth itself as a revelation of God, but also to the training of its future ministers. The

Church is in duty bound to provide for, or at least to supervise, the training of the successive generations of its teachers and pastors. This would seem to be implied in the words of Paul to Timothy: "And the things which thou hast heard from me among many witnesses commit thou to faithful men, who shall be able to teach others also." II Tim. 2:2.

2. THE POTESTAS GUBERNANS. This is divided into the *potestas ordinans* and the *potestas iudicans*.

a. *The potestas ordinans.* "God is not a God of confusion, but of peace," I Cor. 14:33. Hence He desires that in His Church "all things be done decently and in order," vs. 40. This is evident from the fact that He has made provision for the proper regulation of the affairs of the Church. The regulative authority which He has given to the Church includes the power:

(1) *To enforce the laws of Christ.* This means that the Church has the right to carry into effect the laws which Christ has promulgated for the Church. There is an important difference on this point between the Roman Catholic Church and the Protestant Churches. The former virtually claims authority to *enact* laws that are binding on the conscience, and the trangression of which carries with it the same penalty that is annexed to any breach of the divine law. The latter, however, disclaim any such authority, but maintain the right to enforce the law of Christ, the King of the Church. And even so they claim no other than a ministerial or declarative power, regard the law as binding only because it is backed by the authority of Christ, and apply no other censures than those which He has sanctioned. Moreover, they feel that compulsion would conflict with the nature of their power and could never result in real spiritual benefit. All the members of the Church possess this power in a measure, Rom. 15:14; Col. 3:16; I Thess. 5:11, but it is vested in a special measure in the officers, John 21:15-17; Acts 20:28; I Pet. 5:2. The ministerial character of this power is brought out in II Cor. 1:24; I Pet. 5:2,3.

(2) *To draw up canons or church orders.* Numberless occasions arise on which the Church is prompted to make enactments or regulations, often called canons or church orders. Such enactments are not to be regarded as new laws, but merely as regulations for the proper application of the law. They are necessary to give the outward polity of the Church a definite form, to stipulate on what terms persons are permitted to bear office in the Church, to regulate public worship, to determine the proper form of discipline, and so on. General principles for the worship of God are laid down in Scripture, John 4:23; I Cor. 11:17-33; 14:40; 16:2; Col. 3:16(?); I Tim. 3:1-13; but in the regulation of the details of divine worship the churches are allowed great latitude. They may adapt themselves to circumstances, always bearing in mind, however, that they should worship God publicly in the manner best adapted to the purpose of edification. In no case may the regulations of the Church go contrary to the laws of Christ.

b. *The potestas iudicans.* The potestas iudicans is the power that is exercised to guard the holiness of the Church, by admitting those who are approved after examination, and by excluding those who depart from the truth or lead dishonorable lives. It is exercised especially in matters of discipline.

(1) *Scriptural teachings respecting discipline.* Among Israel unintentional sins could be atoned for by a sacrifice, but sins committed "with a high hand" (intentional) were punished with extermination. *The cherem* (the ban or that which is devoted) was not only an ecclesiastical, but also a civil punishment. The uncircumcized, the lepers, and the impure, were not permitted to enter the sanctuary, Lev. 5 f.; Ezek. 44:9. It was only after Israel lost its national independence, and its character as a religious assembly became more prominent, that the ban, consisting in exclusion from the assembly, became a measure of ecclesiastical discipline, Ezra 10:8; Luke 6:22; John 9:22; 12:42; 16:2. Jesus instituted discipline in His Church, when He gave the apostles and, in connection with their word, also the Church in general, the power to bind and to loose, to declare what is forbidden and what is permitted, and to forgive and to retain sins declaratively, Matt. 16:19; 18:18; John 20:23. And it is only because Christ has given this power to the Church, that she can exercise it. Several passages of the New Testament refer to the exercise of this power, I Cor. 5:2,7,13; II Cor. 2:5-7; II Thess. 3:14,15; I Tim. 1:20; Tit. 3:10. Such passages as I Cor. 5:5 and I Tim. 1:20 do not refer to regular discipline, but to a special measure permitted only to the apostles and consisting in giving the sinner over to Satan for temporary physical punishment, in order to save the soul.

(2) *The twofold purpose of discipline.* The purpose of discipline in the Church is twofold. In the first place it seeks to carry into effect the law of Christ concerning the admission and exclusion of members; and in the second place it aims at promoting the spiritual edification of the members of the Church by securing their obedience to the laws of Christ. Both of these aims are subservient to a higher end, namely, the maintenance of the holiness of the Church of Jesus Christ. With reference to diseased members of the Church, discipline is first of all medical in that it seeks to effect a cure, but it may become chirurgical, when the well-being of the Church requires the excision of the diseased member. It is impossible to tell when a process of discipline begins, whether a cure will be effected, or whether the diseased member will finally have to be removed. Probably the Church will succeed in bringing the sinner to repentance —and this is, of course, the more desirable end—; but it is also possible that it will have to resort to the extreme measure of excommunicating him. In all cases of discipline the Church will have to figure with both possibilities. Even in the most extreme measure it should still have the saving of the sinner in mind, I Cor. 5:5. At the same time it should always remember that the primary consideration is the maintenance of the holiness of the Church.

(3) *The exercise of discipline by the officers.* Though the ordinary members of the Church are frequently called upon to take part in the application

of discipline, it is generally applied by the officers of the Church and can be applied *only by them* when discipline becomes censure. There are two different ways in which it may become the duty of a consistory to deal with a matter of discipline. (a) Private sins can become a cause of discipline in the more technical sense of the word in the manner indicated in Matt. 18:15-17. If one sins against a brother, the latter must admonish the sinner; if this does not have the desired effect, he must admonish him again in the presence of one or two witnesses; and if even this fails, then he must notify the Church, and it becomes the duty of the officers to deal with the matter. It should be remembered, however, that this method is prescribed for *private* sins only. The offence given by public sins cannot be removed privately, but only by a public transaction. (b) Public sins make the sinner subject to disciplinary action by the consistory at once, without the formality of any preceding private admonitions, even if there is no formal accusation. By public sins are meant, not merely sins that are committed in public, but sins that give public and rather general offence. The consistory should not even wait until someone calls attention to such sins, but should take the initiative. It was no honor for the Corinthians that Paul had to call their attention to the scandal in their midst before they took action. I Cor. 5:1 ff.; nor was it an honor for the churches of Pergamus and Thyatira that they did not rebuke and exclude the heretical teachers from their midst, Rev. 2:14,15,20. In the case of public sins the consistory has no right to wait until someone brings formal charges; neither has it the right to demand of anyone who finally feels constrained to call attention to such sins that he admonish the sinner privately first. The matter of public sins can not be settled in private.

The disciplinary action of the consistory passes through three stages: (a) The *excommunicatio minor*, restraining the sinner from partaking of the Lord's Supper. This is not public, and is followed by repeated admonitions by the consistory, in order to bring the sinner to repentance. (b) If the preceding measure does not avail, it is followed by three public announcements and admonitions. In the first of these the sin is mentioned, but the sinner is not named. In the second the name is made known in accordance with the advice of classis, which must first be obtained. And in the third the imminent final excommunication is announced, in order that this may have the consent of the congregation. During all this time the consistory, of course, continues its admonitions. (c) Finally, this is followed by the *excommunicatio major*, by which one is cut off from the fellowship of the Church, Matt. 18:17; I Cor. 5:13; Tit. 3:10,11. It is always possible to reinstate the sinner, if he shows due repentance and confesses his sins, II Cor. 2:5-10.

(4) *The necessity of proper discipline.* The necessity of proper discipline is stressed in Scripture, Matt. 18:15-18; Rom. 16:17; I Cor. 5:2,9-13; II Cor. 2:5-10; II Thess. 3:6,14,15; Tit. 3:10,11. The church of Ephesus is praised because it did not bear with evil men, Rev. 2:2, and those of Pergamus and Thyatira are reproved for harboring heretical teachers and heathen abomina-

tions, Rev. 2:14,20,24. On the whole the Reformed churches have excelled in the exercise of Church discipline. They strongly stressed the fact that the Church of Christ must have an independent government and discipline. The Lutheran Churches did not emphasize this. They were Erastian in Church government, and were content to leave the exercise of Church discipline in the strict sense of the word in the hands of the government. The Church retained the right to exercise discipline only by means of the ministry of the Word, that is, by admonitions and exhortations addressed to the church as a whole. This was entrusted to the pastor and did not include the right to exclude anyone from the communion of the Church. At present there is in the Churches round about us a noticeable tendency to be lax in discipline, to place a one-sided emphasis on the reformation of the sinner through the ministry of the Word and—in some instances—through personal contacts with the sinner, and to steer clear of any such measures as excluding one from the communion of the Church. There is a very evident tendency to stress the fact that the Church is a great missionary agency, and to forget that it is first of all the assembly of the saints, in which those who publicly live in sin cannot be tolerated. It is said that sinners must be gathered into the church, and not excluded from it. But it should be remembered that they must be gathered in as saints and have no legitimate place in the Church as long as they do not confess their sin and strive for holiness of life.

3. THE POTESTAS OR MINISTERIUM MISERICORDIAE.

a. *The charismatic gift of healing.* When Christ sent His apostles and the seventy disciples out, He not only instructed them to preach, but also gave them power to cast out devils and to cure all manner of diseases, Matt. 10:1,8; Mark 3:15; Luke 9:1,2; 10:9; 10:9,17. Among the early Christians there were some who had the gift of healing and who could perform miracles, I Cor. 12:9, 10,28,30; Mark 16:17,18. This extraordinary condition, however, soon made way for the usual one, in which the Church carries on its work by the ordinary means. There is no Scriptural ground for the idea that the charism of healing was intended to be continued in the Church of all ages. Evidently, the miracles and miraculous signs recorded in Scripture were intended as a mark or credential of divine revelation, themselves formed a part of this revelation, and served to attest and confirm the message of the early preachers of the gospel. As such they naturally ceased when the period of special revelation came to an end. It is true that the Church of Rome and several sects claim the power of miraculous healing, but the claim is not borne out by the evidence. There are many marvelous stories in circulation of miraculous cures, but before they are given credence it must be proved: (1) that they do not pertain to cases of imaginary sickness, but to cases of real diseases or physical defects; (2) that they do not refer to imaginary or pretended, but to real, cures; and (3) that the cures are actually wrought in a supernatural way, and are not the result of the use of natural means, either material or mental.[1]

---

1. Cf. especially, Warfield, *Counterfeit Miracles.*

b. *The ordinary ministry of benevolence in the Church.* The Lord clearly intended that the Church should make provision for her poor. He hinted at this duty when He said to His disciples: "For ye have the poor always with you," Matt. 26:11; Mark 14:7. By means of a communion of goods the early Church saw to it that no one wanted the necessaries of life, Acts 4:34. It is not impossible that the *neoteroi* of Acts 5:6,10 were the precursors of the later deacons. And when the widows of the Greeks were being neglected in the daily ministration, the apostles saw to it that seven well qualified men were put in charge of this necessary business, Acts 6:1-6. They were to "serve the tables," which seems to mean in this connection, to superintend the service at the tables of the poor, or to provide for an equitable division of the provisions that were placed on the tables. Deacons and deaconesses are mentioned repeatedly in the Bible, Rom. 16:1; Phil. 1:1; I Tim. 3:8-12. Moreover, the New Testament contains many passages urging the necessity of giving or collecting for the poor, Acts 20:35; I Cor. 16:1,2; II Cor. 9:1,6,7,12-14; Gal. 2:10; 6:10; Eph. 4:28; I Tim. 5:10, 16; Jas. 1:27; 2:15,16; I John 3:17. There can be no doubt about the duty of the Church in this respect. And the deacons are the officers who are charged with the responsible and delicate task of performing the work of Christian benevolence with reference to all the needy of the Church. They must devise ways and means for collecting the necessary funds, have charge of the money collected, and provide for its prudential distribution. However, their task is not limited to this offering of material help. They must also instruct and comfort the needy. In all their work they should consider it their duty to apply spiritual principles in the performance of their duty. It is to be feared that this function of the Church is sadly neglected in many of the churches to-day. There is a tendency to proceed on the assumption that it can safely be left to the State to provide *even for the poor of the Church.* But in acting on that assumption, the Church is neglecting a sacred duty, is impoverishing her own spiritual life, is robbing herself of the joy experienced in ministering to the needs of those who suffer want, and is depriving those who are suffering hardships, who are borne down by the cares of life, and who are often utterly discouraged, of the comfort, the joy, and the sunshine of the spiritual ministrations of Christian love, which are as a rule entirely foreign to the work of charity administered by the State.

QUESTIONS FOR FURTHER STUDY: How do the Reformed and the Lutheran conceptions of Christ as the Head of the Church differ? Does the Old Testament contain any indication that Christ is King of the Church? What systems of Church government deny, or detract from, the Head—or Kingship of Christ? How does the Headship of Christ affect the relation of the Church to the State, religious liberty, and liberty of conscience? Is the doctrine that the power of the Church is exclusively spiritual consistent with Romanism and Erastianism? How is the power of the Church overrated by High Church men, and underrated by Low Church men, of various descriptions? How do the Independents view the power of the officers? How is Church power limited? What is the end contemplated in the exercise of Church power? What is meant by the Church in Matt. 18:17? Does the key of discipline shut out only from outward privileges in the Church, or also from a spiritual interest in Christ? By whom and how is discipline exercised in the Roman Catholic, the Anglican, the Methodist, and the Congregational, Church? Can a Church safely discard discipline?

LITERATURE: Bavinck, *Geref. Dogm.* IV, pp. 425-482; Kuyper, *Dict. Dogm., de Ecclesia,* pp. 268-293; id., *Tractaat van de Reformatie der Kerken,* pp. 41-69; Bannerman, *The Church,* I. pp. 187-480; II, pp. 186-200; Hodge, *Church Polity,* cf. Index; Morris, *Ecclesiology,* pp. 143-151; Wilson, *Free Church Principles;* McPherson, *The Doctrine of the Church in Scottish Theology,* pp. 129-224; Gillespie, *Aaron's Rod Blossoming;* ibid., *On Ceremonies;* Bouwman, *De Kerkelijke Tucht;* Jansen, *De Kerkelijke Tucht;* Biesterveld, Van Lonkhuizen, en Rudolph, *Het Diaconaat;* Bouwman, *Het Ambt der Diakenen;* Litton, *Introd. to Dogm. Theol.,* pp. 394-419; Schmid, *Doct. Theol. of the Ev. Luth. Church,* pp. 607-621; Wilmers, *Handbook of the Chr. Rel.,* pp. 77-101; Cunningham, *Discussions of Church Principles;* ibid., *Historical Theology* II, pp. 514-587; McPherson, *Presbyterianism.*

THE MEANS OF GRACE

I. The Means of Grace in General

A. The Idea of the Means of Grace.

Fallen man receives all the blessings of salvation out of the eternal fountain of the grace of God, in virtue of the merits of Jesus Christ and through the operation of the Holy Spirit. While the Spirit can and does in some respects operate immediately on the soul of the sinner, He has seen fit to bind Himself largely to the use of certain means in the communication of divine grace. The term "means of grace" is not found in the Bible, but is nevertheless a proper designation of the means that are indicated in the Bible. At the same time the term is not very definite and may have a far more comprehensive meaning than it ordinarily has in theology. The Church may be represented as the great means of grace which Christ, working through the Holy Spirit, uses for the gathering of the elect, the edification of the saints, and the building up of His spiritual body. He qualifies her for this great task by endowing her with all kinds of spiritual gifts, and by the institution of the offices for the administration of the Word and the sacraments, which are all means to lead the elect to their eternal destiny. But the term may have an even wider scope. The whole providential guidance of the saints, through prosperity and adversity, often becomes a means by which the Holy Spirit leads the elect to Christ or to an ever closer communion with Him. It is even possible to include in the means of grace all that is required of men for the reception and the continued enjoyment of the blessings of the covenant, such as faith, conversion, spiritual warfare, and prayer. It is neither customary nor desirable, however, to include all this under the term "means of grace." The Church is not a means of grace alongside of the Word and the sacraments, because her power in promoting the work of the grace of God consists only in the administration of these. She is not instrumental in communicating grace, except by means of the Word and of the sacraments. Moreover, faith, conversion, and prayer, are first of all fruits of the grace of God, though they may in turn become instrumental in strengthening the spiritual life. They are not objective ordinances, but subjective conditions for the possession and enjoyment of the blessings of the covenant. Consequently, it is better not to follow Hodge when he includes prayer, nor McPherson when he adds to the Word and the sacraments both the Church and prayer. Strictly speaking, only the Word and the sacraments can be regarded as means of grace, that is, as objective channels which Christ has instituted in the Church, and to which He ordinarily binds Himself in the communication of His grace. Of course these may never be dissociated from Christ, nor from the powerful operation of the Holy Spirit, nor from the Church which is the appointed organ for the distribution of the blessings of divine grace. They are in themselves quite ineffective and are productive of spiritual results only through the efficacious operation of the Holy Spirit.

B. Characteristics of the Word and the Sacraments as Means of Grace.

The fact that one can speak of means of grace in a rather general sense makes it imperative to point to the distinctive characteristics of the means of grace in the technical or restricted sense of the word.

1. They are instruments, not of *common* but of, *special* grace, the grace that removes sin and renews the sinner in conformity with the image of God. It is true that the Word of God may and in some respects actually does enrich those who live under the gospel with some of the choicest blessings of common grace in the restricted sense of the word; but it, as well as the sacraments, comes into consideration here only as a means of grace in the technical sense of the word. And the means of grace in this sense are always connected with the beginning and the progressive operation of the special grace of God, that is redemptive grace, in the hearts of sinners.

2. They are *in themselves*, and not in virtue of their connection with things not included in them, means of grace. Striking experiences may, and undoubtedly sometimes do, serve to strengthen the work of God in the hearts of believers, but this does not constitute them means of grace in the technical sense, since they accomplish this only in so far as these experiences are interpreted in the light of God's Word, through which the Holy Spirit operates. The Word and the sacraments are in themselves means of grace; their spiritual efficacy is dependent only on the operation of the Holy Spirit.

3. They are *continuous* instruments of God's grace, and not in any sense of the word exceptional. This means that they are not associated with the operation of God's grace merely occasionally or in a more or less accidental way, but are the regularly ordained means for the communication of the saving grace of God and are as such of perpetual value. The Heidelberg Catechism asks in Question 65, "Since, then, we are made partakers of Christ and all His benefits by faith only, whence comes this faith?" And the answer is, "From the Holy Spirit, who works it in our hearts by the preaching of the holy gospel, and confirms it by the use of the holy sacraments."

4. They are the *official* means of the Church of Jesus Christ. The *preaching* of the Word (or, *the Word preached*) and the *administration* of the sacraments (or, *the sacraments administered*) are the means *officially instituted in the Church*, by which the Holy Spirit works and confirms faith in the hearts of men. Some Reformed theologians limit the idea of the means of grace still more by saying that they are administered only within the visible Church, and that they presuppose the existence of the principle of the new life in the soul.

Shedd and Dabney both speak of them, without any qualification, as "means of sanctification." Says the former: "When the world of unregenerate men are said to have the means of grace, the means of *conviction* under common grace, not of sanctification under special grace, are intended."[1] Honig also distinguishes between the Word of God as a means of grace and the Word as it contains the call to conversion and serves to call Gentiles to the service of the living God.[2] Dr. Kuyper, too, thinks of the means of grace merely as means for the strengthening of the new life when he says: "The *media gratiae* are means instituted by God that He makes use of to unfold, both personally and socially, for and through our consciousness, the re-creation that He immediately established in our nature."[3] There is, of course, a truth in this representation. The principle of the new life is wrought in the soul *immediately*, that is, without the mediation of the Word that is preached. But in so far as the origination of the new life also includes the new birth and internal calling, it may also be said that the Holy Spirit works the beginning of the new life or of faith, as the Heidelberg Catechism says, "by the preaching of the holy gospel."

C. Historical Views Respecting the Means of Grace.

There has been considerable difference of opinion respecting the means of grace in the Church of Jesus Christ. The early Church does not furnish us with anything very definite on this point. There was far more emphasis on the sacraments than on the Word of God. Baptism was rather generally regarded as the means by which sinners were regenerated, while the eucharist stood out as the sacrament of sanctification. In course of time, however, certain definite views were developed.

1. THE ROMAN CATHOLIC VIEW. While the Roman Catholics regarded even relics and images as means of grace, they singled out in particular the Word and the sacraments. At the same time they failed to give due prominence to the Word, and ascribed to it only preparatory significance in the work of grace. As compared with the Word, the sacraments were considered to be the real means of grace. In the system that was gradually developed the Church of Rome recognizes a means that is even superior to the sacraments. The Church itself is regarded as the primary means of grace. In it Christ continues His divine-human life on earth, performs His prophetic, priestly, and kingly work, and through it He communicates the fulness of His grace and truth. This grace serves especially to raise man from the natural to the supernatural order. It is a *gratia elevans*, a supernatural physical power, infused into the natural man through the sacraments working *ex opere operato*. In the sacraments the visible signs and the invisible grace are inseparably connected. In fact, the grace of God is contained in the means as a sort of substance, is conveyed through the channel of the means, and is therefore absolutely bound to the

---

1. *Dogm. Theol.* II, p. 561.
2. *Handboek van de Geref. Dogm.*, p. 611.
3. *Dict. Dogm., De Sacramentis*, p. 7 (translation mine — L.B.).

means. Baptism regenerates man *ex opere operato*, and the even more important eucharist raises his spiritual life to a higher level. Apart from Christ, from the Church, and from the sacrament, there is no salvation.

2. THE LUTHERAN VIEW. With the Reformation the emphasis was shifted from the sacraments to the Word of God. Luther gave great prominence to the Word of God as the primary means of grace. He pointed out that the sacraments have no significance apart from the Word and are in fact merely the visible Word. He did not entirely succeed in correcting the Roman Catholic error as to the inseparable connection between the outward means and the inward grace communicated through them. He, too, conceived of the grace of God as a sort of substance contained in the means and not to be obtained apart from the means. The Word of God is in itself always efficacious and will effect a spiritual change in man, unless he puts a stumblingblock in the way. And the body and blood of Christ is "in, with, and under" the elements of bread and wine, so that they who eat and drink the latter also receive the former, though this will be to their advantage only if they receive them in the proper manner. It was especially his opposition to the subjectivity of the Anabaptists that caused Luther to stress the objective character of the sacraments and to make their effectiveness dependent on their divine institution rather than on the faith of the recipients. The Lutherans did not always steer clear of the idea that the sacraments function *ex opere operato*.

3. THE VIEW OF THE MYSTICS. Luther had to contend a great deal with the mystical Anabaptists, and it was especially his reaction to their views that determined his final view of the means of grace. The Anabaptists, and other mystical sects of the age of the Reformation and of later times, virtually deny that God avails Himself of means in the distribution of His grace. They stress the fact that God is absolutely free in communicating His grace, and therefore can hardly be conceived of as bound to such external means. Such means after all belong to the natural world, and have nothing in common with the spiritual world. God, or Christ, or the Holy Spirit, or the inner light, work directly in the heart, and both the Word and the sacraments can only serve to indicate or to symbolize this internal grace. This whole conception is determined by a dualistic view of nature and grace.

4. THE RATIONALISTIC VIEW. The Socinians of the days of the Reformation, on the other hand, moved too far in the opposite direction. Socinus himself did not even regard baptism as a rite destined to be permanent in the Church of Jesus Christ, but his followers did not go to that extreme. They recognized both baptism and the Lord's Supper as rites of permanent validity, but ascribed to them only a moral efficacy. This means that they thought of the means of grace as working only through moral persuasion, and did not associate them at all with any mystical operation of the Holy Spirit. In fact, they placed the emphasis more on what man did in the means of grace than on what God accomplished through them, when they spoke of them as mere external badges

of profession and (of the sacraments) as memorials. The Arminians of the seventeenth century and the Rationalists of the eighteenth century shared this view.

5. THE REFORMED VIEW. While reaction to the Anabaptists caused the Lutherans to move in the direction of Rome and to bind the grace of God to the means in the most absolute sense — a position also taken by High Church Anglicans —, the Reformed Churches continued the original view of the Reformation. They deny that the means of grace can of themselves confer grace, as if they were endued with a magical power to produce holiness. God and God only is the efficient cause of salvation. And in the distribution and communication of His grace He is not absolutely bound to the divinely appointed means through which He ordinarily works, but uses them to serve His gracious purposes according to His own free will. But while they do not regard the means of grace as absolutely necessary and indispensable, they strongly oppose the idea that these means may be treated as purely accidental and indifferent and can be neglected with impunity. God has appointed them as the ordinary means through which He works His grace in the hearts of sinners, and their wilful neglect can only result in spiritual loss.

D. Characteristic Elements in the Reformed Doctrine of the Means of Grace.

For a proper understanding of the Reformed doctrine of the means of grace the following points deserve special emphasis.

1. The special grace of God operates only in the sphere in which the means of grace function. This truth must be maintained over against the Mystics, who deny the necessity of the means of grace. God is a God of order, who in the operation of His grace ordinarily employs the means which He Himself has ordained. This, of course, does not mean that He has Himself become subservient to the appointed means and could not possibly work without them in the communication of His grace, but only that it has pleased Him to bind Himself, except in the case of infants, to the use of these means.

2. On a single point, namely, in the implanting of the new life, the grace of God works immediately, that is, without the use of these means as instruments. But even so it works only in the sphere of the means of grace, since these are absolutely required in drawing out and nourishing the new life. This is a direct negation of the position of Rationalism, which represents regeneration as the result of moral suasion.

3. While the grace of God generally operates mediately, it is not inherent in the means as a divine deposit, but accompanies the use of these. This must be maintained in opposition to the Roman Catholics, the High Church Anglicans, and the Lutherans, who proceed on the assumption that the means of grace always operate in virtue of an inherent power, though their operation may be made ineffective by the condition or attitude of the recipient.

4. The Word of God may never be separated from the sacraments, but must always accompany them, since they are virtually only a visible representation of the truth that is conveyed to us by the Word. In the Church of Rome the Word retires into the background as having only preparatory significance, while the sacraments, considered apart from the Word, are regarded as the real means of grace.

5. All the knowledge which is obtained by the recipient of divine grace, is wrought in him by means of the Word and is derived from the Word. This position must be maintained in opposition to all kinds of Mystics, who lay claim to special revelations and to a spiritual knowledge that is not mediated by the Word, and who thereby lead us into a sea of boundless subjectivity.

II. The Word as a Means of Grace

A. Meaning of the Term "Word of God" in This Connection.

Roman Catholics can hardly be said to regard the Word of God as a means of grace. In their estimation the Church is the great and all-sufficient channel of grace for sinners, and all other means are subordinate to it. And the two most powerful means which God has placed at the disposal of the Church are prayer and the sacraments. The Churches of the Reformation, however, both the Lutheran and the Reformed, do honor the Word of God as such and even regard it as superior to the sacraments. It is true that the older Reformed theologians, such as the professors of Leyden (Synopsis), Mastricht, à Marck, Turretin, and others, and even some of a more recent date, such as Dabney and Kuyper, do not treat of it separately as a means of grace, but this is largely due to the fact that they have already discussed the Word in other connections. They freely speak of it as a means of grace. And when they consider the Word of God as a means of grace, they are not thinking of the Logos, the personal Word, John 1:1-14. Neither do they have in mind any word of power proceeding out of the mouth of Jehovah, Ps. 33:6; Isa. 55:11; Rom. 4:17, or any word of direct revelation, such as the prophets received, Jer. 1:4; 2:1; Ezek. 6:1; Hos. 1:1. It is the inspired Word of God, the Word of Scripture, which they regard as a means of grace. And even when speaking of this as a means of grace, they contemplate it from a special point of view. The inspired Scriptures constitute the *principium cognoscendi*, the fountain head, of all our theological knowledge, but it is not that aspect which we have in mind when we speak of the Word of God as a means of grace. The Bible is not only the *principium cognoscendi* of theology, but it is also the means which the Holy Spirit employs for the extension of the Church and for the edification and nourishment of the saints. It is pre-eminently the word of God's grace, and therefore also the most important means of grace. Strictly speaking, it is the Word *as it is preached* in the name of God and in virtue of a divine commission, that is considered as a means of grace in the technical sense of the word, alongside of the sacraments which are administered in the name of God. Naturally, the Word of God can also be considered as a means of grace in a more general sense. It may be a real blessing as it is brought to man in many additional ways: as it is read in the home, is taught in the school, or is circulated in tracts. As the *official* means of grace, placed at the disposal of the Church, both the Word and the sacraments can only be administered by the lawful and properly qualified officers of the Church. But in distinction from the sacraments the Word can also be carried out into the world by all believers and operate in many different ways.

B. The Relation of the Word to the Holy Spirit.

There has developed in the course of history quite a difference of opinion respecting the efficacy of the Word, and consequently, as to the connection between the effectual operation of the Word, and the work of the Holy Spirit.

1. Nomism in its various forms, such as Judaism, Pelagianism, Semi-Pelagianism Arminianism, Neonomianism, and Rationalism, deems the intellectual, moral, and æsthetic influence of the Word as the only influence that can be ascribed to it. It does not believe in a supernatural operation of the Holy Spirit through the Word. The truth revealed in the Word of God works only by moral persuasion. In some of its forms, such as Pelagianism and Rationalism, Nomism does not even feel the need of a special operation of the Holy Spirit in the work of redemption, but in its more moderate forms, such as Semi-Pelagianism, Arminianism, and Neonomianism, it considers the moral influence of the Word insufficient, so that it must be supplemented by the work of the Holy Spirit.

2. Antinomianism, on the other hand, does not regard the external Word as necessary at all, and displays a Mysticism which expects everything from the inner word or the inner light, or from the *immediate* operation of the Holy Spirit. Its slogan is, "The letter killeth, but the Spirit giveth life." The external word belongs to the natural world, is unworthy of the really spiritual man, and can produce no spiritual results. While Antinomians of all descriptions reveal a tendency to slight, if not to ignore altogether, the means of grace, this tendency received its clearest expression at the hands of some of the Anabaptists.

3. In opposition to these two views, the Reformers maintained that the Word alone is not sufficient to work faith and conversion; that the Holy Spirit can, but does not ordinarily, work without the Word; and that therefore in the work of redemption the Word and the Spirit work together. Though there was little difference on this point at first between the Lutherans and the Reformed, the former from the beginning stressed the fact that the Holy Spirit works through the Word as His instrument (*per verbum*), while the latter preferred to say that the operation of the Holy Spirit accompanies the Word (*cum verbo*). Later on Lutheran theologians developed the real Lutheran doctrine, that the Word of God contains the converting power of the Holy Spirit as a divine deposit, which is now so inseparably connected with it that it is present even when the Word is not used, or is not used legitimately. But in order to explain the different results of the preaching of the Word in the case of different persons, they had to resort, even though it be in a mild form, to the doctrine of the free will of man. The Reformed indeed regarded the Word of God as always powerful, either as a savour of life unto life or as a savour of death

unto death, but maintained that it becomes efficacious in leading to faith and conversion only by an accompanying operation of the Holy Spirit in the hearts of sinners. They refused to consider this efficaciousness as an impersonal power resident in the Word.

C. The Two Parts of the Word of God Considered as a Means of Grace.

1. THE LAW AND THE GOSPEL IN THE WORD OF GOD. The Churches of the Reformation from the very beginning distinguished between the law and the gospel as the two parts of the Word of God as a means of grace. This distinction was not understood to be identical with that between the Old and the New Testament, but was regarded as a distinction that applies to both Testaments. There is law and gospel in the Old Testament, and there is law and gospel in the New. The law comprises everything in Scripture which is a revelation of God's will in the form of command or prohibition, while the gospel embraces everything, whether it be in the Old Testament or in the New, that pertains to the work of reconciliation and that proclaims the seeking and redeeming love of God in Christ Jesus. And each one of these two parts has its own proper function in the economy of grace. The law seeks to awaken in the heart of man contrition on account of sin, while the gospel aims at the awakening of saving faith in Jesus Christ. The work of the law is in a sense preparatory to that of the gospel. It deepens the consciousness of sin and thus makes the sinner aware of the need of redemption. Both are subservient to the same end, and both are indispensable parts of the means of grace. This truth has not always been sufficiently recognized. The condemning aspect of the law has sometimes been stressed at the expense of its character as a part of the means of grace. Ever since the days of Marcion there have always been some who saw only contrast between the law and the gospel and proceeded on the assumption that the one excluded the other. They based their opinion in part on the rebuke which Paul administered to Peter (Gal. 2:11-14), and partly on the fact that Paul occasionally draws a sharp distinction between the law and the gospel and evidently regards them as contrasts, II Cor. 3:6-11; Gal. 3:2,3,10-14; cf. also John 1:17. They lost sight of the fact that Paul also says that the law served as a tutor to lead men to Christ, Gal. 3:24, and that the Epistle to the Hebrews represents the law, not as standing in antithetical relation to the gospel, but rather as the gospel in its preliminary and imperfect state.

Some of the older Reformed theologians represented the law and the gospel as absolute opposites. They thought of the law as embodying all the demands and commandments of Scripture, and of the gospel, as containing no demands whatsoever, but only *unconditional* promises; and thus excluded from it all requirements. This was partly due to the way in which the two are sometimes contrasted in Scripture, but was also partly the result of a controversy in which they were engaged with the Arminians. The Arminian view, making salvation dependent on faith and evangelical obedience *as works of man*, caused them to go to the extreme of saying that the covenant of grace does not require anything on the part of man, does not prescribe any duties, does not demand or command anything, not even faith, trust, and hope in the Lord, and so on. but merely conveys to man the promises of what God will do for him. Others, however, correctly maintained that even the law of Moses is not devoid of promises, and that the gospel also contains certain demands. They clearly saw that man is not merely passive, when he is introduced into the covenant of grace, but is called upon to accept the covenant actively with all its privileges, though it is God who works in him the ability to meet the requirements. The promises which man appropriates certainly impose upon him certain duties, and among them the duty to obey the law of God as a rule of life, but also carry with them the assurance that God will work in him "both to will and to do." The consistent Dispensationalists of our day again represent the law and the gospel as absolute opposites. Israel was under the law in the previous dispensation, but the Church of the present dispensation is under the gospel, and as such is free from the law. This means that the gospel is now the only means of salvation, and that the law does not now serve as such. Members of the Church need not concern themselves about its demands, since Christ has met all its requirements. They seem to forget that, while Christ bore the curse of the law, and met its demands as a condition of the covenant of works, He did not fulfil the law for them as a rule of life, to which man is subject in virtue of his creation, apart from any covenant arrangement.

2. NECESSARY DISTINCTIONS RESPECTING THE LAW AND THE GOSPEL.

a. As was already said in the preceding, the distinction between the law and the gospel is not the same as that between the Old and the New Testament. Neither is it the same as that which present day Dispensationalists make between the dispensation of the law and the dispensation of the gospel. It is contrary to the plain facts of Scripture to say that there is no gospel in the Old Testament, or at least not in that part of the Old Testament that covers the dispensation of the law. There is gospel in the maternal promise, gospel in the ceremonial law, and gospel in many of the Prophets, as Isa. 53 and 54; 55:1-3,6.7; Jer. 31:33,34; Ezek. 36:25-28. In fact, there is a gospel current running through the whole of the Old Testament, which reaches its highest point in the Messianic prophecies. And it is equally contrary to Scripture to say that there is no law in the New Testament, or that the law does not apply in the New Testament dispensation. Jesus taught the permanent validity of the law, Matt. 5:17-19. Paul says that God provided for it that the requirements of the law should be fulfilled in our lives, Rom. 8:4, and holds his readers responsible for keeping the law, Rom. 13:9. James assures his readers that he who transgresses a single commandment of the law (and he mentions some of these), is a transgressor of the law, Jas. 2:8-11. And John defines sin as "lawlessness," and says that this is the love of God, that we keep His commandments, I John 3:4; 5:3.

b. It is possible to say that in some respects the Christian is free from the law of God. The Bible does not always speak of the law in the same sense.

Sometimes it contemplates this as the immutable expression of the nature and will of God, which applies at all times and under all conditions. But it also refers to it as it functions in the covenant of works, in which the gift of eternal life was conditioned on its fulfilment. Man failed to meet the condition, thereby also losing the ability to meet it, and is now by nature under a sentence of condemnation. When Paul draws a contrast between the law and the gospel, he is thinking of this aspect of the law, the broken law of the covenant of works, which can no more justify, but can only condemn the sinner. From the law in this particular sense, both as a means for obtaining eternal life and as a condemning power, believers are set free in Christ, since He became a curse for them and also met the demands of the covenant of works in their behalf. The law in that particular sense and the gospel of free grace are mutually exclusive.

c. There is another sense, however, in which the Christian is not free from the law. The situation is quite different when we think of the law as the expression of man's natural obligations to his God, the law as it is applied to man even apart from the covenant of works. It is impossible to imagine any condition in which man might be able to claim freedom from the law in that sense. It is pure Antinomianism to maintain that Christ kept the law as a rule of life for His people, so that they need not worry about this any more. The law lays claim, and justly so, on the entire life of man in all its aspects, including his relation to the gospel of Jesus Christ. When God offers man the gospel, the law demands that the latter shall accept this. Some would speak of this as the law in the gospel, but this is hardly correct. The gospel itself consists of promises and is no law; yet there is a demand of the law in connection with the gospel. The law not only demands that we accept the gospel and believe in Jesus Christ, but also that we lead a life of gratitude in harmony with its requirements.

D. The Threefold Use of the Law.

It is customary in theology to distinguish a three-fold use of the law.

1. THE THREE DEFINED. We distinguish:

a. *A usus politicus or civilis.* The law serves the purpose of restraining sin and promoting righteousness. Considered from this point of view, the law presupposes sin and is necessary on account of sin. It serves the purpose of God's common grace in the world at large. This means that from this point of view it cannot be regarded a means of grace in the technical sense of the word.

b. *A usus elenchticus or pedagogicus.* In this capacity the law serves the purpose of bringing man under conviction of sin, and of making him conscious of his inability to meet the demands of the law. In that way the law becomes his tutor to lead him unto Christ, and thus becomes subservient to God's gracious purpose of redemption.

c. *A usus didacticus or normativus.* This is the so-called *tertius usus legis,* the third use of the law. The law is a rule of life for believers, reminding them of their duties and leading them in the way of life and salvation. This third use of the law is denied by the Antinomians.

2. THE DIFFERENCE BETWEEN THE LUTHERAN AND THE REFORMED ON THIS POINT. There is some difference between the Lutherans and the Reformed with respect to this threefold use of the law. Both accept this threefold distinction, but the Lutherans stress the second use of the law. In their estimation the law is primarily the appointed means for bringing men under conviction of sin and thus indirectly pointing the way to Jesus Christ as the Saviour of sinners. While they also admit the third use of the law, they do it with a certain reserve, since they hold that believers are no more under the law. According to them the third use of the law is necessary only because, and in so far as, believers are still sinners; they must be held in check by the law, and should become ever-increasingly conscious of their sins. It is not surprising therefore that this third use of the law occupies no important place in their system. As a rule they treat of the law only in connection with the doctrine of human misery. The Reformed do full justice to the second use of the law, teaching that "through the law cometh the knowledge of sin," and that the law awakens the consciousness of the need of redemption; but they devote even more attention to the law in connection with the doctrine of sanctification. They stand strong in the conviction that believers are still under the law as a rule of life and of gratitude. Hence the Heidelberg Catechism devotes not less than eleven Lord's Days to the discussion of the law, and that in its third part, which deals with gratitude.

QUESTIONS FOR FURTHER STUDY: Why do the Roman Catholics regard the Church as the outstanding means of grace? What accounts for their neglect of the Word as a means of grace? Why are the means of grace in disrespect among the Mystics? What distinguishes the Word and the sacraments as means of grace from all other means? Is it correct to say that they are administered only in the Church and serve, not to originate the new life, but to strengthen it? Is the Word of God exclusively used as a means of grace? How do the law and the gospel differ as different aspects of the Word?

LITERATURE: Bavinck, *Geref. Dogm.* IV, pp. 483-505; Hodge, *Syst. Theol.* III, pp. 466-485; Shedd, *Dogm. Theol.* II, pp. 561-563; Vos, *Geref. Dogm. V. De Genademiddelen,* pp. 1-11; McPherson, *Chr. Dogm.,* pp. 422-427; Dick, *Lect. on Theology,* pp. 447-458; Pieper, *Christl. Dogm.* III, pp. 121-296; Valentine, *Chr. Theol.* II, pp. 282-292; Mueller, *Chr. Dogm.,* pp. 441-484; Raymond, *Syst. Theol.* III, pp. 243-255; Drummond, *Studies in Chr. Doct.,* pp. 399-403.

III. The Sacraments in General

A. Relation Between the Word and the Sacraments.

In distinction from the Roman Catholic Church, the Churches of the Reformation emphasize the priority of the Word of God. While the former proceeds on the assumption that the sacraments contain all that is necessary for the salvation of sinners, need no interpretation, and therefore render the Word quite superfluous as a means of grace, the latter regard the Word as absolutely essential, and merely raise the question, why the sacraments should be added to it. Some of the Lutherans claim that a specific grace, differing from that which is wrought by the Word, is conveyed by the sacraments. This is all but universally denied by the Reformed, a few Scottish theologians and Dr. Kuyper forming exceptions to the rule. They point to the fact that God has so created man that he obtains knowledge particularly through the avenues of the senses of sight and hearing. The Word is adapted to the ear, and the sacraments to the eye. And since the eye is more sensuous than the ear, it may be said that God, by adding the sacraments to the Word, comes to the aid of sinful man. The truth addressed to the ear in the Word, is symbolically represented to the eye in the sacraments. It should be borne in mind, however, that, while the Word can exist and is also complete without the sacraments, the sacraments are never complete without the Word. There are points of similarity and points of difference between the Word and the sacraments.

1. POINTS OF SIMILARITY. They agree: (a) in author, since God instituted both as means of grace; (b) in contents, for Christ is the central content of the one as well as of the other; and (c) in the manner in which the contents are appropriated, namely, by faith. This is the only way in which the sinner can become a participant of the grace that is offered in the Word and in the sacraments.

2. POINTS OF DIFFERENCE. They differ: (a) in their necessity, the Word being indispensable, while the sacraments are not; (b) in their purpose, since the Word is intended to *engender* and to strengthen faith, while the sacraments serve only to strengthen it; and (c) in their extension, since the Word goes out into all the world, while the sacraments are administered only to those who are in the Church.

B. Origin and Meaning of the Word "Sacrament".

The word "sacrament" is not found in Scripture. It is derived from the Latin *sacramentum*, which originally denoted a sum of money deposited by two parties in litigation. After the decision of the court the winner's money was returned, while that of the loser was forfeited. This seems to have been called a *sacramentum*, because it was intended to be a sort of propitiatory offering to the gods. The transition to the Christian use of the term is probably to be sought: (a) in the military use of the term, in which it denoted the oath by which a soldier solemnly pledged obedience to his commander, since in baptism the Christian pledges obedience to his Lord; and (b) in the specifically religious sense which it acquired when the Vulgate employed it as a rendering of the Greek *musterion*. It is possible that this Greek term was applied to the sacraments, because they have a faint resemblance to some of the mysteries of the Greek religions. In the early Church the word "sacrament" was first used to denote all kinds of doctrines and ordinances. For this very reason some objected to the name, and preferred to speak of "signs," "seals," or "mysteries." Even during and immediately after the Reformation many disliked the name "sacrament." Melanchton used *"signi,"* and both Luther and Calvin deemed it necessary to call attention to the fact that the word "sacrament" is not employed in its original sense in theology. But the fact that the word is not found in Scripture and is not used in its original sense when it is applied to the ordinances instituted by Jesus, need not deter us, for usage often determines the meaning of a word. The following definition may be given of a sacrament: *A sacrament is a holy ordinance instituted by Christ, in which by sensible signs the grace of God in Christ, and the benefits of the covenant of grace, are represented, sealed, and applied to believers, and these, in turn, give expression to their faith and allegiance to God.*

C. The Component Parts of the Sacraments.

Three parts must be distinguished in the sacraments.

1. THE OUTWARD OR VISIBLE SIGN. Each one of the sacraments contains a material element that is palpable to the senses. In a rather loose sense this is sometimes called the sacrament. In the strict sense of the word, however, the term is more inclusive and denotes both the sign and that which is signified. To avoid misunderstanding, this different usage should be borne in mind. It explains how an unbeliever may be said to receive, and yet not to receive, the sacrament. He does not receive it in the full sense of the word. The external matter of the sacrament includes not only the elements that are used, namely, water, bread, and wine, but also the sacred rite, that which is done with these elements. From this external point of view the Bible calls the sacraments signs and seals, Gen. 9:12,13; 17:11; Rom. 4:11.

2. THE INWARD SPIRITUAL GRACE SIGNIFIED AND SEALED. Signs and seals presuppose something that is signified and sealed and which is usually called the *materia interna* of the sacrament. This is variously indicated in Scripture

as the covenant of grace, Gen. 9:12,13; 17:11, the righteousness of faith, Rom. 4:11, the forgiveness of sins, Mark 1:4; Matt. 26:28, faith and conversion, Mark 1:4; 16:16, communion with Christ in His death and resurrection, Rom. 6:3, and so on. Briefly stated, it may be said to consist in Christ and all His spiritual riches. The Roman Catholics find in it the sanctifying grace which is added to human nature, enabling man to do good works and to rise to the height of the *visio Dei* (the vision of God). The sacraments signify, not merely a general truth, but a promise given unto us and accepted by us, and serve to strengthen our faith with respect to the realization of that promise, Gen. 17:1-14; Ex. 12:13; Rom. 4:11-13. They visibly represent, and deepen our consciousness of, the spiritual blessings of the covenant, of the washing away of our sins, and of our participation of the life that is in Christ, Matt. 3:11; Mark 1:4,5; I Cor. 10:2,3,16,17; Rom. 2:28,29; 6:3,4; Gal. 3:27. As signs and seals they are means of grace, that is, means of strengthening the inward grace that is wrought in the heart by the Holy Spirit.

3. THE SACRAMENTAL UNION BETWEEN THE SIGN AND THAT WHICH IS SIGNIFIED. This is usually called the *forma sacramenti* (*forma* here meaning essence), because it is exactly the relation between the sign and the thing signified that constitutes the essence of the sacrament. According to the Reformed view this is: (a) not *physical,* as the Roman Catholics claim, as if the thing signified were inherent in the sign, and the reception of the *materia externa* necessarily carried with it a participation in the *materia interna;* (b) nor *local,* as the Lutherans represent it, as if the sign and the thing signified were present in the same space, so that both believers and unbelievers receive the full sacrament when they receive the sign; (c) but *spiritual,* or as Turretin expresses it, *relative* and *moral,* so that, where the sacrament is received in faith, the grace of God accompanies it. According to this view the external sign becomes a means employed by the Holy Spirit in the communication of divine grace. The close connection between the sign and the thing signified explains the use of what is generally called "sacramental language," in which the sign is put for the thing signified or *vice versa,* Gen. 17:10; Acts 22:16; I Cor. 5:7.

D. The Necessity of the Sacraments.

Roman Catholics hold that baptism is absolutely necessary for all unto salvation, and that the sacrament of penance is equally necessary for those who have committed mortal sins after baptism; but that confirmation, the eucharist, and extreme unction are necessary only in the sense that they have been commanded and are eminently helpful. Protestants, on the other hand, teach that the sacraments are not absolutely necessary unto salvation, but are obligatory in view of the divine precept. Wilful neglect of their use results in spiritual impoverishment and has a destructive tendency, just as all wilful and persistent disobedience to God has. That they are not absolutely necessary unto salvation, follows: (1) from the free spiritual character of the gospel dispensation, in which God does not bind His grace to the use of certain external forms, John 4:21,23; Luke 18:14; (2) from the fact that Scripture mentions only faith as the instrumental condition of salvation, John 5:24; 6:29; 3:36; Acts 16:31; (3) from the fact that the sacraments do not originate faith but presuppose it, and are administered where faith is assumed, Acts 2:41; 16:14,15,30,33; I Cor. 11:23-32; and (4) from the fact that many were actually saved without the use of the sacraments. Think of the believers before the time of Abraham and of the penitent thief on the cross

E. The Old and New Testament Sacraments Compared.

1. THEIR ESSENTIAL UNITY. Rome claims that there is an *essential* difference between the sacraments of the Old, and those of the New Testament. It holds that, like the entire ritual of the old covenant, its sacraments also were merely typical. The sanctification wrought by them was not internal, but merely legal, and prefigured the grace which was to be conferred on man in the future, in virtue of the passion of Christ. This does not mean that no internal grace accompanied their use at all, but merely that this was not effected by the sacraments as such, as it is in the new dispensation. They had no objective efficacy, did not sanctify the recipient *ex opere operato,* but only *ex opere operantis,* that is, because of the faith and charity with which he received them. Because the full realization of the grace typified by those sacraments depended on the coming of Christ, the Old Testament saints were shut up in the *Limbus Patrum* until Christ led them out. As a matter of fact, however, there is no *essential* difference between the sacraments of the Old, and those of the New Testament. This is proved by the following considerations: (a) in I Cor. 10:1-4 Paul ascribes to the Old Testament Church that which is essential in the New Testament sacraments; (b) in Rom. 4:11 he speaks of the circumcision of Abraham as a seal of the righteousness of faith; and (c) in view of the fact that they represent the same spiritual realities, the names of the sacraments of both dispensations are used interchangeably; circumcision and passover are ascribed to the New Testament Church, I Cor. 5:7; Col. 2:11, and baptism and the Lord's Supper to the Church of the Old Testament, I Cor. 10:1-4.

2. THEIR FORMAL DIFFERENCES. Notwithstanding the essential unity of the Sacraments of both dispensations, there are certain points of difference. (a) Among Israel the sacraments had a national aspect in addition to their spiritual significance as signs and seals of the covenant of grace. (b) Alongside of the sacraments Israel had many other symbolical rites, such as offerings and purifications, which in the main agreed with their sacraments, while the New Testament sacraments stand absolutely alone. (c) The Old Testament sacraments pointed forward to Christ and were the seals of a grace that still had to be merited while those of the New Testament point back to Christ and His completed sacrifice of redemption. (d) In harmony with the whole Old Testament dispensation, a smaller measure of divine grace accompanied the use

of the Old Testament sacraments than is now obtained through the faithful reception of those of the New Testament.

F. The Number of the Sacraments.

1. IN THE OLD TESTAMENT. During the old dispensation there were two sacraments, namely, circumcision and passover. Some Reformed theologians were of the opinion that circumcision originated among Israel, and was derived from this ancient covenant people by other nations. But it is now quite clear that this is an untenable position. From the earliest times the Egyptian priests were circumcised. Moreover, circumcision is found among many peoples in Asia, Africa, and even Australia, and it is very unlikely that they all derived it from Israel. Only among Israel, however, did it become a sacrament of the covenant of grace. As belonging to the Old Testament dispensation, it was a bloody sacrifice, symbolizing the excision of the guilt and pollution of sin, and obliging the people to let the principle of the grace of God penetrate their entire life. The passover was also a bloody sacrament. The Israelites escaped the doom of the Egyptians by substituting a sacrifice, which was a type of Christ, John 1:29,36; I Cor. 5:7. The saved family ate the lamb that was slain, symbolizing the appropriating act of faith, very much as the eating of the bread in the Lord's Supper.

2. IN THE NEW TESTAMENT. The Church of the New Testament also has two sacraments, namely, baptism and the Lord's Supper. In harmony with the new dispensation as a whole, they are unbloody sacraments. However, they symbolize the same spiritual blessings that were symbolized by circumcision and passover in the old dispensation. The Church of Rome has enlarged the number of the sacraments to seven in a wholly unwarranted manner. To the two that were instituted by Christ it added confirmation, penance, orders, matrimony, and extreme unction. It seeks the Scriptural ground for confirmation in Acts 8:17; 14:22; 19:6; Heb. 6:2; for penance in Jas. 5:16; for orders in I Tim. 4:14; II Tim. 1:6; for matrimony in Eph. 5:32; and for extreme unction in Mark 6:13; Jas. 5:14. Each of these sacraments is supposed to convey; in addition to the general grace of sanctification, a special sacramental grace, which is different in each sacrament. This multiplication of the sacraments created a difficulty for the Church of Rome. It is generally admitted that sacraments, in order to be valid, must have been instituted by Christ; but Christ instituted only two. Consequently, the others are not sacraments, or the right to institute them must also be ascribed to the apostles. Before the Council of Trent many, indeed, asserted that the additional five were not instituted by Christ directly, but through the apostles. The Council, however, boldly declared that all the seven sacraments were instituted by Christ Himself, and thus imposed an impossible task on the theology of its Church. It is a point that must be accepted by Roman Catholics on the testimony of the Church, but that cannot be proved.

Questions for further study: Has the term *musterion* the same meaning in the New Testament as it has in the mystery religions? Are the New Testament teachings respecting the sacraments borrowed from the mystery religions, as a recent school of New Testament criticism claims? Is the assertion of this school correct, that Paul represents the sacraments as effective *ex opere operato*? Why do the Lutherans prefer to speak of the sacraments as *rites* and *actions* rather than as *signs*? What do they understand by the *materia coelestis* of the sacraments? What is meant by the Roman Catholic doctrine of *intention* in connection with the administration of the sacraments? What negative requirement does Rome consider necessary in the recipient of the sacrament? Is it correct to describe the relation between the sign and the thing signified as an *unio sacramentalis*? What constitutes the *gratia sacramentalis* in each of the seven sacraments of the Roman Catholic Church?

Literature: Bavinck, *Geref. Dogm.* IV, pp. 483-542; Kuyper, *Dict. Dogm., De Sacramentis*, pp. 3-96; Hodge, *Syst. Theol.* III, pp. 466-526; Vos, *Geref. Dogm. V. De Genademiddelen*, pp. 1-35; Dabney, *Syst. and Polem. Theol.*, pp. 727-757; McPherson, *Chr. Dogm.*, pp. 422-431; Litton, *Introd. to Dogm. Theol.*, pp. 419-450; Schmid, *Doct. Theol. of the Ev. Luth. Ch.* pp. 504-540; Valentine. *Chr. Theol.* II pp. 278-305: Pieper, *Christl. Dogm.* III, pp. 121-296; Kaftan, *Dogm.*, pp. 625-636; Pope, *Chr. Theol.* III, pp. 294-310; Miley, *Syst. Theol.* II, pp. 389-395; Wilmers, *Handbook of the Chr. Rel.*, pp. 305-314; Moehler, *Symbolism*, pp. 202-218; Schaff, *Our Fathers' Faith and Ours*, pp. 309-315; Bannerman, *The Church* II, pp. 1-41; Macleod, *The Ministry and the Sacraments of the Church of Scotland*, pp. 198-227; Candlish, *The Sacraments*, pp. 11-44; Burgess, *The Protestant Faith*, pp. 180-198.

IV. Christian Baptism

A. Analogies of Christian Baptism.

1. IN THE GENTILE WORLD. Baptism was not something absolutely new in the days of Jesus. The Egyptians, the Persians, and the Hindus, all had their religious purifications. These were even more prominent in the Greek and Roman religions. Sometimes they took the form of a bath in the sea, and sometimes they were effected by sprinkling. Tertullian says that in some cases the idea of a new birth was connected with these lustrations. Many present day scholars hold that Christian baptism, especially as it was taught by Paul, owes its origin to similar rites in the mystery religions, but such a derivation does not even have appearance in its favor. While the initiatory rite in the mystery religions does involve a recognition of the deity in question, there is no trace of a baptism into the name of some god. Nor is there any evidence that the influence of the divine *pneuma*, rather prominent in the mystery religions, was ever connected with the rite of lustration. Moreover, the ideas of death and resurrection, which Paul associated with baptism, do not fit in with the mystery ritual at all. And, finally, the form of the *taurobolium*, which is supposed to be the most striking analogy that can be cited, is so foreign to the New Testament rite as to make the idea of the derivation of the latter from the former seem utterly ridiculous. These heathen purifications have very little in common, even in their external form, with our Christian baptism. Moreover, it is a well established fact that the mystery religions did not make their appearance in the Roman Empire before the days of Paul.

2. AMONG THE JEWS. The Jews had many ceremonial purifications and washings, but these had no sacramental character, and therefore were no signs and seals of the covenant. The so-called baptism of proselytes bore a greater resemblance to Christian baptism. When Gentiles were incorporated in Israel, they were circumcized and, at least in later times, also baptized. It has long been a debatable question, whether this custom was in vogue before the destruction of Jerusalem, but Schuerer has shown conclusively by quotations from the *Mishna* that it was. According to the Jewish authorities quoted by Wall in his *History of Infant Baptism*, this baptism had to be administered in the presence of two or three witnesses. Children of parents who received this baptism, if born before the rite was administered, were also baptized, at the request of the father as long as they were not of age (the boys thirteen and the girls twelve), but if they were of age, only at their own request. Children who were born after the baptism of the parent or parents, were accounted

as clean and therefore did not need baptism. It seems, however, that this baptism was also merely a sort of ceremonial washing, somewhat in line with the other purifications. It is sometimes said that the baptism of John was derived from this baptism of proselytes, but it is quite clear that this was not the case. Whatever historical relation there may have existed between the two, it is quite evident that the baptism of John was pregnant with new and more spiritual meanings. Lambert is quite correct when he, in speaking of the Jewish lustrations, says: "Their purpose was, by removing a ceremonial defilement, to restore a man to his normal position within the ranks of the Jewish community; John's baptism, on the other hand, aimed at transferring those who submitted to it into an altogether new sphere — the sphere of definite preparation for the approaching Kingdom of God. But above all, the difference lay in this, that John's baptism could never be regarded as a mere ceremony; it was always vibrant through and through with ethical meaning. A cleansing of the heart from sin was not only its preliminary condition, but its constant aim and purpose. And by the searching and incisive preaching with which he accompanied it, John kept it from sinking, as it would otherwise have tended to do, to the level of a mere *opus operatum*."[1]

Another question that calls for consideration, is that of the relation of the baptism of John to that of Jesus. The Roman Catholic Church in the Canons of Trent[2] curses those who say that the baptism of John equalled that of Jesus in efficacy, and regards it, along with the Old Testament sacraments, as purely typical. It claims that those who were baptized by John did not receive real baptismal grace in this baptism, and were at a later time re-baptized, or, more correctly expressed, baptized for the first time in the Christian manner. The older Lutheran theologians maintained that the two were identical as far as *purpose* and *efficacy* were concerned, while some of the later ones rejected what they considered to be a complete and essential identity of the two. Something similar may be said of Reformed theologians. The older theologians generally identified the two baptisms, while those of a more recent date direct attention to certain differences. John himself would seem to call attention to a point of difference in Matt. 3:11. Some also find a proof for the essential difference of the two in Acts 19:1-6, which, according to them, records a case in which some, who were baptized by John, were re-baptized. But this interpretation is subject to doubt. It would seem to be correct to say that the two are *essentially* identical, though differing in some points. The baptism of John, like the Christian baptism, (a) was instituted by God Himself, Matt. 21:25; John 1:33; (b) was connected with a radical change of life, Luke 1:1-17; John 1:20-30; (c) stood in sacramental relation to the forgiveness of sins, Matt. 3:7,8; Mark 1:4; Luke 3:3 (comp. Acts 2:28) and (d) employed the same material element, namely, water. At the same time there were several points of difference: (a) the baptism of John still belonged

1. *The Sacraments in the New Testament*, p. 57.
2. Sess. VII. *De Baptismo*.

to the old dispensation, and as such pointed forward to Christ; (b) in harmony with the dispensation of the law in general, it stressed the necessity of repentance, though not entirely to the exclusion of faith; (c) it was intended for the Jews only, and therefore represented the Old Testament particularism rather than the New Testament universalism; and (d) since the Holy Spirit had not yet been poured out in pentecostal fulness, it was not yet accompanied with as great a measure of spiritual gifts as the later Christian baptism.

B. The Institution of Christian Baptism.

1. It was instituted with divine authority. Baptism was instituted by Christ after He had finished the work of reconciliation and this had received the approval of the Father in the resurrection. It is worthy of notice that He prefaced the great commission with the words, "All authority hath been given unto me in heaven and on earth." Clothed with the fulness of that mediatorial authority, He instituted Christian baptism and thus made it binding for all following generations. The great commission is couched in the following words: "Go ye therefore (that is, because all nations are made subject to Me), and make disciples of all nations, baptizing them in the name of the Father and of the Son and of the Holy Spirit: teaching them to observe whatsoever I have commanded you." Matt. 28:19,20. The complementary form in Mark 16:15,16 reads as follows: "Go ye into all the world, and preach the gospel to the whole creation. He that believeth and is baptized shall be saved; but he that disbelieveth shall be condemned." Thus the following elements are clearly indicated in this authoritative command: (a) The disciples were to go out into the whole world and to preach the gospel to all nations, in order to bring people to repentance and to the acknowledgment of Jesus as the promised Saviour. (b) They who accepted Christ by faith were to be baptized in the name of the triune God, as a sign and seal of the fact that they had entered into a new relation to God and as such were obliged to live according to the laws of the Kingdom of God. (c) They were to be brought under the ministry of the Word, not merely as a proclamation of the good news, but as an exposition of the mysteries, the privileges, and the duties, of the new covenant. For the encouragement of the disciples Jesus adds the words, "And lo, I (who am clothed with the authority to give this commandment) am with you always, even unto the end of the world."

2. The baptismal formula. The apostles were specifically instructed to baptize *eis to onoma tou patros kai tou huiou kai tou hagiou pneumatos* (into the name of the Father and of the Son and of the Holy Spirit). The Vulgate rendered the first words *"eis to onoma"* by the Latin "in nomine" (in the name), a rendering followed by Luther's "im namen." The words are thus made to mean "on the authority of the triune God." Robertson gives this as their meaning in his *Grammar of the Greek New Testament*, p. 649, but fails to give any proof for it. The fact is that this interpretation is exegetically untenable. The idea of "on the authority of" is expressed by the phrase *en toi onomati*

or the shorter one *en onomati,* Matt. 21:9; Mark 16:17; Luke 10:17; John 14:26; Acts 3:6; 9:27, etc. The preposition *eis* (into) is indicative rather of an end, and may therefore be interpreted to mean "in relation to," or "into the profession of faith in one and sincere obedience to one." It is quite in harmony with this when Allen says in his commentary on Matthew: "The person baptized was symbolically introduced 'into the name of Christ,' that is, became His disciple, that is, entered into a state of allegiance to Him and fellowship with Him." This is the meaning given by Thayer, Robinson, and, substantially, also by Cremer-Koegel and Baljon, in their Lexicons. It is also that adopted by the commentators, such as Meyer, Alford, Allen, Bruce, Grosheide, and Van Leeuwen. This meaning of the term is fully borne out by such parallel expressions as *eis ton Mousen,* I Cor. 10:2; *eis to onoma Paulou,* I Cor. 1:13; *eis hen soma,* I Cor. 12:13; and *eis Christon,* Rom. 6:3; Gal. 3:27. Dr. Kuyper's argument touching this point is found in *Uit het Woord, Eerste Serie, Eerste Bundel.*[1] It would seem that we should translate the preposition *eis* by "into" or "to" (that is, "in relation to'") the name. The word *onoma* (name) is used in the sense of the Hebrew *shem* as indicative of all the qualities by which God makes Himself known, and which constitute the sum total of all that He is for His worshippers. Deissman in his *Bible Studies*[2] refers to interesting examples of this particular use of the word *onoma* in the papyri. Interpreted in this light, the baptismal formula indicates that by baptism (that is, by that which is signified in baptism) the recipient is placed in a special relationship to the divine self-revelation, or to God as He has revealed Himself and revealed what He will be for His people, and at the same time becomes duty bound to live up to the light of that revelation.

It is not necessary to assume that, when Jesus employed these words, He intended them as a formula to be used ever after. He merely used them as descriptive of the character of the baptism which He instituted, just as similar expressions serve to characterize other baptisms, Acts 19:3; I Cor. 1:13; 10:2; 12:13. It is sometimes said with an appeal to such passages as Acts 2:48; 8:16; 10:48; 19:5, and also Rom. 6:3, and Gal. 3:27, that the apostles evidently did not use the trinitarian formula; but this is not necessarily implied, though it is entirely possible since they did not understand the words of Jesus in the great commission as prescribing a definite formula. It is also possible, however, that the expressions used in the passages indicated served to stress certain particulars respecting the baptism of the apostles. It should be noted that the prepositions differ. Acts 2:38 speaks of a baptism *epi toi onomati Jesou Christou,* which probably refers to a baptism on the confession of Jesus as the Messiah. According to Acts 10:48 those who were present in the house of Cornelius were baptized *en onomati Jesou Christou,* to indicate that they were baptized on the authority of Jesus. All the remaining passages mention a baptism *eis to onoma Jesou Christou* (or *tou kuriou Jesou*), or simply a baptism *eis Christon.* These expressions may simply serve to stress the fact

1. pp. 263 ff.
2. p. 146.

that the recipients were brought into special relationship to Jesus Christ, whom the apostles were preaching, and were thereby made subject to Him as their Lord. But whatever may have been the practice in the apostolic age, it is quite evident that when the Church later on felt the need of a formula, it could find no better than that contained in the words of the institution. This formula was already in use when the Didache (*The Teaching of the Twelve Apostles*) was written (c. 100 A.D.).[1]

C. The Doctrine of Baptism in History.

1. BEFORE THE REFORMATION. The early Fathers regarded baptism as the rite of initiation into the Church, and usually considered it as closely connected with the forgiveness of sins and the communication of the new life. Some of their expressions would seem to indicate that they believed in baptismal regeneration. At the same time it should be noted that in the case of adults they did not regard baptism as efficacious apart from the right disposition of the soul, and they did not consider baptism as absolutely essential to the initiation of the new life, but rather looked upon it as the completing element in the process of renewal. Infant baptism was already current in the days of Origen and Tertullian, though the latter discouraged it on the grounds of expediency. The general opinion was that baptism should never be repeated, but there was no unanimity as to the validity of baptism administered by heretics. In course of time, however, it became a fixed principle not to re-baptize those who were baptized into the name of the triune God. The mode of baptism was not in dispute. From the second century on the idea gradually gained ground that baptism works more or less magically. Even Augustine seems to have considered baptism as effective *ex opere operato* in the case of children. He regarded baptism as absolutely necessary and held that unbaptized children are lost. According to him baptism cancels original guilt, but does not wholly remove the corruption of nature. The Scholastics at first shared Augustine's view, that in the case of adults baptism presupposes faith, but gradually another idea gained the upper hand, namely, that baptism is always effective *ex opere operato*. The importance of subjective conditions was minimized. Thus the characteristic Roman Catholic conception of the sacrament, according to which baptism is the sacrament of regeneration and of initiation into the Church, gradually gained the upper hand. It contains the grace which it signifies and confers this on all those who put no obstacle in the way. This grace was regarded as very important, since (a) it sets an indelible mark on the recipient as a member of the Church; (b) delivers from the guilt of original sin and of all actual sins committed up to the time of baptism, removes the pollution of sin, though concupiscence remains, and sets man free from eternal punishment and from all positive temporal punishments; (c) works spiritual renewal by the infusion of sanctifying grace and of the supernatural virtues of faith, hope, and love; and (d) incorporates the recipient into the communion of the saints and into the visible Church.

1. Cf. Chapter VII.

2. SINCE THE RFEORMATION. The Lutheran Reformation did not entirely rid itself of the Roman Catholic conception of the sacraments. Luther did not regard the water in baptism as common water, but as a water which had become, through the Word with its inherent divine power, a gracious water of life, a washing of regeneration. Through this divine efficacy of the Word the sacrament effects regeneration. In the case of adults Luther made the effect of baptism dependent on faith in the recipient. Realizing that he could not consider it so in the case of children, who cannot exercise faith, he at one time held that God by His prevenient grace works faith in the unconscious child, but later on professed ignorance on this point. Later Lutheran theologians retained the idea of an infant-faith as a precondition for baptism, while others conceived of baptism as producing such a faith immediately. This in some cases led on to the idea that the sacrament works *ex opere operato*. Anabaptists cut the Gordian knot of Luther by denying the legitimacy of infant baptism. They insisted on baptizing all applicants for admission to their circle, who had received the sacrament in infancy, and did not regard this as a re-baptism, but as the first true baptism. With them children had no standing in the Church. Calvin and Reformed theology proceeded on the assumption that baptism is instituted for believers, and does not work but strengthens the new life. They were naturally confronted with the question as to how infants could be regarded as believers, and how they could be strengthened spiritually, seeing that they could not yet exercise faith. Some simply pointed out that infants born of believing parents are children of the covenant, and as such heirs of the promises of God, including also the promise of regeneration; and that the spiritual efficacy of baptism is not limited to the time of its administration, but continues through life. The Belgic Confession also expresses that idea in these words: "Neither does this baptism avail us only at the time when water is poured upon us, and received by us, but also through the whole course of our life."[1] Others went beyond this position and maintained that the children of the covenant were to be regarded as *presumptively* regenerated. This is not equivalent to saying that they are all regenerated, when they are presented for baptism, but that they are assumed to be regenerated until the contrary appears from their lives. There were also a few who regarded baptism as nothing more than the sign of an external covenant. Under the influence of Socinians, Arminians, Anabaptists, and Rationalists, it has become quite customary in many circles to deny that baptism is a seal of divine grace, and to regard it as a mere act of profession on the part of man. In our day many professing Christians have completely lost the consciousness of the spiritual significance of baptism. It has become a mere formality.

D. The Proper Mode of Baptism.

Baptists are at variance with the rest of the Christian world in their position that dipping or immersion, followed by emersion, is the only proper mode of baptism; and that this mode is absolutely essential to baptism, because this

---

1. Art. XXXIV.

rite is intended to symbolize the death and resurrection of Jesus Christ, and the consequent death and resurrection of the subject of baptism with Him. Two questions arise, therefore, and it is best to consider them in the following order: (1) What is the essential thing in the symbolism of baptism? and (2) Is immersion the only proper mode of baptism? This order is preferable, because the former question is the more important of the two, and because the answer to the second will depend in part on that given to the first.

1. WHAT IS THE ESSENTIAL THING IN THE SYMBOLISM OF BAPTISM? According to the Baptists immersion, followed by emersion, is the essential thing in the symbolism of baptism. A surrender of this would be equivalent to giving up baptism itself. The real baptismal idea, they say, is expressed in the going down into, and the coming up out of, the water. That such an immersion naturally involves a certain washing or purification, is something purely accidental. Baptism would be baptism even if one were immersed in something that has no cleansing properties. They base their opinion on Mark 10:38,39; Luke 12:50; Rom. 6:3,4; Col. 2:12. But the first two passages merely express the idea that Christ would be overwhelmed by His coming sufferings, and do not speak of the sacrament of baptism at all. The last two are the only ones that really have any bearing on the matter, and even these are not to the point, for they do not speak directly of any baptism with water at all, but of the spiritual baptism thereby represented. They represent regeneration under the figure of a dying and a rising again. It is certainly perfectly obvious that they do not make mention of baptism as an emblem of Christ's death and resurrection. If baptism were represented here at all as an emblem, it would be as an emblem of the believer's dying and rising again. And since this is only a figurative way of representing his regeneration, it would make baptism a figure of a figure.

Reformed theology has an entirely different conception of the essential thing in the symbolism of baptism. It finds this in the idea of purification. The Heidelberg Catechism asks in Question 69: "How is it signified and sealed unto you in holy baptism that you have a part in the one sacrifice of Christ on the cross?" And it answers: "Thus, that Christ has appointed the outward washing with water and added the promise that I am washed with His blood and Spirit from the pollution of my soul, that is, from all my sins, as certainly as I am washed outwardly with water, by which the filthiness of the body is commonly washed away." This idea of purification was the pertinent thing in all the washings of the Old Testament, and also in the baptism of John, Ps. 51:7; Ezek. 36:25; John 3:25,26. And we may assume that in this respect the baptism of Jesus was entirely in line with previous baptisms. If He had intended the baptism which He instituted as a symbol of something entirely different, He would have indicated this very clearly, in order to obviate all possible misunderstanding. Moreover, Scripture makes it abundantly clear that baptism symbolizes spiritual cleansing or purification, Acts 2:38; 22:16; Rom. 6:4 f.; I Cor. 6:11; Tit. 3:5; Heb. 10:22; I Pet. 3:21; Rev. 1:5. This is exactly the point on which the Bible places all emphasis, while it never represents the going down and coming up as something essential.

2. IS IMMERSION THE ONLY PROPER MODE OF BAPTISM? The generally prevailing opinion outside of Baptist circles is that, as long as the fundamental idea, namely, that of purification, finds expression in the rite, the mode of baptism is quite immaterial. It may be administered by immersion, by pouring or effusion, or by sprinkling. The Bible simply uses a generic word to denote an action designed to produce a certain effect, namely, cleansing or purification, but nowhere determines the specific mode in which the effect is to be produced. Jesus did not prescribe a certain mode of baptism. He evidently did not attach as much importance to it as the Baptists do. Neither do the Biblical examples of. baptism stress any particular mode. There is not a single case in which we are explicitly told just how baptism was administered. The Baptists assert, however, that the Lord did command baptism by immersion, and that all those who administer it in a different way are acting in open disobedience to His authority. To prove their assertion, they appeal to the words *bapto* and *baptizo*, which are used in Scripture for "to baptize." The second word seems to be an intensive or frequentative form of the first, though in general usage the distinction does not always hold. *Bapto* is frequently used in the Old Testament, but occurs in the New Testament only four times, namely, in Luke 16:24; John 13:26; Rev. 19:13, and in these cases does not refer to Christian baptism. Baptists were very confident at one time that this verb means only "to dip"; but many of them have changed their mind since Carson, one of their greatest authorities, came to the conclusion that it also has a secondary meaning, namely, "to dye," so that it came to mean "to dye by dipping," and even, "to dye in any manner," in which case it ceased to be expressive of mode.[1] The question further arose, whether *baptizo*, which is used 76 times, and which is the word employed by the Lord in the words of the institution, was derived from *bapto* in its *primary* or in its *secondary* meaning. And Dr. Carson answers that it is derived from *bapto* in the sense of "to dip." Says he: *"Bapto*, the root, I have shown to possess two meanings, and two only, 'to dip' and 'to dye.' *Baptizo*, I have asserted, has but one signification. It has been founded on the primary meaning of the root, and has never admitted the secondary.... My position is, *that it always signifies to dip; never expressing anything but mode.*"[2] The Baptists must maintain this, if they want to prove that the Lord commanded baptism by immersion.

But the facts, as they appear in both classical and New Testament Greek, do not warrant this position. Even Dr. Gale, who was perhaps the most learned author who sought to maintain it, felt constrained by the facts to modify it. Wilson in his splendid work on *Infant Baptism*, which is partly a reply to the work of Dr. Carson, quotes Gale as saying: "The word *baptizo* perhaps *does not so necessarily express the action of putting under water*, as in general a thing's

1. Carson, *Baptism in its Mode and Subjects*, pp. 44 ff.
2. Op. cit., p. 55.

being in that condition, *no matter how it comes to be so, whether it is put into the water, or the water comes over it*; though, indeed, to put into the water is the most natural way and the most common, and is, therefore, usually and pretty constantly, but it may be not necessarily, implied."[1] Wilson shows conclusively that, according to Greek usage, baptism is effected in various ways. Says he: "Let the baptizing element encompass its object, and in the case of liquids, whether this relative state has been produced by immersion, effusion, overwhelming, or in any other mode, Greek usage recognizes it as a valid baptism." He further goes on to show in detail that it is impossible to maintain the position that the word *baptizo* always signifies immersion in the *New Testament*.[2]

It is quite evident that both words, *bapto* and *baptizo*, had other meanings, such as "to wash," "to bathe," and to "purify by washing." The idea of washing or purification gradually became the prominent idea, while that of the manner in which this took place retired more and more into the background. That this purification was sometimes effected by sprinkling, is evident from Num. 8:7; 19:13,18,19,20; Ps. 51:7; Ezek. 36:25; Heb. 9:10. In Judith 12:7 and Mark 7:3,4 we cannot possibly think of dipping. Neither is this possible in connection with the following passages of the New Testament: Matt. 3:11; Luke 11:37,38; 12:50; Rom. 6:3; I Cor. 12:13; Heb. 9:10 (cf. verses 13,14,19, 21); I Cor. 10:1.2. Since the word *baptizo* does not necessarily mean "to immerse," and because the New Testament does not in any case explicitly assert that baptism took place by immersion, the burden of proof would seem to rest on the Baptists. Was John the Baptist capable of the enormous task of immersing the multitudes that flocked unto him at the river Jordan, or did he simply pour water on them as some of the early inscriptions would seem to indicate? Did the apostles find enough water in Jerusalem, and did they have the necessary facilities, to baptize three thousand in a single day by immersion? Where is the evidence to prove that they followed any other method than the Old Testament mode of baptisms? Does Acts 9:18 indicate in any way that Paul left the place where Ananias found him, to be immersed in some pool or river? Does not the account of the baptism of Cornelius create the impression that water was to be brought and that those present were baptized right in the house? Acts 10:47,48. Is there any evidence that the jailor at Philippi was not baptized in or near the prison, but led his prisoners out to the river, in order that he might be immersed? Would he have dared to take them outside of the city, when he was commanded to keep them safely? Acts 16:22-33. Even the account of the baptism of the eunuch, Acts 8:36,38, which is often regarded as the strongest Scriptural proof for baptism by immersion, cannot be regarded as conclusive evidence. A careful study of Luke's use of the preposition *eis* shows that he used it not only in the sense of *into*, but also in the sense of *to*, so that it is entirely possible to read the relevant statement in verse 38 as follows: "and

---

1.   p. 97.
2.   For the various possible meanings of *baptizo* consult, besides the treatise of Wilson, already referred to, such works as those of Armstrong, *The Doctrine of Baptisms*; Seiss, *The Baptist System Examined*; Ayres, *Christian Baptism*; Hibbard, *Christian Baptism*.

they both went down to the water, both Philip and the eunuch, and he baptized him." And even if the words were intended to convey the idea that they went down *into* the water, this does not yet prove the point, for according to pictorial representations of the early centuries they who were baptized by effusion often stood in the water. It is entirely possible, of course, that in the apostolic age some were baptized by immersion, but the fact that the New Testament nowhere insists on this proves that it was not essential. Immersion is a proper mode of baptism, but so is baptism by effusion or by sprinkling, since they all symbolize purification. The passages referred to in the preceding prove that many Old Testament washings (baptizings) took place by sprinkling. In a prophecy respecting the spiritual renewal of the New Testament day the Lord says: "And I will sprinkle clean water upon you, and ye shall be clean," Ezek. 36:25. The matter signified in baptism, namely, the purifying Spirit, was poured out upon the Church, Joel 2:28,29; Acts 2:4,33. And the writer of Hebrews speaks of his readers as having their hearts sprinkled from an evil conscience, Heb. 10:22.

E. The Lawful Administrators of Baptism.

Roman Catholics consider baptism absolutely essential to salvation; and because they regard it as cruel to make the salvation of anyone dependent on the accidental presence or absence of a priest, they also in cases of emergency permit baptism by others, particularly by midwives. In spite of the contrary view of Cyprian, they recognize the baptism of heretics, unless their heresy involves a denial of the Trinity. The Reformed Churches always acted on the principle that the administration of the Word and of the sacraments belong together, and that therefore the teaching elder or the minister is the only lawful administrator of baptism. The Word and the sacrament are joined together in the words of the institution. And because baptism is not a private matter, but an ordinance of the Church, they also hold that it should be administered in the public assembly of believers. They have generally recognized the baptism of other Churches, not excluding the Roman Catholics, and also of the various sects, except in the case of Churches and sects which denied the Trinity. Thus they refused to honour the baptism of the Socinians and of the Unitarians. In general, they considered a baptism as valid which was administered by a duly accredited minister and in the name of the triune God.

F. The Proper Subjects of Baptism.

Baptism is intended only for properly qualified rational beings, namely, for believers and their children. Rome loses sight of this in so far as it applies the sacrament also to clocks, buildings, and so on. There are two classes to which it should be applied, namely, adults and infants.

1. ADULT BAPTISM. In the case of adults baptism must be preceded by a profession of faith, Mark 16:16; Acts 2:41; 8:37 (not found in some MSS.); 16:31-33. Therefore the Church insists on such a profession before baptizing adults. And when such a profession is made, this is accepted by the Church at its face value, unless she has good objective reasons for doubting its veracity.

It does not belong to her province to pry into the secrets of the heart and thus to pass on the genuineness of such a profession. The responsibility rests on the person who makes it. The method of prying into the inner condition of the heart, in order to determine the genuineness of one's profession, is Labadistic and not in harmony with the practice of the Reformed Churches. Since baptism is not merely a sign and seal, but also a means of grace, the question arises as to the nature of the grace wrought by it. This question is raised here only with respect to adult baptism. In view of the fact that according to our Reformed conception, this baptism presupposes regeneration, faith, conversion, and justification, these surely are not to be conceived as wrought by it. In this respect we differ from the Church of Rome. Even the Lutherans, who ascribe greater power to baptism as a means of grace than the Reformed do, agree with the latter on this point. Neither does baptism work a special sacramental grace, consisting in this that the recipient is implanted into the body of Jesus Christ. The believer's incorporation into mystical union with Christ is also presupposed. Word and sacrament work exactly the same kind of grace, except that the Word, in distinction from the sacrament, is also instrumental in the origination of faith. The sacrament of baptism strengthens faith, and because faith plays an important part in all the other operations of divine grace, these are also greatly benefited by it. Baptism represents primarily an act of the grace of God, but because the professing Christian must voluntarily submit to it, it can also be considered from the side of man. There is in it an offer and gift of God, but also an acceptance on the part of man. Consequently, baptism also signifies that man accepts the covenant and assumes its obligations. It is a seal, not merely of an offered, but of an offered and accepted, that is, of a concluded covenant.

2. INFANT BAPTISM. It is on the point of infant baptism that the most important difference is found between us and the Baptists. The latter hold, as Dr. Hovey, a Baptist author, expresses it, "that only believers in Christ are entitled to baptism, and that only those who give credible evidence of faith in Him should be baptized." This means that children are excluded from the sacrament. In all other denominations, however, they receive it. Several points call for consideration in connection with this subject.

a. *The Scriptural basis for infant baptism.* It may be said at the outset that there is no explicit command in the Bible to baptize children, and that there is not a single instance in which we are plainly told that children were baptized. But this does not necessarily make infant baptism un-Biblical. The Scriptural ground for it is found in the following data:

(1) The covenant made with Abraham was primarily a *spiritual* covenant, though it also had a national aspect, and of this spiritual covenant circumcision was a sign and seal. It is an unwarranted procedure of the Baptists to split this covenant up into two of three different covenants. The Bible refers to the covenant with Abraham several times, but always in the singular. Ex. 2:24; Lev. 26:42, II Kings 13:23; I Chron. 16:16; Ps. 105:9. There is not a single

exception to this rule. The spiritual nature of this covenant is proved by the manner in which its promises are interpreted in the New Testament, Rom. 4:16-18; II Cor. 6:16-18; Gal. 3:8,9,14,16; Heb. 8:10; 11:9,10,13. It also follows from the fact that circumcision was clearly a rite that had spiritual significance, Deut. 10:16; 30:6; Jer. 4:4; 9:25,26; Acts 15:1; Rom. 2:26-29; 4:11; Phil. 3:2; and from the fact that the promise of the covenant is even called "the gospel," Gal. 3:8.

(2) This covenant is still in force and is essentially identical with the "new covenant" of the present dispensation. The unity and continuity of the covenant in both dispensations follows from the fact that the Mediator is the same, Acts 4:12; 10:43; 15:10,11; Gal. 3:16; I Tim. 2:5,6; I Pet. 1:9-12; the condition is the same, namely, faith. Gen. 15:6; (Rom. 4:3); Ps. 32:10; Heb. 2:4; Acts 10:43; Heb. 11; and the blessings are the same, namely, justification, Ps. 32:1,2,5; Isa. 1:18; Rom. 4:9; Gal. 3:6, regeneration, Deut. 30:6; Ps. 51:10, spiritual gifts, Joel 2:28,32; Acts 2:17-21; Isa. 40:31, and eternal life, Ex. 3:6; Heb. 4:9; 11:10. Peter gave those who were under conviction on the day of Pentecost the assurance that the promise was unto them and to their children, Acts 2:39. Paul argues in Rom. 4:13-18; Gal. 3:13-18 that the giving of the law did not make the promise of none effect, so that it still holds in the new dispensation. And the writer of Hebrews points out that the promise to Abraham was confirmed with an oath, so that New Testament believers may derive comfort from its immutability, Heb. 6:13-18.

(3) By the appointment of God infants shared in the benefits of the covenant, and therefore received circumcision as a sign and seal. According to the Bible the covenant is clearly an organic concept, and its realization moves along organic and historical lines. There is a people or nation of God, an organic whole such as could only be constituted by families. This national idea is naturally very prominent in the Old Testament, but the striking thing is that it did not disappear when the nation of Israel had served its purpose. It was spiritualized and thus carried over into the New Testament, so that the New Testament people of God are also represented as a nation, Matt. 21:43; Rom. 9:25.26 (comp. Hosea 2:23); II Cor. 6:16; Tit. 2:14; I Pet. 2:9. Infants were considered during the old dispensation as an integral part of Israel as the people of God. They were present when the covenant was renewed, Deut. 29:10:13; Josh. 8:35; II Chron. 20:13, had a standing in the congregation of Israel, and were therefore present in their religious assemblies, II Chron. 20:13; Joel 2:16. In view of such rich promises as those in Isa. 54:13; Jer. 31:34; Joel 2:28 we would hardly expect the privileges of such children to be reduced in the new dispensation, and certainly would not look for their exclusion from any standing in the Church. Jesus and the apostles did not exclude them, Matt. 19:14; Acts 2:39; I Cor. 7:14. Such an exclusion would seem to require a very explicit statement to that effect.

(4) In the new dispensation baptism is by divine authority substituted for circumcision as the initiatory sign and seal of the covenant of grace.

Scripture strongly insists on it that circumcision can no more serve as such, Acts 15:1,2; 21:21; Gal. 2:3-5; 5:2-6; 6:12,13,15. If baptism did not take its place, then the New Testament has no initiatory rite. But Christ clearly substituted it as such, Matt. 28:19,20; Mark 16:15,16. It corresponds with circumcision in spiritual meaning. As circumcision referred to the cutting away of sin and to a change of heart, Deut. 10:16; 30:6; Jer. 4:4; 9:25,26; Ezek. 44:7,9, so baptism refers to the washing away of sin, Acts 2:38; I Pet. 3:21; Tit. 3:5, and to spiritual renewal, Rom. 6:4; Col. 2:11,12. The last passage clearly links up circumcision with baptism, and teaches that the Christ-circumcision, that is, circumcision of the heart, signified by circumcision in the flesh, was accomplished by baptism, that is, by that which baptism signifies. Cf. also Gal. 3:27,29. But if children received the sign and seal of the covenant in the old dispensation, the presumption is that they surely have a right to receive it in the new, to which the pious of the Old Testament were taught to look forward as a much fuller and richer dispensation. Their exclusion from it would require a clear and unequivocal statement to that effect, but quite the contrary is found, Matt. 19:14; Acts 2:39; I Cor. 7:14.

(5)   As was pointed out in the preceding, the New Testament contains no direct evidence for the practice of infant baptism in the days of the apostles. Lambert, after considering and weighing all the available evidence, expresses his conclusion in the following words: "The New Testament evidence, then, seems to point to the conclusion that infant baptism, to say the least, was not the general custom of the apostolic age."[1] But it need not surprise anyone that there is no direct mention of the baptism of infants, for in a missionary period like the apostolic age the emphasis would naturally fall on the baptism of adults. Moreover, conditions were not always favorable to infant baptism. Converts would not at once have a proper conception of their covenant duties and responsibilities. Sometimes only one of the parents was converted, and it is quite conceivable that the other would oppose the baptism of the children. Frequently there was no reasonable assurance that the parents would educate their children piously and religiously, and yet such assurance was necessary. At the same time the language of the New Testament is perfectly consistent with a continuation of the organic administration of the covenant, which required the circumcision of children, Matt. 19:14; Mark 10:13-16; Acts 2:39; I Cor. 7:14. Moreover, the New Testament repeatedly speaks of the baptism of households, and gives no indication that this is regarded as something out of the ordinary, but rather refers to it as a matter of course, Acts 16:15,33; I Cor. 1:16. It is entirely possible, of course, but not very probable, that none of these households contained children. And if there were infants, it is morally certain that they were baptized along with the parents. The New Testament certainly contains no evidence that persons born and reared in Christian families may not be baptized until they have come to years of discretion and have professed their faith in Christ. There is not the slightest allusion to any such practice.

---

1. *The Sacraments in the New Testament*, p. 204.

(6) Wall in the introduction to his *History of Infant Baptism* points out that in the baptism of proselytes children of proselytes were often baptized along with their parents; but Edersheim says that there was a difference of opinion on this point.[1] Naturally, even if this did happen, it would prove nothing so far as Christian baptism is concerned, but it would go to show that there was nothing strange in such a procedure. The earliest historical reference to infant baptism is found in writings of the last half of the second century. The Didache speaks of adult, but not of infant baptism; and while Justin makes mention of women who became disciples of Christ from childhood (*ek paidon*), this passage does not mention baptism, and *ek paidon* does not necessarily mean infancy. Irenæus, speaking of Christ, says: "He came to save through means of Himself all who through Him are born again unto God, infants, and little children, and boys, and youths, and old men."[2] This passage, though it does not explicitly mention baptism, is generally regarded as the earliest reference to infant baptism, since the early Fathers so closely associated baptism with regeneration that they used the term "regeneration" for "baptism." That infant baptism was quite generally practiced in the latter part of the second century, is evident from the writings of Tertullian, though he himself considered it safer and more profitable to delay baptism.[3] Origen speaks of it as a tradition of the apostles. Says he: "For this also it was, that the Church had from the apostles a tradition (or, order) to give baptism even to infants."[4] The Council of Carthage (A.D. 253) takes infant baptism for granted and discusses simply the question, whether they may be baptized before the eighth day. From the second century on, infant baptism is regularly recognized, though it was sometimes neglected in practice. Augustine inferred from the fact that it was generally practiced by the Church throughout the world in spite of the fact that it was not instituted in Councils, that it was in all probability settled by the authority of the apostles. Its legitimacy was not denied until the days of the Reformation, when the Anabaptists opposed it.

b. *Objections to infant baptism.* A few of the more important objections to infant baptism call for brief consideration.

(1) Circumcision was merely a carnal and typical ordinance, and as such was destined to pass away. To put baptism in the place of circumcision, is simply to continue the carnal ordinance. Such carnal ordinances have no legitimate place in the New Testament Church. In our day this objection is raised by some dispensationalists, such as Bullinger and O'Hair, who claim that the baptism instituted by Jesus is connected with the Kingdom, and that only the baptism of the Spirit has a proper place in the Church. The book of Acts marks the transition from water-baptism to Spirit-baptism. Naturally, this argument would prove all baptism, adult as well as infant, illegitimate. In this representation of the matter the Jewish and Christian dispensations

---

1. *Life and Times of Jesus the Messiah* II, p. 746.
2. *Adv. Haereses* II, 22,4.
3. *De Baptismo*, c. XVIII.
4. *Comm. in Epist. ad Romanos*, lib. V.

are placed over against each other as carnal and spiritual, and circumcision is said to belong to the former. But this argument is fallacious. There is no warrant for placing circumcision altogether on a level with the carnal ordinances of the Mosaic law. Says Bannerman: "Circumcision was independent either of the introduction or abolition of the law of Moses; and would have continued the standing ordinance for admission into the Church of God as the seal of the covenant of grace, had not baptism been expressly appointed as a substitute for it."[1] It may be admitted that circumcision did acquire a certain typical significance in the Mosaic period, but it was primarily a sign and seal of the covenant already made with Abraham. In so far as it was a type it naturally ceased with the appearance of the antitype, and even as a seal of the covenant it made way for an unbloody sacrament expressly instituted by Christ for the Church, and recognized as such by the apostles, since Christ had put an end once for all to the shedding of blood in connection with the work of redemption. In the light of Scripture the position is entirely untenable, that baptism is connected with the Kingdom rather than with the Church, and is therefore Jewish rather than Christian. The words of the institution themselves condemn this view, and so does the fact that on the birthday of the New Testament Church Peter required of those who were added to it that they should be baptized. And if it be said that Peter, being a Jew, still followed the example of John the Baptist, it may be pointed out that Paul, the apostle of the Gentiles, also required that his converts be baptized, Acts 16:15,33; 18:8; I Cor. 1:16.

(2) There is no explicit command that children must be baptized. This is perfectly true, but does not disprove the validity of infant baptism. It should be observed that this objection is based on a canon of interpretation to which the Baptists themselves are not true when they hold that Christians are in duty bound to celebrate the first day of the week as their Sabbath, and that women must also partake of the Lord's Supper; for these are things not explicitly commanded. May not the silence of Scripture be construed for, rather than against, infant baptism? For twenty centuries children had been formally initiated into the Church, and the New Testament does not say that this must now cease, though it does teach that circumcision can no more serve for this purpose. The Lord Himself instituted another rite, and on the day of Pentecost Peter says to those who joined the Church that the promise is unto them and to their children, and further to as many as the Lord Himself shall call. This statement of Peter at least proves that he still had the organic conception of the covenant in mind. Moreover, the question may be raised how the Baptist himself can prove the correctness of his own position by an express command of Scripture. Does the Bible anywhere command the exclusion of children from baptism? Does it command that *all those who are born and reared in Christian families* must profess their faith before they are baptized? Clearly, there are no such commands.

---

1. *The Church of Christ* II, p. 98.

(3) A closely related objection is, that there is no example of infant baptism in the New Testament. It is perfectly true that the Bible does not explicitly say that children were baptized, though it does apprise us of the fact that the rite was administered to whole households. The absence of all definite references to infant baptism finds its explanation, at least to a large extent, in the fact that Scripture gives us a historical record of the missionary work of the apostles, but no such record of the work that was carried on in the organized churches. And here, too, the tables may be easily turned on the Baptist. Will he show us an example of the baptism of an adult who had been born and reared in a Christian home? There is no danger that he ever will.

(4) The most important objection to infant baptism raised by the Baptists, is that, according to Scripture, baptism is conditioned on an active faith revealing itself in a creditable profession. Now it is perfectly true that the Bible points to faith as a prerequisite for baptism, Mark 16:16; Acts 10:44-48; 16:14,15,31,34. If this means that the recipient of baptism must *in all cases* give manifestations of an active faith before baptism, then children are naturally excluded. But though the Bible clearly indicates that only those adults who believed were baptized, it nowhere lays down the rule that an active faith is absolutely essential for the reception of baptism. Baptists refer us to the great commission, as it is found in Mark 16:15,16. In view of the fact that this is a missionary command, we may proceed on the assumption that the Lord had in mind an active faith in those words. And though it is not explicitly stated, it is altogether likely that He regarded this faith as a prerequisite for the baptism of the persons intended. But who are they? Evidently, the adults of the nations that were to be evangelized, and therefore the Baptist is not warranted in construing it as an argument against infant baptism. If he insists on doing this nevertheless, it should be pointed out that on his construction these words prove too much even for him, and therefore prove nothing. The words of our Saviour imply that faith is a prerequisite for the baptism of those who through the missionary efforts of the Church would be brought to Christ, and do not imply that it is also a prerequisite for the baptism of children. The Baptist generalizes this statement of the Saviour by teaching that it makes all baptism contingent on the active faith of the recipient. He argues as follows: Active faith is the prerequisite of baptism. Infants cannot exercise faith. Therefore infants may not be baptized. But in that way these words might also be construed into an argument against infant salvation, since they not only *imply* but *explicitly state* that faith (active faith) is the condition for salvation. To be consistent the Baptist would thus find himself burdened with the following syllogism: Faith is the *conditio sine qua non* of salvation. Children cannot yet exercise faith. Therefore children cannot be saved. But this is a conclusion from which the Baptist himself would shrink back.

c. *The ground for infant baptism.*

(1) *The position of our confessional standards.* The Belgic Confession declares in Art. XXXIV that infants of believing parents "ought to be baptized

and sealed with the sign of the covenant, as the children of Israel formerly were circumcized upon the same promises which are made to our children." The Heidelberg Catechism answers the question, "Are infants also to be baptized?" as follows: "Yes, for since they, as well as adults, are included in the covenant and Church of God, and since both redemption from sin and the Holy Spirit, the Author of faith, are through the blood of Christ promised to them no less than to adults, they must also by baptism, as a sign of the covenant, be ingrafted into the Christian Church, and distinguished from the children of unbelievers, as was done in the old covenant or testament by circumcision, instead of which baptism was instituted in the new covenant."[1] And the Canons of Dort contain the following statement in I, Art. 17: "Since we are to judge of the will of God from His Word, which testifies that the children of believers are holy, not by nature, but in virtue of the covenant of grace, in which they together with their parents are compre- hended, godly parents ought not to doubt the election and salvation of their children whom it pleases God to call out of this life in their infancy (Gen. 17:7; Acts 2:39; I Cor. 7:14)." These statements of our confessional standards are entirely in line with the position of Calvin, that infants of believing parents, or those who have only one believing parent, are baptized on the basis of their covenant relationship.[2] The same note is struck in our *Form for the Baptism of Infants*: "Since, then, baptism has come in the place of circum- cision, the children should be baptized as ·heirs of the Kingdom of God and of His covenant." It will be observed that all these statements are based on the commandment of God to circumcize the children of the covenant, for in the last analysis that commandment is the ground of infant baptism. On the basis of our confessional standards it may be said that infants of believing parents are baptized on the ground that they are children of the covenant, and are as such heirs of the all-comprehensive covenant-promises of God, which include also the promise of the forgiveness of sins and the gift of the Holy Spirit unto regeneration and sanctification. In the covenant God makes over to them a certain grant or donation in a formal and objective way, requires of them that they will in due time accept this by faith, and promises to make it a living reality in their lives by the operation of the Holy Spirit. And in view of this fact the Church must regard them as prospective heirs of salvation, must regard them as under obligation to walk in the way of the covenant, has the right to expect that, under a faithful covenant administration, they, speaking generally, will live in the covenant, and is in duty bound to regard them as covenant breakers, if they do not meet its requirements. It is only in this way that it does full justice to the promises of God, which must in all their fulness be appropriated in faith by those who come to maturity. Thus the covenant, including the covenant promises, constitutes the objective and legal ground for the baptism of children. Baptism is a sign and seal of all that is comprehended in the promises.

---

1. *Lord's Day* XXVII, Q. 74.
2. *Inst.* IV. 16:6,15.

(2) *Differences of opinion among Reformed theologians.* Reformed theologians did not all agree in the past, and are not even now all unanimous, in their representation of the ground of infant baptism. Many theologians of the sixteenth and seventeenth centuries took the position described in the preceding, namely, that infants of believers are baptized, because they are in the covenant and are as such heirs of the rich promises of God including a title, not only to regeneration, but also to all the blessings of justification and of the renewing and sanctifying influence of the Holy Spirit. Others, however, while recognizing the truth of this representation, were not wholly satisfied with it. They stressed the fact that baptism is something more than the seal of a promise, or even of all the covenant promises; and that it is not merely the seal of a future good, but also of present spiritual possessions. The view became rather prevalent that baptism is administered to infants on the ground of presumptive regeneration. But even those who accepted this view did not all agree. Some combined this view with the other while others substituted it for the other. Some would proceed on the assumption that all the children presented for baptism are regenerated, while others would assume this only in connection with the elect children. The difference of opinion between those who believe that children of believers are baptized on the ground of their covenant relationship and of the covenant promise, and those who find this ground in presumptive regeneration persisted up to the present time and was the source of a lively controversy, especially in the Netherlands during the last period of the nineteenth, and the beginning of the twentieth, century. Dr. Kuyper at first spoke of presumptive regeneration as the ground of infant baptism, and many readily accepted this view. G. Kramer wrote his splendid thesis on *Het Verband van Doop en Wedergeboorte* especially in defense of this position. Later on Dr. Kuyper did not use this expression any more, and some of his followers felt the need of more careful discrimination and spoke of the covenant relationship as the *legal,* and presumptive regeneration as the *spiritual,* ground of infant baptism. But even this is not a satisfactory position. Dr. Honig, who is also a disciple and admirer of Kuyper, is on the right track when he says in his recent *Handboek van de Gereformeerde Dogmatiek*:[1] "We do not baptize the children of believers on the ground of an assumption, but on the ground of a command and an act of God. Children must be baptized in virtue of the covenant of God" (translation mine). Presumptive regeneration naturally cannot be regarded as the *legal* ground of infant baptism; this can be found only in the covenant promise of God. Moreover, it cannot be the ground in any sense of the word, since the ground of baptism must be something objective, as the advocates of the view in question themselves are constrained to admit. If they are asked, why they assume the regeneration of children presented for baptism, they can only answer, Because they are born of believing parents, that is, because they are born in the covenant. Naturally, to deny that presumptive regeneration is the ground of infant baptism, is not equivalent to saying

---

1. p. 655.

that it is entirely unwarranted to assume that infant children of believers are regenerated. This is a question that must be considered on its own merits.

It may be well to quote in this connection the first half of the fourth point of the *Conclusions of Utrecht,* which were adopted by our Church in 1908. We translate this as follows: "And, finally, as far as the fourth point, that of *presumptive regeneration,* is concerned, Synod declares that, according to the confession of our Churches, the seed of the covenant must, in virtue of the promise of God, be presumed to be regenerated and sanctified in Christ, until, as they grow up, the contrary appears from their life or doctrine; that it is, however, less correct to say that baptism is administered to the children of believers on the ground of their presumptive regeneration, since the ground of baptism is the command and the promise of God; and that further the judgment of charity, with which the Church presumes the seed of the covenant to be regenerated, by no means intends to say that therefore each child is really regenerated, since the Word of God teaches that they are not all Israel that are of Israel, and it is said of Isaac: in him shall thy seed be called (Rom. 9:6,7), so that in preaching it is always necessary to insist on serious self-examination, since only those who shall have believed and have been baptized will be saved."[1]

(3) *Objection to the view that children are baptized on the ground of their covenant relationship.* It has been said that, if children are baptized on the ground that they are born in the covenant and are therefore heirs of the promise, they are baptized on another ground than adults, since these are baptized on the ground of their faith or their profession of faith. But this is hardly correct, as Calvin already pointed out in his day. The great Reformer answered this objection effectively. The following is a translation of what Kramer says respecting Calvin's position on this point: "Calvin finds occasion here in connection with infant baptism, now that he has taken the standpoint of the covenant, to draw the line farther. Up to this point he has not called attention to the fact that adults too are baptized according to the rule of the covenant. And therefore it might seem that there was a difference between the baptism of adults and that of children. The adults to be baptized on the ground of their faith, infants, on the ground of the covenant of God. No, the Reformer declares, the only rule according to which, and the legal ground on which, the Church may administer baptism, is the covenant. This is true in the case of adults as well as in the case of children. That the former must first make a confession of faith and conversion, is due to the fact that they are outside of the covenant. In order to be admitted into the communion of the covenant, they must first learn the requirements of the covenant, and then faith and conversion open the way to the covenant."[2] The very same opinion is expressed by Bavinck.[3] This means that, after adults find entrance into the covenant by faith and conversion, they receive the sacrament of baptism on the ground

---

1. *Acts of Synod,* 1908, pp. 82 f.
2. *Het Verband van Doop en Wedergeboorte,* pp. 122 f.
3. *Geref. Dogm.* IV, p. 581.

of this covenant relationship. Baptism is also for them a sign and seal of the covenant.

d. *Infant baptism as a means of grace.* Baptism is a sign and seal of the covenant of grace. It does not signify one thing and seal another, but sets the seal of God on that which it signifies. According to our confessional standards and our Form for the administration of baptism, it signifies the washing away of our sins, and this is but a brief expression for the removal of the guilt of sin in justification, and for the removal of the pollution of sin in sanctification, which is, however, imperfect in this life. And if this is what is signified, then it is also that which is sealed. And if it be said, as it is sometimes in our Reformed literature, that baptism seals the promise(s) of God, this does not merely mean that it vouches for the truth of the promise, but that it assures the recipients that they are the appointed heirs of the promised blessings. This does not necessarily mean that they are already in principle in possession of the promised good, though this is possible and may even be probable, but certainly means that they are appointed heirs and will receive the heritage, unless they show themselves unworthy of it and refuse it. Dabney calls attention to the fact that seals are often appended to promissory covenants, in which the bestowment of the promised good is conditional.

But baptism is more than a sign and seal; it is as such also a means of grace. According to Reformed theology it is not, as the Roman Catholics claim, the means of initiating the work of grace in the heart, but it is a means for the strengthening of it or, as it is often expressed, for the increase of grace. This gives rise to a rather difficult question in connection with infant baptism. It can readily be seen how baptism can strengthen the work of faith in the adult recipient, but it is not so apparent how it can operate as a means of grace in the case of children who are entirely unconscious of the significance of baptism and cannot yet exercise faith. The difficulty, with which we are confronted here, naturally does not exist for the small number of Reformed scholars who deny that baptism merely strengthens an antecedent condition of grace, and claim that it "is a means for the impartation of grace in a specific form, and for the specific end of our regeneration and ingrafting in Christ."[1] All the others must, of course, face the problem. Luther also wrestled with that problem. He made the efficacy of baptism dependent on the faith of the recipient; but when he reflected on the fact that infants cannot exercise faith, he was inclined to believe that God by His prevenient grace wrought an incipient faith in them through baptism; and, finally, he referred the problem to the doctors of the Church. Reformed theologians solve the problem by calling attention to three things, which may be regarded as alternatives, but may also be combined. (1) It is possible to proceed on the assumption (not the certain knowledge) that the children offered for baptism are regenerated and are therefore in possession of the *semen fidei* (the seed of

---

1. This position is defended at length in a work entitled *The Divine Life in the Church*, pp. 9-196.

faith); and to hold that God through baptism in some mystical way, which we do not understand, strengthens this seed of faith in the child. (2) Attention may also be called to the fact that the operation of baptism as a means of grace is not necessarily limited to the moment of its administration any more than that of the Lord's Supper is limited to the time of its celebration. It may in that very moment serve in some mysterious way to increase the grace of God in the heart, if present, but may also be instrumental in augmenting faith later on, when the significance of baptism is clearly understood. This is clearly taught in both the Belgic and the Westminster Confession. (3) Again, it may be pointed out, as has been done by some theologians (e.g. Dabney and Vos) that infant baptism is also a means of grace for the parents who present their child for baptism. It serves to strengthen their faith in the promises of God, to work in them the assurance that the child for whom they stand sponsors has a right of property in the covenant of grace, and to strengthen in them the sense of responsibility for the Christian education of their child.

e. *The extension of baptism to children of unbelievers.* Naturally, only children of believers are the proper subjects of infant baptism. In several ways, however, the circle has been enlarged. (1) Roman Catholics and Ritualists of the Anglican Church proceed on the assumption that baptism is absolutely essential to salvation, since it conveys a grace that can be obtained in no other way. Hence they consider it their duty to baptize all children that come within their reach, without inquiring as to the spiritual condition of their parents. (2) Some call attention to the fact that the promise applies to parents and children and children's children, even to the thousandth generation, Ps. 105:7-10; Isa. 59:21; Acts 2:39. In view of these promises they maintain that children whose parents have left the Church have not thereby forfeited their privileges as children of the covenant. (3) There are those who externalize the covenant by making it co-extensive with the State in a State-Church. An English child, has, as such, just as much right to baptism as it has to State protection, irrespective of the question, whether the parents are believers or not. (4) Some have taken the position that the fact that parents are baptized, also assures their children of a title to baptism. They regard the personal relation of the parents to the covenant as quite immaterial. Churches have occasionally acted on that principle, and finally harbored a class of members who did not themselves assume the responsibility of the covenant, and yet sought the seal of the covenant for their children. In New England this was known as the half-way covenant. (5) Finally, the principle of adoption has been applied, in order to obtain baptism for children who were not entitled to it otherwise. If the parents were unfit or unwilling to vouch for the Christian education of their children, others could step in to guarantee this. The main ground for this was sought in Gen. 17:12.

CHRISTIAN BAPTISM

643

QUESTIONS FOR FURTHER STUDY: What are the different meanings of the words *bapto*, *baptizo*, and *louesthai?* Did John the Baptist baptize by immersion? Was the eunuch (Acts 8:38, 39) baptized in that manner? Does the New Testament anywhere emphasize the necessity of one particular mode of baptism? Is the doctrine of infant baptism Biblical? Was its right ever called in question before the Reformation? What accounts for the rise of the Anabaptist denial at the time of the Reformation? What is the Baptist conception of the covenant with Abraham? How do they explain Rom. 4:11? What do our confessional standards say as to the ground on which children are baptized? What is Calvin's position as to the ground on which both children and adults are baptized? What practical dangers are connected with the doctrine of presumptive regeneration? How about Dabney's position that baptism is a sacrament to the parent as well as to the child?

LITERATURE: Bavinck, *Geref. Dogm.* IV., pp. 543-590; Kuyper, *Dict. Dogm. de Sacramentis*, pp. 82-157; id., *E Voto II*, pp. 499-566; III, pp. 5-68; Hodge, *Syst. Theol.* III. pp. 526-611; Dabney, *Syst. and Polem. Theol.*, pp. 728-799; Dick, *Theology*, Lectures LXXXVIII-LXXXIX; Litton, *Introd. to Dogm. Theol.*, pp. 444-464; Vos, *Geref. Dogm., De Genademiddelen*, pp. 36-134; ibid., *De Verbondsleer in de Geref. Theol.*; Strong, *Syst. Theol.*, pp. 930-959; Hovey, *Manual of Theol. and Ethics*, pp. 312-333; Pieper, *Christl. Dogm.*, III, pp. 297-339; Schmid, *Doct. Theol. of the Ev. Luth. Church*, pp. 540-558; Valentine, *Chr. Theol.* II, pp. 305-335; Mueller, *Chr. Dogm.*, pp. 486-505; Wilmers, *Handbook of the Chr. Rel.*, pp. 314-322; Schaff, *Our Fathers' Faith and Ours*, pp. 315-320; Pope, *Chr. Theol.* III, pp. 311-324; Lambert, *The Sacraments in the New Testament*, pp. 36-239; Wilson, *On Infant Baptism*; Carson, *On Baptism*; Ayres, *Christian Baptism*; Seiss, *The Baptist System Examined*; Armstrong, *The Doctrine of Baptisms*; Merrill, *Christian Baptism*; McLeod, *The Sacrament of Holy Baptism* in *The Divine Life in the Church*; White, *Why Are Infants Baptized*; Bannerman, *The Church of Christ* II, pp. 42-127; Kramer, *Het Verband tusschen Doop en Wedergeboorte*; Wall, *History of Infant Baptism*; Wielenga, *Ons Doopsformulier*; Schenck, *The Presbyterian Doctrine of Children in the Covenant*.

V. The Lord's Supper

A. Analogies of the Lord's Supper among Israel.

Just as there were analogies to Christian baptism among Israel, there were also analogies of the Lord's Supper. Not only among the Gentiles, but also among Israel, the sacrifices that were brought were often accompanied with sacrificial meals. This was particularly a characteristic feature of the peace-offerings. Of these sacrifices only the fat adhering to the inwards was consumed on the altar; the wave-breast was given to the priesthood, and the heave-shoulder to the officiating priest, Lev. 7:28-34, while the rest constituted a sacrificial meal for the offerer and his friends, provided they were levitically clean, Lev. 7:19-21; Deut. 12:7,12. These meals taught in a symbolic way that "being justified by faith, we have peace with God through our Lord Jesus Christ." They were expressive of the fact that, on the basis of the offered and accepted sacrifice, God receives His people as guests in His house and unites with them in joyful communion, the communal life of the covenant. Israel was forbidden to take part in the sacrificial meals of the Gentiles exactly because it would express their allegiance to other gods, Ex. 34:15; Num. 25:3,5; Ps. 106:28. The sacrificial meals, which testified to the union of Jehovah with His people, were seasons of joy and gladness, and as such were sometimes abused and gave occasion for revelry and drunkenness, I Sam. 1:13; Prov. 7:14; Isa. 28:8. The sacrifice of the Passover was also accompanied with such a sacrificial meal. Over against the Roman Catholics, Protestants sometimes sought to defend the position that this meal constituted the whole of the Passover, but this is an untenable position. The Passover was first of all a sacrifice of atonement, Ex. 12:27; 34:25. Not only is it called a sacrifice, but in the Mosaic period it was also connected with the sanctuary, Deut. 16:2. The lamb was slain by the Levites, and the blood was manipulated by the priests, II Chron. 30:16; 35:11; Ezra 6:19. But though it is first of all a sacrifice, that is not all; it is also a meal, in which the roasted lamb is eaten with unleavened bread and bitter herbs, Ex. 12:8-10. The sacrifice passed right into a meal, which in later times became far more elaborate than it originally was. The New Testament ascribes to the Passover a typical significance, I Cor. 5:7, and thus saw in it not only a reminder of the deliverance from Egypt, but also a sign and seal of the deliverance from the bondage of sin and of communion with God in the promised Messiah. It was in connection with the paschal meal that Jesus instituted the Lord's Supper. By using the elements present in the former He effected a very natural transition to the latter. Of late some critics sought to cast doubt on the institution of the Lord's Supper by Jesus, but there is no good reason to doubt the testimony of the Gospels, nor the independent testimony of the apostle Paul in I Cor. 11:23-26.

B. The Doctrine of the Lord's Supper in History.

1. BEFORE THE REFORMATION. Even in the apostolic age the celebration of the Lord's Supper was accompanied with *agapae* or love-feasts, for which the people brought the necessary ingredients, and which sometimes led to sad abuses, I Cor. 11:20-22. In course of time the gifts so brought were called oblations and sacrifices, and were blessed by the priest with a prayer of thanksgiving. Gradually these names were applied to the elements in the Lord's Supper, so that these assumed the character of a sacrifice brought by the priest, and thanksgiving came to be regarded as a consecration of those elements. While some of the early Church Fathers (Origen, Basil, Gregory of Nazianze) retained the symbolical or spiritual conception of the sacrament, others (Cyril, Gregory of Nyssa, Chrysostom) held that the flesh and blood of Christ were in some way combined with the bread and wine in the sacrament. Augustine retarded the realistic development of the doctrine of the Lord's Supper for a long time. While he did speak of the bread and wine as the body and blood of Christ, he distinguished between the sign and the thing signified, and did not believe in a change of substance. He denied that the wicked, though receiving the elements, also received the body, and stressed the commemorative aspect of the Lord's Supper. During the Middle Ages the Augustinian view was gradually transplanted by the doctrine of transubstantiation. As early as 818 A.D. Paschasius Radbertus already formally proposed this doctrine, but met with strong opposition on the part of Rabanus Maurus and Ratramnus. In the eleventh century a furious controversy again broke out on the subject between Berenger of Tours and Lanfranc. The latter made the crass statement that "the very body of Christ was truly held in the priest's hand, broken and chewed by the teeth of the faithful." This view was finally defined by Hildebert of Tours (1134), and designated as the doctrine of transubstantiation. It was formally adopted by the fourth Lateran Council in 1215. Many questions connected with this doctrine were debated by the Scholastics, such as those respecting the duration of the change of bread and wine into the body and blood of Jesus Christ, the manner of Christ's presence in both elements, the relation of substance and accidents, the adoration of the host, and so on. The final formulation of the doctrine was given by the Council of Trent, and is recorded in *Sessio* XIII of its *Decrees and Canons*. Eight Chapters and eleven Canons are devoted to it. We can only mention the most essential points here. Jesus Christ is truly, really, and substantially present in the holy sacrament. The fact that He is seated at the right hand of God does not exclude the possibility of His substantial and sacramental presence in several places simultaneously. By the words of consecration the substance of bread and wine is changed into the body and blood of Christ. The entire Christ is present under

each species and under each particle of either species. Each one who receives a particle of the host receives the whole Christ. He is present in the elements even before the communicant receives them. In view of this presence, the adoration of the host is but natural. The sacrament effects an "increase of sanctifying grace, special actual graces, remission of venial sins, preservation from grievous (mortal) sin, and the confident hope of eternal salvation."

2. DURING AND AFTER THE REFORMATION. The Reformers, one and all, rejected the sacrificial theory of the Lord's Supper, and the mediæval doctrine of transubstantiation. They differed, however, in their positive construction of the Scriptural doctrine of the Lord's Supper. In opposition to Zwingli, Luther insisted on the literal interpretation of the words of the institution and on the bodily presence of Christ in the Lord's Supper. However, he substituted for the doctrine of transubstantiation that of consubstantiation, which has been defended at length by Occam in his *De Sacramento Altaris,* and according to which Christ is "in, with, and under" the elements. Zwingli denied absolutely the bodily presence of Christ in the Lord's Supper, and gave a figurative interpretation to the words of the institution. He saw in the sacrament primarily an act of commemoration, though he did not deny that in it Christ is spiritually present *to the faith of believers.* Calvin maintained an intermediate position. Like Zwingli, he denied the bodily presence of the Lord in the sacrament, but in distinction from the former, he insisted on the *real,* though spiritual, presence of the Lord in the Supper, the presence of Him as a fountain of spiritual virtue and efficacy. Moreover, instead of stressing the Lord's Supper as an act of man (either of commemoration or of profession), he emphasized the fact that it is the expression first of all of a gracious gift of God to man, and only secondarily a commemorative meal and an act of profession. For him, as well as for Luther, it was primarily a divinely appointed means for the strengthening of faith. The Socinians, Arminians, and Mennonites saw in the Lord's Supper only a memorial, an act of profession, and a means for moral improvement. Under the influence of Rationalism this became the popular view. Schleiermacher stressed the fact that the Lord's Supper is the means by which the communion of life with Christ is preserved in a particularly energetic manner in the bosom of the Church. Many of the Mediating theologians, while belonging to the Lutheran Church, rejected the doctrine of consubstantiation, and approached the Calvinistic view of the spiritual presence of Christ in the Lord's Supper.

C. Scriptural Names for the Lord's Supper.

While there is but a single name for the initiatory sacrament of the New Testament, there are several for the sacrament now under consideration, all of which are derived from Scripture. They are the following: (1) *Deipnon kuriakon,* the Lord's Supper, which is derived from I Cor. 11:20. This is the most common name in Protestant circles. It seems that in the passage indicated the apostle wants to make a pointed distinction between the sacrament and the *agapae,* which the Corinthians connected with it and which they abused, thus making the two virtually incongruous. The special emphasis is on the fact that this Supper is the Lord's. It is not a supper in which the rich invite the poor as their guests and then treat them niggardly, but a feast in which the Lord provides for all in rich abundance. (2) *Trapeza kuriou*, the table of the Lord, a name that is found in I Cor. 10:21. Corinthian Gentiles offered to idols and after their sacrifices sat down to sacrificial meals; and it seems that some of the Corinthian church thought it was permissible to join them, seeing that all flesh is alike. But Paul points out that sacrificing to idols is sacrificing to devils, and that joining in such sacrificial meals is equivalent to exercising communion with devils. This would be absolutely in conflict with sitting at the table of the Lord, confessing allegiance to Him and exercising communion with Him. (3) *Klasis tou artou*, the breaking of bread, a term that is used in Acts 2:42; cf. also Acts 20:7. While this is a term which, in all probability, does not refer exclusively to the Lord's Supper, but also to the love-feasts, it certainly also includes the Lord's Supper. The name may even find its explanation in the breaking of the bread as this was ordained by Jesus. (4) *Eucharistia*, thanksgiving, and *eulogia*, blessing, terms which are derived from I Cor. 10:16; 11:24. In Matt. 26:26,27 we read that the Lord took the bread and blessed it, and took the cup and gave thanks. In all probability the two words were used interchangeably and refer to a blessing and thanksgiving combined. The cup of thanksgiving and blessing is the consecrated cup.

D. Institution of the Lord's Supper.

1. DIFFERENT ACCOUNTS OF THE INSTITUTION. There are four different accounts of the institution of the Lord's Supper, one in each of the Synoptics, and one in I Cor. 11. John speaks of the eating of the passover, but does not mention the institution of a new sacrament. These accounts are independent of, and serve to complement, one another. Evidently, the Lord did not finish the passover meal before He instituted the Lord's Supper. The new sacrament was linked up with the central element in the paschal meal. The bread that was eaten with the lamb was consecrated to a new use. This is evident from the fact that the third cup, generally called "the cup of blessing" was used for the second element in the new sacrament. Thus the sacrament of the Old Testament passed into that of the New in a most natural way.

2. THE SUBSTITUTION OF BREAD FOR THE LAMB. The paschal lamb had symbolical significance. Like all the bloody sacrifices of the Old Testament, it taught the people that the shedding of blood was necessary unto the remission of sins. In addition to that it had a typical meaning, pointing forward to the great sacrifice which would be brought in the fulness of time to take away the sin of the world. And, finally, it also had national significance as a memorial of Israel's deliverance. It was but natural that, when the real Lamb of God made His appearance and was on the point of being slain, the symbol and type should disappear. The all-sufficient sacrifice of Jesus Christ rendered all further shedding of blood unnecessary; and therefore it was entirely fitting that the

bloody element should make way for an unbloody one which, like it, had nourishing properties. Moreover, through the death of Christ the middle wall of partition was broken down, and the blessings of salvation were extended to all the world. And in view of this it was quite natural that the passover, a symbol with a national flavor, should be replaced by one that carried with it no implications of nationalism.

3. SIGNIFICANCE OF THE DIFFERENT ACTIONS AND TERMS.

a. *Symbolic actions.* All the accounts of the institution of the Lord's Supper make mention of *the breaking of the bread*, and Jesus clearly indicates that this was intended to symbolize the breaking of His body for the redemption of sinners. Because Jesus broke the bread *in the presence of His disciples*, Protestant theology generally insists on it that this action should always take place in the sight of the people. This important transaction was intended to be a sign, and a sign must be visible. After distributing the bread, Jesus took the cup, blessed it, and gave it to His disciples. It does not appear that He poured the wine in their presence, and therefore this is not regarded as essential to the celebration of the Lord's Supper. Dr. Wielinga infers, however, from the fact that the bread must be broken, that the wine must also be poured, in the sight of the communicants.[1] Jesus naturally used unleavened bread, since it was the only kind at hand, and the ordinary wine which was largely used as a beverage in Palestine. But neither the one nor the other is stressed, and therefore it does not follow that it would not be permissible to use leavened bread and some other kind of wine. The disciples undoubtedly received the elements in a reclining position, but this does not mean that believers may not partake of them in a sitting, kneeling, or standing, position.

b. *Words of command.* Jesus accompanied His action with words of command. When He gave the bread to His disciples, He said, "Take, eat." And in issuing this command He undoubtedly had in mind, not merely a physical eating, but a spiritual appropriation of the body of Christ by faith. It is a command which, though it came first of all to the apostles, was intended for the Church of all ages. According to Luke 22:19 (comp. I Cor. 11:24) the Lord added the words: "This do in remembrance of me." Some infer from these words that the Supper instituted by Jesus was nothing more than a memorial meal. It is quite evident, however, especially from John 6:32,33, 50,51; I Cor. 11:26-30, that it was intended to be far more than that; and in so far as it had memorial significance, it was intended as a memorial of the sacrificial work of Christ rather than of His person. There was another word of command in connection with the cup. After distributing the bread the Lord also took the cup, gave thanks, and said, "Drink ye all of it," or (according to Luke), "Take this and divide it among yourselves." It is quite clear that the cup here stands for what it contains, for the cup could not be divided. From these words it is perfectly evident that the Lord intended the Sacrament to be used in both kinds (*sub utraque specie*), and that Rome is wrong in withholding

1. *Ons Avondmaals Formulier*, pp. 243 f.

the cup from the laity. The use of both elements enabled Christ to give a vivid representation of the idea that His body was broken, that flesh and blood were separated, and that the sacrament both nourishes and quickens the soul.

c. *Words of explanation.* The word of command in connection with the bread is immediately followed by a word of explanation, which has given rise to sharp disputes, namely, "This is my body." These words have been interpreted in various ways.

(1) The Church of Rome makes the copula "is" emphatic. Jesus meant to say that what He held in His hand was really His body, though it looked and tasted like bread. But this is a thoroughly untenable position. In all probability Jesus spoke Aramaic and used no copula at all. And while He stood before the disciples in the body, He could not very well say to His disciples in all seriousness that He held His body in His hand. Moreover, even on the Roman Catholic view, He could not truthfully say, "This is my body," but could only say, "This is now becoming my body."

(2) Carlstadt held the novel view that Jesus, when He spoke these words, pointed to His body. He argued that the neuter *touto* could not refer to *artos,* which is masculine. But bread can very well be conceived of as a thing and thus referred to as neuter. Moreover, such a statement would have been rather inane under the circumstances.

(3) Luther and the Lutherans also stress the word "is," though they admit that Jesus was speaking figuratively. According to them the figure was not a metaphor, but a synecdoche. The Lord simply meant to say to His disciples: Where you have the bread, you have my body in, under, and along with it, though the substance of both remains distinct. This view is burdened with the impossible doctrine of the omnipresence of the Lord's physical body.

(4) Calvin and the Reformed Churches understand the words of Jesus metaphorically: "This is (that is, signifies) my body." Such a statement would be just as intelligible to the disciples as other similar statements, such as, "I am the bread of life," John 6:35, and, "I am the true vine," John 15:1. At the same time they reject the view, generally ascribed to Zwingli, that the bread *merely signifies* the body of Christ, and stress the fact that it also serves to seal the covenant mercies of God and to convey spiritual nourishment. To these words Jesus adds the further statement, "which is given for you." These words in all probability express the idea that the body of Jesus is given for the benefit, or in the interest, of the disciples. It is given by the Lord to secure their redemption. Naturally, it is a sacrifice not only for the immediate disciples of the Lord, but also for all those who believe.

There is also a word of explanation in connection with the cup. The Lord makes the significant statement: "This cup is the new covenant in my blood, even that which is poured out for you." Luke 22:20. These words convey an implied contrast between the blood of the Saviour, as the blood of the new covenant, and the blood of the old covenant mentioned in Ex. 24:8. The latter was only a shadowy representation of the New Testament reality. The words "for you" have no wider application than they do in the statement made in connection with the bread, "which is given for you." They are not to be understood in the unrestricted sense of "for all men indiscriminately," but rather in the limited sense of "for you and for all who are really my disciples." The concluding words in I Cor. 11:26, "For as often as ye eat this bread, and drink this cup, ye proclaim the Lord's death till He come," point to the perennial significance of the Lord's Supper as a memorial of the sacrificial death of Christ; and clearly intimate that it should be celebrated regularly until the Lord's return.

E. The Things Signified and Sealed in the Lord's Supper.

1. THE THINGS SIGNIFIED IN THE SACRAMENT. It is one of the character-istics of a sacrament that it represents one or more spiritual truths by means of sensible and outward signs. The outward sign in the case of the Lord's Supper includes not only the visible elements employed, but also the breaking of the bread and the pouring of the wine, the appropriation of bread and wine by eat-ing and drinking, and the partaking of them in communion with others. The following points should be mentioned here:

a. It is a symbolical representation of the Lord's death, I Cor. 11:26. The central fact of redemption, prefigured in the sacrifices of the Old Testament, is clearly set forth by means of the significant symbols of the New Testament sac-rament. The words of the institution, "broken for you" and "shed for many", point to the fact that the death of Christ is a sacrificial one, for the benefit, and even in the place, of His people.

b. It also symbolizes the believer's participation in the crucified Christ. In the celebration of the Lord's Supper the participants not merely look at the symbols, but receive them and feed upon them. Figuratively speaking, they "eat the flesh of the Son of Man, and drink His blood," John 6:53, that is, they sym-bolically appropriate the benefits secured by the sacrificial death of Christ.

c. It represents, not only the death of Christ as the object of faith, and the act of faith which unites the believer to Christ, but also the effect of this act as giving life, strength, and joy, to the soul. This is implied in the emblems used. Just as bread and wine nourish and invigorate the bodily life of man, so Christ sustains and quickens the life of the soul. Believers are regularly represented in Scripture as having their life, and strength, and happiness, in Christ.

d. Finally, the sacrament also symbolizes the union of believers with one another. As members of the mystical body of Jesus Christ, constituting a spiri-tual unity, they eat of the same bread and drink of the same wine, I Cor. 10:17; 12:13. Receiving the elements, the one from the other, they exercise intimate communion with one another.

2. THE THINGS SEALED IN THE LORD'S SUPPER. The Lord's Supper is not only a sign but also a seal. This is lost sight of by a good many in our day, who

have a very superficial view of this sacrament, and regard it merely as a memorial of Christ and as a badge of Christian profession. These two aspects of the sacrament, namely, as a sign and as a seal, are not independent of each other. The sacrament as a sign, or — to put it differently — the sacrament with all that it signifies, constitutes a seal. The seal is attached to the things signified, and is a pledge of the covenanted grace of God revealed in the sacrament. The Heidelberg Catechism says that Christ intends "by these visible signs and pledges to assure us that we are as really partakers of His true body and blood, through the working of the Holy Spirit, as we receive by the mouth of the body these holy tokens in remembrance of Him; and that all His sufferings and obedience are as certainly ours as if we ourselves had in our own persons suffered and made satisfaction to God for our sins."[1] The following points come into consideration here:

a. It seals to the participant the great love of Christ, revealed in the fact that He surrendered Himself to a shameful and bitter death for them. This does not merely mean that it testifies to the reality of that sacrificial self-surrender, but that it assures the believing participant of the Lord's Supper that he personally was the object of that incomparable love.

b. Moreover, it pledges the believing partaker of the sacrament, not only the love and grace of Christ in now offering Himself to them as their Redeemer in all the fulness of His redemptive work; but gives him the personal assurance that all the promises of the covenant and all the riches of the gospel offer are his by a divine donation, so that he has a personal claim on them.

c. Again, it not only ratifies to the believing participant the rich promises of the gospel, but it assures him that the blessings of salvation are his in actual possession. As surely as the body is nourished and refreshed by bread and wine, so surely is the soul that receives Christ's body and blood through faith even now in possession of eternal life, and so surely will he receive it ever more abundantly.

d. Finally, the Lord's Supper is a reciprocal seal. It is a badge of profession on the part of those who partake of the sacrament. Whenever they eat the bread and drink the wine, they profess their faith in Christ as their Saviour and their allegiance to Him as their King, and they solemnly pledge a life of obedience to His divine commandments.

F. The Sacramental Union or the Question of the Real Presence of Christ in the Lord's Supper.

With this question we are entering upon what has long been, and still is, the occasion for considerable difference of opinion in the Church of Jesus Christ. There is by no means a unanimous opinion as to the relation of the sign to the thing signified, that is to say, as to the nature of the presence of Christ in the Lord's Supper. There are especially four views that come into consideration here.

---

1. *Lord's Day* XXIX, Q. 79.

1. THE VIEW OF ROME. The Church of Rome conceives of the sacramental union in a *physical sense*. It is hardly justified, however, in speaking of any sacramental union at all, for according to its representation there is no union in the proper sense of the word. The sign is not joined to the thing signified, but makes way for it, since the former passes into the latter. When the priest utters the formula, *"hoc est corpus meum"*, bread and wine change into the body and blood of Christ. It is admitted that even after the change the elements look and taste like bread and wine. While the substance of both is changed, their properties remain the same. In the form of bread and wine the physical body and blood of Christ are present. The supposed Scriptural ground for this is found in the words of the institution, "this *is* my body", and in John 6:50 ff. But the former passage is clearly tropical, like those in John 14:6; 15:1; 10:9, and others; and the latter, literally understood. would teach more than the Roman Catholic himself would be ready to grant. namely, that every one who eats the Lord's Supper goes to heaven, while no one who fails to eat it will obtain eternal life (cf. verses 53,54). Moreover, verse 63 clearly points to a spiritual interpretation. Furthermore, it is quite impossible to conceive of the bread which Jesus broke as being the body which was handling it; and it should be noted that Scripture calls it bread even after it is supposed to have been trans-substantiated, I Cor. 10:17; 11:26,27,28. This view of Rome also violates the human senses, where it asks us to believe that what tastes and looks like bread and wine, is really flesh and blood; and human reason, where it requires belief in the separation of a substance and its properties and in the presence of a material body in several places at the same time. both of which are contrary to reason. Consequently, the elevation and adoration of the host is also without any proper foundation.

2. THE LUTHERAN VIEW. Luther rejected the doctrine of transubstantiation and substituted for it the related doctrine of consubstantiation. According to him bread and wine remain what they are, but there is in the Lord's Supper nevertheless a mysterious and miraculous real presence of the whole person of Christ, body and blood, in, under, and along with, the elements. He and his followers maintain the *local presence* of the physical body and blood of Christ in the sacrament. Lutherans sometimes deny that they teach the local presence of Christ in the Lord's Supper, but then they ascribe to the word 'local' a meaning not intended by those who ascribe this teaching to them. When it is said that they teach the local presence of the physical nature of Christ, this does not imply that all other bodies are excluded from the same portion of space, nor that the human nature of Christ is nowhere else, as, for instance, in heaven; but it does mean that the physical nature of Christ is locally present in the Lord's Supper, as magnetism is locally present in the magnet, and as the soul is locally present in the body. Consequently, they also teach the so-called *manducatio oralis,* which means that those who partake of the elements in the Lord's Supper eat and drink the Lord's body and blood "with the bodily mouth", and not merely that they appropriate these by faith. Unworthy communicants also receive them, but to

their condemnation. This view is no great improvement on the Roman Catholic conception, though it does not involve the oft-repeated miracle of a change of substance minus a change of attributes. It really makes the words of Jesus mean, 'this accompanies my body', an interpretation that is more unlikely than either of the others. Moreover, it is burdened with the impossible doctrine of the ubiquity of the Lord's glorified human nature, which several Lutherans would gladly discard.

3. THE ZWINGLIAN VIEW. There is a very general impression, not altogether without foundation, that Zwingli's view of the Lord's Supper was very defective. He is usually alleged to have taught that it is a bare sign or symbol, figuratively representing or signifying spiritual truths or blessings; and that its reception is a mere commemoration of what Christ did for sinners, and above all a badge of the Christian's profession. This hardly does justice to the Swiss Reformer, however. Some of his statements undoubtedly convey the idea that to him the sacrament was merely a commemorative rite and a sign and symbol of what the believer pledges in it. But his writings also contain statements that point to a deeper significance of the Lord's Supper and contemplate it as a seal or pledge of what God is doing for the believer in the sacrament. In fact, he seems to have changed his view somewhat in the course of time. It is very hard to determine exactly what he did believe in this matter. He evidently wanted to exclude from the doctrine of the Lord's Supper all unintelligible mysticism, and showed an excessive leaning to the side of plainness and simplicity in its exposition. He occasionally expresses himself to the intent that it is a mere sign or symbol, a commemoration of the Lord's death. And though he speaks of it in passing also as a seal or pledge, he certainly does not do justice to this idea. Moreover, for him the emphasis falls on what the believer, rather than on what God, pledges in the sacrament. He identified the eating of the body of Christ with faith in Him and a trustful reliance on His death. He denied the bodily presence of Christ in the Lord's Supper, but did not deny that Christ is present there in a spiritual manner to the faith of the believer. Christ is present only in His divine nature and in the *apprehension* of the believing communicant.

4. THE REFORMED VIEW. Calvin objects to Zwingli's doctrine of the Lord's Supper, (a) that it allows the idea of what the believer does in the sacrament to eclipse the gift of God in it; and (b) that it sees in the eating of the body of Christ nothing more nor higher than faith in His name and reliance on His death. According to him the sacrament is connected not merely with the past work of Christ, with the Christ who died (as Zwingli seems to think), but also with the present spiritual work of Christ, with the Christ that is alive in glory. He believes that Christ, though not bodily and locally present in the Supper, is yet present and enjoyed in His entire person, both body and blood. He emphasizes the mystical communion of believers with the entire person of the Redeemer. His representation is not entirely clear, but he seems to mean that the body and blood of Christ, though absent and locally present only in heaven, communicate a life-giving influence to the believer when he is in the act of re-

ceiving the elements. That influence, though real, is not physical but spiritual and mystical, is mediated by the Holy Spirit, and is conditioned on the act of faith by which the communicant symbolically receives the body and blood of Christ. As to the way in which this communion with Christ is effected, there is a two-fold representation. Sometimes it is represented as if by faith the communicant lifts his heart to heaven, where Christ is; sometimes, as if the Holy Spirit brings the influence of the body and blood of Christ down to the communicant. Dabney positively rejects the representation of Calvin as if the communicant partakes of the very body and blood of Christ in the sacrament. This is undoubtedly an obscure point in Calvin's representation. Sometimes he seems to place too much emphasis on the literal flesh and blood. Perhaps, however, his words are to be understood sacramentally. that is, in a figurative sense. This view of Calvin is that found in our confessional standards.[1] A very common interpretation of the dubious point in Calvin's doctrine, is that the body and blood of Christ are present only virtually. that is, in the words of Dr. Hodge, that "the virtues and effects of the sacrifice of the body of the Redeemer on the cross are made present and are actually conveyed in the sacrament to the worthy receiver by the power of the Holy Ghost, who uses the sacrament as His instrument according to His sovereign will."[2]

G. The Lord's Supper as a Means of Grace, or Its Efficacy.

The sacrament of the Lord's Supper, instituted by the Lord Himself as a sign and seal, is as such also a means of grace. Christ instituted it for the benefit of His disciples and of all believers. It was clearly the intention of the Saviour that His followers should profit by participation in it. This follows from the very fact that He instituted it as a sign and seal of the covenant of grace. It can also readily be inferred from the symbolical eating and drinking, which point to nourishment and quickening, and from such passages as John 6:48-58 (irrespective of the question, whether this refers directly to the Lord's Supper or not), and I Cor. 11:17.

1. THE GRACE RECEIVED IN THE LORD'S SUPPER. The Lord's Supper is intended for believers and for believers only, and therefore is not instrumental in originating the work of grace in the heart of the sinner. The presence of the grace of God is presupposed in the hearts of the participants. Jesus administered it to His professed followers only; according to Acts 2:42,46 they who believed continued steadfastly in the breaking of bread; and in I Cor. 11:28,29 the necessity of self-examination before partaking of the Lord's Supper is stressed. The grace received in the sacrament does not differ in kind from that which believers receive through the instrumentality of the Word. The sacrament merely adds to the effectiveness of the Word, and therefore to the measure of the grace received. It is the grace of an ever closer fellowship with Christ, of spiritual nourishment and quickening, and of an ever increasing assurance of salvation.

1. Cf. *Conf. Belg.*, Art. XXXV; *Heidelberg Catechism*, Question 75,76, and also in the Form for the celebration of the Lord's Supper.
2. *Comm. on the Confession of Faith*, p. 492.

The Roman Catholic Church names specifically sanctifying grace, special actual graces, the remission of venial sins, preservation from mortal sin, and the assurance of salvation.

2. THE MANNER IN WHICH THIS GRACE IS WROUGHT. How does the sacrament function in this respect? Is the Lord's Supper in any way a meritorious cause of the grace conferred? Does it confer grace irrespective of the spiritual condition of the recipient, or does it not?

a. *The Roman Catholic view.* For the Roman Catholics the Lord's Supper is not merely a sacrament, but also a *sacrifice;* it is even first of all a sacrifice. It is "the unbloody renewal of the sacrifice of the cross." This does not mean that in the Lord's Supper Christ actually dies anew, but that He undergoes an external change, which is in some way equivalent to death. Did not the Lord speak of the bread as His body that was broken for the disciples, and of the wine as His blood that was poured out for them? Roman Catholic controversialists sometimes give the impression that this sacrifice has only a representative or commemorative character, but this is not the real doctrine of the Church. The sacrifice of Christ in the Lord's Supper is considered to be a real sacrifice, and is supposed to have propitiatory value. When the question is raised, what this sacrifice merits for the sinner, Roman Catholic authorities begin to hedge and to speak inconsistent language. The statement of Wilmers in his *Handbook of the Christian Religion,* which is used as a textbook in many Roman Catholic schools, may be given as an example. Says he on page 348: "By the fruits of the sacrifice of the Mass we understand the effects which it produces *for us,* inasmuch as it is a sacrifice of *atonement* and *impetration*: (a) not only supernatural graces, but also natural favors; (b) remission of sins, and of the punishment due to them. What Christ merited for us by His death on the cross is *applied* to us in the sacrament of the Mass." After the sacrifice of the Mass is called a sacrifice of *atonement,* the last sentence seems to say that it is after all only a sacrifice in which that which Christ merited on the cross is applied to the participants.

As far as the Lord's Supper as a sacrament is concerned, the Roman Catholic Church teaches that it works *ex opere operato,* which means, "in virtue of the sacramental act itself, and not in virtue of the acts or disposition of the recipient, or of the worthiness of the minister (*ex opere operantis*)." This means that every one who receives the elements, be he wicked or pious, also receives the grace signified, which is conceived of as a substance contained in the elements. The sacramental rite itself conveys grace unto the recipient. At the same time it also teaches, rather inconsistently, it would seem, that the effects of the sacrament may be completely or partially frustrated by the existence of some obstacle, by the absence of that disposition that makes the soul capable of receiving grace, or by the priest's want of intention to do what the Church does.

b. *The prevailing Protestant view.* The prevailing view in the Protestant Churches is, that the sacrament does not work *ex opere operato.* It is not itself a cause of grace, but merely an instrument in the hand of God. Its effective operation is dependent, not only on the *presence*, but on the *activity*, of faith in the recipient. Unbelievers may receive the external elements, but do not receive the thing signified thereby. Some Lutherans and the High Church Episcopalians, however, in their desire to maintain the objective character of the sacrament, clearly manifest a leaning toward the position of the Church of Rome. "We believe, teach, and confess", says the Formula of Concord, "that not only true believers in Christ, and such as worthily approach the Supper of the Lord, but also the unworthy and unbelieving receive the true body and blood of Christ; in such wise, nevertheless, that they derive thence neither consolation nor life, but rather so as that receiving turns to their judgment and condemnation, unless they be converted and repent (I Cor. 11:27,29).[1]

H. The Persons for Whom the Lord's Supper Is Instituted.

1. THE PROPER PARTICIPANTS OF THE SACRAMENT. In answer to the question, "For whom is the Lord's Supper instituted?" the Heidelberg Catechism says: "For those who are truly displeased with themselves for their sins and yet trust that these are forgiven them for the sake of Christ, and that their remaining infirmity is covered by His passion and death; who also desire more and more to strengthen their faith and amend their life." From these words it appears that the Lord's Supper was not instituted for all men indiscriminately, nor even for all those who have a place in the visible Church of Christ, but only for those who earnestly repent of their sins, trust that these have been covered by the atoning blood of Jesus Christ, and are desirous to increase their faith, and to grow in true holiness of life. The participants of the Lord's Supper must be repentant sinners, who are ready to admit that they are lost in themselves. They must have a living faith in Jesus Christ, so that they trust for their redemption in the atoning blood of the Saviour. Furthermore, they must have a proper understanding and appreciation of the Lord's Supper, must discern the difference between it and a common meal, and must be impressed with the fact that the bread and wine are the tokens of the body and blood of Christ. And, finally, they must have a holy desire for spiritual growth and for ever-increasing conformity to the image of Christ.

2. THOSE WHO MUST BE EXCLUDED FROM THE LORD'S SUPPER. Since the Lord's Supper is a sacrament of and for the Church, it follows that they who are outside of the Church cannot partake of it. But it is necessary to make still further limitations. Not even every one that has a place in the Church can be admitted to the table of the Lord. The following exceptions should be noted:

a. Children, though they were allowed to eat the passover in the days of the Old Testament, cannot be permitted to partake of the table of the Lord, since they cannot meet the requirements for worthy participation. Paul insists on the necessity of self-examination previous to the celebration, when he says: "But

---

1. VII. 7.

let a man prove himself, and so let him eat of the bread and drink of the cup",
I Cor. 11:28, and children are not able to examine themselves. Moreover, he
points out that, in order to partake of the Supper in a worthy manner, it is necessary to discern the body, I Cor. 11:29, that is, to distinguish properly between
the elements used in the Lord's Supper and ordinary bread and wine, by recognizing those elements as symbols of the body and blood of Christ. And this,
too, is beyond the capacity of children. It is only after they have come to years
of discretion, that they can be permitted to join in the celebration of the Lord's
Supper.

b. Such unbelievers as may possibly be within the confines of the visible
Church have no right to partake of the table of the Lord. The Church must require of all those who desire to celebrate the Lord's Supper a credible profession of faith. Naturally, she cannot look into the heart and can only base her
judgment respecting an applicant for admission on his confession of faith in
Jesus Christ. It is possible that she occasionally admits hypocrites to the privileges of full communion, but such persons in partaking of the Lord's Supper will
only eat and drink judgment to themselves. And if their unbelief and ungodli-
ness becomes evident, the Church will have to exclude them by the proper
administration of Church discipline. The holiness of the Church and of the
sacrament must be safeguarded.

c. Even true believers may not partake of the Lord's Supper under all conditions and in every frame of mind. The condition of their spiritual life, their
conscious relation to God, and their attitude to their fellow-Christians may be
such as to disqualify them to engage in such a spiritual exercise as the celebration
of the Lord's Supper. This is clearly implied in what Paul says in I Cor. 11:28-
32. There were practices among the Corinthians which really made their participation in the Lord's Supper a mockery. When a person is conscious of being
estranged from the Lord or from his brethren, he has no proper place at a table
which speaks of communion. It should be stated explicitly, however, that lack
of the assurance of salvation need not deter anyone from coming to the table of
the Lord, since the Lord's Supper was instituted for the very purpose of strengthening faith.

QUESTIONS FOR FURTHER STUDY: Can it be proved that the Lord's Supper took the place
of the Old Testament passover? How? Is it permissible to cut the bread in squares before
the administration of the Lord's Supper, and to use the individual cup? What does the term
"real presence" mean in connection with this sacrament? Does the Bible teach such a real
presence? If it does, does it favor the idea that the human nature of Christ is present in the
state of humiliation, or in that of glorification? What is meant by the Reformed doctrine
of the spiritual presence? Does the discourse of Jesus in John 6 really refer to the Lord's
Supper? How does Rome defend the celebration of the Lord's Supper under one species?
How did the conception of the Lord's Supper as a sacrifice arise? What objections are there
to this notion? Does "eating the body" simply amount to believing in Christ? Is open communion defensible?

LITERATURE: Bavinck, *Geref. Dogm.* IV, pp. 590-644; Kuyper, *Dict. Dogm., De Sacra-
mentis*, pp. 158-238; Vos, *Geref. Dogm. V. De Genademiddelen*, pp. 134-190; Hodge, *Syst.
Theol.* III, pp. 611-692; Dabney, *Syst. and Polem. Theol.*, pp. 800-817; Bannerman, *The
Church of Christ*, II, pp. 128-185; Cunningham, *The Reformers and the Theology of the*

Reformation. pp. 212-291; Valentine, *Chr. Theol.* II, pp. 335-361; *Schmid, Doct. Theol. of the Ev. Luth. Ch.*, pp. 558-584; Browne, *Exposition of the Thirty-Nine Articles*, pp. 683-757; Litton, *Introd. to Dogm. Theol.*, pp. 464-532; Candlish, *The Christian Salvation*, pp. 179-201; Pieper, *Christl. Dogm.* III, pp. 340-458; Pope, *Chr. Theol.* III, pp. 325-334; Wilmers, *Handbook of the Chr. Rel.*, pp. 327-349; Moehler, *Symbolism*, pp. 235-254; Schaff, *Our Father's Faith and Ours*, pp. 322-353; Otten, *Manual of the Hist. of Dogma* II, pp. 310-337; Hebert, *The Lord's Supper*, (two vols.) cf. Index; Ebrard, *Das Dogma vom Heiligen Abendmahl. cf.* Index; Calvin, *Institutes*, Bk. IV, chapters 17 and 18; Wielenga, *Ons Avondmaalsformulier*; Lambert, *The Sacraments in the New Testament*, pp. 240-422; MacLeod, *The Ministry and Sacraments of the Church of Scotland*, pp. 243-300.

THE DOCTRINE OF THE LAST THINGS

Introductory Chapter

A. Eschatology in Philosophy and Religion.

1. THE QUESTION OF ESCHATOLOGY A NATURAL ONE. A doctrine of the last things is not something that is peculiar to the Christian religion. Wherever people have seriously reflected on human life, whether in the individual or in the race, they have not merely asked, whence did it spring, and how did it come to be what it is, but also, whither is it bound? They raised the question, What is the end or final destiny of the individual; and what is the goal towards which the human race is moving? Does man perish at death, or does he enter upon another state of existence, either of bliss or of woe? Will the generations of men come and go in endless succession and finally sink into oblivion, or is the race of the children of men and the whole creation moving on to some divine *telos*, an end designed for it by God. And if the human race is moving on to some final, some ideal, condition perhaps, will the generations that have come and gone participate in this in any way, and if so, how; or did they merely serve as a thoroughfare leading up to the grand climax? Naturally, only those who believe that, as the history of the world had a beginning, it will also have an end, can speak of a consummation and have a doctrine of eschatology.

2. THE QUESTION OF ESCHATOLOGY IN PHILOSOPHY. The question of the final destiny of the individual and of the race occupied an important place even in the speculations of the philosophers. Plato taught the immortality of the soul, that is, its continued existence after death, and this doctrine remained an important tenet in philosophy up to the present time. Spinoza had no place for it in his pantheistic system, but Wolff and Leibnitz defended it with all kinds of arguments. Kant stressed the untenableness of these arguments, but nevertheless retained the doctrine of immortality as a postulate of practical reason. The idealistic philosophy of the nineteenth century ruled it out. In fact, as Haering says, "Pantheism of all sorts is limited to a definite mode of contemplation, and does not lead to any 'ultimate'." Not only did the philosophers reflect on the future of the individual; they also thought deeply on the future of the world. The Stoics spoke of successive world-cycles, and the Buddhists, of world-ages, in each of which a new world appears and again disappears. Even Kant speculated on the birth and death of worlds.

3. THE QUESTION OF ESCHATOLOGY IN RELIGION. It is especially in religion, however, that we meet with eschatological conceptions. Even false religions, the more primitive as well as the more advanced, have their eschatology.

Buddhism has its Nirvana, Mohammedanism, its sensual paradise, and the Indians, their happy hunting-grounds. Belief in the continued existence of the soul appears everywhere and in various forms. Says J. T. Addison: "The belief that the soul of man survives his death is so nearly universal that we have no reliable record of a tribe or nation or religion in which it does not prevail."[1] It may manifest itself in the conviction that the dead are still hovering around and near at hand, in ancestor worship, in seeking intercourse with the dead, in the conception of an underworld peopled with the dead, or in the idea of the transmigration of souls; but it is always present in some form or other. But in these religions all is vague and uncertain. It is only in the Christian religion that the doctrine of the last things receives greater precision and carries with it an assurance that is divine. Naturally, they who are not content to rest their faith exclusively on the Word of God, but make it contingent on experience and on the deliverances of the Christian consciousness, are at a great disadvantage here. While they may experience spiritual awakening, divine illumination, repentance and conversion, and may observe the fruits of the operations of divine grace in their lives, they cannot experience nor see the realities of the future world. They shall have to accept the testimony of God respecting these, or continue to grope about in the dark. If they do not wish to build the house of their hope on vague and indeterminate longings, they shall have to turn to the firm ground of the Word of God.

B. Eschatology in the History of the Christian Church.

Speaking generally, it may be said that Christianity never forgot the glorious predictions respecting its future and the future of the individual Christian. Neither the individual Christian nor the Church could avoid thinking about these and finding comfort in them. Sometimes, however, the Church, borne down with the cares of life, or entangled in its pleasures, thought little of the future. Moreover, it happened repeatedly that at one time it would think more of this, and at another time, more of that particular element of its future hope. In days of defection the Christian hope sometimes grew dim and uncertain, but it never died out altogether. At the same time it must be said that there has never been a period in the history of the Christian Church, in which eschatology was the center of Christian thought. The other loci of Dogmatics have each had their time of special development, but this cannot be said of eschatology. Three periods can be distinguished in the history of eschatological thought.

1. FROM THE APOSTOLIC AGE TO THE BEGINNING OF THE FIFTH CENTURY. In the very first period the Church was perfectly conscious of the separate elements of the Christian hope, as, for instance, that physical death is not yet eternal death, that the souls of the dead live on, that Christ is coming again, that there will be a blessed resurrection of the people of God, that this will be followed by a general judgment, in which eternal doom will be pronounced

---

1. *Life Beyond Death*, p. 3.

upon the wicked but the pious will be rewarded with the everlasting glories of heaven. But these elements were simply seen as so many separate parts of the future hope, and were not yet dogmatically construed. Though the various elements were quite well understood, their interrelation was not yet clearly seen. At first it seemed as if eschatology was in a fair way to become the center of the construction of Christian doctrine, for in the first two centuries Chiliasm was rather prominent, though not as prominent as some would have us believe. As it turned out, however, eschatology was not developed in this period.

2. FROM THE BEGINNING OF THE FIFTH CENTURY TO THE REFORMATION. Under the guidance of the Holy Spirit the attention of the Church was directed from the future to the present, and Chiliasm was gradually forgotten. Especially under the influence of Origen and Augustine, anti-chiliastic views became dominant in the Church. But though these were regarded as orthodox, they were not thought through and systematically developed. There was a general belief in a life after death, in the return of the Lord, in the resurrection of the dead, in the final judgment, and in a kingdom of glory, but very little reflection on the manner of these. The thought of a material and temporal kingdom made way for that of eternal life and the future salvation. In course of time the Church was placed in the center of attention, and the hierarchical Church was identified with the Kingdom of God. The idea gained ground that outside of this Church there was no salvation, and that the Church determined the proper pedagogical training for the future. A great deal of attention was paid to the intermediate state, and particularly to the doctrine of purgatory. In connection with this the mediation of the Church was brought to the foreground, the doctrine of the mass, of prayers for the dead, and of indulgences. As a protest against this ecclesiasticism, Chiliasm again made its appearance in several sects This was in part a reaction of a pietistic nature against the externalism and worldliness of the Church.

3. FROM THE REFORMATION UP TO THE PRESENT DAY. The thought of the Reformation centered primarily about the idea of the application and appropriation of salvation, and sought to develop eschatology mainly from this point of view. Many of the old Reformed theologians treat it merely as an adjunct to soteriology, dealing with the glorification of believers. Consequently, only a part of eschatology was studied and brought to further development. The Reformation adopted what the early Church taught respecting the return of Christ, the resurrection, the final judgment, and eternal life, and brushed aside the crass form of Chiliasm which appeared in the Anabaptist sects. In its opposition to Rome, it also reflected a good deal on the intermediate state and rejected the various tenets developed by the Roman Catholic Church. It can hardly be said that the Churches of the Reformation did much for the development of eschatology. In Pietism Chiliasm again made its appearance. The Rationalism of the eighteenth century retained of eschatology merely the bare idea of a colourless immortality, of the mere survival of the soul after death. Under the influence of the philosophy of evolution with its idea of an

endless progress, it became, if not obsolete, at least obsolescent. Liberal theology entirely ignored the eschatological teachings of Jesus and placed all the emphasis on His ethical precepts. As a result it has no eschatology worthy of the name. Other - worldliness made way for this - worldliness; the blessed hope of eternal life was replaced by the social hope of a kingdom of God exclusively of this world; and the former assurance respecting the resurrection of the dead and future glory was supplanted by the vague trust that God may have even better things in store for man than the blessings which he now enjoys. Says Gerald Birney Smith: "In no realm are the changes of thinking more marked than in the portion of theology which deals with the future life. Where theologians used to speak to us in detail concerning 'last things,' they now set forth in somewhat general terms the reasonable basis for optimistic confidence in the continuance of life beyond physical death."[1] At the present time, however, there are some signs of a change for the better. A new wave of Premillennialism appeared, which is not limited to the sects, but has also found entrance in some of the Churches of our day, and its advocates suggest a Christian philosophy of history, based particularly on the study of Daniel and Revelation, and help to fix the attention once more on the end of the ages. Weiss and Schweitzer called attention to the fact that the eschatological teachings of Jesus were far more important in His scheme of thought than His ethical precepts, which after all represent only an "Interimsethik." And Karl Barth also stresses the eschatological element in divine revelation.

C. The Relation of Eschatology to the Rest of Dogmatics.

1. WRONG CONCEPTIONS WHICH OBSCURE THIS RELATION. When Kliefoth wrote his *Eschatologie,* he complained about the fact that there had never yet appeared a comprehensive and adequate treatise on eschatology as a whole; and further calls attention to the fact that in dogmatical works it often appears, not as a main division uniform with the others, but merely as a fragmentary and neglected appendix, while some of its questions are discussed in other loci. There were good reasons for his complaints. In general it may be said that eschatology is even now the least developed of all the loci of dogmatics. Moreover, it was often given a very subordinate place in the systematic treatment of theology. It was a mistake of Coccejus that he arranged the whole of dogmatics according to the scheme of the covenants, and thus treated it as a historical study rather than a systematic presentation of all the truths of the Christian religion. In such a scheme eschatology could only appear as the finale of history, and not at all as one of the constitutive elements of a system of truth. A historical discussion of the last things may form a part of the *historia revelationis,* but cannot as such be introduced as an integral part of dogmatics. Dogmatics is not a descriptive, but a normative science, in which we aim at *absolute,* rather than at mere *historical,* truth. Reformed theologians on the whole saw this point very clearly, and therefore discussed the last things in a systematic way. However,

---

1. *A Guide to the Study of the Christian Religion,* p. 538.

they did not always do justice to it as one of the main divisions of dogmatics, but gave it a subordinate place in one of the other loci. Several of them conceived of it merely as dealing with the glorification of the saints or the consummation of the rule of Christ, and introduced it at the conclusion of their discussion of objective and subjective soteriology. The result was that some parts of eschatology received due emphasis, while other parts were all but neglected. In some cases the subject-matter of eschatology was divided among different loci. Another mistake, sometimes made, was to lose sight of the theological character of eschatology. We cannot subscribe to the following statement of Pohle (Roman Catholic) in his work on *Eschatology, or the Catholic Doctrine of the Last Things*: "Eschatology is anthropological and cosmological rather than theological; for, though it deals with God as the Consummator and Universal Judge, strictly speaking, its subject is the created universe, i.e. man and the cosmos."[1] If eschatology is not theology it has no proper place in dogmatics.

2. THE PROPER CONCEPTION OF THIS RELATION. Strange to say, the same Catholic author says: "Eschatology is the crown and capstone of dogmatic theology," which is perfectly correct. It is the one locus of theology, in which all the other loci must come to a head, to a final conclusion. Dr. Kuyper correctly points out that every other locus left some question unanswered, to which eschatology should supply the answer. In theology it is the question, how God is finally perfectly glorified in the work of His hands, and how the counsel of God is fully realized; in anthropology, the question, how the disrupting influence of sin is completely overcome; in christology, the question, how the work of Christ is crowned with perfect victory; in soteriology, the question, how the work of the Holy Spirit at last issues in the complete redemption and glorification of the people of God; and in ecclesiology, the question of the final apotheosis of the Church. All these questions must find their answer in the last locus of dogmatics, making it the real capstone of dogmatic theology. Haering testifies to the same fact when he says: "As a matter of fact it (eschatology) does shed a clear light upon every single section of doctrine. Is the universality of God's saving plan, is personal communion with a personal God asserted without reserve, is the permanent significance of the Redeemer upheld, is forgiveness of sin conceived as one with victory over the power of sin — on these points the eschatology must remove all doubt, even when indefinite statements which have been made in the preceding parts could not at once be recognized as such. Nor is it difficult to discover the reason of this. In the doctrine of the last things, the communion between God and man is set forth as completed, and therefore the idea of our religion, the Christian principle, is presented in its purity; not, however, as a mere idea in the sense of an ideal which is never completely realized, but as perfect reality — and it is clear what difficulties are implied in that. It must therefore appear at last, in the presentment of eschatology, if

---

1. p. 1

not sooner, whether the reality of this communion with God has received its unrestricted due."[1]

D. The Name "Eschatology."

Various names have been applied to the last locus of dogmatics, of which *de Novissimis* or *Eschatology* is the most common. Kuyper uses the term *Consummatione Saeculi*. The name "eschatology" is based on those passages of Scripture that speak of "the last days (*eschatai hemerai*), Is. 2:2; Mic. 4:1, "the last time " (*eschatos ton chronon*), I Pet. 1:20, and "the last hour," (*eschate hora*), I John 2:18. It is true that these expressions sometimes refer to the whole New Testament dispensation, but even so they embody an eschatological idea. Old Testament prophecy distinguishes only two periods, namely, "this age" (*olam hazzeh*, Gr. *aion houtos*), and "the coming age" (*ollam habba'*, Gr. *aion mellon*). Since the prophets represent the coming of the Messiah and the end of the world as coinciding, the "last days" are the days *immediately* preceding both the coming of the Messiah and the end of the world. They nowhere draw a clear line of distinction between a first and a second coming of the Messiah. In the New Testament, however, it becomes perfectly evident, that the coming of the Messiah is twofold, and that the Messianic age includes two stages, the present Messianic age and the future consummation. Consequently, the New Testament dispensation may be regarded under two different aspects. If the attention is fixed on the future coming of the Lord, and all that precedes it is considered as belonging to "this age," then New Testament believers are regarded as living on the eve of that important event, the Lord's return in glory and the final consummation. If, on the other hand, the attention is centered on the first coming of Christ, it is natural to consider the believers of this dispensation as already, though only in principle, living in the *future* age. This representation of their condition is not uncommon in the New Testament. The Kingdom of God is already present, eternal life is realized in principle, the Spirit is the earnest of the heavenly inheritance, and believers are already seated with Christ in heavenly places. But while some of the eschatological realities are thus projected into the present, they are not fully realized until the time of the future consummation. And when we speak of "eschatology," we have in mind more particularly the facts and events that are connected with the second coming of Christ, and that will mark the end of the present dispensation and will usher in the eternal glories of the future.

E. The Contents of Eschatology: General and Individual Eschatology.

1. GENERAL ESCHATOLOGY. The name "eschatology" calls attention to the fact that the history of the world and of the human race will finally reach its consummation. It is not an indefinite and endless process, but a real history moving on to a divinely appointed end. According to Scripture that end will come as a mighty crisis, and the facts and events associated with this crisis

---

1. *The Christian Faith*, p. 831.

form the contents of eschatology. Strictly speaking, they also determine its limits. But because other elements may be included under the general head, it is customary to speak of the series of events that is connected with the return of Jesus Christ and the end of the world as constituting general eschatology, — an eschatology in which all men are concerned. The subjects that call for consideration in this division, are the return of Christ, the general resurrection, the last judgment, the consummation of the Kingdom, and the final condition of both the pious and the wicked.

2. INDIVIDUAL ESCHATOLOGY. Besides this general, there is also an individual, eschatology that must be taken into consideration. The events named may constitute the whole of eschatology in the strict sense of the word, yet we cannot do justice to this without showing how the generations who have died will participate in the final events. For the individual the end of the present existence comes with death, which transfers him completely from the present into the future age. In so far as he is removed from the present age with its historical development, he is introduced into the future age, which is eternity. In the same measure in which there is a change in locality, there is also a change of æon. The things touching the condition of the individual between his death and the general resurrection, belong to personal or individual eschatology. Physical death, the immortality of the soul, and the intermediate condition call for discussion here. The study of these subjects will serve the purpose of connecting up the condition of those who die before the parousia with the final consummation.

INDIVIDUAL ESCHATOLOGY

I. Physical Death

The Scriptural idea of death includes physical, spiritual, and eternal death. Physical and spiritual death are naturally discussed in connection with the doctrine of sin, and eternal death is considered more particularly in general eschatology. For that reason a discussion of death in any sense of the word might seem to be out of place in individual eschatology. Yet it can hardly be left out of consideration altogether in an attempt to link up past generations with the final consummation.

A. The Nature of Physical Death.

The Bible contains some instructive indications as to the nature of physical death. It speaks of this in various ways. In Matt. 10:28; Luke 12:4, it is spoken of as the death of the body, as distinguished from that of the soul (psuche). Here the body is considered as a living organism, and the *psuche* is evidently the *pneuma* of man, the spiritual element which is the principle of his natural life. This view of natural death also underlies the language of Peter in I Pet. 3:14-18. In other passages it is described as the termination of the *psuche*, that is, of animal life or living, or as the loss of this, Matt. 2:20; Mark 3:4; Luke 6:9; 14:26; John 12:25; 13:37,38; Acts 15:26; 20:24, and other passages.[1] And, finally, it is also represented as a separation of body and soul, Eccl. 12:7 (comp. Gen. 2:7); Jas. 2:26, an idea that is also basic to such passages as John 19:30; Acts 7:59; Phil. 1:23. Cf. also the use of *exodus* in Luke 9:31; II Pet. 1:15,16. In view of all this it may be said that, according to Scripture, physical death is a termination of physical life by the separation of body and soul. It is never an annihilation, though some sects represent the death of the wicked as such. God does not annihilate anything in His creation. Death is not a cessation of existence, but a severance of the natural relations of life. Life and death are not opposed to each other as existence and non-existence, but are opposites only as different modes of existence. It is quite impossible to say exactly what death is. We speak of it as the cessation of physical life, but then the question immediately arises, Just what is life? And we have no answer. We do not know what life is in its essential being, but know it only in its relations and actions. And experience teaches us that, where these are severed and cease, death enters. Death means a break in the natural relations of life. It may be said that sin

---

1. Cf. Bavinck, *Bijb. en Rel. Psych.*, p. 34.

is *per se* death, because it represents a break in the vital relation in which man, as created in the image of God, stands to his Maker. It means the loss of that image, and consequently disturbs all the relations of life. This break is also carried through in that separation of body and soul which is called physical death.

B. The Connection of Sin and Death.

Pelagians and Socinians teach that man was created mortal, not merely in the sense that he could fall a prey to death, but in the sense that he was, in virtue of his creation, under the law of death, and in course of time was bound to die. This means that Adam was not only susceptible to death, but was actually subject to it before he fell. The advocates of this view were prompted primarily by the desire to evade the proof for original sin derived ·from the suffering and death of infants. Present day science seems to support this position by stressing the fact that death is the law of organized matter, since it carries within it the seed of decay and dissolution. Some of the early Church Fathers and some later theologians, such as Warburton and Laidlaw, take the position that Adam was indeed created mortal, that is, subject to the law of dissolution, but that the law was effective in his case only because he sinned. If he had proved himself to be obedient, he would have been exalted to a state of immortality. His sin brought about no change in his constitutional being in this respect, but under the sentence of God left him subject to the law of death, and robbed him of the boon of immortality, which he might have had without experiencing death. On this view the actual entrance of death, of course, remains penal. It is a view which might be made to fit in very well with the supralapsarian position, but is not demanded by this. In reality this theory merely seeks to square the facts, as they are revealed in the Word of God, with the dicta of science, but even these do not make it imperative. Suppose that science had proved conclusively that death reigned in the vegetable and animal world before the entrance of sin, then it would not yet necessarily follow that it also prevailed in the world of rational and moral beings. And even if it were established beyond the shadow of a doubt that all physical organisms, the human included, now carry within them the seeds of dissolution, this would not yet prove that man was not an exception to the rule before the fall. Shall we say that the almighty power of God, by which the universe was created, was not sufficient to continue man in life indefinitely? Moreover we ought to bear in mind the following Scriptural data: (1) Man was created in the image of God and this, in view of the perfect condition in which the image of God existed originally, would seem to exclude the possibility of his carrying within him the seeds of dissolution and mortality. (2) Physical death is not represented in Scripture as the natural result of the continuation of the original condition of man, due to his failure to rise to the height of immortality by the path of obedience; but as the result of his spiritual death, Rom. 6:23; 5:21; I Cor. 15:56; Jas. 1:15. (3) Scriptural expressions certainly point to death as something introduced into the world of humanity by sin, and as a positive punishment for sin, Gen. 2:17; 3:19; Rom. 5:12,17; 6:23; I Cor. 15:21; Jas. 1:15. (4) Death is not represented as something natural in the life of man, a mere falling short of an ideal, but very decidedly as something foreign and hostile to human life: it is an expression of divine anger, Ps. 90:7,11, a judgment, Rom. 1:32, a condemnation, Rom. 5:16, and a curse, Gal. 3:13, and fills the hearts of the children of men with dread and fear, just because it is felt to be something unnatural. All this does not mean, however, that there may not have been death in some sense of the word in the lower creation apart from sin, but even there the entrance of sin evidently brought a bondage of corruption that was foreign to the creature, Rom. 8:20-22. In strict justice God might have imposed death on man in the fullest sense of the word immediately after his transgression, Gen. 2:17. But by His common grace He restrained the operation of sin and death, and by His special grace in Christ Jesus He conquered these hostile forces, Rom. 5:17; I Cor. 15:45; II Tim. 1:10; Heb. 2:14; Rev. 1:18; 20:14. Death now accomplishes its work fully only in the lives of those who refuse the deliverance from it that is offered in Jesus Christ. Those who believe in Christ are freed from the power of death, are restored to communion with God, and are endowed with an endless life, John 3:36; 6:40; Rom. 5:17-21; 8:23; I Cor. 15:26,51-57; Rev. 20:14; 21:3,4.

C. The Significance of the Death of Believers.

The Bible speaks of physical death as a punishment, as "the wages of sin." Since believers are justified, however, and are no more under obligation to render any penal satisfaction, the question naturally arises, Why must they die? It is quite evident that for them the penal element is removed from death. They are no more under the law, either as a requirement of the covenant of works or as a condemning power, since they have obtained a complete pardon for all their sins. Christ became a curse for them, and thus removed the penalty of sin. But if this is so, why does God still deem it necessary to lead them through the harrowing experience of death? Why does He not simply transfer them to heaven at once? It cannot be said that the destruction of the body is absolutely essential to a perfect sanctification, since that is contradicted by the examples of Enoch and Elijah. Neither does it satisfy to say that death sets the believer free from the ills and sufferings of the present life, and from the trammels of the dust, by liberating the spirit from the present coarse and sensual body. God might effect this deliverance also by a sudden transformation, such as living saints will experience at the time of the parousia. It is quite evident that the death of believers must be regarded as the culmination of the chastisements which God has ordained for the sanctification of His people. While death in itself remains a real natural evil for the children of God, something unnatural, which is dreaded by them as such, it is made subservient in the economy of grace to their spiritual advancement and to the best interests of the Kingdom of God. The very thought of death, bereavements through death, the feeling that sicknesses and sufferings are harbingers of death, and the consciousness of the approach of death, — all have a very beneficial effect on the people of God. They serve to humble the proud, to mortify carnality, to check world-liness and to foster spiritual-mindedness. In the mystical union with their Lord believers are made to share the experiences of Christ. Just as He entered upon His glory by the pathway of sufferings and death, they too can enter upon their eternal reward only through sanctification. Death is often the supreme test of the strength of the faith that is in them, and frequently calls forth striking manifestations of the consciousness of victory in the very hour of seeming defeat, I Pet. 4:12,13. It completes the sanctification of the souls of believers, so that they become at once "the spirits of just men made perfect," Heb. 12:23; Rev. 21:27. Death is not the end for believers, but the beginning of a perfect life. They enter death with the assurance that its sting has been removed, I Cor. 15:55, and that it is for them the gateway of heaven. They fall asleep in Jesus, II Thess. 1:7, and know that even their bodies will at last be snatched out of the power of death, to be forever with the Lord, Rom. 8:11; I Thess. 4:16,17. Jesus said, "He that believeth on me, though he die, yet shall he live." And Paul had the blessed consciousness that for him to live was Christ, and to die was gain. Hence he could also speak in jubilant notes at the end of his career: "I have fought the good fight, I have finished the course, I have kept the faith: henceforth there is laid up for me the crown of righteousness, which the Lord, the righteous Judge, shall give to me at that day; and not to me only, but also to all them that have loved His appearing," II Tim. 4:7,8.

QUESTIONS FOR FURTHER STUDY: What is the fundamental idea of the Biblical conception of death? Is death merely the natural result of sin, or is it a positive punishment for sin? If it is the latter, how can this be proved from Scripture? In what sense was man, as he was created by God, mortal; and in what sense, immortal? How can you disprove the position of the Pelagians? In what sense has death really ceased to be death for believers? What purpose does death serve in their lives? When is the power of death completely terminated for them?

LITERATURE: Dick, *Lect. on Theol*, pp. 426-433; Dabney, *Syst. and Polemic Theol.*, pp. 817-821; Litton; *Introd. to Dogm. Theol.*, pp. 536-540; Pieper, *Christl. Dogm.* III, pp. 569-573; Schmid, *Dogm. Theol. of the Ev. Luth. Church*, pp. 626-631; Pope, *Chr. Theol.* III, pp. 371-376; Valentine, *Chr. Theol.*, II, pp. 389-391; Hovey, *Eschatology*, pp. 13-22; Dahle, *Life After Death*, pp. 24-58; Kenneday, *St. Paul's Conception of the Last Things*, pp. 103-157; Strong, *Syst. Theol.* pp. 982 f.; Pohle-Preuss, *Eschatology*, pp. 5-17.

II. The Immortality of the Soul

In the preceding it was pointed out that physical death is the separation of body and soul and marks the end of our present physical existence. It necessarily involves and results in the decomposition of the body. It marks the end of our present life and the end of the "natural body." But now the question arises, What becomes of the soul: does physical death bring its life to a close, or does it continue to exist and live on after death? It has always been the firm conviction of the Church of Jesus Christ that the soul continues to live even after its separation from the body. This doctrine of the immortality of the soul calls for brief consideration at this point.

A. Different Connotations of the Term "Immortality."

In a discussion of the doctrine of immortality it should be borne in mind that the term "immortality" is not always used in the same sense. There are certain distinctions that are quite essential, in order to prevent confusion.

1. In the most absolute sense of the word immortality is ascribed only to God. Paul speaks of Him in I Tim. 6:15,16 as "the blessed and only Potentate, the King of kings, the Lord of lords, *who only hath immortality.*" This does not mean that none of His creatures are immortal in any sense of the word. Understood in that unrestricted sense, this word of Paul would also teach that the angels are not immortal, and this is certainly not the intention of the apostle. The evident meaning of his statement is that God is the only being who possesses immortality "as an original, eternal, and necessary endowment." Whatever immortality may be ascribed to some of His creatures, is contingent on the divine will, is conferred upon them, and therefore had a beginning. God, on the other hand, is necessarily free from all temporal limitations.

2. Immortality in the sense of continuous or endless existence is also ascribed to all spirits, including the human soul. It is one of the doctrines of natural religion or philosophy that, when the body is dissolved, the soul does not share in its dissolution, but retains its identity as an individual being. This idea of the immortality of the soul is in perfect harmony with what the Bible teaches about man, but the Bible, religion, and theology, are not primarily interested in this purely quantitative and colourless immortality, — the bare continued existence of the soul.

3. Again, the term "immortality" is used in theological language to designate that state of man in which he is entirely free from the seeds of decay

and death. In this sense of the word man was immortal before the fall. This state clearly did not exclude the possibility of man's becoming subject to death. Though man in the state of rectitude was not subject to death, yet he was liable to it. It was entirely possible that through sin he would become subject to the law of death; and as a matter of fact he did fall a victim to it.

4. Finally, the word "immortality" designates, especially in eschatological language, that state of man in which he is impervious to death and cannot possibly become its prey. Man was not immortal in this highest sense of the word in virtue of his creation, even though he was created in the image of God. This immortality would have resulted if Adam had complied with the condition of the covenant of works, but can now only result from the work of redemption as it is completed in the consummation.

B. Testimony of General Revelation to the Immortality of the Soul.

The question of Job, "If a man die, shall he live again?" (Job 14:14) is one of perennial interest. And with it the question constantly recurs, whether the dead still live. The answer to this question has practically always been an affirmative one. Though evolutionists cannot admit that faith in the immortality of the soul is an original endowment of man, yet it cannot be denied that this faith is all but universal, and is found even in the lowest forms of religion. Under the influence of materialism many have been inclined to doubt and even to deny the future life of man. Yet this negative attitude is not the prevailing one. In a recent Symposium on "Immortality," containing the views of about a hundred representative men, the opinions are practically unanimous in favour of a future life. The historical and philosophical arguments for the immortality of the soul are not absolutely conclusive, but certainly are important testimonies to the continued personal and conscious existence of man. They are the following.

1. THE HISTORICAL ARGUMENT. The *consensus gentium* is just as strong in connection with the immortality of the soul, as it is with reference to the existence of God. There always have been unbelieving scholars who denied the continued existence of man, but in general it may be said that belief in the immortality of the soul is found among all races and nations, no matter what their stage of civilization may be. And it would seem that a notion so common can only be regarded as a natural instinct or as something involved in the very constitution of human nature.

2. THE METAPHYSICAL ARGUMENT. This argument is based on the simplicity of the human soul, and infers from this its indissolubility. In death matter is dissolved into its parts. But the soul as a spiritual entity is not composed of various parts, and is therefore incapable of division or dissolution. Consequently, the decomposition of the body does not carry with it the destruction of the soul. Even when the former perishes, the latter remains intact. This argument is very old and was already used by Plato.

3. THE TELEOLOGICAL ARGUMENT. Human beings seem to be endowed with almost infinite capabilities, which are never fully developed in this life. It seems as if most men only just begin to accomplish some of the great things to which they aspire. There are ideals that fall far short of realization, appetites and desires that are not satisfied in this life, yearnings and aspirations that are disappointed. Now it is argued that God would not have conferred upon men such abilities and talents, only to make them fail in their achievements, would not have filled the heart with such desires and aspirations, only to disappoint them. He must have provided a future existence, in which human life will come to fruition.

4. THE MORAL ARGUMENT. The human conscience testifies to the existence of a moral Ruler of the universe who will exercise justice. Yet the demands of justice are not met in this present life. There is a very unequal and seemingly unjust distribution of good and evil. The wicked often prosper, increase in riches, and have an abundant share of the joys of life, while the pious frequently live in poverty, meet with painful and humiliating reverses, and suffer many afflictions. Hence there must be a future state of existence, in which justice will reign supreme, and the inequalities of the present will be adjusted.

C. Testimony of Special Revelation to the Immortality of the Soul.

The historical and philosophical proofs for the survival of the soul are not absolutely demonstrative, and therefore do not compel belief. For greater assurance in this matter, it is necessary to direct the eye of faith to Scripture. Here, too, we must rely on the voice of authority. Now the position of Scripture with respect to this matter may at first seem somewhat dubious. It speaks of God as the only one who hath immortality (I Tim. 6:15), and never predicates this of man. There is no explicit mention of the immortality of the soul, and much less any attempt to prove it in a formal way. Hence the Russellites or Millennial Dawnists often challenge theologians to point to a single passage in which the Bible teaches that the soul of man is immortal. But even if the Bible does not explicitly state that the soul of man is immortal, and does not seek to prove this in a formal way, any more than it seeks to present formal proof for the existence of God, this does not mean that Scripture denies or contradicts or even ignores it. It clearly assumes in many passages that man continues his conscious existence after death. In fact, it treats the truth of the immortality of man very much as it does that of the existence of God, that is, it assumes this as an undisputed postulate.

1. THE DOCTRINE OF IMMORTALITY IN THE OLD TESTAMENT. The assertion has been made repeatedly that the Old Testament, and particularly the Pentateuch, does not teach in any way the immortality of the soul. Now it is perfectly true that this great truth is revealed less clearly in the Old than in the New Testament; but the facts in the case do not warrant the assertion that it is absent from the Old Testament altogether. It is a well-known and generally recognized fact that God's revelation in Scripture is progressive and gradually

increases in clearness; and it stands to reason that the doctrine of immortality in the sense of a blessed eternal life, could only be revealed in all its bearings after the resurrection of Jesus Christ, who "brought life and immortality to light," II Tim. 1:10. But while all this is true, it cannot be denied that the Old Testament implies the continued conscious existence of man, either in the sense of a bare immortality or survival of the soul, or of a blessed future life, in several ways. This is implied:

a. *In its doctrine of God and man.* The very root of Israel's hope of immortality was found in its belief in God as its Creator and Redeemer, its covenant God, who would never fail them. He was to them the living, the eternal, the faithful God, in whose fellowship they found joy, life, peace, and perfect satisfaction. Would they have panted after Him as they did, have entrusted themselves to Him completely in life and death, and have sung of Him as their portion forever, if they felt that all He offered them was but for a brief span of time? How could they derive real comfort from the promised redemption of God, if they regarded death as the end of their existence? Moreover, the Old Testament represents man as created in the image of God, created for life and not for mortality. In distinction from the brute, he possesses a life that transcends time and already contains within itself a pledge of immortality. He is made for communion with God, is but little lower than the angels, and God has set eternity in his heart, Eccl. 3:11.

b. *In its doctrine of sheol.* We are taught in the Old Testament that the dead descend into *sheol.* The discussion of this doctrine belongs to the following chapter. But whatever may be the proper interpretation of the Old Testament *sheol,* and whatever may be said of the condition of those who have descended into it, this is certainly represented as a state of more or less conscious existence, though not one of bliss. Man enters upon the state of perfect bliss only by a deliverance from *sheol.* In this deliverance we reach the real core of the Old Testament hope of a blessed immortality. This is clearly taught in several passages, such as Ps. 16:10; 49:14,15.

c. *In its frequent warnings against consulting the dead or "familiar spirits,"* that is, persons who were able to summon the spirits of the dead and to convey their messages to the inquirers, Lev. 19:31; 20:27; Deut. 18:11; Isa. 8:19; 29:4. Scripture does not say that it is impossible to consult the dead, but rather seems to presuppose the possibility while it condemns the practice.

d. *In its teachings respecting the resurrection of the dead.* This doctrine is not explicitly taught in the earlier books of the Old Testament. Christ points out, however, that it was taught by implication in the statement, "I am the God of Abraham, and the God of Isaac, and the God of Jacob," Matt. 22:32, cf. Ex. 3:6, and chides the Jews for not understanding the Scriptures on this point. Moreover, the doctrine of the resurrection is explicitly taught in such passages as Job 19:23-27; Ps. 16:9-11; 17:15; 49:15; 73:24; Isa. 26:19; Dan. 12:2.

e. *In certain striking Old Testament passages which speak of the believer's enjoyment in communion with God after death.* These are in the main identical with the passages referred to in the preceding, namely, Job 19:25-27; Ps. 16:9-11; 17:15; 73:23,24,26. They breathe the confident expectation of pleasures in the presence of Jehovah.

2. THE DOCTRINE OF IMMORTALITY IN THE NEW TESTAMENT. In the New Testament, after Christ has brought life and immortality to light, the proofs naturally multiply. The passages that contain these may again be divided into various classes, as referring:

a. *To the survival of the soul.* A continued existence of both the righteous and the wicked is clearly taught. That the souls of believers survive, appears from such passages as Matt. 10:28; Luke 23:43; John 11:25 f.; 14:3; II Cor. 5:1; and several other passages make it quite evident that the same can be said of the souls of the wicked, Matt. 11:21-24; 12:41; Rom. 2:5-11; II Cor. 5:10.

b. *To the resurrection by which the body is also made to share in the future existence.* For believers the resurrection means the redemption of the body and entrance into the perfect life in communion with God, the full blessedness of immortality. This resurrection is taught in Luke 20:35,36; John 5:25-29; I Cor. 15; I Thess. 4:16; Phil. 3:21, and other passages. For the wicked the resurrection will also mean a renewed and continued existence of the body, but this can hardly be called life. Scripture calls it eternal death. The resurrection of the wicked is mentioned in John 5:29; Acts 24:15; Rev. 20:12-15.

c. *To the blessed life of believers in communion with God.* There are numerous passages in the New Testament which stress the fact that the immortality of believers is not a bare endless existence, but a rapturous life of bliss in communion with God and with Jesus Christ, the full fruition of the life that is implanted in the soul while still on earth. This is clearly emphasized in such passages as Matt. 13:43; 25:34; Rom. 2:7,10; I Cor. 15:49; Phil. 3:21; II Tim. 4:8; Rev. 21:4; 22:3,4.

D. Objections to the Doctrine of Personal Immortality and Modern Substitutes for It.

1. THE MAIN OBJECTION TO IT. Belief in the immortality of the soul for a time suffered a decline under the influence of a materialistic philosophy. The main argument against it was forged in the workshop of physiological psychology, and runs somewhat as follows: The mind or the soul has no independent substantial existence, but is simply a product or function of brain activity. The brain of man is the producing cause of mental phenomena, just as the liver is the producing cause of bile. The function cannot persist when the organ

decays. When the brain ceases to operate, the stream of mental life comes to a stop.

2. SUBSTITUTES FOR THE DOCTRINE OF PERSONAL IMMORTALITY. The desire for immortality is so deeply implanted in the human soul that even those who accept the dicta of a materialistic science, seek some sort of substitute for the discarded notion of the personal immortality of the soul. Their hope for the future assumes one of the following forms:

a. *Racial immortality*. There are those who comfort themselves with the idea that the individual will continue to live on this earth in his posterity, in his children and grandchildren, to endless generations. The individual seeks compensation for his lack of hope in a personal immortality in the notion that he contributes his share to the life of the race and will continue to live on in that. But the idea that a man lives on in his progeny, whatever modicum of truth it may contain, can hardly serve as a substitute for the doctrine of personal immortality. It certainly does not do justice to the data of Scripture, and does not satisfy the deepest longings of the human heart.

b. *Immortality of commemoration*. According to Positivism this is the only immortality we should desire and look for. Everyone should aim at doing something to establish a name for himself, which will go down in the annals of history. If he does this, he will continue to live in the hearts and minds of a grateful posterity. This also falls far short of the personal immortality which Scripture leads us to expect. Moreover, it is an immortality in which only a few will share. The names of most men are not recorded on the pages of history, and many of those who are so recorded are soon forgotten. And to a great extent it may be said that the best and the worst share it alike.

c. *Immortality of influence*. This is very closely related to the preceding. If a man makes his mark in life, and accomplishes something that is of enduring value, his influence will continue long after he is gone. Jesus and Paul, Augustine and Thomas Aquinas, Luther and Calvin, — they are all very much alive in the influence which they exercise up to the present time. While this is perfectly true, this immortality of influence is but a poor substitute for personal immortality. All the objections that were raised against the immor-tality of commemoration, also apply in this case.

3. THE RECOVERY OF FAITH IN IMMORTALITY. At the present time the materialistic interpretation of the universe is making way for a more spiritual interpretation; and as a result faith in personal immortality is once more gaining favor. Dr. William James, while subscribing to the formula, "Thought is a function of the brain," denies that this logically compels us to disbelieve the doctrine of immortality. He maintains that this conclusion of the scientists is based on the mistaken notion that the function of which the formula speaks is necessarily a *productive* function, and points out that it may also be a *permissive* or *transmissive* function. The brain may merely transmit, and in

the transmission colour, thought, just as a coloured glass, a prism, or a refracting lens, may transmit light and at the same time determine its colour and direction. The light exists independent of the glass or lens; so thought also exists independent of the brain. He comes to the conclusion that one can, in strict logic, believe in immortality. Some evolutionists now base the doctrine of conditional immortality on the struggle for existence. And such scientists as William James, Sir Oliver Lodge, and James H. Hyslop, attach great significance to reputed communications with the dead. On the basis of psychic phenomena the first was inclined to believe in immortality, while the other two embraced it as an established fact.

QUESTIONS FOR FURTHER STUDY: Is the doctrine of immortality found in the Pentateuch? What accounts for the comparative scarcity of proofs for it in the Old Testament? On what did Plato base his belief in the immortality of the soul? How did Kant judge of the usual natural arguments for the doctrine of immortality? Is there any place for belief in personal immortality in either Materialism or Pantheism? Why does the doctrine of so-called "social immortality" fail to satisfy? Is the immortality of the soul in the philosophical sense the same as eternal life? How should we judge of the reputed spiritualistic communications with the dead?

LITERATURE: Bavinck, Geref. Dogm. IV, pp. 645-655; Kuyper, Dict. Dogm., De Consummatione Saeculi, pp. 3-24; Hodge, Syst. Theol. III, pp. 713-730; Dabney, Syst. and Polem. Theol., pp. 817-823; Dick, Lect. on Theol., Lectures LXXX, LXXXI; Litton, Introd. to Dogm. Theol., pp. 535-548; Heagle, Do the Dead Still Live; Dahl, Life After Death, pp. 59-84; Salmond, Christian Doctrine of Immortality, cf. Index; Mackintosh, Immortality and the Future, pp. 164-179; Brown, The Christian Hope, cf. Index; Randall, The New Light on Immortality; Macintosh, Theology as an Empirical Science, pp. 72-80; Althaus, Die Letzten Dinge, pp. 1-76; A. G. James, Personal Immortality, pp. 19-52; Rimmer, The Evidences for Immortality; Lawton, The Drama of Life After Death; Addison, Life Beyond Death, pp. 3-132.

IV. The Intermediate State

A. The Scriptural View of the Intermediate State.

1. THE SCRIPTURAL REPRESENTATION OF BELIEVERS BETWEEN DEATH AND THE RESURRECTION. The usual position of the Reformed Churches is that the souls of believers *immediately* after death enter upon the glories of heaven. In answer to the question, "What comfort does the resurrection of the body afford thee?" the Heidelberg Catechism says: "That not only my soul, after this life, shall be immediately taken up to Christ its Head, but also that this my body, raised by the power of Christ, shall again be united with my soul, and made like the glorious body of Christ."[1] The Westminster Confession speaks in the same spirit, when it says that, at death, "The souls of the righteous, being then made perfect in holiness, are received into the highest heavens, where they behold the face of God in light and glory, waiting for the full redemption of their bodies."[2] Similarly, the Second Helvetic Confession declares: "We believe that the faithful, after bodily death, go directly unto Christ."[3] This view would seem to find ample justification in Scripture, and it is well to take note of this, since during the last quarter of a century some Reformed theologians have taken the position that believers at death enter an intermediate place, and remain there until the day of the resurrection. The Bible teaches, however, that the soul of the believer when separated from the body, enters the presence of Christ. Paul says that he is "willing rather to be absent from the body, and to be at home with the Lord." II Cor. 5:8. To the Philippians he writes that he has a "desire to depart and to be with Christ," Phil. 1:23. And Jesus gave the penitent malefactor the joyous assurance, "To-day shalt thou be with me in paradise," Luke 23:43. And to be with Christ is also to be in heaven. In the light of II Cor. 12:3,4 "paradise" can only be a designation of heaven. Moreover, Paul says that, "if the earthly house of our tabernacle be dissolved, we have a building from God, a house not made with hands, eternal in the heavens," II Cor. 5:1. And the writer of Hebrews cheers the hearts of his readers with this thought among others that they "are come to the general assembly and church of the firstborn *who are enrolled in heaven,*" Heb. 12:23. That the future state of believers after death is greatly to be preferred to the present appears clearly from the assertions of Paul in II Cor. 5:8 and Phil. 1:23, quoted above. It is a state in which believers are truly alive and fully conscious, Luke 16:19-31; I Thess. 5:10; a state of rest and endless bliss, Rev. 14:13.

---

1. Q. 57.
2. Chap. XXXII, I.
3. Chap. XXVI.

2. The Scriptural representation of the state of the wicked between death and the resurrection. The Westminster Catechism says that the souls of the wicked after death "are cast into hell, where they remain in torments and utter darkness, reserved to the judgment of the great day." Moreover, it adds: "Besides these two places (heaven and hell) for souls separated from their bodies, the Scripture acknowledgeth none."[1] And the Second Helvetic Confession continues after the quotation cited above: "In like manner, we believe that the unbelievers are cast headlong into hell, from whence there is no return opened to the wicked by any offices of those who live."[2] The Bible sheds very little direct light on this subject. The only passage that can really come into consideration here is the parable of the rich man and Lazarus in Luke 16, where *hades* denotes hell, the place of eternal torment. The rich man found himself in the place of torment; his condition was fixed forever; and he was conscious of his miserable plight, sought mitigation of the pain he was suffering, and desired to have his brethren warned, in order that they might avoid a similar doom. In addition to this direct proof there is also an inferential proof. If the righteous enter upon their eternal state at once, the presumption is that this is true of the wicked as well. We leave out of consideration here a couple of passages, which are of uncertain interpretation, namely, I Pet. 3:19; II Pet. 2:9.

B. The Doctrine of the Intermediate State in History.

In the earliest years of the Christian Church there was little thought of an intermediate state. The idea that Jesus would soon return as Judge made the interval seem to be of little consequence. The problem of the intermediate state arose when it became apparent that Jesus would not at once return. The real problem that vexed the early Fathers, was how to reconcile individual judgment and retribution at death with the general judgment and retribution after the resurrection. To ascribe too much importance to the former would seem to rob the other of its significance, and *vice versa*. There was no unanimity among the early Church Fathers, but the majority of them sought to solve the difficulty by assuming a distinct intermediate state between death and the resurrection. Says Addison: "For many centuries the general conclusion was widely accepted that in a subterranean Hades the righteous enjoy a measure of reward not equal to their future heaven and the wicked suffer a degree of punishment not equal to their future hell. The intermediate state was thus a slightly reduced version of ultimate retribution."[3] This view was held, though with some variations, by such men as Justin Martyr, Irenæus, Tertullian, Novatian, Origen, Gregory of Nyssa, Ambrose, and Augustine. In the Alexandrian School the idea of the intermediate state passed into that of a gradual purification of the soul, and this in course of time paved the way for the Roman Catholic doctrine of purgatory. There were some,

---

1. Chap. XXXII.
2. Chap. XXVI.
3. *Life Beyond Death*, p. 202.

however, who favored the idea that at death the souls of the righteous immediately entered heaven, namely, Gregory of Nazianze, Eusebius, and Gregory the Great. In the Middle Ages the doctrine of an intermediate state was retained, and in connection with it the Roman Catholic Church developed the doctrine of purgatory. The prevailing opinion was that hell received at once the souls of the wicked, but that only those of the righteous who were free from every stain of sin, were admitted at once into the blessedness of heaven, to enjoy the *visio Dei*. The martyrs were usually reckoned among the favored few. Those who were in need of further purification were, according to the prevalent view, detained in purgatory for a shorter or longer period of time, as the degree of remaining sin might require, and were there purged from sin by a purifying fire. Another idea, that was also developed in connection with the thought of the intermediate state, was that of the *Limbus Patrum*, where the Old Testament saints were detained until the resurrection of Christ. The Reformers, one and all, rejected the doctrine of purgatory, and also the whole idea of a *real* intermediate state, which carried with it the idea of an intermediate place. They held that those who died in the Lord at once entered the bliss of heaven, while those who died in their sins at once descended into hell. However, some theologians of the Reformation period assumed a difference in degree between the bliss of the former and the judgment of the latter before the final judgment, and their final bliss and punishment after the great assize. Among the Socinians and the Anabaptists there were some who revived the old doctrine held by some in the early Church, that the soul of man sleeps from the time of death until the resurrection. Calvin wrote a treatise to combat this view. The same notion is advocated by some Adventist sects and by the Millennial Dawnists. During the nineteenth century several theologians, especially in England, Switzerland, and Germany, embraced the idea that the intermediate state is a state of further probation for those who have not accepted Christ in this life. This view is maintained by some up to the present time and is a favorite tenet of the Universalists.

C. The Modern Construction of the Doctrine of Sheol-Hades.

1. STATEMENT OF THE DOCTRINE. There are several representations of the Biblical conception of *sheol-hades* in present day theology, and it is quite impossible to consider each one of them separately. The idea is quite prevalent at present that the Old Testament conception of *sheol*, to which that of *hades* in the New Testament is supposed to correspond, was borrowed from the Gentile notion of the underworld. It is held that according to the Old Testament and the New, both the pious and the wicked at death enter the dreary abode of the shades, the land of forgetfulness, where they are doomed to an existence that is merely a dreamy reflection of life on earth. The underworld is in itself neither a place of rewards nor a place of punishment. It is not divided into different compartments for the good and the bad, but is a region without moral distinctions. It is a place of weakened consciousness and of slumbrous inactivity, where life has lost its interests and the joy of life is turned into sadness. Some

are of the opinion that the Old Testament represents *sheol* as the permanent abode of all men, while others find that it holds out a hope of escape for the pious. Occasionally we meet with a somewhat different representation of the Old Testament conception, in which *sheol* is represented as divided into two compartments, namely, *paradise* and *gehenna,* the former containing either all the Jews or only those who faithfully observed the law, and the latter embracing the Gentiles. The Jews will be delivered from *sheol* at the coming of the Messiah, while the Gentiles will remain forever in the abode of darkness. The New Testament counterpart of this conception of *sheol* is found in its representation of *hades.* It is not merely held that the Hebrews entertained the notion of such an underworld, nor that the Biblical writers occasionally accommodated themselves formally in their representations to the views of the Gentiles of whom they were speaking; but that this is the Scriptural view of the intermediate state.

2. CRITICISM OF THIS MODERN REPRESENTATION. In the abstract it is, of course, possible that the idea of such a separate locality, which is neither heaven nor hell, in which all the dead are gathered and where they remain, either permanently or until some communal resurrection, was more or less current in popular Hebrew thought and may have given rise to some figurative descriptions of the state of the dead; but it can hardly be regarded by those who believe in the plenary inspiration of the Bible as an element of the positive teachings of Scripture, since it plainly contradicts the Scriptural representation that the righteous at once enter glory and the wicked at once descend into the place of eternal punishment. Moreover, the following considerations can be urged against this view:

a. The question arises, whether the view of *sheol-hades,* now so widely regarded as Scriptural, is true to fact or not. If it was true to fact at the time, when the books of the Bible were written, but is no more true to fact to-day, the question naturally rises, What brought about the change? And if it was not true to fact, but was a decidedly false view—and this is the prevalent opinion —, then the problem at once arises, how this erroneous view could be countenanced and sanctioned and even taught positively by the inspired writers of Scripture. The problem is not relieved by the consideration, urged by some, that the inspiration of Scripture does not carry with it the assurance that the Old Testament saints were correct when they spoke of men entering some subterranean place at death, because not only these saints but also the inspired writers of Scripture employed language which, in itself and irrespective of other clear teachings of Scripture, might be so interpreted, Num. 16:30; Ps. 49:15,16; Ps. 88:3; Ps. 89:48; Eccl. 9:10; Isa. 5:14; Hos. 13:14. Were these inspired writers in error, when they spoke of both the righteous and the wicked as descending into *sheol*? It may be said that there was development in the revelation respecting the future destiny of man, and we have no reason to doubt that on this point, as on many others, that which was first obscure gradually gained in definiteness and clearness; but this certainly does not mean that the true developed out of the false. How could this be? Did the Holy Spirit deem it expedient for man that he first receive false impressions and obtain erroneous views, and then exchange these in course of time for a correct insight into the condition of the dead?

b. If in the Scriptural representation *sheol-hades* is really a neutral place, without moral distinctions, without blessedness on the one hand, but also without positive pain on the other, a place to which all alike descend, how can the Old Testament hold up the descent of the wicked into *sheol* as a warning, as it does in several places, Job 21:13; Ps. 9:17; Prov. 5:5; 7:27; 9:18; 15:24; 23:14? How can the Bible speak of God's anger burning there, Deut. 32:22, and how can it use the term *sheol* as synonymous with *abaddon,* that is, destruction, Job 26:6; Prov. 15:11; 27:20? This is a strong term, which is applied to the angel of the abyss in Rev. 19:11. Some seek escape from this difficulty by surrendering the neutral character of *sheol* and by assuming that it was conceived of as an underworld with two divisions, called in the New Testament *paradise* and *gehenna,* the former the destined abode of the righteous, and the latter that of the wicked; but this attempt can only result in disappointment, for the Old Testament contains no trace of such a division, though it does speak of *sheol* as a place of punishment for the wicked. Moreover, the New Testament clearly identifies paradise with heaven in II Cor. 12:2,4. And, finally, if *hades* is the New Testament designation of *sheol,* and all alike go there, what becomes of the special doom of Capernaum, Matt. 11:23, and how can it be pictured as a place of torment, Luke 16:23? Someone might be inclined to say that the threatenings contained in some of the passages mentioned refer to a *speedy* descent into *sheol,* but there is no indication of this in the text whatsoever, except in Job 21:13, where this is explicitly stated.

c. If a descent into *sheol* was the gloomy outlook upon the future, not only of the wicked but also of the righteous, how can we explain the expressions of gladsome expectation, or joy in the face of death, such as we find in Num. 23:10; Ps. 16:9,11; 17:15; 49:15; 73:24,26; Isa. 25:8 (comp. I Cor. 15:54)? The expression in Ps. 49:15 may be interpreted to mean that God will deliver the poet out of *sheol* or from the power of *sheol.* Notice also what the writer of Hebrews says of the Old Testament heroes of faith in Heb. 11:13-16. The New Testament, of course, speaks abundantly of the joyous outlook of believers on the future, and teaches their conscious happiness in the disembodied state, Luke 16:23,25; 23:43; Acts 7:59; II Cor. 5:1,6,8; Phil. 1:21,23; I Thess. 5:10; Eph. 3:14,15 ("family in heaven," not in "*hades*"); Rev. 6:9,11; 14:13. In II Cor. 12:2,4 "paradise" is used synonymously with "the third heaven." In connection with this clear representation of the New Testament, it has been suggested that the New Testament believers were privileged above those of the Old Testament by receiving immediate access to the bliss of heaven. But the question may well be asked, What basis is there for assuming such a distinction?

d. If the word *sheol* always denotes the shadowy region to which the dead descend, and never has any other meaning, then the Old Testament, while it does have a word for heaven as the blessed abode of God and of the holy angels, has no word for hell, the place of destruction and of eternal punishment. But it is only on the assumption that in some passages *sheol* designates a place of punishment whither the wicked go in distinction from the righteous, that the warnings referred to under (b) have any point. *Sheol* is actually sometimes contrasted with *shamayim* (heavens) as in Job 11:8; Ps. 139:8; Amos 9:2. Scripture also speaks of the deepest or lowest *sheol* in Deut. 32:22. The same expression is also found in Ps. 86:13, but in that passage is evidently used figuratively.

e. Finally, it should be noticed that there was a difference of opinion among scholars as to the exact subject of the descent into *sheol*. The prevailing opinion is that man as a whole is the subject. Man descends into *sheol* and in some obscure fashion continues his existence in a world of shadows, where the relations of life still reflect those on earth. This representation would seem to be most in harmony with the statements of Scripture, Gen. 37:35; Job 7:9; 14:13; 21:13; Ps. 139:8; Eccl. 9:10. There are some which point to the fact that the body is included. There is danger that Jacob's "gray hairs" will be brought down to *sheol*, Gen. 42:38; 44:29,31; Samuel comes up as an old man covered with a robe, I Sam. 28:14; and Shimei's "hoar head" must be brought down to *sheol*, I Kings 2:6,9. But if *sheol* is a place whither all the dead go, body and soul, what then is laid in the grave, which is supposed to be another place? This difficulty is obviated by those scholars who maintain that only the souls descend into *sheol*, but this can hardly be said to be in harmony with the Old Testament representation. It is true that there are a few passages which speak of souls as going down into, or as being in, *sheol*, Ps. 16:10; 30:3; 86:13; 89:48; Prov. 23:14, but it is a well known fact that in Hebrew the word *nephesh* (soul) with the pronominal suffix is often, especially in poetical language, equivalent to the personal pronoun. Some conservative theologians adopted this construction of the Old Testament representation, and found in it support for their idea that the souls of men are in some intermediate place (a place with moral distinctions and separate divisions, however) until the day of the resurrection.

3. SUGGESTED INTERPRETATION OF SHEOL-HADES. The interpretation of these terms is by no means easy, and in suggesting an interpretation we do not desire to give the impression that we are speaking with absolute assurance. An inductive study of the passages in which the terms are found soon dissipates the notion that the terms *sheol* and *hades* are always used in the same sense, and can in all cases be rendered by the same word, whether it be underworld, state of death, grave, or hell. This is also clearly reflected in the various translations of the Bible. The Holland Version renders the term *sheol* by *grave* in some passages, and by *hell* in others. The St. James or Authorized Version employs three words in its translation, namely, *grave*, *hell*, and *pit*. The English Revisers rather inconsistently retained *grave* or *pit* in the text of the historical books, putting *sheol* in the margin. They retained *hell* only in Isa. 14. The American Revisers avoid the difficulty by simply retaining the original words

sheol and *hades* in their translation. Though the opinion has gained wide currency that sheol is simply the underworld to which all men descend, this view is by no means unanimous. Some of the earlier scholars simply identified *sheol* and the *grave;* others regard it as the place where the souls of the dead are retained; and still others, of whom Shedd, Vos, Aalders, and De Bondt may be menticned, maintain that the word *sheol* does not always have the same meaning. It would seem that the last opinion deserves preference, and that the following can be said respecting its different meanings:

a. The words *sheol* and *hades* do not always denote a locality in Scripture, but are often used in an abstract sense to designate the state of death, the state of the separation of body and soul. This state is frequently locally conceived as constituting the realm of death, and is sometimes represented as a stronghold with gates, which only he who has the keys can lock and unlock, Matt. 16:18; Rev. 1:18. This local representation is in all probability based on a generalization of the idea of the grave, into which man descends when he enters the state of death. Since both believers and unbelievers at the termination of their life enter into the state of death, it can very well be said figuratively that they are without distinction in *sheol* or *hades*. They are all alike in the state of death. The parallelism clearly shows what is meant in a passage like I Sam. 2:6: "Jehovah killeth and maketh alive; He bringeth down to *sheol*, and bringeth up." Cf. also Job 14:13,14; 17:13;14; Ps. 89:48; Hos. 13:14, and several other passages. The word *hades* is evidently used more than once in the non-local sense of the state of the dead in the New Testament, Acts 2:27,31; Rev. 6:8; 20:28. In the last two passages we have a personification. Since the terms may denote the state of death, it is not necessary to prove that they never refer to anything that concerns the righteous and the wicked alike, but only that they do not denote a place where the souls of both are gathered. De Bondt calls attention to the fact that in many passages the term *sheol* is used in the abstract sense of *death*, of *the power of death*, and of *the danger of death*.

b. When *sheol* and *hades* designate a locality in the literal sense of the word, they either refer to what we usually call hell, or to the grave. Descent into *sheol* is threatened as a danger and as a punishment for the wicked. Ps. 9:17; 49:14; 55:15; Prov. 15:11; 15:24; Luke 16:23 *(hades)*. The warning and threatening contained in these passages is lost altogether, if *sheol* is conceived of as a neutral place whither all go. From these passages it also follows that it cannot be regarded as a place with two divisions. The idea of such a divided *sheol* is borrowed from the Gentile conception of the underworld, and finds no support in Scripture. It is only of *sheol* as the state of death that we can speak as having two divisions, but then we are speaking figuratively. Even the Old Testament testifies to it that they who die in the Lord enter upon a fuller enjoyment of the blessings of salvation, and therefore do not descend into any underworld in the literal sense of the word, Num. 23:5,10; Ps. 16:11; 17:15; 73:24; Prov. 14:32. Enoch and Elijah were taken up, and did not descend into an underworld, Heb. 11:5 ff. Moreover, *sheol,* not merely as a state, but also as a place, is regarded as in the closest connection with death. If the Biblical conception of death is understood in its deep significance, in its spiritual meaning, it will readily be seen that *sheol* cannot be the abode of the souls of those who die in the Lord, Prov. 5:5; 15:11; 27:20.

There are also several passages in which *sheol* and *hades* seem to designate the grave. It is not always easy to determine, however, whether the words refer to the grave or to the state of the dead. The following are some of the passages that come into consideration here: Gen. 37:25; 42:38; 44:29; 29:31; I Kings 2:6,9; Job 14:13; 17:13; 21:13; Ps. 6:5; 88:3; Eccl. 9:10. But though the name *sheol* is also used for the grave, it does not necessarily follow that this is the original use of the word, from which its use to designate hell is borrowed. In all probability the opposite is true. The grave is called sheol, because it symbolizes the going down, which is connected with the idea of destruction. For believers the Biblical symbolism is changed by Scripture itself. Paul says that they go down in death as a grain is sown in the earth, from which springs a new, a more abundant, a more glorious life. In the Old Testament the word *sheol* is used more often for grave and less often for hell, while in the corresponding use of *hades* in the New Testament the contrary holds.

D. The Roman Catholic Doctrines Respecting the Abode of the Soul After Death.

1. PURGATORY. According to the Church of Rome the souls of those who are perfectly pure at death are forthwith admitted to heaven or the beatific vision of God, Matt. 25:46; Phil. 1:23; but those who are not perfectly cleansed, who are still burdened with the guilt of venial sins and have not borne the temporal punishment due to their sins — and this is the condition of most of the faithful at death — must undergo a process of cleansing before they can enter into the supreme blessedness and joys of heaven. Instead of entering heaven at once, they enter purgatory. Purgatory is not a place of probation, but a place of purification and of preparation for the souls of believers who are sure of an ultimate entrance into heaven, but are not yet fit to enter upon the bliss of the beatific vision. During the stay of these souls in purgatory they suffer the pain of loss, that is, the anguish resulting from the fact that they are excluded from the blessed sight of God, and also endure "the punishment of sense," that is, suffer positive pains, which afflict the soul. The length of their stay in purgatory cannot be determined beforehand. The duration as well as the intensity of their sufferings varies according to the degree of purification still needed. They can be shortened and alleviated by the prayers and the good works of the faithful on earth, and especially by the sacrifice of the mass. It is possible that one must remain in purgatory until the time of the last judgment. The Pope is supposed to have jurisdiction over purgatory. It is his peculiar prerogative to grant indulgences, lightening the purgatorial sufferings or even terminating them. The main support for this doctrine is found in II Maccabees 12:42-45, and therefore in a book that is not recognized as canonical by the

Protestants. But this passage proves too much, that is, more than the Roman Catholics themselves can consistently admit, namely, the possible deliverance of soldiers from purgatory who had died in the mortal sin of idolatry. Certain passages of Scripture are also supposed to favor this doctrine, such as Isa. 4:4; Mic. 7:8; Zech. 9:11; Mal. 3:2,3; Matt. 12:32; I Cor. 3:13-15; 15:29. It is perfectly evident, however, that these passages can be made to support the doctrine of purgatory only by a very forced exegesis. The doctrine finds absolutely no support in Scripture, and moreover, rests on several false premises, such as (a) that we must add something to the work of Christ; (b) that our good works are meritorious in the strict sense of the word; (c) that we can perform works of supererogation, works in excess of the commands of duty; and (d) that the Church's power of the keys is absolute in a judicial sense. According to it the Church can shorten, alleviate, and even terminate the sufferings of purgatory.

2. THE LIMBUS PATRUM. The Latin word *limbus* (fringe) was used in the Middle Ages to denote two places on the fringe or outskirts of hell, namely. the *Limbus Patrum* and the *Limbus Infantum*. The former is the place where, according to the teachings of Rome, the souls of the Old Testament saints were detained in a state of expectation until the Lord's resurrection from the dead. After His death on the cross Christ is supposed to have descended into the abode of the fathers, to release them from their temporary confinement and to carry them in triumph to heaven. This is the Roman Catholic interpretation of Christ's descent into *hades*. *Hades* is regarded as the dwelling place of the departed spirits, having two divisions, one for the righteous and one for the wicked. The division inhabited by the spirits of the righteous was the *Limbus Patrum*, known to the Jews as Abraham's bosom, Luke 16:23, and paradise, Luke 23:43. It is maintained that heaven was not open to any man until Christ had actually made propitiation for the sin of the world.

3. THE LIMBUS INFANTUM. This is the abode of the souls of all unbaptized children, irrespective of their descent from heathen or from Christian parents. According to the Roman Catholic Church unbaptized children cannot be admitted to heaven, cannot enter the Kingdom of God, John 3:5. There was always a natural repugnance, however, to the idea that these children should be tortured in hell, and Roman Catholic theologians sought a way of escape from the difficulty. Some thought that such children might perhaps be saved by the faith of their parents, and others, that God might commission the angels to baptize them. But the prevailing opinion is that, while they are excluded from heaven, they are consigned to a place on the outskirts of hell, where its terrible fires do not reach. They remain in this place forever without any hope of deliverance. The Church has never defined the doctrine of the *Limbus Infantum*, and the opinions of the theologians vary as to the exact condition of the children confined in it. The prevailing opinion is, however, that they suffer no positive punishment, no "pain of sense," but are simply excluded from

the blessings of heaven. They know and love God by the use of their natural powers, and have full natural happiness.

E. The State of the Soul after Death One of Conscious Existence.

1. THE TEACHING OF SCRIPTURE ON THIS POINT. The question has been raised, whether the soul after death remains actively conscious and is capable of rational and religious action. This has sometimes been denied on the general ground that the soul in its conscious activity is dependent on the brain, and therefore cannot continue to function when the brain is destroyed. But, as already pointed out in the preceding (pp. 677 f.), the cogency of this argument may well be doubted. "It is," to use the words of Dahle, "based on the error of confusing the worker with his machine." From the fact that the human consciousness in the present life transmits its effects through the brain, it does not necessarily follow that it can work in no other way. In arguing for the conscious existence of the soul after death, we place no reliance on the phenomena of present day spiritualism, and do not even depend on philosophical arguments, though these are not without force. We seek our evidence in the Word of God, and particularly in the New Testament. The rich man and Lazarus converse together, Luke 16:19-31. Paul speaks of the disembodied state as a "being at home with the Lord," and as something to be desired above the present life, II Cor. 5:6-9; Phil. 1:23. Surely, he would hardly speak after that fashion about an unconscious existence, which is a virtual non-existence. In Heb. 12:23 believers are said to have come to..."the spirits of just men *made perfect*," which certainly implies their conscious existence. Moreover, the spirits under the altar are crying out for vengeance on the persecutors of the Church, Rev. 6:9, and the souls of the martyrs are said to reign with Christ, Rev. 20:4. This truth of the conscious existence of the soul after death has been denied in more than one form.

2. THE DOCTRINE OF THE SLEEP OF THE SOUL (PSYCHOPANNYCHY).

a. *Statement of the doctrine.* This is one of the forms in which the conscious existence of the soul after death is denied. It maintains that, after death, the soul continues to exist as an individual spiritual being, but in a state of unconscious repose. Eusebius makes mention of a small sect in Arabia that held this view. During the Middle Ages there were quite a few so-called Psychopannychians, and at the time of the Reformation this error was advocated by some of the Anabaptists. Calvin even wrote a treatise against them under the title *Psychopannychia*. In the nineteenth century this doctrine was held by some of the Irvingites in England, and in our day it is one of the favorite doctrines of the Russellites or Millennial Dawnists of our own country. According to the latter body and soul descend into the grave, the soul in a state of sleep, which really amounts to a state of non-existence. What is called the resurrection is in reality a new creation. During the millennium the wicked will have a second chance, but if they show no marked improvement during the first hundred years, they will be annihilated. If in that period they give evidence of some amendment of life, their probation will continue, but only to end in annihilation, if they remain impenitent. There is no hell, no place of eternal torment. The doctrine of the sleep of soul seems to have a peculiar fascination for those who find it hard to believe in a continuance of conscious-ness apart from the corporeal organism.

b. *Supposed Scriptural warrant for this doctrine.* Scripture proof for this doctrine is found especially in the following: (1) Scripture often represents death as a sleep, Matt. 9:24; Acts 7:60; I Cor. 15:51; I Thess. 4:13. This sleep, it is said, cannot be a sleep of the body, and therefore must be a sleep of the soul. (2) Certain passages of Scripture teach that the dead are unconscious, Ps. 6:5; 30:9; 115:17; 146:4; Eccl. 9:10; Isa. 38:18,19. This is contrary to the idea that the soul continues its conscious existence. (3) The Bible teaches that the destinies of men will be determined by a final judgment and will be a surprise to some. Consequently, it is impossible to assume that the soul enters upon its destiny immediately after death, Matt. 7:22,23; 25:37-39,44; John 5:29; II Cor. 5:10; Rev. 20:12 f. (4) None of those who were raised from the dead have ever given any account of their experiences. This can best be understood on the assumption that their souls were unconscious in their disembodied state.

c. *Consideration of the arguments presented.* The preceding arguments may be answered as follows in the order in which they were stated: (1) It should be noted that the Bible never says that the soul falls asleep, nor that the body does so, but only the dying person. And this Scriptural representation is simply based on the similarity between a dead body and a body asleep. It is not unlikely that Scripture uses this euphemistic expression, in order to suggest to believers the comforting hope of the resurrection. Moreover, death is a break with the life of the world round about us, and in so far is a sleep, a rest. Finally, it should not be forgotten that the Bible represents believers as enjoying a conscious life in communion with God and with Jesus Christ *immediately after death,* Luke 16:19-31; 23:43; Acts 7:59; II Cor. 5:8; Phil. 1:23; Rev. 6:9; 7:9; 20:4. (2) The passages which seem to teach that the dead are unconscious are clearly intended to stress the fact that in the state of death man can no more take part in the activities of this present world. Says Hovey: "The work of the artisan is arrested, the voice of the singer is hushed, the scepter of the king falls. The body returns to the dust, and the praise of God in this world ceases forever." (3) It is sometimes represented as if man's eternal destiny depends upon a trial at the last day, but this is evidently a mistake. The day of judgment is not necessary to reach a decision respecting the reward or punishment of each man, but only for the solemn announcement of the sentence, and for the revelation of the justice of God in the presence of men and angels. The surprise of which some of the passages give evidence pertains to the ground on which the judgment rests rather than to the judgment itself. (4) It is true that we do not read that any of those who were raised from the dead ever told anything about their experiences between their death and resurrection. But this is a mere argument from silence, which is quite worthless in this case, since the Bible clearly teaches the conscious existence of the dead. It may well be, however, that those persons were silent about their experiences, but this can readily be explained on the assumption that they were not permitted to tell about them, or that they could not give an account of them in human language. Cf. II Cor. 12:4.

3. THE DOCTRINE OF ANNIHILATIONISM AND OF CONDITIONAL IMMORTALITY.

a. *Statement of these doctrines.* According to these doctrines there is no conscious existence, if any existence at all, of the wicked after death. The two are one in their conception of the state of the wicked after death, but differ in a couple of fundamental points. Annihilationism teaches that man was created immortal, but that the soul, which continues in sin, is by a positive act of God deprived of the gift of immortality, and ultimately destroyed, or (according to some) forever bereaved of consciousness, which is practically equivalent to being reduced to non-existence. According to the doctrine of conditional immortality, on the other hand, immortality was not a natural endowment of the soul, but is a gift of God in Christ to those who believe. The soul that does not accept Christ ultimately ceases to exist, or loses all consciousness. Some of the advocates of these doctrines teach a limited duration of conscious suffering for the wicked in the future life, and thus retain something of the idea of positive punishment.

b. *These doctrines in history.* The doctrine of annihilationism was taught by Arnobius and the early Socinians, and by the philosophers Locke and Hobbes, but was not popular in its original form. In the previous century, however, the old idea of annihilation was revived with some modifications under the name of conditional immortality, and in its new form found considerable favor. It was advocated by E. White, J. B. Heard, and the Prebendaries Constable and Row in England, by Richard Rothe in Germany, by A. Sabatier in France, by E. Petavel and Ch. Secretan in Switzerland, and by C. F. Hudson, W. R. Huntington, L. C. Baker, and L. W. Bacon in our own country, and therefore deserves special notice. They do not all put the doctrine in the same form, but agree in tHe fundamental position that man is not immortal in virtue of his original constitution, but is made immortal by a special act or gift of grace. As far as the wicked are concerned some maintain that these retain a bare existence, though with an utter loss of consciousness, while others assert that they perish utterly like the beasts, though it may be after longer or shorter periods of suffering.

c. *Arguments adduced in favor of this doctrine.* Support for this doctrine is found partly in the language of some of the early Church Fathers, which seems to imply at least that only believers receive the gift of immortality, and partly also in some of the most recent theories of science, which deny that there is any scientific proof for the immortality of the soul. The main support for it, however, is sought in Scripture. It is said that the Bible: (1) teaches that God only is inherently immortal, I Tim. 6:16; (2) never speaks of the immortality of the soul in general, but represents immortality as a gift of God to those who are in Christ Jesus, John 10:27,28; 17:3; Rom. 2:7; 6:22,23; Gal. 6:8; and (3) threatens sinners with "death" and "destruction," asserting that they will "perish," terms which are to be taken to mean that unbelievers will be reduced to non-existence, Matt. 7:13; 10:28; John 3:16; Rom. 6:23; 8:13; II Thess. 1:9.

d. *Consideration of these arguments.* It cannot be said that the arguments in favor of this doctrine are conclusive. The language of the early Church Fathers is not always exact and self-consistent, and admits of another inter-pretation. And the speculative thought of the ages has, on the whole, been favorable to the doctrine of immortality, while science has not succeeded in disproving it. The Scriptural arguments may be answered in order as follows: (1) God is indeed the only one that has inherent immortality. Man's immor-tality is derived, but this is not equivalent to saying that he does not possess it in virtue of his creation. (2) In the second argument the bare immortality or continued existence of the soul is confused with eternal life, while the latter is a far richer concept. Eternal life is indeed the gift of God in Jesus Christ, a gift which the wicked do not receive, but this does not mean that they will not continue to exist. (3) The last argument arbitrarily assumes that the terms "death," "destruction," and "perish" denote a reduction to non-existence. It is only the baldest literalism that can maintain this, and then only in connec-tion with *some* of the passages quoted by the advocates of this theory.

e. *Arguments against this doctrine.* The doctrine of conditional immor-tality is plainly contradicted by Scripture where it teaches: (1) that sinners as well as saints will continue to exist forever, Eccl. 12:7; Matt. 25:46; Rom. 2:8-10; Rev. 14:11; 20:10; (2) that the wicked will suffer eternal punishment, which means that they will be forever conscious of a pain which they will recognize as their just desert, and therefore will not be annihilated, cf. the passages just mentioned; and (3) that there will be degrees in the punishment of the wicked, while extinction of being or consciousness admits of no degrees. but constitutes a punishment that is alike for all, Luke 12:47,48; Rom. 2:12.

The following considerations are also decidedly opposed to this particular doctrine: (1) Annihilation would be contrary to all analogy. God does not annihilate His work, however much He may change its form. The Biblical idea of death has nothing in common with annihilation. Life and death are exact opposites in Scripture. If death means simply the cessation of being or consciousness, life must mean only the continuation of these; but as a matter of fact it means much more than that, cf. Rom. 8:6; I Tim. 4:8; I John 3:14. The term has a spiritual connotation, and so has the word death. Man is spirit-ually dead before he falls a prey to physical death, but this does not involve a loss of being or consciousness, Eph. 2:1,2; I Tim. 5:6; Col. 2:13; Rev. 3:1. (2) Annihilation can hardly be called a punishment, since this implies a consciousness of pain and ill-desert, while, when existence terminates, consciousness also ceases. It might at most be said that the dread of annihilation would be a punishment, but this punishment would not be commensurate with the transgression. And naturally the dread of a man who never had within him the spark of immortality, will never equal that of him who has eternity in his heart, Eccl. 3:11. (3) It often happens that people consider the extinction of being and of consciousness a very desirable thing, when they grow tired of life. For these such a punishment would be in reality a blessing.

F. The Intermediate State not a State of Further Probation.

1. STATEMENT OF THE DOCTRINE. The theory of the so-called "second probation" found considerable favor in the theological world of the nineteenth century. It is advocated, among others, by Mueller, Dorner, and Nitzsch in Germany, by Godet and Gretillat in Switzerland, by Maurice, Farrar, and Plumptre in England, and by Newman Smythe, Munger, Cox, Jukes and several Andover theologians in our own country. This theory is to the effect that salvation through Christ is still possible in the intermediate state for certain classes or, perhaps, for all; and that this is offered on substantially the same terms as at present, namely, faith in Christ as Saviour. Christ is made known to all who still need Him unto salvation, and acceptance of Him is urged on all. No one is condemned to hell without being subjected to this test, and only they are condemned who resist this offer of grace. The eternal state of man will not be irrevocably fixed until the day of judgment. The decision made between death and the resurrection will decide, whether one will be saved or not. The fundamental principle on which this theory rests, is that no man will perish without having been offered a favorable opportunity to know and accept Jesus. Man is condemned only for the obstinate refusal to accept the salvation that is offered in Christ Jesus. Opinions differ, however, as to the persons to whom the gracious opportunity to accept Christ will be offered in the intermediate state. The general opinion is that it will certainly be extended to all children who die in infancy, and to the adult heathen who in this life have not heard of Christ. The majority hold that it will even be granted to those who lived in Christian lands, but in this present life never properly considered the claims of Christ. Again, there is great diversity of opinion as to the agency and the methods by which this saving work will be carried on in the future. Moreover, while some entertain the largest hope as to the outcome of the work, others are less sanguine in their expectations.

2. THE FOUNDATION ON WHICH THIS DOCTRINE RESTS. This theory is founded in part on general considerations of what might be expected of the love and justice of God, and on an easily understood desire to make the gracious work of Christ as inclusive as possible, rather than on any solid Scriptural foundation. The main Scriptural basis for it is found in I Pet. 3:19 and 4:6, which are understood to teach that Christ in the period between His death and resurrection preached to the spirits in hades. But these passages furnish but a

precarious foundation, since they are capable of quite a different interpretation.[1] And even if these passages did teach that Christ actually went into the underworld to preach, His offer of salvation would extend only to those who died before His crucifixion. They also refer to passages which, in their estimation, represent unbelief as the only ground of condemnation, such as John 3:18,36; Mark 16:15,16; Rom. 10:9-12; Eph. 4:18; II Pet. 2:3,4; I John 4:3. But these passages only prove that faith in Christ is the way of salvation, which is by no means the same as proving that a conscious rejection of Christ is the only ground of condemnation. Unbelief is undoubtedly a great sin, and one that stands out prominently in the lives of those to whom Christ is preached, but it is not the only form of revolt against God, nor the only ground of condemnation. Men are already under condemnation when Christ is offered to them. Other passages, such as Matt. 13:31,32; I Cor. 15:24-28; and Phil. 2:9-11 are equally inconclusive. Some of them prove too much and therefore prove nothing.

3. ARGUMENTS AGAINST THIS DOCTRINE. The following considerations can be urged against this theory: (a) Scripture represents the state of unbelievers after death as a fixed state. The most important passage that comes into consideration here is Luke 16:19-31. Other passages are Eccl. 11:3 (of uncertain interpretation); John 8:21,24; II Pet. 2:4,9; Jude 7-13 (comp. I Pet. 3:19). (b) It also invariably represents the coming final judgment as determined by the things that were done in the flesh, and never speaks of this as dependent in any way on what occurred in the intermediate state, Matt. 7:22,23; 10:32,33; 25:34-46; Luke 12:47,48; II Cor. 5:9,10; Gal. 6:7,8; II Thess. 1:8; Heb. 9:27. (c) The fundamental principle of this theory, that only the conscious rejection of Christ and His gospel, causes men to perish, is un-Scriptural. Man is lost by nature, and even original sin, as well as all actual sins, makes him worthy of condemnation. The rejection of Christ is undoubtedly a great sin, but is never represented as the only sin that leads to destruction. (d) Scripture teaches us that the Gentiles perish, Rom. 1:32; 2:12; Rev. 21:8. There is no Scripture evidence on which we can base the hope that adult Gentiles, or even Gentile children that have not yet come to years of discretion, will be saved. (e) The theory of a future probation is also calculated to extinguish all missionary zeal. If the Gentiles can decide as to the acceptance of Christ in the future, it can only bring a speedier and increased judgment upon many, if they are placed before the choice now. Why not leave them in ignorance as long as possible?

QUESTIONS FOR FURTHER STUDY: Is the position tenable that *sheol-hades* always designates an underworld whither all the dead go? Why is it objectionable to believe that the Bible in its statements respecting *sheol* and *hades* simply reflects the popular notions of the day? Must we assume that the righteous and the wicked at death enter some temporary and provisional abode, and do not at once enter upon their eternal destiny? In what sense

1. Cf. especially Hovey, *Eschatology*, pp. 97-113, and Vos, Art. *Eschatology of the New Testament* in the *International Standard Bible Encyclopaedia*.

is the intermediate state only transitional? How did the notion of purgatory arise? How do Catholics conceive of the purgatorial fire? Is this fire merely purifying or also penal? What sound element do some Lutherans recognize in the doctrine of purgatory? What mixture of heresies do we meet with in Millennial Dawnism? Does the intermediate state, according to Scripture, represent a third *aion* between the *aion houtos* and the *aion ho mellon?* Is the Scriptural emphasis on the present as "the day of salvation" in harmony with the doctrine of a future probation?

LITERATURE: Bavinck, *Geref. Dogm.* IV., pp. 655-711; Kuyper, *Dict. Dogm., De Consummatione Saeculi*, pp. 25-116; Vos, *Geref. Dogm.* V, *Eschatologie*, pp. 3-14; Hodge, *Syst. Theol.* III, pp. 713-770; Shedd, *Dogm. Theol.* II, pp. 591-640; Dabney, *Syst. and Polem. Theol.* pp. 823-829; Litton, *Introd. to Dogm. Theol.*, pp. 548-569; Valentine, *Chr. Theol.* II, pp. 392-407; Pieper, *Christl. Dogm.* III, pp. 574-578; Miley, *Syst. Theol.* II, pp. 430-439; Wilmers, *Handbook of the Chr. Rel.*, pp. 385-391; Schaff, *Our Fathers' Faith and Ours*, pp. 412-431; Row, *Future Retribution*, pp. 348-404; Shedd, *Doctrine of Endless Punishment*, pp. 19-117; King, *Future Retribution*; Morris, *Is There Salvation After Death?* Hovey, *Eschatology*, pp. 79-144; Dahle, *Life After Death*, pp. 118-227; Salmond, *Chr. Doct. of Immortality*, cf. Index; Mackintosh, *Immortality and the Future*, pp. 195-228; Addison, *Life Beyond Death*, pp. 200-214; De Bondt, *Wat Leert Het Oude Testament Aangaande Her Leven Na Dit Leven?* pp. 40-129; Kliefoth, *Christl. Eschatologie*, pp. 32-126.

GENERAL ESCHATOLOGY

I. The Second Coming of Christ

While the prophets do not clearly distinguish a twofold coming of Christ, the Lord Himself and the apostles make it abundantly clear that the first coming will be followed by a second. Jesus referred to His return more than once towards the end of His public ministry, Matt. 24:30; 25:19,31; 26:64; John 14:3. At the time of His ascension angels pointed to His future return, Acts 1:11. Moreover, the apostles speak of it in numerous passages, Acts 3:20,21; Phil. 3:20; I Thess. 4:15,16; II Thess. 1:7,10; Tit. 2:13; Heb. 9:28. Several terms are used to denote this great event, of which the following are the most important: (1) *apocalupsis* (unveiling), which points to the removal of that which now obstructs our vision of Christ, I Cor. 1:7; II Thess. 1:7; I Pet. 1:7,13; 4:13; (2) *epiphaneia* (appearance, manifestation), a term referring to Christ's coming forth out of a hidden background with the rich blessings of salvation, II Thess. 2:8; I Tim. 6:14; II Tim. 4:1,8; Tit. 2:13; and (3) *parousia* (lit. presence), which points to the coming that precedes the presence or results in the presence, Matt. 24:3,27,37; I Cor. 15:23; I Thess. 2:19; 3:13; 4:15; 5:23; II Thess. 2:1-9; Jas. 5:7,8; II Pet. 1:16; 3:4,12; I John 2:28.

A. The Second Coming a Single Event.

Present day dispensationalists distinguish between a twofold future coming of Christ, though they sometimes seek to preserve the unity of the idea of the second coming by speaking of these as two aspects of that great event. But since these two are in reality represented as two different events, separated by a period of several years, each having a purpose of its own, they can hardly be regarded as a single event. The first of these is the *parousia* or simply "the coming," and results in the rapture of the saints, sometimes represented as a *secret rapture*. This coming is imminent, that is, it can occur at any moment, since there are no predicted events which must precede its occurrence. The prevailing opinion is that at this time Christ does not come down to earth, but remains in the upper air. Those who die in the Lord are raised from the dead, the living saints are transfigured, and together they are caught up to meet the Lord in the air. Hence this coming is also called the "coming *for* His saints," I Thess. 4:15,16. It is followed by an interval of seven years, during which the world is evangelized, Matt. 24:14, Israel is converted, Rom. 11:26, the great tribulation occurs, Matt. 24:21,22, and Antichrist or the man of sin will be revealed, II Thess. 2:8-10. After these events there is another coming of the

Lord *with* His saints, I Thess. 3:13, which is called "the revelation" or "the day of the Lord," in which He comes down to earth. This coming cannot be called imminent, because it must be preceded by several predicted events. At this coming Christ judges the living nations, Matt. 25:31-46, and ushers in the millennial kingdom. Thus we have two distinct comings of the Lord, separated by a period of seven years, of which the one is imminent and the other is not, the one is followed by the glorification of the saints, and the other by the judgment of the nations and the establishment of the kingdom. This construction of the doctrine of the second coming is very convenient for the dispensationalists, since it enables them to defend the view that the coming of the Lord is imminent, but is not warranted by Scripture and carries with it un-Scriptural implications. In II Thess. 2:1,2,8 the terms *parousia* and "day of the Lord" are used interchangeably, and according to II Thess. 1:7-10 the revelation mentioned in verse 7 synchronizes with the parousia which brings the glorification of the saints of which the 10th verse speaks. Matt. 24:29-31 represents the coming of the Lord at which the elect are gathered together as following *immediately after* the great tribulation mentioned in the context, while according to the theory under consideration it should occur *before* the tribulation. And, finally, according to this theory the Church will not pass through the great tribulation, which is represented in Matt. 24:4-26 as synchronizing with the great apostasy, but the representation of Scripture in Matt. 24:22; Luke 21:36; II Thess. 2:3; I Tim. 4:1-3; II Tim. 3:1-5; Rev. 7:14 is quite different. On the basis of Scripture it should be maintained that the second coming of the Lord will be a single event. Happily, some Premillenarians do not agree with this doctrine of a twofold second coming of Christ, and speak of it as an unwarranted novelty. Says Frost: "It is not generally known, and yet it is an indisputable fact that the doctrine of a pretribulation resurrection and rapture is a modern interpretation — I am tempted to say, a modern invention."[1] According to him it dates from the day of Irving and Darby. Another Premillenarian, namely, Alexander Reese, puts up a very strong argument against this whole idea in his work on *The Approaching Advent of Christ.*

B. Great Events Preceding the Parousia.

According to Scripture several important events must occur before the return of the Lord, and therefore it cannot be called imminent. In the light of Scripture it cannot be maintained that there are no predicted events which must still come to pass before the second coming. As might be expected in view of what was said in the preceding, Frost, in spite of his dispensationalism, rejects the doctrine of imminence. He prefers to speak of the coming of Christ as "impending." Support for the doctrine of the imminence of the return of Christ is found in Scripture statements to the effect that Christ is coming after "a very little while," Heb. 10:37; or "quickly," Rev. 22:7; in exhortations to watch and wait for His coming, Matt. 24:42; 25:13; Rev. 16:15; and in the fact that Scripture condemns the person who saith, "My Lord tarrieth" (or,

---

1. *The Second Coming of Christ,* p. 203.

"delayeth his coming"), Matt. 24:48. Jesus did indeed teach that His coming was near, but this is not the same as teaching that it was imminent. In the first place it should be borne in mind that in speaking of His coming, He does not always have in mind the eschatological coming. Sometimes He refers to His coming in spiritual power on the day of Pentecost; sometimes to His coming in judgment in the destruction of Jerusalem. In the second place He and the apostles teach us that several important events had to occur before His physical return at the last day, Matt. 24:5-14,21,22,29-31; II Thess. 2:2-4. Therefore He could not very well regard and represent His coming as imminent. It is evident also that, when He spoke of His coming as near, He did not mean to represent it as *immediately at hand*. In the parable of the pounds He teaches that the Lord of the servants came to reckon with them "after a long time," Matt. 25:19. And the parable of the pounds was spoken for the very purpose of correcting the notion "that the kingdom of God should immediately appear," Luke 19:11. In the parable of the ten virgins the bridegroom is represented as "tarrying," Matt. 25:5. This is in harmony with what Paul says in II Thess. 2:2. Peter predicted that scoffers would arise saying, "Where is the day of His coming?" And he teaches his readers to understand the predictions of the nearness of the second coming from the divine point of view, according to which one day is as a thousand years, and a thousand years as one day, II Pet. 3:3-9. To teach that Jesus regarded the second coming as immediately at hand, would be to represent Him as in error, since almost two thousand years have already elapsed since that time. Now the question can be raised, How can we then be urged to watch for the coming? Jesus teaches us in Matt. 24:32,33 to watch for the coming through the signs: "when ye see all these things, know ye that He is nigh." Moreover, we need not interpret the exhortation to watch as an exhortation to scan the heavens for immediate signs of the Lord's appearance. We should rather see in it an admonition to be awake, to be alert, to be prepared, to be active in the work of the Lord, lest we be overtaken by sudden calamity. The following great events must precede the coming of the Lord.

1. THE CALLING OF THE GENTILES. Several passages of the New Testament point to the fact that the gospel of the Kingdom must be preached to all nations before the return of the Lord, Matt. 24:14; Mark 13:10; Rom. 11:25. Many passages testify to the fact that the Gentiles will enter the Kingdom in goodly numbers during the new dispensation, Matt. 8:11; 13:31,32; Luke 2:32; Acts 15:14; Rom. 9:24-26; Eph. 2:11-20, and other passages. But those indicated above clearly refer to the evangelization of all nations as the goal of history. Now it will hardly do to say that the gospel has already been proclaimed among all peoples, nor that the labors of a single missionary in each one of the nations of the world would meet all the requirements of the statement of Jesus. On the other hand it is equally impossible to maintain that the words of the Saviour call for the preaching of the gospel to every individual of the different nations of the world. They do require, however, that those nations *as nations* shall be thoroughly evangelized, so that the gospel becomes a power in the life of the

people, a sign that calls for decision. It must be preached to them *for a testimony*, so that it can be said that an opportunity was given them to choose for or against Christ and His Kingdom. These words clearly imply that the great commission must be carried out in all the nations of the world, in order to make disciples of all nations, that is, from among the people of all those nations. They do not justify the expectation, however, that all the nations will *as a whole* accept the gospel, but only that it will find adherents in all the nations and will thus be instrumental in bringing in the fulness of the Gentiles. At the end of time it will be possible to say that all nations were made acquainted with the gospel, and the gospel will testify against the nations that did not accept it.

It will readily be understood from what we said in the preceding that many dispensationalists have quite a different view of the matter. They do not believe that the evangelization of the world need be, nor that it will be, completed before the parousia, which is imminent. According to them it will really begin at that time. They point out that the gospel indicated in Matt. 24:14 is not the gospel of the grace of God in Jesus Christ, but the gospel of the Kingdom, which is quite different, the good news that the Kingdom is once more at hand. After the Church has been removed from this earthly scene, and with it the indwelling Holy Spirit has gone — which really means, after Old Testament conditions have been restored —, then the gospel with which Jesus *began* His ministry will again be preached. It will be preached at first by those who were converted by the very removal of the Church, later on perhaps by converted Israel and a special messenger,[1] or, particularly during the great tribulation, by the believing remnant of Israel.[2] This preaching will be wonderfully effective, far more effective than the preaching of the gospel of the grace of God. It is during this period that the 144,000 and the great multitude which no man can number of Rev. 7 will be converted. And in that way the prediction of Jesus in Matt. 24:14 will be fulfilled. It should be remembered that this construction is one which the older Premillenarians did not accept, which is even now rejected by some present day Premillenarians. and which certainly does not commend itself to us. The distinction between a twofold gospel and a twofold second coming of the Lord is an untenable one. The gospel of the grace of God in Jesus Christ is the only gospel that saves and that gives entrance to the Kingdom of God. And it is absolutely contrary to the history of revelation, that a reversal to Old Testament conditions, including the absence of the Church and of the indwelling Holy Spirit, should be more effective than the preaching of the gospel of the grace of God in Jesus Christ and the gift of the Holy Spirit.

2. THE CONVERSION OF THE PLEROMA OF ISRAEL. Both the Old and the New Testament speak of a future conversion of Israel, Zech. 12:10; 13:1;

---

1. Blackstone, *Jesus is Coming*, p. 233.
2. *Scofield's Bible*, pp. 1033,1036; Rogers, *The End from the Beginning*, p. 144; Feinberg, *Premillennialism or Amillennialism*, pp. 134,135.

II Cor. 3:15,16, and Rom. 11:25-29 seems to connect this with the end of time. Premillennialists have exploited this Scriptural teaching for their particular purpose. They maintain that there will be a *national* restoration and conversion of Israel, that the Jewish nation will be re-established in the Holy Land, and that this will take place immediately preceding or during the millennial reign of Jesus Christ. It is very doubtful, however, whether Scripture warrants the expectation that Israel will finally be re-established as a nation, and will as a nation turn to the Lord. Some Old Testament prophecies seem to predict this, but these should be read in the light of the New Testament. Does the New Testament justify the expectation of a future restoration and conversion of Israel as a nation? It is not taught nor even necessarily implied in such passages as Matt. 19:28, and Luke 21:24, which are often quoted in its favor. The Lord spoke very plainly of the opposition of the Jews to the spirit of His Kingdom, and of the certainty that they, who could in a sense be called children of the Kingdom, would lose their place in it, Matt. 8:11,12; 21:28-46; 22:1-14; Luke 13:6-9. He informs the wicked Jews that the Kingdom will be taken from them and given to a nation bringing forth the fruits thereof, Matt. 21:43. And even when He speaks of the corruptions which in course of time will creep into the Church, of the troubles it will encounter, and of the apostasy which will finally ensue, He does not hint at any prospective restoration and conversion of the Jewish people. This silence of Jesus is very significant. Now it may be thought that Rom. 11:11-32 certainly teaches the future conversion of the nation of Israel. Many commentators adopt this view, but even its correctness is subject to considerable doubt. In the chapters 9-11 the apostle discusses the question, how the promises of God to Israel can be reconciled with the rejection of the greater part of Israel. He points out first of all in the chapters 9 and 10 that the promise applies, not to Israel according to the flesh, but to the spiritual Israel; and in the second place that God still has His elect among Israel, that there is among them still a remnant according to the election of grace, 11:1-10. And even the hardening of the greater part of Israel is not God's final end, but rather a means in His hand to bring salvation to the Gentiles, in order that these, in turn, by enjoying the blessings of salvation, may provoke Israel to jealousy. The hardening of Israel will always be only partial, for through all the succeeding centuries there will always be some who accept the Lord. God will continue to gather His elect remnant out of the Jews during the entire new dispensation until the fulness (*pleroma,* that is, the number of the elect) of the Gentiles be come in, and so (in this manner) all Israel (its *pleroma,* that is, the full number of true Israelites) shall be saved. "All Israel" is to be understood as a designation, not of the whole nation, but of the whole number of the elect out of the ancient covenant people. Premillenarians take the 26th verse to mean that, after God has completed His purpose with the Gentiles, the nation of Israel will be saved. But the apostle said at the beginning of his discussion that the promises were for the spiritual Israel; there is no evidence of a change of thought in the intervening section, so that this would come as a surprise in 11:26; and the adverb *houtos* cannot mean "after that," but only "in this manner." With the fulness of the Gentiles the fulness of Israel will also come in.

3. THE GREAT APOSTASY AND THE GREAT TRIBULATION. These two may be mentioned together, because they are interwoven in the eschatological discourse of Jesus, Matt. 24:9-12,21-24; Mark 13:9-22; Luke 21:22-24. The words of Jesus undoubtedly found a partial fulfilment in the days preceding the destruction of Jerusalem, but will evidently have a further fulfilment in the future in a tribulation far surpassing anything that has ever been experienced, Matt. 24:21; Mark 13:19. Paul also speaks of the great apostasy in II Thess. 2:3; I Tim. 4:1; II Tim. 3:1-5. He already saw something of that spirit of apostasy in his own day, but clearly wants to impress upon his readers that it will assume much greater proportions in the last days. Here again present day dispensationalists differ from us. They do not regard the great tribulation as a precursor of the coming of the Lord (the parousia), but believe that it will follow "the coming," and that therefore the Church will not pass through the great tribulation. The assumption is that the Church will be "caught up," to be with the Lord, before the tribulation with all its terrors overtakes the inhabitants of the earth. They prefer to speak of the great tribulation as "the day of Jacob's trouble," since it will be a day of great trouble for Israel rather than for the Church. But the grounds which they adduce for this view are not very convincing. Some of them derive whatever force they have from their own preconceived notion of a twofold second coming of Christ, and therefore have no meaning whatsoever for those who are convinced that there is no evidence for such a twofold coming in Scripture. Jesus certainly mentions the great tribulation as one of the signs of His coming and of the end of the world, Matt. 24:3. It is of that coming (parousia) that He is speaking throughout this chapter, as may be seen from the repeated use of the word parousia, verses 3,37,39. It is only reasonable to assume that He is speaking of the same coming in verse 30. a coming which according to verse 29 will follow immediately after the tribulation. This tribulation will affect also the elect: they will be in danger of being led astray, Matt. 24:24; for their sakes the days of agony will be shortened, verse 22; they will be gathered out of all quarters of the world at the coming of the Son of Man; and they are encouraged to look up when they see these things come to pass, since their redemption draweth nigh, Luke 21:28. There is no warrant for limiting the elect to the elect of Israel, as the Premillenarians do. Paul clearly represents the great falling away as preceding the second coming, II Thess. 2:3, and reminds Timothy of the fact that grievous times will come in the last days, I Tim. 4:1,2; II Tim. 3:1-5. In Rev. 7:13,14 saints in heaven are said to have come out of the great tribulation, and in Rev. 6:9 we find such saints praying for their brethren who were still suffering persecution.[1]

1. For further defense of the position that the Church will pass through the tribulation, we refer to the works of two Premillenarians, namely. Frost, *The Second Coming of Christ*. pp. 202-227; Reese, *The Approaching Advent of Christ*, pp. 199-224.

4. THE COMING REVELATION OF ANTICHRIST. The term *antichristos* is found only in the Epistles of John, namely, in I John 2:18,22; 4:3; II John 7. As far as the form of the word is concerned, it may describe (a) one who takes the place of Christ; then "anti" is taken in the sense of "instead of"; or (b) one who, while assuming the guise of Christ, opposes Him; then "anti" is used in the sense of "against." The latter is more in harmony with the context in which the word occurs. From the fact that John uses the singular in 2:18 without the article, it is evident that the term "antichrist" was already regarded as a technical name. It is uncertain, whether John in using the singular had in mind one paramount Antichrist, of which the others to which he refers were merely harbingers or forerunners, or simply meant to personify the principle embodied in several antichrists, the principle of evil militating against the Kingdom of God. Antichrist clearly does represent a certain principle, I John 4:3. If we bear this in mind, we shall also realize that, though John is the first to use the term "antichrist," the principle or spirit indicated by it is clearly mentioned in earlier writings. Just as there is in Scripture a clearly marked development in the delineation of Christ and of the Kingdom of God, so there is also a progressive revelation of antichrist. The representations differ, but increase in definiteness as God's revelation progresses.

In the majority of the Old Testament prophets we see the principle of unrighteousness working in the ungodly nations which show themselves hostile to Israel and are judged by God. In the prophecy of Daniel we find something more specific. The language used there furnished many of the features of Paul's description of the man of sin in II Thessalonians. Daniel finds the wicked, ungodly principle embodied in the "little horn," Dan. 7:8,23-26, and describes it very clearly in 11:35 ff. Here even the personal element is not altogether wanting, though it is not entirely certain that the prophet is thinking of some particular king, namely, Antiochus Epiphanes, as a type of Antichrist. The coming of Christ naturally calls forth this principle in its specifically *anti-Christian* form, and Jesus represents it as embodied in various persons. He speaks of *pseudoprophetai* and *pseudochristoi*, who take position against Him and His Kingdom, Matt. 7:15; 24:5,24; Mark 13:21,22; Luke 17:23. In order to correct the erroneous view of the Thessalonians, Paul calls attention to the fact that the day of Christ cannot come, "except the falling away come first, and the man of sin be revealed, the son of perdition." He describes this man of sin as "he that opposeth and exalteth himself against all that is called God or worshipped; so that he sitteth in the temple of God, setting himself forth as God," I Thess. 2:3,4. This description naturally reminds us of Dan. 11:36 ff. and clearly points to Antichrist. There is no good reason for doubting the identity of the man of sin, of whom Paul speaks, and the Antichrist mentioned by John. The apostle sees the "mystery of lawlessness" already at work, but assures his readers that the man of sin cannot come forth until that which (or, "he that") restraineth is taken out of the way. When this obstacle, whatever it may be (it is variously interpreted), is removed, he will appear "whose coming is according to the working of Satan with all power and signs and lying wonders," verses 7-9. In this chapter the personal element is presupposed throughout. The book of Revelation finds the anti-Christian principle or power in the two beasts coming up out of the sea and out of the earth, Rev. 13. The first is generally thought to refer to governments, political powers, or some world-empire; the second, though not with the same unanimity, to false religion, false prophecy, and false science, particularly the first two. This opponent, or opposing principle, John in his epistles finally calls "Antichrist."

Historically, there have been different opinions respecting Antichrist. In the ancient Church many maintained that Antichrist would be a Jew, pretending to be the Messiah and ruling at Jerusalem. Many recent commentators are of the opinion that Paul and others mistakenly thought that some Roman emperor would be Antichrist, and that John clearly had Nero in mind in Rev. 13:18, since the letters in the Hebrew words for "emperor Nero" are exactly equivalent to 666, Rev. 13:18. Since the time of the Reformation many, among whom also Reformed scholars, looked upon papal Rome, and in some cases even on some particular Pope, as Anti-Christ. And the papacy indeed reveals several traits of Antichrist as he is pictured in Scripture. Yet it will hardly do to identify it with Antichrist. It is better to say that there are elements of Antichrist in the papacy. Positively, we can only say: (a) that the anti-Christian principle was already at work in the days of Paul and John according to their own testimony; (b) that it will reach its highest power towards the end of the world; (c) that Daniel pictures the political, Paul the ecclesiastical, and John in the book of Revelation both sides of it: the two may be successive revelations of the anti-Christian power; and (d) that probably this power will finally be concentrated in a single individual, the embodiment of all wickedness.

The question of the personal character of Antichrist is still a subject of debate. Some maintain that the expressions "antichrist," "the man of sin, the son of perdition," and the figures in Daniel and Revelation are merely descriptions of the ungodly and anti-Christian principle, which manifests itself in the opposition of the world to God and His Kingdom, throughout the whole history of that Kingdom, an opposition sometimes weaker, sometimes stronger, but strongest toward the end of time. They do not look for any one personal Antichrist. Others feel that it is contrary to Scripture to speak of Antichrist merely as an abstract power. They hold that such an interpretation does not do justice to the data of Scripture, which speaks, not only of an abstract spirit, but also of actual persons. According to them "Antichrist" is a collective concept, the designation of a succession of persons, manifesting an ungodly or anti-Christian spirit, such as the Roman emperors who persecuted the Church and the Popes who engaged in a similar work of persecution. Even they do not think of a personal Antichrist who will be in himself the concentration of all wickedness. The more general opinion in the Church, however, is that in the last analysis the term "Antichrist" denotes an eschatological person, who will be the incarnation of all wickedness and therefore represents a spirit which is always more or less present in the world, and who has several precursors or types in history. This view prevailed in the early Church and would seem to be the Scriptural view. The following may be said in favor of it: (a) The delineation of Antichrist in Dan. 11 is more or less personal, and may refer to a definite person as a type of Antichrist. (b) Paul speaks of Antichrist as "the man of sin" and "the son of perdition." Because of the peculiar Hebrew use of the terms "man" and "son" these expressions in themselves may not be conclusive, but the context clearly favors the personal idea. He opposes, sets himself up as God, has a definite revelation, is the lawless one, and so on. (c) While John speaks of many antichrists as already present, he also speaks of Antichrist in the singular as one that is still coming in the future, I John 2:18. (d) Even in Revelation, where the representation is largely symbolical, the personal element is not lacking, as, for instance in Rev. 19:20, which speaks of Antichrist and his subordinate as being cast into the lake of fire. And (e) since Christ is a person, it is but natural to think that Antichrist will also be a person.

5. SIGNS AND WONDERS. The Bible speaks of several signs that will be harbingers of the end of the world and of the coming of Christ. It mentions (a) wars and rumours of wars, famines and earthquakes in various places, which are called the beginning of travail, the travail, as it were, of the rebirth of the universe at the time of the coming of Christ; (b) the coming of false prophets, who will lead many astray, and of false Christs, who will show great signs and wonders to lead astray, if possible, even the elect; and (c) of fearful portents in heaven involving sun, moon, and stars, when the powers of the heavens will be shaken, Matt. 24:29,30; Mark 13:24,25; Luke 21:25,26. Since some of these signs are of a kind which repeatedly occur in the natural order of events, the question naturally arises in what way they can be recognized as special signs of the end. Attention is usually called to the fact that they will differ from previous occurrences in intensity and extent. But, of course, this does not entirely satisfy, because those seeing such signs can never know, if there be no other indications, whether the signs which they are witnessing may not be followed by other similar signs of even greater extent and intensity. Therefore attention should also be called to the fact that there will be, when the end is near, a remarkable conjunction of all these signs, and that the natural occurrences will be accompanied with supernatural phenomena, Luke 21:25,26. Jesus says: "When ye see *all these things*, know that He is nigh, even at the doors." Matt. 24:33.

C. The Parousia or the Second Coming Itself.

Immediately after the portents just mentioned "the sign of the Son of Man shall be seen coming on the clouds of heaven," Matt. 24:30. In connection with this the following points should be noted:

1. THE TIME OF THE SECOND COMING. The exact time of the coming of the Lord is unknown, Matt. 24:36, and all the attempts of men to figure out the

exact date proved to be erroneous. The only thing that can be said with certainty, on the basis of Scripture, is that He will return at the end of the world. The disciples asked the Lord. "What shall be the sign of thy coming, and of the end of the world?" Matt. 24:3. They link the two together, and the Lord does not intimate in any way that this is a mistake, but rather assumes the correctness of it in His discourse. He represents the two as synchronizing in Matt. 24:29-31,35-44: comp. Matt. 13:39,40. Paul and Peter also speak of the two as coinciding, I Cor. 15:23,24; II Pet. 3:4-10. A study of the concomitants of the second coming leads to the same result. The resurrection of the saints will be one of its concomitants, I Cor. 15:23. I Thess. 4:16, and Jesus assures us that He will raise them up at the last day, John 6:39,40,44,54. According to Thayer, Cremer-Koegel, Walker, Salmond, Zahn, and others, this can only mean the day of the consummation, — the end of the world. Another one of its concomitants will be the judgment of the world, Matt. 25:31-46, particularly also the judgment of the wicked, II Thess. 1:7-10, which Premillenarians place at the end of the world. And, finally, it will also carry with it the restoration of all things, Acts 3:20,21. The strong expression "restoration of all things" is too strong to refer to anything less than the perfect restoration of that state of things that existed before the fall of man. It points to the restoration of *all things* to their former condition, and this will not be found in the millennium of the Premillenarians. Even sin and death will continue to slay their victims during that period.[1] As was pointed out in the preceding, several things must occur before the Lord's return. This must be borne in mind in the reading of those passages which speak of the coming of the Lord or the last day as near, Matt. 16:28; 24:34; Heb. 10:25; Jas. 5:9; I Pet. 4:5; I John 2:18. They find their explanation partly in the fact that, considered from the side of God, with whom one day is as a thousand years, and a thousand years as one day, the coming is always near; partly in the Biblical representation of the New Testament time as constituting the last days or the last time; partly in the fact that the Lord in speaking of His coming does not always have in mind His physical return at the end of time, but may refer to His coming in the Holy Spirit; and partly in the characteristic prophetic foreshortening, in which no clear distinction is made between the proximate coming of the Lord in the destruction of Jerusalem and His final coming to judge the world. Sectaries have often made the attempt to fix the exact time of the second coming, but these attempts are always delusive. Jesus says explicitly: "But of that day and hour knoweth no one, not even the angels of heaven, neither the Son, but the Father only," Matt. 24:36. The statement respecting the Son probably means that this knowledge was not included in the revelation which He as Mediator had to bring.

2. THE MANNER OF THE SECOND COMING. The following points deserve emphasis here:

a. *It will be a personal coming.* This follows from the statement of the angels to the disciples on the Mount of the Ascension: "This Jesus, who was

1. Cf. Thayer, Cremer-Koegel, Weiss, *Bib. Theol. of the N. T.*, p. 194, note.

received up from you into heaven, shall so come in like manner as ye beheld Him going into heaven," Acts 1:11. The person of Jesus was leaving them, and the person of Jesus will return. In the system of present day Modernism there is no place for a personal return of Jesus Christ. Douglas Clyde Macintosh sees the return of Christ in "the progressive domination of individuals and society by the moral and religious principles of essential Christianity, i.e. by the Spirit of Christ."[1] William Newton Clarke says: "No visible return of Christ to the earth is to be expected, but rather the long and steady advance of His spiritual Kingdom. . . . If our Lord will but complete the spiritual coming that He has begun, there will be no need of a visible advent to make perfect His glory on the earth."[2] According to William Adams Brown "Not through an abrupt catastrophe, it may be, as in the early Christian hope, but by the slower and surer method of spiritual conquest, the ideal of Jesus shall yet win the universal assent which it deserves, and His spirit dominate the world. This is the truth for which the doctrine of the second advent stands."[3] Walter Rauschenbusch and Shailer Mathews speak in similar terms of the second coming. One and all, they interpret the glowing descriptions of the second coming of Christ as figurative representations of the idea that the spirit of Christ will be an ever-increasing, pervasive influence in the life of the world. But it goes without saying that such representations do not do justice to the descriptions found in such passages as Acts 1:11; 3:20,21, Matt. 24:44; I Cor. 15:22; Phil. 3:20; Col. 3:4; I Thess. 2:19; 3:13; 4:15-17; II Tim. 4:8; Tit. 2:13; Heb. 9:28. Modernists themselves admit this when they speak of these as representing the old Jewish way of thinking. They have new and better light on the subject, but it is a light that grows rather dim in view of the world events of the present day.

b. *It will be a physical coming.* That the Lord's return will be physical follows from such passages as Acts 1:11; 3:20,21; Heb. 9:28; Rev. 1:7. Jesus will return to earth in the body. There are some who identify the predicted coming of the Lord with His spiritual coming on the day of Pentecost, and understand the *parousia* to mean the Lord's spiritual presence in the Church. According to their representation the Lord did return in the Holy Spirit on the day of Pentecost, and is now present (hence *parousia*) in the Church. They lay special emphasis on the fact that the word *parousia* means *presence.*[4] Now it is quite evident that the New Testament does speak of a spiritual coming of Christ, Matt. 16:28; John 14:18,23; Rev. 3:20; but this coming, whether to the Church on the day of Pentecost or to the individual in his spiritual renewal, Gal. 1:16, cannot be identified with what the Bible represents as *the* second coming of Christ. It is true that the word *parousia* means *presence*, but Dr. Vos correctly pointed out that in its religious

---

1. *Theology as an Empirical Science*, p. 213.
2. *Outline of Christian Theology*, p. 444.
3. *Christian Theology in Outline*, p. 373.
4. This interpretation is found in Warren's *The Parousia of Christ*, and in J. M. Campbell's *The Second Coming of Christ*.

eschatological usage it also means *arrival,* and that in the New Testament the idea of *arrival* is in the foreground. Moreover, it should be borne in mind that there are other terms in the New Testament, which serve to designate the second coming, namely *apokalupsis, epiphaneia,* and *phanerosis,* every one of which points to a coming that can be seen. And, finally, it should not be forgotten that the Epistles refer to the second coming repeatedly as an event that is still future, Phil. 3:20; I Thess. 3:13; 4:15,16; II Thess. 1:7-10; Tit. 2:13. This does not fit in with the idea that the coming was already an event of the past.

c. *It will be a visible coming.* This is intimately connected with the preceding. It may be said that, if the coming of the Lord will be physical, it will also be visible. This would seem to follow as a matter of course, but the Russellites or Millennial Dawnists do not seem to think so. They maintain that the return of Christ and the inauguration of the millennium took place invisibly in 1874, and that Christ came in power in 1914 for the purpose of removing the Church and overthrowing the kingdoms of the world. When the year 1914 passed by without the appearance of Christ, they sought a way of escape from the difficulty in the convenient theory that He remained in hiding, because the people do not manifest sufficient repentance. Christ has come, therefore, and has come invisibly. Scripture does not leave us in doubt, however, as to the visibility of the Lord's return. Numerous passages testify to it, such as Matt. 24:30; 26:64; Mark 13:26; Luke 21:27; Acts 1:11; Col. 3:4; Tit. 2:13; Heb. 9:28; Rev. 1:7.

d. *It will be a sudden coming.* Though the Bible teaches us on the one hand that the coming of the Lord will be preceded by several signs, it teaches on the other hand in an equally emphatic manner that the coming will be sudden, will be rather unexpected, and will take people by surprise, Matt. 24:37-44; 25:1-12; Mark 13:33-37; I Thess. 5:2,3; Rev. 3:3; 16:15. This is not contradictory, for the predicted signs are not of such a kind as to designate the exact time. The prophets pointed to certain signs that would precede the first coming of Christ, and yet His coming took many by surprise. The majority of the people paid no attention to the signs whatsoever. The Bible intimates that the measure of the surprise at the second coming of Christ will be in an inverse ratio to the measure of their watchfulness.

e. *It will be a glorious and triumphant coming.* The second coming of Christ, though personal, physical, and visible, will yet be very different from His first coming. He will not return in the body of His humiliation, but in a glorified body and in royal apparel, Heb. 9:28. The clouds of heaven will be His chariot, Matt. 24:30, the angels His bodyguard, II Thess. 1:7, the archangels His heralds, I Thess. 4:16, and the saints of God His glorious retinue, I Thess. 3:13; II Thess. 1:10. He will come as King of kings and Lord of lords, triumphant over all the forces of evil, having put all His enemies under His feet, I Cor. 15:25; Rev. 19:11-16.

3. THE PURPOSE OF THE SECOND COMING. Christ will return at the end of the world for the purpose of introducing the future age, the eternal state of things, and He will do this by inaugurating and completing two mighty events, namely, the resurrection of the dead and the final judgment, Matt. 13:49,50; 16:27; 24:3; 25:14-46; Luke 9:26; 19:15,26,27; John 5:25-29; Acts 17:31; Rom. 2:3-16; I Cor. 4:5; 15:23; II Cor. 5:10; Phil. 3:20,21; I Thess. 4:13-17; II Thess. 1:7-10; 2:7,8; II Tim. 4:1,8; II Pet. 3:10-13; Jude 14,15; Rev. 20:11-15; 22:12. In the usual representation of Scripture, as already intimated in the preceding, the end of the world, the day of the Lord, the physical resurrection of the dead, and the final judgment coincide. That great turning point will also bring the destruction of all the evil forces that are hostile to the Kingdom of God, II Thess. 2:8; Rev. 20:14. It may be doubted, whether anyone would have read the relevant passages in any other way, if Rev. 20:1-6 had not been set up by some as the standard by which all the rest of the New Testament must be interpreted. According to Premillenarians the second coming of Christ will primarily serve the purpose of establishing the visible reign of Christ and His Saints on earth, and of inaugurating the real day of salvation for the world. This will involve the rapture, the resurrection of the righteous, the wedding of the Lamb, and judgments upon the enemies of God. But other resurrections and judgments will follow at various intervals, and the last resurrection and final judgment will be separated from the second coming by a thousand years. The objections to this view have partly been given in the preceding and will partly be mentioned in the following chapters.

QUESTIONS FOR FURTHER STUDY: Why cannot the term *parousia* simply be rendered 'presence' wherever it is found? In what different senses does the Bible speak of the coming of Christ? How should Matt. 16:28: 24:34 be interpreted? Does the discourse of Jesus in Matt. 24 speak of a single coming? Does the doctrine of the national restoration of the Jews necessarily involve the doctrine of the millennium? Do the following passages teach such a restoration: Matt. 23:39; Luke 13:35; 21:24; Acts 3:6,7? Does Daniel refer to Antiochus Epiphanes as a type of Antichrist in Dan. 11:36 ff.? How are the beasts of Rev. 13 related to Antichrist? Should the man of sin, of which Paul speaks, be identified with Antichrist? What is the restraining power which is mentioned in II Thess. 2:6,7? Did the apostles teach that the Lord might return during their lifetime? Does the New Testament warrant the idea that the phrase "the end" or "the end of the world" simply means 'the end of the age'?

LITERATURE: Bavinck, *Dogm.* IV, pp. 712-753; Kuyper, *Dict. Dogm., De Consummatione Saeculi,* pp. 117-245; Vos. *Geref. Dogm. V, Eschatologie,* pp. 22-23: id., *Pauline Eschatology,* pp. 72-135; Hodge, *Syst. Theol.* III, pp. 790-836; Pieper, *Christl. Dogm.* III, pp. 579-584; Valentine, *Chr. Theol.* II, pp. 407-411; Schmid, *Doct. Theol. of the Ev. Luth. Church,* pp. 645-657; Strong, *Syst. Theol.,* pp. 1003-1015; Pope, *Chr. Theol.* III, pp. 387-397; Hovey, *Eschatology,* pp. 23-78; Kliefoth, *Eschatologie,* pp. 126-147, 191-225; Mackintosh, *Immortality and the Future,* pp. 130-148; Kennedy, *St. Paul's Conceptions of the Last Things,* pp. 158-193; Salmond, *The Chr. Doct. of Immortality,* pp. 241-251; Snowden, *The Coming of the Lord,* pp. 123-171.

II. Millennial Views

There are some who connect with the advent of Christ the idea of a millennium, either immediately before or immediately following the second coming. While this idea is not an integral part of Reformed theology, it nevertheless deserves consideration here, since it has become rather popular in many circles. Reformed theology cannot afford to ignore the wide-spread millenarian views of the present day, but should define its position with respect to these. Some of those who expect a millennium in the future hold that the Lord will return before the millennium, and are therefore called *Premillennialists;* while others believe that His second coming will follow after the millennium, and are therefore known as *Postmillennialists.* There are large numbers, however, who do not believe that the Bible warrants the expectation of a millennium, and it has become customary of late to speak of them as *Amillennialists.* The Amillennial view is, as the name indicates, purely negative. It holds that there is no sufficient Scriptural ground for the expectation of a millennium, and is firmly convinced that the Bible favors the idea that the present dispensation of the Kingdom of God will be followed *immediately* by the Kingdom of God in its consummate and eternal form. It is mindful of the fact that the Kingdom of Jesus Christ is represented as an eternal and not as a temporal kingdom, Isa. 9:7; Dan. 7:14; Luke 1:33; Heb. 1:8; 12:28; II Pet. 1:11; Rev. 11:15; and that to enter the Kingdom of the future is to enter upon one's eternal state, Matt. 7:21,22, to enter life, Matt. 18:8,9 (cf. the preceding context), and to be saved, Mark 10:25,26. Some Premillenarians have spoken of *Amillennialism* as a new view and as one of the most recent novelties, but this is certainly not in accord with the testimony of history. The name is new indeed, but the view to which it is applied is as old as Christianity. It had at least as many advocates as Chiliasm among the Church Fathers of the second and third centuries, supposed to have been the heyday of Chiliasm. It has ever since been the view most widely accepted, is the only view that is either expressed or implied in the great historical Confessions of the Church, and has always been the prevalent view in Reformed circles.

A. Premillennialism.

Since Premillennialism has not always assumed the same form, it may be well to indicate briefly the form which it generally assumed in the past (without noting all kinds of aberrations), and then to follow this up with a more detailed description of the most dominant premillennial theory of the present day.

1. THE PREMILLENNIALISM OF THE PAST. The view of Irenæus may be given as that which best reflects that of the early Christian centuries. The present world will endure six thousand years, corresponding to the six days of creation. Towards the end of this period the sufferings and persecutions of the pious will greatly increase, until finally the incarnation of all wickedness appears in the person of Antichrist. After he has completed his destructive work and has boldly seated himself in the temple of God, Christ will appear in heavenly glory and triumph over all His enemies. This will be accompanied by the physical resurrection of the saints and the establishment of the Kingdom of God on earth. The period of millennial bliss, lasting a thousand years, will correspond to the seventh day of creation, — the day of rest. Jerusalem will be rebuilt; the earth will yield its fruit in rich abundance; and peace and righteousness will prevail. At the end of the thousand years the final judgment will ensue, and a new creation will appear, in which the redeemed will live forever in the presence of God. In general outline this representation is typical of the eschatological views of the early Christian centuries, however these may differ in some details. During all the following centuries and into the nineteenth century, millennial thought remained essentially the same, though there were strange aberrations in some of the sects. Continued study, however, led to further development and to greater clarity in the presentation of some of its particulars. The main features of the common view may be stated somewhat as follows: The coming advent of Christ to the world is near, and will be visible, personal, and glorious. It will be preceded, however, by certain events, such as the evangelization of all nations, the conversion of Israel, the great apostasy and the great tribulation, and the revelation of the man of sin. Dark and trying times are therefore still in store for the Church, since she will have to pass through the great tribulation. The second coming will be a great, single, outstanding, and glorious event, but will be accompanied by several others bearing on the Church, on Israel, and on the world. The dead saints will be raised and the living transfigured, and together they will be translated to meet the coming Lord. Antichrist and his wicked allies will be slain; and Israel, the ancient people of God will repent, be saved, and restored to the Holy Land. Then the Kingdom of God, predicted by the prophets, will be established in a transformed world. The Gentiles will turn to God in great abundance and be incorporated in the Kingdom. A condition of peace and righteousness will prevail in all the earth. After the expiration of the earthly rule of Christ the rest of the dead will be raised up; and this resurrection will be followed by the last judgment and the creation of a new heaven and a new earth. Generally speaking, it may be said that this is the type of Premillennialism advocated by such men as Mede, Bengel, Auberlen, Christlieb, Ebrard, Godet, Hofmann, Lange, Stier, Van Oosterzee, Van Andel, Alford, Andrews, Ellicott, Guinness, Kellogg, Zahn, Moorehead, Newton, Trench, and others. It goes without saying that these men differed in some details.

2. THE PREMILLENNIALISM OF THE PRESENT. In the second quarter of the nineteenth century a new form of Premillennialism was introduced under the influence of Darby, Kelly, Trotter, and their followers in England and America, a Premillennialism wedded to Dispensationalism. The new views were popularized in our country especially through the Scofield Bible, and are widely disseminated through the works of such men as Bullinger, F. W. Grant, Blackstone, Gray, Silver, Haldeman, the two Gaebeleins, Brookes, Riley, Rogers, and a host of others. They really present a new philosophy of the history of redemption, in which Israel plays a leading role and the Church is but an interlude. Their guiding principle prompts them to divide the Bible into two books, the book of the Kingdom and the book of the Church. In reading their descriptions of God's dealings with men one is lost in a bewildering maze of covenants and dispensations, without an Ariadne thread to give safe guidance. Their divisive tendency also reveals itself in their eschatological program. There will be two second comings, two or three (if not four) resurrections, and also three judgments. Moreover, there will also be two peoples of God, which according to some will be eternally separate, Israel dwelling on earth, and the Church in heaven.

The following will give some idea of the Premillennial scheme that enjoys the greatest popularity to-day:

a. *Its view of history.* God deals with the world of humanity in the course of history on the basis of several covenants and according to the principles of seven different dispensations. Each dispensation is distinct, and each one of them represents a different test of the natural man; and since man fails to meet the successive tests, each dispensation ends in a judgment. The theocracy of Israel, founded on Mount Sinai, occupies a special place in the divine economy. It was the initiatory form of the Kingdom of God or the Kingdom of the Messiah, and had its golden age in the days of David and Solomon. In the way of obedience it might have increased in strength and glory, but as the result of the unfaithfulness of the people, it was finally overthrown, and the people were carried away into exile. The prophets predicted this overthrow, but also brought messages of hope and raised the expectation that in the days of the Messiah Israel would turn to the Lord in true repentance, the throne of David would be re-established in unsurpassed glory, and even the Gentiles would share in the blessings of the future Kingdom. But when the Messiah came and offered to establish the Kingdom, the Jews failed to show the requisite repentance. The result was that the King did not establish the Kingdom, but withdrew from Israel and went into a far country, postponing the establishment of the Kingdom until His return. Before He left the earth, however, He founded the Church, which has nothing in common with the Kingdom, and of which the prophets never spoke. The dispensation of the law made way for the dispensation of the grace of God. During this dispensation the Church is gathered out of Jews and Gentiles, and forms the body of Christ, which now shares in His sufferings, but will once, as the bride of the Lamb, share in His glory. Of this Church Christ is not the King, but the divine Head. She has the glorious task of preaching, not the gospel of the Kingdom, but the gospel of the free grace of God, among all the nations of the world, to gather out of them the elect and further to be a testimony unto them. This method will prove to be a failure; it will not effect conversions on any large scale. At the end of this dispensation Christ will suddenly return and effect a far more universal conversion.

b. *Its eschatology.* The return of Christ is imminent now, that is, He may come at any time, for there are no predicted events that must still precede it. However, His coming consists of two separate events, separated from each other by a period of seven years. The first of these events will be the *parousia*, when Christ will appear in the air to meet His saints. All the righteous dead will then be raised up, and the living saints will be transfigured. Together they will be caught up into the air, will celebrate the wedding of the Lamb, and will then be forever with the Lord. The translation of the living saints is called *"the rapture,"* sometimes *"the secret rapture."* While Christ and His Church are absent from the earth, and even the indwelling Holy Spirit has gone with the Church, there will be a period of seven years or more, often divided into two parts, in which several things will happen. The gospel of the Kingdom will again be preached, primarily, it would seem, by the believing remnant of the Jews, and conversions on a large scale will result, though many will still continue to blaspheme God. The Lord will again begin to deal with Israel and it will probably at this time (though some say it will be later) be converted. In the second half of this period of seven years there will be a time of unequalled tribulation, the length of which is still a subject of debate. Antichrist will be revealed and the vials of God's wrath will be poured out upon the human race. At the end of the seven-year period the *"revelation"* will follow, that is, the coming of the Lord down to earth, now not *for* but *with* His saints. The living nations are now judged (Matt. 25:31 ff.), and the sheep separated from the goats; the saints that died during the great tribulation are raised up; Antichrist is destroyed; and Satan is bound for a thousand years. The millennial kingdom will now be established, a real visible, terrestrial, and material kingdom of the Jews, the restoration of the theocratic kingdom, including the re-establishment of the Davidic kingship. In it the saints will reign with Christ, the Jews will be the natural citizens and many Gentiles adopted citizens. The throne of Christ will be established at Jerusalem, which will also again become the central place of worship. The temple will be rebuilt on Mount Zion, and the altar will again reek with the blood of sacrifices, even of sin- and trespass-offerings. And though sin and death will still claim their victims, it will be a time of great fruitfulness and prosperity, in which men's lives will be prolonged and the wilderness will blossom as the rose. In this time the world will speedily be converted, according to some by the gospel, but according to the majority by totally different means, such as the personal appearance of Christ, the envy aroused by the blessedness of the saints, and above all great and terrible judgments. After the millennium Satan will be loosed for a little season, and the hordes of Gog and Magog assemble against the holy city. The enemies are devoured, however, by fire from heaven, and Satan is cast into the bottomless pit, whither the beast and the false prophet have preceded him. After this little season the wicked dead are raised up and appear in judgment before the great white throne, Rev. 20:11-15. And then there will be a new heaven and a new earth.

c. *Some of the variations of this theory.* Premillenarians are by no means all agreed as to the particulars of their eschatological scheme. A study of their literature reveals a great variety of opinions. There is indefiniteness and uncertainty on many points, which proves that their detailed construction is of rather doubtful value. While the majority of present day Premillenarians believe in a coming visible rule of Jesus Christ, even now some anticipate only a spiritual rule, and do not look for a physical presence of Christ on earth. Though the thousand years of Rev. 20 are generally interpreted literally, there is a tendency on the part of some to regard them as an indefinite period of shorter or longer duration. Some think that the Jews will be converted first, and then brought back to Palestine, while others are of the opinion that this order will be reversed. There are those who believe that the means used for the conversion of the world will be identical with those now employed, but the prevailing opinion is that other means will be substituted. There is a difference of opinion also as to the place where the risen saints will dwell during their millennial reign with Christ, on earth or in heaven, or in both places. Opinions differ very much, too, with respect to the continuance of the propagation of the human race during the millennium, the degree of sin that will prevail at that time, and the continued sway of death, and many other points.

3. OBJECTIONS TO PREMILLENNIALISM. In the discussion of the second advent the premillennial view of it was already subjected to special scrutiny and criticism, and the succeeding chapters on the resurrection and the final judgment will offer further occasion for a critical consideration of the premillennial construction of these events. Hence the objections raised at this point will be of a more general nature, and even so we can only pay attention to some of the most important ones.

a. The theory is based on a literal interpretation of the prophetic delineations of the future of Israel and of the Kingdom of God, which is entirely untenable. This has been pointed out repeatedly in such works on prophecy as those of Fairbairn, Riehm, and Davidson, in the splendid work of David Brown on *The Second Advent,* in Waldegrave's important volume on *New Testament Millennarianism,* and in the more recent works of Dr. Aalders on *De Profeten des Ouden Verbonds,* and *Het Herstel van Israel Volgens het Oude Testament.* The last volume is devoted entirely to a detailed exegetical study of all the Old Testament passages that might bear in any way on the future restoration of Israel. It is a thorough work that deserves careful study. Premillenarians maintain that nothing short of a literal interpretation and fulfilment will satisfy the requirements of these prophetic forecasts; but the books of the prophets themselves already contain indications that point to a spiritual fulfilment, Isa. 54:13; 61:6; Jer. 3:16; 31:31-34; Hos. 14:2; Mic. 6:6-8. The contention that the names "Zion" and "Jerusalem" are never used by the prophets in any other than a literal sense, that the former always denotes a mountain, and the latter, a city, is clearly contrary to fact. There are passages in which both names are employed to designate Israel, the Old Testament Church of God, Isa. 49:14; 51:3; 52:1,2. And this use of the terms passes right over into the New Testament, Gal. 4:26; Heb. 12:22; Rev. 3:12; 21:9. It is remarkable that the New Testament, which is the fulfilment of the Old, contains no indication whatsoever of the re-establishment of the Old Testament theocracy by Jesus, nor a single undisputed positive prediction of its restoration, while it does contain abundant indications of the spiritual fulfilment of the promises given to Israel, Matt. 21:43; Acts 2:29-36, 15:14-18; Rom. 9:25, 26; Heb. 8:8-13; I Pet. 2:9; Rev. 1:6; 5:10. For further details on the spiritualization found in Scripture the work of Dr. Wijngaarden on *The Future of the Kingdom* may be consulted. The New Testament certainly does not favor the literalism of the Premillenarians. Moreover this literalism lands them in all kinds of absurdities, for it involves the future restoration of all the former historical conditions of Israel's life: the great world powers of the Old Testament (Egyptians, Assyrians, and Babylonians), and the neighboring nations of Israel (Moabites, Ammonites, Edomites, and Philistines) must again appear on the scene, Isa. 11:14; Amos 9:12; Joel 3:19; Mic. 5:5,6; Rev. 18. The temple will have to be rebuilt, Isa. 2:2,3; Mic. 4:1,2; Zech. 14:16-22; Ezek. 40-48, the sons of Zadok will again have to serve as priests, Ezek. 44:15-41; 48:11-14, and even sin and trespass offerings will again have to be brought upon the altar, not for commemoration (as some Premillenarians would have it), but for atonement, Ezek. 42:13; 43:18-27. And in addition to all that, the altered situation would make it necessary for all the nations to visit Jerusalem from year to year, in order to celebrate the feast of tabernacles, Zech. 14:16, and even from week to week, to worship before Jehovah, Isa. 66:23.

b. The so-called postponement theory, which is a necessary link in the premillennial scheme, is devoid of all Scriptural basis. According to it John and Jesus proclaimed that the Kingdom, that is, the Jewish theocracy, was at hand. But because the Jews did not repent and believe, Jesus postponed its establishment until His second coming. The pivotal point marking the change is placed by Scofield in Matt. 11:20, by others in Matt. 12, and by others still later. Before that turning point Jesus did not concern Himself with the Gentiles, but preached the gospel of the kingdom to Israel; and after that He did not preach the kingdom any more, but only predicted its future coming and offered rest to the weary of both Israel and the Gentiles. But it cannot be maintained that Jesus did not concern Himself with the Gentiles before the supposed turning point, cf. Matt. 8:5-13; John 4:1-42, nor that after it He ceased to preach the kingdom, Matt. 13; Luke 10:1-11. There is absolutely no proof that Jesus preached two different gospels, first the gospel of the kingdom and then the gospel of the grace of God; in the light of Scripture this distinction is untenable. Jesus never had in mind the re-establishment of the Old Testament theocracy, but the introduction of the spiritual reality, of which the Old Testament kingdom was but a type, Matt. 8:11,12; 13:31-33; 21:43; Luke 17:21; John 3:3; 18:36,37 (comp. Rom. 14:17). He did not postpone the task for which He had come into the world, but actually established the Kingdom and referred to it more than once as a present reality, Matt. 11:12; 12:28; Luke 17:21; John 18:36,37; (comp. Col. 1:13). This whole postponement theory is a comparatively recent fiction, and is very objectionable, because it breaks up the unity of Scripture and of the people of God in an unwarranted way. The Bible represents the relation between the Old Testament and the New as that of type and antitype, of prophecy and fulfilment; but this theory holds that, while the New Testament was originally meant to be a fulfilment of the Old, it really became something quite different. The kingdom, that is, the Old Testament theocracy, was predicted and was not restored, and the Church was not predicted but was established. Thus the two fall apart, and the one becomes the book of the kingdom, and the other, with the exception of the Gospels, the book of the Church. Besides, we get two peoples of God, the one natural and the other spiritual, the one earthly and the other heavenly, as if Jesus did not speak of "one flock and one shepherd," John 10:16, and as if Paul did not say that the Gentiles were grafted into the old olive tree, Rom. 11:17.

c. This theory is also in flagrant opposition to the Scriptural representation of the great events of the future, namely, the resurrection, the final judgment, and the end of the world. As was shown in the preceding, the Bible represents these great events as synchronizing. There is not the slightest indication that they are separated by a thousand years, except this be found in Rev. 20:4-6. They clearly coincide, Matt. 13:37-43,47-50 (separation of the good and the evil at "the end," not a thousand years before); 24:29-31; 25:31-46; John 5:25-29; I Cor. 15:22-26; Phil. 3:20,21; I Thess. 4:15,16; Rev. 20:11-15. They all occur at the coming of the Lord, which is also the day of the Lord. In answer to this objection Premillenarians often suggest that the day of the Lord may be a thousand years long, so that the resurrection of the saints and the judgment of the nations takes place in the morning of that long day, and the resurrection of the wicked and the judgment at the great white throne occurs in the evening of that same day. They appeal to II Pet. 3:8... "one day is with the Lord as a thousand years, and a thousand years as one day." But this can hardly prove the point, for the tables might easily be turned here. The same passage might also be used to prove that the thousand years of Rev. 20 are but a single day.

d. There is no positive Scriptural foundation whatsoever for the Premillennial view of a double, or even a three- or fourfold resurrection, as their theory requires, nor for spreading the last judgment over a period of a thousand years by dividing it into three judgments. It is, to say the least, very dubious that the words, "This is the first resurrection" in Rev. 20:5, refer to a physical resurrection. The context does not necessitate, nor even favor this view. What might seem to favor the theory of a double resurrection, is the fact that the apostles often speak of the resurrection of believers only, and do not refer to that of the wicked at all. But this is due to the fact that they are writing to the churches of Jesus Christ, to the connections in which they bring up the subject of the resurrection, and to the fact that they desire to stress the soteriological aspect of it, I Cor. 15; I Thess. 4:13-18. Other passages clearly speak of the resurrection of the righteous and that of the wicked in a single breath, Dan. 12:2; John 5:28,29; Acts 24:15. We shall consider this matter further in the following chapter.

e. The Premillennial theory entangles itself in all kinds of insuperable difficulties with its doctrine of the millennium. It is impossible to understand how a part of the old earth and of sinful humanity can exist alongside of a part of the new earth and of a humanity that is glorified. How can perfect saints in glorified bodies have communion with sinners in the flesh. How can glorified saints live in this sin-laden atmosphere and amid scenes of death and decay? How can the Lord of glory, the glorified Christ, establish His throne on earth as long as it has not yet been renewed. The twenty-first chapter of Revelation informs us that God and the Church of the redeemed will take up their dwelling-place on earth after heaven and earth have been renewed; how then can it be maintained that Christ and the saints will dwell there a thousand years before this renewal. How will sinners and saints in the flesh be able to stand in the presence of the glorified Christ, seeing that even Paul and John were completely overwhelmed by the vision of Him, Acts 26:12-14; Rev. 1:17? Beet truly says: "We cannot conceive mingled together on the same planet some who have yet to die and others who have passed through death and will die no more. Such confusion of the present age with the age to come is in the last degree unlikely."[1] And Brown calls out: "What a mongrel state of things is this! What an abhorred mixture of things totally inconsistent with each other!"[2]

f. The only Scriptural basis for this theory is Rev. 20:1-6, after an Old Testament content has been poured into it. This is a very precarious basis for various reasons. (1) This passage occurs in a highly symbolical book and is admittedly very obscure, as may be inferred from the different interpretations of it. (2) The literal interpretation of this passage, as given by the Premillenarians, leads to a view that finds no support elsewhere in Scripture, but is even contradicted by the rest of the New Testament. This is a fatal objection. Sound exegesis requires that the obscure passages of Scripture be read in the light of the clearer ones, and not *vice versa*. (3) Even the literal interpretation of the Premillenarians is not consistently literal, for it makes the chain in verse

1. *The Last Things*, p. 88.
2. *The Second Advent*, p. 384.

1 and consequently also the binding of verse 2 figurative, often conceives of the thousand years as a long but undefined period, and changes the souls of verse 4 into resurrection saints. (4) The passage, strictly speaking, does not say that the classes referred to (the martyr saints and those who did not worship the beast) were raised up from the dead, but simply that they lived and reigned with Christ. And this living and reigning with Christ is said to constitute the first resurrection. (5) There is absolutely no indication in these verses that Christ and His saints are seen ruling on the earth. In the light of such passages as Rev. 4:4; 6:9, it is far more likely that the scene is laid in heaven. (6) It also deserves notice that the passage makes no mention whatsoever of Palestine. of Jerusalem, of the temple, and of the Jews, the natural citizens of the millennial kingdom. There is not a single hint that these are in any way concerned with this reign of a thousand years. For a detailed interpretation of this passage from the Amillennial point of view we refer to Kuyper, Bavinck, De Moor, Dijk, Greydanus, Vos, and Hendriksen.

B. Postmillennialism.

The position of Postmillennialism is quite the opposite of that taken by Premillennialism respecting the time of the second coming of Christ. It holds that the return of Christ will follow the millennium, which may be expected during and at the close of the gospel dispensation. Immediately after it Christ will come to usher in the eternal order of things. In the discussion of Postmillennialism it will be necessary to distinguish two different forms of the theory, of which the one expects the millennium to be realized through the supernatural influence of the Holy Spirit, and the other expects it to come by a natural process of evolution.

1. DIFFERENT FORMS OF POSTMILLENNIALISM.

a. *The earlier form.* During the sixteenth and seventeenth centuries several Reformed theologians in the Netherlands taught a form of Chiliasm, which would now be called Postmillennialism. Among them were such well-known men as Coccejus, Alting, the two Vitringas, d'Outrein, Witsius, Hoornbeek, Koelman, and Brakel, of which some regarded the millennium as belonging to the past, others thought of it as present, and still others looked for it in the future. The majority expected it toward the end of the world, just before the second coming of Christ. These men rejected the two leading ideas of the Premillenarians, namely, that Christ will return physically *to reign on earth for a thousand years,* and that the saints will be raised up at His coming, and will then reign with him in the millennial kingdom. While their representations differed in some details, the prevailing view was that the gospel, which will gradually spread through the whole world, will in the end become immeasurably more effective than it is at present, and will usher in a period of rich spiritual blessings for the Church of Jesus Christ, a golden age, in which the Jews will also share in the blessings of the gospel in an unprecedented manner. In more recent years some such Postmillennialism was advocated by D. Brown, J. Berg, J. H. Snowden, T. P. Stafford, and A. H. Strong. The last named theologian says that the millennium will be "a period in the later days of the Church militant, when, under the special influence of the Holy Spirit, the spirit of the martyrs shall appear again, true religion be greatly quickened and revived, and the members of Christ's churches become so conscious of their strength in Christ that they shall, to an extent unknown before, triumph over the power of evil both within and without."[1] The golden age of the Church will, it is held, be followed by a brief apostasy, a terrible conflict between the forces of good and evil, and by the simultaneous occurrence of the advent of Christ, the general resurrection, and the final judgment.

b. *The later form.* A great deal of present day Postmillennialism is of an entirely different type, and concerns itself very little about the teachings of Scripture, except as a historical indication of what people once believed. The modern man has little patience with the millennial hopes of the past with their utter dependence on God. He does not believe that the new age will be ushered in by the preaching of the gospel and the accompanying work of the Holy Spirit; nor that it will be the result of a cataclysmic change. On the one hand it is believed that evolution will gradually bring the millennium, and on the other hand, that man himself must usher in the new age by adopting a constructive policy of world-betterment. Says Walter Rauschenbusch: "Our chief interest in any millennium is the desire for a social order in which the worth and freedom of every least human being will be honored and protected; in which the brotherhood of man will be expressed in the common possession of the economic resources of society; and in which the spiritual good of humanity will be set high above the private profit interests of all materialistic groups.... As to the way in which the Christian ideal of society is to come, — we must shift from catastrophe to development."[2] Shirley Jackson Case asks: "Shall we still look for God to introduce a new order by catastrophic means or shall we assume the responsibility of bringing about our own millennium, believing that God is working in us and in our world to will and to work for His good pleasure?" And he himself gives the answer in the following paragraphs: "The course of history exhibits one long process of evolving struggle by which humanity as a whole rises constantly higher in the scale of civilization and attainment, bettering its condition from time to time through its greater skill and industry. Viewed in the long perspective of the ages, man's career has been one of actual ascent. Instead of growing worse, the world is found to be constantly growing better . . . Since history and science show that betterment is always the result of achievement, man learns to surmise that evils still unconquered are to be eliminated by strenuous effort and gradual reform rather than by the catastrophic intervention of Deity.... Disease is to be cured or prevented by the physician's skill, society's ills are to be remedied by education and legislation, and international disasters are to be averted by establishing new standards and new methods for dealing with

---

1. *Syst. Theol.,* p. 1013.
2. *A Theology for the Social Gospel,* pp. 224 f.

the problems involved. In short, the ills of life are to be cured by a gradual process of remedial treatment rather than by a sudden annihilation."[1] These quotations are quite characteristic of a great deal of present day Postmillennialism, and it is no wonder that the Premillenarians react against it.

2. OBJECTIONS TO POSTMILLENNIALISM. There are some very serious objections to the Postmillennial theory.

a. The fundamental idea of the doctrine, that the whole world will gradually be won for Christ, that the life of all nations will in course of time be transformed by the gospel, that righteousness and peace will reign supreme, and that the blessings of the Spirit will be poured out in richer abundance than before, so that the Church will experience a season of unexampled prosperity *just before the coming of the Lord,* — is not in harmony with the picture of the end of the ages found in Scripture. The Bible teaches indeed that the gospel will spread throughout the world and will exercise a beneficent influence, but does not lead us to expect the conversion of the world, either in this or in a coming age. It stresses the fact that the time immediately preceding the end will be a time of great apostasy, of tribulation and persecution, a time when the faith of many will wax cold, and when they who are loyal to Christ will be subjected to bitter sufferings, and will in some cases even seal their confession with their blood, Matt. 24:6-14,21,22; Luke 18:8; 21:25-28; II Thess. 2:3-12; II Tim. 3:1-6; Rev. 13. Postmillennialists, of course, cannot very well ignore entirely what is said about the apostasy and the tribulation that will mark the end of history, but they minimize it and represent it as predicting an apostasy and a tribulation on a small scale, which will not affect the main course of the religious life. Their expectation of a glorious condition of the Church in the end, is based on passages which contain a figurative description, either of the gospel dispensation as a whole, or of the perfect bliss of the external Kingdom of Jesus Christ.

b. The related idea, that the present age will not end in a great cataclysmic change, but will pass almost imperceptibly into the coming age, is equally un-Scriptural. The Bible teaches us very explicitly that a catastrophe, a special intervention of God, will bring the rule of Satan on earth to an end, and will usher in the Kingdom that cannot be shaken, Matt. 24:29-31, 35-44; Heb. 12:26, 27; II Pet. 3:10-13. There will be a crisis, a change so great that it can be called "the regeneration," Matt. 19:28. No more than believers are progressively sanctified in this life until they are practically ready to pass, without much more change, into heaven, will the world gradually be purified and thus made ready to enter upon the next stage. Just as believers must still undergo a great change at death, so must the world suffer a tremendous change when the end comes. There will be a new heaven and a new earth. Rev. 21:1.

c. The modern idea that natural evolution and the efforts of man in the field of education, of social reform, and of legislation, will gradually bring in

---

1. *The Millennial Hope*, pp. 229,238 f.

the perfect reign of the Christian spirit, conflicts with everything that the Word of God teaches on this point. It is not the work of man, but the work of God to bring in the glorious Kingdom of God. This Kingdom cannot be established by natural but only by supernatural means. It is the reign of God, established and acknowledged in the hearts of His people, and this reign can never be made effective by purely natural means. Civilization without regeneration, without a supernatural change of the heart, will never bring in a millennium, an effective and glorious rule of Jesus Christ. It would seem that the experiences of the last quarter of a century should have forced this truth upon the modern man. The highly vaunted development of man has not yet brought us in sight of the millennium.

QUESTIONS FOR FURTHER STUDY: What is the historic origin of Premillennialism? Was it actually the prevailing view in the second and third centuries? What was Augustine's view of the Kingdom of God and the millennium? Are the Kingdom of God and the Church distinct or identical in Scripture? Is the one natural and national, and the other spiritual and universal? Do Luke 14:14 and 20:35 teach a partial resurrection? Will any part of Israel constitute a part of the bride of Christ? Will the bride be complete when Christ returns? Are the Postmillennialists necessarily evolutionists? Is the optimism of the Postmillennialists, that the world is gradually getting better, justified by experience? Does the Bible predict continuous progress for the Kingdom of God right up to the end of the world? Is it necessary to assume a cataclysmic change at the end?

LITERATURE: Bavinck, Geref. Dogm, IV, pp. 717-769; Kuyper, Dict. Dogm., De Consummatione Saeculi, pp. 237-279; Vos, Geref. Dogm. V, Eschatologie, pp. 36-40; id., The Pauline Eschatology, pp. 226-260; Hodge, Syst. Theol. III, pp. 861-868; Warfield, The Millennium and the Apocalypse in Biblical Studies, pp. 643-664; Dahle, Life After Death, pp. 354-418; D. Brown, The Second Advent; Ch. Brown, The Hope of His Coming; Hoekstra, Het Chiliasme; Rutgers, Premillennialism in America; Merrill, Second Coming of Christ; Eckman, When Christ Comes Again; Heagle, That Blessed Hope; Case, The Millennial Hope; Rall, Modern Premillennialism and the Christian Hope; Fairbairn, The Prophetic Prospect of the Jews (by Pieters); Berkhof, Premillennialisme; Riley, The Evolution of the Kingdom; Bultema, Maranatha; Berkhoff, De Wederkomst van Christus; Brookes, Maranatha; Haldeman, The Coming of the Lord; Snowden, The Second Coming of the Lord; Blackstone; Jesus is Coming; Milligan, Is the Kingdom Age at Hand? Peters, The Theocratic Kingdom; West, The Thousand Years in Both Testaments; Silver, The Lord's Return; Bullinger, How to Enjoy the Bible; Waldegrave, New Testament Millenarianism; Feinberg, Premillennialism and Amillennialism; Gaebelein, The Hope of the Ages; Hendriksen, More Than Conquerors; Dijk, Het Rijk der Duizend Jaren; Aalders, Het Herstel van Israel Volgens het Oude Testament; Mauro, The Gospel of the Kingdom, and The Hope of Israel; Frost; The Second Coming of Christ; Reese, The Approaching Advent of Christ; Wyngaarden, The Future of the Kingdom.

III. The Resurrection of the Dead

The discussion of the second advent of Christ naturally leads on to a consideration of its concomitants. Foremost among these is the resurrection of the dead or, as it is sometimes called, "the resurrection of the flesh."

A. The Doctrine of the Resurrection in History.

In the days of Jesus there was a difference of opinion among the Jews respecting the resurrection. While the Pharisees believed in it, the Sadducees did not, Matt. 22:23; Acts 23:8. When Paul spoke of it at Athens, he met with mockery, Acts 17:32. Some of the Corinthians denied it, I Cor. 15, and Hymenæus and Phyletus, regarding it as something purely spiritual, asserted that it was already a matter of history, II Tim. 2:18. Celsus, one of the earliest opponents of Christianity, made especially this doctrine the butt of ridicule; and the Gnostics, who regarded matter as inherently evil, naturally rejected it. Origen defended the doctrine over against the Gnostics and Celsus, but yet did not believe that the very body which was deposited in the grave would be raised up. He described the body of the resurrection as a new, refined, and spiritualized body. While some of the early Christian Fathers shared his view, the majority of them stressed the identity of the present body and the body of the resurrection. The Church already in the Apostolic Confession expressed its belief in the resurrection of the flesh (*sarkos*). Augustine was at first inclined to agree with Origen, but later on adopted the prevalent view, though he did not deem it necessary to believe that the present differences of size and stature would continue in the life to come. Jerome insisted strongly on the identity of the present and the future body. The East, represented by such men as the two Gregories, Chrysostom, and John of Damascus, manifested a tendency to adopt a more spiritual view of the resurrection than the West. Those who believed in a coming millennium spoke of a double resurrection, that of the righteous at the beginning, and that of the wicked at the end of the millennial reign. During the Middle Ages the Scholastics speculated a great deal about the body of the resurrection, but their speculations are mostly fanciful and of little value. Thomas Aquinas especially seemed to have special information about the nature of the resurrection body, and about the order and manner of the resurrection. The theologians of the period of the Reformation were generally agreed that the body of the resurrection would be identical with the present body. All the great Confessions of the Church represent the general resurrection as simultaneous with the second coming of Christ, the final judgment and the end of the world. They do not separate any of these events, such as the resurrection of the righteous and that of the wicked, and the coming of Christ and the end of the world, by a period of a thousand years. The Premillenarians, on the other hand, insist on such a separation. Under the influence of Rationalism and with the advance of the physical sciences some of the difficulties with which the doctrine of the resurrection is burdened were accentuated, and as a result modern religious liberalism denies the resurrection of the flesh, and explains the Scriptural representations of it as a figurative representation of the idea that the full human personality will continue to exist after death.

B. Scriptural Proof for the Resurrection.

1. IN THE OLD TESTAMENT. It is sometimes said that the Old Testament knowns of no resurrection of the dead, or knows of it only in its latest books. The opinion is rather common that Israel borrowed its belief in the resurrection from the Persians. Says Mackintosh: "Strong evidence exists for the hypothesis that the idea of the resurrection entered the Hebrew mind from Persia."[1] Brown speaks in a somewhat similar vein: "The doctrine of individual resurrection first appears in Israel after the exile, and may have been due to Persian influence."[2] Salmond also mentions this view, but claims that it is not sufficiently warranted. Says he: "The Old Testament doctrine of God is of itself enough to explain the entire history of the Old Testament conception of a future life."[3] De Bondt comes to the conclusion that there is not a single people among those with whom Israel came in contact, which had a doctrine of the resurrection that might have served as a pattern for the representation of it that was current among Israel; and that the faith in the resurrection which finds expression in the Old Testament does not find its basis in the religions of the Gentiles, but in the revelation of Israel's God.[4] It is true that we find no clear statements respecting the resurrection of the dead before the time of the prophets, though Jesus found that it was already implied in Ex. 3:6; cf. Matt. 22:29-32, and the writer of Hebrews intimates that even the patriarchs looked forward to the resurrection of the dead, Heb. 11:10,13-16,19. Certainly evidences are not wanting that there was a belief in the resurrection long before the exile. It is implied in the passages that speak of a deliverance from *sheol*, Ps. 49:15; 73:24,25; Prov. 23:14. It finds expression in the famous statement of Job, 19:25-27. Moreover, it is very clearly taught in Isa. 26:19 (a late passage, according to the critics), and in Dan. 12:2, and is probably implied also in Ezek. 37: 1-14.

2. IN THE NEW TESTAMENT. As might be expected, the New Testament has more to say on the resurrection of the dead than the Old, because it brings the climax of God's revelation on this point in the resurrection of Jesus Christ. Over against the denial of the Sadducees, Jesus argues the resurrection of the dead from the Old Testament, Matt. 22:23-33, and parallels, cf. Ex. 3:6. More-

---

1. *Immortality and the Future*, p. 34.
2. *Christian Theology in Outline*, pp. 251 f.
3. *The Christian Doctrine of Immortality*, pp. 221 f.
4. *Wat Leert het Oude Testament Aangaande het Leven na dit Leven*, pp. 263 f.

over, He teaches that great truth very clearly in John 5:25-29; 6:39,40,44,54; 11:24,25; 14:3; 17:24. The classical passage of the New Testament for the doctrine of the resurrection is I Cor. 15. Other important passages are: I Thess. 4:13-16; II Cor. 5:1-10; Rev. 20:4-6 (of dubious interpretation), and 20:13.

C. The Nature of the Resurrection.

1. IT IS A WORK OF THE TRIUNE GOD. The resurrection is a work of the triune God. In some cases we are simply told that God raises the dead, no person being specified, Matt. 22:29; II Cor. 1:9. More particularly, however, the work of the resurrection is ascribed to the Son, John 5:21,25,28,29; 6:38-40, 44,54; I Thess. 4:16. Indirectly, it is also designated as a work of the Holy Spirit, Rom. 8:11.

2. IT IS A PHYSICAL OR BODILY RESURRECTION. There were some in the days of Paul who regarded the resurrection as spiritual, II Tim. 2:18. And there are many in the present day who believe only in a spiritual resurrection. But the Bible is very explicit in teaching the resurrection of the body. Christ is called the "firstfruits" of the resurrection, I Cor. 15:20,23, and "the firstborn of the dead," Col. 1:18; Rev. 1:5. This implies that the resurrection of the people of God will be like that of their heavenly Lord. His resurrection was a bodily resurrection, and theirs will be of the same kind. Moreover, the redemption wrought by Christ is also said to include the body, Rom. 8:23; I Cor. 6:13-20. In Rom. 8:11 we are told explicitly that God through His Spirit will raise up our mortal bodies. And it is clearly the body that is prominently before the mind of the apostle in I Cor. 15, cf. especially the verses 35-49. According to Scripture there will be a *resurrection* of the body, that is, not an entirely new creation, but a body that will be in a fundamental sense identical with the present body. God will not create a new body for every man, but will raise up the very body that was deposited in the earth. This cannot only be inferred from the term "resurrection," but is clearly stated in Rom. 8:11, I Cor. 15:53, and is further implied in the figure of the seed sown in the earth, which the apostle employs in I Cor. 15:36-38. Moreover, Christ, the firstfruits of the resurrection, conclusively proved the identity of His body to His disciples. At the same time Scripture makes it perfectly evident that the body will be greatly changed. Christ's body was not yet fully glorified during the period of transition between the resurrection and the ascension; yet it had already undergone a remarkable change. Paul refers to the change that will take place, when he says that in sowing a seed we do not sow the body that shall be; we do not intend to pick the same seed out of the ground. Yet we do expect to reap something that is in a fundamental sense identical with the seed deposited in the earth. While there is a certain identity between the seed sown and the seeds that develop out of it, yet there is also a remarkable difference. We shall be changed, says the apostle, "for this corruptible must put on incorruption, and this mortal must put on immortality." The body "is sown in corruption; it is raised in incorruption: it is sown in dishonor; it is raised in

power; it is sown a natural body; it is raised a spiritual body." Change is not inconsistent with the retention of identity. We are told that even now every particle in our bodies changes every seven years, but through it all the body retains its identity. There will be a certain physical connection between the old body and the new, but the nature of this connection is not revealed. Some theologians speak of a remaining germ from which the new body develops; others say that the organizing principle of the body remains. Origen had something of that kind in mind; so did Kuyper and Milligan. If we bear all this in mind, the old objection against the doctrine of the resurrection, namely, that it is impossible that a body could be raised up, consisting of the same particles that constituted it at death, since these particles pass into other forms of existence and perhaps into hundreds of other bodies, loses its force completely.

3. IT IS A RESURRECTION OF BOTH THE RIGHTEOUS AND THE WICKED. According to Josephus the Pharisees denied the resurrection of the wicked.[1] The doctrine of annihilationism and that of conditional immortality, both of which, at least in some of their forms, deny the resurrection of the ungodly and teach their annihilation, embraced by many theologians, has also found favor in such sects as Adventism and Millennial Dawnism. They believe in the total extinction of the wicked. The assertion is sometimes made that Scripture does not teach the resurrection of the wicked, but this is clearly erroneous, Dan. 12:2; John 5:28,29; Acts 24:15; Rev. 20:13-15. At the same time it must be admitted that their resurrection does not stand out prominently in Scripture. The soteriological aspect of the resurrection is clearly in the foreground, and this pertains to the righteous only. They, in distinction from the wicked, are the ones that profit by the resurrection.

4. IT IS A RESURRECTION OF UNEQUAL IMPORT FOR THE JUST AND THE UNJUST. Breckenridge quotes I Cor. 15:22 to prove that the resurrection of both saints and sinners was purchased by Christ. But it can hardly be denied that the second "all" in that passage is general only in the sense of "all who are in Christ." The resurrection is represented there as resulting from a vital union with Christ. But, surely, only believers stand in such a living relation to Him. The resurrection of the wicked cannot be regarded as a blessing merited by the mediatorial work of Christ, though it is connected with this indirectly. It is a necessary result of postponing the execution of the sentence of death on man, which made the work of redemption possible. The postponement resulted in the comparative separation of temporal and eternal death, and in the existence of an intermediate state. Under these circumstances it becomes necessary to raise the wicked from the dead, in order that death in its widest extent and in all its weight might be imposed on them. Their resurrection is not an act of redemption, but of sovereign justice, on the part of God. The resurrection of the just and the unjust have this in common, that in both bodies and souls are

---

1. *Ant. XVIII.* 1,3; *Wars* II. 8.14.

re-united. But in the case of the former this results in perfect life, while in the case of the latter it issues in the extreme penalty of death, John 5:28,29.

D. The Time of the Resurrection.

1. THE PREMILLENNIAL VIEW RESPECTING THE TIME OF THE RESURREC-TION. It is the common opinion among Premillenarians that the resurrection of the saints will be separated by a thousand years from that of the wicked. They almost seem to regard it as an axiomatic truth that these two classes cannot possibly arise at the same time. And not only that, but the type of Premillennialism which is now dominant, with its theory of a twofold second coming of Christ, feels the need of positing a third resurrection. All the saints of former dispensations and of the present dispensation are raised up at the parousia or the coming of the Lord. Those still alive at that time are changed in a moment, in the twinkling of an eye. But in the seven years that follow the parousia many other saints die, especially in the great tribulation. These must also be raised up, and their resurrection will occur at the revelation of the day of the Lord, seven years after the parousia. But even at this point Premillenarians cannot very well stop. Since the resurrection at the end of the world is reserved for the wicked, there must be another resurrection of the saints who die during the millennium, which precedes that of the wicked, for the two cannot be raised up at the same time.

2. SCRIPTURAL INDICATIONS AS TO THE TIME OF THE RESURRECTION. According to Scripture the resurrection of the dead coincides with the parousia, with the revelation or the day of the Lord, and with the end of the world, and will immediately precede the general and final judgment. It certainly does not favor the premillennial distinctions with respect to this doctrine. In several places it represents the resurrection of the righteous and that of the wicked as contemporaneous, Dan. 12:2; John 5:28,29; Acts 24:15; Rev. 20:13-15. All of these passages speak of the resurrection as a single event and do not contain the slightest indication that the resurrection of the righteous and that of the wicked will be separated by a period of a thousand years. But this is not all that can be said in favor of the idea that the two coincide. In John 5:21-29 Jesus combines the thought of the resurrection, including the resurrection of the righteous, with the thought of the judgment, including the judgment of the wicked. Moreover, II Thess. 1:7-10 clearly represents the parousia (vs. 10), the revelation (vs. 7), and the judgment of the wicked (vs. 8,9) as coinciding. If that is not the case, language would seem to have lost its meaning. Furthermore, the resurrection *of believers* is directly connected with the second coming of the Lord in I Cor. 15:23; Phil. 3:20,21; and I Thess. 4:16, but it is also represented as occurring at the end of the world, John 6:39,40,44,54 or at the last day. That means that believers are raised up at the last day, and that the last day is also the day of the coming of the Lord. Their resurrection does not precede the end by a period of a thousand years. Happily, there are several Premillenarians who do not accept the theory of a threefold resurrection, but who nevertheless cling to the doctrine of a double resurrection.

3. CONSIDERATION OF THE ARGUMENTS FOR A DOUBLE RESURRECTION.

a. Great emphasis is placed on the fact that Scripture, while speaking in general of the resurrection *ton nekron,* that is, "of the dead," repeatedly refers to the resurrection of believers as a resurrection *ek nekron,* that is, "out of the dead." Premillenarians render this expression, "from among the dead," so that it would imply that many dead still remain in the grave. Lightfoot also asserts that this expression refers to the resurrection of believers, but Kennedy says, "There is absolutely no evidence for this definite assertion." This is also the conclusion to which Dr. Vos comes after a careful study of the relevant passages. In general it may be said that the assumption that the expression *he anastasis ek nekron* should be rendered "the resurrection from among the dead," is entirely gratuitous. The standard lexicons know nothing of such a rendering; and Cremer-Koegel interprets the expression to mean "from the state of the dead," and this would seem to be the most natural interpretation. It should be noted that Paul uses the terms interchangeably in I Cor. 15. Though speaking of the resurrection of believers only, he evidently does not seek to stress the fact that this is of a specific character, for he uses the more general term repeatedly, I Cor. 15:12,13,21,42.[1]

b. Premillenarians also appeal to certain specific expressions, such as "a better resurrection," Heb. 11:35, "the resurrection of life," John 5:29, "the resurrection of the just," Luke 14:14, and "the resurrection of the dead in Christ," I Thess. 4:16, — all of which refer to the resurrection of believers only. These expressions seem to set that resurrection off as something apart. But these passages merely prove that the Bible distinguishes the resurrection of the righteous from that of the wicked and afford no proof whatsoever that there will be two resurrections, separated from each other by a period of a thousand years. The resurrection of the people of God differs from that of unbelievers in its moving principle, in its essential nature, and in its final issue, and can therefore very well be represented as something distinctive and to be desired far above the resurrection of the wicked. The former does, and the latter does not, deliver men from the power of death. In spite of their resurrection unbelievers remain in the state of death.

c. One of the principal proof passages of the Premillenarians for a double resurrection is found in I Cor. 15:22-24: "For as in Adam all die, so also in Christ shall all be made alive. But each one in his own order: Christ the firstfruits; then they that are Christ's, at His coming. Then cometh the end, when He shall deliver up the kingdom to God, even the Father." In this passage they find three stages of the resurrection indicated, namely, (1) the resurrection of Christ; (2) the resurrection of believers; and (3) the end (as they interpret it) of the resurrection, that is, the resurrection of the wicked. Silver puts it rather picturesquely: "In the resurrection Christ and many saints who rise in and around Jerusalem appear as the first band. More than

---

1. *Cf. also Waldegrave, New Testament Millenarianism,* pp. 575 f.

1900 years afterwards 'they that are Christ's, at His coming' appear as the second band. 'Then,' but not immediately, 'cometh the end' (verse 24), the last great body like a band of forlorn creatures ending the procession."[1] It will be noted that the idea "not immediately" is carried into the text. The argument is that because *epeita* (then) in verse 23 refers to a time at least 1900 years later, the word *eita* (then) in verse 24 refers to a time 1000 years later. But this is a mere assumption without any proof. The words *epeita* and *eita* do indeed mean the same thing, but neither one of them *necessarily* implies the idea of a long intervening period. Notice the use of *epeita* in Luke 16:7 and Jas. 4:14, and that of *eita* in Mark 8:25; John 13:5; 19:27; 20:27. Both words can be used for that which will immediately occur and for that which will occur only after some time, so that it is a pure assumption that the resurrection of believers will be separated by a long period of time from the end. Another gratuitous assumption is that "the end" means "the end of the resurrection." According to the analogy of Scripture it points to the end of the world, the consummation, the time when Christ will deliver up the kingdom to the Father and will have put all enemies under His feet. This is the view adopted by such commentators as Alford, Godet, Hodge, Bachmann, Findley, Robertson and Plummer, and Edwards.[2]

d. Another passage to which the Premillenarians appeal is I Thess. 4:16, "For the Lord Himself shall descend from heaven with a shout, with the voice of the archangel, and with the trump of God: and the dead in Christ shall rise first." From this they infer that those who did not die in Christ will be raised up at a later date. But it is perfectly clear that this is not the antithesis which the apostle has in mind. The statement following is not, "Then the dead who are not in Christ shall arise," but, "Then we that are alive, that are left, shall together with them be caught up in the air: and so shall we ever be with the Lord." This is frankly admitted by Biederwolf.[3] Both in this passage and in the preceding one Paul is speaking of the resurrection of believers only; that of the wicked is not in his purview at all.

e. The most important passage to which the Premillenarians refer is Rev. 20:4-6:... "and they lived and reigned with Christ a thousand years. The rest of the dead lived not until the thousand years should be finished. This is the first resurrection." Here the verses 5 and 6 make mention of a first resurrection, and this, it is said, implies that there will be a second. But the supposition that the writer is here speaking of a bodily resurrection is extremely dubious. The scene in the verses 4-6 is evidently laid, not on earth, but in heaven. And the terms employed are not suggestive of a bodily resurrection. The seer does not speak of persons or bodies that were raised up, but of souls which "lived"

---

1. *The Lord's Return*, p. 230.
2. For a further discussion of this whole point cf. Salmond, *Christian Doctrine of Immortality*, pp. 414 f.; Milligan, *The Resurrection of the Dead*, pp. 64 ff.; Vos, *Pauline Eschatology*, pp. 241 ff.
3. *Millennium Bible*, p. 472.

and "reigned." And he calls their living and reigning with Christ "the first resurrection." Dr. Vos suggests that the words, "*This* (emphatic) is the first resurrection," may even be "a pointed disavowal of a more realistic (chiliastic) interpretation of the same phrase."[1] In all probability the expression refers to the entrance of the souls of the saints upon the glorious state of life with Christ at death. The absence of the idea of a double resurrection may well make us hesitate to affirm its presence in this obscure passage of a book so full of symbolism as the Revelation of John. Wherever the Bible mentions the resurrection of the righteous and the wicked together. as in Dan. 12:2; John 5:28.29; Acts 24:15, it does not contain the slightest hint that the two are to be separated by a thousand years. On the other hand it does teach that the resurrection will take place at the last day, and will at once be followed by the last judgment. Matt. 25:31,32; John 5:27-29; 6:39,40,44,54; 11:24; Rev. 20:11-15.

QUESTIONS FOR FURTHER STUDY: Does the Apostolic Confession speak of the resurrection of the body, or of the resurrection of the flesh? How do you account for the change from the one to the other? Do not all Premillenarians have to posit another resurrection of the righteous in addition to those that occur at the parousia and at the revelation? How do Premillenarians construe even Dan. 12:2 into an argument for a double resurrection? How do they find an argument for it in Phil. 3:11? What is the principal argument of modern liberals against the doctrine of a physical resurrection? What does Paul mean, when he speaks of the resurrection body as a *soma pneumatikon,* I Cor. 15:44?

LITERATURE: Bavinck, *Geref. Dogm.* IV, pp. 755-758, 770-777; Kuyper, *Dict. Dogm.,* *De Consummatione Saeculi,* pp. 262-279; Vos, *Geref. Dogm. V. Eschatologie,* pp. 14-22; *ibid. The Pauline Eschatology,* pp. 136-225; Hodge, *Syst. Theol.* III, pp. 837-844; Dabney, *Syst. and Polem. Theol.,* pp. 829-841; Shedd. *Dogm. Theol.* pp. 641-658; Valentine, *Chr. Theol.* II, pp. 414-420; Dahle, *Life After Death,* pp. 358-368, 398-418; Hovey, *Eschatology,* pp. 23-78; Mackintosh, *Immortality and the Future,* pp. 164-179; Snowden, *The Coming of the Lord,* pp. 172-191; Salmond, *The Chr. Doct. of Immortality,* pp. 262-272, 437-459; Kennedy, *St. Paul's Conceptions of the Last Things,* pp. 222-281; Kliefoth, *Eschatologie,* pp. 248-275; Brown, *The Chr. Hope,* pp. 89-108; Milligan. *The Resurrection of the Dead,* pp. 61-77.

---

1. ISBE, Art. *Esch. of the N. T.*

IV. The Final Judgment

Another one of the important concomitants of the return of Christ is the last judgment, which will be of a general nature. The Lord is coming again for the very purpose of judging the living and consigning each individual to his eternal destiny.

A. The Doctrine of the Last Judgment in History.

The doctrine of a final general judgment was from the very earliest times of the Christian era connected with that of the resurrection of the dead. The general opinion was that the dead would be raised up, in order to be judged according to the deeds done in the body. As a solemn warning the certainty of this judgment was stressed. This doctrine is already contained in the Apostolic Confession: "From thence He shall come to judge the living and the dead." The prevailing idea was that this judgment would be accompanied with the destruction of the world. On the whole the early Church Fathers did not speculate much about the nature of the final judgment, though Tertullian forms an exception. Augustine sought to interpret some of the figurative statements of Scripture respecting the judgment. In the Middle Ages the Scholastics discussed the matter in greater detail. They, too, believed that the resurrection of the dead would be followed immediately by the general judgment, and that this would mark the end of time for man. It will be general in the sense that all rational creatures will appear in it, and that it will bring a general revelation of each one's deeds, both good and evil. Christ will be the Judge, while others will be associated with Him in the judgment; not, however, as judges in the strict sense of the word. Immediately after the judgment there will be a universal conflagration. We leave out of consideration some of the other particulars here. The Reformers shared this view in general, but added little or nothing to the prevailing view. The same view is found in all the Protestant Confessions, which explicitly affirm that there will be a day of judgment at the end of the world, but do not enter into details. It has been the official view of the Churches up to the present time. This does not mean that no other views found expression. Kant inferred from the categorical imperative the existence of a supreme Judge who would right all wrongs in some future life. Schelling in his famous dictum, "The history of the world is the judgment of the world," evidently regarded the judgment merely as a present immanent process. Some were not inclined to grant the moral constitution of the universe, did not believe that history was moving on to some moral termination, and thus denied the future judgment. This idea was given a philosophical construction by Von Hartmann. In modern liberal theology, with its emphasis on the fact that God is immanent in all the processes of history, there is a strong tendency to regard the judgment primarily, if not exclusively, as a present immanent process. Says Beckwith: "In his (God's) dealing with men there is no holding in abeyance, no suspension of any attribute of his being. The judgment is, therefore, no more truly future than it is present. So far as God is the author of it, it is as constant and perpetual as his action in human life. To postpone the judgment to a future public hour is to misconceive of justice, as if it were dormant or suspended, wholly bound up with outward conditions. On the contrary the sphere of justice must be sought not first without but within, in the inner life, in the world of consciousness."[1] Dispensationalists believe whole-heartedly in the future judgment. but speak of judgments in the plural. According to them there will be one judgment at the parousia, another at the revelation of Christ, and still another at the end of the world.

B. The Nature of the Final Judgment.

The final judgment of which the Bible speaks may not be regarded as a spiritual, invisible and endless process, which is identical with God's providence in history. This is not equivalent to a denial of the fact that there is a providential judgment of God in the vicissitudes of individuals and nations, though it may not always be recognized as such. The Bible clearly teaches us that God even in the present life visits evil with punishment and rewards the good with blessings, and these punishments and rewards are in some cases positive, but in other instances appear as the natural providential results of the evil committed or of the good done, Deut. 9:5; Ps. 9:16; 37:28; 59:13; Prov. 11:5; 14:11; Isa. 32:16,17; Lam. 5:7. The human conscience also testifies to this fact. But it is also manifest from Scripture that the judgments of God in the present are not final. The evil sometimes continues without due punishment, and the good is not always rewarded with the promised blessings in this life. The wicked in the days of Malachi were emboldened to cry out, "Where is the God of judgment?" Mal. 2:17. The complaint was heard in those days: "It is vain to serve God; and what profit is it that we have kept His charge, and that we have walked mournfully before Jehovah of Hosts? And now we call the proud happy; yea, they that work wickedness are built up; yea, they tempt God and escape," Mal. 3:14,15. Job and his friends were wrestling with the problem of the sufferings of the righteous, and so was Asaph in the 73rd Psalm. The Bible teaches us to look forward to a final judgment as the decisive answer of God to all such questions, as the solution of all such problems, and as the removal of all the apparent discrepancies of the present, Matt. 25:31-46; John 5:27-29; Acts 25:24; Rom. 2:5-11; Heb. 9:27; 10:27; II Pet. 3:7; Rev. 20:11-15. These passages do not refer to a process, but to a very definite event at the end of time. It is represented as accompanied by other historical events, such as the coming of Jesus Christ, the resurrection of the dead, and the renewal of heaven and earth.

---

1. *Realities of Christian Theology*, pp. 362 f.

C. Erroneous Views Respecting the Judgment.

1. THE JUDGMENT PURELY METAPHORICAL. According to Schleiermacher and many other German scholars the Biblical descriptions of the last judgment are to be understood as symbolical indications of the fact that the world and the Church will finally be separated. This explanation serves to evaporate the whole idea of a forensic judgment for the public determination of the final state of man. It is an explanation which surely does not do justice to the strong statements of Scripture respecting the future judgment as a *formal, public, and final declaration.*

2. THE JUDGMENT EXCLUSIVELY IMMANENT. Schelling's dictum that "the history of the world is the judgment of the world" undoubtedly contains an element of truth. There are, as was pointed out in the preceding, manifestations of the retributive justice of God in the history of nations and individuals. The rewards or punishments may be of a positive character, or may be the natural result of the good or evil done. But when many liberal scholars claim that the divine judgment is wholly immanent and is determined entirely by the moral order of the world, they certainly fail to do justice to the representations of Scripture. Their view of the judgment as "self-acting" makes God an otiose God, who merely looks on and approves of the distribution of rewards and punishments. It completely destroys the idea of the judgment as an outward and visible event, which will occur at some definite time in the future. Moreover, it cannot satisfy the longings of the human heart for perfect justice. Historical judgments are always only partial and sometimes impress men as a travesty on justice. There always has been and still is occasion for the perplexity of Job and Asaph.

3. THE JUDGMENT NOT A SINGLE EVENT. Present day Premillenarians speak of three different future judgments. They distinguish: (a) A judgment of the risen and living saints at the parousia or the coming of the Lord, which serves the purpose of vindicating the saints publicly, rewarding each one according to his works, and assigning to them their respective places in the coming millennial kingdom. (b) A judgment at the revelation of Christ (the day of the Lord), immediately after the great tribulation, in which, according to the prevailing view, the Gentile nations are judged *as nations,* according to the attitude they have assumed to the evangelizing remnant of Israel (the least of the brethren of the Lord). The entrance of these nations into the kingdom depends on the outcome. This is the judgment mentioned in Matt. 25:31-46. It is separated from the earlier judgment by a period of seven years. (c) A judgment of the wicked dead before the great white throne, described in Rev. 20:11-15. The dead are judged according to their works, and these determine the degree of punishment which they will receive. This judgment will be more than a thousand years later than the preceding one. It should be noted, however, that the Bible always speaks of the future judgment as a single event. It teaches us to look forward, not to days, but to *the day* of judgment, John

5:28,29; Acts 17:31; II Pet. 3:7, also called "that day," Matt. 7:22; II Tim. 4:8, and "the day of wrath and revelation of the righteous judgment of God," Rom. 2:5. Premillenarians feel the force of this argument, for they reply that it may be a day of a thousand years. Moreover, there are passages of Scripture from which it is abundantly evident that the righteous and the wicked appear in judgment together for a final separation, Matt. 7:22,23; 25:31-46 Rom. 2:5-7; Rev. 11:18; 20:11-15. Furthermore, it should be noted that the judgment *of the wicked* is represented as a concomitant of the parousia and also of the revelation, II Thess. 1:7-10; II Pet. 3:4-7. And, finally, it should be borne in mind that God does not judge the nations *as nations* where eternal issues are at stake, but only individuals; and that a final separation of the righteous and the wicked cannot possibly be made until the end of the world. It is hard to see how anyone can give a tolerable and self-consistent interpretation of Matt. 25:31-46, except on the supposition that the judgment referred to is the universal judgment of all men, and that they are judged, not as nations, but as individuals. Even Meyer and Alford who are themselves Premillenarians consider this to be the only tenable exposition.

4. THE FINAL JUDGMENT UNNECESSARY. Some regard the final judgment as entirely unnecessary, because each man's destiny is determined at the time of his death. If a man fell asleep in Jesus, he is saved; and if he died in his sins, he is lost. Since the matter is settled, no further judicial inquiry is necessary, and therefore such a final judgment is quite superfluous. But the certainty of the future judgment does not depend on our conception of its necessity. God clearly teaches us in His Word that there will be a final judgment, and that settles the matter for all those who recognize the Bible as the final standard of faith. Moreover, the underlying assumption on which this argument proceeds, namely, that the final judgment is for the purpose of ascertaining what should be the future state of man, is entirely erroneous. It will serve the purpose rather of displaying before all rational creatures the declarative glory of God in a formal, forensic act, which magnifies on the one hand His holiness and righteousness, and on the other hand, His grace and mercy. Moreover, it should be borne in mind that the judgment at the last day will differ from that at the death of each individual in more than one respect. It will not be secret, but public; it will not pertain to the soul only. but also to the body; it will not have reference to a single individual, but to all men.

D. The Judge and His Assistants.

Naturally, the final judgment, like all God's *opera ad extra,* is a work of the triune God, but Scripture ascribes it particularly to Christ. Christ in His mediatorial capacity will be the future Judge, Matt. 25:31,32; John 5:27; Acts 10:42; 17:31; Phil. 2:10; II Tim. 4:1. Such passages as Matt. 28:18; John 5:27; Phil. 2:9,10, make it abundantly evident that the honor of judging the living and the dead was conferred on Christ as Mediator in reward for His atoning work and as a part of His exaltation. This may be regarded as one of the crowning honors of His kingship. In His capacity as Judge, too, Christ is saving His people to the uttermost: He completes their redemption, justifies them publicly, and removes the last consequences of sin. From such passages as Matt. 13:41,42; 24:31; 25:31, it may be inferred that the angels will assist Him in this great work. Evidently, the saints will in some sense sit and judge with Christ, Ps. 149:5-9; I Cor. 6:2,3; Rev. 20:4. It is hard to say just what this will involve. It has been interpreted to mean that the saints will condemn the world by their faith, just as the Ninevites would have condemned the unbelieving cities of Jesus' day; or that they will merely concur in the judgment of Christ. But the argument of Paul in I Cor. 6:2,3 would seem to require something more than this, for neither of the two suggested interpretations would prove that the Corinthians were capable of judging the matters that arose in the Church. Though the saints cannot be expected to know all those who appear in judgment and to apportion the penalties, yet they will have some real active share in the judgment of Christ, though it is impossible to say just what this will be.

E. The parties that will be judged.

Scripture contains clear indications of at least two parties that will be judged. It is quite evident that the fallen angels will stand before the tribunal of God, Matt. 8:29; I Cor. 6:3; II Pet. 2:4; Jude 6. Satan and his demons will meet their final doom in the day of judgment. It is also perfectly clear that every individual of the human race will have to appear before the judgment seat, Eccl. 12:14; Ps. 50:4-6; Matt. 12:36,37; 25:32; Rom. 14:10; II Cor. 5:10; Rev. 20:12. These passages certainly leave no room for the view of the Pelagians and of those who follow in their wake, that the final judgment will be limited to those who have enjoyed the privileges of the gospel. Neither do they favor the idea of those sectarians who hold that the righteous will not be called into judgment. When Jesus says in John 5:24, "Verily, verily, I say unto you, He that heareth my word and believeth Him that sent me, hath everlasting life, and cometh not into judgment, but hath passed out of death into life," he clearly means in view of the context, that the believer cometh not into *condemnatory* judgment. But it is sometimes objected that the sins of believers, which are pardoned, certainly will not be published at that time; but Scripture leads us to expect that they will be, though they will, of course, be revealed as *pardoned* sins. Men will be judged for "every idle word," Matt. 12:36, and for "every secret thing," Rom. 2:16; I Cor. 4:5, and there is no indication whatsoever that this will be limited to the wicked. Moreover, it is perfectly evident from such passages as Matt. 13:30,40-43,49; 25:14-23,34-40,46, that the righteous will appear before the judgment seat of Christ. It is more difficult to determine, whether the good angels will be subject to the final judgment in any sense of the word. Dr. Bavinck is inclined to infer from I Cor. 6:3 that they will be; but this passage does not prove the point. It might do this, if the word *aggelous* were preceded by the article, which is not the case. We simply read, "Know ye not that we shall judge angels?" Because of the uncertainty connected with this matter, it is better to be silent. The more so, since the angels are clearly represented only as ministers of Christ in connection with the work of judgment, Matt. 13:30,41; 25:31; II Thess. 1:7,8.

F. The Time of the Judgment.

Though the time of the future judgment cannot be determined absolutely, it can be fixed relatively, that is, relative to other eschatological events. It will clearly be at the end of the present world, for it will be a judgment passed on the whole life of every man, Matt. 13:40-43; II Pet. 3:7. Moreover, it will be a concomitant of the coming (parousia) of Jesus Christ, Matt. 25:19-46; II Thess. 1:7-10; II Pet. 3:9,10, and will follow immediately after the resurrection of the dead, Dan. 12:2; John 5:28,29; Rev. 20:12,13. The question whether it will immediately precede, be coincident with, or immediately follow, the renewal of heaven and earth, cannot be settled conclusively on the basis of Scripture. Rev. 20:11 would seem to indicate that the transformation of the universe will take place when the judgment begins; II Pet. 3:7, that the two will synchronize; and Rev. 21:1, that the renewal of heaven and earth will follow the judgment. We can only speak of them in a general way as concomitants. It is equally impossible to determine the exact duration of the judgment. Scripture speaks of "the day of judgment," Matt. 11:22; 12:36, "that day," Matt. 7:22; II Thess. 1:10; II Tim. 1:12, and "the day of wrath," Rom. 2:5; Rev. 11:8. We need not infer from these and similar passages that it will be a day of exactly twenty-four hours, since the word "day" is also used in a more indefinite sense in Scripture. On the other hand, however, the interpretation of some of the Premillenarians, that it is a designation of the whole millennial period, cannot be regarded as a plausible one. When the word "day" is used to denote a period, it is a period which is, as a whole, characterized by some special characteristic, usually indicated by the genitive that follows the word. Thus "the day of trouble" is the period that is characterized throughout by trouble, and "the day of salvation" is the period which is in its entirety noted for its outstanding display of God's favour or grace. And it certainly cannot be said that the millennial period of the Premillenarians, while beginning and ending with a judgment, is throughout a period of judgment. It is rather a period of joy, of righteousness and of peace. The outstanding characteristic of it is certainly not that of judgment.

G. The Standard of Judgment.

The standard by which saints and sinners are judged will evidently be the revealed will of God. This is not the same for all. Some have been privileged above others, and this naturally adds to their responsibility, Matt. 11:21-24: Rom. 2:12-16. This does not mean that there will be different conditions of salvation for different classes of people. For all those who appear in judgment entrance into, or exclusion from, heaven, will depend on the question, whether they are clothed with the righteousness of Jesus Christ. But there will be different degrees, both of the bliss of heaven and of the punishment of hell.

And these degrees will be determined by what is done in the flesh, Matt. 11:22,24; Luke 12:47,48; 20:47; Dan. 12:3; II Cor. 9-6. The Gentiles will be judged by the law of nature, inscribed in their hearts, the Israelites of the old dispensation by the Old Testament revelation and by that only, and those who have enjoyed, besides the light of nature and the revelation of the Old Testament, the light of the gospel, will be judged according to the greater light which they have received. God will give to every man his due.

H. The Different Parts of the Judgment.

Here we should distinguish:

1. THE COGNITIO CAUSAE. God will take cognizance of the state of affairs, of the whole past life of man, including even the thoughts and secret intents of the heart. This is symbolically represented in Scripture as the opening of the books, Dan. 7:10; Rev. 20:12. The pious of the days of Malachi spoke of a book of remembrance written before God, Mal. 3:16. It is a figurative description which is added to complete the idea of the judgment. A judge usually has the book of the law and the record of those who appear before him. In all probability the figure in this case simply refers to the omniscience of God. Some speak of the book of God's Word as the statute book, and of the book of remembrance as the book of predestination, God's private record. But it is very doubtful whether we should particularize in that fashion.

2. THE SENTENTIAE PROMULGATIO. There will be promulgation of the sentence. The day of judgment is the day of wrath, and of the revelation of the righteous judgment of God, Rom. 2:5. All must be revealed before the tribunal of the supreme Judge, II Cor. 5:10. The sense of justice demands this. The sentence pronounced upon each person will not be secret, will not be known to that person only, but will be publicly proclaimed, so that at least those in any way concerned will know. Thus the righteousness and grace of God will shine out in all their splendor.

3. THE SENTENTIAE EXECUTIO. The sentence of the righteous will convey everlasting blessedness, and that of the wicked everlasting misery. The Judge will divide mankind into two parts, as a shepherd separates the sheep from the goats, Matt. 25:32 ff. In view of what will be said of their final state in the following chapter, nothing more need be added here.

V. The Final State

The last judgment determines, and therefore naturally leads on to, the final state of those who appear before the judgment seat. Their final state is either one of everlasting misery or one of eternal blessedness.

A. The Final State of the Wicked.

There are especially three points that call for consideration here:

1. THE PLACE TO WHICH THE WICKED ARE CONSIGNED. In present day theology there is an evident tendency in some circles to rule out the idea of eternal punishment. The Annihilationists, which are still represented in such sects as Adventism and Millennial Dawnism, and the advocates of conditional immortality, deny the continued existence of the wicked, and thereby render a place of eternal punishment unnecessary. In modern liberal theology the word "hell" is generally regarded as a figurative designation of a purely subjective condition, in which men may find themselves even while on earth, and which may become permanent in the future. But these interpretations certainly do not do justice to the data of Scripture. There can be no reasonable doubt as to the fact that the Bible teaches the continued existence of the wicked, Matt. 24:5; 25:30,46; Luke 16:19-31. Moreover, in connection with the subject of "hell" the Bible certainly uses local terms right along. It calls the place of torment *gehenna*, a name derived from the Hebrew *ge* (land, or valley) and *hinnom or beney hinnom*, that is, Hinnom or sons of Hinnom. This name was originally applied to a valley southwest of Jerusalem. It was the place where wicked idolators sacrificed their children to Moloch by causing them to pass through the fire. Hence it was considered impure and was called in later days "the valley of *tophet* (spittle), as an utterly despised region. Fires were constantly burning there to consume the offal of Jerusalem. As a result it became a symbol of the place of eternal torment. Matt. 18:9 speaks of *ten geennan tou puros*, the gehenna of fire, and this strong expression is used synonymously with *to pur to aionion*, the eternal fire, in the previous verse. The Bible also speaks of a "furnace of fire," Matt. 13:42, and of a "lake of fire," Rev. 20:14,15, which forms a contrast with the "sea of glass like unto crystal," Rev. 4:6. The terms "prison," I Pet. 3:19, "abyss," Luke 8:31, and "tartarus," II Pet. 2:4 are also used. From the fact that the preceding terms are all local designations, we may infer that hell is a place. Moreover, local expressions are generally used in connection with it. Scripture speaks of those who are excluded from heaven

as being "outside," and as being "cast into hell." The description in Luke 16:19-31 is certainly altogether local.

2. THE STATE IN WHICH THEY WILL CONTINUE THEIR EXISTENCE. It is impossible to determine precisely what will constitute the eternal punishment of the wicked, and it behooves us to speak very cautiously on the subject. Positively, it may be said to consist in (a) a total absence of the favor of God; (b) an endless disturbance of life as a result of the complete domination of sin; (c) positive pains and sufferings in body and soul; and (d) such subjective punishments as pangs of conscience, anguish, despair, weeping, and gnashing of teeth, Matt. 8:12; 13:50; Mark 9:43,44,47,48; Luke 16:23,28; Rev. 14:10; 21:8. Evidently, there will be degrees in the punishment of the wicked. This follows from such passages as Matt. 11:22,24; Luke 12:47,48; 20:17. Their punishment will be commensurate with their sinning against the light which they had received. But it will, nevertheless, be eternal punishment for all of them. This is plainly stated in Scripture, Matt. 18:8; II Thess. 1:9; Rev. 14:11; 20:10. Some deny that there will be a literal fire, because this could not affect spirits like Satan and his demons. But how do we know this? Our body certainly works on our soul in some mysterious way. There will be some positive punishment corresponding to our bodies. It is undoubtedly true, however, that a great deal of the language concerning heaven and hell must be understood figuratively.

3. THE DURATION OF THEIR PUNISHMENT. The question of the eternity of the future punishment deserves more special consideration, however, because it is frequently denied. It is said that the words used in Scripture for "everlasting" and "eternal" may simply denote an "age" or a "dispensation," or any other long period of time. Now it cannot be doubted that they are so used in some passages, but this does not prove that they always have that limited meaning. It is not the literal meaning of these terms. Whenever they are so used, they are used figuratively, and in such cases their figurative use is generally quite evident from the connection. Moreover, there are positive reasons for thinking that these words do not have that limited meaning in the passages to which we referred. (a) In Matt. 25:46 the same word describes the duration of both, the bliss of the saints and the penalty of the wicked. If the latter is not, properly speaking, unending, neither is the former; and yet many of those who doubt eternal punishment, do not doubt everlasting bliss. (b) Other expressions are used which cannot be set aside by the consideration mentioned in the preceding. The fire of hell is called an "unquenchable fire," Mark 9:43; and it is said of the wicked that "their worm dieth not," Mark 9:48. Moreover, the gulf that will separate saints and sinners in the future is said to be fixed and impassable, Luke 16:26.

B. The Final State of the Righteous.

1. THE NEW CREATION. The final state of believers will be preceded by the passing of the present world and the appearance of a new creation. Matt.

19:28 speaks of "the regeneration," and Acts 3:21, of "the restoration of all things." In Heb. 12:27 we read: "And this word, Yet once more signifieth the removing of those things that are shaken (heaven and earth), as of things that are made, that those things which are not shaken (the kingdom of God) may remain." Peter says: "But according to His promise, we look for new heavens and a new earth, wherein dwelleth righteousness," II Pet. 3:13, cf. vs. 12; and John saw this new creation in a vision, Rev. 21:1. It is only after the new creation has been established, that the new Jerusalem descends out of heaven from God, that the tabernacle of God is pitched among men, and that the righteous enter upon their eternal joy. The question is often raised, whether this will be an entirely new creation, or a renewal of the present creation. Lutheran theologians strongly favor the former position with an appeal to II Pet. 3:7-13; Rev. 20:11; and 21:1; while Reformed theologians prefer the latter idea, and find support for it in Ps. 102:26,27; (Heb. 1:10-12); and Heb. 12:26-28.

2. THE ETERNAL ABODE OF THE RIGHTEOUS. Many conceive of heaven also as a subjective condition, which men may enjoy in the present and which in the way of righteousness will naturally become permanent in the future. But here, too, it must be said that Scripture clearly presents heaven as a place. Christ *ascended* to heaven, which can only mean that He went from one place to another. It is described as the house of our Father with many mansions, John 14:1, and this description would hardly fit a condition. Moreover, believers are said to be within, while unbelievers are without, Matt. 22:12.13; 25:10-12. Scripture gives us reasons to believe that the righteous will not only inherit heaven, but the entire new creation, Matt. 5:5; Rev. 21:1-3.

3. THE NATURE OF THEIR REWARD. The reward of the righteous is described as eternal life, that is, not merely an endless life, but life in all its fulness. without any of the imperfections and disturbances of the present, Matt. 25:46; Rom. 2:7. The fulness of this life is enjoyed in communion with God, which is really the essence of eternal life, Rev. 21:3. They will see God in Jesus Christ face to face, will find full satisfaction in Him, will rejoice in Him, and will glorify Him. We should not think of the joys of heaven, however, as exclusively spiritual. There will be something corresponding to the body. There will be recognition and social intercourse on an elevated plane. It is also evident from Scripture that there will be degrees in the bliss of heaven, Dan. 12:3; II Cor. 9:6. Our good works will be the measure of our gracious reward, though they do not merit it. Notwithstanding this, however, the joy of each individual will be perfect and full.

QUESTIONS FOR FURTHER STUDY: Why does the moral sense of mankind demand a future judgment? To what historical precursors of the final judgment does Scripture refer? Where will the final judgment take place? What encouragement is there for believers in the fact that Christ will be the Judge? Does not the expression that he who believes on the Son "shall not come into condemnation," John 5:24, prove that believers will not be judged? What works will come into consideration in the final judgment according to Scripture? If all believers inherit eternal life, in what sense is their reward determined by their works? Does the judgment serve the purpose of acquainting God better with men? What purpose does it serve? Will men be finally lost only for the sin of consciously rejecting Christ?

LITERATURE: Bavinck, *Geref. Dogm.* IV, pp. 777-815; Kuyper, *Dict. Dogm., De Consummatione Saeculi*, pp. 280-327; Vos, *Geref. Dogm., Eschatologie* pp. 32-50; Hodge. *Syst. Theol.* III, pp. 844-880; Shedd, *Dogm. Theol.* II, pp. 659-754; ibid., *Doctrine of Endless Punishment;* Dabney, *Syst. and Polem. Theol.*, pp. 842-862; Litton, *Introd. to Dogm. Theol.*, pp. 581-595; Beckwith, *Realities of Chr. Theol.*, pp. 361-382; Drummond, *Studies in Chr. Doct.*, pp. 505-514; Macintosh, *Theol. as an Empirical Science*, pp. 205-215; Dahle, *Life After Death*, pp. 418-455; Mackintosh, *Immortality and the Future*, pp. 180-194; 229-244; King. *Future Retribution;* Hovey, *Biblical Eschatology*, pp. 145-175; Von Huegel, *Eternal Life;* Alger, *History of the Doctrine of a Future Life*, pp. 394-449, 508-549, 567-724; Schilder. *Wat is de Hemel;* Vos, *The Pauline Eschatology*, pp. 261-316; Kliefoth, *Eschatologie*, pp. 275-351.

BIBLIOGRAPHY

DOGMATICS IN GENERAL

Reformed

Barth, *Dogmatik, Prolegomena*, Muenchen, 1927 (officially Reformed); id., *The Doctrine of the Word of God*, New York, 1936.
Bavinck, *Gereformeerde Dogmatiek*, Kampen, 1906-1911.
Breckenridge, *The Knowledge of God, Objectively and Subjectively Considered*, New York 1857-1859.
Brunner, *Our Faith*, New York, 1936.
Calvin, *Institutes of the Christian Religion*, Eerdmans, 1949.
Dabney, *Systematic and Polemic Theology*, St. Louis, 1878.
Dick, *Lectures on Theology*, Cincinnati, 1853.
Gerhardt, *Institutes of the Christian Religion*, New York, 1891-1894.
Heppe, *Dogmatik der evangelisch-reformirten Kirche*, Elberveld, 1861.
Hodge, Charles, *Systematic Theology*, New York, 1892.
Hodge, Archibald A., *Outlines of Theology*, New York, 1878.
Honig, *Gereformeerde Dogmatiek*, Kampen, 1938.
Kuyper, *Dictaten Dogmatiek*, Kampen, 1910.
Marck, *Godgeleerdheid*, Rotterdam, 1741.
Mastricht, *Beschouwende en Practicale Godgeleerdheit*, Rotterdam, 1749.
McPherson, *Christian Dogmatics*, Edinburgh, 1898.
Orr, *Side-Lights on Christian Doctrine*, London, 1909.
Perkens, *Werken*, 1659.
Pictet, *Christian Theology*, Philadelphia, (no date given)
Shedd, *Dogmatic Theology*, New York, 1891-1894.
Smith, H. B., *System of Christian Theology*, New York, 1885.
Synopsis Purioris Theologiae. Leiden, 1881.
Ten Hoor, *Gereformeerde Dogmatiek*, Holland, Mich.
Thornwell, *Collected Writings*, Richmond, Va., 1871-1873.
Turretin, *Institutio Theologiae, Elenchticae*, Edinburgh, 1847.
Vos, *Gereformeerde Dogmatiek* (mimeographed).
Witsius, *Over de Verbonden*, Amsterdam, 1716.

Non-Reformed

Beckwith, *Realities of Christian Theology*, New York, 1906.
Boyce, *Abstract of Systematic Theology*. Philadelphia, 1899.
Brown, *Christian Theology in Outline*, New York, 1906.
Gavin, *Orthodox Greek Thought*, Milwaukee, 1898.
Clarke, *An Outline of Christian Theology*, 1898.
Curtis, *The Christian Faith*, New York, 1905.
Dorner, *System of Christian Doctrine*, Edinburgh, 1897.
Drummond, *Studies in Christian Doctrine*, London, 1908.
Foster, *Christianity in its Modern Expression*, New York, 1921.
Gibbons, *Faith of Our Fathers*. New York, 1917.
Haering, *The Christian Faith*, London, 1915.
Kaftan, *Dogmatik*, Tuebingen, 1920.

Litton, *Introduction to Dogmatic Theology*, London. 1912.
Macintosh, *Theology as an Empirical Science*, New York, 1919.
Martensen, *Christian Dogmatics*, Edinburgh, 1860
Micklem, *What is the Faith*, Nashville, Tenn.
Miley, *Systematic Theology*, New York. 1893.
Mortimer, *Catholic Faith and Practice*, London, 1923.
Mueller, *Christian Dogmatics*, St. Louis, 1934.
Nitzsch, *System of Christian Doctrine*, Edinburgh, 1849.
Pieper, *Christliche Dogmatik*, St. Louis, 1924.
Pohle-Preuss, *Dogmatic Theology*. St. Louis, 12 volumes from 1925 on.
Pope, *Compendium of Christian Theology*, London, 1879.
Rauschenbusch, *A Theology for the Social Gospel*, New York, 1919.
Raymond, *Systematic Theology*, Cincinnati, 1877.
Schleiermacher, *Christlicher Glaube (Glaubenslehre)*, 1821, 1822.
Schmid, *Doctrinal Theology of the Evangelical Lutheran Church*, Philadelphia, 1889
Sheldon, *System of Christian Doctrine*, Cincinnati, 1903.
Strong, A. H., *Systematic Theology*, Philadelphia, 1912.
Strong, T. B., *A Manual of Theology*, London. 1903.
Thomasius, *Christi Person und Work*, Erlangen, 1886-1888.
Valentine, *Christian Theology*, Philadelphia, 1906.
Watson, *Theological Institutes*, London. 1829.
Wilmers, *Handbook of the Christian Religion*, New York, 1921.

THE SEPARATE LOCI

Theology

Adeney, *The Christian Conception of God*, New York.
Baillie, *Our Knowledge of God*, New York, 1939.
Bartlett, *The Triune God*, New York, 1937.
Bates, *The Harmony of the Divine Attributes*, Philadelphia.
Beckwith, *The Idea of God*, New York, 1922.
Boettner, *The Reformed Doctrine of Predestination*, Grand Rapids, 1932.
Brightman, *The Problem of God*, New York, 1930.
Candlish, *The Fatherhood of God*, Edinburgh, 1866.
Charnock, *The Existence and Attributes of God*, New York, 1859.
Clarke, *The Christian Doctrine of God*, New York, 1923.
Cole, *Calvin's Calvinism*, Manchester, 1927.
Comrie en Holtius, *Examen Van Het Ontwerp Van Tolerantie*, Amsterdam, 1753
Crawford, *The Fatherhood of God*. Edinburgh, 1866.
Dijk, *Om't Feuwig Welbehagen*, Amsterdam, 1924; id., *De Voorzienigheid Gods*. Amsterdam, 1927.
Farmer, *Experience of God*, New York, 1929.
Fleming, *Evolution or Creation*. London.
Flint, *Theism*, New York, 1895; id., *Antitheistic Theories*, Edinburgh, 1906.
Girardeau, *Calvinism and Evangelical Arminianism*, Columbia, 1890.
Harris, *God the Creator and Lord of All*, New York, 1896.
Heim, *God Transcendent*, New York, 1936.
Hendry, *God the Creator*, Nashville, 1938.
Illingworth, *Divine Immanence*, New York, 1898; id., *The Doctrine of the Trinity*, London, 1907.
Kerr, *A God-Centered Faith*, New York, 1935.
Kuyper, A., Sr., *De Engelen Gods*, Amsterdam.
Kuyper, A., Jr., *Van de Kennisse Gods*, Amsterdam, 1907.
Mathews, *The Growth of the Idea of God*, New York, 1931.
More, *The Dogma of Evolution*, Princeton, 1925.
Morton, *The Bankruptcy of Evolution*, New York.
Mozley, *Lectures on Miracles*, London, 1886.
Newton, *My Idea of God* (A Symposium), Boston, 1927.
O'Toole, *The Case Against Evolution*, New York, 1926.
Otto, *The Idea of the Holy*, London, 1928.

Pink, *The Sovereignty of God*, Swengel, Pa., 1918.
Polman, *De Praedestinatileer van Augustinus, Thomas van Aquino en Calvijn*, Franeker. 1936.
Pringl-Pattison, *The Idea of God*, London, 1917.
Rimmer, *The Theory of Evolution and the Facts of Science*, Grand Rapids, 1935.
Robinson, *The God of the Liberal Christian*, New York, 1926.
Scheibe, *Calvins Praedestinationslehre*, Halle, 1897.
Shute, *The Fatherhood of God*, Cincinnati, 1904.
Snowden, *The Personality of God*, New York, 1920; id., *The Discovery of God*, New York, 1932.
Steenstra, *The Being of God as Unity and Trinity*, New York, 1891.
Thomas, *The Biblical Idea of God*, New York, 1924.
Thomson, W. D., *The Christian Miracles and the Conclusions of Science*, Edinburgh.
Thomson, W. R., *The Christian Idea of God*, London.
Tolley, *The Idea of God in the Philosophy of Saint Augustine*, New York, 1930.
Warfield, *Biblical Doctrines*, New York, 1929; id., *Calvin and Calvinism*, New York, 1931; ibid., *Studies in Theology*, 1932.
Youtz, *The Enlarging Conception of God*, New York. 1924.
Zanchius, *The Doctrine of Absolute Predestination*.

Anthropology

Aalders, *Het Verbond Gods*, Kampen, 1939.
Ball, *A Treatise on the Covenant of Grace*, London, 1645.
Boston, *The Covenant of Works, Works*, Aberdeen, 1848-1852; id., *The Covenant of Grace, Works*. Aberdeen, 1848-1852.
Brunner, *Man in Revolt*, New York, 1939.
Candlish, *The Biblical Doctrine of Sin*, Edinburgh, 1893.
Cook, *The Origin of Sin*, New York, 1899.
Edwards, *Freedom of the Will, Works*, New York; id., *Doctrine of Original Sin Defended, Works*. New York.
Fleming, *The Origin of Mankind*, London. 1935.
Gib, *Sacred Contemplations (Covenant of Grace)*.
Girardeau, *The Will in its Theological Relations*, New York, 1891.
Gracey, *Sin and the Unfolding Salvation*, London, 1894.
Heard, *The Tri-Partite Nature of Man*, Edinburgh, 1875.
Hendriksen, *The Covenant of Grace*, Grand Rapids, 1932.
Honig, *Creatianisme and Traducianisme*. Kampen. 1906.
Kuyper, A., Jr., *De Vastigheid des Verbonds*, Amsterdam, 1908; id., *De Band des Verbonds*, Amsterdam, 1907; id., *Het Beeld Gods*, Amsterdam, 1929.
Kuyper, H. H., *Hamabdil (Covenant of Grace)*, Amsterdam, 1907.
Laidlaw, *The Bible Doctrine of Man*, Edinburgh, 1905.
Mackintosh, *Christianity and Sin*, New York, 1914.
Moxon, *The Doctrine of Sin*, New York. 1922.
Mueller, *The Christian Doctrine of Sin*, Edinburgh, 1905.
Niebuhr, Reinhold, *The Nature and Destiny of Man*, Scribner, 1941.
Olevianus, *Het Wezen en de Middelen des Genade-Verbonds*, Groningen, 1739.
Orchard, *Modern Theories of Sin*, 1909.
Orr, *God's Image in Man*, New York, 1906.
Owen, *The Covenant of Grace*, Philadelphia, 1862.
Roberts, *God's Covenants with Man*, London, 1657.
Robinson, *The Christian Doctrine of Man*, Edinburgh, 1920.
Strong, *Discourses on the Covenant*, London, 1678.
Talma, *De Anthropologie van Calvijn*, Utrecht, 1882.
Tennant, *The Origin and Propagation of Sin*, Cambridge, 1906; id., *The Concept of Sin*, New York and Cambridge, 1912.
Tulloch, *The Christian Doctrine of Sin*, New York, 1876.
Van den Bergh, *Calvijn over het Genadeverbond*, 's Gravenhage, 1879.
Vos, *De Verbondsleer in de Gereformeerde Theologie*, Grand Rapids, 1887.
Weidner, *The Doctrine of Man*, Chicago. 1912.
Wiggers, *Augustinism and Pelagianism*, Andover. 1840.

Christology

Berkhof, *Christ in the Light of Eschatology*, Princeton Review, Jan. 1927; id., *Vicarious Atonement Through Christ*, Grand Rapids, 1936.
Bruce, *The Kingdom of God*, New York, 1893; id., *The Humiliation of Christ*, New York, 1901.
Brunner, *Der Mitler*, (Eng. tr. *The Mediator*).
Bushnell, *Vicarious Sacrifice*, New York, 1866.
Candlish, *The Kingdom of God*, Edinburgh, 1884.
Cave, *The Doctrine of the Work of Christ*, Nashville, 1937.
Cooke, *The Incarnation and Recent Criticism*, New York, 1907.
Crawford, *The Atonement*, Edinburgh, 1871.
Dale, *The Atonement*, London, 1877.
De Jong, *De Leer der Verzoening in de Amerikaansche Theologie*, Grand Rapids, 1913.
Denney, *The Christian Doctrine of Reconciliation*, New York, 1918.
Emmen, *De Christologie van Calvijn*, Amsterdam, 1935.
Enelow, *A Jewish View of Jesus*, New York, 1920.
Franks, *A History of the Doctrine of the Work of Christ*, New York.
Godet, and others, *The Atonement in Modern Religious Thought* (A Symposium), New York, 1902.
Hodge, *The Atonement*, Philadelphia, 1867.
Honig, *De Persoon des Middelaars in de Nieuwere Duitsche Theologie*, Kampen, 1910.
Hughes, *The Kingdom of Heaven*, New York, 1922.
Kuyper, A., Sr., *De Vleeschwording des Woords*, Franeker, 1887.
Kuyper, A., Jr., *De Middelaar Gods en der Menschen*, Kampen, 1923.
Liddon, *The Divinity of our Lord*, London, 1888.
Macinnes, *The Kingdom of God in the Apostolic Writings*, London, 1924.
Machen, *The Virgin Birth of Christ*, New York, 1930; id., *The Christian View of Man*, New York, 1937.
Mackintosh, *The Doctrine of the Person of Christ*, New York, 1912.
Meeter, *The Heavenly High Priesthood of Christ*, Grand Rapids.
Milligan, *The Ascension and Heavenly Priesthood of Our Lord*, London, 1892; id., *The Resurrection of our Lord*, New York, 1917.
Mozley, *The Doctrine of the Atonement*, New York, 1916.
Orr, *The Virgin Birth of Christ*, New York, 1914; id., *The Resurrection of Jesus*, New York.
Ottley, *The Doctrine of the Incarnation*, London.
Otto, *The Kingdom of God and the Son of Man*.
Relton, *A Study in Christology*, London, 1917.
Ritschl, *Die Christliche Lehre der Rechtfertigung und Versoehnung*, Bonn, 1895-1903.
Robertson, *Regnum Dei*, New York, 1901.
Robinson, *Our Lord*, Grand Rapids, 1937.
Rostron, *The Christology of St. Paul*, New York, 1912.
Sanday, *Christologies Ancient and Modern*, New York, 1910.
Scott, *The Kingdom and the Messiah*, Edinburgh, 1911.
Smith, D., *The Atonement in the Light of History and the Modern Spirit*, New York.
Stafford, *A Study of the Kingdom*, Nashville, 1925.
Stevens, *The Christian Doctrine of Salvation*, New York, 1905.
Stevenson, *Treatise on the Offices of Christ*, Edinburgh, 1845.
Sweet, *The Birth and Infancy of Jesus Christ*, Philadelphia, 1906.
Swete, *The Ascended Christ*, London, 1910.
Symington, *The Atonement and Intercession of Jesus Christ*, New York, 1858.
Tait, *The Heavenly Session of Our Lord*, London, 1912.
Ullmann, *The Sinlessness of Jesus*, Edinburgh, 1901.
Vos, *The Kingdom and the Church*, New York, 1903; id., *The Self-Disclosure of Jesus*, New York, 1926; id., *New Testament Theology* (mimeographed).
Warfield, *Christology and Criticism*, New York, 1929.
Wood, H. G., and others, *The Kingdom of God in History* (A Symposium), New York, 1938.

Soteriology

Ames, *The Psychology of Religious Experience*, New York, 1910.
Bavinck, *Roeping en Wedergeboorte*, Kampen, 1903; id., *De Zekerheid des Geloofs*, Kampen, 1901; ibid., *Algemeene Genade*, Kampen, 1894.
Berkhof, *The Assurance of Faith*, Grand Rapids, 1928.
Brinkman, *De Gerechtigheid Gods bij Paulus*, Rotterdam, 1916.
Broomall, *The Holy Spirit*, New York, 1940.
Buchanan, *The Doctrine of Justification*, Edinburgh, 1867.
Camfield, *Revelation and the Holy Spirit*, New York, 1934.
Candlish, *The Work of the Holy Spirit*, Edinburgh.
Comrie, *Heidelbergsche Catechismus, Zondagen 1-7* [Faith], Amsterdam, 1753; id., *Het A B C des Geloofs*, Sneek, 1860.
Davies, *Treatise on Justification*, Cincinnati, 1875.
Dee, *Het Geloofsbegrip van Calvijn*, Kampen, 1918.
Firey, *Infant Salvation*, New York, 1902.
Flew, *The Idea of Perfection in Christian Theology*, London, 1934.
Gennrich, *Die Lehre von der Wiedergeburt*, Leipzig, 1907.
Girardeau, *Discussion of Theological Questions* [Adoption], Richmond, Va., 1905; id., *Calvinism and Evangelical Arminianism* [Justification], Columbia, S. C., 1890.
Gore, *The Holy Spirit and the Church*, New York, 1924.
Gunkel, *Die Wirkungen des Heiligen Geistes*, Goettingen, 1899.
Hoffmann, *Die Lehre von der Fides Implicita*, Leipzig, 1903.
Hoyle, *The Holy Spirit in St. Paul*, London, 1927.
Impeta, *De Leer der Heiliging en Volmaking bij Wesley en Fletcher*, Leiden, 1913.
Inge, *Faith and Its Psychology*, New York, 1910.
James, *Varieties of Religious Experience*, New York, 1902.
Kerswill, *The Old Testament Doctrine of Salvation*, Philadelphia, 1904.
Koeberle, *The Quest for Holiness*, New York, 1936.
Kuiper, H., *Calvin on Common Grace*, Goes, 1928.
Kuyper, A., Sr., *Het Werk van den Heiligen Geest*, Amsterdam, 1888; id., *De Gemeene Gratie*, Leiden, 1902; id., *Uit het Woord*, 1ste Serie, III, Amsterdam.
Kuyper, A., Jr., *De Band des Verbonds*, Amsterdam, 1907.
Machen, *What Is Faith?* New York, 1915.
Moffatt, *Grace in the New Testament*, New York, 1932.
O'Brien, *The Nature and Effects of Faith*, London, 1863.
Owen, *On Justification*, Philadelphia, 1862; id., *A Discourse Concerning the Holy Spirit*, London, 1852.
Redlich, *The Forgiveness of Sins*, Edinburgh, 1937.
Robinson, H. W., *The Christian Experience of the Holy Spirit*, New York, 1928.
Smeaton, *The Doctrine of the Holy Spirit*, Edinburgh, 1889.
Snowden, *The Psychology of Religion*, New York, 1916.
Stagg, *Calvin, Twisse and Edwards on Universal Salvation of Infants*, Richmond, Va., 1902.
Starbuck, *The Psychology of Religion*, New York, 1911.
Steven, *The Psychology of the Christian Soul*, New York, 1911.
Swete, *The Forgiveness of Sins*, London, 1917; id., *The Holy Spirit in the New Testament*, London, 1919.
Walden, *The Great Meaning of Metanoia*, New York, 1896.
Warfield, *The Plan of Salvation*, Grand Rapids, 1935; id., *Biblical Doctrines*, New York, 1929.
Webb, *The Theology of Infant Salvation*, Richmond, Va., 1907.
Wernecke, *"Faith" in the New Testament*, Grand Rapids, 1934.
Wiersinga, *Gods Werk in Ons*, Kampen.

Ecclesiology

Armstrong, *The Doctrine of Baptisms*, New York, 1857.
Ayres, *Christian Baptism* [dealing with mode], London.
Bannerman, *The Church of Christ*, Edinburgh, 1868.
Barth, *The Church and the Churches*, Grand Rapids, 1936.

Biesterveld, Van Lonkhuizen en Rudolph, *Het Diaconaat*, Hilversum, 1907.
Binnie, *The Church*, Edinburgh.
Bouwman, *Gereformeerd Kerkrecht*, Kampen, 1928; id., *De Kerkelijke Tucht*, Kampen, 1912; id., *Het Ambt der Diakenen*, Kampen, 1907.
Campbell, *Christian Baptism*, St. Louis, 1882.
Carson, *Baptism in its Mode and Subjects*, London, 1884.
Diermanse, *De Uitverkoren Kinderen Wedergeboren. Eisch des Verbonds? Eisch des Doops?* Den Haag, 1906, 1907; id., *Verbond en Kerk, Woord en Doop*, Kampen, 1909; id., *De Beschouwing der Kerkleden*, 's Gravenhage, 1913; id., *De Onderstelling*, Den Haag, 1931.
Dimock, *The Doctrine of the Sacraments*, London, 1908.
Ebrard, *Das Dogma vom Heiligen Abendmahl*, Frankfurt, 1845.
Goode, *The Doctrine of the Church of England as to the Effects of Baptism in the Case of Infants*, London, 1850.
Gore, *The Holy Spirit and the Church*, New York, 1924.
Hatch, *The Organisation of the Early Christian Churches*, Oxford, 1881.
Hebert, *The Lord's Supper: Uninspired Teaching*, London, 1879.
Heyns, *Kybernetiek* (mimeographed); id., *Handbook for Elders and Deacons*, Grand Rapids, 1928.
Hibbard, *Christian Baptism*, New York, 1842.
Hodge, *Church Polity*, New York, 1878.
Hort, *The Christian Ecclesia*, London, 1898.
Jansen, *De Kerkenordening, Van de Diensten*, Nijverdal, 1917; id., *De Kerkelijke Tucht*, Arnhem, 1913; id., *Korte Verklaring Van de Kerkenorde*, Kampen, 1923.
Kramer, *Het Verband van Doop en Wedergeboorte*, Breukelen, 1897.
Kuyper, A., Sr., *Tractaat van de Reformatie der Kerken*, Amsterdam, 1884.
Lambert, *The Sacraments in the New Testament*, Edinburgh, 1903.
Lilley, *Sacraments*, New York, 1929.
Lindsay, *The Church and the Ministry in the Early Centuries*, New York.
Mathews, *The Church and the Changing Order*, New York, 1907.
McPherson, *Presbyterianism*, Edinburgh; id., *The Doctrine of the Church in Scottish Theology*, Edinburgh, 1903.
McGill, *Church Government*, Philadelphia, 1888.
Miller, *Warrant, Nature, and Duties of the Office of the Ruling Elder*, Philadelphia, 1832.
Olthuis, *De Doopspraktijk der Gereformeerde Kerken in Nederland*, Utrecht, 1908.
Schaff, *Church and State in the United States*, New York, 1888.
Schenck, *The Presbyterian Doctrine of Children in the Covenant*, New Haven, 1940.
Seiss, *The Baptist System Examined*, Philadelphia, 1907.
Sillevis Smit, *De Organisatie van de Christelijke Kerk*, Rotterdam, 1910.
Steen, *De Kerk*, Kampen, 1936.
Ten Hoor, *Afscheiding en Doleantie*, Leiden, 1880; id., *Afscheiding of Doleantie*, Leiden, 1891.
Van Dyke, *The Church, Her Ministry and Sacraments*, Philadelphia, 1903.
Visser 't Hooft and Oldham, *The Church and Its Function in Society*, New York, 1937.
Voetius, *Verhandeling over de Zichtbare en Georganiseerde Kerk*, Kampen, 1902; id., *Politica Ecclesiastica*, 1663-1676.
Wall, *History of Infant Baptism*, Oxford, 1836.
White, *Why Infants are Baptized*, Philadelphia, 1900.
Wilson, *Infant Baptism*, London, 1848.
Wilson, Wm., *Free Church Principles*, Edinburgh, 1887.

Eschatology

Addison, *Life After Death in the Beliefs of Mankind*, Boston, 1932.
Aalders, *Het Herstel van Israel Volgens het Oude Testament*, Kampen.
Althaus, *Die Letzten Dinge*, Guetersloh, 1926.
Beet, *The Last Things*, London, 1905.
Berkhof, *Premillennialisme*, Grand Rapids, 1919.

Berkhoff, *De Wederkomst van Christus*, Kampen, 1926; id., *De Christus Regeering*, Kampen, 1929.
Berg, *The Second Advent of Jesus, Not Premillennial*, Philadelphia, 1859.
Brookes, *Maranatha, or the Lord Cometh*, New York, 1889.
Brown, Ch., *The Hope of His Coming*, Anderson, 1927.
Brown, D., *The Second Advent*, Edinburgh, 1867.
Brown, W. A., *The Christian Hope*, New York, 1919.
Bultema, *Maranatha*, Grand Rapids, 1917.
Case, *The Millennial Hope*, Chicago, 1916.
Dahle, *Life After Death*, Edinburgh, 1896.
De Bondt, *Wat Leert het Oude Testament Aangaande het Leven na Dit Leven*, Kampen, 1938
De Jong, *De Komende Christus*, Grand Rapids, 1920.
Doekes, *De Beteekenis van Israels Val*, Nijverdal, 1915.
Dijk, *Het Rijk der Duizend Jaren*, Kampen.
Eaton, *The Millennial Dawn Heresy*, Cincinnati, 1911.
Eckman, *When Christ Comes Again*, Cincinnati, 1917.
Frost, *The Second Coming of Christ*, Grand Rapids, 1934.
Grosheide, *De Verwachting der Toekomst van Jezus Christus*, Amsterdam, 1907.
Heagle, *Do the Dead Still Live?* Philadelphia, 1920.
Hendriksen, *More than Conquerers*, Grand Rapids, 1940.
Hepp, *De Antichrist*, Kampen, 1919.
Hoekstra, *Het Chiliasme*, Kampen, 1903.
Hovey, *Eschatology*, Philadelphia, 1888.
James, A. J., *Personal Immortality*, London, 1922.
King, *Future Retribution*, New York. 1901.
Kliefoth, *Christliche Eschatologie*, Leipzig, 1886.
Kuyper, *Van de Voleinding*, Kampen, 1929-1931. Translation of fourth volume by J. H.
De Vries, Grand Rapids, 1935, entitled: *The Revelation of St. John.*
Lamont, *Issues of Immortality*, New York, 1932.
Lawton, *The Drama of Life After Death*, New York, 1932.
Love, *Future Probation Examined*, New York. 1888.
Mackintosh, *Immortality and the Future*, New York, 1917.
Mauro, *God's Present Kingdom*, New York, 1919; id., *The Gospel of the Kingdom*, Boston, 1928; id.. *The Hope of Israel, What Is It?* Boston, 1929.
McCown, *The Promise of His Coming*, New York, 1921.
Merrill, *Second Coming of Christ*, Cincinnati, 1879.
Milligan, *The Resurrecton of the Dead*, Edinburgh, 1894.
Morris, *Is There Salvation After Death?* New York, 1887.
Peters, *The Theocratic Kingdom*, New York, 1884.
Pieters, *Fairbairn Versus Fairbairn*, Grand Rapids, 1930.
Rall, *Modern Premillennialism and the Christian Hope*, Cincinnati, 1920.
Randall, *The New Light on Immortality*, New York, 1920.
Reese, *The Approaching Advent of Christ*, London, 1937.
Riley, *The Evolution of the Kingdom*, New York, 1913.
Rimmer, *The Evidences for Immortality*, Grand Rapids, 1935.
Rutgers, *Premillennialism in America*, Goes, 1930.
Salmond, *Christian Doctrine of Immortality*, Edinburgh, 1907
Shedd, *Doctrine of Endless Punishment*, New York, 1886.
Silver, *The Lord's Return*, New York, 1914.
Snowden, *The Coming of the Lord*, New York, 1919.
Swedenborg, *Heaven and its Wonders and Hell*, Philadelphia, 1894.
Van Leeuwen, *De Parousie-Verwachting in het Nieuwe Testament*, Utrecht, 1898.
Vos, *The Pauline Eschatology*, Princeton, 1930.
Waldegrave, *New Testament Millenarianism*, London, 1855.
Wyngaarden, *The Future of the Kingdom*, 1934.

INDEX OF AUTHORS

A

Aalders, on days of creation, 154.
Abelard, on the atonement, 386 f.
Addison, on belief in immortality, 662; on intermediate state, 680.
Ames on conversion, 488.
Anselm, on transmission of sin, 238; on original sin, 245; on the atonement, 385 f.
Aquinas, on relation of natural to supernatural revelation, 37; on transmission of sin, 238; on original sin, 245; on regeneration, 466; on justification, 512; on faith, 496; on sanctification, 529 f.
Augustine on: predestination, 109; work of creation, 127, 130; days of creation, 127; image of God, 205; original sin, 244; grace of God, 429; common grace, 432 f.; divine calling, 458; regeneration, 466; faith, 496; justification, 512; sanctification, 529; perseverance, 545; the church, 569; baptism, 626; the Lord's Supper, 645.

B

Barnes, Harry E., on God, 25; on agnosticism, 32.
Barth, Karl, on: God as wholly other, 24, 135; knowledge of God, 33 f., 36; necessity of revelation, 30, 33 f.; innate knowledge, 36; revelation, natural and supernatural, 39; Trinity, 83 f.; predestination, 111; reprobation, 116; immanence of God, 135; image of God in man, 208; origin of sin, 220; narrative of the fall, 223 f.; universality of sin, 239; connection of our sin with that of Adam, 241; original sin, 248 f.; natures of Christ, 316; virgin birth, 336; resurrection of Christ, 349; ascension of Christ, 351; Christ as revealer, 360; common grace, 446; faith, 504; subject of faith, 503; assurance of faith, 498; justified sinner, 514; justification, 525; sanctification, 536 f.; good works, 541; eschatology, 664.
Bateson, on origin of species, 162; on Darwinism, 187.
Bavinck on: names of God, 48; will of God, 78; simultaneous concurrence, 173; ordo salutis, 418 f.; work of redemption, 423; common grace, 434.

Beckwith, on the judgment, 729.
Beet, on the millennium, 715.
Bellarmin: on the image of God in man, 205 f.; on divine calling, 458.
Bergson, on finite God, 25; on creative evolution, 163.
Bonaventura, on transmission of sin, 238.
Bradley, on the absolute and God, 24 f.; 57.
Brown, W. A., on the determination of the divine attributes, 53; on the return of Christ, 705; on the resurrection, 721.
Brown, D., on the millennium, 715.
Brunner on: Schleiermacher's view of God, 24; the Trinity, 83 f.; reprobation, 116; immanence of God,' 135; narrative of the fall, 224; universality of sin, 239; connection of our sin with that of Adam, 241; original sin, 249; the virgin birth, 335 f.; the natures of Christ, 316; mystery of the person of Christ, 322; resurrection of Christ, 349; Christ as revealer, 360; common grace, 446; faith, 498.
Bullinger, H., on second party in the covenant of grace, 273.
Bullinger, E. W., on baptism, 635.
Bushnell on vicarious sacrifice, 376.

C

Calvin on: knowledge of God, 29, 43 f.; persons in the Trinity, 87 f.; predestination, 110; reprobation, 115 f.; angels, 142; origin of soul, 196 f.; image of God in man, 203, 206; image of God in angels, 206; descent into hades, 341, 342; session of Christ, 352; necessity of atonement, 369; common grace, 430, 434; means of common grace, 440, 441; fruit of common grace, 442; divine calling, 459; use of term "regeneration," 466; faith, 497; justification, 514; the church, 560, 564; baptism, 627; ground for infant baptism, 638, 640; the Lord's Supper, 646, 649, 653 f.; sleep of the soul, 688.
Campbell, McLeod, on the atonement, 390 f.
Carson, on *bapto* and *baptizo*, 629.
Case, on the millennium, 717 f.
Charnock, on absolute and ordinate power, 80.

INDEX OF SUBJECTS

O

Obedience of Christ, active and passive, 379 ff.

Obligation not destroyed by voluntary loss of ability, 234.

Offer of salvation: universal, and particular atonement, 397 f.

Officers in the church: apostles, 585; prophets, 585; evangelists, 585; elders, 585; teachers, 586; deacons, 586 f.; calling of, 587; ordination of, 588; laying on of hands on, 588.

Offices of Christ: idea of in history, 356 f.; prophetic, 357 ff.; priestly, 361 ff.; kingly, 406 ff.

Omnipotence: attribute of, defined, 79 f.; limitations of, 80.

Omnipresence, attribute of, defined, 60 f.

Omniscience, attribute of, defined and proved, 67.

Ontological argument, for existence of God, 26.

Opera *ad intra* and *ad extra* defined, 89, 101.

Ordination, of ministers, 588.

Ordo salutis: meaning of term, 415 f.; indicated in Scripture, 416 f.; Reformed view of, 418 ff.; Lutheran view of, 420; Roman Catholic view of, 421; Arminian view of, 421.

Original sin: doctrine of in history, 244 f.; including guilt and pollution, 245 f.; total depravity, 246 f.; total inability, 247 f.; and free will, 248; objections to total depravity and total inability, 249.

P

Pantheism: its conception of God, 24; and immutability of God, 59; and omnipresence of God, 61; and personality of God, 64; and creation, 138 f.; and emanation, 138 f.; and providence, 167; and preservation, 171.

Paradise: the third heaven, 683; not part of hades, 683.

Parousia: designation of second coming, 695, 705; not past, 705.

Pelagianism on: sin, 233 f.; grace, 428 f.; regeneration, 476 f.; physical death, 669.

Perfectionism: defined, 537 f.; scriptural proofs for, 538; different theories of, 538; objections to, 539 f.

Permissive decree: meaning of term, 105.

Perseverance: of elect angels, 121; doctrine of in history, 545; of believers, 545 f.; objections to, 548 f.; importance of doctrine, 549.

Person in Trinity: in what respect different from human person, 87; distinguished from divine essence, 87 f.

Personality of God: and God as absolute, 64; natural proofs for, 64 f.; scriptural proof for, 65.

Personal property: of the Father, 89, 91; of the Son, 89, 93; of the Holy Spirit, 89, 97.

Physical death: punishment for sin, 260, 669; nature of, 668 f.; connection with sin, 260, 669; of believers, 670 f.

Postmillennialism: defined, 716; earlier and later forms of, 716 ff.; objections to, 718 f.

Pre-Adamites, 188.

Predestination: doctrine of in history, 109 ff.; scriptural terms for, 111 f.; author of, 112 f.; distinguished from decree in general, 109; objects of, 113; parts of, 113 ff.; extent of (supra and infra), 118 ff.

Pre-existentianism, theory of, 197.

Premillennialism on: kingdom of Christ, 407, 409, 710 f.; church, 571; Christ as Head of the church, 582; law and gospel, 613; second coming, 695 ff., 704; imminent coming of Christ, 695 ff.; calling of the Gentiles, 698; conversion of Israel, 699; the great tribulation, 700; history, 710 f.; order of eschatological events, 711 f.; literal interpretation, 712 f.; postponement of· kingdom, 713 f.; double resurrection, 714 f., 724 f.; final judgment, 715, 730 f., 733.

Preterition, distinguished from pre-condemnation, 116 f.

Priestly office of Christ: scriptural proof for, 361 f.; sacrificial work connected with, 362 ff.: in modern theology, 366; intercessory work connected with, 400 ff.

Probation: of Adam, 221 f.; second: supposed proofs for, 692 f.; objections to, 693.

Probationary command: nature of and reason for, 222 f.

Procession of the Holy Spirit: defined, 96 f.; different from generation, 97; from both Father and Son, 97.

Prophet: office of, 357 f; elements included in idea of, 358; functions of, 358.

Prophetic office of Christ: ways in which it was administered, 358 f.; scriptural proof for, 359; modern emphasis on, 359 f.

TEXTUAL INDEX

to

SYSTEMATIC THEOLOGY

TEXTUAL INDEX TO SYSTEMATIC THEOLOGY

(Prepared by D. Oosterink, Th.B.)